FINANCIAL MANAGEMENT

V.K. BHALLA

Professor,
Faculty of Management Studies,
University of Delhi,
DELHI

S Chand And Company Limited

(ISO 9001 Certified Company)

S Chand And Company Limited

(ISO 9001 Certified Company)

Head Office: Block B-1, House No. D-1, Ground Floor, Mohan Co-operative Industrial Estate, New Delhi – 110 044 | Phone: 011-66672000

Registered Office: A-27, 2nd Floor, Mohan Co-operative Industrial Estate, New Delhi – 110 044 Phone: 011-49731800

www.**schandpublishing.com**; e-mail: **info@schandpublishing.com**

Branches

Chennai	:	Ph: 23632120; chennai@schandpublishing.com
Guwahati	:	Ph: 2738811, 2735640; guwahati@schandpublishing.com
Hyderabad	:	Ph: 40186018; hyderabad@schandpublishing.com
Jalandhar	:	Ph: 4645630; jalandhar@schandpublishing.com
Kolkata	:	Ph: 23357458, 23353914; kolkata@schandpublishing.com
Lucknow	:	Ph: 4003633; lucknow@schandpublishing.com
Mumbai	:	Ph: 25000297; mumbai@schandpublishing.com
Patna	:	Ph: 2260011; patna@schandpublishing.com

First Edition 2014
Reprint 2019

ISBN: 978-81-219-4321-5 **Product Code:** H8FIM60FINC10ENAA14O

PRINTED IN INDIA

By Vikas Publishing House Private Limited, Plot 20/4, Site-IV, Industrial Area Sahibabad, Ghaziabad – 201 010 and Published by S Chand And Company Limited, A-27, 2nd Floor, Mohan Co-operative Industrial Estate, New Delhi – 110 044

PREFACE

The financial decisions of the firm begin with the choice of a business strategy designed to create value. Finance, the art and science of managing funds, affects the lives of every individual and every organization. Global finance being a reality and to achieve an optimal risk-return trade-off in a highly complex financial world, an integrated strategy is to be designed and implemented by a finance manager. Traditional emphasis on types of securities, fund-raising techniques, and institutional policies is being replaced by intensive study of the optimization of investment and financing decisions under conditions of uncertainty. However, the communication of the new ideas in finance has been hampered by the fact that the important material is scattered among various journals. The most significant contributions need to be brought together and synthesized to make them readily available to the students. Towards this end, an attempt is made in Financial Management to provide a through exposition of the traditional and the modern finance theory. The text, designed in ***Six*** Parts consisting of 33 chapters, concentrates on more than time honored rules of thumb in analyzing *why* companies and financial managers behave the way they do in financial decision making. Throughout the text readers are asked to insert themselves into the role of the firm's financial manager. From this vantage point, they can then envision the entire panorama of the financial setting and the problems and considerations therein. All the material is tied together through the eyes of the financial manager. Each financial function is identified and then discussed so that the reader moves through the organization structure knowing where the function fits, how it interrelates with other functional areas, and what techniques to apply in order to perform appropriately when confronted with the tasks and problems of the function. The aim of the book is to help and enable the readers in developing an understanding of the theory of finance and integrate the knowledge with practice in evaluating the firm's investment, financing and dividend decisions. The various theories have been critically evaluated and compared, with a clear statement of the advantages and disadvantages of each theory, and its contribution in the field of finance.

Part-I introduces the reader to the basic foundations of finance. The intent is to demonstrate that financial decisions are not made in vacuum, but are coordinated with other impacting considerations. It consists of five chapters providing an overview of financial management and policy, financial statements, financial analysis and planning, financial modeling, and profit planning and control. Chapter 1 provides an introduction to the financial management by showing how it relates to the overall management and achievement of appropriate objectives of the business enterprise. Chapter 2 is intended to help the readers to gain insights through the study of financial statements, vital for sound financial decision-making. Since the financial statements comprise the basic data with which the financial analyst works, the ability to understand, interpret and use of this information is basic to an understanding finance. Subsequent Chapter 3, on financial analysis and planning, focuses on the various categories and types of ratios used in analyzing actual and forecasted financial statements and various types of operating budgets. Financial modeling, a fancy buzz word, a meaningful concept absorbed into the body of business knowledge and an integral part of the financial analysis sets forth in chapter 4. Profit planning and control, covered in Chapter 5, occupying a major role within the scope of financial decision-making, is critical both in explaining the goal and relevant measures of achievement to operating management. This requires that management must have information on the changes in volume resulting from adjustments in prices, the effect on costs of variations on volume, the influence on both volume and costs of rearrangements in the product mix, and changes in operating assets. Break-even-analysis, a formal profit planning approach, based on established relations between costs and revenues, provides a much needed 'toolbox' of optimization techniques that can be used to apply the concepts of financial management.

Part-II covers valuation concepts, which includes the time value of money, fundamentals of risk and return, and valuation of securities, in three chapters. Chapter 6, on the time value of money, explains the terminology, computational procedures and tables used in interest theory. In the subsequent Chapter 7, the focus is on risk and return. More precisely, in terms of how risk and return relate to investments, procedures used to measure risk, and the impact of their relationship on decision making. It is shown how a finance manager can reduce expected risk through diversification, why this risk reduction results from *proper* diversification, and how he can estimate the expected return and expected risk of a given portfolio. Chapter 8 covers valuation and rates of return on fixed income securities and on the equity, and all the important characteristics of each of these security types. This structure provides both an institutional understanding of bonds, preference shares, and equity shares, and an understanding of the valuation process of securities in the financial marketplace. The material relates to the various cost of capital estimation models. Capital Asset Pricing Model (CAPM) is presented and discussed in relation to other time tested valuation models.

Part-III, consisting of five chapters, covers capital budgeting decisions and related subjects under certainty, risk, and uncertainty. Chapter 9 covers the most important step in the capital budgeting process, i.e. the estimation of cash flows for potential projects. A detailed discussion of the impact of depreciation method selected and taxation on project cash flows is treated extensively. Chapter 10 deals with the various analytical methods of capital budgeting such as payback, average rate of return, net present value, profitability ratio and internal rate of return, and with the resolution of conflicts that can arise in project ranking. It provides evidence of the superiority of the NPV approach in selecting the set of projects that maximizes shareholders' wealth. The decision -making process becomes more complex as the number of alternatives increases, as these alternatives become interdependent, and as the number of constraints on the decision maker increases. Next three chapters are devoted to capital rationing and capital budgeting decisions under conditions of uncertainty. Chapter 11 expands the discussion of capital budgeting to include multiple project decision making and use of mathematical programming to capture and manipulate the many decision variables and restriction. The focus of the next two Chapters 12 and 13 is on capital budgeting decisions under conditions of uncertainty. They cover a wide variety of specific techniques, ranging from certainty equivalents to the goal programming for the NPV models. These chapters provide the reader with an in-depth treatment of the work of H. Martin Weingartner in mathematical programming applied to the capital budgeting problem setting, and David B. Hertz in the application of Monte Carlo simulation to the capital expenditure decisions.

Part-IV deals with long-term financing and required return in seven chapters. Chapter 14 on cost of capital discusses the various components of the cost of capital and the computation of weighted average and marginal cost of capital. Chapter 15 is on the concept of leverage, emphasizing the use of operating, financial, and total leverage in the financial decision-making. Integration of the capital structure decision-making and problem of the financing mix is the focus of the subsequent Chapter 16. Basic tools of capital-structure management are discussed in the subsequent Chapter 17. The tools and theory of capital structure decision-making have been fully integrated in particular, the role played by the business risk, financial risk, and the degree of operating and financial leverage in establishing an optimal capital structure. Chapter 18 on dividend theories follows up on many of the imperfections first explored in capital structure theory. It examines the effects of dividend policy on the current price of equity, the rate of growth of profits, the rate of growth of dividends per share and the value of the firm. Alternative practical dividend policies, stock dividends and stock splits, institutional and administrative aspects of dividend policy have been focused in Chapter 19. Subsequent Chapter 20 examines the lease vs. purchase decision, first as a financing decision when the assets involved represent mandatory expenditures, and later as a capital budget decision involving discretionary expenditures.

Part-V deals extensively in six chapters with the management of working capital. A theoretical framework on the risk/return trade-off of various approaches applied in the firm's working capital management has been the focus of chapter-21. Remaining five chapters deal with management of cash and marketable securities, forecasting cash flows, receivables management, inventory management, and short-term financing. Chapter 22 devotes itself to the management of cash and marketable securities, while Chapter 23 covers the forecasting of cash flows, highlights design issues relating to forecasting short term cash flows. It covers medium-term; quarterly, monthly and daily cash forecasts and introduces some of the important techniques used in cash forecasting systems. Chapter 24 goes beyond the traditional coverage on receivables management in order to incorporate material on optimum credit policy. The analysis is extended to the point of determining the marginal expected return on investments in receivables. Chapter 25, on inventory management, covers optimal strategies for holding and ordering inventory for firms that choose to use the inventory approach to address some of their problems. It discusses the impact that the inventory management has on the cash cycle of the corporation. Some basic techniques that can be applied by financial manager to effectively manage the important component of cash cycle have been examined. Chapter 26 blends together major sources of short-term financing instruments and techniques to generate a minimum cost structure for current liabilities.

Part-VI, on contemporary topics in finance, includes seven chapters. The first-two chapters deal with mergers and acquisitions, business failure, reorganization and bankruptcy. Chapter 27 provides an analysis of the valuation factors and techniques of which management must be cognizant in order to evaluate properly mergers and acquisitions. It discusses merger accounting and management's choice to purchase or pool. Chapter 28 considers what happens when business experience severe and extended problems that might cause failure. It examines the alternatives available to failing firms. Chapter 29 is on creating wealth, dealing with the corporate financial strategy and decision making. Subsequent chapters are in the international context focusing on multinational business finance and developments in world financial markets. The world view before the crisis was that the growth of the financial sector, in and of itself, was desirable; indeed that real growth can be induced by sheer financial engineering. Hence, the faith in the financial sector grew to such an extent that before the crisis, it was believed that for every real sector problem, no matter how complex, there is a financial sector solution. The crisis changed that. It has now been well recognized that for every real sector problem, no matter how complex, there is a financial sector solution, which is wrong. In the pre- crisis euphoria of financial alchemy, it has been forgotten that the goal of all development effort is the growth of the real economy, and that the financial sector is useful only to the extent it helps deliver stronger and more secure long term growth. Chapter 30 introduces to the world of financial derivatives, covering options, futures, swaps, etc. and the recent developments in these markets. Subsequent Chapter 31 discusses the unique financial considerations in the international financial management. It provides an exposure to the various important aspects of international financial management, including foreign exchange markets, exchange risk management, international capital budgeting, world financial markets, and the economic framework of international financial management. Chapter 32 covers the current global financial crisis and its aftermath. The financial crisis severely tested banking systems, and the deficiencies it revealed warranted a swift and comprehensive official response The crisis revealed that risk can be transmitted through unexpected channels. Final Chapter 33 covers a series of steps introduced through Basel-III to improve the resilience of all banks regardless of complexity and size.

The volume reflects the changes that have taken place in the theory of finance. The text is a product of underlying conviction that the theory of finance can provide guidelines for practical financial management. The objective is not to answer the unanswerable, but rather to spell out an operational framework for reaching the *best attainable* financial decision. The theory of finance is a method rather than a doctrine, a technique of thinking which helps its possessor to draw correct conclusions. Accordingly the practical application of the financial theory in uncertain environments has been emphasized. Further, to facilitate the relative corporate decisions, new illustrative problems, questions, problems, and cases have been added.

The text is based on the courses we have taught for the past two decades at the Faculty of Management Studies, Delhi-University. Keeping in view requirements of the students of MBA/Commerce/Business Economics at various Universitics/ Institutes, Chartered Accountants, Company Secretaries and other professional courses, the text is designed to fill the gap and also transmit some of the excitement of current thinking and controversy. The detailed knowledge gained by the reader should make him more conversant with the discipline and should provide a strong conceptual foundation (both pragmatically and theoretically) on which to build his future financial activities and decisions. Since the book is synthesis, I am indebted to all writers who have contributed to the area of finance. I hope that I have interpreted their views correctly. I have made acknowledgment of every idea whose source I have been able to identify, but some writers may have been missed unintentionally. Finally, I wish to express thanks to the members of the S. Chand & Company Pvt. Ltd. whose high performance standards and in-depth knowledge of publishing have been invaluable in the development of the text.

V.K. BHALLA

CONTENTS

PART-I: FOUNDATIONS OF FINANCE

PART-II: VALUATION

PART-III: CAPITAL BUDGETING DECISIONS

PART -IV: LONG-TERM FINANCING AND REQUIRED RATE OF RETURN

PART-V: THE MANAGEMENT OF WORKING CAPITAL

PART-VI: SELECTED TOPICS IN CONTEMPORARY FINANCE

PART - I

FOUNDATIONS OF FINANCE

This Page has been intentionally left blank

1

FINANCIAL MANAGEMENT AND POLICY: AN OVERVIEW

INTRODUCTION

Financial Management is a goal-oriented activity. It has been described as the blend of art and science through which the important decisions of what to invest in, how to finance it, and how to combine the two in order to maximise some appropriate objective, are taken. The broad and dynamic field of finance affects the financial lives of virtually every business—financial and nonfinancial, private and public, large and small, profit-seeking and nonprofit. The performance of the firm is measured in financial terms; the success of the firm depends on how it is perceived by, and reacts to, external economic markets.The field of finance is much more complicated and faster faced today. New technologies and relaxed regulations are changing the institutional setting. Financial markets are volatile, interest rates can move sharply up or down in a very short-term period. Important and swift development in the field of finance and application of new theories in decision-making environment yield new challenges and opportunities for financial managers. Knowledge of all these developments and their impact is necessary for the effective management and financial viability of the modern business firms. Financial managers need to know how effective decisions can be made, and ineffective ones be avoided. This chapter provides an introduction to the financial management by showing how it relates to the overall management and achievement of appropriate objectives of the business enterprises.

WHAT IS FINANCE ?

In his book *The Theory of Financial Management,* Ezra Solomon has defined the finance function as the study of the problems involved in the use and acquisition of funds by a business. Its main concern is to find a rational basis for answering three question:[1]

(i) What total value of funds should be invested in the business? That is, what size and growth rate should the business aim to achieve?

1. Ezra Solomon, *The Theory of Financial Management,* Columbia University Press (New York), 1963, pp. 8-9.

(ii) What specific assets should the business acquire? That is, in what form the assets be held?

(iii) How should the required funds be financed? Alternatively, how should the liability side of the balance sheet be composed?

Let's look at this definition part by part:

Investing Capital

Coincident with the steady increase in the cost of money over the past decade, financial managers have taken an increasingly active role in coordinating and monitoring their company's investment activities. Investment appraisal is a cooperative effort involving many persons from different parts of an organisation, and certainly the financial manager does not make these decisions singlehandedly. Rather his or her responsibility is usually to determine the financial consequences of alternative use of capital and to ascertain that those investments which are undertaken meet a properly defined standard of economic merit.

Acquiring Capital

Broadly speaking, the financial manager works on the interface between two markets—the product market in which companies sell their goods and services and the financial market in which they raise needed capital. Based on the company's planned activities in the product market, it is the responsibility of the financial manager to estimate his or her firm's need for outside capital and then to raise this capital in the financial market. In addition to estimating the magnitude and duration of the need for outside funds, it is also required that the financial manager decide on the type of capital to raise, whether it should be debt, equity, or some other form, and that he design the particular financial securities to be sold. Furthermore, because the dividends that a company decide to distribute to shareholders affect its need for outside capital, the financial manager must be concerned with dividend policy as well.

Managing Capital

Finally, the financial manager has the primary day-to-day operating responsibility for several of the company's current assets. In addition to determining the size of the company's investment in these assets, the financial manager is also responsible for administering these resources efficiently.

A second way to describe corporate finance is to define it. Depending on one's perspective, corporate finance can be defined in a number to ways, including the following. Corporate finance is:

Management of Money

Business finance can be broadly defined as the activity concerned with the planning, raising, controlling and administering of funds used in the business.[2] Or

2. H. Guthman and H. Dougall: *Corporate Financial Policy* (Englewood Cliffs, N.J. Prentice Hall, Inc., 1940), p. 1.

alternatively, "finance refers to those activities involved in seeing that an individual organisation has the cash with which to pay its bills promptly."[3]

Microeconomics Under Uncertainty

It is the study of the profit maximising firms' output and financing decisions when statements about the future are subject to error,

Part of General Management

Financial management is properly viewed as an integral part of overall management rather than as a staff speciality concerned with fund raising operations. In this broader view the central issue in financial policy is the wise use of funds, and the central process involved is a rational matching of the advantages of potential uses against the cost of alternative sources so as to achieve the broad financial goals which an enterprise sets for itself.[4]

All three of these definitions contain a certain element of truth, however, the last comes closest to the way we will view the topic here. This first definition is too narrow and too passive. It pictures the financial manager as being concerned only with providing capital and simply responding to the financial requirements imposed on him by others. The second definition is too abstract. Economics has much to say about finance (and indeed we shall make considerable use of economic concepts), but finance with its concern for practical decisions, is more than just a branch of micro-economics. The last definition, with its emphasis on the broad, strategic dimensions, of corporate finance, comes closest to capturing the active role of the modern financial manager. At the risk of simply lengthening the list, we might alter this definition a bit to reflect more fully the administrative responsibilities of the financial executive.

Corporate finance is the study of the generation of corporate capital and its allocation among competing investment needs in a manner consistent with company goals. In as much as solvency is certainly one of these goals, this necessarily implies that corporate finance concern itself with the planning and control of cash flows through the organisation.

EVOLUTION OF FINANCIAL MANAGEMENT

The terms *financial management, managerial finance, corporate finance,* and *business finance* are virtually equivalent and are used interchangeably. most financial managers, however, seem to prefer either *financial management* or *managerial finance.* It emerged as a separate branch of economics around the turn of the century. Earlier it was generally taught as an economic subject, with heavy emphasis on the social, rather than the private, viewpoint. The predominantly social viewpoint explains why topics such as investment banking, mergers and consolidations, and public regulation received the greatest attention. Emphasis was also placed on economic institutions,

3. Bion B. Howard and Miller Upton, : *Introduction to Business Finance.* (New York. McGraw Hill Book Company, 1953), p.
4. Ezra Solomon: *The Theory of Financial Management* (New York Columbia University Press, 1963), p. 3.

and courses in finance included much descriptive on stocks, bonds, security exchanges, and risks and generalisation called from practical business experience. Within this financial context, the original purpose of corporation finance as a separate subject was to describe and document the rapidly evolving complex of institutions, instruments, and practices in the capital market. As one of the earlier texts written soon after the turn of the century said: "*Corporation finance aims to explain and illustrate the methods employed in the promotion, capitalisation, financial management, consolidation and reorganisation of business corporations.*" Table-1 summarises the most significant developments in the evolution of financial management.

TABLE 1

Evolution of Financial Management

Period	*Focus*
Pre-1930	Descriptive emphasis on financial markets and securities. Little attention to asset management.
1930s and 1940s	Focus on legal maters dealing with bankruptcy and recognisation and the effects of newly emerging government regulation.
1950s	Increasing emphasis on asset management. Significant theoretical developments in valuation theory.
1960s	Application of mathematical models to allocation of current and fixed assets. Additional theoretical developments in valuation theory, cost of capital, devidend policy, and risk analysis.
1970s	Development of more precise theories and measures of risk. Application of these theories to investment analysis and valuation.
1980s	Increasing application of computer technology to assist in financial decision making.
Late 1980s and 1990s	Reemphasis on value maximisation concepts and the role of competitive, efficient, and complete capital markets.
1990s...	Increased attention to international competition and the management of multinational firms. Renewed concern for the ethical implications of business decisions.

TRADITIONAL CONCEPT OF FINANCE

The traditional concept of finance received its finest expression in the scholarly work of Arthur S. Dewing's *The Financial Policy of Corporation* in 1920.[5] This book established the existing pattern of treatment in the field even more firmly by providing a definitive and scholarly text and a definitive and scholarly basis for academic courses in the field.

The traditional treatment of finance did not go unchallenged. Indeed, it was

5. Arthur S. Dewing, *The Financial Policy of Corporation*. The Ronald Press Company (New York), 1920.

criticised more or less continually throughout the period of its dominance. But what was questioned was not so much the definition of the finance function on which it was based, as matters of treatment and emphasis. In particular, critical attention was directed to four selected aspects of the traditional treatment. *First,* the traditional approach treats the entire subject of finance from the point of view of the investment banker rather than that of the financial decision-maker within an enterprise. The criticism is generally accompanied by a suggestion that at least part of the content of finance should be from the inside looking out rather than from outside looking in. *Second,* the traditional treatment placed altogether for much emphasis on *corporation* finance and too little on the financing problems of noncorporate enterprises. *Thirdly,* the sequence of treatment was built too closely around the episodic but infrequent phases during the life cycle of a hypothetical corporation during which external financial relations happen to be dominant. The argument in the connection in what overemphasis on matters like promotion, incorporation, mergers, consolidation, recapitalisation, and reorganisation left for little room for the problems of a normal growing economy. Finally, critics questioned the heavy emphasis which the traditional approach placed on long-term financing instruments and problems and its corresponding lack of emphasis on problems of working capital management.

These criticisms are not intended to question the reputation of Dewing's book as a classical treatise on the subject of finance. In fact the book is an outstanding representative of the vast amount of finance literature written from the traditional point of view, and we have criticised it only to bring out the difference between the traditional approach to finance and the new approach. The basic difference may be summarised as follows: *Whereas the traditional approach focuses its attention rather narrowly on the acquisition of funds, the new approach expands its focus to encompass both the use and the acquisition of funds in an enterprise.*

Business failures during the *Depression* brought a change in the focus in finance during thirties. While finance continued to be taught as a descriptive discipline, increased emphasis was placed on bankruptcy, liquidity management, and avoidance of financial problems. The political changes that dominated the thirties also influenced the field of finance, bringing increased government regulation and control of both business and the securities market, and the increase requirements to disclose large volume of corporate financial data. These data allowed analysts to assess potential corporate performance more effectively stirring new interest in financial analysis.

In the early years after *World War II*, a switch from external financing to internal financing combined with the freeing of interest rates and some degree of tightening in the money market made the whole question of working capital management more important. Consequently, there was a switch in emphasis from the question of long-term financing to working capital financing and working capital management. The financial manager now dealt with the total funds committed to assets and the allocation of capital to individual assets on the basis of an appropriate and objective acceptance criterion.

TRANSITION TO THE NEW APPROACH

In the years that followed the development of the traditional approach to finance, its shortcomings were perceived by a number of critics firm different points of view. It was attacked for its lack of analytical content and heavy emphasis on descriptive materials. It has also been criticised because it sees the problem of finance from the vantage point of the investment banker rather than from that of the financial manager and because it overemphasises long term financing decisions at the expense of short-term decisions.

Since the mid-1950's, the infusion of new ideas from economic theory and the increased ability of financial writers to apply modern quantitative techniques in their analyses have led to the rapid and widespread acceptance of the new approach to finance. We may conveniently discuss the main developments in this most recent period under three categories: financing decisions, investment decisions, and profit-planning decisions.

The subject of financing decisions has been enlivened by a long controversy over the question of whether a firm's capital structure has any effect on its value and the cost of capital. The argument was touched off by an article written in 1958 by Franco Modigliani and Merton H. Miller in which they contended that value and cost of capital are independent of capital structure.[6] Other theorists, notably David Durand and Ezra Solomon,[7] strongly disagreed with Modigliani and Miller and wrote articles attempting to rebut their conclusions. Although there was some confusion of ideas in the first stages of the controversy, later writings by these authors and by other have clarified the basic areas of disagreement. It is now generally admitted that both theories of capital structure are internally consistent, since they follow logically from their respective assumptions. The validity of these opposing assumptions is a question requiring empirical testing, not simply *a priori* reasoning. A related question is the effect of dividend policy on the value of the firm. Among the important contributors on this subject are Modigliani and Miller, Myron J. Gordon, Irwin Friend and Marshall Puckett.[8] These controversies, which are still unresolved, gave much impetus to the evolution and ascendancy of the new concept of finance because it shifted the main point of view in financial writing from the descriptive to the analytical.

6. *Franco Modigliani and Merton H. Miller*, "The Cost of Capital, Corporation Finance, and the Theory of Investment," *American Economic Review* 48 (June 1958), pp. 261-297.
7. David Durand, "The Cost of Capital, Corporation Finance, and the Theory of Investment: Comment," *American Economic Review* 49 (September 1959), pp. 639-654; Ezra Solomn, "Leverage and the Cost fo Capital," *Journal of Finance* 18 (May 1963), pp. 273-279.
8. Merton H. Miller and Franco Modigliani, "Dividend Policy, Growth, and the Valuation of Shares," *Journal of Business* 34 (October 1961), pp. 411-433; Myron J. Gordon, *The Investment, Financing, and Valuation fo the Corporation* (Homewood, III.: Richard D. Irwin Inc., 1962; Irwin Friend and Marshall Puckett, "Davidends and Stock Prices," *American Economic Review* 54 (September 1964), pp. 656-681.

The period has also seen one of the first applications of linear programming to the costing of funds within a firm. In an article written in 1959, A Charnes, W.W. Cooper, and M.H. Miller[9] showed how linear programming could be used to determine the opportunity cost of funds for a firm with multiple investment opportunities. This concept of the opportunity cost is important because it provides the firm with a basis for deciding whether a particular investment is worth undertaking and whether additional funds are worth acquiring. In a 1965 article, A.A. Robichek, D. Teichroew, and M. Jones[10] considered a firm that experienced pronounced seasonal fluctuations in its cash flows and could choose between several alternative means of financing its needs. A linear programming problem was then set up to find the pattern of financing that minimised the net financing cost to the firm.

In this period the study of financing decisions has been a rapidly expanding field, and the articles we have cited may merely serve to represent the many important analytical contributions that are constantly appearing. On the subject of investment decisions, an important contribution was 1955 article by J. Lorie and L.J. Savage[11] that discussed three problems that arise when a firm allocates its liquid resources among competing investment opportunities. First, they showed that the "internal rate of return" of a project does not always provide a meaningful measure of the investment's profitability. In certain projects the presence of net expenditures subsequent to the initial capital outlay may result in multiple internal rates of return. For such projects, the rate of return becomes an ambiguous concept. Second, they questioned the validity of the method of ranking frequently used by firms forced to choose between competing investments because of fund limitations. In this method all competing projects are ranked in descending order according to their internal rates of return or their net present values, and projects are accepted in that order until the firm's funds are completely exhausted. Lorie and Savage showed that if the projects are indivisible, this ranking method does not necessarily result in the optimal portfolio. In the third place they showed that the ranking method may not result in the optimal portfolio if the project returns are dependent upon each other.

Although Lorie and Savage's article appeared in 1955, no general method for solving the problem of multiple internal rates of return was developed until ten years later. Then in a series of two articles D. Teichroew, A.A. Robichek, and M. Montalbano[12] resolved the problem by viewing projects with multiple returns as a mixture of investment and financing transactions. The problems of independence

9. A. Charnes, W.W. Cooper, and M.H. Miller, "Application of Linear Programming to Financial Budgeting and the Costing of Funds," *Journal fo Business* 32 (January 1959), pp. 20-46.
10. A.A. Robichek, D. Teichroew, and M. Jones, "Optimal Short-term Financing Decision," *Management Science* 12 (September 1965), pp. 1-36.
11. J.H. Lorie and L.J. Savage, "Three Problems in Capital Rationing," *Journal of Business* 28 (October 1955), pp. 229-239.
12. D. Teichroew, A.A. Robichek, and M. Mon Albano, "An Analysis of Criteria for Investment and Financing Decisions Under Certainty," *Management Science* 12 (November 1965), pp. 151-179; and "Mathematical Analysis of Rates of Return Under Certainty," *Management Science* 11 (January 1965), pp. 395-403.

and indivisibility led to the publication of H. Martin Weingartner's award-winning dissertation in 1963.[13] The approach used by Weingartner to solve these two problems was that of mathematical programming. Currently, with the advance of quantitative techniques, the three problems formulated by Lorie and Savage are being resolved by other writers with still more powerful tools.

Whereas the article by Lorie and Savage assumed conditions of certainty, a paper written by Frederick S. Hillier[14] in 1963 dealt primarily with investment decisions under conditions of uncertainty. In this paper Hillier derived formulas for computing the expected value and variance of the net present value of an investment and showed how this probabilistic information can help the firm to optimise investment decisions involving risky projects. Hillier, however, was concerned with the acceptance or rejection of a single investment. If more than one investment may be undertaken, the firm's optimal selection of projects must be based on an examination of all combinations of investments rather than the examination of a series of single isolated investments. Investment analysis taking the broader approach has generally made use of concepts and tools borrowed from Harry M. Markowitz's model of portfolio selection.[15] While Markowitz's original model was concerned with allocating a fixed sum of money among a list of competing securities, his model can be adapted to real investment decisions. Analysis in this area has also benefited from John Lintner's theory of asset valuation under conditions of uncertainty.

On the subject of profit-planning, a Charnes, W.W. Cooper, Y. Ijiri, and others have shown how linear programming can be used to improve the operating programme of a firm. In particular, their writings applied linear programming to break-even analysis: The traditional method of break-even analysis assumes that the firm produces only one product, and if the analysis is to be applied to firms producing more than one product, then the more sophisticated methods of mathematical programming must be used. These writers also extended the application of linear programming to the more general problem of "goal-programming" or "goal analysis." Mention should also be made of the rapid progress that operations researchers have made in developing meaningful inventory models. Since cash may be viewed as an inventory, financial writers have made extensive use of such models in developing their optimal cash management policies.

In 1960s, the major breakthrough was the development of portfolio theory and its application in financial management. First exposited by Markowitz in 1952, the theory showed how to create frontier of investment portfolios, such that each of them had the greatest possible expected rate of return, given their level of risk. The technique was, computationally, very complex, especially given the technology of the time. A student of Markowitz named William Sharpe developed a simplified

13. H. Martin Weingartner, *Mathematical Programming and the Analysis of Capital Budgeting Problems* (Englewood Cliffs, N.J. : Prentice-Hall, Inc., 1963).
14. Federick S. Hillier, "The Derivation of Probabilistic Information for Evaluation of Risk Investments," *Management Science* 9 (April 1963), pp. 443-457.
15. Harry M. Markowitz, *Portfolio Selection* (New York: John Wiley and Sons, Inc., 1959).

version of the technique which is now referred to as the single-index model. The simplified version made portfolio theory practical, even when managing large numbers of securities. In the 1970s, after techniques for estimating the required inputs to the model were perfected, packaged, and marketed as computer software, modern portfolio theory took off in terms of practical application in the real world. *Now the single-index model is widely employed to allocate investments in the portfolio between individual securities. stocks, while the original, more general model of Markowitz is widely used to allocate investments between types of securities, such as bonds, equity shares, venture capital, and real estate.*

Prior to the dissemination of portfolio theory into the real world, three individuals simultaneously and independently asked themselves the following question: "Suppose everyone managed their investments using portfolio theory and invested in the portfolios on the frontier. How would this impact on the pricing of securities?" In answering this question, Sharpe,[16] Lintner,[17] and Mossin[18] developed what is known as the capital asset pricing model (CAPM). This model reigned as the premier model in the field of finance for nearly 15 years. In addition to finding its way into the elementary textbooks in finance, it became widely used in the real world to measure portfolio performance, value securities, make capital budgeting decisions, and even regulate public utilities. In 1976, however, the model was called into question by Richard Roll,[19] who argued that the model should be discarded because it was impossible empirically to verify its single economic prediction. This controversial issue is still the subject of heated debate today. At the same time, an alternative to the capital asset pricing model was being developed by Steve Ross.[20] This model was called the arbitrage pricing theory. This theory argued that expected return must be related to risk in such a way that no single investor could create unlimited wealth through arbitrage. The theory was less demanding in terms of its assumptions, and both Roll and Ross[21] argue that it's testable; at least in principle. At this point, although it is being called into question, the capital asset pricing model is still widely used in the real world. The arbitrage pricing theory, however, seems to be gaining momentum.

The question of how to price option contracts to buy and sell securities long puzzled researchers in finance until a paper by Fisher Black and Myron Scholes was published in 1973. They argued that you can create a riskless hedged position with

16. Sharpe, W.F., A Simplified Model of Portfolio Analysis, *Management Science* (January 1963).
17. Lintner, J., "The Valuation of Risky Assets and the Selection of Risky Investments in Stock Portfolios and Capital Budgets, *Review of Economics and Statistics*, (February 1965).
18. Mossin J., Equilibrium in Capital Market, *Econometrica*, (October, 1966).
19. Roll, R., "Ambiguity when performance is measured by the Security Market Line," *Journal of Finance*, (September 1978).
20. Ross, S.A., "The Arbitrage Theory of Capital Asset Pricing, "*Journal of Economic Theory*, (December 1976).
21. Roll, R., and Ross, S., "A critical Reexamination of the Empirical Evidence on the Arbitrage Pricing Theory: A Reply, "*Journal of Finance*, (June 1984).

an option by taking a position in both the option and the stock it was written on. It will cost you money to set up the hedge, but since it is riskless, the option must be priced relative to the stock so that you get the riskless rate of return on your hedged investment. They developed a model which would price the option so as to produce this result. The Black-Scholes model has since become extremely popular in the investment community. Options have literally exploded in terms of variety and volume of trading. Option traders are extremely sophisticated. The Black-Scholes model remains the most widely used, but since 1973 many alternative models have been developed. Some of these more sophisticated approaches to valuing options are beginning to affect the behaviour of traders and options prices on the floors of the options exchanges.[22]

The introduction of agency costs and the attendant property issues and their implications though were first noted by Berle and Means[23] had further developed by Marris[24] and Penrose,[25], among others, but it was Jensen and Meckling[26] (JM) who were the first to emphasise the role of financial contracts in creating and controlling agency problems. Agency problems arise because of the impossibility of contracting perfectly on the actions of an agent whose action influence both of his own welfare and that of others. JM drew attention to the implications of managerial discretion for the welfare of shareholders and explained low agency cost could be minimised by more fully aligning the interest of shareholders and managers. They also drew attention to the agency problem that exists between shareholders and other claimholders, particularly bondholders. These consideration led to an informal theory of capital structure based on the minimisation of the sum of these agency costs.

A new concept or motive for behaviour introduced in the corporate finance literature is the non-pecuniary benefit allegedly received by those in control of the corporation. This non-pecuniary benefit has implications for the voting structure of the corporation and has been used to justify the assignment of votes to equity on a one-share-one-vote basis.More significantly the non-pecuniary benefits obtained by the manager of an operating corporation may make him reluctant to liquidate the corporation even when it is socially optimal to do so. The infeasibility of writing contracts that will compel the manager to liquidate at the optimal time has led to the development of a line of theory in which the role of capital structure is to ensure socially optimal liquidation. Aghion and Bolton focused on the role securities in re-

---

22. Black, F., and Scholes, M., "The Pricing of Options and Corporate liabilities, *Journal of Political Economy,* (May-June 1973).
23. Berle A.A. and G.C. Means, *The Modern Corporation and Private Property,* Macmillan (New York), 1932.
24. Marris, R., *The Economic Theory of Managerial Capitalism,* Free Press, (London), 1964.
25. Penrose, E.T., The Theory of the Growth of the Firm, Blakwell (Oxfort), 1959.
26. Jensen, M.C. and W.H. Meckling, "They of the firm: Managerial Behaviour, Agency Costs and Ownership Structive, *Journal of Financial Economics,* (October, 1976), pp. 305-360
27. Aghion, P. and P. Botton, "An Incomplete Contracts Approach to Financial Contracting," *Review of Economic Studies,* (July, 1992) pp. 473-494.

allocating control between different contracting parties in a world of incomplete contracts.[27] The non-pecuniary benefits of control and the consequent tendency of managers to continue projects when it would be socially efficient to liquidate them have provided the basis also of theories of debt maturity and the role of financial intermediaries as monitors.Under the standard assumptions, managerial behviour will be influenced by the choice of compensation function as well as by the threat of replacement. Optimal managerial compensation functions that take account of managerial moral hazard have been extensively analysed. One puzzle that has attracted attention is the heavy dependence of executive compensation on accounting earnings rather than stock prices, since it is the stock price that investors are assumed to want to maximize. Paul[28] shows that stock-based compensation can lead to substantial inefficiency because making compensation depend on the stock price constrains the manner in which information about individual project payoffs enters the compensation function. Perhaps a more general limitation of the moral-hazard-based theories of executive compensation is an overly stylised representation of the moral hazard problem itself as one simply of effort aversion: While this may be a major problem in share-cropping on which much of this literature is based, it may well be that shareholders are more concerned with counteracting managerial risk aversion , discouraging the pursuit of grandiose managerial version at their expense or ensuring that managers distribute the rents earned by the firms to shareholders rather than to employees or other groups. As yet, little attention has been directed to the effect of managerial compensation on the ability of the manager to successfully lead a team of employees, or to bargain with other shareholders in the corporation.

The idea that a firm or manager might care about their reputation for quality, skill, or some other attribute, is a new one in corporate finance. Concern with personal reputation may be a consideration in managerial decision-making. A firm's reputation may affect its access to debt markets and demonstrates how this can influence the investment projects it chooses. Boot, Greenbaum, and Thakor[29] argue that limitations in contracting technology may mean that it is efficient to have some contractual provisions that are legally unenforceable and to rely on reputational considerations for enforcement in most but not all states of the world. They cite as an example the behaviour of mutual fund management companies in making voluntary contributions to restore losses on money market funds. Maksimovic and Titman[30] analyse the interaction between a firm's reputation for product quality and its financial structure. The lack of a legal requirement for a firm to pay preferred dividends, and the *prima facie* interest of equity shareholders to suspend them, appears to be a puzzle that may be explicable in terms of reputational considerations.

---

28. Paul, J., "On the Efficiency of Stock-Based Compensation," *Review of Financial Studies,* (Vol. 5, No., 3, 1992), pp. 471-502.
29. Boot, A.W.A., S.I. Greenbaum, and A.V. Thakor, "Reputation and Discretion in Financial Contracting," *American Economic Review,* (December 1993, 1165-1183.
30. Maksimovic, V. and S. Titman, "Financial Policy and Reputation for Product Quality," *Review of Financial Studies* (Vol. 4 No. 1), 1991, pp. 170-200.

However, a difficulty with the reputational concept as applied to firms is that it is unclear precisely where the reputation resides if a firm is no more than a "nexus of contracts;" what is it about firms that makes some "good types" and can this not be changed by a new management?

While outstanding debt can create adverse incentives for investment, which can only be mitigated by the design of appropriate bond indentures several authors have argued that the risk-increasing incentives of debt can be put to creative use by pre-committing the firm to a particular output policy that will give it a competitive advantage in the product market. Empirical evidence of such effects appears to be lacking, however, and some analysts suggest rather the reverse. An important role of debt is to precommit the firm to pay out its free cash flow rather than wasting it on unprofitable investments, and it is argued that the high leverage employed in many takeovers represents a commitment to dispose of assets. On the other side of the coin, a distinction that is sometimes made between bank debt and publicly held debt is that the former can be renegotiated while the latter is very hard to renegotiate. A firm may sometimes wish to precommit not to renegotiate its debt by issuing public debt.

No subject of study better exemplifies the developments that have taken place in the field of corporate finance than that of bankruptcy. Twenty five years ago bankruptcy was a neglected topic in the theory of corporate finance, being taken as virtually synonymous with liquidation, its unverified costs used o provide counterbalance to tax savings in the analysis of capital structure. The absolute priority rule being implicitly assumed to hold, and the details of the legal code neglected. All this has changed. The capital structure theories that relied on bankruptcy costs implicitly neglected the possibility of informal reorganisations and workouts. Modern analyses pay careful attention to the distinction between reorganisation, liquidation, and bankruptcy, and indeed a major focus of concern has become the conditions under which the current bankruptcy code will lead to efficient liquidation. At the same time, reflecting the trend in all aspects of corporate finance, attention is paid to problems raised by asymmetric information about the value of the firm's assets, strategic behaviour, free-rider problems, and to how they can be ameliorated by the bankruptcy code,and more generally, the incentives of the various parties to a bankruptcy or reorganistion. Noteworthy also is the close attention paid to the details of the bankruptcy code. Going beyond positive analyses of the current code, some authors have even proposed modifications which, they argue, will lead to an increase in efficiency.

The implications of corporate and personal taxation for capital structure and dividend policy were a major focus of research 25 years ago. Attention was first directed to the appropriate personal tax rate for analyzing the benefits of corporate debt and the costs of corporate dividends. Miller[31] transformed the debate on capital structure by introducing personal taxes and allowing for adjustments in the supply of debt in a complete markets model; his perfectly elastic supply was modified to

31. Miller, M.H., "Debt and Taxes, *Journal of Finance*, (May 1977), pp. 261-275.

take account of the limited nature of corporate tax deductions. Relatively little progress has been made in testing the new tax-based theories because of the growing recognition of the non-tax effects of debt.

A central concern of neoclassical finance is the valuation of real assets since this is required to implement the net present value(NPV) criterion. At first, the CAPM seemed to offer a practical procedure for calculating discount rates. However, the CAPM was a single-period model and early efforts to derive workable multi-period versions proved nugatory. Moreover, disenchantment with the results of empirical tests of the CAPM, combined with the effect of the Roll[32] critique, has meant that, whereas once finance managers were able to present the material on capital budgeting with the greatest confidence while feeling comparatively diffident about the usefulness of the irrelevance propositions that constituted our knowledge of financial policy, today's manager is likely to feel that he has more to say about financial policy than about capital budgeting; and while the Arbitrage Pricing Theory represents an elegant and more general alternative to the CAPM, its lack of a generally accepted canonical set of factors has so far impeded its widespread adoption.

However, improved understanding of the economics of valuation is beginning to lead to the application of the martingale pricing principle to the pricing of real assets. Pioneers in this effort include Black[33] and Sick.[34] As a special case of martingale pricing, more rapid progress on a narrower front has been made by carrying over directly the principles of the Black-Scholes option pricing model to the pricing of real assets. The trick here was to find a traded security whose return was perfectly correlated with that of the underlying cash flow claim. The option pricing paradigm was also useful in making possible the assimilation of the two old management science techniques of decision trees and Monte Carlo simulation into the mainstream of financial theory. Monte Carlo simulation could be combined with the martingale pricing principle to value financial options—clearly the same principles applied to the pricing of claims to cash flows from real assets. This solved in principle the problems of what discount rate to use in Monte Carlo analyses and how to evaluate the resulting distribution of discounted present value. The growing literature on "real options" has shown how the problem of what discount rate to apply in using decision trees could be solved in principle; it has also brought renewed attention to the relatively neglected topic of the timing of investment outlays and the strategic aspects of investment decisions.

The neoclassical treatment of the capital budgeting problem as essentially one of valuation neglects the incentives of decision makers. Recent work stresses the incentives of privately informed managers and the organisational responses to these incentives. Thus, managers derive utility from the capital resources under their control, the

32. Roll, R., "A Critique of the Asset Pricing Theory's Tests; Part 1: on Past and Potential Testability of the Theory," *Journal of Financial Economics* (March, 1993), 129-176).
33. Black, F. "A Simple Discounting Rule, *Financial Management,* (Summer, 1988), pp. 7-11.
34. Sick, G.A. "A certainty Equivalent Approach to Capital Budgeting", *Financial Management* (Winter, 1986), 23-32.

convexity of the optimal managerial reward function induces excessive risk-taking. The managerial agency problem in these cases is mitigated by capital rationing.

Thus, the focus on capital rationing has come full circle. Twenty-five years ago, attention was directed to devising optimal procedures for capital budgeting in the presence of capital rationing; these approaches fell out of favour both because the information required to implement them was unlikely to be available in practice and because the evidence of Scholes on the elasticity of the demand for stock was taken to imply that capital rationing was unlikely to be important in practice. However, the debt overhang problem and the adverse selection costs of issuing equity make constraints on *external* capital more plausible, while the rationalisation of limited capital budgets as optimal responses to agency problems makes constraints on internal capital allocations more plausible. This cycle is illustrative of the more general trend in corporate finance, the shift away from attempts to *prescribe* normative rules for decision makers that would assist them to take decisions that are optimal from the point of view of shareholders and towards attempts to *describe* more realistically the way that decisions are actually made.

While impressive progress has been made in enriching the corporate finance paradigm, it would certainly be a mistake to think that the work is near to complete. Undoubtedly. new problems, techniques, and avenues of investigation that are as yet hidden to us will appear. One of the more obvious areas that calls for further analysis is the transactions of corporations in efficient capital markets, where they can be expected to possess no informational advantages. The primary examples are the management of corporate pension funds and the explosive growth of corporate hedging in derivatives markets. The second area in which research effort lags practical developments is the proliferation of corporate security types. While general accounts of securities innovation have been offered, there appears as yet to be no systematic study of the nature of the benefits offered by these and other tailored securities. Related to this is the role of marketing in the sale of securities and the implications for corporate policy of the growing institutionalisation of equity markets, which reduces the cost of transacting for the individual investor at the expense of introducing an additional layer of agency problems. The importance of marketing considerations will be enhanced if the supply of funds to the corporation is not as elastic as once believed, is borne out. Further, the growth of those firms whose major asset consists of human rather than physical capital, prominent examples being in computer software and film production, poses a new challenge to theorists and empiricists alike, for the paradigm example underlying most of our theoretical models is the manufacturing firm, which dominated the growth of the economy around mid-century. The new knowledge-based firms have quite different characteristics, since their major assets are autonomous agents rather than inert machines. Finally, relatively little progress has been made in understanding the international dimension of corporate finance. The continuing trend towards the globalisation of business activities suggests that transnational considerations will become more important in the future.

THE OBJECTIVE OF THE FIRM

Decisions are not made in vacuum. Action of the financial manager related to financial analysis and planning, investment decisions, and financing decisions should be taken to achieve the objectives of the firms' owners, its equity shareholders.What objective(s) *should* guide business decisions making? That is, what *should* financial manager try to achieve for the owners of the firm? To achieve the optimal trade-off among the various objectives, the finance manager is to consider the issues such as the potential conflict between the shareholder and action of the management, ethical issues, corporate social responsibility, environment and sustainable development, etc.

MAXIMISING SHAREHOLDER WEALTH

The most widely accepted primary objective of the firm is to maximise the value of the firm for its owners; that is, to maximise equity shareholder wealth. Equity shareholder wealth is represented by the market price of the equity shares of the firm. The shareholder wealth maximisation goal states that management *should* seek to maximise the *present value* of the *expected future returns* to the owners (that is, shareholders) of the firm. These returns can take the form of periodic dividend payments or proceeds from the sale of the equity shares; *Present value* is defined as the value today of some future payment or stream of payments, evaluated at an appropriate *discount rate.* The discount rate takes into account that returns that are available from alternative investment opportunities during a specific (future) time period. The longer it takes to receive a benefit, such as a cash dividend or price appreciation, the lower the value an investor places on that benefit. In addition, the greater the risk associated with receiving a future benefit, the lower the value an investor places on that benefit. Share prices, the measure of shareholder wealth, reflect the *magnitude, timing,* and *risk* associated with future benefits expected to be received by shareholders.

The objective of shareholder wealth maximisation has a number of distinct **advantages.** *First,* this objective explicitly considers the timing and the risk of the benefits expected to be received from stock ownership. Similarly, managers must consider the elements of timing and risk as they make important financial decisions, such as capital expenditures. In this way, managers can make decisions that will contribute to increasing shareholder wealth. *Second,* it is conceptually possible to determine whether a particular financial decision is consistent with this objective. If a decision made by a firm has the effect to increasing the market price of the firm's stock, it is a good decision. *Third,* shareholder wealth maximisation is an *impersonal* objective. Shareholders who object to a firm's policies are free to sell their shares *under more favourable terms* (that is, at a higher price) *than are available under any other strategy* and invest their funds elsewhere. If an investor who has a consumption pattern or risk preference that is not accommodated by the investment, financing, and dividend decisions of that firm, the investor will be able to sell his or her shares in that firm at the best price and purchase shares in a company that more closely meets the investor's needs.

If the managers of a firm accept the goal of maximising shareholder wealth, how should they achieve this objective? To satisfy its commitments to its shareholders, the firm must allocate its resources efficiently in order to show a good return on its investments within the appropriate constraints of risk. If the firm wastes money on overly risky investments or fails to take advantage of profitable opportunities, the stockholders will sell the stock, thus depressing its price. If the firm chooses the wrong type of financing or overburdens the firm with debt, the stockholders will also sell out, even if the debt was used to finance profitable investments. Notice that this corporate goal directly affects the policy decisions of what to invest in and how to finance the investments. When this goal is in force, the objectives of the stockholders and management are compatible.

Notice also that the stockholder wealth maximisation objective is highly compatible with the concept of the perpetual life of the firm. Since the present price of the stock reflects the future benefits to which stockholders are entitled because of their proportional ownership in the firm, management's decisions cannot emphasise short-term profits at the expense of the longer-term health of the firm.

Financial theorists favour the wealth maximisation objective because it serves as a focal point for all the considerations in operating the firm and it is an easily observed measure. Theoretically, if the firm is not making the right investment or financial decisions, the stock price will sink. If it is making the right decisions, its stock price will rise.

There are problems with implementing this objective as a measure of performance. Foremost is the fact that share price is subject to outside influences beyond management's control. A slump in the economy could depress stock prices, yet management has no control over the economy in general. Daily fluctuations in stock prices sometimes draw too much attention from management and distract them, to the detriment of the firm's profit plan. Management may feel frustrated and disillusioned if the stock price performance does not seem to reflect what they consider to be a good effort. While it is a useful goal, shareholder wealth maximisation may be something more to strive for than to achieve.

PROFIT MAXIMISATION

One might be tempted to argue that managers will maximise shareholders wealth if they maximise the profits of the firm. After all, profit maximisation is the predominant objective that emerges from static microeconomic models of the firm. Unfortunately, the profit maximisation objective has too many shortcomings to provide consistent guidance to the practicing manager. Before discussing some of these shortcomings, it is useful to highlight one important managerial decision rule that emerges from the microeconomic profit maximisation model. In order to maximise profits, we learned in microeconomics that a firm should expand output to the point where the marginal (additional) cost (MC) of the last unit produced and sold just equals the marginal revenue (MR) received. To move beyond that output level will result in greater additional costs than additional revenues and hence lower profits.

To fail to produce up to the point where MC = MR results in a lower level of total profits than is possible by following the rule. This fundamental rule, that an economic action should be continued up to the point where the marginal revenue (benefit) just equals the marginal cost, offers excellent guidance for financial managers dealing with a wide range of problems. For example, we shall see that the basic capital expenditure analysis model simply is an adaptation of the MC=MR rule. Other applications appear in the working capital management area and the capital structure area.

From the perspective of economic theory, profit maximisation is simply a criteria of economic efficiency. When markets are reasonably competitive, profits provide a yardstick by which economic performance can be judged. There is also broad agreement that under idealised conditions (generally referred to as perfect competition), where all prices accurately reflect true values and consumers are well informed, profit maximising behaviour by firms leads to an efficient allocation of resources and maximum social welfare. As financial management is concerned with the efficient use of an important economic resource, namely, capital funds, a good case can be made for profit maximisation to serve as the basic criterion for the decisions made by the financial managers of privately owned and controlled firms. In a broad sense, it does. But first it has to be transformed in order to provide the financial manager with an operationally useful guideline.

The reason for such a transformation is that the profit maximisation does not take account of several real world problems we encounter when we seek to make actual decisions about the efficient use of capital funds. Without these transformations, we cannot implement the basic idea which underlies the rationale of Adam Smith's "invisible hand." Let us see why if the profit maximisaiton objective does not provide the proper guidance to managers seeking to maximise shareholder wealth, what rules should these managers follow". It is important to recognise that the maximisation of shareholder wealth is a market concept, not an accounting concept. Managers should attempt to maximise the *market value* of the company's shares, not the accounting or *book value* per share. The book value reflects the historic cost of assets, not the earning capacity of those assets. Also, the book value does not consider the risk associated with the assets.

What factors determine the market value of a company's equity shares? There are three major factors : *The risk of the cash flows*, the *timing* of these cash flows; and the *amount* of the cash flows. *First*, cash flow relates to the actual cash generated or paid by the firm. Only cash can be used to acquire assets, and only cash can be used to make valuable distributions to investors. In contrast, the accounting system focuses primarily on a matching over time of the historic, cost-based revenues and expenses of a company, resulting in a bottom-line earnings figure. But accounting earnings often are misleading because earnings do not reflect the actual cash inflows and outflows of the firm. For example, an accountant records depreciation expense on an asset each period over the depreciable life of that asset over time. However, depreciation itself results in no cash outflow. The entire cash outflow occurred when the asset originally was purchased.The market value of the share is influenced by the perceived risk of the cash flows it is expected to generate. Most rational investors will demand a higher rate of return on an investment when greater risk is associated with the expected returns from that investment. Thus, financial managers also must consider the risk of the cash flows expected to be generated by the firm because investors will reflect this risk in their valuation of the entreprise. The profit maximisation ignores the risk constraints letting management undertake all profitable investments regardless of the associated risk which they might bring to the firm. For having a chemical plant in a politically unstable country that is threatening to expropriate investment without compensation would add considerable risk to the firm's operations. it may not be worth that risk, despite its potential profitability. *Second,* management would ignore the risks associated with the financing of the investment. As long as the investment was profitable, management might borrow in excess, overburdening the firm,just to add profit. In terms of the shareholder wealth model, this would defeat the firm's purpose because shareholders would sell their shares and depress the share price. On the other hand, management's improper use of too little debt, forcing the firm to sell many additional shares to finance would dilute the present shareholders' proportional wealth, not a desirable part of any corporate objective. *Thirdly,* profit-maximisation criterion cannot take account of the fact that timing of benefits expected from investment varies widely. In practice, most investment and financing decisions involve complex patterns of cash flows over many periods. Simply adding the cash flows over time and picking the alternative with the highest total does not solve the problem, because money has time value. Cash flows in early years are valued more highly than equivalent cash flows in later years. The market value of a share is influenced also by the timing of cash flows. If faced with the opportunity of receiving ₹ 100 today or ₹ 100 three years from today,the investor would surely choose the ₹ 100 today, because the investor could invest that ₹ 100 for three years and accumulate substantially more than ₹ 100 in three years. Thus, financial managers must consider both the magnitude of the cash flows they expect to generate and the timing of these cash flows because investors will reflect these dimensions of return in their valuation of the enterprise. Another major shortcoming of the simple profit maximisation criteria concerns ambiguity. Measuring profits is not easy, and profit figures can vary widely depending on the accounting conventions employed.

Despite the excellent insights it offers financial managers, the profit maximisation model is not useful as the central decision-making model for the firm for several limitations. *First,* the standard microeconomic model of profit maximisation is *static;* that is, it lacks a time dimension. Profit maximisation as a goal offers no explicit basis for comparing long-term and short-term profits. Major decisions made by financial managers, however, *must* reflect the time dimension. For example, capital expenditure decisions, which are central to the finance function, have a long-term impact on the performance of the firm. Financial managers must make trade-offs between short-run and long-run returns in conjunction with capital investment decisions.

The *second* limitation has to do with the *definition of profit*. Generally accepted accounting principles result in literally hundreds of definitions of profit for a firm, because of the latitude permitted firms in recognising and accounting for costs and revenues. Even if we could agree on the appropriate accounting definition of profits, it is not clear whether a firm should attempt to maximise total profit, the rate of profit, or earnings per share (EPS).

Consider Ricky Auto Industries (RAI), a firm with 10 crore equity shares issued that currently earns a profit of ₹ 20 crore after tax. If the firm sells an additional 1 crore equity shares and invests the proceeds to earn ₹ 1.5 crore per year, the total profit of the firm will increase from ₹ 20 crore to ₹ 21.50 crore . However, *are shareholders better off* ? Prior to the new equity issue, earnings per share were ₹ 2. After the new equity issue of 1 crore shares, the earnings per share declined to ₹1.95. Although total profit has increased, earnings per share have declined. Equity shareholders are not better off from this action.

This example might lead to conclude that financial manager should seek to maximise earnings per share (for a given number of shares issued). This too, can lead to misleading actions. For example, consider a firm with total costs of ₹ 100 crore at the start of the year, the firm financed entirely with equity (1 crore equity shares issued). After tax earnings are ₹ 15 crore, resulting a return on equity (ROE) of 15 percent, and earnings per share are ₹ 15. The firm decides to retain two-third (i.e. ₹ 10 crore) of this years earnings (increasing assets and equity to ₹ 110 crore) and pay out the balance of ₹ 5 crore in dividend to the equity shareholders. Next year the firm's earnings increases to ₹ 16.25 crore, resulting in earnings per share of ₹ 16.25. *Are shareholders better off because of the decision of the financial manager to reinvest ₹ 10 crore into the firm?* Although the earnings per share has increased from ₹ 15 to ₹ 16.25 per share, the realised return on equity actually has declined from 15 percent to 14.773 percent. In essence, the financial manager of the company has reinvested ₹ 10 crore of equity shareholders' money to earn a return of only 12.5 percent (₹ 16.25 crore of additional earnings divided by ₹ 10 crore of additional investment).

The *third* major limitation associated with the profit maximisation objective is that it provides no direct way for financial managers to consider the risk associated with alternative decisions. For example, two projects generating identical future expected cash flows and requiring identical outlays may be vastly different with respect to the risk of the expected cash flows. Similarly, it often is possible for a firm to increase its earnings per share by increasing the proportion of debt financing used in the firm's capital structure. However, leverage induced increases in EPS come at the cost of increased financial risk. The financial markets will recognise the increased risk of financial distress that accompanies increases in debt financing and will value the resulting EPS accordingly.

Though profits are a necessary conditions for the success of any firm, but they are only one ingredient in the total picture when formulating a corporate objective. Profit maximisation, therefore emphasises only a partial condition for success. Shareholder wealth maximisation is a total picture, although it is difficult to interpret because of its complexity.

BEHAVIOURAL OBJECTIVE

If private wealth maximisation is no longer a necessity, what alternative corporate objectives might the unencumbered modern executive pursue? One possibility suggested by Herbert A. Simon that, because management has very little confidence in estimates of the future returns which may be achieved by the company, it may not attempt to maximise profit but should focus to attain a certain level or rate of profit. As a result of this belief Simon formulated the concept of "satisficing." He argued as follows:

> *In most psychological theories the motive to act stems from drives, and action terminates when the drive is satisfied. Moreover, the conditions for satisfying a drive are not necessarily fixed, but may be specified by an aspiration level that itself adjusts upward or downward on the basis of experience. If we seek to explain business behaviour in terms of this theory, we must expect the firm's goals to be not maximising profit, but attaining a certain level or rate of profit. Holding a certain share of the market or a certain level of sales. Firms would try to "satisfice" rather than to maximise.*[35]

Management informally establishes certain minimum acceptable standards of performance in terms of things like market share, sales growth, and profits, and then tries to do a satisfactory job in meeting all of these standards. Exceeding the standards is fine, but it is not the primary objective.

A related view of the modern manager is offered by Gordon Donaldson.[36] As he sees it, corporate managers are interested primarily in the continued health and strength of their company. In this capacity, management acts much like a mediator resolving the conflicting interests impinging on the company, including those of employees, shareholders, customers, creditors, and the government. In the extremes, management's concern with shareholders is only that they are sufficiently satisfied that proxy fight do not develop, and that the company can raise the new equity capital on reasonable terms, should the need occur. If they do more than this for the shareholder, it would unnecessarily reduce the company's ability to meet other pressing needs and would ultimately weaken the firm.

Satisficing is justified as the only operational goal that can be used by management without exerting undue strain upon the organisation and its ability to work as a cehesive team. As on operational device, satisficing tends to resolve the conflicts among the operating goals. This is particularly true of the conflicts among the internal goals of the firm. For example, the marketing department may want to increase sales at the expense of return on investment. A satisfactory compromise could restore the harmony between the exponents of each objective, although it would sacrifice maximising either one. Further justification is that satisficing is the

---

35. Herbert A. Simon; "Theories of Decision-Making in Economics and Behavioural Science," *American Economic Review*, June 1929, pp. 253.
36. Gordon Donaldson: Financial Goals Management vs. Stockholders *Harvard Business Review*, May-June, 1963.

best we can expect from managers who must make decisions within the constraints of risk. They cannot maximise in the face of uncertainty because the penalties for failure are severe, whereas the panalty for a mediocre job is practically nonexistent.

The major problem with satisficing is that it partially ignores risk, return on investment, profit, dilution of earnings per share, correct financing, proper resource allocation, and the rest of the consideration associated with the maximisation goals. Further, it is vulnerable to competing firms that do maximise when they enter the industry. For this reason, satisficing is more common among well entrenched companies in industries where entry is difficult.

Satisficing firms tend to have vaguely stated corporate goals which emphasise the *status quo* and do not really serve as a focal point for all the considerations that should go into decising what to invest in and how to finance it. Frequently the goals are expressed in terms of a market share or some other measure of size, rather than profitability, for it is important to a satisficing manager that there be no signs of deterioration in the firm's position of importance. Deterioration of importance means loss of prestige and increased vulnerability to attack. Provided there is a modicum of forward progress and no deterioration relative to other firms within the industry, inertia works in the satisficing manager's favour. Satisficing does not allow guidance form the stockholders; once their minimum requirements are pacified, they are forgotten. As a consequence, the stock price of the firm may suffer if stockholders find alternative shares that maximise their position.

On a slightly different tack, William J. Baumol suggested that firm seek to *maximise sales,* that is, total revenue; subject to a minimum profit constraint.[37] An objective of this nature is quite likely in practice, especially if top management is marketing oriented. A motivation for this objective follows naturally from the classic bureaucratic practice of empire building. To the extent that feelings of personal power and prestige are related to the size of the operation that a manager controls, manager will be anxious to increase their empire. One measures of a company's empire is its sales volume. The result of such an objective is that sales revenue could possibly increase at the expense of profits. This is illustrated in Figure-1 where *BB'* represents the profit constraint imposed by management. In this case a total profit *b* will result when total revenue, ₹y, is maximised at a sales volume of *Y* subject to the profit constraint *BB.'* If the maximisation of profit was regarded as the objective of the firms, it would sell *X* units and receive ₹x in sales revenue. However, Baumol argues that management will set a profit constraint which it considers as a satisfactory level of profit and will continue to expand sales provided profit does not fall below this constraint.

37. William J. Baumol; Business Behaviour, Value and growth (New York Harcourt, Brace and world Inc., 1967).

FIGURE-1

MAXIMISATION OF !SALES !REVENUE SUBJECT TO A PROFIT CONSTRAINT

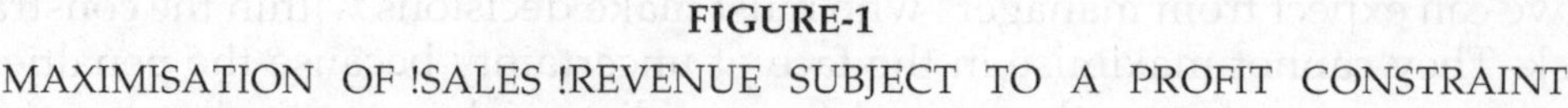

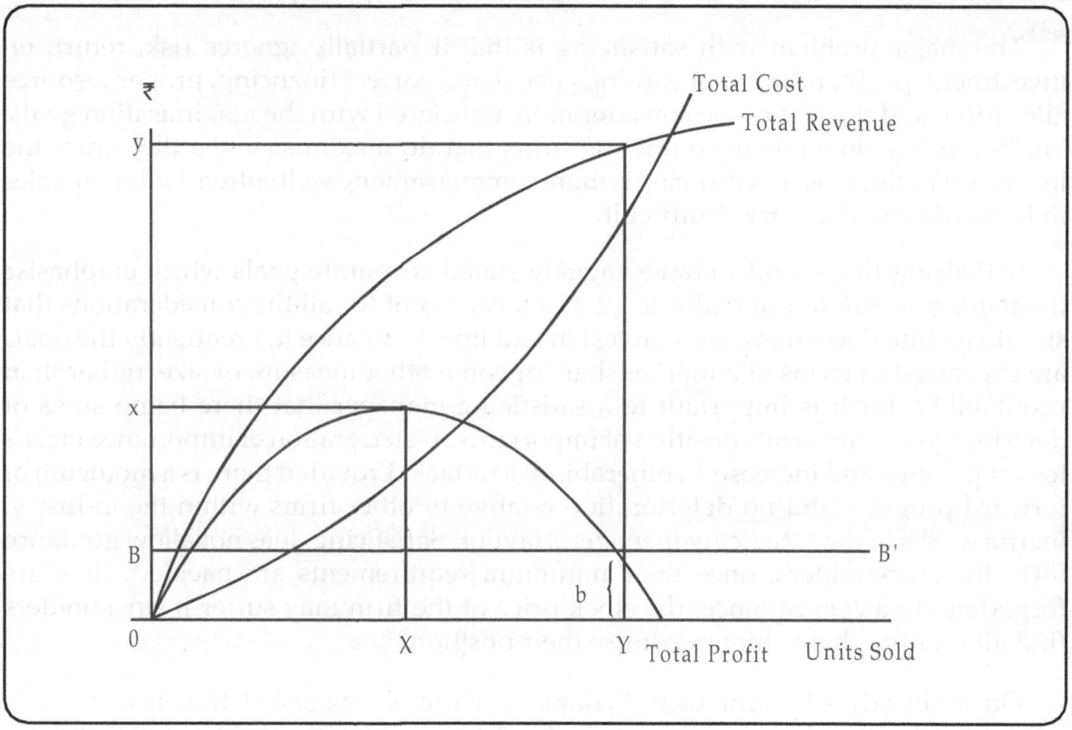

DIVERGENT OBJECTIVES

The goal of shareholder wealth maximisation specifies how financial decisions *should* be made. It has been observed that, in practice, not all management decisions are consistent with this objective. For example, Bennett Stewart has developed an index of managerial performance that measures the success of managers in achieving a goal of shareholder wealth maximisation.[38] Stewart's performance measure considers the difference between the return a firm earns on its invested capital and the cost of that capital. The "market value added" measure used by Stewart is equal to the difference between the market value of a firm and the resources that have been historically invested in the enterprise.

Robin Marris has argued that business behaviour will conform to the manager's own goals. Thus, he has argued that "managers are particularly concerned with the growth rate of the firm subject to minimum constraints on security."[39] Marris ties management's goals of power prestige and salary to the rate of growth of the company, and the desire for security to the rate of return on its assets. He observed

38. G. Bennet Steward, III, *The Quest for Value*, Harper and Row (New York), 1990, Chapter 5.
39. Robin Morris, "A Model of the Managerial Enterprise," *The Quarterly Journal of Economics*, vol. 77, no. 2, May 1963, p. 186.

that managers have a strong and pressing drive toward achievement. Further achievement in the form of promotion is usually restricted for managers in the higher echelons, since transfers from one company to another are difficult, and retirement or sacking of superiors is not common. A manager can, however, gain promotion if the company is growing. The constraint in this model is the rate of return on the company's assets. If, as a result of excessive expansion, the rate of return on the company's assets is permitted to fall to a low level, then the probability of failure becomes too high and the company may be subjected to takeover bids. If a bid is successful, the company's management structure is likely to be reconstructed and the existing managers may be either demoted or dismissed. Thus Marris' managers aim to maximise the firm's rate of growth subject to a minimum rate of return on its assets. This is similar to the position outlined by Baumol. Thus "in place of maximum revenue subject to minimum profit constraint we put maximum growth rate of revenue subject to the same constraint.[40]

In other words, there often may be a divergence between the shareholder wealth maximisation goal and the *actual* goals pursued by management. What is the reason for this divergence?The primary reason has been attributed to *separation of ownership and control* (management) in corporations. Separation of ownership and control has permitted managers to pursue goals more consistent with their own self-interests, subject, of course, to the constraint that they satisfy shareholders sufficiently to maintain control of the corporation. Instead of seeking to maximise some objective (such as shareholder wealth), management is said to "satisfice" or seek acceptable levels of performance, while maximising their own welfare.

Maximisation of their own personal welfare (or utility) may lead managers to be concerned with long-run survival (job security). The concern for long-run survival may lead management to minimise (or limit) the amount of risk incurred by the firm, since unfavourable outcomes can lead to their dismissal or possible bankruptcy for the firm. Likewise, the desire for job security is cited as one reason why management often opposes takeover offers (mergers) by other companies. Giving senior management "golden parachute" contracts to compensate them if they lose their positions as the result of a merger is one approach designed to ensure that they will act in the interests of shareholders in merger decisions, rather than in their own interests. Other firms expect managers and directors to have a significant ownership stake in the firm. Many firms provide to a wide range of key managers significant stock options that increase in value with improvements in the firm's performance in an attempt to align their interests more closely with those of shareholders.

AGENCY PROBLEMS

The existence of divergent objectives between owners and managers is one example of a class of problems arising from agency relationships. *Agency relationships* occur when one or more individuals (the principals) hire another individual the *(agent)* to perform a service on behalf of the *principals*.[41] In an agency relationship,

40. *Ibid.,* p. 205.

decision-making authority is often delegated to the agent from the principals. In the context of finance, two of the most important agency relationships are the relationship between shareholders (owners) and managers and the relationship between shareholders and creditors.

Inefficiencies that arise because of agency relationships have been called *agency problems.* These problems occur because each party to a transaction is assumed to act in a manner consistent with maximising his or her own utility (welfare). The example cited earlier of the concern by management for long-run survival (job security), rather than shareholder wealth maximisation, is an agency problem. Another example is the consumption of on-the-job perquisites by managers who have no (or only a partial) ownership interest in the firm. Shirking by managers is also an agency-related problem.

These agency problems give rise to a number of *agency costs,* which are incurred by shareholders to minimise agency problems. Examples of agency costs include: (1) Expenditures to structure the organisation in such a way as to minimise the incentives for management to take actions contrary to shareholder interests, such as providing a portion of management's compensation in the form of stock of the corporation. (2) Expenditures to monitor management's actions, such as paying for audits of managerial performance and internal audits of the firm's expenditures. (3) Bonding expenditures to protect the owners from managerial dishonesty. (4) The opportunity cost of lost profits arising from complex organisational structures that prevent management from making timely responses to opportunities.

Managerial motivations to act in the interest of shareholders include the structure of their compensation package, the threat of dismissal, and the threat to takeover by a new groups of owners. Financial theory has shown that agency problems and their associated costs can be reduced greatly if the financial markets operate efficiently. Some agency problems can be reduced by the use of complex financial contracts. Remaining agency problems give rise to costs that show up as a reduction in the value of the firm's shares in the marketplace.

Another potential agency conflict arises from the relationship between a company's owners and its creditors. Creditors have a fixed financial claim on the company's resources in the form of long-term debt, bank loans, commercial paper, leases,accounts payable, wages payable, taxes payable, an so on. Because the returns offered to creditors are fixed whereas the returns to shareholders are variable, conflicts may arise between creditors and owners. For example, owners may attempt to increase the riskiness of the company's investments in hopes of receiving greater returns.

41. See Amir Barnca R. Haugen, and L. Senbet, *Agency Problems and Financial Contracting* (Englewood Cliffs, N.J. Prentice-Hall, 1985), for an overview of the agency problem issue. See also Michael Jensen and William Meckling. "Theory of the Firm: Managerial Behaviour, Agency Costs, and Ownership Structure," *Journal of Financial Economics* (October 1976): 305-360, and Eugene Fama, "Agency Problems and the Theory of the Firm." *Journal of Political Economy* (April 1980): 288-307.

When this occurs, bondholders suffer because they do not have an opportunity to share in these higher returns.

In order to protect their interests, creditors often insist on certain protective covenants in a company's bond indentures. These covenants take many forms, such as limitations on dividend payments, limitations on the type of investiments (and divestitures) the company can undertake, poison puts or buy back,[42] and limitations on the issuance of new debt. The constraints on the owner-managers may reduce the potential market value of the firm. In addition to these constraints, bondholders also will demand a higher fixed return to compensate for risks not adequately covered by bond indenture restrictions.

ETHICAL ISSUES

Today, more and more firms are directly addressing the issue of ethics by establishing corporate ethics policies and guidelines and by requiring employee compliance with them. The implementation of pro-active ethics programme is expected to enhance corporate value. Some financial decisions with important ethical dimensions, such as the impact of leveraged buyouts (LBOs)on employees and bondholders or the loan administration policies apparent in many failed savings and loan institutions, command national, high-level attention. However, financial managers encounter day-to-day decisions that have important ethical dimensions. For example, as a new bank loan officer, should you recommend approval of a loan to a longtime friend, even though he does not quite meet the normal loan standards of he bank? As an account executive for a brokerage firm, should you recommend to your clients the securities of firms with poor management records? As a division manager being evaluated in part on a return-on-assets calculation, should you lease assets to keep them out of the asset base for evaluation purposes and thereby enhance your apparent performance? Should your firm aggressively use allowable accounting practices to mask a fundamentally deteriorating level of performance?

This brief sampling of the areas of business and financial management decision making possessing important ethical dimensions provides a feel for the breadth of ethical issues facing financial managers. Most cases, the answers to these questions are not clear-cut. Actual decision making is very complex and involves many trade-offs among parties with competing interests. However, explicitly recognising the costs and benefits associated with each of these decisions and making the decision in an atmosphere of balanced objectivity and fairness can help financial managers avoid apparent or real breaches of their ethical trust.

An important concern for financial managers, who are entrusted with the resources of shareholders and are expected to maximise the value of these resources, is: *How does a concern for ethics in the practice of financial management impact the goal of*

42. A position put or buy-back is an option contained in a bond indenture that permits the bondholder to sell the bond back to the issuing company at face value under certain circumstances such as a leveraged buyout that raises the risk for existing debt holders.

shareholder wealth maximisation? Firms that expect employees to act according to a code of ethics in their business dealings can expect to have reduced litigation and damages expenses. High ethical standards are respected by customers and valued by investors. One could argue that ethical business dealings build long-term value for investors, whereas breaches of standards of business ethics may provide short-term gains at the expense of future returns. Such action, by maintaining and enhancing cash flow and reducing perceived risk (as a result of greater investor confidence), are expected to positively effect that firm's share price. *Ethical behaviour is therefore viewed as a necessary for* achievement of the firm's goal of owners wealth maximisation.

SOCIAL RESPONSIBILITY

Should businesses operate strictly in shareholders' best interests, or are they also partly responsible for the welfare of society at large? There is a conflict between the corporation as an entity in society and as a device for maximising shareholder wealth. The traditional view maintains that the corporation's sole responsibility is to maximise the stockholders' welfare, because the firm will then achieve the most efficient allocation of resources for society as a whole. The argument assumes in its more complete form that certain resources, such as air and water, are held in common ownership by all citizens and that society should therefore bear the cost of these resources when the firm uses them. In turn, the company contributes to the general welfare by producing goods and services in the most efficient manner. Corporations continue to expect that the state will provide roads and educate the labour force. They may expect the state to absorb such costs as the retraining of workers who have been displaced by the corporation's installation of labour saving devices. They may expect help in controlling industrial pollution.

The opposing view sees the corporation as a grant or trust form the state designed to be a relatively efficient way of increasing productivity. As such, it has duties to fulfill to its employes, suppliers, consumers, stockholders, and the general public. Like any individual, it must be a good citizen. It must not dirty the air or foul the streams, and it must not injure the position of any of its constituencies. It must be forced to take on this social responsibility since the competitive system of free enterprise no longer forces corporations to absorb the cost, but allows them to pass such expenses on to the society through oligopoly (a few firms who control their industry) and monopoly pricing.[43] In addition, it is sometimes argued that the corporation owes a debt to society and should bear the cost of some of the external resources it enjoys, such as the roads and the education of its employees.

Exactly how far the corporation social responsibility should go is debatable.[44] It could range anywhere from self-regulation designed to avoid injuring the position of any of its constituencies to the championing of political and moral causes. It has been

43. James Mc Guigan and R. Charles Moyer, *Managerial Economics: Private and Public Sector Decision Analysis,* Dryden Press, Hinsdale, III., 1975, Ch. 20.
44. John G. Simon, Charles W. Powers, and Jon P. Gunneman, *The Ethical Investor,* Yale University Press, New Haven, 1972, p. 26; and Gilbert Burch, "the Hazards of Corporate Responsibility," Fortune, June 1973, 114ff.

suggested that there exists at least a *moral minimum*, which implies that the corporation must at least avoid consciously creating moral and social injury. Perhaps this includes taking affirmative action to correct that which is already present, but it certainly excludes the formulation and perpetration of any new social injury. Corporate social responsibility can also include refusing to cooperate with the government when its requests conflict with *moral righteousness* and making reforms within the corporation that alleviate social injury to one of the corporation's constituencies.

Regardless of what the corporation finally decides is its social responsibility, there will be a conflict among the goals. Any action which the corporation takes to alleviate social injury will cost the firm, for it will now bear the cost that society formerly bore for what the firm formerly used as a free resources. This cost conflicts with profit maximisation, shareholder wealth maximisation, managerial welfare maximisation, and satisficing objectives. Yet the finance manager will have to weigh social responsibility in investment and financing decisions, if nowhere else but in deciding whether to buy pollution-control equipment or to participate in government programmes. To the other major categories of possible corporate objectives, we now have to add social responsibility. And if the overall social and economic policy is an enlightened one, wealth-maximisation by each individual enterprise will also maximise social-economic welfare. If the social-economic framework is not enlightened or wrong, maximum economic welfare cannot be achieved, but the highest attainable level which can be consistently achieved is that associated with an individual company policy based on maximising wealth.

ASSUMPTIONS UNDERLYING THE FINANCIAL OBJECTIVE

A specific problem in the area of finance is the separation of the decisions by a company's managers and the consequences of their decisions, as determined by investors' reactions in the market place (i.e. the effect on the company's share price). The investment, financing and dividend decisions of a company have an effect on investors' expectations of future returns. The investors then choose whether to act in the market place. This pattern of events is represented diagrammatically in Figure 2.

FIGURE 2

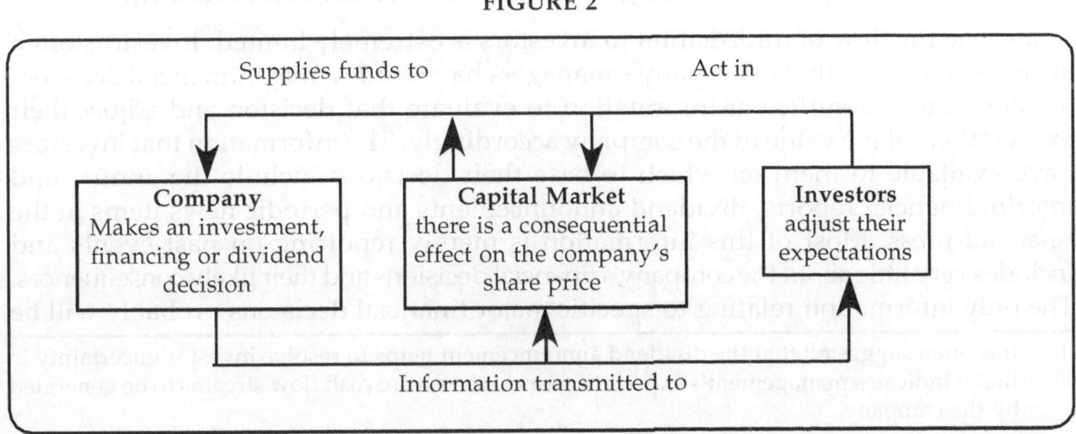

In a situation of perfect certainty, the objective of maximising the market value of the company to its shareholders is operational. A company makes a decision knowing that the decision will cause the value of the company to increase by a specific amount. The company conveys the information to the investors, who also realise hat the company is more valuable by the same specific amount. As a consequence, they act in the capital market causing an increase in the share price which reflects the increased value of the company. For example, a company with one crore shares on issue undertakes a new project which increases, in present value terms, the worth of the company by one ₹ 10 crore. Investors receive the information that the company has undertaken the project and realise that the company is now worth an additional ₹ 10 crore. They then act in the capital market and the company's share price increases by one rupee.

In real world, there are *three reasons* why the chain of events described above may fail to eventuate. *First*, neither management nor investors have perfect certainty. We have previously described how management can evaluate each investment, financing, or dividend decision in relation to its likely effect on the company's share price. The impact of any one of these decisions on the share price is determined by the extent to which the decision alters the cash flow stream generated by the company and/or the risk characteristics of the company. Management cannot be certain of either the effect a particular decision will have on the company's cash flow stream or the way the decision will affect the investors' expectations with regard to future cash flows.[45] In the previous example where there was perfect certainty, the management knew that by undertaking a project the company's net worth would increase by ₹ 10 crore. However, tin reality management can only have expectations about the outcome. Even more importantly, management is not certain that investors will concur with its expectations. For example, investors may expect that the project will reduce the company's net worth by a five crore of rupees causing the share price to fall. Because it is investors and not management who ultimately determine the value of the company in the capital market, management cannot be certain that actively (and even correctly) pursuing a goal of maximising the market value of the company to its shareholders, will ensure that the goal is achieved, at least in the short run.

Second, the flow of information to investors is extremely limited. Investors often are not even aware that a company's managers have made a major financial decision, let alone possess sufficient information to evaluate that decision and adjust their expectations of the value of the company accordingly. The information that investors have available to them on which to base their decisions include the annual and interim financial reports, dividend announcements and periodic news items in the financial press. Most of this information is merely reporting on past events and includes very little about the company's financial decisions and their likely consequences. The only information relating to specific major financial decisions probably will be

45. It is often suggested that the dividend announcement helps to resolve investor uncertainty in that it indicates management's expectations as to the future cash flow streams to be generated by the company.

contained in the directors' report in the company's annual report and in press reports which are generally confined to major decisions made by the larger companies. Of course, the dividend decision is public knowledge and certain other financial decisions such as share issues are also known. However, in most instances (with the exception of the dividend decision), there is insufficient information to enable investors to undertake an analysis similar to that undertaken by management. Therefore, investors' awareness of the consequences of major financial decisions tends to lag behind those decisions by a considerable period as the investors generally have to wait for evidence of the effect of these decisions on the company's cash flow stream.

Third, the goal of maximising the market value of the company to its shareholders presupposes that investors evaluate the value of each company in isolation. This means that we are taking a partial equilibrium approach as we assume that investors evaluate the expected cash flows and risk characteristics of each company independently in order to determine its value. However, investors generally hold shares in a number of companies. The aim of such investors is to obtain the maximum return for any given level of risk from their whole portfolio of investments. This suggests that investors do not value their investment in each company in isolation, but rather they value their portfolio of investments.

The implication of portfolio theory is that investors should hold shares in all companies, that is, they should hold the market portfolio. It follows that management should make decisions which are aimed at maximising the market value of the market portfolio. If we relate this objective to the investment decision, it means that management must work out the interdependencies between each proposed investment and all other possible investments before it can decide which investments should be undertaken. The difficulties that this would entail are so great as to make this approach unfeasible.[46] Further, investors usually hold shares in a limited number of companies rather than in the market portfolio. Consequently, management does not have a clearly defined portfolio whose value it can aim to maximise.

It appears, therefore, that the best that management can achieve is the maximisation of the market value of the company's shares. If the market value of the company's shares is maximised and an investor in the company receives an income stream which is consistent with his investment preferences, then he will be satisfied. If, on the other hand, the market value of the company's shares is maximised but the income stream generated is not consistent with the investor's investment preferences, then the investor can generate the maximum cash flow by selling the shares and investing all or part of the proceeds in assets which will generate the required income stream (provided these market opportunities exist). By maximising the market value of the company's shares, management is providing an investor who is unhappy with the income stream generated by the company with the opportunity of selling his shares at the highest possible market price.

46. Robert W. Johnson, *Capital Budgeting,* Wadsworth Publishing Co., Belmont, California, 1970, pp. 133-134.

MANAGERIAL ACTIONS TO INFLUENCE VALUE

The question of what objective firms actually do pursue is a comparatively new one, for until the turn of this century, competition in the product market and pecuniary self-interest on the part of owner-managers assured that private-wealth maximisation was the only goal. The separation of ownership and control prevalent in many modern corporations and weakening competition in some over product market have led some persons to argue that share-price maximisation is obsolete for the modern corporation. Suggested alternatives include "satisficing" and sales maximisation. However, a careful examination of the empirical evidence shows that most firms appear to have a multidimensional goals. The two most important factors appear to be profitability and risk. The selection of the combination of expected profit and risk which is appropriate for a firm's shareholders is not an easy task, but by taking shareholders' interest as the goal of the firm, an operational method can be found for incorporating both risk and profitability into the firm's goal function. Accordingly, the financial manager focus on making financial decision that can improve the amount, the timing, or the risk profile of a firms cash flow stream, thus leading to increase in shareholder wealth.

How can managers influence the magnitude, timing, and risk of the cash flows expected to be generated by the firm in order to maximise shareholder wealth? Many factors ultimately influence the magnitude, timing, and risk of a firm's cash flows and thus the price of the firm's stock. Some of these factors are related to managers. Other factors can be directly manipulated by the managers. Figure-3 illustrates the factors affecting stock prices. The top panel enumerates some of the factors in the economic environment that have an impact on the strategic decisions managers can make. The economic environment factors largely are outside that direct control of managers, but managers must be aware of how these factors affect the policy decisions under the control of management. The policy decision areas are enumerated in the next panel. Managers make choices regarding the products to be produced, the technology used to produce them, the marketing effort and distribution channels, and the selection of employees and their compensation. In addition, managers establish investment policies, the ownership structure of the firm, the capital structure (use of debt) of the firm, working capital management policies, and dividend policies. The decisions made in these key policy area determine the amount, timing, and risk of the firm in relation to alternative streams of cash flows expected from other firms and ultimately establish the price of the firm's stock. The value of a firm's stock is influenced at any point in time by general conditions in the financial markets, including the level of interest rates, anticipated inflation rates, and the level of investor optimism regarding the future. Financial market conditions also affect the major policy decisions made by management.

It appears, therefore, that the best that management can achieve is the maximisation of the market value of the company's shares. If the market value of the company's shares is maximised and an investor in the company receives an income stream which is consistent with his investment preferences, then he will be satisfied. If, on

FIGURE 3

FACTORS AFFECTING SHARE PRICES

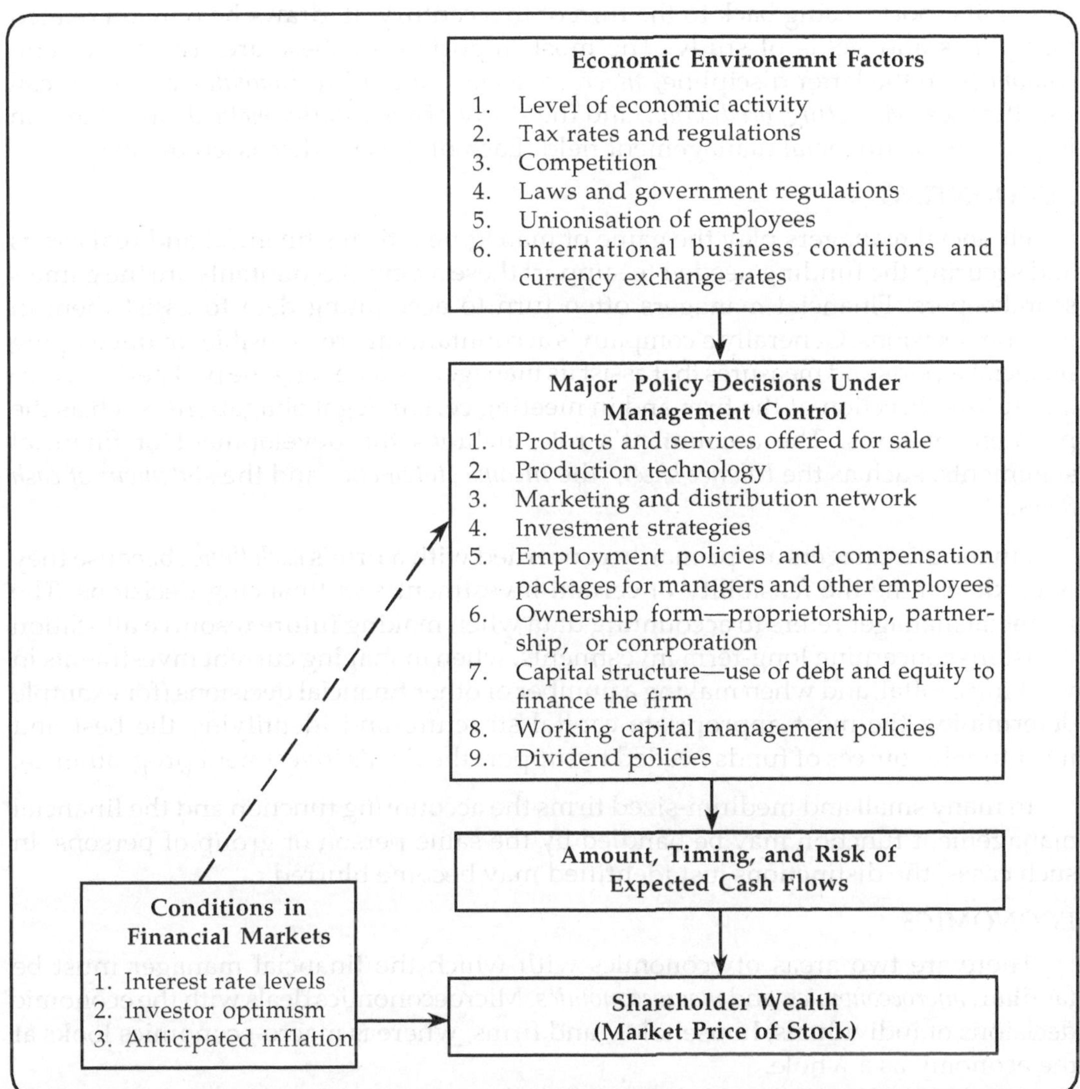

the other hand, the market value of the company's shares is maximised but the income stream generated is not consistent with the investor's investment preferences, then the investor can generate the maximum cash flow by selling the shares and investing all or part of the proceeds in assets which will generate the required income stream (provided these market opportunities exist). By maximising the market value of the company's shares, management is providing an investor who is unhappy with the income stream generated by the company with the opportunity of selling his shares at the highest possible market price.

FINANCIAL MANAGEMENT AND OTHER DISCIPLINES

The study of financial management as a totally independent subject is relatively recent, its roots tracing back to the turn of this century. It draws heavily on related disciplines and fields of study. The most important of these are *accounting* and *economics;* in the latter discipline, *macroeconomics* and *microeconomics* are of special significance. *Marketing, production*, and the study of *quantitative methods* also have an impact on the financial management field. Each of these is discussed below:

ACCOUNTING

Financial managers play the game of managing a firm's financial and real assets and securing the funding needed to support these assets. Accountants are the game's scorekeepers. Financial managers often turn to accounting data to assist them in making decisions. Generally a company's accountants are responsible for developing financial reports and measures that assist its managers in assessing the past performance and future direction of the firm and in meeting certain legal obligations, such as the payment of taxes. The accountant's role includes the development of financial statements, such as the *balance sheet,* the *income statement,* and the *statement of cash flows.*

Financial managers are primarily concerned with a firm's *cash flows,* because they often determine the feasibility of certain investment and financing decisions. The financial manager refers to accounting data when making future resource allocation decisions concerning long-term investments, when managing current investments in working capital, and when making a number of other financial decisions (for example determining the most appropriate capital structure and identifying the best and most timely sources of funds needed to support the firm's investment programmes).

In many small and medium-sized firms the accounting function and the financial management function may be handled by the same person or group of persons. In such cases, the distinctions just identified may become blurred.

ECONOMICS

There are two areas of economics with which the financial manager must be familiar: *microeconomics* and *macroeconomics.* Microeconomics deals with the economic decisions of individuals, households, and firms, whereas macro-economics looks at the economy as a whole.

The typical firm is heavily influenced by the overall performance of the economy and is dependent upon the money and capital markets for investment funds. Thus, financial managers should recognise and understand how monetary policies affect the cost of funds and the availability of credit. Financial managers also should be versed in fiscal policy and how it affects the economy. What the economy can be expected to do in the future is a crucial factor in generating sales forecasts as well as other types of forecasts.

The development of theory of finance began in the 1920s as an offshoot of the study of the theory of the firm in micro-economics. However, two major differences exist between the microeconomist's study of the firm and the financial theorist's. First micro-economists traditionally have focused on the relationship between profit and the value of output while holding the amount of capital invested constant. Financial theorists, on the other hand, have long been interested in the use of capital used.

The financial manager uses microeconomics when developing decision models that are likely to lead to the most efficient and successful modes of operation within the firm. Specifically, financial managers utilise the basic economic notion from microeconomic theory of setting marginal cost equal to marginal revenue when making long-term investment decisions (capital budgeting)and when managing cash , inventories , and accounts receivables (working capital management).Second ,the theory of finance has developed largely under conditions of uncertainty and in the presence of risk- averse behaviour.This contrasts with the study of microeconomics where the inclusion of materials on uncertainty is of relative recent origin.

THE MARKETING, PRODUCTION, AND QUANTITATIVE METHODS

Figure-4 depicts the relationship between financial management and its primary supportive disciplines. Marketing, production, and quantitative methods are indirectly related to the key day-to-day decisions made by financial managers. For example, financial managers should consider the impact of new product development and

FIGURE 4

IMPACT !OF OTHER DISCIPLINES ON FINANCIAL MANAGEMENT

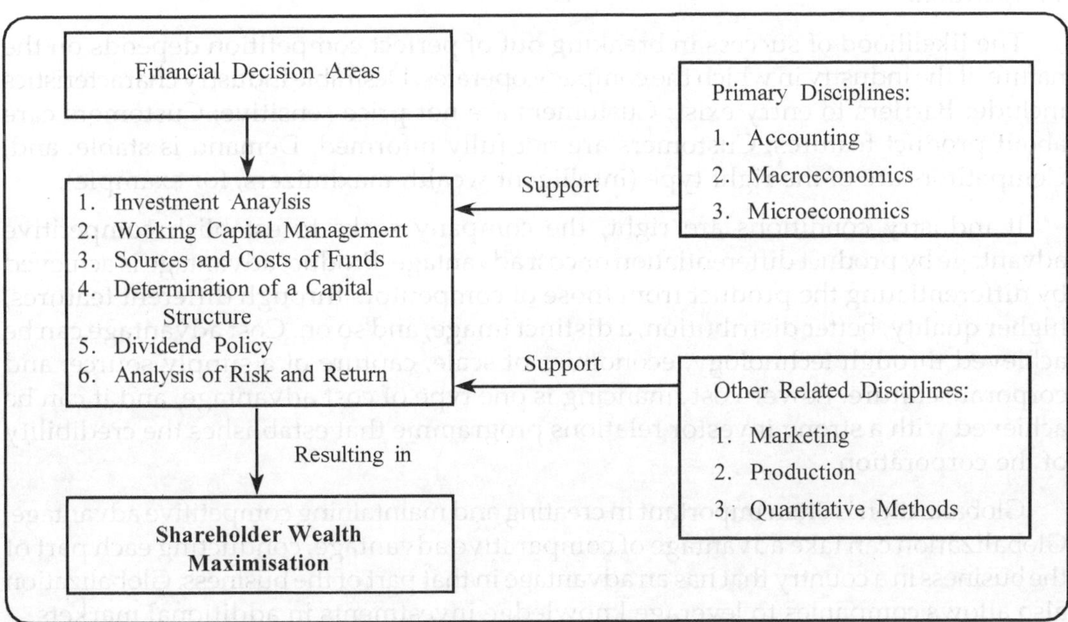

promotion plans made in the marketing area, because these plans will require capital outlays and have an impact on the firm's projected cash flows. Similarly, changes in the production process may necessitate capital expenditures, which the firm's financial managers must evaluate and then finance. And, finally, the tools of analysis developed in the quantitative methods area frequently are helpful in analysing complex financial management problems.

SPECIFIC RESPONSIBILITIES OF FINANCE MANAGER: STRATEGY AND VALUE

In modern business corporations, a chief financial manager's responsibilities have become as diverse and dynamic as they are important. He requires both a thoughful consideration of the changing nature of his job, along with a reliable step-by-step guide to the procedural nuts and bolts. He must manage day-to-day financial activities as well as implementation of a long-term financial strategy, while also keeping abreast of emerging key issues such as outsourcing, shared services best practices, and electronic commerce. He will find that entirely different priorities will apply to individual companies as the targets vary by company, depending on its revenue, its industry, its funding requirements and the strategic intention of its management team.

In a perfectly competitive market, large numbers of producers with identical cost structures compete to sell identical products to customers who are aware of all the other producers and know that all the product nomic profit is possible in this market, and producers must operate at peak efficiency just to survive. Thus, companies seeking to create wealth are of necessity seeking to break out of perfect competition.

The likelihood of success in breaking out of perfect competition depends on the nature of the industry in which the company operates. Desirable industry characteristics include: Barriers to entry exist; Customers are not price sensitive; Customers care about product features; Customers are not fully informed; Demand is stable; and, Competitors are of the right type (intelligent wealth maximizers, for example).

If industry conditions are right, the company seeks to establish competitive advantage by product differentiation or cost advantage. Product advantage is achieved by differentiating the product from those of competitors through different features, higher quality, better distribution, a distinct image, and so on. Cost advantage can be achieved through technology, economies of scale, capture of a supply source, and corporate culture. Lower-cost financing is one type of cost advantage, and it can be achieved with a strong investor relations programme that establishes the credibility of the corporation.

Globalization is often important in creating and maintaining competitive advantage. Globalization can take advantage of comparative advantage, conducting each part of the business in a country that has an advantage in that part of the business. Globalization also allows companies to leverage knowledge investments in additional markets.

The ultimate goals of strategic planning are competitive advantage and economic profit. Strategy is the grand design of the organization, involving the decision as to what business the company are in and how it intends to position itself in relation to others in that business. The major financial decisions of the organization—both investment and financing decisions—follow from and support the organization's strategy.

The strategy of the company defines the business that the company is in and how it intends to position itself within that business. The development of a strategy is based on three major sets of information: (1) a statement of goals, (2) an analysis of the environment, and (3) an analysis of the organization itself.

The objective of most strategic analysis is economic profit: a rate of profit above that just necessary to cover the opportunity cost of capital. To achieve economic profit, the company must avoid operating in perfect competition. Profitability is achieved by creating, enhancing, protecting, and using competitive advantages, either product advantage or cost advantage. Product advantages can include features, quality, image, service, and distribution. Cost advantages can come from economies of scale, technology, corporate culture, or control of the supply of inputs.

A number of conceptual models are used in the process of strategic analysis. These include the product life cycle curve and the strength/attractiveness grid. The conceptual models are used in the process of developing a strategy or grand design. The grand design is then implemented through a number of strategies applied to operation of the business. These include organizational strategies, marketing and distribution strategies, production and processing strategies, personnel strategies, financial strategies, and control strategies.

Financial decisions in support of strategy include both capital investment policy and capital structure policy. Capital investment policy must be designed to assure that the investments chosen are those that will contribute to the corporation's strategy. This requires the design of a capital investment policy and a management reward policy to avoid traps that deflect capital to other uses and encourage the flow of capital to the uses that will generate the greatest value.

Financial structure analysis must go beyond simply minimizing the cost of capital to consider ways in which capital structure can increase the value of the firm by contributing to strategy. Market power, flexibility, and the ability to continue to finance corporate strategy are all affected by capital structure decisions.

A properly developed strategy coordinates decision making from all areas of the organization. Optimal decisions are made in the framework of the corporation's overall objectives, not just in isolation. The result is achievement of overall goals in general and maximization of wealth in particular.

The competitive advantage concepts are applied through strategic planning, because the primary focus of strategy is the positioning of the company so that competitive pressures will not eliminate economic profit and positive net present values. Strategy coordinates the diverse actions of myriad decision makers throughout the organization in achieving the organization's goals. The major financial decisions of the organization—both investment and financing decisions—must be coordinated with and in support of the organization's strategy.

Figure-5 provides an overview of the strategic management process, from development of goals through implementation and monitoring. We begin by assembling the information necessary for a strategy decision. This includes the first three steps: establishment of goals, identification of threats and opportunities in the environment, and analysis of the organization's strengths and weaknesses. Then a strategy is developed. The strategy defines the business that the company is in and how it intends to position itself within that business. Leaders sometimes refer to the strategy

FIGURE-5
THE STRATEGIC MANAGEMENT PROCESS

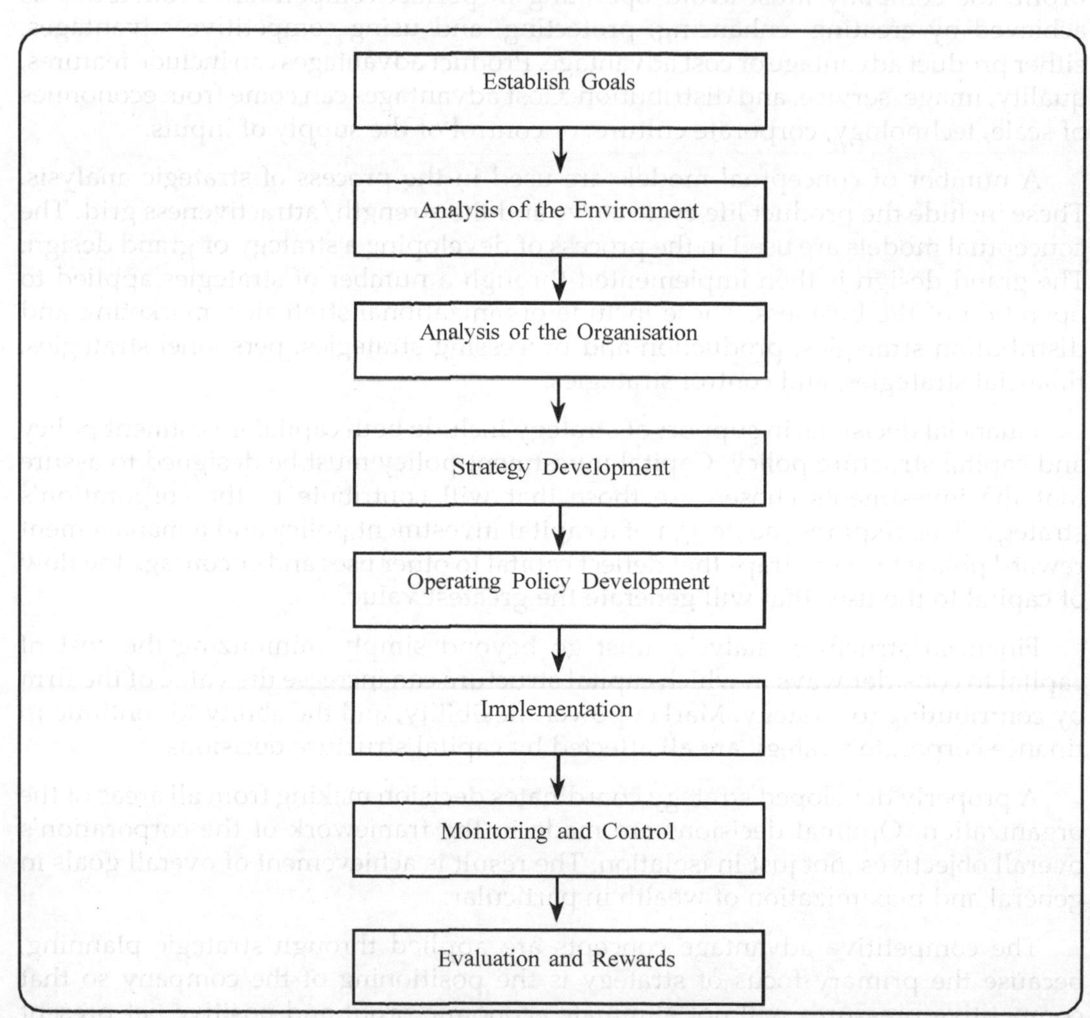

as their *vision* for the organization. The strategy must then be translated into policies for functional areas such as marketing, production, personnel, and finance. These functional area policies are sometimes called operating strategies. Those policies are implemented through plans, budgets, and so on. Performance is monitored and the whole process is continually evaluated so that the organization learns from its experiences and responds quickly to change.

Some of the most common responsibilities of the finance managers are listed below:

1. Pursue Shareholder Value

The top priority for the chief financial manager is the relent less pursuit of the strategy that has the best chance of increasing the return to shareholders. This also includes a wide range of tactical implementation issues designed to reduce costs.

2. Contract Reliable Control Systems

A continuing fear of the chief financial manager is that a missing control will result in problems that detrimentally impact the company's financial results, hence, a need for continous effort to examine the existing systems to control problems. This also implies that he should be deeply involved in the design of controls for new systems, so they go online with adequate control already in place. He typically uses the internal audit staff to assist in uncovering control problems.

3. Understand and Mitigate Risk

A chief financial manager must have a sufficient in-depth knowledge of company system to ferret out any risks occurring in a variety of areas, determining their materiality and likelihood of occurence, and creating and monitoring risk mitigation strategies to keep them from seriously impacting the company. The focus on risk should include include some or all of the following areas:

i) *Loss of key business partners. If* a key supplier or customer goes away, how does this impact the company? The chief finance manager can mitigate this risk by lining up alternate sources of supply, as well as by spreading sales to a wider range of customers.

ii) *Loss of brand image.* What if serious quality or image problems impact a company's key branded product? The chief finance manager can mitigate this risk by implementing a strong focus on rapid management reactions to any brand-related problems, creating strategies in advance for how the company will respond to certain issues, and creating a strong emphasis on brand quality.

iii) *Product design errors.* What if a design flaw in a product injures a customer, or results in a failed product? The chief finance manager can create rapid-response teams with preconfigured action lists to respond to potential design errors. There should also be product design review teams in place whose review methodologies reduce the chance of a flawed product being released. The chief finance manager should also have a product recall strategy in place, as well as sufficient insurance to cover any remaining risk of loss from this problem.

iv) *Commodity price changes.* This can involve price increases from suppliers or price declines caused by sales of commodity items to customers. In either case, the chief finance manager options include the use of long-term fixed-price contracts, as well as a search for alternate materials (for suppliers) or cost cutting to retain margins in case prices to customers decline.

v) *Pollution.* Not only can a company be bankrupted by pollution-related law. suits, but its officers can be found personally liable for them. Consequently, the chief finance manager should be heavily involved in the investigation of all potential pollution issues at existing company facilities, while also making pollution testing a major part of all facility acquisition reviews. He should also have a working knowledge of how all pollution-related legislation impacts the company.

vi) *Foreign exchange risk.* Investments or customer payables can decline in value due to a drop in the value of foreign currencies. The chief finance manager should know the size of foreign trading or investing activity, be aware of the size of potential losses, and adopt hedging tactics if the risk is sufficiently high to warrant incurring hedging costs.

vii) *Adverse regulatory changes.* Changes in local, state, or central laws—ranging from zoning to pollution controls and customs requirements—can hamstring corporate operations and even shut down a company. The chief finance manager should be aware of pending legislation that could cause these changes, engage in lobbying efforts to keep them from occurring, and prepare the company for those changes most likely to occur.

viii) *Contract failures.* Contracts may have clauses that can be deleterious to a company, such as the obligation to order more parts than it needs, to make long-term payments at excessive rates, to be barred from competing in a certain industry, and so on. The chief finance manager should verify the contents of all existing contracts, as well as examine all new ones, to ensure that the company is aware of these clauses and knows how to mitigate them.

ix) *System failures.* A company's infrastructure can be severely impacted by a variety of natural or man-made disasters, such as flooding, lightning, earth. quakes, and wars. The chief finance manager must be aware of these possibilities and have disaster recovery plans in place that are regularly practiced, so the organization has a means of recovery.

x) *Succession failures.* Without an orderly progression of trained and experienced personnel in all key positions, a company can be impacted by the loss of key personnel. The chief finance manager should have a succession planning system in place that identifies potential replacement personnel and grooms them for eventual promotion.

xi) *Employee practices.* Employees may engage in sexual harassment, steal assets, or other similar activities. The chief finance manager should coordinate employee training and set up control systems that are designed to reduce the risk of their engaging in unacceptable activities that could lead to lawsuits against the company or the direct incurrence of losses.

xii) *Investment losses.* Placing funds in excessively high-risk investment vehicles can result in major investment losses. The chief finance manager should devise an investment policy that limits investment options to those vehicles that provide an appropriate mix of liquidity, moderate return, and a low risk of loss.

xiii) *Interest rate increases.* If a company carries a large amount of debt whose interest rates vary with current market rates, then there is a risk that the company will be adversely impacted by sudden surges in interest rates. This risk can be reduced through a conversion to fixed interest-rate debt, as well as by refinancing to lower-rate debt whenever shifts in interest rates allow this to be done.

4. Link Performance Measures to Strategy

The chief finance manager will likely inherit a company- wide measurement system that is based on historical needs, rather than the requirements of its strategic direction. He or she should carefully prune out those measurements that are resulting in behavior not aligned with the strategic direction, add new ones that encourage working on strategic initiatives, and also link personal review systems to the new measurement system. This is a continuing effort, since strategy shifts will continually call for revisions to the measurement system.

5. Encourage Efficiency Improvements Everywhere

The chief finance manager works with all department managers to find new ways to improve their operations. This can be done by benchmarking corporate operations against those of other companies, conducting financial analyses of internal operations, and using trade information about best practices. This task involves great communication skills to convince fellow managers to implement improvements, as well as the ability to shift funding into those areas needing it in order to enhance their efficiencies.

6. Clean up the Accounting and Finance Functions

While most of the items in this list involve changes throughout the organization, the chief finance manager must create an ongoing system of improvements within the accounting and finance functions—otherwise the managers of other departments will be less likely to listen to a chief finance manager who cannot practice what he preaches. To do this, the chief finance manager must focus on the following key goals:

i) *Staff improvements.* All improvement begins with the staff. The CFO can enhance the knowledge base of this group with tightly focused training, cross-training between positions, and encouraging a high level of communication within the group.

ii) *Process improvements.* Concentrate on improving both the accuracy of information that is released by the department as well as the speed with which it is released. This can be accomplished to some extent through the use of increased data-processing automation, as well as through the installation of more streamlined access to data by key users. There should also be a focus on designing controls that interfere with core corporate processes to the minimum extent possible while still providing an adequate level of control. Also, information should be provided through simple data-mining tools that allow users to directly manipulate information for their own uses.

iii) *Organizational improvements.* Realign the staff into project-based teams that focus on a variety of process improvements. These teams are the primary implementers of process changes and should be tasked with the chief finance manager key improvement goals within the department.

7. Install Shared Services

The chief finance manager has considerable control over many administrative tasks, and so can encourage cost reductions in those areas through the use of shared services (where the same task is completed from a central location for multiple company locations). This can result in major cost savings, and is typically completed in coordination with the chief operating officer, who may be responsible for some of the areas being consolidated.

8. Examine Outsourcing Possibilities

A company should focus the attention of its management team on its core activity. The chief finance manager can assist this effort by determining which noncore areas are absorbing large amounts of management time and/or funding, and seeing if they can be prudently outsourced. Though certainly not all noncore areas can be handled in this fashion, the chief finance manager conduct periodic reviews to see how the attractiveness of this option changes over time.

9. Allocate Resources

In its simplest form, the chief finance manager is expected to review the net present value of proposed capital expenditures and pass judgment on whether funding should be allowed. However, the chief finance manager can take a much more proactive stance. For example, he can set aside a block of cash for more radical projects that would not normally make it past the rigorous capital expenditure review process, thereby adding high-risk, high-return projects to the company's portfolio of capital projects. Under this approach, the chief finance manager becomes an internal venture capitalist and mentor to the teams undertaking these high-risk projects.

10. Encourage Innovation

The chief finance manager can modify internal measurement, reporting, and budgetary systems to ensure that some original ideas are allowed to percolate through the company, potentially resulting in the implementation of high-return ideas. It is particularly important to take this approach in mature businesses that are most highly concerned with cost reductions, since an excessive focus on this area can drive out innovation.

Most of the responsibilities noted here rarely fall entirely within the capabilities of the chief finance manager. Instead, he must coordinate activities with other department managers, including such specialized areas as the legal and human resources departments, to ensure that these target areas are addressed. This calls for a strong ability to work with other members of the company who are probably not directly supervised by the chief finance manager.

QUESTIONS

1. The role of finance in the firm has been changing rapidly. Contrast the traditional view of the finance function with the more contemporary view.
2. How has financial thought developed over the past century? What factors have affected it?
3. What are the differences between shareholder wealth maximisation and profit maximisation? If a firm chooses to pursue the objective of shareholder wealth maximisation, does this preclude the use of profit maximisation decision-making rules? Explain.
4. Which type of corporation is more likely to be a shareholder wealth maximiser—one with wide ownership and no owners directly involved in the firm's management or one that is closely held?
5. It has been argued that shareholder wealth maximisation is not a realistic normative goal for the firm, given the social responsibility activities that the firm is "expected" to engage in (such as contributing to the arts, education, etc.). Explain why these social responsibility activities are not necessarily inconsistent with shareholder wealth maximisation.
6. Explain why management may tend to pursue goals other than shareholder wealth maximisation.
7. "Each decision, large or small, can be related to the effect that it will have on the value of the total assets minus the total liabilities and therefore on the shareholders' value." Explain the significance of this statement.
8. What are the major functions of the financial manager? What do these functions have in common?
9. "When I am faced with a financial decision my primary concern is whether or not the result of the action I take is in the shareholders' best interest." (Financial Manager). Discuss critically.
10. Explain what is meant by *agency relationships* and *agency costs.* Give some examples of agency costs incurred by shareholders in the agency relationship between the shareholders (owners) and management of a firm.
11. Why is the financial management function in a firm so important? Do you think that it is going to become more important in the future? Why or why not?
12. "A company cannot maximise sales revenue and the value of the company to its shareholders at the same time." Discuss.

13. Is it true that "if a firm is profitable, its survival is guaranteed?" Explain.
14. Explain the relationship between financial management and (a) microeconomics and (b) macroeconomics.
15. Why is earnings per share not a consistently good measure of a firm's performance? Under what conditions will maximising firm value also enrich society?
16. Corporate governnance is best left to managers because they are much more likely to think about the long term than shareholders. Comment.
17. "Maximising the value of the company to its shareholders is consistent with the company exercising considerable social responsibilities." Discuss.
18. If business firms attempt to maximise profits, are society goals met? Under what circumstances does profit maximisation lead to efficient use of economic resources?
19. How can the adherence to high standards of ethical business practice contribute to the goal of shareholder wealth maximisation?
20. To maximise the price of the firm's stock, what types of actions should management take?
21. Are ethics critical to the financial manager's goal of shareholder wealth maximisation? How are two related? Is the establishment of corporate ethics policies and guidelines, and requiring employee compliance with them, enough to ensure ethical behaviour of employees?
22. If a firm has a goal of shareholder wealth maximisation, does this mean that only cash flows should be considered in decision making and that ethical consideration should be ignored?
23. How can finance manager influence the magnitude, timing, and risk of the cash flow expected to be generated by the firm in order to maximise shareholder wealth?
24. Define the term strategy, as used in financial decision making.
25. Discuss the ways in which the financing decisions can support the corporate's strategy.

2

FINANCIAL STATEMENTS

INTRODUCTION

The ability to gain insights through the study of financial statements is vital to sound financial decision making. The basic data with which the analyst must work are found in the financial statements. Thus, the ability to understand, interpret, and use this information is basic to an understanding of finance. The purpose of this chapter is to discuss the basic nature of financial statements.

OBJECTIVES OF FINANCIAL STATEMENTS

Diverse groups of people are keenly interested in the information found in the firm's financial statements. They study the statements carefully, interpreting the information that relates to the particular interest in the company. The object of all these analyses is some sort of evaluation of the firm's performance. Therefore, the objectives of the financial statements are:

Firstly, the financial statements of business enterprises should provide information, within the limits of financial accounting, that is useful to present and potential investors and creditors in making rational investment and credit decisions. Financial statements should be comprehensible to investors and creditors who have a reasonable understanding of business and economic activities and financial accounting and who are willing to spend the time and effort needed to study financial statements.

Secondly, financial statements of business enterprises should provide information that help investors and creditors assess the prospects of receiving cash from dividends or interest and from the proceeds from the sale, redemption, or maturity of securities or loans. These prospects are affected by (1) an enterprise's ability to obtain enough cash through its earning and financing activities to meet its obligations when due and its other cash operating needs, to reinvest in earning resources and activities, and to pay cash dividends and interest and (2) perceptions of investors and creditors generally about that ability, which affect market prices of the enterprise's securities relative to those of other enterprises. Thus, financial accounting and financial statements should provide information that helps investors and creditors assess the enterprise's prospects of obtaining net cash inflows through its earning and financing activities.

Thirdly, the financial statements of a business enterprise should provide information about the economic resources of an enterprise which are sources of prospective cash inflows to the enterprise; its obligations to transfer economic resources to others, which are causes of prospective cash outflows from the enterprise; and its earnings, which are the financial results of its operations and other events and conditions that effect the enterprise. Since that information is useful to investors and creditors in assessing an enterprise's ability to pay cash dividends and interest and to settle obligations when they mature, it should be the focus of financial accounting and financial statements.

The second objective's emphasis on cash flows is tempered somewhat by this third objective. Objective third says that statements which would be most useful in assessing cash flows should not, in most cases, be prepared from strictly a cash-flows point of view.

BALANCE SHEET

Balance sheet is a statement of financial position or a statement of financial condition of a business on a particular date. In effect, the balance sheet is a listing of what the company owns (assets), what it owes (liabilities) and what the owners have invested (equities), as of a specific point in time. Thus, it provides a snap shot of the company's financial position on a particular date and is a means of judging the company's ability to meet its present obligations and the probability of its continued ability to meet the obligations.

ASSETS

The resources section of the Balance Sheet is usually labelled as "Assets." A definition of assets which will be useful for our purposes follows:

> *Assets are economic resources owned by the business which will provide future service benefits and can be measured objectively in terms of money.*

An economic resource is one which is scarce, a characteristic which gives it value.

Balance Sheet disclosure of assets typically involves sorting them into useful groupings such as: current assets; investments; non-current or fixed assets and other assets (deferred charges).

Current Assets

Current assets are assets which are reasonably expected to be realised in cash or sold or consumed during the normal operating business cycle. The current assets are acquired with the intention of sale or conversion into cash. They include *cash, marketable securities, accounts receivable (debtors), prepaid expenses, inventories* etc. The *cash account* represents the amount of money that the firm has on hand and/or in the bank. Sometimes a firm will have a temporary surplus of cash or will be accumulating money for some majors expenditure and rather than keep the money in a current account (earning no return), the firm will invest in *marketable securities*. These are usually short-term interest-bearing financial instruments with a low degree of risk. *Accounts receivable (debtors)* is the amount owed to the firm for the sale of goods or services on credit. If an agreement to pay is signed by the customer, the account is called bills receivable. *Bills receivable* are the amounts that are owed to the business for which a legal document, called a bill/hundi has been given. A bill is a piece of paper that states that a given amount will be paid at a given date, usually at a specified interest rate. Bills receivable differ form accounts receivable in several ways. *First,* a bill represents a "secured" claim, whereas, an open account is "unsecured." *Second,* a bill usually bears interest. *Third,* it is not necessarily owed by a customer. For example, a bill could represent a loan to an officer or employee. *Prepaid expenses* result from paying an item of expense in advance. For example, inventory account represents the amount of goods that the firm has purchased or produced for sales. This is an asset in the sense that it represents an expenditure that will benefit the business in the future. According to *accrual accounting, outlays for the purchase of goods for sale or costs of producing goods for sale do not become expenses until the goods are sold.* This is known as the *matching principle,* the expenses incurred to generate revenues are matched with revenues, or recorded in the same period as the revenues generated are recorded.

Investments

The second major category of assets are investments. They are bills or securities held by a business for investment purposes. That is to say, the intention is to hold those securities for the long run, at least longer than a year. They are classified separately from short-term marketable securities (which are current assets) because the intent of management regarding the holding period is different.

Fixed Assets

The third major group of assets is called non-current or fixed assets. Non-current assets are those assets that are not expected to be converted into cash in the short-run. Fixed assets are those physical assets that are to be used in the conduct of the business. The expectation is that they will be used rather than sold. Property assets are usually divided into several categories such as land, building, machinery and equipment, delivery equipment, and so forth. Nearly all property assets, except land, are subject to reductions in value over time. The process of accounting for this reduction in value is called "depreciation." The total of this depreciation is called "accumulated depreciation." Fixed assets, therefore, are shown at cost less accumulated depreciation. Depreciation is a process of spreading the depreciable value (cost less estimated future salvage value) over the estimated useful life of an asset in the rational and consistent way. Cost less accumulated depreciation at any intermediate time, thus, may bear little relationship to the asset's sales value at that point. The cost of a fixed asset is frequently called its "gross book value." The cost minus accumulated depreciation is called "net book value" or just "book value."

Other Assets

Other assets refer to payments made in one year, whose usefulness will expire in the future years. These represents assets usually of a intangible nature. The examples of these assets are research and development costs, preliminary expenses etc., and expenses on raising of share capital. These deferred charges are to be amortised or apportioned over the estimated useful life.

LIABILITIES

Liabilities and shareholders' equity constitute the sources of the assets. Liabilities may be defined as:

> '*...obligations to convey assets or perform services, obligations resulting from past or current transactions and requiring settlement in the future, the term "obligations" connotes the claim or series of claims against the business enterprises, each of which has a known or reasonably determinable maturity date and an independent value which is known or reasonable measurable. Settlement of a specific obligation may involve payment in cash or in other assets, or the performance of services. Ultimate settlement may be postponed by the substitution of another obligation.*

Liabilities, then, constitute source for assets for the firm through borrowing. These obligations must be settled at some future time by the delivery of cash, some other asset, or a service. It should be noted that once the asset has been obtained through borrowing it may change form so that it is no longer the same as that which was originally borrowed.

Liabilities typically are not related to a specific asset but are claims against the asset pool. The liabilities may be classified into current and long term liabilities.

Current Liabilities

Current liabilities represent the obligations of the business and arise in the ordinary course of operating business. They are expected to be payable within one year. These liabilities are generally said to have claim over current assets and must be discharged out of current assets. Among the most common current liabilities, the creditors reflect the amounts only include credit sales and credit purchases. If there are other types of short-term assets and liabilities, such as accrued expenses, they will usually be listed separately. If an agreement is signed the account is called bills payable. Short-term *bank loans* represent debts due to bank within one year. *Accrued expenses* refer to expenses incurred that have not been paid.

Long-term Liabilities

These are the obligations which will mature after a period longer than one year. These include company deposits, debentures or bond, long-term loans from financial institutions, etc.

OWNERS' FUND

Owners fund is the sum total of contributed and earned capital. It can be expressed total assets over outsiders liabilities and is called net worth. Contributed capital is the owners investment in the organisation, and it is termed as capital. In company form of organisation, capital is divided into shares of ₹ 10 or ₹ 100 normally. The shares can be preference shares or equity shares.

The balance in profit and loss account, which is often very large, represents the amount of profits that have been retained and reinvested in the business since its inception, the crucial point to remember is that *the balance in profit and loss account does not represent cash or any other resource,* the economic resources owned by the firm are always listed under the various asset accounts. It should also be recognised that the retained earnings account is the means by which the income statement is incorporated into the Balance Sheet.

ACCOUNTING EQUATION

One of the fundamental characteristics of every Balance Sheet is that the total figure for assets always equals the total figure for liabilities (creditors and share capital). This agreement or balance of total assets with total liabilities is one reason for calling this financial statement a Balance Sheet. *But why do total assets equal total equities?* The equity of assets on the one hand and of the claims of the creditors and the owners on the other hand is expressed in the equation:

Liabilities + Owners' Equity = Assets

$$\text{or} \quad L + OE = A \tag{1}$$

where A = Assets, L = Liabilities, OE = Owners' Equity

To emphasise that the shareholders' equity is a residual element secondary to the claims of the creditors, it is often helpful to transpose the terms of the equation, as follows:

$$OE = A - L \tag{2}$$

A Balance Sheet is something more than a detailed statement of this equation. Every business transaction, no matter how simple or how complex, can be expressed in terms of its effect on the accounting equation.

There are two ways to explain this equality. *First,* the accounting process is such that every time an asset account is increased (decreased), there is a corresponding (that is, same amount increase (decrease) in liability or equity account, or a corresponding decrease (increase) in another asset account. The *second* way to explain the equity or balance between assets and liabilities is to recognise that assets are economic resources that are used to generate sales. Liabilities and equities are the sources of these resources (that is, every use of funds must be balanced by corresponding source of funds).

FORMS OF THE BALANCE SHEET

The Balance Sheet can be presented either in the account form or the report form. Balance Sheet presents items in *account form* or horizontal form, when assets are indicated on the right side and the liabilities and capital on the left side. The *report form* of vertical form puts liabilities and capital below assets. Of course, in either form, all assets, liabilities and capital are shown. However, in vertical form, both the net working capital and shareholders' interest available at sight. Under Companies Act 1956, companies are required to present their balance Sheet in horizontal form. As per notification by the Department of Company Affairs (January 12, 1979), a company can prepare its Balance Sheet either in vertical or in horizontal form.

A Balance Sheet in the account form for a hypothetical company is shown in Table-1

TABLE-1

Universal Electronics Limited
Balance Sheet
As at March 31, 2013

Liabilities & Owners' Equity		*Assets*	
Share Capital		**Fixed Assets**	
Authorised Issued subscribed & paid up		Goodwill, Land, Building,	
(5,00,000 equity shares of		Machinery, Patents, etc.	₹ 55,00,000
₹ 10 each fully paid up)	₹ 50,00,000	Less. Depreciation	5,00,000
Reserves and Surplus	₹ 12,50,000		₹ 50,00,000
Secured Loans		**Investments**	₹ 17,50,000
Debentures	₹ 7,50,000	**Current Assets : Loans & Advances**	
Secured Loans	₹ 5,00,000	Debtors	₹ 1,50,000
		Bills Receivables	1,00,000
Current Liabilities & Provisions		Inventories	5,25,000
Bills payable	₹ 1,50,000	Cash and bank balances	4,50,000
Sundary Creditors	₹ 1,00,000	Insurance premium prepaid	1,50,000
Advance payments	₹ 75,000	Other current assets	1,25,000
Unclaimed dividend	₹ 90,000	**Miscellaneous Expenditure**	
Provision for dividend	₹ 1,15,000	(To the extent not written	50,000
Provision for taxation	₹ 1,70,000	off or provided for)	
	₹ 83,00,000		₹ 83,00,000

The report form or vertical form, a step-wise Balance Sheet for a hypothetical company is presented in Table-2.

INCOME STATEMENT *(PROFIT AND LOSS ACCOUNT)*

The most important change in a Balance Sheet between two periods of time is the change of owners equity. It is important that the potential creditor or investor knows not only the amount of this change, but also the principal factors that have contributed to it. One such factor is the operating results of the business. Consequently, in addition to a Balance Sheet, the publicly held companies must also publish an income statement. The income statement, also called Profit and Loss Account, is a statement of revenue and expenses resulting from business operations for a specific period, say a year. This is prepared to show the income or loss, the management has generated over the period from the firm's assets, rather than with the assets themselves. It is prepared on the accrual principle which treats all expenses and revenues relating to the period whether paid or not and records these in the income statement.

TABLE-2
Universal Electronics Limited
Balance Sheet
As at March 31, 2013

(in ₹)

I. Sources of Funds:		
1. Shareholders' Funds		
(a) Equity share capital		50,00,000
(b) Unsecured Loans		12,50,000
		62,50,000
2. Loan Funds		
(a) Secured loans	7,50,000	
(b) Unsecured Loans	5,00,000	12,50,000
Total (a)		75,00,000
II. Application of Funds:		
1. Fixed Assets		
(a) Gross Block	55,00,000	
(b) Less depreciation	5,00,000	
(c) Net Block		50,00,000 (i)
2. Investments		17,50,000 (ii)
3. Current assets Loans & Advances		
Debtors	1,50,000	
Bills receivables	1,00,000	
Inventories	5,25,000	
Cash and bank balances	4,50,000	
Insured premium prepaid	1,50,000	
Other current assets	1,25,000	
Misc. Exp. not written off	50,000	
	15,50,000	
Less Current Liabilities and Provisions		
Bills payable	1,50,000	
Sundry creditors	1,00,000	
Advance payments	75,000	
Unclaimed dividend	90,000	
Provision for dividend	1,15,000	
Provision for taxation	2,70,000	
	8,00,000	
Net Current Assets		7,50,000 (iii)
Total (b) (i) * (ii) + (iii) (a) = (b)		₹ 75,00,000

The purpose of the income statement is to indicate how successful the business has been in meeting this objective. Profits are of primary importance to the board of directors in evaluating the management of company, to shareholders or potential shareholders in making investment decisions, and to banks and other creditors in deciding on action to be taken with respect to loans. Other, things being equal, a profitable company is a good company to invest in, lend money to, work for, and deal with in general. An unprofitable company, on the other hand, presents problem on all of these counts because if the profit situation does not change, it must eventually go out of business. When this happens, most of the persons, or companies dealing with it are likely to be affected adversely. As a result, the income state means of a business are carefully scrutinised by all interested parties.

TABLE-3

Universal Electronics Limited
Income Statement
For the Year Ended March 31, 2013

(in ₹)

Revenues		
Sales	54,00,000	
Less return inward	2,15,000	
Net sales		51,85,000
Expenses		
Cost of goods sold	24,00,000	
General and administration expenses	2,50,000	
Selling expenses	1,50,000	
Interest	1,00,000	
Depreciation	5,00,000	
Non-operating expenses	1,50,000	35,50,000
Net profit (Before Tax)		16,35,000
Provision for tax		2,70,000
Net Profit (after tax)		13,65,000
Appropriation		
Provision for dividend		1,15,000
P & L A/c Bal.		12,50,000
		13,65,000

NATURE OF REVENUES AND EXPENSES

Revenue from primary operations or the business enterprise is the starting point of the income statement. In many businesses important adjustments of the total revenue are recognised. These adjustments include sales returns and allowances and sales discounts given to customers for early payment of their bills. These adjustments may be shown parenthetically rather than as separate totals in the income statement.

Cost of goods sold expense is a major expense in companies that sell products. It does not appear on the statement of a company that sells services. The size of the cost of goods sold expense and its direct relationship to sales are enough to warrant separate disclosure of this item. Some detail of cost of goods sold is often provided.

This detail traces the flow of costs through the business. The cost of goods purchased (net of any returns and allowances) during a period and freight on goods purchased, called "freight inwards, are added to the cost of goods on hand at the beginning of the period (opening inventory), forming a pool of cost of goods that could be sold during the period. This pool of costs is called cost of goods available for sale. The goods left at the end of the period are subtracted to arrive at the cost of goods sold. Purchase returns or allowances or discounts are deducted from purchases as adjustments of the total purchases. This is consistent with the treatment of revenue adjustments described above.

Cost of goods sold expense involves a complicated computation in manufacturing enterprises, where the cost of goods sold figure is the end product of the cost accounting activities. Internal management is usually given a detailed report of the manufacturing activities. Report to investors generally do not carry this detail. A cost of goods sold section in a manufacturing company's report to investors might have one figure, or it might present a short schedule.

Management is provided with a detailed report on the elements of cost that make up the cost of goods manufactured. They include material, labour, and overhead costs.

Operating expense category includes all expenses of the actual operations of the business other than cost of goods sold expense. These expenses are connected with sales, administration, and some of the more general supporting functions in the enterprise. Most of the expenses in this category are matched on a period base.

Other revenue and expenses include revenues and expenses that are not part of the main operating activities. Financial revenues and expenses, such as interest earned and interest expense, often are shown in this category. A company that manufactures products would not necessarily have any interest expense. The expense occurs because of the way the business is financed, not the way it is operated. If a company obtains incidental revenues from sideline activities, such as renting part of the store building or selling display counters, these revenues are shown among the incidental items.

Income tax is usually shown as a separate item on the income statement. Most other taxes, such as property taxes, sale taxes etc. are shown among the operating expenses. Corporate income taxes are deductions from revenues, just like other expenses, but they are unique in two ways: (1) Income taxes are assessed only if a company has a net taxable income. Other expenses are *determinants* of income; income taxes are *determined by* income. (2) Income taxes generally have been substantial. They have a considerable effect on business decisions and planning.

Extraordinary items are generally items of gain or loss which because of their unusual nature and because of their infrequency of occurence, cannot be combined with other revenues and expenses without distorting the income statement, e.g., loss by theft, fire etc.

FORMS OF THE INCOME STATEMENT

Like the Balance Sheet, the Income Statement may be presented in several forms. Two popular forms are: the *step form* and the *account form.* The step form income statement may be single-step or multiple-step. In a *single step income statement,* all revenues and incomes are listed and totalled. Then all expenses, including income taxes, are listed. The total of expense is deducted from revenues to arrive at net income. Extraordinary items are usually handled as a special item at the bottom before arriving at net income. Table-3 illustrates the single-step income statement.

The multiple-step means that several subtotals are obtain before final net income. It makes a distinction between operating revenue and non-operating revenue. Table-4 illustrates the multiple-step income statement for the Universal Electronics Limited.

TABLE-4

Universal Electronics Limited
Income Statement
For the Year Ended March 31, 2013

(in ₹)

Sales		54,00,000
Less: Return inward	2,15,000	
Cost of goods sold	24,00,000	26,15,000
		27,85,000
Gross Profit		
Less: Operating expenses:		
General and administrative expenses	2,50,000	
Selling expenses	1,50,000	
Interest	1,00,000	
Depreciation	5,00,000	10,00,000
Operating profit		17,85,000
Less: Non-operating expenses	1,50,000	1,50,000
Profit before tax		16,35,000
Less: provision for tax		2,70,000
Net Profit after tax		13,65,000
Provision for dividend		1,15,000
P and L A/c Bal.		12,50,000
		13,65,000

The account-form income statement divides the income statement in two sides: the left side is used to record expense items and the right-side lists revenue items. Table-5 illustrates the account form income statement.

RELATIONSHIP BETWEEN BALANCE SHEET AND INCOME STATEMENT

There is an intimate connection between the Income Statement and the Balance Sheet. This follows from the basic notion of income as an excess of revenue over expenses. This excess belongs to the enterprise owners. Net assets can be defined as assets minus liabilities. Because revenues is an inflow of net assets, and expense is an outflow of net assets, net income is a net inflow of net assets and increases owners' equity. A net loss, which occurs when revenue is less than expense, has the opposite effect: a loss reduces net assets and reduces owners' equity.

TABLE-5

Universal Electronics Limited
Income Statement
For the Year Ended March 31, 2013

(in ₹)

Expenses		*Revenues*		
To cost of goods sold	24,00,000	By sales	54,00,000	
To general and administrative		Less:		
To expenses	2,50,000	Return inward	2,15,000	
To selling expenses	1,50,000			51,85,000
To interest	1,00,000			
To depreciation	5,00,000			
To non-operating expenses	1,50,000			
To provision for tax	2,70,000			
To net profit	13,65,000			
	51,85,000			51,85,000
Provision for dividend	1,15,000	By net profit		13,65,000
To P and L A/c. Bal.	12,50,000			
	13,65,000			13,65,000

The fundamental relationship can be stated as follows, beginning with the basic accounting equation:

Liabilities(L) + Owners' Equity(OE) = Assets(A)

Therefore, OE = A – L

or Net Assets = OE

Effect of revenue:

+ Net Assets = + OE

Effect of expenses:

–Net Assets = –OE

Therefore, effect of net income (revenue minus expenses) is:

Net Assets = OE

These relationships are stated in the form of simple equations. The relationships are nevertheless profound and deserve serious considerations.

LIMITATIONS OF FINANCIAL STATEMENTS

First, they are essentially interim reports and, therefore, cannot be final because the actual gain or loss of a business can be determined only when it is sold or liquidated. The allocation of a revenue and costs to an accounting period involves personal judgement. The problem involves the achievement of a satisfactory (but never a perfect) matching of costs with revenues. Revenue and cost transactions flow continuously throughout the life of a business enterprise, yet they must be "cut off" at each balance sheet date. *Second,* the financial statements shows exact amounts, which give an impression of finality and precision. The reader may ascribe to these amounts his own concept of value, whereas the statements may have been set up on the basis of quite different value standards. Rarely does the stated value of an asset represent the amounts of cash that would be realised on liquidation; even the cash balance would be reduced by the expenses incidental to the liquidation process. The Balance Sheet is prepared on the basis of a *going concern'* concept whereby it is assumed that the enterprise will continue in business. Fixed assets are customarily stated at historical cost, and a deduction is made for the amount already charged against revenue in the income statements by way of depreciation (accumulated depreciation); the figures do not, as a rule reflect either the amount for which the fixed assets could be sold or the amount that would have to be expanded to replace them. *Thirdly,* both the Balance Sheet and the income statement reflect transactions that involve money values of many dates. Under inflationary conditions, the depreciation against current revenues by companies may not be enough to replace the plant. The Balance Sheet itself may not be indicative of current economic realities. An increase in sales volume stated in ₹ may or may not be the result of a larger number of units sold. *Fourth,* financial statements do not reflect many factors which affect financial condition and operating results, because they cannot be stated in terms of money. Such factors include: materials, merchandise, and supplies; the reputation and prestige of the company with the public; the credit rating of the company; and the efficiency, loyalty, and integrity of management and employees. Contingent assets and contingent liabilities customarily are not-and usually cannot be stated definitely in ₹. Similarly, some items that involve obligations by the corporation to make future payments are not shown as liabilities, and the debt of unconsolidated affiliated companies are often not fully reflected in financial statements.

CASH FLOW STATEMENT

The purpose of cash flow statement is to provide information about the cash flows of an enterprise so as to enable users of financial statements to assess the ability of the enterprise to generate cash and cash equivalents and the needs of the enterprise to utilise those cash flows.

Preparation and presentation of cash flow statement is governed by Accounting Standard 3 (Revised) issued by institute of Chartered accountants of India. AS 3 (Revised) deals with provisions of information about the historical changes in cash and cash equivalents of an enterprise by means of a cash flow statement which classifies cash flows during the period *from* operating, investing and financing activities.

Under AS 3 (Revised), inflows and outflows of cash and cash equivalents (cash equivalents are short-term, highly liquid investments that are readily convertible into known amounts of cash and which are subject to an insignificant risk of changes in value) are classified into operating, financing and investing activities.

'Operating activities' are the principal revenue-producing activities of the enterprise and other activities that are not investing or financing activities. They generally result from the transactions and other events that enter into the determination of net profit or loss. For example the cash receipts from the sale of goods and the rendering of services; cash receipts from royalties, fees, commissions and other revenue; cash payments to suppliers for goods and services; cash payments to and on behalf of employees; cash receipts and cash payments of an insurance enterprise for premiums and claims, annuities and other policy benefits; cash payments or refunds of income-taxes unless they can be specifically identified with financing and investing activities; cash receipts and payments relating to futures contracts, forward contracts, option contracts and swap contracts when the contracts are held for dealing or trading purposes; cash flows arising from the purchase and sale of dealing or trading securities; and (ix) cash advances and loans made by financial enterprises.

'Investing activities' are the acquisition and disposal of long-term assets and other investments not included in cash equivalents. These activities involve the purchase and sale of long-term productive assets, *e.g.*, plant and machinery, building, etc., that are not meant for resale in the ordinary course of business. Investing activities also include purchase and sale of investments (those which are not classified as cash equivalents). For example, the cash payments to acquire fixed assets (including intangibles). These payments include those relating to capitalised research and development costs and self-constructed fixed assets; cash receipts from disposal of fixed assets (including intangibles); cash payments to acquire shares, warrants or debt instruments of other enterprises and interest in joint ventures (other than payments for those instruments, considered to be cash equivalents and those held for dealing or trading purposes); cash receipts from disposal of shares, warrants or debt instruments of other enterprises and interests in joint ventures (other than receipts from those instruments considered to be cash equivalents and those held for dealing or trading purposes); cash advances and loans made to third parties (other than advances and loans made by a financial enterprise); cash receipts from the repayment of advances and loans made to third parties (other than advances and loans of a financial enterprise); cash payments for futures contracts, forward contracts, option contracts and swap contracts except when the contracts are held for dealing or trading purposes, or the payments are classified as financing activities; and cash receipts from futures contracts, forward contracts, option contracts and swap contracts except when the contracts are held for dealing or trading purposes, or the receipts are classified as financing activities.

'Financing activities' are activities that result in changes in the size and composition of the owners' capital (including preference share capital in the case of a company) and borrowings of the enterprise.' For example, the cash proceeds from issuing shares or other similar instruments; cash proceeds from issuing debentures, loans, notes, bonds and other short or long-term borrowings; and cash payments of amounts borrowed.

Presenting a Cash Flow Statement

Cash Flow Statement should report cash flows during the period of reporting classified by operating, financing and investing activities. Classification in such a manner allows the users of financial statements to assess the impact of those activities on the financial position of the enterprise and the amount of its cash and cash equivalents.

Reporting requirements relating to cash flows from operating activities

Cash flows from operating activities may be reported by the direct method or by the indirect method. *(However, it should be noted that in view of the amendment to clause 32 of listing agreements, listed enterprises should use only indirect method for preparation and presentation of cashflows.)*

Direct Method: Under the direct method, cash receipts from operating revenues and cash payments for operating expenses are calculated and presented on the cash flow statement. The difference between the cash receipts and cash payments is the net cash flow provided by (or used in) operating activities. Really speaking, cash flow statement based on direct method is simply a profit and loss account prepared on cash basis.

Indirect Method: Under the indirect method we adjust net profit for items that affected net profit but did not affect cash. The step-by-step procedure for calculating cash flows from operating activities is as follows:—

Ascertain Net Profit

Add: Non-cash and Non-operating charges (e.g. depreciation, amortization of intangible assets, etc.)

Less: Non-cash and Non-operating credits (e.g. profit on sale affixed assets, interest income, etc.)

Add (Less): Changes in current operating assets and current operating liabilities.

Reporting Requirements Relating to Cash Flows from Investing and Financing Activities

An enterprise should report separately major classes of gross cash receipts and gross cash payments arising from investing and financing activities.

Some Special Cases

Some special cases relating to preparation and presentation of cash flow statement are listed below:

(i) Situations in which cash flows from operating, investing or financing activities may be reported on a net basis

The following cash flows arising from the following operating, investing or financing activities may be reported on a net basis:—

(a) cash receipts and payments on behalf of customers when the cash flows reflect the activities of the customer rather than those of the enterprise, *e.g.*, acceptance and repayment of demand deposits by a bank, funds held for customers by an investment enterprise, etc.;

(b) cash receipts and payments for items in which the turnover is quick, the amounts are large, and the maturities are short, *e.g.*, principal amounts relating to credit card customers, purchase and sale of investments, etc.

Cash flows arising from each of the following activities of a financial enterprise may also be reported on a net basis:—

(a) cash receipts and payments for the acceptance and repayment of deposits with a fixed maturity date;

(b) the placement of deposits with and withdrawal of deposits from other financial enterprises; and

(c) cash advances and loans made to customers and the repayment of those advances and loans.

(ii) Reporting requirements relating to foreign currency cash flows

The cash flows arising from transactions in a foreign currency are to be recorded in the enterprise's reporting currency. For this purpose, the exchange rate on the date of cash flow is to be used. A rate that approximates the actual rate may also be used if the result is substantially the same as would arise if the rates at the dates of the cash flows were used. The effect of changes in exchange rates on cash and cash equivalents held in a foreign currency should be reported as a separate part of the reconciliation of the changes in cash and cash equivalents during the period.

(iii) Reporting requirements relating to extraordinary items

The cash flows associated with extraordinary items are to be disclosed separately as arising from operating, financing or investing activities. It may be noted that these disclosure requirements are in addition to the requirements of AS 5 (Revised).

(iv) Reporting interest and dividends

(a) In case of non-financial enterprises

(a-i) Cash flows from dividend and interest paid are to be classified as a part of financing activities.

(a-ii) Cash flows from dividend and interest received are to be classified as a part of investing activities.

(b) In case of financial enterprises

Cash flows from dividend and interest, whether paid or received are to be classified as a part of operating activities.

(v) Reporting taxes on income

Cash flows arising from taxes on income should be separately disclosed and should be classified as cash flows from operating activities. However, if they can be specifically identified with financing and investing activities then they should be classified as cash flows from financing/investing activities, to the extent they relate to financing/investing activities.

(vi) Reporting non-cash transactions

Investing and financing transactions that do not require the use of cash or cash equivalents should be excluded from a cash flow statement. Such transactions should be disclosed elsewhere in the financial statements in a way that provides all the relevant information about these investing and financing activities. Examples of non-cash transactions are: (a) the acquisition of assets by assuming directly related liabilities; (b) the acquisition of an enterprise by means of issue of shares; (c) the conversion of debt to equity, etc.

ILLUSTRATIVE PROBLEMS

1. Items from the income statement for the year ended March 31, 2013, and the Balance Sheet at March, 31, 2013 of Khanna Sportswear Company Ltd. are listed below:

(in ₹)

Item	Amount	Item	Amount
Share premium account	30,500	Number of Equity shares	10,000
Net sales	2,47,500		
Sundry creditors	52,500	Total current liabilities	54,500
Cash	15,000		
Income tax paid	15,000	Share capital	10,000
Inventory	60,000	Total assets	1,50,000
Accrued expenses	4,500	Accumulated depreciation	9,000
Total liabilities	1,50,000		
Sales returns and allowances	2,500	Bank over draft	15,000
		Net income before taxes	30,000
Net income after taxes	15,000	Administrative expense	30,000
Marketable securities	4,500	Total liabilities	64,500
Gross fixed assets	27,000	Preference Dividends	1,000
Gross profit	1,35,000	Total current assets	1,32,000
Retained earnings	25,000	Secured loan (repayable after one year)	5,000
Net fixed assets	18,000		
Sundry creditors	30,000	Selling expenses	75,000
Cost of goods sold	1,12,500	Gross sales	2,50,000
Secured loan	10,000	Preference share capital	20,000

(a) Prepare the income statement and Balance Sheet in proper form.
(b) Calculate basic earnings per share.

Solution

(a) Label each item as belonging to the income statement or Balance Sheet. The number of equity shares and preference dividends belong to neither, but these items are needed to calculate earnings per share.

Khanna Sportswear Company
Income Statement For the Year Ended March 31, 2013

(in ₹)

Gross sales	2,50,000	
Less sales returns and allowance	2,500	
Net sales		2,47,500
Cost of goods sold		1,12,500
Gross profit		1,35,000
Administrative expenses		30,000
Selling expenses		75,000
Net income before taxes		30,000
Income taxes		15,000
Net income after taxes		15,000
Basic E.P.S.		1.50

Khanna Sportswear Company Ltd.
Balance Sheet as on March 31, 2013

(in ₹)

Liabilities		*Amtount*	*Assets*		*Amount*
Share capital			*Fixed Assets*		
Preference share capital		20,000	G. Fixed assets	27,000	
Equity share capital		10,000	Less accumulated depreciation	9,000	18,000
Reserves and surplus			*Current Assets*		
P and L A/c CR Bal.		25,000	Cash	15,000	
Share premium		30,500	Marketable securities	4,500	132,000
		85,500	S. debators	52,500	
Secured loan (Secured against mortgage).		10,000	Inventory	60,000	
Current liabilities and Provisions					
S. creditors	30,000				
Accrued expenses	4,500				
Bank overdraft	15,000	54,500			
Secured loan (repayable in one year)	5,000				
		1,50,000		150,000	

(b) In published statements earnings per share is listed on the income statement right beneath net income after taxes. If the number of equity shares outstanding varies during the year, an average is employed in making the calculation.

2. Shaloo Syntex Ltd. is interested in opening a handicraft shop. For this, the estimates have been arrived at: (1) Sales will be ₹ 6,00,000 per month and net income after taxes will be ₹ 1,00,000 per month. (2) All goods will be sold on terms of net thirty days. (3) Inventory of ₹ 4,00,000 will be required which is sufficient for one month's sales (i.e. cost of goods solds is ₹ 4,00,000). (4) A minimum cash balance of ₹ 25,000 is required for day-today deed. (5) To house the shop, Shaloo plans make addition to bldg. for ₹ 26,00,000. Furniture and fixtures worth ₹ 2,00,000 will also need to be purchased. Depreciation expense will be ₹ 1,000 per month for the furniture and fixtures for ₹ 9,000 per month for the addition to the bldg.. Depreciation expense was included in the estimate of net income after taxes. (6) Creditors will equal 50% of the inventory level. (7) Shaloo has ₹ 10,00,000 which are planned to be invested in the business. (8) Included with other expenses is an item for ₹ 10,000 which will be paid in the month after incurrence. Income taxes will be paid in the month incurred, (9) There are no dividends: (a) Estimate the funds required to open the business and determine when these funds will be needed. (b) Calculate cash flow from operations for the first month.

Solution

(a) All the assets, except sundry debtors, are needed before business can commence. By the end of the first month, debtors will reach its maximum level of ₹ 6,00,000 since terms are net thirty days. By constructing a Balance Sheet at the end of the first month we can determine the maximum need. What should the firm do at the end of the month when it realises that ₹ 25,05,000 are required to continue operation? Assets are needed to generate sales and assets cannot be obtained without financing, or in other words, assets are uses of funds and every use must have a source.

Shaloo Syntex Ltd.
Balance Sheet
End of Month One

(in ₹)

Cash	25,000	Estimate	4
Debtors	6,00,000	Estimate	1
Inventory	4,00,000	Estimate	3
Net fixed assets	27,90,000	Fixed assets of 2,80,000 less Accumulated depreciation of ₹ 1,000	
Total	38,15,000		
Creditors	2,00,000		
Accrued expenses	10,000	Estimate	6
Equity share			

capital	10,00,000	Estimate	7
Profit from operations	1,00,000	Estimate	9
	13,10,000	Estimate	1 and 9
Need/Funds requirement	25,05,000		
Total	38,15,000		

(b) Cash flow from operations refers to the amount of cash provided by operations. To obtain the amount we should look at the income statement of the first month.

Sales	₹ 6,00,000
Cost of sales	4,00,000
Other expenses	1,00,000
Net income after taxes	₹ 10,00,000

Since all sales were credit sales, no cash flowed in from operations. Cost of goods sold was ₹ 4,00,000 but we know that trade creditors supplied ₹ 2,00,000 which was used for purchasing inventory. Other expenses are ₹ 1,00,000 but we know that this figure includes ₹ 10,000 depreciation and we know that another ₹ 10,000 (the accrual) will not be paid until the following month, so ₹ 80,000 was actually used for other expenses. To summarise:

Gross cash inflows	0
Cash outflows:	
Cost of sales (₹ 4,00,000 - ₹ 2,00,000)	₹ 2,00,000
Other expenses (₹ 1,00,000 - ₹ 20,000)	80,000
	-₹ 2,80,000

Cash flow from operations was a negative ₹ 2,80,000 or in other words cash resources were depleted to that extent.

3. Refer to Problem-2 assume that goods were sold on terms of net sixty days rather than net thirty days. All the other estimates remain the same. Estimate the funds required and determine when these funds will be needed.

Solution

More funds will be needed since S. Debtors will now reach a higher level. However, the peak need will not be reached until the end of the second month. At the end of month one, the need will be ₹ 25,05,000 since S. Debtore will still reach ₹ 6,00,000. However, the Balance Sheet at the end of month two would be:

Shaloo Syntex Limited
Balance Sheet
At the End of Month Two

(in ₹)

S. Creditors	2,00,000	Cash	25,000
Accrued expenses	10,000	S. Debtors	12,00,000
Equity S. capital	10,00,000	Inventory	4,00,000
Earnings from operations	2,00,000	Next fixed assets	27,80,000
	14,10,000		44,05,500
Funds requirements	29,95,000		
Total	44,05,000		

The peak need of ₹ 29,95,000 is reached by the end of the second month. Notice that S. Debtors increased by ₹ 6,00,000 and the need increased by ₹ 4,90,000 (₹ 29,95,500 - ₹ 25,05,500). This difference is due to the fact that operations provided funds (net working capital) of ₹ 1,10,000 (net income after taxes ₹ 1,00,000 +depreciation expense of ₹ 10,000) during the second month.

4. Ignore the revision made in Problem-3, and again assume that creditor terms are net thirty days. Shaloo intends to take out a three-month loan for the needed ₹ 25,05,000 at the beginning of the first month. Also, assume that net income after taxes will still be ₹ 1,00,000. Is Shaloo making a good financing choice? Provide numerical support for your answer.

Solution

Shaloo will not be able to pay off the loan by the end of the third month. This statement can be proved by constructing a Balance Sheet as of the end of the third month showing the bank loan reduced to zero. The loan can be reduced but not eliminated. The need for funds is permanent and a permanent source is required.

Shaloo Syntex Limited
Balance Sheet
End of Month Three

(in ₹)

Liabilities		*Assets*	
Bank loan	0	Cash	25,000
Sundry creditors	2,00,000	S. Debtors	6,00,000
Accrued expenses	10,000	Inventory	4,00,000
Equity share capital	10,00,000	Net fixed assets	27,70,000
Earnings from operations	3,00,000	Total	37,95,000
	15,10,000		
Need	22,85,000		
	37,95,000		

5. Prepare the cash flow statement of XYZ Co. for the year ended 31-3-2013, by using direct method and indirect method.

XYZ Co.
Income Satement

(in ₹)

Revenues	8.40,000
Cost of goods sold	4,80,000
Depreciation	40,000
Interest expense	60,000
Other expense	2,20,000
Dividend	14,000

XYZ Co.
Balance Sheet

	2013 ₹	2012 ₹
Liabilities		
Owner's Equity		
— Share Capital	2,40,000	1,40,000
— Reserves and Surplus	96,000	70,000
Other Liabilities		
— Creditors	1,20,000	1,40,000
— Non-Current Notes Payable	2,00,000	2,00,000
Less: Discount	(16,000)	(20,000)
	6,40,000	5,30,000
Assets		
Non-Current Assets		
— Plant and Machinery	2,40,000	2,00,000
Less: (Accumulated Depreciation)	(80,000)	(40,000)
Current Assets		
— Cash&Bank	2,00,000	1,60,000
— Debtors	2,80,000	2,10,000
	6,40,000	5,30,000

Solution

Preparation of Cash Flow Statement
XYZ Co.
Cash Flow Statement for the year ended 31-3-2013 (Direct Method)

	₹	₹
Cashflows from Operating Activities		
Cash receipts from customers (8,40,000 + 2,10,000 - 2,80,000)	7,70,000	
Cash paid to suppliers and employees (4,80,000 + 2,20,000 - 4,000 + 1,40,000 - 1,20,000)	(7,16,000)	
Net Cash flow from operating activities (A) 54,000		
Cash Flow from Investing Activities		
Purchase of plant and machinery	(40,000)	
Net Cash Used in Investing Activities (B) (40,000)		
Cash flow from Financing Activities		
Issue of share capital	1,00,000	
Payment of interest	(60,000)	
Payment of dividend	(14,000)	
Net cash flow from financing activities (C)		26,000
Net Increase in cash and cash equivalents (A + B + C)		40,000
Cash and cash equivalents at the beginning of the period		1,60,000
Cash and cash equivalents at the end of the period		2,00,000

XYZ Co.
Cash Flow Statement for the year ended 31-3-2013
(Indirect Method)

	₹	₹
Cash Flows from Operating Activities		
Net Profit	40,000	
Adjustments		
— Depreciation	40,000	
— Amortization of discount on note payable	4,000	
— Interest	60,000	
Operating Profit before working capital changes	1,44,000	

Increase in debtors	(70,000)	
Decrease in creditors	(20,000)	
Net cash flow from Operating Activities (A)		54,000
Cash flow from Investing Activities		
Purchase of Plant and Machinery	(40,000)	
Net Cash-Used in Investing Activities (B)		(40,000)
Cash flows from Financing Activities		
Issue of share capital	1,00,000	
Interest paid	(60,000)	
Dividend paid	(14,000)	
Net cash flow from Financing Activities (C)		26,000
Net Increase in cash & cash equivalents (A + B + C)		40,000
Cash and cash equivalents at the beginning of the period		1,60,000
Cash and Cash equivalents at the end of the period		2,00,000

QUESTIONS

1. What are the objectives of reporting financial statements? Briefly explain each of the three basic types of business entities. What are the limitations on the use of financial statements?
2. Identify and briefly discuss the basic information components of each of the three principal financial statements reported by business entities.
3. How would you define an asset, a liability and an owners' equity item? What is the difference between liabilities and owners' equity?
4. Define the following : *(a)* Net sales; *(b)* Cost of goods sold; *(c)* Operating income; *(d)* Net Income.
5. What is the basic accounting equation? Explain the nature of a Balance Sheet in terms of the elements of the accounting equation?
6. How does the Balance Sheet show the sources or resources for a firm?
7. Discuss what the cash flow statement attempts to explain. Does the statement of cash flow eliminate the need for the Balance Sheet and for the income statement? Discuss.
8. What is the purpose of a statement of changes in financial position when prepared on a cash basis? Will cash generated by operations be the same as working capital generated by operations ? Explain.
9. Distinguish between cash flows from operating & financing activities. Give three examples each of (i) operating activities (ii) investing activities & (iii) financing activities.

PROBLEMS

1. All Well Ltd. has paid corporate tax amounting to ₹ 2 crores during the current year. It has also paid Corporate Dividend Tax of ₹ 50 lakhs in the same year. The total tax payment of ₹ 2.50 crores has been classified under operating activities. Comment.

   Hint: Incorrect, ₹ 2 crores to be classified as operating activity and ₹ 50 lakhs as financing activity.

2. In the cash flow statement, how should the following items be classified:

   (i) Loans given by Escorts Finance Ltd.,

   (ii) Deposits by customers in ICICI Bank,

   (iii) Premium received by Subhash Kansal and Co., a stock broker with NSE, in respect of a forward contract entered for purchase of equity shares,

   (iv) Extraordinary item relating to operating activities.

   Hint: All items to be classified as cash flows from operating activities.

3

FINANCIAL ANALYSIS AND PLANNING

INTRODUCTION

Financial analysis and planning are very general managerial activities. Managers may attempt to analyse the historical record of a firm in order to identify factors having a significant influence upon the wealth of shareholders. But various plans aimed at increasing shareholder's wealth are also subject to analysis. For example, managers may subject plans to change the firm's debt-equity ratio or to invest in various capital projects to financial analysis. Financial planning itself pertains to the process of establishing course of action for the firm to guide future activity. For example, a budget is a financial plan.

Financial manager must analyse both the risk and return aspect of past and present financial decisions to *evaluate* what has happened to the firm, to *control* what is happening, and to *assist in planning* what will happen. At the same time, external parties—short and long-term investors, customers, suppliers, employees, financial analysts etc.—whose fortunes are linked with the firm want to analyse the firm and evaluate its financial plans. These parties are concerned that the statements present a fair and accurate picture of a company's financial position (i.e., assets, liabilities, earning, and cash flows).The primary, and sometimes the only, data available for analysis, especially to external parties, are contained in financial statements. In the present context, financial analysis is viewed as the process of reducing a large amount of historical financial data, taken firm financial accounting statements, to a smaller set of information more useful for decision making. Financial ratios comprise an important part of that smaller set of information. In the present chapter, the focus is on the various categories and types of ratios used in analysing actual and forecasted financial statements and various types of operational budgets.

ANALYTICAL PROCESS: *INFORMATION NEEDED FOR FINANCIAL ANALYSIS AND PLANNING*

Financial Analysis and planning rely heavily on standard accounting information normally available to the firm. The balance sheet and income statement of the firm are paramount among the useful types of accounting information and form the basis for this chapter. Use of accounting data is both a strength and weakness. The strength lies in its ready availability. Its weakness is that it is sometimes very difficult to interpret. A financial analysis assists in identifying and indicating whether a firm has enough cash to meet obligation; a reasonable accounts receivable collection period; an efficient inventory management policy; sufficient plant, property, and equipment; and, an adequate capital structure all of which are necessary if the firm is to achieve the goal of maximising shareholder wealth. Financial analysis can also be used to assess a firm's viability as an ongoing enterprise and to determine whether a satisfactory return is being earned for the risk taken.

Financial statement analysis typically follows a series of interrelated steps that leads a user to a meaningful interpretation of financial data. These steps are to specify the purpose of analysis; to identify the measurement base; to collect and process the data; and to compare the processed data with a standard.

In general, the usefulness of financial information is increased when it can be compared with related data. Comparison may be internal (i.e., within one firm). or external (i.e., with another firm). External comparisons may be difficult to make in practice since financial statement of firms may not be readily comparable because of the use of different generally acceptable accounting principles. However, some useful information may be obtained by comparison with industry averages, ratios, etc. or by direct comparison with the statements of another firm.

The financial statements of a particular firm are most useful when they can be compared with related data from within the current period, information from prior periods, or with budgets or forecasts. Comparative statements are useful in providing a standard which facilitates the analysis and interpretation of changes and trends which have occured in elements of the financial statements.

BASIC PROCEDURES

Comparisons of financial statement data are frequently expressed as percentages or ratios. These comparisons may represent: (i) percentage increases and decreases in an item in comparative financial statements; (ii) percentage relationships of individual components to an aggregate total in single financial statement; or, (iii) ratios of one amount to another in the financial statements. Applications of each of these three methods will be illustrated by the use of the comparative financial statements of a hypothetical company, the Shiva Pharma Company. Note, however, that no technique is clearly superior to others. The success of each technique is a function of the analyst's skill.

COMPARATIVE ANALYSIS

In comparative analysis, the financial data for the current year is compared on an absolute basis with the financial data for one or more previous years. In this fashion, the analyst isolates existing trends. The simplest form of comparative analysis contrasts the absolute amount of each item in the current financial statements with the corresponding items in previous years. Generally, this type of analysis discloses both he absolute and percentage changes for the corresponding items in previous years. Generally this type of analysis discloses both the absolute and percentage changes for the corresponding items in comparative statements. Percentage analysis of changes in each live item shown in Table-1 is called horizontal analysis. Note that data from the earliest year's balance (2012 in the example) are used as a base in a horizontal analysis.

Horizontal analysis can provide important insights into financial trends. For example, Table-1 illustrates that the upward trend of sales is not as sharp as the increase in cost of goods sold. That is, the sales growth was relatively expensive in terms of the cost of goods sold and possibly out of control. Further analysis reveal that cuts in administrative expense and interest expense accounts for much for the increase in profits. Although the initial comparative analysis of absolute data appeared favourable, subsequent percentage analysis reveals a different situation.

TABLE-1

Shiva Pharma Company

Comparative Income Statements For the Year Ended March 31, 2013 and 2012

	Year ended March 31		*Increase or Decrease*	
	2013	*2012*	*Amount (₹)*	*Percent*
	(₹)	(₹)		
Sales	80,00,000	60,00,000	20,00,000	33.3
Cost of goods sold	44,50,000	31,00,000	13,50,000	43.5
Gross profit	35,50,000	29,00,000	6,50,000	22.4
Operating expense				45.4
Selling expense	16,00,000	11,00,000	5,00,000	
Administrative expenses	9,00,000	10,50,000	– 1,50,000	– 14.2
	10,50,000	7,50,000	3,00,000	
Interest	40,000	60,000	– 20,000	– 33.3
Net income before taxes	10,10,000	6,90,000	3,20,000	46.3
	4,00,000	2,80,000	1,20,000	42.8
Net income	6,10,000	4,10,000	2,00,000	48.7

Comparative analysis is an important tool in financial statement analysis; however, it is not without limitations. Any trend analysis relies on the assumption that past conditions within a business enterprise change (for instance, the development of the new product and/or a new management), or that conditions within the business environment change (fluctuations in industry or general economic conditions), evaluation of current data becomes more difficult. Unfortunately, the global economic environment is very dynamic; interpretation of financial trends must consider both industry conditions and general economic conditions. To the extent that current conditions are expected to extend into the future, horizontal financial statement analysis may prove to be extremely effective.

COMMON SIZE ANALYSIS

Common-size analysis, sometimes called *vertical analysis*, emphasize relationship between data on the same financial statement. Common-size analysis is relatively simple to effect. Every item on a financial statement is expressed as a percentage of a single base amount. Sales or net sales is commonly used as the base for analysis of an income statement. Table-2 illustrates a common-size analysis of the Shiva Pharma Company Income Statement. Having expressed a set of financial statements in relative terms, the analyst may compare the result with other firm, or another with industry averages.

Common-size analysis suffers from some of the same limitations as does comparative historical analysis. Both evaluations are based on trend assumptions. To the extent, that changes occur in the firm or its environment, both forms of analysis may prove poor predictors of the future. In addition, interpretation of relative data may be ambiguous. For example, if operating expense, expressed as a percentage of sales, is materially higher than industry norms, which element presents the problem? Are operating expenses too high, or did expected sales fail to materialise? A thorough analysis of relative data may be required to derive interpretable results.

TABLE-2
Shiva Pharma Company
Comparative Income Statements
For the Year Ended March 31, 2013 and 2012

Percent	*Year ended March 31, 2013 Amount (₹)*	*Percent*	*Year ended March, 2012*	*Percent*	*Increase or Decrease Amount (₹)*
Sales	80,00,000	100.00	60,00,000	100.0	0
Cost of goods sold	44,50,000	55.6	31,00,00	51.6	4.0
Gross profit	35,50,000	44.4	29,00,000	48.4	– 4.0
Operating expense					
Selling expense	16,00,000	20.0	11,00,000	18.3	1.7
Administrative expense	9,00,000	11.2	10,50,000	17.5	– 6.3
Interest	40,000	0.5	60,000	1.0	– 0.5
Net income before taxes	10,10,000	12.7	6,90,000	11.5	1.2
Taxes	4,00,000	5.0	2,80,000	4.6	0.4
Net income	6,10,000	7.7	4,10,000	6.9	0.8

RATIO ANALYSIS

Ratio is defined formally as "the indicated quotient of two mathematical expressions"—and indeed, a ratio does result from the division of one number into another—and as "the relationship...between two or more things." An operational definition of a financial ratio is the *relationship* between two financial values. The word "relationship" implies that a financial ratio is the result of comparing mathematically two values. And this numerical comparison is important, for these ratios are used as indexes, and as indexes, they are used to make qualitative judgements about the financial health of the firm.

Analysis of the firm by financial ratios enables the financial manager, as well as interested external parties, to evaluate the firm's financial performance and condition rapidly by making comparisons of ratios obtained from the firm with ratios obtained from comparable firms. Financial ratios also present ready comparisons of a firm's financial performance and condition over time as a way of identifying and evaluating performance trends.

Ratio analysis requires considerable judgment and direction by the analyst if it is to serve as a basis for future financial and operating decisions. Rules of thumb and other mechanical interpretations may produce disastrous decisions by those who are ill-informed about the ambiguity of information that may be contained in ratios.

STANDARDS OF COMPARISON

Financial and operating relationships expressed in terms of ratios or otherwise have little significance except as they are judged on the basis of appropriate standards of comparison. Therefore, in interpreting the ratios of a particular business, the analyst cannot determine whether the ratios indicate favourable or unfavourable conditions unless there are available measuring devices or standards of comparison.

In preparing standard ratios for a group of companies, the analyst is confronted with many problems. Certain members of an industry are highly successful and most efficient; other members have an unsatisfactory financial condition and operating performance. Therefore, the decision to include or exclude low, high, or unusual ratios and amounts is an important one. Such items, if included, would bring about a lower or higher average which might not be typical or representative of the industry.

To obtain the most typical financial and operating data for an industry, the analyst must be sure that all the companies included in the summary are homogenous, i.e., own and operate similar properties and businesses and perform almost identical functions or stages of manufacture. However, absolute homogenity is rarely, if ever, attainable.

To be most meaningful and informative, i.e., reliable and representative, standard ratios should be developed for companies of an industry that: 1. Use a uniform accounting system and accounting procedures including a uniform classification of accounts and similar depreciation methods. 2. Follow a uniform accounting period preferable on a natural business year basis. 3. Follow similar asset valuation and amortisation policies. 4. Represent a homogenous group. 5. Adopt and maintain somewhat uniform managerial policies.

In as much as the trade data are merely averages, the analyst may prefer to emphasise a study of historical percentages and ratios for a particular company. Certainly, such data would be more "standard" for the individual business, assuming financial and operating efficiency. The analyst may use both.

Types of Ratios

When standard ratios are not available in published form, the analyst can prepare his own standards. In computing standard ratios, the analyst should: 1. Assemble financial statements of comparable business (having homogenous operations and uniformity of data) within each industry. The problem of determining which companies are comparable is probably the most important and

difficult of the many that have to be solved in the process of computing standard ratios. In other words, it is often stated that the incomparability of the original data represents the most serious difficulty in the development of dependable standard ratios. 2. Compute selected ratios for each business within the various industries. 3. Arrange for each industry and from high to low all pertinent ratios, such as the current ratios, ratios of net income to net sales, ratios of owners' equity to total assets etc. 4. Eliminate the extreme low and high ratios in order to provide a basis for determining the most representative average.

For ease of presentation we shall discuss financial ratios in terms of five basic categories: liquidity ratios, profitability ratios, financial leverage ratios, activity ratios and marketability ratios. Each of these ratio categories relates directly to a particular purpose of financial statement analysis. Each category is discussed through the use of an example set of financial ratios computed using the 2013 financial statements of Shiva Pharma Company (see Table-3).

LIQUIDITY RATIO

Liquidity and short-term solvency ratios are used to judge the firm's ability to meet such current obligations as its accounts payable and the current position of its long-term debt. By interpreting such ratios we can determine the degree to which assets which are quickly convertible to cash exceed the liabilities which require almost immediate cash payment. Liquidity ratios are generally useful to all financial statement users, but are particularly useful to short-term creditors. The most frequently used ratios in this category are the current and the quick (acid test) ratios.

Current Ratio

The current ratio is the traditional ratio used to measure a company's liquidity and is calculated by dividing the total current assets by the total current liabilities. Its use dates back to the last century, and it is still accepted as the best measure of the company's short-term solvency. The current ratio for the Shiva Pharma Company is:

$$\text{Current ratio} = \frac{\text{Total current assets}}{\text{Total current liabilities}}$$

$$= \frac{₹\ 56,50,000}{₹\ 15,80,000} = 3.6$$

This ratios is designed to assist the decision maker in determining a firm's ability to pay its current liabilities. The higher the ratio, the greater the ability of the company to meet its immediate financial obligations. However, the higher this ratio,

TABLE-3
Shiva Pharma Company
Income Statement
For the year ended March 31, 2013

(in ₹)

Sales		80,00,000
Cost of goods sold		44,50,000
Gross profit		35,50,000
Operating expense:		
Selling expense	16,00,000	
Administrative expense	9,00,000	
Interest expense	40,000	
Total expense		25,40,000
Net income before tax		10,10,000
Tax	4,00,000	
Net income		6,10,000
Earnings per share (5,00,000 equity shares)		₹ 1.22

Balance Sheet
As at March 31, 2013

Liabilities and Owners' Equity		*Assets*	
Share capital (₹ 10.00 par value, 5,00,000 shares authorise, issued and outstanding)	50,00,000	Fixed Assets: Equipment	60,00,000
		Less: Accumulated depreciation	18,00,000
Retained earnings	22,70,000		42,00,000
Long-term liabilities:		Investments	5,00,000
Bonds payable (Due 2016)	15,00,000	Current Assets:	
Current Liabilities and Provisions:		Cash	9,00,000
Sundry creditors	9,60,000	Sundry debtors - (net)	6,00,000
Bills payable	5,20,000	Inventory	40,00,000
Accrued wages payable	1,00,000	Prepaid expenses	1,50,000
	1,03,50,000		1,03,50,000

Other Data for 2013
Cash Dividends per share = ₹ .20
Selected Data from the previous year's financial statement
Total assets = ₹ 93,50,000
Total shareholders equity = ₹ 70,60,000
Total number of shares of equity outstanding = 5,00,000 shares
Net sundry debtors = ₹ 5,60,000
Inventory = ₹ 32,00,000

the greater the proportion of the company's resources that is tied up in relatively unproductive assets, which have an adverse effect on profitability. Therefore, regardless of the magnitude of the current ratio, management still bars to make the decision as to the appropriate balance between profitability and liquidity.

Quick (Acid Test) Ratio

A supplementary test of the ability of a business to meet its current obligations is the quick or the acid test ratio. The quick ratio is calculated by dividing the total current assets less inventories by the total current liabilities less bank overdraft. The reason for deducting inventories are regarded as the best liquid of all current assets, and so, this will prove the most difficult to realise at short notice, also, it is unusual for a bank-overdraft to be withdrawn at short notice. Consequently, these items are excluded from the computation of quick ratio. It is guided better than the current ratio as a measure of the company's ability to meet its financial obligations if they become payable in the very short-term.

$$\text{Quick ratio} = \frac{\textit{Cash Marketable securities} + \textit{Interests receivable}}{\textit{Current liabilities}}$$

$$= \frac{\text{Total current assets - Inventories}}{\text{Current liabilities}}$$

$$= \frac{₹\,9{,}00{,}000 + 0 + ₹\,6{,}00{,}000}{₹\,15{,}80{,}000} = 0.95$$

The current ratio and the quick ratio serve as a measure of a company's liquidity position and to have particular application to cash management. The usefulness of these ratios to management has already been questioned, although emprical studies have produced evidence that these and other ratios may assist external parties in estimating the possibility of the future failure of a company. It has also been suggested that a study of the company's future cash flows would be a more suitable method of ascertaining. a company's liquidity position than other based on financial ratios.

Regardless of other criticisms of these ratios, there are serious doubts that they can measure a company's ability to meet its immediate financial obligations. The current ratio is calculated simply by dividing the book value of current liabilities. This does not take into account either the relative liquidity of the various current assets or the relative urgency for repayment of the current liabilities. It is not useful to know that the company has a current ratio of two, if all the liabilities are due to be paid within a week and most of the assets cannot be realised within few months. A further limitation of the current ratio is that it includes inventory valued at historical cost. As it is assumed that inventory can generate liquidity to meet financial obligations, then it may be argued that inventory should be valued at net realisable value, which better represents the asset's contribution to liquidity. Finally, the numerical value of these ratios can be manipulated by management so that the resulting figure will be acceptable to interested parties, This can be easily achieved by delaying purchases or paying off a large amount of the company's current liabilities just prior to the end of the financial year.

PROFITABILITY RATIO

Profitability ratios measure the success of the firm's management in earning a net return from the resources entrusted to them Specifically, profitability ratio can be used to answer such questions as, *How much of each sales was management able to convert into profits? and did the company shareholders receive an adequate return on their investments?* For discussion purposes we shall divide profitability ratios into two groups: profitability in relation to sales and profitability in relation to investment.

Profitability in Relation to Sales

It is important from a profit standpoint that the firm be able to generate adequate profit on each unit of sales, if sales lack a sufficient margin of profit, it is difficult for the firm to cover its fixed costs, fixed charges on debt, and to earn a profit for shareholders. The profit ratios discussed here are commonly referred to as *Profit margins* and include the gross profit margin, operating profit margin, and net profit margin.

(a) Gross Profit Margin

Gross profit margin ratio shows the profits relating to sales after the direct production costs are deducted. It may be used as an Indicator of the efficiency of the production operation and the relation between production costs and selling price. Gross profit margin is calculated as follows:

$$\text{Gross profit margin} = \frac{\text{Sales} - \text{Cost of goods sold}}{\text{Net sales}}$$

$$\frac{₹\ 80,00,000 - ₹\ 44,50,000}{₹\ 80,00,000} = 44.375$$

Thus, Shiva's gross profit constitutes 44.375 percent of firm sales.

(b) Operating Profit Margin

Moving down the income statement, the next statement, the next profit figure encountered is net operating income. This profit figure serves as the basis for computing the operating profit margin.

$$\text{Operating profit margin} = \frac{\text{Net operating figure}}{\text{Sales}}$$

$$= \frac{₹\ 10,10,000}{₹\ 80,00,000} = .12625 = 12.625$$

The operating profit margin reflects the firm's operating expenses as well as its cost of goods sold. Therefore, this ratio serves as an overall measure of operating effectiveness.

(c) Net Profit Margin

The final profit margin considered involves the net after-tax profits of the firm as a percent of sales, Net profit margin is computed as follows:

$$\text{Net profit margin} \; \frac{\text{Net operating figure}}{\text{Sales}}$$

$$\frac{₹\,6{,}10{,}000}{₹\,80{,}00{,}000} = 0.07625 = 7.625$$

By itself, profit margin on sales provides little useful information since it mixes the effectiveness of sales in profits (reflected by the net operating margin) with the effects of the method of financing on profits (since after tax income is after deduction of interest on debt and of taxes, which are reflected by interest).

Profitability in Relation to Investment

This category of profitability ratios attempts to measure firm profits in relation to the capital invested by owners and creditors. If the firm cannot produce a satisfactory profit on its assets base, it may be misusing the assets. Thus, these ratios are very useful in assessing the overall effectiveness of the firm's management.

(a) Rate of Return on Assets

The relationship of the earnings of a business to its total incomes is an important indicator of the effectiveness of management in influencing a return to suppliers of capital, as well as a method of predicting future earnings. It is calculated by dividing net income by average total assets. Net income is found on the current year's income statement average total assets must be calculated as the average of total assets at the end of the previous year and the current year as shown follows:

$$\text{Average total assets} = \frac{\text{(Total assets at the end of last year + Total assets at the end of current year)}}{2}$$

$$= \frac{(₹\,93{,}50{,}000 + ₹\,1{,}03{,}50{,}000)}{2} = ₹98{,}50{,}000$$

$$\text{Rate of return on assets} = \frac{\text{Net income}}{\text{Average total assets}}$$

$$\frac{₹\,6{,}10{,}000}{₹\,98{,}50{,}000} = 6.2\%$$

This calculation is based on average total assets, because profits are assumed to be earned continually throughout the year.

This ratio is regarded as a measure of a company's efficiency in the use of its assets to generate sales. A more efficient company will generate a higher level of sales with a given level of total assets than its less efficient competitor. One weakness of this method is that it is based on the book value of assets which can lead to serious distortions. An extreme case is where a company continues to operate an asset which is no longer efficient and which has been depreciated to zero book value because its use will have favourable effect on the total asset turnover ratio. If the assets were regarded at their current value, the ratio would better reflect the company's use of its available resources.

(b) Rate of Return on Equity

To measure how effectively the resource provided by company shareholders are being utilised, analyst calculate the rate of return on equity shares for potential investors as a rough indication of the long-term return, which they may anticipate the ratio is calculated by dividing net income reduced by dividend on preference share shares by average equity shareholder's equity. Net income is reduced by preference dividends to yield that portion of profits available to equity shareholders. This result is then divided by an average of shareholder's equity for the current end previous year end. Shareholders' equity represents the sum in the equity share, capital additional contributed capital and retained earnings accounts. The rate of return on shareholders equity for company is:

$$\text{Rate of return of equity} = \frac{\text{Net income less preference dividend}}{\text{Average equity share capital}}$$

$$= \frac{₹\,6{,}10{,}000}{(₹\,72{,}70{,}000 - 70{,}60{,}000)/2} = 8.5\%$$

(c) Earnings Per Share

One of the most widely published numbers used in financial statement analysis is the earnings per share ratios since the analysis of earnings from the owner's point of view centres around the *earnings per share* concept in the case of a corporate enterprise. This is simply the relationship of net profit (income) to the number of shares of equity. Since in many corporations the number of shares changes during the year, either from issuance of new shares (new issues of equity, stock dividends, options etc.) it is common practice to use the average number of shares outstanding during the year. Earnings per share is a focal concept to which both management and the investor pay a great deal of attention. It booms large in the valuation of equity share and often is the basis for specific corporate objectives and goals in planning for the future.

$$\text{Earning per share} = \frac{\text{Net income less preference dividend}}{\text{Average number of equity shares}}$$

$$\frac{₹\,6{,}10{,}000}{5{,}00{,}000} = ₹1.22$$

A great deal of current analysis is directed to analysing past earnings per share, both on a quarterly and annual basis. Much of the financial reporting of corporation is built around this figure and are made by the financial community. Fluctuations and trends are watched closely as indicators of strength and weakness. Again, great caution is advised in the interpretation, however, to make allowances for unusal elements both in earnings and number of shares. Any significant changes in the number of equity shares (such as that caused by bonus shares, for example) requires adjustments in past date for computability.

FINANCIAL LEVERAGE RATIOS

Financial leverage ratios, which are also referred to as debt or solvency ratios, are designed to assist the decision maker in judging whether a firm has too little or much debt and then go on to explain the following debt ratios: total debt to total assets; the capitalisation ratio; interest coverage; burden coverage. These ratios are computed either by comparing fixed charges on earnings from the income statement or by relating the debt and equity (shareholders investment) items from the Balance Sheet. These leverage ratios are important to creditors, since they reflect the capacity of firm's revenues to support interest and other fixed charges, and whether there are sufficient assets to pay off the debt in the event of liquidation. Shareholders, are concerned with leverage, since interest payments increases with greater debt. If borrowing and interest are excessive, the company can even experience bankruptcy.

(a) Total Debt to Total Assets Ratio

The ratio of total debt to total assets, generally called the *debt ratio*, measures the percentage total funds provided by creditors. Debt includes current liabilities and all creditors prefer moderate debt ratios, since the lower the ratio, the greater the cushion against creditors' losses in the event of liquidation. In contrast to the creditors preference for low debt ratios, the owners may seek high leverage either (1) to magnify earnings or (2) because raising new equity means giving up some degree of control. If the debt ratio is too high, there is a degree of encouraging irresponsibility on the part of the owners. The stake of the owners can become so small that speculative activity, if it is successful, will yield a substantial percentage return to the owners. If the venture is unsuccessful, however, only a concrete loss is incurred by the owners because there investment is small.

$$\text{Debt Ratio} = \frac{\text{Total debt}}{\text{Total assets}}$$

$$= \frac{₹\ 30{,}80{,}000}{₹\ 1{,}03{,}50{,}000} = 29.75\%$$

(b) Capitalisation Ratio

Another widely used measure of financial leverage is the capitalisation ratio, which is derived by dividing long-term debt by the total of long-term debt plus owner's equity. Since the sum of debt and owner's equity represents the permanent capital of the firm, this ratio indicates the portion of the permanent capital that is financed with debt.

$$\text{Capitalisation Ratio} = \frac{\text{Long-term debt}}{\text{Long-term debt + Net worth}}$$

$$= \frac{₹\ 15{,}00{,}000}{₹\ 15{,}00{,}000 + ₹\ 72{,}70{,}000} = 17.10\%$$

From a lender's point the capitalisation ratio indicates how much of an equity cushion is present.

How could this ratio decline when the total debt to total assets ratio increased? Obviously if a company increase its debt, and this information, together with the declining liquidity ratios should make us very alert to current liabilities as analysis continues. It should be noted that, although ratios do not provide conclusive evidence of performance and profitability, they do indicate where possible problems exist and provide clues to the nature of these problems.

Most lenders are reluctant to become involved in a liquidation. Thus, while they are very concerned with how well protected their loan would be in the event of liquidation, they are more concerned with not becoming involved in such a situation. In other words, if a lender thought that a debt would not be paid in due course, the loan would not be made and while the above ratios assist in determining the lender's protection in the event of liquidation, they really do not help the lender to determine whether the firm can repay. *Coverage ratios* are designed for this purpose.

(c) Earning Coverage Ratio

The earnings coverage ratio is calculated by dividing the company's earnings before interest and taxes (EBIT) by interest on debt finance. Therefore, it is a measure of a company's ability to meet the service charges on its debt finance.

$$\text{Earning per share} = \frac{\text{EBIT}}{\text{Interest expense}}$$

$$= \frac{₹\ 10{,}50{,}000}{₹\ 40{,}000} = 26.25 \text{ times.}$$

This is in many ways a superior measure of financial risk to the leverage ratio as it attempts to measure the company's ability to avoid future financial difficulties which can arise because of its use of debt finance. The larger this ratio, the greater the reduction in the company's earnings which can occur before the company will default on its interest payments.

(d) Ratio of Owners Equity to Total Assets

The ratio of owner equity to total assets shows the percentage of the total investment. This ratio, often called the "proprietory ratio" or "shareholders' equity ratio," is determined, as shown below by dividing the owners' equity by total assets:

$$\text{Ratio of owners' equity assets total (net)} = \left[\frac{\text{Owners' equity}}{\text{Total assets (Net)}}\right]$$

$$= \frac{₹\ 72,70,000}{₹\ 1,03,50,000} = 70.24\%$$

The difference between the foregoing ratio and 100 percent represents the funds supplied by the creditors.

The ratio of owner's equity to total assets and the ratio of liabilities to total sources reflect the relative importance of the sources of borrowed funds and owners' equity and the margin of protection for the creditor claims.

The larger amount of owners' equity indicates an improvement in the long-term financial position, since there is relatively greater margin of safety for outside creditors and less long-term pressure from the point of view of the owners. The most conservative, although not always the most profitable, basis of financing when broad or other long-term obligations are used in place of capital stock is to provide for the gradual retirement of the debt. A high ratio of owners' equity to total liabilities and owners' equity is not necessarily an indication of the most profitable method of financing.

The ratio of owners equity to total liabilities and owner's equity (or to total assets), the proprietory ratio, is at least as important as the current ratio. The former ratio is a rough measure of the relative financial strength and reflects the long-term liquidity (solvency) by showing the presence or absence of long-term liability pressure. The latter gives evidence of the relative liquidity of the business, i.e., a measure of short-term solvency or the liability to meet current debts as they mature. A relatively high proprietary ratio reflects less likelihood of financial difficulty remitting from heavy fixed interest charges and inability to meet measuring debt obligations. A relatively low proprietary ratio reflects a speculative situation because of the possibility of high profit or losses. However, a detailed examination of debt interest burden is superior to any ratio.

From the point of view of the creditors the larger the percentage of assets that is supplied by shareholders, the more satisfactory the financial structure of the business, since owners' equity represents a margin of safety for creditors. In other words, a owner's equity is a "cushion" that first absorbs losses. Periods of business inactivity which are accompanied by financial stress and greatly reduced earnings should prove less burdensome to a business that has a high proprietory ratio. Then, too, a company that has a stable profit or an experienced, successful management is able to operate on a relatively lower proprietary ratio. However an upward trend in this ratio is usually considered by creditors to be favourable; and the larger the percentage of funds supplied by outside creditors, the less "conservative" the financial structure is likely to be, especially in periods of poor business, because of the fixed interest obligations and the necessity of paying or refunding maturing debts. In period of low business, because may not earn its fixed interest charges or may not be able to refinance maturing obligations on favourable terms. When the equity shareholders are quite small in comparison with the creditor's claims, a substantial decline in sales, accompanied by a large operating loss, might reduce owners equity to a dangerously low level and require a financial reorganisation. Owners' equity may be eliminated altogether and heavy losses inflicted upon the creditors.

ACTIVITY RATIOS

Activity ratios reflect the intensity with which the firm uses assets in generating sales. These ratios indicate whether the firm's investments in current and long-term assets are too small or too large. If investment in an asset is too large, it could be that the funds tied up in that asset should be used for more immediate productive purposes. For example, the firm may have unused plant capacity which it could sell and then use the proceeds in some profitable way. If investment is too small, the firm may be providing poor service to customers or inefficiently, producing its product. Some of the activity ratios, which are also referred to as efficiency or turnover are discussed below.

(a) Receivable Turnover

Both the current and the acid test ratio presume that sundry debtors can be converted into cash within enough time to allow the payment of current debits. In the management of assets, a balance must be struck in the creation of sundry debtors. If a firm grants too little credit, it may lose sales as result. On the other hand, if the firm is too generous in the extension of credit, it will soon have much of its short-term assets tied up in slow or uncollectable accounts.

The sundry debtors turnover is a measure of the number of times on the average that receivables turnover each year. This ratio is computed by dividing net credit sales by the average receivable outstanding during the year. Average sundry debtors are calculated by taking the average or the current and previous year-end sundry debtors balances.

$$\text{Debtors turnover} = \frac{\text{Total net sales or credit sales}}{\text{Average net debtors}}$$

$$= \frac{₹\ 80{,}00{,}000}{(₹\ 5{,}60{,}000 + ₹\ 6{,}00{,}000)/2} = 13.8 \text{ times}$$

This ratio indicates that debtors for the Shiva Pharma Company turnover 13.8 times per year. The average period of time required to collect debtors is obtained by dividing the turnover ratio (13.8) into the number of days in a year (360-day is used for simplicity).

$$\text{Average collection period} = \frac{\text{Number of days in year}}{\text{Debtors turnover ratio}}$$

$$= 360/13.8 = 26.1 \text{ days.}$$

On average, Shiva Pharma Company collects its receivables every 26.1 days. This means that Shiva Pharma is providing credit to customers for less than a month. If the terms of credit in this industry call for payment within 30 days of sale, a 26-day collection period may be viewed as a positive one. Comparison with an industry average would help in evaluating these results. A relatively short collection period suggests that most receivables are collectible.

(b) Inventory Turnover Ratio

Another important liquidity ratio is the inventory turnover ratio. Inventory turnover is a measure of the number of times the average inventory has been sold during the year. It is computed by dividing the cost of goods sold by the average inventory balance:

$$\text{Inventory turn ratio} = \frac{\text{Cost of goods sold}}{\text{Average inventory}}$$

$$= \frac{₹\ 44{,}50{,}000}{(₹\ 32{,}00{,}000 + ₹\ 40{,}00{,}000)/2} = 1.236 \text{ times.}$$

The amount of time required to sell the average inventory can be determined by dividing the inventory turnover ratio into the number of days in the year (again, 360 for simplicity).

$$\text{Average inventory turnover days} = \frac{\text{Number of days in the year}}{\text{Inventory turnover ratio}}$$

$$= \frac{360}{1.236} = 291.26$$

The greater the number of times per year that inventory *turns over*, the more efficiently it is being used. The smaller the inventory in relation to annual sales, the greater the sales activity that the inventory is able to support. Ideally, average inventory should be based on a 12-month average; otherwise the average may be distorted by seasonal fluctuations.

Before proper use can be made of this ratio it is necessary for the company to specify an "ideal" ratio at which it can aim. The higher this ratio, the lower will be the amount of funds that the company has tied up in inventory at a particular times, but the more times the company will have to place orders for times of inventory. However, it is unlikely that an ideal inventory turnover ratio can be estimated which will lead to an optimal inventory policy. The reverse is more likely to be true, that is, an optimal policy for each inventory item will result in an optimum turnover ratio.

(c) Total Asset Turnover

Total asset turnover measures the turnover of all the company's assets and is calculated by dividing sales by total assets average.

$$\text{Total asset turnover} = \frac{\text{Sales}}{\text{Average total assets}}$$

$$= \frac{₹\ 80{,}00{,}000}{₹\ 98{,}50{,}000} = .81$$

The calculation for Shiva Pharma Company is based on average total assets because sales are assumed to be incurred continually throughout the year.

(d) Fixed Asset Turnover

The fixed assets turnover ratio is defined as sales divided by fixed assets. This ratio is a measure of how well the firm was its long-term (fixed) assets and shows how many ₹ of sales are supported one ₹ of fixed assets.

$$\text{Fixed asset turnover} = \frac{\text{Sales}}{\text{Fixed asset}}$$

$$= \frac{₹\ 80{,}00{,}000}{₹\ 42{,}00{,}000} = 1.90$$

For Shiva Pharma Company, the asset turnover is 1.90. In general higher than average fixed assets turnover ratios are supposed to reflect better than average fixed asset management, and relatively low fixed assets turnover ratios are supposed to reflect relatively poor fixed assets management. However, since book values of fixed assets may be considerably different than the market value of these assets, the fixed assets turnover may be deceptively low or high. For example, a firm with relatively old but still serviceable plant that has been almost fully depreciated will have a lower book value of fixed assets than a competitor with a new plant, and for similar sales levels the older plant will tend to have a higher fixed assets turnover even though both firms may be utilising their fixed assets at about the same efficiency.

(e) Marketability Ratio

Marketability ratios measure the response of the securities markets to published financial data or to other measures that concern investor decision to purchase securities. Investors and potential investors primarily use these ratios.

(f) Price Earning Ratio

Perhaps the most common marketability ratio is the price earnings ratio, which is popularly referred to as the P.E. ratio. It is an overall measure of the desirability of the firm. The ratio reflects market price of the shares in relation to earnings. The P.E. ratio is given by:

$$\text{P.E. Ratio} = \frac{\text{Market price of share}}{\text{Earning per share}}$$

$$= \frac{₹\ 10}{₹\ 1.22} = 8.2$$

The more attractive the firm is to the investor, the higher its P.E. ratio. Comparison within the industry is an excellent aid in interpreting the P.E. ratio. An unusually low P.E. ratio generally indicates that investors perceive a share to be fairly risky. An unusually high P.E. ratio indicates that investors have high expectations for growth in earnings and share prices.

(g) Dividend Payout Ratio

The dividend payout is the ratio of dividends per share to earnings per share or total dividends to net income. The dividend payout ratio is

$$\text{Dividend payout ratio} = \frac{\text{Cash dividends}}{\text{Net income}}$$

$$= \frac{₹\ 1,00,000}{₹\ 6,10,000} = 16.4$$

This dividend payment ratio reflects the proportion of earnings which are paid to shareholders. As the proportion increases, the amount retained for reinvestment in the firm decreases, theoretically diminishing the future asset base from which further earnings growth may come.

(h) Book Value Per Share

The book value, also known as the net worth, is the assets minus liabilities. In other words, net worth, book value, and shareholders' equity are all similar concepts. The book value per share is a measure of the historical cost value of the firm's assets on a per share basis and is given by dividing the book value or net worth by the number of equity shares.

$$\text{Book value per share} = \frac{\text{Net worth}}{\text{Number of equity shares}}$$

$$= \frac{₹\ 72,70,000}{5,00,000} = ₹\ 14.54$$

Book value per share may be of some consideration if the firm is to be liquidated, its assets sold, and the proceeds distributed to the shareholders, but it rarely reflects the actual market value of the shares or of the assets themselves at auction. Obviously, it has limited uses.

DUPONT SYSTEM OF FINANCIAL ANALYSIS

Around World War I the DuPont Company introduced a method of financial analysis which has general recognition for its usefulness and has, in one form or another been adopted by most firms. Its purpose is to provide management with a measure of performance in the form of a return on investment, ROI. It brings together the activity ratios and profit margin on sales and shows how these ratios interact to determine the profitability of assets. The basic frame work of the system is set out in Figure-1.

FIGURE-1

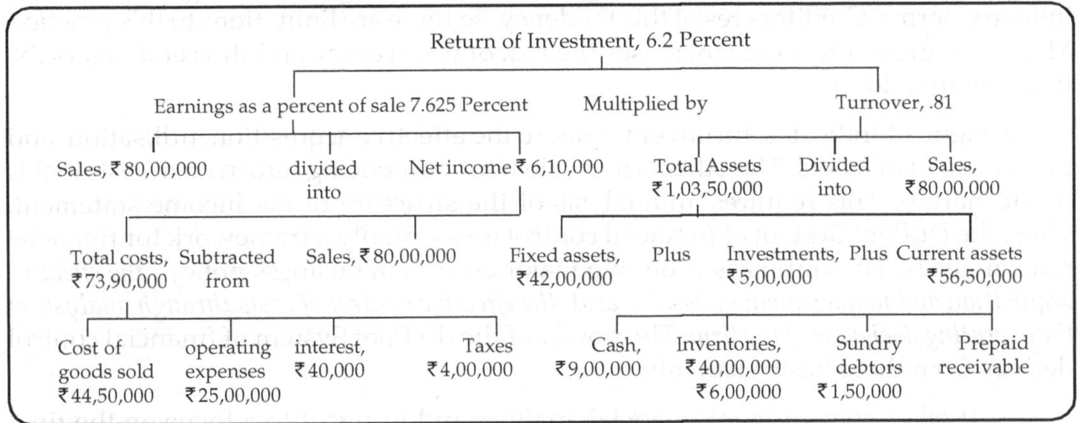

The right side of the figure develops the turnover ratio. That section shows how current assets, when added to fixed assets and investment, gives total investment. Total investment divided into sales gives the turnover of investment.

The left side of the figure develops the profit margin on sales. The individual expense item plus income taxes subtracted from sales to produce net issue after taxes. Net income divided by sales gives the profit margin on sales, when the asset turnover ratio on the right side of Figure—1 is multiplied by the profit margin on sales developed on the left side of the figure, the product is the return on total investments (ROI) to the firm. This can be seen from the

$$\frac{\text{Profit}}{\text{Sales}} \times \frac{\text{Sales}}{\text{Total Assets}} = \text{ROI}$$

Shiva Pharma Company's torunover was seen to be .81 times its profits margin on sales, was 7.625 per cent. Multiplied together, turnover and profit margin produced a return on assets equal to 6.2 percent.

Extending the DuPont System to Include Financial Leverage

To measure the effect of financial leverage on equity shareholders return, formula used is as follow:

$$\text{Rate of return on Net worth} = \frac{\text{Return on assets (ROI)}}{\text{Percent of assets financed by net worth}}$$

$$= \frac{\text{Return on assets (ROI)}}{1.0 - \text{Debt ratio}}$$

$$= \frac{6.2}{1.0 - .2975} = \frac{6.2}{.7025} = 8.825$$

This formula is useful for showing how financial leverage can be used to increase the rate of return on net worth. But increasing returns on net worth by using more and more leverage causes the leverage ratios to rise higher and higher above the industry norms. Creditors resist this tendency, so there are limitations to this practice. Moreover, greater leverage increases the risk of bankruptcy and thus endangers the firm's shareholders.

As Figure-1 indicates, turnover relates to the effective acquisition, utilisation, and management of assets. The other critical element influencing return on investment is profit margin. This requires an analysis of the structure of the income statement. Thus, the DuPont System of financial control is essentially a framework for financial ratio analysis. The emphasis is on two major aspects in business policy : *the effective acquisition and management of assets;* and *the effective control of costs through analysis of the operating decisions of the firm.* The power of the du Pont System of financial control derives from three basic elements:

1. It takes conventional financial analysis and brings it to a focus on the final results of the operations-return on investment. If the return on investment is unsatisfactory, the du Pont System of financial control directs attention to the possible causes of poor performance. Or conversely, it will direct attention to the factors that make for usual success.
2. There is an emphasis in the use of the du Pont System of financial control on a time-trend analysis of the data. It is remarkable how plotting data over time provides insights into the operations of the business firm. An historical record in which time patterns are observed is quite informative. When historical analysis of the date is supplemented by a time trend of ratios, even greater insights may be achieved.
3. The du Pont System of financial control provides a basis for making comparisons. In addition to the time trend analysis, the development of du Pont System of financial analysis provides a basis for comparison with competitors, other firms, and industry composites.

In summary, the du Pont System of financial control is a modified form of financial analysis. One of its greatest strengths is that it focuses on the output of financial analysis.

ILLUSTRATIVE PROBLEMS

1. A firm sells 5,00,000 units of a product at ₹ 25 per unit during a one year period. The cost of each unit is ₹ 20. The firms inventory is 50,000 units. What is the inventory turnover in units and in ₹?

Solution

$$\text{Inventory turnover in units} = \frac{\text{Cost of goods sold}}{\text{Inventory}} = \frac{₹1,00,00,000}{10,00,000} = 10/1$$

$$\text{Inventory turnover in rupees} = \frac{\text{Sales}}{\text{Inventory}} = \frac{₹1,25,00,000}{10,00,000} = 12.5/1$$

2. Roop Saree store has been suffering a severe decline in return on assets (ROA) over the last 5 years, and management has asked you to recommend corrective action. Based on the preliminary information in the table, where would you begin your initial investigative effort?

	2009	*2010*	*2011*	*2012*	*2013*
ROA (percent)	8.4	8.0	7.2	4.8	3.1
Sales (thousands)	₹ 3,500	4,600	6,000	9,200	11,000
Profit after taxes (thousands)	₹ 175	225	280	415	465

Solution

The company is enjoying a healthy increase in sales and profits although the ROA seems to imply that things could be even better. We know that ROA-Margin X turnover and, since we know ROA and can find the margin for the information given, we can solve the turnover:

	2009	*2010*	*2011*	*2012*	*2013*
Margin (per cent)	5.0	4.9	4.7	4.5	4.2
Turnover	1.68	1.63	1.53	1.07	0.74
ROA (per cent)	8.4	8.00	7.2	4.8	3.1

It appears that Roop's problems are due to both declining margins and slower turnover. Part of their rapid sales growth may actually be due to the lower margins and, although this area still warrants further investigation, the more severe problem appears to be in the rapid decline in turnover. The company seems to be employing an inordinate amount of assets, and the investigation should begin there.

3. Modern Hosiery has sales of ₹ 6 crores, asset turnover ratio of 6 for the year, and net profit of ₹ 12,00,000

(a) What is the company's return on assets or earning power?

(b) The company will install new point-of-sales cash registers throughout the stores. This equipment is expected to increase efficiency in inventory control, reduce clerical errors, and improve record keeping throughout the system. The new equipment will increase the investment in assets by 20% and is expected to increase the net profit margin from 2% now to 3%. No change in sales is expected. What is the effect of the new equipment on the return on assets ratio or earning power?

Solution

(a) Total assets = sales/turnover = ₹ 6 crores/6 = ₹ 1 crore

Earning power = net profits/total assets = ₹ 12,00,000/₹ 1 crore = 12%

(b) Total assets = ₹ 1,00,00,000 × 1.2 = ₹ 1,20,00,000

Earnings power = turnover x net profit margin

$$= \frac{₹ 6 \text{ crore}}{₹ 1.20 \text{ crore}} = 15\%$$

4. The data for various companies in the same industry and about the same size follow:

Company	*A*	*B*	*C*	*D*	*E*	*F*
Sales (in thousands)	₹ 10	20	8	5	12	17
Total assets (in thousands)	8	10	6	2.5	4	8
Net income (in thousands)	0.7	2	0.8	0.5	1.5	1

Determine the asset turnover, net profit margin, and earning power for each of the concerns.

Solution

For each of the companies, the asset turnover, net profit-margin and earning power are tabulated below:

Company	*Asset Turnover*	*Net Profit Margin*	*Earning Power*
A	1.25	7%	8.75%
B	2.00	10%	20.00%
C	1.33	10%	13.33%
D	2.00	10%	20.00%
E	3.00	12.50%	37.50%
F	2.12	5.88%	12.50%

QUESTIONS

1. Why must financial statements be analysed? If you were a firm's creditor, which ratios would be especially important to you? Why?
2. Explain the reason for using quick ratio as a measure of firm's solvency rather than the current ratio.
3. Explain how certain profitability and turnover ratios can give misleading indications of financial performance of a firm experiencing rapid sales growth.
4. Indicate why profitability is measured in two ways. Provide examples of types of businesses which would tend to have high profit margins and low returns on assets and vice versa.
5. The three basic groups of financial ratios are liquidity, leverage, and profitability ratios. Discuss the nature of each group and list two example ratios that you would use to measure that aspect of a firm's financial condition.
6. What factors would you, as financial manager, want to examine if a firm's rate of return on assets or on net worth is too low?
7. "The higher the rate of return on investment (ROI), the better the firm's management". Is this statement true for all firms? Explain, if you disagree with the statement, give examples of instances in which it might not be true.
8. Financial ratios are based on historical data. Of what use are they in developing expectations about future?
9. Evaluate the following statement: "Ratio analysis is useless. A firm never paid its trade credit with a current ratio or met a long-term payment with a financial ratio".

PROBLEMS

1. Rama Company has sales of ₹ 40,00,000 and has a gross profit margin of 40 percent. The end of quarter inventories are as follows:

Quarter	1	2	3	5
Inventory	₹ 4,00,000	8,00,000	12,00,000	2,00,000

Calculate the firm's inventory turnover and the average age of inventory.

Ans.: Inventory turnover =3.69; Average age of inventory = 97.53

2. A firm has an earnings before interest of ₹ 10,00,000 interest charges of ₹ 80,000, taxes of ₹ 4,60,000, total assets of ₹ 70,00,000, and total liabilities of ₹ 20,00,000. What is its ROE?

Ans.: = 9.2 per cent

3. A firm has cash of ₹ 25,000, receivables of ₹ 80,000 and inventories of ₹ 88,000,. It has no other current assets, How much can it have in current liabilities and still have a 2/1 current ratio?

Ans.: ₹ 96,500

4. A firm has profit margin of 15 percent and an asset turnover of 2.5. What is its ROI?

Ans.: 37.5 per cent

5. A firm has current liabilities of ₹ 1,00,000, a mortgage of ₹ 1,50,000, and bonds of ₹ 2,50,000. Its total equity is ₹ 7,50,000. What is the debt-equity ratio and debt-asset ratio?

Ans.: Debt-equity ratio = 2/3; Debt-asset ratio = 40 percent.

6. A firm's stock is selling for ₹ 25 per share. It has a 1996 EPS of ₹ 5 and find a dividend of ₹ 2. What is the dividend pay out and dividend yields?

Ans.: = Dividend payout = 2/5; Dividend yield = .08

7. A firm has an earnings before interest and tax of ₹ 27,00,000 and ₹ 60,00,000 in debt at 15 per cent. What is its times interest earned ratio?

Ans.: 3 times

8. A firm has sales of ₹ 2,50,000, a cost of goods sold of ₹ 88,000 and an inventory of ₹ 40,000. What is its inventory turnover?

Ans.: 2.2 times

4

FINANCIAL MODELING

INTRODUCTION

Finance has always been a pivotal segment of the aggregate organisational structure; the art of financial management continues to assume added significance with decision making as the main thrust and sophistication as a necessary ingredient. The financial manager's tasks could be separated into several distinct areas. *First,* it is essential that the financial manager analyse the past and present financial positions of the company in question to ascertain strengths and weaknesses. *Second,* given that analysis, the financial manager must plan the need for funds in order to fortify the strengths, ameliorate the weaknesses, and sustain the presumed course and direction of future business activities. *Third,* management must take the funds information which has been gathered in the planning process and set forth procedures to acquire those funds. Essentially, funds acquisition is the determination of the composition of funds sources. Once the funds have been raised, the *fourth* task is their proper investment. In effect, this fourth step is the determination of the asset composition (mix) of the firm. This sequence of steps provides the foundation from which management performance may be evaluated implicitly or explicitly by current and prospective stockholders and by the board of directors via the return on asset investment (ROI) criterion.

The principal tools of the financial manager are financial statement analysis, operating and financial leverage, cost-volume-profit relationships, fund statements, budgeting and *pro forma* statements, and financial modeling. Financial modeling, fancy buzz word, is a meaningful concept that has gradually, over time, absorbed into the body of business knowledge and become an integral part of the financial planning and control function. Most new techniques are initially oversold to create interest and to overcome the natural forces that resist change. Financial modeling has not been an exception. At present, financial modeling is in its gestation period. There have been many well publicised success stories concerning its benefits; there are also a number of disappointments and failures. Planning is perhaps best conceived as the *ex ante* recognition and identification segment, which is such an integral part of composite financial management performance. This requires the financial manager to be increasingly analytical, decision-oriented, and familiar with operations research (e.g., linear programming and related techniques), management information systems, the computer and its applications, the management science concepts, and the ability to construct viable financial models.

CONCEPTUAL MODELS FOR STRATEGIC DECISION MAKING

Conceptual models are designed to capture the meaning of large amounts of information quickly. Decision makers are often crippled by the existence of too much information. Critical information may be overlooked or the organization may be paralyzed because nobody can decide which information to focus on. Consulting organizations have attempted to overcome these problems by developing conceptual models such as the strength/attractiveness grids and product life cycle models that are discussed in the following sections.

Strength/Attractiveness Grids

Strength/attractiveness grids provide a way to look at each of a company's products or businesses in terms of both the attractiveness of the industry and the position of the company in the industry. A number of these models exist, including the Boston Consulting Group Model and the Hofer Product/Market Evolution Matrix. They all consist of a grid such as that in Figure 1, in which the desirability of the industry is placed on one axis and the competitive strength of the company is placed on the other axis. The fundamental point of all such grids is that we want to be in a strong position in a desirable industry.

The drivetrain business of Eaton would be placed in the upper part of the grid, for example. The industry is attractive to Eaton because barriers to entry are high, quality is more important than price, and so on, so there are opportunities for competitive advantage and economic profit. There is no dominant player other than Eaton. The drivetrain business would be placed on the left side of the grid because Eaton is the dominant player. The upper-left position of

FIGURE 1

STRENGTH/ATTRACTIVENESS GRID

Industry Attractiveness	High	Low
High	Continue to build and maintain competitive strength	Improve competitive position or get out
Low	Milk for cash	Get out or milk for cash

The models differ with regard to the specifics of how the companies measure industry desirability. Some models focus on narrow definitions of desirability, such as growth rate, and narrow definitions of strength, such as market share, but we these limited measures are insufficient. Ultimately, the companies are to consider all the factors that make a market attractive and create the foundation for competitive advantage. Weighing all of those factors and placing a product or business in the matrix necessarily re. quires a major dose of seasoned judgment.

Product Life Cycle Model

Most products pass through a life cycle, and optimal strategy varies by phase of the life cycle. Figure 2 illustrates a typical product life cycle curve. In the development phase, the product does not yet have wide market recognition. Using video-recorders (VCRs) as an example, the units first came on the market priced in the ₹ $20,000, range, with few movies available to rent. Several different formats were being offered by competing companies, which further limited the supply of rental movies. Sales were, needless to say, limited. As less costly production methods were developed and rental movies became available, VCRs entered the growth stage of their life cycle. While sales grew rapidly, the VHS format won dominance, driving other players from the marketplace. Within a few years, households owned VCRs and the product began the transition into the maturity phase. It appeared that the video-recorder market may remain in the maturity phase for some years.

However, new technology such as digital videodisk or DVDs made the existing units obsolete, leading to a new round of growth. Developments in communications technology led to the decline phase by making driving to the video rental shop an obsolete method of gaining access to a movie.

FIGURE 2
PRODUCT LIFE CYCLE CURVE

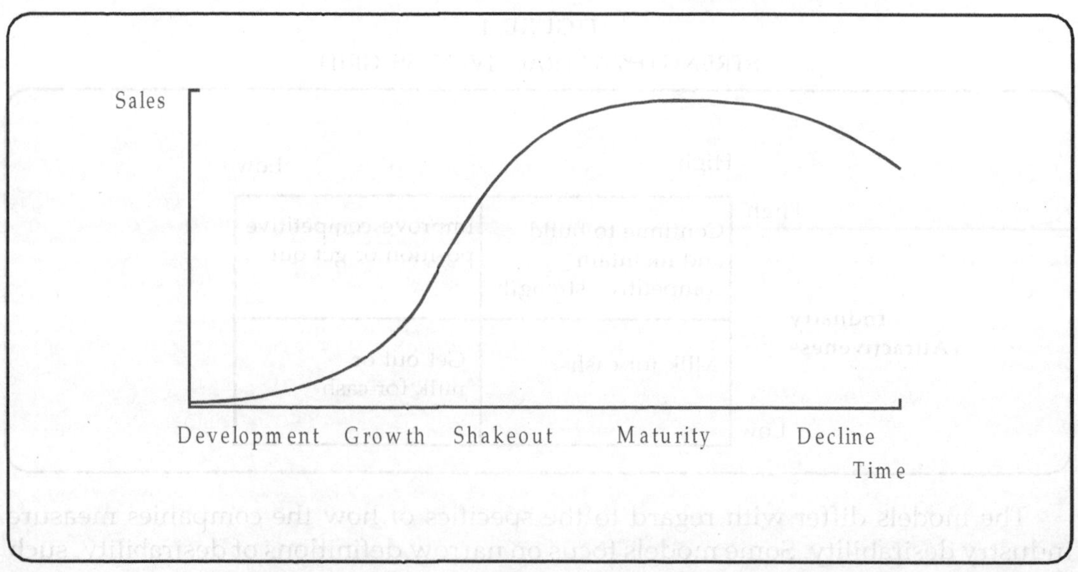

Identification of the position in the life cycle is helpful in identifying industry attractiveness and developing a strategy. In the development phase, for example, companies try to position themselves so that they can become the industry leader when the growth phase begins and to differentiate themselves so that they will not have to rely on pure price competition to develop market share. Their focus is not on current income but on positioning themselves for future profits. This is why several companies were trying to gain dominance for their format during the development stage of the life cycle.

During the growth phase the inability of the industry to keep up with ballooning demand sometimes makes profits easy to come by. Some business advisors have become so enamored as to suggest that the major focus of business strategy should be to stay positioned in the high-growth part of the life cycle. Growth of sales does not, however, produce profitability unless there are restrictions on the rate of supply growth. Thousands of neighborhood video rental stores failed during the rapid growth part of the cycle because there were no barriers to entry and customers preferred larger entrants. If growth temporarily removes competitive pressures on price, it creates a window of opportunity to establish the competitive advantage that will give a company the lead position and continued profitability in the maturity phase. Even a company with no competitive advantage may profit temporarily in this phase before pulling out at maturity. If there are no barriers to entry, supply will catch up with demand eventually, and competitive advantage must be gained and sustained if the company are to continue to create wealth.

If supply cannot keep up with demand during rapid growth, that situation will change as we approach maturity and growth slows. Those who were complacent because of the large profits during the growth stage will fail in this transition period. Successful companies will continue to follow the strategies developed earlier and will not be buffeted or panicked by temporarily low profitability caused by the death throes of competitors. They will often consolidate their power by acquiring failed competitors.

In the maturity or saturation phase, growth stops or is limited by the overall growth of the population and economy. It is not necessarily a bad place to be. The secret of profitability at this stage is to have planned earlier for competitive advantage.

Proper strategy can maximize profitability in the decline phase. Efficiency and cost controls are often critical at this stage. The decline stage may last for decades and provide satisfactory profitability to the industry leaders during that stage. Finally, the most profitable abandonment time must be chosen. Finding the right abandonment time is not always easy.

The conclusion from studies of numerous companies over the product life cycle is that there is no one right place to be. With competitive advantage, the companies can create wealth at any stage. Without competitive advantage, they can lose money at any stage. Nevertheless, it is important to recognize the stage they are in so that they can plan accordingly.

Implementing the Strategy Across the Organization

A change in strategy generally requires changes throughout the organization. Changes include organizational structures, marketing and distribution methods, production methods, and human resource policies. Financial policy, control methods, and reward structures must also be brought in line with the strategy. Like an orchestra conductor, the CEO must bring all the parts together in harmony to support the company's strategy.

THE CONCEPT OF FINANCIAL MODEL

The term, financial modeling, has been defined in many different ways. All too frequently these definition, have created an atmosphere of pseudo-sophistication. Actually, financial modeling is not a complex concept. *It is simply the process of developing financial statements and ratios which deal typically with future projections based upon a defined set of assumptions and logical relationships.*

When an accountant develops a set of assumptions and historical ratios, and then applies normal accounting logic in the preparation and summarisation of spread sheets, we refer to the end product as financial projections or *pro forma* statements. If the same process is followed, except that, instead of pencil, paper and a ten-key adding machine, a computer time-sharing terminal is utilised, the process becomes financial modeling.

As the term is frequently used today, *a financial model is a mechanised way of preparing financial projections.* The advantages of mechanisation in this case are basically threefold: the time required to prepare and revise the projections, the cost of preparation, and the accuracy of the projections.

In terms of mathematical-statistical sophistication, most financial models use the same algebra found in accounting: add, multiply, divide and, of course, debits equal credits. In addition, logic routines normally found in the models relate to depreciation calculations, interest rates, discounting of cash flow, return-on-investment calculations, and growth rates. The output of a financial model is typically a financial statement such while evaluating alternate assumptions, only selected lines of different statements will be printed so as to reduce printing time.

For purposes of decision-making, financial variables may be classified into exogenous and endogenous variables. The exogenous variables are those variables whose values are taken by the decision-maker as given, whereas the endogenous variables are those variables whose value are determined by the model itself. The exogenous variables may in turn be divided into those variables subject to management control and those beyond management control. Given the values assigned to the exogenous variables, the corresponding values of the endogenous variables are determined by the system of relationship within the mathematical model.

The relationships defined by the model also determine how and to what extent endogenous variables are affected by changes in the exogenous variables brought about by new financial decisions. In terms of the model, new financial decisions cause exogenous variables to take on a corresponding set of new values, which in turn causes the endogenous variables to seek their new equilibrium values. If, in addition, there exists an objective function that defines how changes in each variable affect the welfare of the firm, then the financial manager is able to make value judgements among different policies and select that course of action which produces the best results.

Another useful distinction between variables in the mathematical model is the distinction between random variables and deterministic variables. Random variables may be thought of as those variables whose values cannot be predicted with certainty at the time a decision is made. Deterministic variables are simply variables that are not random, that is, variables whose values can be predicted with certainty at the time a decision is made. Since financial decisions must frequently be made under conditions of uncertainty, a number of the mathematical models contain random as well as deterministic variables.

Until a few years ago, mechanisation of projections was not particularly attractive because the programmes required for an in-house computer were expensive to write. Once the programmes were completed, the computer could prepare the projections in a matter of minutes with a very high degree of accuracy. However, there frequently were substantial delays, often in terms of days, in key-punching the data and then scheduling the programme on the computer.

RECENT BREAKTHROUGHS IN FINANCIAL MODELING

By far the most important technological innovation affecting financial analysis and providing the opportunity to greatly expend the use of financial models in recent years has been the advent of inexpensive and readily available computing capacity. A microcomputer is on the desk of virtually every financial analyst at progressive and innovative firms. The primary impact of this cheap computing capacity and user-friendly software has been the case with which previously laborious financial analysis can now be performed and, in particular, the heightened ability of firms to assess risk. Previously, if the firm was going to perform a particularly tedious procedure, such as a forecast for the next year's cash flows for each month, it was quite costly in time and effort to go through the procedure even once. Thus, analysis was often limited to one pass through the algorithm, utilising the best estimates of the input variables. Sensitivity and simulation analysis procedures could be justified only for the most critical decisions. But the microcomputer revolution has changed all that. Now, the changing of input variables and the observation of the effects on output variables takes seconds, not hours. Procedures to assess risk, which in the past were too expensive, can now be performed routinely.

Three types of microcomputer software are currently available and are useful for the analysis of financial decisions: the *spreadsheet*, the *mathematical programming package,* and the *simulation package.* Spreadsheets are now a commodity item; dozens are on the market. Spreadsheets consist of rows and columns. and are useful in the analysis of many types of finance problems. The power of the spreadsheet stems from its *copying feature* and its *quick execution of recalculations.* The former is useful if the financial analysis procedure requires more than a few similar calculations; it makes model building in such circumstances much easier and faster than manual methods. If the analyst wants to see the effect of a deviation from the original estimate on important outcome variables, the quick recalculation feature of the spreadsheet makes substantial analysis feasible; the analyst merely changes the data or formula, and the spreadsheet automatically recalculates all the other cells. However, one note of warning is appropriate. *Spreadsheets are a financial modeling tool, not an end in themselves.* The data outputs they provide are only as good as the estimated input data and the financial algorithms used.

While spreadsheets are very useful in a number of respects, they are tools of *analysis,* not *optimisation.* Some of the problems we study in management are such that an *optimum* solution can be found by the proper application of *mathematical programming techniques,* among them important are *linear programming* (where all the variables may assume noninteger values) and *integer programming* (where only one or several variables may assume integer values), are available. While it is always desirable to accomplish something for less cost, the real value of increased efficiency in programming a financial model is in the end product. The new languages have permitted the development of models that are more comprehensive in nature and more adaptable to the needs of the executives and planners who use the models. Revisions in the models can be made easily and quickly. The models are no longer cast in stone but are adaptable to revisions and refinements.

FINANCIAL MODELS AS A BUSINESS TOOL

The description of a new technique, such as financial modeling, is frequently of intellectual interest. But, for the technique to be of value, it must serve a function. The complexity and sophistication of a technique may intrigue the mind and imagination but in the end it must be evaluated in a practical sense. This seems to have been the problem with many of the earlier attempts at financial modeling. In effect, the models tended to become ends unto themselves rather than useful tools for others to use. They did not meet the critical test in terms of contributing to the achievement of corporate goals.

Financial modeling should be viewed in a functional sense rather than as a technical achievement. How and where can it be used? Some proponents of the technique envision huge corporate models with video-tube displays whereby a captain of industry could plot future courses of action. Eventually such modeling systems may exist. They do not appear to be practical today. *What approaches can a finance manager follow in gaining initial exposure to the actual operations of a financial model?* There are several: through special analysis problems, financial planning models, and corporate models.

Special Analysis

Recent experience indicates financial modeling is very successful when it is initially used in a limited area to solve specific problems. Some examples of such areas are portfolio construction, foreign exchange rates, income tax planning, merger and acquisition analysis, capital equipment evaluation, and analysis of capital structure and bank financing. Real benefits have resulted from financial models applied in these areas. This route also enables financial manager to test the water before deciding whether to jump in—or how deep they should get into it.

FINANCIAL MODELING AND PLANNING

Another approach to financial modeling is to view it as a part of the planning function in an organisation. While this approach has been successful in a number of cases, the chances of success are highly dependent on how well the planning function is organised and accepted by executive management. A finance manager cannot use financial modeling as a substitute for planning, but can use financial modeling to improve planning in an organisation.

It is difficult to generalise about how financial modeling may be used in planning activities because these activities vary so much from company to company and industry to industry. When the emphasis is primarily on the annual plan, the model is usually set up in monthly increments and may be adjusted to reflect monthly operating results and budget revisions. This capability has been particularly useful in industries where prices vary substantially for raw materials. Another important use is in multi-division companies where the clerical-mechanical problems of consolidation limit the use of revised budgets and current outlooks. With a model, consolidations of the budgets of the individual divisions can be accomplished within minutes. With current pressures from investors for earnings projections, a financial model related to the budget may be of considerable value in preparing statement. In addition to the annual planning cycle, most companies today are preparing long-range plans extending over a number of years. In this connection, financial models are useful in evaluating alternate plans and strategies. The *what if* capability of a model is of particular value in this regard.

An example of such a question is: What would be the annual earnings per share if Division Alpha's sales grew at 5 percent instead of 3 percent and Division Omega's sales at 1 percent instead of 7 percent? Of course, such a question could be answered without a model. But, because of short response time and low cost of analysis with a model, more questions are asked, and management tends to get a more comprehensive understanding of the financial implications of different strategies and economic conditions.

CORPORATE MODELS

Financial modeling has also been used in operating management systems. In these situations, the financial model becomes a part (often referred to as a module) of a corporate model which encompasses a number of modules. The nonfinancially oriented modules in a corporate model typically relate to the physical characteristics of production and marketing. For example, the production modules may relate to raw material requirements in tonnes, production capacities in units, and manpower requirements in man-hours. The marketing modules typically deal with factors such as market segments, advertising and promotion programmes, market penetration, price-volume relationships, discounts and allowances, and channels of distribution.

Just as accounting systems eventually tie together the results of the many operating segments of a company in developing financial statements, the financial portion of a corporate model integrates the various modules relating to operations.

COMMUNICATION AND UNDERSTANDING GAP

It is much easier to identify application areas where modeling should be beneficial than to explain why it is not being more widely used today in business decision making. In the technical literature on the subject, there is obviously a broad gap between how the technician thinks modeling should be used and how executives actually use it.

This communication or understanding gap is not new or unique to financial modeling. Executives have always received an abundance of advice from critics who are anxious to tell them how to run their businesses. While technicians criticise management for being backward and resistant to change, they themselves are usually at fault for not communicating more effectively. They persist in using their unique jargon in such a way as to turn off individuals outside their own circle. Jargon also is an excellent screen to hide behind when you don't have an intelligent answer to a good question.

Another reason for the limited use of modeling is the lack of success of early modeling projects. Many of these projects did not succeed, because they were over sold to executive management. Others failed because the models became unnecessarily complex. Some technicians wanted executive management to surrender its decision-making responsibility to the assumed logic of the "black box." When executive management asked what was in the "black box," the answer too often was "that is a technical matter that you won't understand because of your limited background in this area—but I assure you that it will work." The typical executive reaction to such a comment was that the model builder didn't understand the business because of his limited background in executive management—therefore, why pursue the subject any further?

There are ways, however, of narrowing this communication-understanding gap, and they do not involve replacing executive management. The first step is the selection of a person to be responsible for the financial modeling effort. The selection should not be based on technical expertise or years of experience. The right individual will typically be a comer in the organisation who relates primarily to executive management and communicates effectively at this level. He must also be a problem solver with a capability to work with financial data and quantitative analysis. He must be oriented toward making things happen on an orderly and timely basis. The second step in closing the communication-understanding gap relates to executive management. As a group and as individuals, they must define more precisely how the planning function should operate and what role projections and quantitative analysis will play in the decision-making process. Executive management must also analyse its own management style and the management style of the company. A company with an autocratic president who makes seat of the pants decisions will have little need for a financial model. On the other hand, a corporation which emphasises planning and uses financial analysis as a primary means of control will find that financial modeling is a meaningful asset.

ABUSES OF FINANCIAL MODELING

Rather than extol the limitless benefits of financial modeling, it would be more useful to evaluate some reasons why the technique has not been successful in a number of practical business situations.

1. *Don't meander into financial modeling:* A number of companies have launched financial modeling projects without adequate knowledge or a sense of direction. When this happens, the bureaucratic elements inherent in all organisations slowly grab hold of the project. Before, one realises it, *ad hoc* committees may have blurred the objectives of the project and extended the completion dates indefinitely.

2. *Problems of excessive evaluation of computer software:* While it is important to learn about computer software used in financial modeling, this can be overdone. Because of the number of competing software systems available and the rapid technological change in this area, it is easy to lose sight of the forest (the use of the models) because of the trees (the software systems).

3. *Beware of sophisticated statistical models:* A financial model typically is built upon the logic of accounting statements. Some people outside the accounting profession may not be impressed with the complexity of accounting logic. But they usually find it is considerably more difficult to understand than they expect when they are charged with developing financial models. Statistical probability distributions are technically interesting and potentially useful. However, they should not be incorporated into the financial models until the models have been in operation for some time. Generally speaking, these techniques are like candles on a birthday cake. They improve the looks of the cake but not its ultimate use.

4. *Recognise the "future shock" syndrome:* A number of well-conceived financial models have failed because of the reactions of the people who run and use them. The "future shock" or rate at which an organisation can change, must be carefully evaluated and considered in both the design of the models and in the way they are introduced into the organisation. The spread sheet approach to projections may be laburious and ineffective. However, it is a known element to the finance manager who has been working with it during his whole career. The financial model may be a superior technique. But, to many, it may seem to be a threat both to their technical knowledge and their relationship to the organisation.

5. *Financial models are not for everyone:'* There are many situations where financial

modeling would be of very limited use. Before a model can be applied, some form of logical structure must exist and be accepted by the decision-making group. In addition to structure, there must be a means of developing input data and assumptions. The structure of the model may take into account both fixed and variable elements of cost. However, the model will be of little value if there is not a similar breakdown of cost data available for input into the model.

6. *Financial models, budgets, and general ledgers are different:* The potential use of computerised general ledger systems as a financial model has been stressed by some financial managers. While the theory is good, the approach usually is not practical. The level of detail required in a general ledger and the volume of data in the files make it a complex data processing system—even on a monthly closing cycle. Typically, budget data is included in a computer-based general ledger system. However, this is normally at a summary level above the lowest level transaction code. A financial model normally is at a summary level above the budget, but it should be integrated to the budget level. The financial model must operate at an aggregate level in order to keep the number of input elements within reason and to keep the processing time under control.

THE USE AND BENEFITS OF FINANCIAL MODELS

The advent of cost-benefit analysis, which is another new and only partially proven financial tool, means that management must evaluate new systems in a rational manner that compares related costs and benefits. Applying this to financial modeling is difficult, because the most important benefits are those that improve the quality of executive decisions. The problem is to determine how much the quality of executive decisions has been improved and how much of this improvement is due to the financial model and how much to the executives themselves. There are a number of explicit benefits related to financial modeling, but the really important benefits are implicit and imbedded within the executive decision-making process. Most of these benefits can only be evaluated by an executive through first-hand experience. Yet, it can be useful to explore some of them. Here are five particularly pertinent ones.

1. *Increase the breadth of analysis leading to decision making:* In evaluating capital expenditure decisions or a profit plan, it has been fairly common to consider only a few alternate strategies or economic assumptions before reaching a decision. Cost has been one factor limiting the number of contingency plans reviewed, but time to prepare the alternatives has usually been the primary limiting factor.

With a financial model, both the cost and time limitations are greatly reduced. As a result, a decision that might have been based on three or four cycles of analysis might now be predicated on 30 or 40 cycles of analysis. In a similar manner, budget outlooks can be adjusted more frequently to reflect new data and changes in assumptions and forecasts. In effect, the financial model shifts the effort of the financial analyst away from pencil pushing and toward the evaluation of alternate conditions and decisions.

2. *Provide a framework for long-range planning:* The primary problem of long-range planning in industry is that everybody talks about it but few people do anything about it. One reason for this is the lack of structure within the planning process. A financial model may provide a focal point for structuring the planning process. In some cases the financial model and its implications for planning have been used as a vehicle for improving communications between individuals of varied backgrounds within the organisation.

3. *Evaluating new forms and uses of financial information:* In some companies financial modeling has been used to evaluate alternate forms and uses of financial information. Because of the flexibility inherent in modeling and the ability to evaluate the impact of various financial factors on profits, the financial model is used as an experimental lab for testing and evaluating new accounting approaches.

4. *Tool for special problems:* More and more attention is being devoted by management to one-time or temporary problem situations. because they are not of a continuing nature, it is not practical to develop typical data-processing systems for these problems. Financial models can frequently fill this gap. Some recent applications in this area relate to wage-price controls, changes in tax law, exchange rates, and mergers and acquisitions.

5. *Understanding the inherent logic of the financial system:* As a by product of financial modeling, some executives have found that the experience of defining the logic and interaction of the financial system in developing the model was, in itself, a very important and revealing activity. In effect, it forces a soul-searching in terms of "Why do we do it that way?" For the first time, many relationships are recognised a more explicit basis.

It may be observed from experience that financial modeling techniques can be applied effectively in a number of business situations, especially those in which there is a logical structure and where a degree of uncertainty is inherent in the assumptions involved. With business facing the conflicting forces of the energy crisis, environmental constraints, etc., executive management must look for new ways to evaluate alternate courses of action and their impact on profitability. Financial modeling may provide management with important tools for dealing with the increasing complexities and uncertainties facing industry today and tomorrow.

QUESTIONS

1. What is financial modeling? Discuss the recent breakthroughs in financial modeling.
2. Discuss the importance of the microcomputer to modern financial management.
3. "Financial modeling should be viewed in a functional sense rather than as a technical achievement." Do you agree? How and where can it be used?
4. What are the abuses of financial modeling?
5. Discuss the uses and benefits of financial models.
6. Discuss the conceptual models for strategic decision making.

5

PROFIT PLANNING AND CONTROL

INTRODUCTION

Financial planning is interative. Managers explore the future by considering a sries of tentative strategies under different assumptions about the future state of the economy. Finally they come up with a plan that is internally consistent and seems difficult to improve upon. To make such selections requires a knowledge of their probable effects on the applicable economic functions. In the field of profit planning and control, this means that management must have information on the changes in volume resulting from adjustments in price, the effect on costs of variations in volume, the influence on both volume and costs of rearrangements in the product mix, and changes in operating assets.A knowledge of these operating relationships is essential in preparing the details of a specific profit plan. Management is to lay out a financial plan of action establishing the functional relationships between volume of output and sales and potential net profits from operations, keeping in view that certain costs are fixed and the quantity of capital given. Since capital costs are fixed regardless of the level of output and sales, what management is really concerned with in profit planning is maximising net profit after total variable costs and expenses. It is better to sell where some contribution is made to fixed costs than to discontinue sales altogether just because fixed costs are not covered completely. Let us look more closely, at the important point at which the contribution of profits over variable costs just covers fixed charges, in other words, the *break-even point* at which before tax profits are zero, reduced sales would cause a loss, and increased sales would cause a net taxable profit.

BREAK-EVEN ANALYSIS

Break-even analysis which is sometimes called cost volume profit analysis is a formal profit-planning approach based on established relations between cost and revenues. If a firm's costs were all variable, the problem of break-even volume would seldom arise; by having some variable and some fixed costs, the firm must suffer losses until a given volume has been reached. It is a device for determining the point at which sales must cover all costs—those they vary directly with production and those that do not change as production level changes.

OBJECTIVE AND USES

The objective of break-even analysis is to determine the break-even quantity of output by studying the relationship among the firm's cost structure, volume of output, and profit. Alternatively, the breakeven level sales in ₹ that corresponds to breakeven quantity of output can be ascertained. We will develop the fundamental relationship by concentration on units of output and then extend the procedure to permit direct calculation of the break even sales level.

What is meant by the breakeven quantity of output? It is that quantity of output, denominated in units, that results in an earnings before interest and taxes (EBIT) level equals to zero. Use of he breakeven model, therefore, enables the financial manager: 1) to determine the quantity of output that must be sold to cover all operating costs, as distinct from financial costs; and, 2) to calculate the EBIT that will be achieved at various output levels. Actual and potential *applications* of the breakeven approach are wide in scope. Some of these include:

1. *Capital expenditure analysis*: As a complementry technique to discounted cash flow evaluation models, the breakeven model locate in a rough way the sales volume needed to make a project economically beneficial to the firm. It should not be used to replace the time-adjusted evaluation techniques.

2. *Pricing policy*: The selling price of a new product can be set to achieve a target EBIT level. Further, should market penetration be a prime objective, the price could be set that would cover slightly more than the variable costs of production and provide only a partial contribution to the recovery of fixed costs. The negative EBIT at several possible selling prices can then be studied.

3. *Labour contract negotiations:* The effect of increased variable costs resulting from higher wages on the breakeven quantity of output can be analysed.

4. *Cost structure*: The choice of reducing variable costs at the expense of incurring higher fixed costs can be evaluated. Management might decide to become more capital intensive by performing tasks in the production process through use of equipment rather than labourers. Application of the breakeven model can indicate what the effect of this trade-off will be on the breakeven point for the given product.

5. *Financing decision*: Analysis of the firm's cost structure will reveal the proportion that fixed operating costs bear to sales. If this proportion is high, the firm might reasonably decide not to add any fixed financing costs on top of the high fixed operating costs.

TYPES OF COST

The firm's cost of goods sold and its operating expenses contain fixed and variable operating cost components. In some cases, specific costs may have both fixed and variable elements. The resulting three types of costs are defined below:

Fixed costs: These cost are expenditures of a company that *do not vary as output changes.* The cost of office and factory space and equipment, the cost of an executive staff to oversee operations and a production staff to supervise the manufacturing process, real estate property taxes, etc.—all are fixed costs.

Variable costs : These are expenditures of company that *vary with the level of output.* Variable costs include production materials, direct labour, power for production equipment, transport services, and office materials used directly for purchasing and billing.

Semivariable costs: Semivariable costs are partly fixed and partly variable. One example of semivariable cost might be salemen's commissions. These commissions may be fixed over a certain range of value and increase to higher levels for higher volumes. Such a commission schedule would have both fixed and variable cost characteristics.

Some costs may be classified as variable or fixed depending upon the magnitude of the change in output; the amount of time required to change the cost; the length of time the change in output is expected to last. If the expenditure varies with output, the cost is variable, if it does not, the cost is fixed. Besides fixed and variable costs, the essential elements of the breakeven model includes (1) total revenues from sales and (2) volume of output. Total revenue means sales in ₹ and is equal to the selling price unit multiplied by the quantity sold. The volume of output refers to the firm's level of operations and may be indicated as (1) a unit quantity, or (2) as sales in ₹.

DETERMINING THE BREAKEVEN POINT

Finding the breakeven point in terms of units of production can be accomplished in several ways. All approaches require use of the essential elements of the breakeven model. The breakeven model is just a simple adaptation of the firm's income statement expressed in the following analytical format:

Sales—(Total Variable Expenses+Total Fixed Expenses) = Profit ...(1)

On a unit of production basis, it is necessary to introduce (1) the price at which each unit is sold and (2) the variable cost per unit of output. Because the profit item studied in breakeven analysis is EBIT, we will use that acronym instead of the word 'profit.' In terms of units the income statement shown in Equation-I, becomes the *breakeven model by setting EBIT equal* to zero.

[Sales Price Per Unit) (Units Sold)—[(Variable Expenses Per Unit) (Units Sold)+ (Total Fixed Expenses)]=EBIT = ₹.0 ...(2)

To find the number of units that must be produced and sold in order to satisfy Equation-2, that is, to arrive at an EBIT=₹ 0, the use of various approaches is illustrated below by using the same set of circumstances.

TRIAL-AND-ERROR APPROACH

The most cumbersome approach to determining the firm's break-even point is to employ the trial-and-error technique. The process simply involves:1) the arbitrary selection of an output level, and (2) the calculation of a corresponding EBIT amount. When the level of output is found that results in an EBIT=₹ 0, the breakeven point has been located. To illustrate the use of trial-and-error approach, we have taken a hypothetical ABC Company. It can be observed from Table-1 that it is just Equation-2 in worksheet form. For the ABC Company total operating costs will be covered when 5,000 units are manufactured and sold. This tells us that if sales equal ₹ 2,50,000, the firm's EBIT will equal ₹ 0.

TABLE-1

The ABC Company : Sales, Cost and Profit Schedule

Units Sold	10,000	15,000	20,000	25,000	30,000	35,000
Unit sales price	₹ 10	₹ 10	₹ 10	₹ 10	₹ 10	₹ 10
Sales	₹ 1,00,000	₹ 1,50,000	₹2,00,000	₹ 2,50,000	₹ 3,00,000	₹ 3,50,000
Unit variable expenses	₹ 6	₹ 6	₹ 6	₹ 6	₹ 6	₹ 6
Total variable expenses	₹ 60,000	₹ 90,000	₹ 1,20,000	₹ 1,50,000	₹ 1,80,000	₹ 2,10,000
Total fixed expenses	₹ 1,00,000	₹ 1,00,000	₹ 1,00,000	₹ 1,00,000	₹ 1,00,000	₹ 1,00,000
Total expenses	₹ 1,60,000	₹ 1,90,000	₹2,20,000	₹ 2,50,000	₹ 2,80,000	₹ 3,10,000
EBIT	–₹ 60,000	—₹ 40,000	–₹ 20,000	₹ 0	₹ 20,000	₹40,000

ALGEBRAIC PRESENTATION OF BREAKEVEN MODEL

Suppose that the assumptions of a linear cost and revenue function are closely approximated. Let us define the symbols used in our algebraic models as follows:

Q = quantity of output, in units per unit of time

$SPPU$ = selling price per unit of output (assumed to be constant)

TR = $SPPU$ X Q, total revenue

TFC = total fixed costs

TVC = total variable costs

AVC = average variable costs

ACM = average or per-unit contribution margin
= $SPPU - AVC$

TC = total costs, $TFC + TVC$ or $TFC + Q(AVC)$

CP = $TR - TVC = Q(ACM)$, total contribution to profit

NP = $TR - TC$, the total profit from the sale of Q units

B = breakeven output level

Q_B = breakeven sales level

$\%B$ = breakeven utilisation rate

Q_{cap} = plant capacity

By way of definition, the breakeven point occurs when *TR* equals *TC*. Substituting into this equality, we obtain

$$\begin{aligned} \text{TR} &= \text{TC} \\ SPPU \times Q_B &= TFC + TVC \qquad (3) \\ &= \text{TFC} + \text{AVC} \times Q_B \end{aligned}$$

$Q_B\,(SPPU - AVC) \quad = \quad TFC$

Therefore the *breakeven quantity* is given by

$$Q_B = (TFC)/(SPPU - AVC) = (TFC)/ACM) \qquad (4)$$

With this as the basic breakeven model, the breakeven point can be expressed in one of three distinct ways: as a number of units that must be sold, as sales in ₹, or as a percentage of plant capacity. To illustrate, assume that we have a factory that can produce a maximum of 20,000 units of output per month. These 20,000 units can be sold at a price of ₹ 100; variable costs are ₹ 20 per unit and the total fixed costs are 2,00,000.

Computation of the number of units that must be sold to break even implies a direct application of Eq. (4).

$$Q_B = (₹\ 2{,}00{,}000)\ /\ (₹\ 100 - ₹\ 20) = 2{,}500 \text{ units} \qquad (5)$$

To verify this, we could compute the *TR* and the *TC* when output equals 2,500 units as follows:

$$\begin{aligned} TR &= SPPU \times Q \\ &= (100) \times (2{,}500) \\ &= ₹\ 2{,}50{,}000 \\ TC &= TFC + TVC \\ &= TFC + Q(AVC) \\ &= ₹\ 2{,}00{,}000 + (2{,}500)\ (₹\ 20) = ₹\ 2{,}50{,}000 \end{aligned}$$

If the objective is to determine the breakeven level measured in terms of sales in ₹, Eq. (4) must be modified to yield

$$S_B = \frac{TFC}{1-(AVC/SPPU)} = \frac{TFC}{1-(TVC/TR)} \qquad (7)$$

The denominators in these formulations provide a measure of the contribution made to recover fixed costs. For our example, the breakeven level sales in ₹ are:

$$S_B = \frac{₹\ 2{,}00{,}000}{1-(20/100)} = ₹\ 2{,}50{,}000 \qquad (8)$$

which is the same result that was reached in the discussion of breakeven output.

If the objective is to determine the breakeven point in terms of percentage utilisation of plant capacity (%*B*), Eq. (4) can be modified as follows:

$$\%B = \frac{TFC}{(SPPU - AVC) \times Q_{CAP}} \times 100 \qquad (9)$$

Here Q_{cap} refers to the capacity of the plant expressed in units of output. Once again referring to our previous example, the breakeven capacity can be determined as

$$\%B = \frac{₹2,00,000}{(₹100 - ₹\ 20)\ 20,000} \times 100 = 12.5\% \qquad (10)$$

which indicates that the firm can break even by using only 12.5 per cent of its capacity.

GRAPHICAL PRESENTATION OF BREAKEVEN MODEL

Figure-1 presents the most generalised graphical representation of breakeven analysis. The horizontal axis measures the rate of output, and revenues and costs, measured in ₹, are placed on the vertical axis. Figure combines an inverted U-shaped total revenue *(TR)* curve and the familiar S-shaped total cost curve *(TC)* The curvilinear shape of the total revenue curve follows from the assumption that the firm faces a downward-sloping demand curve and must lower its price to sell more. The law of diminishing returns provides the explanation for the curvilinear shape of the total cost curve.

The vertical distance between *TR* and *TC* is a measure of the profit or loss at any specific level of output. To the left of Q_A and to the right of Q_B, total costs exceed total revenues, implying that profits are negative. Between these two points, profits are positive because *TR* exceeds *TC*. The point at which profits are maximized (that is, the point at which the vertical distance between *TR* and *TC* is the largest) is shown as Q_C. (This occurs where marginal revenue equals marginal costs).

The generalised model in Figure-1 is usually simplified to a linear breakeven chart, such as that in Figure-2. Linearity in the total revenue function implies that the firm is selling in a perfectly competitive environment, and hence is a pure price taker

FIGURE-1

BREAKEVEN ANALYSIS: THE GENERALIZED MODEL

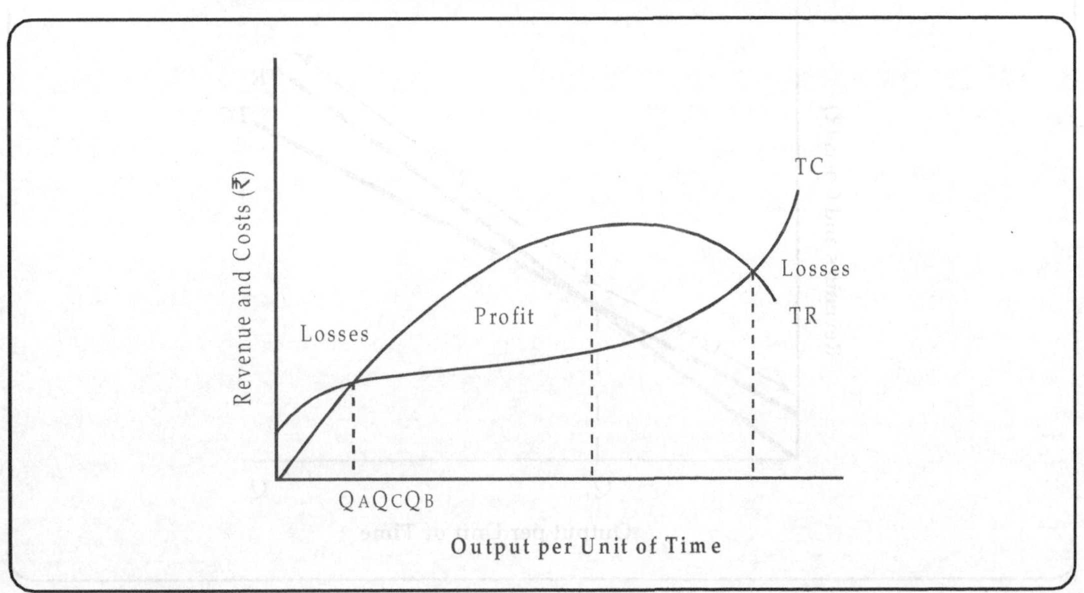

and does not have to lower its price to increase sales. Conversely, linearity in the case of the total cost curve indicates that the firm can expand output without appreciably affecting its average variable costs of production. Although these assumptions may appear to be overly restrictive, they are close approximations of reality when considered within a relatively narrow output range. In addition, the purpose of any model is to provide management with general profit guidelines, not exact answer. With these qualifications in mind, there is much to be said for using the linear breakeven models in the day-to-day business environment.

An interpretation of the linear breakeven chart of Figure-2 is straightforward. The point at which *TR* equals *TC*, point Q_A is the breakeven level of output. The left of this point, the firm incurs losses because *TC* exceeds *TR,* and to right of this point the firm earns profits because *TR* exceeds *TC.* In the decision-making process managers frequently employ a modified breakeven model. The modification follows from the notion that management may not be thinking of profit in the economic sense of total revenues minus total costs. When used for short-run decision making, where a portion of the firm's capital has already been expended in the purchase of fixed capital, a more appropriate measure known as the contribution margin or contribution to profit is used.

CONTRIBUTION MARGIN ANALYSIS

The contribution margin (CM) refers to the amount available to cover fixed costs (FC), and it is hoped, provide profit. The contribution margin can be defined as:

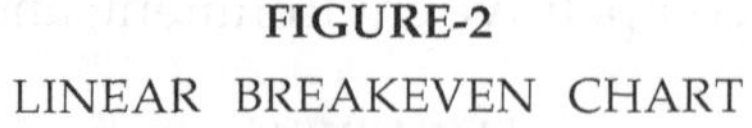

FIGURE-2

LINEAR BREAKEVEN CHART

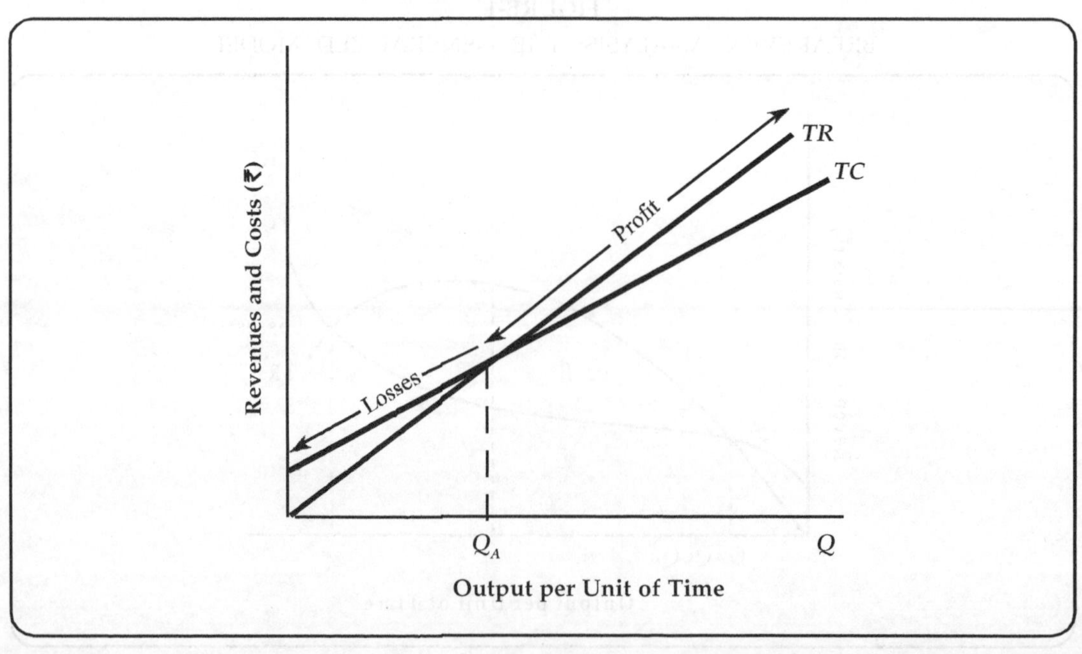

$$CM = \frac{Q\,(SPPU - AVC)}{Q} = SPPU - AVC$$

To illustrate, if a product sells for ₹ 50 per unit and the variable expense is ₹ 30 per unit, each unit sold covers variable cost plus ₹ 20, which can then be applied towards the recovery of fixed expenses.

Among different kind of businesses, contribution margin vary considerable. For instance, new car dealerships might have per unit margin ranging from ₹ 20,000 to ₹ 50,000, depending on the make, model, or other features of the car. Expressed as a per cent of the stocker price, these margin vary usually from model to model. Other businesses, such as food stores, have much smaller margin. Actually the relative size of the margin is only one of several important factors in profit planning. Equally important are the level of fixed costs and the turnover frequency of the inventory.

Figure 3 illustrate a contribution breakeerer charg based on linear cost and revenue curves. NP refers to the total net profit as is defined as the difference between TR and TC. Here, the contribution margin is defined as

$$CM = NP + TFC \tag{11}$$

or

$$CM = TR - TVC \tag{12}$$

FIGURE-3

CONTRIBUTION MARGIN BREAKEVEN CHART

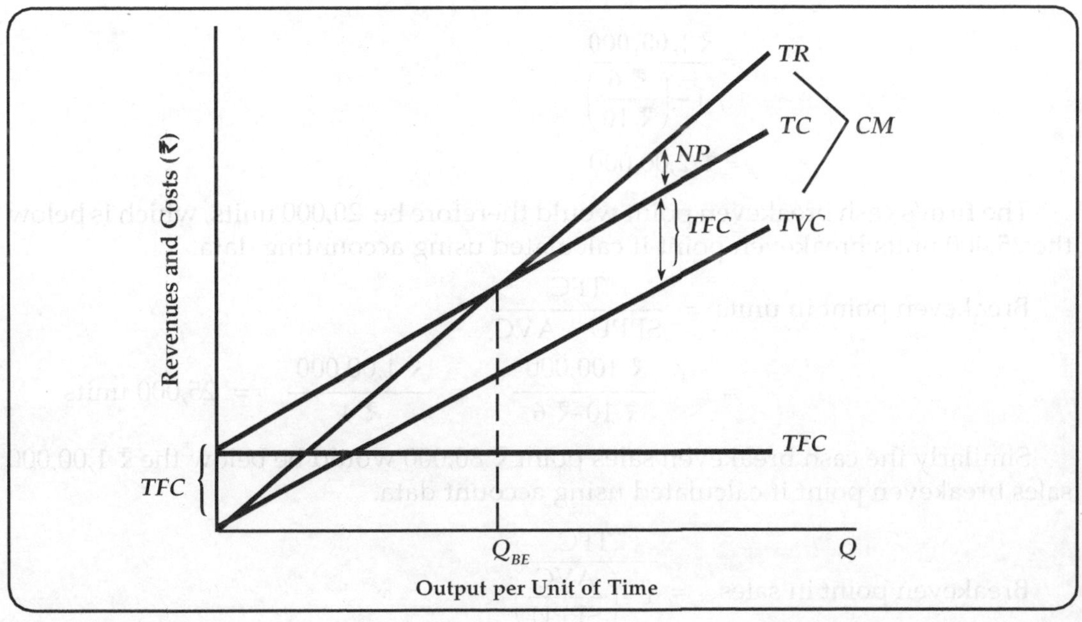

CASH BREAKEVEN ANALYSIS

Some of the firm's fixed costs are noncash outlays, and for a period some of its revenue may be receivables. If the firm's fixed or variable expenses estimates contain allowance for any noncash expenses, then the resultant breakeven point is higher on an accounting profit basis than on a cash basis. This means the firm's production and sales levels do not have to be as great to cover the cash costs of manufacturing the product. *What are these non-cash expenses?* The largest and most significant is depreciation expense. Another category is prepaid expenses. Assuming that the firm has non-cash charges, NC, included in its fixed costs, Equation-4 can be rewritten for the cash breakeven point as given in Equation-13.

$$\text{Cash breakeven point in units} = \frac{TFC - NC}{SPPU - AVC} \qquad (13)$$

To illustrate, assume that ABC Company had included in its fixed expenses of ₹ 1,00,000, ₹ 20,000 of depreciation. Substituting this information along with the firm's ₹ 10 per unit sale price and ₹ 6 per unit variable expenses into Equation—13 yields, the following:

$$\text{Cash breakeven point} = \frac{₹\ 1{,}00{,}000 - ₹\ 20{,}000}{₹\ 10 - ₹\ 6} = 20{,}000 \text{ units}$$

Cash breakeven analysis also can be performed in terms of sales in rupees. The cash breakeven ₹ sales volume can be determined with the following expressions:

$$\text{Cash breakeve sales} = \frac{TFC}{1-\left(\frac{AVC}{SPPU}\right)} \qquad (14)$$

$$= \frac{₹\ 1{,}00{,}000}{1-\left(\frac{₹\ 6}{₹\ 10}\right)}$$

$$= ₹\ 2{,}00{,}000$$

The firm's cash breakeven point would therefore be 20,000 units, which is below the 25,000 units breakeven point if calculated using accounting data.

$$\text{Breakeven point in units} = \frac{TFC}{SPPU - AVC}$$

$$= \frac{₹\ 100{,}000}{₹\ 10 - ₹\ 6} = \frac{₹\ 1{,}00{,}000}{₹\ 4} = 25{,}000 \text{ units}$$

Similarly the cash breakeven sales point ₹ 80,000 would be below the ₹ 1,00,000 sales breakeven point if calculated using account data.

$$\text{Breakeven point in sales} = \frac{TFC}{1-\left(\frac{AVC}{SPPU}\right)}$$

$$= \frac{₹\,1,00,000}{1 - \left(\frac{₹\,6}{₹\,10}\right)}$$

$$= ₹\,2,50,000 \text{ sales}$$

Cash breakeven analysis does not fully represent cash flows for this a cash budget is required. But cash breakeven analysis is useful because it provides a picture of the flow of funds from operations. A firm could incur a level of fixed costs that would result in losses during periods of poor business but large profits during upswings. If cash outlays are small, even during periods of losses the firm might still be operating above the cash breakeven point. Thus the risks of insolvency, in the sense of inability to meet cash obligations would be small. This allows a firm to reach out for higher profits through automation and operating leverage.

APPLICATIONS OF BREAKEVEN ANALYSIS

Adding an Educational Programme

Consider a case of a college which is contemplating the addition of a special weekend MBA programme for non-traditional students. Two different proposals have been put before the Chairman. In the first alternative, the college would incur a fixed cost of ₹ 7,50,000 for microcomputers dedicated to the weekend programme and experience an average variable cost of ₹ 200 per credit hour to cover salaries for additional faculty and the associated incremental expenses. In the second alternative, ₹ 5,00,000 would be spent to augment the capacity of the present mainframe computer in the college, and variable cost per unit is expected to be ₹ 300 per credit hour.

From the perspective of the Chairman, there are two specific question that must be addressed. First, what must the enrollment be for the college to break even with either alternative if the tuition rate is set at ₹ 700 per hour? Second, how high will the volume (credit hours) have to be before the profit level of the high investment project equals the profit level of the low investment alternative? The Chairman's first request contains all of the pertinent information, which can be summarised as follows:

Project 1	*Project 2*
TFC = ₹ 7,50,000	TFC = 5,00,000
AVC = ₹ 200 per credit hour	AVC = ₹ 300 / per credit hour
$SPPU$ = 700/per credit hour	$SPPU$ = ₹ 700/per credit hour

Substituting each of these values into Eq. (4) and solving for the breakeven volumes (Q_1 and Q_2 respectively), we get

$$Q_1 = ₹\,7,50,000/(₹\,700 - ₹\,200) = 1500 \text{ credit hours}$$

$$Q_2 = ₹\,5,00,000/(₹\,700 - ₹\,300) = 1250 \text{ credit hours}$$

Thus the first project might be regarded as riskier because it has higher fixed costs and a higher breakeven level. That is, it requires a larger number of credit hours to cover all of its costs. On the other hand, the contribution margin on a per-unit basis from the first project is ₹ 500 per credit hour versus only ₹ 400 for the second project.

The Chairman's second request was to determine the output level at which the profit from the first project equals that of the second project. This becomes an important issue because the second project can break even at 1250 hours and earn a profit of ₹ 1,00,000 at 1500 hours, whereas the second project must reach 1500 hours before breaking even.

Let

m_1 = profit earned from first investment

m_2 = profit earned from second investment

where

$$m_1 = TR_1 - TC_1 = (700 \times Q) - 7{,}50{,}000 - (200 \times Q) \qquad (15)$$

$$m_2 = TR_2 - TC_2 = (700 \times Q) - 5{,}00{,}000 - (300 \times Q) \qquad (16)$$

To find the volume level at which m_1 equals m_2, we simply set Eq. (15) and (16) equal to each other and solve for Q:

$$\begin{aligned} m_1 &= m_2 \\ 500Q - 7{,}50{,}000 &= 400\,Q - 5{,}00{,}000 \qquad (17) \\ 100Q &= 2{,}50{,}000 \\ Q &= 2{,}500 \text{ credit hours} \end{aligned}$$

Output will have to reach 2500 credit hours for project 1 to be as profitable as project 2. Beyond 2500 hours, the comparative profitability of project 1 becomes greater because of the greater contribution per unit. Conversely, below 2500 hours, project 2 becomes preferable. With this information, the president might very well request an estimate of the likely number of credit hours to be generated by the new programme.

Breakeven Models and Planning for Profit

Suppose that instead of focussing exclusively on the breakeven level of output, management wants an estimate of the volume (Q_T) needed to earn enough not only to cover all costs but earn a "target profit" (*PRT*). If this is the objective, the breakeven equations need to be modified as follows:

$$\begin{aligned} Q_b &= (TFC + m) / (SPPU - AVC) \qquad (18) \\ &= (TFC + m)/ACM \end{aligned}$$

and

$$S_B = \frac{TFC + m}{1 - (AVC/SPPU)} \qquad (19)$$

and

$$\%B = \frac{TFC + m}{(SPPU - AVC)Q_{cap}} \qquad (20)$$

To illustrate this process, we reintroduce the example used in our discussion of the linear breakeven model. A summary of this information is as follows:

$Q_{cap} = 20{,}000$ $SPPU = ₹\ 100$ $AVC = ₹\ 20$ $TFC = ₹\ 2{,}00{,}000$

$Q_B = 2500$ units $S_B = ₹\ 2{,}50{,}000$ $\%B = 12.5$

Now suppose that management wants to earn a target profit of ₹ 50,000. Making the appropriate substitutions into Eq. (18) through (20), we obtain the new levels of $Q_b = 3125$, $S_B = ₹\,3{,}12{,}500$, and $\%B = 15.625$. Adding this target profit to the fixed costs results in increasing the breakeven level of all three factor. The information in this example could be extended so as to make provisions for such factors as payment of taxes or for payment of any other fixed obligations that might be associated with the fixed costs (such as interest payments on a bond issue used to fund the investment).

To illustrate the case or breakeven analysis with taxation suppose that r represents the tax rate percentage, PAT is profits after taxes, and PBT is profits before taxes. The relationship between PAT and PBT can be shown to be

$$PAT = (1 - r)PBT \tag{21}$$

or

$$PBT = PAT/(1 - r) \tag{22}$$

Consider the case when the tax rate is 50 per cent. An after–tax profit of ₹ 50,000 would require a before–tax profit of

$$PBT = ₹\ 50{,}000/(1 - 0.5) = ₹\ 1{,}00{,}000 \tag{23}$$

This figure of ₹ 1,00,000 would then be introduced into the numerator of the breakeven ratio, as was done in Eq. (18) through (20). Essentially, the introduction of taxes or other fixed obligations will result in increasing the breakeven levels of output in unit terms, sales in ₹, and capacity.

Manipulating Cost and Price in the Breakeven Model

One of the most useful managerial applications of breakeven models is in simulating the impact on profits of changes in output and sales levels. An examination of either Figure 1 or Figure 2 indicates that profits could be increased by expanding sales volumes. The problem with this as a short–run alternative is that any increase in volume will be limited by plant capacity. As a short–run alternative, profits can be increased by shifting the breakeven point to a lower level of production or sales. This can be accomplished by manipulating three variables: fixed costs, variable cost, or price.

To illustrate this situation, suppose that we have collected the following information (all tabulated on a per–month basis):

Total fixed costs	=	₹ 600	Plant capacity = 200 units At Capacity		
Price	=	₹ 15			
Average variable cost	=	₹ 9	Total revenue	=	₹ 3000
Breakeven (Q_B)	=	100 units	Total costs	=	₹ 2400

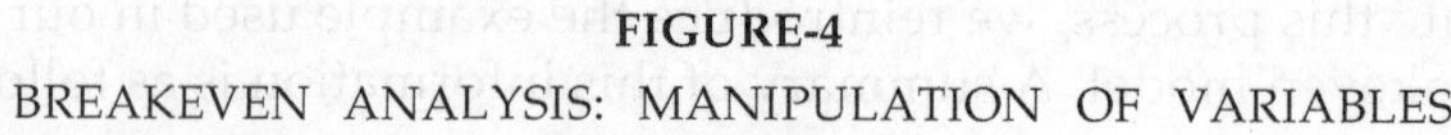

FIGURE-4

BREAKEVEN ANALYSIS: MANIPULATION OF VARIABLES

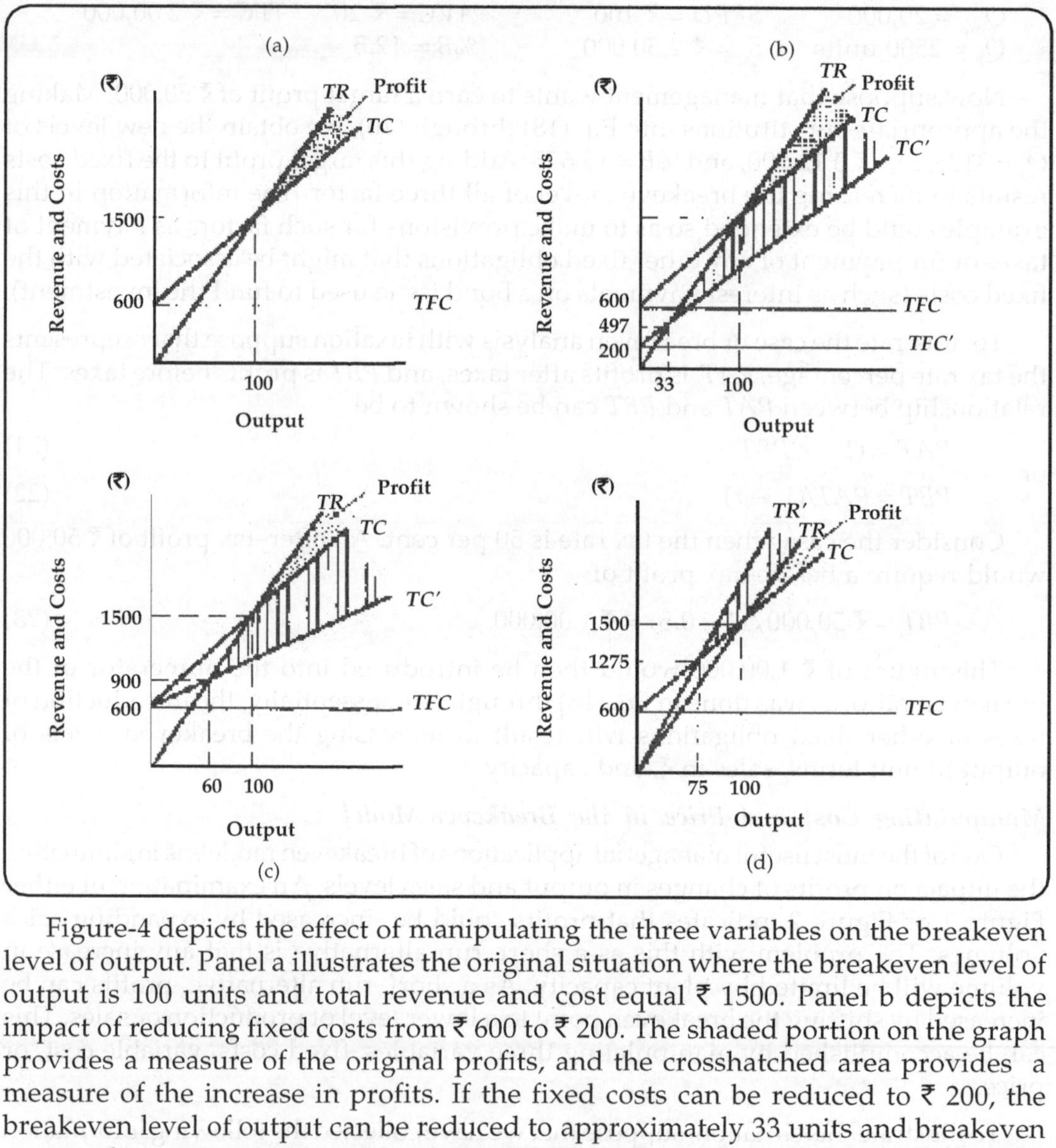

Figure-4 depicts the effect of manipulating the three variables on the breakeven level of output. Panel a illustrates the original situation where the breakeven level of output is 100 units and total revenue and cost equal ₹ 1500. Panel b depicts the impact of reducing fixed costs from ₹ 600 to ₹ 200. The shaded portion on the graph provides a measure of the original profits, and the crosshatched area provides a measure of the increase in profits. If the fixed costs can be reduced to ₹ 200, the breakeven level of output can be reduced to approximately 33 units and breakeven costs and revenues to approximately Rs 497. The impact of reducing variable costs to ₹ 5 is shown in panel c. In this situation, costs and revenues decline to ₹ 900 at the breakeven output level of 60 units. Panel d presents the final option of increasing price to ₹ 17 per unit. When the price is increased, the slope of the total revenue curve changes, with the new breakeven level of output declining to 75 units. An examination of the results of manipulating any one of the three variables indicates that the most promising in terms of profitability is the case where the fixed costs are reduced to ₹ 200.

Margin of Safety

In all of the preceding examples, only one of the variables (price or fixed or variable costs) was changed, but it should be obvious that management may have the power to change all three of them simultaneously. To be able to assess the impact of changing more than one of the variables, a modified version of breakeven analysis is frequently adopted. This modification looks at the ratio of profits to total fixed costs. By focussing on this ratio, we are essentially looking at the margin of profit that the firm is currently making and the losses it would incur should sales fall below the breakeven level. *The larger the ratio of profits to total fixed costs,* the better (from the standpoint of safety)—hence the name that is given to this ratio is the margin of safety.

Algebraically the margin of safety can be written as:

$$MS = \frac{m}{TFC} \quad \text{or} \quad \frac{Q_S - Q_B}{Q_B} \qquad (24)$$

where Q_B refers to the number of units actually sold and Q_s in expected increase in unit sales.

To illustrate the application of the margin of safety in performing the marketing function, suppose that we consider the following information:

Price = ₹ 300 600 units produced and sold per year
Capacity = 850 per year TFC = ₹ 65,000 AVC = ₹ 170

The production manager has suggested a change in a production technique that will increase average variable costs by ₹ 5 per unit. The new item will sell for ₹ 15 less than the old item, and the marketing manager estimates that this price reduction will increase sales to 775 units. However, she also suggests that a ₹ 5,000 advertising campaign should be undertaken to inform potential customers of the price reduction. The task facing management is to decide which of four alternatives is to be preferred: maintaining the *status quo;* adopting the production technique, reducing price, and undertaking the advertising programme; maintaining profits without undertaking the advertising programme; and not reducing the selling price but conducting the advertising programme. The computations for these four alternatives are presented in the succeeding paragraphs.

1. *Maintain status quo:*

$$Q_B = TFC/(SPPU - AVC) = ₹\ 65{,}000/(300 - 170) = 500$$

$$\begin{aligned} \text{Annual profits} = m = {} & Q_s\,(SPPU - AVC) - TFC \\ = {} & 600(300 - 170) - ₹\ 65{,}000 \\ = {} & ₹\ 13{,}000 \end{aligned}$$

$$MS = \frac{Q_S - Q_B}{Q_b} = \frac{600 - 500}{500} = 0.20$$

2. *Undertake all of the options,* i.e., adopt the new production technique; variable

costs increase to ₹ 175 per unit; price is reduced to ₹ 285 and sales increase to 775 units; and expenditure of ₹ 5000 on advertising:

Q_B = (₹ 65,000 + ₹ 5,000)/(₹ 285 – 175) = 636

Annual Profits = (775) (285 – 175) – 65,000 – 5,000 = ₹ 15,250

Thus profits increase by ₹ 2,250:

$MS = (Q_S - Q_B)/Q_B = (775 - 636)/(636) =$ appx 0.2186

3. *Maintain the same level of sales as in option 2 but without the advertising programme:*

Q_B = ₹ 65,000/(285 – 175) = appx 591
Q_S = (₹ 15,250 + ₹ 65,000)/(285 – 175) = appx 730

Note that the projected sales are lower than with the second option because of not undertaking the advertising programme.

$$MS = (Q_s - Q_B)/Q_B$$
$$= (730 - 591)/591$$
$$= 0.2352$$

4. *Maintain the same level of profit as in option 2 but do not lower price and undertake the avertising programme:*

Q_B = ₹ 70,000/(300 – 175) = 560
Q_s = (₹ 15,250 + 70,000)/125 = 682
$MS = (Q_s - Q_B)/Q_B = .2178$

The margin of safety suggests that the third option is preferred. The implication of this higher margin of safety is that management can undertake this option with the knowledge that it can come closer to paying its fixed costs even if the expected level of sales does not materialise.

COMPARISON OF DIFFERENT PRODUCTION TECHNIQUES

One of the primary tasks of the production manager is to make decisions such that costs of production are minimised. Breakeven analysis can be utilised to assist in making cost comparisons among production techniques that involve different fixed and variable cost structures. For example, more capital–intensive methods generally involve a cost structure with greater fixed and lower variable costs. Conversely, labour-intensive production techniques usually imply lower fixed and higher variable costs. Thus the cost advantage of each of these two production techniques depends on the level of output. As a general rule, we can say that the higher the level of output, the more efficient will be the capital-intensive technique, and the lower the level of projected output the more efficient will be the labour-intensive technique.

To illustrate, suppose that the production analyst has derived the following two cost functions for different production techniques:

TC_a = ₹ 170 + ₹ 1.40Q (25)
TC_b = ₹ 520 + ₹ 0.85Q (26)

Technique *a* is the labour-intensive production method and technique *b* the capital-intensive method.

The first step in this type of application is to determine the output level at which the two production techniques are equally efficient. To do this, we simply set the total cost functions equal to each other and solve for *Q* as follows:

$$TC_a = TC_b$$
$$₹\,170 + 1.40Q = ₹\,520 + 0.85Q$$
$$₹\,1.40Q - ₹\,0.85Q = ₹\,520 - ₹\,170$$
$$Q = \text{appx } 636$$

Whenever output is less than 636 units, production technique *a* is more efficient, and when output exceeds 636, production technique *b* will involve a lower cost.

With this information in hand, the production analyst contacts the marketing manager about the projected level of sales. The marketing manager suggests that the most probable level of sales is 700 units with a standard deviation of 250 units and that the distribution of sales is approximated by a normal distribution. This information can be summarised with a graph similar to that depicted in Figure-5. The production analyst can now focus on the question: What is the probability that sales will equal or exceed the breakeven level of 636 units? Graphically, this corresponds to the shaded area under the normal probability curve in Figure-5.

FIGURE-5

COST ADVANTAGE OF PRODUCTION TECHNIQUE B

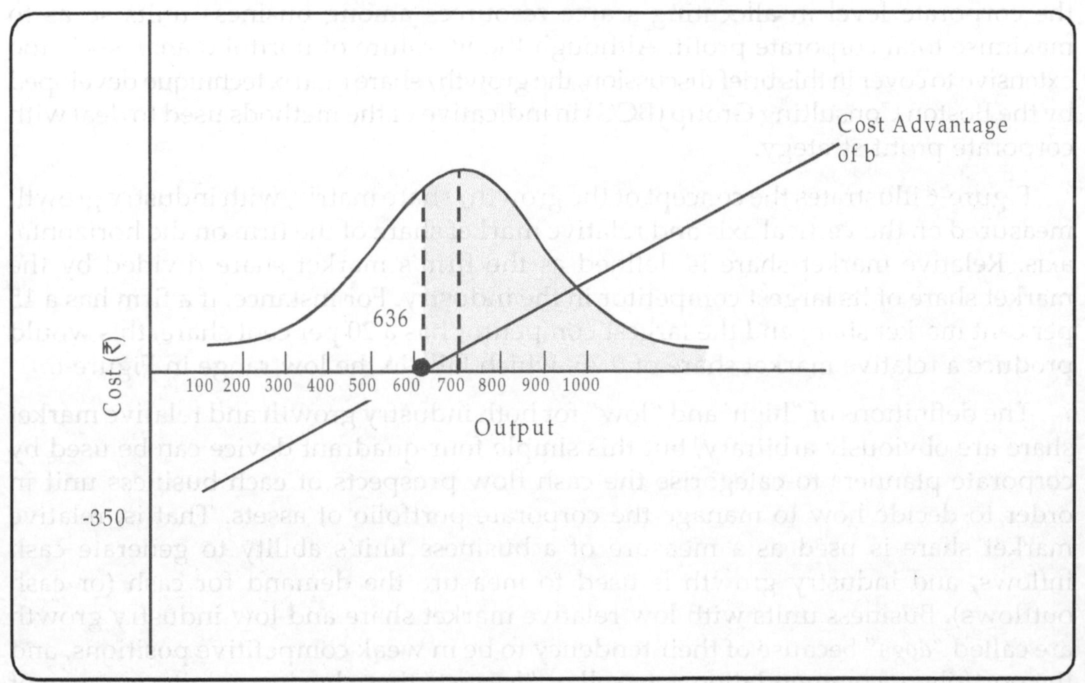

To obtain an exact answer to the question, the first step is to compute the appropriate Z value as follows:

$$Z = \frac{X - \mu}{\sigma} = \frac{636 - 700}{250} = \frac{-64}{250} = \text{appx} - 0.26$$

To find the appropriate percentage of the normal probability curve that corresponds to this Z value, we refer to *Appendix*-Table-5. Corresponding to the Z value of 0.26 is the entry 0.1026. Because 50 per cent of the normal curve is to the right of the mean, the shaded area equals 60.26 per cent (obtained by summing 50 per cent and 10.26 per cent). With this information, the production manager can inform upper management that there is approximately a 60 per cent chance that the capital-intensive plant will lead to a lower level of costs.

This same approach can be utilised to evaluate such proposals such as: 1. Should we buy or lease a piece of equipment? 2. Should we make or buy a part? 3. Should the plant size be expanded?

PROFIT ANALYSIS AND THE GROWTH/SHARE MATRIX

Profit analysis using breakeven techniques isolates company-level variables such as price and average variable cost per unit, but the process of breakeven analysis tends to ignore (or abstract from) broader strategic considerations external to the company. These external considerations must be included when making long-run corporate decisions. Since the late 1960s, a new range of techniques known as portfolio analysis has been developed as a means of assisting business planners at the corporate level in allocating scarce resources among business units so as to maximise total corporate profit. Although the literature of portfolio analysis is too extensive to cover in this brief discussion, the growth/share matrix technique developed by the Boston Consulting Group (BCG) in indicative of the methods used to deal with corporate profit strategy.

Figure-6 illustrates the concept of the growth/share matrix, with industry growth measured on the vertical axis and relative market share of the firm on the horizontal axis. Relative market share is defined as the firm's market share divided by the market share of its largest competitor in the industry. For instance, if a firm has a 15 per cent market share and the largest competitor has a 20 per cent share, this would produce a relative market share of 0.75, which falls in the low range in Figure-6.

The definitions of "high' and "low" for both industry growth and relative market share are obviously arbitrary, but this simple four-quadrant device can be used by corporate planners to categorise the cash flow prospects of each business unit in order to decide how to manage the corporate portfolio of assets. That is, relative market share is used as a measure of a business unit's ability to generate cash inflows, and industry growth is used to measure the demand for cash (or cash outflows). Business units with low relative market share and low industry growth are called *"dogs"* because of their tendency to be in weak competitive positions, and the portfolio recommendation is to sell or *"harvest"* these business units as a way of

FIGURE-6

PROFIT ANALYSIS WITH !A GROWTH/SHARE MATRIX

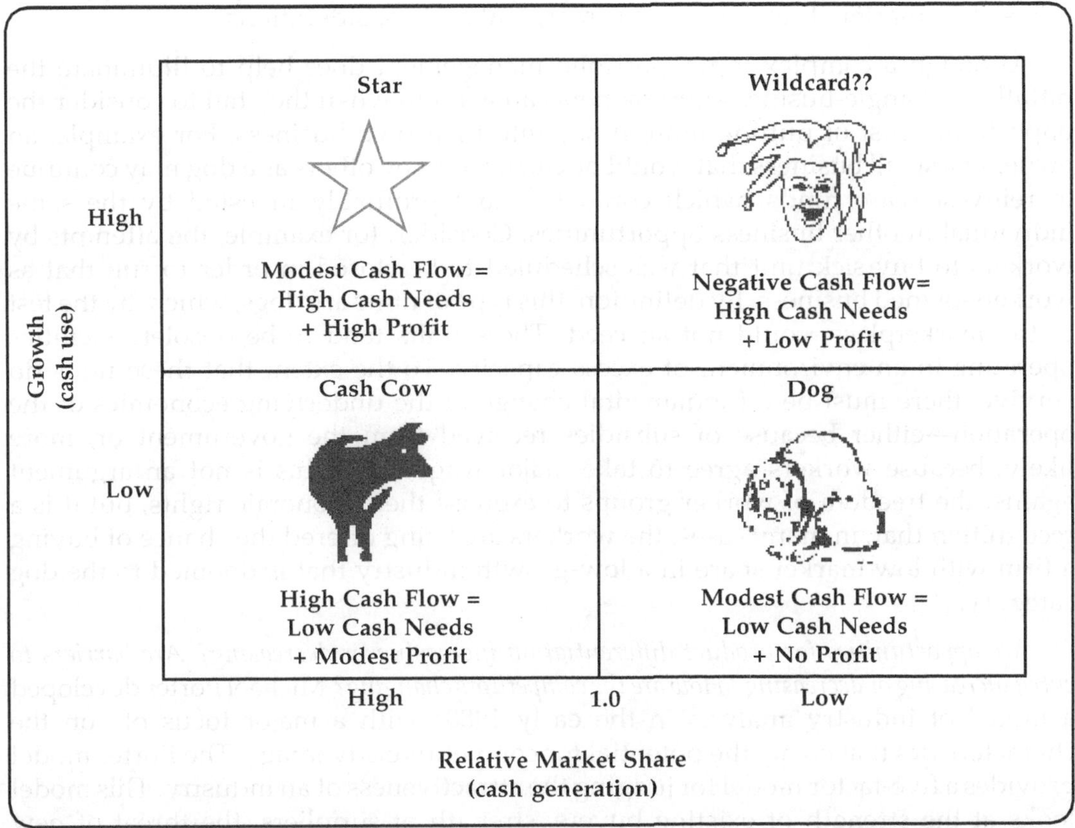

strengthening the profitability of the portfolio. At the other extreme are *"stars,"* which have high relative market share in a rapidly growing industry. Although stars demand a large volume of cash in order to maintain their growth, they hold the potential of high profits. The two remaining categories, *"cash cows"* and *"wildcard,"* represent the essence of the portfolio strategy, which calls for "milking" the excess cash flow from cash cows and using these funds to turn wildcard into stars. That is, because cash flows have high relative market share in low-growth industries, they generate a large positive cash inflow that can be used to fund the cash requirements of wildcards. In this evolutionary cycle, stars will eventually turn into cash cows as the industry matures and falls from high growth to low growth.

Such a simple growth/share matrix may seem crude, but it does high-light the fundamental economic principle of opportunity cost and its relevance to all decision processes. That is, the growth/share matrix forces corporate strategists to consider the opportunity cost of money earned by a cash cow and whether it would be better to invest it in the cash cow or the wildcard. In the portfolio view of asset management, money earned in one quadrant are not necessarily reinvested in the same quadrant.

Rather, there is a constant reassessment of where the highest rate of return can be earned—cash flowing away from quadrants with poor future profit prospects and toward quadrants with better future opportunities. In essence, the portfolio approach is based on marginal revenue versus marginal cost considerations.

Although a complex topic, portfolio management does help to illuminate the pitfalls that single-business-unit owners can get into when they fail to consider the opportunity cost of putting more funds into their own business. For example, an owner of a small business that would be categorised by others as a dog may continue to reinvest scare funds, which could be more profitably invested by the same individual in other business opportunities. Consider, for example, the attempts by workers to buy sick unit that was scheduled to be closed in order to run that as workers-owned business. By definition, this type of units are dogs, which, by the test of the marketplace, could not succeed. These units tend to be obsolete facilities operating in an environment of excess capacity. To the extent that these units do survive, there must be a fundamental change in the underlying economics of the operation—either because of subsidies received from the government or, more likely, because workers agree to take major wage cuts. This is not an argument against the freedom of worker groups to exercise their economic rights, but it is a recognition that, in many cases, the workers are being offered the chance of buying a firm with low market share in a low-growth industry that is doomed to the dog category.

Are opportunities for product differentiation increasing or decreasing? Are barriers to entry increasing or decreasing? How are the competitors changing? Michael Porter developed a model of industry analysis in the early 1980s with a major focus of on the characteristics that create the potential for competitive advantage. The Porter model provides a five-factor model for judging the attractiveness of an industry. This model looks at the strength of existing buyers, strength of suppliers, the threat of new entrants, the threat of substitution, and the degree of rivalry among existing competitors to judge the attractiveness of an industry. Table-2 lists the ways a company can decrease the threat or increase the strength of the factor.

Internal Strengths and Weaknesses

Following environment assessment, some introspection is in order. Managers must identify the organization's strengths and weaknesses, then develop strategy accordingly. The focus of internal analysis is also on sources of competitive advantage, either product advantage or cost advantage. Do our factories make us a high- or low-quality producer, a high- or low-cost producer? A company with products at the leading edge of its industry and with a reputation for quality, service and reliability will develop one strategy. A company that is forced to withdraw a product from the marketplace because of bed publicity over quality will develop quite another strategy.

The most difficult part of the internal analysis process may be an analysis of the top managers and the culture they have created. Top executives who spent their careers in regulated industries are often unprepared to respond quickly and aggressively in a deregulated environment. The bureaucracy that served them so well for decades simply does not work when fast action and risk taking are required.

TABLE-2

PORTER'S FIVE FACTORS FOR EVALUATING AN INDUSTRY'S ATTRACTIVENESS

Factor 1 threat of new entries	**Factor 3—Bargaining Power of the Suppliers**
Economies of scale	Size of the supplier
Patents, copyrights, and trade secrets	Threat of vertical integration
Regulation	Rivalry among suppliers
Switching cost to the customer	Threat that we will substitute inputs
Customer loyalty	Threat of new suppliers entering
Time needed to add capacity	**Factor 4—Threat of Substitutes**
Factor 2—Bargaining Power of the Buyers	The closer the substitutes the more limited the power of the seller
Product differentiation	
Information available to buyers	**Factor 5—Rivalry among Existing Firms**
Customer's interest in features versus price	Goals of competitors—Profit versus size
Price as a percentage of the buyer's income	Strength of competitors—Cost advantage or disadvantage
Switching cost for buyers	
Difficulty of duplicating product advantages	Strength of competitors—Financial strength
	Intelligence of competitors

The combination of environmental and internal analysis is often referred to as SWOT analysis, for Strengths, Weaknesses, Opportunities, and Threats. Once the SWOT analysis is completed, managers can begin the development of a strategy. Managers often apply various conceptual models for this purpose.

EVALUATION OF BREAKEVEN MODELS

Breakeven models are relatively simple to construct and to interpret by both analysts and management. Furthermore, they are inexpensive, especially when compared to more complex models and, given their widespread applicability, the cost advantage can be significant. As a general rule, the needed to apply breakeven analysis is readily available, thus negating the necessity of costly expenditures on data collection. However, like any simplification of reality, breakeven analysis is subject to abuse and mis-interpretation, and the practitioner must be aware of the limitations and qualifications associated with breakeven models.

1. Because most of the data utilised to construct breakeven charts and models are derived from accounting records and statements, analysts must be aware of the limitations and definitions associated with the construction and use of accounting data. In particular, the cost estimates and functions must be adjusted to consider implicit costs, depreciation estimates, and inappropriate assignment of overhead

costs. That is, one must ensure that the measures of total cost represent only those costs that are incured as a result of the decision being considered and that it does not include costs that will be incurred by the firm regardless of the decision made about the problem at hand.

2. Although we have focused on linear applications of the breakeven model, it should be clear that much the same analysis could be applied with curvilinear cost and revenue functions. The specific steps that are generally applied with curvilinear functions are (a) subtract the total cost function from the revenue function to obtain the profit function, (b) take the first derivative of the profit function with respect to output and set this result equal to zero, and (c) solve the respective first derivative for output and conduct the second derivative test. This process may appear to be more sophisticated, but the interpretations and uses of curvilinear models are identical to those in the linear models.

3. The assignment of selling and marketing costs can be difficult and may require some subjective decision making. This follows from the observation that the relationship between output and selling costs is not a one-sided relationship. Furthermore, there is nothing that indicates that the relationship between output and marketing costs is particularly stable over time or over various output ranges.

4. The analysis as presented in all of the preceding examples implicitly assumed that the firm was concerned with only one product. Clearly, there are many situations wherein the firm produces and markets more than one product. How can Zenith add output of personal computers to output of televisions? One possibility would be to assign weights to each of the product lines based on some predetermined trait, such as production hours utilised, and then to aggregate this information into an index number that is used as a proxy for output. A second possibility would be simply to measure output as a percentage of plant capacity. The most common approach for a heterogeneous product mix is to measure output in terms of sales volume in ₹. However, it should be stated that none of these approaches completely overcomes the problems with multiple products.

5. Although the majority of breakeven applications take the price as given, the model can be adapted to consider variable prices simply by computing alternative total revenue functions, one for each price to be considered. This approach has the advantage that the sensitivity of profits to changes in prices and the corresponding outputs can be measured and evaluated.

6. Because breakeven analysis is a short-run decision-making model, multiperiod costs be arbitrarily assigned to the period being considered. For example, to some extent the repair and maintenance costs associated with equipment in the current time period may be related to the rate of utilisation in preceding time periods.

7. Breakeven models should be constructed with taxes and probability distributions taken into consideration. Although these adjustments may appear to complicate the

models, they are needed to compensate for the uncertainty facing decision makers in a dynamic marketplace.

8. In utilising breakeven analysis to consider the introduction of a new product, several adjustments must be made to the basic model. These new product models should take into consideration such diverse concepts as:

a. *Product life cycle.* This refers to the typical pattern of sales experienced by most products over their life span.
b. *Projection of total revenues and costs over the entire life of the product.* This may involve the use of regression estimation techniques or the development of pro-forma statements.
c. *Assignment of appropriate costs to the new product line,* including such items as research and development costs.
d. *Incorporation of probability distribution* of likely sales and cost figures.
e. *Incorporation of learning curve concept* on variable costs as the proficiency of the production process improves over time.

9. Throughout the discussion of breakeven models, we have implicitly assumed that profit depends exclusively on the rate of output. It should be obvious that profit is also affected by the production processes utilised, the state of technology, the effectiveness of selling and marketing program, demand for the product, the general state of economic conditions, and myriad other internal and external factors. This is not meant to suggest that breakeven analysis cannot be used, rather, it should be tempered with good judgment.

BREAK-EVEN FOR INDIVIDUAL PRODUCTS, PLANTS, AND SALES TERRITORIES

Upto this point, the discussion of cost-volume-profit relationship has proceeded on the assumption that only one product is being manufactured and sold. If more than one product is involved, the problem is more complex. Now it becomes necessary to trace variable costs to specific products to determine the contribution that each product is making to fixed cost recovery and profit. Until the different contributions have been calculated, there can be no really sound basis for planning sales promotion to ensure that it is directed toward the most profitable products. Without analysis, sale programmes are made up in the dark and it is more than likely that sales efforts will be misdirected, particularly if the products with the highest selling prices make the smallest contributions.[1]

Because the various products have different profit volume ratios, break-even points and profit patterns change with each change in the proportion, or mix, in which the products are manufactured and sold. We know that in a company with a single product produced in a single plant there is no problem of allocation. All costs are tracable to the product and to the plant. With the facts given in Exhibit-1, the contribution margin per unit and the break-even point can be calculated as shown.

EXHIBIT-1

ONE PRODUCT - ONE PLANT

Fixed costs	₹ 2,65,000
Variable costs	₹ 4.00 per unit
Sales price	₹ 8.50 per unit

Contribution per unit = ₹ 8.50 – ₹ 4.00 = ₹ 4.50

Break-even point = $\frac{2,65,000}{4.50}$ = 58,888 units

TWO PRODUCT-ONE PLANT COMPANY

In a two product—one plant situation some costs will not be traceable to products. These are the common fixed costs. The fixed costs that are traceable to each product can be described as direct fixed costs. With the data given, break-even calculations can be made as shown in Exhibit-2.

EXHIBIT-2

TWO PRODUCTS - ONE PLANT

Break-Even Data		
	Product A	*Product B*
Direct fixed costs	₹ 1,00,000	₹ 1,20,000
Variable costs	₹ 3.00 per unit	₹ 4.00 per unit
Sales prices	₹ 6.00 per unit	₹ 8.50 per unit
Common fixed costs	₹ 45,000	
	Break-Even Calculations	
Contribution per unit	₹ 3.00	₹ 4.50
Break-even point to cover direct fixed costs	$\frac{1,00,000}{3}$ = 33,333 units	$\frac{1,20,000}{4.50}$ = 26,667 units

In order to cover the common fixed costs of ₹ 45,000, there are many possible combinations of sales of Products A and B. Algebraically, one would express the combinations of A and B that would cover the ₹ 45,000 as:

$$3 A + 4.5 B = 45,000$$

Note that the 3 and the 4.5 are the profit contributions per unit of A and B, respectively. The only limits on the solutions to the above equation would be the possibility of limited production capacity and/or limited sales potential.

ONE PRODUCT—TWO PLANT COMPANY

With one produce and two plants some of the fixed costs will not be traceable to plants. Ordinarily these common fixed costs would be the costs of general administration. The data given can be used to calculate break-even points as shown in Exhibit-3.

EXHIBIT-3

ONE PRODUCT - TWO PLANTS

	Break-Even Data	
	Plant I	*Plant II*
Direct fixed costs	₹ 1,10,000	₹ 1,35,000
Variable costs	₹ 4.50 per unit	₹ 4.00 per unit
Sales prices	₹ 8.50 per unit	₹ 8.50 per unit
Common fixed costs	₹ 25,000	
	Break-Even Calculations	
Contribution per unit	₹ 4.00	₹ 4.50
Break-Even point to cover	$\frac{1,10,000}{4} = 27,500$ units	
$\frac{1,35,000}{4.50} = 30,000$ units direct fixed costs		

To cover the common fixed costs of ₹ 25,000 there are many possible combinations of the output of Plants I and II. Algebraically, these combinations can be expressed in the following form:

$$4 \text{ I} + 4.5 \text{ II} = 25,000$$

The 4 and the 4.5 represent the profit contributions of products produced in Plants I and II. Limits on the possible solutions to the above equations would be the possibility of limited production capacity in Plant I and/or II.

TWO PRODUCT-TWO PLANT COMPANY

In a more complex situation with two products and two plant there arise three layers of common fixed costs. These layers represent the costs common to products A and B in Plant I and II and the costs common to the entire operation of all products and all plants. Break-even data and break-even calculations to illustrate the two product—two plant situation are shown in Exhibit-4.

EXHIBIT-4

TWO PRODUCTS - TWO PLANTS

	Break-Even Data			
	Plant I		*Plant II*	
	Product A	*Product B*	*Product A*	*Product B*
Direct fixed costs	₹ 45,000	₹ 50,000	₹ 60,000	₹ 50,000
Variable costs per unit	₹ 3.00	₹ 4.50	₹ 3.50	₹ 4.50
Sale prices per unit	₹ 6.00	₹ 8.50	₹ 6.00	₹ 8.50
Fixed costs common to products	₹ 20,000		₹ 40,000	

Fixed costs common to total operations	₹ 60,000			
	Break-Even Calculations			
	Plant I		*Plant II*	
	Product A	*Product B*	*Product A*	*Product B*
Contribution per unit	₹ 3.00	₹ 4.00	₹ 2.50	₹ 4.00
Break-Even point to cover common fixed costs	$\frac{45,000}{3.00} = 15,000$	$\frac{50,000}{4.00} = 12,500$	$\frac{60,000}{2.50} = 24,000$	$\frac{50,000}{4.00} = 12,500$

₹ 20,000 costs common to Plant I

Any combination of $3A_1 + 4B_1 = 20,000$

₹ 40,000 costs common to Plant II

Any combination of $2.5A_1 + 4B_2 = 40,000$

₹ 60,000 costs common to total operations

Any combination of $3A_1 + 4B_1 + 2.5A_2 + 4B_2 = 60,000$

The subscripts in the equations in Exhibit-4 designate the plants from which products originate. Limits on the possible number of combinations of A and B to cover common fixed costs are the limits of production capacity and sales potential.

ONE PRODUCT—ONE PLANT—TWO TERRITORY COMPANY

When sales territories are considered in break-even analysis, there arises the possibility of fixed costs common to the sales territories as well as the possibility of dealing with variable costs segregated by sales and production. The data and calculations in Exhibit 5 illustrate how such a situation might be handled.

EXHIBIT-5

ONE PRODUCT - ONE PLANT - TWO TERRITORIES

	Break-Even Data		
	Territory I	*Territory II*	*Plant*
Direct fixed costs	₹ 40,000	₹ 57,750	₹ 1,50,000
Variable costs per unit	₹ 1.50	₹ 1.75	₹ 2.00
Sales prices per unit	₹ 8.50	₹ 9.00	
Common fixed costs			
Common to both territories	₹ 15,000+		
Common to all operations		₹ 20,000	
	Break-Even Calculation		
	Territory I	*Territory II*	
Contribution per unit (Sales price minus all variable costs)	₹ 5.00	₹ 5.25	

Break-Even point to cover direct fixed costs of each territory	$\frac{40,000}{5}=8,000$	$\frac{57,750}{5.25}=11,000$
Break-Even point to cover other fixed costs		
₹ 1,50,000 direct fixed costs of production		
Any combination of 51+5.25 II = 1,50,000		
₹ 15,000 costs common to both territories		
Any combination of 51 + 5.25 II = 15,000		
₹ 20,000 costs common to all operations		
Any combination of 51 + 5.25 II = 20,000		

As in previous illustrations, the numbers in the equations in Exhibit 5 represent the profit contributions per unit. Limits on the possible combinations to achieve the various level of break-even are the sales potential in each territory and the production capacity of the plant.

TWO PRODUCT—ONE PLANT—TWO TERRITORY COMPANY

The two product—one plant—two territory situation is quite similar to the preceedding illustration. Actually, the only differences are the extra layers of common fixed costs. The data is Exhibit-6, illustrate the basic problem and its solution.

Subscripts in all of the equations in Exhibit-6 refer to the territories in which products are sold. The limits on the possible combinations to achieve the various levels of break-even again are the sales potential in each territory and the production capacity of the plant.

What is the utility of a break-even chart that attempts to express the multidimensional charter of a business with only three lines, i.e., revenue, fixed costs, and variables costs? When a business is taken apart plant by plant, product by product, and territory by territory, it becomes evident that there is a break-even point related to each and every layer of direct fixed costs and common fixed costs. The existence of multiple break-even points may be frustrating to some people, but others see in it the key issue in cost-volume-profit relationships, that is, the use of production and sales facilities to produce the optimum profit. This optimum profit is produced by obtaining the optimum product mix that is, the combination of products A and B that will produce the greatest profit consistent with the other financial and nonfinancial goals of the enterprise.

In order to deal with the problem of optimum product mix, the preceding illustrations will be enlarged to a two product—two plant—two territory situation. Furthermore, specific consideration will be given to sales potentials, production hours available on special purpose and general purpose equipment, production time requirements for each product, and transportation costs. Exhibit-7 through 11, contain the basic data for this illustration.

EXHIBIT-6

TWO PRODUCT - ONE PLANT - TWO TERRITORIES

Break-Even Data

	Eastern Territory		*Western Territory*		*Plant*	
	Product A	*Product B*	*Product A*	*Product B*	*Product A*	*Product B*
Direct fixed costs	₹ 15,000	₹ 10,000	₹ 30,000	₹ 10,000	₹ 50,000	₹ 55,000
Variable costs per unit	₹ 2.00	₹ 1.50	₹ 2.50	₹ 2.00	₹ 1.00	₹ 2.00
Sales prices per unit	₹ 6.00	₹ 8.50	₹ 6.50	₹ 9.00		
Common fixed costs						
Common to products		₹ 15,000		₹ 20,000		₹ 45,000
Common to territories			₹ 15,000			
Common to all operations					₹ 30,000	

Break-Even Calculations

	Eastern Territory		*Western Territory*		*Plant*	
Contribution per unit (Sales price minus all variable costs)	₹ 3.00	₹ 5.00	₹ 3.00	₹ 5.00		
Break-Even point to cover direct fixed costs in each territory			$\frac{15,000}{3}$	$\frac{10,000}{5}$	$\frac{30,000}{3}$	$\frac{10,000}{5}$
		= 5,000	=2,000	=10,000	=2,000	

Break-Even point to cover other fixed costs

₹ 50,000 direct production costs for Product A
Any combination of $3A_E + 3A_W = 50,000$

₹ 55,000 direct production costs for Product B
Any combination of $5B_E + 5B_W = 55,000$

₹ 45,000 production costs common to both products
Any combination of $3A_E + 3A_W + 5B_E + 5B_W = 45,000$

₹ 20,000 Western Territory costs common to both products
Any combination of $3A_W + 5B_W = 20,000$

₹ 15,000 Eastern Territory costs common to both products
Any combination of $3A_E + 5B_E = 15,000$

₹ 15,000 costs common to both territories
Any combination of $3A_E + 5B_E + 3A_W + 5B_W = 15,000$

TWO PRODUCT—TWO PLANT—TWO TERRITORY COMPANY

In Exhibit-7 through 11, the variable costs are expressed as costs per unit of product for territorial costs and as costs per production hour for production costs. Admittedly, costs could vary with other measures of activity, but use of additional categories of variable costs would make the analysis more complicated than is necessary to illustrate the basic ideas involved.

EXHIBIT-7

PLANT AND TERRITORY COST STRUCTURE

	Plant I		*Plant II*		*Eastern Territory*		*Western Territory*	
	A	B	A	B	A	B	A	B
Direct fixed costs	₹ 30,000	₹ 40,000	₹ 20,000	₹ 15,000	₹ 15,000	₹ 10,000	₹ 30,000	₹ 10,000
Variable costs	₹ 1.00/hr.	₹ 2.00/hr.	₹ 1.50/hr.	₹ 1.00/hr.	₹ 2.00	₹ 1.50	₹ 2.50	₹ 2.00
Common fixed costs								
Products	₹ 20,000		₹ 10,000		₹ 15,000		₹ 20,000	
Plants		₹ 15,000						
Territories						₹ 15,000		
Total firm				₹ 10,000				

EXHIBIT-8

SALES POTENTIALS, SELLING PRICES, AND TRANSPORTATION COSTS

	Eastern Territory		*Western Territory*	
Products	*A*	*B*	*A*	*B*
Sales prices per unit	₹ 6.00	₹ 8.50	₹ 6.50	₹ 9.00
Sales potential (units)	60,000	80,000	50,000	40,000
Transportation costs per unit				
From Plant I	₹ 0.50	₹ 0.50	₹ 1.00	₹ 1.00
From Plant II	₹ 1.00	₹ 1.00	₹ 0.50	₹ 0.50

Since there are two ways (using general purpose or special purpose eqipment) of producing products A and B, two territories in which to sell each product, and two plants that could produce each product, there is no possibility of calculating a specific break-even point for the fixed costs shown in Exhibit-7. All that is possible is to produce a list of the ways of combining the production and sales possibilities that could yield a break-even point for each layer of fixed costs. This list is shown in Exhibit-12.

EXHIBIT-9

PRODUCTION HOUR REQUIREMENTS AND AVAILABILITIES

	Plant I		*Plant II*	
	A	*B*	*A*	*B*
Required Production Hours Per Unit				
Special purpose equipment	0.5	1	1	1.5
or				
General purpose equipment				
Available Production Hours	1.5	1	1.5	1.5
Special purpose equipment	40,000	60,000	20,000	10,000
General purpose equipment—				
can produce A or B	40,00	10,000		

EXHIBIT-10

PROFIT CONTRIBUTION PER UNIT, USING SPECIAL PURPOSE EQUIPMENT

	Product A				*Product B*			
Sold in	*Eastern Territory*		*Western Territory*		*Eastern Territory*		*Western Territory*	
Produced in	*Plant I*	*Plant II*	*Plant I*	*Plant II*	*Plant I*	*Plant II*	*Plant I*	*Plant II*
Sales prices	₹ 6.00	₹ 6.00	₹ 6.50	₹ 6.50	₹ 8.50	₹ 8.50	₹ 9.00	₹ 9.00
Variable costs								
Production	0.50	1.50	0.50	1.50	2.00	1.50	2.00	1.50
Distribution	2.00	2.00	2.50	2.50	1.50	1.50	2.00	2.00
Transportation	0.50	1.00	1.00	0.50	0.50	1.00	1.00	0.50
Contribution per unit of sales	₹ 3.00	₹ 1.50	₹ 2.50	₹ 2.00	₹ 4.50	₹ 4.50	₹ 4.50	₹ 5.00

EXHIBIT-11

PROFIT CONTRIBUTION PER UNIT, USING GENERAL PURPOSE EQUIPMENT

	Product A				*Product B*			
Sold in	*Eastern Territory*		*Western Territory*		*Eastern Territory*		*Western Territory*	
Produced in	*Plant I*	*Plant II*	*Plant I*	*Plant II*	*Plant I*	*Plant II*	*Plant I*	*Plant II*
Sales prices	₹ 6.00	₹ 6.00	₹ 6.50	₹ 6.50	8.50	₹ 8.50	₹ 9.00	₹ 9.00
Variable costs								
Production	1.50	2.25	1.50	2.25	2.00	1.50	2.00	1.50
Distribution	2.00	2.00	2.50	2.50	1.50	1.50	2.00	2.00
Transportation	.50	1.00	1.00	.50	.50	1.00	1.00	.50
Contribution per unit of sales	₹ 2.00	₹ .75	₹ 1.50	₹ 1.25	₹ 4.50	₹ 4.50	₹ 4.00	₹ 5.00

Before examining Exhibit-12 it should be realised that the superscripts S and G refer to special and general purpose equipment, respectively. The subscripts E and W refer to the Eastern and Western Territory, respectively, and the subscripts 1 and 2 refer to Plants I and II, respectively. Thus:

$3A^{S}_{E1}$ = the profit contribution of Product A produced on special purpose equipment in Plant I and sold in the Eastern Territory.

$4B\frac{G}{W2}$ = the profit contribution of Product B produced on general purpose equipment in Plant II and sold in the Western Territory.

Even with only a cursory examination of Exhibit-12 two points should be clear:

1. The various combinations of Products A and B that could cover the various

layers of fixed costs are restricted by the sales potentials shown in Exhibit 8 and the available production hours shown in Exhibit-9.

EXHIBIT-12

COMBINATIONS OF PRODUCTS ABLE TO COVER VARIOUS LAYERS OF FIXED COSTS

₹ 30,000 of direct production costs for Product A in Plant I
Any combination of $3A_{E1}S + 2A_{E1}G + 2.5A_{W1}S + 1.54_{W1}G = 30{,}000$

₹ 40,000 of direct production costs for Product B in Plant I
Any combination of $4.5B_{E1}S + 4.5B_{E1}G + 4B_{W1}S + 4B_{W1}G = 40{,}000$

₹ 20,000 of direct production costs for Product A in Plant II
Any Combination of $1.5A_{E2}S + .75A_{E2}G + 2A_{W2}S + 1.25A_{W2}G = 20{,}000$

₹ 15,000 of direct production costs for Product B in Plant II
Any combination of $4.5B_{E2}S + 4.5B_{E2}G + 5B_{W2}S + 5B_{W2}G = 15{,}000$

₹ 15,000 of direct territory cost for Product A in Eastern Territory
Any combination of $3A_{E1}S + 2A_{E1}G + 1.5A_{E2}S + .75A_{E2}G = 15{,}000$

₹ 10,000 of direct territory costs for Product B in Eastern Territory
Any combination of $4.5B_{E1}S + 4.5B_{E1}G + 4.5B_{E2}S + 4.5B_{E2}G = 10{,}000$

₹ 30,000 of direct territory costs of Product A in Western Territory
Any combination of $2.5A_{W1}S + 1.5A_{W1}G + 2A_{W2}S + 1.25A_{W2}G = 30{,}000$

₹ 10,000 of direct territory costs for Product B in Western Territory
Any combination of $4B_{W1}S + 4B_{W1}G + 5B_{W2}S + 5B_{W2}G = 10{,}000$

₹ 20,000 of production costs common to Products A and B in Plant I
Any combination of $3A_{E1}S + 2A_{E1}G + 2.5A_{W1}S + 1.5A_{W1}G + 4.5B_{E1}S + 4.5B_{E1}G + 4.50B_{W1}S + 4.50B_{W1}G = 20{,}000$

₹ 10,000 of production costs common to products A and B in Plant II
Any combination of $1.5A_{E2}S + .75A_{E2}G + 2A_{W2}S + 1.25A_{W2}G + 4.5B_{E2}S + 4.5B_{E2}G + 5B_{W2}S + 5B_{W2}G = 10{,}000$

₹ 15,000 of territory costs common to Products A and B in Eastern Territory
Any combination of $3A_{E1}S + 2A_{E1}G + 1.5A_{E2}S + .75A_{E2}G + 4.5B_{E1}S + 4.5B_{E1}G + 4.5B_{E2}S + 4.5B_{E2}G = 15{,}000$

₹ 20,000 of territory costs common to Products A and B in Western Territory
Any combination of $2.5A_{W1}S + 1.5A_{W1}G + 2A_{W2}S + 1.25A_{W2}G + 4B_{W1}S + 4B_{W1}G + 5B_{W2}S + 5B_{W2}G = 20{,}000$

₹ 15,000 of production costs common to both Products and Plants
Any combination of $3A_{E1}S + 2A_{E1}G + 1.5A_{E2}S + .75A_{E2}G + 4.5B_{E1}S + 4.5B_{E1}G + 4.5B_{E1}S + 4.5B_{E2}G + 2.5A_{W1}S + 1.5A_{W1}G + 2A_{W2}S + 1.25A_{W2}G + 4B_{W1}S + 4B_{W1}G + 5B_{W2}S + 5B_{W2}G = 15{,}000$

₹ 15,000 of territory costs common to both, Products and Territories
Any combinations of $3A_{E1}S + 2A_{E1}G + 1.5A_{e1}S + .75A_{E2}S + + 4.5B_{E1}S + 4.5B_{E1}G + 4.5B_{E2}S + 4.5B_{E2}G + 2.5A_{W1}S + 1.5A_{W1}G + 2A_{W2}S + 1.25A_{W2}G + 4B_{W1}S + 4B_{W1}G + 5B_{W2}S + 5B_{W2}G + = 15{,}000$

₹ 10,000 of costs common to all operations
Any combination of $3A_{E1}S + 2A_{E1}G + 1.5A_{E2}S + .75A_{E2}G + 4.5B_{E1}S + 4.5B_{E1}G + 4.5B_{E2}S + 4.5B_{E2}G + 2.5A_{W1}S + 1.5A_{W1}G + 2A_{W2}S + 1.25A_{W2}G + 4B_{W1}S + 4B_{W1}G + 5B_{W2}S + 5B_{W2}G = 10{,}000.$

2. Exhibit-12 is quite complicated and perhaps overstresses the idea of covering fixed costs. What should be stressed is *the combination* of Products A and B which will product the optimum profit as opposed to *the many combinations* which could over the various layers of fixed costs.

Each of these points is discussed below:

SALES POTENTIALS AND CAPACITY

Both sales potentials and available production capacity restrict the possible combinations of Products A and B that could cover the various layers of fixed costs.

Sales of Product A would probably not exceed the 60,000-unit potential in the Eastern Territory and the 50,000-unit potential in the Western Territory. In the case of Product B the Eastern Territory unit potential is 80,000 while the Western Territory unit potential is 40,000. See Exhibit-8, for these potentials.

The special purpose equipment of Plant I can produce a maximum of 80,000 units of A and 60,000 units of B. The general purpose equipment of Plant I could produce maximums of either 26,666 units of A or 40,000 units of B. In Plant II special purpose equipment can produce a maximum of 20,000 units of A and 6,666 units of B. General purpose equipment in Plant II could be used to produce a maximum of either 26,666 units of A or 6,666 units of B. Each of these production possibilities can be determined by dividing the total of available production hours by the required production hours per unit, both of which are found in Exhibit-9.

OPTIMUM COMBINATION

Considering all of the preceding data, *how does one approach the determination of that combination of production and sales which will yield the optimum profit*? In this case the problem is easily solved since the profit contribution per unit is greater when special purpose equipment is used than when general purpose equipment is used. Thus, as long as there is capacity on special purpose equipment it will be used. When the special purpose equipment capacity is used up, then the less profitable general purpose equipment will be used. Since there is not enough production capacity on the general purpose equipment to produce at the potential sales level, the available hours on the general purpose equipment will be used on those products that produce the greatest return per production hour as shown in Exhibit-13.

As was mentioned previously, the general purpose equipment capacity is less than the remaining sales potential. This makes hours for general purpose equipment capacity a scarce resource and the optimum usage of a scarce resource is in accordance with its contribution. Thus, the fulfilment of the remaining sales potential by general purpose equipment should be based upon a contribution *per hour production time available* and not a contribution *per unit* of Product A or Product B.

The contribution per hour is calculated by dividing the contribution per unit by the required production hours per unit as shown in Exhibit-14.

Based on these calculations of contribution per production hour the remaining sales potential would be filled by the use of general purpose equipment as shown in Exhibit-15.

Fortunately, in this illustration the optimum combination of products can be derived rather easily by using the contribution data in Exhibits 10 and 11. The reason is that the contribution per sales unit is less when general purpose equipment is used for all production and sales possibilities. If, in any particular situation, the above condition does not hold, one may be forced to express the entire problem in algebraic form. The algebra involved is known as linear algebra since it forms a set of linear equations.

EXHIBIT-13

DETERMINATION OF THE !OPTIMUM COMBINATION OF PRODUCTS

		Plant I production on Special Equipment		
	Product A			*Product B*
Units produced using full capacity	80,000			60,000
Disposal of units produced to most profitable territories*				
Eastern Territory	60,000			60,000
Western Territory	20,000			
		Plant II Production on Special Equipment		
	Product A			*Product B*
Units produced using full capacity	20,000			6,666
Disposal of units produced to most profitable territories*				
Western Territory	20,000			6,666
		Summary of Sales Potential and Its Fulfilment		
	Eastern Territory		*Western Territory*	
	A	*B*	*A*	*B*
Potential sales	60,000	80,000	50,000	40,000
Sales potential filled by special purpose equipment				
Plant I	60,000	60,000	20,000	
Plant II			20,000	6,666
Remaining potential to be filled by general purpose equipment	0	20,000	10,000	33,333

* Units are sent to territories in the order that will produce the greatest contribution per unit as shown in Exhibits-10 and 11.

EXHIBIT-14

CALCULATION OF CONTRIBUTION PER HOUR OF PRODUCTION TIME AVAILABLE

	Product A				*Product B*			
Sold in	*Eastern Territory*		*Western Territory*		*Eastern Territory*		*Western Territory*	
Produced in	*Plant I*	*Plant II*	*Plant I*	*Plant II*	*Plant I*	*Plant II*	*Plant I*	*Plant II*
Contribution per unit of sales (Exhibit 11)	₹ 2.00	₹ .75	₹1.50	₹ 1.25	₹ 4.50	₹ 4.50	₹ 4.00	₹ 5.00
Required production hours	1.5	1.5	1.5	1.5	1	1.5	1	1.5
Contribution per production hour	₹ 1.33	₹ 0.50	₹ 1.00	₹ 083	₹ 4.50	₹ 3.00	₹ 4.00	₹ 3.33

The use of algebra in solving optimum product mix problems is seen as a necessity if some products have greater contributions when produced on general purpose equipment. For example. one might consider using general purpose equipment to th extent of its capacity followed by the use of special purpose equipment when contributions per unit are ₹ 5.00 and ₹ 4.50 per unit, respectively, for Product A. However, this may not produce an optimum if Product B can be produced on general purpose equipment at a contribution of ₹ 4.75 and on special purpose equipment at a contribution of ₹ 4.95 and there is enough special purpose equipment to produce all needs for Product A. As the number of such combinations increases, the optimum product mix becomes less and less observable. Ultimately, there is no alternative but the use of algebra.

EXHIBIT-15

USE OF GENERAL PURPOSE EQUIPMENT

	Eastern Territory		*Western Territory*	
	A	*B*	*A*	*B*
Remaining potential to be filled by general purpose equipment	0	20,000	10,000	33,333
Filled by general purpose equipment				
Plant I		20,000		20,000
Plant II				6,666
Unfilled potential—capacity not available	0	0	10.000	6,667

In this case, the preceding problem is shown in Exhibit-16.

EXHIBIT-16

OPTIMUM PRODUCT MIX PROBLEM

Objective

Maximise $3A_{E1}S + 4.5B_{E1}S + 1.5A_{E2}S + 4.5B_{E2}S + 2.5A_{W1}S + 4B_{W1}S + 2A_{W2}S + 5B_{W2}S + 2A_{E1}G + 4.5B_{E1}G + .75A_{E2}G + 4.5B_{E2}G + 1.5A_{W1}G + 4B_{W1}G + 1.25A_{W2}G + 5B_{W2}G$

Restrictions on Objective

Sales Potential

$A_{E1}S + A_{E2}S + A_{E1}G + A_{E2}G \leq 60{,}000$ Eastern Territory

$A_{W1}S + A_{W2}S + A_{W1}G + A_{W2}G \leq 50{,}000$ Western Territory

$B_{E1}S + B_{E2}S + B_{E1}G + B_{E2}G \leq 80{,}000$ Eastern Territory

$B_{W1}S + B_{W2}S + B_{W1}G + B_{W2}G \leq 40{,}000$ Western Territory

Available Production Hours

$.5A_{E1}S + .5A_{W1}S$	$\leq 40{,}000$	
$B_{E1}S + B_{W1}S$	$\leq 60{,}000$	Plant I
$1.5A_{E1}G + 1.5A_{W1}G + B_{E1}G + B_{W1}G$	$\leq 40{,}000$	
$A_{E2}S + A_{W2}S$	$\leq 20{,}000$	
$1.5B_{E2}S + 1.5B_{W2}S$	$\leq 10{,}000$	Plant II
$1.5A_{E2}G + 1.5A_{W2}G$	$+ 1.5B_{E2}G + 1.5B_{W2}G \leq 10{,}000$	

In the algebraic expression of the problem there is one equation that expresses the objective, that is, to maximize the total profit contribution. This equation is known is the *objective function.* The numbers in the objective function represent the profit contributions for the products produced in various plants and sold in various territories, represented by the letters in the equation.

All the other equations represent restrictions of sales potential and production capacity. These restrictions are all expressed in the form of inequalities since sales potentials and production capacity represent upper limits, and both sales and production could be equal to or less than potential in the optimum solution to the set of eleven equations. Solving these equations means that we desire to derive values for the A's and B's that will produce the maximum total profit contribution. An interesting and distressing point concerning solutions to such a set of equations is that there are situations that will yield no solution, that will yield one solution, and even that will yield many solutions. In our case, we desire the solution that maximises the profit contribution.

Where there is not solution, there is no maximum; where there is one solution, it must be the maximum; where there are many solutions, the maximum must be sought out. Seeking out the maximum may be a long and tedious process since one would never know that we had the maximum if all possible solutions were not tested.

Fortunately, there has been developed a routine technique for deriving the maximum solution (if a solution to the equations exists). This technique, known as the "simplex method," can easily be programmed on electronic compute₹ This process of using linear algebra and the simplex method of solving linear equations have been given the imposing title "Linear Programming."

Linear programming can be used in those many decision-making situations where the objective is to maximise or even minimise a certain value such as revenue or costs. The problem should be expressed algebraically in as precise a manner as possible. A possible objection is that the equations are linear and straight lines may not fully express the cost and revenue functions of a business situations. However, one should remember that a linear equation is probably as close an approximation to real life as the estimates of cost and revenue that will be used in the equations. Why, therefore, should we ask for more precision in the algebra when the precision of the cost and revenue data is probably of the same approximate level of exactitude? Another point to remember is that within the usual range of relevance to specific decisions the cost and revenue functions approximate a straight line.

With linear programming, break-even analysis proves to be much more useful. In fact, linear programming stretches the cost-volume-profit relationships inherent in break-even analysis into a fairly realistic quantitative approach to the incremental cost and revenue concepts of microeconomics.

Much work has already been done by individual firms in the area of linear programming. Those who have yet to learn of it are missing out on one of the most valuable quantitative tools developed in recent yers There is no doubt that more businessmen and accounts should begin to consider the possibility of using linear programming to express cost-volume-profit relationships and to derive the optimum combination of cost, volume, and profit. One need not worry about the size of the equations or the number of equations since computers are readily available to use the simplex method of solving linear equations. Furthermore, there is the possibility that the number of factors and equations could be fewer in some situations than in the illustration presented above.

ILLUSTRATIVE PROBLEMS

1. Punjab Tractors is attempting to develop and market a new small tractor fixed costs to develop and produce the new tractor are estimated to be ₹ 10 crore per year. The variable cost to make each tractor has been estimated at ₹ 20,000. The marketing research department has recommended a price of ₹ 1,00,000 for tractor. (a) What is the breakeven level of output for the new tractor? (b) If management expects to generate a target profit of ₹ 2 crore from tractor each year, how many tractors must be sold?

Solution

$$\text{(a)}\quad Q_b = \frac{FC}{SPPU - AVC}$$

$$= \frac{₹\ 10{,}00{,}00{,}000}{₹\ 1{,}00{,}000 - ₹\ 20{,}000} = 1250 \text{ units / year}$$

(b) Target volume = $\frac{\text{FC + m}}{\text{SPPU – AVC}}$

$= \frac{₹ \text{10 crore} + ₹ \text{2 crore}}{₹ 1,00,000 - ₹ 20,000}$ = 1500 units / year.

2. Nav Jyot Manufacturing sells a single product for ₹ 3 with variable cost per unit of ₹ 1.80. If fixed costs are ₹ 30,00,000, ₹ 9,00,000 of non-cash expenses (depreciation and amortisation), what is the breakeven point on a cash basis?

Solution

The breakeven point in units can be calculated as follows

Breakeven point–units = $\frac{\text{TFC}}{\text{SPPU – AVC}}$

$= \frac{₹ 30,00,000}{₹ 3.00 - ₹ 180}$ = 25,00,000 units

The breakeven point on a cash basis can be calculated as follows:

$\frac{₹ 30,00,000 - ₹ 9,00,000}{₹ 3.00 - ₹ 1.80}$ = 17,50,000 units

3. Vithal Enterprises has determined that the breakeven level of output for its washing machine is 20,000 units. The marketing research department has determined that expected sales will be 22,000 units, with a standard deviation of 4,000 units. What is the probability that Vithal will incur operating losses from the sale of washing machine?

Solution

The probability of having operating losses is the probability of selling 20,000 units or less.

$Z = \frac{20,000 - 22,000}{4,000} = -0.5$

The probability of a Z ≤ 0.5 (i.e., the probability of selling 20,000 units or less) can be determined form Table – 5 as 0.3085, or 30.85%.

4. Vijay Enterprises is in the process of introducing a new product test marketing has been successful, and the product is now entering its production base. The problem in choosing suitable production arrangements. Different plant types have been considered, and the choice has narrowed to type ABC or type XYZ (cost data for each are as follows):

	Plant Type ABC	Plant Type XYZ
Fixed Cost	₹ 16,00,000	₹ 28,00,000
Variable Cost per unit	₹ 60.00	₹ 40.00

The selling price of the new product will be ₹ 140 a unit, and the expected annual volume is ₹ 50,000 units. Management anticipates selecting ABC, although it wants a clear analysis to show that ABC is the most efficient at the expected volume. It also wants to know the range of output where ABC has an advantage over XYZ. In addition, management wants to consider the breakeven point with each production type and the profit levels for each at outputs of 30,000; 50,000; and 70,000 units.

Should plant type ABC be chosen over plant type XYZ?

Solution

Operating Plans : A Comparison

1. Determine Cost Advantage:

Cost relation ABC:	Total Cost = Fixed Cost + Variable Costs
	= ₹ 16,00,000 + ₹ 60 × Q
Cost relation XYZ:	Total Cost = ₹ 28,00,000 + ₹ 40 × Q
Difference XYZ - ABC:	Total Cost = –₹ 12,00,000 – ₹ 20 × Q
Solve for Q:	–₹ 12,00,000 = – ₹ 20 Q
	60,000 = Q

This implies that plant ABC has a cost advantage for all annual outputs from 0 to 60,000 units. When output exceeds this figure, plant XYZ takes the advantage. Since management expects annual output to be 50,000, plant ABC is the better price.

2. Determine the breakeven points.

Type ABC:	Contribution Margin: =	CM XQ = FC
		(₹ 140 – ₹ 60) Q = ₹ 16,00,000
		₹ 80Q = ₹ 16,00,000
		Q = 20,000 units
Type XYZ:		(₹ 140 – ₹ 40) = ₹ 28,00,000
		₹ 100Q = ₹ 28,00,000
		Q = 28,000 units.

3. Determine profit levels:

Type ABC:	Q = 30,000	Profit	= (₹ 80 × 30,000) – ₹ 16,00,000
			= ₹ 8,00,000
	Q = 50,000	Profit	= (₹ 80 × 50,000) – ₹ 16,00,000
			= ₹ 24,00,000
	Q = 70,000	Profit	= (₹ 80 × 70,000) – ₹ 16,00,000
			= ₹ 40,00,000
	Q = 30,000	Profit	= (₹ 100 × 30,000) - ₹ 28,00,000
			= ₹ 2,00,000
Type XYZ:	Q = 50,000	Profit	= (₹ 100 × 50,000) – ₹ 28,00,000
			= ₹ 22,00,000
	Q = 70,000	Profit	= (₹ 100 × 70,000) – ₹ 28,00,000
			= ₹ 42,00,000

Again it can be seen that plant type ABC has a profit advantage at the 30,000 and 50,000 output rates, but that plant type XYZ has the advantage at the 70,000 rate, At 60,000 units, ABC's profit = XYZ's profit = ₹ 32,00,000.

5. Mr. R.P. Verma is planning to open a Modern Variety Store. He has arrived at the following estimates for the first year of operations. Sales will be 80,000 units and the selling price per unit will be ₹ 1.80 for all units All goods are purchased ready for sale and cost-of-goods sold will be ₹ 1.08 per unit for all products, Depreciation expense will be ₹ 1,000/-. Salaries and rent will cost ₹ 15,000 for the year, regardless of the level of sales. The income tax rate will be 40%. All other expenses are variable and equal to 1% of sales.

(a) Calculate the expected level of net income after taxes for the first year of operations.
(b) Calculate the breakeven point in units and ₹.

Solution

(a) The proforma income statement can be calculated follows:

Modern Variety Store

Net sales (80,000 units at ₹ 1.80)	₹ 1,44,000
Cost-of-goods sold	86,400
Gross profit	₹ 57,600
Salaries and rent expense	15,000
Depreciation expense	1,000
Other expense (1%)	1,440
Net income before taxes	₹ 40,160
Income taxes at 40%	16,064
Net income after taxes	₹ 24,096

(b) Before calculating the breakeven points, it would be useful to recast the proforma income statement in the following manner:

Modern Variety Store

Net sales (80,000 units at ₹ 1.80)	₹ 1,44,000
Variable expenses (61%)	87,840
Fixed expenses	16,000
Net Income before taxes	₹ 40,164
Income taxes at 40%	16.064
Net income after taxes	₹ 24096

$$\text{Breakeven—Units} = \frac{₹\ 16{,}000}{₹\ 1.80 - ₹\ 1.098}$$

$$= 22{,}792 \text{ in units}$$

$$\text{Breakeven—₹} = \frac{₹\ 16{,}000}{1\text{–}61\%}$$

$$= \frac{₹\ 16{,}000}{.39} = ₹\ 41{,}025.64$$

The breakeven formulas ignore tax shields. These formulas determine the level of sales at which net income before taxes is zero.

6. Refer to Problem-5, assume that Mr. R.P. Verma arrived at the following optimistic and pessimistic estimates

Optimistic Estimates

Sales will be 1,00,000 units and the selling price per unit will be ₹ 2.00 for all units. Depreciation expense will be ₹ 1,000. Cost of goods sold will be ₹ 1.16 per unit. Salaries plus rent will total ₹ 14,000 for the year. The income tax rate will be 40%. All other expenses are variable and will equal 1% of sales.

Pessimistic Estimates

Sales will be 60,000 units and selling price will be ₹ 1.50 for all units. Depreciation expense will be ₹ 1,000. Cost of goods sold will be ₹ 1.12 per unit. Salaries plus rent will total ₹ 16,000 for the year. The income tax rate will be 40%. All other expenses are variable and will equal 1.5% of sales,

Calculate the breakeven point in units and rupees, for the optimistic and pessimistic estimates.

Solution

We should first summarise selling price per unit, variable expenses per unit, and total fixed expenses for each set of estimates.

Optimistic

Selling price per unit		₹ 2.00
Variable expenses per unit		
Cost-of-goods sold	₹ 1.16	
Other variable	.02	
		1.18
Total fixed expenses		
Salaries and rent	₹ 14,000	
Depreciation expense	1,000	₹ 15,000

The variable expenses to sales ratio can be calculated by dividing variable expenses per unit (₹ 1.18) by selling price per unit.

Pessimistic

Selling price per unit	₹ 1.50
Variable expenses per unit	1.345
Total fixed expenses	₹17,000
Variable expenses to sales ratio	89.6667%

We can calculate the breakeven points.

Optimistic

$$\text{Breakeven–Units} = \frac{₹\ 15,000}{₹\ 2.00 - ₹\ 1.18} = 18292.68 \text{ units}$$

$$\text{Breakeven–Rupees} = \frac{₹\ 15{,}000}{1 - 59\%} = ₹\ 36{,}585.37$$

Pessimistic

$$\text{Breakeven–Units} = \frac{₹\ 17{,}000}{₹\ 1.50 - ₹\ 1.345} = 1{,}09{,}677 \text{ units}$$

$$\text{Breakeven–Rupees} = \frac{₹\ 17{,}000}{1 - 89.6667\%} = ₹\ 1{,}64{,}516.02$$

QUESTIONS

1. Explain how the following may change the classification of a cost into the fixed or variable class: (a) The magnitude of a change in output; (b) The amount of time required to change the cost; (c) The length of time the change in output is expected to last.
2. What benefits can be derived from breakeven analysis? What data are necessary to construct a breakeven chart?
3. To determine the breakeven point, a company plotted total revenues on the X axis and total expenses and total revenues on the Y axis. The president of the firm wanted to know the effect of a 10% increase in price on the breakeven point. The analyst shifted the slope of the revenue line and read off the breakeven point. Comment on this procedure.
4. Discuss the following statement: "If you lower your price, the breakeven point will increase."
5. "Fixed expenses are necessary in order to make it possible for a firm to experience a net loss." Comment.
6. What are the limitations of linear breakeven analysis? How would you try to overcome that?
7. What is the difference between linear and non-linear breakeven analysis? Which is superior and more commonly used? Why is the assumption of linear cost and revenue functions appropriate for most business situations?
8. Explain what is meant by "contribution margin." Why does contribution analysis exclude fixed costs that might otherwise be included in break-even analysis?
9. What is meant by the term *break-even point*? What factors must be taken into consideration in determining this point? Where does the break-even point occur in a graphic representation of break-even analysis? Where are the profits measured?
10. What is the difference between the (ordinary) break-even point and the cash break-even point? Which will be greater?
11. Break-even analysis assumes linear revenue and cost functions. In reality these linear functions over large output and sales levels are highly improbable? Why?
12. For what type of industry might Break-even analysis be most suited? Why? Give an example.
13. Why would a firm's break-even point for operating profit differ from its break-even point on a cash basis?
14. What is the interrelationship between the growth/share matrix and the economic concept of opportunity costs? Does this relationship have any operational implications or is it merely a theoretical concept? Why or why not?

15. How might a business enterprise go about lowering its break-even point? Why might it wish to lower its break-even point?
16. What are the assumptions of break-even analysis for individual products, plants and sales territories?
17. How does production capacity and sales potential affect the break-even analysis?
18. In arriving at an opimum combination of production and sales, what factors justify the use of equipment on the basis of contribution per hour of production time available instead of contribution per unit of individual products?
19. If the objective function and all the restrictions can be expressed in equation form, will linear programming always yield an optimal solution?
20. Would the assumption that variable costs are the only costs relevant to decision-making be valid in most cases? Explain
21. Why is the assumption of linear cost and revenue functions appropriate for most business situations?

PROBLEMS

1. Suppose that a company currently has sales of ₹ 2,50,000 and break-even sales are ₹ 2,00,000. Compute the margin of safety in percentage terms and in term of ₹.
2. The Novex Toys has fixed cost of ₹ 25,000,000 per year and variable costs of ₹ 60 per unit. Its product sells for ₹ 100 per unit and full capacity is 1,00,000 units. (a) Compute the break-even point in units, sales in ₹, and percentage of capacity; (b) Compute the number of units the company must sell if it wishes to have a profit of ₹ 12,00,000.
3. A cosmetics company is considering the introduction of a new product. It is considering three quality levels for the product. The first alternative involves variable costs ₹ 1.25 per unit, the second ₹ 1.875, while the third would involve variable costs of ₹ 2.225 per unit. Fixed costs for the three alternatives would be ₹ 12,00,000, ₹ 18,00,000 and ₹ 25,00,000 respectively. Market research has indicated that the three different products could be priced at ₹ 12.50, ₹ 14.90 and ₹ 19.8 respectively. (a) Calculate the breakeven volumes and ₹ sales levels for each of the three alternatives. (b) What other information would you prefer to have before making your recommendations?
4. DD Enterprise has fixed costs of ₹ 250,000 per year and variable costs of ₹ 6 per unit. Its product sells for ₹ 10 per unit and full capacity is 1,00,000 units. (a) Compute the breakeven point in ₹ sales, units, and percentage of capacity. (b) Compute the number of units the company must sell if it wishes to have a profit of ₹ 11,20,000.
5. Suppose that a company currently has sales of ₹ 2,50,000 and breakeven sales are ₹ 2,00,000. Compute the margin of safety in percentage terms and in terms of ₹.
6. Suppose that a company has a single product that currently sells for ₹ 60, variable costs per unit are ₹ 15 or 25 per cent of selling price, and fixed costs are ₹ 27,000. (a) Compute the breakeven level in terms of number of units and ₹ sales. (b) What would happen to these two breakeven levels if selling price could be increased to ₹ 75? If fixed costs could be reduced to ₹ 24,000? If variable costs could be reduced to ₹ 12 per unit or 20 per cent of selling price?
7. Tanya Collections sells miniature gold-plated replicas. Each miniature is sold for ₹ 2,000. Tanya's fixed cost are ₹ 20,00,000. In 2011, Tanya sold 6000 miniatures. Total variable costs for 2011 were ₹ 60,00,000. (a) What was the company's pretax income in 2011? (b) For 2012, the company expect at 25% increase in fixed cost.

i) What is the new break-even point in units (miniatures) if preice remains at ₹ 2,000?

ii) By how much should the price per miniature be increased in order for the company to make the same profit as in 2011, assuming that variable costs and the number of miniature sold remain at the 2011 level?

PART - II

VALUATION

This Page has been intentionally left blank

6

THE TIME VALUE OF MONEY

INTRODUCTION

The financial manager makes decisions on the cash flows that are expected to occur at various points in time. *Why is it important for the financial manager to somehow quantitatively recognise the differences in the timing of these cash flows?* This is because a firm is viewed as a going concern, its value and the decisions of the financial manager must be assessed in light of both its present and future cash flows. The time value of money is a common denominator for discussing financial transactions and financial opportunities. In a way, the time value of money is a language of finance, a building block, and fundamental in many areas of finance to decide trade-off between risk and return. The chapter explains the terminology, computational procedures and tables used in interest theory. We consider the two common views of time value—future value and present value—and the computational aids that are commonly used to streamline time-value calculations.

INTEREST CALCULATIONS

Interest calculations may be based on interest rates which are either simple or compound.

SIMPLE INTEREST

In order to compute interest it is necessary to know the principal, the rate of interest and the term of the loan. The *principal* is the sum of money borrowed; the *rate of interest* is the percent of the principal which is charged for its use for one period of time, and the *term of the loan* is the number of periods during which the principal is used. Thus, the simple interest (S) on any principal (P) is found by multiplying together the principal, the rate of interest per annum *(i)* and time expressed in years *(n)*.

Thus:

$$S = P \times i \times n \tag{1}$$

Example-1

Assuming a nationalised bank pays 10% on twelve months fixed deposit, what will be the interest on ₹ 10,000 in fixed deposit for a year?

$S = P.\,i.n.$

$S = ₹\ 10{,}000 \times .10 \times 1 = ₹\ 1{,}000$

The accumulated value at the end of the year is found by adding the interest to the principal. That is:

Accumulated value = Principal + Interest

If the accumulated value is designated by the symbol (V) then:

$$V = P + S$$
$$V = P + P.\ i.n.$$
$$V = P\,(1 + i.n.) \qquad (2)$$

Equation (2) is the formula for the accumulated value at simple interest of a principal (P) bearing interest at the rate of i and n years.

Example -2

Calculate the accumulated value for Example-1

$$V = P\,(1 + i.n.)$$
$$V = ₹\,10{,}000\,(1 + .10 \times 1) = ₹\,10{,}000\,(1.10) = ₹\,11{,}000$$

To find the accumulated value of a principal invested at simple interest we use the formula, $V = P\,(1 + i.n.)$. If the accumulated value is known and we wish to calculate the *present value* (principal) we solve Equation-2 for P. Thus, by transformation of Equation-2, we find that:

$$P = \frac{V}{(1 + i.n)} \qquad (3)$$

Equation-3 is the formula for the present value of a future sum of money at simple interest.

Example-3

What is the present value of ₹ 11,000 due in one year's time if money can be invested 10% per annum?

$$P = \frac{V}{(1 + i.n)}$$

$$P = \frac{₹11{,}000}{(1 + .10 \times 1)} = \frac{₹11{,}000}{1.10} = ₹\,10{,}000$$

Thus ₹ 10,000 now and ₹ 11,000 in one year's time at a rate of interest of 10% per annum are *equivalent*.

COMPOUND INTEREST

Compound Interest is similar to receiving interest on interest. The interest earned by the invested capital in any period is accumulated so that simple interest in the next period is paid not only on the original principal but also on the accumulated interest of all the previous periods during which interest was paid.

Example-4

What will ₹ 10,000 amount to in 4 years if interest is 10% per annum compounded annually?

Calculations for the above example are tabulated below:

	Year Amount deposited at beginning of year	*Interest charge for year*	*Amount deposited at end of year*
	₹	₹ ₹	₹
1.	10,000.00	10,000.00 × 0.10 = 1,000.00	11,000.00
2.	11.000.00	11,000.00 × 0.10 = 1,100.00	12,100.00
3.	12,100.00	12,100.00 × 0.10 = 1,210.00	13,310.00
4.	13,310.00	13,310.00 × 0.10 = 1,331.00	14,641.00

The amounted deposited at end of 4 years would be ₹ 14,641,00. In case of simple interest for the same period, it would have been:

$$V_n = P(1+P.i.n.)$$

$$V_4 = ₹\ 10{,}000\ (1+0.10 \times 4) = ₹\ 10{,}000\ (1+.40) = ₹\ 14{,}000$$

The simple interest does not allow for reinvestment of the earned interest. It is calculated on the original principal each year.

Compound Interest Formula

Compound interest is much more often encountered in practice than simple interest. The compounding formula is derived by using the simple interest formula over and over again. Let us use the same symbols as those found in the simple interest formula. An amount paying interest compounded annually will grow to a future sum, V. according to the formula.

$$V = P+Pi$$

$$FV_1 = P(1+i) \text{ for one year} \quad (4)$$

for 2 years we have

$$FV_2 = P(1+i)\,(1+i)$$

$$FV_2 = P(1+i)^2 \quad (5)$$

At the end of n years the original sum deposited will grow to

$$FV_n = P(1+i)^n \quad (6)$$

In the future we will find several uses for Equation-6, not only we will find the future value of an investment, but we also solve for P, i, or n. In any case we will be given three of the four variables and will have to solve for the fourth.

Example-5

Calculate the accumulated value for Example-4 by using Equation-6.

$FV_n = P\ (1+i)^n$

$FV_4 =$ ₹ $10{,}000\ (1+.10)^4 =$ ₹ $10{,}000\ (1.4641) =$ ₹ $13{,}604.90$

Thus, at the end of 4 years, we will have ₹ 14,641.

As the determination of future value can be quite time consuming when an investment is held for a number of years, tables have been compiled for values of $(1 + i).^n$ An abbreviated compound interest table appears in Table-1. (A more comprehensive version of this table appears at the back of this book). Note that the compounding factors given in this table represent the value of ₹ 1 compounded at rate *i* at the end of the *n*th year. To calculate the future value of an initial investment we need only to determine the table value and multiply the times of the initial investment.

Example-6

If we invest ₹ 50,000 in the bank where it earns 8% compound annually. How much will it be worth at the end of 5 years?

Looking in Table-1 in the row n=5 and column i = 8%, we find a value of ₹ 1.469. Substituting this in Equation-6, we find

$FV_n = P\ (1+i)^n$

$FV_5 =$ ₹ $50{,}000\ (1 + .08)^5 =$ ₹ $50{,}000\ (1.4693) =$ ₹ $73{,}465$

TABLE-1

Compound Sum of One Rupee

n	*1%*	*2%*	*3%*	*4%*	*5%*	*6%*	*7%*	*8%*	*9%*	*10%*	*n*
01	1.0100	1.0200	1.03300	1.0400	1.0500	1.0600	1.0700	1.0800	1.0900	1.1000	01
02	1.0201	1.0404	1.0609	1.0816	1.1025	1.1236	1.1449	1.1664	1.1881	1.2100	02
03	1.0303	1.0612	1.0927	0.1249	1.1576	1.1910	1.2250	1.2597	1.2950	1.3310	03
04	1.0406	1.0824	1.1255	1.1699	1.2155	1.2625	1.3108	1.3605	1.4116	1.4641	04
05	1.0510	1.1041	1.1593	1.2067	1.2763	1.3382	1.4026	1.4693	1.5386	1.6105	05
06	1.0615	1.1261	1.1941	1.2653	1.3401	1.4185	1.5007	1.5869	1.6771	1.7716	06
07	1.0721	1.1487	1.2299	1.3159	1.4071	1.5036	1.6058	1.7138	1.8280	1.9487	07
08	1.0829	1.1717	1.2668	1.3686	1.4775	1.5939	1.7182	1.8509	1.9926	2.1436	08
09	1.0937	1.1951	1.3038	1.4233	1.5513	1.6895	1.8385	1.9990	1.1719	2.3580	09
10	1.1046	1.2190	1.3439	1.4802	1.6289	1.7809	1.9672	2.1589	2.3674	2.5937	10
11	1.1157	1.2434	1.3842	1.5395	1.7103	1.8993	2.1049	2.3316	2.5804	2.8531	11
12	1.1268	1.2682	1.4258	1.6010	1.7959	2.0122	2.2522	2.5182	2.8127	3.1384	12
13	1.1381	1.2936	1.4685	1.6651	1.8857	2.1329	2.4098	2.7196	3.0658	3.4523	13
14	1.1495	1.3195	1.5126	1.7317	1.9799	2.2609	2.5785	2.9372	3.3417	3.7975	14
15	1.1610	1.3459	1.5589	1.8009	2.0789	2.3966	2.7590	3.1722	3.6425	4.1773	15
16	1.1726	1.3728	1.6047	1.8730	2.1829	2.5404	2.9522	3.4259	3.9703	4.5950	16
17	1.1843	1.4002	1.6529	1.4479	2.2920	2.6928	3.1588	3.7000	4.3276	5.0545	17
18	1.1962	1.4283	1.7024	2.0258	2.4066	2.8543	3.3799	3.9960	4.7171	5.5596	18
19	1.2081	1.4568	1.7535	2.1069	2.5270	3.0256	3.6165	4.3157	5.1417	5.1156	19
20	1.2202	1.4860	1.8061	2.1911	2.6533	3.2071	3.8697	4.6610	5.6044	6.7275	20

Example-7

How many years will it take for an initial investment of ₹ 10,000 to grow to ₹ 67,275 if it is invested at 10% compounded annually?

Substituting the known values in Equation-6, we find

$$FV_n = P\,(1+i)^n \tag{6}$$

$$₹\ 67{,}275 = ₹\ 10{,}000\ (1+.10)^n$$

$$6.7275 = (1+.10)^n$$

If we look for a table value of 6.7275 in the 10% column, we find that it occurs in the n = 20. Thus, it will take 20 years for an initial investment of ₹ 10,000 to grow to ₹ 67,275 it is invested at 10% compounded annually.

Example-8

At what rate ₹ 10,000 be compounded annually for it to grow to ₹ 45,950 in 16 years?

Substituting into Equation 6, we get:

$$FV_n = P\,(1+i)^n$$

$$₹\ 45{,}950 = ₹\ 10{,}000\ (1+i)^{16}$$

$$4.5950 = (1+i)^{16}$$

By looking in the n=16 row for a table value of 4.5950, we find this in the i = 10% column. Thus, we must invest at 10% if we want the initial investment of ₹ 10,000 to accrue to ₹ 45,950 in 16 years.

Graphic Illustration of Compound Interest

Figure-1 illustrates the effect of compound interest on an initial investment of ₹ 1 over time. Notice how the compounding effect accelerates the increase in the capital value as time passes, particularly when compared to the effect of simple interest over the same interval.

FIGURE-1

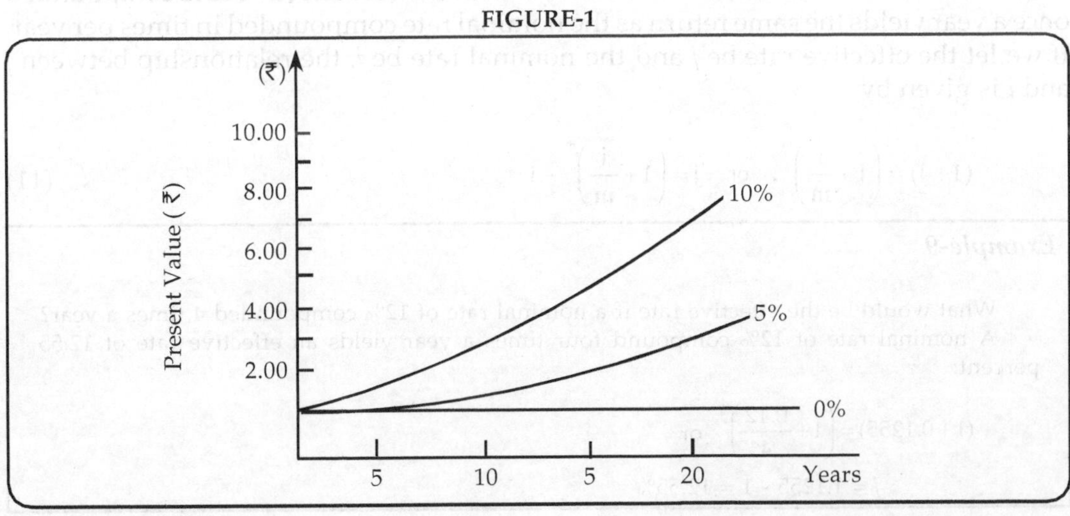

Compounding Interest for Non-annual Periods

Frequently the compounding period is less than a year. We have to adjust the compound interest formula to reflect the increase number of times the compounding will occur in the year. For the more frequently the interest is earned and begins, in turn, to earn further interest, the greater the effective annual compound rate of interest. For example, if interest is compounded quarterly, the amount on deposit at the end of 3 months would be:

$$FV_m = P\left(1+\frac{i}{4}\right) \tag{7}$$

The balance at the end of 6 months is

$$FV_m = P\left(1+\frac{i}{4}\right)\left(1+\frac{i}{4}\right) \tag{8}$$

or $$FV_m = P\left(1+\frac{i}{4}\right)^2$$

and at the end of 1 year

$$FV_m = P\left(1+\frac{i}{4}\right)^4 \tag{9}$$

In general, if interest is compounded m times per year, the amount on deposit at the end of n years will be

$$FV_{mn} = P\left(1+\frac{i}{m}\right)^{mn} \tag{10}$$

The number of times per year interest is compounded may range from once to continuously. The interest rate rate is usually stated on the annual basis and is known as the nominal rate. *When the nominal rate is compounded more than once a year a higher rate of return results, known as the effective rate.* The effective rate compounded once a year yields the same return as the nominal rate compounded in times per year. If we let the effective rate be j and the nominal rate be i, the relationship between j and i is given by

$$(1+j) = \left(1+\frac{i}{m}\right)^m, \text{ or } j = \left(1+\frac{i}{m}\right)^m - 1 \tag{11}$$

Example-9

What would be the effective rate if a nominal rate of 12% compounded 4 times a year?

A nominal rate of 12% compound four times a year yields an effective rate of 12.55 percent:

$$(1+0.1255) = \left(1+\frac{0.12}{4}\right)^4 \text{ or}$$

j = 1.1255 - 1 = 12.55%

Fractional Periods

Where a problem includes fractional periods, it is usual in practice to use simple interest for the fraction of an interest period.

Example-10

Ashok Verma and Suman Gupta invests ₹ 10,000 in each in a joint account. In return for their investment, interest will accumulate at the rate of 8% per annum compounded annually. It is agreed that none of them will withdraw their investment until after the third year. After 3½ years Ashok decides to withdraw his investment; how much will he receive?

Find the compound interest for the first 3 years and add to this simple interest for the half year to solve it. In 3 years the investment would have grown to:

$$FV_3 = ₹\ 10{,}000\ (1.08)^3$$

$$FV_3 = ₹\ 10{,}000\ (1.25971) = ₹\ 12{,}597.10$$

To find the amount of repayment to Ashok:

$$FV_{mn} = ₹\ 12{,}597.10\ (1+½ \times 0.08)$$

$$FV_{mn} = ₹\ 12{,}597.10\ (1.04) = ₹\ 13{,}100.98$$

Interpolation

In many problems the principal, accumulated value and number of compounding periods are known and we wish to calculate the rate of interest. An approximate rate of interest may be found by interpolation. Basically, interpolation assumes that the values in the tables vary uniformly. This is not exactly correct but it is sufficiently accurate for most purposes. Thus, since 2¼% is halfway between the 2% and 2½%, it is expected that 1.025% is approximately halfway between 1.02% and 1.050%.

PRESENT VALUE DISCOUNTING

Present value is the exact opposite or mirror image of future value. While future value shows how much a sum can become at some future date, present value shows what the value is today (at present) of future sums of money. This process of reducing future income payments to their present value is called *discounting. The value today of the sum to be received in the future is called its present value.*

SINGLE PAYMENT

Finding the present value (discounting) of a single payment is the reverse of compounding an initial sum over the same period of time. Dividing both sides of Equation-6, $FV_n = P\ (1+i)^n$ by $(1+i)^n$ where FV is the future sum, P is the amount deposited, and i and n are defined as above, we have

$$P = \frac{FV_n}{(1+i)^n} \tag{12}$$

Rearranging terms and substituting PV for P we have present value:

$$PV = \frac{FV_n}{(1+i)^n} \tag{13}$$

Example-11

At what nominal rate of interest compounded quarterly will ₹ 10,000 amount be ₹ 14,000 in 5 years time?

$$FV_n = P(1+i)^5$$

₹ 14,000 = ₹ 10,000 $(1+i)^{20}$

then:

$$(1+i)^{20} = \frac{₹14,000}{₹10,000} = 1.400$$

Now it is necessary to find the value of i for which $(1=i)^{20}$ is equal to 1.4000. In looking through table we fail to find n = 20 a value of 1.4000. However, we may find the approximate interest rate by linear interpolation which will result in a rate sufficiently accurate for most practical purposes.

In order to find the interest rate we follow along the line n = 20 until we find an entry slightly smaller than 1.4000 and one slightly greater, which we use to set up the following table:

	i		$(1+i)^{20}$	
	0.015		1.3469	
		x	0.0531	
0.0025	?		1.4000	
				0.0679
	0.0175		1.4148	

The interpolation process is performed as follows:

$$\frac{x}{0.0025} = \frac{0.0531}{0.0679}$$

$$x = 0.00196$$

Therefore, the rate of interest per compounding period is 0.015 + 0.00196 = 1.696%. The nominal rate compounded quarterly is $4i$ or 4 × 1.696 = 6.78% approximately.

As the mathematical procedure for determining the present value is exactly the inverse of determining the future value, we also find that the relationships among P, i, and n are just opposite of those we observed with the future value. The present value of a future sum of money in inversely related to both the number of years until the payment will be received at the opportunity rate. Graphically this relationship can be illustrated through Figure-2.

While Equation-13, the present-value equation, is used extensively in evaluating new investment proposals, it should be stressed that Equation—13 is actually the same as Equation—6 where it is solved for P.

FIGURE-2

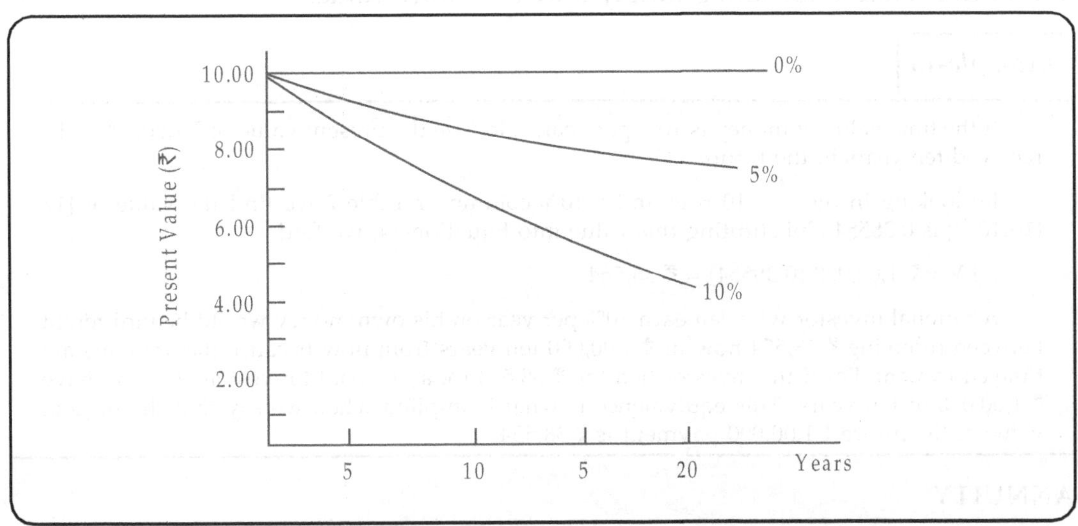

Example -12

What would be the present value of ₹ 1,21,000 to be received in two years when discounted at 10%?

Substituting these values into Equation-13, we get:

$$PV = FV^n \left[\frac{1}{(1+i)^n}\right]$$

$$PV = ₹\ 1{,}21{,}000 \left[\frac{1}{(1+.10)^2}\right]$$

PV = ₹ 1,00,000

Thus, the present value of ₹ 1, 21,000 to be received in 2 year is ₹ 1,00,000.

PRESENT VALUE TABLES

For use in calculating present values, discount tables have been developed to ease the computational work. Discount tables are tables of discount factors. The discount factor is multiplied by the future sum to convert the sum to a present value.

Present value = (Future sum at period n) (Discound factor for i % per period and n periods)

$$PV = (FV_n)\ (DF\ i, n) \tag{14}$$

For convenience, these tables are reproduced at the end of the book. Table-2 is an abbreviated version. A close examination shows that the values in Table-2 are merely the inverse of those in Table-1. This, of course, as it should be, the values in Table-1 are $(1+i)^n$ and those in Table-2 are $[1/(1+i)^n]$. To determine the present value of a sum of money to be received at some future date, we need only to determine the appropriate table value and multiply it by the future value.

Example-13

If the time value of money is 10% per year, calculate the present value of ₹ 1,00,000 to be received ten years in the future.

By looking in the n = 10 row and i=10% column of Table-2 we find the value of $[1/(1+.10)^{10}]$ is 0.38554. Substituting this value into Equation-14, we find

PV = ₹ 1,00,000 (0.38554) = ₹ 38,554

A rational investor who can earn 10% per year on his own money would be indifferent between receiving ₹ 38,554 now or ₹ 1,00,000 ten years from now because the amounts are time equivalent. For if the investor had the ₹ 38,554 today he could invest at 10% and have ₹ 1,00,000 in ten years. This equivalence is what is implied when we say that the present value of the future ₹ 1,00,000 payment is ₹ 38,554.

ANNUITY

An annuity is defined as a series of payments of a fixed amount for a specified number of years. While the process of compounding and determining the present value of an annuity can be dealt with by using the methods we have just described, they can be quite time-consuming, especially for large annuities. Thus we have modified these formulas and developed tables to deal directly with annuities.

TABLE-2

Present Value of One Rupee Due at the End of *n* Years

n	1%	2%	3%	4%	5%	6%	7%	8%	9%	10%	*n*
01	.99010	.98039	.97007	.96154	.95238	.94340	.93558	.92593	.91743	.90909	01
02	.98030	.96117	.94260	.92456	.90703	.89000	.87344	.85734	.84168	.82645	02
03	.97059	.94232	.91514	.88900	.86384	.83962	.81630	.79383	.77218	.75131	03
04	.96098	.92285	.88849	.85480	.82270	.79209	.76290	.73503	.70843	.68301	04
05	.95147	.90573	.86261	.82193	.78353	.74726	.71299	.68058	.64993	.62092	05
06	.94204	.88797	.83748	.79031	.74622	.70496	.66634	.63017	.59627	.56447	06
07	.93272	.87056	.81309	.75992	.71068	.66506	62275	.58349	.54703	.51316	07
08	.92348	.85349	.78941	.73069	.67684	.62741	.58201	.54027	.50187	.46651	08
09	.91434	.83675	.76642	.70259	.64461	.59190	.54393	.50025	.46043	.42410	09
10	.90529	.82035	.74409	.67556	.61391	.55839	.50835	.46319	42241	**.38554**	10
11	.89632	.80426	.72242	.64958	.58468	.52679	.47a9	.42888	.38753	.35049	11
12	.88745	.78849	.70138	.62460	.55684	.49627	.44401	.39711	.25553	.31683	12
13	87866	.77303	.68095	.60057	.53032	.46884	.41496	.36770	.32618	.28961	13
14	.86996	.75787	.66112	.57747	.50507	.44230	.38782	.34046	.29925	.26333	14
15	.86135	.74301	.64186	.55526	.48102	.41726	.36245	.31524	.27454	.23939	15
16	.85282	.72845	.62317	.53391	45811	.39365	.33873	.29189	.25187	.21763	16
17	.84438	.71416	.60502	.51337	.43630	.37137	.31657	.27027	.24107	.19784	17
18	83602	.70016	.58739	.49363	.41552	.35034	.29586	.25025	.21199	.17986	18
19	.82774	.68643	.57029	.47464	.39573	.33051	.27651	.23171	.19449	.16351	19
20	.81954	.67297	.55367	.45639	.37689	.31180	.25842	.21455	.17843	.14864	20

COMPOUND VALUE OF AN ANNUITY

The compound value of an annuity is the total amount one would have at the end of the annuity period if each payment is invested at a certain interest rate and is held to the end of the annuity period.

The procedure can be generalised to

$$FV_a = \left[A \sum_{t=1}^{n} (1+i)^t \right] \tag{15}$$

where FV_a = the future value of the annuity at the end of the nth year,
A = the annuity value deposited at the end of each year,
i = the annual compound interest rate,
n = the number of years for which the annuity will last.

Example-14

A promise to pay ₹ 1,000 a year for three years is a three-year annuity. If you were to receive such an annuity and were to deposit each annual payment at the end of each year in a savings account paying 8% interest how much would you have at the end of three years?

Compounding each of these values, we find that we will have ₹ 3,246.40 at the end of three years.

FV_a = ₹ 1,000 $(1+08)^2$ + ₹ 1,000 (1+.08) + ₹ 1,000
= ₹ 1,000 $(1.08)^2$ + ₹ 1,000 (1.08) + ₹ 1,000
= ₹ 1,166.40 + ₹ 1,080 + ₹ 1,000
= ₹ 3,246.40

PRECALCULATED COMPOUND ANNUITY TABLES

As in the case of the compound interest tables, there are precalculated compound annuities in Table-3 (a more complete version is contained at the back of this book). By selecting the interest rate and the number of periods for which the funds are invested, we can read off the amount to which ₹ 1 deposited annually for n periods will grow at the specific interest rate. Reexamining the previous example-14, in which we determined the value of ₹ 1,000 deposited at the end of each of the next 3 years in the bank at 8%, we can read from Table-3, the factor of 3.2464 which implies:

FV_a = ₹ 1,000 × 3.2464
= ₹ 3,246.40-the same answer we obtained earlier.

Rather than asking how much we will accumulate if we deposit an equal sum in a saving account each year, a more common is how much we must deposit each year in order to accumulate a certain amount of savings. This problem frequently occurs with respect to saving for large expenditures and pension funding obligations.

TABLE-3

Annuity Compound Factor

Period				*Percent (t)*						
n	*1%*	*2%*	*3%*	*4%*	*5%*	*6%*	*7%*	*8%*	*9%*	*10%*
1	1.000	1.000	1.000	1.000	1.000	1.000	1.000	1.000	1.000	1.000
2	2.010	2.020	2.030	2.040	2.050	2.060	2.070	2.080	0.090	2.100
3	3.030	3.060	3.091	3.122	3.153	3.184	3.215	3.246	3.278	3.310
4	4.060	4.122	4.184	4.246	4.310	4.375	4.440	3.506	4.573	4.641
5	5.101	5.204	5.309	5.416	5.526	5.637	5.751	5.867	5.985	6.105
6.	6.152	6.308	6.468	6.633	6.802	6.975	7.153	7.336	7.523	7.716
8	8.286	8.583	8.892	9.214	9.549	9.897	10.260	10.637	11.028	11.436
9	9.369	9.755	10.159	10.583	11.027	11.491	11.978	12.488	13.021	13.759
10	10.462	10.950	11.464	12.006	12.578	13.181	13.816	14.847	15.193	15937
11	11.567	12.169	12.808	13.486	14.207	14.972	15.784	16.645	17.560	18.531
12	12.683	13.412	14.192	15.026	15.917	16.870	17.888	18.977	20.141	21384
13	13.809	14.680	15.618	16.627	17.713	18.882	20.141	21.495	22.953	24.523
14	14.947	15.974	17.086	18.292	19.599	21.015	22.550	24.215	26.019	27.975
15	16.97	17.293	18.599	20.024	21.579	23.276	25.129	27.152	29.361	31.772
16	17.258	18.639	20.157	21.825	23.657	25.673	27.888	30.324	33.003	35.950
17	18.430	20.012	21.762	23.698	25.840	20.213	30.840	33.750	36.974	40.545
18	19.615	21.412	23.414	25.645	28.132	30.906	33.999	37.450	41.301	45.599
19	20.811	22.841	25.117	27.671	30.539	33.760	37.379	41.446	36.018	51.159
20	22.019	24.297	26.870	29.778	33.066	36.786	40.995	45.762	51.160	57.275

Example-15

How much must be deposited in an 10% saving account at the end of each year in order to accumulate ₹ 1,50,000 at the end of 10 years?

Substituting the values into Equation - 15, we find

$$₹\ 1,50,000 = A \sum_{t=1}^{10} (1+.10)$$

$$\frac{₹\ 1,50,000}{15,937} = A$$

$$A = ₹\ 9,412.06$$

Thus, we must deposit ₹ 9,412.06 per year for 10 years at 10% in order to accumulate ₹ 1,50,000.

Example-16

How would an investor know what ₹ 1,000 received at the end of the next 3 years is worth to us given the appropriate discount rate or opportunity rate of 10%? He can simply substitute the appropriate values into Equation-13, such that

$$PV = ₹1,000\left[\frac{1}{(1+.10)}\right] + ₹1,000\left[\frac{1}{(1+.10)^2}\right] + ₹1,000\left[\frac{1}{(1+.10)^3}\right]$$

$$= ₹\ 909.09 + ₹\ 826.45 + ₹\ 751.32$$

$$= ₹\ 2,486.86$$

Thus, the present value of this annuity is ₹ 2,486.86.

PRESENT VALUE OF AN ANNUITY

The present value of an annuity is the lump sum one would need to have on hand today in order to be able to withdraw equal amounts each year and end up with a balance exactly equal to zero at the end of the annuity period.

The mathematics involved, this procedure can also be generalised to:

$$PV_a = A\sum_{i=1}^{n}\frac{1}{(1+i)^t} \quad (16)$$

where A = the annuity received at the end of each year,

i = the annual interest or discount rate,

PV_a = the present value of the future annuity,

n = the number of years for which the annuity will last.

PRECALCULATED PRESENT VALUE OF ANNUITY TABLES

To simplify the process of determining the present value of an annuity, tables are provided at the back of this book for various combinations of i and n; an abbreviated version is given in Table-4.

The product of the annuity discount factor (ADF i,n) and the annuity payment is the present value of the annuity at the stated time value of money:

$$(PV_a =)\ (ADF\ i,n) \quad (17)$$

Solving the example-16, to find the present value of ₹ 1,000 at the end of each of the next 3 years back to the present at 10%, we look in the n = 3 years row and i = 10% column and find a table value 2,486.86. Substituting the appropriate values in Equation-17, we find

$$PV_a = ₹\ 1,000(2.48686)$$

$$= ₹\ 2,486.86$$

TABLE-4

Present Value of One Rupee per Year for *n* Years

n	1%	2%	3%	4%	5%	6%	7%	8%	9%	10%	*n*
01	.9901	.9804	.9709	.9615	.9524	.9434	.9346	.9259	.9174	.9091	01
02	1.9704	1.9416	1.9135	1.8831	1.8594	1.8334	1.8080	1.7833	1.7591	1.7355	02
03	2.9410	2.8839	2.8286	2.7751	2.7233	2.6730	2.6243	2.5771	2.5313	2.4868	03
04	3.9020	3.8077	3.7171	3.6299	3.5459	3.4657	3.3872	3.3121	3.2397	3.1699	04
05	4.8535	4.7134	4.5897	4.4518	4.3295	4.2123	4.1002	3.9927	3.8866	3.7908	05
06	5.7955	5.6014	5.4172	5.2421	5.0757	4.9173	4.7665	4.6229	4.4859	4.3553	06
07	6.7282	2.4720	6.2302	6.0020	5.7863	5.5824	5.3893	5.2064	5.0329	4.8684	07
08	7.6517	7.3254	7.0196	6.7327	6.4632	6.2098	5.9713	5.7466	5.5348	5.3349	08
09	8.5661	8.1522	7.7861	7.4352	7.1078	6.8017	6.5152	6.2469	5.9852	5.7590	09
10	9.4714	8.9825	8.7302	8.1109	7.7217	7.3601	7.0236	6.7101	6.4176	6.1446	10
11	10.3677	9.7868	9.2526	8.7604	8.3064	7.8868	7.4987	7.1389	6.8052	6.4951	11
12	11.2552	10.5753	9.9539	9.3850	8.8632	8.3838	7.9427	7.5361	7.1607	6.8137	12
13	12.1338	11.3483	10.6349	99856	9.3935	8.8527	8.3576	7.9038	7.4869	7.1034	13
14	13.0038	12.1062	11.2960	10.5631	9.8986	9.2950	8.7454	8.2442	7.7861	7.3667	14
15	13.8651	12.8492	11.9379	11.1183	10.3796	9.7122	9.1079	8.5595	8.0607	7.6061	15
16	14.7180	13.5777	12.5610	11.6522	10.8377	10.1059	9.4466	8.8514	8,3125	7.8237	16
17	15.5624	14.2918	13.1660	12.1656	11.2740	10.4772	9.7632	9.1216	8.5436	8.0215	17
18	16.3984	14.9920	13.7534	12.6592	11.6895	10.8276	10.0591	9.3719	8.7556	8.2014	18
19	17.2281	15.2684	14.3237	13.1339	12.0853	11.1581	10.3556	9.6036	8.9501	8.3649	19
20	18.0457	16.3514	14.8774	13.5903	12.4622	11.4699	10.5940	9.8181	9.1285	8.5136	20

This of course, is the same answer we calculated when we individually discounted each cash flow back to the present.

Example-17

How would an investor find the present value of the following cash flow, given the 20% discount rate?

Cash	1	2	3	4	5
Flow	₹ 1,00,000	₹ 2,00,000	–₹ 3,00,000	₹ 5,00,000	₹ 4,00,000

Given a 20% discount rate, the investor would simply merely discount the flows back to the present and total them by adding in the positive flows and subtracting the negative ones. For our example, this is:

PV = [(₹ 1,00,000) (.83333) + (₹ 2,00,000) (.69444) - (₹ 3,00,000),
(.57870) + (₹ 5,00,000) (.48225) + (₹ 4,00,000) (.40188)]
= ₹ 4,50,488

The present value of this series is ₹ 4,50,488.

CAPITAL RECOVERY PROBLEM AND LOAN AMORTISATION

In financial problems it is frequently necessary to find the yearly payment needed to repay a debt such as a mortgage. Present value of an annuity interest factors also can be used to find the annuity amount necessary to recover a capital investment , given a required rate of return on that investment. This is called a *capital recovery problem.* Similarly, present value of an annuity interest factors can be used to find the payments necessary to pay of a loan.

Example-18

Assume you have borrowed ₹ 1,00,000 from XYZ Bank. The loan is for a period of 3 years at an interest rate of 10 percent. It requires that you make three equal, annual end-of-year payments that include both principal and interest on the outstanding balance. To determine the amount of year – end payment, Equation-16 and either Table-4 can be used to solve the problem as follows:

₹ 1,00,000 = A (2.4868)

A = ₹ 40,212.32105

By making 3 annual, end-of-year payments to the bank of ₹ 40,12.32105 each, you will completely pay-off your loan, plus provide the bank with its 10% interest return. This can be seen in the loan amortization table A-1. At the end of each year, you pay the bank ₹ 40,212.32105. During the first year, ₹ 10,000 of this payment is interest (0.10 x ₹ 100,000), remaining balance and the rest (₹ 30,212.32105) is applied against the principal balance owed at the beginning of the year. Hence after the first payment, you owe ₹ 69,787.67895 (₹ 1,00,000 – ₹ 30,212.32105). Similar calculation are done for year 2 and 3.

TABLE A-1

Loan Amortization

End of Year	*Payment*	*Interest 10%*	*Principal Reduction*	*Remaining Balance*
0	—	—	—	₹ 1,00,000
1	₹ 40,212.32105	₹ 10,000	30,212.32105	69,787.67895
2	₹ 40,212.32105	6,978.767895	33,233.55315	36,554.12580
3	₹ 40,212.32105	3,655.41258	36,556.90847	0*

* Due to rounding, the remaining balance is not exactly zero.

PRESENT VALUE OF AN UNEVEN STREAM

If the annual cash flows are not equal and vary in amount from year to year, each of the cash flows has to be discounted at the appropriate interest rate for the number of years for which we have to receive that particular cash flow.

PERPETUITIES

A perpetuity is an annuity or series of periodic payments that runs indefinitely, differing, therefore from the annuities in terms of duration only. The most common example of a perpetuity is the establishment of an endowment, although bonds lacking any maturity also qualify. The value of a perpetuity is determined by dividing the yearly payment by the rate of return being received on the principle. The present value of a perpetuity of ₹ A per year can be expressed as:

$$PV(perpetuity) = \frac{A}{(1+i)} + \frac{A}{(1+i)^2} + ... \frac{A}{(1+i)^\infty}$$

$$= \sum_{t=1}^{\infty} \frac{A}{(1+i)^t} = A\sum_{t=1}^{\infty} \frac{1}{(1+i)^t} \quad (18)$$

By examining expression (16) we can see that

$$\sum_{t=1}^{\infty} \frac{A}{(1+i)^t} = \frac{1}{i} \quad (19)$$

Hence,

$$PV\,(perpetuity) = \frac{₹ A}{i} \quad (20)$$

No tables are required to calculate the present value of a perpetuity.

Example-19

If someone promises to pay ₹ 1,000 each year in perpetuity, what is that promise worth if discount rate is 16%? Substituting into Equation-20, the present value of the promise is:

$$PV\,(perpetuity) = \frac{₹1,000}{0.16} = ₹6,250$$

DETERMINING DISCOUNT RATES

The crux of present value problems is: given a future value, FV_n, and the discount rate, *i*, find the present value, PV. Suppose, instead, we knew both present and future values, but not the discount rate. How would we find this unknown rate? To begin, recall the basic present value formula:

$$PV = \frac{FV}{(1+n)^n} = (FV_n)(DFi, n)$$

Solving for the discount factor, we get

$$DF\,i,n = \frac{PV}{FV_n}$$

Consequently, to find the discount rate that makes future and present values time equivalent we need only to find that rate that corresponds with the discount factor and is consistent with the stated time period, *n*, For example, if PV = ₹ 20,000 and FV_a = ₹ 40,000, DF_{in} = ₹ 20,000/₹ 40,000 = 0.50 and from discount factor table we find the discount rate to be 8% per period.

Now consider the case of an annuity of ₹ A per period. Given the size and duration of the annuity and its present value, how would we find the unknown discount rate? Recall that the present value of an annuity is:

$$PV_a = A\sum_{t=1}^{n}\frac{1}{(1+i)^t} = (A)\,(ADF\ i, n)$$

Therefore:

$$ADF\ i, n = \frac{PV_a}{A}$$

The procedure is the same as before except that annuity discount factor table. If, for example, a ₹ 30,000 annuity lasts eight years and has present value of ₹ 1,50,000. ADF*i* 8 = ₹ 1,50,000/₹ 30,000 = 5.00 and from annuity discount factor table the discount rate is found to be approximately 12% per year.

A more difficult problem arises when there is a series of unequal pyments. Suppose the present value of future receipts, of ₹ 10,000 in year one; ₹ 20,000 in year two, and ₹ 40,000 in year three, is ₹ 50,000, what interest rate is implied by these numbers? Since there are several payments we can't use discount factor table and since the payments are not equal we can't use annuity discount factor table. However, we can set the problem up:

$$PV = \frac{₹10,000}{(1+i)} + \frac{₹20,000}{(1+i)^2} + \frac{₹40,000}{(1+i)^3}$$

= (₹ 10,000) (DF*i* 1) + (₹ 20,000) (DF*i*. 2) + (₹ 40,000) (DF*i*. 3)

Even though there is no direct easy solution we can find by trial and error. First, we choose a trial discount rate, say i = 20%. The present value of the sources of payments at i = 20% is:

PV = (₹ 10,000(0.833) + ₹ 20,000) (0.694) +
(₹ 40,000) (0.578)
= ₹ 8,330 + ₹ 13,880 + ₹ 23,120 = ₹ 45,330

But this calculated present value does not equal the known present value of ₹ 50,000. So let's try another discount rate. We observe that the calculated present value of ₹ 45,330 is too low so we choose a new trial discount rate that will raise calculated present value. Since present value increases as the discount rate decreases, let's try 15%:

PV = (₹ 10,000) (0.870) + (₹ 20,000) (0.756) + (₹ 40,000) (0.685)
= ₹ 8,700 + ₹ 15,120 + ₹ 26,320
= ₹ 50,140

This calculated present value is not exactly equal to ₹ 50,000 but it is very close. Obviously, the correct discount rate is approximately 15%.

This technique illustrated by this example will be used in investment and financing decision work problem later on. In the investment decision work we will refer to such derived discount rates as "internal rates of return," and in financing work we will refer to these derived discount rates as the "cost of capital."

ILLUSTRATIVE PROBLEMS

1. Mr. Raman needs ₹ 1,00,000 for his daughter's marriage in 10 years. How much must be deposited at the end of each year in the bank at 10% compound interest in order to have marriage money ready?

Solution

Using Equation 15. The compound value of an annuity is:

$$₹\ 1,00,000 = A\sum_{i=1}^{10}(1+.10)^{10}$$

$$₹\ 1,00,000 = A(15.9373)$$
$$A = ₹\ 62,745.80$$

Mr. Raman needs to deposit ₹ 62,754.80

2. Find the effective rate of interest for: *(a)* 8% compounded semiannually; *(b)* 8% compounded quarterly; *(c)* 8% compounded monthly

Solution

The solution require the use of Equation—11 to find the effective rate:

(a) $\left(1+\frac{0.08}{2}\right)^2 = 1.0816$ *(b)* $\left(1+\frac{0.08}{4}\right)^4 = 1.0824$ *(c)* $\left(1+\frac{0.08}{12}\right)^{12} = 1.0830$

Effective rate = 8.16% Effective rate = 8.24% Effective rate = 8.30%

3. If ₹ 30,000 is put in a saving account yielding 6% compounded annually and other ₹ 10,000 is added each year, how much it will have accrued in ten years?

Solution

This problem may be solved in two parts. First, calculate how much the original ₹ 30,000 will have increased in ten years. Using Equation—6 we get,

$$FV_n = ₹\ 30,000\ (1.7908) = ₹\ 53,724$$

Next, determine how much the additional ₹ 10,000 will amount to in ten years. Using Equation-15, we get,

$$FV_a = ₹\ 10,000\ (13.1808) = ₹\ 1,31,808$$

The total of the two figures is ₹ 1,85,532.

4. Sharda manufacturing needs ₹ 80,000 for a 3 year period. A local bank will provide a 3 year discount loan at a stated rate of 10%. Determine how much Sharda must borrow in order to have use of the ₹ 80,000. Also calculate the effective rate of interest on the loan.

Solution

Let x equal the amount of the loan. Then $10x$ is the annual interest payment. Since interest rate for 3 years will be subtracted from the total loan, the interest will be $3x$.

$$x - .3x = ₹\ 80,000$$
$$.7x = ₹\ 80,000$$
$$x = ₹\ 1,14,286$$

The total loan would be ₹ 1,14,286. Yearly interest at 10% would be ₹ 11,428.60. The effective rate of interest is therefore:

$$\frac{₹\ 11,428.60}{80,000} = .143 = 14.3\%$$

5. Novelty Industries is establishing a sinking fund to ration a ₹ 50,00,000 bond issue which matures in 15 years. How much do they have to put into the fund at the end of each year to accumulate the ₹ 50,00,000, assuming the funds are compounded at 7% annually?

Solution

The sinking fund is a typical application of a compounded annuity. The interest factor in the 15 year row in the future value of an annuity table is 25.1290.

$$₹\ 50,00,000 = \text{Annuity} \times 25.1290$$

$$\text{Annuity} = \frac{₹\ 50,00,000}{25.1290}\ ₹\ 1,98,973.29$$

Novelty will have to put ₹ 1,98,973.29 into the sinking fund each year.

6. A firm is due to receive ₹ 1,00,000 a year for the next 5 years and ₹ 1,40,000 at the end of the sixth year. Money is worth 12%. What is the present value of the stream?

Solution

The problem may be solved in two parts. First, calculate for the next five years by using Equation-17:

$$PV_a = (A)(ADF\ i,n)$$
$$PV_a = (₹\ 1,00,000)\ (3.6048)$$
$$PV_a = ₹\ 3,60,480$$

Next, determine the present value ₹ 1,40,000 at the end of 6th year by using Equation-14:

$$PV = (FV_n)\ (DF\ i.n.)$$
$$= (₹\ 1,40,000)\ (.50663)$$
$$= ₹\ 70,928$$

The total of the two figures is ₹ 4,31,408.

7. What is the present value of cash flows of ₹ 750 per year forever *(a)* at an interest rate of 8% and *(b)* at an interest rate of 10%?

Solution

The present value of a perpetual stream is the annual flow divided by the discount rate. Using Equation-20, we get:

$$(a)\ \frac{₹\ 750}{0.08} = ₹\ 9,375 \qquad (b)\ \frac{₹\ 750}{0.10} = ₹\ 7,500$$

8. A car dealer extended a 36-month loan to a customer to finance the purchase of a car. The face amount of the loan is ₹ 3,37,500, and the annual percentage rate on the loan is 16 per cent compounded monthly. What are the monthly payment?

Solution

$$\frac{₹\ 3,37,500}{(1/.0133)(1-1/1.0133)^{36}} = ₹\ 11,865.00$$

9. A firm can borrow money at 18 percent interest. It has purchased goods with terms of 1/10 net 60. Should the firm take the discount if it is short of cash?

Solution

$$\text{Effective cost} = \frac{365}{60-10} \times .01 = .073$$

Since of the effective cost of passing up the discount is only 7.3% which is less costly than borrowing at-18 percent, the firm should not take the discount.

QUESTIONS

1. Why does money have time value? How is the concept of 'present value' related to the time value of money?
2. A philosopher once stated that "a bird in the hand is worth two in the bush." Does this statement relate to the time value of money? How?
3. Distinguish between simple interest and compound interest, What happens to the effective rate of interest as the frequency of compounding is increased?
4. What is meant by the present value of the future sum? How are present value and compound interest calculations related?
5. Discuss briefly the statement that "discounting is the reverse of compounding." How are discounting and compounding related mathematically?
6. What effect would a decrease in the interest rate or an increase in the holding period of a deposit have on the future amount available? Why?
7. What is an annuity? Give some examples of annuities. Distinguish between an annuity and a perpetuity.
8. What is meant by the term "compound value of an annuity"? How are the factors in the table for the compound value of an annuity developed, and how may the table be used to find the compound value of an annuity?
9. What is a perpetuity? What relationships exists between discount factors and annuity discount factors? How might the factor for the present value of such a stream of cash flows be determined?

PROBLEMS

1. How much money must be deposited today in a fund paying 8% compounded annually in order to accumulate ₹ 50,000 in 20 years?

Ans.: ₹ 10,725

2. An individual purchases a refrigerator for ₹ 4,500 from a department store. The refrigerator was paid for using the department store's revolving charge account. The store charges 1%on the unpaid monthly balance. If the refrigerator is paid for in 30 months, what will be the size of the monthly payment? What is effective interest rate for the charge account?

Ans.: ₹ 174.18

3. A person deposits ₹ 10,000 in an account each year for 5 years; at the end of 5 years, one half of the account balance is withdrawn; ₹ 20,000 is deposited annually for 5 more years, with the total balance withdrawn at the end of the fifteenth year. If the account earns interest at a rate of 5%, how much money is withdrawn (a) at the end of 5 years? (b) at the end of 15 years.

Ans.: (a) ₹ 27,628; (b) ₹ 1,86,059

4. A processing firm entered into a contract for raw material by agreeing to pay ₹ 50,000 immediately and ₹ 10,000 per year for 5 years beginning at the end of 7 years from the date of the contract. At the end of the fourth year, the firm requested that it be allowed to make a lump sum payment advance for the rest of the contract. What was the amount of the lump sum if interest at the settlement was agreed to be 8%?

Ans.: ₹ 34,329

5. Revenues from a certain project are expected to be ₹ 2,00,000 at the end of the first year and to decrease at the rate of ₹ 10,000 per year through the 15 years life of the project. If interest is 20%, (a) what is the equivalent annual worth of those revenues? (b) what is the equivalent present worth?

Ans.: (a) ₹ 1,60,410 (b) ₹ 7,50,000

6. What is the present worth of operating expenditures of ₹ 1,00,000 per year which are assumed to be incurred continuously throughout in 8 year period if the effective annual rate of interest is 12%?

Ans.: 4,96,764

7. A person deposits ₹ 10,000 per year into an account which pays interest at a continuous compound rate of 5%the first year after the initial deposit. The annual nominal rate increases by 0.25% each year. If the 10 annual deposits are made, what will be the worth of the fund immediately after the last deposit?

Ans.: ₹ 1,34,950

8. An individual deposits ₹ 2,000 in a savings account each year for 5 years. The first year after the initial deposit the account pays interest at a rate of 5% compounded annually; the second year after the initial deposit the interest rate is 5% compounded continuously; the third year the interest rate is 6% compounded annually; an interest rate of 6% compounded semiannually exists the fourth year; and 6% compounded continuously is the interest rate in the fifth year. How much money is accumulated in the account one year after the fifth deposit?

Ans.: ₹ 11,912

9. You need to accumulate ₹ 10,000. To do so, you plan to make deposits of ₹ 1,250 per year, with the first payment being made a year from today, in a bank account which pays 12 per cent interest, compounded annually. Your last deposit will be less than ₹ 1,250 if less is needed to round out to ₹ 10,000. How many years will it take you to reach your ₹ 10,000 goal, and how large will the last deposit be?

Ans.: ₹ 1,106.01; 6 Years.

10. What is the present value of a perpetuity of ₹ 1,000 per year if the appropriate discount rate is 7 per cent? If interest rates in general were to double and the appropriate discount rate rose to 14 per cent, what would happen to the present value of the perpetuity?

Ans.: $PV_{7\%}$ = ₹ 1,428.57; $PV_{14\%}$ = ₹ 714.29

11. Find the present value of ₹ 50,000 due in the future under each of the following conditions: (a) 12 per cent nominal rate, semiannual compounding, discounted back 5 years; (b) 12 per cent nominal rate, quarterly compounding, discounted back 5 years; (c) 12 per cent nominal rate, monthly compounding, discounted back 1 year.

Ans.: (a) ₹ 27,920; (b) ₹ 27,685; (c) ₹ 44,370

12. Find the *present value* of the following *ordinary annuities*. Assume that discounting occurs once a year. (a) ₹ 400 per year for 10 years at 10 pe rcent. (b) ₹ 200 per year for 5 years at 5 per cent.

(c) ₹ 400 per year for 5 years of 0 per cent. (d) Now rework Parts a, b, and c assuming that payments are made at the *beginning* of each year; that is, they are *annuities due.*

Ans.: (a) ₹ 2,457.84; (b) ₹ 2,000; (c) (1) ₹ 2,703.62

13. Find the interest rates, or rates of return, on each of the following: (a) You *lend* ₹ 700 and receive a promise to be paid ₹ 749 at the end of 1 year.(b) Yor borrow ₹ 85,000 and promise to pay back ₹ 2,01,229 at the end of 10 years (c) Yor borrow ₹ 9,000 and promise to make payments or ₹ 2,684.80 per year for 5 years.

Ans.: (a) 7%; (b) 9%; (c) 15%

14. Find the amount to which ₹ 500 will grow under each of the following conditions: (a) 12 per cent compounded annually for 5 years. (b) 12 per cent compounded semiannually for 5 years. (c) 12 per cent compounded quarterly for 5 years. (d) 12 per cent compounded monthly for 5 years.

Ans.: (a) ₹ 881.15; (b) ₹ 895.40; (c) ₹ 903.05; (d) ₹ 908.35

15. Find the future values of the following ordinary annuities: (a) FV of ₹ 40,000 each 6 months for 5 years at a nominal rate of 12 per cent, compounded semiannually. (b) FV of ₹ 20,000 each 3 months for 5 years at a nominal rate of 12 per cent, compounded quarterly. (c) The annuities described in Parts a and b have the same amount of money paid into them during the 5-year period, and both earn interest at the same nominal rate, yet the annuity in Part b earns ₹ 10,160 more than the one in Part a over the 5 years. Why does this occur?

Ans.: (a) ₹ 52,724; (b) ₹ 53,740

16. Your company is planning to borrow ₹ 10,00,000 on a 5-year, 15% annual payment, fully amortised term loan. What fraction of the payment made at the end of the second year will represent repayment of principal?

Ans.: 57.18%

17. (a) It is now January 1, 2002. You plan to make 5 deposits of ₹ 10,000 each, one every 6 months, with the first payment being made *today.* If the bank pays a nominal interest rate of 12 per cent, but uses semiannual compounding, how much will be in your account after 10 years? (b) You must make a payment of ₹ 1,43,202 ten years from today. To prepare for this payment, you will make 5 equal deposits, beginning today and for the next 4 quarters, in a bank that pays a nominal interest rate of 12 per cent, quarterly compounding. How large must each of the 5 payments be?

Ans.: (a) ₹ 1,43,202; (b) ₹ 9,307

18. As the manager of Nico Industry, you want to sell on credit, giving customers 3 months in which to pay. However, you will have to borrow from the bank to carry the accounts payable. The bank will charge a nominal 15 per cent, but with monthly compounding. You want to quote a nominal rate to your customers (all of whom are expected to pay on time) which will exactly cover your financing coasts. What nominal annual rate should you quote to your credit customers?

Ans.: 15.19%

19. While you were a student in college, you borrowed ₹ 12,000 in student loans at an interest rate of 9 per cent, compounded annually. If you repay ₹ 1,500 per year, how long, to the nearest year, will it take you to repay the loan?

Ans.: 15 years.

7

RISK AND RETURN

INTRODUCTION

Investors like returns and dislike risk. Therefore, investors will invest in riskier assets only if they expect to receive higher return. In other words, the investors consider the risk-return trade off in holding various *blends* of *individual* assets since portoflio, which are calculations of these assets, may or may not take on the aggregate characteristics of their individual parts. Portoflio expected return is a weighted average of the expected return of individual securities but portfolio variance, in sharp contrast, can be something less than a weighted average of security variances. As a result an investor can sometime reduce portfolio risk by adding another security with greater individual risk than any other security in the portfolio. This seemingly curious result occurs because risk depends greatly on the covariance among returns of individual securites. We will show how an investor can reduce expected risk through diversification, why this risk reduction results from "proper" diversification, and how the investor may estimate the expected return and expected risk level of a given portfolio of assets. Alongwith defining the terms risk and return more precisely in terms of how they relate to investments, the procedures used to measure risk and the relationship between risk-return have been discussed. Both investors and finance manager are to apply these concepts while taking decisions concerning financial/ real assets.

INVESTMENT RETURNS

The concept of return provides investors with a convenient way to express the financial performance of an investment. An investor invests funds, today with the expectation of earning more money in the future. The expected returns from an investment are the most important part of the valuation and the most important consideration for the management. No matter what has happened to a company in the past, future earnings and expectations about future earnings really determine the current value of the security. This does not mean that investors will necessarily act rationally about future earnings, but they will focus on the earning capability of a company under investigation. Although it may be impossible to forecast future earnings with precision, and despite the uncertainties involved, an estimate must be attempted by anyone who seeks to be successful in investment. This viewpoint is applicable regardless of the type of asset/security being analysed. The amount of future cash flows should be examined in order to estimate the benefits resulting from the investment. To illustrate, suppose an investor buys 100 equity shares of a company for ₹ 1000 today and sells the share for ₹ 1,100 at the end of the year, he will get the return of ₹ 100 (i.e. ₹ 1,100 - ₹ 1,000) or 10%. But if the investor, at the end of the year is able to sell at ₹ 900, his return would be -₹ 100 or -10%. Since it is rarely desirable to invest the entire funds in a single asset or a security, he invest in a portfolio, a combination of assets/securites. Hence it is essential that every security be viewed in a portfolio context. Thus, it seems logical that the expected return of a portfolio should depend on the expected return of each of the security contained in the portfolio. It also seems logical that the amounts invested in each security should be important. Indeed, this is the case. The example of a portfolio with three securities shown in Table-1 A illustrates this point. The expected holding period value- relative for the portfolio is clearly:

$$\frac{₹\ 23{,}000}{₹\ 20{,}000} = 11.55$$

giving an expected holding period return of 15.50%.

Table-1 (B) combines the information in a somewhat different manner. The portfolio's expected holding-period value-relative is simply a weighted average of the expected value-relative of its component securities, using current market values as weights.

The procedure can be used as easily with holding-period returns. Table-l (C) provides an illustration. Holding period return is simply 100 times the value obtained by subtracting one from the holding period value-relative. Thus a weighted average of the former will have the same characteristics as a weighted average of the latter.

Since portfolio's expected return is a weighted average of the expected returns of its securities, the contribution of each security to the portfolio's expected returns depends on its expected returns and its proportionate share of the initial portfolio's market value. Nothing else is relevant. It follows that an investor who simply wants the greatest possible expected return should hold one security: the one which is considered to have the greatest expected return. Very few investors do this, and very vew investment advisers would counsel such an extreme policy. Instead, investors should diversify, meaning that their portfolio should include more than one security. This is because diversification can reduce risk.

RISK

The definition of risk includes the following meanings: "...possibility of loss or injury... the degree or probability of such loss." This conforms to the connotation put on the term by most investors. Professionals often speak of "downside risk" and "upside potential." The idea is straightforward enough: *risk has to do with bad outcomes; potential with good ones.*

As a formal measure of risk, such notions can be criticized on two grounds: vagueness and excessive simplicity. One might measure risk by the probability that

TABLE 1

(a) Security and Portfolio Values

Security	*No. of Shares*	*Current Price Per Share*	*Current Value*	*Expected End-of Period Share Value*	*Expected End-of Period Share Value*
1	2	3	4	5	6
XYZ	100	₹ 15.00	1,500	₹ 18.00	₹ 1,800
ABC	150	20.00	3,000	22.00	3,300
RST	200	40.00	8,000	45.00	9,000
KNF	250	25.00	6,250	30.00	7,500
DET	100	12.50	1,250	15.00	1,500
			₹ 20.000		₹ 23,100

(b) Security and Portfolio Value-Relatives

Security	*Current Value*	*Proportion of current value of Properties*	*Current Price per share*	*Expected End-of-period value per share*	*Expected Holding-period value-Relative*	*Contribution to Portfolio Expected Holding-period value-Relative*
(1)	(2)	3 = (2) ₹ 20,000	(4)	(5)	(6) = (5) / (4)	(7) = (3)x(6)
XUZ	₹ 1,500	.0750	₹ 15,00	₹ 18.00	1.200	0.090000
ABC	3,000	.1500	20.00	2.00	1.100	0.165000
RST	8,000	.4000	40.00	45.00	1.125	0.450000
KNF	6,250	.3125	25.00	30.00	1.200	0.375000
DET	1,250	.0625	12.50	15.00	1.200	0.075000
	20,000	1.0000				1.155000

(c) Security and Portfolio Holding-period Returns

Security	*Proportion of Current Value of Portfolio*	*Expected Holding Period Return (%)*	*Contribution to Portfolio Expected Holding Period Return (%)*
(1)	(2)	(3)	(4)
XYZ	.0750	20.00	.50
ABC	.1500	10.00	1.50
RST	.4000	12.50	5.00
KNF	.3125	20.00	6.25
DET	.0625	20.00	1.25
	1.0000		15.50

return will fall below the expected value. But this could characterize most investments as equally risky, since the probability in question is close to 0.50 in a large number of cases. A more common procedure would focus on the probability of an *negative* return. But even this is an exteremely blunt measure. Which is riskier: an investment with a 0.30 probability of a slight loss or one with a 0.29 probability of a very large loss? A more useful measure of risk takes into account both the probability of an outcome and its magnitude.

QUANTITATIVE MEASURE OF RISK

When risk is considered in capital budgeting decisions each project must be evaluated with respect of both its return and risk. An investor obviously would like to earn a high rate of return, he will not consider that he has sustained a loss unless the return falls below this level. Risk can be measured by the area under the distribution of returns that lies below the target level. In Figure-1, this target level is R.

An investor obviously would like to earn a high rate of return, he will not consider that he has sustained a loss unless the return falls below this level. Risk can be measured by the area under the distribution of returns that lies below the target level. In Figure-1, this target level is T.

Figure-1 shows the distribution of returns offered by three different investments. Distribution A has a smaller standard deviation than distribution *B*. The probability that the return earned on project *A*, will fall below the target level is the dotted area in Figure-1. This area is less than the hatched area, the probability that the return on *B* will fall below the target level. *Project A* is therefore less risky than *B*. *Project C* has the highest standard deviation of the three. However, since the chance that its return will fall below the target level is negligible, it is the least risky project.

FIGURE-1

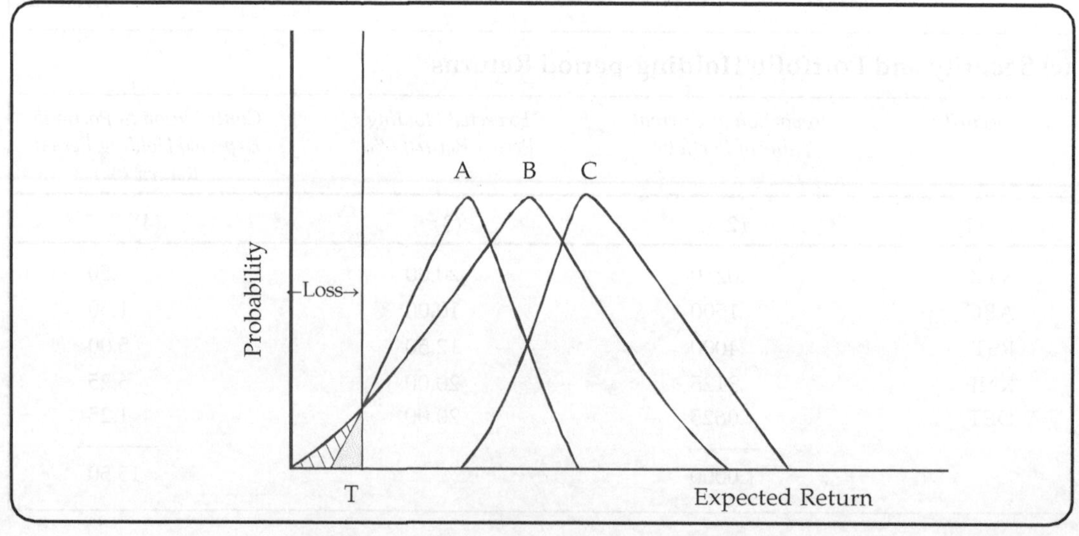

Before describing risk measures, we will explore the probability distributions and the concept of expected return which will serve as our measure of return.

Probability: A Measure of Likelihood

Probability may be described as a measure of someone's opinion about the likelihood that an event will occur. If an event is certain to occur, we say that it has a probability of 1 occuring. If an event is certain not to occur, we say that its probability of occuring is O. All events have a probability of recurrence some what between O and 1. By convention, probabilities follow several rules. Among them are the following:

1. The probability assigned to each possible event must be a positive number between O and 1, where O represents an impossible event and 1 represents a certain event;

2. If a set of events is mutually exhausive and exhaustive (covers all possible outcomes) the probabilities of the events must total 1.

In the approaches we have outlined so far, no attempts has been made to attach probabilities to the possible net cash inflows from a project. Suppose that a company is considering two investment projects which have identical initial costs, the same lives and expected annual net cash inflows of ₹ 10,000. On the basis of our discussion in the preceding Chapters, these projects would be ranked equally. However, assume that probability distributions of the net cash inflows in each year are as as shown in Figure-2.

FIGURE-2

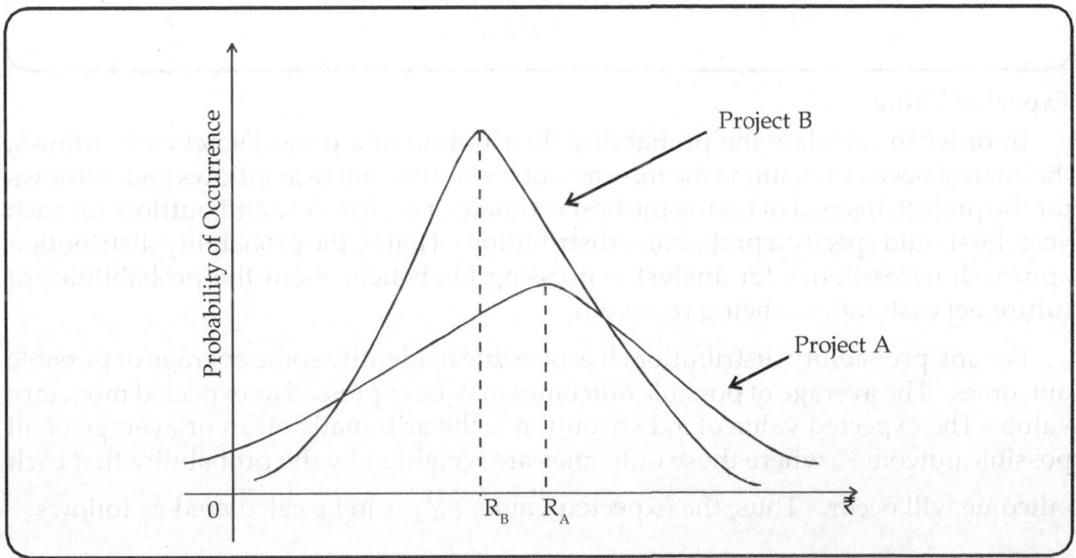

Figure-2 shows that the dispersion of the probability distribution of net cash inflows for project A is greater than for project B, and therefore we cannot assume that management will be indifferent as to which project is undertaken. Thus if we assume that the greater the dispersion the greater the risk, the *project A* is more risky than project B and assuming that management is averse to risk, we would expect it to prefer *project B*.

Assume now that the probability distributions of the net cash inflows of *projects A* and *B* are as shown in Figure-3. Even if the expected value of *project B's* net cash inflows is below that of project A, the company may still choose *B* because it is less risky as indicated by the dispersion about the expected value. Whether management will choose *project B* will depend how strongly risk averse management is in relation to the sacrifice on the expected value necessitated by choosing *B*.

FIGURE-3

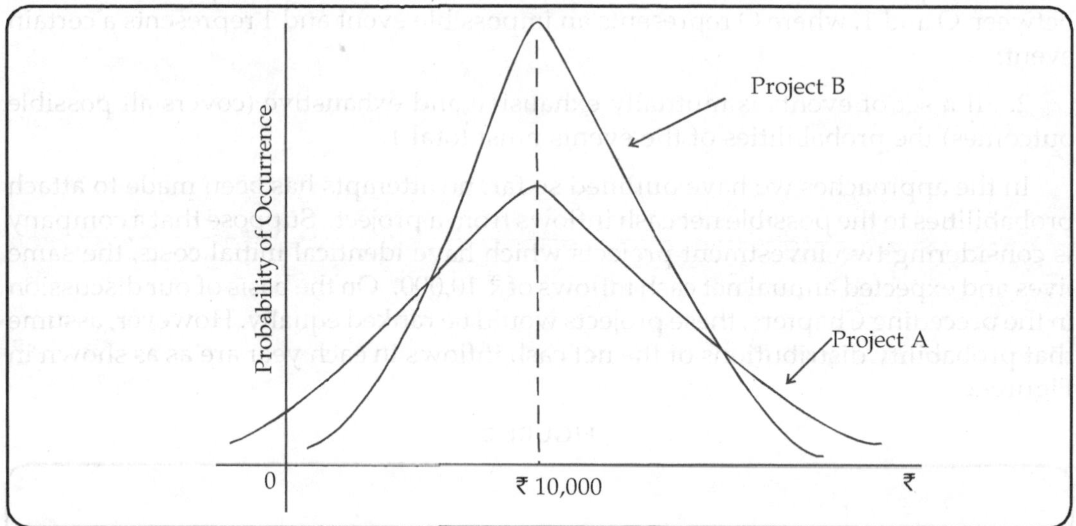

Expected Value

In order to calculate the probability distribution of a project's net cash inflows, the analyst needs to examine the forecasts of the individual cash inflows and outflows for the project; instead of taking the best estimate of each inflow and outflow for each year, he should specify a probability distribution. That is, the probability distribution approach necessitaties for analyst expressing his beliefs about the probabilities of future net cash inflows being received.

For any probability distribution, it is possible to identify some average of possible outcomes. The average of possible outcomes may be expressed as expected monetary value. The expected value of a distribution is the arithmatic mean or average of all possible outcomes, where those outcomes are weighted by the probability that each outcome will occur. Thus, the expected value, $(\overline{X})$, can be calculated as follows:

$$(\overline{X}) = \sum_{t=1}^{n} X_i P_i$$

where n = the number of possible outcomes,
Xi = the value of the ith possible outcomes,
Pi = the probability that the ith outcomes will occur.

To illustrate the computation of the expected value, consider the investment opportunities listed in Table-1.

TABLE-1

Possible Events	*Net Present Value for each event*	*Probability of each event*
a	₹ 3,000	0.10
b	3,650	0.20
c	4,000	0.40
d	4,000	0.20
e	5,000	0.10
		1.00

To determine the expected value of this distribution, we need only to multiply each possible outcome by its probability of occurence and sum as follows:

Expected Value=₹ 3,000 (.10)+₹ 3,650 (.20)+ ₹ 4,000 (.40)+₹ 4,000 (.20)+ ₹ 5,000 (.10)=₹ 3,930

Although this measure of central tendency, the expected value, incorporates more information than simply the most likely outcome in that it gives some weight to the other possible outcomes, the finance manager is likely to be at least as interested in the spread of range of possible outcomes as it tells nothing about the amount of dispersion contained in the probability distribution. To measure dispersion, the standard deviation and coefficient of variation are to be examined.

MEASURES OF DISPERSION

In addition to quantifying the expected value, we can also quantify the risk through various measures of dispersion, the most common of which are standard deviation and the variance.

STANDARD DEVIATION

Standard deviation provides a measure of the spread of the probability of distribution. The large the standard deviation, the greater the dispersion of the distribution. It is calculated by squaring the difference between each outcome and its expected value, weighing each value by its probability, summing over all possible outcomes, and taking the square root of this sum. Thus, the standard deviation becomes

$$\sigma = \sqrt{\sum_{t=1}^{n} (X_i - \bar{x})^2 \, P_i}$$

where:

$\bar{x}$ = the expected value

The calculations for the standard deviation for the probability distribution given in Table-1 are provided in Table-2 below:

TABLE-2

NPV (₹) (1)	Expected value (EV) (2)	Deviations from EV (₹) from EV 3=(1)–(2)		Square Deviations 4=(3)x(3)	Probability (5)	Square Deviations weighted (6)
3,000	4,060	–1,060	=	11,23,600	0.10	1,12,360
3,600	4,060	–410	=	1,68,100	0.20	33,620
4,000	4,060	–60	=	3,600	0.40	1,440
4,600	4,060	+590	=	3,48,100	0.20	69,620
5,000	4,060	+940	=	8,83,600	0.10	88,360
					$\sqrt{\sum_{t=1}^{n}(X_i-\bar{x})^2 P_i}$ =	3,05,400

$$\text{Variance} = \sum_{t=1}^{n}(X_i-\bar{x})^2 P_i$$

$$\text{Standard Deviation} = \sigma = \sqrt{\sum_{t=1}^{n}(X_i-\bar{x})^2 P_i}$$

$$\sqrt{₹3{,}05{,}4000} = ₹\ 552.63$$

Interpretation of the standard deviation: The standard deviation in the normal distribution is unique in that one standard deviation to either side of the mean incorporates 68.3% of all the possible outcomes. We can infer 68.3% certainty that, if the distribution is correctly specified in the first place, the occurence will be within one standard deviation above below the mean. This is illustrated in Figure-4.

$\bar{x} \pm 1\sigma$ = 68.3% of all possible outcomes
$\bar{x} \pm 2\sigma$ = 95% of all possible outcomes
$\bar{x} \pm 3\sigma$ = 99.7% of all possible outcomes

Two standard deviations to either side of the mean implies that we can be 95% certain that one of the possible outcomes within that area will occur. We can extend this to 99.7% certainty by taking the area under three standard deviations to either side of the mean of a normal distribution. Thus, if we are looking at two normal distribution, one with an expected value of ₹ 10,000 and a standard deviation of ₹ 2,500, the other with an expected value of ₹ 25,000 and a standard deviation of ₹ 4,000 we can conclude that the second distribution has more dispersion, hence, more absolute risk associated with it. This does not mean that the second distribution is less desirable, just that it has more absolute risk. While the standard deviation gives us a good measure of a distribution's absolute dispersion, it is also desirable to measure dispersion or risk relative to return to provide the manager with a relative measure of risk. This is the purpose of the co-efficient of variation.

FIGURE-4

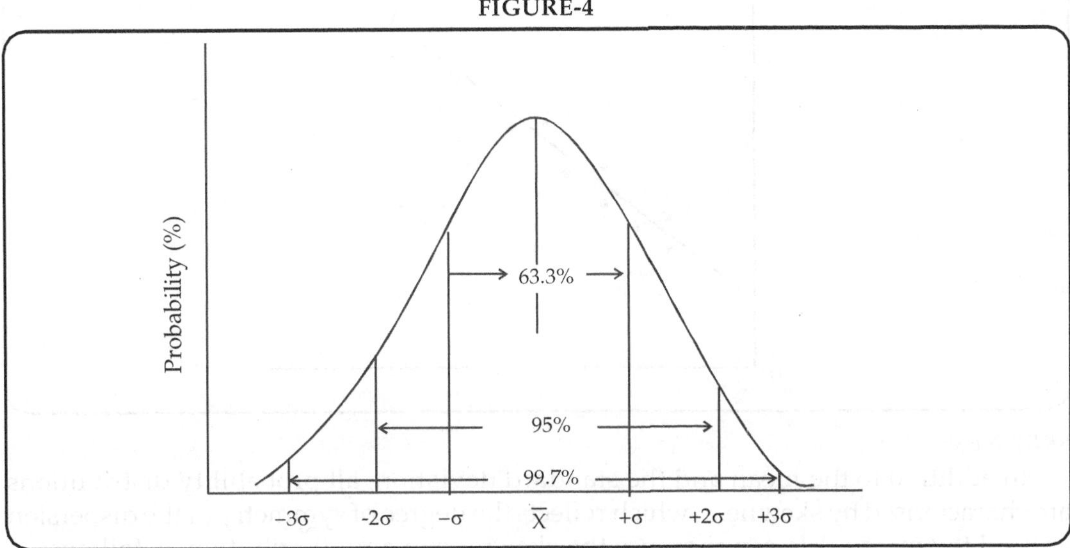

VARIANCE

The variance measures the dispersion around the mean by calculating the weighted average of the square difference between each outcome and the mean, such that:

$$\text{Var} = \sum^{n} (X_i - \bar{x})^2 P_i$$

where;

Var = the variance = σ^2

By substituting the value of our preceding example in the formula we get:

Var = ₹ 3,05,400

The variance increases as the dispersion of the possible outcomes from the mean increases.

Other Measures of Dispersion

The variance and the standard deviation are not the only measures of dispersion that may be useful in interpreting risk, although they are most commonly used. Among the other measures are the standard error of the estimate, skewness and kurtosis.

STANDARD ERROR OF THE ESTIMATE

Standard error of the estimate is the measure of risk associated with the regresson analysis. As illustrated in Figure-5, the regression analysis estimate (Y_x) is the mean of the distribution, whose measure of dispersion is the standard error. We can use this measure as the risk associated with the regression-derived estimate.

FIGURE-5

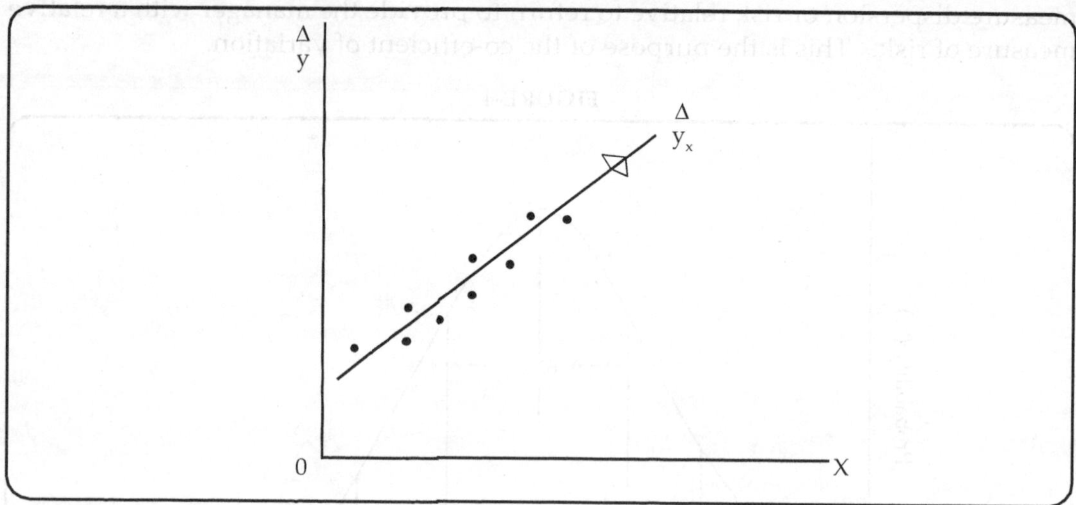

SKEWNESS

In addition to the mean and the standard deviation, all probability distributions are characterised by skewness, which reflects the degree of symmetry of the dispersion around the mean. We can measure the skewness of any distribution as follows:

$$\alpha_3 = \sum_{t=1}^{n} \frac{(X_i - \overline{x})^3 P_i}{\sigma^3}$$

where α_3 = skewness

In the normal distribution there is a perfect symmetry, such that dispersions to both sides of the mean are equal. However, in other distributions the symmetry is not perfect. For example, the probability distribution may be skewed as shown in Figure-6.

In this instance the expected value and standard deviations of the two probability distributions are the same. However, assuming the company's managers are risk averse, they should prefer *Project A* with a probability distribution skewed to the left. The reason for managers prefering *Project A* is that it has a greater chance of generating ₹ amounts much larger that the mean. In other words, *Project A* has a *"tail"* extending the higher ₹ amount than *Project B,* while *Project B* has a *"tail"* extending to lower ₹ amounts than *Project A.*

KURTOSIS

Another measure of the distribution is the kurtosis or the peakedness of the distribution, which is measured as:

$$\alpha_4 = \sum_{t=1}^{n} \frac{(X_i - \overline{x})^4 P_i}{\sigma^4}$$

where α_4 = kurtosis

FIGURE-6

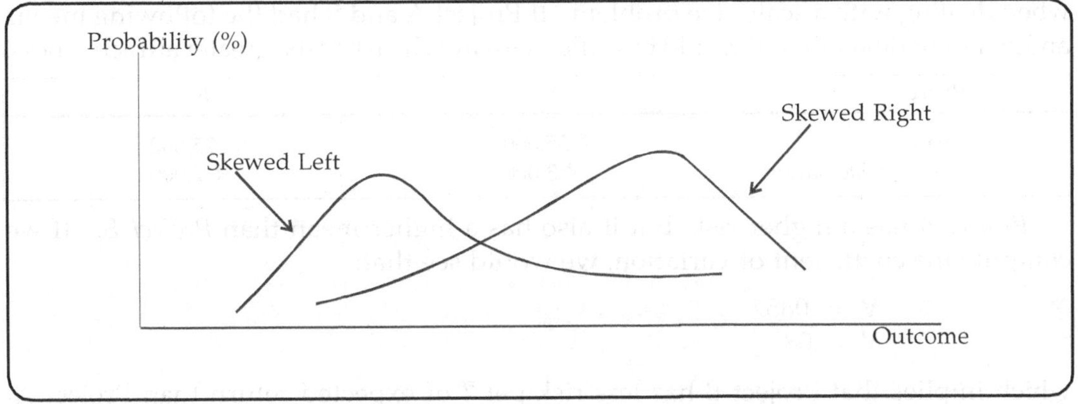

Even with skewness equal to zero, the distributions can have different peakedness, as illustrated in Figure-7.

COEFFICIENT OF VARIATION

The coefficient of variation provides us with a measure of the relative dispersion of probability distribution—that is, the risk per unit of return. Mathematically, it is defined as the standard deviation divided by the expected value,

or $V = \frac{\sigma}{\bar{x}}$

where V = Coefficient of Variation

FIGURE-7

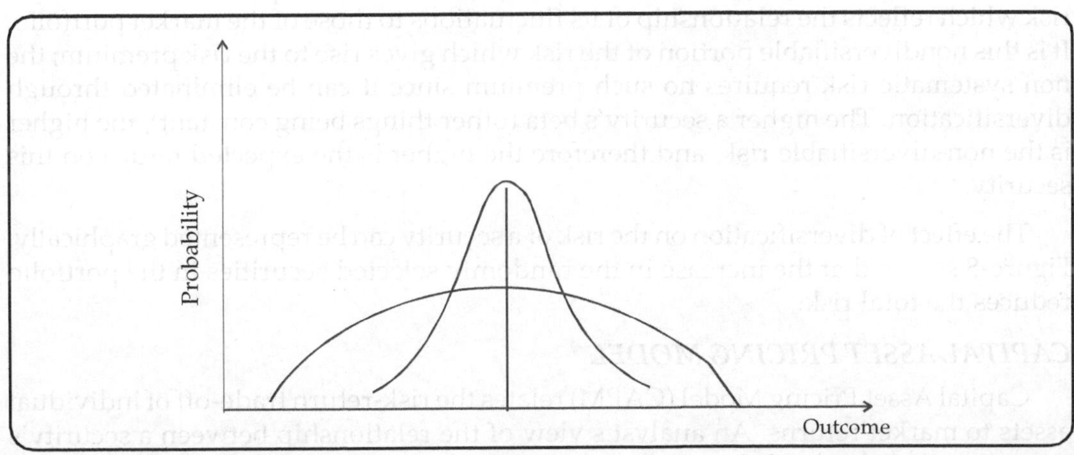

For example, the coefficient of variation of the preceding example would be:

$$V = \frac{₹\ 552.63}{₹\ 4{,}060} = 0.1361$$

The usefulness of the coefficient of variation is derived from the fact that using the standard deviation to compare the riskiness of two projects can be misleading when dealing with a scale size problem. If Project A and B had the following means and standard deviations, it would be difficult to say which has the greater attractiveness.

Project	*A*	*B*
Mean	₹ 35,000	Rs,25,000
Standard Deviation	₹ 3,000	₹ 2,000

Project A has a higher risk, but it also has a higher mean than *Project B*. If we compute the coefficient of variation, we would see that:

$$V_A = .0857$$
$$V_B = .08$$

which implies that Project B has less risk per ₹ of expected return than Project A. This comparison is only possible when we use the coefficient of variation.

IDENTIFYING THE RELEVANT RISK

Total variability of returns is not the relevant risk measure for a security. The risk of each security (or of a portfolio) can be decomposed into two parts. The first component is that part of a security's risk which can be eliminated by combining it in a diversified portfolio. This diversifiable component of risk is often called the non-systematic risk, since no systematic relationship exists between this portion of the risk and the market. The non diversifiable component of a security's risk, i.e. the part of the risk of its returns which can not be eliminated by including the security in a diversified portfolio, is usually called the systematic risk. The latter stems from the general market fluctuations or more specifically from the component of a security's risk which reflects the relationship of its fluctuations to those of the market portfolio. It is this nondiversifiable portion of the risk which gives rise to the risk premium; the non systematic risk requires no such premium since it can be eliminated through diversification. The higher a security's beta (other things being constant), the higher is the non-diversifiable risk, and therefore the higher is the expected return on this security.

The effect of diversification on the risk of a security can be represented graphically. Figure-8 shows that the increase in the randomly selected securities in the portfolio reduces the total risk.

CAPITAL ASSET PRICING MODEL

Capital Asset Pricing Model (CAPM) relates the risk-return trade-off of individual assets to market returns. An analyst's view of the relationship between a security's prospects and those of the market portfolio can be summarised by means of a *characteristic line* Figure-9 shows an example. The vertical axis plots the excess return on the security in question. This is the differences between the holding period return on the security and the riskless rate of interest for that period. In symbols:

$$R_i = T + \beta_i(R_m - T)$$

FIGURE-8

TOTAL UNSYSTEMATIC AND SYSTEMATIC RISK

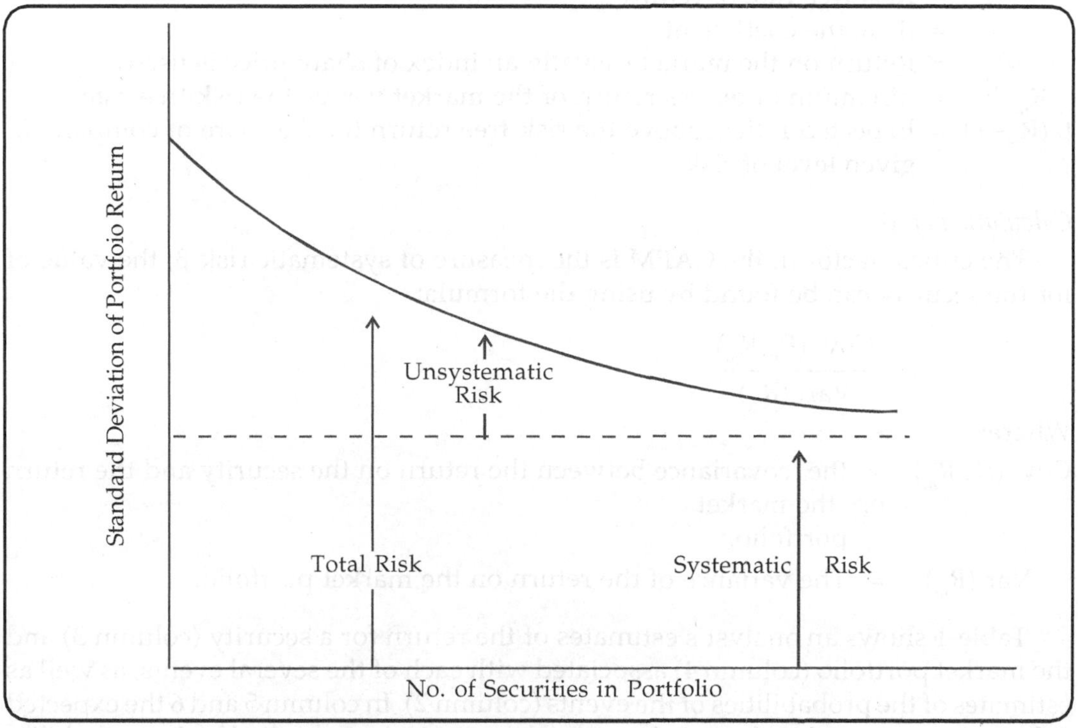

Standard Deviation of Portfoio Return
Unsystematic
Risk
Total Risk
Systematic Risk
No. of Securities in Portfolio

FIGURE-9

A SECURITY CHARACTERISTIC LINE

Excess Return on
Security i
Y
Z
X
Excess Return
on the Market
Portfolio

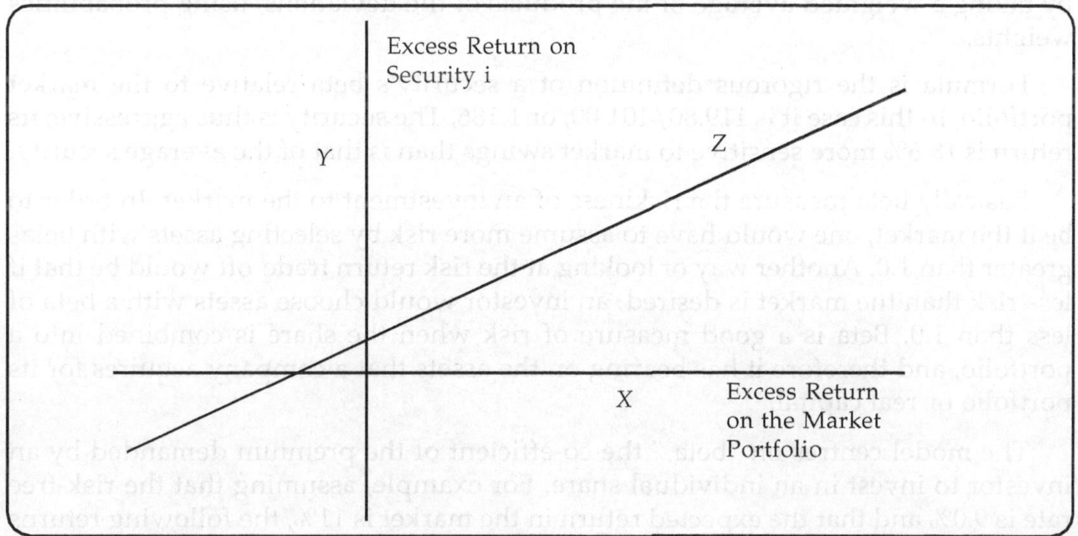

where:

R_1 = Return on individual security of a company

T = Risk free rate of return

β = Beta, the coefficient

R_m = Return on the market (usually an index of share price is used)

$R_m - T$ = Premium or excess return of the market versus the risk free rate

$\beta (R_m - T)$ = Expected return above the risk-free return for the share of company *i*, given level of risk.

Calculation of β

The critical factor in the CAPM is the measure of systematic risk-β, the value of for the security can be found by using the formula:

$$\beta = \frac{\text{Cov. } (R_i, R_m)}{\text{Var. } (R_m)}$$

Where:

Cov. $(R_i . R_m)$ = the covariance between the return on the security and the return on the market portfolio.

Var (R_m) = The variance of the return on the market portfolio.

Table-1 shows an analyst's estimates of the return for a security (column 3) and the market portfolio (column 4) associated with each of the several events, as well as estimates of the probabilities of the events (column 2). In column 5 and 6 the expected values are computed in the usual way; each outcome is multiplied by its probability then summed. The variance of the return on the market portfolio is computed on column 9. Finally, in column 10 the covariance between the two returns is computed by taking a weighted average of the products of the deviations, using probabilities weights.

Formula is the rigorous definition of a security's beta relative to the market portfolio. In this case it is 119.80/101.00, or 1.186. The security is thus aggressive; its return is 18.6% more sensitive to market swings than is that of the average security.

Basically beta measure the riskiness of an investment to the market. In order to beat the market, one would have to assume more risk by selecting assets with betas greater than 1.0. Another way of looking at the risk return trade-off would be that if less risk than the market is desired, an investor would choose assets with a beta of less than 1.0. Beta is a good measure of risk when the share is combined into a portfolio, and therefore it has bearing on the assets that a company acquires for its portfolio or real capital.

The model centres on "beta," the co-efficient of the premium demanded by an investor to invest in an individual share. For example, assuming that the risk-free rate is 9.0% and that the expected return in the market is 11%, the following returns would occur with betas 2,0, 1.0 and 0.5.

TABLE 3
Estimating beta from probabilistic predictions

(1) *Event*	(2) *Probability*	(3) *Excess Return on Security i (%)*	(4) *Excess Return on the Market Portfolio (%)*	(5) = (2) × (3)
a	.10	18.0	13.0	1.8
b	.20	13.0	0.0	2.6
c	.10	8.0	11.0	.8
d	.30	-8.0	-6.0	-2.4
e	.30	25.0	18.0	7.5
				10.3 Expected excess return on security *i*

(6) = (2) × (4)	(7) *Deviation of Excess Return on security i* = (3) – 10.3	(8) *Deviation of Excess Return on the Market Portfolio* = (4) – 6.0	(9) *Weighted Deviation for Market Portfolio squared* = (2) × $(8)^2$	(10) *Weighted Products of Deviations* = (2) × (7) x(8)
1.3	7.7	7.0	4.9	5.39
0.0	2.7	-6.0	7.2	-3.24
1.1	-2.3	5.0	2.5	-1.15
-1.8	-18.3	-12.0	43.2	65.88
5.4	14.7	12.0	43.2	52.92
6.0 Expected excess return on the market portfolio			101.0 Variance of excess return on the market portfolio	119.80 Covariance between the excess return on security *i* and the excess return on the market portfolio

$$\beta_{im} = \frac{119.80}{101.0} = 1.186$$

β 2.0 = 9.0% + 2.0 (11.0% – 9.0%) = 13%
β 1.0 = 9.0% + 1.0 (11.0% – 9.0%) = 11%
β 2.0 = 9.0% + 0.5 (11.0% – 9.0%) = 10%

The CAPM is used to evaluate past and expected future performance of financial assets. It can also apply in the selection of fixed assets by corporation—capital budgeting. A firm or an investor should not expect to be rewarded for all the risks associated with an investment become some risks can be eliminated through diversification. (See Table 4) The involvement risk for which the investors shold be

TABLE-4

Total risk = *	=	Systematic risk	+	Unsystematic risk
	=	Market (economic) risk	+	Firm-specific risk
	=	Nondiversifiable risk	+	Diversifiable risk
	=	Cannot be eliminated	+	Can be eliminated
Relevant risk	=	Nondiversifiable risk	+	~~Diversifiable risk~~ (eliminated)
	=	Systematic risk		

complemented compaensated is that portion of the total risk that caught be diversified away. The specific types and source of risk to which a firm or an investor is exposed an numerous and very counderably depending with situation. (See Table 5).

TABLE-5

	Type of Risk	*Brief Description*
I. Systematic risk (nondiversifiable risk, market risk; relevant risk)	Interest rate risk	When interest rates changes, (1) the values of investments change (in opposite directins) and (2) the rate at which funds can be reinvested also changes (in the same direction).
	Inflation risk	The primary reason interest rates change in because investors change their expectations about future inflation.
	Maturity risk	Long-term investments experience greater price reaction to interest rate change than do short-term bonds.
	Liquidity risk	Reflects the fact that some investments are more easily converted into cash on a short notice at a "reasonable price" than are other securities.
	Exchange rate risk	Multinational firms deals with different currencies, and the rate at which the currency of one country can be I*exchanged* into the currency of another country changes as market conditions change.
	Political risk	Any action by a government that reduce the value of an investment.
II. Unsystematic risks (diversifiable risk; firm-specific risk	Business risk	Risk that would be inherent in the firm's operations if it used no debt—factors such as labour conditions, product safety, quality of manageemnt, competitive conditions, and so forth, affect firm-specific risk.
	Financial risk	Risk associated with how the firm is financed (its credit risk).
	Default risk	Part of financial risk—the chance that the firm will not be able to service its existing debt.

III. Combined risks (some systematicy risk and some unsystematic risk)	Total risk	The combination of systematic risk and unsysmatic risk; also referred to as stand-alone risk, because this is the risk an investor takes if he or she purchases only one investment which is tantamount to "putting all your eggs into one basket."
	Corporate risk	The riskiness of the firm without considering the effect to stockholder diversification; based on the combination of assets held by the firm (inventory, accounts receivable, plant and equipment, and so forth). Some diversification exists because the firm's assets represent a portfolio of investments in real assets.)

RISK-RETURN TRADE-OFF

The concept of required-rate-of return can be examined from a single individual investor's point of view and then be extended to explain how an investor required rate of return relates to the rates prevailing in the market.

Individual Investor's Required Rate of Return

When an investment is to be made, the investor always has alternative opportunities to invest funds. If not, there is no decision to be made. In other words, a prospective investor's examining opportunity with the intention of achieving a required rate of return. It is the rate foregone on the next best alternative investment opportunity. In general, this rate is a function of (1) the time value of money, (2) the riskiness of the investment, and the investor's attitude toward risk. The greater the risk, the greater the compensation required. Figure-10 illustrates the risk-return trade off.

FIGURE-10

RISK-RETURN TRADE-OFF

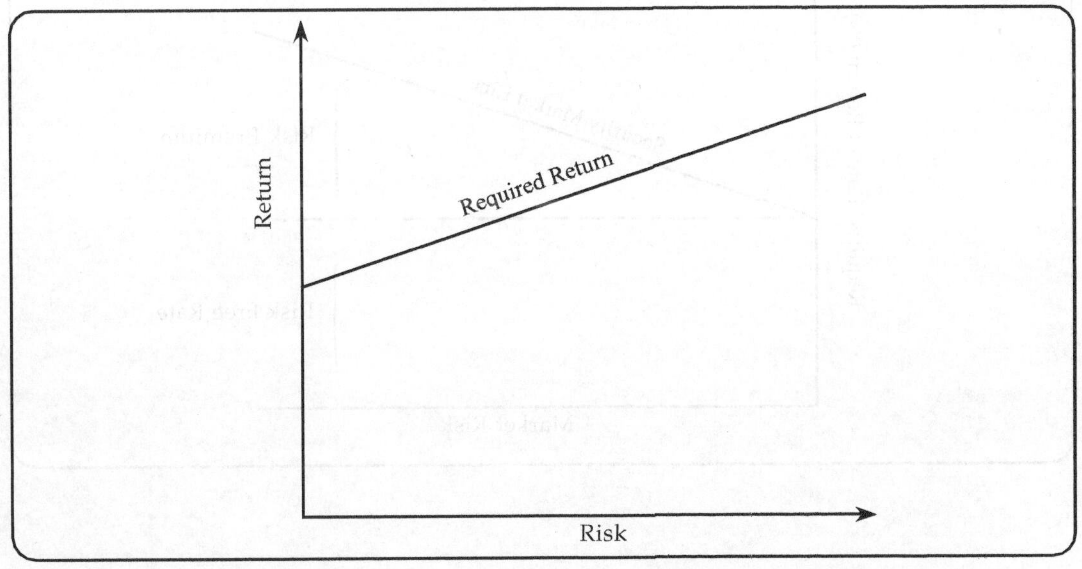

As indicated in Figure-10, for an investment of zero risk the required return is not zero. Investor will require compansation for the passage of time, because the risk-free alternatives are available which offer such a return. The required return compensates the investor for the passage of time and the riskiness of the investment. Thus, the required rate of return is equal to the risk-free rate plus a risk premium.

Required Rates of Return in the Market

A major function of financial markets is to establish prices. Given risk-averse investors, different rates are established for different degrees of risk. The relevant perspective now becomes that of all investors who are actively involved in buying and selling securities. A risk return line may be identified that reflects their attitudes regarding the minimum acceptable rate of return for a given level or risk. One possible description of this relationship, the security market line (SML), is represented graphically in Figure-11. Although the risk-return relationship in the market (SML) is similar in meaning to individual's risk-return preferences, the SML provides an extra dimension. Since the SML results from actual market transactions (buying and selling), the relationship represents not only the risk-return demands of investors in the market, but also the investor's opportunity set. The term opportunity set is used to indicate that this risk-return relationship is actually available for an investor interested in purchasing or selling securities.

FIGURE-11

SECURITY MARKET LINE

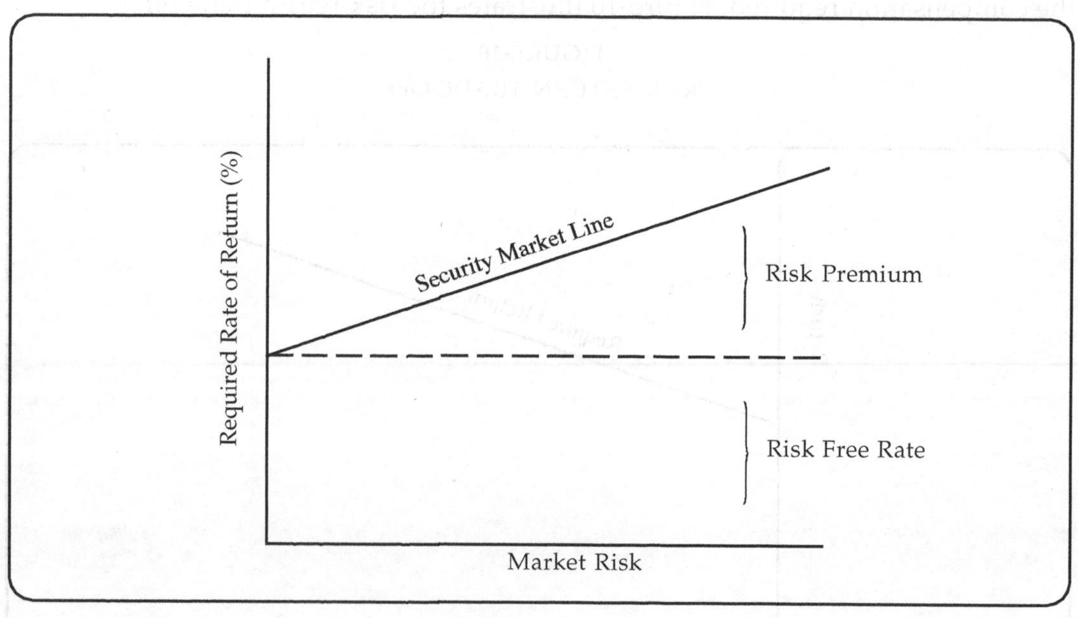

ILLUSTRATIVE PROBLEMS

1. Calculate the returns and standard deviation of a portfolio if half the funds are invested in a project that has a 10% return and a standard deviation of .10 while the other half is invested in a project that has a 20% return and a standard deviation of .2. The covariance of the two projects is –.005.

Solution

Expected return = ½(.10) + ½(.20) = .15

Var (½A + ½B) = $1/4(.1)^2 + (1/4)(.2)^2 + 2(½)(½)(-.005) = .01$

Therefore the standard deviation is .1

2. Indiana Motors is considering two mutually exclusive investment proposals. The following information is relevant:

Expected value of	Standard deviation	net present value
Project X	₹ 6,00,000	₹ 5,00,000
Project Y	₹ 4,50,000	₹ 2,25,000

What is the probability that the actual net present value will be zero or less? which proposal would you accept?

Solution

The standardised differences for a zero cash flow are:

$$\text{Proposal X} = \frac{₹\ 6,00,000-0}{₹\ 5,00,000} = 1.20 \text{ deviations}$$

$$\text{Proposal Y} = \frac{₹\ 4,50,000-0}{₹\ 2,25,000} = 2.00 \text{ deviations}$$

Turning to Table 5 at the back of the book, one finds that these deviations correspond to probabilities of .1151 and .0028. Thus proposal X provides a higher expected value of net present value but significantly greater risks. Which proposal is to be preferred, however, depends on the risk preferences.

3. A firm's required return is 10% on a 3–year project that it is evaluating. The first year return is forecast at ₹ 2,40,000 with a σ of ₹ 20,000, second year return is ₹ 3,00,000 with a σ of ₹ 30,000 and the third year is ₹ 3,60,000 with a σ of ₹ 40,000. The riskless return is 7%. What is the overall standard deviation if the cash flows are independent? If they are perfectly correlated.

Solution

If the cash flows are independent:

$$\sigma = \sqrt{\frac{(20,000)^2}{(1.07)^2} + \frac{(30,000)^2}{(1.07)^4} + \frac{(40,000)^2}{(1.07)^6}} = ₹\ 45,849$$

If perfectly correlated:

$$\sigma = \frac{20{,}000}{(1.07)^1} + \frac{30{,}000}{(1.07)^2} + \frac{40{,}000}{(1.07)^3} = 18{,}700 + 26{,}200 + 32{,}700 = ₹\ 77{,}600$$

4. Stocks A and B have the following historical returns:

Year	*Stock A's Returns, R_A*	*Stock B's Returns, R_B*
2009	(10.00%)	(3.00%)
2010	18.50	21.29
2011	38.67	44.25
2012	14.33	3.67
2013	33.00	28.30

(a) Calculate the average rate of return for each stock during the period 2009 through 2013. Assume that someone held a portfolio consisting of 50 per cent of Stock A and 50 per cent of Stock B. What would have been the realised rate of return on the portfolio in each year from 2009 through 2013? What would have been the average return on the portfolio during this period?

(b) Now calculate the standard deviation of returns for each stock and for the portfolio.

(c) Looking at the annual returns data on the two stocks, would you guess that the correlation coefficient between returns on the two stocks is closer to 0.9 or to −0.9?

(d) If you added more stocks at random to the portfolio, which of the following is the most accurate statement of what would happen to σ_P?

(1) σ_P would remain constant.

(2) σ_P would decline to somewhere in the vicinity of 21 per cent.

(3) σ_P would decline to zero if enough stocks were included.

Solution

(a) The average rate of return for each stock is calculated simply by averaging the returns over the 5-year period. The average return for each stock is 18.90 per cent, calculated for Stock A as follows:

= (−10.00% + 18.50% + 38.67% + 14.33% + 33.00%)/5

= 18.90%.

The realised rate of return on a portfolio made up of Stock A and Stock B would be calculated by finding the average return in each year as R_A (% of Stock A) + R_B (% of Stock B) and then averaging these yearly returns:

Year	*Portfolio AB's Return, R_{AB}*
2009	(6.50%)
2010	19.90
2011	41.46
2012	9.00
2013	30.65
	= 18.90%

(b) The standard deviation of returns is estimated, as follows.

For Stock A:

$$\sigma_A = \sqrt{\frac{(-10.00-18.9)^2+(18.50-18.9)^2+(38.67-18.9)^2+(14.33-18.9)^2+(33.00-18.9)^2}{5-1}}$$

$$= \sqrt{\frac{1,445.92}{4}} = 19.0\%$$

$\sigma B = 19.0$

$\sigma P_{AB} = 18.6$

(c) Since the reduction from diversification is small (σP_{AB} falls only, from 19.0 to 18.6%), the most likely value of the correlation coefficient in 0.9.

(d) If more randomly selected securities were added to the portfolio, σ_P would decline to somewhere in the vicinity of 21%; σ_P would remain constant only if the correlation coefficient were + 1.0, which is most unlikely. σ_P would decline to zero only if the correlation coefficient, *r*, were equal to zero and a large number of securities were added to the portfolio, or if the proper proportion were held in a 2-stock portfolio with r = –1.0.

QUESTIONS

1. What advantage do you see in defining firm risk as the standard deviation of return on a project of average risk undertaken by the firm?
2. In what situation would the variance of an individual asset's rates of return be an appropriate measure of the asset's risk?
3. What is the coefficient of variation? How is it calculated? Why may the coefficient of variation be a better basis for comparing the risk associated with different projects than the standard deviation?
4. What is the relationship between standard deviation and the coefficient of variation? Why do we need two measure of risk?
5. Some financial analysts argue that investment alternative whose return are negatively correlated with market index rates of return are—other things being equal—very desirable investments. Explain this idea.

PROBLEMS

1. A firm is considering two mutually exclusive projects whose annual net flows have the following distribution:

Project A— Net Cash Flow	*Probability of Project A*	*Project B— Net Cash Flow*	*Probability of Project B*
₹ 2,00,000	.1	₹ 2,10,000	.2
3,00,000	.6	3,30,000	.6
4,50,000	.3	4,50,000	.2

Project A requires an initial investment of ₹ 11,00,000 whereas Project B calls for investing ₹ 10,00,000. Both projects would last for 5 years.

Calculate the standard deviation for the net cash flows for both projects. Which one appears to be more risky?

Ans.: SD(A) – ₹ 80,777; SD(B) – ₹ 75,895; Project A is more risky than Project B,

2. A firm is considering two mutually exclusive projects. The initial requirements for both are ₹ 1,00,000. Their annual net cash flows are probabilistic and are given in the following table.

Probability of Project A	*Project A—Net Cash Flow*	*Probability of Project B*	*Project B—Net Cash Flow*
.2	₹ 30,000	.2	₹ 15,000
.5	40,000	.5	43,000
.3	60,000	.3	60,000

Both projects have expected lives of 3 years.

(a) Calculate the expected net cash flows for A and B; (b) Calculate the standard deviations for the net cash flows of A and B.

Ans.: (a) E(A) = ₹ 44,000; E(B) = ₹ 42,500; (b) SD(A) = ₹ 11,136; SD(B) = ₹ 15,596

3. A firm is considering two projects, their cash inflow probability distributions are summarised:

Project A		*Project B*	
Cash Inflow	*Probability*	*Cash Inflow*	*Probability*
₹ 10,000	.10	₹ 10,000	.10
20,000	.20	₹ 30,000	.80
30,000	.40	₹ 50,000	.10
40,000	.20		
50,000	.10		

(a) Determine the expected cash inflow for each project.

(b) Determine the standard deviation of each project's probability distribution of cash inflow.

Ans.: (a) Project A, expected cash Inflow = ₹ 30,000; (b) Project B, standard deviation of expected cash inflow = ₹ 8,944

4. Rama pharmaceutical is in the process of evaluating two mutually exclusive additions to their processing capacity. The firm's financial analysts have developed pessimistic, most likely, and optimistic estimates of the annual cash inflows associated with each project. These estimates are given below:

	Project A	*Project B*
Initial investment	₹ 80,000	₹ 80,000
Cash inflow estimates		
Pessimistic	₹ 2,000	₹ 9,000
Most likely	10,000	10,000
Optimistic	18,000	11,000

(a) Determine the range of annual cash inflows for each of the two projects. Assume the cost of capital for the firm is 10%, and the projects should have 20–year lives

(b) Which project would you recommend and why?

Ans.: (a) Project A, range – ₹ 16,000, Project B, range = ₹ 17,028; (b) Recommend Project B

5. Stocks X and Y have the following probability distributions of expected future returns:

Probability	X	Y
0.1	(10%)	(35%)
0.2	2	0
0.4	12	20
0.2	20	25
0.1	38	45

(a) Calculate the expected rate of return, for Stock Y. (R_x = 12%).

(b) Calculate the standard deviation of expected returns for Stock X. (That for Stock Y is 20.35 per cent). Now calculate the coefficient of variation for Stock Y. Is it possible that most investors might regard Stock Y as being less risky than Stock X? Explain.

Ans.: (a) $E(R_y)$ = 14%; (b) σ_x = 12.20%

8

SECURITIES AND THEIR VALUATION

INTRODUCTION

Valuation is an important factor in the financial manager's decision making process. The study of valuation in competitive markets is important to financial manager because it provides a cut-off criterion for judging the acceptability of new investments, because it is necessary for the proper design and sale of corporate securities and because it is central to the goal of share-price maximisation. The same company can be evaluated by different persons differently to get different values. For example, an accountant may be interested in the *book value,* which is the value of the shareholders' equity. A tax accessor may be interested in the value of the total assets. Both these values differ from the *liquidation value* of a firm that is being dissolved and the *market value* of a potentially profitable firm. The liquidation value is the value that will be received if the firm goes out of business. Under these circumstances, assets are frequently sold for "less than they are worth." If the firm is a *going concern,* a business whose operations are expected to continue, the value of going firm is reflected in the market value. This is the price that willing buyers and sellers agree upon in an open market. Thus the valuation does not take place in a vaccum but rather in a competitive environment in which many companies and private investors are actively seeking the best possible investment.

Without an appreciation of the valuation process, a firm can not establish an efficient set of corporate goals; hence, it has no means by which to evaluate the effectiveness of its decision criteria. This chapter examines the theoretical tenets that explain what determines the value of a security or what it is worth and also explores the manner in which the investor's required rate of return and the expected rate of return for a security is measured.

BASIC DETERMINANTS OF VALUE

The value of financial asset (a security) is defined as the price at which the asset should sell when bought and sold by well informed investors in a market. Value need not be identical to current market price, but the expected value could be related to a market price that is expected to be achieved at *some* point in the future. The value of securities depends on the size and timing of projected cash flows, the riskless rate of interest, the riskiness of the case flows, and investor attitudes toward risk and

1. See Webster's New Collegiate Dictionary, G & C Morriam Co. 1976.

expected return. Expected return and risk are attributable to an investment that can be transferred from one individual to another, in impersonal capital markets. Security analyst must estimate when and under what conditions payment will be received (and, of course, the magnitude of such payments). This typically requires detailed analysis of the company involved, the industry or industries in which the company operates, and the economy as a whole. Once such estimates have been made, the overall value of the security must be determined. This generally requires conversion of *uncertain future* values to equivalent *certain present* values.

BOND VALUATION

A bond is a form of debt characterised by a series of regular interest payments and a final lump sum payment of principal at maturity. The valuation process for a bond, as depicted in Figure-1, requires that we know three essential elements: (1) the amount of the cash flows to be received by the investor, (2) the maturity date of the loan, and (3) investor's required rate of return.

FIGURE-1

BOND VALUATION DATA REQUIREMENTS

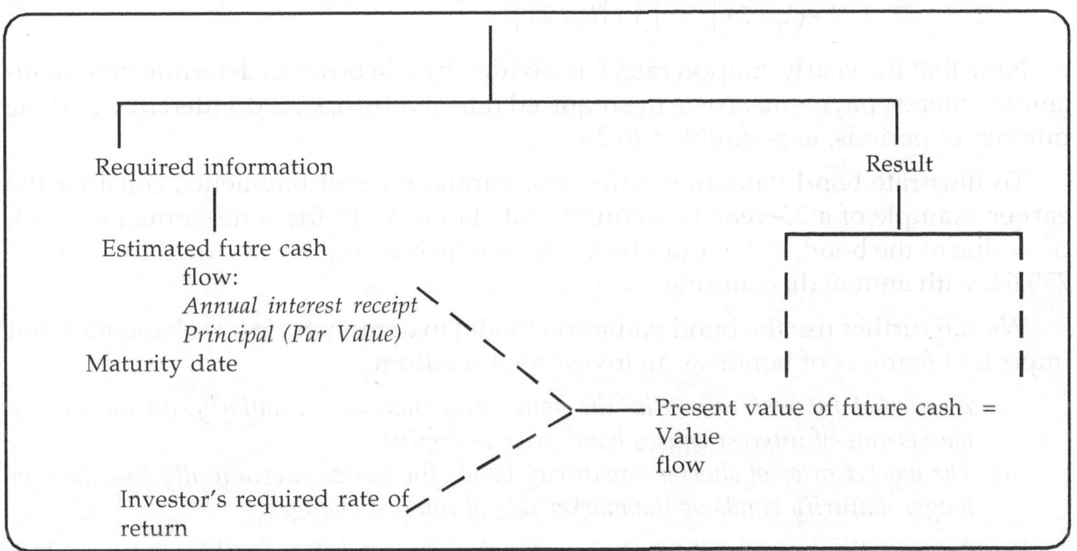

The cash flow from bonds consists of the company's interest payment I, which are fixed, and the principal *P*, which is also set by contract. The period over which the coupons are to be paid and the maturity date *t* for the principal are established by terms of the bond indenture. One can use the following valuation model to solve for the price V_b or the discount rate k_b, which is generally referred to as the yield to maturity:

$$V_b = \frac{I}{(1+k_b)} + \frac{I}{(1+k_b)^2} + ... + \frac{I}{(1+k_b)^t} + \frac{P}{(1+k_b)^t} \quad (1)$$

To see how the equation-1 works let's consider a ₹ 1,000 par bond that has a 12% coupon rate and a 25 year maturity, if this bond has a required rate of return 12% and pays interest annually, its value is:

$$V_b = \frac{₹120}{(1+0.12)^1} + \frac{₹120}{(1+0.12)^2} + ... + \frac{₹120}{(1+0.12)^{25}} + \frac{₹100}{(1+0.12)^{25}}$$

$$= ₹\ 120\ (7.843) + ₹\ 1{,}000\ (0.059) = ₹\ 941.16 + ₹\ 59.00 = ₹\ 1{,}000.16$$

In this example the bond has a current market value of ₹ 1,000, which is exactly equal to its par value. Thus, if the required rate of return is equal to the bond's coupon rate the current market value of a bond is equal, at its par value.[2] The bond then sell, at its par valve of ₹ 1,000.

While some bonds pay interest annually, most pay interest semi-annually. To value bonds with semi-annual interest payments, Eq. 1 is modified as follows:

Value with Semi-annual interest

$$V_b^* = \sum_{t=1}^{2n} \frac{1}{2}\left[\frac{1}{1+(k_b/2)}\right]^t + P\left[\frac{1}{1+(k_b/2)}\right]^{2n} \qquad (2)$$

Note that the yearly coupon rate, I, is divided by 2 in order to determine the semi-annual interest payments. Also, the required rate of return, k_b, is divided by 2 and the number of periods, n, is doubled to $2n$.

To illustrate bond valuation with semi annual interest payments, consider the earlier example of a 25-year 12% coupon rate bond. With the semi-annual interest, the value of the bond, V_b^*, would be ₹ 754.98 which is slightly less then the V_b i.e. ₹ 755.64. with annual discounting.

We can further use the bond valuation model to demonstrate *two* elementary but important features of bonds as an investment medium:

i) *As market interest rate falls, the bond price increases. Similarly, an increase in market rate of interest causes bond price to decline.*
ii) *The market price of shorter—maturity bonds fluctuates substantially less than for longer maturity bonds as the market rate of interest changes.*

Bond generally do not sell for their par value. Instead, they sell for more or less than ₹ 1,000 depending upon current bond market conditions. Suppose, for example, that after the 25-year bond was issued, sharply higher expected inflation cause market interest rates for similar quality and maturity bonds to increase to 16 per cent. The change in market interest rates would cause the required rate of return to increase also—to 16 per cent. This occurs because investors considering the 12 per

---

2. Bond actually sell at their current market price plus accrued interest. For a new issue there is typically little or no accrued interest. However, if it was one-fourth of the way though the bond's interest year, then the actual cost of purchasing the bond would be ₹ 1,000+1/4 (₹ 120) or ₹ 1,030.

cent coupon rate bond would not be willing to settle for less than they could receive in comparable quality, but higher coupon rate newly issued securities. What would the market value of those bonds be? To determine this new market price, the interest and principal are discounted at the new required rate of return of 16 per cent so that the current market price of the bond is ₹ 755.64

An investor purchasing this 12 per cent coupon-rate bond for ₹ 755.64 and holding it for 25 years (to maturity) would receive a return of 16 per cent. This return is composed of two parts—the 12 per cent coupon, which is expected to provide ₹ 120 per year, plus the expected capital appreciation of ₹ 244.36 (₹ 1,000, ₹ – 755.64). The difference between the ₹ 1,000 per value and the current market price of ₹ 755.64 is called the discount on the bond.

Bonds may also sell at a premium to continue our example. if market interest rates drop to 8 per cent on comparable quality and maturity bonds, the current market price of the 12 per cent coupon-rate 25-year bond becomes ₹ 1,427.

Because the coupon rate of 12 per cent is greater than the current market required rate of return of 8 per cent, investors pay a premium of ₹ 427 (₹ 427–1,000) for the bond. The relationship between the current market yield and the market price of these bonds is graphed in Figure-2.

FIGURE-2

RELATIONSHIP BETWEEN A BOND'S MARKET PRICE AND THE CURRENT MARKET RATE OF INTEREST

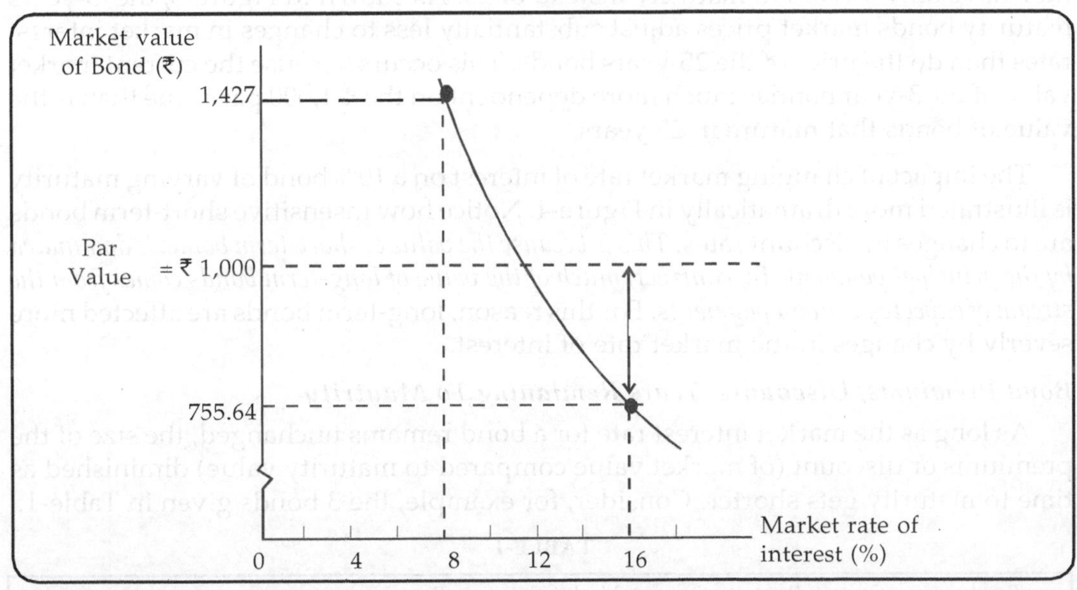

Not only are bond prices influenced by market interest rates, they are also influenced by the length to maturity of the bonds. To see this relationship, consider when happens to the current market price of our 12 per cent coupon-rate bonds if

FIGURE-3

RELATIONSHIP BETWEEN A BOND MARKET PRICE, THE CURRENT MARKET RATE OF INTEREST, AND BOND MATURITY

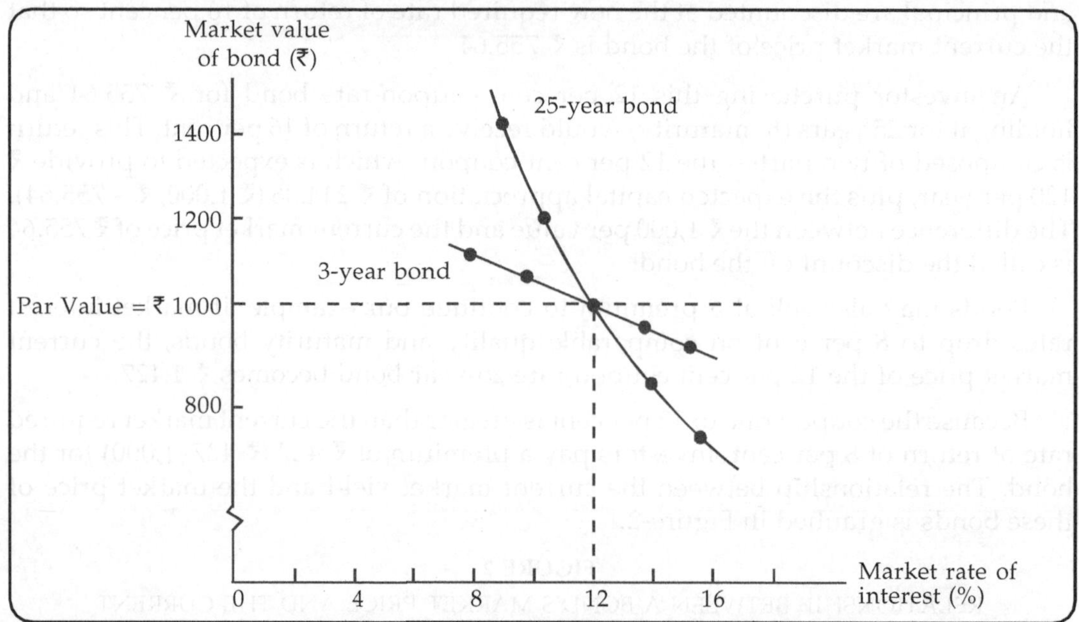

they have only 3 years to maturity instead of 25. As shown in Figure-3, the 3-years maturity bonds market prices adjust substantially less to changes in market interest rates than do the price of the 25-years bonds. This occurs because the current market value of the 3-year bond is much more dependent on the ₹ 1,000 par value than is the value of bonds that mature in 25 years.

The impact of changing market rate of interest on a 10% bond of varying maturity is illustrated more dramatically in Figure-4. Notice how insensitive short-term bonds are to changes in discount rates. *This is because the value of short-term bonds is dominated by the principal payment. By contract, much of the value of long-term bonds comes from the stream of expected coupon payments.* For this reason, long-term bonds are affected more severly by changes in the market rate of interest.

Bond Premiums, Discounts, Years Remianing To Mautrity

As long as the market interest rate for a bond remains unchanged, the size of the premiums or discount (of market value compared to maturity value) diminished as time to maturity gets shorter. Consider, for example, the 3 bonds given in Table-1.

TABLE-1

Bond	*Coupon Rate*	*Market Rate*	*Remaining Years To Maturity*	*Value*
X	10%	8%	10	₹ 1134.20
Y	8	8	10	₹ 1000.00
Z	6	8	10	₹ 865.80

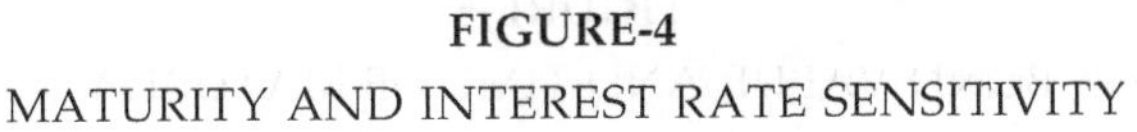

FIGURE-4

MATURITY AND INTEREST RATE SENSITIVITY

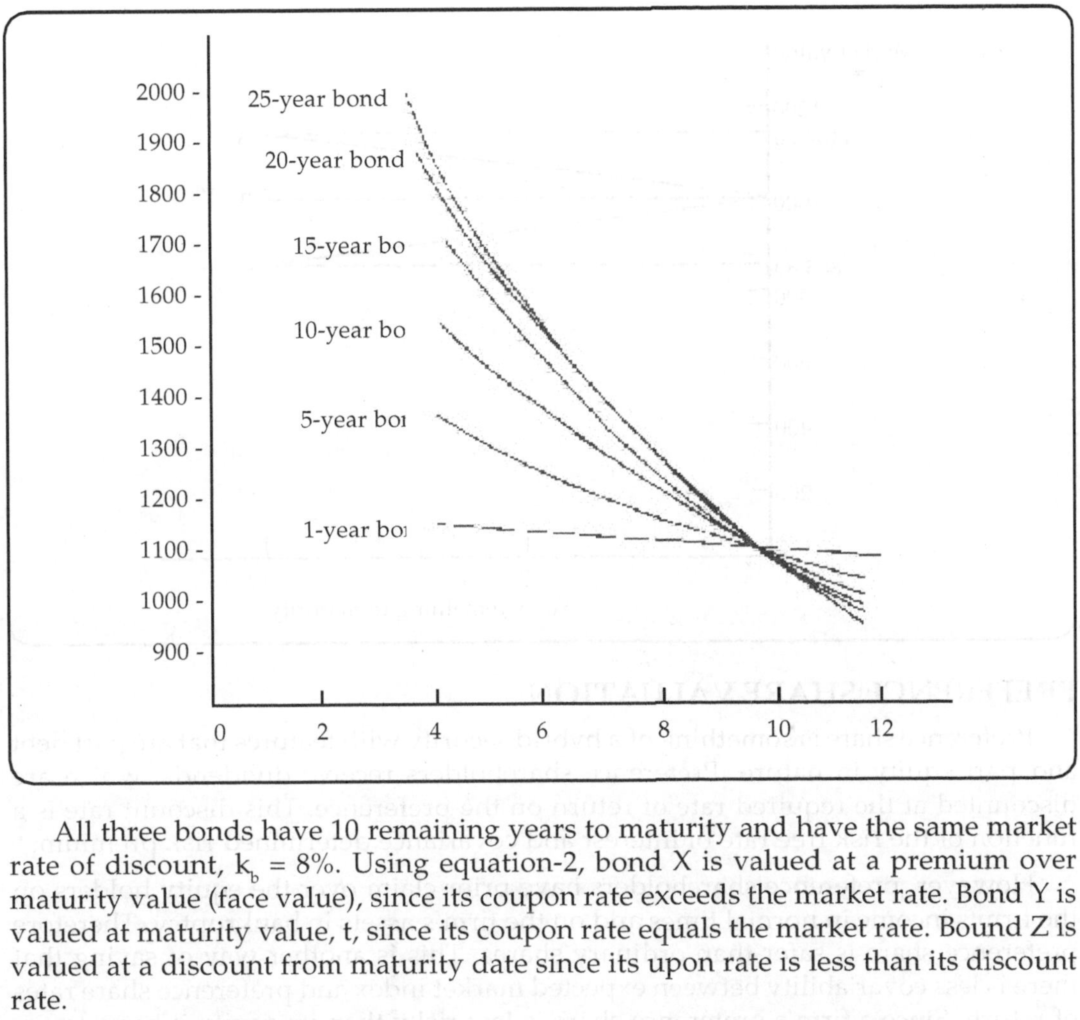

All three bonds have 10 remaining years to maturity and have the same market rate of discount, k_b = 8%. Using equation-2, bond X is valued at a premium over maturity value (face value), since its coupon rate exceeds the market rate. Bond Y is valued at maturity value, t, since its coupon rate equals the market rate. Bound Z is valued at a discount from maturity date since its upon rate is less than its discount rate.

Now if the time to maturity were shorter, and the market interest rate were to remain same, the value of bond X would fall (the premium would diminish) while the value of bound Z would rise until, at maturity, their values equalled maturity value. Bond Y, being valued at maturity value, would remain there until maturity. Figure-5 describes the behaviour of the value of bonds X, Y, Z as remaining time to maturity shortens. We see as maturity shortens, the present value of the fixed principal payment (i.e., is maturity value) increases while that of the interest payments which are diminishing in number decreases. As time of maturity near, maturity value increasingly dominates interest payments until, near maturity, the maturity value is primary remaining cash flow attached to the bond and the primary source of value.

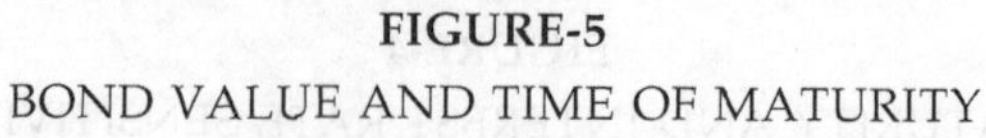

FIGURE-5

BOND VALUE AND TIME OF MATURITY

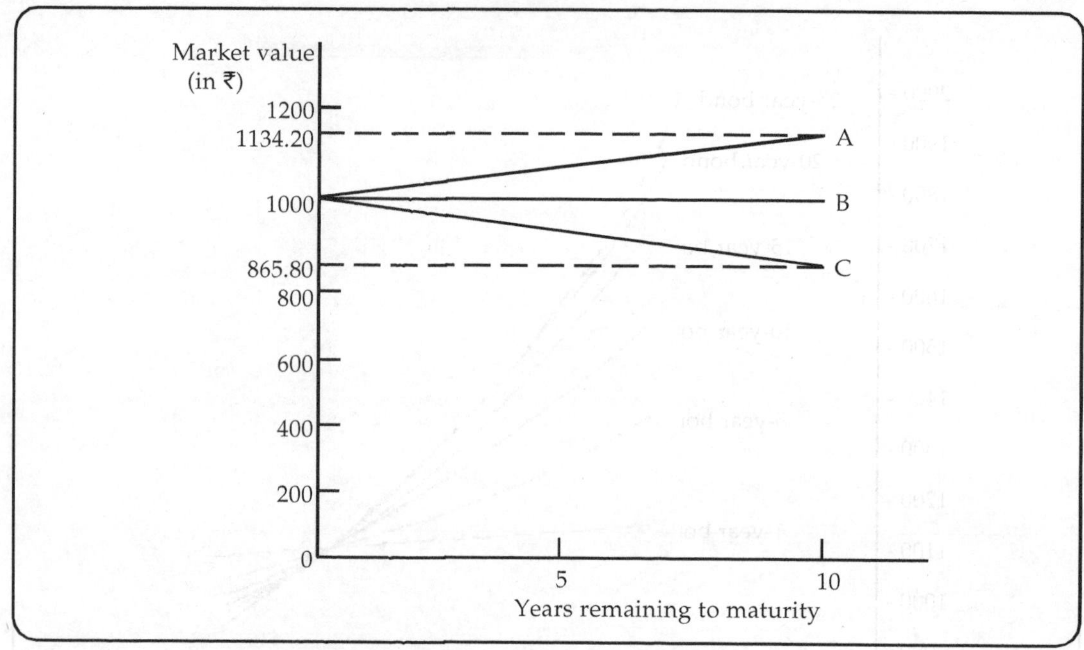

PREFERENCE SHARE VALUATION

Preference share is something of a hybrid security with features that are part debt and part equity in nature. Preference shareholders receive dividends, which are discounted at the required rate of return on the preference. This discount rate is a function of the risk free rate of interest and covariance determined risk premium.

However, preference shareholders have prior claim over the equity holders on the firm's income in normal times and on the firm's assets in bankruptcy. Therefore preference share is safer than ordinary shares. This is another way of saying that there is less covariability between expected market index and preference share rates of return. Since a firm's preference share is less risky than its equity it has a lower required rate of return than the equity. But the preference share is riskier than the firm's bonds (the bonds have first claim to the firm's income and assets), and the required rate of return of the preference is therefore greater than than that of the bonds.

Preference shares offer a level of dividend payment over the life of the security, making the preference share valuation model a type of annuity. In the simplest case, we can write the value of the preference share as a perpetuity:

$$V_p = \sum_{t=1}^{\infty} \frac{A_t}{(1+k_p)^t} = \frac{A}{k_p} \qquad (3)$$

where the A_t is the expected level of annual dividend payment and k_p is the rate of return required by preference shareholders.

For example, if a firm has a ₹ 100 par preference share with a 11% dividend and the current required rate is 15% the current value per share is:

$$V_p = \frac{0.11\ (100)}{0.15} = \frac{₹\ 11.00}{0.15} = ₹\ 73.33$$

EQUITY VALUATION

John Burr Williams developed an early share valuation model in which the value of an equity was the present value of all future cash dividends an owner expect to receive.[3] If all expected cash dividends per share in perpetuity are being evaluated, this valuation model is:

$$V_e = \sum_{t=1}^{\infty} \frac{D_t}{(1+k_e)^t} \tag{4}$$

In this model, D_t is the dividend per share expected by present shareholders at each future data t. The required rate of return for equity k_e, discounts these future dividends to a present value per share.

VALUATION OF DIVIDENDS PER SHARE, NOT TOTAL DIVIDENDS

It is important to emhasise that equation-4 values dividend per share, not total dividends. From the stand point of present shareholders, decisions leading to an increase in total dividends may not lead to proportionate increases in per share dividends with the sale of new shares. Table-2 demonstrates this point. The ABC Company is issuing new shares in each period to finance expansion. Total dividend increased from ₹ 10,00,000 to ₹ 20,00,000 in 4 periods. But initial shareholders, owning 10,00,000 shares in period 0. do not similarly double their dividend receipt. The sale of 5,00,000 new shares to new owners over the periods 4 reduces dividends per share to ₹ 1.33 in period 4 from the level of ₹ 20,00,000/10,00,000 = ₹ 2.00 occurring if the new shares were ignored. Initial share holders increase by only 33 percent their dividend per share (from ₹ 1.00 to ₹ 1.33) and their total dividends to ₹ 13,33,333 from ₹ 10,00,000, as 10,00,000 × ₹ 1.00 = ₹ 10,00,000 and 10,00,000 × ₹ 1.33 = ₹ 13,33,333. The remaining ₹ 20,00,000—₹ 13,33,333 of total dividends is paid to owners of new share at $t = 4$.

Insofar as present owners (at t=0) of shares are concerned, increases in total dividends per share can be quite different things.

3. Williams, John Burr: *The Theory of Investment value,* (Cambridge, M.A., Harvard University Press, 1978) P. 56.

TABLE-2

ABC Company Dividends

(in ₹)

	Period				
	0	*1*	*2*	*3*	*4*
Total Dividends	10,00,000	12,50,000	15,00,000	17,50,000	20,00,000
Equity Shares	10,00,000	11,00,000	12,50,000	14,00,000	15,00,000
Dividends per share	₹ 1.00	₹ 1.14	₹ 1.20	₹ 1.25	₹ 1.33
Total divi dends to owners at Time 0	10,00,000	14,10,000	12,00,000	12,50,000	13,33,333

VALUATION BASED ON DIVIDENDS, NOT EARNINGS

A common objection to this model is that value should be based upon earnings, not dividends. Williams defended the dividend model by arguing that earnings are only a matter to an end; share must derive its value from the cash flows that shareholders expect to receive and the risk attached to those cash flows:

> *If earnings not paid out in dividends are all successfully reinvested at compound interest for the benefit of the stock holders, as critic simply, then these earnings should provide dividends later if not, then they are money lost. Furthermore, if these reinvested earnings will produce dividends, then our formula will take account of them when it takes account of future all dividends; but if they will not, then our formula will rightly refrain from including them in discounted annuity of benefits.*[4]

Although it is possible to properly construct a model based on the valuation of earnings that gives the same per share value as dividend valuation, we adhere to the latter model. But notice that equation-5 requires that every cash dividend in perpetuity be estimated before per share value can be estimated.

Zero Dividend Growth Model

If a firm is expected to pay constant (nongrowing) dividends over the freseeable future, then in terms of the notations already introduced,

$$D_1 = D_2 = \text{........} = D_\infty \tag{5}$$

4. *Ibid.*

Letting D_1 equal the amount of the annual dividend, equation-6 would become[5]:

$$V_b = \sum_{t=1}^{\infty} \frac{D}{(1+k_e)^t} \tag{6}$$

The equation shows that with zero growth, the value of the equity share is equal to the present value of a perpetuity of D_1, discounted at a rate k_e, It should be clear that the form of this equation is identical to that of Euqation-4. which is used to value perpetual bond or preference share. To illustrate, suppose the dividends are expected to be constant at ₹ 2.50 per share forever and the required rate of return on equity is 20 percent, V_e = 2.50/0.20 = ₹ 12.50 per share. Technically, this simplification of the more complex valuation equation-5 is only valid when the assumption by constant dividends and an infinite time horizon are both strictly satisfied. Although there are few instances where these two conditions strictly hold, Equation-6 is very useful because it frequently gives good approximation even when the two assumption are not met. On the other hand, there are many situations where equation-6 is not a good approximation of equation-5. In general, as *-n* gets smaller and/or the expected dividend stream departs. from constancy, the approximation becomes worse.

Constant Growth Rate of Dividends

In another special case, consider what happens if cash dividends are expected to increase at constant (percentage) rate each year. In order to find the discounted present value of this stream of constantly rising dividends, we can use equation-7 which is the constant growth model where:

$$V_e = \sum_{t=1}^{\infty} \frac{D_0(1+g)^t}{(1+k_e)^t} \tag{7}$$

---

5. This is another perpetuity, the derivation of equation-6 from equation-5 is as follows:

$$V_e = \frac{D_1}{(1+k_e)^1} + \frac{D_2}{(1+k_e)^2} + ... + \frac{D_\infty}{(1+k_e)^\infty}$$

Since $D_1 = D_2$ =...............-D_∞. Equation-5 may be rewritten as follows, letting $D=D_1=D_2......=D_\infty$:

$$V_e = D\left[\frac{1}{(1+k_e)^1} + \frac{1}{(1+k_e)^2} + ... + \frac{1}{(1+k_e)^n}\right]$$

Multiplying both sides by $(1+k_e)$ yield:

$$V_e(1+k_e) = D\left[1 + \frac{1}{(1+k_e)^1} + \frac{1}{(1+k_e)^2} + ... + \frac{1}{(1+k_e)^{n-1}}\right]$$

Subtracting the preceding equation from the most recent equation result in:

$$V_e(1+k_e-1) = D\left[1 - \frac{1}{(1+k_e)^n}\right]$$

As $n \rightarrow \infty, \frac{1}{(1+k_e)^n} = O$, so:

and $P_0=D/k_e$: since $D = D_1$: $V_e=D_1/k_e$

and further simplified to[6]:

$$V_e = \frac{D_1}{k_e - g} \qquad (8)$$

This equation tells us that the value of an equity share is equal to the cash dividend in time period I discounted by the difference between the required rate of return required by equity investors and growth rate of dividends. In using equation-4 for a constantly growing series of cash dividends, we must use the cash dividends expected one year hence, or D_1. If we had a share whose current cash dividend (at time t = 0) is ₹ 2.50, the constant compound growth rate in dividends is 15 percent per year and the required rate of return is 20 percent, the value of this share is:

$$V_e = \frac{D_1}{k_e - g} = \frac{D_0(1+g)}{k_e - g}$$

$$= \frac{₹2.50(1+.15)}{0.20-0.15} = ₹73.00$$

Note that this current price of ₹ 73.00 is substantially higher than the ₹ 12.50 when no growth in future cash dividends was assumed. This is as we would expect since, other things being equal, an investor would value a growing cash flow stream at a higher rate than a nongrowing stream. While growth rates for firms are not often

6. We can simplify in this way:

$$V_e = D_o\left[\frac{(1+g)}{(1+k_e)} + \frac{(1+g)^2}{(1+k_e)^2} + \ldots + \frac{(1+g)^n}{(1+k_e)^n}\right] \qquad ...(7.1)$$

Multiply both sides of equation by $(1+k_e)/(1+g)$

$$\left[\frac{(1+k_e)}{(1+g)}\right]V_e = D_o\left[1 + \frac{(1+g)}{(1+k_e)} + \frac{(1+g)^2}{(1+k_e)^2} + \ldots\ldots + \frac{(1+g)^{n-1}}{(1+k_e)^{n-1}}\right] \qquad ...(7.2)$$

Subtract equation (10.1) from equation (10.2)

$$\left[\frac{(1+k_e)}{(1+g)}\right]V_e = D_o\left[1 - \frac{(1+g)^n}{(1+k_e)^n}\right]$$

$$\left[\frac{(1+k_e)-(1+g)}{(1+g)}\right]V_e = D_o\left[1 - \frac{(1+g)^n}{(1+k_e)^n}\right]$$

Assume $k_e > g$ as n approaches infinity; $\left[1 - \frac{(1+g)^n}{(1+k_e)^n}\right]$

approaches 1, which leaves

$$\left[\frac{(1+k_e)-(1+g)}{(1+g)}\right]V_e = D_o$$

which simplified to

$(k_e - g)V_e = D_o(1+g) = 1$ $\qquad$ $D_1 = D_0(1+g)$

$$\therefore \quad V_e = \frac{D_1}{k - g_e}.$$

constant, equation-6 is still useful because of its simplicity.

Variable Growth Rate of Dividends

The last situation we will consider is when a firm grows at a fast rate for a few years and then reverts to a constant or no growth situation. This might occur because a firm made previous investments that produced high cash flows, but increasing, competition is expected to reduce the future growth rate. In this case, the value of firm whose growth rate of dividends varies over time can be determined by the following equation-9.

$$V_e = \sum_{t=1}^{n} \frac{D_0(1+g_x)^t}{(1+k_e)^t} + \sum_{t=n+1}^{\infty} \frac{D_n(1+g_y)^{t-n}}{(1+k_e)^t} \quad (9)$$

where g_x = growth rate of dividends for n year

g_v = growth rate of dividends for year $n + 1$ and beyond.

This equation-9 can be expanded to include any number of growth rate or time periods, the ability to change growth rates allows one to value a share over the life cycle of a firm on the rates of growth change. If the growth rate of dividends is expected to grow at one rate for a period of time and then at a constant rate, the equation for the variable growth rate model is

$$V_e = \sum_{t=1}^{n} \frac{D_0(1+g_x)^t}{(1+k_e)^t} + \frac{D_n+1}{(k_e-g_y)}\left[\frac{1}{(1+k_e)^n}\right] \quad (10)$$

To illustrate the use of the multiple growth rate dividend valuation model in valuing a firm, consider the case of a hypothetical *XYZ* company. The company paid its first cash dividend of ₹ 2.50 today and dividends are expected to grow at a rate of 30% per year for the next 3 years. Thereafter, cash dividends will grow at a 10 percent rate per year. Shareholders expect to earn a 15% return on their investments. Based on these assumptions the steps necessary to calculate the value of the share of *XYZ* Company are presented below:

Step 1

Calculate the present value of dividends for the first 3 years.

$$V_e = \sum_{t=1}^{n} \frac{D_0(1+g_x)^t}{(1+k_e)^t} = ₹\ 8.3473$$

Year	*Dividend* $D_e(1+g_x)^t$ ₹ $2.50\,(1+0.30)^t$	×	*Capitalisation Rate* $k_e = 0.15$	=	*Present Value*
(1)	(2)		(3)		(4) = (2) × (3)
0	₹ 2.500				
1	3.20		0.870		₹ 3.7356
2	4.225		0.756		5.5886
3	5.493		0.658		8.3473

Step 2

Value at the and of 3 years for the remaining live of the company

Dividend in 4th year $D_4 = D_3 (1 + g_v)$

= ₹ 5.493 (1 + 0.10) = ₹ 6.0423

Value at the end of the third year

$$V_3 = \frac{D_4}{k_e - g_v}$$

$$= \frac{6.0423}{0.15 - 0.10} = ₹\ 120.846$$

Step 3

The present value at the end of 3 years (V_3) discounted by the required rate of return, $k_{e\ =\ 0.15}$

$$(V_3) \times \left(\frac{1}{(1+k_e)^3} \right)$$

₹ 120.846 (0.658) = ₹ 79.516668

Step 4

The value per share today equals the present value of dividends for the first 3 years (step 1) plus the present value of the share price at the end of year 3 (Step 3)

Step 1		*Step 2*
V_e = ₹ 8.343	+	₹ 79.516668 = ₹ 87.8639668

Step 5

Multiply the number of share by the price per share to determine the total value of the firm is ₹ 8,78,63,967.

THE RELATIONSHIP OF RISK, RETURN, AND MARKET PRICE

Now that we know how to combine cash flows, time value, and risk to solve for equity and bond values, we are ready to tackle almost any financial management problem. However, before doing that, we pause and do two things: *First,* to see what happens to the required rate of return for equity shares as risk changes, and *second,* to consider how changes in risk and the required rate of return affect the market value of a firm's equity.

RISK ASSESSMENT APPROACH TO COST OF EQUITY

The risk assessment method does not rely on specific estimations of present and future earnings or dividends. Instead, a *normal market return* is developed from published data on financial returns and yields, which is adjusted by a *company-*

specific risk premium or *discount*. The rationale is the assumption that a company's cost of equity in term of shareholder return expectations is related to the *relative riskiness* of its equity. The greater this relative risk, the greater the premium—in the form of an additional economic return over and above a normalised return—that should be expected by an investor. This approach makes intuitive sense and can also be demonstrated statistically. At any time, the securities markets yield a *spread* of rates of return ranging from those on essentially *risk-free* government securities at the low end of the scale to the sizable returns from *highly speculative* securities. The risk/ return trade-off inherent in the many classes of security investments is reflected in this spread. *Risk* is defined for this purpose as the *variability of returns* inherent in the type of security, while *return* is defined as the *total economic return* obtained from it, including both interest or dividends and changes in market value.

A number of specific methods have been developed over the years to express the *risk premium* concept of return on equity—which reflectes the *cost* of equity to a company—as a methodology both theoretically acceptable and practically usable. While no individual method is totally satisfactory in these terms, the most widely accepted is the capital asset pricing model (CAPM).

CAPITAL ASSET PRICING MODEL

The capital asset pricing model (CAPM) *establishes a relationship between risk and the required rate of return.* The *three elements* are required in applying the capital sset pricing model approach, and each must be carefully estimated. The *first* is an expression of the level of return from a *risk-free security.* The purpose is to find the *lowest part* of the range of yields currently experienced in the security markets as the starting point from which to build up the higher, risk-adjusted return specific to the particular equity. Long-term government obligations are commonly used as a surrogate for such a risk-free return. The yields on government obligations are widely quoted and accessible, both for the present and for historical periods. For purposes of analysis, *current* yields, possibly adjusted for expected changes during the next several years, can be used. Precision is not possible here, and reasonable approximations supported by the analyst's judgment are quite sufficient. The *second* element is an estimate of the return from a comparable type of security of *average risk.* This is needed because the CAPM methods develops a specific adjustment for the *relative* riskiness of the particular security *as compared to* an average or baseline. The *third* element required is an expression of relative risk, which is based on the *variability of returns* of the particular security being analyzed. The definition of risk is *very specific* in the CAPM. Risk is *not* defined as *total variability* of returns, but rather, as the *covariance* of the particular stock's returns with those of assets of average risk. The risk measure, in the form of the covariance of an individual stock's return with that of the portfolio of stocks of average risk, is called "beta" (β). It is found by linear regression of *past* monthly total returns of the *particular* security against a *baseline.*

How are the three elements combined to arrive at the expected return and, thus, the company's cost of capital for a particular equity security? The CAPM method defines the cost of equity as the combination of the *risk-free return* and a *risk premium* that has been adjusted for the *specific company risk.*

The CAPM formula appears as follows:

$$k_e = T + \beta(R_m - T)$$

Where

k_e is the cost of capital

T is the risk-free return

β is the company's covariance of returns against the portfolio,

R_m is the average returns on equities

β is expected as a simple factor which is used to multiply the *difference* between the expected return on the average portfolio and the expected risk-free return. This difference of course, is the risk premium inherent in the *portfolio.* The β factor *adjusts* this *average* risk premium to reflecte the *individual* stock's higher or lower relative riskiness. β goes above 1.0 as the relative risk of the stock exceeds the average, and drops below 1.0 when the relative risk is below average.

The calculation itself is quite simple, while deriving the *inputs* is not. To illustrate, we will arbitrarily choose a risk-free rate of return of 9 per cent, an BSE Sensex return estimate of 14.0 per cent, and a company with a farily "risky" β of 1.4. The cost of equity in this hypothetical example would be

$$k_e = 9.0 + 1.4\ (14.0 - 9.0) = 16\%$$

composed of the risk-free return of 9 percent plus the calculated company-specific risk premium of 7 percent, for a total of 16.0 per cent.

What happen, however, to this required rate of return as risk changes? To explore this question, we will employ four-part classification of the sources of risk: *general economic, inflation, firm and issue-specific,* and *international.* As we will see, both general economic and inflation risk tend to affect all firms to a greater or lesser extent. Firm and issue-specific sources of risk, on the other hand, are reflected in the non-diversifiable risk, or beta, of a firm. Finally, international sources of risk may affect all firms or only certain ones.

CHANGE IN GENERAL ECONOMIC RISK

General economic conditions influence the expected return for the economy as a whole as well as for individual firms. As the economy swings from prosperity to recession, the general degree of risk aversion may change. The slope of the security market line reflects the extent to which investors are risk-averse. The steeper the slope, the greater the average investor's aversion to risk.

FIGURE-6

SHIFT IN !SECURITY MARKET LINE (SML) CAUSED BY AN INCREASE IN RISK AVERSION

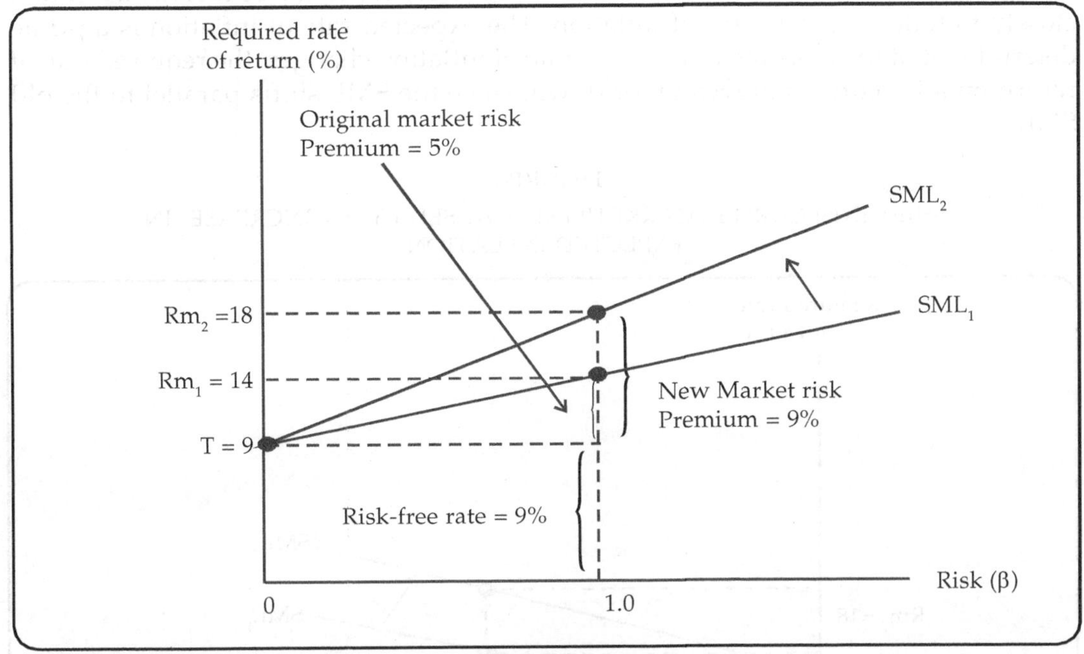

What happens if, due to changing economic conditions, investors become more risk-averse? As this happens, the market risk premium, $R_m - T$, increases with the consequence that the required rate of return on all securities changes. As shown in Figure-6, an increase in risk aversion causing the expected market rate of return to increase from 14 to 18 percent increases the slope of the security market line (SML). The original market risk premium was 5 percent (14% - 9%), whereas the new risk premium is 9 percent (18% - 9%),. Thus, *if the initial risk-free rate remains constant,* the required rate of return increases at all levels of risk.

An increase in risk aversion causes the slope of the SML to increase, with the result that all required rates of return, except T, increase.

How about the required rate of return on our stock with a beta of 1.40? Previously, it had a required return of 16 percent; its required return is now 21.6 percent, where

$$k_{e\ new} = 9\% + 1.40\ (18\% - 9\%)$$
$$= 9\% + 1.40\ (9\%) = 9\% + 12.6\% = 21.6\%$$

When risk aversion in general increases, all securities have a higher required rate of return. Conversely, when investors become less risk averse, all required rates of return fall.

i) Changes in Inflation Risk

The return on government securities, typically treasury bills, is generally employed as a proxy for the risk-free rate of return. Historically, this risk-free return has tended closely to follow actual rates of inflation. The expected rate of inflation is a prime determinant of the risk-free rate. As the rate of inflation changes, the required rate of return on all securities moves up or down, since the SML shifts parallel to the old SML.

FIGURE-7

SHIFT IN SECURITY MARKET LINE CAUSED BY AN INCREASE IN EXPECTED INFLATION

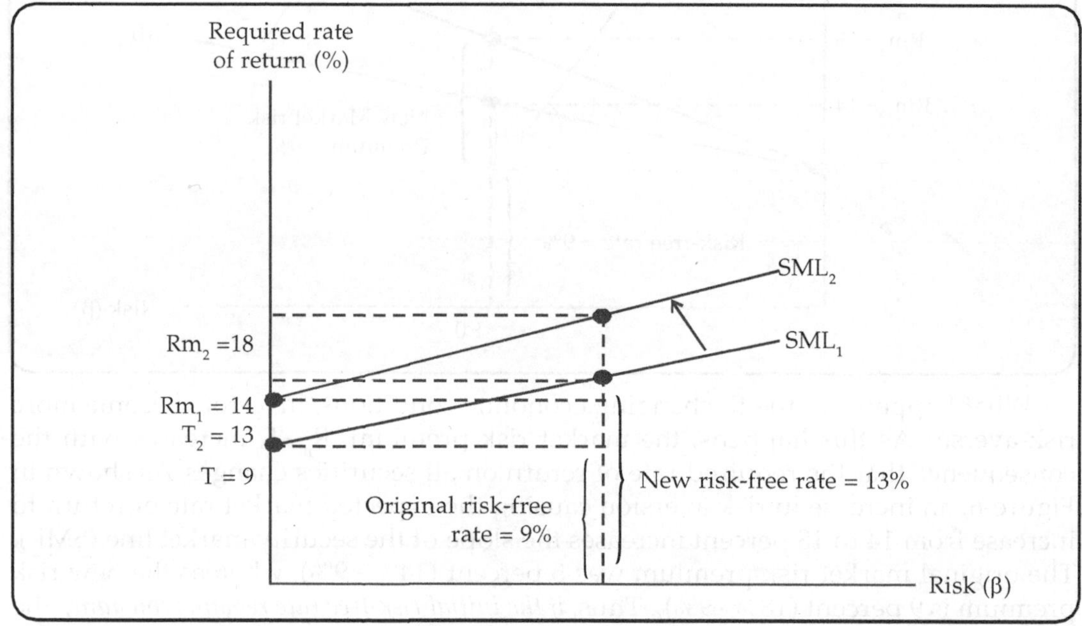

To see this, consider Figure-7, where the expected rate of inflation increases by 4 percent, causing the whole security market line to shift upward correspondingly. Hence, for every degree of risk, the new required rate of return will be 4 percent higher than previously. For our security with a beta of 1.40 and an original required return of 16 percent, the new required rate of return will be 20 percent:

$$
\begin{aligned}
k_{e\ new} &= 13\% + 1.40\ (18\% - 13\%) \\
&= 13\% + 1.40\ (5\%) = 13\% + 7\% = 20\%
\end{aligned}
$$

As expected inflation increases by 4 percent, the risk free rate and all other required rates of return shift upward by 4 percent.

ii) Change in Firm or Issue-Specific Risk

Alternatively, what happens if a firm's nondiversifiable risk changes? How does that change influence the firm's required rate of return? For example, consider our company with a beta of 1.40. What happens if for some reason the firm's nondiversifiable risk increases to 1.80, but the firm's expected cash flows remain the same?" The result is to increase its required rate of return from 16 percent to 18 percent, as follows:

$$k_{e\ new} = 9\% + 1.80\ (14\% - 9\%)$$
$$= 9\% + 1.80\ (5\%) = 9\% + 9\% = 18\%$$

This same effect is graphed in Figure-8. Changes that influence the nondiversifiable riskiness of the firm have the direct impact of increasing or decreasing its required rate of return.

FIGURE-8

IMPACT OF!FIRM'S BETA INCREASING FROM 1.40 TO 1.80.

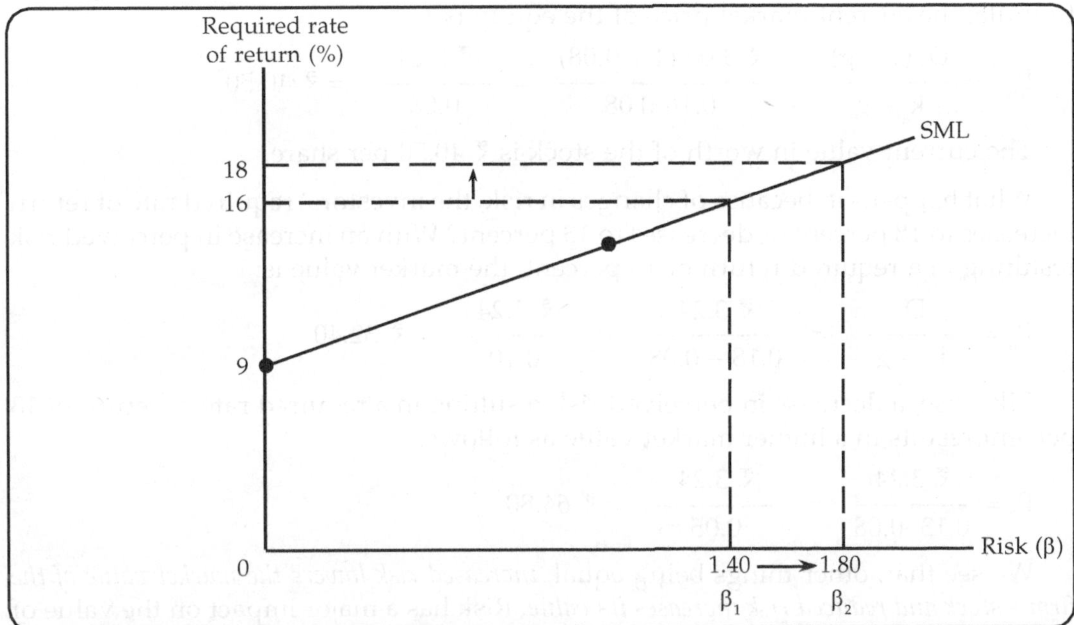

As beta increases, the required rate of return increases: when beta decreases, the required rate of return goes down.

iii) Change in International Risk

Finally let's consider what a change in international risk might do to the required rate of return. If the change in international risk affects all firms because of, say, a large-scale war or serious disruption of the world's oil supply, risk aversion might change with the consequences discussed earlier. Likewise, if worldwide factors directly influence expected inflation, then again we would have consequences similar to those described before.

Although worldwide disruptions can and do occur, often the effects of changes in international risk will be felt by a particular firm or group of firms instead of firms in general. So the firm's nondiversifiable risk as measured by beta will change, and the required rate of return will increase or decrease accordingly. The consideration of international risk can be handled with the ideas just developed for analysing the impact of other kinds of risk on a stock's required rate of return.

IMPACT OF CHANGE IN RISK ON THE VALUE OF THE FIRM

Now that we understand how risk affects the returns required by investors, there is one final step required to tie all this together and relate it to the financial manager's objective of maximising shareholder wealth. That step is the following: *How does a change in the firm's riskiness, and hence the investor's required rate of return, affect the value of the firm?* Suppose a firm is expecting a constant rate of growth in dividends of 8 percent per year, the current cash dividend (at time $t = 0$) is ₹ 3, and the required rate of return demanded by investors is 16 percent. Employing the constant growth formula, the current market price of the equity is:

$$P_u = \frac{D_0(1+g)}{k_e - g} = \frac{₹\ 3.00\ (1+0.08)}{0.16\text{-}0.08} = \frac{₹\ 3.24}{0.08} = ₹\ 40.50$$

The current value in worth of the stock is ₹ 40.50 per share.

What happens if, because of changes in risk, the investors' required rate of return increases to 18 percent or decreases to 13 percent? With an increase in perceived risk resulting in a required return of 18 percent, the market value is:

$$P_0 = \frac{D_1}{k_e - g} = \frac{₹\ 3.24}{0.18 - 0.08} = \frac{₹\ 3.24}{0.10} = ₹\ 32.40$$

Likewise, a decrease in perceived risk resulting in a required rate of return of 13 percent results in a higher market value as follows:

$$P_0 = \frac{₹\ 3.24}{0.13\text{–}0.08} = \frac{₹\ 3.24}{0.05} = ₹\ 64.80$$

We see that, other things being equal, *increased risk lowers the market value of the firm's stock and reduced risk increases its value.* Risk has a major impact on the value of the firm. Financial managers must always be aware of the impact of their actions on the perceived riskiness of the firm's cash flows, as well as on their magnitude and timing. For this is how they can influence the market value of the firm. Only by focusing on these important variables—cash flows, timing, and risk—will the firm be in a position to achieve its goal of maximising the value of shareholder claims by maximizing P_0.

SIMILARITIES BETWEEN SECURITY VALUATION AND CAPITAL BUDGETING

Security valuation involves the same steps that are used in the appraisal of the potential capital budgeting project:

First, determining the price of equity or bond is similar to the finding the cost of the project to be financed.

Second, the security analyst estimates the future dividend or interest payment stream on an equity or bond, along with the equity's expected sale price or the bond's maturity value. This is similar to the estimates of the expected cash flows from the project, including the salvage value of the asset at the end of its expected life.

Third, the riskiness of the projected cash flow must be estimated. For this assessment, management needs information about the probability distribution of the cash flows. Then, given the project's riskiness management determines the cost of the capital at which the cash flows should be discounted. *Fourth,* the expected cash inflows are put on a present value basis to obtain an estimate of the asset's value to the firm. This is equivalent to finding the present value of equity's expected future dividends.

Finally, if an individual investor identifies and invests in a stock or bond whose market price is less than its time value, the value of the investor's portfolio will increase. Similarly, the present value of the expected cash inflows is compared with the required outlay, or cost; if the PV of the cash flows exceeds the cost, the project should be accepted. Otherwise, it should be rejected. Alternatively, the expected rate of return on the project can be calculated, and if the rate of return exceeds the project's cost of capital, the project is accepted. In the words, if a firm identifies (or creates) an investment opportunity with a present value greater than its cost, the value of the firm increase. Thus there is avery direct link between equity value and capital budgeting. Higher the price of the equity—the more effective are the firm's capital budgeting procedures.

ILLUSTRATIVE PROBLEMS

1. Rinky Synthetics has issued a ₹ 100 bond with 15 per cent interest. The bond is to mature in 7 years, and the going interest rate (required rate of return) is currently 14 per cent. If interest is paid semiannually, what would be the present value of bond.

Solution

Substituting the value io equation-1, we get

$$V_b = \sum_{t=1}^{14} \frac{₹\ 7.50}{(1+.07)^t} + \frac{₹\ 100}{(1+.07)^{14}}$$

Equivalently,

$$V_b = ₹\ 7.50 \begin{bmatrix} \text{Table value of} \\ \text{14 periods at} \\ \text{7 per cent} \end{bmatrix} + ₹\ 100 \begin{bmatrix} \text{Table value of} \\ \text{14 periods at} \\ \text{7 per cent} \end{bmatrix}$$

$$= 7.50\ (8.746) + ₹\ 100\ (.388) = ₹\ 65.60 + ₹\ 38.80 = ₹\ 104.40$$

Thus, the value (present value) of a bond paying ₹ 7.50 (15÷2) semiannually, and ₹ 100 at maturity (7 years), is ₹ 104.40, provided the investor's required rate of return is 14 per cent compounded semianually.

2. Hind Rayon's outstanding preference share, provide a ₹ 3.64 in annual dividends. The current yield for the preference share or equivalently, the required rate of return for the share holders, is 8.26 per cent. Calculate the value of the preference share.

Solution

Substituting the given values in the Equation-3 we get:

$$V_p = \frac{₹\ 3.64}{0.0826} = ₹\ 44.07$$

3. Suppose that Hind Chemicals sold an issue of bonds with a 10 year maturity, at ₹ 1,000 par value, a 12% coupon rate and annual interest payments.

(a) What would the market price of bonds be if the going rate of interest on bonds such as these fell to 8% two years after they were issued?

(b) What would the market price of bonds be if the going rate had risen to 14% two years after the initial offering?

Solution

(a) $$\text{Value} = \frac{120}{(1.08)} + \frac{120}{(1.08)^2} + \ldots + \frac{1{,}120}{(1.08)^8}$$

$$= (120 \times 5.7466) + (1000 + 0.5403)$$

$$= ₹\ 1{,}203$$

(b) $$\text{Value} = \frac{120}{(11.4)} + \frac{120}{(1.14)^2} + \ldots + \frac{1{,}120}{(1.14)^8}$$

$$= (120 \times 4.6389) + (1{,}000 \times 0.3506)$$

$$= ₹\ 907$$

4. Arvind Seth has invested in Gujarat Chemicals. The capitalisation rate of the company is 15 percent and the current dividend is ₹ 2.00 per share. Calculate the value of the company's equity share if the company is slowly sinking with an annual decline rate of 5% in the dividend.

Solution

The value of the firm stock is:

$$V_e = \frac{D_1}{k_e - g}$$

$$= \frac{₹\ 2\ (1-0.5)}{0.15 - (-0.05)} = \frac{₹\ 1.90}{0.20} = ₹\ 9.50$$

5. What would be the value of the equity share of Gujarat Chemicals of previous problem-4, if the company shows no growth but is able to maintain its devidend.

Solution

The value of the equity is

$$V_e = \frac{D_1}{k_e - g}$$

$$= \frac{₹\ 2{,}00\ (1 + 0)}{0.15 - 0.00} = \frac{₹\ 2.00}{0.15} = ₹\ 13.33$$

6. Repeat the Gujarat Chemicals problem-4 and assume that it grows at an average rate, which is taken to be an average annual increase in dividend of 7 percent. Compute the value of equity share.

Solution

The value of the equity share is:

$$V_e = \frac{D_1}{k_e - g}$$

$$= \frac{₹\ 2.00\ (1 + 0.07)}{0.15 - 0.07} = \frac{₹\ 2.14}{.08} = ₹\ 26.75$$

7. Ordinary share of R.K. Cotton has been valued by an investor to be worth ₹ 83. If the expected dividend at the conclusion of this year is ₹ 3.32 and dividends and earnings are growing at 20% annual rate, find out the investor's required rate of return.

Solution

The investor's required rate of return would be:

$$k_e = \frac{₹\ 3.32}{₹\ 83} + 20\% = 24 \text{ percent}$$

8. Van Products currently pays a dividend of ₹ 2.00 per share and this dividend is expected to grow at a 15% annual rate for 3 years, then at a 12% rate for the next three years, after it is expected to grow at a 5 per cent rate forever.

(a) What value would you place on the equity if 9% rate of return were required?

(b) Would your calculation change if you expect to hold the equity only 3 years?

Solution

End of Year		*Dividend*		*Dividends*		*Present Value of 9 percent*
1	₹	2.00 (1.15) =	₹	2.30 × 0.9174	=	₹ 2.11
2		2.00 $(1.15)^2$ =		2.64 × 0.8417	=	2.22
3		2.00 $(1.15)^3$ =		3.04 × 0.7722	=	2.35
4		3.04 (1.12) =		3.40 × 0.7084	=	2.41
5		3.04 $(1.12)^2$ =		3.81 × 0.6499	=	2.48
6		3.04 $(1.12)^3$ =		4.27 × 0.5963	=	2.55
					Total	₹ 14.12

Year 7 dividend = ₹ 4.27 (1.05) = ₹ 4.48

Market Value at end of year 6

$$= \frac{4.25}{₹ 11} = ₹ 112$$

Present Value of ₹ 112 with 9% discount rate

= 112 × 0.5963 = ₹ 66.78

Valuation = ₹ 14.12 + ₹ 66.78 = ₹ 80.90

(b) Present Value of Market Value at end of year 3

= ₹ 2.41 + ₹ 2.48 +₹ 2.55 + ₹ 66.78 = ₹ 74.22

Present Value of expected dividend to be received at end of year 1, 2 and 3

= ₹ 2.11 + ₹ 2.22 + ₹ 2.35 = ₹ 6.68

Total Value = ₹ 74.22 + ₹ 6.68 = ₹ 80.90.

Thus, the value is the same for an investor with a 3 year time horizon.

9. The average equity β value for a group of similar companies in the motor industry is 1.32; their average debt to equity ratio is 0.20. The debt-to-equity ratio of Sindhi Motors is 0.30 while the risk-free rate of return is currently 12%. The market risk premium can be assumed to be 9%.

(a) What is the required return on the assets of Sindhi Motors?

(b) What is the required return on the equity of Sindhi Motors?

Solution

(a) Ungear industry group equity bate

$$\beta_A = 1.32\left(\frac{10}{2}\right) = 1.1$$

$$R_A = 12 + 1.1\ (9) = 21.9\%$$

(b) $$\beta_E = 1.1\left(\frac{13}{10}\right) = 1.43$$

$$R_E = 12 + 1.43\ (9) = 24.84$$

10. As an investor in an equilibrium market containing many different assets you currently have 50% of your wealth in a risk-free asset and 50% in the four assets below:

Asset	*Expected return*	*b asset*	*Invested in asset*
A	7.6%	0.2	10%
B	12.4%	0.8	10%
C	15.6%	1.2	10%
D	18.8%	1.6	20%

(a) Calculate the current β and expected return of your portfolio.

(b) Assume that you want an expected return of 12% and intend to obtain it by selling some of the risk-free asset and using the proceeds to buy the market portfolio. Calculate the set of weights in the revised portfolio.

(c) If you hold only the risk-free asset and the market portfolio, what set of weights would give you an expected return of 12%.

Solution

(a) Current beta $= 0.1\,(0.2) + 0.1\,(0.8) + 0.1\,(1.2) + 0.2\,(1.6) + 0.5\,(0)$

$= 0.54$

Expected return $= 0.1\,(7.6) + 0.1\,(12.4) + 0.1\,(15.6) + 0.2\,(18.8) + 0.5\,(6)$

$= 10.32.$

(b) $12 = 0.1\,(7.6) + 0.1\,(12.4) + 0.1\,(15.6) + 0.2\,(18.8) + x\,(6) + (0.5 - x)\,14$

$x = 0.21$, i.e. 21% in rate free asset, 29% in market portfolio.

(c) $12 = x\,(6) + (1 - x)\,14$

$x = 0.25\%$, i.e. 25% in risk-free asset, 75% in market portfolio.

11. The total market value of the equity of Vishnu Electronics is ₹ 6 crore and the total value of its debt is ₹ 4 crore. The beta value of the equity is estimated to be 1.5 and the expected market risk premium is 10%. The risk-free rate of interest is 8%. (a) What is the required return on the Vishnu equity? (b) What is the beta of the company's existing portfolio of assets? (c) Estimate the company's cost of capital. (d) Estimate the discount rate for an expansion of the company's present business. (e) Suppose that the company replaces ₹ 3 crore debt with equity. Does the beta of the equity change? (f) What should the company cost of capital be now? (g) If the company wishes to diversify into another industry with a beta value of 1.2, what would be the required rate of return?

Solution

(a) $R_E = 8 + 1.5\,(10) = 23\%$

(b) $\beta_A = 1.5\left(\frac{6}{10}\right) = 0.9$

(c) $R_A = 8 + 0.9\,(10) = 17\%$

(d) 17%

(e) Yes,

$$\beta_E = 0.9\left(\frac{10}{9}\right) = 1$$

(f) 17%

(g) $R = 8 + 1.2\,(10) = 20\%$

12. Two particular assets A and B are known to lie on the security market line (SML). A, which has a beta of 0.5, carries a risk premium of 4%. B has an expected return of 20% along with a beta of 1.75. In the light of this information, determine whether the securities below are overpriced or underpriced:

Security	*Expected return*	*Beta*
1	20	2.00
2	14	0.75
3	15	1.25
4	5	–0.25
5	31	3.25

Solution

If A with a beta of 0.5 has a risk premium of 4%, the B will have a risk premium of $1.75 \times \frac{4}{0.5}$ = 14%, as the expected return of B is 20% the risk-free rate must be 6% and the expected market return 14%.

The return required for betas given are:

Security	*Beta*	*Return*	
1	2.00	22	Overpriced
2	0.75	12	Underpriced
3	1.25	16	Overpriced
4	–0.25	4	Underpriced
5	3.25	32	Overpriced

13. A firm is considering the following projects and the expected returns calculated by way of IRRs are as follows:

Project	*Beta*	*Expected return*
A	0.5	12%
B	0.8	13%
C	1.2	18%
D	1.6	19%

(a) Which projects have a higher expected return than the firm's current 15% single cost of capital?
(b) Which projects should be accepted?
(c) Which projects could be accepted or rejected incorrectly on the basis of the cost of capital as hurdle rate?

You may assume that the risk-free rate is 8% and the market risk premium is 7%.

Solution

(a) C and D
(b) Project required returns should be calculated using CAPM

$R_A = 8 + 0.5\ (7) = 11.5\%$

$R_B = 13.6\%$

$R_C = 16.4\%$

$R_D = 19.2\%$

Therefore A and C should be accepted, Band D rejected.

(c) Using cost of capital A would be wrongly rejected, while D would be incorrectly accepted.

14. Determine the required return on equity for the following project situations, using the capital asset pricing model.

Situation	*Expected Return Market Portfolio*	*Risk-Free Rate*	*Beta*
1	15%	10%	1.00
2	18	14	.70
3	15	8	1.20
4	17	11	.80
5	16	10	1.90

What generalisations can you make?

Solution

Situation	*Equation*	*Required Return*
1	10% + (15% – 10%) 1.00	15.0%
2	14% + (18% – 14%) .70	16.8
3	8% + (15% – 8%) 1.20	16.4
4	11% + (17% – 11%) .80	15.8
5	10% + (16% – 10%) 1.90	21.4

The greater the risk-free rate, the greater the expected return on the market portfolio and the greater the beta, the greater will be the required return on equity, all other things being the same. In addition, the greater the market risk premium the greater the required return, all other things being the same.

15. Nav Jyot Company presently pays a dividend of ₹ 1. This dividend is expected to grow at a 20 per cent rate for 5 years and at 10 per cent per annum thereafter. The present market price per share is ₹ 20. Using a dividend discount model approach to estimating capital capital costs, what is the company's expected, or required, return on equity?

Solution

Through trial and error, one ends up using 18 per cent and 19 per cent as discount rates.

End of Year	*Dividend per Share*	*Present Value of 18%*	*Present Value at 19%*
1	₹ 1.20	₹ 1.02	₹ 1.01
2	1.44	1.03	1.02
3	1.73	1.05	1.03
4	2.07	1.07	1.03
5	2.49	1.09	1.04
	Present value, 1 - 5 years =	₹ 5.26	₹ 5.13

Year 6 dividend = ₹ 2.49(1.10) = ₹ 2.74

Market prices at the end of year 5 using a perpetual growth dividend valuation model :

$$P_5 = \frac{₹\ 2.74}{.18 - .10} = ₹\ 34.25 \qquad P_5 = \frac{₹\ 2.74}{.19 - .10} = ₹\ 30.44$$

Present value at time 0 for amounts received at end of year 5:

₹ 34.25 at 18% = ₹ 14.97 ₹ 30.44 at 19% = ₹ 12.76

	18%	19%
Present value of 1-5 years	₹ 5.26	₹ 5.13
Present value of 6-∞ years	14.97	12.76
Present value of all dividends	₹ 20.23	₹ 17.89

Therefore, the discount rate is closer to 18 per cent than it is to 19 per cent. interpolating

$$k_e = 18\% + \frac{.23}{20.23 - 17.89} = 18.10\%$$

and this is the estimated return on equity that the market requires.

QUESTIONS

1. Models of security valuation include what elements in addition to the price of time?
2. According to basic valuation theory, what general factors determine security value? Described the basic valuation equation and explain the role return and risk play in this model.
3. Bond prices vary inversely with the required returns on similar risk bonds, leading to bond discounts or bond premiums. Explain how this process works. Why do required returns often differ from bond coupon rates? What effect does the amount of time to maturity have on the size of bond discounts and/or premiums? Explain.
4. Why might a speculator wish to follow a strategy of buying bonds with low coupon when market interest rates are high selling them later when market rates are low?
5. Discuss the relationship between market interest rates and the market price of bonds, why is'not the effect of interest rate changes the same on all bonds?
6. Explain why the required rate of return on equity for a firm is greater than the required rate of return on perference share and bond.
7. The dividend valuation model is a verstile valuation tool. Discuss how it can be adapted to handle no growth situation. constant growth situations, changing growth situation, and negative growth situations.
8. Explain how risk, the required rate of return, and a firm's equity price are related.
9. (a) Describe the CAPM and explain how it may assist in the determination of the discount rate used in the appraisal of capital projects.
   (b) Discuss the major difficulties inherent in its practical application and use.

PROBLEMS

1. Bharat Engineering has some 15 years ₹ 1,000 par bonds which have a coupon interest rate of 9 per cent and pay interest annually. What is the yield to maturity on the bonds if their current market price is:

(a) ₹ 1,181.72; (b) ₹ 795.99; (c) Would you be willing to pay ₹ 795.99 if your minimum required rate of return was 11 per cent? Why or Why not?

Ans.: (a) 7%; (b) 12%; (c) Yes, because the actual return is 12 % which is higher than 11% of required return.

2. What is the current market price of a ₹ 1,000 par 12 per cent coupon-rate bond if interest is paid *(a)* annually, or *(b)* semi-annually, there are 10 years to maturity, and the required rate of return is: (a) 8 per cent; (b) 12 per cent; (c) 14 per cent.

Ans.: (a) ₹ 1,268.20; (b) ₹ 1,000,000; (c) ₹ 895.20

3. Ashoka Enterprises is thinking of issuing a new preference share with a dividend of ₹ 5 per share. Price this issue for Ashoka if the merchant bankers feel it will require a 12 per cent return ; a 10 per cent return; a 14 per cent return. What is the cost of the issue to Ashoka if the issue nets ₹ 40 per share?

Ans.: ₹ 41.67; ₹ 50.00; ₹ 35.71; 12.50%

4. What will be the rate of return on a perpetual bond with a ₹ 1,000 par value, an 8 per cent coupon rate, and a current market price of (a) ₹ 6,000, (b) 8,000, (c) 1,000, and (d) ₹ 1,400? Assume interest is paid annually.

Ans.: (a) 13.3%; (b) 10%; (c) 8%; (d) 5.7%

5. The bonds of the Kindell Corporation are perpetuities with a 10 per cent coupon. Bonds of this type currently yield 8 per cent, and their par value is ₹ 1,000. Assume interest is paid annually. (a) What is the price of the Kindell bonds? (b) Suppose interest rate levels rise to the point where such bonds now yield 12 per cent. What would be the price of the Kindell bonds? (c) At what price would the Kindell bonds self if the yield on these bonds were 10 per cent? (d) How would your answers to Parts a, b, and c change if the bonds were not perpetuities but had a maturity of 20 years?

Ans.: (a) ₹ 1250; (b) ₹ 833.33; (d) At 8%, v = ₹ 1,196.31

6. Suppose RZY Motor Company sold an issue of bonds with a 10-year maturity, a ₹ 1,000 par value, a 10 per cent coupon rate, and semiannual interest payments. (a) Two years after the bonds were issued, the going rate of interest on bonds such as these fell to 6 per cent. At what price would the bonds sell? (b) Suppose that, 2 years after the initial offering, the going interest rate had risen to 12 per cent. At what price would the bonds sell? (c) Suppose that the conditions in Part a existed—that is, interest rates fell to 6 per cent 2 years after the issue date. Suppose further that the interest rate remained at 6 per cent for the next 8 years. What would happen to the price of the RZY Motor Company bond over time?

Ans.: (a) ₹ 1,251.26; (b) ₹ 898.90

7. Gupta Company's bonds have 4 years remaining to maturity. Interest is paid annually; the bonds have a ₹ 1,000 par value; and the coupon interest rate is 9 per cent. (a) What is the yield to maturity at a current market price of (1) ₹ 829 or (2) ₹ 1,104? (b) Would you pay ₹ 829 for one of these bonds if you thought that the appropriate rate of interest was 12 per cent — that is, if k_d = 12%? Explain your answer.

Ans.: (a) YTM at ₹ 825 = 15%

9. Compute the price of a 12% coupn bond with a maturity of 10 years if current interest rates are 8 per cent. Assume that the bond's face value is ₹ 1000 and use annual paymnts and compounding.

Ans.: ₹ 1268.40.

9. Assume that as investment manager of Punjab Electric Company's investment plan (which is exempt from income taxes), you must choose between National bonds and Sony Group preferred stock. The bonds have a ₹ 1,000 par value, they mature in 20 years, they pay ₹ 40 each 6 months, they are callable at National's option at a price of ₹ 1,080 after 5 years (ten 6-month periods), and they sell at a price of ₹ 897.40 per bond. The preferred stock is a perpetuity; it pays a dividend of Rs 2 each quarter, and it sells for ₹ 95 per share. What is the most likely effective annual rate of return (EAR) on the higher-yielding security?

Ans.: National Bond = 9.33%

10. A company has a loan of Rs, 50 crore due to mature in four years time. The company wishes to put aside equal amounts of money each year to enable it to meet the liability when it should fall due. Interest rates are 6% per annum. Say how much money should be set aside at the end of each of the next four years to be able to discharge the debt.

Ans.: ₹ 11,430

11. Lloyd Corporation's 14 per cent coupon rate, semiannual payment, ₹ 1,000 par value bonds which mature in 30 years, are callable 5 years from now at a price of ₹ 1,050. The bonds sell at a price of ₹ 1,353.54, and the yield curve is flat. Assuming that interest rates in the economic are expected to remain at their current level, what is the best estimate of Lloyd's nominal interest rate on new bonds?

Ans.: P_o = ₹ 19.89

12. The Grand Company has two bond issue outstanding. Both bonds pay ₹ 100 annual interest plus ₹ 1,000 at maturity. Bond L has a maturity of 15 years and Bond S a maturity of 1 year. (a) What will be the value of each of these bonds when the going rate of interest is (1) 5 per cent, (2) 8 per cent, and (3) 12 per cent? Assume that there is only one more interest payment to be made on Bond S. (b) Why does the longer-term (15-year) bond fluctuate more when interest rates change than does the shorter-term bond (1-year)?

Ans.: (a) V_L at 5 per cent = ₹ 1,518.97; V_L at 8 per cent = ₹ 1,171.15; V_L at 12 per cent = ₹ 863.79.

13. Madhav International has estimated the following growth pattern: for the first 5 years, Madhav is expected to grow at 30 percent; during the next 5 years Madhav expects a zero growth rate; there after the growth rate is expected to be 10 percent. Madhav currently has a dividend of ₹ 5 per share and shareholders require a 16 percent rate of return. Determine Madhav's share price.

Ans.: ₹ 141.76

14. Punjab Auto has led dividends growth from ₹ 2 to ₹ 5 over the last 5 years. This growth is expected to continut well into the foreseeable future. If the current market price is ₹ 38 per share, what expected rate of return do investors expect to receive from buying Punjab Auto shares?

Ans.: ₹ 35.79%

15. An ordinary share currently pays case dividends of ₹ 4.00 per share (D_0 = ₹ 4.00), and the required rate of return is 12 percent. What is it market value if: (a) There is no future growth in dividends. (b) Dividends growth at 8 percent per year to infinity. (c) D_1 is ₹ 4.20, D_2 is ₹ 4.50, and there is no growth expected after D_2. (d) Growth will be 10 percent for each of two years (for $t = 1$ and $t = 2$), after which the growth will be 5 per cent per year until infinity.

Ans.: (a) ₹ 33.33; (b) ₹ 108.00; (c) ₹ 37.24; (d) ₹ 65.65

16. What price would you pay for National Cables Ltd. share if it pays ₹ 3.50 per share and is forecasted to growth at 12% per year? You require a rate of return 22 percent.

Ans.: ₹ 39.20

17. You buy a share of Handa Enterprise for ₹ 21.40. You expect it to pay dividends of ₹ 1.07, ₹ 1.1449, and ₹ 1.2250 in Years 1, 2, and 3, respectively, and you expect to sell it at a price of ₹ 26.22 at the end of 3 years. (a) Calculate the growth rate in dividends. (b) Calculate the expected dividend yield. (c) Assuming that the calculated growth rate is expected to continue, you can add the dividend yield to the expected growth rate to get the expected total rate of return. What is this stock's expected total rate of return?

Ans.: (a) 7%; (b) 5%; (c) 12%

PART - III

CAPITAL BUDGETING DECISIONS

This Page has been intentionally left blank

9

CAPITAL BUDGETING DECISIONS AND CASH FLOW PRINCIPLES

INTRODUCTION

The field of capital budgeting is both comprehensive and challenging. It clearly plays a vital role in assisting most business firms to achieve there various goals (e.g., profitability, growth, stability, risk reduction, social goals, etc.). It has been closely allied to the economic problem; which is rather broadly defined as the allocation of scarce resources among competing alternatives. Since virtually no unlimited resources situations exist, the firm is placed in the same position as is the aggregate economy—resources must be allocated among the best alternatives. The allocation of funds is, therefore, an important function of financial management as it involves the commitment of funds to assets and activities. Analysis of capital expenditures is predicated on knowledge of the cash outflows needed to acquire assets and the cash inflows that are expected to result from their use. It is the purpose of this chapter to indicate how these cash flows may be determined, based on sales and cost estimates combined with the relevant tax implications of the transactions.

MEANING OF CAPITAL BUDGETING

Capital budgeting may be defined as the planning, evaluation, and selection of capital expenditure proposals. As distinguished from operating expenditures, whose chief benefits are recognised within a period of one year, capital expenditures represent outlay whose principal benefits will be recognised over longer periods of time. Much emphasis has been placed on the proper analysis and evaluation of capital expenditures, because they typically require large cash outlays. Decisions relating to capital expenditures as opposed to those for operating expenditures, are generally irreversible, and they require careful selection techniques and procedures.

Capital budgeting is commonly referred to as fixed -asset management, when integrated with the financial manager's goal of attaining proper combinations of assets (i.e., optimal asset mix), fixed assets assume a great deal of significance. Fixed assets are also frequently termed as the 'earning assets' of the firm since they usually generate large returns. Such returns are contrary to the limited earning power of and returns from short term assets. Management's philosophy may be ascertained to some extent by the relative proportions of fixed assets that are held in the total asset mix. Generally the more fixed assets maintained by a firm the more aggressive is its managerial philosophy and larger the inherent risk.

Since assets are the sources of revenue generation for the firm and fixed assets its principal source, it appears logical that future sales growth is heavily correlated with the expansion of capital expenditure. With increased sales from closely scrutinised capital expenditure selections, the long-range impact on the firm's earnings and dividends theoretically should be referred by a strong performance in the market value of the firm's equity share price. It should be noted, however, that capital budgeting is indeed a specialised process, which very frequently requires highly sophisticated techniques, and rather intricate forecasting for future years. Inaccuracy in the selection of such projects will ultimately decrease the profits, dividends, and share price value of the firm.

SIGNIFICANCE OF CAPITAL BUDGETING

Capital budgeting decisions deserve to be treated in a different manner as there are conceptual problems involved which necessarily makes the decision process more complex, while this makes things more difficult for the decision process maker, it also makes the problem more challenging. There are several practical reasons for placing greater emphasis on capitat expenditure decisions. These are:

Long Time Period: The consequence of capital expenditure extends into the future, and will have to be endured for a longer period than the consequences of current operating expenditures. The decision maker is bound by the decision whether it is good or bad. He has committed the funds of firm and is at the mercy of future developments. To illustrate, in the case of manufacturing firm, capital expenditure decisions are going to determine what plants will be built, where they will be built and how they will be equipped. These factors in turn largely determine what can be made in the plants. Such decisions shape the basic character of the firm, or its "image" and as such may be very important.

Substantial Expenditures: The fact that capital expenditures usually involve large sums of money necessitates a careful job of planning and evaluation. This fact is just as important as the first one, if a firm buys expensive capital assets, the decision to do so had better be a good one. Otherwise, the firm will suffer financially in time to come in two ways: the funds of the firm may have been exhausted and the return from the expenditure will not be rewarding.

Irreversibility: Capital expenditures decisions are quite often irreversible, because there is little or no second hand market for many types of capital goods. The only alternative to continuing to use the asset is to scrap it, recognise the loss, and start a new. Because of these two features, capital expenditures effectively commit the firm to a given technology, and significantly determine the future pattern of operating expenditures.

Over and Undercapacity: To improve the timing and quality of asset acquisition, the capital expenditure decisions must be carefully drawn. An erroneous forecast of asset requirements can result in serious consequences. If the firm has invested too much in assets, it will incur unecessarily heavy expenses. If it has not spent enough on fixed assets, two serious problems may arise. *First,*the firm's equipment may not sufficiently be modern to enable it to produce competitively. *Secondly,* if it has inadequate capacity, it may lose a position of its share of market to rival firms. To regain lost customers typically requires heavy selling expenses, price reduction, product improvements, and so forth.

DIFFICULTIES

There are three basic reasons why capital expenditure decisions pose difficulties for the decision maker. These are:

Uncertainty: The future business success is today's investment decision. The hope for benefits will be derived in the future. The future in the real world is never known with certainty, though it may be convenient for the economic theorists to assume for some purposes that is.

Difficult to Measure in Quantitative Terms: Even if benefits are certain, some might be exceedingly difficult to measure in quantitative terms. This is a problem of particular importance in the case of decisions made by many government agencies.

Time Element: Another problem is to phase properly the availability of capital assets in order to have them come "on stream" at the correct time. Due to intermittant spurts in the demand, a firm may plan to add capacity. By the time additional capacity to be ready, the company may find there is no demand for its increase output other firms had already expanded their operations and had taken on increased share of the market, with the result that demand for this firm had levelled off. In addition, benefits received and costs incurred at different points in time are not comparable because of the time value of money.

CAPITAL BUDGETING DECISION PROCESS

Capital budgeting is the process of selecting capital investments. Capital investment can be physical, financial, or intangible. **Physical assets** such as factories and machinery are familiar capital investments, but computers, airplanes, and highways are also physical assets that qualify as capital investments. *A* **financial asset** is a claim against some other party for monetary payment; examples include savings accounts, bonds, and stock. Financial assets generally have value because money was used to acquire some other asset that will provide cash flows. **Intangible investments** are not physical in nature and do not serve as claims for payment by some other party but are expected to result in future benefits. Examples of intangible assets include a training programme for marketing representatives, a membership drive for a symphony orchestra, and a franchise. The buildings are tangible assets, while the goodwill resulting from the purchases is an intangible investment because the purchases are expected to result in future benefits, even though they do not result directly in an identifiable asset.

The decision process is similar for all capital investments regardless of how those investments are classified. Because capital investments are so important to the success of the organization, most companies have formal policies guiding the decision process. Figure-1 illustrates the typical capital investment process, and a discussion of each step in that process follows.

FIGURE -1

FLOW CHART OF THE CAPITAL BUDGETING PROCESS

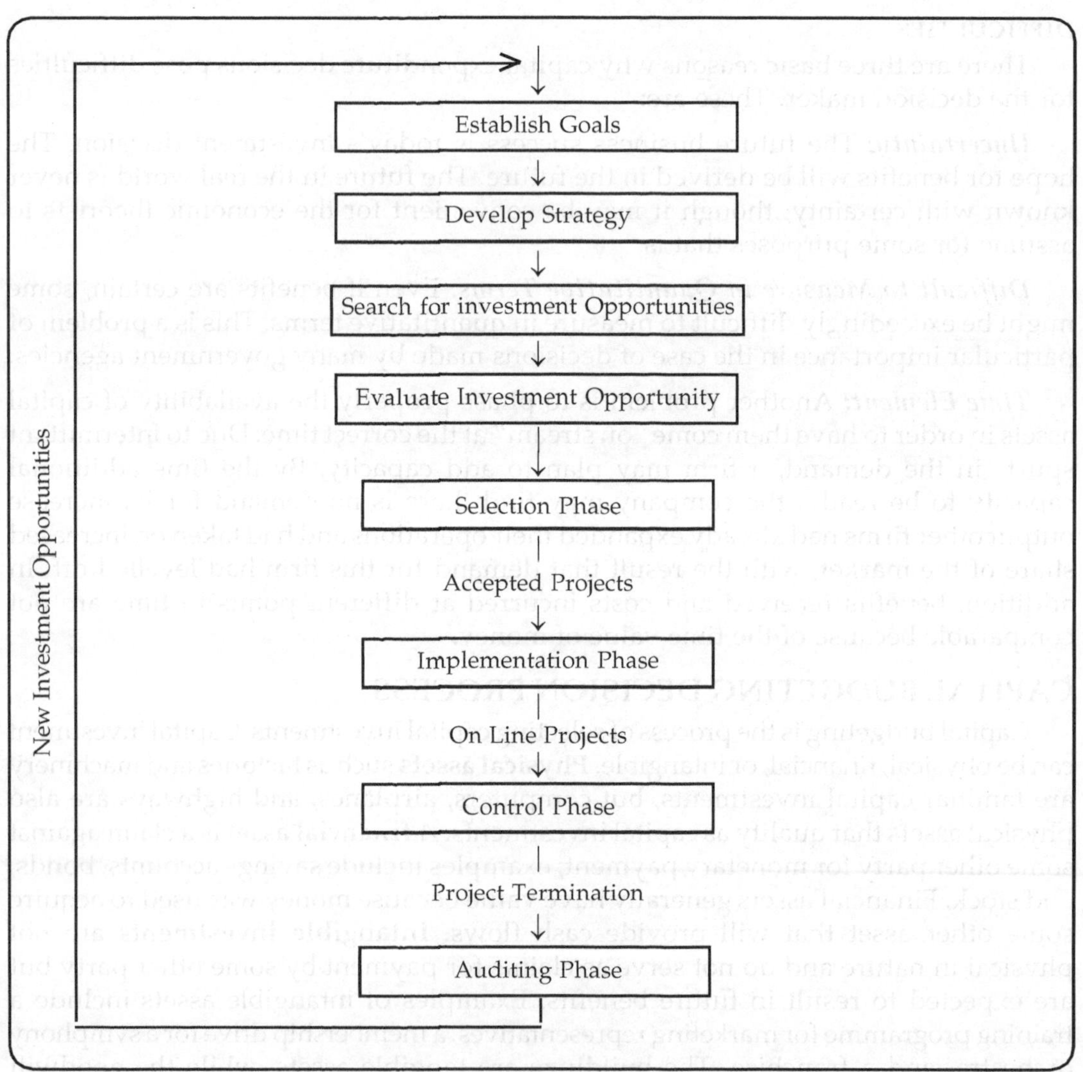

Establish Goals

Wealth creation is generally the overall goal, but wealth creation is abstract. It is difficult to know if shareholder wealth was maximized, for example, because we do not know what share price would have been if we had taken other courses of action. Therefore companies often translate the wealth goal into more concrete goals against which performance can be measured. For example the companies may identify four standards by which progress would be measured: rate of return, size of government contracts, response by financial markets, and ranking among most admired corporations. Ideally, these are the *attainable* goals that companies believe will increase wealth the most. There may also be nonmonetary goals such as reduction of injuries, improved reading ability, or cleaner water. Monetary goals are dominant for businesses, while governmental and nonprofit organizations often focus on nonmonetary goals.

Develop Strategy

Strategy sets the general direction of the organization and provides the frame work within which capital investment opportunities are sought. The goal and strategy of the corporation are typically combined in the vision. The job of the CEO is to "develop a vision" and then oversee a change in the set of shared values and beliefs that make up the organization's culture in order to accomplish it. The job of the boss is also to accumulate and allocate resources in support of that vision. Goals and strategy therefore set the framework for leading people, accumulating resources, and allocating resources.

The major focus of strategy is the generation of wealth through creation and use of competitive advantage. Strategic assessment often begins with an analysis of **opportunities** and **threats** in the environment, followed by an analysis of the company's **strengths** and **weaknesses.** From this analysis, general directions for development are chosen.

Strategy is the foundation of a successful capital budgeting system. Strategy is the framework in which resources are marshaled in pursuit of goals. Strategy also tells members of the organization where to search for profitable capital in. vestments. Successful capital budgeting and wealth maximization are therefore dependent on sound strategy. Likewise, sound strategic planning will not lead to wealth creation unless strategy is implemented with the goal of maximizing wealth. Thus, sound strategic planning, sound capital budgeting, and sound financing plans are essential.

Each strategic decision is in itself a general capital budgeting decision, in that it is based on estimates of wealth creation and other contributions to company goals that can be expected from later capital investments in pursuit of a particular strategy. Goal setting and strategy choice are interactive processes, because goals are often readjusted in response to information about feasibility gained in the strategic assessment process.

Search for Investment Opportunities

The identification of potential capital investments is a critical stage in the capital budgeting process. The remainder of the process can only assure that the best of the proposed investments are selected. Fortunately, companies that want to be successful in identifying capital investment opportunities can organize them. selves for success. The first part of that organization is development of realistic goals, sound strategy, and appropriate rewards for successful managers. Then, specific attention must be devoted to the search process.

A corporate culture that encourages creativity must support the search for in. vestment opportunities; otherwise, there will be no good proposals to evaluate. A successful search process generally requires the commitment of resources. Research, product development, and consumer attitude surveys are all ways to identify investment opportunities. If the strategy involves acquisition of other companies, an acquisition group may be responsible for searching out and evaluating opportunities. These various approaches have in common the willingness to spend money on people to search for attractive capital investments.

Training in support of strategy is another example of organization for a successful search. Executives are increasingly realizing that training of employees is not a sideline activity for good years but an important part of strategy implementation. Managers at all levels must be aware of company goals and strategy if they are to search out the right types of capital investment opportunities. In addition, managers at all levels must have some skill in capital budgeting so that they can perform at least preliminary analysis of potential investments.

A successful search for investment opportunities will be carried out at all levels of the organization. Major capital investments that involve a *change in strategy* will probably be identified at a top management level. **Major investments in support of existing strategy** will typically *be* developed at a high level, such as the senior executive in charge of marketing or production. **Smaller investments** are identified and given preliminary screening by the per. son in a position to perceive a need. Examples include thousands of decisions by industrial engineers to replace or modernize specific pieces of equipment, by supervisors to send employees to training programs, by marketing managers to run advertisements, and so on. Although these investments are smaller in scale, they are vitally important due to their cumulative effect. Because people are involved at all levels, efforts to encourage the search for attractive investments must reach people at all levels of the organization.

Evaluate Investment Opportunities

The ideal corporate culture will result in numerous capital investment proposals, each of which must be evaluated. The fundamental question is whether the present value of the cash benefits or savings to be generated by an investment exceed the present value of the outlays. Identifying these outlays and benefits is by no means a trivial exercise. In fact, project definition and cash flow estimation as the most difficult stage of the evaluation process and generally that estimates are systematically biased. Cash flow estimation requires sales forecasts, cost forecasts, engineering analyses, inflation estimates, tax estimates, and so on. Deciding which cash flows will be affected by a particular investment is a major challenge.

SELECTION PHASE

The firm may now apply more formal selection criteria to the surviving projects. Taking account of the returns and risks of individual projects as well as the cost of capital for the firm, the firm will choose among projects so as to maximise shareholder wealth with its chosen criterion of selection. Projects not expected to meet this criterion are rejected,while accepted projects enter the implementation phase.

IMPLEMENTATION PHASE

When the final selection has been made, the firm must acquire the necessary funds, purchase the assets, and begin operating the projects to implement the decision to accept projects in the capital budget. This phase may concern financial managers relatively little if all prior phases in the capital budgeting process have been correctly performed. For the formal selection procedures should give adequate account of the cost and availability of capital for the firm—given the particular financing mix of debt and equity to be employed by the firm. However, it may be that necessary funds are not available at the specified cost. This contingency will mean that all projects must be re-evaluated at a higher cost of capital than initially used or that some way of selecting projects under a capital constraint will be used to determine the revised size of the capital budget. In either case, higher than expected costs of capital will lead to a shrinkage of the total capital budget, with the result either that fewer projects will be taken than originally planned or that projects will be scaled down in size.

CONTROL PHASE

Once the projects are implemented, the firm will attempt to manage them to insure that assets,labour, and material are efficiently employed. The control phase involves the comparison of actual and expected cash flows and the explanation of differences between actual and expected flows. The attempt to explain such differences will have implications for the firm's planning and evaluation procedures.

AUDITING PHASE

Audits are constructive in purpose. When a project terminates, or even before, the firm should perform an audit on the entire project to explain its success or failure. Like the control phase, the auditing phase may have implications for firm's planning and evaluation procedures. In addition, the audit may produce ideas for new improved proposals gains from operating now-terminated projects. This advantage of audits may be even more important for projects judged to be relative failures. Naturally, no firm should repeat mistakes if it is at all possible to avoid doing so.

Strategic considerations are often on an equal footing with cash flow analysis because investments that are not consistent with the corporation's strategy are not likely to create wealth.

Risk analysis is a standard part of the evaluation of most capital investments. We are estimating future events, and those estimates are almost always fraught with uncertainty. Total project risk is often analyzed by looking at the sources of uncertainty, then estimating the wealth effects of changes in those values. If sales levels are a key variable, for example, analysts may compute net present values using several different sales forecasts. Risk that cannot be diversified away is of particular importance and receives special attention. Results of changes in over.all economic conditions are hard to diversify away, while factors related to a particular project, such as technological life or shifting customer tastes, can be di. versified away when the company or its shareholders spread their money among a number of different projects. Managers must ultimately use this information to decide if the potential benefits are worth the risk.

Other considerations come into play as well. Companies often lack sufficient resources to acquire all attractive investments and must make choices. An investment might have good cash flow characteristics but seriously reduce reported income for several years. Conflicts between accounting income and wealth creation would not occur in a world of perfect information, but these conflicts are sometimes important to managers. An investment may look good in isolation but have disastrous public relations consequences. Because of these and other considerations, the evaluation process commonly includes review by finance, production, engineering, marketing, legal, and public relations departments, The information gained from the evaluation of scores of investment proposlals feeds back into strategy development. If an area of emphasis identified in strategic planning cannot provide attractive investments, it may be necessary to revise the strategy.

GUIDELINES FOR CAPITAL BUDGETING

Guidelines for capital budgeting results from the formulation and implementation of both long and short range plans. Some firms use both long and short range capital budgets. Others use only short range capital budgets, but very infrequently is a firm found that uses long range capital budgets alone. *The long range budget is planning tool; the short range budget is an allocation and rationing device.* The long range plans generally emanate from the firm's upper level of management—the board of directors and the executives of a large firm; and the short-range from the owners and managers of a small firm. Long range plans for capital expenditures result from a thorough analysis of the firm's objectives. Five major areas must be considered: (1) Need and objectives of the owners; (2) Size of the market in terms of existing and proposed product lines and anticipated growth of market share; (3) Size of existing plants and plans for new plant sites and plant expansion; and, (4) Economic conditions which may affect the firm's operations. (5) Business and financial risk associated with the replacement of existing assets or the purchase of new assets.

The same basic areas must be considered in the development of government capital budgeting guidelines. The primary difference lies in the consideration of the group affected rather than of the business as well as the fact that most government agencies operate in a relatively uncompetitive atmosphere, their share of the market is irrelevant. However, market size is important. Business risk is also very important to government capital budgeting decisions since many government agencies actually are "in business."

Short-term plans for capital budgeting generally represent modifications of long range plans. Day-to-day conditions such as competitive activity, sale forecasts, wage rates, material costs, fuel shortages, and similar items provide input into the formulation of short range modification to long range plans. Changes in these factors in economic conditions may have drastic effects on capital budgeting decisions. Firms may be forced to modify long range plans or to restructure them to meet changing conditions.

The extent to which proposed projects cannot be postponed is critical importance. Generally, management will assign priorities to given projects and will plan to allocate funds accordingly. However, in the short-run, equipment failures, rapidly changing market position, rapid inflation, or power shortages can all result in the reordering of priorities.

In the formulation of both long and short range plans it is most important to focus on the key factor in all capital investments; the value of the proposed investment to the firm or government agency depends on the future earning and other cash inflows which will result. Earnings may be measured either in business term of *earnings per share* or in government terms of improved service or cost reduction. Other cash inflows include those which may result from depreciation and the like.

Estimates of the benefits must be made using the best available data pertaining to wage rates, market size and preferences, price levels, etc. Without accurate data, even the application of the most sophisticated capital budgeting techniques will result in poorly formulated plans. Further, benefits expected to result from an investment should be protected over its life since they may vary in amount from year to year.

METHODS OF CLASSIFYING INVESTMENTS

The most useful approach to project classification arranges investment alternatives according to the way benefits from the investment are affected by or affect other possible investments. In evaluating the investment proposals presented to management, it is important to be aware of the possible inter-relationships between pairs of investment proposals. A given investment proposal may be economically independent of, or dependent or, another investment proposal.

INDEPENDENT, DEPENDENT, AND MUTUALLY EXCLUSIVE INVESTMENTS

An independent investment is one that can technically be undertaken whether or not any other investment proposal is accepted and implemented. The benefits and costs of such an investment are not affected by the acceptance or rejection of other proposals. In other words, the investment stands alone and remains virtually unaffected by any concurrent or subsequent investment decision, except, of course, those subsequent investments specifically intended to alter the investment's operating characteristic (for example, investments made to increase efficiency or output or materially change the design of the product). Management must constantly be alert to ways of reducing costs or improving products, and such improvement in previous investments do not keep them from being classified as independent at the time they are first being analysed.

An investment proposal is said to be economically dependent if the cash flows associated for the first investment are affected by the decision to accept or reject the second investment, the first investment is said to be economically dependent on the second. The dependency relationship can be further classified. If a decision to undertake the second investment will increase the benefits expected from the first (or decrease the costs of undertaking the first without changing the benefits), the second investment is said to be *complement* of the first. If the decision to undertake the second investment will decrease the benefits expected from the first (or increase the costs of undertaking the first without changing the benefits), the second is said to be a *substitute* for the first. In the extreme case when the potential benefits to be derived from the first investment will completely disappear if the second investment is accepted, or when it is technically impossible to undertake the first when the second has been accepted, the two investments are said to be *mutually exclusive.* It is also possible to define an extreme case for investments that are complements. Suppose that the second investment is impossible (technologically) or would result in no benefits whatsoever if the first were not accepted. Then the first investment can be said to be a *prerequisite* of the second.

STATISTICAL DEPENDENCE

It is possible for two or more investments to be economically independent but statistically dependent. *Statistical dependence* is said to be present if the cash flows from two or more investments would be affected by some external event or happening whose occurrance is uncertain. For example, a firm could produce high-priced yachts and expensive cars. The investment decisions affecting these two product lines are economically independent. However, the fortunes of both activities are closed, associated with high business activity and a large amount of discretionary income for the rich people. This statistical dependence may affect the risk of investments in these product lines, because the swings of profitability of these two product lines will be wider than those of two product lines having less statistical dependence.

PROFIT (SERVICE) MAINTAINING AND PROFIT (SERVICE) ADDING INVESTMENT

Investments may fall into two basic categories, *profit-maintaining* and *profit-adding* when viewed from the perspective of a business, or *service-maintaining* and *service-adding* when viewed from the perspective of a government agency. The first type include replacement and improvement of existing facilities, while the latter includes new facilities that will increase output, improve product quality, or reduce production costs. Some fall into both categories. For example, the replacement of a worn-out printing press with a new machine having twice the hourly production capacity is both profit maintaining and profit adding. If the new machine had the same output as it predecessor, the investment would have been profit-maintaining. Within the public domain, the widening of a two-lane highway into four lanes is an investment that both maintains and adds service.

Since there is often an overlap in the profit or service maintaining and adding aspects of an investment, it is more convenient to view investments as either replacement or new. These two types are further discussed below:

REPLACEMENT INVESTMENTS

Several important factors should be considered when making a replacement decision. These factors represent an expansion of the underlying considerations in formulating long-range capital budgeting plans. The capital budgeting process is applicable not only to a single piece of equipment, but also to entire plants. As a plant ages, the primary question is not whether to replace individual machines but rather whether improved manufacturing processes and technological changes warrant designing a new plant. Figure-2 exhibits the various options for replacement decision. This basic "decision tree" for a relatively simple decision strongly suggests the need to think through the many alternatives usually surrounding a major capital outlay. It is crucial to select the appropriate alternatives for analysis and to structure the problem in such a way that the analytical tools are applied to the real issue to be decided.

FIGURE 2

OPTION FOR REPLACEMENT DECISION

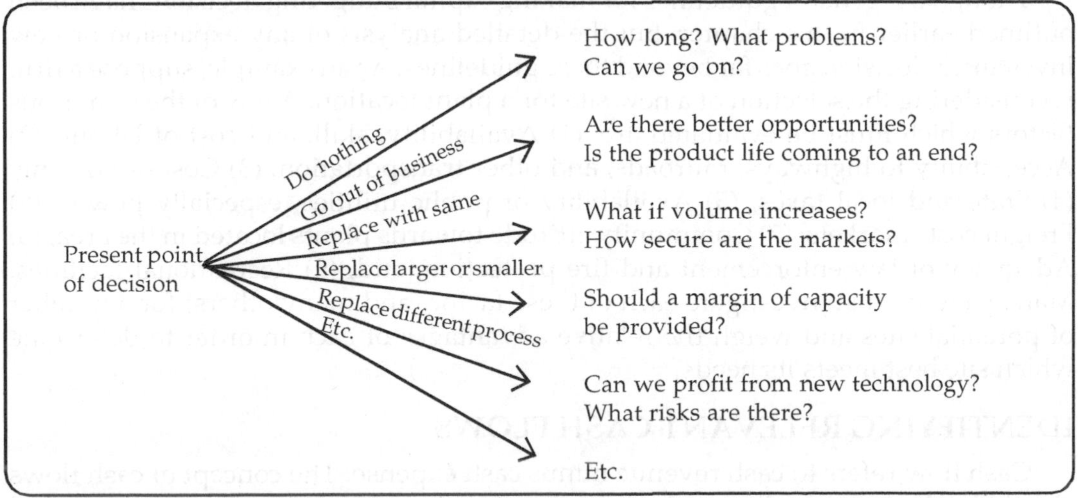

EXPANSION AND NEW PRODUCT INVESTMENT

Expansion and new business investments can generally be divided into four groups:

(1) *Expansion of current production to meet increased demand:* The expansion may lead to more complete utilisation of existing facilities, such as operating three shifts instead of two. Expansion could also involve expanding existing plant size or new site location and plant construction.

(2) *Expansion of production into fields closely related to current operations:* For example, a firm producing household furniture might expand into office furniture. This process is known as *horizontal integration.* Expansion also includes *vertical integration,* which is the purchase or development of supply and

distribution lines for products being manufactured. For example, a company which is currently using the services of a distributor to sell its products may decide to establish retail outlets and sell to the public directly.

(3) *Expansion of production into new fields not associated with the current operations:* Such expansion often comes about by a firm acquiring another business.

(4) *Research and development of new products.*

As a firm enters into areas in which it has had little experience, the capital budgeting decisions become increasingly more difficult and risky. For example, expansion of a current product line to meet existing demand involves little risk. Management has expertise in making the product and knows the demand. Moreover, undertaking basic research and development very risky. Although research may be directed in certain areas, there is no guarantee that the research will ever result in a profitable, marketable product. Since management generally wants to avoid risk, it requires increasingly higher returns from investments as their degree of risk increases.

Though the general guidelines for making capital budgeting decisions have been outlined earlier in this chapter, but the detailed analysis of any expansion or new investment decision goes far beyond these guidelines. As an example, suppose a firm is considering the selection of a new site for a plant location. A few of the numerous factors which must be evaluated are: (1) Availability, skill, and cost of labour; (2) Accessibility to highways, railroads, and other transportation; (3) Cost of housing; (4) State and local taxes; (5) Availability of public utilities, especially power; (6) Freight costs markets; (7) Community attitude towards plants located in the area; (8) Adequacy of law enforcement and fire protection; and, (9) Recreational facilities. Management must investigate each of these factor (and many others) for a number of potential sites and weigh the relative advantages of each in order to determine which site best meets its needs.

IDENTIFYING RELEVANT CASH FLOWS

Cash flow refers to cash revenue minus cash expense. The concept of cash flows should be distinguished from the concept of net income reported in the profit and loss statement. *Since depreciation and other non cash expenses are deducted in the computation of net income, the reported net income understates the cash flow by the amount of these deductions.* In addition, under conditions of uncertianty a distinction should be made between cash flows computed before debt and preference shares financing and those computed after such financing. However, *since the impact of taxation on different investments varies the cash flows associated with each investment should be compared when tax has been deducted, which ever definition of cash flows is employed.*

REASONS FOR USING CASH FLOWS

In evaluating investment projects, the reasons for using cash flows as opposed to using income statement type *earnings flow* which include cash flows such as depreciation, are listed below:

Firstly, the firm is really interested in estimating the economic value of a proposed investment project. This economic value is related to the economic outlays (costs) and inflows (benefits) associated with the project. Only cash flows describe the cash transactions that the firm will experience if the project is accepted. Th firm must pay for a purchased asset with cash, and this cash outlay represents a foregone opportunity to use the cash in other productive economic alternatives. Consequently, the firm should measure the future *net* benefits (revenues minus costs) in cash terms also. Now, if accounting practices were attuned to reporting cash transactions there should be no problem. But standard financial accounting practices are oriented well towards allocating investment costs across useful economic life than in ascribing costs at point of incurrence. Thus, when the firm makes a new investment, traditional accounting procedures spread out the initial investment by capitalising it over the life of the asset and then reducing future net benefits by subtracting an annual depreciation charge. But this accounting treatment does not reflect the original need for cash at the time of investment, nor does the accounting treatment reflect the actual size of the net cash inflows or outflows in later years. Only cash flows reflect the actual cash transactions associated with the project and since investment analysis is concerned with finding out whether future economic inflows sufficiently large to warrant the initial investment, only the cash flow method is appropriate for investment decision analysis.

Secondly, the use of cash flows avoids accounting ambiguities. There are many ways to value inventory, allocate costs, and choose a depreciation schedule to calculate net income, all of which are permissible under generally accepted accounting practices. Thus different net income numbers could be developed for the same project depending upon the accounting procedures followed. But there is only one set of cash flows associated with the project. The firm pays the initial investment and has a single stream of future cash flows. There are far fewer ambiguities in the cash flow stream. Thus more pregmatic reason reinforces the need to use cash flows rather than ambiguous net income flows (accounting approach).

Thirdly, the cash flow approach takes into account the time value of money. A sale on account is an economic event recorded by the accountant and affecting accounting income. But the firm has not yet received the cash, it cannot spend the cash, and the ultimate collection of the cash is uncertain. For purposes of investment analysis we are more interested in the moment when the cash is to be received. At that moment the firm reaches a new decision point. The cash may be return to the shareholders by the payment of a dividend. It may be used to retire debt, increase the working capital, or to acquire new long-lived assets. In other words, accounting data which are quite useful as performance measures often are less useful as decision criteria.

INCREMENTAL CASH FLOW

For any investment project generating either expanded revenues or cost savings for the firm, the appropriate cash flows used in evaluating the project must be incremental cash flow. Since the objective of financial management is to increase the wealth of the present owners, an investment is worthwhile if it enhances the market value of the company's currently outstanding equity. It follows that the attractiveness of any investment proposal should be evaluated in terms of its effect on the size and the quality of the firm's present and future net cash flows. Hence the first requirement in any investment appraisal is an accurate forecast of the incremental cash flows arising from the proposed investment.

In estimating the incremental cash flow from an investment the computation should follow the *"with and without"* principle rather than the *"before and after"* principle. The *"before and after"* method merely compares the present cash flow of the company with the expected cash flow after a certain investment has been made. However, the *"with and without"* principle strives to isolate the effect of the investment from other factors that may cause changes in the firm's cashflow, so it compares the expected cash flow without the investment with the expected cash flow if the investment is made. Thus, project should be evaluated on the basis of the effect specifically attributable to it. In some situations the increase in cash flow might occur in any case, so that the *"before and after"* method would overstate the benefits of the investment and in other situations the investment might have the effect of forestalling a decline, and so the *"before and after"* method would understate the benefits of the investment. The *"with and without"* principle requires that both possible effects be accounted for in the appraisal.

CASH FLOW ESTIMATES

For capital budgeting the estimates must be made of the effect on future cash flows of the various alternatives. Decisions as to what should be included are difficult enough in the context of the firm. It is here that the judgement of the analyst is critical, for once estimates are prepared, application of the decision criterion is almost routine. There are certain ingredients of cash flow streams. The basic principle to be applied in the analysis of these ingredients are outlined below:

TAX EFFECTS

Tax considerations of capital investment decisions are both very important and very complex. There are at least two ways to deal with tax effects in analysing investments. One is to put the cash flows in income statement format. Consider an investment of ₹ 1,00,000 that produces the cash flows shown in Table-1 in the first year. Cash inflow is ₹ 20,000. Cash outflows include ₹ 5,000 for expenses, ₹ 2,000 for taxes, and ₹ 500 for working capital. This gives a net cash inflow of ₹ 12,500.

Note that cash flow from operations, leaving out working capital, is ₹ 20,000 less ₹ 5,000 for expenses and ₹ 2,000 for taxes, or ₹ 13,000. We arrive at the same answer by taking profit after tax and adding back depreciation which is a non-cash charge. This ways we get ₹ 3,000 plus ₹ 10,000 or ₹ 13,000 for cash flow from operations, as before. Profit after taxes plus depreciation is a handy shortent way to get after-tax cash flow from operations, but it is important to understand why it gives the correct answer.

TABLE-1

	Year I
Sales	₹ 20,000*
Cash Expenses	–5,000
Depreciation	–10,000
Profits Before Taxes	₹ 5,000
Tax at 40 percent	–2,000
Profit After Taxes (PAT)	₹ 3,000
Increase in Working Capital	–500
Net cash Flow after Taxes	₹ 12,500

* Cash flow item.

A second method of dealing with taxes, and probably the most direct method after one becomes accustomed to it, is to convert each cash flow to its *after-tax equivalent*. Applying this method to the above example, we get another Table-2. Note that we get the same result as before. With respect to sales revenue, we receive ₹ 20,000 but taxes increase by ₹ 8,000, leaving ₹ 12,000 net after taxes. We pay ₹ 5,000 in expenses, but as a result, the tax bill declines by ₹ 2,000 for a net after tax expense of ₹ 3,500.

TABLE-2

	Pre-tax	*Tax Effect*	*After-tax Equivalent*
Sales	₹ 20,000	(1—0.40)	₹ 12,000
Cash Expenses	–5,000	(1—0.40)	–3,000
Depreciation tax shield	10,000	(0.40)	4,000
Working Capital	–500		–500
		Net cash flow after taxes	₹ 12,500

The depreciation charge of ₹ 10,000 provides a depreciation tax shield, that is, a reduction in taxes, of ₹ 4,000. The working capital increase has no effect on taxes. From the preceding examples, we derive the general rules in Table-3. In Table-3, T is the tax rate applicable to the cash flow in question. Remember that changes in items such as working capital do not affect taxes. Remember also that non-cash expenses reduces taxes, so the tax shields is an inflow, not an outflow.

TABLE-3

Type of Item	*Calculation*
For cash items: Sales, Cash Expenses, etc.	Pre-tax amount × (1–T) = After-tax equivalent
For non-cash items: depreciation, etc.	Pre-tax amount × T = Tax shield

It is important to keep in mind that tax effects may be quite different if the firm is losing money at the time and therefore paying no taxes. Tax laws permit carrying losses forward to be applied against future income. In such cases, tax consequences still may be very important, but the actual cash flows due to tax effects may take place in years other than the current one.

WORKING CAPITAL EFFECTS

An investment in plant assets will usually lead to funds being tied up in working capital. This will include the cash necessary to meet payroll and other bills, funds invested in raw materials, work-in-process and finished-goods inventory, and receivables from customers. The size of these items will depend on the exact nature of the capital investment, but all the previously mentioned funds requirements will usually accompany an investment in long-lived assets. The one possible exception would be an investment that would decrease the use for working capital by increasing efficiency. Examples of this nature are accounting machines that expedite the billing to customers or storage facilities and inventory-control devices that reduce the amount of inventory which must be kept on hand.

A working capital increase has the effect of increasing the investment outflow today. Ignoring this factor will lead toward the acceptance of investments that should be rejected. If the investment has a limited life and the working capital is expected to be recovered at the end of the life of the investment, the recovery of the working capital in the last period should be considered as cash proceeds and treated in the same manner as the other cash flows are treated. It should not be thought that ignoring the working capital investment and the recovery of working capital will balance each other out. The factor that must be considered is the required return on the working capital during the period of use.

TIME HORIZON EFFECTS

Over what time period should an investment opportunity be analysed? The answer depends on the nature of decision, the decision maker, the size and importance of decision, the time and effort that justifiably can be devoted to the analysis, and the time period over which incremental cash flows will be generated.

A possible criterion for project time horizon is the maximum *physical life* of the assets contained in the project. A horizon constructed on this basis is very long indeed for may assets, since continued repair can keep many assets functioning nearly indefinitely if the costs of repair can be borne. The latter point is crucial in suggesting a more important criterion—the *economic life* of assets. Because assets become obsolete due to technological advance and because repair and maintenance costs rise with age, the economic life of an asset is shorter than physical life. For example, a firm producing some product may find it desirable to purchase new productive assets to replace old assets even though the old productive assets are not physically worn out. *The economic life of the new assets will determine the project time horizon of cash flows.* However, a project involving the production of the additional or new product will have an economic life based not on equipment used to produce the product but upon the number of years the *product* will be produced. Product like productive assets, become obsolete and have their own economic lives. Product life may equal, exceed, or be less than asset life. In either case, determination of the economic life of a project is a problem of optimisation. As a definition, we may regard economic life as that time horizon maximising the increase in shareholder wealth caused by the project. Finally, the concept of *depreciable life* of assets is sometimes used to define the time horizon for project cash flows. Depreciable life is the length of time over which an asset may be depreciated for tax purposes. Only by coincidence will depreciable and economic life be the same thing.

In general economic life is the proper concept to use in defining the project time horizon of cash flows. Physical life has relatively little meaning for defining time horizons nor, except, for computing depreciation charges and income taxes, does depreciable life. Yet, while economic life is significant for cash flow determination purposes, it is sometimes difficult to estimate with any precision. The consequences of this lack of precision are varied. Given the time value of money, it is evident the errors made in estimating the economic life of short-lived assets will be more costly than errors made with long-lived assets. This result occurs because additional years of cash flows in the *near* term are not discounted to a high degree.

EXTERNAL EFFECTS

The external effects of a project are those benefits and costs which do not accrue to the decision-making unit. While they occur both within the public sector and the private, indeed the relative importance of external effects is one of the major reasons for the incorporation of certain activities. Where they occur within the private sector, they may lead to troublesome discrepencies between private and social costs which prevent the attainment of an efficient allocation of resources through the functioning of the market mechanism.

Ideally, from the point of welfare economies, all decision making unit should take account of the external consequences of their acts and behave accordingly, for it is only in such conditions that an ideal allocation of resources will be attained. Costs that cannot be directly identified with activities are allocated to those activities for accounting purposes. Allocation sometimes is done on the basis of number of workers involved in the activity, floor space used, sales revenue, or some similar common factor. However, overhead allocation to cash flows of projects are improper to the extent that the overhead represents the sunk costs. *Sunk costs are prior expenditures being allocated to the current time period.* Prior plant and equipment expenditures or past research and development outlays are examples of such costs. These costs cannot be affected by current activity and are irrelevant to the decision affecting future cash flows. In the long run, all costs are variable. The incremental cash flow rule gives the right answer, but in the case of overhead it is difficult to apply, for often it is not easy to identify the overhead expenses that really will change, and when the changes will occur.

Keeping Operating and Financing Flows Separate

When financing sources are closely related to the investment there may be the temptation to include interest and principal payments among the cash flows to be discounted. Such imputed interest is not a cash flow (if it is, the project and its financing are hopelessly scrambled up and should be separated), and its inclusion as an expense results in an understatement of the desirability of the project. The appropriate allowance for interest is included in the analysis when cost of capital is computed as part of the decision process. Putting it anywhere else counts it twice. A safer procedure is to discount the operating cash flows, of the project, that is, all flows other than interest, principal, and dividend payments. Operating cash flows are defined as those attributable to the project without regard to sources of funds.

Effect of Inflation

An increasing amount of attention has been focused on the problem of price level changes, particularly inflation, in recent years. That these produce distortions in reported incomes, using conventional accounting standards, is reasonably clear. Unless care is taken, they may also distort the decision making process and lead to inappropriate choices.

EFFECT OF DEPRECIATION PROCEDURES

Depreciation enters into capital budgeting computations only because of the effect on taxes. The timing of the depreciation charge affects the timing of the tax payments and therefore the timing of the cash inflows. For this reason, the depreciation method is pertinent to capital budgeting decisions.

Depreciation Methods

The most commonly used depreciation methods are listed below:

(i) Straight-Line Depreciation

At one time, the most commonly used method for computing tax depreciation expenses was the straight line method. *With the straight-line method, it is assumed that the asset decrease in value at a constant annual rate throughout its life, and, therefore, the total depreciation expense is divided by the asset's life to obtain the annual depreciation expense that can be claimed as a deductible expense.*

(ii) Sum-of-the Year's-Digits Depreciation (SYD)

The sum-of-the-year's-digits method is an alternative depreciation method for achieving accelerated write-off during the years of life of an asset. The first step in this approach is to compute the value of the total depreciation expense. As before, this is the difference between the total cost and the estimated salvage value of the asset.

(iii) Declining-Balance Depreciation

The sum-of-the-year's-digits method is considered to be an accelerated method of depreciation, as compared with the straightline method, because its results in the asset's being depreciated at a faster rate. Another such method is the double rate declining balance method. This double rate is applied as follows: *The depreciation expense for any given year is found by multiplying the asset's book value at the beginning of that year by the double rate, which is obtained by dividing the asset's life, n, into 2.*

(iv) Sinking Fund Deprecation

The sinking fund depreciation method is of more interest in some special types of economy studies than for its use for normal accounting and income tax purposes. It historical origin stems from times when it was fairly common for public utilities and other regulated companies to set aside depreciation charges in an interest-bearing account so that the accumulated charges and interest would just equal to estimated depreciable part of the asset investment as of the end of the investment life.

The total depreciation charge for any year is the sinking fund deposit plus accumulated interest for that year. It is also the difference in book value for that year and the previous year.

COMPARISON OF DEPRECIATION METHODS

To provide a common basis for comparing the four methods of depreciation, table below shows year-by-year depreciation charges for a typical asset which costs ₹ 16,000 and is expected to last 5 years, and then can be sold for a net of ₹ 1,000

(in ₹)

End of Year	*Straight Line*	*Double declining Balance*	*Sum-of-year's Digits*	*Sinking funds 10%*
1.	3,000	6,000	5,000	2,457
2.	3,000	3,750	4,000	2,703
3.	3,000	2,344	3,000	2,973
4.	3,000	1,465	2,000	3,270
5.	3,000	1,441*	1,000	3,597
Total	1,5000	15,000	15,000	15,000

* Based on exercising option of switching to straight line depreciation to adjust to final salvage value. In this example, the change in method occurs in the fifth year.

COMPUTING CASH FLOWS

Decisions concerning the purchase of fixed assets must obviously be based upon the effect of future cash flows. Since a long time span in involved. estimates have considerable room for error. In general, a project's cash flows will fall into one of three categories:

(1) Cash outlays for investments

(2) Cash inflows from investments

(3) Terminal cash flow

Cash Outlays for Investments

Determining the amount of cash outflow involved in the purchase of a fixed or other long-term asset may appear to be simple. However, in this part of the problem,

Example-1

In order to clarify the calculation of the initial outlay, consider an example of a company in the 50% marginal tax bracket. This company is considering the purchase of a new machine for ₹ 90,000 which will be depreciated using the straight-line method down to a salvage value of zero in 10 years. The new machine will replace an existing machine originally purchased for ₹ 30,000 ten years ago. The existing machine is being depreciated by the straight-line method down to zero over its expected life of 20 years. In order to put this machine in running order, it is necessary to pay transportation charges of ₹ 1,500 and installation charges of ₹ 7,500. Because the new machine will work faster than the old one, it will require an increase in goods-in-process inventory of ₹ 11,250. Finally, the old machine can be sold for ₹ 18,000 to a scrap dealer.

The installing cost of the new machine would be the ₹ 90,000 plus ₹ 1,500 transportation and ₹ 7,500 installation fees, for a total of ₹ 99,000. Additional outflows are associated with taxes incurred on the sale of the old machine and with increased investment in inventory. Although the old machine had a book value of ₹ 15,000, it was sold for ₹ 18,000. The increased taxes on resulting capital gain will be equal to selling price of the old machine less its depreciated book value time the firm's marginal tax rates, or (₹ 18,000 - ₹ 15,000) (.50) or ₹ 1,500. The effect of their assets in the block has been ignored. The increase in goods in process inventory of ₹ 11,250 must also be considered part of the initial outlay, with an offsetting inflow of ₹ 11,250 corresponding to the recapture of this inventory occuring at the termination of the project. In effect, the firm invests ₹ 11,250 in inventory now, resulting an initial cash outlay, and liquidates this inventory in 10 years, resulting in a cash inflow at the end of the project. The total outlays associated with the new machine are ₹ 99,000 for its installed cost, ₹ 1,500 in increased taxes, and ₹ 11,250 in investment in inventory, for a total of ₹ 1,11,750. This is somewhat offset by the sale of old machine for ₹ 18,000. Thus, the net initial outlay associated with this project is ₹ 93,750. These calculations are summarised in Table-5.

TABLE-5

Calculations of Initial Outlays

Outflows:		
Purchase price	₹ 90,000	
Shipping fee	1,500	
Installation fee	7,500	
Installed cost of machine		₹ 99,000
Increased taxes (₹ 18,000 – ₹ 15,000) (.50)		1,500
Increased investment in inventory		11,250
Total outflows		₹ 1,11,750
Inflows:		
Salvage value of old machine		18,000
Net initial outlay		₹ 93,750

care must be exercised. What must be figured is the *net cash outflow*. Some offsetting cash inflows will often result from the purchase (as contrasted with the use) of an asset and will be received at approximately the same time that the payments for the investment are made. *Tax* rules are such that if the old machine is traded in rather than sold the book loss adds to the depreciable base of the new machine. In this events, the tax saving occurs during the life of the new machine and therefore, affects the cash inflows over the life new machine rather than the initial outflow.

In focussing attention on outlays for plant and equipment it is possible to lose sight of the fact that the *working capital* needed to operate the investment project should also be included in computing the investment outlays. Because residual working capital is recoverable at the termination of operations, this leads to the investment having a net terminal value that should be taken into consideration. The term working capital is used here in a net sense, and applicable current liabilities are subtracted from the increase in current assets to compute the use of cash. It is assumed that the additional current liabilities do not change the proportion of current liabilities to other sources of capital.

Cash Inflows from Investments

The amount of future cash inflows expected from an investment may be difficult to calculate accurately. These flows may continue for a very long period, and obviously, the degree of accuracy in the estimate is somewhat function of time. By using cash flows rather than profit, one incorporates the same concept into capital budgeting.

The cash flows can be calculated either before or after the added taxes resulting from the added taxable profit. Obviously a consistent approach must be adhered to either before or after tax figures must be used for all projects being compared and for both the cost of capital and cash flows. Because of the nature of tax regulations, using after-tax figures throughout will make the calculations simpler and reduce the chances for inaccuracy.

The added cash flow expected from a project may come either from increase in revenues or from reduction in expenses. There is really little analytical difference between a machine that will increase the net annual cash flow and a machine that will reduce the annual operating cost. The pertinent figure is the expected net incremental cash flow. The source is quite irrelevant except in terms of risk.

In most cases, the net incremental cash will be received throughout the year. There is a difference in present value between an expected inflow of ₹ 1 each day for a year and an expected inflow of ₹ 365 at the end of the year. This difference will be ignored for the sake of simplicity, and the assumption will be made that all cash inflows are expected at the end of each year.

Cash outflows related to the cost of money will be treated different from other cash outflows. The cost of capital will he used either as a hurdle rate that must be exceeded by the anticipated rate of return or as the rate of discount. If cash outflows connected with the financing of a project were deducted from anticipated net incremental inflows, this would constitute a double counting.

Example 2

Extending the Example-1, which illustrated the calculations of the initial outlay, suppose that purchasing the machine is expected to reduce salaries by ₹ 18,000 per year and fringe benefits by ₹ 1,500 annually, because it will take only one man to operate, whereas the old machine requires two operators. In addition, the cost of defects will fall from ₹ 9,000 per year to ₹ 1,500. However, maintenance expenses will increase by ₹ 1,500 annually. The annual depreciation on this new machine is ₹ 9,900 per year, while the depreciation expense lost with the sale of the old machine is ₹ 1,500 for each of the next 10 years. Annual depreciation on the new machine is determined by taking its depreciable value—that is, the cost of the new machine plus any expenses necessary to put it in operating order-subtracting out the salvage value, and dividing by the machine's expected life. For the new machine these calculations are reflected in Table-6.

TABLE-6

Calculation of Depreciation for the New Machine

New machine purchase price	₹ 90,000
Transportation charges	1,500
Installation fee	7,500
Total depreciable value	₹ 99,000
Less : Salvage value	0
Divided by expected life	₹ 99,000/10
Equals: Annual Depreciation	₹ 9,900 year

Since the depreciation on the old machine is ₹ 1,500 per year, the increase depreciation will be from ₹ 1,500 per year to ₹ 9,900 per year, or an increase of ₹ 8,400 per year. Although this increase in depreciation expenses is not a cash flow item, it does affect cash flows by reducing book profits, which in turn reduces taxes.

In order to determine the annual net cash flows resulting from the acceptance of the project, the net savings before taxes using both book profit and cash flows must be found. The additional taxes are then calculated based upon the pre-tax book profit. For this example, Table-7 shows the determination of the differential cash flows on an after-tax basis, thus the differential cash flows over the project's life are ₹ 16,950.

TABLE-7

Calculation of the Differential Cash Flow

	Book Profit	*Cash Flow*
Savings:		
Reduced salary	₹ 18,000	₹ 18,000
Reduced fringe benefits	1,500	1,500
Reduced defects (₹ 9,000-₹ 1,500)	7,500	7,500
Costs:		
Increased maintenance expenses–1,500		–1,500
Increased depreciation expenses (₹ 9,900-₹ 1,500)	–8,400	
Net savings before taxes	₹ 17,100	₹ 25,500
Taxes (50%)	8,550	–8,550
Net cash flow after taxes		₹ 16,950

Terminal Cash Flow

When an asset's economic life is terminated there is frequently some value left in the asset. The asset may still be useable in its current form. For example, a pump on a depleted oil well may transfer the pump and saves the purchase price of another pump or if the firm sells the pump to another firm there is a cash inflows created. In the transfer case this case inflow is in the form of a cost savings and in the case of the sale the cash salvage cash flow before tax created. Alternatively, if the asset is worn out there may be some scrap value associated with it. If, for example, the pump is worn out and beyond repair it may still have value as scrap metal. The sale of the asset as asset creates a salvage cash flow before tax in the year of abandonment. Additionally the firm will recover any increased net working capital that was committed to the project in the initial time period.

Example 3

Extending the examples-1 and 2 to termination, the depreciated book value of the machine at the termination date will be equal to zero. However, there will be a cash flow generated from the liquidation of the ₹ 11,250 in work-in-process inventory. Therefore, the expected total terminal cash flow equals ₹ 11,250. If we are to draw a cash flow diagramme from this example (Figure-3), it would have an initial outlay of ₹ 93,750, differential cash flows during years 1 through 10 of ₹ 16,950, and an additional terminal cash flow at the end of year 10 of ₹ 11,250. The cash flow occuring in year 10 is ₹ 28,200, the sum of the differential cash flow in year 10 of ₹ 16,950, and the terminal cash flow of ₹ 11,250. In Figure-3, arrows above the time line indicating cash inflow and arrows below the time line denoting cash outflows.

FIGURE-3

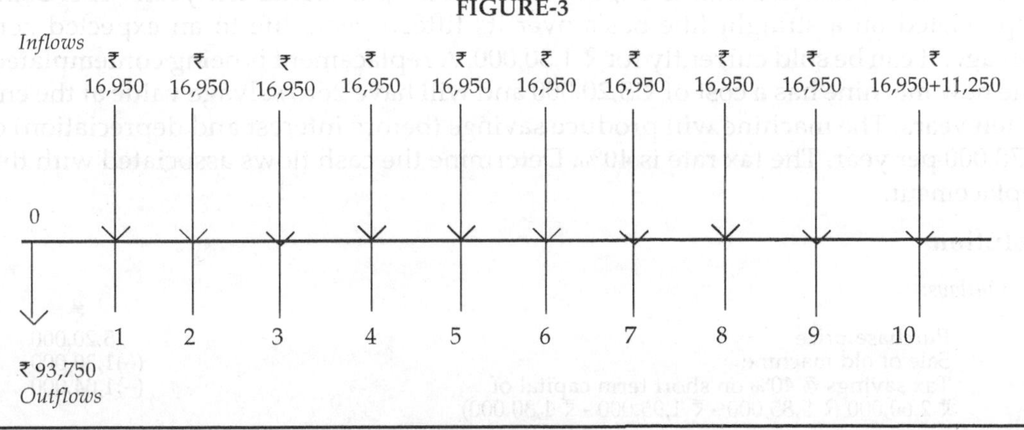

While the above calculations for determining the incremental after tax, net cash flows do not cover all possible cash flows, they do set up a framework under which almost any situation can be handled.

ILLUSTRATIVE PROBLEMS

1. NIMCO is purchasing an asset to replace an existing asset. The purchase price is ₹ 6,00,000 plus an additional ₹ 80,000 to transport and install it. It will operate much more quickly than the asset it replaces and therefore will tie up additional inventory worth ₹ 1,20,000. The firm has an existing asset that can be sold for ₹ 90,000, but it will cost ₹ 30,000 to remove it so that it can be delivered to the buyer. The book value of the existing asset is ₹ 80,000. What is the net initial outlay for the new asset? Tax rate is 50%.

Solution

Calculation of initial net outlay is tabulate follows:

Outflows:		
Purchase price	₹ 6,00,000	
Transport and Installation cost	80,000	
Installed cost of machine		₹ 6,80,000
Increased investment in inventory		1,20,000
Total outflows		₹ 8,00,000
Inflows:		
Salvage value of old machine (₹ 90,000 – ₹ 30,000)		60,000
Tax savings @ 50% on short term capital less of 10,000 ₹ 20,000 (₹ 80,000 – ₹ 60,000)		10,000
Net initial outlay		₹ 7,30,000

Net initial outlay for the new asset is ₹ 7,30,000.

2. Wadhwa Industries is using a machine whose original cost was ₹ 5,85,000. The machine is 5 years old and is expected to last an additional ten years. It is being depreciated on a straight line basis over its fifteen years life to an expected zero salvage. It can be sold currently for ₹ 1,30,000. A replacement is being contemplated. The new machine has a cost of ₹ 5,20,000 and will have zero salvage value at the end of ten years. The machine will produce savings (before interest and depreciation) of ₹ 78,000 per year. The tax rate is 40%. Determine the cash flows associated with this replacement.

Solution

	₹
Outlays:	
Purchase price	5,20,000
Sale of old machine	(–)1,30,000
Tax savings @ 40% on short term capital of ₹ 2,60,000 (₹ 5,85,000 - ₹ 1,95,000 - ₹ 1,30,000)	(–)1,04,000
Net cash outlay	2,86,000
Cash benefits	
Savings	78,000
Incremental depreciation	(–)13,000
Taxable income	65,000
Less: Tax	26,000

Earnings after taxes	39,000
Add: back depreciation	13,000
Cash flow (Yrs. 1-10)	52,000

3. Ravi Instruments is considering the purchase of a machine tool to replace an existing tool that has a book value of ₹ 24,000, and can be sold for ₹ 12,000. The salvage value of the old machine in four years is zero, and it is depreciated on a straightline basis. The proposed machine will perform the same function that the old machine is performing; however improvements in technology will enable the firm to reap cash benefits (before depreciation and taxes) of ₹ 56,000 per year in materials, labour, and overhead. The new machine has a four year life, costs ₹ 1,12,000 and can be sold for an expected ₹ 16,000 at the end of the fourth year. Assuming straight-line depreciation and a 40% tax rate, compute the cash flows associated with this replacement.

Solution

(1) Calculation of net initial outlay:

Outlays:	
Purchase price	₹ 1,12,000
Inflows	
Salvage of old machine	12,000
Tax savings @ 40% on short term capital loss	4,800
Net initial outlay	₹ 95,200

(2) Calculation of differential cash flows:

	Book profits		*Cash flow*
Saving:			
Cash benefits	₹ 56,000		₹ 56,000
Costs:			
Increased depreciation expense (₹ 24,000-₹ 6,000)	18,000		
Net savings before taxes	₹ 38,000		₹ 56,000
Taxes (40%)	15,200	———>	15,200
Net cash flow after taxes			40,800

In addition, there is a ₹ 16,000 cash flow at the end of year four from sale of new machine.

Period	*Cash flow*	
0	–₹ 95,200	
1	40,800	
2	40,800	
3	40,800	
4	56,800	(40,800 + 16,000)

4. Management of Andhra Pulp and Paper Company is trying to decide whether it should replace a manually operated machine with a fully automatic version of the same machine. The existing machine, purchased ten years ago, had an accounting book value of ₹ 2,40,000 and a projected life of 20 years. The projected salvage value was ₹ 40,000 at the time of purchase. The machine has recently begun causing problems with breakdowns and is costing the company ₹ 20,000 per year in maintenance expenses. The company has been offered ₹ 1,00,000 for the old machine as a trade-in on a newer model which has a delivered price (before allowance for trade-in) of ₹ 2,20,000. It is expected to have a ten-year life and a salvage value of ₹ 20,000. The new machine will require installation modifications of ₹ 40,000 to the existing facilities, but it is projected to have a cost savings in production materials of ₹ 80,000 per year. Maintenance costs are included in the purchase contract and are borne by the machine manufacturer. The tax rate is 40%. Straight line depreciation over ten years will be used. Construct a summary table of relevant cash flows.

Solution

The cost of the new machine (accounting book value) is ₹ 2,20,000 + ₹ 40,000 = ₹ 2,60,000. Since ₹ 1,00,000 is received on trade-in the year 0 cash flow becomes ₹ 2,60,000 - ₹ 1,00,000 = ₹ 1,60,000. To Calculate the incremental benefits of depreciation tax shields, we require both values of depreciation:

$$\text{Depreciation (old)} = \frac{₹\ 2{,}40{,}000 - ₹\ 40{,}000}{20} = ₹\ 10{,}000$$

$$\text{Depreciation (New)} = \frac{₹\ 2{,}20{,}000 + ₹\ 40{,}000 - ₹\ 20{,}000}{10} = ₹\ 24{,}000$$

Incremental depreciation = ₹ 24,000 – ₹ 10,000 = ₹ 14,000

Incremental tax benefit = ₹ 14,000 × 0.40 = ₹ 5,600 per year

The new machine reduce maintenance expense by ₹ 20,000 and production costs by ₹ 80,000 for a total reduction of ₹ 1,00,000. Thus, this yields in incremental cash flows of ₹ 1,00,000 (1–0.40) = ₹ 60,000 per year. Additional flows are all concerned with salvage values. First the book value of the old machine is currently ₹ 2,40,000–₹ 1,00,000 = ₹ 1,40,000. We thus recognise a loss of ₹ 1,40,000 – ₹ 1,00,000 = ₹ 40,000, which represents a year 0 tax shield of ₹ 40,000 × 0.40 = ₹ 16,000. Next, the firm would have received a ₹ 40,000 salvage value on the old machine in year 10, so this represents a year 10 outflow of ₹ 40,000. Finally, we will receive a salvage value on the new machine of ₹ 20,000 in year 10.

Summarising

Year	*0*	*1-9*	*10*
Outlay for new machine	–₹ 1,60,000		
Depreciation tax shield		₹ 5,600	₹ 5,600
Cost reduction		60,000	60,000
Tax savings on loss	16,000		
Old salvage			–40,000
New salvage			20,000
Totals	–₹ 1,44,000	₹ 65,600	₹ 45,600

5. R.K. Synthetics has an opportunity to replace an existing plant with a new machine that performs a particular manufacturing operation more efficiently. Given the following information determine the cash flows associated with the replacement:

Existing Situation:

Two full-time machine operators—salaries	₹ 25,000 each/per year
Cost of maintenance	₹ 2,500 per year
Cost of defects	₹ 20,000 per year
Original cost of old machine	₹ 37,500
Expected life	15 years
Age	5 years
Expected salvage value	₹ 0
Depreciation method	Straight line
Tax rate	40%
Current market value of old machine	₹ 37,500

Proposed Situation:

Fully automated machine no operator necessary	
Cost of machine	₹ 75,000
Installation fee	₹ 7,500
Transportation fee	₹ 5,000
Cost of maintenance	₹ 12,500
Cost of defects	₹ 7,500
Expected life	Ten years
Salvage value	₹ 0
Depreciation method	Straight line
Increase in inventory	₹ 12,500

Solution

Net initial outlay is to be ₹ 67,500 as the following table shows:

Outflows:		
Cost of machine	₹ 75,000	
Installation fee	7,500	
Transportation fee	5,000	
Installed cost of machine		₹ 87,500
Increased taxes (₹ 37,500—25,000) (0.40)		5,000
Increased investment in inventory		12,500
Total outflows		₹ 1,05,000
Inflows:		
Salvage value of old machine		37,500
Net initial outlay		₹ 67,500

Calculations of depreciation for the new machine is given below:

New machine purchase price	₹ 75,000
Installation fee	7,500
Transportation fee	5,000
Total depreciable value	87,500
Less: Salvage value	0
Divided by expected life	₹ 87,500/10
Equals: Annual depreciation	₹ 8,750 per year

Determination of the differential cash flows in tabular form is presented below:

	Book Profit		*Cash Flow*
Savings:			
Reduced Salary	₹ 25,000		₹ 25,000
Reduced defects (₹ 20,000 – ₹ 7,500)	12,500		12,500
Costs:			
Increased maintenance expense	10,000		10,000
Increased depreciation expense (₹ 8,750 - ₹ 2,500)	6,250		
Net savings before taxes	₹ 21,250		₹ 27,500
Taxes (40%)	–8,500	—>	–8,500
Net Cash flow after taxes			19,000

From the liquidation of the ₹ 12,500 investment in work-in-process inventory, there will be a terminal cash flow of ₹ 12,500.

Summarising

Year	*Investment outlay*	*Incremental funds flow*	*Incremental net working capital*		*Incremental cash flow*
0	– ₹ 67,500			=	– ₹ 67,500
1		₹ 19,000		=	19,000
2		19,000		=	19,000
3		19,000		=	19,000
3		19,000		=	19,000
5		19,000		=	19,000
6		19,000		=	19,000
7		19,000		=	19,000
8		19,000		=	19,000
9		19,000		=	19,000
10		19,000	12,500	=	31,500

QUESTIONS

1. Why is the capital budgeting decision such an important process? Why are capital budgeting errors so costly?
2. The novice to capital budgeting may interpret the term 'project' to mean only a new investment in plant and equipment. Evaluate this assumption as it relates to the overall theory of the firm.
3. Would it be beneficial for firm to review its past capital expenditures and capital budgeting procedures? Why?
4. Strictly speaking, all activities of a firm are interdependent that is, they affect one another's cash flows. Therefore any new investment in some way-directly or indirectly-affects the cash flows of every other investment the firm adopts. Since this is so, how can we justify ever evaluating a new investment by itself, i.e., without considering how it affects the cash flows of every other investment we are considering? What are the advantages and disadvantages of ignoring inter-dependencies?
5. "The most useful approach to project classification arranges investment alternatives according to the way benefits from the investment are affected by or affect other possible investment." Comment.
6. Are all investment projects interdependent? Suggest some projects that are relatively independent. What kind of firm is most likely to have independent projects?
7. Many firms continue to use obsolete machinery long after new more efficient equipment is available. Under what circumstances would this represent poor financial planning?
8. How should working capital be treated in analysing investment opportunities?
9. To calculate a capital budgeting problem, one must calculate the net incremental cash flow resulting from the proposed investment for each year of the asset's expected life.
   (a) Why is cash flow used instead of net profit?
   (b) What is meant by "net incremental cash flow"?
   (c) Why must one calculate this for each year of the asset's life rather than merely using a total figure for the entire use period?
10. In identifying relevant cash flows, the object normally is to determine after-tax flows rather than pre-tax cash flow? Why is it best to deal with after-tax rather than pre-tax flows?
11. Why do we focus on cash flows rather than on actual profit in making our capital budgeting decisions? Why are we interested only in incremental cash flows rather than total cash flows?
12. Why might economic life of an asset be shorter than its actual, physical, and expected life?
13. Describe the importance of steps involved in the capital budgeting process.

PROBLEMS

1. The installed cost of a new piece of equipment is ₹ 5,00,000. The machine will have a 5-year service life at which time it will have a book value of ₹ 25,000. Using the straight-line method, compute the annual depreciable cost of the machine.

Ans.: ₹ 95,000 annual depreciation cost.

2. Allied Products is considering a new machine. It will cost ₹ 50,000 and will replace an existing machine that can be sold for its book value of ₹ 20,000. An investment tax credit of ₹ 3,000 will be allowed. Either machine will last for 5 years and will be depreciated to zero over that period. The new machine will reduce the material waste by ₹ 7,000 a year. Allied Products is facing a 48% tax rate. Compute the annual after-tax flow to purchase the new machine.

Ans.: Annual After-tax Cash Flow is ₹ 6,520

3. Omega Chemicals is evaluating a new labour saving machine. The machine will cost Rs: 40,000. It will replace a machine with a book value and salvage value of ₹ 10,000. An investment tax credit of ₹ 2,000 will be allowed. Either machine will last 10 years from now and will be depreciated to zero over that time. The new machine will reduce labour expense by ₹ 7,000 a year. Compute the annual after-tax cash flow.

Ans.: Annual After-tax Cash Flow is ₹ 5,080

4. Shiva Pharma has an asset that currently generates annual revenues of ₹ 34,00,000 and incurs annual costs of ₹ 14,00,000. These costs do not include ₹ 2,40,000 of depreciation. If a replacement machine is purchased, the revenues would rise to ₹ 38,00,000 and the costs would drop to ₹ 12,80,000. but depreciation on the new machine would be ₹ 3,20,000 per year. What are the annual after tax cash flows on each machine?

Ans.: Cash Flow After-tax (Present Machine) = ₹ 11,20,000; Cash Flow After-tax (New Machine) ₹ 14,20,000

5. Royal Blue Company is considering a new automatic drill press. The drill press will cost ₹ 5,00,000. It has a five-year life and a zero salvage value. The machine will reduce labour expense by ₹ 1,20,000 a year. The company faces a 48% tax ate. What will be the annual after-tax cash flow generated by the machine?

Ans.: Annual After-tax Cash Flow is ₹ 1,10,400

6. Gupta Engineering is considering an investment in a new product. The information for one year is as follows:

Sales	₹ 2,00,000
Manufacturing costs of sales (includes ₹ 20,000 of depreciation)	80,000
Selling and administrative expenses (directly associated with the product)	40,000
Equipment purchase	10,000
Decrease in contribution of other products	5,000
Increase in accounts receivable	15,000
Increase in inventories	20,000
Increase in current liabilities	30,000
Income taxes associated with product income	12,000
Interest on debentures expected to be used in financing	18,000

Compute the cash flows that can be used in the present value computations of this investment.

Ans.: Net cash flow is ₹ 68,000

7. Surya Group is considering the construction of a new plant to replace its existing facilities. Pertinent information relating to the current plant is listed below:

	Book Value	*Sale Price*
Land	₹ 1,00,000	₹ 25,00,000
Building	2,75,000	–60,000 *
Machinery	5,00,000	3,75,000

* Cost to demolish old building.

Cost Factor for the new plant are as follows:

	Purchase Price	*Related Costs*
Land	₹ 20,00,000	₹ 2,50,000 real estate fees. ₹ 80,000 interest during construction.
Building	₹ 36,00,000	₹ 60,000 property taxes during construction. ₹ 1,00,000 interest during construction.
Machinery and equipment	₹ 16,00,000	₹ 4,00,000 installation
Additional working capital	₹ 2,50,000	

All equipment and machinery has a life exceeding 7 years. The corporation is in the 48% marginal tax bracket. Determine the net-out-of-pocket cost to purchase the new plant if the capital gains taxes are 30% and the investment tax credit is 10%.

Ans.: The Group would have to pay ₹ 57,67,800 to purchase the new plant.

10

CAPITAL BUDGETING DECISIONS UNDER CONDITIONS OF CERTAINTY

INTRODUCTION

Capital budgeting is a process for analysing and selecting appropriate long term investment projects. At times this pursuit represents art more than science; in many cases, factors determining a capital investment project's ultimate success (general economic condition, competition, interest rates, government regulations, etc.) are beyond a company's control.[1] Also, the time horizon for many capital projects extended too far into the future, so projecting the timing and benefit of these investment activities can be a highly uncertain process. Since in all organisations the amounts of funds available for capital expenditures is limited, *the financial manager is faced with the dual problem of establishing some basic criteria for the acceptance, rejection, or postponement of proposed investments, and the ranking the projects that meet the criteria for acceptance in order of their value to the firm.*

In this chapter, we shall consider five commonly used criteria for determining acceptability of investment proposals. The first two are the least sophisticated, in that they do not incorporate the time value of money into the calculations; the final three do take account of it. Conflict ranking, resulting from differences in the magnitude and timings of cash flows, will be examined in the subsequent section.

CAPITAL BUDGETING: ANALYTICAL METHODS

NONDISCOUNTED CASH FLOW CRITERIA FOR CAPITAL BUDGETING DECISIONS

Two nondiscounted techniques, used fairly often in capital budgeting analysis, are the payback period and the average rate of return.

PAYBACK PERIOD (PP)

Payback is a measure of the rapidity with which the project will return the original capital outlay. The payback period is the number of years it takes the firm to recover the original outlay from the cash inflows of the project. *Projects offering a*

1. David Quirin: *The Capital Expenditure Decision*, Richard D. Irwin, Inc., Homewood III, 1967,

payback period less than some firm determined number of years (N) are accepted and those projects with a payback period (PP) greater than that acceptable number of years are rejected. In symbols:

$$PP \leq N \quad \text{accept}$$
$$PP > N \quad \text{reject}$$

For example, assume a certain investment project will result in an initial cash outflow of ₹ 25,000. It will result in a cash inflow of ₹ 5,000 per year for eight years. To determine the payback period divide the cash inflow per year into the cash outflow

$$\frac{₹\ 25{,}000}{₹\ 5{,}000} = 5 \text{ years}$$

It will take 5 years to recover the ₹ 25,000 investment. If the firm determined number of years are five or more, the proposed project would be accepted.

To illustrate further the nature of the problem, consider a certain project has yearly after-tax outflows and inflows as tabulated below :

Time		*Expected Cash Flows*
Present	–	₹ 15,000
1	–	6,000
2-6	+	4,500
7-15	+	9,000
15*		

*Recovery of working capital

In this case, since the cash flows are not constant over the life of the project, the payback period may be found using the tabular form as follows:

Time		*Expected Cash Flow*		*Net Cash Outflow*
Present	–	₹ 15,000	–	₹ 15,000
1	–	6,000	–	21,000
2	+	4,500	–	16,500
3	+	4,500	–	12,000
4	+	4,500	–	7,500
5	+	4,500	–	3,000
6	+	4,500	+	1,500

The total investment is recovered during the sixth year. Since ₹ 3,000 remains outstanding at the start of the sixth year, and ₹ 4,500 is expected to be received during the sixth year, the total investment will be recovered, two-thirds of the way through the sixth year. The payback period is thus 5 years and 8 months.

The payback period method for choosing among alternative proposals is very popular among corporate managers.

The main **advantages** of payback period are:

1. It is easy to understand, compute, and communicate to others. Its quick computation makes it a favourite among finance managers who prefer snap answers.
2. It is only used as a quick method of approximation for screening proposals. To the extent that it is used only lightly, the harm may not always be great; although as we shall see, it can result in bypassing profitable investment opportunities.
3. It is an adequate measure for firms with very profitable internal investment opportunities, whose sources of funds are limited by internal low availability and external high costs. Thus it is said that if shortage of funds limits the company to the acceptance of projects with a small payback, say two years, the use of more refined methods of selection might not change the composition of selected projects.
4. It is useful for approximating the value of risky investments where the income from the investment is highly uncertain and its life expectancy more. Under such circumstances, payback may become important, not so much as a measure of profitability but as a means of establishing an upper hand on the acceptable degree of risk. When one can appraise the near future with some confidence, but is completely in the dark about longer term prospects, a short payout period may be an adequate guarantee against loss, investment being undertaken as a sporting proposition in the hope that some of the projects will last long enough to make the whole operation profitable. It examplifies the importance of liquidity and control as goals of business behaviour, while also pointing to *satisficing* rather than *maximising* objectives.
5. When the payback period is set at a large number of years, and income streams are uniform for each year, the payback criterion is a good approximation to the reciprocal of the internal rate of return. However, since the payback period is purposely set at a low values, this conditional advantage lacks generality.

For every advantage claimed by the advocates of payback, there is a disadvantage claimed by its opponents, often based on same information. Let us explore some of its ***disadvantage***:

1. Even if the utilisation of the method is justified at times for certain firms under special conditions, these firms are in the minority. Hence the generality of the technique is severely constrained.
2. It overlaps the importance of liquidity as a goal of the capital expenditure decision. While no firm can ignore its liquidity requirements with impunity, there are more direct and less costly means of safeguarding liquidity levels. This disadvantage, of course, overlooks the possibility that liquidity or satisficing, or even survival, may indeed be the primary managerial goal in capital budgeting decisions.

3. It ignores capital wastage and economic life by restricting consideration to the project's gross earnings (before depreciation).
4. It fails to consider the earnings from an investment *after* the pay back period, thus treating them as a windfall. Assume that two projects are being considered by a firm. Each requires an investment of ₹ 10,00,000. The firm's marginal cost of capital is 15%. The net cash flows (net operating income after taxes plus depreciation) from investments X and Y are shown in Table-1.

TABLE-1

Net Cash Flows

Year	X	Y
1.	₹ 4,00,000	₹ 3,00,000
2.	3,00,000	2,50,000
3.	2,00,000	2,00,000
4.	1,00,000	1,50,000
5.	—	1,00,000
6.	—	50,000

Since the cost is ₹ 10,00,000 the payback period is 4 years for project X and 5 years for project Y. If the firm is employing a four-year payback period, project X would be accepted and project Y would be rejected. Thus, the payback ignores the income beyond the payback period.

5. Another weakness in the use of the payback method for ranking investment proposals lies in its *failure* to take into account the *time value of money.* To illustrate, consider the assets A and B each costing ₹ 9,00,000 and each having the following cash flows,

Year	A	B
1.	₹ 6,00,000	₹ 3,00,000
2.	3,00,000	6,00,000
3.	3,00,000	3,00,000

Each project has a two year payback, each appearing equally desirable. However, we know that a rupee today is worth more than a rupee next year, so project A, with its faster cash flow, is certainly more desirable.

To summarise, under conditions of certainty, payback is a poor method of ordering the attractiveness of projects. Under conditions of uncertainty, however, the measure may have some value as one of the constraints that limit a firm's range of options. More important, it can be a rough guide to reduce the degree of uncertainty associated with a project, since if a project has a quick payback, the decision-maker is left only with the problem of whether the useful life of the project beyond the payback period is long enough to make it attractive. If a project has a long payback period, the firm may not even recover its costs let alone a return on its investment.

ACCOUNTING RATE OF RETURN (AROR)

Some corporations measure project profitability as an annual percentage of capital employed. These expost measures are derived from financial statements and are intended to present a so-called *true rate of returns.*

The first most elaborate version, and the most thoroughly consistent one, take average income, as measured by a series of proforma income statements, as a percentage of average investment, *i.e.*, average book value after deducting depreciation. To illustrate, the calculations for a project costing ₹ 50,000 with scrap value of ₹ 10,000 and annual incomes for a hypothetical company XYZ are shown in Table-2.

TABLE-2
Accounting Rate of Return: Version 1

	Year 1	*Year 2*	*Year 3*	*Year 4*	*Average*
	₹	₹	₹	₹	₹
Cash income	15,000	20,000	25,000	30,000	22,500
Depreciation	10,000	10,000	10,000	10,000	10,000
Net income	5,000	10,000	15,000	20,000	12,500
Book Value :					
Jan. 1	50,000	40,000	30,000	20,000	35,000
Dec. 31	40,000	30,000	20,000	10,000	25,000
Average	45,000	35,000	25,000	15,000	30,000

$$\text{Rate of Return} = \frac{12,500}{30,000} \times 100 = 41.7\%$$

The second version uses original cost rather than average book value as the denominator, i.e., (12,500/50,000)100=25%. This is a little less consistent, in that income is averaged but investment is not. As an approximation to the internal rate of return, this usually gives better results than using average investment.

A second type of accounting measure is the single year rate of return. This, as the name implies, is a measure of profit in a single year, which may be the first year, the "first full year" or some other equally elusive standard. It may be applied either against average investment over the life of the project, against average investment in the year selected for study, or simply against initial cost. Table-3 shows in the calculations for these six variants, for the project analysed in Table-2 *assuming year one is the first year and year two "first full year."*

Now, this may seem very confusing, and indeed it is. The widely varying results point to the desirability of ensuring uniformity of practice if an accounting measure is to be employed. These versions ignore all years other than the one studied. Their dangers when applied to projects having anything except a stable income are too obvious to require elaboration. Moreover, the diverse concepts of earnings, whether before or after taxes, as well as whether original or average investment is selected, provide varying rates of return under the accounting or financial statement method. In addition, the initial determination of what part of the project will be expensed currently and what part will be capitalised also affects the rate of return. For example, had more of the cost of the project above been expensed and less capitalised, the rate of return could have changed considerably owing merely to a variation of accounting technique.

TABLE-3

Accounting Rate of Return : Version III, IV

	Version III (First Year)	*Version IV (First full year)*
Cash Income	₹ 15,000	₹ 20,000
Depreciation	10,000	10,000
Net income	₹ 5,000	₹ 10,000
Book Value :		
Jan. 31	50,000	40,000
Dec. 31	40,000	30,000
Average	45,000	35,000
Rate of return :		
(a) On lifetime average investment	$\frac{5,000}{30,000} \times 100$	$\frac{10,000}{30,000} \times 100$
	= 16.7	=33.7%
(b) On average investment in year studied	$\frac{5,000}{45,000} \times 100$	$\frac{10,000}{35,000} \times 100$
	=11.1%	=28.5%
(c) On initial cost	$\frac{5,000}{50,000} \times 100$	$\frac{10,000}{50,000} \times 100$
	10.0%	=20%

The chief limitation of this financial statement method is that it does not allow for the time element in the return of funds. It gives the same weight to future money as it gives to current. New and distant earnings are asumed to have the same value, and this is, of course, contrary to fact. The time value of money is ignored and the same value is given to receipt of the last as to the first year.

Inspite of the foregoing criticism, the accounting rate of return has been a very popular tool for capital budgeting analysis, primarily because accounting measures are very useful for purposes of performance measurement and management control. How much did we earn last year? Were last year's earnings above or below the prior year's earnings? Were they above or below profit plan? What has been the trend in earnings? What has been the trend in AROI? Are investments be more profitable or less in terms of profit per rupee of outlay? Accounting measures such as profit after tax, earnings per share, and return on investment are very useful for answering such questions.

DISCOUNTED CASH FLOW CRITERIA FOR CAPITAL BUDGETING DECISIONS

Discounted cash flow methods use cash flows such as are calculated not only for the payback period, but for the whole life of the project; do not need to differentiate 'capital' from income flows, and can accommodate all cash flows inwards or outwards whenever they occur; and take account of the rate of return on the capital invested in the project by discounting all the cash flows to their present value equivalent. We will examine below three discounted cash flow capital budgeting techniques—*the net present value, the profitability index, and the internal rate of return.*

NET PRESENT VALUE (NPV)

The net present value of a project is defined as the difference between the present value of all cash outflows and the present values of the expected cash inflows when discounted at a rate of return, which may be firm's cost of capital or another rate developed using capital asset pricing model. The net present value of an investment proposal is

$$\text{NPV} = \sum_{t=1}^{n} \frac{A_t}{(1+k)^t} - 10 \qquad (1)$$

where,

A_t = the cash inflow for period t.

k = the appropriate discount rate, that is required rate of return or the cost of capital.

IO = the initial cash outlay.

n = the project's expected life.

The following example illustrates the basic computations for discounted cash flows, that is, adjusted future cash flows for the time value of money, using the net present value method.

Assume that there is an investment opportunity with following cash flows :

Period	*Cash Flow*
0	– ₹ 64,320
1	20,000
2	25,000
3	28,000
4	24,000

We want first to compute the present value of this investment using 15% as the discount rate. The present value of :

₹ 1 due 0 period from now discounted at any interest rate is 1.000.

₹1 due 1 period from now discounted at 15% is .8696
₹ 1 due 2 periods from now discounted at 15% is .7561
₹1 due 3 periods from now discounted at 15% is .6575
₹1 due 4 periods from now discounted at 15% is .5718.

The net present value of the investment is the algebriac sum of the present values.

Period	*Cash Flow*	*Present Value Factor*	*Present Value*
0	– ₹ 64,320	1.0000	– ₹ 64,320
1	20,000	.8696	17,392
2	25,000	.7561	18,903
3	28,000	.6575	18,410
4	24,000	.5718	13,723
		₹ 4,108	

The net present value is positive, indicating the investment is acceptable. Any investment with a net present value equal to or greater than zero is acceptable using this single criterion.

Let us look into the net present value method in some greater detail. To begin with, the measure can apply to three generalised subcases: (1) The maximisation of the present value from a sequence of future earnings flows in a single project. (2) The maximisation of the present value of a combination of projects through their productive transformations. (3) The adoption of an incremental project when NPV>0. The first case suggests that we take every possible opportunity that will assure us the highest level of wealth. The second suggests that we accept opportunities that increases the value of the combination of projects. The third suggests that we should accept every opportunity so long as its net present value is positive. The third case, involving incremental projects, can be used only if the project under consideration is independent of all other projects in the firm's plans.

With regard to the business firm, one may well feel that a more appropriate approach might be to assume that the firm seeks to maximise (rather than minimise) the wealth of its shareholders. Note that this wealth-maximising behaviour is an assumption and not a conclusion of the analysis, and is not intended to imply a normative prescription for the behaviour of the firm or of individual investors. But given this goal, we can devise a consistent set of optimal risks for reaching the goal, and these decision rules should provide a good explanation, and prediction of the firm's investment decisions in practice.

Given the assumptions of wealth maximisation and perfect certainty, the following decision rules should be adopted.

when the NPV>0 *accept the project*
when the NPV<0 *reject the project*

The present values are calculated using a discount rate which reflects the alternative use of capital, that is its opportunity cost. Given the assumption of certainty, the opportunity cost will be equal to the riskless rate of interest. Thus the firm will accept those proposals whose net present values are positive, and will reject those projects whose net present values are negative. These decision rules follows directly from the assumption that firm operate to maximise the wealth of their shareholders, since under the assumed condition certainty the prices of all assets, including equity, are determined by their discounted present values.[2] These decision rules results in an optimal choice of projects since, under the assumed conditions, no other set of projects can be found which will increase the value of the firm.

So the NPV evaluation technique is more than just a good investment criterion. For accept-reject problems the NPV always provides theoretically correct decisions, and we will see that for mutually exclusive choice problems the NPV method is the best decision criterion.

The primary difficulty encountered with NPV is in deciding the appropriate rate of return (the hurdle rate) to use in discounting the cash flows. While the firm's cost of capital may be used as the discount rate, there exist questions as to how the cost of capital should be calculated. Also, there may be difficulty involved in obtaining the data needed to perform the calculations, even after procedural questions are resolved.

PROFITABILITY INDEX (BENEFIT/COST RATIO)

The profitability index or, benefit/cost ratio, is the ratio of the present value of the future net cash flows to the initial outlay. The profitability index (PI) can be expressed as follows:

$$\text{PI} = \frac{\sum_{t=1}^{n} \frac{A_t}{(1+k)^t}}{\text{IO}} \tag{2}$$

The decision criterion with respect to the profitability index is to accept the project if the PI is greater than 1.00, and to reject the project if the PI is less than 1.00. However, if the PI exactly equals 1.00, we are indifferent between acceptance and rejection of the project. The accept reject criterion is illustrated below :

PI>1.0	Accept
PI≤1.0	Reject

Looking closely at this criterion, we see that it will always gives the same accept-reject decision as does the net present value criterion. Whenever the present value of the project's net cash flow is greater than its initial cash outlay, the project's net present value will be positive, signalling an accept decision. While this is true, then the project's profitability index will also be greater than one, as the present value of

2. A formal proof of this proposition is given in Paul A. Samualson: Some Aspects of the Pure Theory of Capital, *Quarterly Journal of Economic, 51.* (May, 1973); pp. 469-96.

the net cash flows (the PI's numerator) is greater than initial outlay (the PI's denominator).

These relationships may be summarised as :

If NPV>0 then PI>1
If NPV=0 then PI=1
If NPV<0 then PI<1

However, it should be noted that while these two decision criteria will always yield the same accept-reject decision, they will not necessarily rank acceptable projects in the same order.

To illustrate, consider the following two mutually exclusive investment opportunities with the present value of cash flows as shown :

Year	*Project A*	*Project B*
0	– ₹ 1,00,000	– ₹ 70,000
1	80,000	60,000
2	80,000	60,000
NPV (.15)	30,000	27,600
PI (.15)	1.3	1.4

Notice that both projects are acceptable if the cost of capital is 15% as both NPV>0 and PI>1. However, when ranked by NPV, project A is more attractive while project B is better when ranked by PI. A conflict in NPV and PI rankings can only occur when the *initial investments of the two projects are not the same,* which is the situation with project A and B. Because the NPV methods nets the original cost from the present value of the future cash flows while the PI method divides the present value of future cash flows by original cost, projects with different initial investments (different scales of investment) may have different rankings under the two evaluation methods.

When there is conflict in rankings which project should the firm accept? The NPV technique is superior and project A is a better project (at least when k=0.15). The best project will add the most new value to the shareholder's wealth, and this is the project that has the highest positive net present value. Since the NPV method, by definition, always selects the project with highest positive net present value. The NPV method is a better mutually exclusive choice evaluation technique than PI.

Since the net present value and profitability index criteria are essentially the same, they have the same advantages over the other criteria examined. They both employ cash flows, recognising the timing of the cash flows, and are consistent with the goal of maximisation of shareholders' wealth. The major disadvantage of this criterion, as of the net present value criterion, is that it requires long, detailed cash flow forecasts.

INTERNAL RATE OF RETURN (IRR)

The internal rate of return utilises present value concepts but seeks to avoid the arbitrary choice of a rate of interest in evaluating an investment proposal. This technique is also known as yield, interest rate of return, return on investment, present value return on investment, discounted cash flow, investor's method, time-adjusted rate of return, and marginal efficiency of capital.

The internal rate of return is that rate of discount that equates the present value of the expected after tax cash inflows with the present value of the after-tax outflows. In other words, the internal rate of return is the rate of discount that sets the net present value equal to zero. The net present value has to be zero if the present value of the project's income streams is equal to the present value of the project's cash outlay. Mathematically, the internal rate of return is defined as the value r in the following equation :

$$\text{IRR} = \sum_{t=1}^{n} \frac{A_t}{(1+r)^t} - \text{IO} = 0 \qquad (3)$$

Notice that the internal rate of return formula is simply the NPV formula solved for that particular value of r that causes the NPV to equal zero. In other words, the same basic equation is used for both methods, but in the NPV method the discount rate (k) is specified and the NPV is found, while in the IRR method, the NPV is specified to equal zero and the value of r that forces the NPV to equal zero is found.

We will illustrate the internal rate of return calculation using the example of the previous section where the investment had a net present value using .15 as the discount rate.

We want to find the rate of discount that causes the sum of the present values of the cash flows to be equal to zero. Assume our first choice (on arbitrary guess) is.15. In the preceding situation we found that the net present value using .15 is a positive ₹ 4,108. We want to change the discount rate so that the present value is zero. Should we increase or decrease the rate of discount for our second estimate? To decrease the present value of the future cash flow, we should increase the rate of discount (thus causing the present value of future cash flows that are positive to be smaller).

Let us try .20 as the rate of discount.

Period	*Cash Flow*	*Present Value Factor*	*Present Value*
0	– ₹ 64,320	1.0000	– ₹ 64,320
1	20,000	.8333	16,666
2	25,000	.6944	17,360
3	28,000	.5787	16,204
4	24,000	.4623	11,095
			Net Present value = – ₹ 2,995

The net present value is negative, indicating that the .20 rate of discount is too large. Assume that we try .18:

Period	*Cash Flow*	*Present Value Factor*	*Present Value*
0	– ₹ 64,320	1.0000	– ₹ 64,320
1	20,000	.8475	16,950
2	25,000	.7182	17,950
3	28,000	.6086	17,041
4	24,000	.5158	12,379
		Net Present Value	= 0

The net present value is zero, using .18 as the rate of discount, which by definition means that .18 is the internal rate of return of the investment. This degree of computational difficulty has discouraged many users, despite access to computers that can perform the arithmatic in seconds.

However, when all cash flows are equal, the calculation of a project's internal rate of return is relatively very simple. To illustrate this annuity type problem of even cash flows, consider a firm with a required rate of return of 10% and a project that involves an initial outlay of ₹ 45,555. If the investment is taken, the after-tax flows are expected to be ₹ 15,000 per annum over the project's four-year life. In this cash, the internal rate of return is equal to the following equation:

$$₹\ 45{,}555 = \frac{₹\ 15{,}000}{(1+r)^1} + \frac{₹\ 15{,}000}{(1+r)^2} + \frac{₹\ 15{,}000}{(1+r)^3} + \frac{₹\ 15{,}000}{(1+r)^4}$$

By considering the present value of an annuity, this equation can be reduced to

$$₹\ 45{,}555 = ₹\ 15{,}000 \left[\sum_{t=1}^{n} \frac{₹\ 1}{(1+r)^t} \right]$$

Use of table values for $\left[\sum_{t=1}^{n} 1/(1+i)^t \right]$ for various combinations of i and t, further reduces this equation to :

$$₹\ 45{,}555 = ₹\ 15{,}000 \left[\begin{array}{c} \text{Table Value} \\ \text{4 years} \\ \text{IRR percent} \end{array} \right]$$

Dividing both sides by ₹ 15,000, this becomes

$$₹\ 3.037 = \left[\begin{array}{c} \text{Table Value} \\ \text{4 years} \\ \text{IRR percent} \end{array} \right]$$

Hence, we are looking for a table value of 3.037 in the four year row. This value occurs when *i* equals 12%, which means that 12% is the internal rate of return for the investment.

If a firm is considering various proposals having differential cash flows, the projects having greater IRR than the firm's required rate of return should be selected. To illustrate, assume again a firm with a required rate of return of 10% is considering three investment proposals and the differential cash flows:

Period		*Cash Flow*	
	Proposal A	*Proposal B*	*Proposal C*
0	–₹ 1,00,000	–₹ 1,00,000	–₹ 1,00,000
	33,620	0	10,000
	33,620	0	30,000
	33,620	0	60,000

Because project A is an annuity, we can easily calculate its internal rate of return by determining the table value necessary to equate the present value of the future cash flows with the initial outlay. This computation is done as follows:

$$IO = A_t \left[\sum_{t=1}^{n} \frac{1}{(1+r)^t} \right] \tag{4}$$

The uneven nature of the future cash flows associated with project C necessitates the use of the trial-and-error search method. The internal rate of return for project C is equal to the value of IRR in the following equation :

$$₹\ 1,00,000 = \frac{₹\ 10,000}{(1+r)^1} + \frac{₹\ 30,000}{(1+r)^2} + \frac{₹\ 60,000}{(1+r)^3} + \frac{₹\ 70,000}{(1+r)^4}$$

Arbitrarily selecting a discount rate of 15% and substituting it into above equation for IRR reduces the right-hand side of the equation to ₹ 1,10,855. Therefore, since the present value of the future cash flows is larger than the initial outlay, we must raise the discount rate in order to find the project's internal rate of return. Substituting 20% for the discount rate, the right-hand side of the above equation now becomes ₹ 97,648. As this is less than the initial outlay of ₹ 1,00,000, we must now decrease the discount rate. In other words, we know that internal rate of return for this project is between 15% and 20%. Since the present value of the future flows discounted back to present at 20% was only ₹ 2,352 too low a discount rate of 19% is selected. A discount rate of 19% reduced the present value of the future inflow down to ₹ 1,00,102, which is approximately the same as the initial outlay.

COMPUTING THE IRR FOR PROJECT C

1. Try r = 15%

Period	*Net Cash Flow*	*Present value factor at 15 percent*	*Present value*
1	₹ 10,000	.8696	₹ 8,696
2	30,000	.7561	22,683
3	60,000	.6575	39,450
4	70,000	.5717	40,026
Present Value of Inflows			₹ 1,10,855
Initial Outlay			₹ 1,00,000

2. Try r =20%

Period	*Net Cash Flow*	*Present value factor at 20 percent*	*Present value*
1	₹ 10,000	.8333	₹ 8,333
2	30,000	.6944	20,832
3	60,000	.5787	34,722
4	70,000	.4823	33,761
Present Value of Inflows			₹ 97,648
Initial Outlay			₹ 1,00,000

3. Try r=19%

Period	*Net Cash Flow*	*Present value factor at 19 percent*	*Present value*
1	₹ 10,000	.8403	₹ 8,403
2	30,000	.7062	21,186
3	60,000	.5934	35,604
4	70,000	.4987	34,909
Present Value of Inflows			₹ 1,00,102
Initial Outlay			₹ 1,00,000

However, if desired, the actual rate can be more precisely approximated through interpolation as follows :

	Discount rate	Present value
	19%	₹ 1,00,102
	20	97,648
Difference	1%	₹ 2,454
Proportion ₹ 102 is of ₹ 2,454		
$\frac{₹102}{₹2,454} = 0.04\%$		
19%+0.04% =19.04%		

Consequently, project's internal rate of return is 19.04%. Since the internal rate of return is greater than the firm's required rate of return of 10%, this investment should be accepted.

Notice too that r is the internal to the project itself, in contrast to the external nature of the given cost of capital, k, used in the NPV analysis. The projects are accepted or rejected by comparing the internal rate of return (r) to the required rate of return (k) under the following decision rule :

IRR (r) > RRR (k)	*Accept*
IRR (r) < RRR (k)	*Reject*
IRR (r) = RRR (k)	*Indifferent*

Thus projects earnings as internal rate of return in excess of the cost of capital are accepted while those earnings less than the cost are rejected. If the internal rate of return is equal to the cost of capital, accepting the project should not result in any change in the firm's share price. This is because the firm is earning exactly the rate that its shareholders are requiring. On the other hand, if the project yields or internal rate of return are greater than the investor's required rate of return, its acceptance should increase the firm's share price. Similarly, the acceptance of a project with an internal rate of return below the investor's required rate of return will decrease the firm's share price.

The IRR criterion appeals to many firms because r is expressed as a percentage and is readily comparable to the firm's computed cost of capital, k, which is also expressed as a percentage. Further, a few feel that the seperation of the IRR calculation from the cost of capital presents a better position from which to judge the proposed project on its own operating merits, independently of the cost of capital, which appears to the few to fluctuate widely, frequently, and beyond their control.

RELATIONSHIP BETWEEN THE IRR AND NPV: INDEPENDENT PROJECTS

Clearly the IRR and NPV methods are closely related. To bring out this relationship let us consider the set of all "conventional" investment projects, where a conventional project is defined as one in which the initial outlay is followed by a stream of net receipts of the form: –+++ (or if the outlay takes place, over more than one year we have cash flows of the form: ––+++). The necessary and sufficient condition for a project's inclusion in the set of conventional investment projects is that there will be only one *change* in sign in the cash flow. Thus a project with large terminal costs: – +++– is precluded since there are *two* changes in sign: the first following the initial investment outlay and the second preceding the terminal year.

The IRR for any conventional project can be written as :

$$NPV = \sum_{t=1}^{n} \frac{A_t}{(1+r)^t} - IO \tag{5}$$

where r denotes the IRR.

The NPV for the *some* project can be written as

$$NPV = \sum_{t=1}^{n} \frac{A_t}{(1+k)^t} > IO, \text{ if the NPV } > 0 \tag{6}$$

or

$$NPV = \sum_{t=1}^{n} \frac{A_t}{(1+k)^t} < IO, \text{ if the NPV } < 0 \tag{7}$$

If we assume that the project has a positive NPV, equation (5) and inequality (6) must hold simultaneously. This implies that the left hand side of (5) is smaller than the left hand side of (6). Since by definition their numerators are identical, this implies r>k, and conversely for the assumption of a negative NPV. Thus, the IRR and NPV methods imply the same investment decision. *If a project is acceptable by the NPV rule (i.e., NPV>0), it is also acceptable by the IRR rule since we have just shown that r>k; but if project fails the NPV test, that is, its NPV is negative, it will also be rejected by the IRR rule since in such a case r<k.*

NPV > 1	Accept	IRR (r) > RRR (k)
NPV < 1	Reject	IRR (r) < RRR (k)
NPV = 0	Indifferent	IRR (r) = RRR (k)

This relationship is also shown in Figure-1, which graphs the NPV of a conventional investment project as a function of the discount rate. When the discount rate=0 (at the intercept with the vertical axis) the NPV equals the algebraic sum of the stream of net receipts minus the initial outlay, $\sum_{t=1}^{n} A_t$—10; as the discount rate approaches infinity the NPV is reduced zero, i.e. PV = 10. Since we have assumed the project to be conventional in form, the function slopes downward monotonically as the discount rate increases. For every increase in the discount rate the positive cash flow is reduced while the initial investment outlay remains constant, and therefore the NPV declines. (In general, this function is a n-degree polynomial, and therefore will *not* be linear except in the limiting case where n=1, that is, in the case of a one period investment project). The intercept with the horizontal axis denotes the internal rate of return, r, since by definition r is that rate of discount which reduces the NPV of a project to zero.

FIGURE-1

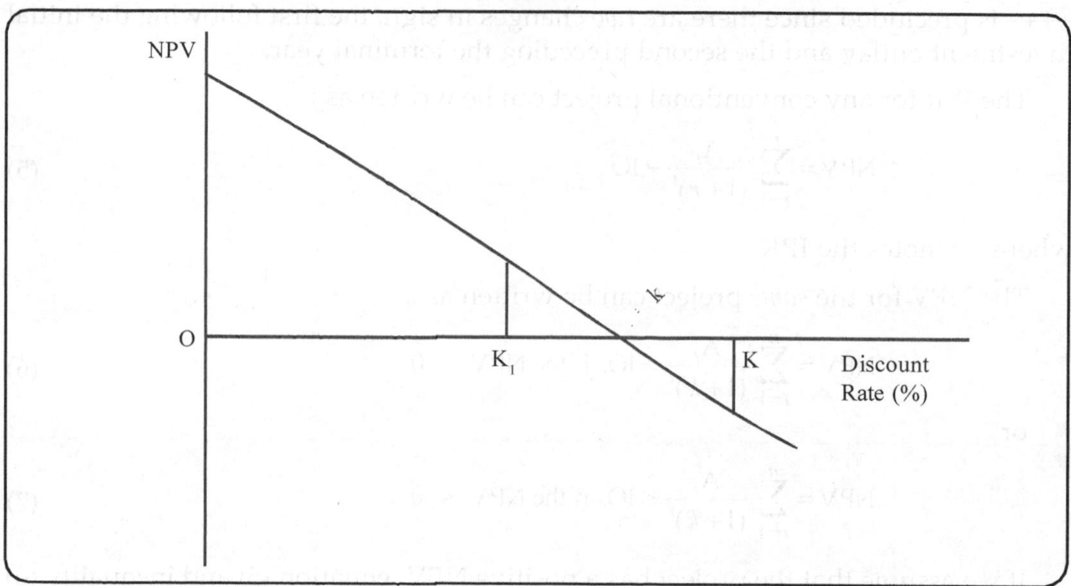

From Figure-1 we can again see that where the NPV is positive for example, at a discount of K_1, $r>k$. Conversely, where the NPV is negative, for example, using a discount rate equal to K, $r<k$. In sum, both methods give the same accept-reject decisions. If a project is profitable by the NPV criterion it will also be profitable by the IRR criterion, and vice versa. Thus, faced with the problem of differentiating acceptable from unacceptable investments, both decision criteria yield the same answers.

RANKING INVESTMENT PROPOSALS

Despite the fact that both the NPV and the IRR criteria result in the same accept and reject decisions, this equivalence does not necessarily hold for the *ranking* of investment proposals. Consider, for example, the cash flows of the following two investment projects.

Project	*Project A*	*Project B*
0	– ₹ 10,000	– ₹ 10,000
1	1,000	6,500
2	2,000	6,500
3	20,000	6,500

The internal rates of return of the projects are

$r_A = 35\%$

r_B = 42 to 43%

Their NPV's, using a 10% discount rate are

NPV_A = ₹ 7,581.00

NPV_B = ₹ 6,165.50

To clarify this differential ranking, we graph the NPV of each of the projects as a function of discount rate in Figure-2. The ranking of the projects by their internal rate of return is constant, and does *not* depend on the discount rate used-clearly 42 to 43% always exceed 35%. But it is equally from Figure-2 that the ranking of projects by the NPV need not be constant, and that it does depend on the discount rate used. If the two functions cross in the positive quadrant of the diagramme, and such is the case in Figure-2 the dominance of one project over another will not be absolute. In our example, if the discount rate is less than R_o, project A is ranked first, but for higher discount rates project B is ranked ahead of A.

Which ranking is to be preferred? On the surface the difference in ranking might not seem too serious. After all, a maximising firm will not accept the first five or ten projects, but will choose to those whose NPV's are positive. And as we have already shown, this set of projects, despite differences in the relative rankings, is identical to the set which results when we use the IRR. Unfortunately, the world is not always so simple as to permit a straight-forward accept-reject decision. For a variety of reasons, the firm may be confronted with two or more mutually exclusive investment projects, projects which if accepted imply the rejection of other proposals. Where this is true, the firm must choose *between* the two alternatives, and the ranking becomes crucial. Clearly, if A and B in our example are mutually exclusive, the NPV and IRR rankings indicate different orders of priority. At a 10% discount rate the firm would prefer A by the NPV rule; however, should it use the IRR rule, B would be preferred.

FIGURE-2

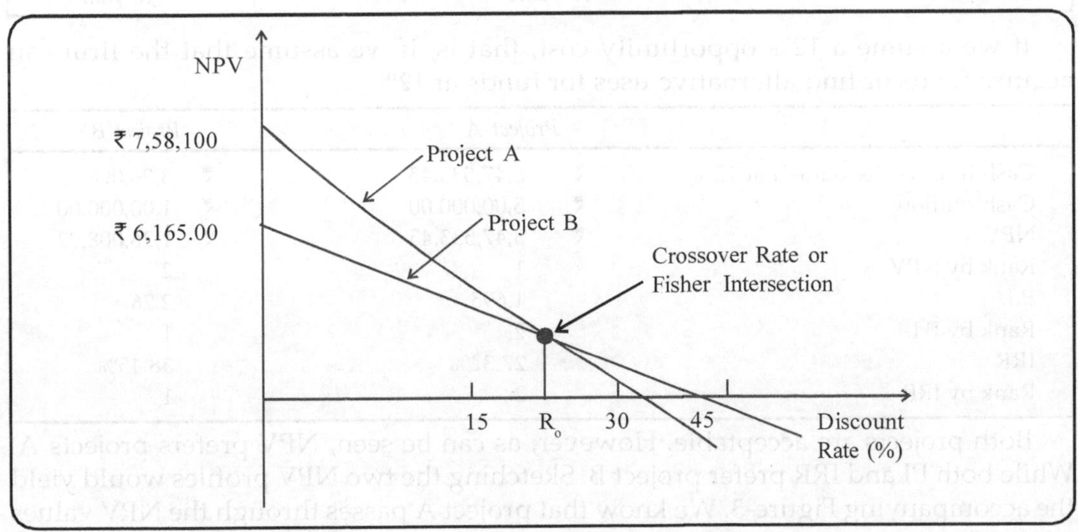

The problems raised by the possible existence of mutually exclusive projects cannot be brushed aside with the remark that they are theoretical curiousities. It should be noted that even where the initial decision is not inherently mutually exclusive, the firm often must choose among a number of alternative means of carrying out the project, and these alternatives are mutually exclusive.

RELATIONSHIP BETWEEN IRR AND NPV: DEPENDENT PROJECTS

When the relationships among projects create mutually exclusive choice situation, the relative ranking of projects becomes important. In this context the fact that the IRR ranks projects one-and-for-all without regard to the discount rate, that is, without regard to the opportunity cost of the capital, is cause for concern. This will become clear if we consider a number of examples.

SIZE DISPARITY PROBLEM

The size disparity problem occurs when mutually exclusive projects of unequal size are examined. Under such conditions there *could be* conflicts in the rankings assigned to the various projects by NPV, PI, and IRR. The major reason that such conflicts exist is that the NPV measures the absolute magnitude of the excess of discounted cash inflows over discounted cash outflows (which could form larger investments) whereas PI measures relative profitability of the discounted cash inflows per rupee of discounted cash outflow, and IRR measures the compounded rate of return earned on the original investment of the discount rate, which equates discounted cash inflows to discounted cash outflow (both of the latter techniques usually favour smaller investments). Consider the cash flows of the following two projects :

	Project A	*Project B*
Original investment	– ₹ 5,00,000	– ₹ 1,00,000
Cash inflows each year	1,50,000	40,000
Useful life	10 years	10 years

If we assume a 12% opportunity cost, that is, if we assume that the firm can acquire funds or find alternative uses for funds at 12%.

		Project A		*Project B*
Cash inflows discounted at 12%	₹	8,47,533.45	₹	3,26,008.92
Cash outflow	₹	5,00,000.00	₹	1,00,000.00
NPV	₹	3,47,533.45	₹	1,26,008.92
Rank by NPV		1		2
P.I.		1.695		2.26
Rank by P.I.		2		1
IRR		27.32%		38.45%
Rank by IRR		2		1

Both projects are acceptable. However, as can be seen, NPV prefers projects A. While both PI and IRR prefer project B. Sketching the two NPV profiles would yield the accompanying Figure-3. We know that project A passes through the NPV values

FIGURE-3

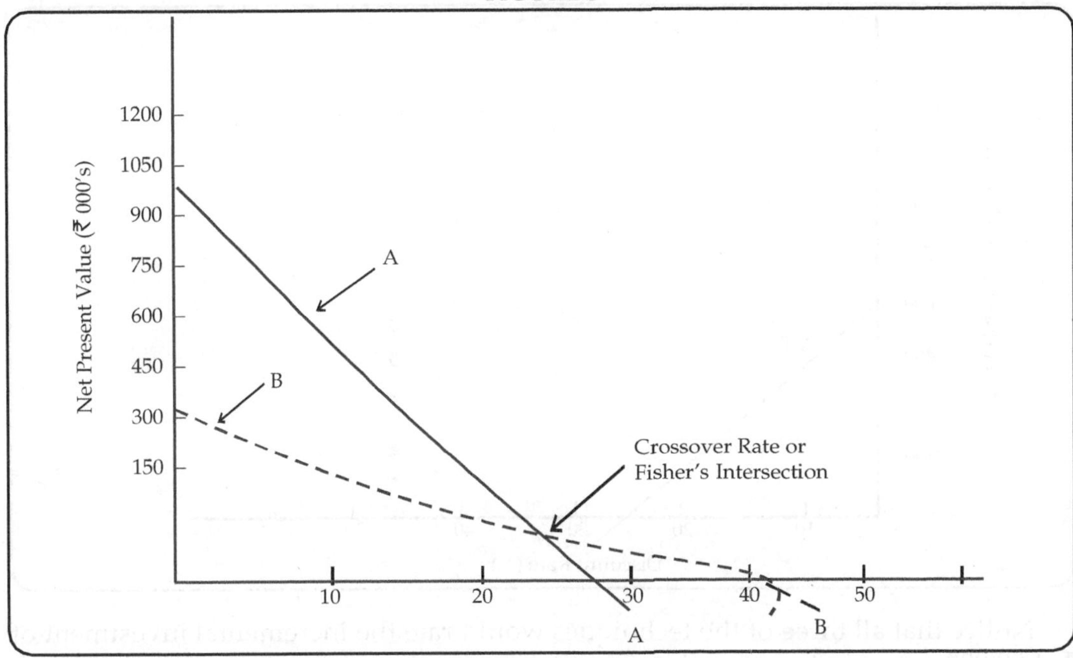

of ₹ 10,00,000 at 0% ₹ 3,47,533 at 12%, and ₹ 0 at 27.32%. Project B, on the other hand, passes through the NPV values of ₹ 3,00,000 at 0%, ₹ 1,26,008.92 at 12%, and ₹ 0 at 38.45%. The Fisher's intersection occurs between 24% and 25% with an NPV of ₹ 45,454.

How is the conflict between NPV and PI and IRR resolved? The resolution depends upon what conditions are faced by the firm in making its capital expenditure decisions. If capital rationing exists, we must evaluate the returns on the incremental investment in the larger project. If the incremental investment required by the larger project is available and if it offers a positive NPV at the appropriate required rate, the larger project should be considered for acceptance. The larger project should be accepted if the incremental investment in the larger project cannot be placed into another project or projects which offers a greater aggregate NPV at the appropriate required rate. To illustrate this process, consider again the two mutually exclusive projects from preceding example. For the incremental investment, in project A, the computation of the NPV, PI, and IRR is done in the following table and shown in Figure-4.

	Project A	*Project B*	*Incremental Flows A-B*
Original investment	– ₹ 5,00,000	– ₹ 1,00,000	₹4,00,000
Cash inflows each year	₹ 1,50,000	₹ 40,000	₹1,10,000
NPV at 12%			2,21,524.53
PI			1.554
IRR			24.4%

FIGURE-4

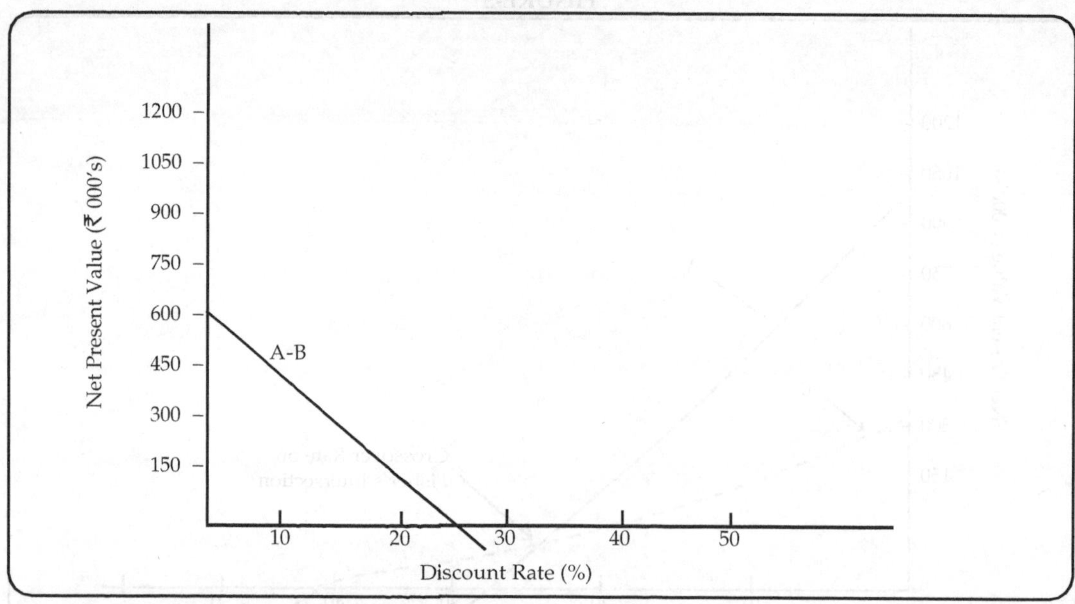

Notice that all three of the techniques would rate the incremental investment of ₹ 4,00,000 in project A as being justified by the incremental returns generated. Finally, project A would be accepted if alternatives available for the commitment of the incremental ₹ 4,00,000 would not generate an aggregate NPV of more than ₹ 2,21,524.53. This is equivalent to saying that if all the firm can invest is ₹ 5,00,000, then project A should be accepted unless some other feasible combination of projects generate an NPV in excess of ₹ 3,47,533.45 (the NPV for project A).

In concluding this example, consider the NPV profile of the incremental investment A-B. As might be expected, this profile is merely the geometric difference between the profiles for project A and project B. Notice that the IRR (24.4%) for the incremental project is precisely equal to the rate of return over cost (Fisher's intersection). It is often much easier to find the IRR for the incremental project than it is to solve for the rate of return over cost (designated r^*) directly. To solve for r^* directly for projects A and B would require solution of the following equation for r^* :

NPV of project A at r^*=NPV of project B at r^*

$$-5,00,000\sum_{t=1}^{10}+\frac{₹\ 1,50,000}{(1+r^*)^t}=-₹\ 1,00,000+\sum_{i=1}^{10}\frac{₹\ 40,000}{(1+r^*)^t}$$

The solution of this equation is simplified by the equal annual cash inflows, which enables the use of the present value of an annuity factor. Notice that upon simplification the preceding expression becomes:

$$\frac{₹\ 1{,}50{,}000 - ₹\ 40{,}000}{(1+r^*)^t} = ₹\ 4{,}00{,}000$$

This is exactly the IRR of the incremental investment in project A

TIME DISPARITY PROBLEM

In addition to the projects that vary as to size of original investment, firms often have to evaluate mutually exclusive projects wherein differences exists with respect to the sequence of the time of cash flows. These time disparities, coupled with differing implicit assumptions about the rate of return that can be earned on intermediate cash inflows, can lead to conflicts in ranking between NPV (or PI) and IRR). Again, this problem may be illustrated through the use of an example of a firm whose cost of capital is 15% and is considering two mutually exclusive projects A and B, whose characteristics are as follows:

Period	*Cash Flow*	
	Project A	*Project B*
0	– ₹ 3,50,000	– ₹ 3,50,000
1	50,000	2,50,000
2	1,00,000	2,00,000
3	1,50,000	1,00,000
4	2,25,000	50,000
6	3,00,000	50,000
Total Cash flows	₹ 8,25,000	₹ 6,50,000

By examining the discounted cash flow methods, we notice that project B has a significantly higher IRR than project A. However at the firm's cost of capital of 15%. Project B has a lower NPV than project A. The IRR technique favours projects that have high cash inflows early in the life of the project (*i.e.*, such cash flows significantly increase the internal rate of return because it was assumed that they can be reinvested at this higher rate). The NPV method, on the other hand, assumes reinvestment at a lower rate (*i.e.*, the firm's cost of capital) and hence assesses a smaller penality for cash inflows received later in the project's life compared to the IRR technique. Project A has greater cash inflows ₹ 4,95,312 over its life than project B (₹ 4,87,820) and at lower reinvestment rates (such as the cost of capital) this difference more than compensates for the bulk of the cash inflows occuring in the last two years of its useful life. Thus, the NPV profiles for the two projects demonstrates that project A is preferred to B at all discount rates less than 16.1% to play an important role in resolving the conflict between NPV and IRR.

	Project A	Project B
Discounted cash inflows at 15%	₹ 4,95,312	₹ 4,87,820
NPV	₹ 1,45,312	₹ 1,37,820
Rank by NPV	(1)	(2)
PI	1.415	1.394
Rank by PI	(1)	(2)
IRR	27.2%	37.55%
Rank by IRR	(2)	(1)

The compound interest process of the internal rate and present value methods assumes that at the end of each period the cash inflow (including both recovery of principal and return on investment) is reinvested from period to period at a relevant rate. In particular, NPV assumes that the funds are reinvested at the discount rate applied to the project (usually a weighted cost of capital). By contrast, the IRR approach assumes that the funds are reinvested at the project's internal rate of return. If cash inflows can be reinvested at a rate that exceeds the firm's cost of capital, the NPV method understates the value of the investment. Conversely, if the cash flows can only be reinvested at a rate below the internal rate of return, the IRR model overstates the true rate of return on the project. However, the NPV and PI will always produce consistent project rankings under time disparities since the two methods make the same reinvestment assumption, *i.e.*, the cash flows over the life of the project can be reinvested at the required rate of return.

The conflict between NPV and IRR (which can occur when a time disparity exists between mutually exclusive projects) can be resolved by explicitly incorporating a reinvestment rate into both the NPV and IRR approaches. This is accomplished by calculating the terminal value of the project, given that intermediate cash inflows can be reinvested at a specified rate. Then, the terminal value can be discounted to the present value using the NPV method. Similarly, the true internal rate of return can be found by ascertaining the discount rate that equates the terminal value to the discounted cash outflows.

UNEQUAL LIVES PROBLEM

Many capital budgeting problems involve decisions between mutually exclusive projects having unequal useful lives. Such projects are not directly comparable, because they usually suffer from both a size disparity and a time disparity. Hence, under this combination of the two disparities, conflicts in ranking *could occur* among NPV, PI and IRR. The critical question here is what will take place at the end of the shorter-lived project. Will it be replaced by another asset of similar profitability, or will the funds be *reinvested* elsewhere in the firm at a relevant rate?

One common situation wherein mutually exclusive projects exhibit both a time and size disparity as well as having unequal useful lives involves the decision between replacing equipment versus rebuilding equipment. In general, replacement will have higher NPV, owing to its longer life, even though the initial cost is greater. On the other hand, rebuilding could very well have a higher IRR and PI, because of its smaller cost. To illustrate, consider a firm (whose cost of capital is 18%) which is evaluating the A and B, two projects:

Period	*Cash Flow*	
	Project A	*Project B*
0	– ₹ 5,00,000	– ₹ 5,00,000
1	3,00,000	2,00,000
2	3,00,000	2,00,000
3	3,00,000	2,00,000
4	—	2,00,000
5	—	2,00,000
6	—	2,00,000

The NPVs, PIs, and IRRs are as follows:

	Project A	*Project B*
Discounted cash inflows at 18%	₹ 8,52,281	₹ 6,99,520
NPV	1,52,281	1,99,520
Rank by NPV	(2)	(1)
PI	1.304	1.399
Rank by PI	(2)	(1)
IRR	35.5%	32%
Rank by IRR	(1)	(2)

Notice that NPV and PI indicate that project B is better project, while the internal rate of return favours project A. This ranking inconsistency is caused by the different life spans of the projects being compared. In this case the decision is a difficult one because the projects are not comparable.

This problem of incomparability of projects with unequal useful lives is not merely a result of different lives; rather it arises because further profitable investment proposals are affected by the decision currently being made. If it can realistically be assumed that at the end of the life of each project it will be replaced by another of like profitability, then for ranking the projects correctly a replacement chain to equalise the life spans is to be created. On the other hand, if cash flows from the short-lived project can be assumed to be reinvested at the relevant rate uptil the termination of the longer-lived asset, we should compute the terminal value and expected NPV. If capital rationing does not exist, then the project with the greater expected NPV should be accepted (as long as this value is positive). If capital rationing does exist, we have to evaluate various sets of feasible (satisfying both budget requirements and mutually exclusive conditions) assets so that the set that maximised expected NPV can be selected.

NON CONVENTIONAL INVESTMENT: MULTIPLE RATES OF RETURN PROBLEM

The NPV and IRR methods could also make conflicting selections because the IRR method, when applied to cash flows of a proposal, may produce more than one internal rate of return. No unique internal rate of return then exists. The decision-maker does not know which internal rate of return to utilise, and, in selecting anyone of the rates found to compare to the cost of capital, may make a decision inconsistent with maximising shareholders' wealth.

The possibility that more than one internal rate of return exists arises whenever the sequence of cash flows of a proposal has more than one reversal of sign. When more than one reversal of sign exists, the cash flow pattern is called a *broken* cash flow series. To illustrate, consider a company having following cash flow series :

Proposal	*Year*					
	0	*1*	*2*	*3*	*4*	*5*
A	—	—	—	+	+	+
B	—	+	+	+	—	+
C	—	+	+	+	+	+
D	—	+	—	+	—	+

Proposals A and C are examples of *standard* cash flow series. In such series one or more cash outflows is followed by an unbroken stream of cash inflows. Only one reversal of sign occurs. Consequently, a unique internal rate of return exists for a standard cash flow series.

Broken cash flows can be observed for proposals B and D. For proposal B the outlay at t=0 is followed by a cash inflows at t=1 (one reversal of sign). Cash inflows continue until t=4 when an outflow (reversal of sign) again occurs. At t=5 an inflow (another reversal of sign) again appears. Altogether, three reversals of sign occur and therefore proposal B may have as many as three internal rates of return. Proposal D may have as many as five internal rates of return since, with alternate outflows and inflows, five reversals of sign exist. In general a broken cash flow series may, as an upper limit, have as many different internal rates of return as there are reversals of sign.

As an example of a proposal having more than one rate of return, consider the following proposal of an oil company which is trying to decide whether or not to install a high-speed pump on a well that is already in operation. The estimated incremental cash flows are given below :

Year	*Estimated Cash Flow*
0	– ₹ 1,60,000
1	10,00,000
2	–10,00,000

The pump will cost ₹ 1,60,000 to install. During the first year of operation it will produce ₹ 10,00,000 more oil than the pump which is currently in place. But during the second year, the high-speed pump produces ₹ 10,00,000 less oil because the well has been depleted. The question is whether or not to accept the rapid pumping technique, which speeds up cash flows in the near term at the expense of cash flows in the long-term. Figure-5 shows the NPV of the project for different discount rates. If the opportunity cost of capital is 10% the NPV rate would reject the project because it has negative NPV at that rate. If we are using the IRR rule, the project has two IRRs, 25% (A) and 400% (B). Since both exceed the opportunity cost of capital, the project would probably be accepted.

FIGURE-5

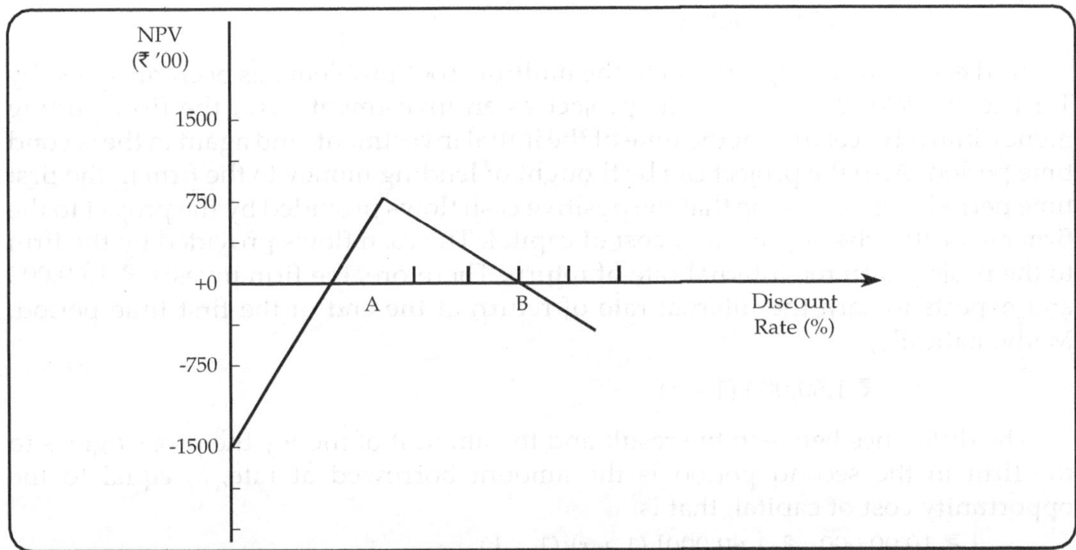

Mathematically, the multiple IRRs are a result of Descartes' rule of signs, which implies that every time the cash flow changes signs there will be a new root to the problem solution. For the above example, the signs of cash flows change twice. The IRR is the rate which causes the discounted value of the cash flows to equal zero. Hence we solve the following equation for IRR.

$$NPV = 0 = \frac{-₹\ 1,60,000}{(1+r)^0} + \frac{₹\ 10,00,000}{(1+r)^1} + \frac{-₹\ 10,00,000}{(1+r)^2}$$

$$NPV = 0 = \frac{-₹\ 1,60,000(1+r)^2 + ₹\ 10,00,000\ (1+r) - ₹\ 10,00,000}{(1+r)^2}$$

$$₹\ 1,60,000\ (1+r)^2 + ₹\ 10,00,000\ (1+r) - ₹\ 10,00,000 = 0$$

This is clearly a quadratic equation and has two roots, it has the general form :

$$ax^2 + bx + c = 0$$

and can be solved using the quadratic formula:

$$x = \frac{-b \pm \sqrt{b^2 - 4ac}}{2a}$$

Therefore, for our example, the roots are:

$$(1+r) = x = \frac{₹\ 10,00,000 \pm \sqrt{10,00,000^2 - 4(₹\ 1,60,000)(₹\ 10,00,000)}}{2\ (1,60,000)}$$

$$(1+r) = \frac{₹\ 10,00,000 \pm ₹\ 6,00,000}{₹\ 3,20,000}$$

$$r = 25\% \text{ or } 400\%$$

And economic interpretation to the multiple root problem has been provided by Teichroew.[3] We can think of the project as an investment, with the firm putting money into it twice: first, at the time of the initial investment, and again in the second time period. Also the project can be thought of lending money to the firm in the first time period. Let us assume that the positive cash flows provided by the project to the firm are at 10% the opportunity cost of capital. The cash flows provided by the firm to the project earn the internal rate of return. Therefore, the firm invests ₹ 1,60,000 and expects to earn the internal rate of return at the end of the first time period. Mathematically,

$$₹\ 1,60,000\ (1 + r)$$

The difference between the result and the amount of money the project gives to the firm in the second period is the amount borrowed at rate, k, equal to the opportunity cost of capital, that is,

$$[₹\ 10,00,000 - ₹\ 1,60,000]\ (1 + r)\ (1 + k)$$

The firm then repays ₹ 10,00,000 at the end of the second period :

$$₹\ 10,00,000 = [₹\ 10,00,000 - ₹\ 1,60,000]\ (1+r)](1+k)$$

Recalling that k=10%, we can solve for the rate of return on investment :

$$\frac{₹\ 10,00,000 - ₹\ 11,00,000}{₹\ 17,60,000} = 1 + r$$

$$-43.18\% = r$$

This way of looking at the cash flows of the project solves the multiple root problem because positive cash flows provided by the project are assumed to be lent at a known rate of return equal to the opportunity cost of capital. This makes it possible to insolate the rate of return on money invested in the project. This rate can be thought of as the internal rate of return. From the example on the oil pump we see that when it is viewed properly, the IRR gives the same answer as the NPV. We

3. D. Teichroew: *An Introduction to Management Science: Deterministic Models*, Wiley, New York, 1964, pp. 78-82.

should reject the project because the rate of return on investment is less than the opportunity cost of capital.

APPROPRIATE DECISION CRITERION

The choice of the appropriate decision criterion depends on the circumstances surrounding the decision and on the customary practices of the firm. It requires a method general enough to make choices that are always consistent with the goal of maximising shareholders wealth. Out of the nondiscounted cash flow criteria and discounted cash flow criteria, the later criteria typically works best for a firm that has a shareholder-wealth-maximisation objective and that recognises that the present value of the firm is enhanced by projects with discounted cash flow in excess of the project's cost. The less sophisticated non-discounted cash flow criteria for capital budgeting decisions are hard to relate to any particular corporate objective. For instance, payback criterion can be appropriately used for the firm with an overriding consideration for liquidity a very short-term spurt in earnings. But it cannot be recommended in any situations since the criterion ignores the time value of money, the timing of the cash flows, the life expectancy of the project, and the value of the inflows beyond the acceptance year. Similarly, though the accounting rate of return criterion is best applied by firms with profit-maximisation objectives, but it is not very effective criterion. Like the payback criterion, it ignores the life expectancy of the project, the cash generation of the depreciation, the time value of money, and the timing of the income stream. Only under those unusual circumstances in which the firm is looking for a net income return figures which approximates an average annual return might use this criterion.

Out of the discounted cash flow criteria for capital budgeting decisions, a significantly greater number use IRR than either NPV or PI. However, there is widespread confusion about what the internal rate of return really shows and whether it is an appropriate criterion to use as a surrogate for maximising shareholders' wealth. *Four reasons are usually advanced in favour of IRR.*

First, the IRR is an internally generated rate which does not rely on an externally derived discount rate, and therefore avoids the difficulties involved in calculating that rate. However, before a decision can be made on the basis of IRR, it has to be compared with a criterion discount rate. In addition, IRR is unreliable, when used to rank investment by a straight comparison of IRRs. Nevertheless, it might be an advantage to delay the use of a criterion discount rate until late in the decision process and to be able to make a judgement as to whether or not the unknown discount rate is likely to be above or below the known IRR.

Second, the IRR is a relative measure, relating initial cash outflows and subsequent cash inflows to produce an average rate of return, and thus is able to compare investments of substantially different sizes. NPV is an absolute measure which is consistent with the assumed objective of maximising an absolute figure of wealth rather than a rate of return. It would distinguish between the large investment with a very high return. Nevertheless, there may be circumstances, such as resources rationing, in which return per unit of outlay is relevant, NPV may be converted into a relative measure, the benefit-cost ratio or profitability index or present value index.

Third, its proponents argue that IRR can take risk and uncertainty into account more effectively than can NPV, because the 'safety margin' between IRR and the criterion rate of discount can readily be identified and its adequacy assessed. Without anticipating the discussion of risk and uncertainty, it may be said that although there is some merit in the argument, there is little which cannot be accomplished by using the NPV method.

Lastly, the businessmen find dealing with rates of return easier and work comprehensible than dealing with absolute cash figures. They are, it is argued, used to dealing with percentage returns—but notice that these percentage returns are likely to be very closely allied to the accounting rate of return, about which there are serious reservations. If the argument is correct and this is an empirical question, misunderstandings and misconceptions may arise in managers' mind over nodiscounted 'accounting' rates and discounted cashflow rates. However, when the basic ideas behind each are explained to managers, they are more in sympathy with NPV than with IRR, partly because NPV is in fact easier to understand and its calculations are tidier than the trial and error methods often used to approximate IRR.

At this juncture one might question why such difficulties are experienced in the use of IRR. It could be said that the IRR does a good job of measuring the *compounded rate of return over time on the funds that remain invested in an asset, but the problem is that this figure has nothing at all to do with maximising shareholders' wealth.* A firm that attempted to maximise IRR could very well find that the highest IRR project had an original cost of ₹ 1,000 and a return on next year of ₹ 1,500 leading to a 50% IRR, shareholders would be pleased over the ₹ 500 return, but would raise more questions about how the remaining portion of the capital budget was invested. If management replied that they did not want to invest any more than ₹ 1,000 because to do so would deteriorate the IRR below the very attractive 50% level achieved, they would be looking for new jobs. *The NPV criterion shows, clearly and unambiguously the impact of projects on shareholders' wealth or the present value of the firm. However, the same is obviously not true for IRR.*

If three projects have NPVs of ₹ 1,00,000, ₹ 1,40,000 and ₹ 1,60,000, these figures show the magnitudes of the increase in shareholders' wealth if the respective investments are accepted. On the other hand, if these projects have IRRs of 40%, 30%, and 25% and PIs of 1.68, 1.22 and 1.53 respectively, we have no idea which of the three will lead to the greatest increase in shareholders' wealth by looking at these IRRs and PIs. In fact, the increase in shareholders' wealth can be opposite of the rankings indicated by either the IRR or PI criterion. In an informative and hard-hitting article, Keane points out :

4. S.M. Keane: 'Let scrap IRR once and for All!", *Accountancy*, February 1974, pp. 78-82.

The internal rate of return, therefore, is invalid not because of any implicit reinvestment assumption or because of the possibility of producing multiple yields, but simply because a rate of return expressed in percentage terms is inappropriate for discriminating between projects of different sizes. All but identical projects have different sizes whatever their initial outlays or expected lives may suggest, and although the rate of return method might appear at times to give correct investment advise, it is never in fact correct in principle.[4]

Weingartner[5] also has a number of uncomplimentary things to say about the profitability index. He demonstrates that given a size disparity between two mutually exclusive projects, there will be a conflict between NPV and PI whenever.

$$\frac{b_1}{b_2} < \frac{c_1}{c_2} \tag{8}$$

where

b_j = net present value of product j

c_j = cost of project j

Assume that $b_1 > b_2$, which means that the NPV criterion prefers project 1. Under the condition specified above, the PI will rank project 2 higher than 1, which is in conflict with NPV. This can be seen by noting that since all the b's and c's are positive, the following inequality exists.

$$\frac{b_1}{c_1} < \frac{b_2}{c_2} \tag{9}$$

The relationship between the PIs is as follows :

$$\text{PI}_1 = \frac{b_1 + c_1}{c_1} < \frac{b_2 + c_2}{c_2} = \text{PI}_2 \tag{10}$$

To obtain this expression, we simply added unity to both sides of the inequality. In such circumstances, as Weingartner[6] points out, the PI criterion *would lead to selection of the project with the lower net present value which would make a lower contribution to the wealth of the owners of the firm.* Finally, Weingartner concludes his article by stating :

Our examples of mutually exclusivee alternative reinforce the conclusion that PI does not provide aid in the choice among such alternatives. In two examples, ranking by means of PI and by IRR led to the same incorrect choice. In the third example, these rankings are different, and the PI criterion resulted in the wrong choice. In all these instances, the NPV criterion and Fisher's rate of return yielded similar answers which are correct in the absence of capital rationing or more complex interrelationships between investments.[7]

5. H. Martin Weingartner, "The Excess Present Value Index—A Theoretical Basis and Critique, *Journal of Accounting Research,* Autumn 2963, pp. 223-224.
6. *Ibid.,* p. 270.
7. *Ibid.,* p. 224.

ALIGNING CAPITAL BUDGETING WITH CORPORATE STRATEGY

Strategy should guide decisions about where to look for capital investment opportunities and which types of investments are most likely to have positive net present values. A decision to expand in a particular direction will not be implemented unless capital investment proposals are generated. Expertise and manpower are required to generate capital investment proposals. Thus, the strategic decision must often be backed up with research-and-development staffs, an acquisition unit, and so on. These units will increase the probability of a flow of proposals from areas expected to generate competitive advantage.

Capital budgeting policies are often biased against strategically important capital investments. The bias is typically unintentional, which makes it that much more difficult to correct. Recognizing some of the forms of this bias is helpful in designing appropriate capital investment policies to support corporate strategy.

One common type of bias is a policy favouring replacement decisions, which often lead to continuation of "business as usual." These investments are viewed as low risk by managers who often approve them with less rigorous justification than is required for investments involving departures from the past. While adjusting required returns for risk makes sense, the required returns for investments involving new ways of doing business are often set artificially high. These policies may leave managers continually frustrated in their attempts to implement corporate strategy.

An undue focus on short-term results also inhibits implementation of strategy. Companies sometimes set a limit such as three years on the payback period, the time it takes a project to return the amount invested. The justification is often that they do not want to take too much risk. A high discount rate and a short payback-period requirement favour assets with short lives, while investments of major strategic importance may take years to begin paying off. Thus, a policy designed to assure profitability may inadvertently assure that an economic profit is never achieved.

A narrow or shortsighted view is another culprit hindering implementation of strategy. Strategic investments must be evaluated in the context of their impacts on other investments now and in the future. Capital investment analysis will lead to the wrong decision if it does not include the value of future investment opportunities that may be created by the investment currently under consideration. A test-market investment may, for example, include such high costs that it loses money in even the most favourable scenario. But the purpose of the test market is not to make money. If the test market confirms an adequate customer demand, nationwide investment opportunities are thereby created. A potential source of conflict between the strategists and the capital investment analysts often arises in the recognition of potential future investment opportunities or embedded or real options created by the current investment.

Investing in growth for growth's sake is another impediment to strategy implementation. Growth is often desirable because it takes advantage of economies of scale, creates barriers to entry, and so on. But companies that want to grow simply to be bigger may find funds diverted from the activities that create economic profits. The stock market is full of examples of declining stock prices in the face of rapid growth because investors do not believe the company's growth will lead to economic profits.

Failure to give up is another barrier to strategy implementation. When a business can no longer generate an economic profit, it should be sold or abandoned. But giving up is often seen as failure. Furthermore, managers and employees in the unprofitable area will develop one scheme after another for returning the business to profitability. The decision that a viable scheme is unlikely is a painful one and is often avoided for years while capital and attention are diverted from strategically important capital investments.

Allocating capital among divisions according to past profitability is another potential detriment. First, accounting profitability is the wrong measure. A division with a functional factory that is fully depreciated for accounting purposes will have an extremely high accounting return on investment, while a division with a new factory will have a lower return on capital. Even more fundamentally, historical performance is the wrong measure. A division that requires a capital investment to become profitable is forever doomed while capital is allocated to divisions with historical profitability and no opportunities for profitable new investment.

Capital investment analysis that ignores market dynamics is another blow to implementation of strategy. One of the more common errors is forgetting that competitors will change too. A proposal for a "business as usual" capital investment will overstate profitability if it ignores declining competitive advantage. The "business as usual" investment may beat out a capital investment that would help the company improve its competitive advantage and generate economic profits.

Finally, the management reward system should be consistent with the profitability goals of the company. Many companies give lip service to profitable capital investments but base the management reward system entirely on this year's sales or accounting income. This focuses attention on short-term results rather than on the capital investments that create wealth. A compensation system based on longer-term profitability helps.

ILLUSTRATIVE PROBLEMS

1. A certain project has yearly after-tax cash outflows and inflows as tabulated below :

Period	*Outflow*	*Inflow*
0	– ₹ 25,000	0
1	– 12,500	₹ 7,500
2	0	10,000
3-6	0	12,500

Determine the payback period.

Solution

The total outflow is ₹ 37,500. To determine how many years it will take to pay this back, a table such as the one shown below may be employed.

Period		*Total Outflow*	*Total inflow*		*Difference*
0	–	₹ 25,000	0	–	₹ 25,000
1	–	37,500	₹ 7,500	–	30,000
2	–	37,500	17,500	–	20,000
3	–	37,500	30,000	–	7,500
4	–	37,500	42,500		5,000
5	–	37,500	55,000		17,500
6	–	37,500	67,500		30,000

At the end of the third year, all but ₹ 7,500 will have been recovered. An additional ₹ 12,500 in cash inflows will be generated during the fourth year. Three-fifths of this ₹ 12,500 will be needed to recover the remaining ₹ 7,500. Thus, it will take three and three-fifths years (just over three years and seven months) to recover the total of ₹ 37,500 outflow.

2. A proposed investment having an after-tax cost of ₹ 25,000 is expected to produce after-tax cash inflows as shown in table below. If the firm's hurdle rate (cost of capital) is 12%, should the investment be made?

Period	0	1	2	3	4	5
Cash Flow	– ₹ 25,000	5,000	5,000	7,500	7,500	10,000

Solution

The problem may be easily solved by constructing a solution table as shown below:

Solution Table for 12%

Time (1)	*Amount* (2)	*Discount Factor* (3)	*Present Factor* (4) = (2) (3)
0	– ₹ 25,000	1.0000	– ₹ 25,000.00
1	5,000	.8929	4,464.50
2	5,000	.7972	3,986.00
3	7,500	.7118	5,338.50
4	7,500	.6355	4,766.25
5	10,000	.5674	5,674.00
		Net Present Value =	– ₹ 771.25

The NPV is negative in this problem. Hence, the investment should not be made.

3. Rajan Textiles is considering two investments, each of which requires an initial investment of ₹ 1,80,000. The total cash inflows, that is, profits after taxes and depreciation charges, for each project are :

Year	1	2	3	4	5	6	7
Project X	₹ 30,000	50,000	60,000	65,000	40,000	30,000	16,000
Project Y	₹ 60,000	1,00,000	65,000	45,000	—	—	—

Rajan's cost of capital is 8%. Rank these investments by their excess present values. Which is the most profitable ?

Solution

Present values of both the projects are tabulated below:

Present Value at 8%

Year	Cash Flow		Discount Factor at 8%	PV of X	PV of Y
	Project X	Project Y			
0	– ₹ 1,80,000	– ₹ 1,80,000	1.000	– ₹ 1,80,000	– ₹ 1,80,000
1	30,000	60,000	.926	27,777	55,554
2	50,000	1,00,000	.857	42,865	85,750
3	60,000	65,000	.794	47,628	51,597
4	65,000	45,000	.735	47,775	33,075
5	40,000	—	.681	27,224	—
6	30,000	—	.630	18,906	—
7	16,000	—	.583	9,336	—
			Excess Present Value =	₹ 41,511	₹ 45,956

Project Y is most profitable.

4. Hind Machine Tools is considering replacing an existing machine with a new machine costing ₹ 20,000. The older machine was fully depreciated to its actual salvage value of ₹ 2,000 prior to 2013. The new machine will be depreciated over its ten-year projected life using straight-line depreciation and will have a ₹ 3,000 salvage value. It is anticipated that the new machine will reduce labour costs by ₹ 3,000 per year. Hind's income statement for 2011 is as shown below. Their cost of capital is 14% and their marginal tax rate is 40%.

Hind's Income Statement 2013

Sales:		₹ 2,50,000
Materials	₹ 75,000	
Labour	1,00,000	
Administration	21,000	
Depreciation	19,000	
Total expense :		–2,15,000
Earnings before taxes		₹ 35,000
Income tax		–14,000
After tax profit		₹ 21,000

If Hind requires an after-tax return on investment of 14% should they buy the new machine?

Solution

Calculate the after-tax cash outflow needed to purchase the machine. It costs ₹ 20,000, but the old machine can be sold for ₹ 2,000. Therefore, the actual cash outflow will be ₹ 18,000.

Calculate the increase in the after-tax cash inflows which will result from using the machine. The current yearly cash inflow, based on the 2001 income statement is the sum of the after-tax profit plus depreciation cash throw-off :

₹ 21,000 + ₹ 19,000 = ₹ 40,000

Using a depreciable value of ₹ 20,000– ₹ 3,000= ₹ 17,000 for the new machine, the depreciation will be ₹ 1,700 per year for the machine's projected ten-year life. However, labour costs will be reduced by ₹ 3,000 per year. The changes are incorporated into the proforma income statement below:

Proforma Income Statement

Sales:		₹ 2,50,000
Materials	₹ 75,000	
Labour	97,000	
Administration	21,000	
Depreciation	20,700	
Total expenses:		–2,13,700
Earnings before taxes		₹ 36,300
Income tax		–14,520
After-tax profits		₹ 21,780

The yearly cash inflow is expected to be ₹ 21,780 + ₹ 20,700 = ₹ 42,480. The yearly after-tax cash inflow has been increased, to ₹ 42,480 from ₹ 40,000. This amounts to a yearly increase of ₹ 2,460. Keeping in mind that the ₹ 3,000 salvage value will be recovered in the tenth year, a solution table can be constructed.

Solution Table for 14%

Period	*Amount*	*Discount Factor*	*Present value*
0	– ₹ 18,000	1.0000	– ₹ 18,000
1	2,480	.8772	2,175
2	2,480	.7695	1,908
3	2,480	.6750	1,674
4	2,480	.5921	1,468
5	2,480	.5194	1,288
6	2,480	.4556	1,129
7	2,480	.3996	991
8	2,480	.3506	869
9	2,480	.3075	763
10	5,480	.2697	1,478
			NPV = – ₹ 4,257

Since the NPV is negative, the machine does not yield the required 14% and should not be purchased.

5. Refer to problem 4 and solve the problem using present value from annuity tables.

Solution

Reconstruct the solution table as shown below :

Solution table for 14%

Period	*Amount*	*Discount Factor*	*Present value*
0	– ₹ 18,000	1.000	– ₹ 18,000
1-9	2,480	4.9464	12,267
10	5,480	.2697	1,478
			NPV= – ₹ 4,255

6. Refer to Problem-5, and assume that the old machine could be sold for ₹ 6,000 and originally cost ₹ 10,000. And the tax rate is increased to 48%. However would this affect the profitability of the project?

Solution

The sale of the machine for ₹ 6,000 would result in a recapture of depreciation of ₹ 4,000, based on a salvage value of ₹ 2,000. The ₹ 4,000 would be taxed at 48%. The result is ₹ 1,920 goes in tax. Thus, ₹ 4,080 of the original ₹ 6,000 would remain. Based on the cost of the new machine of ₹ 20,000, the actual outflow of cash required to buy it would be ₹ 20,000— ₹ 4,080= ₹ 15,920. The ₹ 15,920 would replace the ₹ 18,000 and the solution table would appear as follows :

Solution Table for 14%

Period (1)	*Amount* (2)	*Discount Factor* (3)	*Present value* (4) = (2) × (3)
0	– ₹ 15,920	1.0000	– ₹ 15,920
1-9	2,376	4.9464	11,753
10	5,376	.2697	1,450
			NPV = – ₹ 2,717

Based on the 14% cost of capital, the project would still be rejected.

7. Adarsh Manufacturing owns a machine which is six years old and has an estimated remaining physical life of two years. The following cash flow estimates have been made for the machine:

End of year	*Net Cash Inflow*	*Salvage value*
6	—	₹ 1,20,000
7	₹ 80,000	60,000
8	50,000	0

Management wishes to determine whether the machine should be retained for one more year. The company's required rate of return is 10%.

Solution

Net cash inflow in year 7	₹ 80,000
Interest on salvage value forgone year 6	
= (0.1) (₹ 1,20,000)	12,000
+ Decline in salvage value year 6 to year 7	
= (₹ 1,20,000– ₹ 60,000)	60,000
	₹ 72,000

Therefore, ₹ 80,000 exceeds ₹ 72,000 by an amount of ₹ 8,000. As it is assumed that the flows are received at the end of the year, the ₹ 8,000 should be discounted to present value. Thus :

₹ 8,000(0.90909) = ₹ 7,272.

Alternative the problem could have been analysed as a simple net present value calculation. Thus:

NPV = – ₹ 1,20,000 + (₹ 80,000+ ₹ 60,000) (DF)
NPV = – ₹ 1,20,000 + (₹ 1,40,000) (.90909)
NPV = – ₹ 1,20,000 + ₹ 1,27,272 = ₹ 7,272

That is, the company is foregoing ₹ 1,20,000 current salvage value in order to obtain net cash inflows of ₹ 80,000 and salvage value of ₹ 60,000 in one year's time. The analysis, therefore, indicates that the machine should be retained for at least one more year.

8. Refer to Problem-7 and assume that the management may also be interested in finding out whether, given the current forecasts, the machine should be retained for the remaining two years of its life.

Solution

If this is done the company will forego ₹ 1,20,000, which is the current salvage value, and receive in lieu net cash inflows in year 7 and 8 or ₹ 80,000 and ₹ 50,000 respectively. There is no salvage value at the end of year 8. Thus :

NPV = – ₹ 1,20,000+(₹ 80,000) (0.90909)+(₹ 50,000) (0.82645)
NPV = – ₹ 1,20,000+ ₹ 72,727+ ₹ 41,323 = – ₹ 5,950

Therefore, it seems that unless there is some upward revision in the estimates of cash inflows for year 8, the machine will be retired at the end of the seventh year.

9. One of the largest and most profitable companies in the country is faced with the prospect of having to replace a large stamping machine. Two machines currently being marketed will do the job satisfactorily. The Superior Stamping machine costs ₹ 50,000 and will require cash running expenses of ₹ 20,000 per year. The Peerless machine costs ₹ 75,000 but running expenses are only expected to be ₹ 15,000 per year. Both machines have a ten-year useful life with no salvage value and would be depreciated on a straightline basis.

(a) If the company pays a 50% tax rate and has a 10% after tax required rate of return, which machine should it purchase?

(b) Would your answer be different if the required rate of return were 8%?

Solution

	Peerless	*Superior*	*Differential*
Initial outlay	₹ 75,000	₹ 50,000	₹ 25,000
Operating expenses	15,000	20,000	5,000
Depreciation	7,500	5,000	2,500
Expenses savings-depreciation			2,500
Tax on the above			1,250
Cash flow			3,750
(Expense savings of ₹ 5,000-tax)			
Present value of ` 1 received cash year for 10 years = 5.6502.			
₹ 3,750 × 5.65 = ₹ 21,188			

As the present value of the incremental cash flow benefits, ₹ 21,188 is less than the differential cash outlay of ₹ 25,000 the additional cost of the Peerless machine cannot be justified. The superior machine should be purchased.

(b) Present value of ` 1 received each year for 10 years at 8% = 6.7101,
₹ 3,750 × 6.7101 = ₹ 25,163

As the present value of incremental benefits, ₹ 25,163, now exceeds the incremental outlay of ₹ 25,000 the Peerless machine should be purchased.

10. Sardar Transport has ₹ 25,00,000 allocated for capital budgeting purposes. The following proposals and associated profitability indexes have been determined:

Project	*Amount*	*Profitability Index*
1	₹ 12,50,000	1.22
2	8,75,000	1.25
3	5,00,000	1.20
4	3,75,000	0.95
5	11,25,000	1.18

(a) Which of the above investments should be undertaken?

(b) Would the firm be maximising the price of the equity shares by turning down projects having an index large than one?

Solution

(a) Selecting these projects with the highest index values would indicate

Project	*Amount*	*P.I.*	*Net present value*
1	₹ 12,50,000	1.22	₹ 2,75,000
2	8,75,000	1.25	2,18,750
	₹ 21,25,000		₹ 4,83,750

However, utilising the full budget will be better, even though one of the most profitable projects is foregone.

Project	Amount	P.I.	Net present value
2	₹ 8,75,000	1.25	₹ 2,18,750
3	5,00,000	1.20	1,00,000
5	11,25,000	1.18	2,02,500
	₹ 25,00,000		₹ 5,21,250

(b) The firm would not be maximising the price of the equity share by turning down projects having an index larger than one. The firm should accept all projects with a positive NPV. If capital is not available to finance them at the discount rate used, a higher discount rate should be used which more adequately reflects the costs of financing.

11. Gujarat Rayon is subject to a 50% tax rate and a 10% cost of capital. The company is considering a new finishing machine. The machine will cost ₹ 1,00,000 and will reduce materials waste by an estimated ₹ 25,000 a year. The machine will last 10 years and will have a zero salvage value. Straight line depreciation will be used. There is no investment tax credit in effect.

(a) Identify the relevant cash flows.
(b) Compute the present value, net present value, and profitability index.
(c) Is this an attractive project?

Solution

(a) The cash outlay to purchase the new machine will be ₹ 1,00,000.

Annual depreciation will be ₹ 1,00,000/10 (i.e., ₹ 10,000).

Annual cash flows can be identified as follows :

Annual material savings	₹ 25,000	₹ 25,000
Increased depreciation	10,000	
Increased profit before tax	₹ 15,000	
Increased tax	7,500	7,500
Increased profit after-tax	₹ 7,500	
Increased annual after-tax cash flows		₹ 17,500

(b) Computation for present value are presented below :

Present value at 10% discount rate

Period	Cash Flow	Present value factor	Present value
1-10	₹ 17,500	6.145	₹ 1,07,538

Present value = ₹ 1,07,538

Net present value = ₹ 1,07,538 – ₹ 1,00,000 = ₹ 7,538
Profitability index = ₹ 1,07,538/ ₹ 1,00,000=1.075

(c) This is an attractive project as its net present value is greater than zero.

12. Madras Udyog is considering a new automatic blender. The new blender would last for 10 years and would be depreciated to zero over the 10 year period. The old blender would also last for 10 more years and would be depreciated to zero over the same 10 year period. The old blender has a book value of ₹ 10,000 but could be sold for ₹ 15,000 (the original cost was ₹ 20,000). The new blender would cost ₹ 50,000. It would reduce labour expense by ₹ 6,000 a year. The company is subject to a 50% tax rate on regular income and a 30% tax rate on capital gains. Their cost of capital is 8%. There is no investment tax credit in effect.

(a) Identify all the relevant cash flows for this replacement decision.
(b) Compute the present value, net present value and profitability index.
(c) Is this an attractive project?

Solution

(a) *Tax on the sale of the old machine :*

Original cost	₹ 20,000	
Sale price	15,000	
Book value	10,000	
₹ 5,000 × .50	₹ 2,500	tax on sale.

After-tax cash receipts from sale of old machine :

Sale price	₹ 15,000
Taxes on sale	2,500
After-tax cash receipts	₹ 12,500

Net cash flow to replace old machine with new :

Cost of new machine	₹ 50,000
After-tax receipt from sale of old machine	12,500
Net cash flow to replace old machine with new	₹ 37,500

Depreciation on new machine = ₹ 50,000/10 = ₹ 5,000
Depreciation on old machine = ₹ 10,000/10 = ₹ 1,000

	Book value	*Cash flow*
Annual labour savings	₹ 6,000	₹ 6,000
Increased depreciation (₹ 5,000- ₹ 1,000)	4,000	
Increased earnings before tax	₹ 2,000	
Increased tax	1,000	1,000
Increased earnings after tax	₹ 1,000	
Increased after-tax cash flow		₹ 5,000

(b) Calculation of present value at 8% discount rate are tabulated below :

Year	*Cash flow*	*Present value factor*	*Present value*
1-10	₹ 5,000	6.710	₹ 33,550

Present value = ₹ 33,550

Net present value = ₹ 33,550– ₹ 37,500 = – ₹ 3,950

Profitability index = ₹ 33,550/ ₹ 37,500 = .895

(c) Since the net present value is negative and profitability index is less than one, the project is *not* an attractive project.

13. Blue Star is considering replacing a machine that has a current market value of ₹ 40,000. This machine as purchased five years ago for ₹ 1,00,000 and is being depreciated on a straight-line basis over a ten-year life to a zero salvage value. The machine will last another five years. The replacement will cost ₹ 1,20,000 and will produce labour savings of ₹ 34,000 per year for five years. The replacement machine will be depreciated on a straight line basis over a five-year to a zero salvage value and the level of net working capital required to support sales will not be affected. Finally the firm has on income tax rate of 40% and its required return is 14%. Use the internal rate of return method to determine whether the new machine is economically acceptable.

Solution

The cost of the new machine is ₹ 1,20,000 and the old machine will be sold for ₹ 40,000. Thus, the net outflow before considering the tax effects of the sale of the old machine is ₹ 80,000. If a capital asset is sold for more than its book value, then a gain is experienced if an asset is sold for less than its book value, then a loss is experienced.

Selling price	₹ 40,000
–Book value	50,000
= Loss	₹ 10,000

This loss will create a tax shield of ₹ 4,000 given the tax rate of 40%. The net cash outflow can be determined as follows :

Cash outlay for new machine	₹ 1,20,000
Cash from sale of old machine	–40,000
Tax shield created by sale of old machine	4,000
Net cash outflows	₹ 76,000

We can now turn to the effect on funds flow :

Issue-Statement Items	*Amount*	*Effect on profits before and expenses that do not use net working Capital*	*Effect on income taxes*		*Effect on funds flows*
Labour Expense	₹ 34,000	₹ 34,000	– ₹ 13,600	=	₹ 20,400
Depreciation - New	24,000		9,600	=	9,600
Depreciation-old	10,000		4,000	=	4,000

The new machine creates tax shield of ₹ 9,600 but the firm will lose the tax shield of ₹ 4,000 on the old machine.

We can now calculate the investment's incremental cash flows.

Year	*Investment + outlay*	*Change in net + working capital*	*Change in funds flow*	=	*Incremental cash flows*
0	– ₹ 76,000			=	– ₹ 76,000
1-5			₹ 26,000	=	₹ 26,000

Let us try 18% to determine the internal rate of return.

Year	*Cash flows*	×	*PV at 18 to*	=	*PV*
0	– ₹ 76,000	×	1.0000	=	– ₹ 76,000
1-5	₹ 26,000	×	3.1272	=	₹ 81,310
					₹ 5,310

We find that 18% is too low. Let us try 20%

Year	*Cash flows*	×	*PV at 20 to*	=	*PV*
0	– ₹ 76,000	×	1.0000	=	– ₹ 76,000
1-5	₹ 26,000	×	2.9906	=	₹ 77,760
					₹ 1,760

Since 20% is too low, let us try 21%

Year	*Cash flows*	×	*PV at 21% to*	=	*PV*
0	– ₹ 76,000	×	1.0000	=	– ₹ 76,000
1-5	₹ 26,000	×	2.9260	=	₹ 76,080
					₹ 80

The internal rate of return on this investment is approximately 21%. The investment is economically acceptable since the internal rate of return is greater than the required rate of 14%

Issue-Statement Items	Amount	Effect on profit before taxes and expenses that do not use working capital	Effect on income tax		Effect on funds flow
Labour expense	₹ 34,000	₹ 34,000	₹ 13,600	=	₹ 20,400
Depreciation expense	₹ 14,000		– ₹ 5,600	=	₹ 5,600
					₹ 26,000

We should clarify the effect of depreciation on funds flow. Depreciation expense on the new machine will be ₹ 24,000 per year. However, depreciation expense on the old machine would have been ₹ 10,000, so the incremental amount of depreciation expense will be ₹ 14,000 and the net tax shield is ₹ 5,600 (40% time ₹ 14,000). Some analysts find it more convenient to deal seperately with each depreciation expense.

14. Super Silver Manufacturing is evaluating an investment of ₹ 76,50,000 to build a refinery to process silver and speciality products. The terms of the construction agreement would require an initial cost of ₹ 27,00,000 an January 1, another ₹ 27,00,000 payment one year after, and a final ₹ 22,50,000 one year after the second payment. The firm's required return is 12%. After the third payment, the refinery would be operational and should produce cash inflows of ₹ 9,00,000 per year after taxes for 15 years. Compute the internal rate of return, net present value and profitability index.

Solution

Rate of return is just over 6%

Year	Cash flow	Factor	Present value
–2	– ₹ 27,00,000	1.254	– ₹ 33,85,800
–1	– 27,00,000	1.110	– 30,24,000
0	– 22,50,000	1.000	– 22,50,000
			– ₹ 86,59,800

To get the present value of the net cash benefits, we use :

$$₹ 86,59,800 = ₹ 9,00,000 \left[\sum_{i=1}^{n} \frac{1}{(1+r)^t}\right]$$

₹ 86,59,800 = ₹ 9,00,000 [Table value 15 years IRR per cent]

9.622 = [Table value 15 years IRR per cent]

This is just lower than the 6%, 15-year present value factor so the return is just above 6%.

Net present value = ₹ 9,00,000 × 6.811 – ₹ 86,59,800
= ₹ 61,29,900– ₹ 86,59,800
=– ₹ 25,29,900

$$\text{Profitability Index} = \frac{₹\,61,29,900}{₹\,86,59,800} = .7079$$

15. Narendra Textile receives ₹ 15,00,000 a year after taxes from an investment in an automatic plant that has 12 more years of service life. The firm's required return is 12%. The firm can make improvements to the plant to raise its service life to 20 years and its annual after tax cash flow of ₹ 48,00,000 per year. These investments would cost ₹ 2,10,00,000. With the improvements, the plant's after tax value at the end of 12 years would rise from ₹ 7,50,000 to ₹ 75,00,000. Would the improvements produce a return satisfactory to the firm?

Solution

Calculation of the present value of the present value of the existing stream :

₹ 15,00,000 ×	6.194 =	₹ 92,91,000
₹ 7,50,000 ×	.257 =	₹ 1,92,750
		₹ 94,83,750

Calculation of the present value of new stream :

₹ 48,00,000 ×	6.194 =	₹ 2,97,31,200
₹ 75,00,000 ×	.257 =	₹ 19,27,500
		₹ 3,16,58,700

Differential stream of present value :

₹ 3,16,58,700– ₹ 94,83,750 = ₹ 2,21,74,950

Net present value is :

₹ 2,21,74,950 – ₹ 2,10,00,000 = ₹ 11,74,950

Since the NPV is positive ₹ 11,74,950, the improvements produce a return satisfactory to the firm.

16. A firm is evaluating two mutually exclusive but rather profitable projects :

Period	*Project A*	*Project B*
0	– ₹ 10,000	– ₹ 10,000
1	0	+ 20,000
2	+ 40,000	+ 10,000

(a) Compute the internal rate of return for both projects.

(b) Determine the Fisher's intersection.

(c) Show that for any intersection less than Fisher's intersection (say 10%), the firm would be sacrificing wealth by following the IRR criterion rather than the NPV criterion.

Solution

(a) $$IRR_A = \frac{-₹\,10,000}{(1+r)^0} + \frac{0}{(1+r)^1} + \frac{₹\,40,000}{(1+r)^2} = 0$$

Therefore, r_A = 100%

$$IRR_B = \frac{-₹10,000}{(1+r)^0} + \frac{₹20,000}{(1+r)^1} + \frac{₹10,000}{(1+r)^2} = 0$$

Therefore, r_B = 141.4%

(b) Of course, Fisher's intersection would be the *discount rate* (r^*), where the NPV of the two projects equaled each other:

$NPV_A = NPV_B$

$$\frac{-₹10,000}{(1+r^*)^0} + \frac{₹0}{(1+r^*)^1} + \frac{₹40,000}{(1+r^*)^2} = \frac{-₹10,000}{(1+r^*)^0} + \frac{₹20,000}{(1+r^*)^1} + \frac{₹10,000}{(1+r^*)^2}$$

$$\frac{-₹10,000}{(1+r^*)^1} + \frac{₹30,000}{(1+r^*)^2} = 0$$

Therefore,

r^* = 50%

(c) Based on the information above, we see that Project B has the higher IRR but Project A would be preferred using the NPV criterion at any cost of capital less than 50% (Fisher's intersection).

Some IRR proponents might argue that Project B is preferred because it gives the ₹ 20,000 inflow in period 1 which can be used for reinvestment in attractive opportunities. However, if such attractive opportunities exist, the firm would still be better off by accepting Project A and borrowing ₹ 20,000 in period 1 at the cost of capital of 10% and repaying the loan in period 2 with part of the ₹ 40,000 cash inflow. The comparison is as follows :

Period		*Project A*		*Project B*
	Original	*Loan*	*Revised*	
0	– ₹ 10,000	0	– ₹ 10,000	– ₹ 10,000
1	0	+ ₹ 20,000	20,000	20,000
2	+ ₹ 40,000	– ₹ 22,000*	18,000	10,000

*This value includes ₹ 2,000 of interest plus the ₹ 20,000 principal.

We can see that the revised Project A again clearly dominate project B.

17. An investment has an outlay of ₹ 2,00,000 today, an inflow of ₹ 12,50,000 at the end of one year, and an outflow of ₹ 12,50,000 at the end of two years. What is its internal rate of return? If the initial outlay were ₹ 3,12,500, what would be its IRR?

Solution

Setting the problem up using the quadratic formula :

$$\frac{-₹12,50,000}{(1+r)^2} + \frac{₹12,50,000}{(1+r)} - ₹2,00,000 = 0$$

$$\frac{1}{(1+r)} = \frac{-b \pm \sqrt{b^2 + 4ac}}{2a}$$

$$\frac{1}{(1+r)} = \frac{-₹\,12,50,000 \pm \sqrt{(₹\,12,50,000)^2 - 4(₹\,250,00,00,00,000)}}{-2(₹\,250,00,00,00,000)}$$

$$\frac{1}{(1-r)} = \frac{-₹\,12,50,000 \pm ₹\,7,50,000}{₹\,25,00,000}$$

$$\frac{1}{(1+r)} = .20,\ .80$$

$(1+r) = 1/.20 = 5$

$1/.80 = 1.25$, $r = 400\%$ and 25%

Thus, the problem has dual rates of return. With an initial outlay of ₹ 3,12,500, we have:

$$\frac{1}{(1-r)} = \frac{-₹\,12,50,000 \pm \sqrt{(₹\,12,50,000) - 4(390,62,50,00,000)}}{-₹\,25,00,000}$$

$$\frac{1}{(1-r)} = \frac{-₹\,12,50,000 \pm 0}{₹\,25,00,000}$$

$$\text{or } \frac{1}{(1+r)} = .5$$

$$\frac{1}{(1+r)} = \frac{1}{.5} = 2$$

Therefore

$r = 100\%$

Thus, a unique IRR is implied here. The problem serves to illustrate the pitfalls of multiple internal rates of return and of financing projects in general.

18. A company is faced by the following five investment opportunities:

Investment no.	*Profitability index*	*Initial outlay*
1	1.3	5,00,000
2	1.4	1,00,000
3	1.1	4,00,000
4	1.5	2,00,000
5	1.6	1,50,000

The company has ₹ 7,50,000 available for investment. Projects 3 and 4 are mutually exclusive. All the projects are divisible. Which group should be selected in order to maximise NPV? What is the NPV figure that results?

Solution

First of all, divide the investments up into two mutually exclusive sets. Set A (containing investment 3) consists of 1, 2, 3 and 5. Set B (which contains investment 4) comprises, 1, 2, 4 and 5. Now find the best selection that can be made from each set. Thus for set A we obtain:

Investment	*PI*	*Σoutlay*	*ΣNPV*
5	1.6	₹ 1,50,000	₹ 90,000
2	1.4	2,50,000	1,90,000
1	1.3	7,50,000	4,15,000

where we note that the NPV of any project is found as outlay multiplied by PI minus one. Thus with set A the best that can be done is a total NPV of 4,15,000. For set B we have:

Investment	*PI*	*Σoutlay*	*ΣNPV*
5	1.6	₹ 1,50,000	₹ , 90,000
4	1.5	3,50,000	2,65,000
2	1.4	4,50,000	4,45,000
1 $(\frac{3}{5})$	1.3	7,50,000	5,80,000

Thus set B provides by far the better result with the selection of 5, 4, 2 and 3/5 of 1 giving a total NPV of ₹ 5,80,000.

19. Determine which of the following two projects would be selected by the return on capital method.

	A	B
t=0	– ₹ 20,000	– ₹ 25,000
t=1	2,000	10,000
t=2	4,000	6,000
t=3	10,000	2,000
t=4	5,000	10,000
t=5	3,000	3,000
t=6	5,000	6,000

Solution

Rate of return on capital is expressed as the ratio of average return to average capital. Taking 'average capital' to be one-half of the initial outlay, the results are as follows: For project A the total of undiscounted returns is ₹ 29,000 achieved over six years—giving an average of 4,833.33—so that return on capital is:

$$\left(\frac{4,833.33}{10,000}\right) \times 100 = 48.33\%$$

For project B the total of undiscounted returns is ₹ 37,000, an average of ₹ 6,166.66 over the six years. So return on capital in this case is:

$$\left(\frac{6,166.66}{12,500}\right) \times 100 = 49.33\%$$

There is very little to choose between the two projects on the basis of return on capital defined as above. The measure is unlikely to be used in isolation and ideally is solely a matter of report. The case for project B is strengthened by the fact that its net present value is ₹ 2,632 in comparison to a net present value of ₹ 737 for project A, whilst in terms of yield, B has a yield of 13.92% against A's yield of 11.17%.

QUESTIONS

1. Explain and illustrate the payback period as a method of investment appraisal. What are the theoretical short-comings of this method and what are the practical justifications for its frequent use in industry?
2. "If the economic life of a project is long relative to its payback period it gives a reasonable estimates of a project's rate of profit." Illustrate this statement with a numerical example.
3. What weaknesses are commonly associated with the use of the payback period to measure an investment's worth? What factors are usually used to justify the reciprocal of the payback period? In what situation it is justifiable?
4. Evaluate the accounting rate of return (AROR) approach as a capital budgeting decision rule.
5. How can either the average rate of return or the payback period of an investment be used to make accept-reject decision? What additional data is required?
6. How are the capital budgeting techniques based on the payback period and the average rate of return difficult?
7. If evaluating a project by the NPV criterion, given the cost of capital, k, if NPV>0, the project is accepted, and NPV<0, the project is rejected.
   (a) What decision should the firm take if NPV=0? Explain your answer.
   (b) What is the analogous IRR situation?
8. How can the present value of the mixed stream of cash flows be determined?
9. How are benefit-cost ratios calculated? What is the criterion for judging the acceptability of investments when using B/C ratios? What do B/C ratios signify? What is an investment's B/C ratio when its net present value equals zero?
10. Do the benefit-cost ratio and the net present value approaches to capital budgeting always agree with respect to both the acceptability and ranking of investments? Why or why not?
11. What is the internal rate of return of an investment? How is it used to determine the acceptability of a project?
12. Define the internal rate of discount. What aspects of investment performance does it measure? Compare it to the net present value criterion.
13. In attempting to find the internal rate of return for a project, what must one do if the present value of inflows discounted at a given rate is greater than the initial investment? Why?
14. Under what conditions would the internal rate of return and net present value always give a similar accept-reject decision on a project.
15. When two projects of different economic lives are ranked according to their IRR's, management implicitly assumes that the firm's reinvestment rate is at least as high as the IRR of the longer-lived project. Do you agree with this statement? Why or why not?
16. Distinguish between decision criterion and performance measure.
17. "The trouble with discounted cash flow technique is that they ignore depreciation." Do you agree?
18. Why is it necessary to rank investment alternatives and what are the problems inherent in this approach?
19. What causes the time disparity ranking problem? What reinvestment rate assumptions are associated with the net present value and internal rate of return as capital budgeting criteria?
20. When might two mutually exclusive projects having unequal lives be incomparable? How should this problem be dealt with?

21. Why does the net present value (NPV) method, when improperly applied; tend to give incorrect choices among unequal lived competing proposals?
22. Describe the advantages and disadvantages of discounted and non-discounted capital budgeting methods.
23. What is the underlying cause of conflicts between the NPV and IRR methods? If a conflict exists, should the capital budgeting decision be made on the basis of the NPV or the IRR ranking? Why?
24. What is the "multiple IRR problem," and what condition is necessary for the occurrence?
25. Does not present value analysis has role in strategic planning ? Explain.
26. Discuss some ways in which capital budgeting policy can inadvertently thwart corporate strategy and thereby limit profitability.
27. If an investment has a positive net present value, it will also have a profitability index greater than 1.0 and internal rate of return in excess of the required rate of return. Likewise, an investment with a negative net present value will also have a profitability index less than 1.0 and an internal rate of return less than the required return. Since all three measures give the same accept-reject signals, why do companies bother to corporate all three of these measures ?

PROBLEMS

1. Gujarat Cork Industries has just obtained a new cork cutter for ₹ 1,14,000. The future case flow and profit generated by the cork cutter are:

Year	*Cash flow*	*Profit*
1	₹ 57,000	₹ 19,000
2	57,000	19,000
3	57,000	19,000

Compute the following : (a) Payback period, (b) Accounting rate of return, (c) Net present value using a cost of capital of 12%, and (d) Internal rate of return.

Ans.: (a) Payback period-2 years; (b) Accounting rate of return 16.667%; (c) Net present value = ₹ 22.924;(d) Internal rate of return = 23%

2. Standard Textiles is considering two mutually exclusive investments with the following cash flows :

Period	*Project X-Cash flow*	*Project Y-Cash flow*
0	– ₹ 1,62,727	– ₹ 90,000
1	1,90,909	20,000
2	60,000	1,60,000

which of the two investments do you prefer if the firm's time value of money is : (a) 0.05; (b) 0.20; (c) 0.30?

Ans.: Y is to be perferred at 0.5 and 0.30

3. U. Special Laundries is considering the purchase of new wash and dry equipment in order to expand its operations. Two types of options are available: a low-speed system with a ₹ 14,000 initial cost and a high-speed system with a ₹ 23,000 initial cost. Each system has a twenty-year life and no salvage value. The net cash flows associated with each investment are :

	Low speed system	*High speed system*
Initial cost	₹ 14,000	₹ 23,000
Annual cash flow for years 1 through 20	2,000	3,100
Compute NPV for each project at discount rate of 10%.		

Ans.: NPV (low-speed system) = ₹ 3,028 NPV (High-speed system) = ₹ 3,393

4. Orient Paper owns a machine that has been fully depreciated to ₹ 20,000, but has a market value and can sold for ₹ 50,000. A new machine costing ₹ 2,00,000 is available to replace the old machine. It is expected to reduce costs by ₹ 32,000 annually while being depreciated to ₹ 30,000 salvage value over its 10-year life. If Orient Paper has a 22% tax rate, a 14% required rate of return, and uses straight-line depreciation, decide if the new machine should be purchased.

Ans.: Since NPV is ₹ 21,190, purchase the machine.

5. Modern Limited are considering replacing an existing machine with a new one to reduce operating and maintenance cost. The new machine will cost ₹ 40,000 and is expected to last ten years with only negligible value by that times. The existing machine can be sold for ₹ 5,000 now. Operating and maintenance costs are currently ₹ 25,000 for the existing machine but will fall to only ₹ 18,000 each year for the new machine. Modern Limited require a return of at least 15% before sanctioning such investment.

Ans.: NPV is ₹ 133. Hence, the new machine is acceptable.

6. A firm is faced with deciding between the following two investment alternatives. Assume a cost of capital of 10%

Year	*Project A*	*Project B*
0	– ₹ 20,000	– ₹ 20,000
1	5,000	17,000
2	9,000	5,000
3	16,000	5,000

(a) Determine the NPV and IRR for both projects.
(b) In this situation, which is the better selection criterion? Why?

Ans.: (a) NPV_A = ₹ 4,005; NPV_B = ₹ 3,343 IRR_A = 19%; IRR_B = 22%; (b) Obviously, Project A is preferred.

7. Suraj Tubes is attempting to choose between two different machines that accomplish essentially the same task (the machines are mutually exclusive). A comparison of cash flows of the two machines shows that if the less expensive of the two machines is chosen, there will be a saving of ₹ 10,000 at the time of purchase, but there will be additional outlays of ₹ 3,330 per year over the five-year life of the machines. The cost of money of the Suraj Tubes is 10%. Compute the internal rate of return of the incremental cash flows and determine whether or not the cheaper of the two machines should be purchased. Make the same decision using the present-value procedure.

Ans.: The more expensive of two machines is more desirable.

8. H.O. Company is considering purchasing a machine in order to produce a new product. The new product will generate revenues of ₹ 5,00,000 per year for five yea ₹ The cost of materials and labour needed to generate these revenues will total ₹ 3,00,000 per year and other cash expenses will be ₹ 50,000 per year. Net working capital of ₹ 50,000 will be required immediately and this amount will be freed-up at the end of the fifth year.

The machine will cost ₹ 2,50,000. It will be depreciated on a straight line basis over its five-year life to zero salvage value. Finally, the firm's tax rate is 48% and its required return is 10%.

Using the net present value method, determine whether the investment in the new machine is economically acceptable.

Ans.: NPV is ₹ 1,17,710. Hence the investment is economically acceptable.

9. Manjit Cotton is considering the two mutually exclusive investments. Which of the two investments be chosen using the index of present value? Assume a cost of money of 10%.

Period	*Project X-Cash flow*	*Project Y-Cash flow*
0	– ₹ 4,00,000	– ₹ 4,00,000
1	11,00,000	– 10,00,000
2		21,00,000

Ans.: Index of present value (X) = 2.5; Index of present value (Y) = 1.46. But same NPV. Choose Project X.

10. Determine the internal rate of return of the following investment :

Period	*Cash flow*
0	– ₹ 91,200
1	10,000
2	50,000
3	1,00,000

Ans.: IRR is 25%.

11. A firm plans to invest in one of the following projects

Period	*Cost*	*Annual cash inflow*	*Project (life in years)*
A	₹ 46,000	₹ 7,500	10
B	53,000	8,450	9
C	61,600	9,600	13

The annual cash inflows include depreciation charges. Rank projects by their internal rates of return.

Ans.: (C) 12%; (A) 10%; (B) 8%

12. A project costing ₹ 5,60,000 is expected to produce annual net cash benefits of ₹ 80,000 over a period of 15 years. Estimate the internal rate of return (IRR). Also find the payback period and obtain the IRR from it.

Ans.: IRR = 11.5% Payback period=7 years.

13. Compute the internal rate of return of the following investments :

Investments	*Period*			
	0	1	2	3
X	– ₹ 1,00,000	₹ 47,470	₹ 47,470	₹ 47,470
Y	–1,00,000			1,72,800

Compare the two investments. Which do you prefer? Are you making any assumption about the reinvestment of the cash flows?

Ans.: Both investments have an internal rate of return of 20%.

14. The Filips Corporation, which has a 50% tax rate and a 10% after-tax cost of capital, is evaluating a project which will cost ₹ 1,00,000 and will require an increase in the level of inventories and receivables of ₹ 50,000 over its life. The project will generate additional sales of ₹ 1,00,000 and will require cash expenses of ₹ 30,000 in each year of its 5 year life; it will be depreciated on a straight-line basis. What are the net present value and internal rate of return for the project?

Ans.: NPV = ₹ 51,643; IRR = 21.27%

15. Accept or reject the following independent investment proposals, using the internal rate of return and present value procedures, and a cutoff rate of 10%.

Investment	*Period*		
	0	*1*	*2*
X	– ₹ 1,00,000	₹ 20,000	₹ 1,20,000
Y	–1,00,000	1,05,000	
Z	1,00,000	–1,20,000	

Ans.:

	IRR	NPV	
X	.20	₹ 17,350	Accept
Y	.05	–4,540	Reject
Z	.20	–9,590	Reject

16. Sunrise Manufacturing is considering an investment that has the following case flows :

Period	*0*	*1*	*2*
Cash flow	₹ 10,000	— ₹ 21,600	₹ 11,600

The investment has IRRs of 0 and .16. Assume that the firm has a time value of .10 (it can borrow at .10). Divide the investment into two components, a fictitious borrowing of ₹ 10,000 at time zero and an investment of ₹ 10,600 at time 1. Determine whether the basic investment is desirable.

Ans.: The IRR of the investment is 0.094 which is less than 01.100, thus reject.

17. Carriers Limited are trying to decide between two transporters which are both satisfactory from a technical viewpoint but which have different costs and benefits. Model a costs ₹ 40,000 and its payload is expected to earn ₹ 10,200 in each of the next ten years. Model B costs ₹ 30,000 but its earning capacity is only ₹ 8,400 each year for the same life. Carriers management want to know which is the better buy.

Ans.: Model B is better than Model A because on the former the IRR is 25% whereas in the case of latter, i.e., Model A, the IRR is 22%.

18. The management of a company has two alternative projects under consideration. Project A requires a capital outlay of ₹ 1,20,000 but Project B needs ₹ 1,80,000. Both are estimated to provide a cash flow for five years: A— ₹ 40,000 per year and B— ₹ 58,000 per year. The cost of capital is 10%. Show which of the two projects is preferable from the view-point of (i) Net present value and (ii) Internal rate of return.

Ans.: (i) NPV (Project A) = ₹ 31,640; NPV (Project B) = ₹ 39,878; Project B is preferable over A.

(ii) IRR (Project A) = 19.80%; IRR (Project B) = 18.35%; Project A is preferred over B.

19. A particular home was worth ₹ 5,00,000 on January 2013. The increase in the general level of prices (inflation was 5% during the year from January 1, 2013 to June 30, 2013).

(a) If the real value of the house (value in terms of purchasing power was the same as on June 30, 2013 as on January 31, 2013, what were the rupee value of the house on June 30, 2013?

(b) If the real value of the house was 4% greater on June 30, 2013 than it was on January 1, 2013, what was the rupee value of the house on June 30, 2013 ?

Ans.: (a) ₹ 5,25,00; (b) ₹ 5,46,000

20. Certain new machine is estimated to cost ₹ 1,20,000 installed. It is expected to reduce net annual operating disbursements by ₹ 24,000 per year for 10 years and to have ₹ 20,000 salvage value at the end of the tenth year. What is the before tax rate of return? If the ordinary income tax rate is 48%, and straight line depreciation is used, compute the after-tax rate of return.

Ans.: Before-tax rate of return = 16.2%; After-tax rate of return = 8.9%

21. Raj Kamal House is evaluating the purchase of a new machine costing ₹ 1,50,000. The machine would be depreciated on a straight-line basis over 5 years towards a zero salvage value. The machine is expected to increase revenues by ₹ 1,00,000 and operating costs (not including depreciation) by ₹ 40,000 annually. Raj Kamal's tax rate is 48% and it uses a 10% discount rate. (a) Calculate the net present value of the decision to purchase the machine; (b) Calculate the internal rate of return for the machine.

Ans.: (a) NPV = ₹ 22,860; (b) IRR = 15.81%

22. The Novex Publishing Company is considering two mutually exclusive expansion plans: *Plan A* calls for the expenditure of ₹ 4 crore on a large-scale, integrated plant which will provide an expected cash flow stream of ₹ 6.4 crore per year for 20 years. *Plan B* calls for the expenditure of ₹ 12 crore to build a somewhat less efficient, more labour-intensive plant which has an expected cash flow stream of ₹ 2.72 crore per year for 20 years. Novex's cost of capital is 10 per cent.

(a) Calculate each project's NPV and IRR.

(b) Graph the NPV profiles for Plan A and Plan B. From the NPV profiles constructed, approximate the crossover rate.

(c) Give a logical explanation, based on reinvestment rates and opportunity costs, as to why the NPV method is better than the IRR method when the firm's cost of capital is constant at some value such as 10 per cent.

Ans.: (a) NPV_A = ₹ 14,48,68,080; NPV_B = ₹ 11,15,68,930; IRA_A = 15.03%; IRA_B = 22.26%

23. Project KRS costs ₹ 15,00,000 and is expected to produce benefits cash flows) of ₹ 4,50,000 per year for 5 years. Project NTL costs ₹ 37,50,000 and is expected to produce cash flows of ₹ 11,10,000 per year for 5 years. Calculate the two projects' NPVs and IRRs, assuming a cost of capital of 14 per cent. Which project would be selected, assuming they are mutually exclusively, using each ranking method? Which should actually be selected?

Ans.: NPV_{KRS}= ₹ 44,886; IRR_{KRS} = 15.24%; NPV_{NTL} = ₹ 60,720; IRR_{NTL}= 14.67%

NATIONAL TRAINING COLLEGE: *A CASE*

National Training College founded by D. C. Patel in 1992, has dealt primarily in personal and professional motivational courses particularly for corporate employees. Patel and his associates have developed several programmes that have proven successful in their reception by the individuals completing the courses. At the present time, extensive thought and considerations are being committed to a new programme (Executive Development Programme Plan) to be used by financial services and insurance as a client service. In this regard, K.D. Arora, the executive vice-president, has identified a strong potential market for such courses for both business executives actively involved in the management of large amounts of corporate funds as well as persons having little experience in the proper management of money.

In analysing the prospects of the investment, Patel and Arora consider the basic product to have an expected life of approximately five years (Plan A). However, this estimate could be significantly lengthened, provided either an extensive marketing campaign was conducted in subsequent years (Plan B) or a major revision in the course package is developed in the fifth year (Plan C). In this regard, the options under consideration may be summarised as follows:

Plant A: This first strategy requires an investment at the present time totaling ₹ 3 crore. This amount would afford the necessary funds for production equipment as well as working capital requirements of ₹ 50,00,000. The working capital portion of the investment may be liquidated upon the termination of the course. The expected life of the project is five years.

Plant B: The second alternative would permit an increase in the expected life of the course to 10 years. Based upon experience with prior investments of a similar type, the firm's management considers the feasibility of a project in terms of length of life to be quite sensitive to increased efforts in customer awareness in the latter years of the programme. Thus, the extension of the product life would come from an intensive marketing campaign in years 6 through 10. The capital investment would be similar to the amount under Plan A in that the same equipment would be needed; however, ₹ 1 crore in working capital would have to be maintained, as opposed to only ₹ 50,00,000 for Plan A.

Plan C: The final analysis to be performed relates to a two-phase investment in which the initial investment of ₹ 3.50 crore is committed, including ₹ 1 crore in working capital, and ₹ 2 crore must be expended on equipment at the conclusion of the fifth year. This investment would result in substantive modifications and improvements in the programme. While time is of essence in going to the market, within the next few years several major improvements in educational equipment is expected. Such a two-phase investment would permit receiving the benefits of these developments.

Succinctly stated, the management is considering two basic approaches for promoting Executive Development Programmes: (1) a concentrated effort with the intent being to saturate the market during a 5-year period (Plan A) or (2) and extended investment in Executive Development Programmes with the prolonged life being the result of a marketing campaign in years 6 through 10 (Plan B) or a major revamping of the course structure in the fifth year (Plan C).

The estimates of the annual receipts and operational expenses for the three plans are given follows in Table A-1.

TABLE A-1

(₹ in crore)

Year	*Sales*		
	Plan A	*Plan B*	*Plan C*
1.	1.00	0.75	0.75
2.	3.00	1.25	1.25
3.	4.50	2.00	2.00
4.	4.50	2.80	2.80
5.	4.50	3.50	3.50
6.		4.00	4.75
7.		4.25	5.00
8.		4.75	5.00
9.		4.50	5.00
10.		2.50	5.00
Years	*Marketing Expenses per Year*		
	Plan A	*Plan B*	*Plan C*
1-5	₹ 35,00,000	₹ 25,00,000	₹ 25,00,000
6-7		50,00,000	25,00,000
8-9		70,00,000	25,00,000
10		25,00,000	25,00,000

Additional data thought to bear on the decision are:

1. The production of the material will require the use of a portion of an existing plant not included in the capital investment figures quoted above. This part of the plant, which represents excess floor space, could be considered to have a book value of ₹ 1.50 crore and a corresponding annual depreciation of ₹ 10,00,000 per year. However, this segment of the plant could not be used otherwise due to the floor plan of the building.
2. Cost of goods sold of similar programmes has generally been a variable cost approximating 60 percent of sales.
3. Administrative expenses for the company will be ₹ 10,00,000 annually, which has been the level of administration expenses for the past year. However, only ₹ 4,00,000 of this amount will be allocated via the cost accounting system to the new plan.

4. The bank has agreed to finance ₹ 1 crore of the investment at an interest rate of 8 percent, with the interest being payable yearly and the principal coming due at the end of the project life.
5. The company is in a 40 percent tax rate and uses straight line depreciation (no salvage) for all expenditures.

Questions

1. Determine the costs of the three alternatives.
2. Compute the annual after-tax cash flows for the three plans.
3. Compute the net present value, the profitability index, and the internal rate of return for each plan. Assume a cost of capital of 8 percent.
4. Which course of action should be taken by the firm? Explain.

HIND PLASTIC COMPANY: *A CASE*

On January 11, 2001 the finance committee of Hind Plastic Company (HPC) met to consider eight capital budgeting projects. Present at the meeting were R. Venkat, president and founder, C. Ganesh, finance manager, and P. Jhamil, head of research and development. Over the past five years. this committee has met every month to consider and make final judgment on all proposed capital outlays brought up for review during the period.

HPC was founded in 2000 by R. Venkat to produce plastic parts and molding for the automakers. For the first 10 years of operations, HPC worked solely as a subcontractor for the automakers, but since then has made strong efforts to diversify in an attempt to avoid the cyclical problems faced by the auto industry. By 2005 this diversification attempt had led HPC into the production of over 1,000 different items, including kitchen utensils, camera housings, phonographic and recording equipment. It also led to an increase in sales of 500 percent during the 2005 to 2010 period. As this dramatic increase in sales was paralleled by a corresponding increase in production volume, HPC was forced, in late 2009, to expand production facilities. This plant and equipment expansion involved capital expenditures of approximately ₹ 10.5 crore and resulted in an increase of production capacity of about 40 percent. Because of this increased production capacity, HPC has made a concerted effort to attract new business, and, consequently, has recently entered into contracts with a large toy firm and a major discount department store chain. While nonautomotive related business has grown significantly, it still only represents 32 percent of HPC's overall business. Thus, HPC has continued to solicit nonautomotive business, and as a result of this effort and its internal research and development, the firm has four sets of mutually exclusive projects to consider at this month's finance committee meeting.

Over the past 10 years, HPC's capital budgeting approach has evolved into a somewhat elaborate procedure in which new proposals are categorised into three areas: profit, research and development, and safety. Projects falling into the profit or research and development area are evaluated by using present value techniques, assuming a 15 percent opportunity rate; those falling into the safety classification are evaluated in a more subjective framework. Although research and development projects have to receive favourable results from the present value criteria, there is also a total limit assigned to projects of this category, typically running about ₹ 95,00,000 per year. This limitation was imposed by Venkat primarily because of the limited availability of quality researchers in the plastics industry, Venkat felt that if more funds than this were allocated, "We simply couldn't find the manpower to administer them properly." The benefits derived from safety projects, on the other hand, are not in terms of cash flows; hence, present value methods are not used at all in their evaluation. The subjective approach used to evaluate safety projects is a result of the pragmatically difficult task of quantifying the benefits from these projects into money terms. Thus, these projects are subjectively evaluated by a management-worker committee with a limited budget. All eight projects to be evaluated in January are classified as profit projects.

The first set of projects listed on the meeting's agenda for examination involve the utilisation of HPC's precision equipment. Project A calls for the production of vacuum containers for thermos bottles produced for a large discount hardware chain. The containers would be manufactured in five different size and colour combinations. This project would be carried out over a three-year period, for which HPC would be guaranteed a minimum return plus a percentage of the sales. Projects B involves the manufacture of inexpensive photographic equipment for a national photography outlet. Although HPC currently has excess plant capacity, both of these projects would utilise precision equipment of which the excess capacity is limited. Thus, adopting either project would tie up all precision facilities. In addition, the purchase of new equipment would be both prohibitively expensive and involve a time delay of approximately two years, this making these projects mutually exclusive. The cash flows associated with these two projects are given in Exhibit - 1.

EXHIBIT - 1

Cash Flows

Year	*Project A*	*Project B*
0	– ₹ 9,50,00,000	– ₹ 9,50,00,000
1	3,00,00,000	6,30,00,000
2	5,00,00,000	6,30,00,000
3	10,00,00,000	6,30,00,000

The second set of projects involves renting computer facilities over a one-year period to aid in customer billing and perhaps inventory control. Project C entails the evaluation of a customer billing system proposed by Super Computer Consultants. Under this system, all of the bookkeeping and billing presently being done by HPCs accounting department would now be done by Super. In addition to saving costs involved in bookkeeping, Super would provide a more efficient billing system and do a credit analysis of delinquent customers, which could be used in the future for in-depth credit analysis. Project D is proposed by Best Computer Consultants and includes a billing system similar to that offered by Super, and, in addition, an inventory control system that will keep track of all raw materials and parts in stock and reorder when necessary, thereby reducing the likelihood of material stockouts, which has become more and more frequent over the past three years. The cash flows for these projects are given in Exhibit - 2.

EXHIBIT - 2

Cash Flows

Year	*Project C*	*Project D*
0	– ₹ 1,00,00,000	– ₹ 2,50,00,000
1	1,50,00,000	3,50,00,000

The third decision that faces the financial directors of HPC involves a newly developed and patented process for molding hard plastics. HPC can either manufacture and market the equipment necessary to mold such plastics or they can sell the patent rights to Polyplastics Industries. The cash flows for projects E and F are shown in Exhibit - 3. At present, the process has not been fully tested, and if HPC is going to market it itself, it will be necessary to complete this testing and begin production of plant facilities immediately. On the other hand, selling these patent rights to Polyplastics would involve only minor testing and refinements, which could be completed within the year. Thus, a decision on the proper course of action is needed immediately.

EXHIBIT - 3

Cash Flows

Year	*Project E*	*Project F*
0	– ₹ 4,50,00,000	– ₹ 37,50,00,000
1	37,50,00,000	12,00,00,000
2		12,00,00,000
3		12,00,00,000
4		12,00,00,000
5		12,00,00,000
6		12,00,00,000
7		12,00,00,000
8		12,00,00,000
9		12,00,00,000
10		12,00,00,000

The final set of projects up for considerations revolved around the replacement of some of the machinery. HPC can go in one of two directions. Project G suggests the purchase and installation of moderately priced, extremely efficient equipment with an expected life of 5 years; project H advocates the purchase of a similarly priced, although less efficient machine with life expectancy of 10 years. (The cash flows for these alternatives are shown in Exhibit-4.)

EXHIBIT - 4

Cash Flows

Year	*Project G*	*Project H*
0	– ₹ 50,00,00,000	– ₹ 50,00,00,000
1	22,50,00,000	15,00,00,000
2	22,50,00,000	15,00,00,000
3	22,50,00,000	15,00,00,000
4	22,50,00,000	15,00,00,000
5	22,50,00,000	15,00,00,000
6		15,00,00,000
7		15,00,00,000
8		15,00,00,000
9		15,00,00,000
10		15,00,00,000

As the meeting opened, debate immediately centered on the most appropriate method for evaluating all of the projects. Venkat suggested that since the projects to be considered were mutually exclusive, perhaps their usual capital budgeting criteria of net present value was inappropriate. He felt that, in examining these projects, perhaps they should be more concerned with relative profitability of some measure of yield. Both Ganesh and Jhamil agreed with Venkat's point of view, with Ganesh advocating a profitability index approach and Jhamil preferring the use of the internal rate of return. Ganesh argued that the use of the profitability index would provide a benefit-cost ratio, directly implying relative profitability. Thus, they merely need to rank these projects and select those with the highest profitability index. Jhamil agreed with Ganesh point of view but suggested that the calculation of an internal rate of return would also give a measure of profitability and perhaps be somewhat easier to interpret. To settle the issue, Venkat suggested that they calculate all three measures, for they would undoubtedly yield the same ranking.

From here the discussion turned to an appropriate approach to the problem of differing lives among mutually exclusive projects E and F and projects G and H. Jhamil argued that there really was not a problem here at all, that as all of the cash flows from these projects can be determined, any of the discounted cash flow methods of capital budgeting will work well. Ganesh on the other hand, argued that although this was true, he felt that some compensation should be made for the fact that the projects being considered did not have equal lives.

Questions

1. Was Venkat correct in stating that the NPV, PI, and IRR necessarily will yield the same ranking order? Under what situations might the NPV, PI and IRR methods provide different rankings? Why is it possible?
2. What is the NPV, PI, and IRR for projects A and B? What has caused the ranking conflicts? Should project A or B be chosen? Might your answer change if project B is a typical project in the plastic molding industry? For example, if projects for HPC generally yield approximately 12 percent, is it logical to assume that the IRR for project B of approximately 33 percent is a correct calculation for ranking purposes?
3. What is the NPV, PI and IRR for projects C and D? Should project C or D be chosen? Does your answer change if these projects are considered under a capital constraint?
4. What is the NPV, PI, and IRR for projects E and F? Are these projects comparable even though they have unequal lives? Why? Which project should be chosen? Assume these projects are not considered under a capital constraint.
5. What is the NPV, PI, and IRR for projects G and H? Are these projects comparable even though they have unequal lives? Why? Which project should be chosen? Assume these projects are not considered under a capital constraint.

11

CAPITAL BUDGETING DECISIONS UNDER CONDITIONS OF CAPITAL RATIONING

INTRODUCTION

The investment decision making process becomes more complex as the number of alternatives become interdependent, and as the number of constraints on the decision maker increases. In the proceeding chapter, we considered investment appraisal without in situations where the decision-maker's achievement of objective was limited only by the range of opportunities that were open. To all intents and purposes the cash flow and other financial data were known with certainty and capital availability for investment was limited only by the ability to repay. In this chapter we consider a range of methods that can be useful to management when the choice is restricted by limitations on finance available. The functional relationship between the effectiveness and the structure of the constraint matrix for an integer programming formulation will be examined. We shall concentrate on problems in which the constraints that arise are financial in character, although the principles of the methods apply whatever the nature of the scarce resource or constraint.

MEANING OF CAPITAL RATIONING

A capital rationing problem is defined as a situation where insufficient funds can be made available to finance all the *prime facie* profitable projects.[1] What subset of projects should the firm select, given the set of available projects? An inter-relationship exists between projects because of the assumption of a common scarce source : *capital*. The firm is to maximise shareholder's wealth, so it should invest in the group of projects that collectively have the largest net present value. Such a group must be selected without violating the stated budget constraint. The question becomes how to identify that best group of projects out of the larger set of acceptable proposals. Which investment criterion will identify this optimum group?

To illustrate, suppose that a firm has only a limited amount of funds-say ₹ 1,00,000/- to spend on various projects. The returns and cost of four pieces of equipment are presented, in Table-1. If only one of each machine can be purchased,

1. See J.H. Lorie and L.J. Savage. Three Problems in "Rationing Capital," *Journal of Business*, 28, 4, October, 1955, pp. 229-239.

which should the firm buy? How should it allocate its ₹ 1,00,000 among these potential investments to earn as high a rate of return as possible?

Suppose that the company first purchase machine I because it has the highest internal rate of return. With only ₹ 40,000 left, the firm will have to forgo machine 2 and 3, each of which cost ₹ 50,000 and can purchase only machine 4. The firm's average return on its total investment in machine 1 and 4 will be 22%:

Average rate of return = (.6) (.30) +(.4) (.1) = .22

TABLE-1

Potential Investment Opportunities

Machine	*Cost*	*Internal Rate of Return*
1.	₹ 60,000	30%
2.	50,000	26%
3.	50,000	24%
4.	40,000	10%

The firm could follow another strategy, however, and bypass machine 1. It would then have enough funds to purchase 2 and 3. Its return on investment, under this strategy would be 25%, 3% more than under the first strategy.

Determining which investments to make and which to reject to earn the highest rate of return was easy in this example. Not all finance problems, however, are so trivial. It is therefore worthwhile to spend some time analysing the structure and solution of this simple problem.

First, note that the capital investment question was cast in a technical format. It was stated as a problem of maximising returns subject to the constraints of limited resources. The scarce resources were to be distributed among alternative investment to achieve a particular goal to a maximum rate of return on the entire ₹ 1,00,000. The problem was not one of choosing goals. We did not ask whether it was desirable for the firm to try to maximise its average rate of return or whether it should set some other goal, such as a large market share. Nor was the problem one of discovering whether all the firm's alternatives were included in the model. We took the four purchase options as given and did not search for another investment that might yield 30% and cost ₹ 1,00,000. Both these problems, setting goals for the firm and establishing the range of options are important problems of corporate management. They are not, however, part of the technical problem posed here.

Second, the problem that was posed can be divided into a statement of the objective and a statement of the constraints. This is the classical format for decision problems; readily available mathematical procedures, or algorithms, can be used to find the solution to problems set up this way.

Not all business problems will fit this technical economic format. Policy questions, for example, can seldom be decided in this way. A different methodology is also needed to solve social, political, and legal problems. For example how to handle employees grievances concerning work rules is a recurring business problem whose resolution depends on principles that are more legal than economic. Still other business problems, such as motivating employees and improving job performance, may be solved by applying sociological or psychological principles.

Third, it is important to stress that the rational solution to the technical economic problem of maximising some function subject to constraints frequently conflicts with the intuitive solution. In the example, the highest rate of return on the firm's total investment was achieved by rejecting the investment with the highest return and selecting the next two options. (This result arose because of the integer and budget constraints. The firm could not purchase part of a machine, nor could it buy more than one of each. If it purchased machines 1 and 2, it would exceed its budget. Whether the constraints are considered really binding or merely guidelines for is a matter of company policy and is not a issue here.)

CAUSES OF CAPITAL CONSTRAINTS

It may seem unrealistic and certainly non-maximising to ration capital so that not all profitable projects are undertaken, but it is argued that firms, in fact, do ration or limit capital. This, although not maximisation in the total economic sense, requires us to examine the various causes of capital rationing both external as well as internal.

(A) CAPITAL CONSTRAINTS ARISING IN THE MARKET

If capital markets were such that a firm could lend or borrow as much money as it desired at the going rate of interest, this rate of interest would be the same for both the borrowing and lending transactions. The goal of profit maximisation would then require that the firm accept all independent investments whose present values were positive, using this rate of interest. With such capital markets the choice of investments would not be dependent on the amount of funds available to the firm, because by an appropriate combination of borrowing and lending, each firm could finance investments that has positive present values.

This theoretical situation is an ideal never encountered in practice. There will almost be some divergence between the rates of interest at which the firm can lend surplus funds and the rates at which it can borrow funds. The size of the gap may vary for many reasons, including the effects of the flotation costs of raising new money and the fact that there may be hidden costs or risks connected with one or other of the investments. Another reason is that money-lenders may prefer firms having certain characteristics, thus driving up the cost of borrowing by firms that lack these characteristics.

If the borrowing rate and the lending rate are almost equal, little is lost by neglecting the difference and speaking of a market rate of interest. If the difference is large, it cannot be ignored in determining the investment and financial policies of the firm. This gives rise to the situation we describe as external capital rationing a result of the market imperfections or transaction costs.

We may see the influence of high flotation cost in Figure-1. There, the internal rates of returns for a firm's available independent investment projects are arranged in a step diagramme. The line K_1 shows the cost of capital to the firm based upon a given desired debt/equity mix and assuming that equity funds are provided by currently retained earning and, say, debt issued. If the company could finance all projects at the K_1, projects M, N, O and P would be accepted in an unconstrained determination of the capital budget. However, if taking that number of projects required that the firm go into the open market and issue additional debt/equity, the cost of capital, adjusted for flotation cost, will increase. Suppose that this point occurs at X in Figure-1 and that the firm is a small one. The increase in the cost of capital due to flotation costs may, because of the fixed element of flotation costs that is independent of the size of the transaction, be very large. Such behaviour is described by the dashed line K, in Figure-1. The large increase in the cost of capital at point X technically means only that additional capital is available at a much higher price. The increase is so great that the lower return projects are rendered much less desirable if they are desirable at all. Under these circumstances, it may be reasonable to treat the point X as if it were a capital constraint imposed by the market and to employ capital rationing techniques to select among available projects.

FIGURE-1

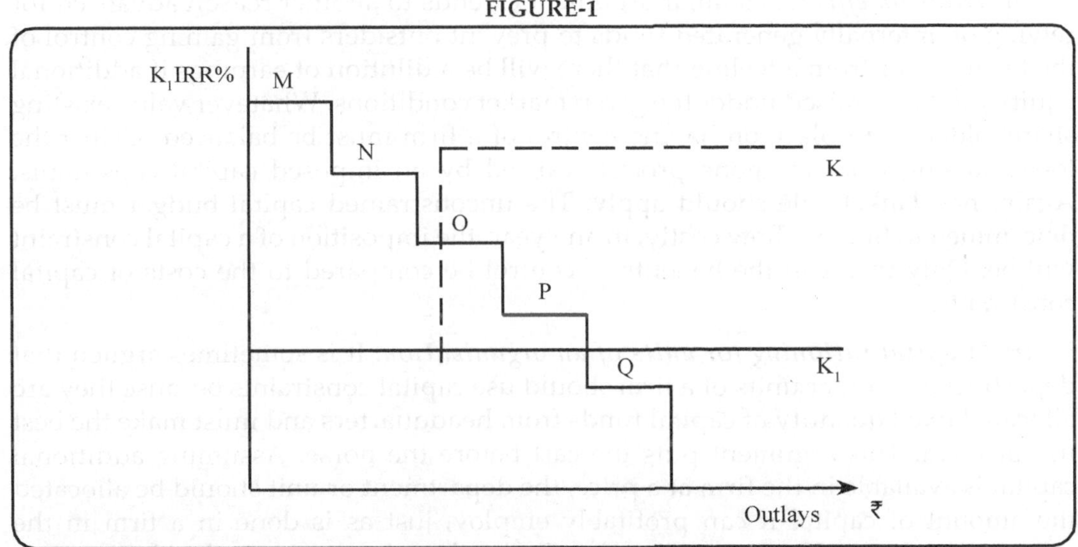

(B) MANAGERIAL IMPOSED CAPITAL CONSTRAINTS

Assuming that additional capital is available, perhaps at a higher cost, what arguments exists for managerially imposed capital constraints that leave behind unexploited, desirable investment projects and fail to maximise increases in wealth for shareholders? Such arguments are made and should at least be recorded here because of their widespread existence.

(i) Reliance on internally generated funds: Some firms have a policy of financing investment projects only from internally generated funds. Under no circumstances will they permit debt to be employed to finance projects, nor are any new equity issues to be sold. The scale of investment is then confined to available, currently retained earnings plus accumulated cash and short-term investments not needed for operations. If more desirable projects exists than can be financed by internally generated funds, then it is argued that capital constraints should be imposed.

The problem with this argument is that it implies a blanket rule without any qualifications. It may be, for example, that a firm relies solely on internally generated funds because the shareholders are averse to the risks of debt. No one can argue against their risk preference. Yet, the costs in terms of foregone wealth increase caused by desirable projects being not undertaken due to a capital constraint must be measured and weighed against whatever benefit being free from debt has for these shareholders. In some years at least, the losses in foregone wealth against from unexploited projects may be so high that the prohibition against debt might well be voluntarily abandoned. Once that possibility is admitted, no blanket rule for internally generated funds can be allowed. At least initially, capital budgets should be determined without managerially imposed capital constraints in order to measure the cost of imposing capital constraints in any given year.

(ii) Dilution effect: A similar argument extends to another reason advanced for relying on internally generated funds to prevent outsiders from gaining control of the business, or from a feeling that there will be a dilution of earnings if additional equity funds are raised under the given market conditions. Whatever value existing shareholders may place on having control of a firm must be balanced against the losses arising from foregone projects caused by an imposed capital constraints. Again, no blanket rule should apply. The unconstrained capital budget must be determined to find out how costly, in any year, the imposition of a capital constraint will be. Only then can the benefits of control be compared to the costs of capital constraints.

(iii) Capital rationing for units of an organisation: It is sometimes argued that departments or other units of a firm should use capital constraints because they are allocated fixed quantity of capital funds from headquarters and must make the best use of them. This argument puts the cart before the horse. Assuming additional capital is available in the firm at a price, the department or unit should be allocated the amount of capital it can profitably employ, just as is done in a firm in the unconstrained capital budgeting situation. To do otherwise may mean that departments having many desirable projects will end up excluding some because of the managerially imposed constraint. Further, departments having few desirable projects may undertake undesirable projects simply to use up their quota of capital funds. Neither action is consistent with the goal of maximising shareholder wealth.

(iv) Higher cutoff rate: Sometimes the firms set a cut off rate for investments that is higher than the firm's cost of money. Suppose a firm require investments must have a positive present value at 15%, even though the firm's cost of money is only 10%. In this case, the same cutoff rate in future years will be known, and the firm can evaluate all investments as if the cost of money were 15%.

But although a definite cut off rate is available, the logic of using that rate to discount cash flows is no longer completely correct. The rate of discount used should measure the alternative uses of funds available to the firm. In the present instance however, it indicates only that an investment yielding less than 15% will not be undertaken. If next year the company has more internally generated funds than it is willing to invest following the 15% cutoff rule, then extra funds that become available next year will have an opportunity cost that is less than 15%. How much less will depend on what use the firm makes of the "excess" cash that it will not invest.

(v) Organisation limits on the growth of the firm: Where the number of desirable investment projects is larger relative to the existing size of the firm, it is sometimes thought that the firm will be unable to exploit all of the projects because of short-run constraints on the availability of managerial talent and inertia involved in changing the organisation of the firm to adjust to growth. Consequently, it is argued that capital constraints are justified to prevent the firm from undertaking more activity within a given time period than it can manage.

The argument is really not an argument for capital constraints as much as it is for proper specification of the costs associated with investment projects. If, as is often true, firms experience managerial difficulties with growth caused by investment projects, then the costs of this growth should be estimated and the returns of all projects scaled downward accordingly. Given the cost of capital, fewer projects will then be undertaken, not because of capital constraints, but because apparent project returns were initially estimated at too high a level.

AN UNRESOLVED PROBLEM

The fact is that capital constraints sometimes are managerially imposed even though theories predicted on the goal of maximising shareholder wealth suggest that such actions are inconsistent with that goal. Resolution of this apparent conflict between theory and practice is not easy. Perhaps other concerns, such as preserving control of a firm by using only internal financing, are sufficiently important goals for some shareholders, in which case concentration solely on the shareholder wealth maximisation goal not sufficient. Or, for reasons yet unknown, the market-determined cost of capital may suddenly increase greatly when a firm's demand for capital reach a certain level. Even if the cost of capital does not become infinitely high as capital constraints imply, it may become so high that the capital constraint is a reasonable approximation of market conditions.

When we release the assumption that the financial manger has access to as much capital as he needed, we found that the capital allocation problem became even more complex. Hence, real-world capital market conditions tend to force financial managers to ration the capital they have. The basic rationale for capital allocation remains the same, however, for investment projects should add to the present value of the firm in order for them to be acceptable.

SINGLE PERIOD CONSTRAINTS

The simplest capital rationing situation is one in which the expenditure constraint lasts for a single period only. This case is of practical as well as theoretical interest; however, because many (if not most) firms do not have sufficient knowledge of their future investment opportunities to apply the more sophisticated models.

The easiest way of selecting projects, assuming they are of similar risk, for inclusion in a limited budget is to rank them in descending order of attractiveness, then to accept the projects from the top of the list and work down until the funds are exhausted. Mutually exclusive projects are handled by breaking into a basic project and supplementary projects.

However, there are a number of ways of ranking projects, and these do not always give the same results. Some firms select investment projects by the joint use of two separate selection criteria. Among such firms, the combination of the payback method with either of the net present value (NPV) or internal rate of return (IRR) methods is especially prevalent. When two criteria are used, an investment project must be selected by both criteria to be accepted. Selection by only one criterion is insufficient for project acceptance.

If the two selection criteria used by a firm always agree in selecting or rejecting projects, then the practice of using joint criteria is a harmless, if redundant, action. However, if the criteria sometimes disagree and only one of the criteria may be considered consistent with the goal of maximising shareholder wealth, then the resulting capital budget may be too small and not contain the proper combination of projects. An example of the tendency is given in Table-2.

TABLE-2

Capital Budgets Evolved from Joint Use of Net Present Value and Payback Method

Project	*Outlay*	*Available Projects NPV*	*Payback period in years*
A	₹ 1,00,000	₹ 10,000	2.8
B	50,000	7,000	2.0
C	75,000	11,000	4.0
D	1,20,000	–4,000	2.5
E	60,000	5,000	1.6

There the net present value and payback method are used to evaluate a set of available investment projects. Of the available projects shown in Table-2, D is not acceptable because by the NPV method application we get the negative NPV (i.e. ₹ 4,000) at the prevailing cost of capital. With a maximum allowable payback period of three years, only project C with an estimated four-year payback period is unacceptable

Capital Budget

NPV Method Alone			*Both NPV and Payback*		
Project	*Outlay*	*NPV*	*Project*	*Outlay*	*NPV*
A	₹ 1,00,000	₹ 10,000	A	₹ 100,000	₹ 10,000
B	50,000	7,000	B	50,000	7,000
C	75,000	11,000	E	60,000	5,000
E	60,000	5,000		₹ 2,10,000	₹ 22,000
	₹ 2,85,000	₹ 33,000			

by the payback method. Using the NPV method alone, the capital budget would consist of projects A, B, C and E, with a total outlay of ₹ 2,85,000 and a total net present value of ₹ 33,000. Using both criteris, the failure of the project C to pass the payback test reduces the budget to projects A, B and E, with the smaller total outlay and net present value of ₹ 2,10,000 and ₹ 22,000, respectively. Shareholder wealth does not increase as much as it would if only the NPV method were followed and total capital outlay is reduced. If shareholders wealth maximisation is the goal, then the NPV method should be used.

Artifically High Discount Rates

Still other use some sort of discounted cash flow method to evaluate projects but employ an artificially high discount rate in that method. For example, suppose that a firm estimates its cost of capital to be 12% and that the risk premium included in that cost of capital is appropriate for the firm requires an after tax return of 20% for all projects and computes net present values on that should be accepted. Table-3 describes such a case. If the cost of capital is 12% to evaluate projects, then projects E and F will be rejected. Use of the high discount rate both lowers the total size of capital budgets, favours short-lived investments and results in foregone increases in shareholder wealth caused by omitted project.

TABLE-3

Effect of Using Artificially High Discount Rates

Project	*Outlay*	*NPV at 20% Discount Rate*	*NPV at 12% Cost of Capital*
A	₹ 1,00,000	₹ 4,000	₹ 8,571
B	1,00,000	5,000	12,500
C	40,000	1,333	4,286
D	75,000	1,280	6,696
E	50,000	-1,667	1,786
F	85,000	-4,250	1,518

The real question raised by the practice of artificially high discount rates is, what is the cost of capital ? If 12% represents the best estimate of the firm's cost of capital there can be no justification for using the artificially high 20% discount rate. To argue that the 20% discount rate is to allow for uncertainty concerning the cost of capital estimate is an argument for improving cost of capital estimates. If the firm really believes that the cost of capital is more than 12% it should estimate that higher rates and not, arbitrarily, use some artificially higher figure such as 20%.

A Profit-Planning Model

The investment projects the firms adopt will, of course, have an impact on the financial statements, they give to their shareholders. In determining which projects to adopt and which to reject, it is not unreasonable for a financial manager to consider the explicit impact of each project on the profit figures the firm will report in the year ahead.

Assume that the firm has prepared estimates of the cashflow of various projects and that it has determined a cost of capital figure which it uses to discount these flows. The problem the financial manager then faces is to select from the firm's set of investment opportunities the projects that will both maximise the firm's net present value and generate profits subject to the constraint that profits follow a specified growth pattern through time.

The objective function in this capital-budgeting problem, then, is to select the projects that yield a maximum total return over the cost of the funds that the firm has committed to them. When the excess present value of all the projects is maximised, the return to the firm's shareholders will be at a peak. The logic of the profit constraint is equally apparent. If the firm reports rising earning through time and the firm's shareholders attribute this to careful planning by management, the price of the firm's securities is likely to appreciate.

For any investment proposal or project to be potentially acceptable, its NPV must be positive—as must be its profitability index. If NPV is zero, the index is also zero and if NPV is negative, then so is the index.

In using the profitability index to select investments proposals under a capital constraint, four steps are required :

(1) Compute the index for all proposals.

(2) For competing proposals, retain the proposal having the highest (and positive) index. Reject other competing proposal (s).

(3) Rank the remaining proposals in the order of their index values.

(4) Beginning with the proposal having the highest index value, accept proposals until their accumulated total outlays exhaust the available capital.

Suppose we are comparing two projects which have the same life. Project A costs ₹ 10,00,000 and has a net present value of ₹ 10,000, while Project B costs ₹ 1,000 and has a net present value of ₹ 5,000. It is very tempting to argue that project B is better because it returns more net present value per ₹ of cost. However, the NPV rule is very clear. If these are mutually exclusive projects, the correct decision is to take the one that has the highest NPV, i.e., project A.

But let us assume that there is a meaningful capital constraint imposed on the firm. How should the NPV rule be modified to consider projects of different scale. Table-4 shows the present value of the cash inflows and outflows of four independent projects which have identical lives. If there were no constraint we would accept all four projects because they all have positive NPV s. Project 1 has the highest NPV, followed by Project 3, then 2, and, finally 4. Suppose that there is a capital constraint which limits our spending to ₹ 3,00,000 or less. Now we could accept only projects 2 and 3 because they have the greatest NPV among those combinations of projects which use not more than ₹ 3,00,000. The logic leading to this decision is formalised by what is known as the profitability index.

TABLE-4

Profitability Index

Project	*PV of*	*Current inflows*	*PI outflow*	*NPV*
1.	₹ 2,30,000	₹ 2,00,000	1.15	₹ 30,000
2	1,41,250	1,25,000	1.13	16,250
3.	1,94,250	1,75,000	1.11	19,250
4.	1,62,000	1,50,000	1.08	12,000

When used correctly, the PI is equivalent to maximising the NPV of a set of projects subject to the constraint that projects outlays be less than or equal to the firm's budget. The PI for each project is given in Table-4. The PI of excess funds, not invested in any of the projects, is always assumed to be equal to 1.0 (why ?).

The object is to compare all sets of projects which meet the budget and which meet the budget and find the one which maximises the weighted average PI. For example, if project 2 and 3 are selected, the weighted average PI is

$$PI = \frac{1,25,000}{3,00,000}(1.13) + \frac{1,75,000}{3,00,000}(1.11) = 1.1183$$

It is computed by multiplying the PI of each project by the percentage of the total budget allocated to it. If project 1 is selected, no additional project can be undertaken.

Therefore the PI for Project 1 is

$$PI = \frac{2,00,000}{3,00,000}(1.15) + \frac{1,00,000}{3,00,000}(1.00) = 1.100$$

Project 1 is not preferred to Projects 2 and 3 because ₹ 1,00,000 must be invested in marketable securities which have a PI of 1.0 (*i.e.,* their cost is always equal to the present value of their cash inflows).

The PI can be used to solve simple problems where there is a one period capital constraint. It can also be used to compare mutually exclusive projects of different scale although a simple comparison of NPV's provides the same result. For example, refer to projects A and B. The first project cost only ₹ 10,00,000 and had NPV of ₹ 10,000 while the second cost only ₹ 1,000 and had NPV of ₹ 5000. If these are the only two project available to the firm and if they are mutually exclusive, we can evaluate them by comparing their PI's with the assumption that the firm has a ₹ 10,00,000 budget.

The PI of Project A is:

$$\frac{10,00,000}{10,00,000}\left(\frac{10,10,000}{10,00,000}\right)=(1.01)$$

and the PI of Project B is:

$$\frac{1,000}{10,00,000}\left(\frac{6,000}{1,000}\right)+\frac{9,99,000}{10,00,000}(11.0)=1.005$$

Because Project A has a higher PI it is superior. The PI solution is exactly the same as the NPV solution; that is, we take the project with the highest NPV. The PI merely helps to highlight the assumption that if the project really are mutually exclusive, then the extra ₹ 9,99,000 which is not invested in Project B must be invested in marketable securities with a PI of 1.0.

Usually, the project to be compared are not so exaggerated as the above example ; however, it does help to illustrate the meaning of a capital constraint. If a strict budget exists, then the PI should be used. Otherwise the firm should accept all projects with positive NPV.

MULTIPERIOD CAPITAL CONSTRAINT

A fixed one-period constraint is highly artificial. Seldom will a budget be set so rigidly that it does not provide for some flexibility. In addition, the cost of certain investment projects may be spread over several years. Consequently, we must consider more than just a one-period constraint. With a multiperiod analysis, the capital constraint problem can be extended to consider budget constraints in many future time periods. If we assume that it is possible to undertake fractions of projects then the problem may be formulated using linear programming. If projects are indivisible, then integer programming may be used. With binding capital constraints, it is conceivable that a project with negative NPV may be accepted in the optimal solution if it supplies the funds needed during a later time period to undertake very profitable projects.

Mathematical programming can be used to allocate capital under conditions of capital rationing. The most comprehensive treatment of the problem has been provided by Weingartner. However, much of the initial impetus for the development of mathematical programming models in capital budgeting was provided by famous Lorie—Savage (LS) Problems.

In particular, L and S were concerned with several sub-problems which must be faced when a fixed capital budget is to be divided among a number of competing projects. The first sub-problem was "lumpiness", or discontinuties, which as they noted, was not a major problem to most corporations.

For large firms the vast majority of investment proposals constitute such a small proportion of their capital budget that the problem created by discontinuities can be disregarded at only significant cost, especially when the imprecision of the estimates of income is taken into account. When a project constitute a large proportion of the capital budget, the problem of discontinuities may become serious, though not necessarily difficult to deal with. This problem can become serious because of the obvious fact that accepting the large proposal, because it is "richer" than smaller proposals, may preclude the possibility of accepting two or more smaller and less rich proposals which, in combination, have a greater value than the large proposals.

A second and "more serious", subproblem was the necessity to choose among several investment projects, some of which required outlays in more than one budget period. To illustrate the complexity of this problem, L-S presented a capital budgeting problem in which there were nine projects, labelled "1" to "9", for each project its net present value and cash outlays for the first two years were given in Table-5.

TABLE-5

Two-Period Capital Constraint

Project	*Perioa-I outlay*	*Period-2 outlay*	*NPV*
1	₹ 12	₹ 3	₹ 14
2	54	7	17
3	6	6	17
4	6	2	15
5	30	35	40
6	6	6	12
7	48	4	14
8	36	3	10
9	18	3	12

Let us examine that cashflows cannot be transferred between time periods, that projects are infinitely divisible, and that the cash budget in period 1 is ₹ 50 while in period 2 it is ₹ 20. The problem is to find the set of projects which maximises NPV and satisfies the cash constraints. Weingartner solved the problem by using linear programming[2] The model seek to maximise the present value, as of the current date, of the excess of present values over costs resulting from the adoption of a particular budget. This is expressed in the objective function which is to

$$\text{Maximise NPV} = \sum_{t=1}^{n} b_j \, X_j \; (\textit{Primal Problem}) \tag{1}$$

where X_j = percent of of project *j* that is accepted

b_j = net present value of project *j* over its useful life when discounted at the cost of capital (market capitalisation rate).

Each project is expected to involve cash outlays having present values C_{jt} in one or more of the periods to under consideration. These are regarded as fixed and not subject to alteration, i.e., by rescheduling the project. There are fixed budget constraints K_t, the present value today of the actual constraints in the tth period. This gives us a set of budget constraint inequalities

$$\sum_{j=1}^{n} X_j C_{jt} \leq K_t \tag{2}$$

one for each period being considered.

It is impossible to construct a negative project, or to construct it more than once, so we have a third set of constraints:

$$0 \leq X_j \leq 1 \tag{3}$$

This is the basic model.

The objective is to choose the set of weights, X_j, which maximises the combined NPV of all projects. The constraints require (1) that the set of projects undertaken use less cash than is budgeted and (2) that no more than 100% of any project be undertaken.

Every linear programming problem has a counterpart called the *dual problem* where the primal constrains appear in the dual objective function and the primal decision variables become dual constraints. The dual for this problem can be written as:

Minimise

$$\sum_t P_t K_t + \sum_j U_j \tag{4}$$

Subject to

$$P_t C_{jt} U_j \geq b_j \qquad \textit{(Dual Problem)} \tag{5}$$

$$\text{and } P_t \geq 0 \qquad t = 1,2,....,T \tag{6}$$

$$U_j \geq 0 \qquad j = 1, 2....,n \tag{7}$$

P_t and U_j are new variables, called "dual variables," and the definition of the other variables remains unchanged. When one of the projects enters into the primal solution (that is, (X_j >0), then the corresponding constraint in the dual problem is binding. Thus the dual constraint can be written as an equality

$$\Sigma P_t C_{ij} + U_i = b_j$$

or, solving for U_j, we have

$$U_j - b_j = \Sigma P_t C_{tj} \quad (8)$$

Therefore U_j may be thought of as the difference between the NPV of a project's cashflows, b_j, and the imputed value of the outlays needed to undertake the project, $\Sigma P_t C_{tj}$. Conceptually, it is similar to the PI in the single-period problem because it is a measure of the benefit (NPV) minus the imputed cash cost of a project.

Finally, P_t may be thought of as the implicit one-period discount rate caused by the cash constraints in the linear programming problem. It is the value of relaxing the cash constraint by one ₹, the shadow price. This can be demonstrated by using Equation (8) and noting that for fractionally accepted projects, where the constraint is binding, $U_j = 0$. Therefore Equation (8) becomes

$$\Sigma P_t C_{tj} = bi$$

This says that the NPV of a project, b_j, equals the discounted' value of tits cashflows. Consequently P_t is the one period discount rate,

$$P_t = \frac{1}{(1+O^{ri+1})}$$

Table-6 shows the complete formulation of this problem and its solution. The maximum present value of the nine projects is ₹ 70.27. This result is achieved by adopting by adopting projects 4, 3, 1 and 9 in full and portions of projects 6 and 7.

TABLE-6

Linerar-Programming Model and Solution to the Lorie-Savage Problem

Maximise:

$14x_1 + 17x_2 + 17x_3 + 15x_4 + 40x_5 + 12x_6 + 14x_7 + 10x_8 + 12x_9$

Subject to:

$12x_1 + 54x_2 + 6x_3 + 6x_4 + 30x_5 + 6x_6 + 48x_7 + 36x_8 + 18x_9 + s_1 = 50$

$3x_1 + 7x_2 + 6x_3 + 2x_4 + 35x_5 + 6x_6 + 4x_7 + 3x_8 + 3x + s_2 = 20$

$x_1 + q_1 = 1$	$x_4 + q_4 = 1$	$x_7 + q_7 = 1$
$x_2 + q_3 = 1$	$x_5 + q_5 = 1$	$x_8 + q_8 = 1$
$x_3 + q_3 = 1$	$x_6 + q_6 = 1$	$x_9 + q_9 = 1$

Solution :

$x_1 = 1.0$	$x_4 = 1.0$	$x_7 = .045$
$x_2 = 0$	$x_5 = 0$	$x_8 = 0$
$x_3 = 1.0$	$x_6 = .970$	$x_9 = 1.0$

Total present value : ₹ 70.27

Shadow Prices : $P_1 = .136$ $P_2 = 1.864$

The project with the greatest net "benefit" is project 4 with $U_n = 10.45$. Although it has a smaller NPV than several of the other projects, it also uses less cash than the others. Finally comparison of the dual variables, P_1 and P_2, tells us that the value of relaxing the second period constraint is greater. In other words, providing extra cash in the second period would increase the firm's NPV more than providing extra cash in the first period. We can use the value of P_t to calculate one period implicit interest rates:

$$ {}_1r_2 = \frac{1-P_1}{P_1} = 635\% $$

$$ {}_2r_3 = \frac{1-P_2}{P_2} = -46.4\% $$

Linear programming solutions to capital budgeting have great verstality and have been applied to many types of problems. However, it is difficult to justify the existence of capital constraints consideration, linear programming models fail to adequately handle it. For these and other reasons, linear programming models have become less popular in recent years.

INTEGER PROGRAMMING APPLIED TO THE CAPITAL BUDGETING PROBLEM

In his pioneer work, Weingartner also suggested an integer programming approach to the capital budgeting problem in addition to the LP models discussed above. The main motivations for the use of integer programming (ILP) in the capital budgeting setting are as follows:

(1) Difficulties imposed by the acceptance of partial projects in ILP are eliminated, since ILP requires that project either be completely accepted or rejected.
(2) All the projects interdependencies can be formally included in the constraints ILP, while the same is not true for LP, due to the possibility of accepting partial projects.

The general ILP formulation for the capital budgeting problem is shown in Equations (10) through (12):

Maximise NPV

$$ \sum_{j=1}^{N} b_j X_j \qquad (10) $$

Subject to

$$ \sum_{j=1}^{N} X_j C_{jt} \leq K_t \qquad t = 1, 2, \ldots N \qquad (11) $$

$$ X_j = (0,1) \qquad j = 1, 2, \ldots N \qquad (12) $$

Notice that the only change in the formulation mentioned above compared to the primal LP formulation shown in Equations (1), (2), and (3) is that Equation (12) replaces Equation (3). Equation (12), which is the zero—one condition of ILP, guarantees that each project is either completely accepted ($X_j = 1$) or that it is rejected ($X_j = 0$).

The second attractive feature of the ILP mentioned above deserve elaboration. In using the simple capital budgeting models (NPV, IRR, PI, etc.), it is assumed that all the investment projects are independent of each other (i.e., that project cash flows are not related to each other and do not influence or change one another dependencies can be incorporated in the model by means of the special constrains discuss below. The three types of project dependencies—mutually exclusive, pre-requisites, and complementary projects—can be handled in a straightforward manner. Each will be discussed in turn.

Recall that *mutually exclusive* projects are defined as a set of projects wherein the acceptance of one project in the set precludes the simultaneous acceptance of any other projects in the set. The existence of such a set of projects is incorporated in an ILP model by the following constraint:

$$\sum_{j \in J} X_j \leq 1 \tag{13}$$

where J = set of mutually exclusive projects under consideration
$j \in$J = that project j is an element of the set of mutually exclusive projects J.

Note that the constraint states that *at most* one project from set J can be accepted; this means that the firm could choose not to accept any project from set J. on the other hand, if it was necessary to select one project from the set, constraint (13) would appear as a strict equality:

$$\sum_{j \in J} X_j = 1 \tag{14}$$

Another important application of this constraint is the situation wherein a firm is considering the possibility of delaying a project for one or more years. For example, consider project X which has the following characteristics:

Period	Cash Flows Project X
0	–₹ 10,000
1	7,500
2	7,500
3	7,500

The NPV of this project at 10% is ₹ 8,653. If the firm wants to determine whether it would be desirable to delay project X either 1 or 2 years, the following two new projects, X^I and X^{II}, respectively, can be defined:

Period	Cash Flow	
	Project X^I	Project X^{II}
0	₹ 0	₹ 0
1	–10,000	0

2	7,500	−10,000
3	7,500	7,500
4	7,500	7,500
5		7,500

The NPVs (with a cost of capital of 10%) that would be included in the objective function for project X^{I} and X^{II}, respectively, are ₹ 7,866 and ₹ 7,147. These values differ from the NPV of project X because of the 1-and-2-year delays, respectively, in the cash flows, which necessitates multiplying project X's NPV by 1/1.10 to arrive at the NPV for X^{I} and by $1/(1.10)^2$ to arrive at the NPV for X^{II}. Of course, the ₹ 10,000 cash outflow would be shown in the budget constraint for year 0 for project X, year 1 for project X^{I}, and year 2 for project X^{II}. Finally, to show that at most one of these versions of project X could be accepted, the following constraint would be included in the ILP formulation :

$$X + X^{I} + X^{II} \leq 1$$

Pre-requisite (or contingent) projects are two or more projects wherein the acceptance of one project necessitates the prior acceptance of some other project (s). For example, if project A cannot be accepted unless project Z is accepted, we would say that project Z is a pre-requisite project for acceptance of project A; alternatively, we could also say that acceptance of project A is contingent upon the acceptance of project Z. Again, the representation of the above project inter-relationships in ILP is immediate:

$$X_A \leq XZ \qquad (15)$$

where X_A and X_Z are decision variables denoting projects A and Z. Note in Equation (15) that if project A is accepted (i.e., $X_A = 1$), then necessarily, project Z must be accepted also. However, project Z can be accepted on its own and project A rejected. Of course, there may be many possible variations, to constraints (13), (14), and (15).

The final type of project interrelationship is that of *complementary projects* wherein the acceptance of one project enahances the cash flows of one or more other projects. This synergistic effect is reflected in the ILP formuation by using the strategy outlined below.

Consider that we have two complementary projects, 7 and 8. Either of these projects can be accepted in isolation. However, if both are accepted simultaneously.

(1) The cost will be reduced by say 10%.

(2) The net inflow will be increases by say 15%. To handle the problem, a new project (call it 78) would be constructed having a cost equal to 90% of the cost of project 7 plus project 8 and net cash inflows equal to 115% of those of project 7 plus project 8. In addition, we would need the following constraint to preclude acceptance to both project 7 and 8 as well as 78, because the later is the composite project consisting of the two former projects:

$$X_7 + X_8 + X_{78} \leq 1$$

Two significant shortcomings of the ILP methodology are: firstly the ability to include the various types of constraints for project inter-relationships adds to the realism of the problem representation using ILP as compared to LP which encounters difficulty handling such constraints). Furthermore, the existence of partial projects in the optimal LP solution raises questions about how realistic the problem representation is. However, the question arises whether the price that has to be paid in moving to ILP is worth the benefits gained, considering the difference, in solution, time and the lack of meaningful shadow prices in ILP compared to LP.

The second shortcoming of ILP formulations and solutions is perhaps more devastating: meaningful shadow prices (which show incremental change in the right-hand sides of various constraints) are not available in ILP. That is, many of the constraints on ILP problems which are not binding on the optimal integer solution will be assigned shadow prices of zero, which indicates that these resources are "free goods." In reality, this is not true since the objective function would clearly decrease if the availability of such resources were decreased. Furthermore, Baumol, who was one of the pioneers in the area of dual variables in ILP, summarises the problem of shadow prices in ILP quite well:

However, we must be careful here—the preceding interpretation amounts to our thinking of these dual prices as the marginal revenue of these inputs. In integer programming case, this concept runs into difficulties. In integar programming, inputs must be clearly thought of as coming in indivisible units. For that reason we cannot speak, e.g., of the marginal profit contribution of a small change input, i.e., we must deal with $\Delta R/\Delta X$ rather than dR/dX (as we do in LP) where ΔX is an indivisible unit of input X and R is total profit. But a dual price represents dR/dX, which may change over the range of a unit change in X, and hence it may well give an incorrect evaluation of the marginal revenue of input X (Emphasis added).[3]

Thus, the ILP model, in trying to handle the problem of indivisibilities, runs into problems itself because the feasible region consists only of points that have integer values for all decisions variables. This same problem of "gaps in the feasible region" is the culprit in creating both of the problems cited above: computer time required to solve ILP problems and difficulties in interpreting the shadow price in ILP.

ILLUSTRATIVE PROBLEMS

1. Model M. makes ₹ 25 per unit profit and model N makes ₹ 15 per unit profit Model M requires 7material units and 1 hour labour. Total materials available are 700 units and total available labour is 300 hours. Formulate problem as a linear programming.

Solution

Maximise

$$25 \text{ M} = 15 \text{ N}$$

Subject to

$$7 \text{ M} + 1 \text{ N} \leq 700$$

$$1\,M + 3\,N \leq 300$$
$$M, N \geq 0$$

2. Given the following data, what are the totals of present value of net cash benefits in period "t" and "$t + 1$," if the data reflects the optimal solution under the Lorie and Savage Linear programming algorithm?

× (A) = .85 NPV(A) = 480 PVNCO(A) = 400 PVNCO(A) $t + 1 = 60$

× (B) = 1.00 NPV(B) = 60 PVNCO(B) = 48 PVNCO(B) $t + 1 = 10$

× (C) = 0 NPV(C) = 25 PVNCO(C) = 30 PVNCO(C) $t + 1 = 5$

× (D) = .60 NPV(D) = 120 PVNCO(D) = 90 PVNCO(D) $t + 1 = 20$

Solution

The net present value of the benefits is ₹ 540; the outlay in period "t" has a present value of ₹ 442 and in "t+1" of ₹ 73, as follows:

Proposal	*Present Value*	*PV Outlay Period "t"*	*PV Outlay Period 2t+1"*
A	480 × .85 = 408	400 × .84 = 340	60 × .85 = 51
B	60 × 1.00 = 60	48 × 1.000 = 48	10 × 1.00 = 10
C	25 × 0 = 0	30 × 0 = 0	5 × 0 = 0
D	120 × .60 = 70	90 × .60 = 54	20 × .60 = 12
	Total = ₹ 540	Total = ₹ 442	Total = ₹ 73

3. Laxman Machine Tools has determined certain risk profiles for investment projects after making a careful study of the risk preferences of its management. These risk profiles show the maximum standard deviation of profitability index that is tolerable for particular expected value of profitability index. The risk profiles for various profitability indexes are as follows:

Expected PI	1.00	1.05	1.10	1.15	1.20	1.25
Maximum S.D.	0	0.04	0.10	0.15	0.21	0.26

The company is considering two new investment proposals, which are expected to have two following characteristics:

Proposal A Cost = ₹ 2,00,000		*Proposal B Cost = ₹ 5,00,000*	
NPV	*Probability of Occurrence*	*NPV*	*Probability of Occurrence*
₹ –5,000	0.10	–₹ 40,000	0.10
0	0.20	₹ 10,000	0.15
50,000	0.40	₹ 50,000	0.50
1,00,000	0.20	₹ 90,000	0.15
1,50,000	0.10	₹ 1,40,000	0.10

Knowing the risk profiles of the company, would you accept either or both of the two proposals?

Solution

Proposal A

Expected value of NPV = ₹ 50,000

Expected value of PI = ₹ 2,50,000/ ₹ 2,00,000 = 1.25

Standard deviation (000 omitted)

$= [0.1(1{,}500-500)]^2]+0.2(0-500)^2 + 0.2(1000-500)^2$
$+0.1[1{,}500-500)^2]^{1/2}$ = ₹ 547.7

Standard Deviation of PI = ₹ 547.7/₹ 2,000 = .274

Given the maximum standard deviation of .26 for a PI of 1.25, Proposal A would be rejected. It exceeds the risk tolerances of management.

Proposal B

Expected value of net present value = ₹ 50,000

Expected value of PI = ₹ 5,50,000/₹ 5,00,000 = 1.10

Standard deviation (000 omitted) = $[0.1(-400-500)^2+0.15$
$(100-500)^2 + 0.15\ (900-500)^2 + 0.10(1{,}400-500)^2]^{1/2}$ = ₹ 458.3.

Standard deviation of PL = ₹ 458.3/ ₹ 5,000 = .09. For a Pl of 1.10, the maximum standard deviation is 0.10. As the standard deviation is slightly below this maximum, Proposal B would be accepted.

4. Suraj Transport has two goals; it wants to maximise the present value of the cash flows of the projects it adopts and it wants to report a 10 percent rise in earnings per year. To meet its goals, it has decided to use linear programming. The relevant facts about the projects it has under consideration are presented below. No earnings will result if no new investments are made. Structure the capital budgeting problem of Suraj Transport.

		Planned Earnings		
Project	*Present Value*	*Period 1*	*Period 2*	*Period 3*
A	₹ 20	₹ 5	₹ 7	₹ 8
B	15	10	9	8
C	30	3	6	9

Solution

Maximise:

$$20x_1 + 15x_2 + 30x_3$$

Subject to:

$$(7x_1 + 9x_2 + 6x_3)—(1.10)(5x_1 + 10x_2 + 3x_3) \geq 0$$
$$(8x_1 + 8x_2 + 9x_3)-(1.10)(7x_1 + 9x_2 + 6x_3) \geq 0$$

These constraints can be rewritten as:

$$1.5\ x_1 - 2x_2 + 2.7x_3$$
$$-3x_1 - 1.9x_2 + 2.4x_3 \geq 0$$

5. The Rapid Growth Company has decided to structure its capital-budgeting procedures so that Linear-programming technique can be applied. The company is considering the purchase of three machines, each of which will require some outlays is the next two periods. According to the management's best estimates, the firm will have ₹ 20,000 available to spend in each of these periods. Data about each of the three projects are presented below. Rapid Growth Company wants to maximise the present value of the projects it has under review. Structure the capital budgeting problem for them.

Machine	*Present Value of Investment Period-1*	*Present Value of outlay in*	*Present Value of outlay in Period-2*
A	₹ 10,000	₹ 8,000	₹ 8,000
B	₹ 12,000	₹ 2,000	₹ 12,000
C	₹ 15,000	₹ 14,000	₹ 6,000

Solution

Maximise:

$$10{,}000x_1 + 12{,}000x_2 + 15{,}000x_3$$

Subject to:

$$8{,}000x_1 + 2{,}000x_2 + 14{,}000x_3 \le 20{,}000$$
$$8{,}000x_1 + 12{,}000x_2 + 6{,}000x_3 \le 20{,}000$$
$$x_1 \ , x_2 \ , \ x_3 \le 1$$
$$x_1 \ , x_2 \ , \ x_3 \ge 0$$

6. Lucky Shareholder Company estimated that the utility schedule of its shareholders was as follows: $U_1 = 1$, $U_2 = .87$, $U_3 = .75$, and $U_4 = .66$ (where the subscript stand for the year). It has allocated ₹ 1,00,000 for new projects and it does not plan to spend any more funds in later periods for investment projects. It is considering the purchase of projects with the following cash flows:

Project	*Cash Flows in Various Years (000 Omitted)*			
	1	2	3	4
A	–₹ 50	₹ 6	₹ 20	₹ 100
B	–50	50	50	50
C	–40	–40	100	200

Construct a linear-programming problem for the firm that will help decide which project to adopt.

Solution

Maximise

$$1U_1 + .87U_2 + .75U_3 + .66U_4$$

Subject to:

$$50x_1 + 50x_2 + 40x_3 + U_1 \le 100$$

$$-60x_1 - 50x_2 + 40x_3 + U_2 \leq 0$$
$$-20x_1 - 50x_2 - 50x_3 + U_3 \leq 0$$
$$-100x_1 - 50x_2 - 200x_3 + U_4 \leq 0$$
$$x_1, x_2 x_3 \geq 0$$
$$x_1, x_2 x_3 \leq 1$$

QUESTIONS

1. What is meant by "capital rationing?" Is it unusual for firm to ration capital? Why or why not?
2. What reasons are commonly given for capital rationing? Is capital rationing rational?
3. What does the imposition of a capital constraint imply about the cost of capital to the firm?
4. When capital must be rationed? How should investment opportunities be selected?
5. Why does the existence of a capital constraint mean that economically dependent investment proposals must be evaluated in different combinations?
6. Is it reasonable to assume that a capital budgeting decision will be affected by the volume of funds the firm has available to spend? Is it reasonable to think that if one company has abundant funds while a second company has a limited amount, additional funds will be worth less to the first company than to the second? Will the cost of capital of the two companies be different? Will they value comparable investment projects differently?
7. What are the likely effects if a firm uses multiple investment selection criteria or artificially high discount rates in accepting or rejecting investment projects?
8. Critique the following statement. "We employ a capital constraint because we finance all projects internally."
9. "If we undertook every project available to our firm, we'd break under stress. An organisation can only absorb so much new task at a time." What does this statement suggest that this firm should do in evaluating investment projects?
10. What are the internal rate of return, net present value, profitability index, and integer programming approaches to capital rationing? Which method, if any, is preferable?
11. Formulate a programme for optimal selection of projects in a capital rationing situation. How can the dual of this programme be used?
12. Why does a fixed budget constraint in the Lorie-Savage problem give rise to questions about the present value of projects?

PROBLEMS

1. Minerva Products, has the following independent Investments under examination:

Project	*Initial investment per year*	*After-tax cash flows (years)*	*Life of the project*
A	₹ 1,00,000	₹ 39,000	4
B	50,000	12,000	6
C	80,000	39,000	3
D	60,000	15,000	7
E	75,000	25,000	5
F	90,000	25,000	6

Minerva Products required rate of return is 14 percent:

(a) In the absence of capital rationing, which projects should be selected? What is the size of the capital budget? The total NPV of all of the projects selected?

(b) Now suppose a limit of ₹ 2,50,000 is placed on new capital projects. Which projects should be selected?

(c) What is the total NPV determined in (b)? What is the loss to Minerva Products due to the capital rationing constraint?

Ans.: (a) NPV_A = ₹ 13,646; NPV_B = ₹ 3,332, NPV_C = ₹ 10,554, NPV_D = ₹ 4,320; NPV_E = ₹ 10,825; and NPV_F = ₹ 7,225; Accept all but B; (b) Project – A, D, and E; (c) NPV : ₹ 28,791, Loss : ₹ 17,783.

2. Ranade Group is studying a number of capital projects. It has allocated ₹ 10,00,000 for capital budgeting purposes. The following proposals and associated profitability indexes have been determined. The projects themselves are independent of one another.

Project	*Amount*	*Profitability Index*
A	₹ 5,00,000	1,21
B	3,50,000	1.20
C	4,50,000	1.18
D	4,50,000	1.05
E	1,50,000	0.95
F	2,00,000	1.20

(a) With strict capital rationing, which of the above investments should be undertaken?

(b) Is this an optimal strategy?

3. The XYZ Company has more investment opportunities than it can use. Management estimated that the investment cutoffs for the next two years will be as follows:

Year	*Cutoff*
0-1	.20
1-2	.30

It is attempting to choose between two mutually exclusive alternatives both of which will require an initial outlay now and payoff at the end off two periods. what discount rate should be used in evaluating the mutually exclusive investments? What rate would you use if the investment had a life of one year?

4. The Datmax Company has recently become enthrilled with linear programming and wants to utilise it in determining the optimal product mix for its two product lines. The relevant information about its products is as follows:

	Product x	*Product y*
Selling price	₹ 16.000	₹ 23.00
Standard material cost	₹ 1.50	₹ 2.25
Standard labour cost	6.60	8.00
Standard transport cost	100	1.00
Maximum demand	None	500 Units
Minimum requirements	100 Units	None

In addition, Datamax has several constraints that cannot be violated:

Raw material constraint		
Labour hours constraint	1,200	hours at 4.00 standard cost
Machine hours constraint	2,800	hours at 1.50 standard cost
Transport-capacity constraint	650	units at 1.00 standard cost

Formulate this linear programming problem and solve it using the graphical technique.

Ans.: 133.3 units product x, 500 units product *y*, ₹ 3,649.99 profit.

12

CAPITAL BUDGETING DECISIONS UNDER CONDITIONS OF UNCERTAINTY–I

INTRODUCTION

The capital budgeting techniques enable us to make rational decisions, under condition of complete certainty, on the cash flows resulting from undertaking an investment. But the world we live in is one of change and uncertainty, and financial managers know that they are not omniscient. In fact, they play a mixed game of skill and chance, the average result of which the players are not known. When a potential investor calculates that a proposed venture offers the prospect of a return of x percent per annum, he is fully aware that unforeseen events may invalidate his estimate. The purpose of this chapter is to ensure that the investor is able to analyse situations in which it is appropriate to supplement the simple decisions rules of the present value procedure with an analysis of risk.

CERTAINTY, RISK, AND UNCERTAINTY

A decision maker may be faced with conditions of certainty, risk, and uncertainty. ***Certainty*** *postulates that the decision maker knows in advance the precise values that all the parameters that may affect the decision will take on.* ***Risk*** *postulates that the decision maker is aware of all possible future states of the economy, business and so on, which may occur and thereby affect relevant decision parameters and is able to place a probability on the value of the occurence of each of these states.* ***Uncertainty*** *postulates that the decision maker may or may not be aware of all the possible states that affect the decision and may or may not be able to place a probability distribution on the occurence of each.*

The classical distinction between risk and uncertainty is that an element or analysis involves risk of the probabilities of the alternative, possible outcomes are known, while it is characterised by uncertainty if the frequency distribution of the possible outcomes is not known. Another less restrictive distinction between risk and uncertainty is that risk is the dispersion of the probability distribution of the element being estimated or calculated outcome (s) being considered, while uncertainty is the degree of lack of confidence that the estimated probability distribution is correct. The word risk can be used to apply to the outcome if any element or measure of merit. Colloquially, the word is often used merely to denote variability of outcome, and often times the only variability which is of concern is variability in an unfavourable direction.

CAUSES OF RISK AND UNCERTAINTY

Risk and uncertainty in project investment decisions are attributable to many possible sources. A brief description of some main causes is as follows:

(1) Insufficient numbers of similar investments: In general, a firm will have only a few investments of a particular type. This means that there will be insufficient opportunity for the result of particular investment type to "average out", *i.e.*, for the effect of unfavourable outcomes, to be virtually cancelled by favourable outcomes. This type of risk is dominant when the magnitude of the individual investment commitment is large compared to the financial resources of the firm.

(2) Bias in the data and its assessment: It is common that individuals making or reviewing economic analysis have biases of optimism or are unconciously influenced by factors which should not be a part of an objective study. A pattern of consistent optimism or pessimism on the part of an anayst should be recognised through analysis review procedures.

(3) Changing external economic environment, invalidating past experiences: Whenever estimates are made of future conditions that usual bases rare past result for similar quantities, whenever available. While the past information is often valuable, there is risk in using it directly without adjustment for expected future conditions.

(4) Misinterpretation of data: Misinterpretation may occur if the underlying factors behind elements to be estimated are so complex that the relationship of one or more factors to the desired elements is misunderstood.

(5) Errors of analysis: Errors can occur either in analysis of the technical operating characteristics of project or in the analysis of the financial implications of a project.

(6) Managerial talent availability and emphasis: The performance of an industrial investment project or set of projects usually depends in substantial part on the availability and application of managerial talent once the project has been undertaken. In general, management talent is a very limited resources within a firm; hence, it follows that the results of some projects are going to suffer compared to the results of other project. Thus, there is risk due to lack of availability or neglect in needed managerial talent applied to investment projects.

(7) Salvageability of investment: Of prime consideration in judging risk is the relative recoverability of investment commitments if a project, for performance considerations or otherwise, is to be liquidated. For example, an investment in a special purpose equipment which would have a high percentage salvage value if sold because of poor operating results of descriptive synonym is "bail-outability."

(8) Obsolescence: Rapid obsolescence, change and progress are characteristic of a dynamic economy. Not only do products become superseded, thus rendering

production facilities for those products less needed or useless, but also changes in process technology can render existing facilities obsolete.

ANALYSING RISKY INVESTMENTS

Although there is now a large literature on the theory of investment, much of it is confined merely to decision making under conditions of certainty. The procedures for risk anaylsis suggested in this literature have tended to offer rather crude solutions for the problems they were to solve.

CRUDE PROCEDURES

PAYBACK PERIOD

The payback period is probably one of the most widely used methods of conveying information about risk to managers. When applied to risky investments, the concept of the payback period assumes that an investment has assured net cash flows during its payback period, but that its subsequent net cash flows are so uncertain that they may be regarded as virtually non-existent for purposes of investment analysis. Undoubtedly, investment risks sometimes do contain this elements of uncertainty. For example, in government subsidised industries where it is likely that such subsidies may be substantially reduced or even eliminated. But as A.J. Merrett and Allen Sykes point out, *"the usual risks in business are not that a project will go on as forecast for a period and than collapse altogether. Rather the risks are that a given project will have lower sales, higher costs, unsuspected teething troubles etc.—the risk that all will not go as planned."*[1]

For these usual business risk, the payback period method, with its all-or-nothing assumption, is too crude an instrument for reaching sound investment decision.

EXPECTED MONETARY VALUE

Another crude approach used by businessmen for appraising risky investment is the expected monetary value (EMV). This method views *the net cash flow from an investment in each period as a random variable capable of taking on any one of many possible values. The expected value is then computed for each random variable and the investment appraised as if the expected net cash flows were certain to be realised.*

The EMV method is easy to understand and simple to apply, but it suffers from the disadvantage of not making full use of all available risk information. The EMV average out the positive and negative elements in a situation without offering any explicit measue of the risk of investment. This suppression of risk information might not constitute a serious disadvantage in decisions involving small investments. Behavioural studies have shown that when the sum at stake is small, the optimal decision is not sensitive to risk consideration. In terms of utility analysis, this means that since an investor's utility of money is approximately linear when small sums are involved, a decision that maximises the EMV also tends to maximise the expected

1. A.J. Merrett and Allen Skyes: The Finance and Analysis of Capital project", John Wiley & Sons, Inc., N.Y. 1963.

utility value. In such instances the expected monetary value approach despite its theoretical shortcomings, is acceptable as a practical method for appraising risky investments.

However, when the sum at stake is large, the optimal investment decision is sensitive to risk considerations. The investors are averse to risk and uncertainty; that is, their utility curves are concave downward. If an investor's utility function is quadratic and concave downward, he will choose his investments on the basis of the expected value and the variance of return. It is quite conceivable, therefore, that faced with two investments with differing returns and risks, a firm may choose the one with the lower expected monetary gain, provided of course, it also has the lower variance of monetary gain. In such instances strict adherence to the EMV method of appraisal may lead to non-optimal investment decisions.

REFINED PROCEDURES

There are many approaches to the incorporation of risk into capital budget. Their applicability varies among the decision criteria and situations. Basically, there are two major competing method for making risky long-term investment decisions: *the risk adjusted discount rate approach* and *the certainty equivalent approach.*

RISK-ADJUSTED DISCOUNT RATE APPROACH

The risk adjusted discount rate approach is based on the promise that the riskiness of a project may be accounted for by adjusting the discount rate (cost of capital). Relatively risky projects would have relatively high discount rates and relatively safe projects would be assigned relatively low discount rates.

When the finance manager consider other possible investments besides the risk-free government securities, it is necessary to adjust the cost of capital (discount rate) in the present value capital budgeting procedures to reflect additional risk such that:

$$k_a = T + \alpha_a \qquad (1)$$

where k_a = the risk-adjusted cost of capital for project *a*

T = the risk-free rate

α_a = the risk-adjustment premium

The risk-adjustment premium added to the risk free rate (T) reflects the greater risk attached to this projects than attached to a government debt obligation. As the risk increase, the risk-adjustment premium also increases and the risk-adjusted cost capital to the project rises.

In order to get some feel for the size of the risk adjustment, the finance manager will again turn to the dispersion in the distribution of cash flows. As the dispersion increases, α_a and k_a also increases. In fact, we can express α_a as a function of the proportional relationship between the standard deviation of the total firm's cash flows, such that:

$$\alpha_a = \left(\frac{V_a}{V_{firm}}\right)\alpha_{firm} \tag{2}$$

where α_a = the risk premium to project *'a'*

V_a = the coefficient of variation of project *'a'*

V_{firm} = the coefficient of variation of the firm.

α_{firm} = the risk premium associated with the entire firm.

In a some what arbitrary fashion, the finance manager will determine the risk premium for the entire firm (α_{firm}) in comparison to the risk free rate. The next step is to divide the coefficient of variation of the project (V_a) by the coefficient of variation of the firm's cash flows (V_{firm}) and decide if the project has a greater or lesser risk than the entire firm. This relationship between V_a and V_{firm} will proportionally increase k_a above or below the risk free rate (T) such that if:

$$\frac{V_a}{V_{firm}} > 1 \text{ then } k_a > k_{firm}$$

and if:

$$\frac{V_a}{V_{firm}} < 1 \text{ then } k_a < k_{firm}$$

If the coefficient of variation of the project is less than that of the firm's, then the risk-adjusted discount rate for the project is less than that of the firm, and vice-versa.

Using the expected value of the cashflow distributions ($\overline{A}_t$) for each year in the project's life and the risk-adjusted discount rate, the finance manager will find the risk-adjusted net present value for the project. For example, if:

$$NPV = \sum_{t=1}^{n} \frac{\overline{A}_t}{(1+k_a)^t} - IO \tag{3}$$

The symbols used have the following meanings and values:

NPV = net present value of the project

$\overline{A}_t$ = net cash flows per year from the project

k_a = cost of capital applicable to the project

n = number of years the net cash flows are received

IO = required investment outlay for the project

and the following figures are available on the firm and the project:

TABLE-1

Year	$(\overline{A}_t)$	T	V_{firm}	V_a	α_{firm}	$k_a = T + \frac{V_a}{V_{firm}} \alpha_{firm}$
1.	₹ 3,000	7%	.16	.08	.06	.10
2.	₹ 3,000	7%	.16	.08	.06	.10
3.	₹ 3,000	7%	.16	.08	.06	.10

and if, in this example, the project costs ₹ 5,000, then its risk adjusted NPV would be:

$$\text{NPV} = ₹\ 5{,}000 + \frac{₹\ 3{,}000}{(1+.10)^1} + \frac{₹\ 3{,}000}{(1+.10)^2} + \frac{₹\ 3{,}000}{(1+1.10)^3} = ₹\ 2{,}461.00$$

We would undertake this project because its risk-adjusted NPV is greater than zero. If the risk-adjusted NPV were less than zero. We would reject the project.

CERTAINTY-EQUIVALENT APPROACH

Some financial theorists object to a risk adjusted discount rate to evaluate risky proposals. The objection goes like this. There are two important things to account for in the valuation process, the time value of money and risk attitudes. But these two concepts should be logically seperated in the valuation process. Specifically, use of a discount rate that lumps together the risk free interest rate and a risk premium is wrong. That is, discounting for the futurity of cash flows should *only* include time value considerations and *not* risk consideration. Adding the risk premium into discount rate leads to a *compounding* of risk over time, which is a questionable practice.

Proponents of this argument advocate an alternative evaluation method that avoid the problem of including a risk premium in the discount factor. This approach is called certainty equivalent approach. The decision rule associated with the certainty equivalent approach is to undertake the project if its certainty-equivalent NPV is greater than zero. For any of the other present value decision criteria, the rule is similarly altered to reflect the present value of the certainty-equivalent cashflows in relation to the projects' cost.

We can calculate certainty equivalent of the cashflow (A_t) in several ways. First we can reduce the cashflow estimate by a sufficient number of standard deviations to ensure that under the normal distribution, the occurence will be certain to occur. This can be done by taking the mean of the cashflow estimates for each period and reducing it by three standard deviations as follows;

$$CE_t = \overline{A}_t - 3\sigma \qquad (4)$$

where CE_t = the certainty equivalent for-period t

Reduction of the mean by three standard deviations makes us 99.7% certain that the occurence will be at least equal to the certainty equivalent. Of course, we could use any multiple of standard deviation that produce certainty. For example, if:

$\bar{A}_t$ = ₹ 3,000

σ = ₹ 500

then CE_t = ₹ 3,000–3 (₹ 500) = ₹ 1,500

If the project had a 3-year life, no salvage value, cost ₹ 5,000 and the risk-free discount rate were 7%, the project certainty-equivalent NPV would be:

$$NPV = \frac{₹\,1{,}500}{(1+.07)^1} + \frac{₹\,1{,}500}{(1+.07)^2} + \frac{₹\,1{,}500}{(1+.07)^3} - ₹\,5{,}000 = -₹\,1{,}063.55$$

Since the certainty-equivalent NPV is negative, we would reject the project. Notice that the discount factor used was the risk-free rate of 7% but that the reduced cashflow estimates more than offset the lower rate of discount.

A second method of calculating the certainty equivalent is to reduce the estimate by a factor (B) that reflects financial manager particular willingness to trade the risky estimates for the certainty equivalent.

$$B_t = \frac{\text{Certain cashflow}_t}{\text{Estimated cashflow}_t}$$

B_t increases as the certainty equivalent increases relative to any estimate for the period. If there is great certainty of the estimating occuring, B_t will be close to (if not exactly) 1.0, implaying that the certain cashflow and the estimated cashflow are equal. As financial manager become less certain that the estimated cashflow and the certain cashflow are equal, B_t decreases; in the extreme, it sinks to zero.

This B_t factor is then applied to the numerator of the NPV formula, reducing the estimated cashflows to certainty and forcing the discount factor in the denominator to be the risk-free rate. In our example, if the risk-free discount rate were 7% and B_t was:

$$B_t = \frac{₹\,2{,}000}{₹\,3{,}000} = .67$$

then the NPV would be:

$$NPV = -₹\,5{,}000 + \frac{.67(₹\,3{,}000)}{(1+.07)^1} + \frac{.67(₹\,3{,}000)}{(1+.07)^2} + \frac{.67(₹\,3{,}000)}{(1+.07)^3} = ₹\,274.88$$

A third method of calculations of the certainty equivalent is the time adjusted method. If financial manager felt less certain of estimated cashflow as the length of time over which he has to estimate increases, he might want to increase B_t to account for any increased uncertainty, associated with the futurity of the estimate. For example, instead of having B_t remain constant at .67, he might want to have B_t decline as time progresses such that:

B_1 = .67; B_2 = .50; B_3 = .40

The NPV would be:

$$\text{NPV} = -₹\,5{,}000 + \frac{.67(₹\,3{,}000)}{(1+.07)^1} + \frac{.50(₹\,3{,}000)}{(1+.07)^2} + \frac{.40(₹\,3{,}000)}{(1+.07)^3} = ₹\,831.75$$

We would now the B_t factor effectively decreases the certainty equivalent of the estimated cashflow overtime. Of course, the finance manager has great flexibility in determining the exact value of the B_t factor, since this is basically done by any subjective feel. The degree to which risky cashflow are scaled down, that is how small the B_t is,will depend upon: (a) the amount of risk dispersion associated with subjective probability distribution assigned to the expected annual cashflow, more risk, the lower the B_t value; (b) the decision maker's feeling about attractiveness of the distribution's form: the more attractive the distribution, the higher the B_t values; and (c) to what extent the random variations in the annual cashflows from this project are expected to cancel out with variations in flows from other projects: the more variations that are canceled out, the higher the B_t values.

Markowitz[2] modifies the certainty-equivalence approach along the following lines:

1. It incorporates the notion of constraints as the type of the use of mathematical programming.
2. It incorporates the notion of interactive effects of the expected returns from a group of investments by the use of covariances.
3. It incorporates the notion of diversification and the selection of investment combinations (portfolio) that will minimise risk (variance) at the specified levels of expected return.

Markowitz proved that the rationale that underlies the certainty-equivalence approach, a preference of expected returns and an aversion towards risks can lead to the construction of balanced or diversified portfolio. It is portfolios, and not individual assets, which define the real set of available investment opportunities.

IMPACT OF INFLATION ON CAPITAL BUDGETING PROCEDURES

What effects does inflation have on the results of capital budgeting analysis? To examine the impact of inflation on capital budgeting procedures. We will use comprehensive example to clarify the influences introduced.

Let us begin with the standard capital budgeting case in which inflation is absent. The expression for calculating the NPV of the investment is shown in Equation (3):

2. Harry M. Markowitz: "Porfolio Selection", *Journal of Finance March*, 1952, pp. 17-91.

$$NPV=\sum_{t=1}^{n}\frac{\overline{A}_t}{(1+k)^t}-10$$

The symbols used have the following meanings and values:

NPV = net present value of the project
$\overline{A}_t$ = net cash flows per year from the project = ₹ 26,500
k = cost of capital applicable to the project = 9%
n = number of years the net cash flows are received = 5
IO = required investment outlay for the project = ₹ 1,00,000
t = applicable tax rate of 50%

By substituting the data in Equation (3), we put:

$$NPV_0 = \sum_{t-1}^{n} \frac{₹\ 26,500_t}{(1.09)^t} - ₹\ 1,00,000$$

$$NPV_o = ₹\ 26,500\ (3.8896) - ₹\ 1,00,000 = ₹\ 1,03,074 - ₹\ 1,00,000 = ₹\ 3,074$$

We find that the project has an expected NPV of ₹ 3,074 and under the simple conditions assumed, we would accept the project. Now let us consider the effects of inflation. Suppose that inflation at an annual rate of 6% will take place during the five years of the project. Note that we assume that the future inflation rate is known with certainty.

Since investment and security returns are based on expected future returns, the anticipated inflation rate will be reflected in the required rate of return on the project or the applicable cost of capital for the project. This relationship has long been recognised in financial economics and is known as the Fisher effect. In formal terms we have:

$$(1+K)\ (1+p) = (1+K_n) \qquad (5)$$

where K_n is the required rate of return in nominal terms and p is the anticipated annual inflation rate over the life of the project. For our example, Equatiun (5) would be:

$$(1+.09)\ (1+.06) = (1+.09+.06+.0054)$$

If the cross-product term .0054, is included in the addition, we would have .1554 as the required rate of return in nominal terms. However, since the cross-product term in generally small and since both K_n the required rate of return in real terms and the anticipated inflation rate are estimates, it is customary to make a simple addition of the real rate and the inflation rate. The required nominal rate of return that would be used in the calculation would therefore be 15%. Note, then, that the applicable discount rate to reflects the summation of 6% anticipated inflation rate to the 9% rate of return in real terms to obtain the total of 15%.

The market returns will include a factor for the uncertainty associated with the future rate of inflation. The nominal returns provided by market data will therefore, in addition to the Fisher effect for anticipated inflation include an additional uncertainty adjustment factor for the uncertainty of the future inflation rate. However, no analytic solution to the problem of uncertain inflation exists. Therefore, we must ignore it here.

It is at this point that some biases in capital budgeting under inflationary conditions may be introduced. The market data utilitsed in the estimated current capital costs will include the premium for anticipated inflation. But while the market remembers to include an adjustment for inflation in the capitalisation factor, the cashflow estimate used by the firm in the capital budgeting analysis may fail to include an element to reflect future inflation. Conceptually, the decision maker can correct for inflation either by (*a*) adding an estimate of inflation to the cashflow in the numerator or (*b*) expressing the numerator without including an adjustment for inflation and subtracting an inflationary factor from the market rate in the denominator.

It is more natural to utilise market data and to explicitly incorporate estimate of the anticipated inflation rate in the cash flow in the numerator. Without an adjustment for inflation in the cash flows, the analysis would appear as in the following calculations for NPV_1:

$$NPV_1 = \sum_{t-1}^{n} \left[\frac{₹\ 26,500}{(1.09)^t + (1.06)^t} \right] - ₹\ 1,00,000$$

$$= \sum_{t-1}^{n} \frac{₹\ 26,500}{(1.15)^t} - ₹\ 1,00,000$$

$$= ₹\ 26,500\ (3.3522) - ₹\ 1,00,000 = ₹\ 88,833 - ₹\ 1.00,000 = -₹\ 11,167$$

It now appears that the project will have a negative NPV of ₹ 11,167. With a negative NPV of substantial magnitude the project would be rejected. However, a sound analysis required that the anticipated inflation rate also be taken into account in the cash flow estimates. Initially, for simplicity, let us assume that the same inflation rate of 6% is applicable to the net cash flow. We take this step setting forth the expression for NPV_2 as follows:

$$NPV_2 = \sum_{t=1}^{n} \frac{₹\ 26,500\ (1.06)^t}{(1.09)^t (1.06)^t} - ₹\ 1,00,000$$

$$= \sum_{t=1}^{n} \frac{₹\ 26,500}{(1.09)^t} - ₹\ 1,00,000$$

Since the inflation factors are now in both the numerator and the denominator are the same, they can be cancelled. The result for the calculation of NPV_0 will therefore be the same as for NPV_2 which was a positive ₹ 3,074. Thus when anticipated in the inflation is properly reflected in both the cash flow estimates in the numerator and the required rate of return from market data in the denominator, the resulting, the resulting NPV calculation will be both in real and nominal terms. In other words, if inflation is reflected in both the cash flow estimates and in the required rate of return, the resulting NPV estimate will be free of inflation bias.

To this point we have purposely kept the analysis simple to focus on the basic principles since controversy has erupted over the issues involved. We may expect that the effect of the anticipated inflation on the required rate of return will differ from that on the cash flow estimates. Indeed, the components of the net cash flows, the cash outflows and the cash inflows, may themselves be influenced to different degrees by the anticipated inflation. These complications will not, however, change the basic method of analysis, only the specifics of the calculations. The nature of the more complex case is illustrated in Equation (6):

$$NPV_0 = \sum_{t=1}^{n} \frac{[(\text{inflows})_t\,(1+pi)^t - (\text{outflows})^t(1+po)^t](1-t)+(\text{dep.})^t(t)}{(1+k)^t} - IO \quad (6)$$

The cash inflows may be subject to a rate of inflation *pi* that is different from the rate of inflation in the cash outflows *po*. Both may differ from the anticipated rate of inflation reflected in the required rate of return in the denominator. Some illustrative data will demonstrate the application of Equation (6).

TABLE-2

(in ₹)

	Year 1	*Year 2*	*Year 3*	*Year 4*	*Year5*
Expected cash inflows	53,000	53,000	53,000	53,000	53,000
Expected cash outflows	20,000	20,000	20,000	20,000	20,000
Earnings before taxes	33,000	33,000	33,000	33,000	33,000
Multiplied by (1–*t*)	16,500	16,500	16,500	16,500	16,500
Earnings after taxes	16,500	16,500	16,500	16,500	16,500
Depreciation tax shelter	10,000	10,000	10,000	10,000	10,000
Expected net cash flows	26,500	26,500	26,500	26,500	26,500

The pattern of the expected net cash flows without inflation effects is constant ₹ 26,500 per year for five year years as in the original example. Data for expected cash flows without inflation effects is tabulated in Table-2.

The estimates of expected net cash flows including inflation effects are presented below in tabluar. The cash inflows are subject to a 6% inflation rate while the cash outflows are subject to a 7% inflation rate. The resulting expected net cash flows are shown in the bottom line of the table. The required rate of return of 15% is assumed to reflect a 6% inflation rate as before in Table-3.

TABLE-3

(in ₹)

	Year 1	*Year 2*	*Year 3*	*Year 4*	*Year5*
Expected cash inflows (p=6%)	56,180	59,551	63,124	66,912	70,927
Expected cash outflows (p=7%)	21,400	22,898	24,501	26,216	28,051
Earnings before taxes	34,870	36,653	38,623	40,696	42,876
Multiplied by (1–t)	17,390	18,326.5	19,311.5	20,348	21,438
Earnings after taxes	17,390	18,326.5	19,311.5	20,348	21,438
Depreciation tax shelter	10,000	10,000	10,000	10,000	10,000
Expected net cashflows	27,390	28,326.5	29,311.5	30,348	31,438

The calculation of the expected NPV (NPV_3) is shown in Table-4. Taking all the inflation influences into account, we find that NPV_3 is a negative ₹ 2,507. The project would be rejected. In this example, the inflationary forces on the cash outflows were greater than on the cash inflows.

TABLE-4

Year	*Cash flow*	*Discount factor 15%*	*PV*
(1)	(2)	(3)	(4)=(2)(3)
1.	₹ 27,390	.8696	₹ 23,818
2.	28,326	.7561	21,418
3.	29,311	.6575	19,272
4.	30,348	.5718	17,353
5.	31,438	.4972	15,631
		NPV_3=₹ 97,493	–₹ 1,00,000
			=-₹ 2,507

The situation we illustrated initially was that failure to take inflation into account in the expected cash flows resulted in an erroneous capital budgeting analysis. A project was rejected which, when measured correctly, produced a return exceeding the required rate of return. The allocation of capital would be unsound if the bias in the analysis due to inflation had not been taken into account. In our second and more complex example, inflation caused the cash outflows to grow at a higher rate than the cash inflows. As a consequence the expected NPV of the project was negative. Making the inflation adjustment does not always necessarily result in a positive NPV for the project—it simply results in a more accurate estimate of the net benefit from the project, positive or negative.

RISK ADJUSTED DISCOUNT RATE VERSUS CERTAINTY-EQUIVALENT APPROACH

These two approaches to risky project evaluation both have strengths and weaknesses. The risk adjusted discount rate approach is an intuitively appealing method. It seems very logical to apply a higher discount rate to more risky proposals and lower discount rate to less risky proposals. Also, the theory behind determining the risk adjustment cost of capital is well developed and provides some concrete guidence about how to find risk adjusted discount rates; thus the method is both plausible and operationally tractable. On the disadvantage side, the use of a risk adjusted discount rate clearly equates discounting for time with discounting for risk. This implies that risk necessarily increases with time since the discount factor for year $t+1$ is less than the discount factor for year t. Certainty equivalent proponents argue that in some years risk may be the same. Handling risk by increasing the discount rate necessarily implies that risk increases with time, and instance where risk does not increase with time may not be properly evaluated by the risk adjusted cost of capital method.

Because the certainty equivalent method can properly account for cash flow patterns that do not exhibit increasing risk with time, it is a more flexible model and has more generality. And this is the outstanding feature of the certainty equivalent approach. On the negative side, the certainty equivalent approach is not as intuitively appealing to as the risk adjusted discount rate method. It is more difficult to both understand and explain the certainty equivalent adjustment made in the numerator of the expected cash flows. Also, implementation of the approach is more difficult. As opposed to the risk adjusted discount rate approach, which in addition to expected cash flows, requires estimation of only one other parameter i.e. risk-adjusted discount rate, while the certainty equivalent approach requires the analyst to estimate a certainty equivalent factor for *each* year.

In summary, both methods have good and bad features. The essence of the difference between the two methods is that the risk adjusted discount rate method accounts for risk by adjusting the discount rate in the *denominator* of the expected net present value formula, while the certainty equivalent approach accounts for risk by adjusting the expected cash flows in the *numerator* of the expected net present value formula.

ILLUSTRATIVE PROBLEMS

1. A corporation has a cost of capital of 15% and the risk–free rate of return is 7.5%. A project falling within the firm' normal risk posture is being evaluated. It has a 1–Year life and an expected cash flow of ₹ 25,000 to be received in one year. Determine the certainty coefficient value for this project.

Solution

Using the net present value method, we would first determine the present value of the project's cash flow, as follows:

$$PV = \frac{₹\ 25,000}{1+0.15} = ₹\ 21,739.13$$

The value of the corresponding certainty equivalent coefficient may be found using this present value.

$$\frac{B_t.₹\ 25,000}{1+0.075} = ₹\ 12,739.13$$

$$B_t = \frac{(₹\ 21,739.13)(1.075)}{25,000} = 0.9193$$

2. Suppose that the estimated cash flows for a project, the risk free rates of return, and the certainty equivalent co–efficients are as follows:

Time	B_t	$\overline{A_t}$	*Risk-free Return*
Present	1	– ₹ 30,000	—
1	0.95	10,000	0.05
2	0.92	15,000	0.06
3	0.89	17,000	0.07

Determine the expected certainty equivalent value $(\overline{C,E.}_t)$ over the life of the project.

Solution

$$\overline{CE_t} = -₹\ 30,000 + \frac{0.95₹10,000)}{(1+0.05)} + \frac{0.92\ (₹15,000)}{(1+0.05)(1+0.06)} + \frac{0.89(₹17,000)}{(1+0.05)(1+0.06)(1+0.07)}$$

$$= -\ ₹\ 30,000 + ₹\ 9,050 + ₹\ 12,400 + ₹\ 12,700 = ₹\ 4,150$$

3. An investor is considering the purchase of two businesses. One, a racing stable, has an expected annual return of ₹ 5,00,000 and a standard deviation about this value of ₹ 1,00,000. The second, a nursing home, has an expected return of ₹ 4,00,000 and a standard deviation about this value of ₹ 40,000. The investor is moderately averse to risk in the sense that his B coefficient in the certainty–equivalent formula is .5. He has a four-year horizon and expects that the salvage value of both investments at the end of this period will be zero. If he wants to earn a 15% on his money, how much should he offer the sellers of each investments?

Solution

Year	Present value of ₹ 1 at 15%	Certainty Equivalent of Stable's Cash Flows	Present value of Stable's Cash Flows
1	.87	₹ 4,50,000	₹ 3,91,500
2	.75	₹ 4,50,000	₹ 3,37,500
3	.66	₹ 4,50,000	₹ 2,97,000
4	.57	₹ 4,50,000	₹ 2,56,500
			₹ 12,82,500

Year	Present value of ₹ 1 at 15%	Certainty Equivalent of Nursing Home Cash Flows	Present value of Nursing Home Cash Flows
1	.87	₹ 3,80,000	₹ 3,30,600
2	.75	₹ 3,80,000	₹ 2,85,000
3	.66	₹ 3,80,000	₹ 2,50,000
4	.57	₹ 3,80,000	₹ 2,16,600
			₹ 10,83,000

Thus he should offer ₹ 12,82,500 for the racing stable and ₹ 10,83,000 for the nursing home.

4. Consider project Alpha, which has an original cost of ₹ 200 thousand, a 3–year useful life, and cash inflows distributions as follows:

(₹ '000 ommited)

Outcome	Period 1		Period 2		Period 3	
	R_{A1}	P_{A1}	R_{A2}	P_{A2}	R_{A3}	P_{A3}
1	₹ 100	0.10	₹ 40	0.13	₹ 10	0.10
2	120	0.20	80	0.25	60	0.30
3	140	0.40	120	0.30	100	0.30
4	160	0.20	160	0.25	160	0.20
5	180	0.10	200	0.10	270	0.10

The risk–free rate is 6% . Compute σ^2C.E. under the assumption that *(a)* cash inflows are independent over Alpha's useful life and *(b)* cash inflows are perfectly correlated over Alpha's useful life.

Solution

Computing the standard deviation for each of the 3 years above, we would find: $\sigma_1 = 21.91$, $\sigma_2 = 45.61$ and $\sigma_3 = 69.54$. These three standard deviations are now used to compute σ^2C.E.

a) Assuming independent cash inflows:

$$\sigma^2 CE = \sum_{t=0}^{n} \frac{\sigma t^2}{(1+i)^{2t}}$$

$$= \frac{(21.91)^2}{(1+0.6)^2} + \frac{(45.61)^2}{(1+0.6)^4} + \frac{(69.54)^2}{(1+.06)^6} = 5{,}484.07$$

or

σCE = ₹ 74.05

(*b*) Assuming perfectly correlated cash inflows:

$$\sigma^2 CE = \left[\sum_{t=0}^{n} \frac{\sigma_t}{(1+i)^t}\right]^2$$

$$= \left[\frac{21.91}{(1.06)} + \frac{45.61}{(1.06)^2} + \frac{69.54}{(1.06)^3}\right]^2$$

$$= (20.67 + 40.59 + 58.39)^2 = (119.65)^2 = 14{,}016.1225$$

or

σCE = ₹ 119.65

Of course, it can be seen that σCE assuming perfectly correlated cash inflows is significantly greater than σCE where cash inflows are assumed to be independent. This is due to the risk-intensifying result produced by high positive correlation among the cash flows over the life of the project rather than the canceling-out effect of independent (zero correlation) cash inflows over the project's life.

5. A firm is considering the adoption of a project which has the cash flows as shown by the following distribution:

		Cash Inflows			
Original cost		*Years 1–5*		*Years 6–10*	
Probability	*Amount*	*Probability*	*Amount*	*Probability*	*Amount*
0.3	₹ 13,000	0.2	₹ 2,000	0.2	₹ 2,609
0.4	14,000	0.4	2,400	0.6	3,200
		0.3	2,800	0.1	3,400
0.3	15,000	0.1	3,400	0.1	3,600

The firm's cost of capital is 14. Determine the risk–adjusted net present value.

Solution

First determine the mean value for each cash flow equation and incorporate into the following eqquation:

$$NPV = -₹\ 14{,}000 \sum_{t=1}^{5} + \frac{₹2{,}540}{(1.14)^t} + \sum_{t=6}^{10} + \frac{₹31{,}000}{(1.14)^t}$$

$$= -₹\ 14{,}000 + ₹\ 8{,}720 + ₹\ 5{,}599 = ₹\ 319$$

Since the NPV is positive, the project is accepted.

QUESTIONS

1. What is the difference between risk and uncertainty? Are business problems those where risk or uncertainty is likely to be present?
2. What is the underlying rationale of probabilistic methods in dealing with uncertainty and risk?
3. How can a risk–return function be used to determine the risk–adjusted discount rate used in evaluating a project? What must be known in order to determine the risk–adjusted discount rate? Why?
4. Using the NPV framework, what changes are necessary to utilise the certainty equivalent approach to evaluate risky capital expenditures?
5. In comparing the risk adjusted discount rate method to the certainty equivalent method: *(a)* What similarities are there between the two methods? *(b)* Explain the fundamental conceptual difference between the two methods. *(c)* Explain the comparative advantages and disadvantages of each.
6. Why must inflation be taken into account in evaluating investment opportunities in a firm?

PROBLEMS

1. Determine the certainty coefficient value for a proposed project whose expected risky cash flow is ₹ 2,300, to be received in one year. The corporation's cost of capital is 15% and the risk free rate of return is 8%.

Ans.: Bt = 0.939

2. A manufacturing company is evaluating two alternative projects. Project A consists of an expansion of the same business by building a new facility at the same location. The total project cost is estimated to be ₹ 30,000. Project B consists of an acquisition of another firm selling products unrelated to the company's primary business. The total cost of the project is ₹ 40,000. The following table shows the cash inflows distribution.

Outcome	*Project A (Cash Flow, ₹ '000)*						Outcome	*Project B (Cash Flow, ₹ '000)*					
	RA_1	PA_1	PA_2	PA_2	RA_3	PA_3		RA_1	PA_1	RA_2	PA_1	RA_3	PA_3
1	10	0.3	15	0.2	10	0.3	1	15	0.2	20	0.3	15	0.2
2	15	0.5	20	0.6	25	0.6	2	20	0.6	25	0.5	30	0.6
3	20	0.2	25	0.2	30	0.1	3	25	0.2	30	0.2	40	0.2

(a) Compute the expected certainty value for both projects.
(b) Compute σCE for both projects based on the assumption that cash flow are independent and cash flows are perfectly correlated.

Assume that the risk–free rate is 6%, constant over the life of the projects, and that the company considers cash flows for the first 3–year period.

Ans.: (a) $\overline{CE_A}$ − 8.6; $\overline{CE_B}$ = 8.48; (b) Independent σA = 7.54; σB = 7.98

3. BKN Company must decide between two mutually exclusive investment projects. Each project costs ₹ 6,75,000 and has an expected life of 3 years. Annual net cash flows from each project begin 1 year after the initial investment is made and have the following probability distributions:

Project A		Project B	
Probability	*Net Cash Flows*	*Probability*	*Net Cash Flows*
0.2	₹ 6,00,000	0.2	₹ 0
0.6	6,75,000	0.6	6,75,000
0.2	7,50,000	0.2	18,00,000

BKN has decided to evaluate the riskier project at a 12 per cent rate and the less risky project at a 10 per cent rate. (a) What is the expected value of the annual net cash flows from each project? What is the coefficient of variation (CV)? (b) What is the risk-adjusted NPV of each project? (c) If it were known that Project B was negatively correlated with other cash flows of the firm whereas Project A was positively correlated, how would this knowledge affect the decision? If Project B's cash flows were negatively correlated with gross domestic product (GDP), would that influence your assessment of its risk?

Ans.: (a) Expected CF_A = ₹ 6,75,000; CV_A = 0.0703, Expected CF_B = ₹ 7,65,000; (b) NPV_A = ₹ 10,03,700; NPV_B = ₹ 11,62,400

BERRY COAL ENTERPRISES: *A CASE*

On August 15, 2011, the Berry Coal Enterprises (BCE) was investigating the feasibility of two mutually exclusive projects. The first prospective investment involved a strip mining operation in eastern India. The second investment also involved the extraction of coal, but this expenditure would be on underground site.

For the past several months Jayant Das had been involved in the development of revenue and expense projections for the two projects. In his analysis, sufficient data existed from prior investments to provide relatively accurate cost data. After having drawn upon this information, Das made projections as to investment costs for each operation shown in Table-1.

TABLE - 1

	Strip Mining	*Underground Mining*
Leasehold Investment	₹ 4,00,00,000	₹ 3,00,00,000
Equipment	30,00,00,000	15,00,00,000
Additional Working Capital Requirements	2,00,00,000	2,00,00,000
Total	₹ 36,00,00,000	₹ 20,00,00,000

With respect to these figures, experience suggests that a 10-year life may be expected on either of the two prospective investments, with the practice being to expense the leasehold investments on a straight line basis over the life. Furthermore, the equipment would be depreciated over the same life on a straight line basis. However, the projected salvage value for the strip mining operation would be ₹ 6,00,00,000, while the equipment for the underground plant could be expected to have a residual value of ₹ 1,50,00,000. The exigency for incremental working capital as a result of the investment would arise at the time of the investment, but could be released upon the termination of the project, with only a negligible chance of the full amount not being recovered.

In addition to the cost estimates, the engineers, based upon studies of the subsurface formations, were able to make projections on the revenues that could be generated from the two fields. As a result of their studies, expected earnings after taxes for the two investments would be as follows:

TABLE - 2

	Years	*Expected Earnings After Taxes per Year*
Strip Mining	1-4	₹ 4,00,00,000
	5-7	2,20,00,000
	8-10	1,00,00,000
Underground Mining:	1-4	3,60,00,000
	5-7	2,30,00,000
	8-10	1,30,00,000

Upon receiving the above information, Das questioned the reliability of the anticipated earnings. In response, Suman Dubey head of the engineering staff at BCE, informed him that both projects would have to be considered to be more risky than the firm's typical investment. Furthermore, the personnel conducting the analysis indicated that the expected cash flows from the underground mining operation were subject to considerably more uncertainty than the strip mining. In fact, Dubey considered the extraction of coal through the underground facility to be twice as risky as that of the strip mining alternative. For this reason, he recommended that the strip mining project be discounted at a 15 percent rate and that the underground mining proposal be analysed with a 25 percent criteria. Das questioned Dubey's logic because the company's cost of capital had been computed to be 12 percent. He believed this figure reflected the shareholder's required rate of return, and for that reason should be used as the discount rate for both projects.

In support of his position on the riskiness of the two proposed investments, Dubey developed some in-depth worksheets for Das, which suggested other possible returns depending on the amount of coal actually extracted from the mines. As a summary measurement of the possible deviations from the expected values, the engineering staff further calculated the standard deviation of the earnings before the taxes. These computations also represent the standard deviations for each flows after taxes. These calculations are shown below:

TABLE - 3

	Years	*Standard Deviations of Earnings After Taxes*
Strip Mining:	1 - 4	₹ 3,40,00,000
	5 - 7	2,50,00,000
	8 - 10	1,90,00,000
Underground	1 - 4	3,15,00,000
	5 - 7	2,76,50,000
	8 - 10	2,36,00,000

In addition to the standard deviation of these reported earnings, the engineering personnel estimated the standard deviation relating to the salvage value of each project to be ₹ 3,00,00,000 or the strip mining facility and ₹ 1,35,00,000 or the underground mining equipment.

In reviewing the engineering department's work Das was very pleased with the results. However, a question remained in his mind about the soundness of using the various discount rates as suggested by Dubey. Das had been particularly interested in this question even before the two projects in question had been brought before him. As an alternative to adjusting the discount rate for dissimilar investments in terms of risk, he had been conducting some informal seminars with top management in the hopes of establishing a pattern of its attitude toward risk. From these session, he was able to specify the relationship between the level of risk and the willingness of management to accept such uncertainty, as reflected by "certainty-equivalent factors." The results of these meetings are depicted in Table-4. With this information, he felt that a better approach would be to adjust the cash flows by the appropriate certainty-equivalent factor and to discount these adjusted flows at the firm's cost of capital. However, Dubey is of the opinion that the risk-free rate, which is currently 8 percent, would be more appropriate for such an analysis. At this point, the investigation has been temporarily halted until the questions confronting the men have been resolved.

TABLE - 4

Management's Risk-Return Profile

*Coefficient of Variation**	*Certainty-Equivalent Factor***
.5	.95
.6	.93
.7	.91
.8	.88
.9	.85
1.0	.82
1.1	.78
1.2	.74
1.3	.70
1.4	.64
1.5	.58
1.6	.52
1.7	.43
1.8	.33
1.9	.15

* The coefficient of variation is a relative measure of dispersion; it is calculated by dividing the standard deviation by the expected value.

** The factor states the amount management would accept for certain in lieu of ₹ 1 expected return.

QUESTIONS

1. Given both the expected values of returns and a measure of the risk accompanying these returns for two mutually exclusive projects, can an individual determine the better investment to accept? ("Better" is defined as the investment that may be identified as being unequivocably preferable for any decision maker.)
2. Specifically define the "certainty-equivalent factor." How does it differ from the probability of an event occuring?

3a. Calculate the net present value for each investment by using (a) the certainty-equivalent approach and (b) the risk-adjusted rate of return method.

3b. Are the results of the certainty-equivalent methodology and the risk-adjusted rate approach consistent, that is, do both techniques indicate acceptance of the same project? If an inconsistency does exist, explain the reasons(s) why.

4. Under what condition(s) should the decision maker use the risk-adjusted discount rate or an adjustment of cash flows by a certainty-equivalent factor as opposed to simply discounting the expected cash flows by the cost of capital?
5. Set up the solution (but do not solve) for determining the risk-adjusted rate of return that would provide identical results as the certainty-equivalent approach for the strip mining project.

13

CAPITAL BUDGETING DECISIONS UNDER CONDITIONS OF UNCERTAINTY–II

INTRODUCTION

While analysing the risk associated with a capital expenditure, it is important to distinguish between the *total project risk* and the *portfolio risk,* or *beta, risk* of that investment. By total project risk we mean the chance that a project will perform below expectation—possibily resulting in losses from the project and for the firm. In the worst case, these losses could be so severe as to cause the firm to fail. In contrast, a project that has a high level of total project risk may not affect the portfolio risk of the firm at all. From a capital budgeting perspective, the beta risk of a project certainly is important, because the beta of a firm influence the returns required by investors in that firm and hence the value of the firm's shares. Consequently, in the evaluation of the investment, it is important to consider both the total project risk and the impact of the project on the beta risk of the firm. We continue this chapter with a discussion on a number of techniques to be used in capital budgeting decisions under uncertainty.

CONCEPTUAL METHOD: THE SHACKLE APPROACH

G.S.L. Shackle[1] has proposed a subtle approach to handle the problems of risk and uncertainty by focusing on the mental and psychological process involved in the investment decision. Shackle argues that decision makers do not explore all possible outcomes to a proposals but instead tend to characterise the risk inherent in an important decision in term of two extreme outcomes: one focused on a representative potential gain (called the *focus gain*) and another focused on a representative potential loss (called the *focus loss*). Shackle is thus a precursor to what is now called the *satisficing goal.*

Shackle discards the notion of risk discounting in a favour of a concept called *potential surprise.* This assumes that decision makers conceive the consequences of their actions in terms of a measure that classifies their potential surprise at the occurence of unexpected outcomes. He suggests that the occurence of an outcome to which we had subjectively assigned a low probability contains a high elements of

1. G.S.H. Shackle: *Expectations of Economics*, Cambridge University Press, London, 1952.

surprise. Conversely, the occurence of one outcome with a high probability contains very little surprise. Finally, the occurence of one of two equiprobable outcomes holds no surprise for the decision maker. Again, we must point out that Shackle predated modern efforts to apply the concepts of information theory to business decisions. An additional characteristic of Shackle's approach is its total reliance on subjective probability. He defends his approach by arguing that the decision involving a number of mutually exclusive investment opportunities in term of considering what might occur in the future, is inescapably subjective.

PROBABILSTIC METHOD: SINGLE PROJECT

The constraint of single-project consideration, aside from its pedagogic value, is theoretically acceptable under the following conditions; (1) If the investment in consideration will constitute the only asset entering the firm's production function within its planning horizon. And (2) if the other assets possessed by the firm are considerably smaller than the one contemplated. Then, the other assets can be omitted from the analysis and the single asset technique will yield approximate results of practical value. We shall review here two example using probabilistic method for the analysis of investment decision. Both cases will be limited to the consideration of single-project decisions. The first case, by Hillier, utilise *analytical* techniques, while the second one by Hertz, employs *simulation.*

INVESTMENT DECISIONS WITH THE DERIVATION OF PROBABILITY INFORMATION

HILLIER'S MODEL

Frederick S. Hiller proposed an approach for specifying information about an investment proposal in a more explicit manner.[2] This approach is meant to apprise management of the variety of consequences involved in a decision; thus it is intended as complement, rather than a substitute, to existing evaluation procedures.

Hillier combines the assumption of mutual independence and perfect correlation in developing a model to deal with mixed situations. The model enable the analysis of investment proposal in which some of the expected cash flows over time are closely related and others are fairly independent. To illustrate the model, suppose, that a firm is considering the introduction of a new product with returns expected over the next five years. Because the product's market receptions uncertain, management feels that if initial receptions exceeds expectations, reception in later year also will exceed expectations, in about the same proportion. We could say that, if the periods are correlated, once it starts to deviate from the expected, it would continue to deviate again in the next period making the total deviation over the entire life of the project rather large, since the deviations would cumulate.

The decision-makers should at least be aware of this possibility. The financial

2. Frederick S. Hillier: "The Derivation of Probability information for the Evaluation of Risky Investments", *Management Science,* 9, April, 1963, pp. 443-454.

manager can make them aware of it be specifying the correlation coefficient (r) among the cashflows of the different periods as:

$$r = \frac{\text{Cov}(A_t, A_{t+1})}{\sigma A_t \sigma A_{t+1}} \tag{1}$$

where r = the correlation coefficient which can go from 0 to + 1 in the case.

COV $(A_t)(A_{t+1})$ = the covariance or the degree to which the outflow of one period moves in union with the cashflow of the next period.

σA_t = the standard deviation of the cashflow in the period t.

When the correlation coefficient equals zero, the cashflow are independent between period, and can use the simple mean standard deviation approach. When the correlation coefficient reaches one, the cashflows in the different periods are perfectly positively correlated so that as this period's cashflow deviates from its expected value, next period's cashflow will also deviate from its expected value by a proportional amount. If the cashflows are perfectly positively correlated, the effect of the deviations from the expected value causing a relatively large deviation from the expected value for the entire project. We must also account for this in our calculations of the expected NPV and standard deviation.

The expected NPV for the project does not change even with perfectly positively correlated cashflows between periods so we can continue to calculate the expected NPV as:

$$\overline{NPV} = \sum_{t=1}^{n} \frac{\overline{A}_t}{(1+k)} - IO \tag{2}$$

The presence of a perfectly positive cashflow stream does, however, change the assumptions for the variance and its square root, the standard deviation, such that for the two periods case, the variance is:

$$\sigma^2 NPV = \sigma^2 A_0 + \frac{\sigma A_1}{(1+k)^2} + \frac{\sigma^2 A_2}{(1+k)^4} + \frac{2}{(1+k)} \text{Cov}(A_0, A_1)$$
$$+ \frac{2}{(1+k)^2} \text{Cov}(A_0, A_2) + \frac{2}{(1+k)^2} \text{Cov}(A_1, A_2) \tag{3}$$

which since Cov A_t, $A_{t+1} = \sigma A_1 \sigma A_2$ when r=1 reduces to:

$$\sigma^2 NPV = \sigma^2 A_0 + \frac{\sigma^2 A_1}{(1+k)^2} + \frac{\sigma^2 A_2}{(1+k)^4} + \frac{2\sigma A_0 \sigma A_1}{(1+k)} + \frac{2\sigma A_0 A_2}{(1+k)^2} + \frac{2\sigma A_1 \sigma A_2}{(1+k)^3} \tag{4}$$

$$= \left[\sigma A_0 + \frac{\sigma A_1}{(1+k)} + \frac{\sigma A_2}{(1+k)^2}\right]^2 \tag{5}$$

All we have done in the above equation is to include the covariance in our calculation of the standard deviation as we first computed it in the simple mean-standard deviation approach. If we take the square root of equation—5, we get the standard deviation. We now have the expected NPV and the standard deviation of that NPV if the cashflows are correlated.

Notice, also, that the incorporation of the covariance has forced us to consider the correlation among the cashflows of different periods so that we are not taken by surprise if we are below estimates and keep getting worse. Even if financial manager may not explicitly incorporate this correlation between periods, it is advisable to at least recognise the possibility that an initial deviation from expectation may only worsen in the next periods instead of correcting itself. In fact, contingency budgets reflect this possibility.

HERTZ'S MODEL

In an important contribution to evaluating risky investments David B. Hertz proposed the use of a simulation model obtain the expected return and dispersion about this expected return for an investment proposal.[3] It has enjoyed widespread acceptance in practice because of the analytical power it makes possible without the necessity for complex mathematics. It is especially adaptable to computation by digital computers. Indeed, computer languages have been developed especially to facilitate Monte Carlo simulation. The technique is sometimes descriptively called the *method of statistical trials.* It invloves first, the random selection of an outcome for each variable (element) of interest, the combining of these outcomes with any fixed amounts, and calculation if necessary to obtain one trial outcome in terms to the desired answer (measure of merit). This, done repeatedly, will result in enough trial outcomes to obtain a sufficiently close approximation of the means, variance, distribution shape, or other characteristic of the desired answer.

The key requisite of the simulation technique is that the outcomes of all variables of interest be *randomly* selected, *i.e.*, that the probability of selection of all possible outcomes be in exact accord with their respective probability distributions. This is accomplished through the use of tables of random numbers and relating these numbers to the distributions of the variables. Random numbers are numbers which have been generated in such a way that there is an equal probability of any number appearing each time, regardless of what sequence is experienced at any prior time. To illustrate, assume we had the following possible outcomes,their associated probabilities and the assigned numbers as shown in Table-1.

Each outcome is assigned one or more of the random numbers *depending on its probability*. If, as in this example, there is a 1 in 10 chance of the occurence being ₹ 10,000, that possible outcome is assigned 1 out of 10 possible random numbers. Similarly, since the ₹ 20,000 possible outcome has a 40% chance of occuring, it is

3. David B. Hertz: "Risk Analysis in Capital Investments" Harvard Business Review, 42, January-February, 1964, pp. 95-196.

TABLE-1

Possible outcomes	*Associated Probabilities*	*Assigned random numbers*
₹ 10,000	.10	1
15,000	.20	5 and 10
20,000	.40	2, 3, 4 and 9
25,000	.20	7 and 6
30,000	.10	8

assigned 4 out of 10 possible numbers. In Monte Carlo simulation each possible outcome assigned a random number corresponding to those on a roulette wheel. As the wheel turns, one of the ten number is selected as the outcome for this round of simulation. Of course, those outcomes with more assigned number have a large chance of being selecting an occurence until we have a sufficient number such that the average of all the selected occurrences truly reflects what might actually occur if the situation were composed of random occurrences.

Each outcome is assigned one or more of the random numbers *depending on its probability*. If, as in this example, there is a 1 in 10 chance of the occurence being ₹ 10,000, that possible outcome is assigned 1 out of 10 possible random numbers. Similarly, since the ₹ 20,000 possible outcome has a 40% chance of occuring, it is assigned 4 out of 10 possible numbers. In Monte Carlo simulation each possible outcome assigned a random number corresponding to those on a roulette wheel. As the wheel turns, one of the ten number is selected as the outcome for this round of simulation. Of course, those outcomes with more assigned number have a large chance of being selecting an occurence until we have a sufficient number such that the average of all the selected occurrences truly reflects what might actually occur if the situation were composed of random occurrences.

When Monte Carlo simulation is applied to capital budgeting, the procedure remains the same. It evolves through three interlocking stages, as follows:

1. The management uses the best methods available to estimate the range of values for each of the relevant independent variables (both *endogenous* and *exogenous*). Each value is associated with its likelihood of occurence. Thus management develops a detailed data bank about the probability distributions of such variables as sales, range of selling price, inventories, present and future outlays, and so forth. One of these controlling distributions, perhaps sales will determine the shape of the distribution of returns.
2. Since each relevant variable has been defined in stage I by its distribution, for example, normal, uniform, and so on, management can use standard statistical sampling techniques to select a specific value for each variable, combine all values and compute the rate of return or some other criterion. The combination of the variable value should account for such things as the dependence of the expected flows, the range of values for strategic variables, and other important decision criteria. Each combination is technically called an *iteration*.

3. Stage 2 is repeated through a prespecified number of *iterations* to define and evaluate the probabilities of occurence for each possible rats of return, or some other criterion. The number of *iterations* will be determined by the desired accuracy of the results, within the constraint of time and computational costs. Each *iteration* is stored in an array, in which certain characteristics are also computed (e.g. frequency distribution, cumulative distribution function, measures of location, scale, skewness, kurtosis, and other details). When all *iterations* are completed, the programme lists all the possible rates of return in the range defined within estimated maximum losses and maximum gains. The average expected rate of return is from the weighted outcomes. When the average expected computed return and variability for each of the proposals have been estimated, management can use of its specified decision criterion for acceptance or rejection of single proposals. Hertz utilises nine input variables, defined by their probability density functions which are eventually combined into three categories:

THREE CLASSES OF VARIABLES

(a) *Market analysis*, which include the market size and its rate of growth, selling prices, and the firm's market share. Various combinations of these variables generate different values for expected sales revenue.

(b) *Investment costs analysis*, which includes service life, operating cost characteristics, and other technological factor that introduce uncertainty into the division process.

(c) *Operating and fixed costs analysis*, which include information about the firm's production function.

The major advantage of the simulation technique is that we now have normal distribution from which we can get a mean and a standard deviation for use in other analysis or for use in our decision to accept or reject the project. The appealing characteristics of the distribution is that it incorporates all the areas that impact the NPV decision criterion with the subjective opinions of the experts in the area, yet it let us coordinate those diverse opinions into easily communicated and uniform measurements upon which a decision can be made.

Although the simulation model computes the average rate of return on investment, the method could easily be modified to calculate the internal rate of return on investment, the net-present value, or the profitability index. In addition although Hertz allows for dependency among the nine factors, the model presented treats the factors as though they were independent. To the extent that dependency exists among factors, it must be taken into account in determining the probability distributions. For example, there is likely to be significant correlation between the market size and the selling price. These interrelationships add considerable complexity to the estimating procedure. Notwithstanding the added complexity of estimating and specifying the relationships between factore, it must be done if the model is to provide realistic results. These estimates may be based upon empirical testing when such testing is feasible. Once the relationships are incorporated in the model, those factors that are correlated would be simulated jointly. Rates of return for the simulated trials would be calculated and a frequency distribution of simulated trials formed in the same manner as before.

SENSITIVITY ANALYSIS

Sensitivity analysis are performed when conditions of uncertainty exist for one or more parameters. The objectives of a sensitivity analysis are to provide the decision-maker with information concerning, 1) the behaviour of the measure of economic effectiveness due to errors in estimating various values of the parameters and 2) the potential for reversals in the preferences for economic investment alternatives. The term sensitivity analysis is derived from the desire to measure the sensitivity of a decision to changes in the values of one or more parameters.

Sensitivity analysis is not really a risk-reducing or risk measuring technique. It is a technique for evaluating the robustness of a given model by relaxing some of its assumptions through "what it" type questions. In its mathematical sense, it is a study to determine how changes errors in the value of the parameters affect the output of a model. For example, if we are estimating the cashflow in period t and using the following model to do so:

$$A_t = (m \times s) - (m \times u) + \frac{(c)}{(n)} \qquad (6)$$

where m = market size

s = the selling price per unit

u = the unit cost of the product

c = the cost of the machine

n = the life of the machine in years

The following values would give a cashflow estimate of ₹ 28,334 in period t:

m = 1,00,000 units

s = ₹ 1

u = ₹ .75

c = ₹ 10,000

n =3

What would be the effect on the cashflow during the period of raising the selling price per unit (s) to ₹ 1.25? Sensitivity analysis will pre-test this on the model, to give an indication of what the effect might be. If, in the opinion of the marketing expert, the increase in the selling price will also cause a decline in demand to 80,000 units, the cashflow for the period will be:

A_t= (80,000 × ₹ 1.25)–(80,000 × ₹ 0.75)+(₹ 10,000/3) =₹ 43,334

In this particular case, the increase in the selling price will apparently have a favourable impact on the cashflow during the period. Therefore, judging from the sensitivity analysis, the selling price should be raised. Of course, the analysis may also reveal that the impact is unfavourable or that the change in the variable's value has no significant impact and that it would be a waste of time for the firm to devote any of its resources to analysing or considering it. Finally, analysis of this type often reveals that the riskiness of the project by highlighting the fact that a small miscalculation in a highly sensitive area can have a effect on the occurence. Thus, a sensitivity analysis would be particularly helpful on projects that are large and will therefore have a substantial impact on the firm.

DECISION TREES AND SEQUENTIAL INVESTMENT DECISIONS

Decision trees, also commonly called decision flow networks and decision diagrammes, are powerful means for depicting and facilitating the analysis of important problems, especially those that involve sequential decisions and variable outcomes over time. Decision trees have great usefulness in practice because they make it possible to look at a large complicated problem in terms of a series of smaller simple problems and they enable objective analysis and decision making which includes explicit consideration of the risk and effect of the future.

The name decision tree is descriptive of the appearance of a graphical portrayal, for it shows branches for each possible alternative for a given decision and branches for each possible outcome (event) which can result from each alternative. Such networks reduce abstract thinking to a logical visual pattern of cause and effect. When costs and returns are associated with each branch and probabilities are estimated for each possible outcome, then analysis of the flow network can clarify choices and risks.

In business, decision trees may be used to clarify problems involving a whole sequence of decision in which the alternative and their relative attractiveness at one stage depends on the decision taken at the stage before. In each case the consequence of the decision depends on the outcome of some chance event. The outcome of the chance event cannot be known at the time the decision is taken, though a probability distribution can subjectively be assigned to it. For example, the financial manager might have to decide between immediately launching a full scale project and undertaking small pilot project now with a second stage decision about going full scale to be made later. The small scale pilot project, if successful, could lead to a larger investment, immediate full-scale production, if successful could capture the market ahead of the competition. The question is to decide which alternative under the conditions of risk is more acceptable, if either.

In such a situation, it is often more realistic to examine the future cashflows under different assumed conditions such as different levels of demand. That is, we can assume different conditions under which different possible outcomes might occur during the next period. We can make another set of different assumptions concerning the period after that, and so on. Then we can examine the possible outcomes in each period to evaluate the project.

To illustrate the analysis of a small pilot project versus immediate full-scale production, assume the cost of a project is ₹ 20,000 which can be invested immediately in full-scale production or ₹ 5,000 in stage 1 and ₹ 15,000 in stage 2, 2years later. At the end of the second year, we have to make a decision to either remain small or go into full-scale production. The assumed life-expectancy of either alternative is 5 years. Figure-1 shows that at stage 1, the initial decision, the firm can expect a high, medium or low demand response for either alternative. Whether the firm chooses the pilot project or full-scale production, it has a 0.5 chance of encountering a high demand, a 0.1 chance of encountering low demand, and 0.4 chance of encountering a medium demand. These are the possible demand outcomes and their associated probabilities, based on estimates made at the initial decision point.

The possible demand outcomes and probabilities of the full scale production alternative holds for the entire 5-year period as shown in Figure-1. The possible demand outcomes and probabilities for the pilot project cover only first 2 year of stage 1. We must also estimate, at the initial decision point, the possible demand outcomes and their associated probabilities that could occur during stage 2, if we move into full-scale production. Figure-1 shows that if demand were high for the pilot project through stage 1, the probability that demand will remain high during stage 2 is assigned a relatively high value of .7—against relatively probabilities of .2 for medium demand and .1 for low demand.

FIGURE-1

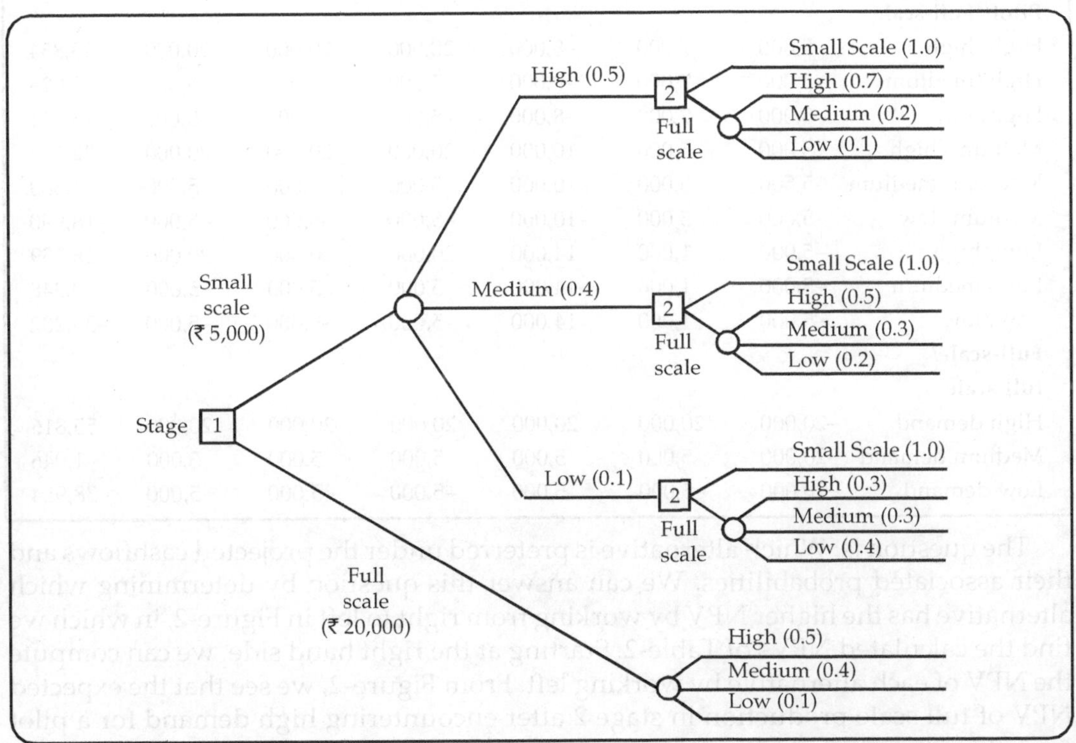

If, on the other hand, the pilot project encounters only medium demand during stage 1, then the probability of encountering high demand during state 2 is estimated to be only .5. The probability of medium demand is estimated at .3, and the probability of low demand is estimated at .2. If the pilot project encounters low demand stage 1, the probabilities for stage 2 would be .3 for high demand, .3 for medium demand, and .4 for low demand. Of course, at the end of stage 1 we also have the choice of remaining at the pilot project (small-scale) level during stage 2, which would assure us of continuing at the same level as in stage 1, whether that level was small, medium, or high demand. This is represented by a certain probability of 1.0 in Figure-1.

Table-2 shows the 5-year costflows stream for each alternative and the NPV of those streams at a cost of capital of 10 percent.

TABLE-2

(Amount in ₹)

Demand	*Year*						
Stage 1/Stage 2	0	1	2	3	4	5	*NPV*
Pilot/pilot							
High demand	–5,000	7,000	7,000	7,000	7,000	7,000	21,536
Medium demand	–5,000	5,000	5,000	5,000	5,000	5,000	13,954
Low demand	–5,000	1,000	1,000	1,000	1,000	1,000	–1,210
Pilot/ Full-scale							
High/high	–5,000	7,000	–8,000	20,000	20,000	20,000	35,854
High/medium	–5,000	7,000	–8,000	5,000	5,000	5,000	5,029
High/low	–5,000	7,000	–8,000	–5,000	–5,000	–5,000	–15,521
Medium/high	–5,000	5,000	–10,000	20,000	20,000	20,000	32,385
Medium/medium	–5,500	5,000	–10,000	5,000	5,000	5,000	1,560
Medium/low	–5,000	5,000	–10,000	–5,000	–5,000	–5,000	–18,990
Low/high	–5,000	1,000	–14,000	20,000	20,000	20,000	26,359
Low/medium	–5,000	1,000	–14,000	5,000	5,000	5,000	–9,348
Low/low	–5,000	1,000	–14,000	–5,000	–5,000	–5,000	–33,202
Full-scale/ full scale							
High demand	–20,000	20,000	20,000	20,000	20,000	20,000	55,816
Medium demand	–20,000	5,000	5,000	5,000	5,000	5,000	–1,046
Low demand	–20,000	–5,000	–5,000	–5,000	–5,000	–5,000	–38,954

The question is: Which alternative is preferred under the projected cashflows and their associated probabilities. We can answer this question by determining which alternative has the higher NPV by working from right to left in Figure-2, in which we find the calculated NPVs of Table-2. Starting at the right hand side, we can compute the NPV of each alternative by working left. From Figure-2, we see that the expected NPV of full scale production in stage 2 after encountering high demand for a pilot project in stage 1 is:

$\overline{\text{NPV}}$ (high demand/full scale) =.7 (₹ 35,854)+.2(₹ 5,029)+ .1 (–₹ 15,521) =₹ 24,552

We can do this for each possible pilot project demand outcome in stage 1 followed by full-scale production in stage 2 such that:

Stage 1 demand	=	$\overline{\text{NPV}}$
High	=	₹ 24,552
Medium	=	.5 (₹ 32,385)+.3 (₹ 1,560)+.2(–₹ 18,990) =₹ 12,862
Low	=	.3 (₹ 26,359)+.3 (–₹ 9,348)+ .4(–₹ 33,202)= –₹ 8,177

On the other hand, the NPV's for initiating a pilot project in stage 1 and remaining with it through stage 2 are:

Stage 1 demand	=	$\overline{\text{NPV}}$
High	=	₹ 21,536
Medium	=	₹ 13,954
Low	=	–₹ 1,210

Notice that if only a high demand occurs during the stage 1 pilot project, is it worth going into full-scale production during stage 2? For the expected NPV under full-scale production in stage 2, after encountering either medium or low demand during the stage-1 pilot, is less than if we remained at the pilot project level throughout stage 2. We have two alternatives. We either go into immediate full-scale production, or we start with a pilot project which will shift to full-scale production only if the stage 1 demand is high; otherwise it will stay as a pilot project during stage 2.

FIGURE-2

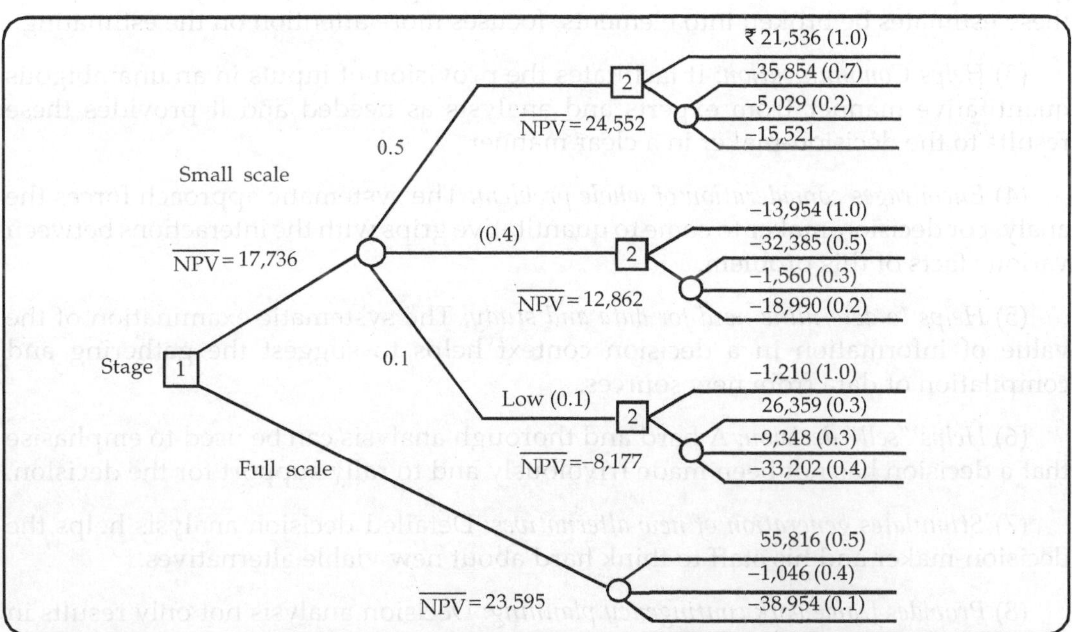

The selection of the better alternative on the expected NPV's of the alternatives, which are:

$\overline{\text{NPV}}$ = .5 (₹ 55,816)+.4(–₹ 1,046)+.1(–₹ 38,954)
= ₹ 23,595 for the immediate full scale project.

$\overline{\text{NPV}}$ = .5 (₹ 24,552)+.4(₹ 13,954)+.1(–₹ 1,210)
= ₹ 17,736 for running the pilot project first.

Obviously, in this particular example, we would go immediately into full-scale production, because the expected NPV of that alternative is higher than expected NPV of any pilot project/full scale alternative.

How does one find his way through this maze and select the best sequence of decisions? The decision maker assigns probabilities and monetary values of each of the outcomes in the tree. Than, he calculates expected monetary values of each of the paths, and working from right to left, chooses that path (that set of decisions) that has the highest expected monetary value.

The systematic approach of decision tree analysis has it merits and demerits. Indeed, what is a pro to some analysis and decision-maker may well be a con to others. The following is a synthesis of often claimed **advantages**:

(1) *Makes uncertainty explicit:* The uncertainty which the analyst feels about estimates or projects is recognised and incorporated in the analysis.

(2) *Promotes more reasoned estimating procedures:* By requiring that estimates be given as probability distributions rather than as single values, and by requiring that these estimates be broken into elements, focuses more attention on the estimating.

(3) *Helps Communication:* It facilitates the provision of inputs in an unambigous quantitative manner from experts and analysts as needed and it provides these results to the decision-maker in a clear manner.

(4) *Encourages consideration of whole problem:* The systematic approach forces the analyst or decision-maker to come to quantitative grips with the interactions between various facts of this problem.

(5) *Helps to determine need for data and study:* The systematic examination of the value of information in a decision context helps to suggest the gathering and compilation of data from new sources.

(6) *Helps "sell" decision:* A hard and thorough analysis can be used to emphasise that a decision has not been made frivolously and to rally support for the decision.

(7) *Stimulates generation of new alternatives:* Detailed decision analysis helps the decision-maker and his staff to think hard about new viable alternatives.

(8) *Provides framework contingency planning:* Decision analysis not only results in

an initial decision but it can be used as a basis for continuous re-evaluation of a decision problem that has a distant time horizon.

The following is a synthesis of often claimed **disdvantages**:

(1) *Tends to exclude consideration of intangibles:* Because a well-done decision analysis is thorough, there is a tendency to place great reliance on the quantitative results.

(2) *The clear basic questions are often difficult:* Often the decision-maker would rather take refuge in the fuzziness and complexity of real life situations than reveal preferences in a number of broken-down or starkly simple decision situations.

(3) *Requires expert articulation of the thought process:* A decisions-maker may be a great synthesizer of interconnected considerations through sub-conscious thinking, but he may be unable to give a verbal description of his thought process, thus making it appear that he is much more restricted in the complexity of his analysis than is actually true.

(4) *Decision analysis tend to lack compassion:* Persons who elect to get into formalised systematic analysis are so prone to attach numbers to everything that they tend to exclude many human and artistic qualities and therefore they inhibit creativity.

ABANDONMENT VALUE IN CAPITAL BUDGETING

A critical aspect of the capital-budgeting is the consideration of the residual value of the investment assets. The residual values will be known only at some future date so they are necessarily uncertain at the time investments are being made. However, for investments such as land and buildings, values may actually increase with inflation in future years. For machinery and equipment, subject to a high rate obsolescence, the residual value may drop to virtually nothing even before the end of the expected life of the machine used in the initial capital-budgeting analysis.

Clearly, the residual value of an investment asset may be substantial. Hence to make a capital-budgeting decision without taking residual value into account may lead to serious errors. In addition, for a number of reasons, the sales value or abandonment value of an asset may be greater than the present value of the continued use of the asset by the firm which owns the asset.

Thus there are two aspects of the abandonment decision. One aspect is to take the resale value or abandonment value of the analysis. The second is the requirement that the analysis consider the optimal period at which abandonment of the asset or its sale at its current market value should take place.

The first article emphasising the importance of taking abandonment value into account was published by Robichek and Van Horne in 1967, who proposed that the project be abandoned in the first year that its abondonment value exceeds the present value the remaining expected cash flow associated with the continued operation of the investment. They pointed out that considering abandonment before the end of the life of a project could increase the project's NPV so that an otherwise unacceptable project would become desirable.[4]

In a comment on the Robicheck-Van Horne analysis, Dyl and Long[5] in 1969 point out that there may be an even greater advantage to abandonment in a period subsequent to the first instance when abandonment value exceeds the present value of continued operations. They argue that it is necessary to consider future abandonment possibilities in addition to the year in which abandonment value may exceed the present value of continued operations. Consideration of future abandonment values will provide a measure of maximum present value resulting from the selection of the optimum abandonment timing.

Robicheck-Van Horne acknowledge that deferred abandonment may be preferred to present abandonment. However, they observe that future operating cashflows and abandonment values are not known with certainty. They suggest that a practical operational procedure does not require a forecast over the full estimated economic life of the investment, and go on to offer a revised formulation which requires only one period for which the present value of continued operations exceeds abandonment value. If such an instance exists, the project is held another year and then re-evaluated. The re-evaluation would be based on the new formulation of expectations made at that time. Thus it is not required that the decisions provide a complete enumerations of all possible present values of continued operations and of abandonment values in future years. The benefits of a sequential decision process can be obtained.

To formulate a clear statement of the revised Robicheck-Van Horne abandonment value algorithm, let

A_t = expected operating cash flow in year t
k_0 = Cost of capital
n = maximum expected feasible life of project
AV_a = expected abandonment value in period a

Step 1. Set a=1

Step 2. Compute NPV_a, where

$$NPV_a = \sum_{t=1}^{a} \frac{A_t}{(1+k_0)^t} + \frac{AV_a}{(1+k_0)^a} - IO \tag{7}$$

=NPV of project, given abandonment in period a

Step 3. If NPV_a> O, accept, if NPV_a <O, go to step 4

Step 4. Repeat steps 2 and O for a=2,3, ..., n until either

---

4. A.A. Robichek and J.C. Van Horne: "Abandonment Value and Capital Budgeting," *Journal Finance,*March, 1969, pp. 88-95.

5. E.A. Dyl and H.W. Long: "Abandonment Value and Capital Budgeting: Comment." *Journal of Finance,* March, 1969, pp. 88-95.

$NPV_a > O$ for some a: accept
or $NPV_a < O$ for all a: reject

The basic decision decision is weather to relinquish now or to hold it for one more period. A decision to keep the asset requires only one instance where the present value of continuing to hold the asset exceeds the abandonment value. The same analysis applies to currently owned assets. The decision to abandon leads to immediate abandonment. Otherwise the asset will be held for one additional year and keep-vs.-abandon decision will then again be made. At that time revision in estimates of expected future operating cash flows and abandonment value may be made.

The foregoing analysis is applicable to accept-reject decisions for independent investments. However, if mutually exclusive project are being compared, it is necessary to make the analysis over the full planning horizon for each to determine which of the projects dominates. Hence an exhaustive search for abandonment possibilities over a full planning horizon will be required utilising the Dyl-Long approach. Formulation for this abandonment algorithm is as follows:

Step 1. Compute NPV_a for a=1, 2, ...n for each project
Step 2. Select the maximum value of NPV_a for each project, and select that project with the largest positive maximum value for NPV_a.

A comparison of this accept-reject decision approach with the mutually-exclusive choice decisions is illustrated utilising the data presented Table-3.

TABLE-3

Series of flows	*Period*				
	1	2	3	4	5
1. Estimated present values of project in period a if operated for remaining years of life and then abandoned.	₹ 11,000	₹ 11,000	₹ 11,000	₹ 10,000	₹ 9,000
2. Estimated present value of abandonment in period a	₹ 4,000	₹ 6,000	₹ 12,000	₹ 13,000	₹ 8,000

The investment costs of the project are assumed to be ₹ 10,000. Present value estimates are made for two series of flows. Line 1 is the estimated present value of the project in period a if operated for its remaining years of life and then abandoned. Line 2 is the estimated present value of the project if abandoned in period a. A plausible real world counterpart to such a pattern of flows could be an investment in a furniture workshop. With such an investment there is always the alternative of selling the annual product from the furniture worpshop or to sell the furniture workshop at various time periods. The values from selling the product of the workshop may fluctuate with estimates of demand and supply conditions in those markets in particular years. In addition, there may be a demand for the furniture for decorative or other purposes which will be sensitive to fluctuations in demand conditions in individual years, and over longer periods of time supply conditions may change as well. Thus a wide variety of patterns in gains from selling the product of the workshop, selling the furniture for future product yields, or selling the furniture for immediate decorative purposes could create a wide variety of year-by-year present value estimates.

Let us first illustrate the accept-reject decision. The first column of figures in the table provides a basis for undertaking the investment and deferring the abandonment decision for at least one year. The estimated present value of the project at the beginning of period is ₹ 11,000. Hence the net value of the project is positive. In addition the NPV of the project with deferred abandonment is greater than estimated present value of abandonment of the project in period 1. At the beginning of period 2, another assessment of future prospects could be made. If the estimates are as indicated in column 2, the decision would be to continue to operate the project another year.

At the beginning of the third year another analysis is made with the estimates as indicated in the column for period 3. Now the estimated present value of the project given abandonment in period 3 is ₹ 12,000. The estimated present value of the project in period 3 if operated for the remaining years of its life and then abandoned is seen to be only ₹ 11,000. According to the Robichek-Van Horne formulation as revised, the project would then be abandoned in the third year. However, the Dyl-Long criticism still seems to be valid. Before such a determination could be made, a complete enumeration would be required over the remaining years of the investment planning horizon. For example, if in the fourth year the estimated present value of abandonment in period 4 were ₹ 13,000, then it would have been even more favourable to deffer the abandonment until the fourth year rather than to abandon the project in the third year. Thus the Dyl-Long comment remains valid even where the accept-reject decision is involved. Complete enumeration can be avoided for any individual year until the year in which a tentative decision to abandon the project is made. Then it is still necessary to make an analysis for the remaining years of the planning horizon to determine the year in which the abandonment will yield the highest present value.

Thus so far in the analysis the discussion has been in terms of best estimates of the cash flows over the time pattern of years. The analysis could be extended by an additional step which would consider estimates of probabilities of various levels of cash year and then show the calculations of expected values and their standard deviations. To illustrate, assume a financial manager's expectations for a two year project costing ₹ 10,000 at a cost of capital of 10 are as given in Table-4.

TABLE-4

Year 1		*Year 2*	
Cash flow	*Associated Probability*	*Cash flow*	*Associated probability*
₹ 7,000	.9	₹ 10,000	.7
		9,000	.3
₹ 2,000	.1	2,000	.5
		1,000	.5

It is clear from the table that financial manager is forecasting a 90% probability that the first year's cashflow will be ₹ 7,000 and a 10% probability that the first year's cashflow will be only ₹ 2,000. The forecast for the second years is obviously influenced by whatever happens in the first year, such that a small cashflow in the first year leads to a forecast for a small cashflow in the second year. If the first year's larger forecast is the one to occur, the financial manager is projecting a 70% probability of ₹ 10,000 second year cashflow or a 30% probability of ₹ 9,000 second year cashflow. If the first year's smaller forecast is the one to occur, the financial manager is forecasting a 50% probability of either ₹ 2,000 or ₹ 1,000 cashflow in the second year.

The possible outcomes and associated probability for the entire two years of the project are:

Combined cashflows	*Associated probability*
₹ 7,000+10,000	(.9) (.7)=.63
7,000+9,000	(.9) (.3)=.27
2,000+2,000	(.1) (.5)=.05
2,000+1,000	(.1) (.5)=.05
	1.00

The NPV's for each possible combined cashflow discounted at a cost of capital of 10% are:

NPV= – ₹ 10,000 + ₹ 7,000 (.909) + ₹ 10,000 (.826) = ₹ 4,623
NPV= – 10,000+ 7,000 (.909)+ 9,000 (.826) = ₹ 3,797
NPV= – 10,000+ 2,000 (.909)+ 2,000 (.826) = –₹ 6,530
NPV= – 10,000+ 2,000 (.909)+ 1,000 (826) = –₹ 7,356

The expected NPV_0 and the standard deviation (σNPV) are calculated as they were for the mean-standard approach, such that:

$\overline{NPV_0}$ = 4,623 (.63)+3,797 (.27)–6,530 (.05)–7,356 (0.5) = ₹ 3,242

$\overline{\sigma NPV}$ = $(4{,}623–3{,}242)^2(.63)+(3{,}797–3{,}242)^2(.27)+$
$(–6{,}530–3{,}242)^2 (0.05)+(-7{,}356–3{,}242)^2(.05)$ = 3,416.9

If the project has an expected salvage value of ₹ 3,000 at the end of period 1, then the expected cashflow would be:

Combined cashflows		*Probability*
Year 1	*Year 2*	
–₹ 10,000 + 7,000 +	10,000	.63
–10,000 + 7,000 +	9,000	.27
–10,000 + 5,000 +	0	.05
–10,000 + 5,000 +	0	.05

In the last two combinations the second year cashflow have been forfeited in favour of abandoning the project and receiving the ₹ 3,000 salvage value, because the salvage value at the end of year 1 exceeded the present value of the subsequent year's expected cashflow in the last two combinations.

Under the circumstances, the NPV's at a 10% cost of capital are:

NPV= – ₹ 10,000+7,000 (.909) +10,000 (.826) = ₹ 4,623
NPV= – 10,000+7,000 (.909) +9,000 (.826) = 3,797
NPV= – 10,000+5,000 (.909) + 0 = –5,455
NPV= – 10,000+5,000 (.909) + 0 = –5,455

Then the expected NPV and associated standard deviation are:

$$\overline{NPV} = ₹\ 4{,}623\ (.63)+3{,}797\ (.27)-5{,}455\ (.05)-5{,}455\ (.05) = ₹\ 3{,}392$$

$$\overline{\sigma NPV} = ₹\ (4{,}623-3{,}392)^2(.63)+(3{,}797-3{,}392)^2(.27)+(-5{,}455-3{,}392)^2(.05) +(-5{,}455-3{,}392)^2(.05) = ₹\ 2{,}970.9$$

Notice that the explicit in corporation of the abandonment alternative has increased the expected NPV and simultaneously decreased the associated risk. Specifically, we have substituted the abandonment value for the second–year operating cashflow in the last two combinations. Explicit consideration of the abandonment alternative is obviously a useful device for financial planning.

UTILITY THEORY AND CAPITAL BUDGETING

How does the financial manager adjust capital budgeting techniques to include considerations and the risk measurement we have just discussed? In this problem-setting, as in most under conditions of risk, the statistics provide additional information about the alternatives, but they do not specify which should be selected by all decision makers. None of the alternatives is dominant, which would mean that it simultaneously has a higher expected value and a lower level of risk. The final decision would have to be made in terms of the decision maker's utility function, that is, his specification of preferences considering all relevant aspects of the problem setting.

One way to link the expected return and the variation in the return of a project is to assume that an investor's utility curve depends on both of these factors rather than on the project's expected return alone. Utility theory is an attempt to formalise rational decision making, wherein preferences among alternatives are specified by a given decision maker. The utility value attached to various alternatives represents an integration of all aspects relevant to the decision.

When faced with a decision, the decision maker must consider the following within the framework of personal preferences.

1. The opportunity set of all relevant goals and objectives.
2. The hierarchy of goals and acceptable trade-offs of goals within the hierarchy.
3. The perceptions of risk per se and risk-return preference (i.e., the incremental expected return required to justify acceptance of an additional unit of risk.
4. The preferences for current versus future consumption as affected by present wealth position, liquidity requirements, and so on.

In order to be able to specify and differentiate among various classes of risk preference (or aversion), it is useful to define the decision maker's utility function with respect to required return and risk. This necessitates acceptance of the *axioms of coherence.*[6]

1. Given any two pay offs (which may involve nonmonetary as well as monetary values), a decision maker can specify preference of one over the other or indifference between the two.
2. If a given decisions maker prefers pay off P_1 to P_2 and P_2 P_3, then necessarily P_1 is preferred to P_3 (*transitivity or consistency of preferences*).
3. If a decision maker prefers P_1 to P_2 and P_2 to P_3, there is some mixture of P_1 and P_3 which is preferred to P_2, some other mixture of P_1 and P_3 which is inferior to P_2 and a third mixture of P_1 and P_3 which will leave the decision maker indifferent relative to P_2.
4. If a decision maker prefers P_1 to P_2 and P_3 is some other pay off, a probabilistic mixture of P_1 and P_3 will be preferred to the same probabilistic mixture of P_2 and P_3.
5. If a decision maker is indifferent between payoffs P_4 and P_5, they may be substituted for each other in any decision setting.
6. If a decision maker prefers P_1 to P_2, two probabilistic mixtures of P_1 and P_2 will find the former preferred if, and only if the former has a larger proportion of P_1.

If the decision maker accept the axioms of coherence, it is reasonable to assume that he or she will act so as to maximise utility. This means selection of those available decision alternatives that will lead to the greatest level of satisfaction. Since preferences are necessarily subjective, the exact specification of a decision maker's utility function is fraught with operational difficulties. Further, individual utility preferences are likely to change overtime. However, we can specify three general

6. Robert L. Winkler: *Introduction to Bayesian Inference and Decision*, Holt and WInston, Inc., N.Y., pp. 260-264.

categories of decision makers based on their risk preferences: *risk-averse, risk-indifferent,* and *risk-taking*. The utility functions for each category of decision maker are shown in Figure-3.

With respect to risk, decision makers may be classified as follows;

1. *Risk-averse* decision makers have a decreasing marginal utilities for increases in wealth. For the risk-averse decision maker, the chances to enjoy additional wealth are less attractive than the possibility of the pain associated with a decrease in wealth or income.

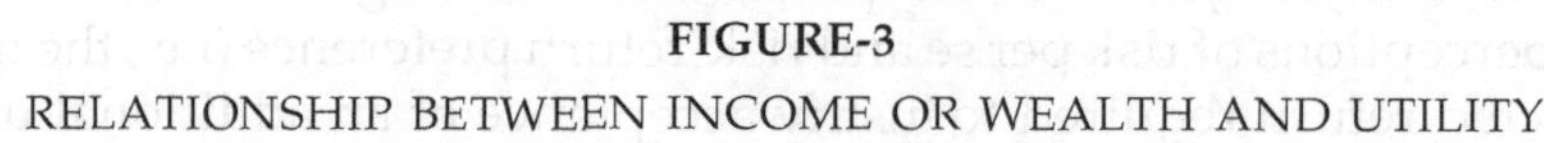

FIGURE-3

RELATIONSHIP BETWEEN INCOME OR WEALTH AND UTILITY

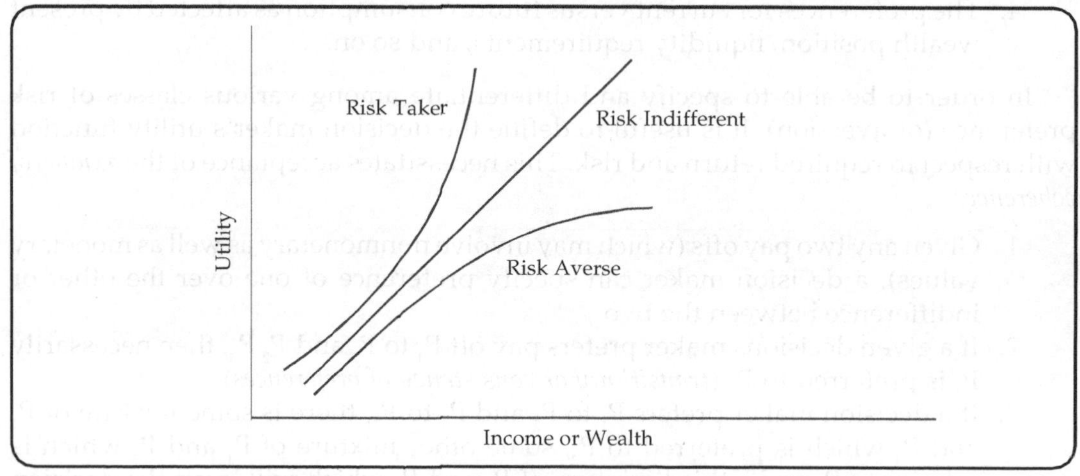

2. *Risk-indifferent* decision makers have constant marginal utilities; hence, their utility curves are linear.

3. *Risk-taking* decision makers have increasing utilities for larger potential increases in wealth.

Within each of the categories, decision makers demonstrate varying degrees of preference or aversion to risk. Thus we can anticipate different utility function for each individual decision maker. Further, each decision maker has a whole family of nonintersecting utility curves, showing successively higher levels of satisfaction. To maximise expected utility, the decision maker will strive to achieve the highest feasible curve within the available alternatives and constraints.

Within the area of capital investment decision making, experience indicates that the great majority of managers are risk averters, but again the specific degree of aversion varies over a wide spectrum. Figure-4 shows risk-return utility functions (indifference curves) for managers. Manager A is less risk-averse than manager B. Both managers are willing to accept a 10% risk-free-rate of return, but manager B requires increasingly returns as risk increases than does manager A. Figure-4 shows the risk-return preferences for two managers at one point in time.

FIGURE-4

RISK RETURN INDIFFERENCE CURVES

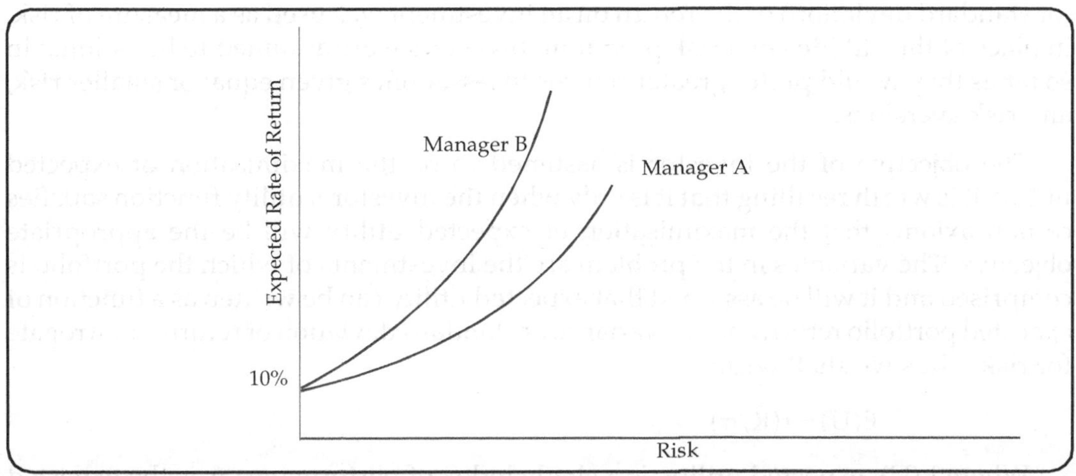

As described above, each manager has a whole set of indifference curves, indicating successively higher levels of satisfaction. Such a family of indifference curves is shown in Figure-5. As we move to the right, each curve indicates a higher level of satisfaction.

FIGURE-5

A FAMILY OF INDIFFERENCE CURVES FOR ONE MANAGER

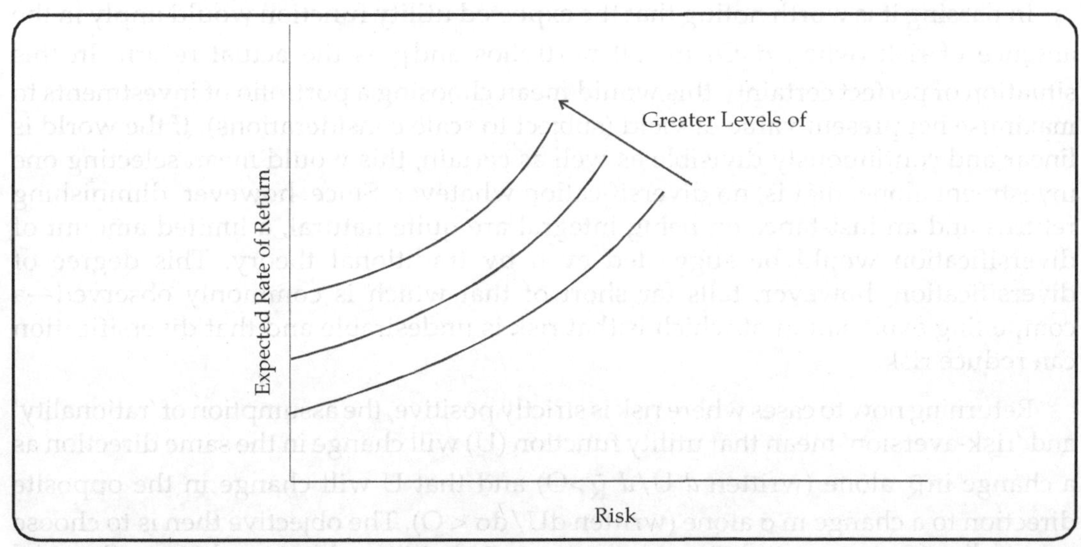

PORTFOLIO THEORY AND CAPITAL BUDGETING

Modern approaches to the problem of portfolio selection began with Markowitz and nowadays most theorists take his work as a starting point. The principle advance that Markowitz made over preceding theories of portfolio selection was the manner in which the risk associated with investments were taken into account. The variance (or standard deviation) of the return on an investment was used as a measure of risk, in place of the old idea of a risk premium. Investors were assumed to be rational in so far as they would prefer greater returns to lesser ones given equal or smaller risk, and risk aversions.

The objective of the investor is assumed to be the maximisation of expected utility. It is worth recalling that it is only when the investor's utility function satisfies certain axioms that the maximisation of expected utility will be the appropriate objective. The variables in the problem are the investments of which the portfolio is comprised and it will be assumed that expected utility can be written as a function of expected portfolio return and the variance or standard deviation of return as surrogate for risk. Thus we shall write:

$$E(U) = f(\tilde{R}, \sigma)$$

Where E(U), expected utility, is a single index of performance, $\tilde{R}$ is the expected return on the portfolio as a whole and σ is the associated standard deviation of return. The function 'maps' a two-dimensional measure into one dimension. Although the function relates to a single time period this is the entire planning horizon. More involved models may include several time periods. Note that in maximising E(U), we shall be maximising what we expect 'utility' to be and what it will actually turn out to be since this is unknown at the time the decisions has to be taken.

In passing it is worth noting that the expected utility function would imply in the absence of risk (when σ=O) for all portfolios and $\tilde{R}$ is the actual return. In this situation of perfect certainty this would mean choosing a portfolio of investments to maximise net present value of yield (subject to scale considerations). If the world is linear and continuously divisible as well as certain, this would mean selecting one investment alone, that is, no diversification whatever. Since, however, diminishing returns and an insistance on being integral are quite natural, a limited amount of diversification would be suggested even by traditional theory. This degree of diversification, however, falls far short of that which is commonly observed—a compelling explanation of which is that risk is undesirable and that diversification can reduce risk.

Returning now to cases where risk is strictly positive, the assumption of 'rationality' and 'risk-aversion' mean that utility function (U) will change in the same direction as a change in $\tilde{R}$ alone (written $dU/d\tilde{R}$>O) and that U will change in the opposite direction to a change in σ alone (written $dU/d\sigma$ < O). The objective then is to choose a portfolio of investments that maximises expected utility subject to whatever financial and other constraints may apply. It is clear that a portfolio which maximises expected utility must satisfy the following condition: *the portfolio of investments must have maximum expected return for all risk levels (measured by standard deviation here) not exceeding its own, and it must have minimum standard deviation of return for levels of return not lower than its own.*[7]

There will in general be many portfolios which satisfy the above condition. These are known as the *mean variance efficiency portfolios.* Graphically the mean-variance efficient portfolios lie on a line such as FF′—the efficiency frontier—in Figure-6. All portfolios in the shaded area to the left of FF′ are mean-variance inefficient—that is to say there are other portfolios (nearer to FF′) which have greater expected returns. $U_1U_1^1$, U_2U^12, and $U_3U_3^1$ in the figure are indifference curves. All points on any one such curve are combinations of risk and return which are equally satisfactory for the investor. Curves further to the right correspond to greater levels of utility, that is $u_3>u_2>u_1$. They possess the curvature (convex to the risk axis), as drawn, if investors have a diminishing marginal rate of substitution between expected and risk. This would mean that investors were decreasingly willing to accept higher returns to compensate for greater risk. If all assets are risky, the optimal portfolio is portfolio M, at a point of tendency between indifference curve and the efficiency frontier.

FIGURE-6

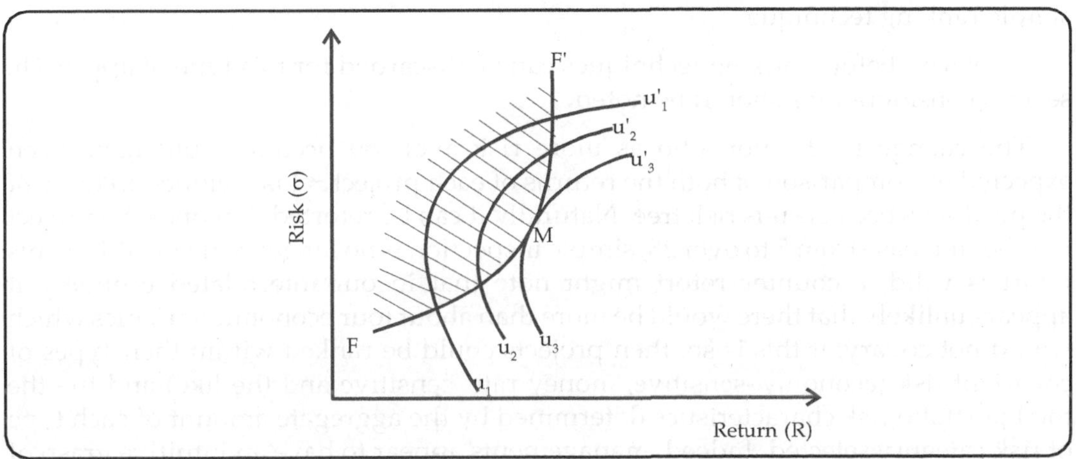

Recently Weingartner, Mao and others have begun to advocate this approach for the selection of a "portfolio" of capital projects that is both efficient in the Markowitz sense and representative of the risk preference of the company's decision makers.[8] Such efficiency requires that a portfolio of investments be the one with the smallest variance of return among all portfolios with the same expected return, and that it has the largest expected returns among all those with the same variance.

7. See Harry M. Markowitz: *"Portfolio Selection: Efficient Diversification of Investment;"* John Wiley & Sons, Inc., N.Y., 1959.
8. See H. Martin Weingartner; "Capital Budgeting of Interrelated Projects: Survey and SYnthesis," *Management Science,* March, 1966 and also James C.J. Mao: *Quetiattizs Analysis of Financial Decisions,* Macmillan Co., N.Y., 1969.

Using the criteria, Weingartner formulated the portfolio selection problem for capital budgeting as an integer quadratic programming model to:

Maximise

$$U^{*}-\lambda\ \sigma p^{2}$$

subject to

$$d_{11}x_1+d_{12}x_2+...d_{in}x_n \leq D_1,$$
$$d_{T1}x_1+d_{T2}x_2+...d_{Tn}x_n \leq D_T,$$
$$0 \leq r_1 \leq \text{for } i = 1,2, ..., nx_i \text{ is integer}$$

where U* is the expected values of a prortfolio, σ^2 is the variance of that portfolio, λ is the firm's trade-off coefficient between risk and return x_1 is I if project *i* is accepted and 0 if it is rejected, d_{ti} is the net cash flow of project *i* in time period *t*, and D_t is the budget constraint in period *t*.

To illustrate the use of the model, Mao developed and ran the hypothetical data (see Table-5).[9] As can be seen from the variation in the efficient portfolio mixes for different value of λ, it would be virtually impossible to obtain accurate results by a simple ranking technique.

However, before ranking techniques can be discarded for this type of approach, several considerations should be noted.

The change in the portfolio as more risk aversion occurs, could have been expected by comparison of both the returns of each project ≠ 4 is included in three of the portfolios because it is risk free. Naturally it can be retorted that once the project number increase from 5 to over 25, simple inspection is no longer realistic. While this retort is valid, a counter–retort might note that in our interrelated economy it appears unlikely that there would be more than about four economic variables which would not covary; if this is so, then projects could be ranked within their types of covariant risk (economy–sensitive, money rate–sensitive and the like) and the the total portfolio risk characteristics determined by the aggregate amount of each type of risk category selected. Indeed, managements appear to have an intuitive grasp of an individual project and how its outcome interrelates with the outcomes of other projects. Yet they may not be able to quantify the intuitive "feel" without making unjustified assumptions. Great care must be taken in making such "hard" number estimates since others may invest them with a degree of accuracy that is totally insupportable. It may be better to operate non–quantitatively under such circumstances. Still, the principle of diversification can and should be applied, even if it must be limited to as simplistic a principle as *"Don't put all your eggs in one basket."*

---

9. See J.C.. Mao; "Essentials of Portfoio Eiversification Strategy, *Journal of Finance*, June, 1970.

TABLE-5
Mao's Data and Results

Project Number	*Net present value*	*Cash outlay year 1*	*Cash outlay year 2*		*Covariance* ≠1	≠2	≠3	≠4	≠5
1	₹ 10	20	20	≠ 1	1.0	3.0	0.1	0	0.5
2	20	30	15	≠ 2	3.0	36.1	2.0	0	0.0
3	5	15	5	≠ 3	0.1	2.0	1.0	0	0.5
4	3	10	7	≠ 4	0.0	0.0	0	0.0	0.0
5	2	5	4	≠ 5	0.5	0.0	0.5	0	1.0

Budget – ≠65, ≠46
Mutually Exclusive Projects –1, 2

Portfolio λ	*Results Selection*
0.0	2, 3
0.1	2, 4, 5
0.3	1, 4, 5
1.1	1,4

GOAL PROGRAMMING

Goal programming is a special type of linear programming developed and extended by A. Charnes, W.W. Cooper, and Yuji Ijiri.[10] In ordinary linear programming, only one goal is incorporated into the objective function to be maximised or minimised. If management has multiple goals, then the goals not incorporated into the objective function are treated as *constraints* of the problem. The computational procedure then picks from the set of all solutions that satisfy the constraints the one (or ones) that maximises or minimise the objective function. Since the firm is striving for the highest value of the objective function, it is said to be adopting an optimising behaviour. In goal programming approach, all goals, whether one or many are incorporated into the objective function, and only the true environmental conditions are treated as constraints. Generally, the priorities are expressed as either ordinal or cardinal priorities. In the case of ordinal priorities, the most important goal is satisfied first, followed by the satisfaction of as many other goals as possible; in rank order. When a cardinal scale is used, it is typically assumed that "goal attainment" is additive and an aggregate linear objective function is developed.

In terms of capital investment decision–making it is generally the case that managers have multiple goals. Although the number or reported applications of the use of goal programming in capital budgeting is small, the approach seems promising. For this reason, to illustrate the technique of goal programming, let us consider a

10. See A. Chernes, W.W. Cooper, and Y. Ijiri: Breakeven Budgeting and Programming to Goals," Journal of Accounting Research, Vol. 1, April 1963, pp. 16-43.

production manager who must schedule the production of two products on three machines. The unit profits, machining times, and production capacities of the equipment are summarised below:

Product	*Machines*			
	1	*2*	*3*	
1	0.2 hr	0.4 hr	0.3 hr	Time/unit
2	0.4 hr	0.1 hr	0.3 hr	Time/unit
Capacity	40 hr	40 hr	40 hr	Time/unit

Product	*Maximum Demand*	*Profit*
1	80/week	₹ 5/unit
2	80/week	₹ 20/unit

The linear programming formulation of the production scheduling problem is given below:

$$\begin{aligned} \text{Maximise} \quad & 5x + 20y \\ \text{Subject to} \quad & 0.2x + 0.4y \leq 40 \\ & 0.4x + 0.1y \leq 40 \\ & 0.3x + 0.3y \leq 40 \\ & x \leq 80 \\ & y \leq 80 \\ & x \geq 0 \quad y \geq 0 \end{aligned}$$

As depicted in Figure-7, the optimum solution is $x = 40$ and $y = 80$. The unused

FIGURE-7

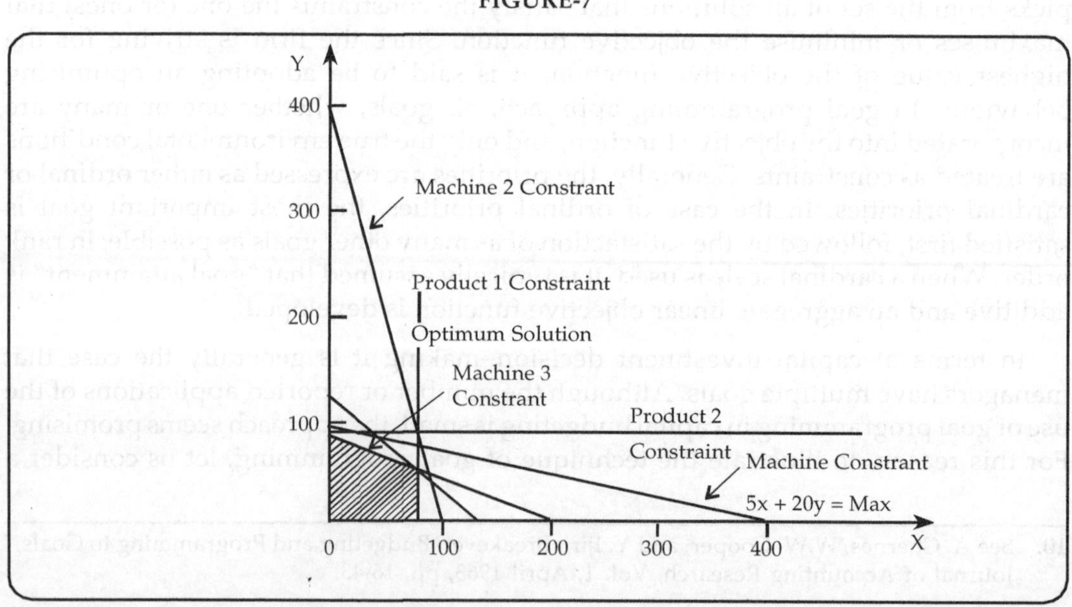

machining capacities for the machines are 0.16, and 4 hours per week, respectively. Hence, machine 2 will be only 60% utilised.

The manager is concerned not only with the utilisation of the machines but also with profits realised for the firm. He also recognises that the market forecasts of 80 units per week for the products could be in error.

The manager would prefer to have there machines equally loaded, but he does not want to sacrifice profits unduly. The maximum profit condition (x=40, y=80) would result in an ₹ 1,800 profit. He feels that a satisfactory minimum profit level be ₹ 1,500.

The following alternative formulation is being considered.

Minimise $(d_1^-, d_2^- d_3^- d_4^-)$

subject to $5x + 20y + d_1^- - d_1^- =$ ₹ 15,000

$0.2x + 0.4y + d_2^- = 40$

$0.4x + 0.1y + d_3^- = 40$

$0.3x + 0.3y + d_4^- = 40$

$x \qquad \leq 80$

$y \leq 80$

$x, y, d_j^-, d_j^+ \leq 0$

The slack variable, d_2^-, and surplus variable $dj+$, measure the deviation from the right–hand side of the constraints. (Since the upper limit of 40 hours production capacity cannot be exceeded, the surplus variables are omitted for j = 2, 3, 4). The objective function is expressed using an ordinal sealing of the project goals (make at least ₹ 1,500 profit) and the machine balance goal (minimise the sum of unused capacities). To solve the problem, the set of optimum solution is determined using the following objective: Minimise d_1^-, the resulting set of solutions is directed in Figure-8, for $d_1^- = 0$.

Next, the following linear programming problem is solved:

Minimise $d_2^- + d_3^- + d_4^-$

Subject to $0.2x + 0.4y \_ d_2^- = 40$

$0.4x + 0.1y + d_3^- = 40$

$0.3x + 0.3y + d_4^- = 40$

$0.5x + 20y + d_1^+ = 1{,}500$

$x \qquad \leq 80$

$y \qquad \leq 80$

$x, Y, dj^-, d_1^+ \geq 0$

FIGURE-8

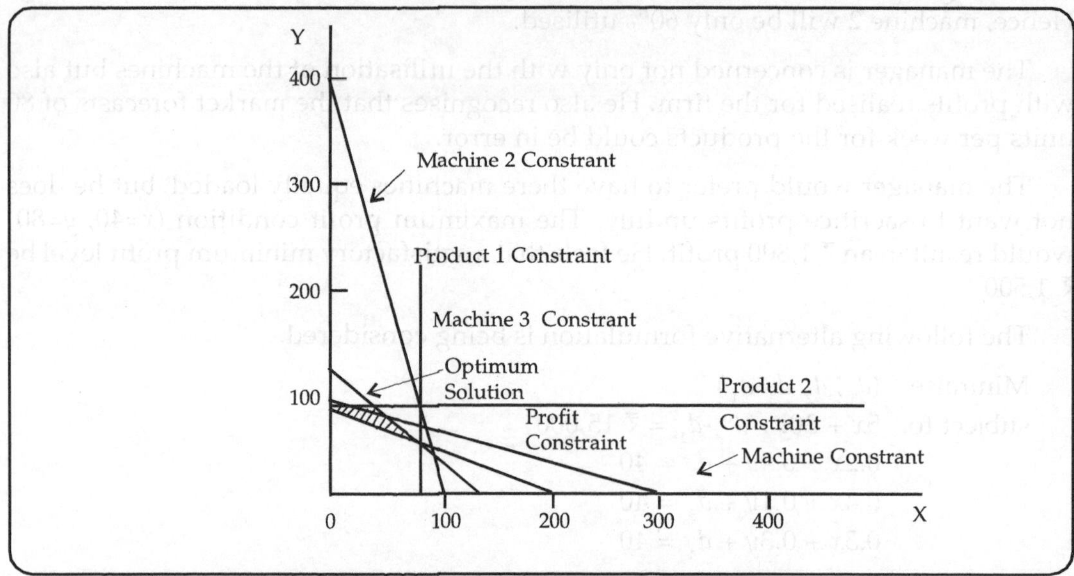

The optimum solution is $x = 700/9, y = 500/9, d_2^- = 20/9, d_3^- = 10/3, d_1^- = 0$, and $d_1^+ = 0$. Hence, the profits obtained is ₹ 1,500, with machine utilisation of 99.44%, 91.67%, and 100%

An alternative expressions of the machine balance goal is to minimise the maximum difference in the dj^- values, i.e.

Minimise maximum

$$(\mid d_2^- - d_3^- \mid, \mid d_2^- - d_4^- \mid, \mid d_3^- - d_4^-)$$

subject to
$$0.2x + 0.4y + d_{-2} = 40$$
$$0.4x + 0.1y + d_3^- = 40$$
$$0.3x + 0.3y + d_4^- = 40$$
$$5x + 20y - d_1^+ = 1{,}500$$
$$x \leq 80$$
$$y \leq 80$$
$$x, y, dj^-, d_1^+ \geq 0$$

Letting z denotes the maximum absolute deviation among the slack variables, the formulation becomes:

Minimise z

subject to
$$z \leq \mid d_2^- - d_3^- \mid$$
$$z \geq \mid d_2^- - d_4^- \mid$$
$$z \geq \mid d_3^- - d_4^- \mid$$
$$0.2x + 0.4y + d_2^- = 40$$

$$0.4x + 0.1y + d_3^- = 40$$
$$0.3x + 0.3y + d_4^- = 40$$
$$5x + 20y - d_1^+ = 1{,}500$$
$$x \leq 80$$
$$y \leq 80$$
$$x, y, dj^-, d_1^+ \geq 0$$

The first three constraints insure that the minimum value of z will equal the maximum absolute deviation among the slack variables. A constraint of the form

$$| u - v | \leq w$$

can be written as two linear constraints:

$$u - v \leq w$$
$$u - v \geq -w$$

Therefore, the optimisation problem can be written :

Minimise z

subject to $d_2^- - d_3^- - z \leq 0$

$$-d_2^- + d_3^- - z \leq 0$$
$$d_2^- - d_4^- - z \leq 0$$
$$-d_2^- + d_4^- - z \leq 0$$
$$d_3^- - d_4^- - z \leq 0$$
$$-d_3^- + d_4^- - z \leq 0$$
$$0.2x + 0.4y + d_{-2} = 40$$
$$0.4x + 0.1y \mid \mid d_{-3} = 40$$
$$0.3x + 0.3y + d_4^- = 40$$
$$5x + 20y - d_1^+ = 1{,}500$$
$$x \leq 80$$
$$y \leq 80$$

A linear programming solution to the above problem yields the following values for the decision variables: $x = 700/9, y = 500/9, d_1^+ = 0, d_2^+ = 20/9, d_3^+ = 10/3, d_3 = 0$ and z = 10/3. Hence, a profit of ₹ 1,500 is obtained, along with machine utilisations of 94.44%, 91.67% and 100%. For this example, the same solution is obtained for the goal programming problem using a minimax objective of minimising the sum of the deviations.

Goal programming problems are special cases of multi–criterion optimisation problem. In the past decade considerable research has been performed on the general class of multi–criterion optimistic problems. Although multi–criterion optimisation offers considerable potential for improved decision making in capital budgeting, further development is required before it will receive widespread application.

MISCELLANEOUS DECISION RULES FOR COMPLETE UNCERTAINTY

Various decision rules or principles have been developed for choosing among alternatives in situations in which there is complete uncertainty about certain probabilities. These decision rules apply to situations in which there are a number of alternatives (courses of action) and a number of possible outcomes (states of nature), and in which the *result* (effect) of each alternative on each possible outcome is not known.

The most difficult aspect of using these decision rules is deciding which one to use for making a decision. In effect, these decision rules reflect various degrees of optimism or pessimism and should be chosen according to which reflect certain management views involving intuition and appropriateness for a particular situation. The greatest defense for the use of any of these rules is that their use will promote explicitness and consistency in decision-making under complete uncertainty. A representation of a typical problem is given by the payoff matrix Table-6.

TABLE-6

Payoff Matrix

	Recession	*Normal*	*Boom*	*State of Nature*
NPV_A	0	₹ 10,000	₹ 25,000	
NPV_B	–₹ 10,000	₹ 25,000	₹ 80,000	

The financial manager's opinion about the net present values of project A any project B under the three possible levels of economic activity show that during recession, the NPV_A would be ₹ 0. while the NPV_B would be –₹ 10,000. The payoff in terms of NPV during a normal period would be:

NPV_A = ₹ 10,000 NPV_B = ₹ 25,000

while during a boom period the payoff would be:

NPV_A = ₹ 25,000 NPV_B = ₹ 80,000

Which project should be undertaken? The following section will explain and illustrate each of several decision rules for this type of problem.

MAXIMIN OR MINIMAX RULE

The maximin rule suggests that the decision–maker determine the minimum profit (payoff) associated with each alternative and then select the alternative which maximises the minimum profit. Similarly, in the case of costs, the minimax rule suggests that the decision–maker determine the maximum cost associated with each alternative and select the alternative which minimises the maximum costs. These decision rules are conservative and pessimistic, for they direct attention to the worst outcome and then make the worst outcome as desirable as possible. In our example, the maximin or minimax rule would lead us to undertake project A, because under the worst state of nature, the lowest we can get is zero net present value.

MAXIMAX OR MINIMIN RULE

The maximax or minimin rules are direct opposites of their counterparts, and thus reflects extreme optimism. The maximax rule suggests that the decision–maker determine the maximum profit associated with each alternative and then select the alternative which maximises the maximum profit. Similarly, in the case of costs, the minimin rule indicates that the decision–maker should determine the minimum cost associated with each alternative and then select the alternative which minimises the minimum cost. Obviously this is a very optimistic strategy. In our example, the maximax criterion leads us to undertake project B because it has the highest possible outcome of ₹ 80,000. In contrast, we could never get that high a NPV with project A, regardless of the state of nature. As in the maximin strategy, we reached this decision without specifying the probabilities.

LAPLACE PRINCIPLE OR RULE

The Laplace rule simply assumes that all possible outcomes are equally likely and treat one can choose on the basis of expected outcomes as calculated using equal probabilities for all outcomes. There is a common tendency toward this assumption in situations where there is no evidence to the contrary, but the assumption (and, therefore, the rule) is of highly questionable merit. For example, if financial manager felt 50% sure that the boom would occur, *a* would equal .50 and its complement (1–*a*) would equal .50. Assigning each of those to maximum and the minimum payoff for each project would give the expected NPV:

$$E(NPV_A) = .5(₹\ 25{,}000) + .5(0) = ₹\ 12{,}500$$

$$E(NPV_B) = .5(₹\ 80{,}000) + .5(-₹\ 1{,}0000) = ₹\ 35{,}000$$

In this example, project B would be undertaken because the expected net present value based on the assigned probabilities is larger.

HURWICZ PRINCIPLE OR RULE

The Hurwicz rule is intended to reflect any degree of moderation between extreme optimism and extreme pessimism which the decision–maker may wish to choose. The rule may be stated explicitly as:

Select an index of optimism, a, such that $0 < a \leq 1$. *For each alternative, compute the weighted outcome : ax (value of profit or cost most favourable outcome occurs) (1–2) × (value of profit or cost if least favourable outcome occurs). Choose the alternative which optimises the weighted outcome.*

We want to be put in a position where we are equally as well off with either strategy over a series of repeated trials. If *a* equals that percentage of the time we are investing in equity–share strategy, (1–*a*) equals the percentage of time we are investing in bonds, and the equity share strategy must equal the bond strategy, the payoff matrix might be as shown below:

	Market down	*Market up*
Return on equity share	–10%	+30%
Return on bonds	+7%	+8%

If the bond and the equity share strategies have to return the same, and *a* is the percentage of time we are investing in equity shares.

$a(-.10) + (1-a).30 = a(0.7) + (1-a)(.08)$

$a = 56.4\%$

The optimum mixed strategy is to be invested in equity share 56.4% of the time, and the remainder of the time in bonds. As those percentage we would be equally well off in bonds or in equity share and would minimise our position. A word of caution is appropriate in the example: the mixed strategies method assumes the state of nature occurs randomly, that bond and equity–share returns are random occurences.

A practical difficulty of the Hurwicz rule is that it is difficult for the decision–maker to determine a proper value for *a*, the weighting factor. The Hurwcz rule also lacks several of the desirable properties of a good decision rule, and it can even lead to results which are obviously counter to one's institution.

MINIMAX REGRET RULE

The minimax regret rule, proposed by L.J. Savage is similar to the minimax and maximin rules but is intended to counter some of the ultra conservative results given by those rules. This rule suggests that the decision–maker examine the maximum possible regret (loss because of not having chosen the best alternative for each possible outcome) associated with each alternative and then select the alternative which minimises the maximum regret.

We can construct the regret matrix to tell us the difference between each payoff and the maximum payoff that could occur for that project. Each regret payoff in each box reflects how much NPV is to be missed if the boom does occur. The following table also reflects that nothing is to be missed and have no regrets if the boom occurs under either project.

Regret Matrix

	Recession	*Normal*	*Boom*	*State of Nature*
NPV_A regret	₹ 40,000	₹ 20,000	0	
NPV_B regret	₹ 1,40,000	₹ 65,000	0	

However, if the recession occurs, the financial manager has only ₹ 40,000 worth of regret the project A, but ₹ 1,40,000 worth of regret with project B. In order to minimise the regret, apply the minimax strategy to the regret matrix and, in this example, find the project A to minimise the regret because the most regret that financial manager can have is ₹ 40,000 while the largest regret in project B is ₹ 1,40,000.

REAL OPTIONS

Traditional capital budgeting theory says nothing about the actions that can be taken after the project has been accepted and placed in operation that might cause the cash flows to increase. In reality, however, uncertainty plays a continuing role throughout the life of the project and managers are to respond to changing market conditions and to competitors' actions. Opportunities to respond to changing circumstances are called *managerial options* because they give managers the option to influence the outcome of a project. They are also called *strategic options* because they are often associated with large, strategic projects rather than routine maintenance projects. Finally ,they are called *real options* .which are differentiated from financial options because they involve real, rather than financial assets.

A real option is a right ,but not the obligation ,to take an action(e.g., deferring expanding .contracting ,or abandoning)at a predetermined cost called the exercise price ,for a predetermined period of time-the life of the option. Many projects include a variety of embedded options that can dramatically affect the true NPV. Examples of embedded options include *investment timing options* that allow a firm to delay a project; *growth options* that enable a firm to manage its capacity in response to changing market conditions; *abandoning options; flexibility options* that allow a firm to modify its operations overtime; and .finally *.rainbow options*-driven by multiple sources of uncertainty.

An investment timing option involves not only the decision of whether to proceed with a project but also a decision when to proceed with it. This opportunity to affect a project's timing can dramatically change its estimated value. Option to delay is valuable only if it more than offsets any harm that might have come from delaying. The option to delay is usually more valuable to firms with proprietary technology , patents , licenses, or other barriers to entry, because these factors lessen the threat to competition. The option to delay is valuable when market demand is uncertain , but it is also valuable when during periods of volatile interest rates, since ability to wait can allow firms to delay raising capital for projects until interest rates are lower.

A growth option occurs if an investment creates an opportunity to make other potentially profitable investments that would not be otherwise possible . These include options to expand output, options to enter a new geographical market, and option to introduce complementary products or successive generation of products.

Many projects contain an abandonment option. The abandonment option is the ability to abandon the project if the operating cash flows and / or abandonment value turn out to be lower than expected. It reduces the riskiness of a project and increases its value . Instead of a total abandonment, some options allow a company to reduce capacity or temporarily suspend operations .Such options are common in the natural resource industry, including mining, oil, timber, etc. They are be reflected in the analysis when NPV rae being estimated

A flexible option is the option to modify operations depending on how conditions develop during a project's life , especially the type of output produced or inputs used.

Rainbow options, driven by multiple sources of uncertainty, require many real-world situations applications. For example, exploration and production , research and development, and new product development are all compound rainbow options.

Real options have the greatest value when three factors come together. When there is high uncertainty and when managers have flexibility to respond it, real options are important. But value of real options relative to NPV is large when the NPV is close to zero, in the gray area. If the NPV is high then most options that provide additional flexibility will have a very low probability of being exercised , and therefore have a low relative value. Conversely, if the NPV is extremely negative, no amount of optionality can rescue the project . It is in making the tough decisions — those where the NPV is close to zero ——that the additional value of flexibility makes a big difference.

Some of the possible procedures applied to deal with real options are : use discounted cash flow valuation and ignore real options by assuming their values are zero; use discounted cash flow valuation and include a qualitative regulation of any real option's value; use decision tree analysis(*however, decision tree should not use the original project's cost of capital although finance theory has not provided a way to estimate the appropriate cost of capital for a decision three .sensitivity analysis can identify the effect that different costs of capital have on a project's value)*; use a standard model ,such as Black-Scholes, for a financial option . There are also other number of financial models which include the option to exchange one asset for another, the option to purchase the minimum or the maximum of two or more assets , the option on average of several assets , and even an option on an option for a variety of options . Given the large number of standard models for existing financial options, it is often possible to find a financial option that resembles the real option being analysed ; develop a unique project specific model using financial engineering techniques in case real option don't resemble any financial option.

Why the time has come for practical applications of real option analysis ? The modern breakthrough in valuation of options was made in the early 1970s by Robert Merton, Fischer Black, and Myron Scholes. The early applications were almost exclusively in the securities pricing arena where the data was plentiful and where the market price of the underlying securities was directly observable .And theoretician found it convenient to use stochastic equations as a tool of choice for publishing their advances. This was not a particularly friendly environment for management applications for real options. However, at the beginning of the new millennium, the application of real option has taken off since the speed and capacity of personal computers have advanced so rapidly that the managers had at their disposal enough easy-to-access computer power to bring realism and transparency. No longer is Ito calculus a necessary tool. Instead, use of lattices and algebraic solutions that are easy to implement and easy to understand can be used. Next, early pioneers assumed that real options required that the early users identify an underlying asset that are traded in the marketplace of the world. Now, it has been realised that real options can be applied to almost any situation where it is possible to estimate the NPV of the underlying project without flexibility. It is now possible to understand and to value real value for many realistic applications including those that are compound options and that have multiple sources of uncertainty.

ILLUSTRATIVE PROBLEMS

1. A firm must choose between constructing a large or small factory to produce a new line of products. The large plant would be needed if the future brings a high demand for new products. But the large plant would have net cash inflows below the ₹ 10,00,000 outlay, if demand is medium or low. The present value cash flows are ₹ 14,00,000 with high demand, ₹ 9,00,000 with medium demand, and ₹ 6,00,000 with low demand. The smaller plant produces a lower return if demand is high but has positive net present values at medium demand. It would cost ₹ 2,00,000 as a cash outlay and would return a present value inflow of ₹ 3,20,000 with high demand, ₹ 2,70,000 with medium demand, and ₹ 1,80,000 with low demand. What is the net present value of each alternative if there is a 40% chance of high demand and a 20% chance of low demand?

Solution

₹ 40,000 for the large plant and ₹ 72,000 for the small plant, as follows:

Decision	*Branching Probabilities*	*Present Value Of Cash Flows*		*Expected Returns*
Build ₹ 10,00,000 plant	high demand	.40 × ₹ 14,00,000	=	₹ 5,60,000
	med. demand	.40 × 9,00,000	=	3,60,000
	low demand	.20 × 6,00,000	=	1,20,000
	Expected Return		=	₹ 10,40,000
Decision Point				
Build ₹ 2,00,000 plant	high demand	.40 × ₹ 3,20,000	=	₹ 1,28,000
	med. demand	.40 × 2,70,000	=	1,08,000
	low demand	.20 × 1,80,000	=	36,000
				₹ 2,72,000

The net present values for the two choices indicate that the small factory is a better investment at the present time. This decision would not necessarily preclude a future expansion, should the high demand materialise.

2. A firm is considering an investment proposal that requires the rental of a warehouse. The building can be rented for 5 years for ₹ 52,500 per year at a fixed rate. Or, alternatively, it can be rented for ₹ 25,000 per year plus the actual costs of maintenance and power charges. The previous year's maintenance was ₹ 16,000 and the power bill was ₹ 9,000. How sensitive is the second method to one percent rate of inflation? At what inflation rate would the two alternatives involve the same cost to the firm if the firm's required return for this kind of decision is 10%?

Solution

Since one-half of the initial ₹ 50,000 is exposed to inflation with the second method, a 1% rate the first year will cost the firm ₹ 50,250 (₹ 25,000 + ₹ 25,000 x 1.01, or ₹ 50,000 x 1.0005). Compounding this effect and then taking the present value at 10%, we get a stream with a present value of ₹ 1,92,179 with a 1% annual inflation.

Year	*Value with 1%*	*Present Value at 10% Annual Inflation*
1	₹ 50,250	₹ 45,677
2	50,501	41,714
3	50,754	38,116
4	51,008	34,838
5	51,263	31,834
	Total Present Value =	₹ 1,92,179

With no inflation, the present value of the stream would be n = 5, i = 10, PMT = ₹ 50,000, PV = ₹ 1,89,539. Therefore, 1% inflation costs ₹ 2,640 (₹ 1,92,179–₹ 1,89,539). The fixed payment of ₹ 52,500 has a present value of n = 5, i = 10, PMT = ₹ 52,500, PV = ₹ 1,99,016. This is ₹ 9,477 more than the second alternative at zero inflation (₹ 1,99,016–₹ 1,89,539). At ₹ 2,640 per 1% of inflation, the difference would be eliminated with a 3.6% rate of inflation (₹ 9,477/₹ 2,640). The two alternatives involve equal costs at 3.6% rate of inflation.

3. A project offers after–tax cash flows of ₹ 4,50,000 a year for 3 years and ₹ 2,50,000 a year for 3 additional years, after which time it must be scrapped to net ₹ 2,00,000 after taxes. The firm's after tax required return is 8% on this kind of project. The project can be abandoned today to net ₹ 16,00,000 after taxes or in 3 years when it would be net ₹ 9,00,000 after taxes. When should the project be abondoned?

Solution

The three possibilities are;

ABANDON NOW ₹ 16,00,000

ABANDON in Three Years

n = 3, i = 8%	PAT = ₹ 4,50,000,	PV =	₹ 11,59,694
n = 3, i = 8%	FV = ₹ 9,00,000,	PV =	₹ 7,14,449
			₹ 18,74,143

ABANDON IN SIX YEARS

n = 3, i = 8%	PAT = ₹ 4,50,000,	PV =	₹ 12,59,694
n = 4, i = 8%	FV = ₹ 2,50,000,	PV =	₹ 1,83,758
n = 5, i = 8%	FV = ₹ 2,50,000,	PV =	₹ 1,70,1462
n = 6, i = 8%	FV = ₹ 2,50,000,	PV =	₹ 1,57,542
n = 6, i = 8%	FV = ₹ 2,00,000,	PV =	₹ 1,26,034
			₹ 17,97,174

The project should be abandoned after 3 years when it will be its maximum present value to the firm.

4. A project requires an outlay of ₹ 12,000 and runs for three years. The discount rate is 10%. Return are independent between years and in each of the years are given by

Probability	*Return*
0.06	₹ 1,500
0.17	₹ 2,000
0.22	₹ 4,500
0.29	₹ 6,000
0.16	₹ 7,500
0.10	₹ 9,400

Given the digits

8 7 0 5 6 9 0 5 8 1 9 4 2 7 1 4 2 1 8 7 7 4 9 5 3 1 5 8 0 4

conduct a simulation exercise (five runs) to estimate expected net present value (ENPV). Use the information obtained to estimate the coefficient of variation.

Solution

The first step in the simulation procedure is to allocate blocks of two-digit number to the alternative outcomes. This is done as shown below.

Probability	*Return*	*Nos allocated*
0.06	₹ 1,500	00-05
0.17	2,000	06-22
0.22	4,500	23-44
0.29	6,000	45-73
0.16	7,500	74-89
0.10	9,400	90-99

Of course, the digits *could* have been allocated in any other way that gave 6% of the total to correspond to the 1500 returns, 17% to correspond to the 2000 return, and so on. Although the particular details will differ depending upon how the allocation is done, in practice there should be a sufficiently large number of runs, so that these differences are immaterial.

Now, using the digits given, in pairs from left to right to generate return data for the first run, we obtain the results:

Random no.	*Return*
87	₹ 7,500
05	1,500
69	6,000

Thus the NPV be given by:

$$- ₹\ 12{,}000 + \frac{₹\ 7{,}500}{(1.1)} + \frac{₹\ 1{,}500}{(1.21)} + \frac{₹\ 6{,}000}{(1.331)} = ₹\ 565.74$$

The data for the full five runs are given below:

		Cash flow (returns)			NPV
Run no.	1	₹ 7,500	1,500	6,000	₹ 565.14
	2	1,500	7,500	9,400	2,624.34
	3	4,500	2,000	2,000	– 4,753.57
	4	7,500	7,500	9,400	8,078.89
	5	4,500	6,000	1,500	– 1,823.44
					Σ = ₹ 4,691.96

where, in run two, the numbers used are 05, 81, 94. For the remaining runs the digits are used in a similar fashion beginning with 27. The total NPV for the five runs is ₹ 4,691.96 which gives an average of ₹ 938.39. This is the simulation estimate of ENPV.

Having obtained the estimate of ENPV, we can go on the estimate the variance and hence the standard deviation and coefficient of variation. The variance will be:

$$\frac{\Sigma(\text{NPV} - \text{ENPV})^2}{4}$$

The workings are:

NPV	(NPV – ENPV)	(NPV – ENPV)²
₹ 565.74	–₹ 372.65	₹ 1,38,868
2,624.34	1,685.95	28,42,427
– 4,753.57	–5,691.96	3,23,98,409
8,078.89	7,140.50	5,09,86,740
–1,823.44	–2,761.83	76,27,705
		9,39,94,149

Thus variance, $\sigma^2 = \frac{9,39,94,149}{4}$ = Rs. 2,34,98,537

so that the coefficient of variation, CV, is given by:

$$\text{CV} = \frac{\sqrt{(2,34,98,547)}}{938.39} = 5.17$$

5. For an investment project, the following tentative initial estimates have bene made:

		Sales volumes	
Outlay	₹ 1,00,000		
Sales price	₹ 30	Year 1	4000 units
Unit cost	₹ 20	Year 2	6000 units
Discount rate	10% p.a.	Year 3	3000 units
Life3 years			

The ₹ 1,00,000 purchases equipment which will manufacture a product produced at the above unit cost and selling at the sales price in the volumes indicated.

(a) Calculate the maximum tolerable unfavourable change (as a percentage of the original estimated value) in (i) sales price, (ii) unit cost, (iii) sales volume, (iv) initial outlay and (v) project lifetime. Comment on the results. Could the sales volumes be treated *separately* in the analysis?

(b) Now suppose that government anti-inflation policy will allow sales prices to rise by 10% per annum compound, but unit costs are expected to rise at an annual rate of 20% compound (both starting at $t = 0$). What initial cash subsidy would be necessary to retain variability for the project.

Solution

With sales price p, unit cost c and sales volume v, in any year the return will be R. where:

$$R = v(p - c)$$

Thus in the first year of the project where p = ₹ 30, c - ₹ 20 and $v = 4000$ the return will be ₹ 40,000. On the basis of the original estimates the cash flow will be – ₹ 1,00,000; 40,000; 60,000; 30,000, so that net present value will be:

$$\text{NPV} = -₹\ 10{,}00{,}000 + \frac{₹\,40{,}000}{(1.1)} + \frac{₹\,60{,}000}{(1.21)} + \frac{₹\,30{,}000}{(1.331)} = ₹\ 8.490$$

Thus the project is worthwhile. Now, if the revenues changed in such a way that gross present volume came down from ₹ 1,08,490 to 1,00,000, the project would break even with zero NPV, Now, although the revenues are unequal in the three years, they will all be affected in *equal proportion* by a change in v or a change in $(p - c)$. In particular, if the value of $p - c$ was halved to ₹ 5, then GPV would be halved. Similarly, if $p - c$ was replaced by:

$$\frac{₹\,60{,}000}{₹\,1{,}08{,}490}(p-c)$$

then GPV would be 1,00,000, giving zero NPV. If c remains constant at ₹ 20, then if p was such that the margin was:

$$\frac{₹\,10{,}000 \times ₹\,10}{₹\,1{,}08{,}490}$$

then NPV would be zero. Thus p must be such that the margin is ₹ 9.22. The minimum value of p, *ceteris paribus*, is ₹ 29.22. This represents a fall of 0.78 or just 2.60%. On the other hand, given p = ₹ 30 the value of c required to give a margin of ₹ 9.22 is ₹ 20.78, which would represent a rise of 3.90%.

In respect of sales volume, if each year was affected in the same *proportion* and if all volume figures stood at:

$$\left[\frac{₹\,8{,}490}{₹\,1{,}08{,}490}\right] 100\%$$

of the original values, then NPV would be zero. Thus the requisite percentage fall in v is:

$$\left[\frac{₹\,8{,}490}{₹\,1{,}08{,}490}\right] 100\% = 7.83\%$$

If GPV remains at 1,08,490, then the initial outlay must not exceed this figure. Obviously this would represent a rise of 8.49%.

In analysing the effects of variation in the project's lifetime we start by considering the present values if the project only ran for *two* years. This would be:

$$\text{NPV (2 years)} = -\,₹\,1{,}00{,}000 + \frac{₹\,40{,}000}{(1.1)} + \frac{₹\,60{,}000}{(1.21)}$$

$$= -\,₹\,14{,}050$$

Thus for viability the project needs to run for such a part of the third year that the present value of the part return is ₹ 14,050, which would bring NPV up to zero level. A fairly plausible assumption about happenings in the third year is that if the project runs for some fraction, f, of the year, then the return achieved will be 30,000 f and the timing of the return would be after 2 + f years. Thus we require that f be such that:

$$\frac{₹\,30{,}000\,f}{(1.1)^{2+f}} = ₹\,14{,}050$$

$$\frac{\text{Rs. } 30{,}000f}{(1.1)^{2+f}} = \text{Rs. } 14{,}050$$

With x representing the present value of the third year return, calculations produce the following results:

f	x
0.65	₹ 15,147.6
0.64	14,928.79
0.63	14,709.54
0.62	14,489.86
0.61	14,269.74
0.6	14,049.2
0.59	13,828.22

Thus, on the basis of the assumptions made, if the project ran for 2.6 years instead of a 3 years, then breakeven would be achieved. This would represent a reduction in lieftime of 13.33%.

The results in total are as follows:

Factor	*% variation*
Price	2.60
Unit cost	3.90
Sales volume	7.83
Outlay	8.49
Lifetime	13.33

We could conclude form this that the project is sensitive to all factors but particularly so in respect of price and cost. If, as is often the case, these are volatile parameters, the variability of the project could easily be jeopardized. Of course, we cannot specify a particular percentage variation, in general, which represents the boundary point for sensitivity. An arbitrary, but informed, decision has to be made in the light of particular cases. However, judging by typical payback periods in practice anything below 20% or 30% would be regarded as sensitive.

Sales volumes in the individual years can be easily examined. For instance, assuming that everything is as originally estimated in years 2 and 3, and the sales volume in year 1 is v,then v_1, must be such as to produce zero NPV; thus :

$$\frac{10v_1}{(1.1)} + \frac{60,000}{(1.21)} + \frac{30,000}{(1.331)} = ₹\ 1,00,000$$

This equation solves for v_1 = 3,066, a reduction of 23.35%. For year 2 the equation is:

$$\frac{40,000}{(1.1)} + \frac{10v_2}{(1.21)} + \frac{30,000}{(1.331)} = ₹\ 1,00,000$$

which solves for v_2 = 4,973, a reduction of 17.12%. Finally, for year 3;

$$\frac{40,000}{(1.1)} + \frac{60,000}{(1.21)} + \frac{10v_3}{(1.331)} = ₹\ 1,00,000$$

solves for v_3 = 1870, a reduction of 37.67%. It would appear, then, that the project is most sensitive to sales performance in the second year, and least sensitive in the third year.

Now consider the inflation scenario. The calculations necessary to ascertain present value are shown below:

t	*p*	*c*	*p - c*	*R*	*pv*
1	₹ 33.0	₹ 24.00	9.00	₹ 36,000	₹ 32,727.27
2	36.30	28.80	7.50	45,000	37,190.08
3	39.93	34.56	5.37	16,110	12,103.68
					₹ 82,103.03

It will be seen that the margin starts to decline at once and in increasing absolute amounts. The gross present value plunges to ₹ 82,021. Therefore, a subsidy sufficient to bring this figure up to ₹ 1,00,000 would be needed for economic viability. Thus the subsidy required would be ₹ 17,797.

6. A project has a initial outlay fixed at 1500. The return in year 1 could be 1350 with probability 0.4 or 900 with probability 0.6. If in year 1 the 900 return transpires, then in year 2 there can be 1200 (p = 0.2) or 1050 (p = 0.8). If the year 1 return had been 1350, then in year 2 there is a 0.7 chance of 600 and a 0.3 chance of 150. Find the coefficient of variation. The interest rate is 10%.

Solution

First, draw up a tree diagram, as shown below. The column headed '*p*' shows the probability of each stream of returns. Thus the stream –1500, 900, 1200 has probability 0.12 of arising. The next column shows the NPV of each stream. Note that the probability of the project

				p	NPV	pNPV
	0.4	1350	0.7	600	0.28	223.14	62.48
			0.3	150	0.12	–148.76	–17.85
–1500							
	0.6	900	0.2	1200	0.12	309.92	37.19
			0.8	1050	0.48	185.95	89.26
						ENPV =	171.08

NPV-ENPV	$(NPV\text{-}ENPV)^2$	$p(NPV\text{-}ENPV)^2$
52.06	2710.24	758.87
–319.84	102297.63	12,275.72
138.84	19276.55	2,313.19
14.87	221.12	106.14
		σ^2_{NPV} = 15,453.92

making a loss is 0.12. The ENPV emerges in the usual fashion as 171.08. The remaining three columns give the variance calculations. The variance emerges as 15,453.92, so that the coefficient of variation is given by:

$$CV = \frac{\sqrt{(15,433.92)}}{171.08} = 0.7266$$

QUESTIONS

1. Under what circumstances might the decision tree technique in capital budgeting analysis be useful?
2. What is the advantage of analysing investment expenditure as a single component within a sequence of investment decisions rather than as an isolated period decisions? Use your answer to illustrate the statement that "decision free are especially effective in showing the interplay between a present decision, chance events, and possible future decisions and their consequences."
3. Many firms continue to use obsolete machinery long after new, more efficient equipment is available. Under what circumstances would this represent poor financial planning?
4. What decision rule can be used to determine whether an investment project should be continued or abandoned?
5. What is the basic simulation approach for dealing with project risk? How does simulation provide the decision maker with the useful decision–making inputs?
6. In what ways does the Hillier Model complement the standard approaches to risk and uncertainty?
7. "To some degree, simulation and sensitivity analysis provide similar information to the financial analyst, although simulation is a more comprehensive form of analysis." Comment on the statement.
8. What is meant by utility? Do you feel that financial managers should be risk–averse? Why or why not?
9. Provide examples of risk–averse and risk preferent behaviour. Can a single individual be both risk–averse and risk–preferent?

10. Why should the firm be viewed as having a portfolio of projects? Why is the correlation between project returns important?
11. (*a*) Define and graphically illustrate an efficient frontier.
    (*b*) Define and graphically illustrate an indifference curve map for a risk averter.
    (*c*) How are the efficiency frontier and indifference map useful in selecting a portfolio of projects? Illustrate graphically.
12. Why are diversification effects relevant in analysing investment opportunities?
13. Is it possible for the risk attached to a combination of a number of projects to be less than the risk attached to a single investment project? Why?
14. What is a payoff matrix? What are the two dimensions of this matrix? How can a payoff matrix be used to evaluate risk?
15. Discuss the capital budgeting techniques without probabilities.

PROBLEMS

1. The initial installed cost of a compressor is ₹ 60,000. Operation and repair costs are ₹ 10,000 for the first year and increase by ₹ 3,000 each year thereafter. The expected salvage value is ₹ 36,000 after 1 year and decreases by ₹ 4,000 each year thereafter until the compressor reaches a maximum life of 8 years. If the minimum required rate of return is 10% before taxes, determine, by before-tax annual cost analysis, the most economical year in which to replace the compressor. Assume indefinite planning horizon.

Ans.: 5 years.

2. A machine originally costs ₹ 1,00,000. Operating and maintenance costs for year *j* are equal to ₹ 10,000 + ₹ 1000 (*j*–1). A 50% tax rate, 10% investment tax credit, straight–line depreciation, zero salvage value at all times, 10% minimum required rate of return after taxes, and indefinite planning horizon are to be assumed. The machine must be used for at least 5 years and cannot be used more than 10 years. Determine the optimum replacement interval under the assumption of identical replacements.

Ans.: 10 years.

3. Consider the project ABC has the following cash flows and abandonment value over its useful life.

Period	*0*	*1*	*2*	*3*	*4*	*5*
Cash Flows	– ₹ 7,500	2,000	2,000	2,000	2,000	2,000
Abandonment Values		– ₹ 6,200	5,200	4,000	2,200	0

The firm's cost of capital is 10%. Determine the optimal time for project ABC to be abandoned if it is accepted.

Ans.: The NPV (i.e. ₹ 476) is maximised by abandoning project ABC at the end of period 3.

4. Given the following matrix of equivalent annual costs (in ₹ thousands) for three alternatives as follows:

Alternatives	*State of nature*		
	Kind	*Erratic*	*Perverse*
X	20	28	40
Y	25	25	25
Z	11	27	45

Show which alternative should be chosen using each of the following decision rules or principles: *(a)* Minimax rule; *(b)* Minimin rule; *(c)* Laplace principle; *(d)* Hurwicz principle, with 0.8 index of optimism; and *(e)* Minimax regret rule.

Ans.: (a) Y; (b) Z; (c) Z

5. Given the following matrix of net present values for four alternatives, show which alternative should be chosen using each of the following decision rules or principles: (a) Minimax rule; (b) Minimax rule; (c) Laplace principle; (d) Hurwicz principle, with 0.5 optimism; and (e) Minimax regret rule.

Alternatives	*Business Conditions*		
	S_1	S_2	S_3
I	30	25	– 15
II	15	15	15
III	35	30	– 15
IV	45	10	– 5

Ans.: (a) II; (b) III; (c) III; (d) IV; (e) III or IV

6. Sandhya Corporation's present capital structure, which is also its target capital structure, calls for 50 per cent debt and 50 per cent equity. The firm has only one potential project, an expansion programme with a 10.2 per cent IRR and a cost of ₹ 20 crore which is completely divisible; that is, Sandhya can invest any amount up to ₹ 20 crore. The firm experts to retain ₹ 3 crore of earnings next year. It can raise up to ₹ 5 crore new debt at a before-tax cost of 8 per cent, and all debt after the first ₹ 5 crore will have cost of 10 per cent. The cost of retained earnings is 12 per cent, and the firm can sell amount of new equity desired at a constant cost of new equity of 15 per cent. The firm's marginal tax rate is 40 per cent. What is the firm's optimal capital budget?

Ans.: ₹ 10 crore

7. The risk-free rate of return is 9 per cent, and the market risk premium is 5 per cent. The beta of the project under analysis is 1.4, with expected net cash flows estimated to be ₹ 15,00,000 per year for 5 years. The required investment outlay on the project is ₹ 45,00,000.

(a) What is the required risk-adjusted return on the project?

(b) Should the project be accepted?

Ans.: (a) = 1.6%; (b) NPV = ₹ 4,11,111; Accept

8. Suppose T = 5%, R_m = 10%, and R_A = 12%.

(a) Calculate Stock A's beta.

(b) If Stock A's beta were 2.0, what would be A's new required rate of return?

Ans.: (a) β_A = 1.40; (b) R_A = 15%

9. Suppose T = 99%, R_m = 14%, and b_i = 1.3.

(a) What is R_i, the required rate of return on Stock i?

(b) Now suppose T (1) increase to 10 per cent or (2) decreases to 8 per cent. The slope of the SML remains constant. How would this affect R_m and R_i?

(c) Now assume T remains at 9 per cent but R_m (1) increases to 16 per cent or (2) falls to 13 per cent. The slope of the SML does not remain constant. How would these changes affect R_i?

Ans.: (a) R_A = 15.5%; (b) R_m = 15%; R_i = 16.5%; (c) R_i = 18.10%

PART - IV

LONG-TERM FINANCING AND REQUIRED RATE OF RETURN

This Page has been intentionally left blank

14

COST OF CAPITAL

INTRODUCTION

The discounted cash flow techniques used to evaluate alternative investments measure cash flows in term of required rate of return to determine their acceptability. The required rate of return applied may be the cost of capital adjusted for project risk differing from that of the normal risk complexion of the firm. But what exactly is the cost of firm, and how do we go about for determining it? These are the questions that can be addressed by examining the composition of the sources of financing. The funds needed to finance an investment may be obtained by a company in a variety of ways—by making a new equity issue, using retained earnings, by issuing debt such as debentures, by allowing short term liabilities to increase, an so on. Each of these sources has a cost and it may be argued, therefore, the cost of the particular sources of fund used to finance a proposal should be used to finance a cut-off rate. However, a particular source of fund, used to finance a particular investment project, should not be regarded as the cost of capital. From the point of view of the share market, there is no such thing as investment financed by a new issue of equity or an investment financed by debt. In the share market, price is influenced by the combined effect of all the company's investment and financing decisions. Therefore, it is necessary to calculate an overall cost of capital for company to use as its cut-off rate in investment decision-making. The!return is to be approximated by the weighted average of the cost of each type of finance. In turn, the weight for each type of finance will be given by the proportion of each source of finance that the company intends to employ to finance future investments. It is assumed throughout that these proportions are equal to the proportions of each source of finance in the optimum capital structure. Besides initially utilising the traditional methodology, we will apply capital asset pricing model (CAPM) and use it to determine the cost of equity capital based upon systematic risk, the value of a project to the firm based on the market price of risk, the value of the firm after acceptance of a project, and, the firm's average cost of capital after acceptance of the project.

FACTORS DETERMINING THE COST OF CAPITAL

The primary factors determining the cost of capital are listed below:

GENERAL ECONOMIC CONDITIONS

The general economic conditions determine the demand for and supply of capital within the economy, as well as the level of expected inflation. This economic variable is reflected in the riskless rate of return. This rate represents the rate of return on riskfree investments, such as the interest rate on short-term government securities. In principal, as the demand for money in the economy changes relative to the supply, investors change their required rate of return. For example, if the demand for money increases without an equivalent increases in supply, creditors will raise their required rate of interest. At the same time as inflation is expected, there would be deterioration in the purchasing power of the money, investors require a higher rate of return to compensate for this anticipated loss.

RISK AND COST OF CAPITAL

If an investor is purchasing a security where the risk of the investment is significant, the opportunity for additional returns is necessary to make the investment attractive. The risk elements is composed of five aspects that are closely inter-twined: business risk, financial risk, purchasing power risk, money rate risk (also called interest rate risk), and market (or liquidity) risk. *Business risk* is the variability in return on assets and is affected by the company's investment decisions. *Financial risk* refers to the proportion of debt and equity with which a firm is financed. *Purchasing power risk* refers to the change in the purchasing power of money measured by price level changes. *Money rate risk* refers to the premium in yield demanded by suppliers of capital to cover the risk of an increase in future interest rates. *Market (or liquidity) risk* refers to the ability of a supplier of funds to sell his holdings quickly.

AMOUNT OF FINANCING REQUIRED

As management approaches the market for large amount of capital relative to the size of the firm, suppliers of capital become hesitant to grant relatively large amounts of funds without evidence of management's capability to absorb the capital into business. For additional funds, therefore, the investors may ask for higher required rate of return.

FLOTATION COSTS

Flotation costs represent a financial market-distortion which makes the new issues more expensive form of financing. They are defined as the cost of marketing new securities. They include all costs involved in moving new securities from the issue to the ultimate investor. They include legal fees, printing expenses, sales commissions, and profit to the underwriting syndicate, among other things. Flotation costs are so called because they are incurred in *floating new securities*. They are also sometimes called *underwriting costs* or *issuance costs*.

Flotation costs can be included in the cost of capital buy adjusting the market rate of return. The cost of capital including flotation costs is figured as:

$$\text{Cost of Capital} = \frac{\text{Market rate of return}}{1 - \text{Flotation cost percentage}} \quad (1)$$

To illustrate, assume a firm issues an equity share of ₹ 100, if flotation cost are 2 per cent, the issuing firm will receive only ₹ 98 on per equity share. However, reduction of proceeds when flotation costs are incurred is not accompanied by a reduction in the return to the capital suppliers. Consider a corporation that issues a ₹ 1,000 bond that promises 12.00 per cent return. The issue promises to pay ₹ 120 interest each year, that is:

$$.12 \times ₹\ 1{,}000 = ₹\ 120$$

Without flotation costs, the corporation is to earn only 12.00 per cent before taxes on his assets to pay the bondholder, other things equal. But when flotation costs are introduced, the picture changes. Assume that it costs ₹ 20 to market each bond. This mean that the firm gets proceeds of only ₹ 980 (₹ 1,000—₹ 20). But the bondholders are still expecting a ₹ 120 return for each bond. Ignoring the tax affects momentarily, the corporation must earn ₹ 120 over the net proceeds of ₹ 980, that is:

$$\frac{₹\ 120}{₹\ 980} = 12.24\%$$

TAXES

In capital budgeting, all cash flows are evaluated on an after-tax basis. In order to be consistent with this capital budgeting framework, the cost of capital, which is to discount the cash flows in determining net present values and benefit-cost ratios and as the cut-off-rate for internal rates of return must also be measured on an after tax basis. The specific cost of capital that actually requires any type of tax adjustment is the cost of debt.

COMPONENTS OF COST OF CAPITAL

The overall cost of capital of a firm is comprised of the costs of the various components of financing, Techniques for determining the specific costs of each of these sources, i.e., debt, preferences shares, retained earnings, and equity shares, are presented in the following pages. Although the techniques presented tend to develop precisely calculated values of specific as well as weighted average costs, it is important to recognise that the resulting values are at best rough approximations due to the numerous assumptions and forecasts that underlie them.

COST OF DEBT

The cost of capital for debt is the return that potential investors require of the firm's debt securities, such as its bonds. The cost of debt has two basic components: one is the annual interest and the other arises from the amortisation of discounts or premium paid or received when the debt is initially issued.

Since the interest payments and the return of principal remain constant regardless of the change in investors' required rate of return, only the bond price and the cost of debt can change. a financial manager can pinpoint the exact cost of debt after the price change by calculating k_d in generalise equation:

$$P_o = \sum_{t=1}^{n} \frac{IP_t}{(1+k_d)^t} + \frac{P_n}{(1+k_d)^n} \qquad (2)$$

where:

P_o = the observed market price of the bond
IP_t = the interest payments on the principal
P_n = the return of principal
k_d = the cost of debt (after-tax)
n = the number of years until the bond matures.

Since interest is a tax-deductible expense, we have to consider the after-tax cost of debt, especially if we want to judge its impact on the firm's after-tax profitability or compare it to the cost of other types of securities which a company can offer whose cash flow streams are not—deductible, such as preference and equity shares. We can calculate the after-tax cost of debt by adjusting the pre-tax for the tax rate such that:

$$k_d = k_i (1-t) \tag{3}$$

where

k_d = the after-tax cost of debt
k_i = the pre-tax cost of debt
t = the tax rate.

For example, look at the data in Table—1. There are two firms X and Y, which have indentical earnings before interest and taxes. Firm 'X' has no debt, where as firm 'Y' has ₹ 250 crore in outstanding debt and pays interest rate of 12 per cent. The firms' incomes are calculated using three tax

TABLE-1

Tax Rate and the Effective Rate on Debt

(₹ in crore)

	0% tax rate		*25% tax rate*		*50% tax rate*	
	Firm X	*Firm Y*	*Firm X*	*Firm Y*	*Firm X*	*Firm Y*
	₹	₹	₹	₹	₹	₹
Earnings before interest and taxes (EBIT)	100	100	100	100	100	100
Interest	0	30	0	30	0	30
Earnings before taxes (EBT)	100	70	100	70	100	70
Tax	0	0	25	17.50	50	35
Earnings after taxes (EAT)	100	70	75	52.50	50	35
Difference1	3 0		22.50		15	
Effective rate[2]		12%		5%		6%

(1) Net income of firm X-Net income of firm Y
(2) Difference in net income/₹ 250 crore of outstanding debt for firm Y.

rates, 25 and 50 per cent, and the resulting values of the net income are compared. If no taxes were paid, the only difference between the net incomes of the two firms would be due to the interest expense incurred by firm 'Y' of ₹ 30 crore. In this case we would say that the effective rate on debt was equal to the interest rate of 12 per cent the effective rate on debt was equal to the interest rate of 12 per cent (₹ 30 crore /₹ 250 crore =12 per cent). If the tax rate is 25 per cent, the impact of debt interest on net income is only ₹ 12.50 crore due to tax deductibility of interest. The effective rate on debt is therefore only ₹ 12.50 crore/₹ 250 crore = 5 per cent. Similarly, at a 50 per cent tax rate the effective rate is only ₹ 15 crore/ ₹ 250 crore =6 per cent. The general formula for effective rate is

Effective rate=interest rate (1.0–tax-rate)

In many instances, individuals or corporations may borrow from more than one source. The amounts of loans and their interest rates often differ quite appreciably. As a result, the average interest rate must be calculated. Since the amounts of the loans differ, a weighted average must be taken.

Example - 1 (₹ in crore)

Mukund Industries has the following outstanding debts:

Debt	*Amounts*	*Pretax Interest Rate*
Bonds, *Series A*	₹ 2,000	10.00%
Mortgage	₹ 3,000	10.50
Bonds, *Series B*	₹ 2,500	11.00
Bonds, *Series C*	₹ 4,000	11.50
	₹ 11,500	

Determine the weighted average pre-tax interest rate.

Solution

First, determine the proportion of each type of debt. This is accomplished by dividing the amount of each debt by the total debt. In this example, the total is ₹ 11,500.

Bonds, Series A	:	₹ 2,000/₹ 11,500	=	.174
Mortgage	:	₹ 3,000/₹ 11,500	=	.261
Bond, Series B	:	₹ 2,500/₹ 11,500	=	.217
Bond, Series C	:	₹ 4,000/₹ 11,500	=	.348
			Total =	1.000

Next multiply the proportion of each type of debt by its interest rate (expressed in decimal form). Then add the sum to obtain the weighted average cost of debt. These calculation in tabular form are shown follows:

Debt	Amounts	Proportion	Pre-tax interest		Weighted costs Rate (cost)
Bonds, Series A	2,000	.174	.100	=	.0174
Mortgage	3,000	.261	.105	=	.0274
Bonds, Series B	2,500	.217	.110	=	.0239
Bonds, Series C	4,000	.348	.115	=	.0400
	11,500	1.000			.1087

The weighted average pre-tax cost of debt (interest rate) is 10.87%

Example-2

Refer to example-1 and assume that Mukund Industries has a marginal income tax-rate of 40%. Determine the after-tax weighted average cost of debt.

Solution

The weighted average pre-tax cost of debt (interest rate) is 10.87%. Employing equation-3 the after tax cost of debt may be calculated:

$$k_d = k_i (1-t)$$

$$= .1087\ (1-.40) = .06522 = 6.522\%$$

The after tax weighted average cost of debt is 6.522%.

Flotation-costs (F) for new issues of debt drive the cost up. The greater the flotation cost, other things being equal, the higher the cost of debt. The following formulation accounts for the incidence of flotation cost and tax effects:

$$k_d = \frac{k_i(1-t)}{(1-F)} \qquad (4)$$

Example-3

Refer to example-2, calculate the after-tax weighted average cost of debt for Mukund Industries, assuming the flotation costs for bonds to be 2 per cent.

Solution

To determine the after-tax weighted average cost of debt, equation (4) is to be applied to take the incidence of flotation costs. By using equation (4), we get:

$$k_d = \frac{.1087\ (1\text{-}.40)}{(1\text{-}.02)} = 6.655\%$$

Yield To Maturity (YTM)

The calculation of the k_d which we performed also give us the yield to maturity, which is synonymous with the cost of debt. We can continue to calculate the k_d as above, using such aids as the present-value tables or we can resort to the approximation method:

The formula for yield to maturity is:

$$\text{Approximate YTM} = \frac{\text{Average Annual Return}}{\text{Average investment}}$$

$$[C+(M-P)/n]/\ [(M+P)/2] \tag{5}$$

where:

C = the annual coupon
M = the maturity or the par value of the bond
P = the purchase price
n = the number of years remaining to maturity

Example-4

Grand Company issued bonds with par value of ₹ 1,000 at 10 per cent at 5 per cent discount for 10 years. Calculate the YTM.

Solution

Substituting the information of bond into the equation (5), we have:

YTM =[100+(1000-950)/10] /[(1000+950)/2] = 105/975 = 10.77 per cent

COST OF PREFERENCE SHARE

The cost of preference share is represented by a fixed dividend payment carrying a higher order of precedence than equity share dividends, but not the binding contractual obligation as of interest on debt. Preference share, being a hybrid security, has neither the ownership privilege of equity nor the legally enforceable provisions of debt. The cost of preference share is found by dividing the annual preference share dividend by net proceeds from the sale of preference share. The net proceeds represent the amount of money to be received minus flotation costs.

$$k_p = \frac{D}{P_p - F} \tag{6}$$

where

k_p = the cost of preference share
D = the preference share dividend
P_p = the market price of preference share
F = the flotation or selling costs.

For example, if:

(i) $D = ₹ 8; P_p = ₹ 100$
then:

$$k_p = \frac{₹ 8}{₹ 100} = 8\%$$

If:
(ii) F = ₹ 1

then:

$$k_p = \frac{₹ 8}{₹ 100 - ₹ 1} = 8.08\%$$

If, the preference is selling at a premium, say, ₹ 110:

$$k_p = \frac{₹ 8}{₹ 110 - ₹ 1} = \frac{₹ 8}{₹ 109} = 7.34\%$$

If, the preference share is selling at a discount, say, ₹ 90:

$$k_p = \frac{₹ 8}{₹ 90 - ₹ 1} = \frac{₹ 8}{₹ 89} = 8.99\%$$

Example-5

In 2013, Atul Enterprises issued preference shares for ₹ 100 per share. The share pays a yearly dividend of ₹ 7.50. Atul Enterprises received ₹ 99 for each share. Determine the cost of the 2013 issue of preference share.

Solution

The selling price was ₹ 100 and the amount Atul Enterprises received was only ₹ 99, because the flotation cost was ₹ 1. Using equation 6, the cost is calculated below:

$$k_p = \frac{₹ 7.50}{₹ 100 - ₹ 1} = \frac{₹ 7.50}{₹ 99} = 7.58\%$$

$$k_p = \frac{₹ 7.50}{₹ 100 - ₹ 1} = \frac{₹ 7.50}{₹ 99} = 7.58\%$$

The cost of the 2013 issue of preference share equity financing is 7.58%

Even though preference share is a mean to obtain financial leverage, the increased cost of this financial leverage argues for the use of debt securities to obtain financial leverage. In recent years there has been relatively little preference share financing (unless the preference shares are issued as convertible).

COST OF RETAINED EARNINGS

The cost of retained earnings is closely related to the cost of equity shares. If earnings are not retained they will be paid out to the equity shareholders as dividends.

Retained earnings are often looked on as fully subscribed issue of new equity, since they increase the shareholders' equity in the same way that a new issue of equity shares would. The cost of retained earnings must therefore be viewed as the opportunity cost of the foregone dividends to the existing equity shareholders. In other words, when the company retain earnings, it assumes that the shareholders cannot earn as much on the money elsewhere through reinvestment.

The cost of funds obtained by retained earnings can be defined as *the rate of return shareholders require on the firm's equity shares.*

The value of an equity share depends, ultimately on the dividends paid on the share:

$$P_o = \frac{D_1}{(1+k_r)^1} + \frac{D_2}{(1+k_r)^2} + \ldots\ldots \quad (7)$$

where:

P_o = the current price of the share
D_1 = the dividend expected to be paid at the end of year t
k_r = the required rate of return

If dividends are expected to grow at a constant rate, equation (7) reduces to

$$P_o = \frac{D_1}{k_r - g} \quad (8)$$

where: g = growth rate.

In equilibrium, the expected and required rates of return must be equal, so we can solve k_r to obtain the required rate of return on equity:

$$P_o = \frac{D_1}{P_o} + \text{expected g} \quad (9)$$

To illustrate this, consider a firm expected to earn ₹ 20 a share and to pay a ₹ 10 dividend during the coming year. The company's earnings, dividends and share prices have all been growing at about 10 per cent a year, and this growth rate is expected to continue indefinitely. If the current price of the equity share is ₹ 100, then k_r would be estimated as follows:

$$k_r = \frac{₹\ 10}{₹\ 100} + 10\% = 20\%$$

If the firm refrains from meeting investment and pays all its earnings in dividends, it will cut its growth rate to zero. However, the price of the share will not fall, because investors still get the required 20 per cent rate of return on their shares.

$$= \frac{₹\ 20}{₹\ 100} + 0 = 20\%$$

If a firm earns required rate of return, k_r ,and it decides to retain earnings and invest them in its operation, its current share price will not change as a result of this financing and investment. However, if it earns less than k_r the share price will fall, if it earns more, the price will rise.

Based on the fact that *individuals* are taxed on dividends and that they must pay brokerage fees, to reinvest their funds, the firms need not obtain as great a return on retained earnings as they must obtain on equity capital. A firm obviously do as well as the owners could do for themselves. Hence in determining the cost of retained earnings, the firm may discount the investor's tax rate and brokerage fees. The result is equation 10 which provides the cost of retained earnings:

$$k_r = k_e (1-t)(1-B) \tag{10}$$

where

k_r = the cost of retained earnings
k_e = the cost of equity capital
t = the owner's marginal-tax rate
B = the average brokerage fee

But the use of equation (10) requires that the financial manager must be able to estimate be owner's marginal tax rate and brokerage fees.

Example-6

Standard Products has a cost of equity capital of 20%. While the owners' marginal tax rates vary among industries due to different types of investors attracted, approximate value for Standard Products of t and B are established at 40% and 3% respectively. Using the average value for the owners, marginal tax rates and brokerage fees, determine the cost of retained earnings for Standard Products.

Solution

Employ equation (10):

$$K_r = .20\ (1-.40)\ (1-.03) = .20\ (.60)\ (.97) = .1164$$

The cost of retained earnings is 11.64%

COST OF EQUITY

The cost of equity can be generally stated as the rate at which investors discount the expected dividend of the firm in order to determine the market price of an ownership interest in the firm. The cost of new issues of equity can easily be calculated by determining the percentage reduction in the current market price attributable to flotation costs. If we let F represent the percentage reduction in the current market price expected as a result of underpricing and underwriting charges on a new equity-issue, the cost of the new equity issue, k_e, can be expressed as follows:

$$k_e = \frac{D_1}{P_o(1-F)} + g \tag{11}$$

Here F is the percentage cost of selling the issue, so $P_o (1-F) = P_n$ is the net price received by the firm.

Example-7

The market price of Arvind Products equity share is ₹ 550 per share and the flotation costs are ₹ 10 per share. If the dividend is ₹ 25 and has been growing at an annual rate of 20%, determine the cost of equity capital.

Solution

Using equation (11), the cost of equity share is determined as follows:

$$k_e = \frac{₹\,25}{₹\,550 - ₹\,10} + g$$

$$= \frac{₹\,25}{₹\,540} + .20 = .0463 + .20 = .2463$$

The cost equity capital is 24.63%

WEIGHTED AVERAGE COST OF CAPITAL (WACC)

The weighted average cost of capital (WACC) summarises the after tax cost of the entire capital structure. It is used as the discount rate in calculating the net present value of investment proposals. Any projects with internal rates of return less than the weighted-average cost cannot be accepted.

COMPUTATION OF WACC

The WACC is found by weighing the cost of each specific type of capital by the *historical, target, or marginal proportions* of each type of capital used. *Historical weights* are based on the firm's existing capital structure, *target weights* are based upon the proportions of the various types of capital the firm wishes to maintain, whereas *marginal weights* consider the actual proportions of each type of capital expected to be used in financing a given project.

HISTORICAL WEIGHTS

The use of historical weights for calculating the firm's weighted average cost of capital is quite common. The use of these weights is based on the assumption that the firm's existing mix of funds (i.e. capital structure) is optimal and therefore should be maintained in the future. Two types of historical weights can be used: *book value weights and market value weights.*

Book Value Weights

The book value weights in calculating the firm's weighted average cost of capital assumes that new financing will be raised using exactly the same proportion of each type of financing as the firm currently has in its capital structure. The calculations involved can be illustrated by a simple example.

Table-2 shows an example of calculation of the weighted-average cost of capital. Column 1 lists the type of capital-bonds, preference shares, retained earnings, and equity shares. Column 2 contains the book value of each capital source. These figures will be used to determine the relative importance of each capital source. The values in column 3 are calculated by dividing the amount of each type of capital by the total capital figure. For example, bonds contribute 30 per cent of the capital (i.e., ₹ 3,000 crore/₹ 10,000=.30). Since the percentage of total capital base is being calculated, the weight must sum to unity, 1.0.

TABLE-2

Calculating the Weighted Average Cost of Capital (Book-Value Weights)

(₹ in crore)

Capital Component	*Book Value*	*Book Value Weight (2)÷10,00,00,000*	*Before-tax Cost*	*After-tax Cost**	*Weighted Cost of Capital*
1	2	3	4	5	6
Bonds	₹ 3,000	.30	.10	.06	.0180
Preference Shares	500	.05	.08	.08	.0040
Retained Earnings	1,500	.15	.15	.15	.0225
Equity Shares	5,000	.50	.18	.18	.0900
Total	₹ 10,000	1.00			WACC= .1345

* Tax rate=40%

Column 4 contains the before-tax cost of each type of capital. The figure in column 5 contains the after-tax cost of each type of capital. This figure is calculated by applying the tax rate to the before-tax cost. The only type of capital in Table 2 whose cost is tax-deductible is debt. Applying the 40 per cent tax rate to the before-tax cost of debt of .10, leaves an after tax cost of .060.

The costs of preference shares, retained earnings and equity shares are not tax-deductible,therefore their after-tax cost is the same as of before-tax cost.

Column 6 is very important one. Column 6 contains the weighted cost of each type of capital source. It is calculated by multiplying the capital source's weight (column 3) by its after-tax cost (column 5). This process of weighting each component of the capital structure accounts for relative importance of each. For example, the cost of debt accounts for 30 per cent of the total, and so forth. Summing column 6 gives the weighted average cost of capital (WACC) for the firm. It is an index figure, an average, that summarises th entire capital structure. It says that, taking into account that relative importance of each capital source, the average cost of capital is 13.45 per cent.

Market Value Weights

The use of market value weights for calculating the firm's weighted average cost of capital is theoretically more appealing than the use of book value weights since the market value of the securities closely approximate the actual to be received from their debt. Moreover since the cost of the various types of capital are calculated using prevailing market prices, it seems only reasonable to use market value of a firm's sources of equity financing (i.e. preference, retained earnings, and equity) than to use book values. It is practically difficult to allocate a market value to the firm's retained earnings. The weighted average cost of capital based on the market value weights is typically greater than the weighted average cost of capital based on book value weights, since it is not unusual for preference and equity shares to have market values that are above their book value. Since these sources of long-term funds have higher specific costs than debt, the overall cost of capital normally increases when market value instead of book value weights are used.

Table-3 is based upon market-value weights. Column 2 contains the market value of the firm's capital rather than its book value. The market value of bonds is calculated by multiplying the number of bonds outstanding by each one's current market value. In Table-3, each of the company's bond sells for ₹ 950, and there are 3 crore bonds outstanding, for a total market value of bonds of ₹ 2,850 crore. There are 5 crore shares of preference, each with a market value of ₹ 90, for a total value of ₹ 450 crore. Likewise, there are 10 crore shares of equity, each with a market value of ₹ 600, for a total of ₹ 6,000 crore . By definition retained earnings have no explicit market value, but again, the key to their valuation is taken from equity shares. Since equity shares are selling for 20 per cent more than its book value (₹ 6,000/₹ 5,000), we impute the same increased value to retained earnings, and increase their value by 20 per cent, from ₹ 1,500 crore to ₹ 1,800 crore. Thus, we now have market value weights instead of book value weights.

TABLE-3

Calculating the Weighted—Average Cost of Capital (Market-Value Weights)

(₹ in crore)

Capital Component (1)	*Market Value* (2)	*Market Value Weight* (3)	*Before Tax Cost* (4)	*After Tax Cost* (5)	*Weighted Cost of Capital* (6)
Bonds	₹ 2,850	.26	.10	.06	.0156
Preference Shares	450	.04	.08	.08	.0032
Retained earnings	1,800	.16	.15	.15	.0240
Equity Shares	6,000	.54	.18	.18	.0972
Total	11,100	1.00			.1400

*Tax rate=50%

The remainder of Table-3 has been left the same a Table-2 in order to trace out only the impact of change in weight: Note that when market-value weights are used, higher-cost equity and retained earnings assume a greater role, and lower-cost debt and preference shares assume a smaller role. This has to result in a higher WACC, and so it does, 14.00 per cent as opposed to 13.45 per cent.

Using market-value weights in lieu of book-value weights is dependent upon the availability of current and reliable market price for the firm's securities. If such market price are available, market-value weights may be used.

Book Value Weights Vs. Market-Value Weights

Table-2 is constructed using book-value weights. i.e., the values for the various kinds of capital listed on the position statement, taken from the accounting records ("books") of the firm. Some argue that this is inaccurate, since the book value of capital is not necessarily its current value. These people argue that the cost of capital is used in future-oriented decisions, and to use historical book costs is inaccurate. They suggest that book-value weights be replaced by market-value weights.

TARGET WEIGHTS

Another approach for weighting the various components of a firm's capital structure in order to calculate the weighted average cost of capital is the use of target capital structure weights. If the firm has determined the capital structure they believe most consistent with their goal of owner wealth maximisation, and they are directing their financing towards achievement of this 'optimal' capital structure, then the use of these target capital structure weights may be appropriate. Because of the fluctuations expected in the market value of the capital components, these target weights are typically based upon historic book value rather than market values. Although, in theory, the use of market value weights makes more sense, the practical difficulty associated with their use causes them to be operationally impractical. Target weights based upon historic book values are therefore much more commonly utilised. Often, firms believing that the existing capital structure is optimal, will use existing book value proportions as target capital structure proportions. Unless a firm's existing capital structure significantly differs from the optimal capital structure, the weighted average cost of capital using historic book value weights is not expected to differ greatly from the weighted average cost of capital calculated using capital structure proportions. When one considers the some what approximate nature of these calculations, the choice of weights may not be as critical as was believed initially.

If the optimal capital structure is one which consists of 35 per cent debt, 7.5 per cent preference shares, 15-per cent retained earnings, and 42.5 per cent equity shares, By comparing these target proportions to the actual book value proportions in column 3 of Table-2, it should be clear that the target proportions only differ slightly from the book value proportions. Using the target proportions and the specific costs calculated earlier, the weighted average cost of the capital is calculated in Table-4.

Comparing the weighted average cost of 12.60 per cent to the weighted average cost of 13.45 per cent and 14.00 per cent resulting from the use of historic book value and market value proportions respectively, it can be seen that the use of target proportions results in a lower cost. Of course, such a relationship would be expected since the fact that the target proportions differ from the historic ones implies that a better capital structure exists. The achievement of such a structure would be expected to reduce the firm's weighted average cost of capital since it reflects a more nearly optimal mix of financing.

TABLE-4

Calculating the Weighted—Average Cost of Capital (Target-Value Weights)

(₹ in Crore)

Capital Component (1)	*Book Value (2)*	*Target-Value weights (3)=(2)÷10,00,00,000*	*Before Tax Cost (4)*	*After Tax Cost (5)*	*Weighted Cost of Capital (6)=3×5*
Bonds	₹ 3,500	.35	.10	.06	.0210
Preference Shares	750	.075	.08	.08	.0060
Retained earnings	1,500	.15	.15	.15	.0225
Equity shares	4,250	.425	.18	.18	.0765
Total	₹ 10,000	1.00			.1260

*Tax-rate=50%

MARGINAL WEIGHTS

An alternative to the use of historical weights, based on the firm's current capital structure as measured by either book values or market values or target weights based upon the desired capital structure proportions is to use marginal weights. The use of marginal weights involves weighting the specific costs of various types of financing by the percentage of the total financing expected to be raised via each method. In using historical weights we have assumed that the proportion of each type of financing in the firm's capital structure would remain the same. In using target weights we have assumed that the firm is trying to develop what is believed to be an optimal capital structure reflected by certain desired proportions of capital. In using marginal weights we are concerned with the actual amounts of each type of financing used.

The use of marginal weights is more attuned to the actual process of financing projects. It recognises that the funds actually raised in discrete amounts, using the various sources of long-term funds.

MARGINAL COST OF CAPITAL

The marginal cost of capital is calculated by taking a weighted average of the marginal costs of each component in proportion to the respective amounts of each that the firm will raise. The process is demonstrated in Example-8.

Example-8

A corporation plans to raise ₹ 4,000 crore of new capital as follows:
Current liabilities: ₹ 200 crore at 12% (assume no floatation or service change)
Long-term debt: ₹ 500crore at 10% (floatation costs, 2%)
Preference shares ₹ 300crore, floatation cost (F) estimated at 2%; sold at ₹ 32 per share with a stated dividend of ₹ 2.50

Equity shares: ₹ 3,000 crore, floatation cost (F) estimated at 2.50%, dividend ₹ 4.50 per share; market price ₹ 50 per share, anticipated growth rate of dividend, 12%.

The firm's marginal tax rate is 40%. Determine the cost of each component and the marginal cost of capital.

Solution

Cost of long-term debt:

$$k_i = \frac{I(1-t)}{P(1-F)} = \frac{₹\ 50\ crore(1-.04)}{₹\ 500\ crore(1-.02)} = \frac{₹\ 30\ crore}{₹\ 490\ crore} = 0.0612$$

Cost of preference:

$$k_p = \frac{D_p}{P_p(1-F)} = \frac{₹\ 2.50}{₹\ 32\ (1-0.02)} = \frac{₹\ 2.50}{₹\ 31.36} = 0.0797$$

Cost of new equity

$$k_e = \frac{D_1}{P_0(1-F)} + g = \frac{₹\ 450}{₹\ 50\ (1-.025)} = \frac{₹\ 4.50}{₹\ 48.75} + .12 = .2123$$

Marginal Cost of Capital

(₹ *in Crore*)

	Market Values	*Market Weights*	*After-Tax Cost*	*Weighted After Tax Cost*
Current liabilities	₹ 200	0.050	0.0720	0.0036
Long-term debt	500	0.125	0.0612	0.0077
Preference shares	300	0.075	0.0797	0.0059
New equity	3,000	0.750	0.2123	0.1592
	₹ 4,000	!!!!!!!!!!!!!!Marginal cost of capital=		0.1764

The marginal cost of capital is approximately 17.64%

WEIGHTED MARGINAL COST OF CAPITAL (WMCC)

The weighted average cost of capital may vary at any time depending on the volume of financing the firm plans to raise. As the volume of financing increases, the costs of the various types of financing will increase, thereby raising the firm's weighted average cost of capital. *A schedule or graph relating the firm's weighted average cost of capital to the level of new financing is called weighted marginal cost of capital (WMCC).* These increasing costs are attributable to the fact that suppliers of capital—long-term debt, preference shares and equity shares will require greater returns in the form for the interest, dividends, or growth, in order to compensate them for the increase risk introduced as larger volumes of new financing are incurred. A second factor contributing to the increased cost relates to the use of equity financing. The portion of new financing provided by equity shares will be taken from available retained earnings until exhausted, and then obtained through new equity financing. Since the retained earnings are a less expensive form of equity financing than the sale of new equity shares it should be clear that once retained earnings have been exhausted, the weighted average cost of capital will rise with the addition of more expensive new equity shares. Because firms will utilise all retained earnings financing available prior to selling new equity shares, it is best to view the firm as having three types of capital: (1) long term debt, (2) preference shares and (3) equity shares, which includes both retained earnings and new equity shares financing.

USE OF WMCC FOR DECISION MAKING

The WMCC should be used in conjunction with the firm's available investment opportunities in order to choose investments to be implemented. *As long as a project's internal rate of return is greater than the weighted marginal cost of capital, the project should be accepted.* As a firm increases the amount of money available for investment, in capital projects, the return on the projects will decrease since generally the first project accepted would have the highest return, next project selected would have second highest return, and so on. In other words, the return on investment will decrease as the firm accepts additional projects. At the same time as more projects are accepted, the weighted marginal cost of capital will increase since greater amounts of new financing will be required. The firm would therefore accept projects up to the point where the marginal return on its investment just equals its weighted marginal cost of capital, since beyond that point its investment return will be less than its capital cost.

The WACC concept is valid to use, if all existing projects and proposals of the firm are homogeneous with respect to risk. When this is not the case, the use of the firm's WACC may result in erroneous decisions. When the firm's existing investment projects and proposals differ with respect to risk, reject-or-accept decision criteria must be formulated for each project. Here the capital asset pricing model (CAPM) provides a mean for evaluation.

Having gone to the effort of calculating a company's weighted oost of capital, the finance manager know the cost of all corporate funding, but this is the cost of funding that has already been incurred. *How does this relate to the cost of capital for any upcoming funding that has not yet been obtained? What if a company wants to change its blend of fun ling sources, and how will this impact the cost of capital? What about using it to discount the cash flows from existing projects?*

The trouble with the existing weighted cost of capital is that it reflects the cost of debt and equity only at the time the company obtained it. For example, if a company obtained debt at a fixed interest rate during a period in the past when the prime rate offered by banks for new debt was very high, the resulting cost of capital, which still includes this debt, will be higher than the cost of capital if that debt had been retired and refunded by new debt obtained at current market rates, which are lower. The same issue applies to equity, for the cost of equity can change if the underlying return on risk-free debt has changed, which it does continually. Similarly, a company's beta will change over time as its overall risk profile changes, possibly due to changes in its markets, or internal changes that a ter its mix of business. Accordingly, a company may find that its carefully calculated weighted cost of capital does not bear even a slight resemblance to what the same cost would be if recalculated based on current market conditions, Furthermore, it is also important to determine management's intentions in regard to the new blend of debt and equity, for changes in the proportions of the two will alter the weighted cost of capital. If a significant alteration in the current mix is anticipated, the new proportion should be factored into the weighted cost of capital calculation. For example, management may be forced by creditors or owners to alter the existing proportion of debt and equity. This is most common when a company is closely held, and the owners do not want to invest any more equity in the company, thereby forcing it to resort to debt financing. Alternatively, if the debt to equity ratio is very high, lenders may force the addition of equity in order to reduce the risk of default, which goes up when there is a large amount of interest and principal to pay out of current cash flow. In short, the incremental cost of capital is the most relevant hurdle rate figure when using new funds to pay for new projects.

ALTERNATIVE APPROACH: THE CAPITAL ASSET PRICING MODEL (CAPM) IN CAPITAL BUDGETING

The marginal cost of capital captures the risk position of the firm in its entirety. However, when used as a hurdle rate in the selection of capital projects, it does not reflect the risk of the particular project or projects under consideration. One potential difficulty encountered with the application of conventional methods for risk adjustment is increasing, or racheting upward, the firm's cost of capital. This could come about by accepting projects having risk postures in excess of the firm's risk complexion and thereby increasing the firms risk posture. If this were to happen, the firms marginal cost of capital would increase to reflect the firms new risk structure. If, however, the conventional methods are correctly applied, the firm will also accept projects having a lower risk complexion than the firm overall, and the racheting effect should not take place. Put another way, the average cost of capital represents a strategic rate that management strives to earn on the totality of the operation; management accepts some projects with higher and others with lower risk-return levels, but the average risk-return posture approximates that embodied in the marginal cost of capital.

The capital asset pricing model (CAPM) can also be used to calculate a market-based hurdle rate, risk-adjusted to the project under evaluation (see chapter - 6 for computations). The methodology relates a projects expected returns to an index representing a broad-based measure of economic activity. In Exhibit-3, a project's expected return, $E(R_j)$, and the expected return on the index, $E(R_m)$, are computed based upon different states of the economy and their respective probability of occurrence.

In Table A of Exhibit-3, the returns from the index, R_m, and four projects (*a, b, c,* and *d*) are shown for four possible states of the economy. The probability of each state of the economy is denoted by P_s. All of the forecasted returns (R_m, R_a, R_b, R_c and R_d) and probabilities in Table A represent estimates for single periods for each of the projects and the market index. Estimates may be the result of projections from historical data or simulation. The data in Table A are the results of economic forecasts.

EXHIBIT-3

PROJECT EVALUATION USING CAPM

TABLE A

State of the Economy	P_s	R_m	R_a	R_b	R_c	R_d
Revival (S_1)	0.20	20%	15%	40%	15%	10%
Prosperity (S_2)	0.50	30%	20%	30%	40%	15%
Recession (S_3)	0.20	6%	13%	00%	00%	–6%
Depression (S_4)	0.10	0%	3%	– 30%	00%	– 3%
	1.00					

TABLE B

State of the Economy	P_s	R_m	$P_s \times R_m$	$[R_m - E(R_m)]$	$[R_m - E[R_m]]^2$	$[R_m - E(R_m)]^2 P_s$
S_1	0.20	0.20	0.040	– 0.002	0.000004	0.0000008
S_2	0.50	0.30	0.150	+ 0.098	0.009604	0.004802
S_3	0.20	0.06	0.012	– 0.142	0.020164	0.0040328
S_4	0.10	0.00	0.000	– 0.202	0.040804	0.0040804
		$E(R_m)$	= 0.202			$\sigma_m^2 = 0.0129160$
						$\sigma_m = 0.1136485$

TABLE C

State of	P_s	R_a	$P_s \times R_a$	d_a $R_a - E(R_a)$	d_m $R_m - E(R_m)$	$d_a d_m$	$d_a d_m P_s$
S_1	0.20	0.15	0.030	– 0.009	– 0.002	+ 0.000018	+ 0.0000036
S_2	0.50	0.20	0.100	+ 0.041	+ 0.098	+0.004018	+ 0.0020090
S_3	0.20	0.13	0.026	– 0.029	–0.142	+ 0.004118	+ 0.0008236
S_4	0.10	0.03	0.003	– 0.129	– 0.202	+ 0.026058	+ 0.0026058
		$E(R_a)$ =	0.159				Cov (R_a, R_m) =+ 0.0005442

$$\beta_a = \frac{\text{Cov}(R_a, R_m)}{\sigma_m^2} = \frac{+0.005442}{0.012916} = 0.421$$

TABLE D

$E(R_a) = 0.159$	$\text{Cov}(R_a, R_m) = +\ 0.005442$	$\beta_a = 0.421$
$E(R_b) = 0.20$	$\text{Cov}(R_b, R_m) = +\ 0{,}02062$	$\beta_b = 1.596$
$E(R_c) = 0.23$	$\text{Cov}(R_c, R_m) = +\ 0.019543$	$\beta_c = 1.513$
$E(R_d) = 0.08$	$\text{Cov}(R_d, R_m) = +\ 0.00962$	$\beta_d = 0.745$

Table B is a summary of the calculations needed to obtain the expected return, variance, and standard deviation for the market index. Note that the estimated returns for the market index, R_m, are expressed in decimal form in Table B rather than as percentages as in Table A. The results show that the expected return on the market index is 20.2%, with a standard deviation of 11.36%.

Table C derives the necessary inputs to determine the required return from investment *a*, consistent with its risk characteristics. The results for all four projects are shown in Table D.

Based on the inputs of Table D, it is possible to compute the required return for each project, R_j. In our computation we will assume that the risk–free rate of return, T, is 8%:

		R_j	$E(R_j)$
$R_a =$	0.08 + (0.202 – 0.08)0.421	= 13.14%	15.0%
$R_b =$	0.08 + (0.202 – 0.08)1.596	= 27.47%	20%
$R_c =$	0.08 + (0.202 – 0.08)1.513	= 26.46%	23%
$R_d =$	0.08 + (0.202 – 0.08)0.745	= 17.09%	8%

Using the CAPM approach, only project *A* would be accepted, since its expected return exceeds its required return.

Figure-1 shows where each project falls relative to the market price of risk line [i.e., the security market line (SML)]. Only project *A* falls below the SML, indicating that it offers a rate of return sufficient to compensate for its risk. The other three projects fall above the SML, since their returns are not sufficient to cover the market-related risk.

Several aspect of the capital asset pricing approach illustrated above warrant attention.

1. The possible states of the economy over the life span of the projects must be forecasted. It should be noted that intermediate and long-term forecasting as commonly practiced by business firms have larger variances than do short-term projections.

2. The probabilities related to different states of the economy can be derived from historical data on cyclical behaviour and/or by simulation.

3. Based upon these variables, the forecaster can project returns on the broad-based market index. It will suffice that the market index consists of assets comparable or meaningfully related to the projects. Alternatively, the analysis could have employed

historical data on the relationship between similar projects and the market index to calculate Beta.

FIGURE-1

PROJECT SELECTION USING CAPITAL ASSET PRICING

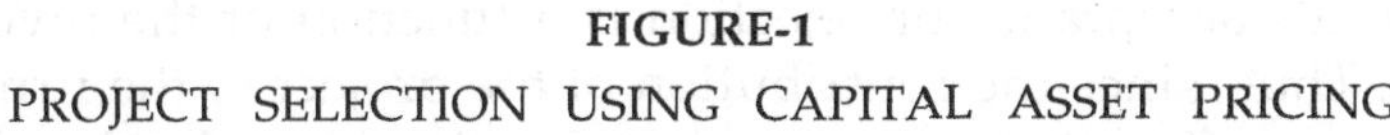

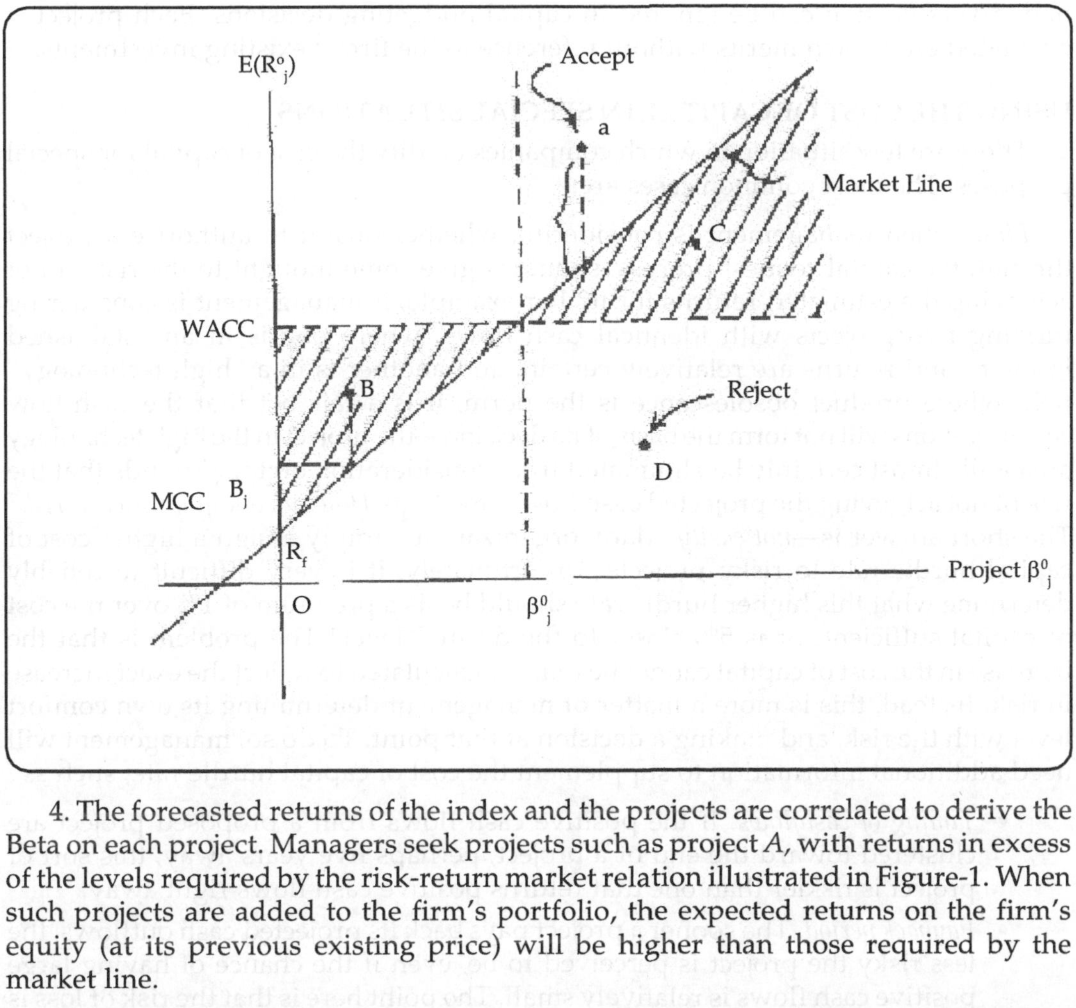

4. The forecasted returns of the index and the projects are correlated to derive the Beta on each project. Managers seek projects such as project *A*, with returns in excess of the levels required by the risk-return market relation illustrated in Figure-1. When such projects are added to the firm's portfolio, the expected returns on the firm's equity (at its previous existing price) will be higher than those required by the market line.

5. In practical implementation, the success of the method hinges on the stability of Beta. Empirical evidence here points to instability when a few time periods are utilised in the calculation, but the variance in Beta tends to decrease as the number of time periods increases.

6. CAPM provides an alternative approach for estimating the firm's cost of equity capital. If we know the Beta of the firm, then the cost of equity capital can be defined using Equation (12):

$$K_e = T + \beta_j\,[E(R_m - T] \qquad (12)$$

Equation (12) may be used to determine the firm's cost of equity capital in place of the dividend valuation model.

7. The project's acceptance or rejection is a function of the investment's own systematic risk. Thus, since the contribution of the project to the firm's variance of equity rate does not affect the accept or reject decision given by the security market line, diversification can be ignored in capital budgeting decisions. Each project is evaluated on its own merits without reference to the firm's existing investments.

USING THE COST OF CAPITAL IN SPECIAL SITUATIONS

There are few situation in which companies modify the cost of capital for special purposes. The most common cases are:

First, when management is considering whether or not to authorise a project through the capital request process, should it give some thought to the risk of not achieving the estimated returns for it? For example, if management is considering funding two projects with identical cash flows, where one is in an established industry and returns are relatively certain, and another is in a "high technology" field where product obsolescence is the norm, it is a fair bet that the cash-flow considerations will not form the basis of its decision—the project in the high technology area will almost certainly be eliminated from consideration on the grounds that the risk of not achieving the projected cash flow is too high. *How can one quantify this risk?* The short answer is—*not easily.* Many organizations simply assign a higher cost of capital hurdle rate to risky projects. Unfortunately, it is very difficult to reliably determine what this higher hurdle rate should be. Is a premium of 1% over the cost of capital sufficient, or is 5% closer to the desired level? The problem is that the increase in the cost of capital cannot be reliably calculated to reflect the exact increase in risk. Instead, this is more a matter of management determining its own comfort level with the risk, and making a decision at that point. To do so, management will need additional information to supplement the cost of capital hurdle rate, such as:

- *Timing of cashflows.* If the positive cash flows from a proposed project are clustered toward the end of a project, perhaps five years away, this sort of project is riskier than one that returns positive cash flows right away.
- *Payback period.* The sooner a project pays back its projected cash outflows, the less risky the project is perceived to be, even if the chance of having large positive cash flows is relatively small. The point here is that the risk of loss is reduced with a quick payback.
- *Level of expected competition.* If a number of competitors are clustering their efforts in the same area, it is a fair bet that there will be price competition when everyone's projects are completed and start to spew new products into the marketplace, resulting in reduced profits for all competitors. One can quantify this risk somewhat by modeling a range of profit scenarios based on a number of different product price points. A further degree of sophistication is to include in the cash-flow analysis the estimated dates at which product

pricing is anticipated to drop, based on when competing projects are estimated to be completed, resulting in high competition.

- *History of previous projects in this area.* If a company has funded a number of projects in the same area, and the majority of them have not done well, this is certainly a consideration in determining the level of project risk. Unless management thinks it can improve the situation by bringing in new project managers or doing something else to improve the probability of success, a project with this type of history should be assigned a higher degree of risk.

Thus, it is not necessary to blindly increase the hurdle rate, as defined by the cost of capital, to evaluate a new capital project, since a higher hurdle rate does not sufficiently define the level of risk. Instead, it is better to provide management with a range of supplemental data that provide more information about the likely level of project riskiness.

Second, special situation in which the cost of capital can be modified is when it is used in a large corporation with multiple divisions that bear no close relationship to one another in terms of the markets they serve, the products they sell, or their methods of obtaining funding. The most common example of this is a conglomerate, which is an assemblage of unrelated businesses that are frequently brought together under one corporate umbrella because they have uniformly high returns on investment, or because they have offsetting cash flows — in other words, one subsidiary may have strong cash flows that match swings in the business cycle, while a fellow subsidiary has cash flows that track the inverse of the business cycle. When combined, the cash flows of the two entities theoretically result in even cash flows at all times, and a reduced level of risk for the conglomerate as a whole. In such situations, the conglomerate is the entity that obtains financing, and this results in a specific cost of capital. However, the levels of risk of all the component subsidiaries may diverge wildly from the overall level of risk, resulting in the application of a conglomerate-wide hurdle rate to all subsidiaries that is either too high or too low for each individual subsidiary. For example, a subsidiary with a very high risk of return on its projects will be subject to a hurdle rate that is compiled from the conglomerate as a whole, which may have been assembled for the express purpose of achieving a very low level of variability in cash flows, which of course results in a low cost of equity, and consequently a low cost of capital. When this happens, nearly all the projects of the risky subsidiary will be approved, since the hurdle rate is so low, without any consideration for the high degree of risk. A probable outcome is that the cash flows from many of these projects will be substandard, resulting in low future performance by this subsidiary. Alternatively, using the same hurdle rate for a different subsidiary with extremely low-risk projects will result in the rejection of some projects that are quite capable of generating an adequate return on investment. Thus, using an average hurdle rate for subsidiaries is not a good idea.

Instead, one can determine an average hurdle rate from information about the competitors in each subsidiary's industry. By doing so, one can compile the cost of capital of the industry, or of selected competitors within each industry, and use that as the hurdle rate for applicable subsidiaries. Though not as accurate as determining the specific cost of capital of the subsidiary (which is not possible, since it has no equity or debt of its own — that is held by the corporate parent), it is still much more accurate than the overall cost of capital of the entire organization. This is the preferred method for calculating the cost of capital of a corporate subsidiary.

Third, special financing facilities at concessional rates may be available for certain projects in particular areas. For project evaluation, in case of special financing, adjustments are to be made in the weighted average cost of capital taking into consideration the amount and maturity of such financing since it may not coincide with the optimal financing mix for the investment. To simplify the calculations in such cases, the NPV is first computed as if no special financing is added to the NPV to compute unadjusted NPV. The formula for the net advantage of special financing (NASF) is:

$$\text{NASF} = \text{Amount of special financing} - \left[\sum_{t=1}^{n} \frac{P_t + Int_t(1-Tc)}{(1+k_d)^t}\right] \tag{13}$$

where P_t and Int_t are the principal and interest payments on the special financing. T_c is the corporate tax rate and k_d is the cost of the company's regular debt.

This approach is particularly easy to use if the investment's risk is the same as the average risk of the company for which the weighted average cost of capital has already been determined. The net advantage of financing is the present value of the difference between the after tax principal and interest payments for special financing and what would be required for regular financing with the same maturity.

To illustrate, assume ABC Co. has a weighted average cost of capital of 15%. The corporate tax rate is 35% and the company can borrow at interest cost of 10%. The company is considering a new project that would cost ₹ 50 crore and would generate year-end cash flows of ₹ 7 crore after tax but before considering interest. The new project would have the same average risk as the company's other projects and would have a 20-year life. The net present value is therefore:

NPV = ₹ 7 crore $PV_{20\ years,}$ 15% - ₹ 50 crore
= 43.8151 crore - ₹ 50 crore
= –₹ 6.1849 crore

The investment is therefore unattractive. However, the government is willing to subsidise the project to the extent of ₹ 40 crore loan with a 7% interest cost and the entire principal due in 10 years. The net advantage of the special financing is ₹ 40 crore, minus the present value of the principal payment and after-tax payments, discounted at the after tax cost of the company's regular debt:

NASF = ₹ 40 crore – ₹ 40 crore x .07 (1 - .35) $PV_{10\ yes,}$ 7%– ₹ 40 crore/1.07^{10}
= ₹ 40 crore – ₹ 12.7829 crore – ₹ 20.3339
= ₹ 6.8832 crore

The NPV with special financing is then:

NPVSF = NPV + NASF

= -₹ 6.1849 crore + ₹ 6.8832 crore

= ₹ 0.6983 crore

If the subsidise loan is raised to ₹ 45 crore, the NASF will be:

NASF = ₹ 45 crore - ₹ 14.3808 crore - ₹ 22.8757 crore

= ₹ 7.7435 crore

The NPV with special financing is then:

NPVSF = - ₹ 6.1849 crore + ₹ 7.7435 crore

= ₹ 1.5586 crore

Thus, the net present value with special financing will increase with the subsidised loan increase from ₹ 40 crore to ₹ 45 crore. The special financing achieves the project viability which was unviable without it by showing a negative NPV of ₹ 6.1849 crore. The subsidised investment help in increase in the shareholders' wealth.

ALTERNATIVE METHODS FOR DEALING WITH FINANCING MIX

There are several formulations of the NPV that recognise the impact of leverage. Some of the alternative methods for dealing with the financing mix are discussed below:

Standard Net Present Value

The alternative methods, to evaluate the investment purposely, should be compared to the standard NPV method. To put everything in comparable term, the NPV method using the WACC is:

$$NPV = \sum_{t=1}^{n} \frac{EBIT_t\,(1 - T_c) + Dep_t}{(1 + k_0)^t} - I_O \quad (14)$$

Where $EBIT_t$ is the earnings before interest and tax in period t, Dep_t is depreciation in period t, T_c is the corporate tax rate, and I_O is the initiate outlay. K_o is the marginal cost of capital, based on the WACC concept. For k_o to remain constant, it is necessary that the debt ratio and risk remain constant over the life of the project. Depreciation is added because it was deducted in arriving at EBIT even though it was not a cash expense.

Arditti-Levy Net Present Value [NPV(AL)]

Arditti-Levy Net Present Value approach, an alternate to the standard NPV, is often used by pubic utilities. NPV(AL) formula is:

$$NPV(AL) = \sum_{t=1}^{n} \frac{(EBIT_t - Int_t)\,(1 - T_c) + Dep_t + Int_t}{(1 + k_{AL})^t} - I_O \quad (15)$$

Where $k_{AL} = w_{kd} / 1-T_c) + (1-w) k_e$. In this equation, $k_d / (1-T_c)$ is the before tax marginal cost of debt for the investment. Int_t is the increase interest expense as a result of the investment, and k_e is the marginal cost of equity for the project.

The difference between the standard NPV and NPV(AL) weighted average cost of capital is that the tax saving from interest is recognised in the numerator rather than denominator. The NPV(AL) method gives the same NPV as the standard NPV if the debt is held at constant percent of value throughout the asset's life.

Public utilities generally aim for NPV of zero, based on the NPV(AL) method. After the estimate of k_{AL}, the rates are set so that k_{AL} is achieved. The public utilities use k_{AL} to evaluate projects.

Adjusted Present Value

To consider interaction between investment and financing decisions, Stewart C. Myers developed adjusted present value (APV) method. The formula for the APV is:

$$APV = \sum_{t=1}^{n} \frac{EBIT_t\ (1-T_c) + Dep_t}{(1+k_u)^t} - I_O + \sum_{t=1}^{n} \frac{T_c\ Int_t}{(1+R_d)^t} \qquad (16)$$

When:

K_u is the required return appropriate an unleveraged investment, and R_d is the interest rate on the corporation's debt.

$$R_d\ (1-T_c) = k_d$$

Though the cash flows discounted in the APV and those of discounted in the NPV(AL) approach are the same but the difference is that one required return is used for the interest tax shield and another is used for other cash flows. The APV avoids the necessity of assuming that debt remains constant percent of value but it requires estimation of the debt ratio for each future period to estimate interest expense in future periods. This may be difficult since interest expense is not limited to debt specifically used to finance the investment, but depends on the investments contribution to the corporation's debt capacity each period. Further, the implied assumption in the model is that debt results in tax shields, ignoring other costs or benefits associated with debt (e.g. agency costs, bankruptcy costs etc. assumed to be unaffected by debt changes).

Equity Residual Net Present Value: NPV(ER)

NPV(ER) method treats financing alternatives by focusing entirely on the cash flows to equity holders, the formula for the NPV(ER) is:

$$NPV(ER) = \sum_{t=1}^{n} \frac{(EBIT_t\ - Int_t)\ (1-T_c) + Dep_t + (D_t - D_{t-1})}{(1+ke)} - (I_O - D_o) \qquad (17)$$

where D_t is the amount of debt supported by the investment at time t, and D_o is the initial amount of debt used to finance the investment.

NPV(ER) is the same as the standard NPV if debt is constant percent of value throughout the asset's life. Further, the NPV(ER) is like the APV as it provides a method for dealing with the changes in the capital structure over the life of the asset. It also provides a method of dealing with differences in contribution to debt capacity between assets.

ILLUSTRATIVE PROBLEMS

1. An issue of 15 per cent irredeemable debenture is currently priced at ₹ 112. Assume the rate of corporate tax is (a) zero and (b) 40 per cent. Calculate the cost of debt.

Solution

The cost of debt is:

(a) $K_d = \dfrac{₹\,15}{₹\,112} = 13.39\%$

(before tax)

(b) k_d (after tax) $= ki\,(1 - t)/₹\ 112$
$= 15(1 - .40)/₹\ 112 = 9/₹\ 112 = 8.04\%$

2. An issue of 12 per cent preference shares, value of ₹ 100.00 has a current shares price of ₹ 68.00 ex-dividend. Compute the cost of these preference shares to the company.

Solution

The cost of these preference shares to the company is:

$$K_p = \frac{₹\ 12}{₹\ 68.002} = 17.65\%$$

3. In 2011, Candy Industries sold preference shares for ₹ 65 per shares. Candy paid a yearly dividend of ₹ 7.60 per share. Candy received ₹ 62 for each share. Determine the cost of the 2011 issue of preference.

Solution

The cost of the Candy is:

$$K_p = \frac{₹\ 7.60}{₹\ 62.00} = 0.1226 = 12.26\%$$

4. The market price of ABC company is ₹ 25.00 per share. If the dividend is ₹ 2.50 and has been growing at an average rate of 4%, determine the cost of equity.

Solution

The cost of equity is determined as follows:

$$K_e = \frac{₹\ 2.50}{₹\ 25.00} + 0.04 = 0.10 + 0.04 = 0.14 = 14.00\%$$

5. XYZ Company is attempting to determine the cost of a new issue of equity shares. The prevailing market price of the firm's equity share is ₹ 64 per share and the flotation cost of the new ordinary share is ₹ 2.50 per share. The firm expects to pay a dividend on the new issue of ₹ 3 at the first years. The dividends paid on the currently outstanding equity over the past six years (i.e., 2006-2011) are given below. The firm maintained a fixed dividend payout from 2006-2011.

Year	*2011*	*2010*	*2009*	*2008*	*2007*	*2006*
Dividend	₹ 2.86	2.75	3.65	2.54	2.43	2.34

Solution

Using a compound interest table, we can find an annual growth to be approximately 4%. The proceeds to the firm are expected to be only ₹ 61.50 since flotation cost of ₹ 2.50 must be paid. The flotation costs of ₹ 2.50 represents 3.91 per cent (i.e. 2.50/₹ 64) of the price of the outstanding equity.

Substituting D_1 = ₹ 3, P_o = ₹ 64, and g = 4 per cent into equation results in a cost of equity, k_r, of 8.69 per cent:

$$K_r = \frac{₹\ 3}{₹\ 64} + .04 = 0.0469 + 0.04 = 0.0869$$

By substituting F = 3.91%, D_1 = ₹ 3.00, Po = ₹ 64, and g = 4 per cent into equation we can find the cost of the new equity, k_e, which is 8.88 per cent.

$$K_r = \frac{₹\ 300}{(₹\ 64.00)(1 - .0391)} + .04 = 0.0488 + 0.04 = 0.0888 = 8.88\%$$

6. Chaman Enterprises currently pays an equity dividend of ₹ 3.50 per share. The price of equity share is ₹ 60. Analysts have forecast that earnings and dividends will glow at an average annual rate of 6.8 per cent for the foreseeable future. (a) What is the marginal cost of retained earnings? (b) What is the marignal cost of new equity if the issuance costs per share are ₹ 3.

Solution

$$\text{(a) } k_r = \frac{D_1}{P_0} + g$$

$$= \frac{₹\ 3.50(1 + 0.068)}{₹\ 60} + 0.068 = 0.13 \text{ or } 13\%$$

$$\text{(b) } k_e = \frac{₹\ 3.50(1 + 0.068)}{₹\ 60 - ₹\ 3} + 0.068 = 0.134 \text{ or } 13.4\%$$

7. Vikas Group of Industries has a beta estimated value of 1.3. The current risk-free rate (short term) is 7.5 per cent and the market risk premium is 8.6 percent. What is the cost of equity capital for Vikas?

Solution

$$k_e = T + \beta (R_m - T)$$
$$= 7.5\% + 1.3 (8.6\%) = 18.7\%$$

8. Amit Equipment has a capital sturcture target of 60 per cent equity, 15 per cent of preference, and 25 per cent of long-term debt. Amit's financial analysts have estimated the marginal, after-tax cost of debt, preference shares, and equity to be 9 percent; 15 per cent, and 18 per cent, respectively. What is weighted marginal cost of capital for Amit Equipment?

Solution

$$k_o = 0.60 (k_e) + 0.15 (k_p) + 0.25 (k_e)$$
$$= 0.60 (18\%) + 0.15 (15\%) + 0.25 (9\%) = 15.3\%$$

9. Assume perfect markets except for corporate taxes at a rate of 50%. PLC is an all-equity company and has cost of equity of 16%. The risk-free rate is 10% and the expected market return is 15%. PLC's management decides to move to a capital structure such that debt-to-equity, in market-value terms, will equal 0.5. At that level, debt is still considered risk free. (a) Estimate the cost of equity for PLC in the revised capital structure, explaining the reasons for the change in equity cost. (b) Estimate the weighted-average cost of capital for PLC and explain the circumstances in which this would be appropriately used as a discount rate for capital investment analysis.

Solution

(a) Using data given $16 = 10 + \beta_E (15–10)$

$$\beta_E = 1.2$$

At present $\beta_E = \beta^*$

with new capital structure,

$$1.2 = \frac{\beta^*}{1 + \frac{1}{2}(1 - .50)}$$

$$\beta^* = 1.5$$

Revised return on equity

$$= 10 + 1.5 (15 - 10) = 17.5\%$$

Risk of equity increases as debt is added to capital structure; this is mitigated to some extent by the tax deductibility of debt interest.

(b) $\text{WACC} = 17.5 \left(\frac{2}{3}\right) + 5 \left(\frac{1}{3}\right) = 13.3\%$

We need to assume that all project appraised have the same level of risk as average risk of projects currently being undertaken; that the company is at its target level of gearing and any new project will be financed by the same mix of debt and equity; and that all cash flows are perpetual as is debt.

10. Wadhwa Enterprises has the following capital structure, which is considers to be optimal under the present and forecasted conditions:

Debt	30%
Equity	70%
Total capital	100%

For the coming year, management expects to realise net income of ₹ 1,05,00,000. The past dividend policy of paying out 50 per cent of earnings will continue. Present commitments from its banker will allow the firm to borrow at a rate of 8 per cent.

The company's tax rate is 40 percent; the current market price of its equity is ₹ 50 per share; its *last* dividend was ₹ 1.85 per share; and its expected constant growth rate is 8 per cent. External equity (new) can be sold at a flotation cost of 15 per cent. The firm has the following investment opportunities for the next period:

Project	*Cost*	*IRR*
A	₹ 50,00,000	12 %
B	15,00,000	11
C	20,00,000	10
D	50,00,000	9

Management asks you to help them determine what projects (if any) should be undertake. You proceed with this analysis by following these steps: (a) Calculate the WACC using both retained earnings and new equity. (b) Which projects should the firm accept? (c) What implicit assumptions about project risk are embodied in this problem? If you learned that Projects A and B were of above-average risk, yet the firm chose the projects which you indicated in part B, how would this affect the situation? (d) The problem stated that the firm pays out 50 per cent of its earnings as dividends. How would the analysis change if the payout ratio were change to 100 percent.

Solution

(a) Cost using retained earnings:

$$k_r = \frac{D_1}{P_0(1-F)} + g = \frac{(₹\ 1.85)(1.08)}{₹\ 50} + 0.08 = .12.0\%$$

$$\text{WACC}_1 = 0.3(8\%)(0.6) + 0.7(12.0\%) = 9.84\%.$$

Cost using new equity.

$$k_r = \frac{D_1}{P_0(1-F)} + g = \frac{(₹\ 1.85)(1.08)}{(₹\ 50)(0.85)} + 0.08 = .12.7\%$$

$$WACC_2 = 0.3(8\%)(0.6) + 0.7\ (12.7\%) = 10.33\%.$$

Break point:

$$\text{Break point} = \frac{₹\ 1{,}05{,}00{,}000}{₹\ 0.7} = ₹\ 75{,}00{,}000$$

(b) We conclude that the firm should definitely undertake projects A and B, assuming that these projects have about "average risk" in relation to the rest of the firm. Now, to evaluate Project C, recognise that one half of its capital would cost 9.84 per cent, while the other half would cost 10.33 per cent. Thus, the cost of the capital required for Project C is 10.09 per cent:

$$0.5(9.84\%) + 0.5(10.33\%) = 10.09\%.$$

Since the cost is greater than Project C's return of 10 per cent, the firm should not accept Project C.

(c) The solution implicitly assumes (1) that all of the projects are equally risky and (2) that these projects are as risky as the firm's existing assets. If the accepted projects (A and B) were of above-average risk, this could raise the company's overall risk, and hence its cost of capital. Taking on these projects could result in a decline in the company's value.

(d) If the payout ratio were lowered to zero, this would shift the break point to the right, from ₹ 75,00,000, to ₹ 1,50,00,000.

$$\text{Break point} = \frac{₹\ 1{,}05{,}00{,}000(1.0)}{₹\ 0.7} = ₹\ 1{,}50{,}00{,}000$$

As the problem is set up, this would make Project C acceptable. If the payout were changed to 100 per cent, the break point would shift to the left, from ₹ 75,00,000 to ₹ 0:

$$\text{Break point} = \frac{₹\ 1{,}05{,}00{,}000(0.0)}{₹\ 0.7} = ₹\ 0$$

The optimal capital budget would still consist of Projects A and B. This assumes that the change in payout would not affect k_e or k_d; however, this assumption may not be correct.

11. A colleague has been taken ill. Your managing director has asked you to take over from the colleague and to provide urgently needed estimates of the discount rate to be used in appraising a large new capital investment. You have been given your colleague's working notes, which you believe to be numerically accurate.

Estimates for the next five years (annual Average)

Stock market total return on equity	16%
Own company dividend yield	7%
Own company share price rise	14%
Standard deviation of total stock market return on equity	10%
Standard deviation of own company total return on equity	20%
Correlation coefficient between total own company return on equity and total stock market return on equity	0.7

Correlation coefficient between total return on the new capital investment and total market return on equity 0.5

Growth rate of own company earnings 12%

Growth rate of own company dividends 11%

Growth rate of own company sales 13%

Risk-free security yield 12%

The company's gearing level (by market values) is 1:2 debt to equity, and after-tax earnings available to equity shareholders in the most recent year were ₹ 54,00,000 of which ₹ 21,40,000 was distributed as ordinary dividends. The company has 10,00,000 issued equity shares which are currently trading on the Stock Exchange at ₹ 32.10. Corporate debt can be assumed to be risk free. The company pays tax at 35% and personal taxation can be ignored.

Estimate the company's weighted average cost of capital using: (a) the dividend valuation model; (b) the capital asset pricing model.

Under what circumstances would these models be expected to produce similar values for the weighted average cost of capital? State clearly any assumptions that you make.

Solution

(i) *Dividend valuation model*

Cost of equity may be estimated using

$$k_e = \frac{D_1}{P} + g$$

Dividend per share is

$$\frac{₹\ 21,40,000}{10,00,000} = ₹\ 2.14$$

Given an 11% growth rate D_1 is 2.14 (1 + 0.11) = 2.375

$$k_e = \frac{2.375}{32.10} + 0.11 = 0.184 \text{ or } 18.4\%$$

Cost of debt (k_d) as corporate debt is assumed to be risk free, is 12%, the risk-free secuirty yield

The after-tax cost is 12(1 − 0.35) = 7.8%.

The weighted average cost of capital (WACC) is the cost of debt after tax x proportion of debt financing + cost of equity x proportion of equity financing.

$$\text{WACC} = 7.8\% \times \frac{1}{3} + 18.4 \times \frac{2}{3} = 14.87\%$$

(ii) *The capital asset pricing model*

Cost of equity may be estimated using

$$E(R_e) = T + [E(R_m) - T]\ \beta_e$$

$$\beta_e = \frac{\sigma e r_{em}}{\sigma m}$$

Where r_{em} is the correlation coefficient between total company returns and total market returns.

$$\beta_e = \frac{20\% \times 0.7}{10\%} = 1.4$$

$$E(R_e) = 12\% + (16\% - 12\%)\ 1.4 = 17.6\%$$

$$k_d = 7.8\% \text{ as in part (i)}$$

$$\text{WACC} = 7.8\% \times \frac{1}{3} + 17.6\% \times \frac{2}{3} = 14.33\%$$

If the stock market is in equilibrium, and the inputs into the models are correctly specified (i.e. the dividend valuation model reflects only systematic risk), then the cost of equity k_e, from the dividend valuation model should approximately equity and expected return on equity $E(R_e)$ of the CAPM.

12. Sunny Computers is not subject to taxation and has calculated its cost of equity and debt capital as follows:

	Total amounts		*Cost*
	Book values (₹ crore)	*Market values (₹ crore)*	*%*
Equity— 10 crore shared issued	500	800	15
Debt— irredeemable debentures	200	200	10

Sunny wishes to invest in a new project which will provide equal expected annual cash flows in perpetuity. Investment in the project can be at several different levels. The project will be financed entirely from the net proceeds of the issue of 3 crore shares (issue costs, ₹ 6 crore) and ₹ 60 crore 10% debentures issued at par (issue costs, ₹ 4 crore). Issue costs will be borne by Sunny at the time that the issue of securities is carried out. The price and method of issuing share are still not determined. Three specific possibilities are under consideration: (a) shares issued at their current market value; (b) share issued to existing shareholders at a discount of 25% from current market value; (c) shares issued to entirely new shareholders at a discount of 25% from current market value.

The financial director estimates that, because of the additional risks involved, undertaking the project will increase the cost of all issued equity to 16% but will not alter the cost of debt. For each of the three possibilities concerning the issue price and method for Sunny's new equity, determine the minimum expected internal rate of return required from the *net* investment in the proposed project if the wealth of the existing shareholders is not to be reduced.

Solution

Sunny Computers

(a) *Equity*

3 crore shares issued at a market price of ₹ 80	₹ 240 crore
Debt	₹ 60 crore
	₹ 300 crore

The gearing is therefore 4/5 equity, 1/5 debt. The same as existing gearing at market values.

Cost of equity

Net proceeds ₹ 234 crore

This has to earn a return of 16% on ₹ 240 crore, i.e. ₹ 38.4 crore

Therefore cost : $\frac{38.4}{234} \times 100 = 16.41\%$

Cost debt

Net proceeds ₹ 56 crore

This has to earn a return of 10% on ₹ 60 crore.

Therefore cost : $\frac{6}{56} \times 100 = 10.7\%$

Therefore cost of capital and minimum required internal rate of return equals:

$$\left(\frac{4}{5}\right) 16.41 \left(\frac{1}{5}\right) 10.70 = 15.27\%$$

(b) The same minimum rate of return, i.e. 15.27%.
Because it is existing shareholders who benefit from discount on new rights issue, the cost of capital for new project will not change.

(c) The amount of equity raised is now 3 crore share at ₹ 60 per share

	₹ 180 crore
New debt	₹ 60 crore
	₹ 240 crore

The price of all equity share will fall after the rights issue to :

$$\left(₹\ 80 \times \frac{10}{13}\right) + \left(₹\ 60 \times \frac{3}{13}\right) = ₹\ 75.40$$

The market value of existing shareholders' shares will fall to ₹ 75.4 crore, with existing projects they will be receiving a 15% return, this gives ₹ 113.10 crore.

The existing shareholder will, however, want 16% return on ₹ 800 crore, i.e. ₹ 128 crore. The new project must therefore make up for this difference, i.e. ₹ 15 crore.

Alternative A

Cost of equity

Net proceeds ₹ 234 crore

This has to earn 16% on

₹ 240 crore i.e.	₹ 38.4 crore
Plus extra 1% on existing equity capital, i.e. ₹ 800 crore × 1%	₹ 8.0 crore
	₹ 46.4 crore

Therefore cost: $\frac{₹\ 46.4}{₹\ 234.0} = 19.83\%$

Therefore overall cost:

$$\left(\frac{4}{5}\right) 19.83 \left(\frac{1}{5}\right) 10.70 = 18\%$$

Alternative B

Share price before fall ₹ 80: cost of capital	15%
Because of higher risk now	16%
Share price falls to ₹ 75.4	

Now need to earn on existing equity to raise price to pre-issue levels:

$$\frac{80.0}{75.40} \times 16\% = 16.98\%$$

Cost of this to new investment:

1.98% × ₹ 754 crore = ₹ 14.9 crore
say = ₹ 15.0 crore

Cost of capital on new project:

Net proceeds ₹ 174 crore	
This has to earn 16% on	
₹ 180 crore, i.e.	₹ 28.8 crore
plus	15 crore
	₹ 43.8 crore

Therefore equity cost:

$$\frac{43.8}{174.00} \times 100 = 25.17\%$$

Cost of debt 10.7%

The new gearing level is:

Equity 13 crore shares at ₹ 75.4	=	₹ 980	(79%)
Debt		₹ 260	(21%)
		₹ 1240	

Therefore overall cost:

(79% × 25.17) + (21% × 10.7) = 22.4%

13. Punjab Agro Instruments is an agricultural equipment specialists manufacturer. The firm's most recent balance sheet along with the market values of each source of financing are represented in Exhibit-1. The management attempts to maintain a relatively constant capital structure mix in terms of the market value of the securities . The most recent earnings per share (2013) was ₹ 5.00, which was twice the earnings per share in 2007, and this represents a growth rate of 12 per cent.* Dividends and the market price of the firm's equity shares have grown at the same rate. The dividend payout ratio, which equals the ratio of equity dividends to earnings available to equity shareholders, has been 50 per cent, and management intends to keep this dividend policy in the future. Six potential investments are being examined by the company for 2014. The costs and the expected internal rate of return for these projects are provided in Exhibit-2. To finance these projects, the company expects to have ₹ 1000 crore from 2014 retained earnings available for reinvestments. Also management has conferred with representatives of merchant banks, and it is believed that the following issues can be sold:

EXHIBIT-1

PUNJAB AGRO INSTRUMENT: MARCH 31, 2013

(₹ in crore)

Total Liabilities and Equity	*Balance Sheet Data*		*Market Value Data*	*Market Value Percentages*
Bonds (8 crore, 12% ₹ 100 par, maturing in 2021)		₹ 800	₹ 720	30.0%
Preference shares 8%, 2 crore shares ₹ 100 par)		200	180	7.5%
Equity shares:				
Par Value (₹ 100				
Shares 6 crore	₹ 600			
Paid-up capital	150			
Earnings Retained	250	1,000	1,500	62.5%
		₹ 2,000	₹ 2,400	100.0

Market price: ₹ 90 for bonds; ₹ 90 per share for preference shares; and ₹ 250 per share for equity shares.

Bonds: An amount not exceeding ₹ 480 crore could be issued in new bonds. The issue, after considering the effect of flotations costs, would have an effective before-tax cost of 12 per cent, if additional debt is required, the effective yield would have to be increased to 12.50%. Tax rate is 40 per cent.

Preference shares: New preference shares could be issued by Punjab Agro with a par value of ₹ 100, paying a ₹ 8.00 annual dividends. The market price of the security is ₹ 90, but ₹ 2.00 per share in flotation costs would be incurred for an issue size of

₹ 210 crore or less. For raising funds in excess of ₹ 210 crore through preference shares at ₹ 90; however, the flotation costs would be ₹ 2.50 per share.

Equity Shares: Equity shares can be sold at the existing ₹ 250 market price, if the issue size is not greater than ₹ 750 crore, a ₹ 4.00 flotation cost would result. For any additional equity issue, the flotation costs will increase to ₹ 4.80.

EXHIBIT-2

PUNJAB AGRO INSTRUMENTS 2014 INVESTMENT OPPORTUNITIES

(*₹ in crore)*

Investment	*Estimated cost*	*Project Internal Rate of Return*
	₹	
A	900	21.0%
B	1,000	17.25%
C	850	20.0%
D	700	17.20%
E	950	19.5%
F	650	17.00%
	5,000	

Solution

Weighted marginal cost of capital can be computed from the market weights presented in Exhibit-1 and the amount of capital available at each cost, we can compute the points at which breaks in the marginal cost will occur. These calculations are presented in Exhibit-3, with the results indicating two breaks in the costs. The increase in the marginal cost of capital arise as the amount of total financing raised reaches (1) ₹ 1,600 crore (cost of debt and equity shares simultaneously increase), and (2) ₹ 2,800 crore cost of preference shares increases and cost of equity shares increases again).

The next step in determining the weighted cost of capital requires computing the individual costs of capital from the various sources of financing. The procedure is presented in Exhibit-4, with the amount of capital and the costs for these funds being provided. For debt, the costs need only to be adjusted by Punjab Agro is marginal income tax rate. For a 40 per cent income tax rate the 12 per cent costs of debt have an effective after-tax cost of 7.20 per cent [(1-.4)12%] and 7.50 per cent [(1-.4) 12.50%], respectively, the cost of preference shares, which equals the dividends relative to the net price per share received by the company, equals 9.09 per cent for the first ₹ 210 crore and 9.14 per cent for any greater amounts. The cost of retained earnings equals the dividend yield (the forthcoming dividend per share/price) plus the expected growth in dividends. An annual compound growth rate of 12 per cent is estimated from the past growth in earnings per share. The dividend yield plus the 12 per cent growth rate produces a 23.20 per cent cost of internally generated equity. The costs of new equity share are easily determined by adjusting the required rate of return of the equity shareholders by the flotation costs in issuing the shares.

EXHIBIT-3

PUNJAB AGRO INSTRUMENT: BREAKS IN MARGINAL COST OF CAPITAL

1. *Debt:*

$$\text{Total financing available with the cheaper debt} = \frac{\text{Total debt available at lower cost}}{\text{percentage of debt financing}}$$

$$= \frac{₹\ 480 \text{ crore}}{.30}$$

$$= ₹\ 1{,}600 \text{ crore}$$

2. *Preference shares:*

$$\text{Total financing available with cheaper preference share} = \frac{\text{Total preference shares available at lower cost}}{\text{Percentage of preference shares}}$$

$$= \frac{₹\ 210 \text{ crore}}{.075}$$

$$= ₹\ 2{,}800 \text{ crore}$$

3. *Equity shares:*

$$\text{Total financing available with retained earnings} = \frac{\text{Total internal retaining earnings available}}{\text{Percentage of retained earnings financing}}$$

$$= \frac{₹\ 100 \text{ crore}}{.625}$$

$$= ₹\ 1{,}600 \text{ crore}$$

$$\text{Total financing available with both internal retained earnings and with cheaper new equity shares} = \frac{\text{Total internal retained earnings plus new equity shares financing}}{\text{Percentage of equity shares financing}}$$

$$= \frac{₹\ 100 \text{ crore} + ₹\ 75 \text{ crore}}{.625}$$

$$= ₹\ 2{,}800 \text{ crore}$$

EXHIBIT-4

PUNJAB AGRO INSTRUMENTS: AMOUNT AND COSTS OF INDIVIDUAL SOURCES

Source	*Amount Available*	*Cost Calculation*
(i) Debt		$\begin{pmatrix}\text{After - tax}\\ \text{cost of debt}\end{pmatrix} = \begin{pmatrix}\text{Before - tax}\\ \text{cost of debt}\end{pmatrix}(1-\text{tax–rate})$
		$k_d = k_i\,(1-t)$
	(a) ₹ 480 crore	$k_d = 12\%\ (1-.40) = 7.20\%$
	(b) Over ₹ 480 crore	$k_d = 12.50\%\ (1-.40) = 7.5\%$
(ii) Preference shares		
		$(\text{Cost of perference shares}) = \dfrac{\text{Dividend per share}}{\text{Market price per share less flotation costs}}$
		$= \dfrac{\text{D}}{\text{MPPS}}\text{-F}$
	(a) ₹ 210 crore	$k_p = \dfrac{₹\ 8.00}{₹\ 90\text{-}₹\ 2.00} = 9.09\%$
	(b) Over ₹ 210 crore	$k_p = \dfrac{₹\ 8.00}{₹\ 90\text{-}₹\ 2.50} = 9.14\%$
(iii) Equity financing		
(A) Retained earnings		
$\text{Cost of Retained earning} = \dfrac{\text{Dividend in one year}}{\text{Market price per share}} + \text{Growth}$		
$k_p = \dfrac{₹\ 25(1+.12)}{₹ 250\text{-}₹ 4} + .12 = 23.20$		
(B) New equity shares		
$\text{Cost of equity shares} = \dfrac{\text{Dividend in one year}}{\text{Market price per share less flotation cost}} + \text{Growth}$		
(a) ₹ 28,00,00,000 $k_e = \dfrac{₹\ 25(1+.12)}{₹ 250\text{-}₹ 4} = 23.38$		
(b) Over ₹ 28,00,00,000 $k_e = \dfrac{₹\ 25(1+.12)}{₹ 250\text{-}₹ 4.80} + .12 = 23.42$		

The weighted marginal cost of capital relative to the funds raised may be determined with this much information. Exhibit-5 presents the necessary calculations. The first portion of the exhibit identifies the weighted marginal cost of capital, provided that the total amount of capital does not exceed ₹ 1,600 crore . The remaining parts of the exhibit reflect the incremental weighted costs as the individual costs increases. For example, the difference between the 17.34 and the 17.54 per cent weighted costs of capital results from the simultaneous increases in the cost of equity. The third weighted cost of capital in Exhibit-5, 17.58 per cent, corresponds to new financing in excess of ₹ 2,800 crore.

The weighted marginal costs of capital in Exhibit–5 are to be used in determining whether to accept any or all of the investment prospects being reviewed by Punjab Agro Instruments. From the ranking of the projects, taken from Exhibit-2, and a comparison of the returns against the weighted costs of capital, given in Exhibit–5, it is evident that Punjab Agro Instrument's optimal capital budget for 2014 is ₹ 2,700 crore. The particular investments that should be included in the budget are projects A, C and E with the return for projects, B, D and F falling short of the weighted cost of capital hurdle rate.

EXHIBIT-5

PUNJAB AGRO INSTRUMENTS: WEIGHTED MARGINAL COST OF !CAPITAL

(₹ in crore)

Source (1)	*Maximum Amount of Capital* (2)	*Proportions* (3)	*Cost of Capital* (4)	*Weighted Cost of Capital* (5)
Weighted marginal Cost of Capital for ₹ 0 – ₹ 1,600 crore Funds Raised				
Bonds	480 (a)	30.0%	7.20%	2.16%
Preference Shares	120 (a)	7.5%	9.09%	0.68%
Equity	1,000 (a)	62.5%	23.20%	14.50%
	₹ 1,600	100.00%		17.34%
Weighted Marginal Cost of Capital for ₹ 1,600 crore - ₹ 2,800 crore Funds Raised				
(1)	(2)	(3)	(4)	(5)
Bonds	840	30.0%	7.50% (b)	2.25%
Preference Shares	210 (a)	7.5%	9.09%	0.68%
Equity	1,750	62.5%	23.38 (b)	14.61%
	₹ 2,800	100.0%		17.54%
Weighted Marginal Cost of Capital for more than ₹ 2,800 crore Funds Raised				
(1)	(2)	(3)	(4)	(5)
Bonds	840	30.0%	7.50% (b)	2.25%
Preference Share	210	7.5%	9.14 (b)	0.69%
Equity	1,750	62.5%	23.42 (c)	14.64%
	₹ 2,800	100.0%		17.58%

(a) Maximum amount without an increase in the cost
(b) Cost increase from the previously weighted cost of capital computation.
(c) Cost of equity for more then ₹ 2,800 crore.

14. Birender Group is developing a new personal computer with an expected life of three year. The investment has a total initial cost of ₹ 283 crore, of which ₹ 106 crore will be provided from internally generated funds, ₹ 90 crore from a right issue and the remainder from a fixed rate term loan at 12% per annum. The proportion represented by the term loan reflects the optimum debt capacity of the company.

Issue costs are estimated at 3.5% for the right issue and 1% for the term loan. Corporate taxes are payable at a rate of 40% on net operating cash flows in the year that the cash flows occur. The treasury bill yield is 9%, the market return is 14% and an appropriate asset beta for the investment is believed to be 1.5. The project net operating cash flows (after tax) are as follows:

Year 1	*Year 2*	*Year 3*
₹ 89 crore	₹ 198 crore	₹ 59 crore

Additionally, a residual value of ₹ 28 crore (after all taxes) is expected at the end of year three.

Estimate the adjusted present value of the investment and recommend whether the investment should be undertaken.

Solution

(a) It is often assumed in capital budgeting that investment decisions can be made independently of financing decisions and that there are no interactions between them. In a world with no taxes, transaction costs or other form of market imperfections, this would be a valid assumption, but where such factors exist the level of gearing, dividend policy and other financing choices are likely to affect shareholder wealth. The adjusted present value technique attempts to directly allow for relevant financing effect by, first of all, estimating the net present value of the project as if it were all—equity financed and then adjusting this 'base case' net present value for all of the individual financing side-effects of the project.

The net present value technique can try to take into account the financing side-effects by an adjustment of the discount rate. However, there is no generally accepted means of accurately making the appropriate adjustment.

(b) An estimate of the base case NPV requires cash flows to be discounted at a rate appropriate to all-equity financing. This rate can be found by using the beta asset value (equals beta equity for an ungeared company) in the capital asset pricing model equation.

$$\text{Discount rate} = T + (E(R_m) - T)\beta$$
$$= 9\% + (14\% - 9\%)\ 1.5 = 16.5\%$$

(The risk-free rate is assumed to be the Treasury Billy yield).

The base case NPV therefore is:

$$\frac{89}{1.165} + \frac{198}{(1.165)^2}\frac{87}{(1.165)^3} - 283 = ₹\ 5.7 \text{ crore}$$

The use of debt has a financing side-effect as interest on debt is a tax allowable expense.

Interest payable per year is ₹ 87 crore × 12% = ₹ 10.44 crore per year.

The tax relief on this interest payment is: ₹ 10.44 crore × 0.4 = ₹ 4.176 crore per year.

The present value of this tax saving for the three years of the project (discounted at the cost of debt) is:

₹ 4.176 crore × 2.4018 = ₹ 10.03 crore

Issue costs are:

₹ 90 crore × 3½% for the right issue	=	₹ 3.15 crore
₹ 87 crore × 1% for the term loan	=	₹ 0.87 crore
		₹ 4.02 crore

The adjusted present value is estimated to be the base case NPV, plus the PV tax shield less the issue costs, or ₹ 0.31 crore.

On the basis of this information, the project has a positive adjusted present value and should therefore be accepted. However, the positive adjusted present value is very small when compared to the size of the project, and further analysis (including sensitivity analysis) is recommended before a final decision is made.

15. ABC Co. is considering a new ₹ 100 crore investment in an auto dye plant. For simplicity, assume the dye plant will last for only two years and will have no salvage value. The plant will generate earnings before interest and tax of ₹ 15 crore a year. ABC maintains debt equal to 75% of value, using the present value of future cash flows to represent value. ABC can borrow at 12%, and its required return on equity is 15%. The tax rate is 35%. Compute the standard NPV, Arditti-Levy Net Present Value (NPV-AL) and the Equity Residual Net Present Value (NPV : ER).

Solution

The weighted average cost of capital = .75 (.12) (1-.35) + .25 (.15)
= .0960

The annual cash flow and standard net present value will be:

Annual cash flow = ₹ 15 crore (1-.35) + ₹ 50 crore
= ₹ 59.75 crore

$$\text{NPV (WACC)} = \frac{₹\ 59.75 \text{ crore}}{1.096} + \frac{₹\ 59.75 \text{ crore}}{1.096} - ₹\ 100$$

= ₹ 4.258 crore

To find the NPV (AL), the amount of debt outstanding each period is computed. Based on the assumption that ABC Co. maintains debt equal to 75% of the present value of future cash flows, the debt and interest payments for each period are shown as:

(₹ in crore)

Year	*0*	*1*	*2*
Cash flow	-₹ 100	59.75	59.75
PV of remaining cash flows k_o = 9.6%	104.26	54.52	0
Debt at end of period	78.19	40.89	0
Interest (12% of debt at the end of previous period	9.38	4.91	

The discount rate and NPV (AL) are then:

k_{AL} = .75(.12) + .25(.15) = .1275

$$\text{NPV (AL)} = \frac{(15-9.38)(1-.35)+50+9.38}{1.1275} + \frac{(15-4.91)(1-.35)+50+4.91}{(1.1275)^2} - \text{IO}$$

$$= \frac{3.65+50+9.38}{1.1275} + \frac{6.56+50+4.91}{(1.1275)^2} - 100$$

= 55.90 + 48.35 - 100 = ₹ 4.25 crore

To find the APV, the cost of capital for unleverage firm is 15 per cent. The APV is then:

$$\text{APV} = \frac{15(1-.35)+50}{1.15} + \frac{15(1-.35)+50}{(1.15)^2} + \frac{.35(9.38)}{(1.12)} + \frac{.35(4.91)}{(1.12)^2} - 100$$

= 51.96 + 45.18 + 2.93 + 2.62!-100

= ₹ 2.69 core

The NPV (ER) is then:

NPV (ER) =

$$\left[\frac{(15-9.38)(1-.35)+50+(40.89-78.19)}{1.15} + \frac{(15-4.91)(1-.35)+50+(0-40.89)}{(1.15)^2} - (100-78.19)\right]$$

$$= \frac{3.65+50-37.30}{1.15} + \frac{6.56+50-40.89}{(1.15)^2} - 21.81$$

= 14.21 + 11.85 - 21.81 = ₹ 4.25 crore.

The justification for the standard NPV is based on the assumption that risk and optimal capital structure are not affected by the investment under consideration and remain constant in future periods. To justify further the standard NPV, it can further be assumed that debt remains a constant percentage of the remaining value of cash flow throughout the life of the assets. If these assumptions hold, the standard NPV equals the NPV(AL) and the NPV (ER). However, the APV is consistent with the standard NPV only with the additional assumption about the relationship between the leveraged and the unleveraged cost of capital. When the assumptions needed to justify the NPV are not met, it is necessary to consider the interactions between the investment and financing decisions of the firm in capital budgeting.

QUESTIONS

1. Why do we calculate a firm's cost of capital? What are the uses and limitations of cost of capital to the financial manager?
2. "The cost of capital is a function of management preferences." Discuss this statement.
3. How do the company's tax rate and the flotation costs associated with a new security issue affect a firm's cost of capital?
4. How can the use of debt increases the value of the firm? In what ways the cost of debt similar to the cost of preference capital? Are there any differences?
5. Do you think a firm's cost of newly issued equity should differ from the cost of existing equity?

6. How would one calculate the cost of preference share? Why do we concern ourselves with the net proceeds from the sale of the share instead of the sale price?
7. How is the cost of retained earnings calculated? What are the practical and theoretical difficulties in estimating this cost?
8. What is the principal criticism of the use of the marginal cost of capital as opposed to the weighted average cost of capital to the book values?
9. It has been repeatedly stated that as long as a firm has a *productive use* for them, earnings should be retained, what do you think the term "productive use" means?
10. Define the expression marginal cost of capital. Why is the marginal cost of capital be the appropriate investment criterion?
11. Why do funds generated by retained earnings appear 'free' when the weighted-average-cost-of-capital approach is used? Is it advisable and theretically correct to have a "different criterion apply if a project were financed with retained earings as apposed to external equity"? Why? What are the long–term profitability implications of such a decision rule?
12. What is the separation principle? Why has this principle been important in capital budgeting? What are the main exceptions to this principle?
13. Differentiate between projects that transfer wealth from one financing source to another, ones that As a finance manager, what is your ethical responsibility when you have an opportunity to transfer wealth from creditors to equity shareholders?created wealth, and ones that do both.
14. Why might special low-cost financing be available for a specific investment but not available for other investments being considered by the firm?
15. Explain the separation principle in regard to wealth created from investing in positive NPV projects versus wealth transferred or created from changing the capital structure (or financing mix).
16. What are the advantages and disadvantages of the equity residual net present rule is comparison to the standard net present value as a capital budgeting tool?
17. Describe the logic underlying the use of target capital structure weights and compare and contrast this approach to the use of historic weights. Recognise situations that may have an investment and financing interaction. How would you calculate an Arditti-Levy net present value that adjusts for a change in the financing mix?
18. Why must dividend payments be included in the analysis in order to calculate a firm's cost of capital?
19. What are the advantages and disadvantages of the adjusted present value in comparison to the standard net present value as a capital budgeting tool?
20. "The standard net present value, Arditti-Levy net present value, and the equity residual net present value are identical if debt is held at a constant proportion of value and cost of capital is estimated using weights the amounts of each components as a percent of value." Do you agree?
21. Other things equal, explain how the following events would affect the firm's average cost of capital: (a) The corporate income tax rate is increased. (b) The firm begins to make substantial new investment in assets that are considerable riskier than the firm's presently owned assets.
22. The weighted average cost of capital may be computed using "book" or "market" weights. Briefly describe how each set of weights is calculated. Compare the advantages

and disadvantages of using book weights rather than market weights in calculating the firm's weighted average cost cost of capital.

23. In terms of risk and required rate of return, why did the market value of the outstanding debt decreases with the announcement of the leveraged buyout? Can wealth be created or transferred with the leveraged buyout?

PROBLEMS

1. MNT Steel is planning to issue a 12 per cent 10-year bond that pays interest annually and has a face value at maturity of ₹ 100.00. MNT will receive ₹ 96.70 per bond and will have a marginal tax rate of 40 per cent. Compute the before and after cost of debt for MNT

Ans.: 12.474%, 7,484%

2. RGF Engineerings are increasing their capital with an issue of preference shares. The issue will be priced at ₹ 60 per share to investors and pay a dividend of ₹ 9.00 per share. The flotation cost is ₹ 4.00 per share for bringing the issue to the market. Compute the cost of the preference issue to the Company.

Ans.: 16.07%

3. Kohinoor Manufacturers provide the following information.

	Balance Sheet Data	*Market Value*
Bonds	₹ 4,00,00,000	₹ 3,60,00,000
Preference shares	1,00,00,000	80,00,000
Ordinary shares	5,00,00,000	7,60,00,000

Compute both historical and market weights for the Kohinoor's capital structure.

4. You are given the following information about the Suman Company:

Tax rate	50%
Cost of equity capital	16%
Market value of equity	₹ 5,00,00,000
Market value of debt	₹ 5,00,00,000
Yield to maturity or debt	8%

The company has an investment opportunity costing ₹ 9,00,00,000 and yielding an annual cash flow after tax of ₹ 10,00,000 in perpetuity. What is the company's weighted average cost of capital?

Ans.: 10%

5. Basic Metals has a target capital structure that consists of 50 per cent long-term debt, 10 per cent preference shares, and 40 per cent equity (internally generated funds or new equity). The firm's marginal tax rate is 40 per cent, and it expects to raise ₹ 3,00,00,000 in new capital this year. New funds can be acquired as follows:

Debt: Any amount of 7-Year, ₹ 1000 par value bonds having a 12 per cent coupon rate can be sold to net the firm ₹ 980 per bond.

Preference Shares: 10 per cent preference shares, ₹ 100 par value can be sold in any amount, with proceeds to the firm being ₹ 95 per share.

Equity Shares: The current market price of the equity share is ₹ 50 per share, the past dividend yield, Do/Po, is 6 per cent, and equity shares can be sold to net the firm ₹ 42 per share. Internally generated fund available are expected to total ₹ 1,00,00,000.

(*a*) Calculate the explicit cost for each source of financing.

(*b*) What is the breaking point in new total financing associated with the exhaustation of internally generated funds?

(*c*) Determine the weighted MCC for each of the two MCC schedule segments.

Ans.: (a) k_d = 7.37% *kp* = 10.53% *kr* = 13.42% *ke* = 14.64%. (b) ₹ 2,50,00,000 (c) MCC_1 = 10.11% MCC_2 = 10.59%

6. The management of Premier Products is considering further expansion. The present capital structure, which is considered optimal, is:

	Book Value	*Market Value*
Debt	₹ 50,00,000	₹ 40,00,000
Preference	₹ 10,00,000	₹ 5,00,000
Equity	₹ 30,00,000	₹ 55,00,000
	₹ 90,00,000	₹ 1,00,00,000

The anticipated opportunities are these : *Debt* can be issued with a 15% before-tax cost. *Preference share* will be of ₹ 100 per value, carry a dividend of 13 per cent, and can be sold to net the firm ₹ 96 per share. The cost of *equity* capital is 18 per cent. (a) If the firm's tax rate is 40 per cent, what is its marginal cost of capital? (b) What happens to its MCC if Premier's marginal tax rate is zero?

Ans.: (a) 14.18% (b) 16.58%

7. Calculate Sandhya Steel's weighted average cost of capital, when you have the following information about the company:

The compare rate on the company's debt is 3.75 per cent. The yield to maturity on this debt is 8%. The annual principal repayment is ₹ 10,00,000. The book value of the company's debt-to-equity ratio is 60 per cent. The same ratio in terms of market weights is 40 per cent. The company's tax rate is 40%. The minimum acceptable rate of return to be equity shareholders to Sandhya is 16 per cent.

Ans.: (12.58%)

8. Bhinder Company's EPS was ₹ 6.50 in 2011 and ₹ 4.42 in 2006. The company pays out 40 per cent of its earnings as dividends, and the equity share sells for ₹ 36. (a) Calculate the past growth rate in earnings. (Hint: This is a 5-year growth period). (b) Calculate the *next* expected dividend per share, D_1. (D_0 = 0.4(₹ 6.50) = ₹ 2.60). Assume that the past growth rate will continue. (c) What is the cost of retained earnings, k_r, for the Bhinder Company?

9. The earnings, dividends, and equity share price of KINO Technologies Inc. are expected to grow at 7 per cent per year in the future. KINO's equity share sells for ₹ 23 per share, its last dividend was ₹ 2.00, and the company will pay a dividend of ₹ 2.14 at the end of the current year. (a) Using the discounted cash flow approach, what is its cost of retained earnings? (b) If the firm's beta is 1.6, the risk-free rate is 9 per cent, and the average return on the market is 13 per cent, what will be the firm's cost of equity using the CAPM approach? (c) If the firm's bonds earn a return of 12 per cent, what will k_e, be using the bond-yield-plus-risk-premium approach? (Hint: Use the midpoint of the risk premium range).

Ans.: (a) 16.3%; (b) 15.4%; (c) 16%.

10. Madhev Electric Company (MEC) uses only debt and equity. It can borrow unlimited amounts at an interest rate of 10 per cent as long as it finances as its target capital structure, which calls for 45 per cent debt and 55 per cent equity. Its last dividend was ₹ 2.00; its expected constant growth rate is 4 per cent; its equity share sells at a price of ₹ 25; and new stock would net the company ₹ 20 per share after flotation costs. MEC's tax rate is 40 per cent, and it expects to have ₹ 10 crore of retained earnings this year. Two projects are available ; Project A has a cost of ₹ 20 crore and a rate of return of 13 per cent, while Project B has a cost of ₹ 12.5 crore and a rate of return of 10 per cent. All of the company's potential equity shares projects are equally risky. (a) What is MEC's cost of equity from newly issued equity? (b) What is MEC's marginal cost of capital, i.e., what WACC cost rate should it use to evaluate capital budgeting projects (these two projects plus any others that might arise during the year, provided the cost of capital schedule remains as it is currently)?

Ans.: (a) k_e = 14.40%; (b) WACC = 10.62%

11. A company's 6 per cent coupon rate, semiannual payments, ₹ 1,000 par value bond which matures in 30 years sells at a price of ₹ 515.16. The company's tax rate 40 per cent. What is the firm's component cost of debt for purposes of calculating the WACC? (Hint: Base your answer on the *nominal* rate).

Ans.: 7.2%

12. Hansa Company's financing plans for next year include the sale of long-term bonds with a 10 per cent coupon. The company believes it can sell the bonds at a price that will provide a yield to maturity of 12 per cent. If its tax rate is 35 per cent, what Hansa's after-tax cost of debt?

Ans.: 7.80%

13. Trivoli Industries plans to issue some ₹ 100 par preference shares with an 11 per cent dividend. The stock is selling on the market for ₹ 97.00, and Trivoli must pay flotation costs of 5 per cent of the market price. What is the cost of the preference share for Trivoli?

Ans.: 11.94%

14. Diwan Company's next expected dividend, D_1, is ₹ 3.18; its growth rate is 6 per cent; and the equity share now sells for ₹ 36. New equity can be sold to net the firm ₹ 32.40 per share. (a) What is Diwan's percentage flotation cost, F? (b) What is Diwan's cost of new equity, k_e?

Ans.: (a) F = 10; (b) k_e = 15.8%

15. ABC Company expects earnings of ₹ 3 crore next year. Its dividend payout ratio is 40 per cent, and its debt/assets ratio is 60 per cent. ABC uses no preference shares. (a) What amount of retained earnings does ABC expect next year? (b) At what amount of financing will there be a break point in the MCC schedule? (c)If ABC can borrow ₹ 1.2 crore at an interest rate of 11 per cent, another 1.2 crore a rate of 12 per cent, and any additional debt at a rate of 13 per cent, at what points will rising debt costs cause breaks in the MCC schedule?

Ans.: (a) ₹ 1.8 crore; (b) ₹ 4.5 crore; (c) Break points (i) ₹ 2 crore; (ii) ₹ 4 crore

16. On January 1, 1998, the total assets of the XYZ Company were ₹ 27 crore. The firm's present capital structure, which follows, is considered to be optimal. Assume that there is no short-term debt.

Long-term debt	₹ 13,50,00,000
Equity	13,50,00,000
Total liabilities	₹ 27,00,00,000

New bonds will have a 10 per cent coupon rate and will be sold at par. Equity share, currently selling at ₹ 60 a share, can be sold to net the company ₹ 54 a share. Shareholders' required rate of return is estimated to be 12 per cent, consisting of a dividend yield of 4 per cent and an expected growth rate of 8 per cent. (The next expected dividend is ₹ 2.40, to ₹ 2.40/₹ 60 = 4%). Retained earnings are estimated to be ₹ 1.35 crore. The corporate tax rate is 40 per cent. Assuming that all asset expansion (gross expenditures for fixed assets plus related working capital) is included in the capital budget, the amount of the capital budget, ignoring depreciation, is ₹ 13.5 crore. (a) To maintain the present capital structure, how much of the capital budget must XYZ finance by equity? (b) How much of the new equity funds needed will be generated internally and externally? (c) Calculate the cost of each of the equity components. (d) At what level of capital expenditure will there be a break in MCC schedule. (e) Calculate the WACC (1) below and (2) above the break in the MCC schedule.

Ans.: (a) ₹ 6,75,00,000; (b) k_r = 12%; k_e = 12/4%; (c) ₹ 2,71,00,000; (e) WACC = 9.1% $WACC_2$ = 9.2%

HINDWIRE INDUSTRIES LIMITED: *A CASE*

Hind Wires Industries Limited was incorporated in 1st October 1947, under the Indian Companies Act 1913 and obtained the Certificate of commencement of business on 19th December, 1947. The objects of the company are to carry on business of manufacturing of steel wires and other wire products. The company has an Industrial licence bearing No. A/1A(7)/N-302/69/LC dated 8.12.69 for manufacture of 15,000 tonnes and C.O.B. Licence No. 8 (76) dated 30.1.76, for manufacture 9,500 metric tonnes of steel wire. The company has total installed capacity for manufacturing 37,000 tonnes of all types of wires. Production of the New Unit under C.O.B. Licence No. IL : 5 No. 8(76) dated 30.1.1976 commenced from March, 1978.

In view of the growing value of business of the company there has been an ever increasing need for augmenting the resources of the company. The need for additional funds arises also on account of continuously rising price of inputs, the higher level of inventories and outstandings despite vigorous controls, replacement of ageing equipment and the commitments to rehabilitate the sick units recently amalgamated with the company. Hind's partial balance sheet is shown in exhibit-1, the asset side of the balance sheet is excluded from the exhibit-1. On January 1, 2013, Mr. Ramesh Chand Gupta, vice president of the company, sought information he wanted to utilise in finalising the firm's capital budget for 2013. He knew that one set of projects required outlays of ₹ 98 crore would provide a rate of return of 25 per cent. A second set of projects required ₹ 92 crore and provide a 22 per cent return. The third set of projects required ₹ 80 crore and expected return were 18 per cent. The fourth set of projects would return 16 per cent and require ₹ 70 crore. Mr. Gupta knew that depreciation shielded funds

EXHIBIT-1

HIND WIRE INDUSTRIES LIMITED PARTIAL BALANCE SHEET MARCH 31, 2013

(₹ in lakhs and percents)

Current liabilities:				
Accounts payable	₹ 40.6			
Taxes payable	30.7			
Current maturity-long-term debt	50.6			
Total current liabilities		₹ 121.9	5.37%	
Long-term debt:				
12.5 bonds, due 2023	304.9		13.43%	
15.0 bonds, due 2025	426.5		18.79%	37.59%
Total long-term debt		₹ 731.4		
Total liabilities:		853.3		
Preference share, 12% par		97.6	4.30%]	4.30%
Net Worth:				
Equity share ₹ 10 par				
12 crore authorised	120		5.29%	
Paid-up capital excess over par	300.5		13.24%	
Reserves for retirement of 'X' plant	350.6		15.44%	58.11%
Retained earnings	548.0		24.14%	
Total net worth		₹ 1319.1		100.00%
Total liabilities and net worth		₹ 2270		

* The per cent figures are based on the sum of all interest bearing debt, preference shares and net worth. Retained earnings exclude additions from earnings in 2012.

would provide ₹ 70 crore; the rest of the funds would have to come from retained earnings and new external financing, Mr. Gupta, being an ardent follower of the company equity share, knew that its current price is ₹ 65.00 per share. Also, in keeping with company policy of paying 60 per cent of earnings in dividends, the company had just paid to shareholders 60 per cent of 2011 net income available to equity shares of ₹ 200 crore.

Just a few days ago, Mr. Gupta had reiterated his previous statements that the company's growth rate was expected to remain at 6 per cent. In talking with representative of an investment banker he found that additional shares of equity could be sold to net the ₹ 59.50 per share. He also learned that bonds similar to the ones currently issued could be sold at par with a coupon rate of 15 per cent. He noticed that the firm's preference share was selling for ₹ 84 a share. Issuing new preference shares would carry flotation cost of 2 per cent at selling price. Mr. Gupta felt that in book value terms, the firm's capital structure was an optimal. The firm's corporate tax rate was 50 per cent. Mr. Gupta was interested in finding the marginal and average cost of capital. In addition, he wanted to know the size of the capital budget.

Solution

Calculating the Component Costs

In calculating component costs, only those components that are expected to provide investors or lenders a return are considered. The appropriate components of financing to be considered are debt, preference, and equity share.

Cost of debt : Cost of debt by applying equation-3:

$$k_d = k_i\ (1\text{-}t)$$

$$k_d = 15(1 - .50) = 7.5\%$$

Cost of Preference shares: Since dividends and selling price is not given, k_p cannot be calculated directly. However, the new preference share could be, for all practical purposes, the same as the existing preference shares and hence would have the same k_p. By using euqation-6, we find that the investor to buy the new preference share, requires a yield or return of:

$$k_p = \frac{D}{(P_p - F)}$$

$$k_p = \frac{12}{84(1-.02)} = 14.58\%$$

Cost of Retained Earnings: Exhibit-1 indicates that the firm has 12 crore equity shares. Dividends per share in 2010, D_o, were

$$D_o = \frac{₹\ 200 \text{ crore} \times 0.60}{12 \text{ crore}} = ₹\ 10 \text{ per share}$$

D_1 then becomes

$$D_1 = D_o\ (1 + g) = ₹\ 10(1 + 0.06) = ₹\ 10.60 \text{ per share}$$

k_r may now be calculating by using equation-9.

$$k_r = \frac{D_1}{P_o} + g$$

$$= \frac{₹\ 10.60}{₹\ 65} + .06 = 22.31\%$$

Cost of External Equity: Cost of external equity is calculated by using equation-11, keeping in mind that $P_o(1-F)$ figures is already provided.

$$k_e = \frac{D_1}{P_o(1-F)} + g$$

$$= \frac{₹\,10.60}{₹\,59.50} + .06 = 23.81\%$$

In calculating both k_r and k_e caution should be exercised in identifying the right D_1 figure to use—these are current period dividends paid at the end of the period.

Component weights

A few remarks are in order on the per cent weights associated with the various permanent financing instruments. First, Mr. Gupta includes the current portion of long-term debt as a permanent source of financing. Second, there is no perceived difference in the two bond issues. Thus all long-term debt amount to ₹ 731.40 crore. Third, equity section shows four entries. There is no financial differences in the entries whether they be called paid-up capital, excess, surplus, reserve, or retained earnings. Thus total equity is ₹ 1319.10 crore. Fourth, the retained earnings figure of ₹ 548 crore does not include 2010 addition to retained earning of ₹ 200 crore—120 crore =₹ 80 crore. The weight are as follows:

Debt	37.59
Preference shares	4.30
Equity shares	58.11

Marginal Cost of Capital

Since the Hind's marginal cost of capital (MCC) is going to shift upward when the firm exhausts internally generated equity and has to utilise external equity, the budget at which this occurs has to be identified—refer to this budget as the break-even budget. It may be calculated as

$$\text{Break-even budget} = \frac{\text{Retained Earnings}}{\text{Equity weight}} + \text{Depreciation}$$

$$= \frac{₹\,80\text{ crore}}{.5811} + 70\text{ crore} = ₹\,207.67\text{ crore}$$

The MCC for any budget amount up to ₹ 207.67 crore is :

Source	*Per cent*	*Cost*	*Contribution*
Debt	37.59	0.0750	2.82
Preference	4.30	0.1458	.63
Equity	58.11	0.2231	12.96
			MCC = 16.41

The equity cost used here is that for retained earnings. The marginal cost of capital for any budget amount in excess of ₹ 207.67 crore is:

Source	*Per cent*	*Cost*	*Contribution*
Debt	27.59	0.0750	2.82
Preference	4.30	.1458	.63
Equity	58.11	0.2381	13.84
			MCC = 17.29

The equity cost used here is that for new equity. The cumulative project amounts are shown below:

Set Number	*Cumulative Investment (₹ in crore)*	*Return (Per cent)*
One	98	25
Two	190	22
Three	270	18
Four	340	16

If it is assumed that the projects within the sets are independent and either all or none within a set would be undertaken, the data in the preceding exhibit indicates that the firm should undertake the first three sets of projects, since return would be in excess of MCC. The returns for the fourth set are 16 per cent, and project in this set should not be undertaken. Thus the firm's capital budget is ₹ 207.67 crore and its MCC is 17.50 per cent.

Average Cost of Capital

The average cost of capital equal to marginal cost of capital for any budget up to ₹ 207.67 crore. Beyond that it slowly increases and approaches MCC. Hind's budget is ₹ 270 crore, of which ₹ 70 crore are financed by depreciation-shielded funds. Thus its equity financing will equal ₹ 200 crore × 0.5811 = ₹ 116.22 crore. Of this amount, retained earnings provide for ₹ 80 crore. Thus equity financing equals ₹ 36.22 crore. The 58.11 per cent equity component may be divided into internal ₹ 80 crore/₹ 200 crore = 18.11 per cent. The average cost of capital for Hind Wires is:

Source	*Per cent*	*Cost*	*Contribution*
Debt	37.59	0.075	2.82
Preference	4.30	.1458	.63
Equity:			
Internal	40.00	0.2231	8.92
External	18.11	.2381	4.31
			ACC = 16.68

The average cost of capital for the Hind Wires is 16.68 per cent. Thus, it can be observed that for any budget up to ₹ 207.67 crore MCC = ACC = 16.41 per cent. For any budget in exess of ₹ 207.67 crore. MCC is 17.29 per cent However, ACC only slowly increases from 16.41per cent and moves toward 16.68 per cent. Thus Hind Wires' optimal capital budget for 2013 is 207.67 crore. It should be allocated over projects in sets one, two, and three, with the returns for projects in set fourth falling short of the weighted cost of capital hurdle rate.

VARUN FERTILISERS: *A CASE*

Tarun Fertilisers Pvt. Ltd., incorporated on 16th June, 1984, was changed to the present one, i.e. Varun Fertilisers Ltd., on 27th July, 1987 and later converted into a public limited company on 20th December, 1987. Engaged in petrochemicals, plastics, fibres, fertilisers, industrial gases etc., the company lays great emphasis on activities to accelerate modernisation of agriculture. Some of the prominent activities, being undertaken in this field, are establishment of green house to demonstrate advantages of high-tech methods for agriculture, propagating Tissue Culture and Bio-fertilisers production in a big way. After a modest beginning in Tissue Culture of Bananas, this year the Company is proposing to sell 60,000 such plants. These activities besides demonstration farms, soil testing and other traditional agricultural expansion activities undertaken by the Company will go a long way in helping the farmers.

The new economic regime, in terms of globalising the national economy has vastly accelerated the growth process. It has unleashed new and exciting investment opportunities. The winds of liberalisation sweeping through the country have perhaps irreversibly changed the way Indian corporations conducted their business both in domestic as well as international market place. These changes resulted in a faster moving economy, rapid industrial growth, booming exports and buoyant exchange reserves. Changing economic environment and all round business activities have compelled restating the principles of corporate governance. In pursuing the objectives of profitability and growth, the corporations should conduct themselves as economic institutions, operating to achieve corporate profits and these should be conditioned by social imperatives and needs, including protection and conservation of ecology and shaping appropriate ethical standards.

Sweeping economic reforms and opening up of economy to foreign investors have considerably changed the old equations. With the advent of multinationals, Indian companies are gearing up to face competition in the domestic market from stronger and more efficient market players. As a result they are finding it increasingly necessary to operate in global terms in order to expand their business beyond the domestic boundaries and also to survive in the local market. Varun Fertilisers has initiated measures to successfully meet these challenges.

The Hon'ble Finance Minister has accorded priority to strengthening the agriculture sector and supporting investments in infrastructure. He has continued the process of tax reforms initiated by the previous Government. The reduction of surcharge on corporate tax and intended changes in the Companies Act are moves in the right direction. However the introduction of Minimum Alternate Tax and reduction in the customs duty on imported Caprolactam is likely to bring pressure on the growth and profitability of the Company. Appropriate representation has been made to the Government of India. At the same time, Varun Fertilisers is also taking appropriate steps to meet the situation arising out of reduction of customs duty on Caprolactam.

The excellent results achieved by the Varun fertilisers during the 2010-11 are reflected in net Profit @ ₹ 206 crores, representing increase of 81% over last year; an all time high turnover of ₹ 1819 crores as against ₹ 1572 crores in the previous year reflecting an increase of 16%; this consists of: 52% (₹ 945.88 crores) from Fertilisers and 48% (₹ 873.12. crores) from Petrochemicals and other Industrial Products. Consequently the Company has been able to revise the dividend substantially from 33% to 40%.

During the period of 9 months from April to December, 2011, all Fertiliser Plants are operating above the installed capacity. Operation of other plants is also satisfactory. The aggregate sales turnover during the 9 months has been ₹ 897 crores as compared to ₹ 802 crores for the same period during the last year. Quantitywise, there has been an appreciable increase in the sale of Caprolactam. As compared to the sale of 18337 MTs. during the 9 month period of the last year, this year the sale of Caprolactam during the corresponding period has been 22774 MTs. recording an increase of 24%. The sale of fertilisers of other products has been satisfactory.

As present, the Varun Fertilisers is considering four projects in a capital expansion programme to utilise the Jetty at Sikka for importing and handling materials like Benzene, Cyclohexanone and other Hydrocarbons in addition to the present import of Amonia Phosphoric Acid for the DAP Plant at Sikka. These facilities when created would enable the company to further improve profitable and commercial utilisation of Jetty at Sikka.

EXHIBIT-1A

SUMMARY OF INFORMATION

(1) State of world (s)	(2) Subjective probability ($*_s$)	(3) Market return (R_{ms})	(4) Proj. #1	(5) Project rates of return Proj. #2	(6) Proj. #3	(7) Proj. #4
s = 1	.1	–.30	–.46	–1.00	–.40	–.40
s = 2	.2	–.10	–.26	–.50	–.20	–.20
s = 3	.3	–.10	–.46	.00	.00	.60
s = 4	.4	–.30	.00	1.00	.70	.00

The Vice-President of Finance has estimated that the firm's weighted average cost of capital (WACC) is 12 per cent. The Economics Staff projected the future course of the market portfolio over the estimated life span of the projects under each of the four states-of-the-world (first three columns in Exhibit-1A); it recommended the use of a risk-free rate of return of 4 per cent. The Finance Department considered the four states-of-the-world with respect to future prospects for real growth in Gross National Product. State 1 represents a relatively serious recession, State 2 is a mild recession, State 3 is a mild recovery and State 4 is a strong recovery. The probabilities of these alternative future states-of-the-world are set forth in column 2 of Exhibit-1A. Estimates of market returns and project rates of return are set forth in the remaining columns. The Finance Department also provided the estimates of project returns conditional on the state-of-the-world (columns 4 through 7 in Exhibit-1A). Each project involves an outlay of approximately ₹ 50,00,000.

Assuming that the projects are independent and that the firm can raise sufficient funds to finance all four projects, which projects would be accepted using the WACC and MPR criteria?

Solution

In Exhibit-2A the data provided by market relationships are utilised to calculate the expected return on the market along with its variance and standard deviation. The probabilities of the future states-of-the-world are multiplied by the associated market returns and their products are summed to obtain the expected market return $E(R_m)$ of 10 per cent.

EXHIBIT-2A

CALCULATION OF MARKET PARAMETERS

(1) P_s	(2) R_m	(3) P_s	(4) $R_m - E(R_m)$	(5) $[R_m - E(R_m)]^2$	(6) $P_s[R_m - E(R_m)]^2$
.1	–.30	–.03	–.40	.16	.016
.2	–.10	–.02	–.20	.04	.008
.3	.10	.03	0	0	0
.4	.30	.12	.20	.04	.016
		$E(R_m) = 10$		Var R_m = .040	σ_m = .20

The expected market return $E(R_m)$ is used in calculating the variance and standard deviation of the market returns. This is shown in columns 4 through 6. The expected return is deducted from the return under each state, and deviations from $E[R_m]$ in column 4 are squared in column 5. In column 6 the squared deviations are multiplied by the probabilities of each expected future state (which appear in column 1). These products are summed to give the variance on the market return. The square root of the variance is its standard deviation.

EXHIBIT-3A

CALCULATION OF EXPECTED !RETURNS AND COVARIANCES FOR THE FOUR HYPOTHETICAL PROJECTS

(1) Project number	(2) P_s	(3) R_i	(4) $P_s R_i$	(5) $[R_i - E(R_i)]$	(6) $[R_m - E(R_m)]$	(7) $[R_i - E(R_i)]$ $[R_m - E(R_m)]$	(8) $P_s[R_i - E(R_i)]$ $[R_m - E(R_m)]$
P1	.1	– .46	– .046	.50	– .40	.200	.0200
	.2	– .26	– .052	– .30	– .20	.060	.0120
	.3	.46	.138	.42	.00	.000	.0000

	.4	.00	.000	.04	.20	−.008	−.0032
			$E(R_1) = .040$				$Cov\ (R_1, R_m) = .0288$
P2	.1	− 1.00	− .10	− 1.20	− .40	.480	.0480
	.2	− .50	− .10	− .70	− .20	.140	.0280
	.3	0	.00	−.20	.00	.000	.0000
	.4	1.00	.40	0.80	.20	.160	.0480
			$E(R_2) = .20$				$Cov\ (R_2, R_m) = .1400$
P3	.1	− .40	− .04	− .60	− .40	.240	.0240
	.2	− .20	− .04	− .40	− .20	.080	.0160
	.3	.00	.00	− .20	.00	.000	.0000
	.4	+ .70	.28	.50	.20	.100	.0400
			$E(R_3) = .20$				$Cov\ (R_3, R_m) = .0800$
P4	.1	− .40	− .04	− .50	− .40	.200	.0200
	.2	− .20	− .04	− .30	− .20	.060	.0120
	.3	.60	.18	.50	.00	.000	.0000
	.4	.00	.00	− .10	.20	−.020	−.0080
			$E(R_4) = .10$				$Cov\ (R_4, R_m) = .0240$

A similar procedure is followed in Exhibit-3A for calculating the expected return and the covariance for each of the four individual projects. The expected return is obtained by multiplying the probability of each state times the associated forecasted return. The deviations of the return under each state from the expected return are next calculated in column 5. The deviations of the market returns from their mean are repeated for convenience. In column 8, the deviations of project returns are multiplied by the deviations of the market returns and by the probability factors to determine the covariance for each of the four projects.

EXHIBIT-4A

CALCULATION OF THE BETAS

$\beta_1 = .0288/.04 = 0.72$

$\beta_2 = .1400/.04 = 3.50$

$\beta_3 = .0800/.04 = 2.00$

$\beta_4 = .0240/.04 = 0.60$

In Exhibit-4A, the beta for each project is calculated as the ratio of its covariance to the variance of the market return, and they are employed in Exhibit-5A to estimate the required return on each project in terms of the market line relationship. The risk-free rate of return is assumed to be 4 per cent and market risk premium of 6 per cent.

EXHIBIT-5A

CALCULATION OF EXCESS RETURNS

(1) *Project number*	*(2)* *Measurement of required return*	*(3)* *Estimated return*	*(4)* *Excess return*
P1	$E(R_1) = .04 + .06(0.72) = .083$	.040	–.043
P2	$E(R_2) = .04 + .06(3.50) = .250$	.200	–.050
P3	$E(R_3) = .04 + .06(2.00) = .160$	.200	.040
P4	$E(R_4) = .04 + .06(0.60) = .076$	.100	.024

Required returns as shown in column 2 of Exhibit 5A are deducted from the estimated returns for each individual project to derive the "excess returns." These relations are depicted graphically in Figure-1A.

FIGURE-1A

APPLICATION OF THE ASSET EXPANSION CRITERION

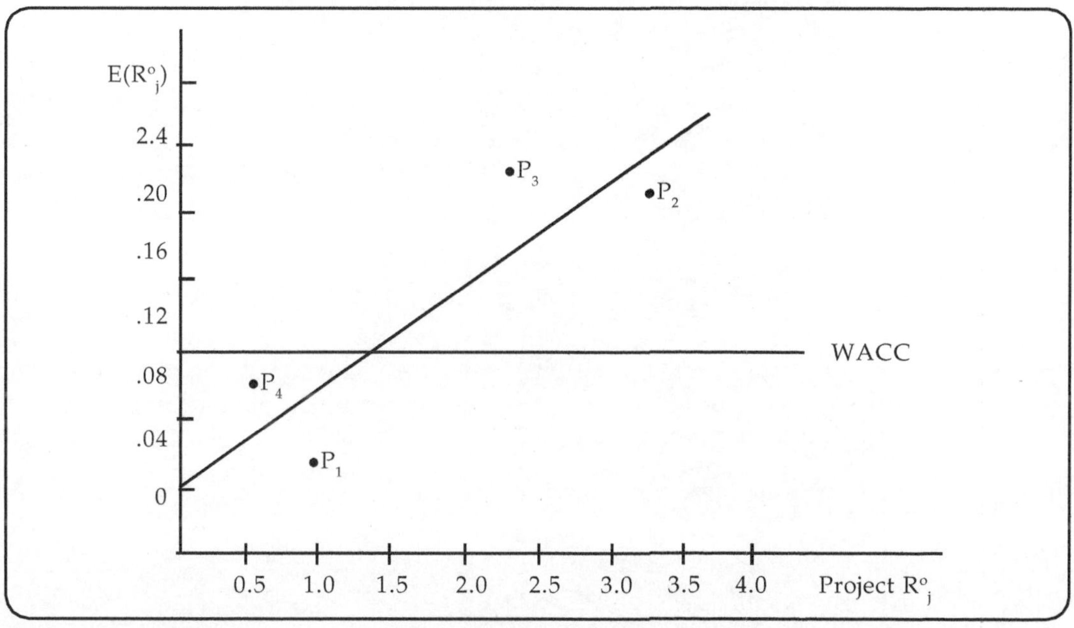

The MPR criterion accepts the projects with positive excess returns which appear above the MPR line. It rejects those with negative excess returns (plotted below the MPR line). The WACC criterion as portrayed in Figure-1A accepts projects with returns above 12 per cent and rejects those with returns less than 12 per cent. The two ceiteria give conflicting results for Project 2 and for Project 4.

It may be argued with justice that projects with different risk are in different risk classes and, therefore, the WACC line cannot be employed in this frame. This emphasises the direct adjustments of the MPR criterion for risk differences and its development of the appropriate return-risk relations for making a determination of whether to accept or reject an individual project.

15

LEVERAGE

INTRODUCTION

Leverage has been defined as the action of a lever and the mechanical advantage gained by it. A lever is defined as the rigid piece that transmits and modifies force or motion when forces are applied at two points and it turns around a third.In finance, the term leverage is used to describe the firm's ability to use fixed-cost assets or funds to magnify the returns to its owners. The financial manager is to find the trade-off between risk-return, an optimal investment-financing mix, to maximise the value of the firm to its shareholders.

This chapter is concerned with the firm's underlying cost factors that affect profits. We will examine, first, the concepts of operating and financial leverage; second, the impact on the firm's earnings stream from combining operating and financial leverage in various degrees. Our immediate tasks are to distinguish between two types of risk that confront the firm and to clarify some other concepts that will be used throughout the financial mix decisions.

RISK

In studying capital budgeting techniques we referred to risk as the likely variability associated with expected revenue streams. As our attention is now focused on the firm's financing decision, it is useful to separate the income-stream variations attributable to (1) the exposure to business risk and (2) its decision to incur financial risk.

BUSINESS RISK *VERSUS* FINANCIAL RISK

Business risk, which is sometimes called operating risk, is the risk associated with the normal day to day operations of the firm. *Financial risk* is created by the use of fixed-cost securities (that is, debt and preference shares). Looking at the two categories in a sources and uses context, business risk represents the chance of loss and variability of return created by a firm's uses of funds. Financial risk is the chance of loss and the variability of the owners return created by a firm's sources of funds.

To clarify this important distinction between business and financial risk, let us examine the income statement of XYZ company in Table-1.

Earnings before interest and taxes can be viewed as the operating profit of the firm that is, the profit of the firm before deducting financing charges and taxes. *Business risk is concerned with earnings before interest and taxes and financial risk is concerned with earnings available to equity share holders. The two components of business risk are* (i) the chance that the firm will fail because of the inability of the assets of the firm to generate a sufficient level of earnings before interest and taxes and (ii) the variability of such earnings. *The two components of financial risk* are (i) the chance that the firm

TABLE-1

XYZ Company
Income Statement For the Year 2010-11

(*₹ in Crore*)

Net Sales	₹ 2,500
Cost of goods sold	1,000
Gross profit	₹ 1,500
Selling expenses	625
Earnings before interest and taxes (EBIT)	₹ 875
Interest	125
Earnings before taxes (EBT)	₹ 750
Income taxes at 40%	300
Earnings after taxes (EAT)	450
Preferred dividends	50
Earnings available to equity shareholders (EATES)	₹ 400
Number of equity shares	100
Earnings per share (EPS)	₹ 4.00

will fail because of the inability to meet interest and/or principal payments on debt, and (ii) the variability of earnings available to equity shareholders caused by fixed financing charges (that is, interest expense and preferred dividends). Putting it another way, this second component of financial risk, is the extent to which earnings available to equity shareholders vary at a greater rate than earnings before interest and taxes. Note that if a firm does not employ debt or preference shares, their will be no financial risk-the total risk of the firm will equal its business risk.

OPERATING LEVERAGE

The operating leverage is the percentage change in pretax profits which will accompany a given percentage change in output and sales. The concept of operating leverage is useful since management is concerned with the effect of changes in output and sales on pretax profit.

Operating leverage arises whenever a firm can expand output and sales without a proportionate increase in costs. Under these circumstances, operating profits, those directly related to the firm's production and sales, increase proportionately more than sales increase. Of course, if output decreases, without an accompanying proportionate decrease in costs, the firm's operating profits shrink proportionately more than the decrease in sales. Looking as it another way, operating leverage is concerned with the *relationship between sales and operating income* (that is, earning before interest and taxes). We may also define operating leverage *as the effect of fixed expenses on the level of net income, the rate of change of net income, and the level of business risk.* Fixed expenses do not include interest charges incurred from the firm's use of debt financing. These costs will be incorporated into the analysis when financial leverage is to be discussed.

FIXED EXPENSES AND THE LEVEL OF NET INCOME

Fixed expenses are necessary in order to make it possible for a firm to experience a net loss. To illustrate this, assume that Mr. R.D. Gupta is going to open a retail firm, which he will call the Gupta Company. After having examined various economic data and having discussions with people in the same line of business, Mr. Gupta arrives at the following estimates for the first year:

(1) Sales will be ₹ 100 crore for the first year. Only one product will be sold and the selling price per unit will be ₹ 100, Mr. Gupta expects to sell 1crore units at ₹ 100 each.

(2) All goods will be purchased ready for sales and Mr. Gupta will pay suppliers ₹ 75 for each unit. Stated alternatively cost of goods sold be 75 per cent of sales.

(3) The fixed assets required will produce an annual depriciation expenses of ₹ 3 crore ; however, these fixed assets will support a sales volume of 3 crore units so that if volume increases in subsequent years no fixed assets will be required (until volume exceeds 3 crore units).

(4) One hundred employees will be needed to operate the business. Total salaries will be ₹ 20 crore per year. Mr. Gupta estimates that these employees can support a sales level upto 2.50 crore units. If sales exceed this amount, then additional employees must be employed.

(5) There are no other expenses and for simplicity only we shall assume that there are no income taxes. Expected net income for the first year is ₹ 2 crore . This amount is derived as shown in Table-2.

TABLE-2

Gupta Company Projected Income Statement For Year One

(₹ in Crore)

Net sale (1 crore units at ₹ 100)	₹ 100
Cost-of goods sold (₹ 75 per unit)	75
Salaries	20
Depreciation	3
Net Income	₹ 2

What if sales are less than 1crore units? If the sales estimate is reduced to 0.75 crore units for example, the revised pro-forma income statement would be as shown in Table-3.

TABLE-3

Gupta Company Projected Income Statement For One Year

(*₹ in Crore)*

Net sales (0.75 crore units at ₹ 100)	₹ 75.00
Cost-of-goods sold (₹ 75 per unit)	56.25
Salaries	20.00
Depreciation	3.00
Net Income	- ₹ 4.25

It would be impossible for the Gupta Company to experience a net loss if all expenses are variable. To illustrate this, let us assume that Mr. Gupta is able to arrange with a department store to supply his product, which the department store will sell for ₹ 100 per unit. The department store will pay for all expenses except cost-of-goods sold and will receive a fee from Mr. Gupta equal to 23 per cent of sales. Let us now examine what happen to net income at various levels of scale. Table-4 shows that if the only expenses were cost-of-goods sold and fees, then the Gupta Company could not experience a net loss.

TABLE-4

(*₹ in Crore)*

Units	*Sales in ₹*	*Cost of goods Sold (₹ 75.00 per unit)*	*Fee Expenses (23% of Sales) ₹*	*Net Income*
1.00 crore	₹ 100	₹ 75.00	₹ 23.00	₹ 2.00
0.75 crore	75	56.25	17.25	1.50
0.50 crore	50	37.50	11.50	1.00
0.10 crore	10	7.50	2.30	2.00
0.05 crore	5	3.75	1.15	0.20
0.00 crore	0	0	0	0.10

The above finding, while not surprising, is very important and deserves further attention. If sales decline, then total expenses will decline by the same proportion; for example, if sales are ₹ 75.00 crore or 25 per cent less than expected level, expenses will be ₹ 73.50crore (98 per cent times ₹ 75.00 crore) which is less ₹ 5.75 crore of the first situation when cost of good (75% of sale price), fixed services (₹ 20.00 crore) and depreciation (₹ 3.00 crore) are considered together. Salaries and depreciation are fixed even if sales are below 1 crore units. These expenses will still be ₹ 23.00 crore. Consequently, at some sales level (below break-even point), the firm will experience a net loss.

Hence, if the variable expense rate is greater than sales, a firm would experience a net loss even with no fixed expenses. However, we would not normally expect a firm to sell product if its selling price is less than its variable expense. On the other hand, a firm might sell a product if its price it greater than its variable expenses but less than its total expenses. The reason is that there would at least be contribution to fixed expenses. Very often the difference between net sales and variable expenses is referred to as *contribution margin* that is, the contribution of net sales to fixed expenses and net income.

FIXED VERSUS VARIABLE EXPENSES

Let us now assume, that Mr. Gupta's employees intends to work on commissions equal to 20 per cent of sales rather than on salaries i.e. work for zero salaries. Assume also that this substitution will not not effect the factors that influence sales. Should Mr. Gupta accept the offer? Despite the reduction in business risk, however, it is not obvious that Mr. Gupta should choose the variable however, it is not obvious that Mr. Gupta should choose the variable salaries alternative. A finance manager cannot consider risk alone. It is always risk in relations to return that is relevant. *Is there anything to be gained from bearing the additional risk?* To answer this question, let us compare the levels of net income for both alternatives for sales levels higher than 1crore units. Table-5 shows income based on 1.25 crore units and 1.50 crore units.

TABLE-5

(₹ in Crore)

	Fixed Salaries	*Variable Salaries*
Net sales (1.25 crore units @ ₹ 100)	₹ 125.00	₹ 125.00
Cost-of-goods sold (75%)	93.75	93.75
Fixed salaries	20.00	—
Variable salaries	—	25.00
Depreciation expense	3.00	3.00
Net income	8.25	3.25
Net sales (1.50crore units @ ₹ 100)	150.00	150.00
Cost of goods sold (75%)	112.50	112.50
Fixed salaries	20.00	—
Variable salaries	—	30.00
Depreciation expenses	3.00	3.00
Net income	14.50	4.50

We can see from Table–5 that fixed expenses can be advantageous to a firm, if sales are above a certain determinable level, the use of fixed expenses will provide a higher level of net income than the use of variable expenses.

INDIFFERENCE POINT

A finance manager, in making a decision regarding the use of fixed versus variable expenses, would certainly want to know the level of sales at which the net incomes under both alternatives would be equal. The procedure used to determine this point is simple and we will use the Gupta Company as an example to illustrate it. The level of net income for each alternative at any level of sales can be determined as follows:

Fixed Salaries

(Net sales–.75 net sales)–₹ 23.00 crore = Net income

Variable Salaries

(Net sales–.95 net sales)–₹ 3 crore = Net income

Setting the left hand side of the two equations equal to each other and solving for net sales will give the level of net sales at which the level of net income under each alternative will be equal. To demonstrate:

Net sales–.75 Net sales–₹ 23.00 crore = Net sales–.95 Net sales–₹ 3 crore

.20 Net sales=₹ 20 crore

Net sales = 100 crore

To check the answer:

(₹ in Crore)

	Fixed Salaries	*Variable Salaries*
Net sales	₹ 100	₹ 100
Cost-of-goods sold	75	75
Fixed salaries	20	—
variable salaries	—	20
Depreciation expense	3	3
Net income	2	2

Thus, it can be noted that the fixed salaries alternative will provide a higher level of net income at any sales level above ₹ 100 crore, while at any sales below ₹ 100 crore net income will be higher under the variable salaries alterantive.

FIXED EXPENSES AND THE RATE OF CHANGE OF NET INCOME

In analysing the extent to which fixed expenses should be employed, manager must also consider the effect that fixed expenses can have on the rate of change of net income over times. To illustrate this important point. We will use a more convenient example of a Jain Company rather than of Gupta Company.

Assume that the Jain Company sold 1 crore units during 2012-13 at a price of ₹ 100 per unit. All expenses were variable and were equal to ₹ 90 per unit. Table-6 shows the 2012-13 income statement of the Jain Company, it is estimated that sales can be 50 per cent higher (1.50 crore units) or 50 per cent lower (0.50 crore units) during 2013-14. If sales are 50 per cent higher, net income will be ₹ 150 crore which is 50 per cent higher than the level of net income earned in 2012-13. If sales are 50 per cent lower, net income will be ₹ 50 crore, which is 50 per cent lower than the level of net income earned in 2012-13. The same rate of change for sales and net income is due to the fact that the firm has only variable expenses. To generalise, *if a firm has only variable expenses, the rate of change of net income will always be identical to the rate of change of sales.*

TABLE-6

Jain Company
Income Statement (2012-13)

Net sales	₹ 100 Crore
Expenses	₹ 90 Crore
Net Income	₹ 10 Crore

Let us now assume that on April 1, 2012, the Jain Company installed a machine that created fixed expenses of ₹ 10 crore per year but reduced variable expenses to ₹ 75 per unit. The revised income statement for 2012-13 is shown in Table -7.

TABLE-7

Jain Company
Income Statement
(2012-13)

Net sales	₹ 100 Crore
Variable expenses	₹ 75 Crore
Fixed expenses	₹ 10 Crore
Net Income	₹ 15 Crore

The firm has achieved a higher level of net income by substituting fixed expenses for variable expenses. However the breakeven point is 0.40 crore units versus zero units of all the variable expense. The firm has increased the level of income but has also increased the level of business risk. What will happen to the level of income in 2013-14 if sales increases or decreases by 50 per cent from 2012-13's level. Table-8 shows proforma income statements.

TABLE-8
Jain Company
Pro-forma Income Statement
2013-14

Net Sales	50.00	150.00
Variable expenses (75%)	37.50	112.50
Fixed expenses	10.00	10.00
Net Income	₹ 2.50	₹ 27.50

If sales increases by 50 per cent, net income will increase by 83.3 per cent (increase in net income of ₹ 12.50 crore in 2013-14 divided by net income of ₹ 15.00 crore in 2012-13). If sales decline by 50 per cent then net income will decline by 83.3 per cent (a decrease of ₹ 12.50 crore in net income divided by net income of ₹ 15.00 crore in 2012-13). The rate of change in net income is greater than the change in net sales and this will always be the case when a firm has fixed expenses. *In other words, given the existence of fixed expenses, if sales are growing at a certain rate, income will grow at a greater rate, the use of fixed expenses creates the opportunity to magnify the rate of growth in net income. On the other hand, if sales are declining by a certain rate, income will decline at a greater rate.*

To continue, let us assume that sales for the Jain company again increase by 50 per cent (to 2.25 crore units). What sill happen to net income in 2014-15, if sales increased further by 50 percent ? The pro-forma income statement for the 2014-15 is shown in Table-9.

TABLE-9

Jain Company
Pro-forma Income Statement
20014-15

(₹ in Crore)

Net sales	225.00
Variable expenses (75%)	168.70
Fixed expenses	10.00
Net income	46.25

With net sales further increase by 50 per cent in 2014-15, net income will increase by 68.2 per cent (₹ 18.75/₹ 27.50). Note that net income will increase at a greater rate than sales but at a lower rate than the rate of growth in net income in 2013-14 (that is, 68.2 per cent versus 83.3 per cent). This diminution is due to the fact that *the degree of operating leverage (DOL) declines as the level of sales moves further from the breakeven point*. The *degree of operating leverage is defined as the percentage change in net income that will be produced by each one per cent change in sales at a given level of sales*. For example, at a sales level of ₹ 100 crore for the Jain Company, the degree of operating leverage is 1.67. A change in sales from the ₹ 100 crore level will produce a proportionate change in net income 1.67 times as large; if sales change by 10 per cent, net income will change by 16.7 per cent (1.67 times 10 per cent).

MEASURING THE DEGREE OF OPERATING LEVERAGE (DOL)

To calculate the degree of operating leverage (DOL) at any level, we calculate the rate of change in net income for all per cent change in sales. The degree of operating leverage for the Jain Company at a sales level of ₹ 100 crore is calculated as follows:

	–1%	Given	+1%
Net sales	99.00	100.00	101.00
Variable expenses	74.25	75.00	75.75

Fixed expenses	10.00	10.00	10.00
Net income	₹ 14.75	15.00	₹ 15.25
	- ₹ 0.25 crore / ₹ 15.00 crore = - 1.67%		₹ 0.25 crore / ₹ 15.00 crore + 1.67%

At sales level of ₹ 150 crore for the Jain Company, the degree of operating leverage is calculated as follows:

	–1%	Given	+1%
Net sales	₹ 148.500	₹ 150.000	₹ 151.500
Variable expenses	111.375	112.500	113.625
Fixed expenses	10.000	10.000	10.000
Net income	₹ 27.125	₹ 27.500	₹ 27.875
	– ₹ 0.375 / ₹ 27.50 = – 1.36%		₹ 0.375 / ₹ 27.50 = + 1.36%

The degree of operating leverage at a sales level of ₹ 150 crore is 1.36, which means that any percentage change in sales from this level will produce a change in net income 1.36 times as large.

Many analysts prefer to rely on the following formula to calculate the degree of operating leverage:

$$\text{DOL} = \frac{\text{Q (SPPU–VEPU)}}{\text{Q (SPPU–VEPU) – FE}}$$

Where:

DOL = Degree of operating leverage
Q = Volume in units
SPPU = Selling price per unit
VEPU = Variable expenses per unit
FE = Total fixed expenses.

We will illustrate this formula by calculating the degree of operating leverage at a sales level, of 1,00,000 units for the Jain Company:

$$\text{DOL} = \frac{\text{1 crore units (₹ 100.00-₹ 75.00)}}{\text{1 crore units (₹ 100.00—₹ 75.00 crore)-₹ 10.00 crore}} = 1.67$$

Implications

The above computations indicate that the degree of operating leverage will be different at each sales level. It is highest near the firm's break-even level of sales. The degree of operating leverage will change at each sales level if the firm's break-even point changes. The factors that affect a firm's break-even point can also affect the degree of operating leverage at each sales level. Recall that these factors are: (1) selling price per unit (2) variable expenses per unit, (3) total expenses, and (4) a combination of the preceding three factors.

An understanding of the operating leverage concept can assist the manager in production planning. For example, the company may have the opportunity to change its cost structure by introducing labour-saving machinery and thereby increasing fixed capital costs and reducing variable labour costs. This rise in fixed costs and decline in variable costs will increase DOL. In this case, a financial manager would want to evaluate the probability that sales will be high so that the firm can enjoy the increase earnings of increased DOL—or that sales will be low in which case the higher fixed costs and higher leverage would be disadvantageous. The greater the likelihood of high sales, the more attractive will be the shift to a higher DOL (higher fixed cost and lower variable cost) method of production.

Operating leverage, is often incorrectly used as a synonym for "business risk." *Business risk refers to the uncertainty or variability of the firm's EBIT.* A company with a higher unpredictable EBIT is regarded as having high business risk. It is true that the greater is the DOL, the more sensitive is EBIT to a given change in unit sales and that, everything else being equal, a higher DOL means higher business risk. But *risk also depends on two other factors; the variability of the firm's sales and the variability of the firm's cost and price structure.* Let's examine these two other factors.

Assume first that output price and the company's cost structure are known. The DOL, indicates how EBIT will change with sales: but to evaluate the variability of EBIT (the company's risk), we must also know something about the variability of sales. A company with large fixed and low variable costs will have large DOL, but it may have extremely stable revenue and consequently a stable EBIT and low risk. Conversely, a firm with low fixed costs and high variable costs, and therefore a low DOL, may have very unpredictable sales and highly unpredictable or variable EBIT—for example, a construction firm with most of its costs being wages, material purchases, and equipment rentals.

EBIT can vary not only because sales fluctuate but also because of change in the company's output price and unit costs. Indeed, unit sales might remain fixed while EBIT gyrates widely because of cost or price variations. Notice also that with prices and costs uncertain, DOL is uncertain since DOL is defined in term of SPPU, FE, and VEPU. In such cases, the use of DOL in evaluating business risk is some what limited.

The main point here is that DOL is only one measure that can be useful in some situations for determining the behaviour of EBIT. The analysis must also examine sales variability, and in many instances must take into account uncertainty regarding output, price and cost structure.

FINANCIAL LEVERAGE

Financial leverage is defined as *the effect of fixed cost securities (debt and preference shares) on the level of EPS, the rate of change of EPS overtime, and financial risk.* Financial leverage is created when the firm finances with sources of capital that have fixed charges that must be met. Since financial leverage is involved with financing increments of assets with debt instead of equity, leverage is also sometimes called "trading on the equity" because the existence of equity permits the incremental issuance of low-cost debt—that is the low-cost relative to equity.

The object of using financial leverage is to finance incremental asset acquisition with relatively cheap debt and thereby magnify the returns to the equity owners. However, increased leverage reduces commercial flexibility and increases the probability of financial distress. Choosing the appropriate level of debt involves a trade-off among these operating factors. The optium debt level is that which maximises the total value of the firm, equity and debt together.

FIXED COST SECURITIES AND EPS

To illustrate the effect of fixed cost securities on EPS, suppose Rama Watch Company with long term capitalisation of ₹ 10,000 crore, consisting entirely of equity, wishes to raise another ₹ 5000 crore for expansion through one of three possible financing plans. The company may finance with (1) all debt, at 12 per cent interest; (2) all preference shares 8 per cent dividend rate: or (3) all equity shares. Present annual earnings before interest and taxes (EBIT) are ₹ 4,000 crore, the income tax rate is 50 per cent, and 100 crore shares of equity are presently issued new equity shares can be sold at ₹ 100 per share under financing option 3, i.e., 50 crore additional shares of equity. The expansion plan in expected to increase earnings before interest and taxes to ₹ 4,000 crore.

Let us now analyse the effect of each alternative on earnings after taxes (EAT), earnings available to equity shareholders (EATES) and earning pershare (EPS) for the hypothetical level of EBIT. Calculation of earnings per share under three financing alternatives are presented in Table-10.

TABLE-10

(₹ in crore)

	Debt	*Preference*	*Equity*
Earnings before interest and taxes (EBIT)	₹ 4,000	₹ 4,000	₹ 4,000
Interest (I)	600	—	—
Earnings before taxes (EBT)	₹ 3,400	₹ 4,000	₹ 4,000
Income taxes at 40% (T)	1,360	1,600	1,600
Earnings after taxes (EAT)	₹ 2,040	₹ 2,400	₹ 2,400
Preferred dividends	—	400	—
Earnings available to equity shareholders (EATES)	₹ 2,040	₹ 2,000	₹ 2,400
Number of equity shares	100 crore	100crore	150crore
Earnings per share (EPS)	₹ 20.40	₹ 20.00	₹ 16.00

Table-10 contain the desired calculations if EBIT were ₹ 4,000 crore. We can see that the debt alternative produces the lowest level of earnings after taxes but the highest level of EPS. The preference alternative produces a level of the lowest level of earnings available to equity shareholders. The equity alternative produces the highest level of earnings available to equity holders but the lowest level of EPS.

FIXED-RUPEE COST VERSUS FIXED-PERCENTAGE DILUTION

Will debt and preference always provide a higher level of EPS than equity. If so, why? If not, why not? To answer these important questions we will leave the Rama Watch Company and establish a more convenient example. Assume that R.C. Mehra opened a business that reported EBIT and EPS of ₹ 2,000 crore and ₹ 10 respectively for the first year. The income tax rate is 50 per cent. There is no debt or preference shares issued and there are 100 crore shares of equity which are all owned by Mr. Mehra, who has an opportunity to expand his business. The expansion will cost ₹ 5,000 crore and is expected to increase EBIT by ₹ 1,600 crore to ₹ 3,600 crore. He can either borrow the funds at 12 per cent or sell equity shares to a group of investors who are willing to supply ₹ 5,000 crore for 50 per cent ownership (that is, there would be 200 crore shares of equity outstanding and Mr. Mehra and the group of investors would each own 100 crore shares).

If equity shares are issued and earnings before interest and taxes are ₹ 3,600 crore, earnings available to equity shareholders (EATES) will be ₹ 1,800 crore and EPS will be ₹ 9.00. The new suppliers of capital would own 50 per cent of the equity shares and would be entitled to 50 per cent of earnings available to equity shareholders. But what if earnings before interest and taxes (EBIT) varies (see Table-11).

TABLE-11

(₹ in crore)

EBIT	*EATES*	*EPS*	*Suppliers % Shares of EATES*
₹	₹	₹	
0	0	0	50
200	100	.50	50
1,000	500	2.50	50
2,000	1,000	5.00	50
4,000	2,000	10.00	50
5,000	2,500	12.50	50

No matter what the level of earnings available to equity shareholders, the new suppliers' proportionate share is 50 per cent. Note the new equity share are entitled to a fixed proportionate share of the total amount of earnings and not just a proportionate share of the incremental earnings with the new funds.

To generalise when a firm issues equity shares, the new shares are entitled to a fixed proportionate share of all the earnings available to equity shareholders. This proportionate share can be determined as follows:

$$\text{Fixed proportionate share owned by new shares of equity} = \frac{\text{Number of new shares of equity}}{\text{Existing shares + New Shares}}$$

$$= \frac{\text{Number of new shares of equity}}{\text{Total number of equity shares}}$$

For example, if a firm has 8 crore shares and issues 1crore new shares, the new shares would be entitled, to 11.1 per cent (1 crore shares/9 crore shares) of earnings available to equity shareholders. This fixed proportion will always be 11.1 per cent lower than it would have been had the new shares not been issued. For example, if the firm had an EPS level of ₹ 10 prior to the issue, the new shares would dilute EPS by ₹ 1.11 (11.1 per cent times ₹ 10) to ₹ 8.89.

To continue if 12 per cent debt is issued and EBIT is ₹ 3,600 crore , earnings available to equity share holders will be 1,500 . EPS will be ₹ 15 (versus an EPS of ₹ 9 produced by the equity alternative at an earnings before interest and taxes level of ₹ 3,600 crore). But what if earnings before interest and taxes (EBIT) is not ₹ 3,600 crore ? Let us calculate EPS under the debt alternative for each of the EBIT levels assumed in Table-11. Table-12 gives these calculations. No matter what the level of earnings before interest and taxes, the suppliers of capital are entitled to interest of ₹ 600 crore.

TABLE-12

EBIT	*Interest Expense*	*EATES**	*EPS*
!!0	₹ 600 crore	-₹ 600 crore	-₹ 6.00
200	600	-400	-4.00
1,000	600	200	2.00
2,000	600	700	7.00
4,000	600	1,700	17.00
5,000	600	2,200	22.00

*The negative earnings available to equity shareholders figures and the negative EPS figures the tax shield that the loss would create.

Let us now compare in Table-13 the levels of EPS produced by each alternative.

TABLE-13

EBIT	*EPS-Equity*	*EPS-Debt*
₹ 0	₹ 0	-₹ 6.00
200	.50	- 4.00
1,000	2.50	2.00
2,000	5.00	7.00
4,000	10.00	17.00
5,000	12.50	22.00

At low levels of earnings before interest and taxes the equity alternative produces a higher level of EPS, but at high levels, the debt alternative produces a higher level of EPS. The reason is that the *equity creates a percentage dilution and debt is a fixed-cost security*. That is, debt requires a fixed ₹ amount.)We should note that preference shares also requires a fixed ₹ amount).

FINANCIAL LEVERAGE AND THE RATE OF CHANGE OF EPS

The use of fixed cost securities can also effect the rate of change of EPS overtime. If earnings before interest and taxes is changing and a firm is employing fixed cost securities, then EPS will change at a greater rate than EBIT. To illustrate this point, let us take the following case of the Gold Star Company.

1. Earnings before interest and taxes for the firm's first five years of operations are estimated to be as follows:

(*₹ in crore)*

Periods	*Earning Before Interest and Taxes*
Year 1	₹ 2500
Year 2	3250
Year 3	4500
Year 4	5400
Year 5	6000

2. External permanent capital of ₹ 10,000 crore is needed immediately. This amount will be sufficient to support operations for the first five years.

3. The firm intends to issue no preference shares.

4. The income tax rate is 40 per cent.

Let us initially assume that the firm decides to finance 100 per cent with equity and issue 40 crore shares in order to raise the desired amount. Given the above estimate, we can calculate the estimates of EPS for the five-year period as follows:

Periods	*EAT*	*EPS*
Year 1	₹ 1,500 crore	₹ 37.50
Year 2	1,950	48.75
Year 3	2,750	67.50
Year 4	3,240	81.00
Year 5	3,600	90.00

Let us now compare the annual rates of growth for the estimated levels of earnings before interest and taxes (EBIT) and EPS.

Periods	*EBIT*	*EPS*
Year 1	—	—
Year 2	30.00%	30.00%
Year 3	38.46%	38.46%
Year 4	20.00%	20.00%
Year 5	11.11%	11.11%

The growth rates are identical. This will always be the case when a firm does not employ financial leverage (that is fixed cost securities). More specifically, if a firm does not use fixed cost-securities then a given percentage change in EBIT will produce an identical percentage change in EPS.

To continue, let us assume that instead of issuing 40 crore shares, the Gold Star Company decides to issue 20 crore shares and to borrow ₹ 5000 crore at 12 per cent. We will assume that no principal payments will be made during the five-year period. The EPS estimates for this alternative can be calculated as shown in Table-14.

TABLE-14

Period	*Earnings before Interest and Taxes*	*–Interest =*	*Earnings before Taxes*	*–Taxes*	*Earnings after / taxes and Earnings Available to Equity Shareholders*	*Number of Share*	*=EPS*
1	2	3	4=(2)–(3)	5	6=(4)–(5)	7	8=(6)÷(7)
	₹	₹	₹	₹	₹		₹
!Year 1	2,500 crore-	600crore=	1,900crore -	760crore =	1,140 crore ÷	20 crore =	57.00
!Year 2	3,250 -	600 =	2,650 -	1,060 =	1,590 ÷	20crore	=79.50
!Year 3	4,500 -	600 =	3,900 -	1,560 =	2,340 ÷	20crore =	117.00
!Year 4	5,400 -	600=	4,800 -	1,920 =	2,880 ÷	20crore =	144.00
!Year 5	6,000 -	600 =	5,400 -	2,160 =	3,240 ÷	20crore =	162.00

Let us now calculate and compare the rates of growth for earnings before interest and taxes (EBIT) and EPS for this financing alternative:

Periods	*EBIT*	*EPS*
Year 1	—	—
Year 2	30.00%	39.47%
Year 3	38.46%	47.17%
Year 4	20.00%	23.08%
Year 5	11.11%	12.50%

We can see that EPS will grow at a greater rate than earnings before interest and taxes, and this will always be the case when a firm employs financial leverage. More specifically, *if a firm employs fixed—cost securities, a given percentage change in earnings before interest and taxes will produce a greater percentage change in EPS.*

MEASURING THE DEGREE OF FINANCIAL LEVERAGE (DFL)

To obtain useful information regarding the sensitivity of EPS to such changes, we can calculate the degree of financial leverage, which is defined *as the percentage change in EPS produced by a given percentage change in earnings before interest and taxes.* This sensitivity measure can be determined by calculating the percentage change in EPS produced by a 1 per cent change in earnings before interest and taxes at a given level of EBIT. To illustrate, we will calculate the degree of financial leverage for the

Gold Star Company at an earnings before interest and taxes (EBIT) level of ₹ 2500 crore

	EBIT	*EPS*	
-1%	₹ 2,475 crore	56.25	-1.32%
	2,500	57.00	
+ 1%	2,525	57.75	+ 1.32%

At an EBIT level of ₹ 2,500 crore, the degree of financial leverage is 1.32. A given percentage change from ₹ 2,500 crore (EBIT) level will produce a percentage change in EPS 1.32 as large. For example, a 10 per cent change in EBIT from ₹ 2,500 crore will produce a 13.2 per cent change in EPS. To show how this sensitivity measure varies, we will use it to calculate EBIT levels of ₹ 4,500 crore and ₹ 6,000 crore.

	EBIT	*EPS*	
-1%	₹ 4,455 crore	₹ 115.65	1.15
	4,500	117.00	
+ 1%	4,545	118.35	1.15
	EBIT	*EPS*	
-1%	5,940	160.20	1.11
	6,000	162.00	
+ 1%	6,060	163.80	1.11

We can see how the degree of financial leverage declines as earnings before interest and taxes increases.

Many analysts prefer to rely on the following formulas to calculate the degree of financial leverage:

DFL = EBIT/ EBIT – F

Where:

DFL = Degree of financial leverage.
EBIT = Earnings before interest and taxes.
F = Annual interest expense plus the before-tax cost of preference share dividends.

We will illustrate this formula, using the ₹ 2500 crore earnings before interest and taxes level for the Gold Star Company.

$$\text{DFL} = \frac{₹\ 2500}{₹\ 2{,}500 \text{ crore} - ₹\ 600 \text{ crore}} = 1.316$$

COMBINING OPERATING AND FINANCIAL LEVERAGE: TOTAL LEVERAGE

Decisions regarding the level of fixed expenses to income and the amount of debt to employ are interrelated. To clarify this important point, it is useful to examine the dual effect of operating and financial leverage on the rate of change of EPS.

Assume the following for the ABC Company.

(1) Sales will be ₹ 1000 crore during the first year of operations.
(2) All expenses are variable and are equal to 80 per cent of sales.
(3) There are no taxes.
(4) The firm employs no debt or preference shares.
(5) There are 10 crore shares of equity.

Given these estimates, EPS can be calculated as shown in table 15.

TABLE-15

ABC Company - Pro-Forma Income Statement for Year One

(₹ in crore)

Net sale	₹ 1,000
Variable expenses	800
Fixed expenses	0
Earnings before interest and taxes	₹ 200
Interest expense	0
Earnings before taxes	₹ 200
Income Taxes	0
Earning after taxes	₹ 200
Preferred dividends	0
Earnings available to equity shareholders	₹ 200
Number of equity shares	10 crore
Earnings per share	₹ 20.00

Let us now examine what will happen to EPS as sales changes. In Table-16, we assume a 10 per cent increase and a 10 per cent decrease in sales. A 10 per cent decrease in sales produces a 10 per cent decrease in EPS, while a 10 per cent increase in sales produces a 10 per cent increase in EPS.

TABLE-16

ABC Company
Pro-Forma Income Statement for Year One

(₹ in crore)

	-10%	*+10%*
Net sales	₹ 900	₹ 1,100
Variable expenses	720	880
Fixed expenses	0	0
Earnings before interest and taxes	₹ 180	₹ 220
Interest expenses	0	0
Earnings before interest and taxes	₹ 180	₹ 220

Interest expenses	0	0
Earnings before taxes	₹ 180	₹ 220
Preferred dividends	0	0
Earnings available to equity shareholders	₹ 180	₹ 220
Number of equity shares	10crore	10crore
Earnings per share	₹ 18.00	₹ 22.00

This will always be the case when a firm does not employ operating and financial leverage. More specifically, *in the absence of operating and financial leverage, a given percentage change in sales will produce an identical percentage change in EPS.*

Next, let us assume that the ABC company substitutes a part of fixed expenses by variable expenses, fixed expenses will be ₹ 200 crore and variable expenses will be 60 per cent of sales instead of 80 per cent of sales. Table-17 shows that at a sales level of ₹ 1000 crore earnings before interest and taxes and EPS will still be ₹ 200 and ₹ 20 respectively.

TABLE-17

ABC Company
Pro-Forma Income Statement For Year One

(₹ in crore)

	–10%	*Given*	*+ 10%*
Net sales	₹ 900	₹ 1,000	₹ 1,100
Variable expenses	540	600	660
Fixed expenses	200	200	200
Earnings before interest and taxes	₹ 160	₹ 200	₹ 240
Interest expenses	0	0	0
Earning before taxes	₹ 160	₹ 200	₹ 240
Income taxes	0	0	0
Earning after taxes	₹ 160	₹ 200	₹ 240
Preferred dividends	0	0	0
Earnings available to equity shareholders	₹ 160	200	240
Number of equity shares	10crore	10crore	10 crore
Earnings per share	₹ 16.00	₹ 20.00	₹ 24.00

A 10 per cent increase in sales produces a 20 per cent increase in both earnings before interest and taxes and EPS, while a 10 per cent decrease in sales produce a 20 per cent decrease in both. However, *the earning before interest and taxes and EPS changes at the same rate because the firm uses no financial leverage.*

Let us now assume that the ABC Company will be financed 50 per cent by debt and 50 per cent by equity rather than 100 per cent by equity. Let us assume that interest expenses on the debt will be ₹ 100 crore and that only 5 crore shares must be issued to rise the desired amount of equity capital. We will still assume that fixed expenses are ₹ 200 crore and that variable expenses will be 60 per cent of sales. Table-18 presents the results with a 10% change in sales.

A 10 per cent increase in sales produces a 40 per cent increase in EPS, while a 10 per cent decrease in sales produces a 40 per cent decrease in EPS.

We can calculate the combined degree of operating and financial leverage that is the percentage change in EPS produced by a given percentage change in sales at a certain level of sales. This combined sensitivity measure can be determined by calculating the percentage change in EPS produced by a 1 per cent change in sales from a certain level. For example, it can easily be varified from Table-18 that at a sales level of ₹ 1,000 crore , the degree of operating time financial leverage is four. In other words, a given percentage change in sales from the ₹ 1,000 crore level will produce a percentage change in EPS four times as large.

TABLE-18

ABC Company

Pro-Forma Income Statement For Year One

(₹ in crore)

	-10%	*Given*	*+10%*
Net sales	₹ 900	₹ 1,000	₹ 1,100
Variable expenses	540	600	660
Fixed expenses	200	200	200
Earnings before interest and taxes	₹ 160	₹ 200	₹ 240
Interest expenses	100	100	100
Earnings before taxes	₹ 60	₹ 100	₹ 140
Income taxes	0	0	0
Earning after taxes	₹ 60	₹ 100	₹ 140
Preferred dividends	0	0	0
Earnings available to equity shareholders	₹ 60	₹ 100	₹ 140
Number of equity shares	5crore	5crore	5crore
Earnings per share	₹ 12	₹ 20	₹ 28

It is possible to ascertain the degree of combined leverage in a direct fashion, without determining any percentage fluctuations or the separate leverage values, we need only to substitute the appropriate values into the following equation:

$$DCL = DOL \times DFL$$

$$\text{or DCL} = \frac{\text{Q (SPPU – VEPU)}}{\text{Q (SPPU – VEPU)–FE}} \times \frac{\text{EBIT}}{\text{EBIT–F}} \qquad (13)$$

Using the information in Table-18, we get:

$$\text{DCL} = \frac{\text{10 crore units (₹ 100 – ₹ 60)}}{\text{10 crore units (₹ 100 – ₹ 60) – ₹ 200 crore}} \times \frac{\text{₹ 200 crore}}{\text{₹ 200 crore –₹ 100 crore}}$$

$$= \frac{\text{₹ 400 crore}}{\text{₹ 400 crore – 200 crore}} \times \frac{\text{₹ 200 crore}}{\text{₹ 100 crore}}$$

$$= \frac{\text{₹ 400 crore}}{\text{₹ 200 crore}} \times \frac{\text{₹ 200 crore}}{\text{₹ 100 crore}}$$

= 4 times

IMPLICATIONS

The total risk exposure that the firm assumes can be managed by combining operating and financial leverage in different degrees. When a firm is considering the substitution of fixed expense for variable expenses, or vice versa, it must take into account the extent to which financial leverage is employed. Moreover, when a firm is considering the addition of fixed-cost securities, it must take into account the extent to which it is employing operating leverage. Second, the variability of sales is the key to the variability of EPS. In other words, if sales do not change, EPS, will not change, regardless of the level of operating and financial leverage. Some firms with large amounts of both operating and financial leverage have experienced stability of EPS over time because sales for these firms have been stable over time.

ILLUSTRATIVE PROBLEMS

1. Three financing plans are available to Ahuja Products, which needs ₹ 10,00,000 for construction of a new plant. Ahuja wants to maximise EPS. Currently the equity share is selling for ₹ 30 per share. The EBIT resulting from the plant operation is ₹ 1,50,000 per year. Ahuja's marginal tax rate is 50%. Money can be borrowed at the rates indicated:

Up to ₹ 1,00,000 at 10%

Over ₹ 1,00,000 to ₹ 5,00,000 at 14%

Over ₹ 5,00,000 at 18%

The three financing plans are as follows:

Plan X: Use ₹ 1,00,000 debt; Expected EBIT = ₹ 2,50,000

Plan Y: Use ₹ 3,00,000 debt Expected EBIT = ₹ 3,50,000

Plan Z: Use ₹ 6,00,000 debt; Expected EBIT = ₹ 5,00,000

Determine the EPS for these three plans and indicate the financing plan which will result in the highest EPS.

Solution

Plan Z results in the highest EPS as the following solved table shows:

	Plan-X	*Plan-Y*	*Plan-Z*
EBIT	₹ 2,50,000	₹ 3,50,000	₹ 5,00,000
Interest	– 10,000	–38,000	– 84,000
EBT	₹ 2,40,000	₹ 3,12,000	₹ 4,16,000
Taxes	1,20,000	1,56,000	2,08,000
EAT	₹ 1,20,000	₹ 1,56,000	₹ 2,08,000
No of shares	30,000	23,333	13333
EPS	₹ 4.00	₹ 6.69	₹ 15.64

2. Assume that a firm is considering expanding assets by ₹ 5 crores and has determined that it can finance the expansion either through a bond issue carrying a 15% interest rate or through a new issue of equity shares which can be sold to net the company ₹ 20 per share. The firm currently has 40,00,000 shares issued and ₹ 6 crores with a 12% coupon. The tax rate is 50%.

(a) Calculate the EPS for each alternative at EBIT levels of ₹ 2 crores and ₹ 7.5 crores.

(b) What can be said from this analysis regarding the choice between bonds and equity shares?

Solution

(a) For debt financing

Total debt interest = 0.15 (₹ 5,00,00,000) + 0.12 (₹ 6,00,00,000) = 1,47,00,000

Shares issued = 40,00,000

(₹ in Thousand)

EBIT	20,000	75,000
Interest	14,700	14,700
EBT	5,300	60,300
Taxes	2,650	30,150
EAT	2,650	30,150
EPS	0.6625	7.5375

For equity financing:

Interest = 0.12 (₹ 6,00,00,000)
= ₹ 72,00,000

Total Share = New Shares + Existing Shares

Total Shares = (₹ 5,00,00,000 / ₹ 20) + 40,00,000
= 65,00,000

(₹ in thousand)

EBIT	20,000	75,000
Interest	7,200	7,200
EBT	12,800	67,800
Taxes	6,400	33,900
EAT	6,400	33,900
EPS	0.9846	5.2154

(b) The answer here depends on the expected level of EBIT and its variance. At higher EBIT, debt produce higher EPS.

3. Hind Company has the following income statement for 2013:

Sales	₹ 500 crore
Variable operating costs	₹ 100 crore
Fixed operating costs	₹ 200 crore
EBIT	₹ 200 crore
Interest	50 crore
EBT	₹ 150 crore
Tax (at 40%)	60 crore
EAT	₹ 90 crore
Preferred dividends	10 crore
Earnings available to equity shareholders	₹ 80 crore
Equity share issued	10 crore share

(a) Compute Hind's DOL, DFL, and DCL.

(b) If sales increase to ₹ 55,00,000, what is your forecast of EPS?

Solution

(a) $$\text{DOL} = \frac{\text{Sales - Variable costs}}{\text{FC}}$$

$$= \frac{₹\,500 \text{ crore} - ₹\,100 \text{ crore}}{₹\,200 \text{ crore}} = 2.0$$

$$\text{DFL} = \frac{\text{EBIT}}{\text{EBIT} - I - D_p / (1-T)}$$

$$= \frac{₹\,200 \text{ crore}}{₹\,200 \text{ crore} - ₹\,50 \text{ crore} - \dfrac{₹\,10 \text{ crore}}{(1\text{-}0.4)}}$$

$$= \frac{₹\,200 \text{ crore}}{₹\,133.33} = 1.5$$

$$\text{DCL} = \frac{\text{Sales} - \text{Variable Costs}}{\text{EBIT} - I - D_P \;/ (1 - \text{T})}$$

$$= \frac{₹\,500 \text{ crore} - ₹\,100 \text{ crore}}{₹\,200 \text{ crore} - ₹\,50 \text{ crore} - \dfrac{₹\,10 \text{ crore}}{(1\text{-}0.4)}} = 3.0$$

Check = DOL × DFL

= 2.0 × 1.5 = 3.0

(b) Current EPS $= \dfrac{₹\,500 \text{ crore}}{10 \text{ crore shares}} = ₹\,8.00$

A sales increase to ₹ 600 crore represents a 12% increase in sales. Hence, EPS should increase by 36% (12% × 3.0), to ₹ 10.88.

4. Fidex Electronics Inc. produces stereo components which sell for P = ₹ 100. Fidex's fixed costs are ₹ 2,00,000; 5,000 × components are produced and sold each year; EBIT is currently, ₹ 50,000; and Fidex's assets (all equity financed) are ₹ 5,00,000. Fidex estimates that it can change its production process, adding ₹ 4,00,000 to investment and ₹ 50,000 fixed operating costs. This change will (1) reduce variable costs per unit by ₹ 10 and (2) increase output by 2,000 units, but (3) the sales price on all units will have to be lowered to ₹ 95 to permit sales of the additional output. Fidex has tax loss carry-forwards that cause its tax rate be zero. Fidex uses no debt, and its average cost of capital is 10 per cent.

(a) Should Fidex make the change?

(b) Would Fidex's degree of operating leverage increase or decrease if it made the change? What about its breakeven point?

(c) Suppose Fidex were unable to raise additional equity financing and had to borrow the ₹ 4,00,000 to make the investment at an interest rate of 10 per cent. Use the Du Pont equation to find the expected ROA of the investment. Should Fidex make the change if debt financing must be used?

Solution

(a) (1) Determine the variable cost per unit at present, using the following definitions and equations:

Q = units of output (sales) = 5,000.

P = average sales price per unit of output = ₹ 100.

F = fixed operating costs = ₹ 2,00,000.

V = variable costs per unit.

$$\begin{aligned} \text{EBIT} &= \text{P(Q)} - \text{F} - \text{V(Q)} \\ ₹\,50{,}000 &= ₹\,100(5{,}000) - ₹\,2{,}00{,}000 - \text{V}(5{,}000) \\ 5{,}000\text{V} &= ₹\,2{,}50{,}000 \\ \text{V} &= ₹\,50. \end{aligned}$$

(2)Determine the new EBIT level if the change is made:

$$\text{New EBIT} = P_2(Q_2) - F_2 - V_2(Q_2)$$
$$= ₹\,95(7{,}000) - ₹\,2{,}50{,}000 - ₹\,40(7{,}000)$$
$$= ₹\,1{,}35{,}000.$$

(3) Determine the incremental EBIT:

$$\Delta EBIT = ₹\,1{,}35{,}000 - ₹\,50{,}000 = ₹\,85{,}000.$$

(4)Estimate the approximate rate of return on the new investment:

$$\Delta ROA = \frac{\Delta EBIT}{\text{Investment}} = \frac{₹\,85{,}000}{₹\,4{,}00{,}000} = 21.25\%$$

Since the ROA exceeds Fidex's average cost of capital, this analysis suggests that Fidex should go ahead and make the investment.

(b) $$DOL = \frac{Q(P-V)}{Q(P-V)-F}$$

$$DOL_{Old} = \frac{5{,}000(₹100 - ₹50)}{5{,}000(₹100 - ₹50)\ ₹\,2{,}00{,}000} = 5.00$$

$$DOL_{New} = \frac{7{,}000(₹95 - ₹40)}{7{,}000(₹95 - ₹40)\ ₹\,2{,}50{,}000} = 2.85$$

This indicates that operating income will be less sensitive to changes in sales if the production process is changed; thus, the change would reduce risks. However, the change would increase the breakeven point. Still, with a lower sales price, it might be easier to achieve the higher new breakeven volume.

$$Old: Q_{BE} = \frac{F}{P\text{-}V} = \frac{₹\,2{,}00{,}000}{₹100 - ₹50} = 4{,}000 \text{ units}$$

$$New: Q_{BE} = \frac{F}{P_2\text{-}V_2} = \frac{₹\,2{,}50{,}000}{₹95 - ₹40} = 4{,}545 \text{ units}$$

(c) The incremental ROA is:

$$ROA = \frac{\Delta Profit}{\Delta Sales} \times \frac{\Delta Sales}{\Delta Assets}$$

Using debt financing, the incremental profit associated with the investment is equal to the incremental profit found in Part *a* minus the interest expense incurred as a result of the investment:

$$\Delta Profit = \text{New profit} - \text{Old profit} - \text{Interest}$$
$$= ₹\,1{,}35{,}000 - ₹\,50{,}000 - 0.10(₹\,4{,}00{,}000) = ₹\,45{,}000.$$

The incremental sales is calculated as:

$$\Delta Sales = P_2Q_2 - P_1Q_1$$
$$= ₹\,95(7{,}000) - ₹\,100(5{,}000)$$
$$= ₹\,6{,}65{,}000 - ₹\,5{,}00{,}000 = ₹\,1{,}65{,}000.$$

$$\text{ROA} = \frac{₹\,45,000}{₹\,1,65,000} \times \frac{₹\,1,65,000}{₹\,4,00,000} = 11.25\%$$

The return on the new equity investment still exceeds the average cost of capital, so Fidex should make the investment.

5. Gentry Motors Inc., a producer of turbine generators, is in this situation: EBIT = ₹ 4 crore; tax rate = T = 35%; debt outstanding = D = ₹ 2 crore; k_i = 10%; k_r = 15%; shares of equity issued = N_o = 60,00,000; and book value per share = ₹ 10. Since Gentry's product market is stable and the company expects no growth, all earnings are paid out as dividends. The debt consists of perpetual bonds.

(a) What are Gentry's earnings per share (EPS) and its price per share (P_o)?
(b) What is Gentry's weighted average cost of capital (WACC)?
(c) Gentry can increase its debt by ₹ 8 crore, to a total of ₹ 10 crore, using the new debt to buy back and retire some of its shares at the current price. Its interest rate will be 12 per cent (it will have to call and refund the old debt), and its cost of equity will rise from 15 per cent to 17 per cent. EBIT will remain constant. Should Gentry change its capital structure?
(d) If Gentry did not have to refund the ₹ 2 crore of old debt, how would this affect things? Assume that the new and the still outstanding debt are equally risky, with k_i = 12 per cent, but that the coupon rate on the old debt is 10 per cent.
(e) What is Gentry's times-interest-earned (TIE) coverage ratio under the original situation and under the conditions in Part c of this question?

Solution

EBIT	₹ 4,00,00,000
Interest (₹ 2,00,00,000 × 0.10)	₹ 20,00,000
Earnings before taxes (EBT)	₹ 3,80,00,000
Taxes (35%)	₹ 1,33,00,000
Net income	₹ 2,47,00,000

EPS = ₹ 2,47,00,000/60,00,000 = ₹ 4.12.
P_o = ₹ 4.12/0.15 = ₹ 27.47.
Equity = 60,00,000 × (₹ 10) = ₹ 6,00,00,000
Debt = ₹ 2,00,00,000.
Total capital = ₹ 8,00,00,000

$$\text{WACC} = w_i k_i (1 - T) + w_e k_e$$
$$= (2/8)(10\%)(1 - 0.35) + (6/8)(15\%) = 1.63\% + 11.25\% = 12.88\%.$$

EBIT	₹ 4,00,00,000
Interest (₹ 10,00,00,000 × 0.12)	1,20,00,000
Earnings before taxes (EBT)	₹ 2,80,00,000

Taxes (35%)	₹ 98,00,000
Net Income	₹ 1,82,00,000

Shares bought and retired:

$$\Delta N = \Delta Debt/P_o = ₹\ 8,00,00,000/₹\ 27.47 = 29,12,268.$$

New outstanding shares:

$$N_1 = N_o - \Delta N = 60,00,000 - 29,12,268 = 30,87,732$$

New EPS:

$$EPS = ₹\ 1,82,00,000/30,87,732 = ₹\ 5.89.$$

New price per share:

$$P_o = ₹\ 5.89/0.17 = ₹\ 34.65 \text{ versus } ₹\ 27.47.$$

Therefore, Gentry should change its capital structure.

d. In this case, the company's net income would be higher by (0.12 – 0.10) (₹ 2,00,00,000) (1 – 0.35) = ₹ 2,60,000 because its interest charges would be lower. The new price would be

$$P_0 = \frac{(₹1,82,00,000 + ₹2,60,000)/30,87,732}{0.17} = ₹\ 35.18$$

In the first case, in which debt had to be refunded, the bondholders were compensated for the increased risk of the higher debt position. In the second case, the old bondholders were not compensated; their 10 per cent coupon perpetual bonds would now be worth

$$₹\ 100/0.02 = ₹\ 833.33,$$

or ₹ 1,66,66,667 in total, down from the old ₹ 2 crore, or a loss of ₹ 33,33,333. The stockholders would have a gain of

$$(₹\ 35.18 - ₹\ 34.65)\ (30,87,732) = ₹\ 16,36,498.$$

The gain would, of course, be at the expense of the old bondholders. (There is no reason to think that bondholders' losses would exactly offset stockholders' gains).

$$TIE = \frac{EBIT}{I}$$

$$\text{Original TIE} = \frac{₹4,00,00,000}{₹\ 20,00,000} = 20 \text{ times}$$

$$\text{New TIE} = \frac{₹4,00,00,000}{₹\ 1,20,00,000} = 20 \text{ times.}$$

6. Abhishek Industries Ltd. (AIL) manufactures a line of power tools used in the construction industry, its state of the art plant gives it a competitive operating advantage over its competitors during boom periods, but unfortunately, leads to heavy excess capacity during slow downs and recessions. Business activity has been brisk in recent years, prompting AIL's finance manager to consider refinancing its current financial structure. As the data below in Table-1 indicate, AIL presently has considerable long-term debt and preference shares. Arun Verma, the finance manager, is proposing that an issue of 2,00,000 equity shares be sold for ₹ 50 a share and that the proceed be used to retire both the debt and the preference shares. He feels that the refinancing would reduce the company's risk exposure but that it might also lower its EPS. Verma intends to evaluate the situation by determining EPS amounts with the present structure and with the proposed all equity structure. He decides to consider two other sales levels—₹ 40,00,000 and ₹ 60,00,000. Finally, he will determine the financial indifference point between the two arrangements as an analytical aid.

Table-1

AIL: Income Statement for upcoming years

(Existing Financial Structure)

Sales	₹ 50,00,000
Less: Fixed Costs	12,80,000
Variable Costs (0.20 of sales)	10,00,000
EBIT	27,20,000
Interest (12% rate on ₹ 60,00,000)	7,20,000
EBT	20,00,000
Taxes (40% rate)	8,00,000
EAT	12,00,000
Preferred dividends (9% rate on 40,00,000)	3,60,000
EATES	8,40,000
EPS (4,00,000 shares issued)	₹ 2.10

Should the All Equity Plan be Adopted?

Solution

FINANCING PLANS: A COMPARISON

1. Calculate EBIT for the ₹ 40,00,000 and ₹ 60,00,000 sales levels:

Sales	₹ 40,00,000	₹ 60,00,000
VC (0.2 of sales)	8,00,000	12,00,000
FC	12,80,000	12,80,000
EBIT	₹ 19,20,000	₹ 35,20,000

2. Calculate EPS for each EBIT level for each financing plan

	Present Financing			*All Equity*	
EBIT	₹ 19,20,000	₹ 35,20,000	₹ 19,20,000	₹ 27,20,000	₹ 35,20,000
I	7,20,000	7,20,000			
EBT	₹ 12,00,000	₹ 28,00,000	₹ 19,20,000	₹ 27,20,000	₹ 35,20,000
T	₹ 4,80,000	11,20,000	7,68,000	10,88,000	14,08,000

EAT	₹ 7,20,000	₹ 16,80,000	₹ 11,52,000	₹ 16,32,000	₹ 21,12,000
Div. to PS	₹ 3,60,000	₹ 3,60,000	0	0	0
EATES	₹ 3.60.000	₹ 13,20,000	₹ 11,52,000	₹ 16,32,000	₹ 21,12,000
No. of Shares Issued	₹ 4,00,000	4,00,000	6,00,000	6,00,000	6,00,000
EPS	₹ 0.90	₹ 3.30	₹ 1.92	₹ 2.72	₹ 3.52

As the data indicate, the all equity produces higher EPS amounts for the three EBIT levels considered (the ₹ 27,20,000) level and the related 2.10 EPS for the existing arrangement). If these levels seem not realistic to Verma, the all—equity plan should be adopted and the refinancing accomplished.

$$EPS\ Plan_A \qquad EPS\ Plan_B$$

$$\frac{(EBIT - I)(1 - T) - P}{4{,}00{,}000} = \frac{EBIT(1 - T)}{6{,}00{,}000}$$

$$\frac{0.6\ EBIT - ₹\ 7{,}92{,}000}{4{,}00{,}000} = \frac{0.6\ EBIT}{6{,}00{,}000}$$

$$6{,}00{,}000\ [0.6\ (EBIT) - ₹\ 7{,}92{,}000] = 4{,}00{,}000\ [0.6\ (EBIT)]$$

$$1.5\ [0.6\ (EBIT) - ₹\ 7{,}92{,}000] = 0.6\ (EBIT)$$

$$0.3\ (EBIT) = ₹\ 11{,}88{,}000$$

$$EBIT = ₹\ 39{,}60{,}000$$

At this level of EBIT, EPS for each plan is ₹ 3.96. Verma must consider the likelihood of EBIT exceeding the amount. If there is a good chance that it will, the present financing arrangement is more desirable than the all-equity plan.

QUESTIONS

1. What is meant by the term "leverage"? With what type of risk is leverage generally associated?
2. How can breakeven analysis be used in financial leverage planning?
3. Define the term *operating leverage,* What type of effect occurs when the firm uses operating leverage?
4. Distinguish between business risk and financial risk. What gives rise to, or course, each type of risk?
5. Define the term financial leverage. Does the firm use financial leverage if preference shares are present in the capital structure?
6. Should a firm avoid incurring fixed expenses? Why?
7. Evaluate the following statement: "An increase in fixed expenses always increases the level of business risk."
8. Define the degree of financial leverage (DFL). Explain why it is a measure of risk.
9. What is the relationship between operating leverage and operating risk? How is each of these related to the firms breakeven point and risk-return trade-off?
10. Define the degree of combined leverage (DCL) and explain how DCL depends on operating and financial leverage.

11. Discuss the similarities and differences of financial and operating leverage.
12. Comment of the following statement: "The use of fixed-cost securities will always affect the rate of change of EPS."
13. Financing with either debt or preference shares creates leverage. However, if the leverage is positive, debt financing will cause higher earnings per share for the equity shares than with preference shares financing even if the interest and dividends rates are the same. Why is this so?
14. What is the difference between positive and negative financial leverage?
15. What is the relationship between financial leverage and financial risk? How is each of these related to the firm's financial breakeven point and risk-return trade-off?
16. What is the general relationship between operating financial leverage and the total leverage of the firm? Do both types of leverage complement each other? Why or why not?
17. Other things beings equal, what effect would the following changes have on a firm's degree of combined leverage? Explain your answer.
    (a) The firm's EBIT level increases
    (b) Sales price increases, but volume remains the same
    (c) Fixed operating costs decline.
18. What is the relationship of total leverage to total risk? How is each of these related to the firm's total breakeven point and overall risk-return trade-off? How does one measure the degree of total leverage?

PROBLEMS

1. The Bush Company sells its finished product for ₹ 9.00 per unit. Its fixed operating cost are ₹ 20,000 and the variable operating cost per unit is ₹ 5.00. Compute the firm's earnings before interest and taxes (EBIT) for sale of 10,000 units.

Ans.: ₹ 20,000

2. PQR Company has estimated that for a new product its breakeven point is 2,000 units if the item is sold for ₹ 1,400 per unit and the cost accounting department has correctly identified variable costs of ₹ 9.00 per unit. Calculate the degree of operating leverage for sales volume of 1,500 units and 2,500 units.

Ans.: DOL = -3

3. Usha Electronics has 4,00,000 shares of equity and ₹ 1,00,000 of bonds outstanding. The firm has a 40% tax rate. (a) Calculate the financial breakeven point if the interest rate on the bonds is 10%; (b) What is the financial breakeven if the firm has 1000 shares of outstanding preference and the dividend per share is ₹ 5.40?

Ans.: (a) ₹ 10,000 (b) ₹ 20,000

4. Vinay Textiles is trying to evaluate the profitability of a new venture that would require an investment of ₹ 12,00,000 in fixed assets. Items produced would be sold for ₹ 200 each and would require variable costs of ₹ 120 per unit. (a) What are the breakeven points in units and in sales for this venture? (b) What would happen to the breakeven point if, as a result of inflationary pressures, variable costs per unit could be expected to rise to ₹ 140 and the selling price to ₹ 210 per unit.

Ans.: (a) 15,000 units, (b) ₹ 36,00,000.

5. Ajay Tools Company has ₹ 1,20,00,000 of 8% bonds outstanding, 1,50,000 shares of preference paying ₹ 5.00 dividends per share, and 4,00,000 shares of equity outstanding. Assume the firm has a 40% tax rate, compute the earnings per share for the ₹ 24,00,000 level of EBIT.

Ans.: ₹ 0.375.

6. If a firm can sell 5,00,000 units at ₹ 10 and 8,00,000 units at ₹ 9, and has variable costs of ₹ 6, fixed costs of ₹ 3,00,000 and interest of ₹ 60,000, which selling price yields the highest net income after taxes?

Ans.: At ₹ 10 NIAT is ₹ 8,20,000
At ₹ 9 NIAT is ₹ 10,20,000

7. Firm XYZ has a contribution margin of ₹ 3 per unit, fixed costs of ₹ 60,000 and sells 1,00,000 units. Interest is ₹ 1,00,000 per year. Firm ABC has a contribution margin of ₹ 15 per unit, fixed costs of ₹ 6,25,000 and sells 1,00,000 units. Interest is ₹ 1,75,000 per year. Assume both firms are in the 40% tax bracket. Compute the degree of combined leverage for both the firm.

Ans.: DCL of XYZ = 2.14; DCL of ABC = 2.14

8. The Bright Auto Co. will begin operations next year to produce a single product at a price of ₹ 12 per unit. Bright has a choice of two methods of production: Method A, with variable costs of ₹ 6.75 per unit and fixed operating costs of ₹ 6,75,000; and Method B, with variable costs of ₹ 8.25 per unit and fixed operating costs of ₹ 4,01,250. To support operations under either production method, the firm requires ₹ 22,50,000 in assets, it has established a debt ratio of 40 per cent. The cost of debt is k_i = 10 per cent. The tax rate is irrelevant for the problem, and and fixed *operating* costs do not include interest. (a) The sales forecast for the coming year is 2,00,000 units. Under which method would EBIT be more adversely affected if sales did not reach the expected levels? (b) Given the firm's present debt, which method would produce the greater percentage increase in earnings per share for a given increase in EBIT?

Ans.: (a) DOL_A = 2.80; $DOL_{B'}$ = 2.15; Method A; (b) DFL_A = 1.32; DFL_B = 1.35; Method B

9. The firms HL and LL are identical except for their leverage ratios and interest rates on debt. Each has ₹ 20 crore in assets, earned ₹ 4 crore before interest and taxes in 1998, and has a 40 per cent tax rate. Firm HL, however, has a leverage ratio of 50 per cent and pays 12 per cent interest on its debt, whereas LL has a 30 per cent leverage ratio and pays only 10 per cent interest on debt. (a) Calculate the rate of return on equity (net income/equity) for each firm. (b) Observing that HL has a higher return on equity, LL's treasurer decides to raise the leverage ratio from 30 to 60 per cent, which will increase LL's interest rate on all debt to 15 per cent. Calculate the new rate of return on equity for LL.

Ans.: (a) ROE_{LL} = 14.6% ; ROE_{HL} = 16.8%; (b) ROE_{LL} = 16.5%

10. Medico offers patient-ordered magnetic resonance scans to examine hearts. Traditionally, this test is ordered by physicians; however, in this case, patients solicit the exam without medical intervention and receive results without medical interpretation. The magnetic resonance machine (MRM) cost ₹ 25,00,000 and the company estimates that the machine's installation will cost ₹ 46,000. The procedure requires a nurse who is paid ₹ 50 per hour, a technician who is paid ₹ 30 per hour, and a physician who is paid ₹ 150 per hour. Patients are billed ₹ 900 for the procedure, compared with ₹ 700 for a traditional x-ray series. How many patients must the company treat to break even?

Ans.: Patients 3800

11. Winny Communications Corporation (WCC) supplies headphones to airlines for use with movie and stereo programmes. The headphones sell for ₹ 288 per set, and this year's sales are expected to be 45,000 units. Variable production costs for the expected sales under present production methods are estimated at ₹ 1,02,00,000 and fixed production (operating) costs at present are ₹ 15,60,000. WCC has ₹ 48,00,000 of debt outstanding at an interest rate of 8 per cent. There are 2,40,000 shares of equity outstanding, and there is no preferred stock. The dividend payout ratio is 70 per cent, and WCC is in the 40 per cent tax bracket.

The company is considering investment of ₹ 72,00,000 in new equipment. Sales would not increase, but variable costs per unit would decline by 20 per cent. Also, fixed operating costs would increase from ₹ 15,60,000 to ₹ 18,00,000. WCC could raise the required capital by borrowing ₹ 72,00,000 at 10 per cent or by selling 2,40,000 additional shares at ₹ 30 per share. (a) What would be WCC's EPS (1) under the old production process, (2) under the new process if it uses debt, and (3) under the new process if it uses equity? (b) Calculate DOL, DFL, and DCL under the existing setup and under the new setup with each type of financing. Assume that the expected sales level is 45,000 units, or ₹ 1,29,60,000. (c) At what unit sales level would WCC have the same EPS, assuming it undertakes the investment and finances it with debt or with stock? (d) At what unit sales level would EPS = 0 under the three production / financing setups—that is, under the old plan, the new plan with debt financing, and the new plan with stock financing? (e) On the basis of the analysis in Parts a through d, which plans is the riskiest, which has the highest expected EPS, and which would you recommend? Assume here that there is a fairly high probability of sales falling as low as 25,000 units, and determine EPS_{Debt} and EPS_{Equity} at that sales level to help assess the riskiness of the two financing plans.

Ans.: (a) EPS_{old} = ₹ 2.04; New: EPS_{D} = ₹ 4.74; EPS_{e} = ₹ 3.27; (b) DOL_{old} = 2.30; DOL_{new} = 1.60; DFL_{old} = 1.47; $DFL_{new\ stock}$ = 1.15 $DCL_{New,\ debt}$ = 2.53; (c) 33,975 units; (d) $Q_{new,\ debt}$ = 27,225 units.

12. Shilpi Corporation produces tea kettles, which it sells for ₹ 15 each. Fixed costs are ₹ 7,00,000 for up to 4,00,000 units of output. Variable costs are ₹ 10 per kettle. (a) What is the firm's gain or less at sales of 1,25,000 units and at 1,75,000 units? (b) What is the breakeven point? (c) What is Shilpi's degree of operating leverage at sales of 1,25,000 units, at 1,50,000 units and at 1,75,000 units?

Ans.: (a) (1) –₹ 75,000 (2) ₹ 1,75,000; (b) R_{BE} = 1,40,000; (c) (1) –8.3; (2) 15.0; (3) 5.0.

13. Neel Company wishes to calculate next year's return on equity under different leverage ratios. Neel's total assets are ₹ 140 crore, and its tax rate is 40 per cent. The company is able to estimate next year's earnings before interest and taxes for three possible states of the world: ₹ 42 crore with a 0.2 probability, ₹ 28 crore with a 0.5 probability, and ₹ 7 crore with 0.3 probability. Calculate Neel's expected return on equity, standard deviation, and coefficient of variation for each of the following leverage ratios, and evaluate the results:

Leverage *(Debt/Total Assets)*	*Interest Rate*
0%	—
10	9%
50	11
60	14

Ans.: No leverage : ROE = 10.5%; S.D. = 5.4%; CV = 0.51; 60% Leverage: ROE = 13.7%; S.D. = 13.5%; CV = 0.99.

14. Gold Watch Company manufactures ladies' watches which are sold through discount houses. Each watch is sold for ₹ 2,500, the fixed costs are ₹ 1,40,00,000 for 30,000 watches or less: variable costs are ₹ 1,500 per watch. (a) What is the firm's gain or loss at sales of 8,000 watches and at 18,000 watches? (b) What is the breakeven point? (c) What is Gold's degree of operating leverage at sales of 8,000 units and at 18,000 units? (d) What happens to the breakeven point if the selling price rises to ₹ 3,100? What is the significance of the change to the financial manager? (e) What happens to the breakeven point of the selling rices rises to ₹ 3,100 but variable cost rise to ₹ 2,300 a unit?

Ans.: (a) (1) – ₹ 60,00,000; (b) Q_{BE} = 14,000; (c) (1) – 1.33

15. The following relationships exist for Sham Industries, a manufacturer of electronic components. Each unit of output is sold for ₹ 45; the fixed costs are ₹ 1,75,000; variable costs are ₹ 20 per unit. (a) What is the firm's gain or loss at sales of ₹ 5,000 units and at ₹ 12,000 units? (b) What is the breakeven point?

Ans.: (a) (2) ₹ 1,25,000; (b) Q_{BE} = 7,000

ARVIND GENERAL PRODUCERS: *A CASE*

Arvind General Producers (AGP) is a medium-sized, public corporation that until recently consisted of two divisions. The Retail Furniture Group (RFG) has eight locations in northern India. These retail outlets generate sales of traditional and contemporary furniture. Additionally, casual and leisure furniture lines are carried by the stores. The other (old) division of AGP is its Concrete Group (CG). The CG operates three plants in western India. These plants produce precast concrete wall panels. The headquarters of AGP is located in Delhi.

AGP was started ten years ago as Arvind Producers by its current president and board chairman, Tersem Singh Ahluwalia. During the firm's existence it has enjoyed periods of both moderate and strong growth in sales, assets, and earnings. Key managerial decisions have always been dominated by Ahluwalia who openly boasts of the fact that his company has never suffered through a year of negative earnings despite the often cyclical nature of both the retail furniture (RFG) and concrete (CG) divisions.

Recently Ahluwalia decided to acquire a third division for his firm. The division manufactures special machinery for the seafood processing industry and is appropriately called the Seafood Industry Group (SIG). The financial settlement for the acquisition took place yesterday. Currently, the SIG consists of one manufacturing plant. A single product is to be manufacutred, assembled, and transported from the facility. That product, however, represents a design breakthrough and carries with it a projected contribution margin ration of 0.40. This is greater than that enjoyed by either of AGP other two divisions.

Recent income statements for the older divisions of AGP are contained in Exhibits-1 and -2. Ahluwalia has now decided to assess more fully the probable impact of the decision to establish the SIG upon the financial condition of AGP. Ahluwalia knew that such figures should have been generated prior to the decision to enter this special machinery field, but this seasoned judgment led him to the quick choice. He has requested several pieces of information, detailed from his finance manager.

EXHIBIT 1

ARVIND GENERAL PRODUCERS

Retail Furniture Group

Income Statement, for the Year 2012-13

Sales	₹ 1,20,00,000
Less: total variable costs	79,20,000
Revenue before fixed costs	₹ 40,80,000
Less: total fixed costs	25,44,000
EBIT	₹ 15,36,000
Less: interest expense	1,92,000
Earnings before taxes	13,44,000
Less: taxes @ 50%	6,72,000
Net Profit	₹ 6,72,000

EXHIBIT 2

ARVIND GENERAL !PRODUCERS

Concrete Group

Income Statement, for the Year 2012-13

Sales	₹ 80,00,000
Less: total variable costs	59,20,000
Revenue before fixed costs	₹ 20,80,000
Less: total fixed costs	6,40,000
EBIT	₹ 14,40,000
Less: interest expense	80,000
Earnings before taxes	₹ 13,60,000
Less: taxes @ 50%	6,80,000
Net Profit	₹ 6,80,000

QUESTIONS AND PROBLEMS

1. Using last year's results, determine the breakeven point in ₹ for AGP (i.e., before investing in the new SIG). The breakeven point is defined here in the traditional manner where EBIT = ₹ 0. (Hint: Use an aggregate contribution margin ratio in your analysis).
2. Using last year's results, determine what volume of sales must be reached in order to cover all before-tax costs.
3. Next year's sales for the SIG are projected to be ₹ 40,00,000. Total fixed costs will be ₹ 6,40,000. This division will have no outstanding debt on its balance sheet. AGP uses a 50 percent tax rate in all of its financial projections. Using the format of Exhibits-1 and -2 construct a proforma income statement for the SIG.
4. After the SIG begins operations, what will be AGP's breakeven point in ₹ (a) as traditionally defined and (b) reflecting the coverage of *all* before-tax costs? Base the new sales mix on last year's sales performance for the older divisions plus that anticipated next year for the SIG. Using your answer to part (b) of this question, construct an analytical income statement demonstrating that earnings before taxes = ₹ 0.
5. Using next year's anticipated sales volume for AGP (including the SIG), compute (a) the degree of operating leverage, (b) the degree of financial leverage, and (c) the degree of combined leverage. Comment on the meaning of each of these statistics.
6. Using projected figures, determine whether acquisition of the SIG will increase or decrease the vulnerability of AGP's earnings before interest and taxes (EBIT) to cyclical swings in sales. Show your work.
7. Review the key assumptions of cost-volume-profit analysis.

16

THEORY OF CAPITAL STRUCTURE

INTRODUCTION

Perhaps no area of financial management has commanded as much attention as the capital structure problem. Simply put, a firm's capital structure represents the mix of securities that it has sold in order to finance its asset acquisitions. The capital structure problem, then, deals with the firm's choice of the types of securities to issue. In the current market-oriented policies, the corporate financial managers have been motivated to use more debt financing for several powerful reasons. On the one hand, owners, including the ever more powerful institutional investors, have confronted management with increased demands for performance generally expressed as a desire for continuously increasing earnings per share. On the other hand, low-debt usage companies are extremely attractive to leverage-minded conglomerate managers. Increased use of leverage often offers a way to improve a company's earnings and at the same time remove some of the attractiveness of the firm as a takeover target.

Demands for more finely tuned performance by management calls for astute decision making, and many managers are, or probably will be, working with the firm's optimal financing mix. The firm's optimal financing strategy is that which maximises the market value of the firm. The finance manager must evaluate the possible adverse effects of debt if it becomes a proportionally larger part of the capital structure. The increased volatility of earnings produced by high fixed charges may decrease price earnings ratios, another source of attraction for the acquisition-minded. In the extreme case, there is the potential of insolvency. Hence, the financial manager must determine that level of debt which offers increased profitability to the firm's owners without unduly increasing the risk of insolvency and at the same time makes the firm a less attractive target for merger or takeover. Any deviation in either direction from the optimal financing mix will induce a decline in value of the equity shares, and hence in the market value of the firm. The current chapter is directed to the question of *what happens to the total value of the firm and to the cost of capital when the ratio of debt to equity, or degree of leverage, is varied.* Three major views on the question of capital structure have been outlined.

FINANCIAL STRUCTURE *VERSUS* CAPITAL STRUCTURE

Financial structure is the mix of all items that appears on the left-hand side of the company's balance sheet. *Capital Structure* is the mix of the long-term sources of funds used by the firm. In equation form, the relationship between financial and capital structure can be expressed as:

Financial Structure – Current Liabilities = Capital Structure (1)

Prudent financial-structure design requires answers to the following *two* questions.

(1) What should be the maturity composition of the firm's sources of funds?

(2) In what proportions relative to the total should the various sources of permanent financing be utilised?

The first of these questions concerns the division of total funds sources into short-term and long-term components. The major influence on the maturity structure of the financing plan is the nature of the assets owned by the firm. A company heavily committed to real capital investment represented primarily by fixed assets on its balance sheet should finance those assets with permanent (long-term) types of financial capital. Furthermore, the permanent portion of the firm's investment in current assets should likewise be financed with permanent capital. Alternatively, assets held on a temporary basis are to be financed with temporary funds sources.

Table-1 presents equation-1, in terms of a simplified balance sheet format. It helps us in visualising the overriding problem of capital structure management. While equation-1 quite accurately indicates that the corporate capital structure may be viewed as an *absolute amount*, the real capital structure problem is one of balancing the array of funds sources in a proper manner. However, this financing mix is one of the many relevant dimensions of the capital structure. Other dimensions involve the investment decisions of the firm, and the optimal use of leverage, within the constraints imposed by the internal and external environmental conditions. These conditions, in turn, affect the decisions of the firm with respect to the timing of investment and financing transactions, as well as the acceptable levels of risk and liquidity. As such the problem of capital structure can be dealt with at three different levels of complexity.

TABLE-1

Balance Sheet

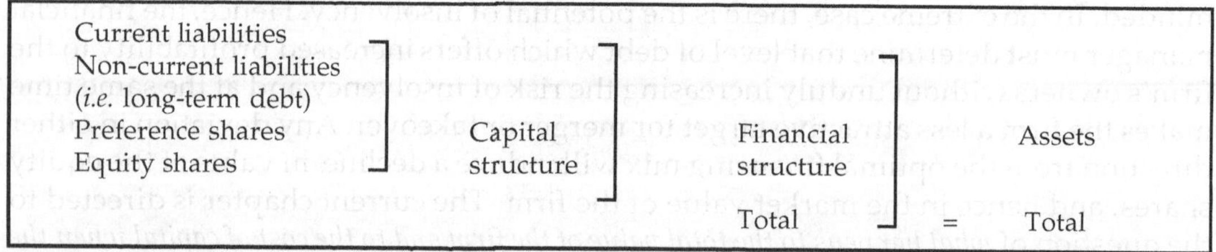

Current liabilities Non-current liabilities (*i.e.* long-term debt) Preference shares Equity shares	Capital structure	Financial structure		Assets
		Total	=	Total

THREE LEVELS OF COMPLEXITY

The Static View

The first level views the existence of an optimal asset structure as a static proposition requiring a unique solution for the capital for each choice of capital structure. Essentially the static approach suggests that, given the relevant information about the firm's asset structure, the quality of expected earnings, and capital market conditions, management should obtain that mix of financial claims that minimises the cost of capital-provided, of course, there is such a mix. Hence capital structure is viewed as the *active policy variable.*

The Comparative Static View

The second level views capital structure as a comparative static proposition yielding different values for the cost of capital and capital structure as some of the underlying parameters change. Thus changes in the existing asset structure, the quality of expected earnings, and the capital market conditions generate new equilibrium solutions between the financing mix and the cost of funds.

The Dynamic View

The third level views capital structure as a dynamic process of interdependent investment and financing decisions that yield optimal values within the constraints at the time and place when the decisions were made. That is, the firm's management continually makes financing decisions based on its retention policies and available information about the environmental conditions. Hence the existing capital structure reflects the sequential decisions of the past and as such, it is no longer the active decisions variable but rather the by product of the continual process of matching sources and uses of funds.

The first and second levels of complexity are subject of the dynamic process that conditions the allocation of the firm's resources. By the same token, these levels are easy to treat analytically for the pedagogic purposes on hand; hence we shall confine our analysis to the simple static level.

CAPITAL STRUCTURE THEORY

Even a casual review of the literature brings one quickly to the key question of whether the way in which investment proposals are financed *matters* and if it does matter, *what is optimal capital structure?*

Capital structure can be properly defined as that combination of debt and equity that attains the *stated* managerial goals, in our case, the maximisation of the firm's market value. In other words, the optimal capital structure is also defined as that combination of debt and equity that minimises the firm's cost of capital. Hence the existence of an optimal capital structure also implies the simultaneous optimisations of two other important variables namely, cost of capital and market value.

However, the existence of an optimal capital structure, which leads to maximum market valuation and minimum cost of capital is not accepted unequivocally. As in many other controversial issues, there are two extreme views and the inevitable intermediate version. To wit on the one hand of the spectrum, we have the traditional view that argues consistantly and convincingly that there is an optimal capital structure defined by a range of values acceptable to the capital markets. On the other hand, we have the view of F. Modigliani and M.H. Miller, who argue, also consistently and convincingly, that under certain acceptable assumptions there can be no leverage effect on the market value of the firm; hence there is *no optimal capital structure* as such. Between these two extremes we have the intermediate view of the net-operating-income approach that argues that changes in the capital structure do not changes the overall risk content of the firm; rather, they redistribute this risk among the claim holders. Hence there is *no* leverage effect in this sense. However, there is an optimal capital structure and its effect, which derive from the tax treatment of debt and market imperfections. These frictional elements can lead to higher market values and lower cost of capital (for given levels of risk) when the firm's management employs a judicious combination of financial claims. All three views are internally consistent, that is given their assumptions we can logically derive their conclusions; worse, empirical tests to date have not substantiated any of these views in a clear-cut manner.

DEFINITIONS AND ASSUMPTIONS

Leverage can be defined in many ways. We can measure leverage as:

$$L_1 = \frac{B}{S} \quad \text{– the ratio of debt to equity, at market prices} \tag{2}$$

$$L_2 = \frac{B}{(B+S)} \quad \text{– the ratio of debt to total capital, at market prices} \tag{3}$$

$$L_3 = \frac{F}{O} \quad \text{– the ratio of debt charges to net operating income} \tag{4}$$

Some measures are more convenient for certain purposes and some, for other. For the present we will use the first of these alternatives and measure L as the ratio of bonds to equity, with both values computed at market prices.

Using Solomon's symbols[1] we are concerned with the following three rates:

$$k_i = \frac{F}{B} = \frac{\text{Annual interest charges}}{\text{Market value of debt}} \tag{5}$$

In the equation-5, k_i is the yield on the company's debt, assuming the debt to be perpetual.

$$k_e = \frac{E}{B} = \frac{\text{Earnings available to equity shareholders}}{\text{Market value of equity}} \tag{6}$$

The required rate of return for investor in a firm whose earnings are not expected to grow and that has 100 per cent dividend-payout.

The final rate we consider is:

1. Solomon, Ezra: "Leverage and the Cost of Capital, *Journal of Finance*, 18 (May, 1963), pp. 273-79.

$$k_o = \frac{O}{V} = \frac{\text{Net operating earnings}}{\text{Total market value of the firm}} \tag{7}$$

where $V = B + S$, Here k_o is an overall capitalisation rate for tthe firm. It is defined as the weighted average cost of capital and may also be expressed as:

$$k_o = k_i \frac{B}{(B+S)} + k_e \frac{S}{(B+S)} \tag{8}$$

Our concern will be with what happens to k_o, k_e and k_i as the degree of leverage is changed. To get this we need to compare the level of k_i, k_e and k_o at one capitalisation structure with their level at some different structure, with all other factors constant.

To simplify the analysis, we make the following facilitating **assumptions**:

No Income Taxes : Income taxes with be ignored here to simplify the analysis, but the absence of taxes does not detract from the general relationships. Without taxes the after tax cost of debt, k_d, and the before-tax cost of debt, k_i, are equal.

Financing through bonds and equity: We assume that the sources of financing available to the firm are bonds and equity. Specific types of bonds or shares are not isolated. This assumption simplifies graphical representation of the analysis, since only two dimensions are required.

A 100—per cent dividend payout: The firm is assumed to pay out all earnings in the form of dividends. The assumption supports the preceding assumption by eliminating retained earnings as a source of financing.

Constant earnings before interest and taxes (EBIT): The distributions of future EBIT are known and the mean value of each annual EBIT distribution is constant. This provides for the determination of an optimal capital structure. Changes in expected EBIT would therefore result in a different "optimum" capital structure for each level of EBIT.

Constant operating risk: Operating risk is held constant by assuming that all assets acquired are such that the line of business of the firm remains unchanged. Holding operating risk constant let us isolate the effects of financial risk (i.e. financial leverage).

Changes in financial leverage: The firm decreases its financial leverage by selling shares and using the proceeds to retire bonds. The firm's leverage is increased by issuing bonds and using the proceeds to retire equity. In other words, the firm's total book financing (i.e. equity plus bonds) remains fixed over the period being considered. The second assumption also supports this strategy. Keeping the total financing constant makes it easier to isolate the effects of a changing capital structure on the firms' value.

CAPITAL STRUCTURE AND VALUATION: *THREE APPROACHES*

NET INCOME APPROACH[2]

Net income approach assumes that the only cost of debt finance is the interest rate and that there are no hidden or implicit costs. Thus the value of the firm is expected to increase with changes in the debt-to-equity ratio. To illustrate the net income approach, assume that a firm is expected to generate net operating earnings of ₹ 700 crore which market capitalise at the rate, k_e, at 0.15 or 15 per cent . Assume that it has ₹ 1,000 crore in debt at 10 per cent interest. Given this information, the value of the firm may be calculated as shown in Table-2.

TABLE-2

(₹ in crore)

Net operating earnings	(O)	₹ 700
Interest on debt	(F)	100
Earnings available to equity shareholders.	(E)	₹ 600
Assumed equity capitalisation	(*ke*)	.15
Market value of equity	(S)	₹ 4,000
Market value of debt	(B)	1,000
Total value of firm	(V)	₹ 5,000

The implied over all capitalisation rate now is:

$$k_o = \frac{O}{V} = \frac{₹\ 700 \text{ crore}}{₹\ 5{,}000 \text{ crore}} = 14\%$$

The net income approach suggests that the explicit and implicit costs of debt are one and the same. The use of more debt does not change the firm's cost of equity. Using more debt which is explicitly cheaper than equity will lower the firm's overall cost of capital, k_o. Assume now that the firm increases its debt from ₹ 1,000 crore to ₹ 2,500 crore and uses the proceeds of the debt issue to repurchase shares. Also assume that the interest rate on debt remains unchanged at 10 per cent . The value of the firm then is shown in Table-3.

2. The net income and net operating income approaches were first presented in comprehensible form by David Durand, "Cost of Debt and Equity Funds for Business: Trends and Problems of Measurement," *Conference on Research in Business Finance* (New York; National Bureau of Economic Research, 1952), reprinted in *The Management of Corporate Capital,* Ezra Solomon, ed, (New York, Free Press, 1959), pp. 91—116. The leading proponents of the independence hypothesis is in its various forms are professors Modigliani and Miller. See Franco Modigliani and Merton H. Miller, "The Cost of Capital. Corporation Finance and The Theory of Investment." *American Economic Review* 48 (June 1958), pp. 261—97; Franco Modigliani and Merton H. Miller, "Corporate Income Taxes and the Cost of Capital; A Correction, "*American Economic Review,* 53 (June 1983), pp. 433—43 and Merton H. Miller, "Debt and Taxes, "*The Journal of Finance,* 32 (May 1977), pp. 261—75.

TABLE-3

(₹ in crore)

Net operating earning	(O)	₹ 700
Interest on debt	(F)	250
Earnings available to equity shareholders	(E)	₹ 450
Assumed equity-capitalisation rate	(k_e)	.15
Market value of equity	(S)	₹ 3.000
Market value of debt	(B)	2,500
Total value of firm	(V)	₹ 5,500

The implied overall capitalisation rate now is:

$$k_o = \frac{O}{V} = \frac{₹\ 700\ \text{crore}}{₹\ 5{,}500\ \text{crore}} = 12.73\%$$

So changing the financing mix lowered the overall cost of capital from 14.00 per cent to 12.73 per cent . This also implies that the company's ordinary share price will rise with increased leverage use. The ingredients of net income approach are illustrated in Figures-1 and-2.

FIGURE-1

CAPITAL COSTS AND FINANCIAL LEVERAGE *NI APPROACH*

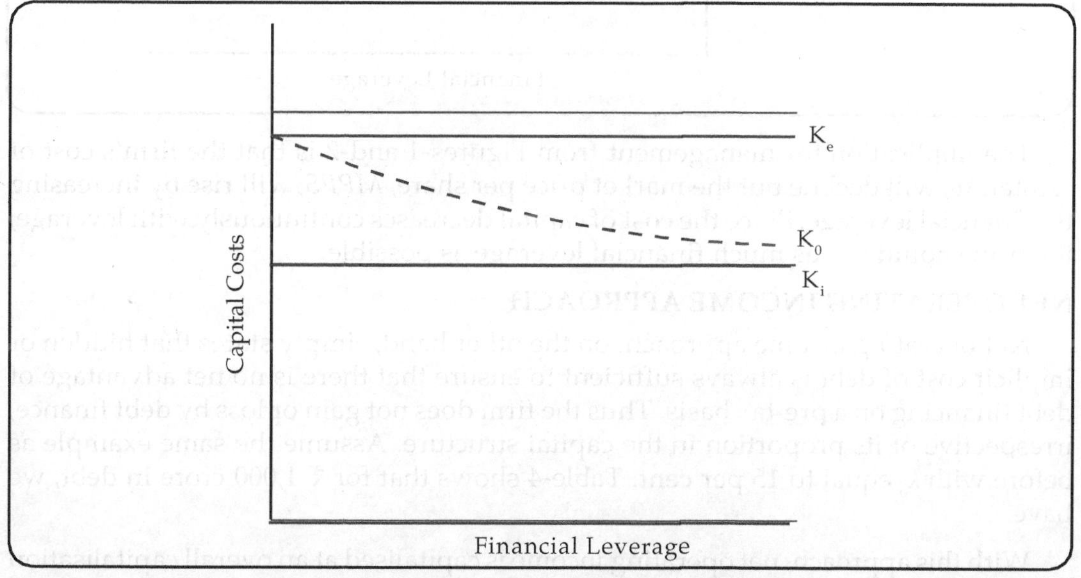

Thus the firm is able to increase its total valuation, *V*, and lower its overall cost of capital, *ko*, by increasing the degree of financial leverage. Notice that the total market value of the firm's securities has risen to ₹ 5,500 crore from the ₹ 5,000 crore level that existed before. As a result, the market price per share increases. To illustrate, assume in our example that the firm with ₹ 1,000 in debt has 10 crore shares of equity outstanding. Thus, the market price per share is ₹ 400 (₹ 4,000crore/10 crore shares). The firm issues ₹ 1,500 crore in additional debt and, at the same time, repurchases equity shares worth ₹ 1,500 at ₹ 400 a share, or 3.75 crore shares in total. It then has 6.25 crore shares outstanding. We saw in the example the total market value of the firm's equity after the change in capital structure is ₹ 3,000 crore/6.25 crore = ₹ 480.00, where before it was ₹ 400.

FIGURE-2

SHARE PRICES AND FINANCIAL LEVERAGE: *NI APPROACH*

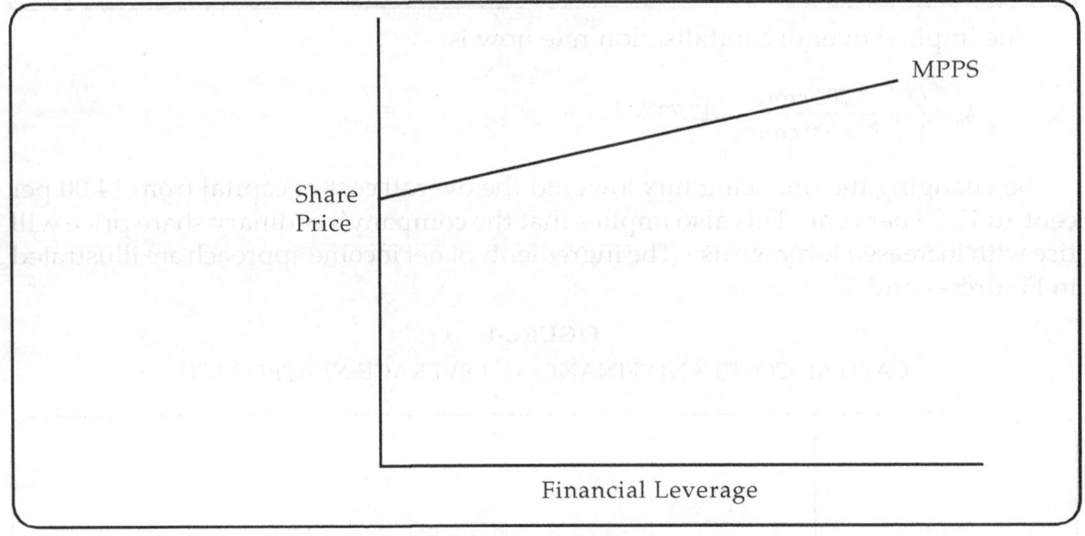

The implication for management from Figures-1 and-2 is that the firm's cost of capital, *ko*, will decline but the market price per share, *MPPS*, will rise by increasing the financial leverage. Since the cost of capital decreases continuously with leverage, the firm should use as much financial leverage as possible.

NET OPERATING INCOME APPROACH

Net operating income approach, on the other hand, simply states that hidden or implicit cost of debt is always sufficient to ensure that there is no net advantage of debt financing on a pre-tax basis. Thus the firm does not gain or loss by debt finance, irrespective of its proportion in the capital structure. Assume the same example as before with k_o equal to 15 per cent. Table-4 shows that for ₹ 1,000 crore in debt, we have.

With this approach, net operating income is capitalised at an overall capitalisation rate to obtain the total market value of the firm. The market value of the debt then is deducted from the total market value to obtain the market value of the equity.

In this framework the use of a greater degree of financial leverage may result in greater earnings and dividends but the firm's cost of equity will rise at precisely the same rate as the earnings and dividends. The critical assumption with this approach is that k_o is constant regardless of the degree of leverage.

TABLE-4

(₹ *in crore)*

Net operating earnings	(O)	₹ 700
Assumed overall capitalisation rate	(K_o)	.15
Market value of firm	(V)	₹ 4,666.67
Market value of debt	(B)	₹ 1,000.00
Market value of equity	(S)	₹ 3,666.67

Implied equity-capitalisation rate in this case is:

$$k_e = \frac{E}{S} = \frac{₹\ 600 \text{ crore}}{₹\ 3,666.67 \text{ crore}} = 16.36 \text{ per cent}$$

Suppose as before that the firm increases the amount of debt from ₹ 1,000 crore to ₹ 2,500 crore and uses the proceeds of the debt issue to repurchase equity. The valuation of the firm then is indicated in Table-5.

TABLE-5

Net operating income	(O)	₹ 700
Overall capitalisation rate	(k_0)	.15
Total value of firm	(V)	₹ 4,666.67
Market value of debt	(B)	₹ 2,500.00
Market value of equity	(S)	₹ 2,166.67

The implied equity capitalisation rate is:

$$k_e = \frac{E}{S} = \frac{₹\ 450 \text{ crore}}{2,166.67} = 20.77\%$$

The implied equity-capitalisation rate, ke, rises with the degree of financial leverage. This approach implies that the total valuation of the firm is unaffected by its capital structure. Graphically this approach is shown in Figures-3 and 4.

In Figure-3 the firm's costs of capital, k_o is shown to be unaffected by an increased use of financial leverage. If more debt is used in the capital structure, the cost of equity will rise at the same rate additional earnings are generated. This will keep the over all cost of capital to the corporation unchanged. Figure-4 shows that since the cost of capital will not change with leverage use, neither will the firm's equity price.

FIGURE-3

CAPITAL COSTS AND FINANCIAL LEVERAGE: *NOI APPROACH*

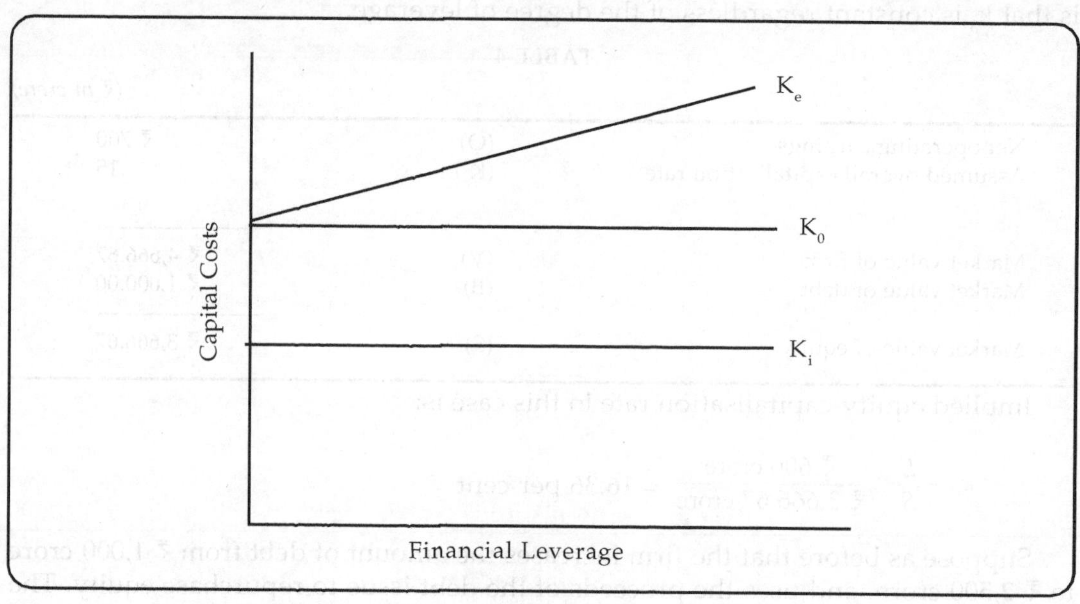

FIGURE-4

SHARE PRICES AND !FINANCIAL !LEVERAGE: *NOI APPROACH*

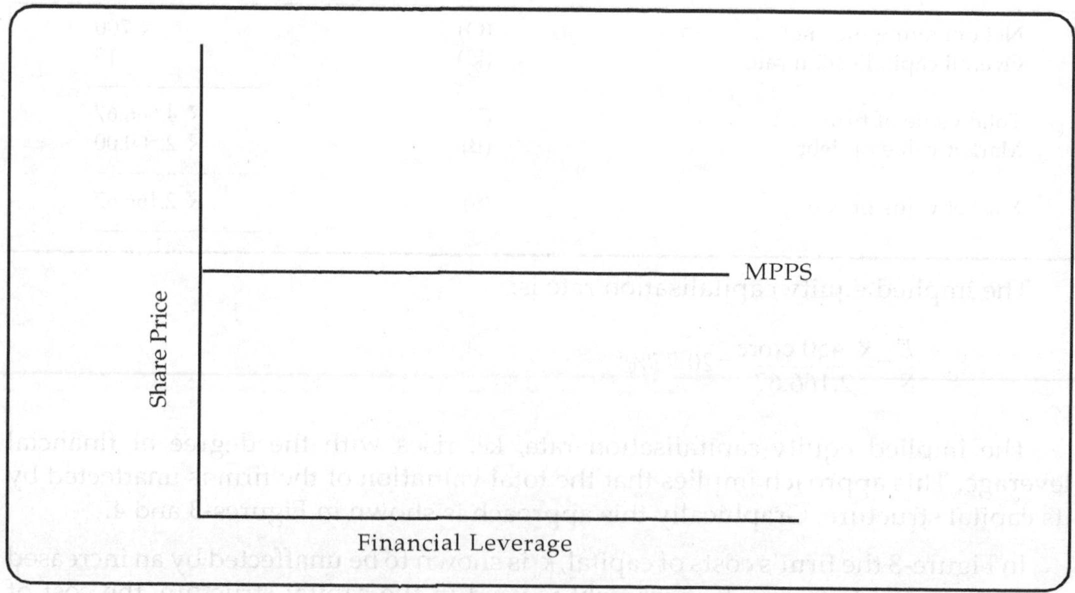

Thus, the net operating income approach states that the real cost of debt and the real cost of equity are the same, namely, k_o. The cost of debt has two parts: the explicit cost represented by the rate of interest and the implicit cost which is the change in the cost of equity brought on by using financial leverage (additional debt). The real cost of debt is the sum of these explicit and implicit costs. In general the real cost of any source of capital is its explicit cost plus the change that it induces in the cost of any other source of funds. This will keep the overall cost of funds constant. The implication for management is that one capital structure is as good as any other. In other words, all capital structures are optimal, for market price per share does not change with leverage. To illustrate, assume again that our example firm with ₹ 1,000 crore in debt has 10 crore shares of equity outstanding. The market price per share in this case is ₹ 3,666.67 crore/10 crore shares =₹ 366.67 . With the ₹ 1,500 crore in additional debt, the firm repurchases equity shares worth ₹ 1,500 crore at ₹ 366.67 a share, or 4.09 crore shares, in total. Therefore the market price per share after the change in capital structure is ₹ 2,166.67 crore / 5.91 crore shares, i.e., (10 crore shares - 4.09 crore shares = ₹ 366.67, the same as before. Thus capital structure would be a mater of indifference to the investor).

TRADITIONAL APPROACH

The traditional approach encompasses all the ground between the net income approach and the net operating income approach. The traditional position implies that the *cost of capital is not independent of the capital structure of the firm.* Implicitly, or more rarely explicitly, traditional doctrine assumes that there does exists an optimal point of leverage for any given firm. The objective may be stated as a balanced capital structure (which) deserves the proper relationship between debt and equity, or as one adapted to the level of business uncertainty involved. It is clearly logical that the greater the inherent business risk, the less should be financial risk, the thicker should be the equity and the less the leverage. The traditional position is that the market value of a company's securities will rise as the amount of leverage in its financial structure is increased from zero to some point determined by the capital market's evaluation of the level of business uncertainty involved. Beyond this point and up to a second point, changes in leverage have very little effect *i.e.,* within this range of leverage the total market value of the company is unchanged as leverage changes. Beyond this range of "acceptable" leverage, the total market value of securities will decline with further increases in leverage.

The actual location of the optimum leverage point or range for any given firm will vary with the amount of business uncertainty involved in its operations and with the attitude of the capital markets toward this uncertainty. This in turn is made up of the composite of expectations with regard to a company's product markets and prices, the fixity of its costs, the liquidity and marketability of its assets, and the opinion of the market with respect to the firm's management. As far as those elements of instability and uncertainty are concerned, a firm is likely to resemble other firms in the same industry. But interindustry differences are likely to be significant. Because of this, each industry group can be expected to have a different optimum range as far as leverage is concerned. This optimum range occurs at a higher level of leverage for stable industries than for unstable industries.

The traditional view of the hypothetical reaction of firm's total market value as leverage is increased from zero is that there are three discernible phases involved.

1. During the first phase, increase in leverage increases market value. In this phase, k_e, the rate at which the market capitalises net earning rises, with increasing leverage but does not rise fast enough to offset the increase in the net earnings rate achieved through the increased use of lower cost of debt capital. For most of this range the cost of borrowing, k_i, is either constant or rises only negligibly because actual and potential creditors regards the debt proportions involved as being within the sound limits. The combined effect of increasing leverage on F, E, k_i, k_e, w_1* and w_2** is such that total market value $V = (E/k_e) + (F/k_i)$ rises. A corollary of this is that the combined cost of capital $k_e w_1 + k_i w_2$ falls with increase in leverage. Since $k_o = k_e w_1 + k_i w_2$ the overall capitalisation rate k_o, also falls as leverage rises.

2. After a certain degree of leverage is reached, further moderate increases in leverage have little or no effect on total market value. During this middle range the changes brought about on F, E, k_e and k_i, offset one another so that total market value $V = (E/k_e) + (F/k_i)$ remains virtually constant as leverage is increased. Likewise the combined cost of capital $k_e w_1 + k_i w_2$ and the overall capitalisation rate k_o are also virtually constant.

3. Beyond a certain critical point, still further increases in leverage are unwise. The reaction of the capital market will be such that k_e and k_i rise rapidly. And this results in a fall in V and a rise in overall cost of capital, k_o.

To illustrate one variation of the approach, assume that our hypothetical firm has ₹ 1,000 crore , debt and the equity-capitalisation rate is 16 per cent rather than the 15 per cent. The valuation of the firm is presented in Table-6.

TABLE-6

(₹ in crore)

Net operating earning	(O)	₹ 700.00
Interest on debt	(F)	100.00
Earnings available to equity on share-holders	(E)	₹ 600.00
Assumed equity capitalisation rate	(*ke*)	.16
Market value of equity	(S)	₹ 3,750.00
Market value of debt	(B)	1,000.00
Total value of firm	(V)	₹ 4,750.00

The implied overall capitalisation rate is

* $w_1 = S/V$

** $w_2 = B/V$

$$k_o = \frac{O}{V} = \frac{₹\ 700 \text{ crore}}{₹\ 4{,}750} = 14.73\%$$

This example suggests that the firms can lower its cost of capital and decrease the total value of the firm and share price by leverage. Although investors raise the equity-capitalisation rate, *ke*, as the firm becomes more financially risky with leverage. The increase in *ke* does not offset entirely the benefit using cheaper debt funds. As a result, total valuation and share price increase and the cost of capital decrease. With ₹ 2,500 crore in debt and 10 crore shares outstanding, the market price per share is ₹ 3,750.00 crore/ 10.00 crore shares = ₹ 375.00. This contrasts with ₹ 366.67 under the assumption of net operating income approach to valuation.

The traditional approach implies that *ke* rises at an increasing rate with leverage beyond some point. Moreover, *ki* also may rise beyond some point. To illustrate, suppose now that the firm increases its debt from ₹ 1,000 crore to ₹ 2,500 crore and uses the proceeds of the debt issue to repurchase stock. Assume also that the average rate of interest on all debt rises to 12.50 per cent and that the equity-capitalisation rate, *ke*, at that degree of leverage is 20 per cent . Table-7 provides the valuation of the firm.

The implied overall capitalisation rate is

$$k_o = \frac{O}{V} = \frac{₹\ 700 \text{ crore}}{₹\ 4{,}437.50 \text{ crore}} = 15.77\%$$

TABLE-7

(*₹ in crore*)

Net operating earning	(O)	₹ 700.00
Interest on debt	(F)	312.50
Earnings available to equity on share-holders	(E)	₹ 387.50
Assumed equity capitalisation	(*ke*)	.20
Market value of equity	(S)	₹ 1,937.50
Market value of debt	(B)	2,500.00
Total value of firm	(V)	₹ 4,437.50

Thus the total valuation of the firm is lower and its cost of capital slightly higher than when the amount of debt was ₹ 1,000 crore . The result is due to the increase in *ke* and to a lesser extent, the increase in *ki* with ₹ 2,500 crore in debt and 6 crore shares (i.e. 10 crore shares minus 4 crore shares) outstanding, the market price per share is (₹ 1,937.50 / 6 crore shares) ₹ 322.92. This contrasts with ₹ 366.67 under the assumption of a net operating income approach to valuation. From these two observations we know that the optimal capital structure in this example occurs before a debt to equity ratio of ₹ 2,500.00 crore /₹ 1,937.50 crore or 1.29.

Graphically, the traditional view of the relationship between financing mix and the firm's cost of capital is depicted in Figure-5. The result is a saucer shaped (or U—shaped) average cost of capital curve, k_o.The firm's average cost of equity, k_e, is seen to rise over all positive degrees of financial leverage use. For a while the firm can borrow funds at a relatively low cost of debt, k_i. Even though the cost of equity is rising: it does not rise at a fast enough rate to offset the use of the less expensive debt financing. Thus, the average cost of capital declines and share price rises between points O and A on the financial leverage axis. Eventually the threat of financial distress causes the cost of debt to rise. In figure-5 this increase in the cost of debt shows up in the average cost of debt curve k_i, at point A. Between point A and B, mixing, debt and equity funds produces an average cost of capital that is (relatively) flat. The firm's optimal range of financial leverage use lies between points A and B.

All capital structure between these two points are optimal because they produce the firm's lowest overall cost of capital. Beyond point B, the additional fixed-charge capital can be attracted only at very costly interest rates. At the same time, the excessive use of financial leverage would cause the firm's cost of equity to rise at a faster rate than previously. Thus, point B signifies the firm's debt capacity beyond which the overall cost of capital rises quite rapidly and the firm's share price would decline.

FIGURE-5

CAPITAL COSTS AND FINANCIAL LEVERAGE: *THE TRADITIONAL VIEW*

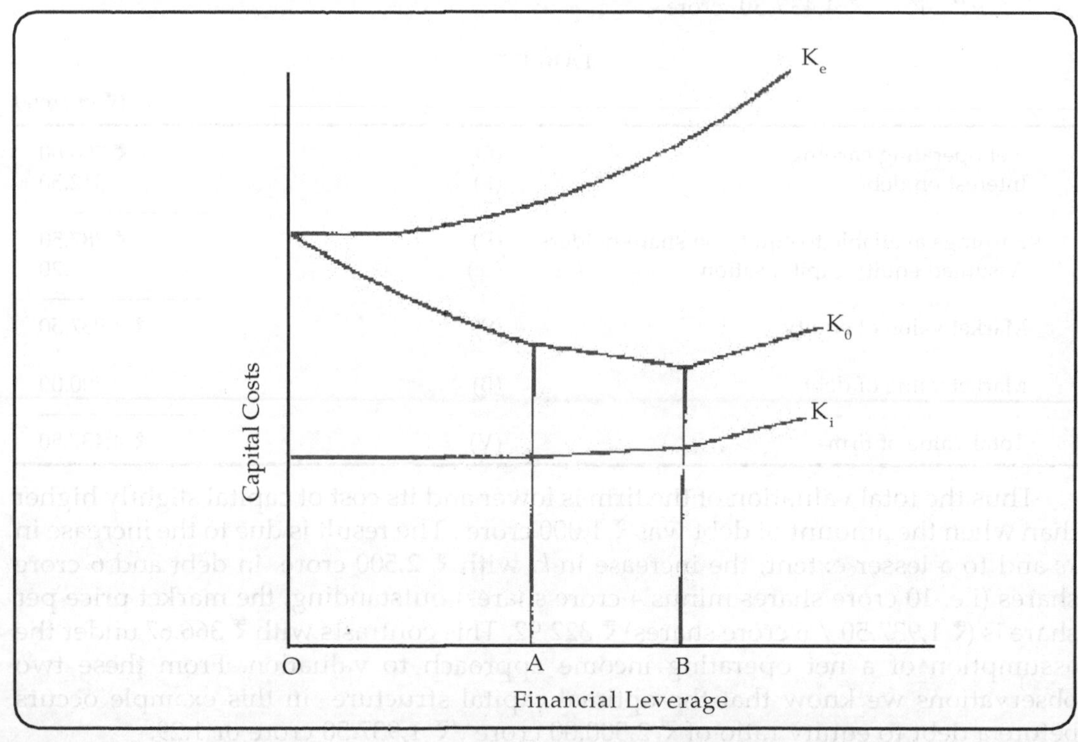

Figure-5 showing the relationship between the cost of capital and capital structure points out that, all other things being equal, investors in debt consider the debt less risky if the firm has a low, rather than high, proportion of debt in its capital structure. As the proportion of debt in th capital structure increases, investors require a higher return on the more risky debt. And because the firm's cost of capital is the investor's required return, the cost of debt increases as the proportion of debt increases.

The precise relationship between the cost of debt and the debt ratio is difficult to determine. This is because it is impossible to observe the cost of debt at two different capital structures (at the same time) for a single firm. Nevertheless, there is good evidence, that the cost of debt increases rather slowly for moderate amounts of debt. There is a point at which the capital markets consider any new debt "excessive" and therefore much more risky. The cost of debt curve k_i, in Figure-5 illustrates such a relationship. The actual region where the cost of debt begins to increase more rapidly varies by firm and industry depending on the firm's level of business risk.

The next step in this analysis focuses on the relationship between the cost of equity capital and capital structure. When a firm has low financial leverage, that is, a low debt-to-equity ratio, any equity employed is less risky than equity used when the firm is financed with a relatively high proportion of debt. The greater the fraction of debt used, the greater is the variability in earnings per share. In addition, the greater the fraction of debt used, the greater is the risk of bankruptcy. Because the returns expected by shareholder in the form of present and future dividends depend partly on current earnings, it can be concluded that variability in earnings per share can result in variability of the returns and the cost of equity capital increase as the relative amount of debt used to finance the firm increases.

Once again, the exact nature of the relationship between the cost of equity and financial leverage is difficult to determine in practice. However, there is agreement that the cost of equity capital increases at a relatively slow rate as the debt proportion increases up to moderate amounts. Then, in the range where additional debt is viewed as "excessive" and much more risky, the cost of equity increases more rapidly. This is shown in Figure-5. As is true in the debt illustration, the region where the cost of equity capital, k_e, begins to increase more rapidly varies by firm and industry.

The relationship between the weighted cost of capital, k_o, and financial leverage now can be considered. The following equation:

$$k_o = k_i \frac{B}{(B+S)} + k_e \frac{S}{(B+S)}$$

can be used to calculated k_o for any level of financial leverage, provided that the values of k_e and k_i at the level of financial leverage are known. (*B* is the market value of debt, and *S* is the market value of equity in the firm's capital structure.) Because the relationships between financial leverage and k_i and k_e have been developed, the relationship between k_o and financial leverage follow accordingly. The k_o curve, shown in Figure-5, begins at $k_o = k_e$, because, by definition the weighted cost of capital for an all-equity firm equals the cost of equity. As even small increments of debt are used, k_o becomes lower; as the debt proportion continues to increase from moderate to excessive, k_o "bottoms out" and then begins to increase. The resulting saucer-shaped curve contains a point at which the firm's overall cost of capital is mainimised and its value maximised. This point is the firm's *optimal capital structure.* If the firm is thought of as a cash flow generator, it can be seen that the lower the discount rate (the weighted cost of capital), the higher is the firm's value.

MODIGLIANI-MILLER POSITION

In 1958, Modigliani and Miller (M-M) wrote an important article which provided an ingeneous and rigorous basis for the Net Operating Income Approach. They suggested that, aside from the question of tax, the debt-to-equity mix did not change the value of the firm. They reasoned that in a competitive capital market the shareholder would 'arbitrage' until the Net Operating Income of all firms in the same risk class would fetch the same price in the market, regardless of financing arrangements made by individual firms. As their *assumptions* are extremely important, it is necessary to spell them out:

1. *Capital markets are perfect.* Information is costless and readily available to all investors, there are no transaction costs, and all securities are infinitly divisible. Investors are assumed to be rational, and to behave accordingly.

2. *The average expected future operating earnings of a firm are represented by a subjective random variable.* It is assumed that the expected values of the probability distributions of all investors are the same. Implied in the MM illustration is that the expected values of the probability distributions of expected operating earnings for all future periods are the same as present operating earnings.

3. *Firms can be categorised into equivalent return classes.* All firms within class have the same degree of business risk.

4. *The absence of corporate income taxes is assumed.* MM removes this assumption later.

MM draws essentially the same conclusion of the net operating income approach. Their **three basic *propositions*** are listed below:

1. *The total market value of the firm and its cost of capital are independent of its capital structure.* The total market value of a firm is given by capitalising the expected stream of operating earnings at a discount rate appropriate for its risk class.

2. The expected yields of a share of stock, k_e, is equal to the capitalisation rate of a pure equity stream, plus a premium for financial risk equal to the difference between the pure equity capitalisations rate and k_i times the ratio *B/S*. In other words, k_e *increase in a manner to offset exactly the use of cheaper debt funds.* This can be illustrated using the weighted-average cost-of-capital formula previously examined (see equation-8). If k_u is the return required on equity of an unlevered firm, then we know that this

is equal to the weighted-average cost-of-capital of all geared firms in the same risk-class. We can write

$$k_o = k_u = k_i \frac{B}{B+S} + k_e \frac{S}{B+S}$$

Multiplying throughout by B+S we obtain:

$$k_u B + k_u S = k_i B + k_e S$$

Dividing by S gives

$$k_e = k_u + \frac{k_u B}{S} - \frac{k_i B}{S}$$

$$k_e = k_u + \frac{B}{S}(k_u - k_i)$$

This expression shows that the expected return on the equity of a levered company is equal to the expected return on a pure equity stream plus a risk premium dependent on the level of debt in the capital strucutre. The effect on the cost of equity of introducing debt into the capital structure is that the cost of equity rises linearly to offset the lower-cost debt directly, giving a constant weighted-average cost of capital irrespective of the level of gearing.

3. The cut-off rate to be used in investment appraisal is the rate of return appropriate to an all-equity firm. This is the case because in an MM world the weighted-average cost of capital is constant and equal to the cost of equity in an all-equity firm. Hence, the *cut off rate for investment purposes is completely independent of the way in which an investment is financed.* This proposition along with the first implies a complete separation of the investment and financing decisions of the firm.

Given these assumptions, Modigliani and Miller argue that while companies in different industries face different risks which will result in their earnings being capitalised at different rates, it is not possible for these companies to affect their market values, and therefore their overall capitalisation rate, k_o, by the use of leverage. That is, for a company in a particular risk class, the total market value must be the same irrespective of the proportion of debt in the company's capital structure.

The behavioural support for the Modigliani and Miller position stems from a process known as 'arbitrage' which prevents perfect substitutes from selling at different prices in the market. Thus, in a perfect capital market, the arbitrage process prevents the total market values of two or more companies in the same risk class that differ only in terms of their capital structure from being different. Arbitrage works as follows:

> *Suppose that there are two companies in an 'equivalent return' set; company A is financed entirely by equity and company B has a capital structure which includes debt. If there is a disequilibrium so that B has a higher market value than A, market participants would take advantage of the difference by selling equity in B, borrowing money to equate their personal leverage to the degree of corporate leverage in B, in the*

equity of which they had higher to invest (thus maintaining to their desired level of 'financial risk') and using these funds to buy into the unlevered and lower valued company, A. Pressure on the price of B's equity will force down its price until the market value of B's debt and equity combine equals the market value of the all-equity company, A. This sector of the market is thereby returned to equilibrium, and no further gains are possible. Any similar future movement apart of the total market values of two companies, which are identical except for 'financial risk,' will immediately probe an 'arbitrage' response to bring them back into line.

Consider, for example, that B and A both have identical business risks and the same expected level of earnings before interest and taxes. We assume that all business risk is based on the probability distribution of EBIT and that these two firm are identical in every respect that company A is not levered and company B has ₹ 1,000 crore of 10 per cent bonds outstanding. According to the traditional approach, company B would have lower overall cost of capital, *ko* and higher total value than company A. Data on the two companies are shown in Table-8. MM maintain that this position cannot continue, for arbitrage will drive the total values of the two firms together. To illustrate the process, suppose that a rational investor owned 1 per cent of company B, the levered firm, worth ₹ 37.50 crore value. Given this situation, he should:

1. Sell his shares of company B for ₹ 37.50 crore.
2. Borrow ₹ 10 crore at 10 per cent interest. This personal debt is equal to 1 per cent of the debt of company B-his previous proportional ownership of the company.
3. Buy 1 per cent as the shares of company A, the unlevered firm, for ₹ 46.67 crore.

TABLE-8

(*₹ in crore*)

		Company A	*Company B*
Net operating income	(O)	₹ 700	₹ 700
Interest on debt	(F)	—	100
Earnings available to equity shareholders	(E)	₹ 700	600
Equity-capitalisation rate	(*ke*)	**.15**	**.16**
Market value of equity	(S)	₹ 4,666.67	3,750
Market value of debt	(B)	—	1,000
Total value of firm	(V)	₹ 4,666.67	4,750
Implied overall capitalisation rate	(*ko*)	15%	14.74
Debt-to-equity ratio	(B/S)	0	26.67%
Thus, his net ₹ return is:			
Return on investment in company A ₹ 7 crore			
Less Interest (₹ 10 crore x 0.10)			1crore
			₹ 6 crore

Prior to this series of transaction, the investor's expected return on investment in company A was 15 per cent on an investment of ₹ 46.67 crore or ₹ 7 crore . Whereas the expected return on investment in company B was 16 per cent on a ₹ 37.50 investment or ₹ 6 crore. From this return, he must deduct the interest charges on his personal borrowings.

We see then that his ₹ return, ₹ 6 crore , is the same as it was for his investment in company B. However, his cash outlay of ₹ 36.67 crore (₹ 46.67 crore less personal borrowings of ₹ 10.00 crore) is less than by ₹ 0.83 crore (₹ 37.50 crore - ₹ 36.67 crore) investment in company B, the levered firm. The action of a number of rational investors undertaking similar arbitrage transactions will tend to drive up the price of Company A shares, and lower its *ke* and drive down the price of Company B, increasing its *ke*. This arbitrage process will continue until there is no further opportunity for reducing one's investment outlay and achieving the same ₹ return. At this requilibrium, that total value of the two firms must be at the same. As a result their overall cost of capital, *ko*, also must be the same. The principle involved is simple that the investment opportunities available to investors are not altered by changes in the capital structure of the firm.

Given Modigliani and Miller's assumptions the same conclusions apply no matter how many companies are included in a particular risk class.[3] As a result, there is no way in which a company is able to increase its total market valuation (or reduce its overall capitalisation rate) by introducing debt into its capital structure. Therefore, the financing decision is irrelevant from the point of view of achieving the goal of maximising shareholders' wealth.

ARGUMENTS AGAINST THE MODIGLIANI-MILLER HYPOTHESIS

There have been many arguments advanced against the Modigliani-Miller hypothesis. Most of the criticisms stem from the critics concern with the Modigliani-Miller assumption of a perfect capital market. Clearly if perfect capital markets are assumed, then the arbitrage process assures the validity of the Modigliani-Miller hypothesis that the weighted average cost of capital and total market value of company are independent of its capital structure. If the capital market is not perfect, it seems that their hypothesis losses its behavioural justification.

However, the MM's assumptions and the existence of perfect capital markets, their conclusions follow logically. Therefore, to dispute the MM propositions we must examine the assumptions to determine if there are systematic market imperfections

3. See Robert S. Hamada, "Portfolio Analysis, Market Equilibrium and Corporation Finance," *Journal of Finance* 24 (March 1969), pp. 13-31; Robert A. Haugen and James L. Pappas, "Equilibrium in the Pricing of Corporate Assets, Risk-Bearing Debt Instruments and the Question of Optimal Capital Structure," *Journal of Financial and Quantitative Analysis* 6 (June 1971), pp. 943-953; and Yutaka Imai and Mark E. Rubinstein, "Comment," and Haugen and Pappas, "Reply" *Journal of Financial and Quantitative Analysis* 7 (September 1971), pp. 2001-2003; 2005-2008.

that would impede the equilibrium process. After investigating some of the basic assumptions, we introduce corporate taxes. Then we discuss bankruptcy costs, agency costs, personal taxes, and end with a brief review of relevant empirical testing.

RELAXING SOME OF THE PERFECT MARKET ASSUMPTIONS

EXISTENCE OF HOMOGENEOUS RISK CLASSES

MM originally introduced the idea of risk classes because at the time of their original study no market equilibrium pricing model (such as the CAPM) existed. However, with the capital asset pricing model nondiversifiable (or beta) risk, β, is the only relevant measure of risk; thus, the cost of equity capital for a levered firm k_{eL} is:

$$k_{eL} = k_{eu} + (k_{eu} - k_d)\ B/S \tag{9}$$

where:

k_{eu} = Cost of equity capital for unlevered firm

k_{eL} = Cost of equity capital for levered firm

which is exactly the same relationship specified by MM. An increase in the debt-to equity ratio increases not only the expected return of a stock but also its beta. In perfect markets, both increase proportionally, so that they offset each other with respect to their effect on share price. Since share price is being invariant with respect to leverage, once the CAPM is introduced, the existence of homogeneous risk classes as originally specified by MM is unncessary.[4]

SUBSTITUTION OF PERSONAL FOR CORPORATE LEVERAGE

Implied in the MM analysis is the condition that personal and corporate leverage are perfect substitutes. Critics argued that personal leverage is not equivalent to the leverage of a company because when a company borrows funds, the individual shareholder is protected by the concept of limited liability, whereas with personal leverage the individual carries full personal liability. As a result, the individual's risk exposure is greater when he incurs personal leverage and invests in the unlevered company than when he simply invests in the levered company. Modigliani and Miller well may be incorrect in assuming that personal and company leverage are perfect substitutes. Hence, because of the existence of limited liability for corporations, increased perceived personal risk from margin calls, and greater inconvenience, investors may not view personal leverage as a perfect substitute for corporate leverage. The arbitrage, however, need not occur in terms of investors actually borrowing at the market rate or using margin; all that is required is that there be

---

4. The MM propositions can be illustrated in the context of the CAPM. See Mark E. Rubinstein, "A Mean-Variance Synthesis of Corporate Financial Theory," *Journal of Finance* 28 (March 1973), pp. 167-181; and Jack Becker, "General Proof of Modigliani-Miller Propositions I and II Using Parameter-Preference Theory," *Journal of Financial and quantitative Analysis* 13 (March 1978), pp. 65-69.

sufficient investors who have they ability to adjust their holdings, of bonds.[5] In addition, institutions as well as individuals are assumed to engage in this process. So although personal and corporate leverage may not be perfect substitutes, it appears that this difference is not enough, by itself, to invalidate the MM proposition.

DIFFERENT COST OF BORROWING

Also implied in the MM analysis is the condition that the cost of borrowing is the same for individuals and coropration. Due to market imperfections however, the effective cost of borrowing may be higher for individual investors than for corporations. But, as just mentioned, the arbitrage process may be carried out simply by investors varying their holdings of bonds. Also, since institutional investors can often borrow on a basis very similar to the corporate rate, the impact of this imperfection does not appear to seriously weaken the MM propositions.

INSTITUTIONAL RESTRICTIONS

The arbitrage process depends on a sufficient number of personal or institutional investors being capable of engaging in the process, or at least being able to restructure their portfolios through the purchase or sale of bonds. Because of restriction on margin transactions, short sales, and limitations imposed by regulatory authorities on the bonds or stocks acceptable for investment, institutional investors appear to be able only partially to participate in the arbitrage process envisioned by MM.[7] Although the total impact of these restrictions is not clear, it appear they may have some effect on the MM arbitrage process. The combined impact of these four items suggests that the arbitrage process may not operate as efficiently as MM envisioned. However, it is not clear that the four (separately or jointly) are sufficient to invalidate the MM propositions.

THE MM PROPOSITIONS WITH CORPORATE TAXES

Once corporate taxes are introduced, MM's position is that the value of the firm can increase (and k_0 decrease) as new debt is added to its capital structure.[8] In essence, their position is very similar to the net-income approach since firms can increase their total value and reduce their marginal cost of capital by increasing the use of debt.

---

5. See David Durand, "The Cost of Capital, Corporation Finance and the Theory of Investment: Comment," *American Economic Review* 49 (September 1959), pp. 639-655; Joseph E. Stiglitz, "A Re-Examination of the Modigliani-Miller Theorem," *American Economic Review* 69 (December 1969), pp. 784-793; and Peter R. Lloyd-Davies, "Optimal Financial Policy in Imperfect Markets," *Journal of Financial and Quantitative Analysis* 10 (September 1975), pp. 457-481.
6. See Stiglitz, "A Re-Examination of the Modigliani-Miller Theorem; and David P. Baron, "Default Risk, Homemade Leverage, and the Modigliani-Miller Theorem," *American Economic Review* 64 (March 1974), pp. 176-182.
7. See Durand, "The Cost of Capital, Corporation Finance and the Theory of Investment: Comment"; and David W. Glenn, "Super Premium Security Prices and Optimal Corporate Financing Decisions," *Journal of Finance* 31 (May 1976), pp. 507-524).
8. Franco Modigliani and Merton H. Miller, "Corporate Income Taxes and the Cost of Capital: A Correction," *American Economic Review* 53 (June 1963), pp. 433-443.

To examine this, consider the cash flow streams that exist for unlevered versus levered firms. Table-9 illustrates that the expected value of annual net operating income for two companies is ₹ 700 crore before taxes, the corporate income tax rate is 40 per cent , the after-tax capitalisation rate is 15 per cent for both companies, and that company ABC has no debt, whereas company XYZ has ₹ 1,000 crore in 10% bonds. Accordingly to the MM position, the total value of the two companies is shown in table-9. The respective portion of the two companies show the impact of corporate taxes, i.e. debt is providing a benefit to company XYZ because of the tax deductibility of interest payments.

TABLE-9

(₹ in crore)

	Company ABC	Company XYZ
1. Net operating income	₹ 700	₹ 700
2. Taxes@40%	280	280
3. Profits before interest, but after taxes	₹ 420	₹ 420
4. After-tax capitalisation rate for debt-free company	0.15	0.15
5. Capitalised value of (3)	₹ 2,800	₹ 2,800
6. Interest on debt	0	100
7. (I-Tax Rate) (6)	0	60
8. Tax savings on interest	0	40
9. Interest rate	—	.10
10. Capitalised value of (8)	0	400
11. Total value of firm (5)+(10)	2,800	3,200

We can now state that the market value of the levered firm is equal to the market value of the unlevered firm plus the present value of the tax shield:

$$\text{Market value of levered firm} = \text{Market value of unlevered firm} + \text{Present value of tax shield}$$

From this equation, we can conclude that the value of the firm increases linearly as the amount of debt in the capital structure increases, as shown in Panel (a) of Figure-6. This result implies that a firm should increase its level of debt to the point at which the capital structure consists entirely of debt. In other words, the market value of the firm is maximised and its optimal capital structure is achieved when capital structure is all debt. As shown in Panel (b) of Figure-6, the weighted cost of capital, k_o, declines with increases in finacial leverage.

In practice, we *normally* do not observe companies with extremely high levels of debt in their capital structures. Even in the face of leveraged buyouts, however, we still do not observe many companies that approach a 100 per cent debt-financed capital structure. Hence, other factors must be influencing the determination of an optimal capital structure. Two of the most important factors are bankruptcy and agency costs.

BANKRUPTCY COSTS

From a practical viewpoint, a firm cannot expect to gain the benefits associated with the tax deductibility payments without also increasing certain costs. One significant cost category is the costs of financial distress, or bankruptcy. As a firm increases the proportion of debt in its capital structure, there is likely to be an increased possibility of liquidation because of its inability to pay its creditors. There are administrative and other costs associated with liquidation costs means that investors in the company will receive less in the event of its liquidation than if there were no liquidation costs. Others things being equal, it seems reasonable to expect that the possibility of liquidation for the levered company is greater than for the unlevered company which in turn may result in the levered company being less attractive to investors than the unlevered company. If this is is so it is likely that high levels of leverage which may increases the chance of liquidation will be detrimental to the market value of the company.[9] Even if there is virtually no possibility of the company being forced into liquidation, the fact that it has a high proportion of debt in its capital structure may force a change in its investment and financing strategies. For example, because of its high level of debt the company may find it difficult to finance its investments causing it to forgo profitable investment opportunities. Such a change in its investment strategy would be unfavourable to the company's total market value. If capital market were perfect it would not be necessary for the company to modify its investment strategy as funds could always be obtained for profitable investments.

Altman[10] has measured the size of bankruptcy costs for industrial firms. He defines *bankruptcy cost* to consist of *direct costs* (costs paid by debtors in the bankruptcy and restructuring process) and *indirect costs* (costs associated with the loss of customers, suppliers, and key employees plus the managerial effort expended to manage the firm in its distressed condition). Altman found evidence that the direct costs of bankruptcy average about 6 per cent of firm value at the time of filling for bankruptcy. Direct plus indirect cost as a per cent of firm value averaged 12.1 per cent three year prior to filling and 16.7 per cent at the time of filling. Thus, it appears that bankruptcy costs are significant, even if one adjusts for the expected time of occurrence and the probability of occurrence. Castanias[11] offers evidence that supports this conclusion when he finds small firms in industries with high failure rates tend to use less financial leverage.

The likelihood of bankruptcy is not a linear function of a firm's debt. Rather, there is evidence that it increases at an increasing rate beyond some threshold level. Accordingly, bankruptcy costs also become more important beyond this threshold debt ratio.

---

9. Sec. Joseph E. Stiglitz, "A Re-examination of the Modigliani and Miller Theorem," *American Economic Review,* December 1969, pp. 784-793.
10. Edward Altman, "A Further Empirical Investigation of the Bankruptcy Cost Question," *Journal of Finance* 39 (1984) : 1067-1089.
11. Richard Castanias" Bankruptcy Risk and Optimal Capital Structure," *Journal of Finance* 38 (1983) 1917-1635.

FIGURE-6

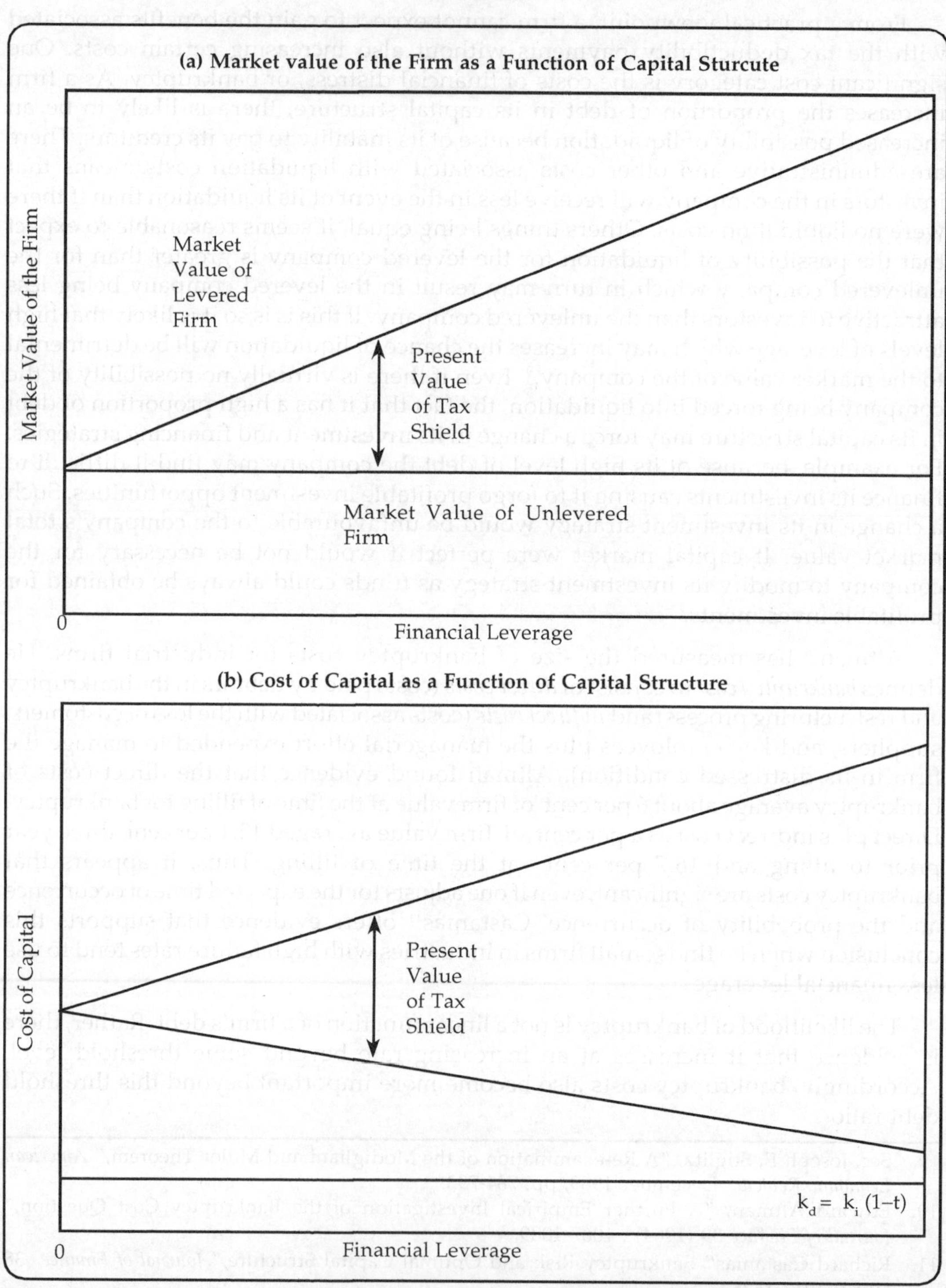
(a) Market value of the Firm as a Function of Capital Sturcute
Market Value of the Firm
Market Value of Levered Firm
Present Value of Tax Shield
Market Value of Unlevered Firm
0
Financial Leverage
(b) Cost of Capital as a Function of Capital Structure
Cost of Capital
Present Value of Tax Shield
k_d = k_i (1–t)
0
Financial Leverage

AGENCY COSTS

Recently, the importance of agency costs to a firm's optimal capital structure has received attention in the literature.[12] An *agency relationship* is defined as a contract under which one or more principals engage agents to perform some service on their behalf by delegating some decision-making authority to the agent. The costs associated with the agency agreement consist of monitoring expenditures by the principal, bonding expenditure by the agent, and other residual losses that arise because the agent's decisions often are not the decisions that would maximise the wealth of the principal. Given the separation of ownership and control that exists for virtually all corporations, and the use of both external debt and equity, the modern firm is involved in numerous agency relationships. On the one hand, there are monitoring costs associated with the firm's use of equity. If a firm is owned exclusively by a single individual (the owner-manager), he or she will obviously makes only those decisions that are wealth-maximising. However, if some of this ownership rights are sold to new shareholders, obvious conflicts in interest may arise. The new shareholders, will have to incur monitoring costs in one form or another to ensure that the co-owner-manager makes decisions that are in the stockholders' best interests. These costs are borne by the firm's shareholders as a reduction in the value of the firm.

Further, there is a problem associated with the issuance of debt. The interest of the owner-manager may lead to investment decisions that are in the shareholders' interests but at the expense of the bondholders interests. This happens because the cost of investments that maximise the firm's total (combined bond and equity) value is not the same as the cost of investments that maximises share value. Complete protection requires specification of an extermely detailed set of protective covenants and high enforcement costs. All these monitoring costs reduce the value of the firm. ultimately, however incurred, the costs of monitoring are borne by the shareholders, and they cause the value of the firm to be less than the discounted present value of the expected cash flows from operations.

Agency costs act as an incentive for the firm to balance the amount of debt and equity in its capital structure. With increased agency costs, as the amount of debt in a firm's capital structure increases, there is an incentive for the firm to limit the amount of debt.

At low debt levels, bondholders do not demand extensive protective covenants and monitoring arrangements, because the risk exposure for the bondholders viewed as being quite limited.[13] Also , at low debt levels, the interest cost of debt financing

12. See Michael C. Jenson and William H. Mickling, "Theory of th Firm: Managerial Behaviour, Agency Costs and Ownership Structure," *Journal of Financial Economics* 3 (October 1976), pp. 305-360.
13. If the capital markets are not perfect, all security holders a must protect themselves against capital structure changes that would erode their position. These "me-first" rules ensure that one party cannot gain at the expense of another. See E. Han Kim, John J. McConnell, and Irwin H. Silberman, "Capital Structure Rearrangements and Me-First Rules in an Efficient Capital Market," *Journal of Finances* 32 (June 1977), pp. 789-810; and Eugane F. Fama, "The Effects of a Firm's Investment and Financing Decisions on the Welfare of Its Security Holders," *American Economic Review* 68 (June 1978), pp. 272-284.

will be low. As the amount of debt increases as a proportion of the total capital structure, bondholders find themselves subject to increased risk that managers (acting on behalf of shareholders) may make investments or take financing actions that could harm the current bondholders. Accordingly, monitoring costs are assumed to increase with increase in a firm's financial leverage, resulting in an increase in the *implicit* cost of debt, including the cost of monitoring and lost operating efficiency. This increase in the cost of debt has the effect of reducing the total value of the firm's securities.

In summary, agency costs are an increasing function of the proportion of debt in the capital structure of a firm. Because of this, agency costs represent another powerful reason, in addition to the increased bankruptcy potential at higher debt ratios, a firm will choose a value-maximizing capital structure that is less than the 100 per cent debt corner solution implied by the MM analysis.

THE VALUE MAXIMISING CAPITAL STRUCTURE

The preceding discussion of the impact of taxes, bankruptcy costs, and agency costs indicates that the market value of a levered firm can be represented by the following equation:

Market value of levered firm	=	Market value of unlevered firm	+	Present value of tax sheld	−	Present value of bankruptcy costs	−	Present value of agency cost

Figure-7 illustrates this relationship graphically. As indicated in this figure and in Equation the present value of expected bankruptcy costs and the agency costs associated with debt financing offset the present value of the tax shield accruing from debt—resulting in an optimal (value-maximising) amount of debt, B, and an optimal capital structure, B/S.

CAPITAL STRUCTURE DECISIONS IN PRACTICE

Following the traditional approach, a company would increase the proportion of debt in its capital structure until an optimal position is reached. The company would then seek to finance future investment proposals in roughly the same proportions as the optimal capital structure. Clearly, the financial manager should endeavour to finance the company's investments so as to minimise the weighted average cost of capital. That is, he should use the available sources of finance in order of their cost. However, this does not mean that all companies should always finance their investments by using first the cheapest source of finance. There are clearly many factors influencing a company's financing decisions, and cost is only one of them. These factors include personal tax effects, industry effects, signaling effects, and managerial preference effects.

PERSONAL TAX EFFECTS

The MM tax case led to the conclusion that, in the absence of bankruptcy and agency costs, the firm should attempt to minimise its taxes by empolying the

FIGURE-7

VALUE OF THE FIRM AS A FUNCTION OF CAPITAL STRUCTURE (WITH CORPORATE INCOME TAX BANKRUPTCY COSTS, AND AGENCY COSTS)

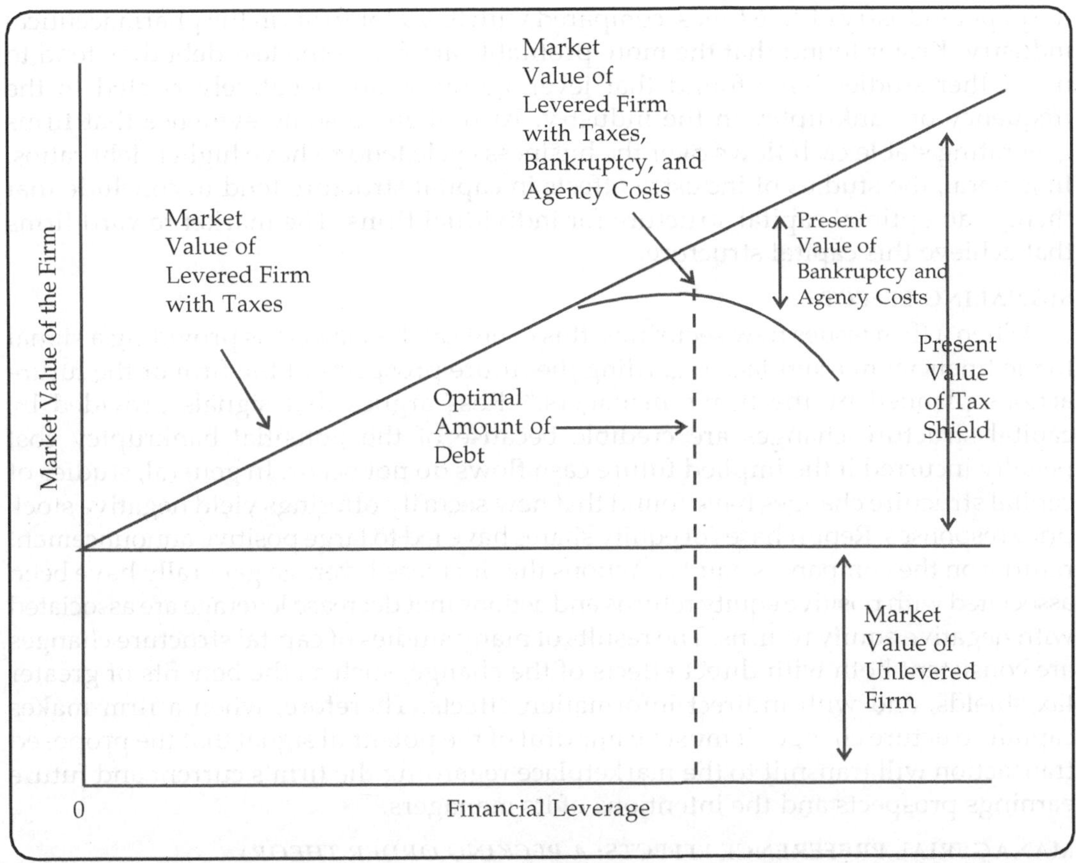

maximum amount of debt. The MM tax case did not consider the effect of personal income taxes, however. Miller[14] has extended the tax case analysis to include both corporate and personal income taxes. Miller argued that although a firm can save taxes by increasing its debt ratio, individual investors would pay greater taxes on their returns from the firm if these returns were predominantly interest, rather than dividends and capital appreciation on equity. Historically, the tax code has favoured capital gains income from equity over interest income, because capital gains generally have been taxed at a lower rate than ordinary income (including interest income) and because taxes on capital gains are deferred until the capital gain is realised.

Miller concluded that when both personal and corporate income taxes are considered, there is no optimal debt ratio for an individual firm, although there is an optimal amount of total debt in the marketplace, reflecting the difference in corporate and personal tax rates.

14. M.H. Miller, "Debt and Taxes," *Journal of Finance,* 32 (May 1977): 261-276.

INDUSTRY EFFECTS

A number of studies have found significant capital structure differences among industries. For example, a study by Kester[15] shows a debt to equity ratio for firms in the paper industry of 1.36 times, compared with 0.079 for firms in the pharmaceutical industry. Kester found that the more profitable are firms, the less debt they tend to use. Other studies have found that leverage ratios are negatively related to the frequency of bankruptcy in the industry. Also, there is some evidence that firms generating stable cash flows over the business cycle tend to have higher debt ratios. In general, the studies of industry effects in capital structure tend to conclude that there is an optimal capital structure for individual firms. The market reward firms that achieve this capital structure.

SIGNALING EFFECTS

When a firm issues new securities, this event can be viewed as providing a signal to the financial marketplace regarding the future prospects of the firm or the future actions planned by the firm's managers.[16] Ross argues that signals provided by capital structure changes are credible because of the potential bankruptcy cost penalty incurred if the implied future cash flows do not occur. In general, studies of capital structure changes have found that new security offerings yield negative stock price responses. Repurchases of equity shares have led to large positive announcement returns on the company's equity. Actions that increase leverage generally have been associated with positive equity returns and actions that decrease leverage are associated with negative equity returns. The results of many studies of capital structure changes are consistent both with direct effects of the change, such as the benefits of greater tax shields, and with indirect information effects. Therefore, when a firm makes capital structure changes it must be mindful of the potential signal that the proposed transaction will transmit to the marketplace regarding the firm's current and future earnings prospects and the intentions of its managers.[17]

MANAGERIAL PREFERENCE EFFECTS: *A PECKING ORDER THEORY*

Myers[18] has suggested that there may be no particular target capital structure. *Myers's pecking order theory implies that firms prefer to finance internally.* Myers argued that managers modify dividend payouts to avoid the need for external equity sales while avoiding major changes in the dividend amount. If external financing is required, Myers suggested that the safest securities are issued first. Debt tends to be the first. Debt tends to be the first security issued and external equity the security of

15. W.C. Kester, "Capital and Ownership Structure: A Comparison of United States and Japanese Manufacturing Corporation," *Financial Management* (Spring 1986): 5-16.
16. Stephen Ross, "The Determination of Financial Structure: The Incentive-Signaling Approach," *Bell Journal of Economics* 8 (1977): 23-40.
17. See Ronald W. Masulis, *The Debt/Equity Choice,* (Cambridge, Mass.: Ballinger Publishing. 1988) for an excellent discussion and review of the signaling literature as it relates to capital structure decisions.
18. S.C. Myers, "The Capital Structure Puzzle," *Journal of Finance,* 39 (July 1984): 575-592.

last resort. The preference for internal financing is based on a desire to avoid the discipline and monitoring that occurs when new securities are sold publicly. In addition, Myers argued that the pecking order of financing may reflect the relative issue costs for various security types. The pecking order theory helps to explain why profitable firms tend to have low debt ratios.

ETHICAL ISSUES: LBO STAKEHOLDER IMPACTS

The rapid pace of mergers and acquisitions has raised may interesting issues regarding the rights of the various corporate stakeholders in these transactions. Leveraged buyouts result in dramatic increases in the amount of debt used to finance a firm—up to 95 per cent of the capital structure in some cases. The use of this large amount of debt permits a small group of investors to acquire ownership and control of a large firm with a relatively small equity investment. By concentrating ownership and control, the equity agency problems associated with separation of ownership from control are largely eliminated. Also, the heavy burden of fixed charges from the debt financing forces managers to increase dramatically the efficiency of operations of the acquired firm. These benefits from LBOs are well-documented.[19]

However, these benefits do not come without significant costs. For example, increased operating efficiency often is achieved by eliminating jobs, reducing other payroll expenses, and closing inefficient plants. LBOs raise important ethical questions. How are the competing interests of stakeholders to be resolved in LBOs and other significant financial transactions? These questions rarely have simple answers, however. Some issues to consider when debating the ethics of LBOs are:

1. Is it in the long-run interest of employees to maintain staffing levels and operate facilities that are inefficient and reduce the company's ability to compete with other enterprises?
2. Are bondholders truly harmed in LBO transactions, considering the bond covenants for which they contracted when they purchased the bonds and the relationship between bond yields and covenant protection?

MANAGERIAL IMPLICATIONS OF CAPITAL STRUCTURE THEORY

The rich body of theoretical and empirical capital structure studies provides important insights for financial mangers. When finance managers, analysts, and investors evaluate the projects that firms undertake, they generally have the assumption that long-term capital expenditure decisions can be separated from capital structure decisions. This assumption, however, does not hold. Wealth created or transferred from changing the capital structure (or financing mix) versus the wealth created from investing in the net present value projects are strategic financial decisions, discussed under Seperation Principle.

19. See for example, G.P. Baker and K.H. Wruck, "Organization Changes and Value Creation in Leveraged Buyouts: The Case of O.M. Scott and Sons Company," *Journal of Financial Economics* 25 (1989): 163-190.

SEPARATION PRINCIPLE

The separation principle states that the selection of capital investments is independent of the selection of financing methods. In other world, the attractiveness of a capital investment is independent of how that particular investment is financed. There are sound reason for this principle, as a general guidelines, but there are situations in which an investment affects the optimal debt ratio and/or the components costs of the capital. A review of the reasons for the separation principle creates the foundation for dealing with exceptions. The principle gained prominence in the capital budgeting as a response to erroneous attempts to make undesirable investment look viable by tying them with debt financing. To illustrate suppose Vijaya Group, a company with ₹ 100 crore of capital, is financed with 40% debt and 60% equity. The after tax costs of debt and equity are 8% and 15%, respectively. The internal rate of return of the group is 12.1 per cent and the company has plans for expansion which requires ₹ 200 crore. Can the expansion plans be financed entirely with debt? The finance manager justifies the investment entirely by debt by computing the weighted average cost of capital (WACC) of the Group. Which is 12.2% = .6(.15) + .4 (.08). But there is a fallacy in finance manager's justification and here comes the importance of separation principle. Assume again that Vijaya Group's existing capital structure is optimal and if there is a increase in financial leverage (50:50), the cost of equity rises to 16% and the cost of debt to 9%. After the new asset is required, the WACC will be 12.5% = .5(.16) + .5 (.09). Hence, Vijaya Group must earn 12.5% on ₹ 1200 crore of assets as against the previous requirement of 12.2% on ₹ 1000 crore of assets. Thus the required after tax benefit must increase by ₹ 28 crore.

Increase in required benefit = .125 (₹ 1200 crore) - .122 (₹ 1000 crore)
= ₹ 28 crore.

This means the Marginal Cost of Capital (MCC) is

= ₹ 28 crore / ₹ 200 crore
= 14%

Vijaya Group minimises its MCC for a new project by financing with the existing mix. If the existing financing mix is not optimal, the Group can gain the benefit of moving to the optimal capital structure. Thus, the company can maximise the shareholders wealth by applying the separation principle and in the process create the capital structure of minimise the weighted average cost of capital.

A company may move around the optimal capital structure, issuing debt one time and issuing equity the next time because of flotation costs and the economies of scale in securities issues. The separation principle still hold in these cases because any movement away from optimal capital structure is purely temporary and only for the purpose of minimising transaction costs.

The separation principle is an important response to what otherwise be erroneous decisions. But, like most simple rules, it does not always hold. Wealth transfer are one case in which the separation principle does not hold.

Wealth Transfers from Shareholders to Creditors

A finance manager may transfer wealth from shareholders to creditors, or vice versa, and this wealth transfer must be considered in capital budgeting. Some investments create opportunities for special financing which may in turn change the risk characteristics of the firm by changing the financing mix. To see how the wealth transfer might occur, assume that Vijaya Group from the previous example has ₹ 400 crore of long-term debt and ₹ 600 crore of equity issued. The company can issue ₹ 200 crore of new debt. The increased debt ratio makes the old debt more risky—the required rate of return will increase and the share price falls—but Vijaya need not to pay the higher required rate of return because the interest rate is already contractually set. The existing creditors simply lose wealth. The necessary after tax benefit before the expansion was:

= .15 (₹ 600 crore) + .08 (₹ 400 crore)
= ₹ 122 crore

The necessary after tax benefit on new financing of ₹ 200 crore asset with new debt is:

= .16 (₹ 600 crore) + .08 (₹ 400 crore) + .09 (₹ 200 crore)
= ₹ 146 crore

The marginal cost of capital (MCC) is:

MCC = (₹ 146 crore - ₹ 122 crore) ÷ ₹ 200 crore = 12%.

Thus, the wealth transfer effect makes the otherwise a particular unviable project an attractive one since the MCC is 12%, below the WACC at the optimal capital structure. If it is necessary to pay the high rate of invest to all creditors, the all-debt financing world result in a 14% MCC, well above the 12.2% cost of the optimal capital structure. Hence, one must be cautious in assigning the benefit of wealth to a particular investment by decreasing the MCC for that investment. If new debt is to be issued to reduce the proportion of equity in total financing by buying back the equity, the same wealth transfer can be allowed independent of investment decision. Even if wealth transfer is through acquisitions of assets, the benefit will generally be available regardless of which asset is acquired. Consequently, the MCC based on wealth transfer must generally be applied to all proposed investments in choosing the alternative investments. The wealth transfer benefit would accrue to a particular investment only if there was some characteristic of that investment that meant that it alone could be used to capture the wealth transfer benefit. This could be the case if one particular investment created the opportunity for secured financing. Further, the restrictive covenants associated with debt issues eliminates the opportunities for wealth transfer. For instance if the covenants put the limit of total debt to 50% of capital, the company must retire the old debt and replace it with the new debt. This means the MCC may be higher if the new debt is raised at higher cost. The only way to reduce the WACC is to change the capital structure to meet the increased needs for financing the additional asset acquisition in future periods.

Continuing with the example of Vijaya Group, assume that existing assets will generate a perpetuity of ₹ 250 crore. The proposed new assets will generate an after tax flow of ₹ 100 crore at the end of each year for 3 years. The debt with an 8% after tax interest cost must be repaid over the first 2 years. Table-1 shows the present value of all future cash flows for Vijaya Group *with and without* an attempt by finance manager to transfer wealth from existing creditors by increasing the debt ratio.

It can be observed from Table-10 that discount rates changes from period to period with the changed leverage alternative. The present value computed for 3 years are:

$$\text{Year 1 flow:} \quad \frac{₹\ 350\ \text{crore}}{1.121} = ₹\ 311.94\ \text{crore}$$

$$\text{Year 2 flow:} \quad \frac{₹\ 350\ \text{crore}}{1.121 \times 1.121} = ₹\ 278.02\ \text{crore}$$

$$\text{Year 3 flow:} \quad \frac{₹\ 350\ \text{crore}}{1.121 \times 1.121 \times 1.125} = ₹\ 247.78\ \text{crore}$$

At the start of year 4, Vijaya Group will have an annuity of ₹ 250 crore year forever. The value of this annuity, as of the end of year 3 or the beginning of year 4, is ₹ 250 crore ÷ .125 = ₹ 2000 crore. With the changed leverage, the value of that annuity, as of now is:

$$\text{Present value of annuity} = \frac{₹\ 2000\ \text{crore}}{1.121 \times 1.121 \times 1.125} = ₹1414.71\ \text{crore}$$

Thus the higher cost of capital off-sets the benefit of lower cost in the initial period. However, the wealth transfer way sufficient to off-set the longer-term detrimental effects of the change in the leverage.

INFORMATION ASYMMETRY AND WEALTH TRANSFER

Information asymmetary may also lead to wealth transfer. To illustrate, assume that investors expectations differ from the management of ABC Co. The company has annual income of ₹ 100 crore and has 10 crore equity shares issued. Hence, the EPS is ₹ 10. If all earnings are distributed among the shareholders and they require a 20% return, the price of each share in the market will be ₹ 50. The price of the share will double if the earnings and dividends are double next year without any new investment. If a new opportunity arise before ABC Co., requiring new investment of ₹ 100 crore, that ensures a perpetual issue and dividend of ₹ 30 a year. The new investment obviously has a positive NPV with a 20% required rate of return. But to raise additional funds for new investment, the company must issue 2 crore new equity shares. After earnings from existings investments double, the EPS and anticipated equity share price will be:

TABLE-10

Present Value With and Without A Capital Structure Slight

Year	1	2	3	4
Cash Flows				
Existing assets	₹ 250 crore	₹ 250 crore	₹ 250 crore	₹ 250 crore
New assets	100	100	100	—
Total cash flow	₹ 350 crore	₹ 350 crore	₹ 350 crore	₹ 350 crore
Unchanged Leverage				
Required return	12.2%	12.2%	12.2%	12.2%
Total cash flows	₹ 350 crore	₹ 350 crore	₹ 350 crore	₹ 250 crore
Present value	₹ 311.94 crore	₹ 278.02 crore	₹ 247.79 crore	₹ 1450.78 crore
Total present value	= ₹ 2868.84 crore			
Changed Leverage				
Required return	12.2%	12.2%	12.2%	12.2%
Present Value	₹ 312.22 crore	₹ 278.52 crore	₹ 247.57 crore	₹ 1414.71 crore
Total Present Value	₹ 2253.02 crore			

EPS = ₹ 230 crore ÷ 12 crore = ₹ 19.2
Expected equity share price = ₹ 19.2 ÷ .20
= ₹ 96.0

The equity share price a year later is depressed because the investors are uninformed and the current share price is unchanged by the investments. This problem arises where investors do not correctly recognise future investment opportunities. Wealth is created by the new investment, but that wealth and more is transferred from old to new shareholders.

CHANGE IN THE RISK CHARACTERISTICS OF THE FIRM

To consider the impact of unsystematic risk on required return for an individual capital investment the finance managers should examine both. The change in the components costs of debt and equity and the change in optimal mix of debt and equity simultaneously.

First, the finance manager examining the simplest case of changing debt capacity, the component costs remain unchanged, but the optimal debt ratio increases due to low or negative correlation between cash flows for the new investment and cash flows for the company's existing investments. In this case, the MCC for the investment is based on the increase in the total optimal amount of debt if the investment is accepted:

$$\text{MCC} = \frac{k_d \times \text{Increased Debt} + \text{ke} \times \text{Increased Equity}}{\text{Total Investment Required}}$$

Where k_d and Ke are respective after tax cost of debt and equity.

To illustrate, Vijaya Group's existing capital structure of debt (40%) and equity (60%) is considered to be optimal for current base with 8% after tax cost of debt and 15% of equity. Vijaya is considering ₹ 200 crore of additional investment to improve the stability of cash flow and profit. If the enhanced investment increase the optimal debt ratio to 0.45, the new debt is:

New debt = .45 (₹ 1200 crore) - .40 (₹ 1000 crore)
= ₹ 540 crore - ₹ 400 crore
= ₹ 140 crore

and the new equity will be:

₹ 200 crore - ₹ 140 crore = ₹ 60 crore.

In other word, the marginal financing for the new investment will be 70% debts and 30% equity. Assuming the component costs do not change, the required return for this investment is :

MCC = .70 (.08) + .30 (.15)
= 10.1 %

But the investments that change the optimal debt ratio will also have an impact on the components costs of funding. The component costs will also change with the change in the company's optimal debt ratio.

In the second case, the MCC is guideline. The finance manager analyses the investments that changes the optimal debt ratio and component. The marginal cost of the increase in debt as a result of new investment will be:

$$\text{Marginal cost of debt} = \frac{k_{dn}\ \text{Debt}_n - k_{do}\ \text{Debt}_o}{\text{Debt}_n - \text{Debt}_o}$$

Where k_{dn} and k_{do} are respective costs of debt of new and old optimal debt ratios. Debt_n and Debt_o are the optimal debt amounts of debt funds new and old investments.

The marginal cost of equity is defined in a similar way.

$$\text{Marginal cost of equity} = \frac{k_{en}\ \text{Equity}_n - k_{eo}\ \text{Equity}_o}{\text{Equity}_n - \text{Equity}_o}$$

Where k_{en} and k_{eo} are respective costs of equity under new and old investments. Equity_n and Equity_o are the optimal amounts of equity under new and old investments.

In illustrate, assume again that Vijaya Group has no opportunity to transfer wealth from existing creditors to shareholders or vice versa. If the proposed new investments increase the optimal debt ratio from 0.40 to 0.45. With acquisition and optimal financing of the new asset, the after tax cost of debt will increase to 8.5% and the cost of equity to 16%. The marginal costs of debt and equity are therefore:

$$\text{MC of debt} = \frac{.085 \times ₹\ 540 \text{ crore} - .08 \times ₹\ 400 \text{ crore}}{₹\ 540 \text{ crore} - ₹\ 400 \text{ crore}}$$

$$= \frac{₹\ 45.9 \text{ crore} - ₹\ 32 \text{ crore}}{₹\ 140 \text{ crore}}$$

$$= 9.928\%$$

$$\text{MC of equity} = \frac{.16 \times ₹\ 660 \text{ crore} - .15 \times ₹\ 600 \text{ crore}}{₹\ 660 \text{ crore} - ₹\ 600 \text{ crore}}$$

$$= \frac{₹\ 105.6 \text{ crore} - ₹\ 90 \text{ crore}}{₹\ 60 \text{ crore}}$$

$$= 26\%$$

Since the ₹ 200 crore increase in assets results an increase of ₹ 140 crore in the optimal amount of debt, the debt ratio for the investment is 0.7 and the MCC for the investment is:

$$MCC = .7 \times .09928 + .3!x .26$$
$$= .06949!!+ .078 = .14749$$
$$= 14.75\%$$

The MCC can also be found without computing the component costs by finding the required earnings (after tax but before interest) with and without new investment. This can be expressed as the required earnings as a % of the increase in assets:

$$MCC = \frac{[(.085 \times ₹\ 540 \text{ crore} + .16 \times ₹\ 660 \text{ crore}) - (.08 \times ₹\ 400 \text{ crore} + .15 \times ₹\ 600 \text{ crore}]}{₹\ 1200 \text{ crore} - ₹\ 1000 \text{ crore}}$$

$$= 14.75\%$$

The component costs of debt may differ with the debt maturity, risk, and liquidity. For instance, the component costs of debt for an investment with 2-year life and another with 7-year life are likely to be different. Liquidity essentially gives the company an option to change the debt amount if conditions change and vice versa is the case with the creditors. Further, the company may be required to rely on equity financing unless it agrees to restrictive covenants limiting its ability to sell assets without lenders' permission.

It is clear that the capital structure decision is one of the centrally important decisions facing financial managers. There is little doubt that changes in capital structure result in changes in the market value of the firm. The benefits of the tax shield from debt lead to increased firm value, at least up to the point that increased bankruptcy and agency costs begin to offset the debt advantage. The optimal capital structure is influenced heavily by the business risk facing the firm. Finally, it can be what that when managers make explicit changes in a firm's capital structure, these actions transmit important information to investors.

ILLUSTRATIVE PROBLEMS

1. A company with a debt-equity ratio of 2 : 3 has a level of business risk which gives it a weighted average cost of capital of 18%. The cost of debt is 10 per cent . What is the cost of equity?

Solution

The cost of equity can be calculated as below:

$$k_e = k_o + (k_o - k_i)\ 2/3$$
$$= 18\% + (18\% - 10\%)\ 2/3 = 23.3\%$$

2. Repeat the Problem-1 and assume that the company increases the level of debt-equity to 100 per cent .

Solution

Increase in the financial risk will cause the cost of equity to rise as follows:

k_e = 18%(18% – 10%) 1/1 = 26%

3. Company XYZ is unlevered and has a cost of equity of 20 per cent and a total market value of ₹ 10,00,00,000. Company ABC is identical to XYZ in all respects except that it uses debt finance in its capital structure with a market value of ₹ 4,00,00,000 and a cost of 10 per cent . Find the market value of equity, weighted average cost of capital and cost of equity of ABC if the tax advantage of debt is 25 per cent .

Solution

Total market value

$V_{ABC} = V_{XYZ} + B.t.$

Where:

V_{ABC} = the weighted average cost of capital of leveraged company.
V_{XYZ} = The weighted average cost of capital of unlevered company.
B = The market value of debt.
t = The pre-tax cost of debt.

By inserting the given values in above equation we get:

= ₹ 100 crore + (₹ 400 crore x 0.25)
= ₹ 100 crore + ₹ 10 crore = ₹ 110 crore

The market value of equity (s):

= ₹ 110 crore—₹ 40crore = ₹ 70 crore

$$\text{Weighted average cost of capital} = k_{o(\text{ABC})} = k_{o(\text{XYZ})}\left(1-\frac{\text{B.t.}}{\text{B+S}}\right)$$

$$= 20\%\left(1\text{-}\frac{₹\ 40 \text{ crore x } 0.25}{₹\ 11 \text{ crore}}\right)=18.18\%$$

Cost of equity=

$$k_e = k_{e(\text{XYZ})} + (k_{e(\text{ABC})} - k_t)\frac{\text{B}(1-t)}{\text{S}_{(\text{ABC})}}$$

$$=20\%+(20\%\text{-}10\%)\frac{₹\ 40 \text{ crore } (1\text{-}0.25)}{7 \text{ crore}}=24.28$$

The alternative calculation of the weighted average cost of capital is:—

$$k_o = k_i(1-t)\frac{B}{B+S} + k_e\frac{S}{B+S}$$

$$=10\% \ (1\text{-}0.25)\ \frac{₹\ 40}{₹\ 110} + 24.28\%\ \frac{₹\ 70}{₹\ 110} = 18.18\%$$

4. Bharat and National Industries have the same of business risk. Illustrate any arbitrage gains which may be possible using the data below:

	Bharat	*National*
Market Values:		
Equity	₹ 5,00,00,000	₹ 7,50,00,000
Debt	3,00,00,00	—
	₹ 8,00,00,000	₹ 7,50,00,000
Earnings	₹ 1,50,00,000	₹ 1,50,00,000
Interest	30,00,000	—
Dividends	₹ 1,20,00,000	₹ 1,50,00,000

All earnings are distributed. Assume Mr. K.L. Rao owns 1 per cent of the equity in both Bharat and National industries.

Solution

The weighted average cost of capital of each company is as follows:

$$\text{Bharat} = \frac{₹\ 1,50,00,000}{₹\ 8,00,00,000} = 18.75\%$$

$$\text{National} = \frac{₹\ 1,50,00,000}{₹\ 7,50,00,000} = 20.0\%$$

Mr. Rao should keep his investment in National and transfer his investment from Bharat to National. Current income from Bharat Industries is

=1% × ₹ 1,20,00,000 = ₹ 1,20,000

Mr. Rao should sell shares for

1% × ₹ 5,00,00,000 = ₹ 5,00,000

In order to maintain the same level of financial risk assuming that Mr. Rao decides to borrow at 10% which is same as of Bharat Industries' cost of debt:

₹ 5,00,000 × 3/5 = ₹ 3,00,000

and the total of ₹ 8,00,000 should be invested in National Industries.

Income from National Industries after transfer:

$$\text{Dividends} = \frac{₹\ 8,00,000}{₹\ 7,50,00,000} = ₹\ 1,60,000$$

Less: interest payable on personal borrowings:

₹ 3,00,000 × 10% = ₹ 30,000

Hence, Mr. Rao's income is:

₹ 1,60,000–₹ 30,000=₹ 1,30,000

Thus, Mr. Rao increased his income by ₹ 10,000.

5. Assume that A Ltd., B Ltd. and C Ltd. are three companies which fall *in the same risk category* in a particular capital market. A Ltd. has an all-equity capital structure whilst B Ltd. and C Ltd. have both equity and debt funds in their structure. Assume also that our capital market is perfect (no taxation and no transaction costs). The ordinary share of A Ltd. (which currently earn a 12% return on capital) and the debenture capital market are both in equilibrium. The following information about earnings, dividends, interest payments and market values of Companies B and C are temporarily as follows:

	Company B	*Company* C
Total market value of equity	₹ 1,00,000	₹ 1,60,000
Total market value of debt	₹ 1,00,000	₹ 3,20,000
	₹ 2,00,000	₹ 4,80,000
	Years *1–∞*	*Years* *1–∞*
Annual dividends	₹ 13,000	₹ 53,600
Annual interest	₹ 5,000	₹ 16,000
Annual earnings	₹ 18,000	₹ 69,600

(a) (i) Determine the weighted-average cost of capital of companies B and C; then comment whether these two companies' ordinary shares are in equilibrium or not.

(ii) What do you think is the best decision for shareholders in both company B and company C to make?

(iii) Assume that Madan Lal holds ₹ 450 worth of ordinary shares in B Ltd. Assume also that he can borrow money at an annual interest rate of 5%. Show Madan Lal how he can improve his financial position whilst keeping his current level of financial risk unchanged.

(b) Discuss the implications of your calculations above for the determination of the optimal financial structure of a firm from a practical point of view.

Solution

	Co. B	*Co. C*
(a) (1) Return on debentures:	$\frac{₹\ 5,000}{₹\ 1,00,000} \times 100 = 5\%$	$\frac{₹\ 16,000}{₹\ 3,20,000} \times 100 = 5\%$
Return on equity:	$\frac{₹\ 13,000}{₹\ 1,00,000} \times 100 = 13\%$	$\frac{₹\ 53,600}{₹\ 1,60,000} \times 100 = 33.5\%$

WACC: $5\% \times \frac{1}{2} + 13\% \times \frac{1}{2} = 9\%$ $5\% \times \frac{2}{3} + 33.5\% \times \frac{1}{3} = 14.5\%$

In the MM world the WACC of all three companies should be the same as they all fall in the same risk category. As the ordinary shares of A and the debenture market are in equilibrium, then clearly the ordinary shares in B and C cannot be in equilibrium. The equity in B is overvalued and that in C undervalued.

(2) If this situation existed, then 'arbitrage' should take place with shareholders migrating from the overvalued company to the undervalued company. This arbitrage activity would result in the returns of both companies attaining equilibrium levels. Therefore shareholders in B should sell their holdings and reinvest the proceeds in C whilst keeping their level of financial risk constant. Shareholders in C should hold or increase if possible their shareholdings as the value should increase as arbitrage takes place.

(3) In line with advice given in (2), above, Madan Lal should move his investment from B to C whilst keeping the level of financial risk constant.

At present Madan Lal receives 13% × 450 = ₹ 58.50 on his investment in B. He should sell his shares for ₹ 450, borrow ₹ 450, making his personal gearing the same as that faced in B, and invest the ₹ 900 in C's equity and debt in proportion to their market values—one-third in equity, two-thirds in debt.

Madan Lal's income would then be:			
On C equity	33.5% × ₹ 300	=	100.50
On C debt	5% × ₹ 600	=	30.00
			130.50
Less: Interest on personal debt:			
	5% × ₹ 450	=	22.50
			₹ 108.00

Madan Lal increases his income by ₹ 49.50 (108–58.50) whilst maintaining his current level of financial risk.

(b) Part (a) calculations and discussion were conducted under the restrictive assumptions necessary to support MM's irrelevancy theorem, that is where firms of identical risk category exist in perfect market conditions the capital structure will not change the overall return demanded by financial markets. WACC will remain the same for all firms in the same risk class irrespective of differences in financial structure. However, when the assumptions are relaxed the position is less clear. Corporate taxation provides valuable tax shields on interest paid which increase the value of the firm. Bankruptcy costs are likely to become more significant as the level of gearing increases. In addition the interaction of personal and corporate taxes as suggested by Miller may also be important.

6. Super Star Co. is soon to be incorporated. Its promoters are considering five different possible capital structures for the new company. An analysis of comparable companies with equivalent business risks has been undertaken. This analysis shows that, if the before-tax cost of debt is a constant 10% irrespective of the capital structure, then the cost of equity capital, after corporation tax, will be as follows:

Gearing ratio (debt capital/total capital) (%)	*Cost of equity capital (%)*
0	20.000
20.0	21.250
40.0	23.333
50.0	25.000
60.0	27.500

The above predictions for the equity cost of capital also assume that the earnings of the Super Star Co. will be taxed at a rate of 50% and that the debt interest is an allowable expense for tax purposes. The promoters expect that the company will generate a steady annual earnings stream of ₹ 12.6 crore, before the payment of debt interest, for the foreseeable future.

(a) Calculate the effective after-tax weighted-average cost of capital and the total market value for each of the five possible capital structures, assuming that the before-tax annual cost of debt will be a constant 10% (irrespective of the capital structure chosen).

(b) Interpret the results of your calculations in (a) above and explain their significance in financial management.

(c) Discuss the possible consequences to a company of having a capital structure containing a high gearing ratio.

Solution

(a) *After-tax WACC for each capital structure:*

After tax cost of debt = 50% × 10% = 5%

Gearing ratio	WACC		
0%			20%
20%	(0.2 × 5%) + (0.8 × 21.25%)	=	18%
40%	(0.4 × 5%) + (0.6 × 23.333%)	=	16%
50%	(0.5 × 5%) + (0.5 × 25%)	=	15%
60%	(0.6 × 5%) + (0.4 × 27.5%)	=	14%

Total market capitalisation of firm:

In each case this is:

$$\frac{\text{Annual earnings before tax} \times (1\text{–tax rate})}{\text{WACC}}$$

as follows:

Gearing ratio	*Market capitalisation*		*₹ crore*
0%	12.6 × (1–0.5) ÷ 0.2	=	31.5
20%	12.6 × (1–0.5) ÷ 0.18	=	35.0
40%	12.6 × (1–0.5) ÷ 0.16	=	39.375
50%	12.6 × (1–0.5) ÷ 0.15	=	42.0
60%	12.6 × (1–0.5) ÷ 0.14	=	45.0

(b) The cost of equity capital and firm value at different levels of gearing agree with Modigliani and Miller's propositions with tax. With taxation they proposed that:

Total market value = MV of ungeared firm + PV of interest tax shield

Assuming perpetual debt:

Total MV = MV of ungeared firm + tax rate × MV debt

also:

$$\text{WACC} = \text{cost of equity if ungeared} \times \left(\frac{\text{MV equity} + (1-t)\ \text{MV debt}}{\text{total MV of firm}}\right)$$

With corporate taxes, MM proposed that WACC decreased and market value increased with levels of debt taken on due to tax shield on interest payments. In this scenario the highest level of gearing attainable would be optimal.

(c) When probability of bankruptcy is admitted, the position changes. If bankruptcy occurs, then costs will be increased. The greater the level of gearing, the greater the probability of bankruptcy occurring and the PV of bankruptcy costs must be set against the PV of the tax shield on debt interest.

Gearing will only be of value if taxable profits exist to take advantage of tax shield. As level of gearing increases probability of profit being high enough to absorb interest payments decreases. Cost of borrowing will increase as level of gearing increases as will cost of equity. All these factors imply that marginal benefit to be gained from borrowing decreases at higher levels of gearing.

7. Gita Industries and Rita Industries are two firms which operate in the same industry and are both considered to be in the same risk class. Both companies have gross operating profit of ₹ 1,00,000 per annum. Gita relies on equity sources in its finance while Rita uses both loan and equity sources. Their capital structure is as follows

Gita: equity	: ₹ 7,00,000	(market value)
Rita: equity	: ₹ 4,00,000	(Market value)
8% debenture	: ₹ 4,00,000	(nominal value – currently traded at par)
	₹ 8,00,000	

At the present time you hold 4% of Rita's share capital. Assume that both companies pay out all their profit after interest in dividends.

(a) Determine the weighted-average cost of capital of both companies; then comment whether these two companies' ordinary shares are in equilibrium or not.

(b) Show how you may gain from arbitrage whilst keeping your current level of financial risk constant. Assume that you can borrow money at an annual interest rate of 8%.

(Ignore taxation).

Solution

(a) Gita Industries:

$$\text{Return of equity} = \frac{₹\ 1{,}00{,}000}{₹\ 1{,}00{,}000} \times 100 = 14.29\%$$

$$= \text{WACC (all equity)}$$

Rita Industries:

$$\text{Return of debit} = \frac{₹\ 32{,}000}{₹\ 4{,}00{,}000} \times 100 = 8\%$$

$$\text{Return of equity} = \frac{₹\ 1{,}00{,}000 - ₹\ 32{,}000}{₹\ 4{,}00{,}000} = 17\%$$

$$\text{WACC} = 8\% \times \frac{₹\ 4{,}00{,}000}{₹\ 8{,}00{,}000} + 17\% \times \frac{₹\ 4{,}00{,}000}{₹\ 8{,}00{,}000} = 4\% + 8.5\% = 12.5\%$$

The total value of Rita exceeds that of Gita, despite the operating cash flows of both companies being equal and of the same risk class. In an MM world the value of both companies should be the same and therefore the ordinary shares of Rita and Gita must be misvalued—i.e. Gita's shares undervalued, Rita's overvalued.

(b) As a holder of 4% of Rita's share capital, the strategy should be to sell at market value, take on personal borrowing to make financial risk the same as faced by shareholders in Rita and to invest the total in Gita shares:

4% of Rita shares would sell for:	₹ 16,000
Personal borrowing at 8%	₹ 16,000
Invested in Gita shares	₹ 32,000
Income from Gita shares:	
$\frac{₹\ 32{,}000}{₹\ 7{,}00{,}000} \times ₹\ 1{,}00{,}000$	₹ 4,571
Less: Interest on personal borrowing: ₹ 16,000 × 8%	₹ 1,280
	₹ 3,291
Previous income from Rita shares: 16000 × 17%	₹ 2,720
Gain from arbitrage	₹ 571

8. Anupam Company and Zenith Calculators are identical except for capital structures, has 50 per cent debt and 50 per cent equity, while Zenith has 20 per cent debt and 80 per cent equity. (All per cent ages are in market-value terms.) The borrowing rate for both companies is 13 per cent in a no-tax world, and capital markets are assumed to be perfect.

(a) (1) If you own 2 per cent of the stock of Anupam what is your return if the company has net operating income of ₹ 3,60,000 and the overall capitalization rate of the company, k_0, is 18 per cent ? (2) What is the implied required rate of return on equity? (b) Zenith has the same net operating income as Anupam. (1) What is the implied required equity return of Zenith? (2) Why does it differ from that of Anupam?

Solution

1. a. (1)

Net operating income	₹ 3,60,000
Overall capitalization rate	.18
Total value of firm	₹ 20,00,000
Market value of debt (50%)	10,00,000
Market value of stock (50%)	₹ 10,00,000
Net operating income	₹ 3,60,000
Interest on debt (13%)	1,30,000
Earnings to equity	₹ 2,30,000
2% of ₹ 2,30,000 = ₹ 4,600	

(2) Implied required equity return = ₹ 2,30,000/₹ 10,00,000 = 23%

b. (1)

Total value of firm	**₹ 20,00,000**
Market value of debt (20%)	4,00,000
Market value of equity (80%)	₹ 16,00,000
Net operating income	₹ 3,60,000
Interest on debt (13%)	52,000
Earnings to equity	₹ 3,08,000

Implied required equity return = ₹ 3,08,000/ ₹ 16,00,000 =19.25%

9. MM Enterprises has earnings before interest and taxes (EBIT) of ₹ 3 crore and a 40 per cent tax rate. Its required rate of return on equity in the absence of borrowing is 18 per cent.

(a) In the absence of personal taxes, what is the value of the company in an MM world (1) with no leverage? (2) with ₹ 4 crore in debt? (3) with ₹ 7 crore in debt?

(b) Personal as well as corporate taxes now exist. The marginal personal tax rate on equity income is 25 per cent and the marginal personal tax rate on debt income is 30 per cent . Determine the value of the company for each of the three debt alternatives in part (a). Why do your answers differ?

Solution

(a) (1) Value if unlevered

(*₹ in '000)*

EBIT	₹ 30,000
Profit before taxes	30,000
Taxes	12,000
Profit after taxes	₹ 18,000
* required equity return	.18
Value of unlevered	₹ 1,00,000 (₹ 10 crore)

(2) Value with ₹ 4 crore in debt:

Value = Value if unlevered + Value of tax shield

Value = ₹ 10 crore + .40 (₹ 4 crore) = ₹ 11.60 crore

(3) Value with ₹ 7 crore in debt :

Value = ₹ 10 crore + .40(₹ 7 crore) = ₹ 12.80 crore

Due to the tax subsidy, the firm is able to increase its value in a linear manner with more debt.

b. (1) Value if unlevered the same as before, namely, ₹ 10 crore. (2) Value with ₹ 4 crore in debt:

$$\text{Value} = ₹\ 10\ \text{crore} + \left[1 - \frac{(1-.40)(1-.25)}{1-.30}\right] ₹\ 4\ \text{crore} = ₹\ 11.429\ \text{crore}$$

(3) Value with ₹ 7 crore in debt:

$$\text{Value} = ₹\ 10\ \text{crore} + \left[1 - \frac{(1-.40)(1-.25)}{1-.30}\right] ₹\ 7\ \text{crore} = ₹\ 12.50\ \text{crore}$$

The presence of personal taxes reduces the tax advantage associated with corporate debt. As long as the personal tax on stock income is less than that on debt income, however, the net tax advantage to debt is positive. As a result, the value of the firm rises with more debt, but not as rapidly as if there were no personal taxes or if the personal tax rate on stock and debt income were the same.

10. Trident Resorts is considering various levels of debt. Presently, it has no debt and a total market value of ₹ 150 crore. By undertaking leverage, it believes that it can achieve a net tax advantage (corporate and personal combined) equal to 20 per cent of the amount of the debt. However, the company is concerned with bankruptcy and agency costs as well as lenders increasing their interest rate if it borrows too much. The company believes that it can borrow up to ₹ 50 crore without incurring any of these costs. However, each additional ₹ 50 crore increment in borrowing is expected to result in the three costs cited being incurred. Moreover, they are expected to increase at an increasing rate with leverage. The present-value cost is expected to be the following for various levels of debt:

Debt (in crores)	₹ 50	₹ 100	₹ 150	₹ 120	₹ 250	₹ 300
PV cost of bankruptcy, agency, and increased interest rate (in crores)	0	6	12	20	32	50

Is there an optimal amount of debt for the company?

Solution

(₹ in crore)

(1) Level of Debt	(2) Firm Value Unlevered	(3) PV of Tax Shield (1) x 0.20	(4) PV of Bankruptcy, Agency, and increased Interest Cost	(5) Value of Firm (2) + (3) - (4)
0	150	0	0	150
50	150	10	0	160
100	150	20	6	164
150	150	30	12	168
200	**150**	**40**	**20**	**170**
250	150	50	32	168
300	150	60	50	160

The market value of firm is maximized with ₹ 200 crore in debt.

QUESTIONS

1. What is the objective of capital-structure management?
2. What is the theory of the capital structure of a firm? Of what importance is it to financial manager?
3. How might a firm go about determing its *optimal* capital structure?
4. Why might you suspect that the optimal capital structure would differ significantly from one industry to another? Would the same factors produce differing optimal capital structure within all industry grouping?
5. What are the uses and limitations of the optimal capital structure model?
6. Contrast the David Durand net operating income approach with the Modigliani-Miller approach to the theory of the capital structure.
7. In the simplified world of 'no taxes', there are two competing theories that purport of describe how stock prices are related to capital structure.
   (a) Identify these two theories.
   (b) Briefly describe these two theories
   (c) What main impact does including taxes have on the debate?
8. Integrate the financial leverage approach with the following approaches to the capital structure:
   (a) Net income
   (b) Net operating income
   (c) Traditional
   (b) Modigliani-Miller
9. A financial manager might say that the firm's composite cost of capital is saucer-shaped or U-shaped what does this mean?

10. If there were no imperfactions in financial markets, what capital structure should the firm seek? Why are market imperfections important in finance? Which imperfections are most important?
11. Define the following terms:
    (a) Financial structure
    (b) Capital structure
    (c) Optimal capital structure
    (d) Debt capacity
12. How would the development of a truly comprehensive and accurate theory of capital structure help policy-makers and corporate executive around the world?
13. Discuss the difference between the direct-indirect costs of corporate bankruptcy. Can the threat of deadweight (out-of-pocket) costs entering into the bankruptcy process affect capital structure decision?
14. Indicate the effect of the occurrences on the cost of debt (k_d), the cost of equity (k_e), and the weighted average cost of capital (k_o) for Firms A and B respectively if there is increase in inflation; downturn in economic activity; more stable industry demand; and, lastly, Firm B increase its leverage.
15. Develop an example of 'home-made' leverage showing (i) initial capital structure disequilibrium, (ii) the specific arbitrage process involved in correcting this disquilibrium, and (iii) the new capital structure equilibrium that will result from this process.
16. Describe how certain projects can change the overall risk of the firm in such away that the optimal mix of debt and equity may change and the cost of debt and / or equity may change.
17. Explain the separation principle in regard to wealth created from investing in positive NPV projects versus wealth transferred or created from changing the capital structure (or financing mix).
18. Why might special low-cost financing be available for a specific investment but not available for other investments being considered by the firm?
19. Differentiate between projects that transfer wealth from one financing source to another, ones that created wealth, and ones that do both.
20. As a finance manager, what is your ethical responsibility when you have an opportunity to transfer wealth from creditors to equity shareholders?

PROBLEMS

1. Surat Chemicals is selling for an aggregate market value of ₹ 12,00,00,000. It currently has no debt outstanding. At the annual general meeting, discussion has turned to capital structure—what added debt will do to the ordinary share price. The firm, which is in a 54 per cent tax rate, is considering raising ₹ 2,00,00,000 in new debt using the proceeds to retire some of its equity. You are asked what the theoretical effect of this action will be on the value of the firm in the absence of bankruptcy risks, by how much will the value of the firm change as result of this increase in leverage?

Ans.: ₹ 1,08,00,000

2. Pandhi Industries is an unlevered firm with net operating income of ₹ 20 crores, a cost of equity capital of 12. 5 per cent , and a corporate tax rate of 40 per cent . (a) What is the after-tax cash flow and total value for the unlevered firm? (b) If Pandhi decides to change its capital structure to become a levered firm by issuing debt and buying back its equity shares. The before-tax cost of debt is 10 per cent . Determine the cost of capital of the levered firm for the following amounts of debt issued at per: (i) ₹ 1,00,00,000; (ii) ₹ 6,00,00,000; (iii) ₹ 11,00,00,000.

Ans.: (a) Cash flow after tax : ₹ 12,00,00,000 Total value of unlevered firm : ₹ 96,00,00,000; (b) Debt=₹ 1,00,00,000; k_o=12%, Debt=₹ 6,00,00,000; k_o=10%, Debt=₹ 11,00,00,000; k_o=8.57%

3. Vijaya Steel Tubes has net operating income, NOI, of ₹ 50,00,000 and pays a coupon rate of 10 per cent on all debt. Assume there are no taxes and all debt is issued at par.

(a) Under the net income (NI) approach, assuming a cost of equity capital of 15 per cent , compute the value of the firm and overall cost of capital for: (i) An all-equity capital structure; (ii) Debt of ₹ 2,30,00,000; (iii) An all debt capital structure.

(b) Under the net operating income (NOI) approach, assuming a cost of capital of 12.5 per cent , compute the value of the firm, the cost of equity capital, and the over all cost of capital based on for: (i) An all-equity capital structure; (ii) Debt of ₹ 2,30,00,000; (iii) An all-debt capital structure.

(c) Graph K_i, k_e and k_o as financial leverage increases for both the NI approach and the NOI approach.

(d) Why is the capital structure issue important under the NI approach and only a "mere detail" under the NOI approach?

Ans.:	*(a)*	*(i)*15.00%	*(ii)*12.20%	*(iii)*10.00%
	(b)	*(i)*12.50%	*(ii)*12.50%	*(iii)*12.50%

4. The Universal Plast Ltd. and the Bharat Plast Ltd. comprise a single risk class. These firms are identical in every respect except that the Universal Plast is not levered, while the Bharat Plast has ₹ 10,00,000 in 15% bonds outstanding. The valuation of the two firms is assumed to be the following:

	Universal	*Bharat*
Net operating income	₹ 7,50,000	₹ 7,50,000
Interest on debt	—	1,50,000
Earnings to equity	₹ 7,50,000	₹ 6,00,000
Equity capitalisation rate	.20	.21
Market value of equity shares	37,50,000	28,57,143
Market value of debt	—	10,00,000
Total value of the firm	37,50,000	38,57,143
Implied overall capitalisation rate	20%	19.48%
Debt/equity ratio	0	35%

(a) An investor owns ₹ 10,000 worth of Bharat equity. Show the process and the amount by which he could reduce his outlay through the use of arbitrage.

(b) According to Modigliani and Miller, when will this arbitrage process cease?

(c) What arguments can be raised against this hypothesis?

5. Shiva paper Ltd. has net operating earnings of ₹ 25,00,000 and ₹ 50,00,000 of debt with a 15 per cent interest charge. In all cases, assume no taxes: (a) Using Durand's net income method and an equity-capitalisation rate of 25 per cent , compute the total value of the firm and the implied overall capitalisation rate. (b) Next, assume that the firm issues an additional ₹ 25,00,000 in debt and uses the processed to retire the equity, the interest rate and equity capitalisation rate remains the same. Compute the new total value of the firm and overall capitalisation rate. (c) Using Durand's net operating income concept and an overall capitalisation rate of 20 per cent , compute the total market value, the equity-market value, and the implied equity capitalisation rate for the Shiva Paper Ltd. Prior to the sale of additional debt. (d) Determine the answer to (c) if the company were to sell the additional ₹ 25,00,000 in debt.

17

BASIC TOOLS OF CAPITAL STRUCTURE MANAGEMENT

INTRODUCTION

In planning its capital structure, the first major policy decision facing the firm is that of determining the appropriate level of debt. For some firms, the decision involves a choice between long term debt and equity. Firms without access to the equity markets also must decide how much debt they prudently can use. The choice of an appropriate debt policy involves tradeoff between tax benefits and the costs of financial distress. The optimal debt level depends to an important extent on the firm's operating risk. The greater the operating risk, the less debt the firm should use. Therefore, a firm's financing policy should be tailored to its commercial strategy. The question is: *Given the set of investments, what is the appropriate mix of debt and equity for financing?* Financial theory talks in terms of an optimum. The theory is precise in concept and gives valuable qualitative guidance, but it is quite difficult to apply quantitatively. It seems more realistic to speak of an appropriate debt ratio. In this Chapter, the focus is on the appropriate mix of debt and equity.

EBIT-EPS ANALYSIS

The use of EBIT-EPS analyses indicates to management the projected EPS for different financial plans. Generally, management wants to maximise EPS if doing so also satisfies the primary goal of financial management-maximisation of the owner's wealth as represented by the value of business, i.e. the value of the firm's equity. If a firm attempts to use excessive amounts of debt, shareholders (who are risk-averters) may sell their shares, and thus its price will fall.

While the use of large amounts of debt may result in higher EPS, it may also result in a reduction in the price of the firm's equity. The optimum financial structure for a firm (that is, the use of debt in relationship to equity and retained earnings as sources of financing) should be one which maximises the price of the equity.

Given the importance of earnings per share (EPS) as a measure of firm performance, analysis of the impact of financing alternatives on EPS is an important first step.

Essentially, this method involves the comparison of alternative methods of financing under various assumptions at a level of EBIT.

Example-1

Suppose a firm requires a total of ₹ 1,000 crore and may select between two financing mixes: *(i)* all equity shares, *(ii)* half equity shares and half debt at 10 per cent effective interest rate. Suppose further that the firm can sell equity shares for ₹ 100 per share, has a tax rate of 40 per cent, and expects EBIT of ₹ 250. Determine the earnings per share (EPS) using each of the possible financial mixes.

Solution

The interest of ₹ 50 crore was obtained by multiplying ₹ 500 crore by 10 per cent. The number of shares was determined by dividing the amount to be financed by issuing equity at ₹ 10 per shares. Thus, when half equity or ₹ 500 crore was used, the number of shares is ₹ 500 crore/ ₹ 100 = 5 crore shares.

(*₹ in crore*)

	Plan A *All Equity*	*Plan B* *Half Equity and half Debt*
EBIT	₹ 250	₹ 250
Less Interest	0	50
EBT	₹ 250	₹ 200
Less Taxes	100	80
After-tax Profit	₹ 150	₹ 120
Share of equity crore	10 crore	5
EPS	₹ 15	₹ 24

Graphic Analysis

By way of EBIT-EPS analysis, it is often useful to examine the relationship between EPS and EBIT using graphical method. An EBIT-EPS chart shows the behaviour of EPS in response to variations in EBIT. A moment's reflection reveals that EPS is a linear function of EBIT. An EBIT-EPS line can be developed for each financing plan available to the firm.

Example-2

Using the Example-1, graph the EBIT-EPS line for half equity and half debt under the assumption of an EBIT of ₹ 250 crore.

Solution

To draw a line, two points are required. For plan B, one point has already been determined. EBIT is ₹ 250 crore and EPS is ₹ 24. To obtain the second point necessary for the construction of the EBIT-EPS line, it is convenient to choose a value of EBIT which exactly equals the interest. Selection of a value for EBIT which just equals the interest cost will result in zero EPS. Thus, a second point is where EBIT is ₹ 50 crore and EPS is 0. For equity, the intercept is zero. We then plot earnings per share for both alternatives. When we connect the intercepts with the appropriate EPS points at an EBIT level of ₹ 250 crore, we obtain the straight line, shown in Figure-1. They tell us the earnings per share for the two financing alternatives that will occur under varying levels of EBIT.

FIGURE-1

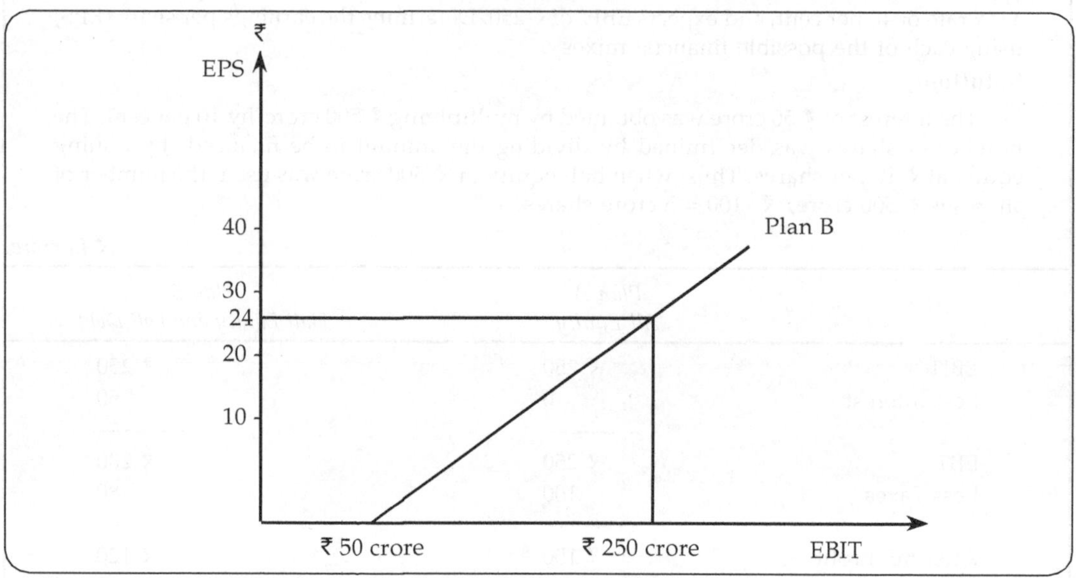

COMPUTING THE INDIFFERENCE POINTS

Indifference point identifies the EBIT at which the EPS will be the same regardless of the financing plan chosen by the financial manager. This point, sometimes called the breakeven point, has major implications for financial planning. At amounts excess of the EBIT-EPS indifference level, the more heavily levered financing plan will generate a higher EPS. At amounts below the EBIT-EPS indifference level, the financing plan involving less leverage will generate a higher EPS. It is important to know the EBIT-EPS indifference level.

In order to determine the EBIT-EPS break-even, or indifference, points between the various financing alternatives, we begin by calculating earnings per share for some hypothetical level of EBIT. EPS at any level of earning before interest and taxes (EBIT) can be calculated as follows for each alternative.

Debt alternative:

$$\frac{(\text{EBIT}-\text{I})\ (\text{I} - t)-\text{P}}{\text{E}_b} = \text{EPS}$$

Equity alternative:

$$\frac{(\text{EBIT}-\text{I})\ (1 - t) - \text{P}}{\text{E}_s} = \text{EPS}$$

The mathematical formula for determining the indifference point is given below in equation-1.

$$\underset{\textit{EPS : Bond Plan}}{\frac{(\text{EBIT}-\text{I})\,(1-t)-\text{P}}{\text{E}_b}} = \underset{\textit{EPS : Equity Plan}}{\frac{(\text{EBIT}-\text{I})\,(1-t)-\text{P}}{\text{E}_s}} \qquad (1)$$

Where :

EBIT = earnings before interest and taxes

I = total interest expenses-this amount includes both existing interest on currently outstanding debt plus interest on the proposed debt.

t = tax rate

P = total preference dividends—if preference share were being considered, this amount would include existing preference dividends on currently outstanding preference shares plus the preferred dividends on the proposed preference shares issue.

E_s = the number of shares under the equity plan

E_b = the number of equity shares issued under the equity and bond plans.

Example-3

Utilise the information given in Example-1, to calculate the indifference points between alternatives. Which financing alternative do you prefer? Why?

Solution

Using the Equation - 1, we calculate the indifference level of EBIT as:

$$\frac{(\text{EBIT}-₹\ 50\text{ crore})\,(1-0.40)-0}{5\text{ crore}} = \frac{(\text{EBIT}-0)\ (1-0.40)}{10\text{ crore}}$$

$$\text{EBIT} = ₹\ 100\text{ crore}$$

When the expression above is solved for EBIT, we obtain ₹ 100 crore. If EBIT turns out to be ₹ 100 crore then EPS will be ₹ 6.00 under both plans.

To check our answer:

	Debt Plan	*Equity Plan*
Earnings before interest and taxes (EBIT)	₹ 100	₹ 100
Interest	50	—
Earnings before taxes	50	₹ 100
Income taxes (40 percent)	20	40
Earning after taxes	₹ 30	₹ 60
Preference dividends	—	—
Earning available to equity share holders	₹ 30	₹ 60
Number of equity shares	5 crore	10 crore
	₹ 6.00 per share	₹ 6.00 per share

The break-even EBIT-EPS occurs at ₹ 100 crore. At that point, EPS is equal under the two plans. If EBIT turns out to be above ₹ 100 crore, EPS will be higher under the bond plan. If EBIT is below ₹ 100 crore, the equity plan produces higher EPS.

Effects of leverage can be observed in graphic form in Figure-2. The slope of the bond line is steeper than that of the equity line indicating that, with leverage, EPS is more sensitive to changes in EBIT. *The steeper slop is advantageous if EBIT rises, and disadvantageous if it falls.*

FIGURE-2

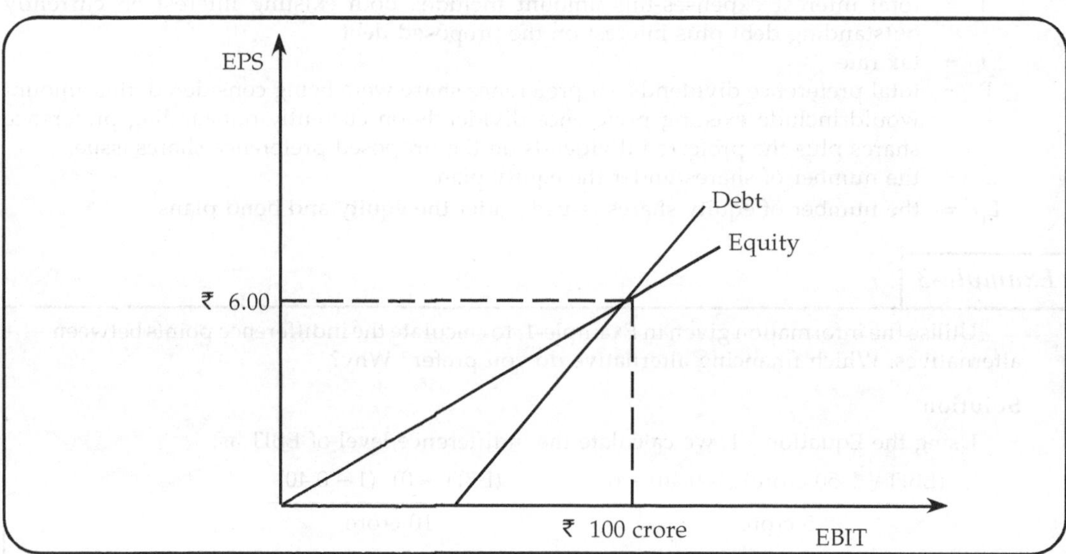

So far, we have assumed that the firm had no preference share outstanding. The term earnings per share is interpreted as earnings available to equity share holders per share. If preference share were issued, its dividend requirements would be subtracted before dividing by the number of shares to calculate earnings per share.

Example-4

Anand Enterprises is considering expanding assets by ₹ 500 crore and has determined that it can finance the expansion either through the selling of 5 crore preference shares at 8 per cent to net ₹ 100 per share or through a new issue of equity shares which can be sold to net the company ₹ 50.00 per share.

The tax rate is 40 per cent. The firm currently has 20 crore equity shares.

Solution

Total preference dividend = 0.08 (₹ 500 crore) = ₹ 40 crore

Equity shares = (₹ 500 crore/ ₹ 50.00 per share)+ 20 crore shares

10 crore shares + 20 crore shares = 30 crore shares

EPS break-even:

EPS: Preference share Plan = *EPS: Equity share Plan*

$$\frac{(\text{EBIT} - 0)\ (1 - 0.40) - ₹\ 40 \text{ crore}}{20} = \frac{(\text{EBIT} - 0\ (1 - 0.40)}{30}$$

Solving for EBIT, we find break-even at EBIT = ₹ 200 crore. At that level, EPS= ₹ 6.00 under both plans.

To check our answer:

	Preference Share	*Equity Share*
Earnings before interest and taxes	₹ 200	₹ 200
Interest	—	—
Earnings before taxes	₹ 200	₹ 200
Income taxes (40 percent)	80	80
Earnings after taxes	₹ 120	₹ 120
Preference dividends	40	—
Earnings available to equity share holders	₹ 80	₹ 120
Number of equity shares	20 crore	30 crore
Earnings per share	₹ 4.00 per share	₹ 4.00 per share

At any earnings before interest and taxes (EBIT) level above ₹ 200 crore EPS will be higher under the preference shares alternative, at any level of earnings below ₹ 200 crore EPS will be higher under the equity alternative. Graphic presentation of the above conclusion regarding EPS at levels of earnings before interest and taxes above and below equivalency level is illustrated in Figure-3.

FIGURE-3

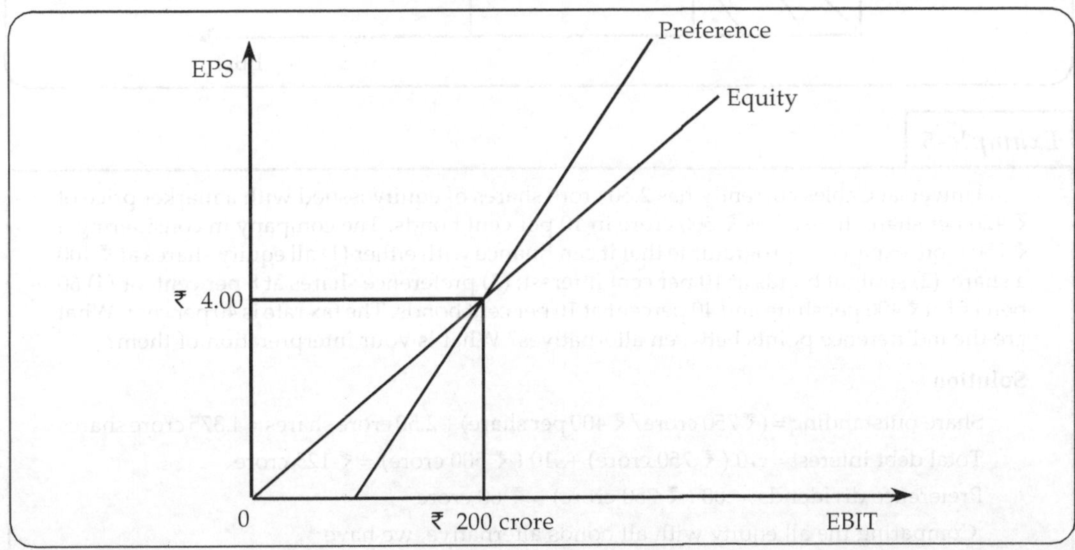

At what level of EBIt will the debt and preference shares alternatives produce the same level of EPS? An equivalency level of earnings before interest and taxes (EBIT) does not exist between these two preference alternatives. Since the after-tax ₹

amounts for the debt and shares alternatives will be different at all levels of earnings before interest and taxes, the preference shares and debt lines on the chart do not intersect, indicating that there is no equivalency level for these two alternatives. This is illustrated in Figure-4.

FIGURE-4

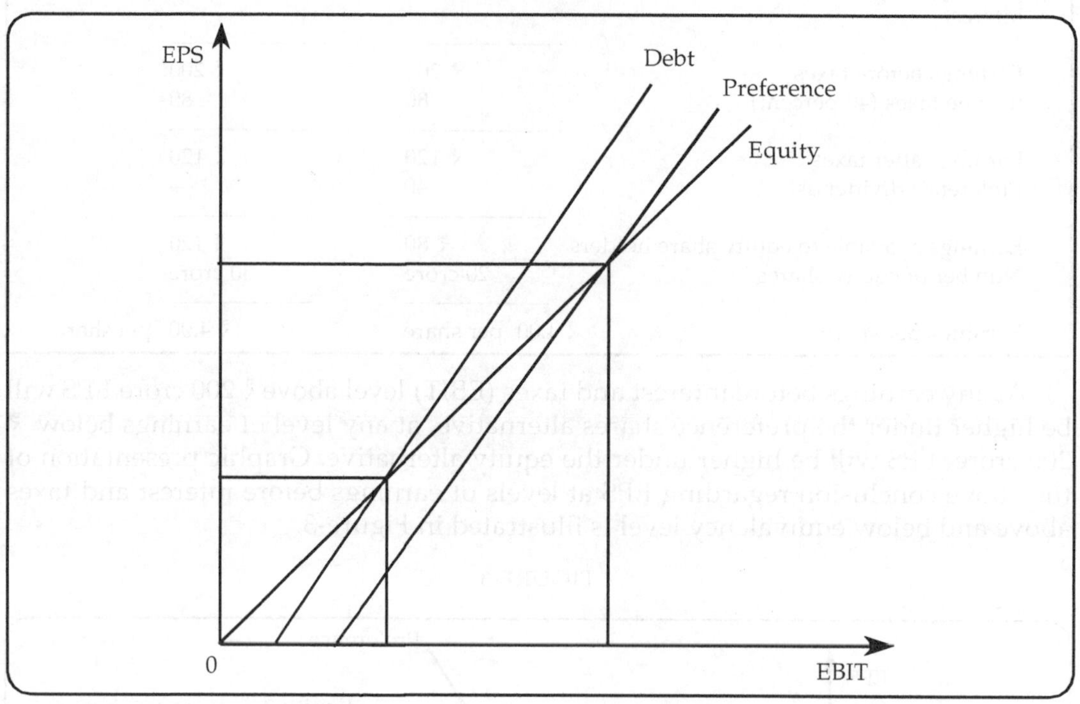

Example-5

Universal Cables currently has 2.50 crore shares of equity issued with a market price of ₹ 420 per share. It also has ₹ 500 crore in 10 per cent bonds. The company in considering a ₹ 750 crore expansion programme that it can finance with either (1) all equity shares at ₹ 400 a share; (2) straight bonds at 10 per cent interest; (3) preference shares at 8 per cent, or (4) 60 percent at ₹ 400 per share and 40 percent at 10 per cent bonds. The tax rate is 40 per cent. What are the indifference points between alternatives? What is your interpretation of them?

Solution

Share outstanding = (₹ 750 crore/ ₹ 400 per share) + 2.50 crore shares = 4.375 crore shares

Total debt interest = .10 (₹ 750 crore) + .10 (₹ 500 crore) = ₹ 125 crore

Preference dividends = .08 (₹ 750 crore) = ₹ 60 crore.

Comparing the all equity with all bonds alternative, we have

EPS: Bond Plan		*EPS: Equity Plan*
(EBIT– ₹ 125 crore) (1 – 0.40) / 2.50 crore	=	(EBIT – ₹ 50 crore) (1-.40) / 4.375 crore

(0.6 EBIT - ₹ 75 crore) 4.375 crore = (0.6 EBIT - ₹ 30 crore) 2.50 crore

2.625 EBIT - ₹ 328.125 = 1.5 EBIT - ₹ 75 crore

1.125 EBIT= 253.125

EBIT = ₹ 225 crore

Thus, we find the break-even at EBIT is ₹ 225 crore. At that level EPS is ₹ 24 under both plans.

For the all equity, all preference comparison, we have:

$$\underset{\text{EPS : Preference shares}}{\frac{(\text{EBIT} - ₹\ 50\ \text{crore})(1 - 0.40) - ₹\ 60\ \text{crore}}{2.50\ \text{crore}}} = \underset{\text{EPS : Equity shares}}{\frac{(\text{EBIT} - ₹\ 50\ \text{crore})(1 - 0.40)}{4.375\ \text{crore}}}$$

EBIT = ₹ 283.33 crore.

Solving for EBIT, we find break-even at EBIT = ₹ 283.33. crore.

At that level EPS = ₹ 32 under both plans.

Above ₹ 283.33 crore , preference shares is more favourable and below ₹ 283.33 crore equity is more favourable.

For the all equity, 60 percent equity-40 percent bonds comparison, we have

$$\underset{\text{EPS : Equity Plan}}{\frac{(\text{EBIT} - ₹\ 50\ \text{crore})(1 - 0.40)}{4.375\ \text{crore}}} = \underset{\text{EPS: 60\% Equity-40\% Bonds}}{\frac{(\text{EBIT} - ₹\ 80.50\ \text{crore})(1 - 0.40)}{3.75\ \text{crore}}}$$

EBIT = ₹ 260 crore

At break-even EBIT = 260 crore, the EPS is ₹ 28.80 under both plans.

The preference plan is not attractive. At all levels of EBIT it will result in lower EPS than will the bond plan. Figure-4 also illustrates this. These exact indifference points can be used to check graph approximations.

UNCOMMITTED EARNINGS PER SHARE AND INDIFFERENCE POINTS

So far the calculations that permitted us to solve for EBIT-EPS indifference point made no explicit allowance for the repayment of bond principal. This procedure is not that unrealistic. It only presumes the debt will be perpetually outstanding. This means that when the current bond issue matures, a new bond issue will be floated. The proceeds from the newer issue would be used to pay off the maturity value of the older issue.

Many bond contracts, however, require that sinking fund payment be made to a bond trustee. A sinking fund is a real cash reserve that is used to provide for the orderly and early retirement of the principal amount of the bond issue. Most often sinking-fund payment is a mandatory fixed amount and is required by a clause in the bond indenture. Sinking-fund payments can represent a sizable cash drain on the firm's liquid resources. Moreover, sinking-fund payment are return of borrowed principle, so they are not tax deductible to the firm.

Because of the potentially seriousness of the cash drain caused by sinking-fund requirements, the financial manager might be concerned with the uncommitted earnings per share (UEPS) related to each financing plan. The calculation of UEPS recognise that sinking-fund commitments have been honoured. UEPS can be used, then, for discretionary spending such as the payment of cash dividends to equity shareholders or investment in capital facilities.

If we let S_f be the sinking fund payment required in a given year, the EBIT-UEPS indifference point can be calculated as

$$\underset{\textit{UEPS : Bond Plan}}{\frac{(\text{EBIT} - 1)(1 - t) - P - S_f}{E_b}} = \underset{\textit{UEPS : Equity share Plan}}{\frac{(\text{EBIT} - 1)(1 - t) - P - S_f}{E_s}} \quad (2)$$

We should note that if the firm had other debt issue outstanding, interest and principal (sinking fund) payments on those issues should be considered in calculating break-even points. In calculating EPS break-even, old interest payments would appear on both sides of equation-1. Likewise, old sinking fund payments would appear on both sides of equation-2. If preference shares were outstanding, its dividend (and sinking fund, if any) requirements would be subtracted before dividing by E_s and E_b. Lastly, the indifference level of EBIT based on UEPS will always exceed that based on EPS.

Example-6

The current balance sheet for Ravi Enterprises shows ₹ 1,000 crore of 10.00 per cent bonds and ₹ 1,800 crore of ₹ 100 par value equity share. Total current sales of ₹ 15,000 crore per year are to the Patel Instruments on a 10 year contract. National Engineers has offered a similar 10 years contract for ₹ 10,000 crore per year. The company has accepted the new contract and now must raise ₹ 2,000 crore from external sources in order to expand their production facilities. The financing could be accomplished through a debt issue carrying a 12 per cent caupon rate, or by selling shares of equity to net the company ₹ 160 per share. EBIT is 3.0 per cent of sales and the tax rate is 40 per cent.

(a) Calculate the EPS beak-even level of EBIT (*i.e.* the level of EBIT at which EPS is equal under the two financing schemes).

(b) Assuming that a ₹ 50 crore per year sinking fund payment would be required on the new debt issue, calculate the UEPS break-even level of EBIT.

Solution

Total debt interest = .10(₹ 1,000 crore)+.12(₹ 2,000 crore) = ₹ 340 crore

Shares issued = ₹ 1,800 crore / ₹ 100 = 18 crore equity shares

Total equity shares issued = 18 crore shares + $\dfrac{₹\ 2000\ \text{crore}}{₹\ 160\ \text{price per share}}$

= 30.50 equity shares

a) EPS Break-Even:

$$\frac{\text{EPS-Bond Plan}}{\frac{(\text{EBIT} - ₹\ 340\text{ crore})(1 - 0.40)}{18\text{ crore shares}}} = \frac{\text{EPS-Equity Plan}}{\frac{(\text{EBIT} - ₹\ 100\text{ crore})(1 - 0.40)}{30.50\text{ crore share}}}$$

EBIT = ₹ 685.60 crore

At the break-even level, EBIT is 685.60 and EPS under both the plans are equal to ₹ 11.52.

b) UEPS Break-Even:

$$\frac{\text{UEPS-Bond Plan}}{\frac{(\text{EBIT} - ₹\ 340\text{ crore})(1 - 0.40) - ₹\ 50\text{ crore}}{18\text{ crore share}}} = \frac{\text{UEPS-Equity Plan}}{\frac{(\text{EBIT} - ₹\ 100)(1 - 0.40)}{30.50\text{ shares}}}$$

EBIT = ₹ 888.93

At the UEPS break-even, EBIT is ₹ 888.93 and EPS under both alternatives are ₹ 15.52.

The necessity to cover sinking fund payments makes equity shares relatively more attractive.

WEAKNESS OF EBIT-EPS ANALYSIS

EBIT-EPS analysis provides management slow indication of the likely impact of an issue of senior securities on the possible returns to the company's shareholders. However, in undertaking such an EBIT-EPS analysis, the financial manager should recognise the implicit costs associated with an issue of senior securities. For instance, the real cost of debt includes not only the explicit interest costs but also the implicit costs representated by the decline in the share price as a result of the increased financial risk. Consequently, because of the increasing risk, investors will tend to place a lower value on the firm's earnings—that is, the price-earnings ratio will decline. If a small amount of debt is employed, however, the price-earnings ratio might not decline, because investors will consider the increase in risk to be minor. In fact the price-earnings ratio might actually increase because of the higher potential growth of EPS caused by the use of fixed-cost securities. However, as the level of debt increases, the price-earnings ratio will begin to decline and then decline more rapidly because of the increasing levels of risk.

Figure-5 is a graphic example of how one might expect the price earnings ratio, market price per share, and EPS to behave as the level of debt increases. At the outset the firm is employing no debt in its capital structure. This illustration assumes that financial leverage is favourable in terms of EPS; that is, EBIT is at such a level that the use of debt instead of equity will result in a higher level of EPS. Initially, the price-earnings ratio does not decline (upto point X) because the increased risk is considered minor. As debt is increased beyond point X, the market price per share continues to rise (up to point Y). The reason is that the increase in EPS more than offsets the decrease in the price-earnings ratio. However, beyond point Y, the decrease in the price-earnings ratio, more than offsets the increase in EPS, and hence, the market price per share begins to decline.

Thus, a financial manager must be concerned with the effect of fixed cost securities on both EPS and the price-earnings ratio. An increase in risk has a depressing influence on a price-earnings ratio while an increase in growth will tend to increase the price-earnings ratio. Fixed cost securities affect both risk and growth. If the growth effect outweighs the risk effect, then the price-earnings ratio will increase. If the risk effect outweighs the growth effect, then the price-earnings ratio will decline. In fact, this type of analysis must be used in conjunction with other basic tools in achieving the objective of optimal capital structure.

FIGURE-5

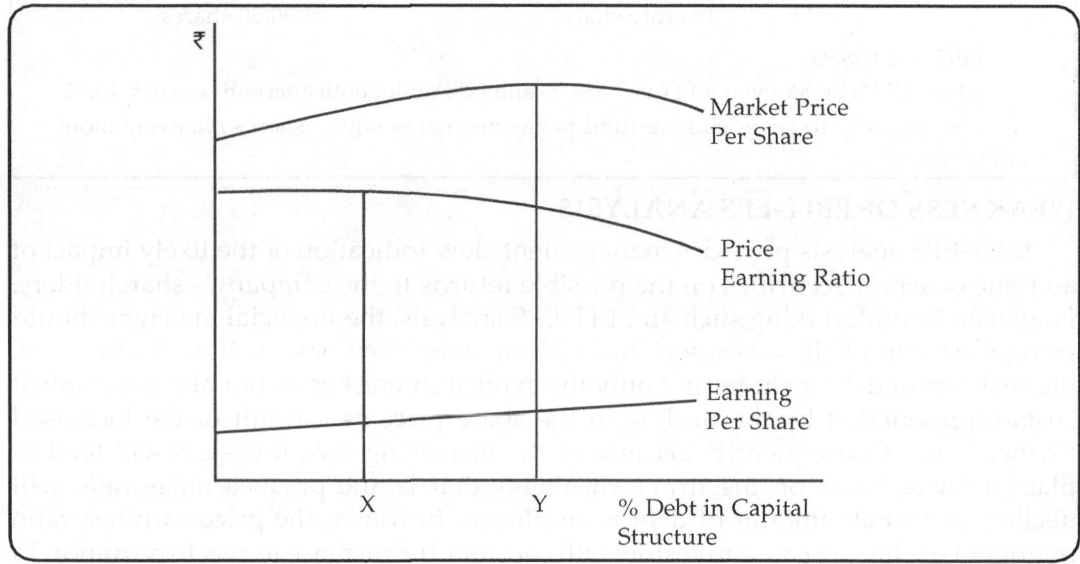

EARNINGS COVERAGE STANDARD

It has also become customary to express the limits of debt in terms of income statement data. The earnings coverage ratio is the relationship of the net income available for debt services to the total amount of annual interest plus sinking fund charges. By relating fund requirements for long-term debt to net earnings available for servicing the debt, it sheds light on the question of whether earnings will be adequate under varying conditions to meet debt services requirements. No new long-term debt will be assumed unless the net income available for debt servicing is equal to or in excess of some multiple of debt service requirements, such as 2 to 1 or 3 to 1, so that there is a margin of safety to allow for a decline of earnings and yet still permit the firm to continue its debt service. The greater the fluctuation in earnings, the higher the ratio should be to provide a large enough custom to meet debt services under adverse circumstances. However, high coverage ratios, compared to a standard, imply unused capacity. Table-1 is a simple work-sheet used to analyse the key coverage ratios.

The variability of EBIT points up a major short coming of coverage ratios in general. Which EBIT do we use to calculate coverage? To draw really meaningful conclusion regarding the safety of various payments that the firm is committed to make would require some knowledge of the likelihood of a decline in EBIT to levels at which the payments are threatened. We can calculate coverage at several different levels of EBIT. If we could construct a probability distribution over all possible values of EBIT, we then would have a better feel for the adequacy of various coverage levels.

TABLE-1

Coverage Ratios

Coverage	*Computation Method*	*Existing Ratio*	*Ratio with New Equity Financing*	*Ratio with New Debt Financing*
Times interest earned	$\dfrac{\text{EBIT}}{\text{Annual Interest Expenses}}$	–Times	–Times	–Times
Times burden covered	$\dfrac{\text{EBIT}}{\text{Interest} + \dfrac{\text{Sinking Fund}}{(1 - t)}}$	–Times	–Times	–Times
Cash flow overall coverage ratio	$\dfrac{\text{EBIT+Lease expense+depreciation}}{(\text{interest} + \text{lease expense}) + \left(\dfrac{\text{Preference dividends}}{(1 - t)}\right) + \left(\dfrac{\text{Preference Payments}}{(1 - t)}\right)}$	–Times	–Times	–Times

CASH ADEQUACY STANDARD

Before a company incurs new debt commitments, the financial manager must also ascertain the company's, ability to meet the fixed charges associated with the issue. This may be achieved by a detailed analysis of the company's future cash flows. Such an analysis is essential, because the company's inability to meet these fixed charges may result in the company being placed in the hands of a receiver and eventually liquidated.

Example-7

Utilising the information given in Example—6, analyse the coverage ratios for Ravi Enterprises under each of the two financing alternatives.

Solution

We can calculate the coverage ratios for an expected level of EBIT of ₹ 750 crore (0.03 × ₹ 25,000 crore) as follows:

Coverage	*Pre tax Burden*		*Times Covered at EBIT = ₹ 750 crore*
Interest (Bond plan)	₹ 340 crore	(EBIT/I)	2.21
Interest (plus sinking fund)	₹ 423.33 crore	$\dfrac{EBIT}{I + \dfrac{S_f}{(1-t)}}$	1.54
Interest (equity plan)	₹ 100		7.50

The table shows that the inclusion of a sinking fund payment under the bond plan results in a lower coverage ratio.

Cash budget indicates that the demands on the company's cash resources are many and varied. Some of these demands may be regarded as discretionary such as the payment of dividends and research and development expenditures. Other demands on the company's cash resources are non discretionary. One of the non-discretionary demands on the company's cash is the servicing of the company's debt. As a result, before a company increases any of its fixed commitments, including the fixed charges associated with an increase in the company's debt, the financial manager should study the company's projected cash flows. This should be done in order to ascertain whether the company will have sufficient cash resources to cover the increased fixed commitment at the dates they become due.

The cash flows recorded in a cash budget are, in effect, managements best estimates of the company's flows. In addition to a budget prepared under the "most likely" operating conditions, cash budgets may also be prepared assuming optimistic operating conditions and pessimistic operating conditions. The cash flows ability of the company to service debt under these varying assumptions is, from the financial manager's point of view, probably the best method of analysing the company's ability to meet its commitments.

Donaldson attacks the problem in a similar way.[1] He argues that if management is contemplating an increase in the amount of debt in the company's capital structure, it should look at the chances of the company's running out of cash as a result of the increase in the fixed debt charges, particularly in recession periods. This requires an

1. For a more detailed discussion of Donaldsom's approach, see Gordon Donaldson, *Corporate Debt Capacity,* Division of Research, Harvard Business School, Boston, 1961, and also G. Donaldson, "Stretegy for financial Emergencies, *Harvard Business Review*, pp. 67-71, November-December 1969.

analysis of the primary factors which cause variations in cash flow and a measure of the limits, of their behaviour in recession periods in terms of adverse effects on the company's cash position. From this is derived an estimate of the *maximum* and *most probable adverse limits* of recession cash flows and balances. These figures provide an approximate measures of the magnitude of the risk associated with given amount of debt servicing. It is then left to the financial manager to judge whether the risks should be incurred and, if so to what extent.

Donaldson's analysis centres on the behaviour of cash flows during recession periods in order to determine the firm's capacity to bear incremental fixed cash outflows either for debt or for other purposes. The recession cash flows analysis provides tests for *cash solvency* and for *cash adequacy.* The former measures the risk of running out of cash in a recession for absolute essentials like debt services which will precipitate insolvency. The latter recognises that there are other essential minimum requirements, such as a given level of dividends, basic research and development expenditures, and the like, which could be sacrificed to avoid insolvency if absolutely unavoidable but which management regards as necessary and which should therefore fall within the range of adequate cash availabilities, even in recession.

The analysis starts by identifying for the individual firm the primary key factors, such as sales volume, which may produce variations and particularly contractions in cash flow. The next step is to observe the behaviour of these factors over time and particularly in recessions. In the case of sales, for example, it may be found that a decline in volume of not less than 4 per cent not more than 32 per cent is to be expected. The behavioural limits for the key factors are thus translated into a range of estimates of cash flow in future recession periods based on all possible combinations of factors. It is then possible to estimate the total amount of additional or incremental fixed cash charges which the company can assume without any threat of insolvency (cash insolvency standard) or without any threat of impairing the company's ability to meet the other minimum cash outflow requirements which management considered essential (cash adequacy standard). Making some assumptions about the nature and terms of the debt to be incurred, the figure for the total amount of additional fixed cash charges which may be incurred can be converted into the principal amount of additional debt which can be assumed with a reasonable expectation of complete safety.

Viewed in this way, the debt capacity question is seen as part of a broder problem of determining the capacity of a business to assume additional fixed cash outflows, for any of a variety of purposes. In this sense, debt competes with lease payments, dividends, research expenditures, and so forth. The commitment of cash to servicing a long-term lease is equivalent to the commitment of the same amount of cash for debt servicing and if management is contemplating an increase with amount of debt in the company's capital structure it should look at the chances of the company running out of cash as a result of the increase in the fixed debt charges. The financial manager should look at this in two ways. *First,* he should estimate the probability of cash insolvency, that is, of the company being unable to meet the non-discretionary demands on its cash resources. *Second*, he should estimate the probability of cash inadequacy, that is, of the company having insufficient cash to continue meeting those discretionary cash payments which the financial manager considers to be essential. Donaldson suggests that the financial manager should study the probability of cash insolvency and cash inadequacy under the most adverse economic conditions. These, according to his definition, are recession conditions. The recession cash flow analysis provides tests for cash solvency and cash adequacy.

NONDISCRETIONARY CASH DISBURSEMENTS AND TESTING FOR CASH INSOLVENCY

The financial manager should assess the probability of cash insolvency by calculating a probability distribution of the company's future cash flows under the most adverse conditions that could reasonable be expected. Estimates of cash flows should include collections from sales, other cash inflows and those cash disbursements which are vital to the company's survival, including payments for raw materials, payroll and other nondiscretionary disbursements. Once the probability distribution of recession cash flows is calculated, it is combined with the cash balances at the commencement of the recession period to obtain the probability distribution of cash balances during a recession.

FIGURE-6

PROBABILITY DISTRIBUTION !OF RECESSION CASH BALANCES INCLUDING ONLY NONDISCRETIONARY CASH DISBURSEMENTS

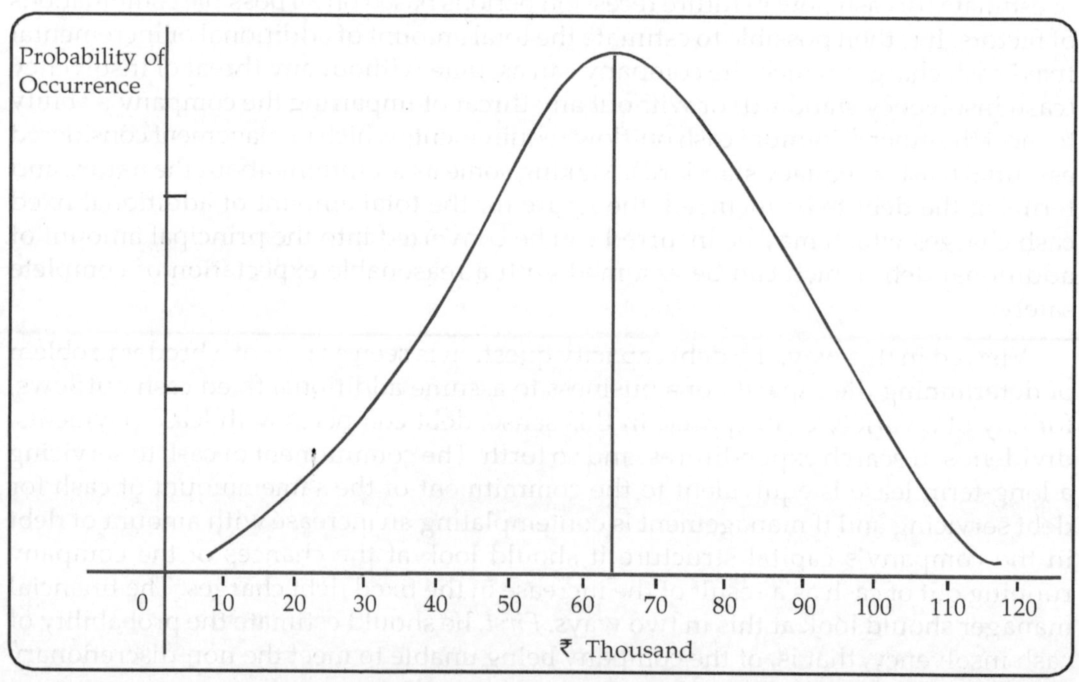

Thus:

Cash balance during a recession = Cash balance at start of recession + Net cash Flows during the recession

This is illustrated in Figure-6

Assuming a normal distribution of recession cash balances Figure-6 indicates that the most likely recession cash balances is ₹ 62,000 while, addition, the dispresion of the probability distribution indicates that there is no likelihood of the company becoming insolvent during the recession period.

If management is contemplating a new issue of debt, it would calculate the probability of the company running out of cash when the new fixed charges are included. For example, a new debenture issue of ₹ 10 lakhs at an interest rate of 15% per year will increase the non-discretionary cash out flows by ₹ 1,50,000 per year, and the probability of running out of cash with these additional fixed charges should be calculated. If the increase in fixed charges increase the probability of running out of cash, then the acceptability of the new debenture issue will depend on management risk preferences.

FIGURE-7

PROBABILITY DISTRIBUTION !OF RECESSION CASH BALANCES INCLUDING DISCRETIONARY CASH DISBURSEMENTS

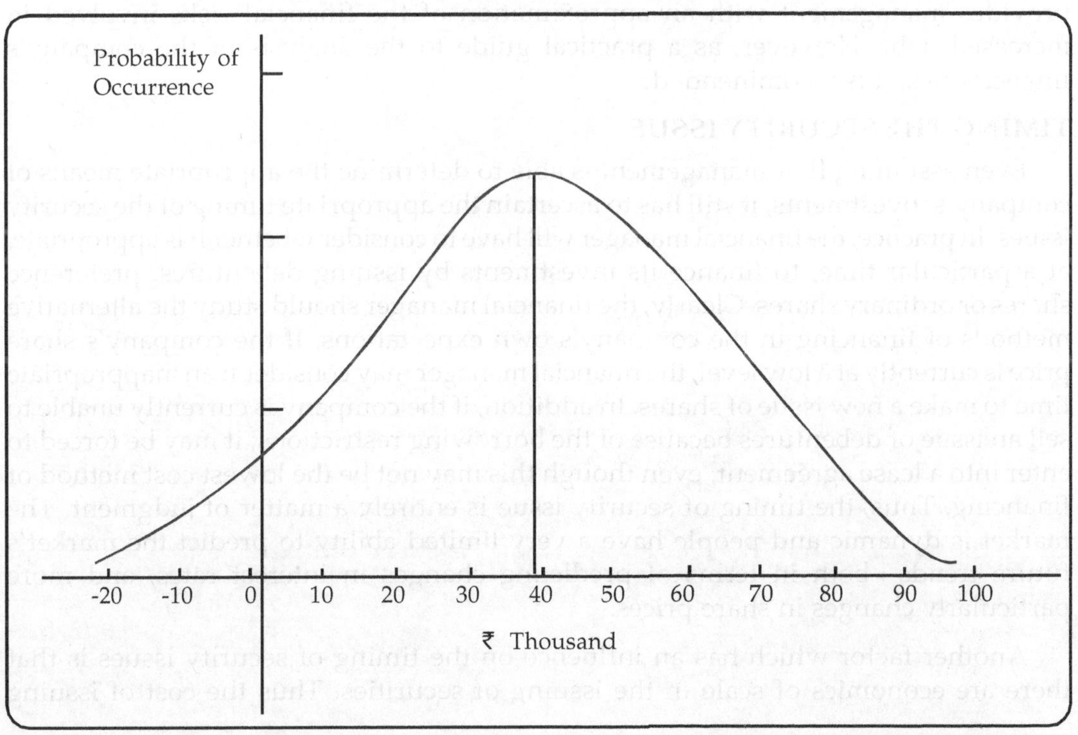

DISCRETIONARY CASH DISBURSEMENTS AND TESTING FOR CASH INADEQUACY

So far the analysis has concentrated on cash disbursements which are non-discretionary and therefore vital to the company's survival. However, management may also test for cash inadequacy by including the outflows which management believes should be maintained in the company's best interest such as dividend payments, research and development expenditures, and capital expenditures. This does not mean that the expenditures will be maintained at their non-recession level during a recession, but that there is some level below which management believes these expenditures should not fall. Once management has decided what the minimum level should be, then these cash outflows are simply added to the outflows of the previous analysis. Clearly, this reduces the company's ability to assume additional fixed cash outflows. Thus, while there may be no risk of cash insolvency, there may be considerable risk of cash inadequacy, especially if a new debenture issue is made. This may be demonstrated in Figure-7, which shows the probability distribution of recession cash balances when the minimum level of discretionary cash disbursements is included in the cash outflow data.

As a result of this type of analysis, management is provided with much more information on the ability of the company to service increased fixed charges, including the interest expense on a new issue of debentures. Management now has information on the risk of cash inadequacy and cash insolvency which it could not possibly obtain from a study of the conventional ratios. Admittedly the analysis is crude, and only provides management with an approximation of the financial risks involved in increased debt. However, as a practical guide to the analysis of the company's financial risk, it is recommended.

TIMING THE SECURITY ISSUE

Even assuming that management is able to determine the appropriate means of company's investments, it still has to ascertain the appropriate timing of the security issues. In practice, the financial manager will have to consider whether it is appropriate, at a particular time, to finance its investments by issuing debentures, preference shares or ordinary shares. Clearly, the financial manager should study the alternative methods of financing in the company's own expectations. If the company's share price is currently at a low level, the financial manager may consider it an inappropriate time to make a new issue of shares. In addition, if the company is currently unable to sell an issue of debentures because of the borrowing restrictions, it may be forced to enter into a lease agreement, even though this may not be the lowest cost method of financing. Thus, the timing of security issue is entirely a matter of judgment. The market is dynamic and people have a very limited ability to predict the market's future trends—both in terms of predicting changes in interest rates, and more particularly changes in share prices.

Another factor which has an influence on the timing of security issues is that there are economics of scale in the issuing of securities. Thus the cost of issuing securities as a percentage of the total amount of the issue decline as the size of the issue increases. This is true for all types of securities although the issue costs vary from one type of security to another. For example, the costs of issuing debentures are less than the costs of issuing shares. Consequently, the financial manager should plan the company's financing methods well in advance and issue securities relatively infrequently.

ILLUSTRATIVE PROBLEMS

1. Jindal Products is considering to expand its assets by ₹ 25,00,00,000 and determined that it can finance the expansion either through a debenture issue carrying a 15 per cent interest rate or through a new issue of equity shares which can be sold to net the company ₹ 25 per share. The firm currently has 50,00,000 shares of equity issued and ₹ 30,00,00,000 of debentures with a 12 per cent coupon. The tax rate is 50 per cent. *(a)* Calculate the EPS for each alternative at EBIT level of ₹ 10,00,00,000 *(b)* Calculate the EPS break-even point. *(c)* What can be said from this analysis regarding the choice between debentures and equity shares? Which financing alternative would you recommend? Why?

Solution

(a) For debt financing:

Total debt interest = 0.15 (₹ 25,00,00,000) + 0.12 (₹ 30.00.00.000) = ₹ 7,35,00,000

Equity Shares issued = 50,00,000

EBIT	₹ 10,00,00,000
Interest	7,35,00,000
EBT	₹ 2,65,00,000
Taxes (.50)	1,32,50,000
No. of shares issued	50,00,000
EPS	₹ 2.65

For equity financing:

Interest = 0.12 (₹ 30,00,00,000) = ₹ 3,60,00,000

Equity Shares issued = ₹ 25,00,00,000/ ₹ 25 + 50,00,000 = 1,50,00,000

EBIT	₹ 10,00,00,000
Interest	₹ 3,60,00,000
EBT	6,40,00,000
Taxes (.50)	3,20,00,000
EAT	₹ 3,20,00,000
No. of shares issued	1,50,00,000
EPS	₹ 2.13

(b) EPS Break-even point calculations are shown below

$$\frac{(\text{EBIT} - 1_B)(1 - t)}{E_b} = \frac{(\text{EBIT} - 1_B)\,1 - t)}{E_s}$$

This can be simplified to:

$$\text{EBIT}_{BS} = \frac{E_s 1_B - E_b 1_s}{E_s - E_b}$$

Thus,

$$\text{EBIT}_{BS} = \frac{1{,}50{,}00{,}000(₹\ 7{,}35{,},00{,}000) - 50{,}00{,}000(₹\ 3{,}60{,}00{,}000)}{1{,}50{,}00{,}000 - 50{,}00{,}000} = ₹\ 9{,}22{,}50{,}000$$

(c) The answer here depends on the expected level of EBIT and its variance. Above EBIT of ₹ 9,22,50,000 equity gives higher EPS. The EBIT - EPS analysis makes explicit the risk - return trade off, but does not identify the superior plan.

2. Assuming that the firm in Problem-1 has a third financing alternative, that of selling 31,25,000 shares of 14 per cent preference to net ₹ 80 per share, beginning in the fifth year after issuance, the firm would make an annual sinking fund payment of ₹ 2,00,00,000 for retirement of the preference share over a 10 year period. *(a)* Add to the EBIT/EPS chart in Problem-1 above lines representing the reference shares alternative in year 1 and 5; *(b)* Calculate EPS and UEPS break-even points for the preference share plan compared with the equity-share plan; *(c)* How attractive is the preference-share plan?

Solution

(a) For preference-share financing
Total debt interest = 0.12 (₹ 30,00,00,000) = ₹ 3,60,00,000
Total preference dividend =.14 (₹ 25,00,00,000) = ₹ 3,50,00,000
Equity share issued = 50,00,000

Sinking fund payment (beginning year 5) = ₹ 2,00,00,000

At EBIT = ₹ 10,00,00,000

$$\text{EPS} = \frac{(1\text{–}0.50)\ (₹\ 10{,}00{,}00{,}000 - ₹\ 3{,}60{,}00{,}000) - ₹\ 3{,}50{,}00{,}000}{50{,}00{,}000} = -\ ₹\ .60$$

In year UEPS -EPS

Beginning in year 5:

At EBIT = ₹ 10,00,00,000

$$\text{UEPS} = \frac{(1 - 0.50)\ ₹\ 10{,}00{,}00{,}000 - ₹\ 3{,}60{,}00{,}000) - ₹\ 3{,}50{,}00{,}000 - ₹\ 2{,}00{,}00{,}000}{50{,}00{,}000} = -\ ₹\ 4.60$$

EPS break even:

EPS Preference Share	*EPS—Equity Share*
(EBIT – ₹ 3,60,00,000) (1 – 0.50)	(EBIT – ₹ 3,60,00,000)

$$\frac{- ₹\ 3.50,00,000}{50,00,000} = \frac{(1 - 0.50)}{1,50,00,000}$$

$EBIT_{BE}$ = ₹ 14,10,00,000

EPS_{BE} = 3.50

UEPS break-even :

UEPS—Preference-Share | *UEPS—Equity-Share*

$$\frac{- ₹\ 3,50,00,000 - ₹\ 2,00,00,000 \quad (EBIT - ₹\ 3,60,00,000)\ (1 - 0.50)}{50,00,000} = \frac{(EBIT - ₹\ 3,60,00,000)\ (1 - 0.50)}{1,50,00,000}$$

$EBIT_{BE}$ = ₹ 20,10,00,000

$UEPS_{BE}$ = ₹ 5.50

(c) The preference-share plan is not attractive. At all levels of EBIT, it sill result in lower EPS than will the bond plan.

3. Arvind Transport currently has 10,00,000 shares of equity outstanding with a market price of ₹ 50 per share. It also has ₹ 4 crore in 12 per cent bonds. The company is considering a ₹ 5 crore expansion programme that it can finance either (1) all equity shares at ₹ 40 a share (2) straight bonds at 15 per cent interest (3) preference shares at 14 per cent or (4) half equity shares at ₹ 40 per share and half 15 per cent bonds.

(a) For a hypothetical EBIT level of ₹ 2,50,00,000 after the expansion programme, calculate the earnings per share for each of the alternative methods of financing. Assume a corporate tax rate of 50 per cent.

(b) What are the indifference points between alternatives? Calculate the EPS at these indifference points? What is your interpretation of these?

Solution

(a) For a hypothetical EBIT level of ₹ 2,50,00,000, earnings per share for each of the alternatives are calculated and shown in exhibit-1.

EXHIBIT-1

	Existing Capital Structure	*All Equity*	*All Bonds*	*All Preference*	*Half Equity-Half bonds*
EBIT	₹ 2,50,00,000	₹ 2,50,00,000	₹ 2,50,00,000	₹ 2,50,00,000	2,50,00,000
Interest	48,00,000	48,00,000	1,23,00,000	48,00,000	85,50,000
EBT	₹ 2,02,00,000	₹ 2,02,00,000	₹ 1,27,00,000	₹ 2,02,00,000	₹ 1,64,50,000
Taxes	1,01,00,000	1,01,00,000	63,50,000	1,01,00,000	82,25,000
Dividend to Preference shareholders	—	—	—	70,00,000	—
Earnings available to					

equity share-holders.	₹ 1,01,00,000	₹ 1,01,00,000	₹ 63,50,000	₹ 31,00,000	₹ 82,25,000
No. of equity shares	10,00,000	₹ 22,50,000	10,00,000	10,00,000	16,25,000
Earnings per share	₹ 10.1	₹ 4.49	₹ 6.35	₹ 3.10	₹ 5.06

Comparing the all equity with the all bonds alternative, we have:

$$\underset{\textit{All Equity}}{\frac{(\text{EBIT} - ₹\ 48{,}00{,}000)\ (0.5)}{22{,}50{,}000}} = \underset{\textit{All Bonds}}{\frac{(\text{EBIT} - ₹\ 1{,}23{,}00{,}000)\ (0.5)}{10{,}00{,}000}}$$

(.5 EBIT – ₹ 24,00,000) 10,00,000 = (.5 EBIT – ₹ 61,50,000) 22,50,000

$EBIT_{BE}$ = ₹ 1,83,00,000

EPS_{BE} = ₹ 3.00

Above ₹ 1,83,00,000, debt is more favourable and EPS would be higher and vice versa.

For the all equity, all preference comparison, we have:

$$\underset{\textit{All Equity}}{\frac{(\text{EBIT} - ₹\ 48{,}00{,}000)\ (0.5)}{22{,}50{,}000}} = \underset{\textit{All Preference}}{\frac{(\text{EBIT} - ₹\ 48{,}00{,}00)\ (0.50) - ₹\ 70{,}00{,}000}{10{,}00{,}000}}$$

[(.5 EBIT – ₹ 24,00,000) (10,00,000)] = [(.5 EBIT – 24,00,000) – (₹ 70,00,000)] (22,50,000)

$EBIT_{BE}$ = ₹ 3,00,00,000

EPS_{BE} = ₹ 5.6

Above ₹ 3,00,00,000, preference share financing will yield higher level of earnings per share and vice versa.

For the all equity, half equity-half bonds comparison, we have

$$\underset{\textit{All Equity}}{\frac{(\text{EBIT} - ₹\ 48{,}00{,}000)\ 0.50)}{22{,}50{,}000}} = \underset{\textit{Half-Equity Half-Bonds}}{\frac{(\text{EBIT} - ₹\ 85{,}50{,}000)\ (0.50)}{16{,}25{,}000}}$$

[(.5 EBIT – ₹ 24,00,000) 16,25,000] = [(.5EBIT – 42,75,000) 22,50,000]

$EBIT_{BE}$ = ₹ 1,83,00,000

$EBIT_{EPS}$ = ₹ 3.00

Hence, for the all equity and half equity-half-bonds comparison, the indifference point is again ₹ 1,83,00,000 and earnings per share are ₹ 3.00.

For the all preference shares and half-equity half bonds. we have:

$$\underset{\textit{All Preference}}{\frac{(\text{EBIT} - ₹\ 48{,}00{,}000)\ (0.5) - ₹\ 70{,}00{,}000)}{10{,}00{,}000}} = \underset{\textit{Half-Equity Half-Bond}}{\frac{(\text{EBIT} - ₹\ 85{,}50{,}000)\ (0.5)}{16{,}25{,}000}}$$

$$[(.5EBIT - ₹\ 24,00,000) - ₹\ 70,00,000)]\ (16,25,000) = [(.5\ EBIT - ₹\ 42,75,000)\ 10,00,000]$$

$$EBIT_{BE} = ₹\ 3,52,00,000$$

$$EPS_{BE} = ₹\ 8.2$$

Above ₹ 3,52,00,000, preference share financing in more favourable; below, half-equity half-bonds in more favourable.

4. ABC Company and XYZ Company have the following EBIT and debt-servicing burden:

	ABC	*XYZ*
Expected EBIT	₹ 10,00,00,000	₹ 24,00,00,000
Annual Interest	4,00,00,000	6,00,00,000
Annual Principal payment on debt	4,00,00,000	8,00,00,000

The tax rate for ABC is 40 per cent and for XYZ the tax rate is 50 per cent. Compute the times-interest-earned ratio and the debt-service coverage ratio for the two companies, with which company you would be more comfortable if you were a lender? Why?

Solution

ABC Company:

Times interest earned $= ₹\ 10,00,00,000 / ₹\ 4,00,00,000 = 2.50$

$$\text{Debt service coverage} = \frac{₹\ 10,00,00,000}{₹\ 4,00,00,000 + \dfrac{₹\ 4,00,00,000}{(1\text{-}.40)}} = 0.714$$

XYZ Company:

Times interest earned $= ₹\ 24,00,00,000 / ₹\ 6,00,00,000 = 4.00$

$$\text{Debt service coverage} = \frac{₹\ 24,00,00,000}{₹\ 6,00,00,000 + \dfrac{₹\ 8,00,00,000}{(1\text{-}.50)}} = 1.091$$

The question of with which company one feels more comfortable depends on business risk. Inasmuch as a company has stable cash flows and XYZ is large, it is no doubt it is safer for loan.

5. Mazda Textiles was registered in 1983 at Calcutta. Its total current sales of ₹ 50,00,000 per year are to a leading public sector unit, KLYZ. This year Mazda has got a similar 10 years contract of ₹ 15,00,00,000 per year from KLYZ. The company has accepted the new contract. The current balance sheet for the company shows ₹ 10,00,00,000 of 12 per cent bonds and ₹ 8,00,00,000 of ₹ 10 per value equity shares. The company now must raise ₹ 7,50,00,000 from external sources in order to expand their production facilities so that contract can be fulfilled. For the expansion plan, the company is to decide that whether the financing should be accomplished through a debt issue carrying a 15 per cent coupon rate, or by selling shares of equity to net the company ₹ 15.00 per share. EBIT is 10 per cent of sales and the tax rate is 50 per cent.

(a) Calculate the EPS break-even level of EBIT, that is, the level of EBIT at which EPS is equal under the two financing alternatives.

(b) Assuming that a ₹ 75,00,000 per year sinking fund payment would be required on the new debt issue, calculate the Uncommitted Earnings Per Share (UEPS) break-even level of EBIT.

(c) Calculate the coverage ratio for Mazda Textiles under each of the two financing alternatives.

(d) What conclusions can you draw.

Solution

Total number of equity shares issued:

$$E_s = \frac{₹\,8{,}00{,}00{,}000}{₹\,10} + \frac{₹\,7{,}50{,}00{,}000}{₹\,15} = 1{,}30{,}00{,}000 \text{ equity shares}$$

Interest on Existing Debt :

$$I_s = 0.12\ (₹\ 10{,}00{,}00{,}000) = ₹\ 1{,}20{,}00{,}000$$

Total number of existing equity shares,

$$E_b = \frac{₹\,8{,}00{,}00{,}000}{₹\,10} = 80{,}00{,}000$$

Total interest on debt including new issue of bonds:

$$I_B = 0.12\ (₹\ 10{,}00{,}00{,}000) + 0.15\ (₹\ 7{,}50{,}00{,}000) = ₹\ 2{,}32{,}50{,}000$$

$$EBIT_{BE} = \frac{[1{,}30{,}00{,}000\ (₹\ 2{,}32{,}50{,}000) - (80{,}00{,}000)\ (₹\ 1{,}20{,}00{,}000)]}{1{,}30{,}00{,}000 - 80{,}00{,}000} = ₹\ 4{,}12{,}50{,}000$$

(b) $EBIT_{BE}$ for the sinking fund payment of ₹ 75,00,000 on new debt:

$$EBIT_{BE} = \frac{EBIT - ₹2{,}32{,}50{,}000(1-0.50) - ₹75{,}00{,}000}{8{,}00{,}000} = \frac{EBIT - ₹1{,}20{,}00{,}000(1-0.50)}{1{,}30{,}00{,}000}$$

$$EBIT_{BE} = ₹\ 8{,}02{,}50{,}000$$

$$EPS_{BE} = ₹\ 2.625$$

The necessity to cover sinking fund payments makes equity shares relatively more attractive. In fact since after tax earnings are only ₹ 2,08,75,000 at the projected level of sales, the ₹ 75,00,000 sinking fund payment would increase the firm's risk of not being able to meet contractual obligations.

(c) The coverage ratio for Mazda's expected level of EBIT of ₹ 6,50,00,000 (.10 × ₹ 65,00,00,000) is calculated below:

Coverage		*Pre-tax Burden*	*Times covered*
Interest (bond plan)	$\frac{EBIT}{I}$	₹ 2,32,50,000	2.79
Interest plus sinking fund	$\frac{EBIT}{I+(SF/0.5)}$	2,82,50,000	1.69
Interest (equity plan)		1,20,00,000	5.42

The table shows that inclusion of a sinking fund payment under the bond plan results in a lower coverage ratio.

6. Suraj Auto Company presently has ₹ 36 crore in debt outstanding bearing an interest rate of 10 per cent. It wishes to finance ₹ 40 crore expansion programme and is considering three alternatives:additional debt at 12 per cent interest, preferred stock with an 11 per cent dividend, and the sale of equity shares ₹ 16 per share. The company presently has 8,00,000 equity shares issued and is in a 40 per cent tax bracket.

(a) If earnings before interest and taxes are presently ₹ 15 crore, what would be earnings per share for the three alternatives, assuming no immediate increase in profitability?

(b) Develop a break-even, or indifference, chart for these alternatives. What are the approximate indifference points? To check one of these points, what is the indifference point mathematically between debt and equity.

(c) Which alternative do you prefer? How much would EBIT need to increase before the next alternative would be best?

Solution

(a) *(in thousands)*

	Debt	*Preferred Stock*	*Equity*
EBIT	₹ 1,50,000	₹ 1,50,000	₹ 1,50,000
Interest on existing debt	36,000	36,000	36,000
Interest on new debt	48,000	—	—
Profit before taxes	₹ 66,000	₹ 1,14,000	₹ 1,14,000
Taxes	26,400	45,600	45,600
Profit after taxes	₹ 39,600	₹ 68,400	₹ 68,400
Preferred stock dividend	—	44,000	—
Earnings available to equity shareholders	₹ 39,600	₹ 24,400	₹ 68,400
Number of shares	80,000	80,000	1,05,000
Earning per share	₹ .495	₹ .305	₹ .651

(b) Approximate indifference points: debt and equity ₹ 24 crore in EBIT; preferred and equity, ₹ 33 crore in EBIT; debt dominates preferred by the same margin throughout, there is no indifference point. Mathematically, the indifference point between debt and equity is:

$$\frac{\text{EBIT}^* - ₹\ 8,40,00,000}{80,000} = \frac{\text{EBIT}^* - ₹\ 3,60,00,000}{1,05,000}$$

$$\text{EBIT}^*\ (1,05,000) - ₹\ 8,40,00,000\ (1,05,000) = \text{EBIT}^*\ (80,000) - ₹\ 3,60,00,000\ (80,000)$$

$$25,000\ \text{EBIT}^* = ₹\ 59,40,00,00,000$$

$$\text{EBIT}^* = ₹\ 23,76,00,000$$

Note that for the debt alternative, the total before-tax interest is ₹ 8,40,00,000 and this is the intercept on the horizontal axis. For the preferred stock alternative, we divide ₹ 4,40,00,000 by (1 – .40) to get ₹ 7,33,33,333. When this is added to ₹ 3,60,00,000 in interest on existing debt, the intercept becomes ₹ 10,93,33,333.

(c) For the present EBIT level, equity is clearly preferable. EBIT would need to increase by ₹ 23,76,00,000 - ₹ 15,00,00,000 = ₹ 8,76,00,000 before an indifference point with debt is reached. One would want to be comfortably above this indifference point before a strong case for debt should be made. The lower the probabilityu that actual EBIT will fall below the indifference point, the stronger the case that can be made for debt, all other things the same.

QUESTIONS

1. What general concepts underlie the use of the EBIT-EPS approach for evaluating capital structure? Does this approach reflect the firm's overall goal of owner wealth maximisation?
2. What information is provided by a complete analysis—of cash flows that normally is provided by EBIT-EPS and coverage analysis?
3. What is the relationship between leverage and the firm's cost of debt? How is leverage measured in this case?
4. Suppose you discovered a firm that does not have any debt in its capital structure because the chairman of the board of directors is averse to borrowing. As its financial manager, you are asked to prepare an argument in favour of borrowing moderate amounts in the market.
5. What is uncommitted earnings per share (UEPS)?
6. What information is provided by a complete analysis of cash flows that normally is not provided by EBIT/EPS and coverage analysis?
7. Distinguish between (a) balance sheet ratios and (b) coverage ratios. Give two examples of each and indicate how they would be computed.

PROBLEMS

1. Punjab Equipment has recently been reorganised to produce garden equipment. It is in the process of establishing a financial policy. Two alternative financing plans have been suggested. The tax rate is 20 per cent.

Plan A: 2,50,000 shares of equity at ₹ 10/- share,
₹ 20,00,000 business loan at 12 percent

Plan B: 5,00,000 shares of equity at ₹ 10/-share,
₹ 10,00,000 business loan at 11 per cent.

The founders of Punjab Equipment have projected the following EBITs.

Economic Plan	*Probability*	*EBIT*
Best	.2	₹ 2,00,000
Normal	.6	₹ 3,50,000
Poor	.2	₹ 5,00,000

(i) Compute the expected EPS for each financial plan.
(ii) Compute the level of EBIT where the EPS are equal for the two plans.
(iii) Draw a graph for each plan illustrating the relationship between EBIT and EPS.
(iv) Which plan for both is acceptable if the firm desires a 75 per cent chance of earning a profit?

Ans.: (i) EPS_A = ₹ .352; (ii) EPS_B = ₹ .384 (iii) ₹ 3,70,000 (iv) Both

2. Novex Tools is looking at alternative financial structure. Currently, it uses 25 per cent debt in its book value capital structure. However, its debenture issue is coming due and it must decide whether a change in structure would be beneficial. The firm's tax rate is 40 per cent.

(₹ in Thousands)

	Current	*Plan 1*	*Plan 2*
Equity (₹ per share)	₹ 6000	₹ 6000	₹ 6,000
Debt	₹ 2000 at 12%	₹ 1000 at 10%	₹ 0
Preference	0	₹ 1000 at 12 %	₹ 2000 at 10%

(a) Compute the EPS for each plan if EBIT is ₹ 3,00,000 and ₹ 8,00,000.
(b) Prepare EBIT-EPS analysis.
(c) Which plan is most risky? Why?

Ans.: (a) EPS_0 = ₹ 60, ₹ 5.60; (b) EPS_1 = ₹ .00, ₹ 5,00; *(c)* EPS_2 = ₹ .333, ₹ 4.47

3. GND Metals is an expanding firm. It is currently financed with trade credit and owner equity. GND is planning an expansion of ₹ 1,00,00,000 and is trying to determine how to finance the expansion. An EBIT equal to ₹ 20,00,000 is fore casted. Assume taxes are 50 per cent. (a) Determine the EPS of GND if half of the ₹ 1,00,00,000 is financed with debt at 14 per cent interest cost and half with equity shares at ₹ 10 per share net. Assume 5,00,000 shares exist before the new issue. (b) Determine the EPS if GND Metals 75 per cent of the ₹ 1,00,00,000 is financed with debt (same rate). (c) At what level of EBIT do the two financing plans have equal EPS?

Ans.: (a) ₹ 1.05 (b) ₹ 1.17 (c) ₹ 15,00,000

4. Rantex Group is planning to diversify and for this needs ₹ 50,00,00,000 by issuing either 50,00,000 shares of equity, or bonds (at par) with 12 per cent coupon rate. Its present income statement is:

Sales	₹ 20,00,00,000
Operating costs	₹ 15,00,00,000
EBIT	₹ 5,00,00,000

Interest	₹ 50,00,000
EBT	₹ 4,50,00,000
Taxes	₹ 1,80,00,000
EAT	₹ 2,70,00,000

Earnings per share on the currently outstanding 25,00,000 shares are therefore ₹ 1.80. After the new financing, Group's financial managers estimate the EBIT will be ₹ 5,00,00,000, ₹ 7,00,00,000 or ₹ 10,00,00,000, with probabilities of 0.4, 0.5, and 0.1 respectively. (a) Determine the EPS for each level of EBIT for the two financing glans. (b) What is the expected EPS, its standard deviation, and the coefficient of variation of EPS for each plan? (c) Which plan should Rantex Group choose? Why? What other factors should be considered?

5. ABC Company currently has 15,00,000 shares of equity issued, with a market price of ₹ 50 per share. It has ₹ 2,00,00,000 in 9 per cent coupon rate bonds outstanding. ABC is considering a ₹ 3,00,00,000 expansion programme that it will finance with *(i)* all equity shares that can be sold to net the firm ₹ 40 per share; *(ii)* preference shares sold at par, with a 8% dividend rate; *(iii)* debentures sold at par, with a 9% coupon rate; or *(iv)* a combination of half equity shares and half 9 per cent coupon-rate debenture (sold at par). The firm is in the 40 per cent marginal tax bracket and estimates with a probability of .50 that EBIT will be ₹ 10,00,000, and with a probability of .50 that EBIT will be ₹ 2,00,00,000. (a) Calculate the EPS for each level of EBIT for all four plans. Also, calculate the mean or expected EPS for each financing plan. (b) Draw an EBIT-EPS chart showing the four possible financing plans. From the chart, estimate the indifference points between all equity shares and each of the other three plans. (c) Calculate the exact indifference points. Why is the indifference point between the equity shares and debt financing plans the same as the indifference point between equity shares plan and the combination equity shares and debt financing plan? (d) The cost of equity capital, k_e, is 10 per cent if equity shares financing employed, 10.5 per cent if the combination plan is employed, and 11 per cent if either the preference shares or debt financing plans are employed. What is the total value of ABC Company under each of the four alternative plans, using the mean or expected EPS calculated in (a) ? Assume all earnings are paid out as dividends. (e) Which of the plans should ABC Company select? Why?

Ans.: (a) *Plan:* Equity (EPS) ₹ 3.25; Preference (EPS) ₹ 3.68 Debt (EPS) ₹ 4.20; Equity/Debt (EPS) ₹ 3.79. (c) Estimated indifference points: Equity versus preference = ₹ 1,38,00,000; Equity versus debt - ₹ 99,00,000; Preference versus Equity/Debt = ₹ 1,64,00,000

6. Bharat Chemicals has current P/E ratio of 12.5 times and its present financial status is as follows:

Balance Sheet		*Income Statement*	
Total Assets	₹ 20,00,00,000	Sales	₹ 40,00,00,000
Debentures 15%	₹ 4,00,00,000	Operating cost	₹ 31,60,00,000
Equity shares (₹ 10 par)	₹ 4,80,00,000	EBIT	₹ 8,40,00,000
		Interest	40,00,000
Retained earnings	₹ 11,20,00,00	EBT	₹ 8,00,00,000
Total liabilities			

and shareholders equity	₹ 20,00,00,000	Taxes	₹ 3,20,00,000
		EAT	₹ 4,80,00,000

Bharat is considering three financing plans to raise ₹ 5,00,00,000. Its marginal tax rate is 60%. The three financing plans: *(i)* issue equity shares *(ii)* issue more 15% coupon rate debentures; *(iii)* issue 8% dividend rate preference shares. (a) Determine Bharat's current EPS and market price. (b) Determine the number of shares of equity to be issued if it is sold at its current market price (Plan *i*), as well as the interest or dividends (Plans *ii* or *iii*). (c) Determine the indifference EBIT between plan *(i)*, plans *(i)* and *ii*, and (2) *i* and *iii*. Explain why there is no indifference point between plans *ii* and *iii*. (d) If the EBIT/sales ratio stays the same after the expansion as before, determine the EPS under each plan for sales of ₹ 60,00,00,000. (e) If the P/E ratio stays at 12.5 for equity-share financing but drops to 12 under plan *ii* and *iii*, which plan should be chosen if sales are ₹ 60,00,00,000? Is there any other information you would want before making your decision? Explain.

Ans.: (a) EPS : ₹ 1.00; Market price = ₹ 12.50; (b) Equity shares : 40,00,000 : Interest : 75,00,000 Dividends: 40,00,000; (c) Plans *ii* and *ii* 6,90,00,000; Plans *i* and *iii* 9,06,66,667; Plans *ii* and *iii*; No solution is possible because plan *ii* dominates plan *iii* for any level of EBIT; (d) ₹ 1.41; ₹ 1.46; ₹ 144; (e) Equity-share plan.

PREM AUTO INDUSTRIES: *A CASE*

Prem Auto Industries (PAI) is located in Ludhiana, Punjab. The firm was founded in 1969 by R. K. Sharma, who served as a firm's President and Chairman of the board until his death in early 1985. Both positions are now filled by P. D. Sharma, the grandson of the R. K. Sharma, who is carrying on his grandfather's dogmatic tradition of *high-quality products for a quality industry*. A.K. Anand, vice-president of finance, often argued formally and informally against the total emphasis contained in the latter four words of that phrase which trademarked all of PAI's advertisements. Anand simply felt that by concentrating on supplying component parts to only the auto industry an undue exposure to basic business risk was assumed by the enterprise.

PAI manufacturers a very wide range of component parts, subassemblies, and final assemblies for sale to the major automobile producers that are largely concentrated in Delhi. Standard items in the product line include hubs, rims, brakes, antiskid units, and mirrors.

Sharma's family interests own 51 percent of the equity of PAI. Over the years outside financing has almost been completely shunned by the organisation. The PAI annual reports for the past four years contain this statement: "We will continue to finance corporate growth primarily through the internal generation of funds." Recent auto industry trends, however, have necessitated a shift by PAI management away from strict adherence to that policy. A national recession saw last year's motor vehicle factory sales of passenger cars drop 24 percent from the previous annual period. This in turn adversely affected the profitability and funds-generating capacity of PAI. On top of this the officials of PAI have decided upon a major product mix shift. The firm underestimated the demand for disc brakes, which have been installed on about 84 to 86 percent of passenger cars in recent years (see Exhibit-1). PAI's capacity to produce in this area will be increased during the next year. The volume achieved on the sale of antiskid units are proved to be disappointment. Accordingly, some factory space and equipment devoted to this product line will be used for other more profitable activities.

EXHIBIT - 1

Prem Auto Industries

Factory Installations of Selected Equipment
(Percent of Total Units Installed Upon)

Automobile Equipment	*Most Recent Year*	*One Year Earlier*
Power brakes, 4-wheel drum	2.4	1.0
Power brakes, 2-or 4-wheel disc	64.8	74.5
Disc brakes manual	19.2	11.2
Skid control device	0.9	1.9
Rer window defogger	21.5	16.4

Noting the public's acceptance of rear window defoggers, the firm has developed the technology necessary to be competitive in this product. To effect this expertise, however, substantial equipment purchases will be required within the next six months. The end result is that PAI must raise ₹ 500 crore in the capital markets through either the sale of new equity or the issuance of debentures. The new equity shares could be sold to net the firm ₹ 50 per share. The equity share price of PAI shares in the marketplace is now ₹ 56. C. P. Gupta, who is a partner in the investment company long-used by PAI, has assured Anand that the new debenture issue could be placed with a 12 percent interest rate. Gupta's counsel has always been highly valued by both Anand and other members of the PAI top management team.

EXHIBIT - 2

Prem Auto Industries

Abbreviated Balance Sheet, December 31, Last Year

(₹ in crore)

Assets	
Current assets	₹ 1,736
Net plant and equipment	2,015
Other	175
Total assets	₹ 3,926
Liabilities and Equity	
Current liabilities	₹ 488
Long-term debt:	
First mortgage bonds, 20 years to maturity, at 7%	300
Equity shares stock, ₹ 10 par	500
Capital surplus	1,200
Retained earnings	1,438
Total liabilities and equity	₹ 3,926

A preliminary meeting took place one week ago with Anand, Gupta and Sharma in attendance. The only topic discussed was the ₹ 500 crore financing choice facing PAI. Exhibits 2, 3, and 4 were analysed at length. Anand felt that the firm's owners would benefit if the asset expansion were financed with debt capital. Also, Sharma liked having total control over the firm's operations. With 51 percent of the equity shares family owned, Sharma knew that he could personally choose a course of action when a tough situation faced PAI.

EXHIBIT - 3

Prem Auto Industries

Income Statement, December 31, Last Year

(₹ in crore)

Sales	₹ 11,500
Variable costs	8,967
Fixed costs (excluding interest)	850
Interest expense	21
Earnings before taxes	₹ 1,662
Taxes (at 40%)	665
Net profit	₹ 997

Anand pointed out to Sharma that apart from the family, no "public" investor controlled as much as 5 percent of the issued equity shares. Thus Anand noted that effective control of the firm's operations would remain with the Sharma family should the new equity shares alternative be elected. Anand did not think it would be prudent to elect the debt alternative *only* because it would ensure Sharma family control over PAI in the strictest sense.

Both Anand and Sharma were concerned with the effect of additional financial leverage on the firm's price/earnings ratio. To partially deal with this question Sharma had his staff prepare Exhibit 4. Gupta suggested to Sharma that his firm prepare for the *worst that could happen*. He stated that PAI's price/earnings ratio might remain unchanged from its present level of 9.33 times if the debt alternative were chosen. He did not, however, believe such an occurrence to be highly likely. Gupta offered that his best guess is PAI's price/earnings ratio will fall to 9.11 times if debentures are sold and will rise to 10 times if the equity shares alternative is selected.

EXHIBIT - 4

Prem Auto Industries

Main Competitors' Selected Financial Relationships

Firm	*Debt Ratio**	*TIER***	*P/E Ratio ****
Hind Auto Components	32.7%	7	7.5
Autonite	20.1%	38	9.5
National Auto Ltd.	24.2%	14	9.0
K.D. Parts	26.8%	14	9.0
Suraj Auto Limited	19.0%	29	11.0
Simple average	24.6%	20.4	9.2

* Total debt divided by total assets.

** Times interest earned ratio.

*** Price to earnings ratio.

Prior to taking the question before the entire board of directors, Mr. Sharma wanted to review a more substantial body of analysis with Mr. Anand and Mr. Gupta. He gave Anand a week to prepare the information requested below.

QUESTIONS

1. Anand has projected that the firm's variable cost to sales ratio will be .76 after the ₹ 800 crore expansion is effected. In addition, fixed costs apart from interest will rise to an annual level of ₹ 1200 crore. Calculate the level of sales that will equate earnings per share regardless of whether the subject ₹ 800 crore is financed with debentures or equity shares.
2. Set up income statements for debenture-financing and equity financing by using the sales volume determined above, and demonstrate that earnings per share will indeed to be the same under the assumed conditions.
3. Use last year's results as the base period. Compute earnings per share under each financing alternative for sales levels equal to (a) 60 percent, (b) 80 percent, (c) 100 percent, (d) 110 percent, and (e) 120 percent of the base period results.
4. Using the price/earnings ratios, project the equity share prices for each financing choice at the sales levels just analysed.
5. Again taking "best guess" price/earnings ratios, determine the sales level that will equate market price per share regardless of the financing source chosen.
6. After reviewing recent marketing department forecasts of sales levels, P. D. Sharma concluded, "Rarely will PAI experience revenues below the ₹ 12,500 crore crore mark". If Sharma is correct, which financing alternative do you recommend?

18

DIVIDEND THEORIES

INTRODUCTION

Corporate dividend policy deals with the firm's decision about how much of its earnings to pay out to its equity shareholders in cash dividends. Since earnings paid out to equity shareholders are not available for financing new investments, the corporate dividend policy decisions is intertwined with corporate financial policy. The effect of a firm's dividend policy on the current price of its shares is a matter of considerable importance, not only to the corporate officials who must set the policy, but to investors planning portfolios and to economists seeking to understand and appraise the functioning of the capital markets. Do companies with generous distribution policies consistently sell at a premium over those with niggardly payouts? Is the reverse ever true? If so, under what conditions? Is there an optimum payouts ratio or range of ratios that maximises the current worth of the shares? The fundamental theoretical question is *why does a firm's dividend policy affect (or not affect) the wealth of the firm's equity shareholders?* If, for example, dividend policy affects the corporation's stock market value—and particularly if an increase in dividends increase that value — the owners will prefer that earnings be paid to them in dividends and that new investments be financed through the sale of new securities (debt and/or equity). When financial theorists have held the firm's investment policy constant (so as to isolate the impact of its dividend policy), they generally have found that its dividend policy does not impact on equity value. However, some theorists have argued that the firm's dividend policy decision affects the firm's willingness to undertake its investment opportunities (for example, where there exists a differential cost of retaining earnings versus paying dividends and raising equity funds via the sale of new equity shares). Under this circumstance dividend policy will have impact on firm value, *albeit indirectly*.

In this chapter we focus attention on a question which has occupied the attention of leading financial experts: why do firms almost universally pay out a substantial portion of their earnings as cash dividend? The key to this problem can be found in the answers to two additional albeit related questions:

(a) *What impact (if any) does dividend policy have on the market prices of a firm's equity share? Essentially the question asks whether dividend policy is a significant factor in determining the market value of the shareholders investment.*

(b) *If dividend policy does affect shareholder's wealth (the market value of equity-share), what constitute the firm's optimal dividend policy?*

Dividend policy has been (and remains today) a subject of considerable controversy. The basic conflict in the dividend policy issue is between those theorists who hold that, the rate of return required by the shareholders, is affected by dividend policy and those who hold that dividend policy has no effect on the required rate of return. Those who hold that dividend policy is immaterial usually view share price as the present value of future earnings. However, since they believe that the rate of capitalisation is unaffected by the dividend policy, they would presumably accept the dividend formula as an alternative basis for calculating share price. For those who hold that dividend policy does matter, the dividend formula is clearly the only appropriate means for calculating value. Therefore we can properly call them the *dividend theorists,* and for convenience we may call the other group the *earning theorists*. The objective of the management is to resolve this apparent conflict by evolving a dividend policy that balances shareholders needs for the current income against the demand for expected future growth in such a way that maximise the value of the firm.

Dividend policy should be seen in its proper perspective as a decision involving legal as well as economic considerations. To be legal, dividend payments must meet the conditions stipulated by the law of the nation in which the company is incorporated. Judging the importance of dividend policy requires consideration of various hypotheses on dividend policies. This chapter begins with an investigation of dividend payment under perfect capital market assumptions, Then follows a systematic analysis of the implications of various market imperfections. The chapter itemizes what the firm in practice should analyse in approaching a dividend decision.

DIVIDEND-PAYOUT RATIO

Dividend policy like all business decisions, can be optimised only in terms of the objectives that the financial management of the company is trying to achieve. Chapter-1 states that the objective of financial management is to maximise the firm's net present worth. This objective is a valid guide to financial decisions for all transactions not involving the transfer of assets between the corporate entity and the shareholders. For these external transactions the maximisation of the firm's net present worth naturally results in the maximisation of the shareholders' wealth. However, in the case of dividend policy, since cash is transferred from the corporate entity to its shareholders, the wealth of the shareholders is measured not only by the value of their shares, but also by the amount of cash dividends that they receive. Therefore, *maximisation of the firm's net present worth may not result in the maximisation of the shareholder's wealth.* For example, it is possible that a company can maximise its net worth and share prices by not paying any dividends at all. But such a dividend policy could actually reduce the wealth of the shareholders if the return on the retained earnings is lower than the rate at which investors capitalise the earnings of the company.

Share-price-maximisation is a necessary but not a sufficient condition for shareholder's wealth maximisation. The reason for going beyond the share-price-maximisation goal is that dividend payments can at times reduce the market share price, and yet increase the shareholder's wealth. Shareholders' wealth maximisation is a more fundamental goal since dividend payments are not meant to enlarge the supply of funds to the owners, but to increase their wealth. Let us see how the goals of share-price and wealth maximisation[1] can be reconciled:

Let P_1 = market share price before dividend declaration.

P_2 = market share price after dividend declaration but before actual cash payment.

P_3 = market share price after cash dividend payment.

K_1 = market discount rate associated with P_1

K_2 = market discount rate associated with P_2

K_3 = market discount rate associated with P_3

D_c = planned current dividend per share.

D_f = estimated future dividend stream before decision to pay current dividends.

CF_f = future cash flows per share, associated with source used to pay dividend

By using the simple terminology above, we can specify the conditions under which the firm should pay dividends. Specifically, the firm should pay dividends so long as the resulting price decline is less than the amount of dividend that is, so long as

$$D_c > P_1 - P_3 \quad (1)$$

Notice that it is not the share price after the declaration of dividends that is of interest here, rather, it is the market price after the payment of the dividend. The decision criterion used for the dividend payment can also be used to decide the size of the dividend. To wit, in order to maximise shareholder's wealth, the firm must try to maximise the sum $D_c + P_3$. In marginal terms, the dividend D_c must be increased to the point where the last increment results in an equal decline in P_3,

$$\Delta D_c = -\Delta P_3 \quad (2)$$

The dividend-decision criterion in effect answers the simple question of whether or not to pay a cash dividend. This is equivalent to the accept or reject situation, and does not lend itself to the ranking of alternatives. However, it can be slightly modified to account for the case where the dividend decision is but one of many competing investment opportunities. This can be done by first establishing the optimal size of dividends, that is, when $\Delta D_c = -\Delta P_3$. Then the firm must compare the expected increase in market price per share invested, $\Delta P/P$, resulting from the acceptance of a project, with the same factor for the payment of dividends, $(D_c \pm \Delta P_3)/D_c$. The answer is given in the following relationships:

1. James T. Porterfield: *Investment Decisions and Capital Costs*, Prentice-Hall. Inc., Englewood Cliffs N.J., 1965, pp. 87-93.

$$\text{If } \frac{\Delta P}{P} > \frac{D_c + P_3}{D_c} \quad \text{invest in the project}$$

$$\text{If } \frac{\Delta P}{P} < \frac{D_c + P_3}{D_c} \quad \text{pay the cash dividend} \tag{4}$$

$$\text{If } \frac{\Delta P}{P} = \frac{D_c + P_3}{D_c} \quad \text{take either action} \tag{5}$$

Thus, the dividend policy represents the link between the theory of capital budgeting and the theory of cost of capital. James E. Walter developed a formula to illustrate that dividend policy cannot be separated from the investment policy of the firm.

WALTER'S FORMULA

Walter's model is one of the earliest dividend models and certain later models correspond to this one. The nature of his contribution may be indicated by his formula suggesting the fundamental factors which influence the market value of a firm's equity shares. Operating with the objective of maximising the wealth position of the equity shareholder, Walter made following adjustments in the formula for equity share valuation to include dividend policy. Gordon formula[2] for valuation of an equity share is:

$$V_e = \frac{D}{k_e - g} \tag{6}$$

where

V_e = Value of an equity share
D = initial dividend,
k_e = capitalisation rate appropriate to the risk.
g = expected growth rate of earnings.

To reflect earnings retention, Walter adjusted the equation—6 as:

$$V_e = \frac{D}{k_e - rb} \tag{7}$$

where

b = percentage of earnings retained, (E-D)/E
r = expected rate of profitability

V_e, D and k_e are as defined above.

In other words, the rate of growth of dividends (*g*) is the product of the rate of profitability of retained earnings (*r*) multiplied by the earnings retention percentage (*b*).

---

2. Myron J. Gordon, *The Investments Financing and Valuation of the Corporations*, Richard D. Irwin, Homewood, all; 1962

Translating Formula for Equity Share Value to Operational Form

Equation-7 is basically accepted by almost all who have been engaged in discussion on the theory of dividend policy, but it falls far short of being a complete treatment of all the variables affecting dividend policy, and it is not operational as it stands.

In an effort to put equation—7 into operational form, Walter[3] has developed the formula

$$V_e = \frac{D+(R_a/R_c)(E-D)}{R_c} \tag{8}$$

where

V_e = market value of a share of equity
R_a = return on investment
R_c = market capitalisation rate
V_a = rate of profit of retained earnings
E = earnings per share
D = dividends per share

In this formula the rate of capitalisation (Re) is taken as the rate of capitalisation of a broad group of equity shares. The rate of profit on retained earnings can be measured as the increase in earnings per share of the firm over a recent period, such as three years, divided by the change in book value per share over that period. The other terms of the formula are readily available for any particular firm.

The Walter formula can be recast into the form

$$V_e = \frac{D}{R_c} + \frac{R_a - R_c}{R_c^2}(E - D) \tag{9}$$

for the purpose of bringing out the fact that the price or value of share of a particular firm will deviate from what would be indicated by the price-earnings ratio of the average

---

3. J.E. Walter, "Dividend Policies and Common Stock Prices," *Journal of Finance*" (March 1956), pp. 29-41. The transition from equation—1 to equation—8 is as follows Restating equation—6.

We have

$$k_e = \frac{D}{V_e} + g$$

since $g = \frac{\Delta V_e}{V_e}$, $k_e = \frac{D}{V_e} + \frac{\Delta V_e}{V_e}$

and since $V_e = \frac{R_a}{R_c}(E - D)$ and $k = R_c$

hence $V_e = \frac{D + (R_a / R_c)(E - D)}{R_c}$

E = earning per share
D = dividends per share

equity share according to the role played by the second term of equation-9. The second term of the right-hand side brings out the role of dividend policy and the earning rate on new investment.

It should be emphasised that both forms of the Walter formula given in equation-8 and-9 assume that the rate of profitability of new investment (R_a) will continue indefinitely into the future. As a practical matter, this rate is likely to drop as the firm grows and diminishing returns set in. But if the drop in R_a occurs far in the future, the effect is less because the drop will be time-discounted. Hence what is desired for use in the formula is a time-weighted average of R_a far into the future. Furthermore, it is apparent that a change in dividend policy in the future will have a similar effect and hence what is desired is the average future dividend pay out.

Finally, the Walter formula permits the ready incorporation of two practical aspects. The first is the desire of the shareholders for diversification. As an investment develops favourably, particularly if an equity share is a large segment of an investor's portfolio, the investor will seek some diversification with the profits of the investment. This practice entails costs of diversification, which include commission and a capital gains tax. These costs, defined as p and measured as a rate, can be readily incorporated into the basic formula to compute the value of the share to the particular investor.

$$V_e = \frac{E}{R_c} + \frac{R_a - R_c}{R_c^2}(E-D) \qquad (10)$$

As this value falls below the market price, the investor will sell.

The second practical aspect involves the tax differential between the capital gains and the marginal rate of personal income tax on the ordinary income of the investor. To reflect this aspect, the formula becomes.

$$V_e = \frac{D+[(t/s)R_c](E\text{-}D)}{R_c} \qquad (11)$$

where

s = 1 minus the tax rate of capital gains

t = 1 minus the marginal rate on ordinary income.[4]

---

4. Clearly this involves the statement that

$$R_a = \frac{t}{s} R_c$$

which simply means that to the particular investor the rate of profitability of reinvested funds is to be adjusted for the fact that a lower dividend payout ratio improves the tax position of the investor relative to his position under a higher payout ratio. Thus the individual investor seeks equivalence of the retention situation to his personal tax rate on ordinary income. This requires that

$$s\frac{R_a}{R_c} = t$$

This is the same thing as stating

$$R_a = \frac{t}{s}(R_c)$$

ILLUSTRATION OF THE INTERPLAY OF DIVIDEND POLICY AND KEY VARIABLES

CASE-1

Illustrations of Professor Walter's formula brings out the interplay of dividend policy and the key variables. Thus if a company's earning rate on recent investment (R_a) is 10 per cent and the average market rate of equity share (R_c) is 10 per cent and the company is earnings ₹ 5.0 per share with a 60 per cent payout of ₹ 3.00 per share, the indicated market value of a share using equation-8 is:

$$V_e = \frac{₹\ 3 + (0.1/0.1)(2)}{0.1} = ₹\ 50$$

Then, if we shift the dividend payout to 50 per cent or ₹ 2.50 per share, the market value remains

$$V_e = \frac{₹\ 2.50 + (0.1/0.1)(₹\ 2.50)}{0.1} = ₹\ 50$$

Here we have an average company (its $R_a = R_c$), and shifting the dividend payout ratio will not affect the market value of a share of its equity. The shareholder would gain nothing by leaving retained earnings with the company, since such money earns only the average rate available elsewhere.

Hence it follows that in the case where retained earnings yield no more than the average of equity shares, the dividend payout policy will have no effect on the price or value of the particular equity share.

CASE-2

If we assume a growth company in which we leave all the values as they stood in our first case with R_a now taken as 20 per cent (and we pay out 60 per cent of earnings), we have

$$V_e = \frac{₹\ 3 + (0.2/0.1)(₹\ 2)}{0.1} = ₹\ 70$$

And if we reduce the dividend payout to 50 per cent, the market price becomes

$$V_e = \frac{₹\ 2.50 + (0.2/0.1)(₹\ 2.50)}{0.1} = ₹\ 75$$

This follows because earnings kept in the firm will earn double what they would if the shareholder received them in dividends and invested them at the market rate.

Then if we cut the dividend payout to 25 per cent, the market price becomes

$$V_e = \frac{₹\ 1.25 + (0.2/0.1)(₹\ 3.75)}{0.1} = ₹\ 87.50$$

Hence it follows that if $R_a > R_c$, the value of the equity-share will vary inversely with dividend payout per cent.

CASE-3

If we examine a declining company in which earnings on new investment opportunities fail to meet the average rate of capitalisation of equity shares and leave all the values as they stood in our first example but with R_a now taken to be 5 per cent (and payout 60 per cent of earnings), we have

$$V_e = \frac{₹\,3 + (0.05/0.1)(₹\,2)}{0.1} = ₹\,40.00$$

But if we shift the dividend payment to 50 per cent of ₹ 2.50 per share, the market value becomes

$$V_e = \frac{₹\,2.50 + (0.05/0.1)(₹\,2.50)}{0.1} = ₹\,37.50$$

Hence it is apparent that if $R_a < R_c$, capital assets and liabilities the value of the equity share will vary directly with the dividend payout percentage.

Thus, the Walter's Formula spotlights the return on retained earnings relative to the average market rate of return on investment (market capitalisation rate) as the critical determinant of dividend policy. A high rate of return on retained earnings indicates a low payout ratio, whereas a low rate relative to the market average indicates the desirability of a high payout ratio to increase the price of the equity shares.

DIVIDENDS AS A PASSIVE RESIDUAL

The most prominent dividend policy prescription to evolve from the theory that internal financing is cheaper than external financing is referred to as the residual dividend policy. The residual theory holds that dividends should be the residual of the capital investment process. The capital investment decision making concepts indicated that in any decision-making period, capital investment project should be accepted whenever their expected rates of return exceeded their required rates of return (risk-adjusted cost of capital). The overall cost of capital (k_o) in turn, is a weighted average cost of debt (k_d) and the cost of equity (k_e) where the appropriate weights reflect the target capital structure proportions. The cost of equity (k_e) may have two components, the cost of retained earnings (k_r) and the cost of new equity (k_{ne}). The cost of retained earnings (k_r) is an opportunity cost reflecting the rate of return available to shareholders if earnings were paid to them in dividends and invested in other securities of comparable risk. This cost k_r, is lower than k_{ne} because the latter includes flotation costs. Thus the shareholders would appear to be better off if available earnings were retained to provide the required equity financing of approved capital investments than if dividends were paid and the firm then had to issue additional equity shares at a higher cost. This is the line of reasoning underlying the residual theory of dividends.

Dividends are therefore merely a residual remaining after all equity investments need are fulfilled. Notice carefully that a residual policy minimises the use of external equity financing (sale of new shares) since, by this policy, equity investment has a higher-priority claim to earnings than do dividend.

Companies have employed three general approaches in putting the residual dividend policy into practice. Before describing these approaches, we will define the following variables:

D_t = dividend paid in year t

l_t = investment in year t that is financed from equity sources (retained earnings and equity sales).

E_t = earnings in year t.

q_t = dividend payout ratio in year t $\left(\text{i.e.,} \frac{D_t}{E_t}\right)$

Pure residual dividend policy: Following this policy, the company will set the dividend paid each year as the amount of that year's earnings left after the year's equity investments is deducted. This can be expressed as :

$$D_t = E_t - l_t \quad (12)$$

Fixed dividend payout ratio: Dividends set under this method are equal to a constant proportion (q_t) of yearly earnings. This can be expressed as:

$$D_t = q_t \cdot E_t \quad (13)$$

If the percentage paid in dividends is 40 per cent, for example, this would equal:

$$D_t = q_t E_t = 0.4\ E_t$$

The percentage q_t is set so that dividend are equal to earnings minus equity-investment over the long-run.

Smoothed residual dividend policy. Under this method, yearly dividends are set at a constant value. Dividends are set so that over the long run they will be equal to earnings minus equity investment. Table-1 shows the dividend for five years paid out by a company using each of these methods. In the second method, the ratio (percent) used is 40 per cent.

The pure residual dividend policy can produce highly volatile dividends, particularly if investment and earnings move in opposite directions from period to period (from years 2 to 3 an from year 3 to 4 in the Table-1). The fixed dividend payout ratio residual dividend policy lets dividends fluctuate directly with earnings and will be as volatile as those earnings.The smoothed residual dividend strategy generally produces the most stable dividend.

TABLE-1
Earnings, Equity Investment, and Dividends of a Company Using a Residual Payout Policy

₹ '000

	Year					
	1	*2*	*3*	*4*	*5*	*Total*
Earnings (E_t)	₹ 350	₹ 450	₹ 325	₹ 500	₹ 375	₹ 2,000
Equity Investment (I_t)	200	150	325	275	250	1,200
Pure residualdividend (D_t)	150	300	0	225	125	800
Fixed dividend payout ratio dividend (D_t) (ratio = 0.4)	140	180	130	200	150	800
Smoothed residual dividend (D_t)	125	150	150	175	200	800

In a period in which earnings exceed dividends plus equity investment (years 1, 2 and 4 in Table-1), the firm increases its holdings of liquid assets (cash and marketable securities). These holdings are used later for dividends and investment in periods in which dividends plus investment exceed earnings (year 3 and 5). Observe that the smoothed residual policy provides both a minimisation of dependence on external financing of equity investment and the benefits of a stable dividend.

Thus, dividend policy is a passive result (or residue) of the capital investment decision-making process. Only the earning that are left over from financing capital investment projects should be paid out in dividends. A pure residual policy does not seek stability. Whereas the fixed dividend payout ratio and the smoothed residual dividend policy achieves stability in terms of the level of dividends.

The treatment of dividend policy as a passive residual determined solely by the availability of acceptable investment proposals implies that dividends are irrelevant, the investor is indifferent between dividends and retention by the firm. The critical question is whether dividends are more than jut a means of distributing unused fund. Should dividend policy be an active decision variable as opposed to a passive one? To answer these questions, we must examine more thoroughly the argument that dividends are irrelevant, so that changes in the payout ratio (holding investment opportunies constant) do not effect shareholder wealth.

IRRELEVANCE OF DIVIDENDS

The *earnings theorists* holds that investors are (or should be) indifferent to the payment (or lack of payment of dividends). According to this school of thought the price of a share varies only with the size of earnings, not with the distribution of earnings between dividends and reinvestment. However, since current earnings are subject to temporary disturbances, they can provide only a rough approximation of expected earnings. For Franco Modigliani and Merton Miller (M-M), leading proponents for the school of thought that argues that dividends are irrelevant, the dividend payout ratio is a mere detail.[5] Shareholders' wealth is neither created nor destroyed by dividend policy.

BASIC ASSUMPTIONS

The critical assumptions of the M-M are perfect capital markets; rational behaviour, absence of flotation costs, tax-free world; no transactions costs, infinitely divisible securities; given investment policy; and, finally, perfect certainty. Although the terms "perfect markets," "rational behaviour," and "perfect certainty" are widely used throughout economic theory, it may be helpful to start by spelling out the precise meaning of these assumptions in the present context.

(1) In "perfect capital markets," no buyer or seller (or issuer) of securities is large enough for his transactions to have an appreciable impact on the then ruling price. All traders have equal and costless access to information about the ruling price and about all other relevant characteristics of shares. No brokerage fees, transfer taxes, or other transaction costs are incurred when securities are brought, sold, or issued, and there are no tax differentials either between distributed and undistributed profits or between dividends and capital gains.

(2) "Rational behaviour" means that investors always prefer more wealth to less and are indifferent as to whether a given increment to their wealth takes the form of cash payments or an increase in the market value of their holdings of shares.

(3) "Perfect certainty" implies complete assurance on the part of every investor as to the future investment programme and the future profits of every corporation. Because of this assurance, there is, among other things, no need to distinguish between stocks and bonds as sources of funds at this stage of the analysis. We can, therefore, proceed as if there were only a single type of financial instrument which, for convenience, we shall refer to as shares of stock.

Assuming a given investment plan for the company, Miller and Modigliani argue that *dividend policy is irrelevant for determining the company's market value because market value is determined by the return on the company's assets and not by the division of this return between dividends and retained earnings. The problem facing the financial manager is to find the optimal investment plan, and dividend policy is irrelevant to the choice of an optimal investment plan.* In the capital structure theories, Modigliani and Miller argued that in the absence of the tax deductibility of interest payments on debt, the company's proportion of debt to equity is irrelevant in determining its value.[6] Their contention that dividend policy is irrelevant also rests on their argument that the proportions of debt to equity in the capital structure are irrelevant. Given their assumptions, the payment of dividends cannot of itself be assumed to affect shareholders' wealth. *The payment of dividends simply helps to alter the financing proportions of the company.* For example a company's decision to borrow in order to

5. Merton H. Miller and Franco Modigliani, *Dividend Policy, Growth, and the Valuation of Shares* Journal of Business 34, (October 1966), pp. 411-33.
6. Miller and Modigiliani, *op. cit.*

pay dividends has the effect of substituting debt for equity in the company's capital structure. If, as Modigliani and Miller state, the company's capital structure is irrelevant to the determination of shareholders' wealth, then this substitution of debt for equity is also irrelevant. Therefore, shareholders will be indifferent to alternative investment plans that will produce identical net present values, even if the plans entail radically different patterns of dividend payments, and therefore different patterns of financing.

In a perfect capital market, the reason for shareholder's indifference to different patterns of dividend payments is that the effect of dividend payments on shareholders wealth is offset exactly by other means of financing such as a new share issue or a new debt issue. A company may decide to pay a dividend and make a new share issue of the same amount in order to finance the company's proposed investments. Miller and Modigliani argue that there would be a decline in the company's share price as a result of the new issue which would, in effect, exactly offset the effect of the payment of the dividend. Under these circumstances shareholders would be indifferent between the payment of dividends and the retention of earnings.

Miller and Modigliani's argument goes as follows. The market price of a company's shares at the beginning of any period (t_o) is equal to the present value of the dividend it will pay at the end of the period (D_1) plus the ex-dividend price of the share at the end of the period (P_1). Thus:

$$P_0 = \frac{1}{1+k_e}[D_1 + P_1] \tag{14}$$

where

P_o = market price per share at t_o

k_e = required rate of return on equity capital for a company in that risk class.

Then they consider what will happen if the company pays a dividend and at the same time makes a new share issue equal to the amount of that dividend. Let n equal the number of shares outstanding at t_o and let D_n equal the number of new shares sold at t_1. Rewriting equation (14) to reflect the total market value of equity at to they get:

$$nP_0 = \frac{1}{1+k_e}[nD_1 + (n+\Delta n)P_1 - \Delta nP_1] \tag{15}$$

The total value of the new issue of shares (ΔnP_1) will depend on the amount of new investment (I), th profit earned during the period (Y), and the dividends paid on the outstanding shares (D_nD_1). Thus:

$$\Delta nP_1 = 1 - (Y - nD_1) \tag{16}$$

Substituting Equation (16) into Equation (15) they find that:

$$nP_o = \frac{1}{1+k_e}\ [(n + \Delta n)P_1 \text{-} I + Y] \tag{17}$$

As the nD_1 term has cancelled out, D_1 does not appear in Equation (17). Furthermore as the other variables in Equation (17) are assumed to be independent of D_1, Miller and Modigliani conclude that P_o is not a function of the company's dividend decision. We will illustrate their hypothesis by means of the following example.

Comprehensive Example

The ABC Company currently has 1 crore shares on issue which have a current market price of ₹ 100 per share. Therefore, shareholder's wealth is equal to ₹ 100 crore. The company is considering the possibility of paying a dividend of ₹ 5 per share one year from now. The required rate of return (k_e) is 10 per cent.

If the dividend is paid the share price at the end of the period (P_1) will be equal to:

$$P_o(1 + k_e) - D_1 = P_1 \text{ (from Equation (14))}$$

$$₹\ 100\ (1.10) - ₹\ 5 = P_1$$

$$₹\ 105 = P_1$$

If no dividend is paid P_1 ₹ 110. Now we will assume that the company is expected to earn an annual net profit of ₹ 10 crore and has new investments amounting to ₹ 50 crore. If the company pays the dividend of ₹ 5.00 per share, then in order to finance its investments it must issue ₹ 42,85,714 new shares. Thus:

$$\Delta nP_1 = I - (Y - nD_1)$$

$$\Delta n(105) = 50 \text{ crore} - (₹\ 10 \text{ crore} - ₹\ 5 \text{ crore})$$

$$\Delta n = \frac{₹\ 45 \text{ crore}}{₹\ 105 \text{ per share price}}$$

$$\Delta n = 42{,}85{,}714$$

If no dividend is paid the company will only needed to issue 36,36,364 shares in order to finance the investments. Thus:

$$\Delta n = \frac{₹\ 40 \text{ crore}}{₹\ 110 \text{ per share price}}$$

$$\Delta n = 36{,}36{,}364$$

It follows that if the dividend is ***paid***, shareholders' wealth (nP_o) is equal to:

$$nP_o = \frac{1}{1+k_e}\ [(n + \Delta n)\ P_1 - 1 + Y]$$

$$nP_o = \frac{1}{1.10}\ [(1{,}42{,}85{,}714)\ (₹\ 105) - ₹\ 50 \text{ crore} + ₹\ 10 \text{ crore}]$$

$$nP_o = 0.90909\ [₹\ 150 \text{ crore} - ₹\ 50 \text{ crore} + ₹\ 10 \text{ crore}] = ₹\ 100 \text{ crore}$$

If the dividend is ***not paid***, shareholders' wealth remains the same. Thus :

$$nP_o = \frac{1}{1.10}\ [(1{,}36{,}36{,}364)\ (₹\ 110) - ₹\ 50 \text{ crore} + ₹\ 10 \text{ crore}]$$

$$nP_o = 0.90909\ [₹\ 150 \text{ crore} - ₹\ 50 \text{ crore} + ₹\ 10 \text{ crore}] = ₹\ 100 \text{ crore}$$

Given their assumptions, therefore, it appears that the payment of a dividend by the company is irrelevant in determining shareholders' wealth.

If it is now assumed that the company proposes to issue debentures in order to finance the dividend, Miller and Modigliani maintain that this financing strategy will also leave shareholders' wealth unchanged. They claim that this result is achieved by means of the arbitrage process which we described in chapter-24.[7] They argue that in the absence of taxes there can be no change in shareholders' wealth as a result of changes in capital structure. As issuing debentures to pay dividends is simply a means of substituting debt for equity in the company's capital structure, it can have no effect on shareholders' wealth.

The proposition that dividends are irrelevant is based, therefore, on the proposition that the company's capital structure is not important in determining shareholders' wealth. If both dividends and leverage are irrelevant, the company's financial manager would be indifferent to financing the company's investments by using debt, retained earnings or a new share issue. One method of financing is as good as any other method of financing.

RELEVANCE OF DIVIDENDS

Even after they drop the assumption of certainty, Miller and Modigliani still claim that as a result of the ability of investors to arbitrage, a company's dividend policy is irrelevant in determining shareholders' wealth.[8] However, arguments have been advanced that the dividends can actively influence the value of the firm and shareholder wealth. In such a case, there is reason for management to concern itself with the development and implementation of a dividend policy. In this section, we examine some of the arguments in support of the position that dividends are relevant to stock valuation and that dividend policy is an active decision variable.

RESOLVING INVESTOR UNCERTAINTY

The school of thought on relevance of dividends maintains that investors will not be indifferent about receiving dividends so long as uncertainty, differential tax rates, and market imperfections exist. Most investors would prefer to receive a cash dividend today as opposed to some time in the future, since *a bird in the hand is worth two in the bush.* Current dividend payments reduce investor uncertainty and, other things being equal, increased the market price of a share of stock. Reduced risk exposure means a lower required rate of return and according to the basic stock valuation model a higher value for the firm's stock. The dividend relevance school's leading proponents Myron J. Gordon, suggest that shareholders do have a preference for current dividends — that, in fact, there is a direct relationship between th dividend policy of a firm and its market value. They argues that investors are generally risk-averse and therefore attach less risk to current as opposed to future dividends or capital gains. John Emmett Kirshmann made one of the earliest and the most concise statements of this argument when he said:[9]

7. The arbitrage process for dividend decisions is illustrated by James E. Walter, *Dividend Policy and Enterprise Valuation*, Wadsworth Publishing Company Inc., Belmont, California, 1967, pp. 106-110.
8. Miller and Modigliani, *op. cit.*, pp. 426-430. See also Michael Brennan, "A Note on Dividend Irrelevance and the Gordon Valuation Model," *Journal of Finance,* pp. 1115-1121, December 1971.
9. Johan Emmett Kirshmann : *Principles of Investment,* McGraw-Hill, New York, 1933 p. 737.

Of two stocks with identical earnings, records, and prospects, but the one paying a larger dividend than the other, the former will undoubtedly command a higher price merely because stockholders prefer present to future values. Myopic vision plays a part in the price-making process. Stockholders often act upon the principle that a bird in the hand is worth two in the bush and for this reason are willing to pay a premium for the stock with the higher dividend rate, just as they discount the one with the lower rate.

A view similar to Kirshmann's is held by Benjamin Graham and David L. Dodd who states.[10]

The typical investor would most certainly prefer to have his dividend today and let tomorrow take care of itself. No instances are on record in which the withholding of dividends for the sake of-future profits has been hailed with such enthusiasm as to advance the price of the stock. The direct opposite has invariably been true. Given two companies in the same general position and with the same earnings power, the one paying the larger dividend will always sell at the higher prices.

The bird-in-the hand argument of Kirshmann, Graham, and Dodd has beerobably the best known of all contemporary advocates of the dividend hypothesis.[11] Gordon's mathematical formulation is useful not only because of its theoretical foundation in uncertainty, but also because it clearly brings out the essential point at issue between the earnings theorists and the dividend theorists.

To demonstrate the dividend effect, Gorden tested the following simple valuation expression:

$$P = a_0 + a_1 D + a_2 \text{ RE} + e$$

where

P = Current share price
D = Dividends
RE = Addition to retained earnings
a_0, a_1, a_2 = Regressions coefficients
e = A random-error term

Gordon found that although the estimate of a_1 and a_2 were significantly positive in most cases, a_1 was consistently larger than a_2. From this he concluded that cash dividends are generally worth more to investors than of retained earnings; a conclusion that is clearly contrary to the irrelevance proposition.

Although this argument seems intuitively logical it has led to counter arguments. In one case it was shown that if a firm follows a rational capital expenditure policy and accept all projects with an Internal Rate of Return (IRR) equal to or greater than

10. Benjamin Graham and David L. Dodd, *Security Analysis*, McGrawHill, Inc., 1st ed., 1934, pp. 327.
11. Myron J. Gordon, "Optimal Investment and Financing Policy." *Journal of Finance* (May 1963), pp. 264-272, and Gordon, "The Savings, Investment and valuation of a Corporation," *Review of Economics and Statistics* 40 (February 1962), pp. 37-51.

the first Marginal Cost of Capital (MCC), then higher dividends, other things being equal, will force the firm to acquire more external capital to compensate for the higher payout ratio. In a world of rational investors, even with uncertainly, the value of an equity share will adjust to the firm's current payout ratio and its expected future dividend stream only so long as the firm's investment policy is unaffected by any changes in its dividend policy.[12] That is, if the firm still accepts all capital expenditure for which the IRR is greater than the firm's MCC, the value of the firm is not affected by the dividend payout ratio. Only if the firm acts in a manner to make its investment and dividend decisions interdependent will the dividends payout ratio influence its value.

On the slightly different tack, Professor Van Horne and McDonald present evidence on the optimality of a residual payout policy. If the residual payout policy is optimal, companies paying dividends and also issuing new equity capital should sell at discount. Conversely, if a non residual dividend policy is optimal, these companies should sell at a premium.[13] Others have suggested that if shareholders want to have a cash income stream which differs from that offered by the firm, they can achieve it by periodically liquidating some shares or by reinvesting the dividend proceeds.[14] *Since in the perfect market in the absence of taxes, these "homemade" dividends are perfect substitutes for corporate dividends, a firm's dividends policy is not a thing of value for investors.* Whether or not dividends resolve in vestor uncertainty and therefore affect share valuation depends in large part on whether the firm can do something for invgestors that they cannot do for themselves. Clearly, the dividend policies of many firms seem to intimate that they feel they can do just that.

CLIENTELE EFFECTS

There are many reasons why particular investors may prefer one payout policy to another. The market is so diverse that while some investors actively pursue firms with high dividend rates, others couldn't care less about them. The clientele effect, as originally discussed by Miller and Modigliani[15] suggests that if investors have preferences for different dividend policies, they will be attracted to firms that have policies consistent with their objectives. Likewise, firms will find it advantageous to adjust their dividend policies to the needs of their target investors. Clientele effect proponents argue that every firm has an implied, if not formal, dividend payment pattern which attracts stockholders whose preferences with respect to the payment and stability of dividends correspond to those of the firm. Any attempt on the part of the firm to abruptly alter its dividend payment pattern will lead to price changes (some of which may be severe), as investors alter their holdings to compensate for

---

12. Michael Brennan; A Note on Dividends Irrelevance and the Gordon Valuation Model, *Journal of Finance* 26 (Dec., 1971), pp. 115-1121.
13. James C. Van Home and McDonald, John G.: "Dividend Policy and New Equity Financing." *Journal of Finance,* May 1971, pp. 507-19.
14. Robert C. Higgins: Dividend policy and increasing Discount Rates: A Clarification, *Journal of Financial and Quantitative Analysis* (June 1972), pp. 1757-1762.
15. Miller and Modigliani, "Dividend Policy Growth, and the Valuation of Shares," p. 429.

the changes. There is some empirical evidence that a clientele effect does exist, though its magnitude is not felt to be large.[16] The existence of even relatively small effects, however, may in part explain a firm's reluctance to alter established patterns.

In equilibrium, the dividend payouts of corporations will match the desires of investors groups. At this point, no company would be able to affect its share price by altering its dividend. As a result, even with taxes, dividend payout would be irrelevant. Black and Scholes are principal proponents of the neutral position, based on corporations adjusting the supply of dividends to take advantage of any mispricing of stocks in the marketplace.[17] Another argument against clientele effects is that investors can use combinations of put and call options to isolate movements in stock price. By so doing, the investor effectively strips the dividend from the capital gains component of the stock. If investors are able to separate dividends from capital gains to suit there needs, the tax-induced clientele argument for particular stocks is weakened.

INFORMATION COST

Shareholders always face uncertainty about the future profitability of a firm. Contrary to the assumption of perfect markets, information that might reduce that uncertainty is not free. Indeed, some investors may incur substantial costs to obtain information about the prospects of the firm. But even those who have the resources and are willing to pay may not be able to obtain all the information they desire. They must make do with titbits provided by management, market letters, the opinion of professional analysis. Financial data from authentic and other less common sources, all of which are likely to have some cost in cash or in use of scarce time.

In the face of costly information, one source to which investors turn is the firm itself. However they are likely to be wary of simply believing everything that management say (and do not say). After all it is in the manager's personal economic interest to make investors think that all is well with the firm and management is doing a good job. In addition,earnings, sales, and cost figures, historical or projected, are subject to various forms of manipulation—most of which are not specifically

---

16. Edwin J. Elton and Martin J. Gruber, "Marginal Stockholder Tax Rates and the Clienate Effect," *Review of Economics and Statistics* 52 (February 1970), pp. 68-74; R. Richardson Pettit, 'Taxes, Transactions Costs and the Clientele Effects of Dividends," *Journal of Financial Economics* 5 (December 1977), pp. 419-436; and Wilbur G. Lewellen, Kenneth L. Stanley, Ronald C. Lease, and Gary G. Schlarbaum, "Some Direct Evidence of the Dividend Clienatele Phenomenon," *Journal of Finance* 333 (December 1978), pp. 1385-1399.

17. Fischer Black and Myron Scholes, "The Effects of Dividend Yield and Dividend Policy on Common Stock Prices and Returns," *Journal of Financial Economics,* 1 (May 1974), 1-5. Rosita P. Chang and S. Ghon Rhee, 'The Impact of Personal Taxes on Corporate Dividend Policy and Capital Structure Decisions," *Financial Management,* 19 (Summer 1990), 21-31, find a significant degree of correlation between financial leverage and dividend-payout ratio, which is consistent with the simultaneous occurrence of leverage and dividend tax clientele effects.attempting to empirically test a version of the CAPM that contained a dividend influence, Litzenberger and Ramaswamy[20] concluded that dividends were highly

intended to deceive. In such a situation investors may look to dividend and dividend policy to provide information about the future.

INFORMATION CONTENT

Another argument for the relevance of dividends is based on the premise that the mere payment of dividends imparts certain information to shareholders. Known as the information content of dividends theory, this idea implies that dividends have an impact on share prices because they communicate information to investors about the firm's profitability. An increase in the dividend rate, for example, says favourable things about the future outlook of the company. It has been suggested that implicit in the MM dividend irrelevance argument is this assumption that the market knows a company's expected return stream exactly, and discounts this stream to determine the value of the firm. Advocates of information content argue that what is really valued in the marketplace is the perceived return stream. If this is the case, then changes in dividend policy will alter the market's perception about the firm and therefore affect the valuation process. Tests for an information content effect have uncovered some short-run impact on share prices due to changes in dividend policy, though little long-lasting effect was founded.[18]

If investors truly attribute unambiguous information content to dividend policy, it would seem that any dramatic and/or erratic changes in a firm's dividend rate or payout ratio will heighten investor uncertainty and influence stock prices. It is reasonable to conclude, therefore, that regardless of the dividend policy chosen, the practice of stability is recommendable. Major dividend changes are likely to be perceived as containing substantial information and hence should be made only after careful consideration of the consequences.

At first blush, dividend policy may appear to offer on exceedingly inefficient way to communicate with shareholders, but if one believes the old adage that *money speaks louder than words,* there may be some logic in practice. In a risky world, anything management can do to reduce shareholder uncertainty about the future is worthwhile. Of course, management can communicate directly with owners through quarterly and annual reports. But according to the "talk-is-cheap" philosophy, a much more convincing way for management to convey their expectations is with money—that is, with dividend policy. In any case, it seems clear that once dividends begin to carry an information content, subsequent erratic changes in dividends will heighten investor uncertainty and, in the case of dividend cuts, will probably reduce the share price. An example of the effects of erratic dividend streams will demonstrate this point.

Consider two new firms, United Motor Ltd. and National Motor Ltd., alike in all respects except dividend policy. Their earnings and dividends are shown in Table-2. Assume that both companies have investment opportunities requiring that, on

---

18. R. Richardson Pettit, "Dividend Announcements, Security Performance, and Capital Market Efficiency, "*Journal of Finance* 27 (December 1972) pp. 993-1007; and Ross Walls. 'The Information Content of Dividends," *Journal of Business* 46'April 1973), pp. 191-211.

average, 40 per cent of earnings be retained. Average annual earnings over the 6-year period are ₹ 6.00 per share for booth companies, and average dividends per share are ₹ 3.60. As of 2013, both managements believe that ₹ 6.00 per share for represents the level of expected annual earnings per share in future years.

TABLE-2

	United Motor Ltd.			*National Motor Ltd.*		
	Dividends per share	*Earnings per share*	*Payout ratio*	*Dividends per share*	*Earnings per share*	*Payout ratio*
2008	₹ 2.40	₹ 4.00	0.60	3.60	₹ 5.00	0.72
2009	3.00	5.00	0.60	3.60	7.50	0.48
2010	3.60	6.00	0.60	3.60	6.00	0.60
2011	4.20	7.00	0.60	3.60	6.40	0.56
2012	4.80	8.00	0.60	3.60	4.50	0.80
2013	3.60	6.00	0.60	3.60	6.60	0.54
Average	3.60	6.00	—	3.60	6.00	0.60

Suppose that investors of both firms view dividends as an indicator of the future profitability of those firms. Neither set of shareholders knows what management's expectations of the future are. *With its stable dividend of ₹ 3.60 per year, National Motor might convey management expectations of future profitability more effectively through dividend policy than can United Motor.* United's dividend fluctuates with earnings from period to period. Even though dividends are always 60 per cent of realised earnings, it would be difficult for investors to discern, after observing a particular 60 per cent payout, whether management's expectations of the future had changed. National's management could, because dividends have been historically stable, signal its expectations by raising or lowering the ₹ 3.60 dividend.

To the extent that dividends are viewed as an important source of information by both investor and managers, those policies that convey information easily should be preferred. Such policies may reduced both the preceived risk and cost of obtaining information. If so they should increase the price that investors are willing to pay for the firm's shares. That is, one might expect the shares of National to sell at slightly higher prices then that of United Motor.

From the discussion above it is possible to discover how a firm wishing to convey maximum information to the market, might set dividend policy. First management would assess future profitability and form expectations about future earnings level. These expectations in mind, management might set a target payout ratios. The target ratio is the proportion of permanent earnings that will be paid out, regardless of fluctuations in actual earnings. If dividend policy is set in this way, there are two reasons for altering dividends per share. *First*, expectations about permanent earnings might change. *Second*, even though permanent earnings were unchanged, the target payout might be altered by changes in the financial and operating environment of the firm.

As a practical matter it may still be difficult for investors to determine the real reason for change in dividends. They can never be certain why dividends increased or decreased; but given the company history and management practices of a specific firm that constitute generally available information, a reasonable assessment should be possible.

The information content of dividend policy varies from firm to firm. Availability of alternative sources of information as well as specific circumstances facing a firm may make dividend policy an efficient and highly ambiguous source of information. Also, we should recognise that managerial attempts to fool the market and maintain dividends when their expectation of permanent earning are falling may only create future problems for management. Maintaining dividends when earnings decline might convey a temporary sense of security regarding the profitability of the firm. However, as actual earnings continue to decline perhaps irregularly shareholders will realise that the current dividend cannot be maintained and will expect a decline in future dividends. When that expectation commonly held, share price will fall even if high dividends are temporarily maintained.

Finally, we should note that the possibility of information content in dividends reinforces the argument made in discussing the clientcle effect. Not only may such a policy reduce trading costs, it should also reduce shareholder uncertainty about the prospects of the firm. When a firm suddenly change, policies, investors may s reassess existing information. As a result, the value of shares may be more unstable and shareholder wealth may decline.

DIVISIBILITY OF SECURITIES

In addition to transaction and flotation costs, we must consider the problem of divisibility. The notion of a perfect market presumes that financial securities can be sold in any amounts. Most publicly held firms have lakhs of shares outstanding and one share represents a very small, ownership claim, so their equity is divisible into relatively small parts. However, small investors having shares in some firms will find difficulty in creating homemade dividends because fractional shares cannot be sold and the cost of selling a very few shares on an organised exchange is relatively large.

TAX EFFECTS

A key premise of the irrelevance argument is that investors are indifferent as to whether they receive their return in dividend income or share price appreciation. In the absence of personal taxes, this premise is reasonable. However, once differential personal tax rates are considered, there may well be a preference for long-term capital gains, since they are taxed at lower rates than cash dividends. Moreover, the tax on capital gains is deferred until an investor actually disposes of the shares. Thus, once personal taxes are considered, it follows that for a given level of risk, investors will require a higher total return on a security the larger the proportion of its return attributable to dividends, since dividend are subject to a higher tax rate than long-term capital gains. This implies that not only are share prices influenced by dividends, they are influenced in a negative way—high dividends actually hurt share prices.

Another alternative explanation for observed dividend behaviour can be found by applying the portfolio principle. In recent paper Feldstein and Green use the idea that shareholders, risk-aversion provides a limit to corporate growth. They consider an economy with shareholders in diverse tax situations, i.e., two groups of taxable individuals and untaxed institutions, but the same line of reasoning holds for investors in "low" and "high" tax brackets. Firms can either distribute their profits as dividends or reinvest them and grow larger, eventually distributing these funds to shareholders are capital gains. Under certainty, this would lead to a segmented market in which taxable individuals invest only in firm which forgo dividend payments, while untaxed institutions would prefer the firm which pay dividends. However, if we assume that investors regard each firm's return as uncertain, they will desire to diversify their holdings. Feldstein and Green demonstrate that in such a market share price maximisation implies that each firm must attract both types of investors and this in in turn implies that some fraction of earnings must be distributed as dividends. Market equilibrium of the segmented form can take place only in the case of little or no uncertainty or if we assume a constraint on investors' ability to diversify risk.[19]

This proposition has also important theoretical and empirical implications for the capital asset pricing model (CAPM) because it suggests that dividend payout should be included as a second factor in explaining the equilibrium rate of return on securities. In attempting to empirically test a version of the CAPM that contained a dividend influence, Litzenberger and Ramaswamy[20] concluded that dividends were highly significant. Specifically, they found that as cash dividends increased, investors raised their before-tax returns by bidding down the price of the shares. In assence, investors sought more preferentially taxed capital gains as the way to maintain a desired after-tax rate of return. Such findings suggest a definite relationship between dividend policy and expected returns, and provide evidence that the differential tax on dividend and capital gains creates a preference for capital gain.[21]

In a different attack, Miller and Scholes argue that it is possible for investors to

19. Martin Feldstein and Jerry Green: Why Do Companies Pay Dividends? *National Bureau of Economic Research*, Working Paper 413 December 1979.
20. Robert H. Litzenberger and Ramaswamy, Krishna: The Effect of Personal Taxes and Dividends on Capital Asset Prices, *Journal of Financial Economics 1* (June 1979), pp. 163-195.
21. Other studies have been conducted to show that even in the face of differential tax rates, dividend policy is still irrelevant, however, these studies continue to rely on major theoretical assumptions. See, for example, Merton H. Miller and Meron S. Scholes, Dividends and Taxes; *Journal of Financial Economics* 8 (Dec. 179) pp. 333-364. Merton H. Miller and Myron S. Scholes, "Dividends and Taxes," *Journal of Financial Economics,* 6 (December 1978), 333-64.

avoid paying taxes on dividends.[22] With such avoidance, of course, any tax bias in favour of retention of earnings disappears. The Miller and Scholes "tax dodge" involves a shareholder borrowing a sufficient amount of funds of produce one equivalent amount of interest expense for the amount of dividend income. The amount borrowed is invested in a single-payment annuity or some other type of tax-deferred investment. The interest expense is offset against dividend income, so the investor pays no immediate tax. The capital gain on the investment of the borrowed funds is sheltered. If this gain is postponed until the time of death, no capital gains tax would be paid. Thus, the argument is one of investors transforming dividends into capital gains that are postponed.

Suppose an investor invested ₹ 20,000 in the equity of XYZ Co. and the share has an 8 per cent dividend yield. The investor receive ₹ 1,600 in dividends. In addition to dividend yield, the share is expected to show annual price appreciation of 6 per cent. Now the investor borrow ₹ 40,000 at 12 per cent interest and invest the proceeds of the loan in additional equity of the XYZ Co. The interest on this loan is deductible for tax purposes. As a result, the investor tax position would be:

Ordinary Income	*Appreciation*	*Expected Price*
Dividends received (₹ 60,000 × .08)	₹ 4,800	(₹ 60,000 × .60) = ₹ 3,600
Less: Interest expense (₹ 40,000 × .12)	4,800	
Net ordinary income	₹ 0	

Thus, the dividend income is neutralised by the interest expense. As the share is not sold, the price appreciation will go unrealised for tax purposes. Consequently, no taxes will be paid. We see that dividend income is transformed into capital gains. Of course, borrowing funds increases the overall risk of the investor position. The investor cannot get something (incremental price appreciation of ₹ 2,400 above the ₹ 1,200 the investor otherwise would expect) for nothing. The added return is the result of increased risk. If the investor wishes to bear no more risk than before, Miller and Scholes suggest that the investor should use an insurance annuity. Instead of borrowing ₹ 40,000, borrow ₹ 13,333, again at 12 per cent interest. Then take the ₹ 13,333 and invest it in a risk-free insurance annuity. Such an annuity implies that the insurance company invests the funds in a risk-free asset and agrees to repay, at some future date, the ₹ 13,333 plus compound interest at the risk-free rate. Thus, the risk-free asset offsets the investors' borrowing, and he incurs no increase in risk on his overall position. At the outset, the investor balance sheet includes the following items:

22. Merton H. Miller and Myron S. Scholes, "Dividend and Taxes," *Journal of Financial Economics*, 6 (December 1978), 333-64.

Liabilities	*Assets*	
Borrowings ₹ 13,333	XYZ Co. Equity	₹ 20,000
	Single-time insurance annuity	13,333
	Your current tax return would be	
	Dividends received	
	(₹ 20,000 x .08)	₹ 1,600
	Less : Interest expense	
	(₹ 13,333 x .12)	1,600
	Net taxable income	₹ 0

Thus, the investor will pay no taxes on his dividend income. When the annuity is realised, he will have to pay tax, but this realisation is off in the future, and presumably he will postpone it. Instead of an insurance annuity, he might increase his contribution to a pension fund. In both cases, the institutions involved are not taxed on their investment income, so they provide vehicles for the postponement of taxes. The idea is to borrow so that interest payments offset dividends received; as a result, no taxes are paid. The second step is to neutralise the risk of borrowing and to postpone the realisation of capital gains.

Although the steps just outlined work to reduce the tax bias that favours retention over dividends, there is some question about how easy they are to accomplish. Often it is difficult to find insurance or other vehicles by which taxes can be conveniently postponed. Moreover, the specific tax provision that allows such a tax dodge may be highly restrictive.

OTHER MARKET IMPERFECTIONS

Many other market imperfections exist, but we will concentrate on two: (1) flotation costs, and (2) other legal or institutional factors that cause markets to be less than perfectly efficient. The dividend irrelevance position is based on the idea that firms can issue or repurchase securities at will, and at no cost, to undertake desired capital expenditures, and use whatever dividend payout policy they feel is worthwhile. However, *equity flotation costs incurred by firms cause them to favour the retention of earnings.* For every amount paid out in the form of cash dividends, the existence of flotation costs means that the firm has to issue more than the amount worth of new financing. Also, financing is "lumpy," in the sense that small issues are more difficult and more expensive to market than large ones. Such factors will of course, cause firms to prefer retention of earnings.

Institutional restrictions may also inhibit the perfect market dividend process. First, the tax treatment of dividends received by firms creates a demand for current dividends. Also, some institutional investors are restricted by law to investing only in stocks that appears on "approved lists." Since a common standard for admission to an approved list is the duration of cash dividends paid by the firm, these investors are forced to favour shares of dividend-paying firms. Many trusts, estates, and endowment funds have restrictions governing the liquidation of principal and the distribution of the income earned. Also, the income beneficiaries are often different from the principal beneficiaries, so to the extent that current income is needed by the income beneficiaries, there is clearly an institutionally derived preference for high dividend-paying stocks. All these factors create demand for dividend-paying stocks.

It is obvious that there is no clear-cut consensus on the relevance of dividend policy. On the one hand, theory plainly demonstrates that in the absence of taxes, transaction costs, and other market imperfections, a firm's dividend policy has no effect on its value. Once taxes are introduced, however, we see that the firm can maximise shareholder wealth by paying no cash dividends, so long as the personal tax rate on dividend income is higher than the rate on capital gains. Moreover, because of vastly different tax circumstances and a variety of other market imperfections, there is the possibility that a clientele effect may exist, wherein shareholders choose the firm with the dividend payout policy they prefer. At this point, the empirical evidence is contradictory concerning whether dividend policy has any effect on the value of the firm. But so long as it does, or so long as there is the remotest chance that it does, it follows that dividend policy is a decision variable which should be taken seriously by financial management.

ILLUSTRATIVE PROBLEMS

1. The shareholders of GATA Group are in the 70% marginal income tax bracket for dividend income. The Group earned ₹ 35 crores after taxes in the current year. With 10,00,000 shares outstanding earnings per share were ₹ 35.00. The stock recently has been traded at ₹ 720 per share, among the current shareholders—₹ 20 of this value is accounted for by investor anticipation of a cash dividend. As financial manager of GATA Group, you have contemplated the alternative of repurchasing the company share by means of an offer at ₹ 720 per share. (a) How much shares could the firm repurchase if this alternatives were selected? (b) Ignoring taxes, which alternative should be selected? (c) Considering taxes, which alternative should be selected?

Solution

(a) Net profit after taxes ₹ 3,50,00,000
Number of shares 10,00,000

Earnings per share ₹ 35

Market price, ex-dividend ₹ 700

P/E ratio 20
Contemplated value of cash dividend = ₹ 20 × 10,00,000 share = ₹ 2,00,00,000

(b) If these shares were purchased, EPS would become ₹ 36.00 *i.e.* $\left(\frac{₹\ 3{,}50{,}00{,}000}{9{,}72{,}222}\right)$. With a multiple of 20, the price of the share would remain at ₹ 720 (20 × ₹ 36.00). If taxes are ignored either alternative is acceptable. If the dividend were paid, the stock dividend would be worth ₹ 700, and shareholders would have ₹ 20 in cash dividends. If the shares were purchased, the share would be worth ₹ 720 per share.

(c) Consideration of taxes, however, makes the repurchase alternative more attractive. After tax value of ₹ 20 capital gains would be:

$$₹ 20 - (₹ 20 \times .70) = ₹ 6$$

2. XYZ Company expects with some degree of certainty to generate the following net income and to have the following capital expenditure during the next five years (in thousands):

Year	*1*	*2*	*3*	*4*	*5*
Net income	₹ 5,000	₹ 4,000	₹ 2,500	₹ 2,000	₹ 1,500
Capital expenditure	2,000	2,500	3,200	4,000	5,000

The company currently has 10,00,000 shares of equity and pays dividneds of ₹ 5 per share. (a) Determine dividends per share if dividend policy is treated as a residual decision. (b) Determine the amounts of external financing that will be necessary if the present dividend per share is maintained. (c) Determine dividends per share and the amounts of the external financing and will be necessary if a dividend payout ratio of 50% is maintained. (d) Under which of the three dividend policies are aggregate dividends maximised and external financing minimised?

Solution

(a)

Year	*Income Available for Dividends*	*Dividends Per Share*	*External Financing*
1	₹ 30,00,000	₹ 3	0
2	15,00,000	1.5	0
3	0	0	₹ 7,00,000
4	0	0	20,00,000
5	0	0	35,00,000
	₹ 45,00,000		₹ 62,00,000

(b)

Year	*Net Income*	*Dividends Expenditure*	*Capital Financing*	*External*
1	₹ 50,00,000	₹ 50,00,000	₹ 20,00,000	₹ 20,00,000
2	40,00,000	50,00,000	25,00,000	35,00,000
3	25,00,000	50,00,000	32,00,000	57,00,000
4	20,00,000	50,00,000	40,00,000	70,00,000
5	15,00,000	50,00,000	50,00,000	85,00,000
	₹ 2,50,00,000			₹ 2,67,00,000

(c)

Year	*Net Income*	*Dividends*	*Dividends Per Share*	*Capital Expenditure*	*External Financing*
(1)	*(2)*	*(3)*	*(4)*	*(5)*	*(6)-(3)+ (5)-(1)*
1	₹ 50,00,000	₹ 25,00,000	₹ 2.50	₹ 20,00,000	—
2	40,00,000	20,00,000	2.00	25,00,000	₹ 5,00,000
3	25,00,000	12,50,000	1.25	32,00,000	19,50,000
4	20,00,000	10,00,000	1.00	40,00,000	30,00,000
5	15,00,000	7,50,000	0.75	50,00,000	42,50,000
	₹ 74,50,000				₹ 97,00,000

(d) Aggregate dividends are highest under alternative b, external financing is minimised under alternative c, a constant dividends payout policy.

3. A firm has new investment opportunities requiring an aggregate outlay of ₹ 10,00,000. The firm has decided that the appropriate debt/equity ratio, given the nature of its business and its operating risk, is 0.30. Historically, it has paid out 65% of its earnings as dividends. Its earnings for the period just ended were ₹ 12,00,000. Determine for each of the four policy alternatives the external financing requirements (debt and equity) and the debt and equity levels after external financing is completed.

Solution

The solution table shows the firm treat all three decisions as active, that is, it sets each at the desired level.

(₹ in thousands)

	No external equity			
	No residual	*Investment residual*	*Debt/equity residual*	*Dividends residual*
Before external financing				
Debt	3,000	3,000	3,000	3,000
Equity	10,000	10,000	10,000	10,000
Debt/equity	0.30	0.30	0.30	0.30
Investment opportunities	1,000	550	1,000	550
Earnings	1,200	1,200	1,200	1,200
Payout ratio	0.65	0.65	0.65	0.36
Dividends	780	780	780	430
Earnings retained	420	420	420	770
External financing				
Debt	230	130	580	230
Equity	350	0	0	0
After external financing				
Debt	323	313	358	323
Equity	1,077	1,042	1,042	1,077
Debt/equity (optimum=0.30)	0.30	0.30	0.34	0.30

4. The expected earnings and capital expenditure for Venkat Industries are shown in the following table; the company presently has 20,00,000 (2 milllion) equity shares issued and pays a dividend of ₹ 1.50 per share

(₹ in million)

Year	*Net Income*	*Capital Expenditure*
1	₹ 40	₹ 25
2	30	30
3	36	28
4	48	36
5	42	44
	196	163

a. Determine the dividend per share for the next five years assuming residual dividend policy.

b. Determine the amount of external financing that will be necessary if the present dividend is maintained for the next five years.

c. Determine the amount of external financing and the dividends per share over the next five years which would result from a 50 per cent dividend payout ration.

d. Of the three dividend policies (residual, constant, current in ₹ and constant payment ratio), which will miximize dividends paid out and minimize external financing?

Solution

a. Under a resideual dividend policy, after all acceptable capital projects have been budgeted for, any remaining earnings are distributed among shareholders as dividends.

(₹ in million)

Year	*Net Income*	*Capital Expenditure*	*Residual*	*Dividend per Share*
1	₹ 4.0	₹ 2.5	₹ 1.5	₹ 0.75
2	3.0	3.0	0	0.00
3	3.6	2.8	0.8	0.40
4	4.8	3.6	1.2	0.60
5	4.2	4.4	-0.2	0.00

b. External financing is necessary every year as shown below.

(₹ in million)

Year	*Net Income*	*Capital Expenditure*	*Residual*	*Needed for ₹ 1.50 Dividend*	*External Financing Needed*
1	₹ 4.0	₹ 2.5	₹ 1.5	₹ 3.0	₹ 1.5
2	3.0	3.0	0	3.0	3.0

3	3.6	2.8	0.8	3.0	2.2
4	4.8	3.6	1.2	3.0	1.8
5	4.2	4.4	(0.2)	3.0	3.2

c. Under a 50 per cent dividend payout, one-half of all earnings are paid out as dividends, with any extra funds neede to finance capital expenditures being reaised externally.

(₹ in million)

Year	*Net Income*	*Capital Expenditure*	*Dividends*	*External Financing*
1	₹ 4.0	₹ 2.5	₹ 2.0	₹ 0.5
2	3.0	3.0	1.5	1.5
3	3.6	2.8	1.8	1.0
4	4.8	3.6	2.4	1.2
5	4.2	4.4	2.1	2.3
			9.8	6.5

d. From part b we can determine that total dividends paid out are ₹ 15 million and total external financing necessary under a residual dividends approach is ₹ 2,00,000.

From part c, under a constant payout ratio, total dividends paid out are ₹ 9.8 million and external financing necessary is ₹ 6.5 million.

If the ₹ 1.50 per share dividend (₹ 3.0 million total) is maintained total dividends paid out are ₹ 15.0 million and total external financing necessary is ₹ 11.7 million.

The following table summarizes:

	Residual	*Constant Ratio*	*Constant Amount in ₹*
Net income	₹ 19.6	₹ 19.6	₹ 19.6
Capital expenditure	(16.3)	(16.3)	(16.3)
Dividends	(3.5)	(9.8)	(15.0)
	₹ 0.2	₹ 6.5	₹ 11.7

The constant policy would maximise dividends paid while the residual policy minimises the external financing necessary.

5. Mehta Textiles has traditionally followed a no-dividend policy, yet in recent years its shareholders have been putting pressure on management to distribute some of the earnings because the company is maturing and cash flow is fairly substantial. Its shareholders generally pay no taxes. Mehta considering either a cash dividend of ₹ 2 a share or a stock repurchase of 10 per cent of the sotck. The following financial information is available for the company.

Balance Sheet

Assets		*Liabilities and Equity*	
Current	₹ 30	Debt	₹ 60
Fixed	50	Common Equity	20
	₹ 80	Retained Earnings	₹ 80

Net income—₹ 16 crore
Current share price—₹ 10

a. As an individual shareholder owning 200 shares of Mehta, paying no taxes, is the dividend decision of the firm relevant to year total wealth position?

b. Suppose that the firm ignores the demands for earnings distrbution. Short of throwing management out, what can shareholders do to receive a cash return from their shares in Mehta? Is there any effect on total wealth of investors? Show numerically using a 200-share ownership position.

Solution

a. In the absence of personal taxes the total wealth of the investor is unrelated to the form of earnings distrbution; thus the investor is indifferent:

	Current	*Dividend*	*Repurchase*
End position, number shares	200	200	180
End share price	₹ 10	₹ 8	₹ 10
Stock position	₹ 2,000	₹ 1,600	₹ 1,800
Cash/div. received	—	400	—
Shares sold/tendered	—	—	20
Proceeds	—	—	200
Cash position	—	400	200
Total wealth	₹ 2,000	₹ 2,000	₹ 2000

b. If the firm chooses to retain all earnings, then, as an investor, you should be able to create your own dividends, referred to in the text as homemade dividends. In the case of Mehta, to create for yourself the 20 per cent cash dividend that would have been paid you must sell 20 per cent of your stock:

200 x 0.20	=	40	shares
	x	10	
		₹ 400	homemade dividend

6. KEC Syntex is all equity financed. Some 10,00,000 equity share of par value ₹ 10 are in issue and dividends (just paid) amount to ₹ 1.20 per share. All earnings are distributed and no growth is anticipated. A new major investment is available with an outlay of ₹ 10,00,000 in 1 year's time which will produce cash inflows of ₹ 2,00,000. KEC Syntex's cost of a equity is 20 per cent.Calculate the current share price, and the share price if the investment is undertaken if no external finance is available, using the present value of dividends model.

Solution

The current share price is

$$P = \frac{D}{k_e} = \frac{₹\,1.20}{₹\,0.20} = ₹\,6.00$$

The new project will be financed by producing dividends in years 1 to:

$$\frac{₹\,2,00,000}{10,00,000} = ₹\ 0.20 \text{ per share}$$

Dividend in years 2—will then be:

$$₹\,1.20 + \frac{₹\,2,00,000}{10,00,000} = ₹\,1.40$$

The share price is:

$$P = \frac{₹\,0.20}{1.20} + \frac{₹\,1.40}{0.20} + \frac{1}{1.20} = ₹\,8.00$$

7. Again using the KEC data as in Problem-6 show, using the present value of dividend model, the new share price if the project was financed by ₹ 10,00,000 of perpetual debt at 10%. Assume that an "M-M no-tax world" exists.

Solution

Current earning (10,00,000 × ₹ 1.20)	₹ 12,00,000
New earnings	2,00,000
	₹ 14,00,000
Less interest on new debt finance =₹ 10,00,000 × .10	1,00,000
New Dividends	₹ 13,00,000

$$\text{New dividends per share} = \frac{₹\,13,00,000}{₹\,10,00,000} = ₹\,1.30$$

Due to increase in financial leverage the cost of equity will have risen, and this can be calculated from :

$$k_e = k_0 + (k_0 - k_d)\frac{D}{E}$$

In an M-M world with no tax k0 will remain constant at 20%. The market value of equity will, however, have increased due to the NPV of the new project:

$$\text{NPV} = \left(\frac{₹\ 2,00,000}{0.20} \times \frac{1}{1.20}\right) - \left(\frac{₹\ 1,00,000}{1.20}\right) = ₹\ 74,999$$

$$\text{E} = (10,00,000 \times ₹\ 8.00) + ₹\ 74,999 = ₹\ 80,74,992$$

$$k_e = 20\% + (20\% - 10\%) \times \frac{₹\ 1,00,000}{₹\ 80,74,000} = 20.12\%$$

New share price at year $1 = \frac{D}{k_e}$

$$= \frac{₹\ 1.30}{0.2012} = ₹\ 646$$

New share price at year 0

$$= \frac{₹\ 1.20}{1.20} + \frac{₹\ 6.46}{1.20} = ₹\ 6.38$$

8. Using the same data an in Problem-6, show how an investor can increase income next year whilst maintaining income constant thereafter.

Solution

Assumption an investor owns 10,000 shares in KEC Syntex (any assumption could be made).

Current income = ₹ 1.20 × 10,000

= ₹ 12,000 p.a.

The number of shares needed to maintian income in years 2—after selling shares in year 1 are:

$$= \frac{₹\ 12,000}{₹\ 1.40} = 8,571$$

Therefore, 10,000-8,571 = 1,429 shares can be sold in year 1. Share price next year:

$$\frac{₹\ 1.40}{₹\ 0.20} = ₹\ 7.00$$

Income in year 1:

= dividends 10,000 × ₹ .20 + sale of shares 1,429 × ₹ 7.00

= ₹ 2,000 + ₹ 10,003 = ₹ 12,003

9. An all equity financed company has 10,00,000 ordinary shares of face value ₹ 10 in issue with a current share price of ₹ 25 ex-dividend. Annual earnings, are ₹ 4.50 per share and in the absence of new investments will remain constant in perpetuity all earnings are distributed at present. A new investment is available which will cost ₹ 35,00,000 in 1 year's time and will produce annual cash inflows thereafter of ₹

7,00,000. Analyse the effect of the new project on dividend payments and the share price.

Solution

The cost of equity is:

$$k_e = \frac{D}{P} = \frac{₹\ 4.50}{₹\ 25.00} = 18\%$$

Current earnings = ₹ 4.50 × 10,00,000 = ₹ 45,00,000.

The new project can be financed by retaining ₹ 35,00,000 of the ₹ 45,00,000 earnings next year, reducing the dividend payment to ₹ 10,00,000, or:

$$\frac{₹\ 10,00,000}{10,00,000} = ₹\ 1.00 \text{ per share}$$

In the following years dividends will increase due to the cash generated by the new project. Dividends per share in year 2 to × will be :

$$\frac{₹\ 45,00,000 + ₹\ 7,00,000}{10,00,000} = ₹\ 5.20$$

The new share price can be calculated by finding the present value of the revised dividend payments:

$$P = \frac{₹\ 1.00}{1.18} - \left(\frac{₹\ 5.20}{0.18} \times \frac{1}{1.18}\right) = ₹\ 25.33$$

An alternative method of calculating the effect of the new project is simply to calculate its net present value:

$$NPV = \left(\frac{₹\ 7,00,000}{0.18} \times \frac{1}{1.18}\right) - \frac{₹\ 35,00,000}{1.18} = ₹\ 32,95,668.50 - ₹\ 29,66,101.60 = ₹\ 3,29,566.90$$

The new share price is therefore

$$₹\ 25.00 + \frac{₹\ 3,29,566.90}{10,00,000} = ₹\ 25.33$$

10. Repeating the Problem-9, let us assume that an investor own; 20,000 shares in the all equity financed company. The investor prefers to receive a consistent income, each year.

Solution

The investor's income if the new project was not undertaken is:

20,000 × ₹ 4.50 = ₹ 90,000 p.a.

Income if the new project is undertaken will be:

Year 1 : 20,000 × ₹ 1.00 = ₹ 20,000

Year 2 : 20,000 × ₹ 5.20 = ₹ 1,04,000

In order to maintain income in year 1 at its previous level, the investor can sell some shares. The share price in 1 year's time will, however, be different from the share price calculated in Problem-9.

The share price at year 1 will be the present value of dividends in year 2 to ∞

$$\frac{₹\ 5.20}{0.18} = ₹\ 28.89$$

The investor should, therefore, sell the following number of shares to make up the income difference of ₹ 70,000 in year 1:

$$\frac{₹\ 70,000}{₹\ 28.89} = 2,423 \text{ shares}$$

The income receivable in year 2—∞ will now be reduced to dividends being received on fewer shares, but it will still be higher than the original ₹ 90,000 p.a., reflecting the positive NPV of the new project undertaken.

Income in year 2 – ∞

=(20,000-2,423) × ₹ 5.20

= ₹ 91,400

11. The board of directors of United Groceries is in the process of approving a capital budget for the upcoming year. However, it faces a dilemma in deciding on acceptable investments, their financing, and the amount of dividends to pay on the equity. Amit Tandon, Vice President of Finance, has analysed five possible investments, as follows:

Project	*Needed Funds (₹ crore)*	*Expected IRR*
A	₹ 100	16%
B	40	20
C	80	13
D	200	12
E	60	25

The company has a target capital structure of 70% equity and 30% debt. It adheres to a stable dividend policy, which calls for a cash dividend of ₹ 50 crore.

Tandon believes that the year will have unusually large cash inflows and that ₹ 250 crore will be available before taking dividends into consideration. The cost of retained earnings is estimated at 16%, and the after-tax cost of debt is estimated at 10%. The company has 40 crore shares of equity outstanding, with a market price of ₹ 40 a share. An *EPS* of ₹ 5 is estimated for the upcoming year.

Tandon proposes to the board that all profitable investments be undertaken, that the D/A ratio remain unchanged, and that ₹ 50 crore in dividends be paid. He suggests that excess internal funds be used for a share repurchase with a tender offer of ₹ 50 a share. He presents details to the board, including an analysis of participating and nonparticipating shareholders (assumed to own 100 shares).

Determine the optimal total investments, the amount of debt and equity financing, any excess internal funds, the number of shares repurchased, and the after-repurchase position of participating shareholders.

Solution

1. Determine the weighted average cost of capital, K_a

   $k_a = (0.70 \times 0.16) + (0.30 \times 0.10) = 0.112 + 0.030 = 0.142$
2. Arrange the projects by descending *IRR* values to determine acceptable investments, which are E, B and A. Projects C and D have returns less than 14.2%.

Project	*IRR (%)*	*Needed Funds (₹ crore)*	*Cumulative Needed Funds (₹ crore)*
E	25	60	60
B	20	40	100
A	16	100	200

3. Since total investment (in crore of ₹) is ₹ 200, needed internal equity funds are ₹ 140 (0.70 × ₹ 200) and borrowed funds are ₹ 60 (0.30 × ₹ 200). Finally, since total internal funds are ₹ 250 and since cash dividends are ₹ 50, excess internal funds are ₹ 60 (₹ 250 – ₹ 140 – ₹ 50).
4. With excess funds of ₹ 60 crore and an offer price of ₹ 50 a share, a repurchase acquires 1.2 crore shares (₹ 60 crore), or 3% of all outstanding shares (1.2 crore/ 4crore). Total company earnings are ₹ 200 crore (₹ 5 × 40 crore); so *EPS* after the repurchase is ₹ 5.155 (₹ 200 crore/ 38.8 crore). And, assuming the P-E ratio of 8 is constant (₹ 40/₹ 5 before the repurchase), the market price should increase to ₹ 41. 24 (8 × ₹ 5.155). Then, the participating shareholder's position is as follows:

Before the repurchase	100 × ₹ 40	=	₹ 4,000
After the repurchase	97 × ₹ 41.24	=	4,000
	+ 3 × ₹ 50	=	150
	Total	=	₹ 4,150

QUESTIONS

1. What is a dividend? Who has the power to declare a dividend? When does a share begin trading ex-dividend? Why?
2. How does dividend policy relate to management's responsibility to maximise the wealth of the firm's shareholders in the long run?
3. Discuss the residual dividend theory and how it relates to the value of the firm.
4. Explain the logic underlying the indifference theory of dividends. Upon what critical assumptions is the indifference theory based?
5. Explain the logic of the bird-in-the hand theory of dividend. What assumption regarding risk (uncertainty) is inherent in the bird-in-the-hand theory?
6. What is meant by the "information content" of a dividend policy? Does a dividend policy have to be stated explicitly to have information content? Explain.
7. Explain how, in theory, the residual theory of dividends leads to the proposition that dividends are irrelevant. Be sure to specify.

8. What is the clientele effect? Is the clientele effect inconsistent with the abstract concept of the irrelevance of a dividend policy? Explain.
9. Explain why a residual dividend payout ratio may be the optimal dividend payout for many firms.
10. How might the lack of consistent dividend policy of a firm tend to reduce share price when market imperfections exist?
11. Explain why the firm should treat the dividend decision as a longer residual, subject to short-run constraints.
    (i) List and briefly discuss the constraints and factors that should be taken into consideration when establishing a dividend policy.
    (ii) Does this imply that dividend policy is relevant or irrelevant to the value of the firm?
12. Under what conditions, if any, will the rational investors want a firm to pay dividend?
13. Explain why you agree or disagree with the following statement: "The Irrelevance of dividends argument says that:
    (i) A company's share price not change on the day it distributes a dividend.
    (ii) A company's share price will be the same today and in all future periods, regardless of its dividend policy."
14. What do Modigliani and Miller say about the effect of dividends on stock price? Do they believe that dividends affect stock prices?
15. Why is the primary consideration with respect to dividend policy its effect on the firm's owners? How may the tax status of the owners affect a firm's dividend policy?
16. "An increase in dividends operates as a positive financial signal?" Explain this statement. Is there empicial evidence to support it?
17. Given the assumption needed for dividends to be irrelevant, what types of firms are most likely to find that their values are unaffected by their dividend policies?
18. Describe how housemade dividends can undo the firm's dividend policy.
19. Respond to the following:

    Modern corporate finance theory does not apply to firms that currently pay no dividends because the market is obviously pricing their stock based on something other than dividends.

PROBLEMS

1. Usha strips has income after taxes of ₹ 80,00,00,000 in 2011 and retains ₹ 5,00,00,000. If Usha has 20,00,000 equity shares, compute the dividend per share paid to Usha's equity shareholders in 2011.

Ans.: ₹ 15

2. Mittal leasing has a dividend reinvestment plan for its equity shareholders. Mittal currently has a payout of 60 per cent of earnings. However, on average, 40 per cent of its equity shareholders use the reinvestment plan. Compute Mittal's actual cash payment ratio.

Ans.: 36%

3. Sagar Lamps has earned ₹ 1,00,00,000 in 2011 and plants to distribute 60 per cent to its equity shareholders. Sagar has 5,00,000 equity share outstanding, currently trading at ₹ 200 per share. Compute the dividends per share.

Ans.: ₹ 12.00

4. Sangam Instruments Company treats dividends as a residual decision. It expects to generate ₹ 20,00,000 in net earnings after taxes in the coming year. The company has an all-equity capital structure and its cost of equity capital is 15%. The company treats this cost as the opportunity cost of retained earnings. because of flotation costs and underwriting the cost of equity financing is higher. It is 16%. (a) How much in dividends (out of ₹ 20,00,000 in earnings) should be paid if the company has ₹ 15,00,000 in project whose expected return exceeds 15%? (b) How much in dividends should be paid if it has ₹ 20,00,000 in projects whose expected return exceeds 15%? (c) How much in dividends should be paid if it has ₹ 30,00,000 in projects whose expected return exceeds 16%? What else should be done?

Ans.: a = ₹ 5,00,000; b = 0, c = Dividends to be zero. Company should also raise on additional ₹ 10 lakhs through an issue of equity.

5. A firm has had the following indicated earnings per share

Year	*Earnings per share*
2013	₹ 4.00
2012	3.80
2011	3.20
2010	2.80
2009	3.20
2008	2.40
2007	1.20
2006	1.80
2005	- .50
2004	.25

(a) If the firm's dividend policy was based on a constant payout ratio of 40% for all years with positive earnings and a zero payout otherwise, determine the annual dividend for each year.

(b) If the firm had a dividend payout of ₹ 1.00 per share, increasing by ₹ .10 per share whenever the dividend payout fell below 50% for two consecutive years, what annual dividend did the firm pay each year?

(c) If the firm's policy was to pay ₹ .50 per share each period except when earnings per share exceed ₹ 3.00. when an extra dividend equal to 80% of earnings beyond ₹ 3.00 would be paid, what annual dividend did the firm pay each year?

Ans.: (a) 2005 = ₹ 0.00; 2009 = ₹ 1.28; (b) 2010 = ₹ 1.00; 2012 = ₹ 1.40; (c) 2007 = ₹ 0.50; 2010 = ₹ 1.30

6. Financial data on two companies is presented below. What differences reflected in the data give insight into dividend policy and valuation?

	ABC Co.			XYZ Co.		
	Earnings Per share	Dividends per share	Range P/E ratio	Earning per share	Dividends per share	Range P/E ratio
2013	₹ 5.25	2.60	10-15	₹ 4.25	₹ 0.25	20-25
2012	5.15	2.60	12-18	4.30	0.22	24-29
2011	5.00	2.60	15-20	4.05	0.18	28-32
2010	4.25	2.60	13-18	3.85	0.10	31-35
2009	4.75	2.60	16-22	3.50	0.12	35-40
2008	4.80	2.60	15-19	3.10	0.10	32-37
2007	5.10	2.90	14-18	2.85	0.28	33.38
2006	5.25	2.60	17-23	2.40	0.30	31-36
2005	5.20	2.60	16-11	2.10	0.40	28-33
2004	4.80	2.60	12-18	1.95	0.35	26-31

7. United Tubes is trying to set dividend policy to maximise the value of the firm. United has a cost of equity 14 per cent and can earn 16 per cent on investments. The firm earned ₹ 6 per share this past year, (a) Determine the market price per share if dividend are ₹ 4 per share. (b) Determine the market price per share if dividends are ₹ 2 per share. (c) What dividend policy maximises share price?

Ans.: (a) ₹ 44.90 (b) ₹ 46.94 (c) ₹ 0

8. SIMCO is considering seven proposed capital expenditures as follows:

Capital Investment	Cash Flow After-taxes	Return
A	₹ 20,00,000	25%
B	₹ 30,00,000	22%
C	₹ 15,00,000	17%
D	₹ 45,00,000	16%
E	₹ 35,00,000	14%
F	₹ 25,00,000	12%
G	₹ 10,00,000	9%

The firm's target capital structure is 30 per cent debt and 70 per cent equity, SIMCO's cost of capital is 15 per cent, and there is ₹ 1,20,00,000 available in internally generated funds that can be reinvested in the firm or paid out in the form of cash dividends. (a) Which capital budgeting projects should be accepted? If the firm follows a residual dividend policy, how much is available to be paid out in form of cash dividends? (b) How does your answer change if SIMCO's cost of capital is only 11 percent?

Ans.: (a) Project A, B, C and D, would be accepted. Funds available for cash dividends are ₹ 43,00,000. (b) Projects A, B, C, D, and F are accepted. It has ₹ 1,00,000 left for cash dividend.

9. Trishul Soap has a current stock market value of ₹ 1,00,00,000 and it has debt with a market value of ₹ 1,00,00,000. It has 10,00,000 equity shares outstanding and currently pays no cash dividends. Two dividend policies are under consideration : Plan I is to continue paying no cash dividends. Plan II involves selling 5,00,000 of new equity shares (with no flotation costs) and immediately paying the ₹ 50,00,000 to the existing (but not the new) shareholders. Since there are presently 10,00,000 shares of equity outstanding, every current shareholder would receive ₹ 5.00 per share in cash dividends. The new shares would have to be sold at ₹ 35.00 per share (the current market value of ₹ 4,00,00,000 divided by the current 10,00,000 shares, less the case dividend of ₹ 5.00). (i) How many shares will have to be issued to raise the ₹ 50,00,000? Compare the par value of the current share-holders' holdings, taking into account both market price and dividends under Plan 1 versus Plan II (ignore taxes). (ii) Now assume that Trishul also has to incur flotation costs of ₹ 2 per share, so the new share will sell at ₹ 33.00 share. How many shares now will have to be issued to raise the ₹ 50,00,000? Compare the total per share value of the current shareholders' holdings for both plans now. (iii) By comparing your answer to (i) and (ii), what can you say about the impact of flotation costs on the dividend (and valuation) decision?

Ans.: (i) Per share value of ₹ 40 with either plan. There is no preference. (ii) Plan I : ₹ 40.00 Plan II : ₹ 39.70; (iii) Flotation costs cause plan I to be preferred.

10. Ghai's Corporation expects next year's net income to be ₹ 15 crore. The firm's debt ratio is currently 40 per cent. Ghai has ₹ 12 crore of profitable investment opportunities, and it wishes to maintain its existing debt ratio. According to the residual dividend policy, how large should Ghai's dividend payout ratio be next year?

Ans.: Payout ratio = 52%.

11. In 2012 the Handa Company paid dividends totaling ₹ 3,60,00,000 on net income of ₹ 10 crore. 2012 was a normal year, and for the past 10 years, earnings have grown at a constant rate of 10 per cent. However, in 2013, earnings are expected to jump to ₹ 14.4 crore and the firm expects to have profitable investment opportunities of ₹ 8.4 crore. It is predicted that Handa's will not be able to maintain the 2012 level of earnings growth —the high 2013 earnings level is attributable to an exceptionally profitable new product line introduced that year — and the company will return to its previous 10 per cent growth rate. Handa's target debt ratio is 40 per cent.

(a) Calculate Handa's total dividends for 2013 if it follows each of the following policies. (1) Its 2013 dividend payment is set to force dividends to grow at the long-run growth rate in earnings. (2) It continues the 2012 dividend payout ratio. (3) It uses a pure residual dividend policy (40 per cent of the ₹ 8.4 crore investment is financed with debt). (4) It employs a regular-dividend-plus-extras policy, with the regular dividend being based on the long-run growth rate and the extra dividend being set according to the residual policy. (b) which of the preceding policies would you recommend? Restrict your choices to the ones listed, but justify your answer. (c) Assume that investors expect Handa to pay total dividends of ₹ 9 crore in 2013 and to have the dividend grow at 10 per cent after 2013. The total market value of the stock is ₹ 180 crore. What is the company's cost of equity? (d) What is Handa's long-run average return on equity? [Hint: g = (Retention rate) (ROE) = (1.0 - payout rate) (ROE).] (e) Does a 2013 dividend of ₹ 9 crore seem reasonable in view of your answers to Parts c and d? If not, should the dividend be higher or lower?

Ans.: (a) (1) ₹ 3.96 crore, (2) ₹ 4.80 crore, (3) ₹ 9.36 crore, (4) Regular= ₹ 3.96 crore; Extra = ₹ 5.4 crore; (c) 15%; (d) 15%

12. Diamond Company's optimal capital structure calls for 50 per cent debt and 50 per cent equity. The interest rate on its debt is a constant 10 per cent; its cost of equity from retained earnings is 14 per cent; the cost of equity from new equity is 16 per cent; and its tax rate is 40 per cent. Diamond has the following investment opportunities:

Project A : Cost = ₹ crore; IRR - 20%.
Project B : Cost = ₹ crore; IRR - 12%.
Project C : Cost = ₹ crore; IRR - 9%.

Diamond expects to have net income of ₹ 7,28,75,000. If Diamond bases its dividends on the residual policy, what will its payout ratio be?

Ans.: Payout ratio = 31.39%.

19

DIVIDEND POLICY

INTRODUCTION

The effect of a firm's dividend policy on the current price of its shares is a matter of considerable importance, not only to the corporate officials who must set the policy, but to investors for planning portfolios and for appraising the functioning of the capital markets. The precise question to be asked is: *"what is the effect of a change in cash dividend paid, given the firm's capital budgeting and borrowing decision?"* If a firm's investment outlays and borrowings are fixed, then the only possible source to raise the funds is an issue of stock. Hence, the dividend policy is a trade-off between retaining earnings on the one hand and paying out cash and issuing new shares on the other. The companies may schedule a stock issue with every dividend payment. They could avoid the stock issues by paying lower dividneds. While formulating their dividend policies, the companies are to design for their dividend policies respective the optimal trade-offs.

ALTERNATIVE PRACTICAL DIVIDEND POLICIES

Possible alternative dividend policies are almost infinite. A firm's management unit carefully select one to encompass consideration of both its internal needs and there of its shareholders. Several basis types of dividend policies may be considered by managers to establish one that meets that needs of their firms. These basic types that will be discussed are (1) stable dividend, (2) target payout ratio and the (3) regular and extra dividends.

STABLE DIVIDENDS

Investors may place a premium on the shares of a company which pays stable dividends and only increases its dividend payment when it believes that increase can be maintained. It seems reasonable to expect that a stable dividends policy will lead to higher price, because shareholders will value more highly dividends they believe they are certain to receive. This may be compared with a company which has a dividend policy of paying a fixed percentage of its earnings, which will give rise inevitably to fluctuations in dividends. In this case the investors' likelihood of receiving a particular amount of money as a dividend payment is reduced and they may discount the share price accordingly.

Investors are said to prefer dividend stability for reasons which are similar to those suggested as possible reasons for investors preferring current dividends to retention of earnings. Thus, stable dividends may be viewed as conveying useful information to investors. For example, it is argued that if there is a decline in a company's net profit but the dividend payment remains the same, then market confidence in the company's shares is not likely to be hurt to anywhere near the same extent as if there had been a simultaneous reduction in dividends. The stable dividend may convey to investors management's view that the future of the company is better than the fall in profit suggests. Clearly this can be a short run effect, for if investors observe that there is a permanent downward trend in earnings, management will not be able to convince investors of a bright future for the company, even if management continues to maintain a stable dividend. Similarly an increase in the dividend payout not based upon a real change in the prospects for the company can have only a temporary effect on share prices.

Another reason investors may prefer stable dividends is their desire for current income. If shareholders want a specific annual income, they will prefer a company with a stable dividend policy to one that adjusts its dividend payments to fluctuations in profit even though, apart from their dividend policy, the companies are identical in every respect.

In addition, a stable dividend may be advantageous from the legal standpoint of permitting certain institutional investors to buy the corporate securities. Various governmental bodies prepare legal lists of securities in which financial institutions and others may invest. These institutions generally invest in the shares of those companies which have an uninterrupted pattern of dividends.

TARGET PAYOUT RATIO

Although there is reason to believe that stable dividends have a positive effect on a company's share price, many firms set a bench-mark target payout ratio (or range), deviating from his target as appropriate to achieve relatively stable dividends or stable and occasionally increasing ones. Linter[1] contends that companies seek to maintain a target dividend payout ratio over the long run, but only with a lag. The basic perameters in Lintner's model area target payout ratio, *r*, and speed-of-adjustment coefficient, *c*, letting Y_t. represent the firm's earnings in year *t*, the company's target dividend is defined as:

$$D_t^* = rY_t \tag{1}$$

But the firm does not actually distribute its target dividend every period because the resulting dividend stream would be too volatile, Instead, Lintner suggested that firms maintain dividend stability by changing dividends in each year by only a fraction of the change indicated by the target. This fraction is the speed-of-adjustment coefficient. In symbols, Lintner's model states that the actual year to year change in dividend is:

$$D_t - D_{t-1} = a + c\,(D_t^* - D_{t-1}) \tag{2}$$

1. John Lintner: Distribution of Income of Corporations Among Dividends. Retained Earnings, and Taxes: *American Economic Review,* May 1956, pp. 97-113.

where $D_t^*-D_{t-1}$ is the dividend change implied by the new target. The positive constant, *a*, appears in this equation to allow for the presumed greater reluctance to cut dividends than to raise them. Thus when *a* is positive, D_t^* must be enough-below D_{t-1} to offset *a* before dividends will be cut.

Substituting for D_t^* from equation 2 and rearranging terms, Lintner's partial adjustment model implies the following regression equation for aggrevate corporate dividends:

$$D_t = a + b_1 Y_t + b_2 D_{t-1} + e_t \qquad (3)$$

where a, b_1 and b_2 are constants and e_t is an error term. The values of b_1 and b_2 are *cr* and 1-*c*, respectively. According to this equation, aggregate corporate dividends in year *t* depend linearly upon the year's profits and last year's dividends.

To illustrate the Lintner model, suppose XYZ Co. has a target payout ratio equal to 60 per cent, and that it changes its dividends each year by 30 per cent of the change indicated by its target. Then, if last years dividend, D_{t-1} was ₹ 10,00,000 and this year's earnings are ₹ 30,00,000. XYZ's target dividend for this year is:

$$D^*_t = .60\ (₹\ 30,00,000) = ₹\ 18,00,000$$

If earnings remains at ₹ 30,00,000, the company will eventually reach this target; however, because XYZ's speed-of-adjustment coefficient, *c*, is only 30 per cent, the actual change in dividends, assuming *a* equals 0, predicted by the Lintner model is:

$$D_t - D_{t-1} = (.30)\ (₹\ 18,00,000 - ₹\ 10,00,000) = ₹\ 2,40,000$$

Alternatively, the dividend for this year as indicated by equation—3, assuming a and e_t equal 0. is:

$$D_t = (.30)\ (.60)\ (₹\ 30,00,000) + (1 - .30)\ (₹\ 10,00,000) = ₹\ 12,40,000$$

In empirical tests, the Lintner model has proven remarkably accurate in predicting aggregate dividends, Subsequent studies by Britain[2] and by Fama and Babick[3] extend and improve Lintner's original model in some respects but do not change its basic structure.[4] It thus remains a powerful expression of the importance of dividend stability to corporations.

2. John A. Britain : *Corporate Dividend Policy*. The Brooking Institution, Washington, D.C. 1966.
3. Eugene F. Fama and Harvey Babick: Dividend Policy: An Empirical Analysis, *Journal of American Statistical Association*, December, 1966, pp. 1132-61.
4. Although there is reason to believe that stable dividends have a positive effect on a company's share price, Lintner has observed that companies seek to maintain a target dividend payout ratio over the long run. It is Lintner's contention that after earnings increase, dividends increase also but only after a lag. Generally, this contention has been supported. Thus, only after an increase in profit appears to be relatively permanent are dividends increased. Once a company's dividends have been increased there is a reluctance to reduce the amount of the dividend payments and a company will make every effort to maintain dividends at the new level. If there is a fall in the company's profit, the Board of Directors will endeavour to maintain dividends at their previous level until it is clear that a recovery in profit will not take place in the foreseeable future.

So far we have discussed only the factors affecting the determination of an optimum dividend payout ratio. However, it should also be realised that, other things being equal investors may place a premium on the shares of a company which pays stable dividends and only increases its dividend payment when it believes the increase can be maintained. It seems reasonable to expect that a stable dividend policy will lead to higher share prices, because shareholders will value more highly dividend; they believe they are certain to receive. This may be compared with a company which has a dividend policy of paying a fixed percentage of its earnings, which will give rise inevitably to fluctuations in dividends. In this case the investors' likelihood of receiving a particular amount of money as a dividend payment is reduced and they may discount the share price accordingly.

REGULAR AND EXTRA DIVIDENDS

A few firms that have relatively outstable earnings and/or capital investment requirements lable their dividends "regular" and "extra." This policy recognises the information contents of dividends. The regular dividend is set at a level that management believes can be maintained regardless of fluctuations in earnings and capital investment requirements. Then, in years when additional cash is available because earnings are exceptionally high or capital investment requirements are not pressing, an extra dividend is declared at year-end. Such a policy sends the clear message to investors that regular dividends are expected to be sustained but that the extra dividend should not be counted on the future. This labeling of dividends is designed to its downword market fluctuations when the extra dividend must be reduced or eliminated.

STOCK DIVIDENDS AND STOCK SPLITS

An integral part of dividend policy is the use of stock dividends and stock splits. Unlike cash dividends which distribute corporate assets to shareholders and reduce the shareholder's investments correspondingly, the stock dividends and stock splits are just recapitalisations; they do not distribute assets or change the total investment, although they change the equity accounts.

STOCK DIVIDENDS (BONUS SHARES)

A stock dividend is the payment to shareholders of additional shares of equity rather than cash. For example, the declaration of a 10 per cent stock dividend by XYZ Company on the date of record will receive 10 new shares of equity for every 100 shares already owned. Thus, a shareholder retains his proportionate ownership of the company.

Nevertheless some investors do not understand that they have more paper representing the same proportionate share of ownership, and they believe their wealth has increased. One reason for the confusion is that some companies pay cash dividends in addition to giving the investors additional shares of equity. If the company continues to pay the same cash dividend per share, the investors will receive a greater monetary return on the shares. However, the investor is not better off because more shares are held. To clarify this point, assume that in year 1, a company has 10,00,000 shares of equity and pays ₹ 20,00,000 in dividends which amount to dividends of ₹ 2.00 per share. In the following year, the company gives shareholders an additional 10,00,000 shares of equity and increases the dividends to ₹ 40,00,000.The increased equity shares permit the dividend per share to remain the same. The shareholder is better off because the dividends increased from ₹ 20,00,000 to ₹ 40,00,000, but not because the number of shares doubled.

Stated otherwise, an investor holding 100 shares of equity in year 1 received ₹ 200 in cash dividends. In the following year, the investor received ₹ 200. If the number of shares had not doubled, the investor still would have received ₹ 200 because the cash dividends increased.

Accounting treatment: The accounting effect of a stock dividend is to permanently capitalise retained earnings equal to th market value of the shares issued. To illustrate, the capital structure of a hypothetical company XYZ is given in Table-1.

TABLE - 1

Equity share capital (10,00,000 shares, ₹ 10 par)	₹ 1,00,00,000
Paid-up capital	₹ 2,00,00,000
Retained earnings	4,00,00,000
Total net worth	₹ 7,00,00,000

Assume the company XYZ pays a stock dividend of 10 per cent and at the time of the stock dividend declaration the fair market price per share is ₹ 50. The impact of stock dividend upon the shareholders equity section of balance sheet is shown in Table-2.

TABLE - 2

Equity share capital (11,00,000, shares, ₹ 10 par)	₹ 1,10,00,000
Paid-up capital	2,40,00,000
Retained earnings	3,50,00,000
Total net worth	₹ 7,00,00,000

Note that the retained earnings account, from which dividends may be paid, has been reduced by the number of shares times the market value per share of the equity paid out in dividends, ₹ 50,00,000. This amount has been permanently capitalised. Administrative costs of issuing stock dividends are relatively high and are not allowable expense for tax purposes.

STOCK SPLITS

Closely related to the stock dividend is a stock split. From a purely economic viewpoint, a stock split is nothing but a giant stock dividend. Like stock dividends, the number of shares with a stock split increase through a proportional reduction in the per value of the shares. Thus a 2-for-1 stock split is recorded as a doubling of the number of shares outstanding and having of the par value of the share. As a result, the equity share capital, paid-up capital, and retained earnings accounts remain unchanged. The net worth, of course, also stays the same; the only change is in the par value of the share.[5]

Accounting treatment: Accounting for a stock split differs from that for a stock dividend in that retained earnings are not permanently capitalised. For example, if the company XYZ split its stock 2 for 1, only the number of shares and the par value would be changed as indicated in table-3. Yet despite this disimilarity in accounting treatment, we should remember that from an investor's point of view there is practically no difference between a stock dividend and a stock split. In both cases, the corporation gives the shareholder more share of equity in the same company. Both are analogous to owning a pie and cutting it into more slices. The overall size of the investor's share of the pie does not change, but the shareholders has more slices.

TABLE - 3

Before		*After*	
Equity share capital (10,00,000 share, ₹ 10 par)	₹ 10,00,000	Equity share capital (20,00,000 share, ₹ 5 par)	₹ 1,00,00,000
Paid up capital	2,00,00,000	Paid-up capital	2,00,00,000
Retained earnings	4,00,00,000	Retained earnings	4,00,00,000
Total new worth	₹ 7,00,00,000	Total net worth	₹ 7,00,00,000

REVERSE SPLIT

Sometimes a firm reduces the number of shares outstanding by effecting a reverse split. Each shareholder is required to exchange with the corporation the shares owned for a smaller number of shares, e.g., to exchange each 4 shares owned for one share in return. This action frequently follows a decline in the price of the company's shares due to adverse earnings performance over several years.

Often stock splits or reverse splits are made before a closely held firm "goes public." The effects of a stock dividend or a stock split can be summarised as: (i) There is no change in the firm's assets or liabilities or in shareholders, equity (assets less liabilities), and there is no change in the total market value, of the firm's shares. (ii) There is a fall in per share earnings, book value, and market price, and an offsetting rise in the number of shares held by each shareholder. Each shareholder therefore, has no change in the total book value, total earnings, or total market value of all shares held since he or she owns the same percentage of the firm after the stock dividend as before.

5. The New York Stock Exchange arbitrarily defines a stock dividend greater-than 25 per cent as stock split. There are, however, some minor difference in the accounting treatment of two.

A stock dividend or split does not change the assets of the firm, since nothing is received by the firm for new share issued. The firm's debt is also unchanged by the stock dividend or split, since the debt is in no way involved. It follows that the shareholder's equity (the firm's total assets less debt) is also unchanged. Since shareholders each retain their old percentage of the total shareholders' interest, each has the same claim to real assets after the stock dividend or split as before. The total value of a shareholders' shares will consequently be the same as before and after the new shares are issued. The shareholders therefore do not gain or loss as a result of the new share.

RATIONALE FOR A STOCK DIVIDEND OR SPLIT

Although stock dividends and splits occur far less frequently than cash dividends, a significant number of companies choose to use these share distributions either with or in lien of cash dividends. In view of our earlier conclusion that no economic benefits results, how do corporations justify these distribution? The reason most frequently given for distributing stock dividends or resorting to stock splits are listed below:

Agreeable-trading range: The "agreeable-trading-range" philosophy is based on the idea that shares are most attractive to investors when they sell somewhere in the range of about ₹ 10 to ₹ 100 per share. It has been argued that additional shares may benefit shareholders reducing the share's price and thereby allowing investors to purchase round lots (multiples of 100 shares) rather than add lots (less than 100 shares). The advantage here would be to reduce the brokerage fees since they are greater on odd lot purchase than on round lot purchase.

Listing Requirements: Sometimes the companies have to increase the number of shares outstanding in order to qualify for stock-exchange listing. It may be noted that one of the requirements for listing on an organised stock exchange, is that the company have outstanding at least a minimum number of shares. The easiest way to increase the number of shares outstanding is to non cash dividend. Hence the declaration of the stock dividends or split rather than cash dividends may be pursued to increase the number of shares in order to qualify for stock-exchange listing and to get all the advantages of listing. Thus, the essential requirements for listing may be achieved without losing the control over company.

Tax considerations: As with cash dividends, tax considerations have an important bearing on the decision to issue a stock dividend. This factor is particularly more important for shareholders who are already in high tax brackets.

Psychological value: It is argued that stock dividends and splits convey positive information to investors about the recent performance of the company. If nothing else, the publicity surrounding the split might be helpful in attracting buyer interest.

Loan agreement restrictions that prohibit or limit the declaration of cash dividends: Under stringent cash difficulty and the loan agreement restrictions the company may not be left with any option except to declare stock dividends. The declaration of the stock dividends will simply be an exercise to maintain the confidence of the shareholders in the company.

Desire to broaden the shareholder base: Sometimes the companies may resort to stock dividend or split practices in order to broaden the shareholder base to bring consistency in the policy. The existing management can keep control over the company by keeping intact the proportion of ownership.

To conserve cash: Although companies claim various motives for paying stock dividends, a common justification is that management wants to conserve cash and therefore is unwilling to pay cash dividend. But at the same time they want to give the shareholders something in recognition of the firms continued dividend-paying ability.

To indicate higher future profits: Stock dividends are usually an indication of higher profits. Since stock dividends are the recognition of the fact that some retained earnings have been permanently committed to the business (for example, by investment in expanded facilities). In addition some companies state that they have declared stock dividends when the amount of their retained earnings has grown disproportionately large in relation to the capital contributed by shareholders. If the regular cash dividend is continued after an extra stock dividend is declared, the shareholders will receive an increase in cash dividends in future.

Despite the arguments offered in support of stock dividends and splits, the opponents of this practice cite following **reasons to oppose non cash dividends**, i.e. stock dividends and splits. The main objection is that stock dividends are unnecessary if a company has enough cash to distribute to its shareholders. But beyond this some feel that stock dividends can have serious **disadvantages** for the company as well as for the shareholders. *Firstly*,the principle disadvantage to the company, according to opponents of stock dividends, is that a "permanent liability" for future dividend payments is created, Presumably, the old dividend rate is expected to be maintained after the additional shares are issued. If so, an additional strain is placed on the company's future earnings without any real addition to the company's earning power in the form of new capital. *Secondly,* issuing stock dividends, especially if fractional shares are involved, is considerably expensive, time consuming, and troublesome. Some companies, however, avoid the fractional share problem by issuing cash in lieu of the fractional shares; and sometimes, they are able to make the dividend large enough so that fractional shares need not be considered. *Thirdly,* the stock dividends tend to depress the market price of the company's shares. In many cases, this depress in the market value may be a disservice to the shareholders and not a benefit as the share market is mainly a psychological market. *Fourthly,* the stock dividends are not really satisfactory to shareholders, particularly who rely on dividends for income. While such shareholders can sell their dividend shares to get cash, this dilutes their equity in the company and they thus trade one disavantage for another. *Finally,* the accounting requirement that the full market value of the dividend shares, not merely their par or stated value, must be capitalised in market value for beyond their par value. In paying a stock dividend, they would be required to set aside out of their earned surplus the difference between par value and market price. In such cases where the stock is so highly priced in relation to its relation to its par value means that if they paid many stock dividends their earned surplus would soon evaporate. As a result, they are boxed in on stock dividends.

INSTITUTIONAL AND ADMINISTRATIVE ASPECTS OF DIVIDEND POLICY

Once a long-term target payout ratio has been established, financial manager is then in a position to spell out the details of the firm's policy and carry it out in the face of short-run corporate and market developments. The actual execution of dividend policy is influenced by a number of factors, all of which affect in one way or another the final dividend decisions of the firm.

FACTORS INFLUENCING THE DIVIDEND DECISIONS

The corporate, insitutional and legal factors that influence the dividend decision of a firm include the growth and profitability of the firm its liquidity position, the cost and availability of alternative forms of financing concerns about the managerial control of the firm, the existence of external (largely legal) restriction and the impact of inflation of cash flow.

Growth and Profitability

The amount of growth a firm can sustain and its profitability are related to its dividend decisions, so long as the firm (because of managerially imposed to external market constraints) cannot issue additional equity. To see that this relationship exists consider the model developed by Higgins.[6] He relates the sustainable growth (g^*) in sales to the firm's dividend policy, capital structure, and profitability, such that:

$$g^* = \frac{p(1\text{-}d)(1\text{-}L)}{t\text{-}\,p(1\text{-}d)(1\text{-}L)} \tag{4}$$

where

g^* = sustainable growth in sales
p = after-tax profit margin on new and existing sales
d = target dividend payout ratio
L = target total debt to total equity ratio
t = ratio of total assets to net sales, applicable to new and existing sales

For example, assume a firm had a profit margin (p) of 10 per cent, a target dividend payout ratio (d) of 60 per cent, and target capital structure ratio (L) of 80 per cent. If it required ₹ 73 of assets to support ₹ 100 of sales, than according to the Higgins model, the firm's maximum sustainable growth in sales (g^*) would be 10.94 percent

6. Robert C. Higgins, "How Much Growth Can a Firm Afford? *Financial Management* 6 (Fall 1977), pp. 7-16.

$$g^* = \frac{(.10)(.40)(1.80)}{.73-[(.10)(.40)(1.80)]} = 10.94$$

However, consider the interdependency that exists if, for example, the firm's profit margin is only 8 per cent instead of 10 per cent. The drop in the firm's profitability causes its sustainable growth to decrease to 8.57 per cent, unless there is a decrease in the dividend payout ratio or an increase in its financial leverage, or unless the firm increases its turnover and is able to generate more sales per ₹ of assets employed. Similar interrelations exist if any of the other policy variables in the Higgins model are changed. We can see from this why firms with strong growth prospects maintain low target payout ratios. In essence, firms that experience above-average growth rates are expected to have low dividend payout ratios since, in line with the residual theory of dividends, a greater number of profitable investment opportunities should result (other things being equal in a greater need for earnings retention. This interrelationship among the firm's growth, its profitability, and its investment, financing, and dividend decisions cannot be overemphasized.

Liquidity

The liquidity position of a firm is often an important consideration in dividend decisions. Since dividends represent a cash outflow, it follows that the better the cash position and overall liquidity of the firm, the greater is the firm's ability to pay (and maintain) a cash dividend. A growing, profitable firm may not be liquid, since it needs funds for new capital expenditures and to build up its permanent working capital position. Likewise, firms in cyclical industries may experience times when they lack liquidity due to general economic conditions. Hence, the degree of liquidity is a variable of concern when a firm's dividend policy is being assessed.

Cost and Availability of Alternative Forms of financing

The ability of a firm to raise money externally will have a direct bearing on the level of dividends paid to shareholders. Clearly, a company that has easy access to the capital markets, and that can conveniently and economically raise funds in a number of alternative ways, will have greater latitude in setting dividend policy than a firm that has to rely heavily on earnings retention as a source of financing. In essence, the key question is whether or not a firm can (if the need arises) finance its dividend payments externally. Those that can are likely to set higher dividend levels than those that cannot.

Two aspects that tend to work against this approach to dividend payments are the cost of financing and issue expenses. Financing dividends externally may have merit so long as the cost of financing is relatively low. However, when interest rates rise, the idea of financing dividends begins to lose its appeal. Moreover, issue expenses and other flotation costs will lower desired payout ratios, since they raise the cost of financing. This is particularly true when the amount of external financing involved is fairly small, for flotation costs are inversly related to the size of the issue and tend to rise rapidly as the size of an issue declines.

Managerial Control

In some cases, control of the firm may be a factor to consider when establishing dividend policy. Suppose a fairly substantial proportion of the firm is owned by a controlling group, and the remainder of the stock is publicly held. Under these circumstances, the higher the payout ratio, the more likely that a subsequent issue of equity may be needed to finance capital expenditures. Those in control might prefer to minimise the likelihood of an offering of equity to avoid any dilution in their ownership position. Hence, they would prefer a low payout policy. On the other hand, a firm may establish a relatively high dividend payout ratio (if it believes that is what shareholders desire) as a way to keep the firm from being acquired in a merger or acquisition.

Legal constraints

The legal rules act as a boundaries within which a company can declare dividends. In general, cash dividends must be paid from current earnings or from previous earnings that have been retained by the corporations after providing for depreciation. However, a company may be permitted to pay dividend in any financial year out of the profits of the company without providing for depreciation. Though the dividends should be paid in cash, but it doesn't prohibit a company from capitalising its profits or reserves (retained earnings) for the purpose of issuing fully paid bonus shares (stock dividend).

Access to the Capital Market

Another matter for consideration by management in setting an appropriate dividend policy is the company's ability to obtain cash on relatively short notice. This may be achieved by the company negotiating for a bank overdraft limit or having access to other short-term sources of funds. However, if a company's ability to make a new issue of shares or to issue debt is restricted, it is likely that it will retain a higher proportion of its profits than a company which has ready access to funds from the capital market. Companies which are likely to have difficulties raising funds on the capital market include small companies, new companies, and companies in what may be termed venture capital fields.

Inflation

Inflation must be taken into account when a firm establishes its dividend policy. On the one hand, investors would like to receive larger cash dividends because of inflation. But from the firm's viewpoint, inflation causes it to have to invest substantially more to replace existing equipment, finance new capital expenditures, and meet permanent working capital needs. Thus, in inflationary times, there may be a tendency to hold down cash dividends.

External Restrictions

The protective convenants in a bond indenture or loan agreement often include a restriction on the payment of cash dividends. This restriction is imposed to preserve the firm's ability to service its debt. These restrictions may be in the form of coverage ratio, sinking fund etc. Presence of these restrictions force a company to retain earnings and follow a low payout.

DIVIDEND PAYMENT PROCEDURES

After the firm's dividend policy has been structured, several procedural details must be arranged. For instance, *how frequently are dividend payments to be made? If a shareholder sells the shares during the year, who is entitled to the dividend?* To answer these questions, we need to understand the dividend—payment procedures.

Generally, cash, the most common type of dividend, is one of several types of dividends that corporate directors can declare. The cash dividend is the only monetary dividend that shareholders of equity shares receive. The directors of a corporation are charged with the responsibility of making the formal decision to pay dividends. In the cash of bonus shares, their decision may be subject to shareholder approval. Once the decision to pay a dividend is made, four dates become important: date declared, date of record, ex-dividend date, and date payable. The *Date declared* is the date on which the directors of a company declare that a dividend is going to be paid. Such announcements are frequently reported in the financial press and elsewhere. At the same time, the directors announce the date of record. Only shareholders who are recorded on the transfer books of the company on the *date of record* are entitled to receive the dividend. It takes about four business days from the time one buys shares until one's name is recorded on the company's transfer books. Therefore a date must be established to let potential buyers know that they will be eligible to receive the dividend because their names are on the company books. Those who buy the shares after it has gone *ex-dividend* are not entitled to the dividend because there is not sufficient time to get their names on the books before the date of record and the dividend is paid. The *date payable* is the date when the dividend is paid. The time between the date declared and the date payable varies from company to company.

ILLUSTRATIVE PROBLEMS

1. A firm has 2,40,000 shares of equity at ₹ 10 par, a premium account of ₹ 6,50,000 and a retained earnings account of ₹ 29,20,000. The firm declares a 20 per cent stock dividend at a time when the fair market value of the equity share is ₹ 40 per share. Prepare the equity section of the balance sheet before and after the dividend.

Solution

Equity section of the balance sheet before and after the dividend is presented below:

	Before the dividend	*After the dividend*
Equity share capital (₹ 10 par)	₹ 24,00,000	₹ 28,80,000
Share premium	6,50,000	20,90,000
Retained earnings	29,20,000	10,00,000

2. Refer to Problem 1, assume the firm declared a 100% stock split. Prepare the balance sheet before and after the dividend.

Solution

Balance sheet before and after the dividend is given below:

	Before the dividend	*After the dividend*
Equity share capital (₹ 5 par)	₹ 24,00,000	₹ 24,00,000
Reserves premium	6,50,000	6,50,000
Retained earnings	29,20,000	29,20,000

3. Wadhwa Group had a capitalisation shown below:

Equity share capital (₹ 10 per, 5,00,000 shares)	₹ 50,00,000
Paid up capital	1,25,00,000
Retained earnings	2,25,00,000
Total owners' equity	₹ 4,00,00,000

Wadhwa split their stock four for one. Show their new capitalisation.

Solution

Equity share capital (₹ 2.50 per, 20,00,000 shares)	₹ 50,00,000
Paid up capital	1,25,00,000
Retained earnings	2,25,00,000
Total owners' equity	₹ 4,00,00,000

Usually when a stock is split, the cash dividend per share is reduced proportionately. Thus, if Wadhwa's dividend were four for one before the split, it would probably be reduced to after the split.

4. On January 2 Amtex Industries declared a 20 per cent stock dividend payable on February 15 to shareholders of record January 31. The stock is currently selling for ₹ 40 per share and you own 200 shares.

a. If you decided to sell your stock on January 17, what price would you expect to receive?

b. If you held the stock until February 17, what price would you expect to receive?

c. If you elected to hold onto the stock, how many shares would you own after the stock dividend is paid?

d. What would you expect the total value of your Amtex Industries stock to be before and after the payment of the stock dividend?

Solution

a. Since a stock dividend has no value, there should be no change in the price of the stock in the market.

b. The price after the stock dividend has been paid should drop by just enough to leave the total value of stock outstanding unchanged:

$$P = \frac{200}{240} \times 40 = ₹\ 33.33$$

c. A 20 per cent stock dividend entitles the stockholder to receive a number of shares equal to 20 per cent of the current holding; in this case, the stock would be equal to 40 shares:

$200 \times 0.2 = 40$ new shares

d. You now have 20 per cent more shares, which have a lower market value; therefore your total value is unchanged:

before: 200 @ ₹ 40 = ₹ 8,000
after: 240 @ ₹ 33.33 = ₹ 8,000

5. You hold 200 equity shares of Bindra Group. The Group has just had another profitable year and will continue to pay its regular cash dividend. It was announced that Bindra's dividend for this year would be raised to ₹ 1.50.

a. What will be your total dividend income for the year from your Bindra's stock?
b. If the company elected instead to have a stock dividend of 10 per cent, what would be your new holdings in Bindra Group?
c. Bindra's stock is trading at ₹ 90, and the Board of Directors feels a lower price might encourage liquidity. Thus it is proposing a 3 for 1 stock split. How many shares will you hold and what will be your total dividend for the year after the stock split?

Solution

a. The total dividend is simply the dividend per share time the total shares held:

$300 \times ₹\ 1.50 = ₹\ 300$

b. If Bindra declared a 10 per cent stock dividend rather than a cash dividend, your holdings would increase by 10 per cent

$200 \times 1.1 = 220$ shares

c. When the stock is split, the dividend is normally split in the same proportion, so there is no change in dividend income:

before:	200 × ₹ 1.50	=	₹ 300
after:	200 × 3	=	600
	₹ 1.50/3	= ×	0.50
			₹ 300

6. Super Industries had capitalisation as shown:

Equity share capital (₹ 10 per, 10,00,000 shares)	₹ 1,00,00,000
Paid up capital	5,00,00,000
Retained earnings	14,00,00,000
Total owners' equity	₹ 20,00,00,000

Super paid a 20% stock dividend. At the time of the stock dividend, the stock was selling at ₹ 60 per share. Show the new capitalisation.

Solution

A 20% stock dividend would represent 2,00,000 new shares (20% of 10,00,000 shares outstanding). At ₹ 60 per share, the totalo the equity share capital and paid-up capital accounts. The equity share capital account is allocated ₹ 10 per share (the par value) or a total of ₹ 20,00,000. The paid-up capital account is allocated the remaining ₹ 1,00,00,000. The result is shown below:

Equity share capital (₹ 10 per, 2,00,000 shares)	₹ 1,20,00,000
Paid up capital	6,00,00,000
Retained earnings	12,80,00,000
Total owners' equity	₹ 20,00,00,000

The total reamins constant, and only the distribution of amounts by account changes.

QUESTION

1. Distinguish between declaration date; date of record, ex-dividend date, and payment date.
2. Company ABC has a very stable dividend overtime where as company XYZ's is more volatile. To what firm characteristics would you attribute this difference?
3. How does the constant percentage payout policy differ from the regular-plus-extra dividend policy from the view of shareholders?
4. It is readily observed that companies distribute differing proportions of earnings as dividends. To what firm characteristics would you attribute these differences?
5. A dividend decision is "the other side of the coin" of a financing decision. Explain.
6. Under what conditions are the investment, financing and dividend decisions of a firm interrelated? Explain how these variables are related to a firm's sustainable growth.
7. A stock split should have no effect on value, but it does seem to affect a firm's stock price. How would you reconcile this contradiction?
8. To what extent do you agree or disagree with the following statement? "A company's dividend decision can be viewed most accurately as just part of its investment decision."
9. Some people think that stock dividends are unrealistic and unnecessary, since they give the investor what he has already received. Comment.
10. What are (i) a constant payout-ratio policy? (ii) a regular dividend policy, and (iii) a low regular-and-extra-dividend policy? What are the ramifications of these policies?
11. A company that has an excess cash on hand is trying to decide whether to pay out the cash as a regular dividend or a special dividend or to repurchase stock with it. What are some of the considerations that would enter into this decision?
12. What are the advantages of a stock split or dividend over a cash dividend?
13. What is the relationship between dividend policy and the investment decision and between dividend policy and the cost of capital?
14. Why do companies with high growth rates tend to have low dividend payout ratios, and companies with low growth rates high payout ratios?

15. Evaluate the following quotation: "As long as management is presumed to be acting in the best interests of stockholder, retained earnings can be regarded as equivalent to a fully subscribed, pre-emptive issue of common stock. Hence for present purposes, the division of the stream between cash dividends and retained earnings in any period is a mere detail."
16. Some firms do reverse stock splits in which investors receive one share for every three or four they own. What might be the rationale for a reverse stock split, and what effect will it have on stock prices?

PROBLEMS

1. Kunal Electrical earns ₹ 5.40 per share and pays a ₹ 1.50 dividend. This year they have increased the cash dividend to ₹ 1.60 and gave a 5 per cent bonus share. If the share sold for ₹ 40 per share before the dividends, compute the increase in yield to the equity shareholders and the change in the firm's payout ratio.

Ans.: Yield 3.75% to 4.20%; Payout ratio .2778 to .2963

2. Hind press is meeting to establish a tentative dividend policy to complement their new 5-year operating plan. Selected information from this plan appears below:

Year	*1*	2	3	*4*	5
Sales	₹ 60,00,000	70,00,000	75,00,000	85,00,000	90,00,000
Profits	₹ 3,00,000	3,50,000	4,00,000	4,50,000	5,00,000
Number of equityshares	1,00,000	1,00,000	1,00,000	1,00,000	1,00,000
Net fixed assets	₹ 40,00,000	46,00,000	53,00,000	54,00,000	59,00,000
Investment (net of de-preciation)	₹ 2,00,000	6,00,000	7,00,000	1,00,000	5,00,000
Depreciation	₹ 6,00,000	7,00,000	7,00,000	8,00,000	8,00,000

In fixing the tentative dividend policy, Hind management would like to: (i) maintain a target debt-to-equity ratio of 50 per cent. (ii) pay the same dividend every year insofar as possible. What annual dividends would you recommend the company plan on distributing?

Ans.: Average annual dividend = ₹ 1,18,600

3. Goldens Tobacco Company has for many years enjoyed a moderate but stable growth in sales and earnings. However, cigar consumption, and consequently Golden's sales, have been falling recently, primarily because of an increasing awareness of the dangers of smoking to health. Anticipating further declines to tobacco sales for the future, Golden's management hopes eventually to move almost entirely out of the tobacco business and into a newly developed, diversified product line in growth-oriented industries. The company is especially interested in the prospects for pollution-control devices, because its research department has already done much work on the problems of filtering smoke. Right now, the company estimates that an investment of ₹ 15 crore is necessary to purchase new facilities and to begin operations on these products, but the investment could be earning a return of about 18 per cent within a short time. The only other available investment opportunity totals ₹ 6 crore and is expected to return about 10.4 per cent.

The company is expected to pay a ₹ 3.00 dividend on its 3 crore issued shares, the same as its dividend last year. The directors might, however, change the dividend if there are good reasons for doing so. Total earnings after taxes for the year are expected to be ₹ 14.25 crore; the equity share is currently selling for ₹ 56.25; the firm's target debt ratio (debt/assets ratio) is 45 per cent; and its tax rate is 40 per cent. The costs of various forms of financing are as follows:

New bonds, k_i = 11%. This is a before-tax rate.

New equity sold at ₹ 56.25 per share will net ₹ 51.25.

Required rate of return on retained earnings, k_r = 14%.

(a) Calculate Golden's expected payout ratio, the break point at which MCC rises, and its marginal cost of capital above and below the point of exhaustion of retained earnings at the current payout. (Hint: k_r is given, and D_1/P_0 can be found. Then, knowing k_r and D_1/P_0, g can be determined). (b) How large should Golden's capital budget be for the year? (c) What is an appropriate dividend policy for Golden? How should the capital budget be financed? (d) How might risk factors influence Golden's cost of capital, capital structure, and dividend policy? (e) What assumptions, if any, do your answers to the preceding parts make about investors preferences for dividends versus capital gains (in other words, what are investors' preferences regarding the D_1/P_0 and g components of k_r)?

Ans.: (a) Payout ratio = 63.16%; Break point = ₹ 9.35 crore, $WACC_1$ = 16.67%; $WACC_2$ = 10.96%. (b) ₹ 15 crore.

4. The Andhra Corporation declared a 6 per cent stock dividend plus a cash dividend of ₹ 9.00 per share. The cash dividend was paid on both the old shares and the new shares received from the stock dividend. Construct a pro-forma balance sheet showing the effect of these actions; use one new balance sheet that incorporates both actions. The stock was selling for ₹ 37.50 per share, and a condensed version of Andhra's balance sheet as of March 31, 2011, before the dividends, follows:

Debt	₹ 15,000 crore	Cash	₹ 1,125 crore
Equity (90 crore shares authorised, 75 crore shares issued at ₹ 10 par)	₹ 750 crore	Other assets	₹ 28,875 crore
Paid-in capital	₹ 3,000 crore		
Retained earnings	₹ 1,1250 crore		
Total liabilities and equity	₹ 30,000 crore	Total assets	₹ 30,000 crore

Ans.: Equity = ₹ 795 crore; Paid in capital = ₹ 4,642.50 crore; Retained earnings = ₹ 8,847 crore

5. After a 5-for-1 stock split the XYZ Company paid a dividend of ₹ 7.5 per new share, which represents a 9 per cent increase over last year's pre-split dividend. What was last year's dividend per share?

Ans.: D_0 = 34.40

20

LEASING

INTRODUCTION

Leasing, like long-term debt, is a process by which a firm can obtain the use of certain fixed assets for which it must make a series of contractual, periodic, tax-deductible payments. *Why would financial managers frequently compare the economics of a lease to the alternative of borrowing to purchase a needed asset?* In this chapter, we discuss the basic types of leases including definitions of some key terms encountered in the leasing industry; the advantages and disadvantages of leasing; the lease agreement; the risk in leasing; the lease quote; lease-versus-purchase decision; and, fully, a lease purchase model that can be used to evaluate the economic consequences of leasing versus purchasing an asset.

THE CONCEPT OF LEASING

Leasing is an alternative to purchase an asset in order to acquire the services of that asset. By leasing an asset the lessee essentially acquires its use value from the lessor, who actually purchased and owns (retains title to) the asset. Simply stated, ownership of a productive asset conveys two types of 'property rights' to the owner (1) to use the asset throughout its productive life and (2) to sell or dispose of it for its salvage value. In this context, the lessee acquires all or a portion of the "use value" of the asset in return for making a set of rental payments to the lessor. The lessor retains title to the asset and, hence, the right to sell or dispose of it for its salvage value. Thus, leasing distributes the rights of ownership by separating the asset's use value from its salvage value.

TYPES OF LEASING

The ever growing complexity of the law and the various diverse circumstances of the "lessees" and "lessors" lead to a number of variations in the standard financial and operating leases. These leases have come into picture in the various parts of the world and are practised according to the convenience of the lessor and lessee. Broadly, leases can be categorised as follows:

Financial Lease

A financial lease is a contract that is non-cancellable and the lease period is usually shorter than the useful life of the asset being leased. During the life of the contract all of the cost of the property plus financing and servicing charges should be recovered through periodic payments. The lease assumes complete financial responsibility for the leased asset; and, if operated successfully, the lessor or owner will recover the original investment.

In this kind of 'lease agreement' the leasing company will act simply as a financial institution. The lessee will specify the equipment needed and act as the lessor's agent in the matters of ordering it, inspecting it and maintaining it. The lessor is simply interested in the equipment as its legally owned asset. The lessor will raise the money, accept the invoice from the supplier and pay accordingly.

Certain circumstances relating to change of the structure of the finance economy, particular requirement of the lessee, government rules and regulation, have led to creative finance lease writing. Some of them are listed below:

(a) **Floating rental rate lease contracts.** World financial circles have experienced a very volatile phase of interest rates in the last few years. Keeping in view, these aspects a number of lessees and lessors have written the leases in a way whereby the lease rentals are reduced or increased according to the borrowing interest rates by the lessor. This kind of lease permits a lessee to undertake the risk and awards of interest rate variations.

(b) **Non-tax base leasing.** Lessor, in general, enjoys the benefits of tax deductions and various grants extended by governments to the new capital investment in the industry. But sometimes the leases are written in such a way that lessors are forced to abandon tax benefits in favour of the lessees. The lease written in this fashion is categorised under the non-tax base leasing.

(c) **Net Lease.** In a net lease, the lessee pays the costs associated with partnership. These costs include property taxes, insurance premiums, and capital and maintenance expenses.

USE VS. OWNERSHIP

Financial leasing is a means of financing the use rather than the ownership of an asset. From this essential feature, which distinguishes leasing from other methods of financing capital equipment, all its characteristics flow. The two concepts involved, separating use from ownership and differentiating between long-term use as a method of financing equipment and short-term use of an asset, establish a distinct place for financial leasing as a business practice. Financial leasing is *sui generis.*

However, there is no clear dividing line between use and ownership. Different distinctions apply for different purposes. Under a hire-purchase arrangement, for example, legal ownership does not pass to the user until the hirer exercises the purchase option after the last instalment payment is made, whereas he may be considered to have economic ownership throughout the period of hire. Economists and accountants argue that there is frequently no substantive difference between owning an item of equipment and having the right to use it for all its useful life.

Although use and economic ownership are often indistinguishable, the existence of an option to acquire title to equipment is the definite dividing line between a financial lease and hire-purchase. This distinction is clear cut because of the different tax treatments. Lessors as owners are entitled to claim the capital allowances on the equipment and are also eligible for those incentives, such as government development grants, which are payable to purchasers of qualifying equipment. On the other hand, users of equipment financed by hire-purchase claim the allowances and grants—ownership is imputed in circumstances where a firm enters into a contract which provides that it shall or may become the owner of the equipment.

Operating Lease

Operating leasing is a service available for which there is an established leasing and second-hand market. Computers and television sets are the items most widely leased on an operating basis in the commercial and consumer fields, respectively. Assets are leased over periods from around six months, shorter periods being more in the nature of plant hire, up to three years for most types of equipment. Longer terms are available for aircraft and ships and for certain other items, subject to the lessee having a right to cancel the lease either unilaterally or in the event of an increase in rentals.

An operating lease may be attractive when a firm requires a machine for a relatively short period because, for example, of the anticipated early development of more advanced machinery. In industries where the rate of technological change is rapid, there is much uncertainty about the future economic life of equipment. The operating lessor's function in assuming the obsolescence risk in these circumstances is comparable to an insurance contract. The lessor collects a premium from each lessee and the sum total of all the premiums collected is sufficient to cover the cost of the losses arising from the unrecovered value of the obsolete machines. Lessees are willing to permit the lessor to earn a profit for this risk-taking because it reduces their exposure to a potentially larger individual loss. For items of equipment such as computers, the lessor is frequently also the manufacturer. He is then in a better position to estimate the extent of obsolescence and, in fact, may to some extent control when it occurs.

Operating lessors usually confine their activities to a particular specialised area and purchase a large number of similar types of machines. They are then able to offer attractive terms by reflecting economies of scale in the rentals. These include purchase discounts, higher sale proceeds, and savings in maintenance and reconditioning costs. As in the case of financial lease, various circumstances have led to different kinds of operating lease writing. Some of them are listed below:

(a) Service lease

A service lease resembles to *'Contract Hire'* but has a different legislative outlook. In this kind of lease, the 'lessor' renders the services of the equipment, generally automobiles, office and domestic equipment, for a relatively short period. The rentals do not have any direct correlation towards the *recovery* of capital costs, interest and lessors' profit in the lease period. Lessors' primary objective while offering the lease rentals is to have a regular income and the interest on the capital. Moreover these rentals are fixed keeping in view the useful working life of the equipment.

(b) Captive lease

This kind of leasing was introduced by certain manufacturers who wanted to contest the second-hand market of the equipment which they are manufacturing to maintain the monopoly of their products in the market. This type of leasing is significantly popular in computers, machine tools, etc.

Sale and Lease Back

Sale and lease back leasing was designed as an alternative to the 'hypothecation' of fixed assets to raise funds by an organisation in the traditional financial circles. Under this type a sole and leaseback arrangement consists of the sale of machinery, equipment, or building by a firm to a financial institution that in turn leases the assets back to the firm. The financial institution may be a company that specialises in the leasing business, or it may be a bank. Assets that have been used by the firm for some time may be made and leased back. Sometimes there are tax advantages to this arrangement.

New assets are frequently sold and leased back. For example, a firm may be building a new plant. During the construction period, the firm takes construction loans from a bank to handle the financing. When the plant is completed, it is sold according to a prearranged plan to a leasing company or a bank. The firm uses the proceeds from the sale to repay the construction loans. This type of lease will typically be a financial lease arranged on a net basis. It is the equivalent of doing term financing of the new plant.

Almost any type of fixed asset can be leased. The arrangement can be a sale and leaseback, or the financial institution can purchase an asset directly, with the specifications set by the lessee. There may be little if any net differences.

Leverage Lease

Under a leverage lease the 'lessee' assigns his interest in a purchase order to 'lessor' who agrees to advance only a portion of the total equipment cost, and arranges to borrow the remaining portion from institutional lenders. Many leading corporations of the world has been using leverage lease to aid their capital expenditure requirements. Traditional leverage leases contain three basic characteristics which separate them from other financing concepts: i) lessors are required to structure transaction which produce overall profits and have reasonable cash flows, both on a pre-tax basis; ii) lessors are required to maintain at least a certain percent of permanent investment, say 20%, in leased assets throughout the lease term. Such investment may be in the future residual value remaining at the conclusion of the lease term; and iii) finally, the lessors must accept the risk of equipment ownership and cannot insure themselves or otherwise protect themselves against lessee bankruptcies or debt forgiveness consequences.

There are number of *participants* in a leverage lease and the role of each is described below:

(a) Broker: A leverage lease is organised and managed by a broker. Once the broker has found a company interested in acquiring an asset by means of a leverage lease, he has to find two other parties to participate in the financing of the asset: a **lender** prepared to lend long-term debt funds to a *lessor* which then adds sufficient of its own funds to the borrowed funds in order to purchase the required asset. Apart from arranging the parties to, and the terms of, in the leverage lease the broker will also handle the legal documentation and keep accounts for all parties during the term of the lease. In return, the broker receives a certain percent of the cost of the asset as fee.

(b) Lender: This role is performed by one, or more, institutional lenders which lend a major proportion of the cost of the asset to the lessor. The lender will receive interest and principal repayments paid out of the lease payments. While the interest rate will approximate the current rate on long-term mortgages, the precise rate charged depends upon the credit standing of the lessee. The lender receives a registered first mortgage over an asset leased as well as a first charge over the lease payments received from the lessee.

(c) Lessor (equity participants): The lessor comprises one or more banks or finance companies with sufficient profits to take the full tax advantage, of the depreciation charges and investment allowances allowable on the asset. The lessor provides the additional funds not provided by the lender and purchases the asset. The lessor receives only a very small cash flow from the lease payments as the major proportion of the lease payments is paid out as interest and principal repayments to the lender. However, as the lessor receives the tax benefits of ownership, the lessor is prepared to accept a low return on the funds it provides.

(d) Lessee: The lessee enters into a normal lease agreement agreeing to lease the asset for a specified period of time and to make specified lease payments. Usually, the period of the lease is shorter than the economic life of the asset.

If the lease runs its normal course, the asset reverts to the lessor (as owner). In the case of default by the lessee any money obtained either as a result of action against the lessee or from the sale of the asset will be used to repay the lender which has a first mortgage over the asset and a first charge over the lease payments.

Thus, the *special attractions* of a leverage lease are : (i) the lessor can obtain a high rate of return with very little risk, and because of the tax savings the lessor can recover its contribution. (ii) The lessee can lease very expensive assets for a long period of time at a low interest cost; and, (iii) the lender appears to benefit the least from a leverage lease. However, the lender can obtain return either equal to above that is available from alternative forms of lending with very little risk of default if the lessee is a good credit risk.

Sale-Aid Leasing

By the advent of intensive competition in product marketing, a number of companies adopted this technique as a marketing tool because under this scheme, a manufacturer directly extends facility of leasing either by one of his own subsidiaries or through a third party, a leasing company. This kind of leasing arrangements normally have a very strong psychological advantage even where the lessee is in a position to raise lease finance through their own contracts. Normally a customer, when he is offered lease finance by the manufacturer, feels that the manufacturer is offering his goods on a monthly payment basis spread out on a very long period. It is worthwhile reiterating at this stage that the sales plus that the salesman can put to his customer in support of this facility are: (1) The instrument can be installed and operational without the need for capital expenditure. (2) The equipment can be replaced or updated at any time during the lease term.

The leasing enables a manufacturer, who join ventures with the leasing company: (1) The leasing can make the sale an on the spot decision and one made by a manager authorised to commit the revenue expenses. (2) Immediate payment of invoices and elimination of bad debt risks. (3) An on-going laison with the customer leading to more regular updating or replacement of equipment, thus, providing improved sales opportunities. (4) Personalised documentation, drawn up and supplied by the leasing company, retains the manufacturer's identity and reinforces their trading position throughout the negotiations.

A few variations which have come into the picture for sales-aid leasing are in the form of leasing by dealers. A number of large distributors and dealers have been offering leasing facilities to their customers. In such kind of leasing a part of the profit of the vehicle sale is normally passed on the lessee whereby reducing the cost of equipment to the lessee.

It is worthwhile to point out here that the most distinguishing factor of this kind of lease arrangement is that a customer gets the entire deal as a package i.e., purchase, contracts, arrangements of finances and all other things are done by one company itself. Therefore, it reduces a number of operational expenses and time consumed in various negotiations.

Tax Benefit Transfer lease

The objective of these kind of leases is to make the economically distressed companies to encash the benefits of investment tax credits and other various fiscal incentives which they were not in a position to enjoy because of the non-tax paying conditions of the company. In this kind of leasing, the lessor pays a down payment on the capital cost of the equipment and execute a note exactly identical to the lease rentals to be received from lessee. Thus, these notes are equal to the amount to be repaid to the financial institutions towards their loan repayment and the interest to be accrued during the contract period. Thus, no money is to be repaid by the lessor to the financial institution. Accordingly, the lessee's cost of the equipment is reduced by the initial payment made by the lessor to the financial institution.

Cross Border Lease

When a lessor leases an equipment to a lessee who is not falling in the jurisdiction of the lessor's territory then the lease written is known as Cross Border leasing. Equipment financed by cross border leasing displays one or more of the following characteristics: (i) undisputed title (giving rise to registration); (ii) used in an economically essential sector with strong and lasting profitability; (iii) long life and a good second hand value in many different countries; and, (iv) relative mobility.

The reason for recourse to cross border leasing are first of all financial : in the majority of cases such a operation serves to finance an international commercial transaction and the user not only procures 100% financing which he can also obtain through direct purchase by means of export and complementary financial credits-but also, finance which is generally of balance sheet, and covers a longer period than government export credits, which are limited by international agreements.

Financial institutions on the other hand believe that the possession of title to equipment, which theoritically should be easily recovered in the event of breach of the contract by the lessee, and which conserves a good second hand value on the international market, enables them to take the added risk of extending the term of their assistance. However this risk of taking is—with the complexity of the operation—one of the reasons which justifies the generally better margin commanded by cross border deals compared with domestic deals of a comparable size.

ADVANTAGES AND DISADVANTAGES OF LEASING

Advantages

The merits of leasing from a potential lessee's point of view are set out below. Normally, only a few of the **advantages** will be important on any given occasion.

1. *Equipment procurement:* Leasing may be the cheapest (or only) means of obtaining the use of the most suitable equipment because of import or export controls or the existence of patent rights or other form of monopolistic restriction on the free supply of the equipment by way of sale.
2. *Additional source of finance:* By leasing, the use of equipment is obtained *without capital outlay.* Leasing extends the range of methods of financing the acquisition of capital equipment. Many companies adopt a mixed financing strategy with leasing one of several facilities which they employ simultaneously to finance their capital investments.
3. *Debt capacity:* As an additional source of finance, leasing may enable a firm to increase its overall debt-raising capacity, notwithstanding the fact that rental commitments are now frequently disclosed in published accounts. A lessor's security is the asset financed and a leasing facility does not necessarily adversely affect a company's ability to arrange general credit lines.

4. *Certainty :* The fixed nature of a leasing contract applies to the lessor as well as to the lessee. A lease is a medium-term facility which unlike a loan repayable on demand, cannot be withdrawn or curtailed in the event of a credit squeeze or a change in economic conditions. Except as a consequence of default by the lessee, the lessor cannot seek to accelerate the payment of rentals during the primary lease period.
5. *Availability:* Leasing may be the only suitable form of external finance available to a firm. Leasing facilities on fixed terms have recently been obtainable at times when it has not been possible for an industrial concern to arrange a comparable loan for a five-year or longer period, either at a fixed interest rate or, on some occasions, on any terms.

   Leasing may also provide financial institutions with the additional security or reward necessary to encourage them to offer asset financing facilities for new types of risk, such as financing the equipment required for the development of basic infrastructure. Ownership of an asset may be preferable to security obtainable by way of a mortgage or charge for which enforcement may be difficult and the cost of registration, if available, high. Financial lessors are able to earn additional profits by retaining or sharing in the residual value of leased equipment.
6. *Taxation:* The 100 per cent first year capital allowance available on the purchase of most types of plant and machinery is claimed by the lessor and the benefit of the tax deferment is normally reflected in the calculation of rentals. This reduction in rentals is attractive to those companies whose taxable profits are insufficient for them to obtain immediate and full benefit from the allowances to which they would be entitled if the equipment were purchased.
7. *Flexibility:* Leasing arrangements are very flexible. Leasing companies have proved more adaptable than banks and financing institutions with regard to contract structures. In fact the typical lease does not have the restrictive provision of the term loan. The firm does not unduly restricts its ability to undertake a change of plans or unchanged action in order to grasp a sudden profit opportunity or adjust to a changing operating environment. The simple fact that the lessee may not require the prior approval of the lessor, whereas the term loan probably does, mean a speadier reaction time.
8. *Limited claims in the event of bankruptcy or re-organisation:* Lease also offered the firm a small advantage if bankruptcy occurs. They are less burdensome to the firm at that time, because the title is with the lessor. The asset cannot be seized by the firm's creditors. The firm can readily break the lease by simply returning the asset to the lessor (with one to three years' payments, depending on the circumstances). This makes it considerably easier for the financial manger to reorganise the firm.
9. *Hedging risks:* To the extent that rentals fixed in relation to changes in money costs are available, lessees are able to hedge against inflation—payments are

made in fixed money terms out of future earnings, which will rise with inflation.

10. *Convenience:* Leasing is often regarded by lessees as a simple and convenient method of financing the acquisition of capital equipment. Book-keeping is streamlined and the regular nature of rental payments may assist expense budgeting and cash flow forecasting. Leases can be arranged on tailor-made terms to reflect the particular needs of individual lessees. Rentals may also be related to the earning power of the leased equipment; the opportunity to match cash flows over the expected life of an asset provides an element of financial stability.
11. *Avoidance of the risk of obsolescence:* The lease arrangement also lets the firm avoid the risk of rapid obsolescence. Since the firm does not own the asset, a deterioration in its value because of changing technology does not affect the firm's asset value. If the asset does not have any salvage value at the end of the lease, despite original expectations that it would, the lessor suffers the loss, not the firm.
12. *Increase in liquidity*: The use of sale-lease back arrangements may permit the firm to increase its liquidity by converting an existing asset into the cash which can be used as working capital. A firm short of working capital or in a liquidity squeeze can sell an owned asset to a lessor and lease the asset back for a specified number of years. The benefits of the increase in current liquidity are therefore tempered somewhat by the added fixed financial payments incurred through the lease.
13. *Step-by-step financing:* Some firms expand in step-wise fashion as in building a chain of supermarkets. Here lease financing can be utilised to advantage. As each new location is added, a lease can be arranged for constructing the building. Large sums obtained from earlier security issues are not left in low-yielding investments waiting for new locations to be identified. One alternative to leasing is short-term temporary financing or open-ended loans that permit additional borrowing as needed. Letter the temporary loans can be refinanced. This *'double'* financing can be costly both in time and money and alternately, may be more expensive than lease financing.
14. *Flotation costs:* Leasing avoids the costs involved in under-writing and floating bonds and shares issue as well as the public disclosure of financial information which is required when companies sell securities to the public.
15. *Disposal problem:* There is no disposal problem associated with the equipment or other facilities at the end of the lease. Of course, this can work to the disadvantages of lessee, if, over the period of the lease, the facilities have increased in value. The lessor will benefit from any increase in value which is likely to occur when real estate is involved, but this increase seldom occurs with equipment.
16. *Higher incomes:* An operating lease will tend to inflate the incomes of early

years of life compared with the expenses resulting from buying the asset. Of course, there might be lower incomes in later years, but management taking a short-run point of view might lease in the hopes of inflating the incomes of the next few years.

17. *A well-defined cost:* For certain purposes (for example, in the case of governmental contract), it is useful to have the well defined costs offered by a lease contract. Buying an asset requires estimating the asset's life, its salvage value, and its depreciation per year. With leasing, one only has to produce the cancelled cheque showing the amount paid to the lessor. With buying, there are differences of opinion.
18. *Maintenance is cheap and certain:* With leasing the maintenance may be contracted. The certainty of maintenance and the fact that its cost is certain is said to make leasing attractive. More exactly, these characteristics make maintenance contracts attractive. These contracts can generally be obtained with purchases as well as with leasing. They do not affect the merit of leasing compared with buying but, rather, are a separate decision.

Disadvantages

The advantages of leasing over other forms of medium-term finance in any given circumstances need to be weighed against the possible **disadvantages**. The disadvantages are listed below:

1. *Ownership flexibility:* A purchaser of equipment avoids any of the restrictions found in leasing agreements concerning the operation of the equipment and the requirement to obtain the lessor's approval to the insurance arrangements. However, the restrictions are not normally onerous and the need to consider such matters carefully by reason of the lease provisions may be a useful safeguard; leasing companies are able to advise lessees about ways of protecting the equipment and the adequacy of insurance coverage.
2. *Residual value:* A lessee gives up some or all of the benefit of the residual value of the equipment at the end of the lease period. For certain types of assets, this may be significant, and the current value of this forgone future benefit needs to be compared with the possible cost savings during the primary lease period.
3. *Taxation:* A company able to take immediate advantage of the 100 per cent first year capital allowance on equipment purchased gives up a part of the value of this investment incentive by leasing, since leasing companies do not normally reflect the whole of the benefit in the calculation of rentals.
4. *Early disposal:* Financial leasing may not be appropriate if a firm foresees only a short-term requirement for an asset. If a lease is cancelled early in the primary lease period, there may be an additional cost to reflect the reduction in the period.
5. *Security value:* A lessee (unlike a firm which buys equipment and is not

required to charge the asset as security for a loan to acquire it) is unable to include the leased equipment in a pool of assets which is then available as security for general borrowing.

6. *Understatement of assets:* The right to use equipment for a major part of its useful life is an intangible asset which is not shown on a lessee's balance sheet unless leased assets are capitalised at economic values. A firm leasing equipment may thus be understating its assets, with the consequence that shareholders, and other users of the firm's accounts, including a possible bidder for its shares or assets, may undervalue the business.
7. *Prestige:* Ownership may be thought to be prestigious and to give an emotive sense of satisfaction denied to lessees! On the other hand, this may become a disadvantage; ownership of a fully depreciated asset can sometimes have the effect of delaying the replacement of outdated equipment by preventing a clear appreciation of the considerations relevant to a replacement decision.
8. *High cost of leasing:* Cost of financing by means of leasing will generally be more costly, on the face value, than other sources, primarily because:
   (a) Leasing Company must pay interest at the market rates from its borrowing sources and must charge a premium or its profits to the 'lessee,"
   (b) The leasing company employs the specialists to design particular lease and also employs people who are thoroughly knowledgeable on all aspects of equipment technically as well as financially. The cost of these people is to be included in the lease rentals. Also the management cost is passed on to the 'lessee'.
9. *Prohibited property improvements:* Under a lease, the lessee is generally prohibited from making improvements on the leased property without the approval the lessor. If the property were owned, this difficulty would not arise. Related to this disadvantage is the fact that it is often hard to obtain financing for improvements on leased property since it is difficult for the lender to obtain a security interest in the improvements. On the other hand, the lessor may agree in the initial lease contract to finance or make certain lease hold improvements specified by the lessee.
10. *Obsolescence considerations:* If a lessee leases (under financial lease) an asset that subsequently become obsolete, it still has to make lease payments over the remaining life of the lease. This is true even if it is unable to use the leased assets. For example, if the firm entered into a 20 years lease on a retail store, which after two years in operation proved unprofitable and had to be abandoned, the firm remains obligated to pay 18 more years of rent.

LEASING AGREEMENT

In recent years, the leasing agreements used by different leasing companies have tended to become broadly alike, but it is unlikely that any form of standard lease generally acceptable to majority of lessors will appear in the near future. Lessors' interpretations of their legal positions are not identical and there will continue to be differences between their individual commercial requirements.

The main features of a financial leasing agreement are: (i) The lessor agrees to purchase an asset for leasing to the lessee who in turn agrees to take the asset on lease. (ii) The lessee takes on the responsibility for checking the condition of the asset at the time of delivery and normally accepts it on the lessor's behalf. The lessor gives no warranty to the lessee as to fitness of the equipment but, where there is no direct contractual arrangement between the lessee and supplier, there is provision in the lease for action to be taken by the lessor on the lessee's behalf against the supplier. (iii) The lessee is afforded possession or quiet enjoyment (the legal term) of the leased asset subject to paying the prescribed rentals and complying with the other lease terms and conditions. (iv) The lessee covenants to insure and maintain the equipment during the period of the lease. (v) The lessee acknowledges that title to the asset remains with the lessor and he is not to dispose of the equipment or do anything to jeopardise the lessor's interest in the equipment. (vi) As user of the equipment, the lessee indemnifies the lessor against any claims made by third parties arising out of the lessor's ownership of the asset. (vii) The leasing agreement stipulates the lessor's rights of action in the event of a default by the lessee during the lease period. (viii) The agreement provides either for the return of the equipment to the lessor at the end of the lease period or the sale of the equipment by the lessee, acting as agent for the lessor.

RISKS IN LEASING

A leasing company entering into a financial lease looks to the lessee for the recovery of the full, or at least a major part of, the outlay on a leased asset. The lessor needs to be assured that the user of the equipment is in a position to meet the rentals payable during the primary lease period as they fall due.

In the event of premature termination of the lease before the end of the primary period, because of default by the lessee or in other circumstances such as a total loss of the equipment, the lessor will require the outstanding capital cost of the equipment to be paid as a lump sum. In the absence of insurance proceeds, the lump sum terminal payment has to be found by the lessee. The terminal payment is usually calculated by discounting future rentals from their due dates to the date of measurement at a rate specified in the lease and, except in the case of total loss of the leased equipment, by deducting therefrom an amount related to its market value. For most types of equipment, it is unlikely that its second-hand value at the date of termination will be high enough to eliminate the outstanding capital cost, so that an unrecovered balance will remain to be paid by the lessee; from time to time there are exceptions (such as aircraft and ships in a period of rapid inflation and other items of equipment in limited supply) which retain a sufficiently high market value.

From a creditworthiness viewpoint, a financial lease is akin to a medium-term loan secured on the equipment. Leasing companies need to make the same enquiries and obtain the same information regarding the credit standing of prospective lessees as banks and other financial institutions do for loan applications.

A credit appraisal is necessarily a subjective assessment of the solvency of a potential lessee. Although the past cannot be ignored, leasing companies place particular emphasis on a lessee's future viability. Criteria taken into account by lessors include: (i) The nature of the lessee's business. (ii) The quality of management. (iii) Future prospects, particularly the adequacy of the forecast future cash flow to meet rentals and other outgoings. (iv) The financial position shown by the latest accounts. (v) The likely value over the primary lease period of the equipment to be leased.

There are several specific factors which may make the overall risk in leasing different from that in other forms of finance. Ways financial leasing may increase the risk include the following.

1. *The inherent risks of ownership:* As owner of the equipment, a lessor may be liable for claims from third parties for losses arising out of the use of the leased asset. In some situations, both the owner and the user are legally responsible. In other cases, the law is uncertain and a lessor may well be involved in expense in defending an action for damages; injured parties may prefer to institute proceedings directly against a leasing company, part of a large financial group, rather than a lessee-what is known as 'deep pocket' syndrome. Although a lessor is normally indemnified by the lessee against any such claims, and may be entitled to the proceeds of insurance covering the equipment against third party liabilities, there will be occasions when the lessee has insufficient resources to meet the indemnity and there is inadequate insurance cover.
2. *Default claims:* The law applying to a claim for repayment of a loan following a default by a borrower is more certain and tested than the corresponding claim by a financial lessor for recovery of the unamortised cost of equipment.
3. *Collateral:* A lessor is financing the acquisition of an individual item of equipment and may be unable to enjoy the benefit of additional security in the same way as a lender who also provides comprehensive banking services to a customer. The lender may have previously arranged collateral security such as a floating charge.
4. *Interest and tax assumptions:* For leases without variation clauses, there is a risk that an adverse change in interest rates or taxation is more detrimental to the lessor's return than the element, if any, included in the rental to compensate the lessor for assuming these risks. In particular, a lessor's cash flow is more sensitive to a change in the rate of corporation tax or in the general basis of taxation than a corresponding medium-term loan. For leases with interest or tax variation clauses, a change may result in higher rentals, which increase the lessor's overall exposure.

There is also the danger for a leasing company that there will be insufficient taxable capacity within its group to obtain immediate benefit of the first year capital allowance (which may have been assumed for rental calculation purposes).

On the other hand, leasing may reduce the level of risk.

1. *Asset recovery:* It may be easier and cheaper for a lessor as owner to repossess leased equipment following a default by the lessee than it would be for a mortgagee or chargee.
2. *Productive investment:* A lessor is leasing income-producing or expense saving equipment and not just augmenting a firm's general body of assets. A lessor is less likely to be propping up a lame duck than a lender.
3. *Value of investment incentive:* A lessee unable to take immediate advantage of the 100 per cent first year capital allowance that would be available if he purchased the equipment receives a benefit to the extent that the capital allowance claimed by the lessor is reflected in the rentals.

The lessor's risk is thus less than that of a lender providing an equivalent medium-term loan. This is a result of the actual reduction in rentals and the improvement in the lessee's overall financial position as a consequence of his paying less for the use of the equipment concerned.

LEASE PROPOSAL ANALYSIS

The lease-*versus*-purchase problem is a hybrid capital budgeting problem that forces the analyst to consider the consequences of alternative forms of financing on the investment decision. Capital budgeting decision implies that all new financing would be undertaken in accordance with firm's optimal capital structure. When analysing an asset that is to be leased, the analysis must be altered to consider financing through leasing as opposed to the use of the more traditional debt and equity sources of funds. Thus, the lease-*versus*- purchase decision requires a standard capital-budgeting type of analysis, as well as an analysis of two alternative financing packages.

Thus, the lease-purchase decision can be viewed as consisting of two separate issues:

(i) *Should the asset be purchased using the firm's optimal financing mix?*

(ii) *Should the asset be leased?*

The answer to the first question can be obtained through an analysis of the project's net present value. However, there are three basic problems in analysing buy *versus* lease decisions. One is the definition of the cash flows to be used. The second is the choice of the rate of discount. The third problem is to match the appropriate rate of discount with the choice of the cash flow.

A major problem with the cash flow calculation is the inclusion or exclusion of the debt component of the lease flows. The objective is to make the lease analysis comparable in terms of debt characteristics with the buy analysis. Generally this means extracting elements of the lease cash flows.

There are *three* basic choices for the rate of discount to be used: (ii) the after-tax borrowing rate; (ii) the before-tax borrowing rate; and (iii) some type of risk-adjusted rate such as the weighted average cost of capital.

If we assume that there are four possible sets of cash flows (there are more) and three discount rates (again, there are more), there are then twelve different ways of combining the two elements. If we then recognise the possibility of using different rates of discount to discount different types of cash flows for either the buy or the lease components, we can readily see why there has not been agreement on analysing buy *versus* lease decisions.

Finally, there is the matter of comparing the cash flows of one alternative (buy) with the other alternative (lease). However, regardless of whether the asset should or should not be purchased, it may be advantageous for the firm to lease it. That is, the cost savings accruing through leasing might be so great as offset a negative net present value or add to a positive value. In addition, while a "lessee" is in the process of decision, whether to purchase the equipment (either with own generated cash or with borrowed funds), or to lease it there are many other aspects to be considered. For example, in some cases it is exceedingly difficult to borrow funds, in order to finance the purchase of the equipment by an organisation. This position may have arrived because of government policy, credit rating of the company, adverse debt-equity ratio, time factor to get the sanction from financial institutions, and lastly, the opportunity to utilise companies capital for more profitable use and its capital cost. Normally a growing enterprise has a higher return on its own capital than the prevailing rate of interest on borrowing. In other words the capital cost of company's funds is higher than the borrowed funds. In the case of acquiring the equipment by owning either with the complete finance provided by the company or 30% is provided by the company and balance is financed by borrowing, the overall capital cost in these cases will be: (i) in case of own funds, the cost will be equivalent to the total returns on the capital of the enterprise; (ii) in case of borrowed funds, the cost will be: interest of 70% of the cost of equipment; plus enterprise's capital cost on 30% of the cost of capital. Therefore while computing the net cash outflows it is essential to include firms capital cost also. There situations encourage the use of leveraged leasing.

Thus, provided the financial manager recognises the major aim of the lease agreement it is quite easy for him to classify a lease as either a financing decision or investment decision. In some cases the asset to be leased or purchased will represent a mandatory investment: the project must be accepted, and the only decision is whether to acquire the asset by purchase or by lease. In such cases, lease analysis is essentially a financing decision, and we attempt to evaluate the lease against alternative ways of financing the asset. In other cases the lease arrangement itself is important in deciding whether to accept or reject a capital project. For example, some capital projects may only be available by lease: in other cases, it may not be sound financially to buy an asset but leasing the same assest may be quite attractive. In this situation, lease proposals are incorporated in the capital budget as discrete projects, and the evaluation process should permit management to properly rank all proposed capital expenditures (including lease projects) in order of desirability.

ESTABLISHING A LEASE QUOTE

The lessor seeks to maximise present worth and will strive to negotiate a lease such that the present value of the lease payments plus the present value of the residual equal or exceeds the cost of the equipment. The lessor applies a gross discount rate to the cash flow (or quotes a lease rate) to cover the cost of capital and any additional expenses of leasing (maintenance, operating. and insurance costs, if assumed). The process of determining a lease quote by a lessor is demonstrated in Example-1.

Example-1

A lessor may purchase equipment for ₹ 1,00,000. It has a five-year life and the lease will be for 5 years. The projected salvage value is ₹ 10,000 to be discounted at 25% owing to higher rate of uncertainty connected to the estimate. The company is earning 10% (after– taxes) on its marginal investments. Hence, a 10% discount rate is to be used in computing present values of debt financing and lease financing. Determine the annual lease payments made at the start of each year and then at the end of each year.

Solution

First, determine the present value of the salvage using 25% rate.

PV =₹ 10,000 × 0.32768 = ₹ 3,276.8

Next determine the annual lease payments if they are made in advance. This requires finding the amount of payment which when discounted at 10% for 5 years will equal the cost of the amount less the present value of the salvage value (₹ 1,00,000–₹ 3,276.80)=₹ 96,723.20.

₹ 96,723.20=initial lease payment plus present value of lease payments made at start of each successive years up to 1 to 5th year.

₹ 96,723.20=lease payment+lease payment (3.169865)

$$\text{lease payment} = \frac{₹\ 96,723.20}{4.169865} = ₹\ 23,195.76$$

3.169865 is the present value factor for 4 years at 10%. Last, determine the annual lease payment if it is made at the end of each year.

₹ 96,723.20=lease payment (3.790787)

$$\text{lease payment} = \frac{₹\ 96,723.20}{3.790787} = ₹\ 25,515.33$$

3.790787 is the present value factor for 5 years at 10%.

Several observations should be made relating to developing a lease quote:

(1) A higher expected residual value lowers the minimum acceptable rental, and vice versa.

(2) The residual value is discounted at a higher rate due to the uncertainty attached to the estimate. With an asset having a longer life, this uncertainty would probably be greater.

(3) If the lessee assumed the operating, maintenance, or insurance, the lessor might lower his bid.

(4) If the lessor had tax advantages, economies of large-scale operation, or lower financing charges, some portion might be passed to the lessee in the form of lower lease payments.

(5) The timing of the lease payments, whether at the beginning or end of the period, whether monthly or quarterly, affects the amount of payment.

(6) Many items are negotiable and depend upon the position of both lessor and lessee.

LEASE *VERSUS* PURCHASE: A FINANCING DECISION

Suppose a firm decides that the purchase of a certain asset desirable but prefers not to finance the acquisition solely with equity funds. The firm can pay for the assets either with borrowed funds or with a financial lease. To choose between these two methods of financing requires consideration of following factors:

1. *Capital adequacy:* It is important that a firm has adequate shareholders' equity for its planned level of trading. Any possible problems should be eliminated by issuing new capital, or retaining a greater proportion of earnings, rather than taking on further debt obligations (assuming loan or lease finance were to be available).

2. *Financing strategy:* The method of finance to be selected for a new project should be compatible with a firm's overall financing strategy. It may be appropriate to provide for a mix of financial instruments in order to reduce risk. Companies may wish to structure debt payments so as to avoid loan maturities coinciding and to arrange sources of finance so as not to be unduly dependent on particular types of debt, such as foreign currency loans giving risk to possible exchange losses. The part to be played by leasing in a firm's overall financing strategy may well depend on the view taken concerning the extent to which leasing may enable the firm to increase its overall debt-raising capacity.

3. *Liquidity:* A firm needs to retain sufficient liquidity to meet any sudden unexpected shortfall in cash inflows or additional operating or capital expenditure.

4. *Availablity* The initial availability of the various types of finance should be ascertained. Fixed-rate finance for the period required might, for example, only be available by leasing the equipment rather than through loan

arrangements. Firms should also assess the importance of a guaranteed continuing availability of the finance, as in the case of a financial lease, rather than the possibility of repayment on demand as normally stipulated in overdraft and certain other types of loan arrangements.

5. *Marshalling of security:* There may be ways of arranging finance secured on the assets of a firm, including fixed or floating charges and leasing, which increase its overall debt capacity.
6. *Benefit eligibility:* Although most types of investment incentives are equally available for purchased and leased equipment, it is important that the method of finance does not adversely affect a firm's eligibility for government grants and other benefits.
7. *Restrictions:* The chosen method of finance needs to comply with all restrictive covenants and governmental regulations. There may be borrowing restrictions in a firm's Memorandum or Articles of Association or in a debenture trust deed. Additional borrowing may not be permitted under exchange control regulations.
8. *Administrative convenience:* Firms may be attracted to those methods of finance, including leasing, which simplify book-keeping procedures and assist expense budgeting and cash flow forecasting.

The second stage in the financing decision is the comparison of the costs of the various available sources of finance. To simplify the financial evaluation, it is necessary to make certain assumptions concerning the characteristics of the leasing and borrowing cash flows.

The principal assumptions made (usually on an implicit basis) when comparing the costs of leasing and borrowing are as follows.

1. The decision to acquire the equipment has already been taken by the firm carrying out the evaluation.
2. Lease finance is equivalent to borrowing and does not increase debt capacity.
3. The firm has sufficient other borrowing requirements to remain in a debt situation. There are not periods of overall cash surplus.
4. Rentals and interest rates equally reflect the firm's creditworthiness.
5. Lease finance and the available forms of borrowing have similar risk characteristics, i.e., there are no differences in the types of security interest in the equipment afforded to the providers of the finance or in other terms such as a lender's right to require repayment on demand.
6. Inflation may be disregarded. All of the cash flows are money rather than real cash flows.
7. Any uncertainty about future corporation tax rates is ignored, so that tax cash flows may be discontinued at the same rate as other cash flows.
8. There are no economies of scale achievable by leasing, for example, as a

consequence of the lessor negotiating with the supplier a reduction in the cost of the equipment or of being able to obtain a higher selling price for the equipment at the end of the lease period.

9. Leasing provides the best means of a firm taking advantage of any first year capital allowances from which, because of a lack of taxable capacity, it cannot itself immediately benefit.

CONVENTIONAL METHOD OF ANALYSIS

Discounted Cash Flow Criteria

The conventional method of comparing the merit of leasing with those of debt financing is to compare the discounted present value of the cash disbursements associated with these two alternatives. Since the operating revenues from the asset being acquired are unaffected by the source of funds used to acquire it, the policy that minimises the cost of financing necessarily maximises net present value.

Below is a list of symbols that will be used to explain this conventional method of analysis:

P = loan payment: interest and amortisation of principal

L_t = lease payment in period t

I_t = interest payment in period t

D_t = depreciation in period t

O_t = incremental operating costs of ownership in period t

t_c = firm's tax rate on ordinary income

t_g = tax rate applicable to gains and losses on the disposal of fixed assets

S_N = expected cash value of asset in period N

K_d = explict after tax cost of new debt capital

B = book value of asset in period N

K_s = discount rate applied to residual value of the asset

The cost to lease is the sum of the after-tax lease payments discounted by the after-tax cost of debt capital, as expressed in equation (1):

Cost to lease with end-of-period payments

$$= \sum_{t=1}^{N} \frac{L_t(1-tc)}{(1+K_d)^t} \qquad (1)$$

If lease payments are made at the start of each period, we would sum from t=0 to t=N–1. This would have the effect of reducing the lease payment.

The cost of the borrow and purchase alternative is the sum of loan payment for each period plus operating expenses less interest, depreciation, and operating expense tax shields, less the after-tax salvage value discounted to present value at a discount rate appropriate to the cash flows. The cost of borrowing and purchasing is expressed in equation (2):

$$\text{Cost of purchase} = \sum_{t=1}^{N} \frac{P + O_t - (I_t + D_t + O_t)tc}{(1+k_d)^t} = \frac{SN - (SN - B)tg}{(1+k_s)^N} \quad (2)$$

According to the NPV criterion, if cost to lease is less than the cost to purchase, the company should resort to leasing; and if the costs to lease is greater than cost to purchase, it should resort to debt financing. The methodology for comparison is demonstrated in Example-2.

Example-2

Assume the conditions and solutions to example 1 and that the machine may also be purchased by the company at ₹ 1,00,000 financed through a 16% bank loan, and depreciated on straight-line basis over its 5-year life. The loan would be paid back in five *equal* annual instalments. The tax rate is 50%. Determine the NPVs of the three alternatives: lease with start-of-year payments, lease with end-of-year payments, and purchase, assuming that the operating costs are the same whether the machine is leased or purchased.

Solution

First, consider the lease with start-of-year payments. The present value cost (after-taxes) of lease is tabulated below:

TABLE-1

(1) *Year*	(2) *Lease cost*	(3) *Tax shield*	(4) *Cash outflow*	(5) *Discount factor*	(6) *Present value of lease*
0	₹ 23,196	₹ 11,598	₹ 11,598	1.00000	₹ 11,598.80
1	23,196	11,598	11,598	.925926	10,738.89
2	23,196	11,598	11,598	.857339	9,943.42
3	23,196	11,598	11,598	.793821	9,206.74
4	23,196	11,598	11,598	.735030	8,524.88
					₹ 50,011.93

Next, consider the lease with end-of-year payments. The present value cost (after-taxes) of lease is tabulated below:

TABLE-2

(1) *Year*	(2) *Lease cost*	(3) *Tax shield*	(4) *Cash outflow*	(5) *Discount factor*	(6) *Present value of lease*
1	₹ 25,515	₹ 12,757.5	₹ 12,757.5	0.925926	₹ 11,812.50
2	25,515	12,757.5	12,757.5	0.857339	10,937.50
3	25,515	12,757.5	12,757.5	0.793821	10,127.17
4	25,515	12,757.5	12,757.5	0.735030	9,377.15
5	25,515	12,757.5	12,757.5	0.680583	8,682.54
					₹ 50,936.86

The loan schedule is the amount needed to amortise ₹ 1,00,000 over a 5-year period at 16%.

Loan repayment = ₹ 1,00,000 (0.30540938)
= ₹ 30,541

The loan interest payments and depreciation represent tax deductible expense as would be operating costs, which are not considered in this example. The yearly cash flows are determined in tabular fore as shown in table-3. The table shows that the present value of the cash outflow is ₹ 63,734.82; the present value of the salvage is ₹ 3,276.80 (discounted at 25%), so the present value of the net cash outflow is ₹ 60,458.02 if the machine is purchased.

In this cash the present value of the net cash outflow of the purchases is greater than the present value of either of the two lease plans, so leasing represents the better choice.

TABLE-3

Present Value Cost (After-taxes) of Debt Plau

(Amount in ₹)

(1) Year	(2) Loan Repayment	(3) Principal	(4) Interest	(5) Balance	(6) Depre-ciation	(7) Tax shield [(4)+(6)](0.5)	(8) Cash out-flow (1)-(7)	(9) Present value at 8%
1	30,541	14,541	16,000	85,459	18000	17,000.00	13,541.00	12,537.96
2	30,541	16,868	13,673	68,591	18,000	15,836.50	14,704.50	12,606 74
3	30,541	19,566	10,975	49,025	18,000	14,487.50	16,053.50	12,743.60
4	30,541	22,697	7,844	26,328	18,000	12,922.00	17,169.00	12,619.73
5	30,541	26,328	4,213	—	18,000	11,106.50	19,434.50	13,226.79
								63,734.82

Criticism of the discounted cash flow approach

The use of the discounted cash flow approach has been criticised by Richard F. Vancil[1] on the ground that the costs so computed reflect the intermingled effects of tax savings and the amount of funds provided. Usually, leasing and debt financing provide the company with different amounts of financing over the life of the capital asset. But Vancil feels that since alternative sources of financing are always available to the company, any method that purports to compare the costs of leasing and borrowing should not be influenced by the amount of financing provided under each plan. He claims, therefore, that the discounted cash flow method gives management a misleading comparison of the true costs of leasing and borrowing.

The following quotations from Vancil's article give the gist of his argument:[2]

Recognising that other sources of money are available (means that it is desirable to eliminate the difference in the amounts of financing provided when comparing specific proposals.

1. Richard F. Vancil, "Lease of borrow—New Method of Analysis "*Harvard Business Review* (September-October, 1961), pp. 138-159.
2. Ibid., pp. 138-159.

Holding constant the amount of financing provided.....allows us to isolate one of the most important differences between debt and lease financing: the difference in permissible income-tax deductions.

In the second quotation, Vancil states explicitly that the key consideration in a decision to lease or borrow is the difference in tax savings. To isolate the tax affect in lease-or-borrow decisions, Vancil has devised the Basic Interest Rate (BIR) method, which we shall describe below.

There is, in addition, a still more serious objection to the discounted cash flow approach. Since leasing provides more financing than debt the company will have more fixed charges under the lease plan than under the debt plan. These higher fixed charges may prompt investors to discount the earnings (or dividends) of the company at a higher rate. The discounted cash flow method, however, fails to make allowance for the resulting difference in the effect of the two financing alternatives on the cost of equity funds. The Basic Interest Rate (BIR) approach, on the other hand, compares leasing with borrowing only after it has removed the difference in the amount of funds provided by the two financing plans. Hence, although the Basic Interest Rate method was originally designed to focus on the different tax effects, its particular merit lies in its ability to remove any difference in the effects of leasing and debt financing on the firm's capital structure.

BASIC INTEREST RATE APPROACH

If a company is to decide whether to borrow or to lease a particular piece of equipment and it is to earn a return of k on its marginal investments, but can borrow funds from the equipment manufacturer or a bank at a lower interest rate of r. This borrowing rate of, r, which we shall designate on the company's "basic interest rate" plays an important part in removing the difference in the amounts of financing provided by leasing and borrowing.

TABLE-4

Case—I: Lease Payment Made in Advance

Present Value Cost (After Taxes) of Leasing *(Amount in ₹)*

Price of capital asset							₹ 1,00,000.00
Tax savings provided by lease payments in case of imputed interest							
(1) Year	*(2) Lease Cost*	*(3) Loan Payment*	*(4) Interest [(3)x16]*	*(5) Cash outflow [(2)—(4)]*	*(6) Tax shield [(2)-(4)×.50]*	*(7) Present value of lease at 10%*	
0	23,196	1,00,000.00	—	23,196.00	11,598.00	11,598.00	
1	23,196	76,804.00	12,288.64	10,907.36	5,453.68	4,957.89	
2	23,196	65,896.64	10,543.46	12,652.54	6,326.27	5,228.31	
3	23,196	53,244.10	8,519.06	14,676.94	7,338.47	5,513.24	
4	23,196	38,567.16	6,170.75	17,025.25	8,512.63	5,814.24	33,111.94
Total present value cost (after taxes) of leasing							
66,888.06							

Under the BIR method, the cost of leasing is equal to the price of the capital asset minus the present value of the tax savings provided by the noninterest portion of the lease payment. Both the interest and noninterest portions of each rental payment are tax deductible. However to remove the difference in the amount of financing provided by leasing and borrowing, the BIR method focuses on the tax savings associated with the noninterest portion of the leases payments. Applying this approach to the preceding numerical example, we find that after eliminating the tax effects of imputed interest expenses, the present value cost of leasing are ₹ 66,888.06 in Case I and ₹ 75,883.77 in Case II respectively. (See Table-4 and-5).

TABLE-5

Case—II : Lease Payment Made at End of the Period

Present Value Cost (After Taxes) of Leasing *(Amount in ₹)*

Price of capital asset							₹ 1,00,000.00
Tax savings provided by lease payments in case of imputed interest							
(1) Year	(2) Lease Cost	(3) Loan Payment	(4) Interest [(3) x .16]	(5) Cash outflow [(2)—(4)]	(6) tax shield [(2)–(4)×.50	(7) Present value of lease at 10%	
1	25,515	1,00.000.00	16,000 00	9,515.00	4,757.50	4,324.99	
2	25,515	90,485.00	14,474.60	11,037.40	5,518.70	4,560.93	
3	25,515	79,444.60	12,711.14	12,80.86	6,401.93	4,809.83	
4	25,515	66,640.74	10,602.52	14,852.48	7,426.24	5,072.20	
5	25,515	51,788.26	8,286.12	17,228.88	8,614.44	5,348,88	24,11623
			Total present value cost (after-taxes) of leasing				75,883.77

Next, for purposes of comparison, the cost of debt financing must to be determined. Accordingly the case of preceding numerical example is tabulated below:

TABLE-6

Present-Value Cost (After-taxes) of Debt Financing

Price of capital asset				₹ 1,00,000.00
Tax savings provided by depreciation				
(1) Year	(2) Depreciation	(3) Depreciation after taxes	(4) Present value of own	
1	₹ 18,000	₹ 9,000	₹ 8,181.82	
2	18,000	9,000	7,438.02	
3	18,000	9,000	6,761.83	
4	18,000	9,000	6,147.12	
5	18,000	9,000	5,588.30	₹ 34,117.09
	Total present value cost (after taxes) of debt financing			₹ 65,882.91

We find that the present value cost of debt financing to be ₹ 65,882.91; the present value of the salvage is ₹ 3,276.80, so the present value of the net cash outflow is ₹ 62,606.11 if the machine is purchased. Thus, present value cost of leasing of either of the two lease plans after eliminating the tax effects of imputed interest expense is higher than the present value cost of debt financing. It may be noted that the discounted cash flow approach applied to the same problem earlier showed the leasing plans to be cheaper than debt financing. This disparity occurs because the discounted cash flow approach reflects the combined effects of financial leverage and tax savings, while the BIR approach reflects only the effects of tax savings.

BOWER-HERRINGER-WILLIAMSON METHOD

In yet another approach to evaluate lease *versus* borrowing, Bower, Herringer, and Williamson (BHW) divide the payments streams into two parts: the cash flows associated with financing and the cash flow associated with tax savings.[3] As in our present-value example, they assume that the loan payment schedule is of the same configuration as the lease payment schedule. This assumption places the loan on an equivalent basis with the lease.

Analysing the cash flows associated with financing first, Bower, Herringer, and Williamson measure the incremental impact of a loan by subtracting the present value of lease payments from the present value of loan payments. Where both are discounted at the debt rate. For our example problem, the financial advantage of leasing is determined as follows:

Present value of loan payment	₹ 1,00,000.00
Present value of lease payment	96,725.00
Financial Advantage	₹ 3,275.00

TABLE-7

Calculation of decrease in tax payments with leasing— BHW Method

End of year	*Leasing tax shield**	*Borrowing tax shield***	*Decrease in tax payments with leasing*	*Present value of of decreases (10%)*
1	₹ 12,757.5	₹ 17,000.00	–₹ 4,242.50	–₹ 3,856.82
2	12,757.5	15,836.50	–3,079.00	–2,544.63
3	12,757.5	14,487.50	–1,730.00	–1,299.98
4	12,757.5	12,922.00	–346.50	–236.66
5	12,757.5	11,106.50	1,469.00	912.13
				–₹ 7,025.96

* From Table-2 **From Table-3

3. Richard S. Bower, Herringer, F.C., and Williamson, Peter J. "Lease: Evaluation," *Accounting Review* 41 (April 1 1966) pp. 257-266.

The present value of the lease payments is determined by discounting the lease payments in column (2) of Table-1 by 10%.

The next step is to determine the incremental present value of the tax savings associated with leasing. The calculations are presented in table-7. When these decreases in tax payments are discounted by the cost of capital rate, we obtain what BHW call the *operating advantage* of the lease.

The decision to lease or borrow is made on the basis of whether the operating advantage of the lease exceeds its financial disadvantage. If so, lease financing should be used; if not, debt financing should be employed. In our case, there is actual operating advantage associated with leasing. Therefore the former holds, and lease financing should be employed, according to the analysis.

LEASE *VERSUS* PURCHASE: A CAPITAL BUDGETING DECISION

In lease versus purchase as a financing decision, it is indicated that the capital budgeting decision has been made (the acquisition was mandatory), and our concern lay in selecting the optimum mode for financing. Thus, we presumed conditions of certainty as to the financing and lease payment cash flows, and discounted them at the after-tax cost of debt. *By contrast, if the firm were considering the lease proposal as a distinct capital project to be ranked against all other projects, the cash flows would not be considered-certain. Sales and operating costs change, tax-rates and the like change frequently with business conditions, and sometimes lease payments also vary with business conditions. In this case, the financial manager would discount the separate cash flows of ownership or leasing at a rate appropriate to the level of risk.*

Moreover, it is axiomatic in capital budgeting that the return on investment be computed independently of the cost of financing yet in Example—2 interest charges were explicitly included in the ownership calculation. *The reason for including interest in the calculation was the need to find the difference in the after-tax cash flows between the leasing and borrowing alternatives. The project had already been accepted, and the decision was made independently of financing.* We had to look directly to those cash flows which would affect the financing decision.

JOHNSON-LEWELLEN APPROACH

Johnson-Lewellen viewed the question of purchase or lease as two distinct, independent, and mutually exclusive projects.[4] Further, it is not necessary to make any assumption of borrowing to *meet the purchase price of the asset.* These modificator change the structure of the calculations in three ways;

(1) It is necessary to calculate the differences between net present value of ownership and the net present value of leasing as a basis for the decision.

(2) The approach follows the general rule in capital budgeting of separating the

4. W. Johnson and Lewellen, W.G.: Analysis of the Lease or buy decision. "*Journal of Finance,* vol. 27., September 1972, pp. 815-823.

return on a project from the cost of financing. Specifically, we delete the interest charges from the costs of ownership in determining net present value.

(3) Allowance is made for the uncertainties of the operating cash flows, tax shields, and residuals by discounting the first two by the firm's cost of capital and the latter by a rate appropriate to the risk level.

The net present value anticipated from purchase of the asset, then, is the sum of the present value of the net after-tax operating profits (revenues less operating costs) plus the discounted after-tax cash proceeds from salvage less the cost of the asset. Similarly, the net present value of the leasing project would be the present value of the revenues less the lease payments and other costs, if any, associated with leasing. In comparing the net present values of the two alternatives, the revenues are assumed to be the same in both cases, which allows their deletion from the analysis.

In practice, two steps are required. We first determine whether the project is acceptable if purchased. Then we compare the net present values of ownership versus leasing using Equation (3):

$$\Delta NPV = NPV\ (purchase) - NPV\ (lease)$$

$$= \sum_{t=1}^{N} \frac{tc(D_t) - O_t(1-tc)}{(1+K)^t} + \frac{SN-(SN-B)tg}{(1+K_s)N} - C + \sum_{t=1}^{N} \frac{L_t(1+t_c)}{(1+K_d)^t} \qquad (3)$$

where

ΔNPV=difference between NPV (purchase) and NPV (lease)

K=firm's marginal cost of capital. Excluding revenues from both NPV calculations the net present value of ownership is the sum of depreciation tax shield, $t_c(D_t)$ is the after-tax operating costs, $O_t\ (1-t_c)$, for each period discounted at the firm's cost of capital (r) plus the after-tax salvage SN–(SN–B)tg discounted at some higher rate (K_s) less the cost of equipment (c). The present value of leasing in the comparison (again excluding revenues) is the sum of after tax rented for each period, $L_t\ (1-t_c)$, discounted at the cost of debt capital (K_d). This amount is added to the present value of ownership since it represents a negative NPV because the lease involves exclusively cash outflows. If ΔNPV is positive, purchasing is preferred while if ΔNPV is negative, leasing is preferred.

The process of deciding between purchasing and leasing is demonstrated in example 3 and 4. In example 3 we examine only the purchase, while in example 4 we determine the difference in the purchase and lease costs using Equation (3) to determine which is preferable.

Example-3

A corporation may purchase or lease equipment costing ₹ 1,00,000 and having a salvage value of ₹ 10,000. If purchased, the equipment would be depreciated using straight line method of depreciation over its 5-year life. If leased, the lease payment would be made at year's and the cost would be ₹ 28,773.40. In either case operating revenues would be increased by ₹ 50,000 per year and if the equipment is purchased operating costs would be increased by ₹ 5,000. The corporation's tax rate is 50%, its cost of capital 16%, risk adjusted discount rate for salvage 20%, and its after-tax cost of debt 5%. Assume that investment tax credits are the same if purchased or leased and committed for (the sake of simplicity in this example), and determine the NPV of the purchase.

Solution

The change in corporation's income statement and cash flows are tabulated below:

TABLE-8

Changes in Corporation's Income Statement

	Year 1	*Year 2*	*Year 3*
Revenues	₹ 50,000	₹ 50,000	₹ 50,000
Operating expenses	– 5,000	– 5,000	– 5,000
Depreciation	– 18,000	– 18,000	– 18,000
Earnings before taxes	₹ 27,000	₹ 27,000	₹ 27,000
Taxes at 50%	– 13,500	– 13,500	– 13,500
Earnings after taxes	₹ 13,500	₹ 13,500	₹ 13,500

Change in Corporation's Cash Flows

	Year 1	*Year 2*	*Year3*
Depreciation	₹ 18,000	₹ 18,000	₹ 18,000
Earnings after taxes	13,500	13,500	13,500
Cash Flow	₹ 31,500	₹ 31,500	₹ 1,500

The cash flow are shown discounted to present value below. The 10% rate is applied to the operating cash flows, while 20% is applied to the salvage value.

TABLE-9

Time	*Amount*	*Discount factor*	*Present Value*
Present	–₹ 1,00,000	1,00,000	–₹ 1,00,000
1.	31,500	.86207	27,155
2.	31,500	.74316	23,409
3.	31,500	.64066	20,181
4.	31,500	.55229	17,397
5.	31,500	.47611	14,997
6.	10,000	.40188	4,019
			NPV = ₹ 7,158

Since the NPV of the purchase is positive, the purchase should be acceptable. However, the lease may be better than purchase. This determination is made using Equation (3), as demonstrated in Example-4.

The analysis illustrates the impact of choosing discount rates unique to the cash flows of ownership and leasing. A higher degree of risk surrounds the cash flows associated with ownership; therefore, these are discounted at the firm's cost of capital and at higher rates for salvage values. The lease cash flows, supported by contractual agreements, are discounted at the after-tax cost of debt capital.

Example-4

Using the information provided in Example—3, determine the ΔNPV of the lease and purchase employing Equation (3).

Solution

Employing Equation (3) in a sequential manner, we have the following:

$$\sum_{t=1}^{5} \frac{t_c(D_t)-O_t(1-t_c)}{(1+K)^t}$$

= ₹ 9,000 – ₹ 2,500) (.86207) + (₹ 9,000 – ₹ 2,500) (.74316) + (₹ 9,000 – ₹ 2,500) (.64066) + (₹ 9,000 – ₹ 2,500) (.55229) + (₹ 9,000 – ₹ 2,500) (.47611) = ₹ 5,603.46 + ₹ 4,830.54 + ₹ 4,164.29. + ₹ 3,589.88 + ₹ 3,094.22

= ₹ 21,282.89

$$\frac{\text{SN - (SN - B)}tg}{(1+K_S)\text{N}} = ₹\ 10{,}000(0.401878)$$

= ₹ ₹ 4018.78 C = 1,00,000

$$\sum_{t=1}^{5} \frac{L_t(1-tc)}{(1+K_d)^t} = ₹\ 14386.5(.9524) + ₹\ 14386.5(.9070)+$$

₹ 14386.5 (.8638) + ₹ 14386.5 (.8227) ₹ 14386.5 (.7835)

= ₹ 13,701.70 + ₹ 13,048.55 + ₹ 12,427.05 + ₹ 11,835.77 + ₹ 11271.82

= ₹ 62,284

Δ NPV = ₹ 21,282.89 + ₹ 4,019 – ₹ 1,00,000 + ₹ 62,284.92

=–₹ 12,413.19

The negative NPV means that leasing is preferable to purchasing:

The analysis is not limited to net present value; internal rate of return may used following the same guidelines in comparison of the lease *versus* borrow-purchase financial decision and discretionary lease *versus* purchase decision.

INTERNAL-RATE-OF-RETURN ANALYSIS

Instead of computing the present value of cash outflows for the two financing alternatives, we would compute the internal rate of return. This approach avoids the problem of having to choose a discount rate. In general, the managers feel more comfortable in comparing percentages than they do in comparing present values. The methodology for comparison of lease is demonstrated in Example-5.

Example-5

Modern Industries is considering the leasing of special handling equipment for a period of 20 year. The lease will cost ₹ 20,000 per year, with payments in advance. As a result of using the machine, costs will be reduced by ₹ 23,000 per year. If Modern has a marginal tax rate of 48%, determine the internal rate of return of the machine.

Solution

Determine the cash flows for each year, noting that the lease payments are made in advance.

	Income Statement		*Cash Inflow (year-end)*
Reduction in cost	₹ 23,000		₹ 23,000
Lease payment	–20,000		
Added EBT	₹ 3,000		₹ 23,000
Added taxes	–1,440		–1,440
After tax profit	₹ 1,560	Cash Inflow	–₹ 21,560

Since the lease payment is made at the beginning of the year the firm would pay ₹ 20,000 at the beginning and get ₹ 21,560 back at the end. The solution table is presented below:

Time	*Amount*		*Discount factor*		*Present Value*
Present	– ₹ 20,000	×	1	=	– ₹ 20,000
1-19	1,560	×	Unknown	=	Unknown
20	21,560	×	Unknown	=	Unknown

As a first estimate of the IRR, consider only the ₹ 1,560 cash flow per year for 19 years:

₹ 1,560, DF= ₹ 20,000

DF = ₹ 20,000/₹ 1,560

= 12.82

This corresponds to approximately 5%. Since an added ₹ 21,560 will be received in the twentieth year, a good first estimate could be 7%. A solution table using 7% is presented below

Solution Table for 7%

Time	*Amount*		*Discount factor*		*Present Value*
Present	–₹ 20,000	×	1	=	–₹ 20,000
1-19	1,560	×	10.3356	=	16,123
20	21,560	×	.2584	=	5,571
					NPV = ₹ 1,694

Since the NPV is positive, a higher rate must be used. The solution table for 8% is given below:

Solution Table for 8%

Time	*Amount*		*Discount factor*		*Present Value*
Present	– ₹ 20,000	×	1	=	–₹ 20,000
1-19	1,560	×	9.6036	=	14,982
20	21,560	×	.2145	=	4,624
				NPV =	₹ 394

The actual IRR lies between 7% and 8%. Linear interpolation can be used to determine the actual values as shown in Figure-1. Note that at the actual IRR the NPV = 0. The width of the lower scale is ₹ 394 + ₹ 1,694 = ₹ 2,088, as shown. The zero value is ₹ 394/₹ 2088 = .189 of the way from 8%. Therefore the internal rate of return is 8% – .189% = 7.811%.

FIGURE-1

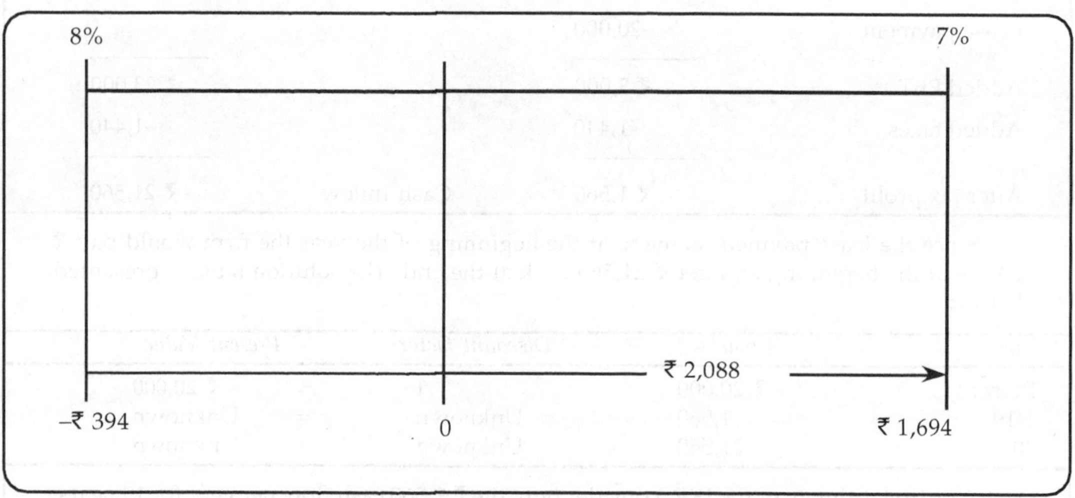

ILLUSTRATIVE PROBLEMS

1. PSEB has decided to buy a special generator plant costing ₹ 12,00,000. It can finance the project with a ten-year mortgage bond issue. The interest rate would be 12%, and the loan is payable at the beginning of each of the ten years. In essence, the first payment serves as a down payment. The company's tax rate is 33.33%, and the investment tax credit of 10% is available at the outset. The company uses straight-line depreciation, but the asset has an economic life of 15 years and falls into the 15-year property category for depreciation purposes. At the end of 10 years, however, the company expects to sell the asset at its then existing book value. In addition to financing the project with debt, PSEB is considering a sale and leasebank arrangement with Power Finance Company. The generator plant would be sold, and lease payments of ₹ 1,00,000 per year would be required at the beginning of each of the next 10 years. On the basis of the present value of cash outflows, which of the two financing alternative is better?

Solution

Present value of the total cash flows under lease alternative is presented below:

(1) End of year	(2) Lease Payment	(3) Tax shield (1) (0.333)	(4) Cash outflow (2)-(3)	(5) Present value of Cash Outflows (8%)
0	₹ 1,60,000	—	₹ 1,60,000	₹ 1,60,000
1-9	1,60,000	₹ 53,333	1,06,667	6,66,338
10	—	53,333	–53,333	–24,703
				Present value of total cash outflows = ₹ 8,01,635

* After-tax cost of debt = 12% (1 – 0.333) = 8%.

Mortgage payment required at the beginning of each year:

₹ 12,00,000—investment tax credit of ₹ 1,20,000

$$= \sum_{t=1}^{n} \frac{x}{(1+.12)^t}$$

₹ 10,80,000 = $x + 5.3282x$

$$x = \frac{₹\ 10,80,000}{6.3282}$$

x = ₹ 1,70,665

Depreciator = ₹ 12,00,000/15

= ₹ 80,000 per year

Residual value at the end of year 10

= ₹ 12,00,000–(10 × ₹ 80,000) = ₹ 4,00,000.

The debt alternative has a lower present value of cash outflows and is best as shown in the table.

(in ₹)

(1) End of year	(2) Loan payment	(3) Principal owing at end of year	(4) Annual Interest	(5) Depre-ciation	(6) Tax Shield [(4)+(5)].333	(7) Residual Value	(8) Cash outflowss after taxes (2)–(6)–(7)]	(9) Present cash outflows (8%)
0	1,70,665	9,09,335	0	0	0	—	1,70,665	1,70,665
1	1,70,665	8,47,790	1,09,120	80,000	63.040	—	1,07,625	99,653
2	1,70,665	7,78,860	1.01,735	80,000	60,578	—	1,10,087	94,382
3	1,70,665	7,01,658	93,463	80,000	57,821	—	1,12,844	89,579

4	1,70,665	6,15,192	84,199	80,000	54,733	—	1.15,932	85,213
5	1,70,665	5,18,350	73,823	80,000	51,274	—	1,19,391	81,255
6	1,70,665	4,09,887	62,202	80,000	47,401	—	1,23,264	77,677
7	1,70,665	2,88,408	49,186	80,000	43,062	—	1,27,603	74,455
8	1,70,665	1,52,352	34,609	80,000	38,203	—	1,32,462	71,565
9	1,70,634*	0	18,282	80,000	32,761	—	1,37,873	68,971
10	0	0	0	80,000	26,667	4,00,000	– 4,26,667	–1,97,629
								7,15,786

* This payment is smaller than the others because it is residual.

2. Sandhya Enterprises is attempting to decide whether to lease or buy a new machine costing ₹ 10,000. The machine is to be depreciated on straight-line basis over five year period. The tax rate is 22%. The operating income of the company will increase by ₹ 3,000 per year. The machine would also be paid at the beginning of each year. Salvage value of the machine will be zero. Determine which method of financing is better.

Solution

First, consider the purchase. Determine the cash flow of the machine.

Statement	*Income*		*Cash Flow (year end)*
Increase income	₹ 3,000		
Depreciation	–2,000		₹ 2,000
EBT	₹ 1,000		
Taxes	–220		
After tax profit	₹ 780		780
		Cash Flow	₹ 2,780

The machine will result in a cash flow of ₹ 2,780 per year for five years if purchased.

Determine the IRR of the machine.

Solution Table for 10%

Time	*Amount*	*Discount factor*	*Present Value*
Present	–₹ 10,000	1	–₹ 10,000
1-5	2,780	3.791	10,539

NPV = ₹ 539

Since the NPV is positive, it can be concluded that 10% is too low, so try 12%

Solution Table for 12%

Time	*Amount*	*Discount factor*	*Present Value*
Present	–₹ 10,000	1	–₹ 10,000
1-5	2,780	3.605	10,022
			NPV = ₹ 22

The NPV is ₹ 22, which is very close to zero. Therefore, the actual return is just over 12%.

Next, consider the lease. Determine the cash flow of the machine.

Income	*Cash Flow (year end)*	*Statement*
Increased income	₹ 3,000	₹ 3,000
Lease payment	–2,600	
Earning before tax	₹ 400	
Taxes	–88	–88
After-tax profit	₹ 312	₹ 2,912

The lease payment of ₹ 2,600 is made at the beginning of each year. At the end of the year, the firm would get the ₹ 3,000 less taxes of ₹ 88, or ₹ 2,912. Thus, it would pay out ₹ 2,600 at the start of each year and get back ₹ 2,912 at the year's end.

Solution Table for 10%

Time	*Amount*	*Discount factor*	*Present Value*
Present	–₹ 2,600	1	–₹ 2,600
1-4	312	3.170	989
5	2,912	.621	1,808
			NPV = ₹ 197

10% is too low. Try 12%.

Solution Table for 10%

Time	*Amount*	*Discount factor*	*Present Value*
Present	–₹ 2,600	1	–₹ 2,607
1-4	312	3.037	948
5	2,912	.567	1,651
			NPV = – ₹ 1

The return is almost exactly 12%. Since the IRR of the lease is almost exactly 12% and the IRR of the purchase is just over 12%, the purchase is financially preferable to the lease. However, the returns are very close. Therefore, it would be wise for management to carefully consider all of the other advantages and disadvantages of leasing before making a final decision.

3. A firm can lease a ₹ 2,50,000 machine for five years at ₹ 62,500. It can purchase the machine for ₹ 50,000 down and the balance in five equal payments at 10% interest. The firm qualifies for a ₹ 20,000 tax credit in year zero if it purchases. The machine will be depreciated at straight line calculations to a book value of ₹ 50,000 at the end of year five. The cash value at that time will be zero. The cost of debt is 10% and the cost of capital is 12%. Should machine be leased or owned?

Solution

(*a*) Loan repayment schedule:

Year	*10% of Loan Payment*	*Annual Interest*	*Principal Reduction*	*Balance Out*
0			₹ 50,000	₹ 2,00,000
1	₹ 52,757 **	₹ 20,000	32,757	1,67,243
2	52,757	16,724	36,033	1,31,210
3	52,757	13,121	39,636	91,574
4	52,757	9,157	43,600	47,974
5	52,757	4,797	47,960	14*

*Due to rounding, **–₹ 2,00,000/3.91 = ₹ 52,757

(*b*) Investment tax credit savings-given at ₹ 20,000

(*c*) After tax cash salvage value—A ₹ 50,000 book value; therefore a loss of ₹ 50,000 or a tax savings of ₹ 25,000. An additional advantage of owning.

(*d*) After-tax cost of owning

Year	*Loan Payment*	*Depre-ciation*	*Interest*	*Total (2)+(4)*	*Tax Savings*	*After-tax cost of owning*
0	₹ 50,000				₹ 20,000	₹ 30,000
1	52757	₹ 40,000	₹ 20,000	₹ 60,000	30,000	22,757
2	52757	40,000	16,724	56,724	28,362	24,395
3	52757	40,000	13,121	53,121	26,560	26,196
4	52757	40,000	9,157	49,157	24,578	28,178
5	52757	40,000	4,797	44,797	22,398	30,358
6						–25,000

(*e*) After-tax lease cost:

Lease payment times (1–tax rate)

= ₹ 62,500 × 0.50%

= ₹ 31,250

(*f*) Present value advantage to owning

Year	*After-tax Lease Costs*	*After tax-Owning Cost*	*Advantage to own*	*Present value Factor at 10%*	*Present value*
0	—	₹ 30,000	–₹ 30,000	1.000	–₹ 30,000
1	31,250	22,757	8,493	.909	7,720
2	31,250	24,395	6,855	.826	5,662
3	31,250	26,196	5,054	.751	3,796
4	31,250	28,178	3,072	.683	2,098
5	31,250	30,358	892	.621	554
6	—	–25,000	25,000	.567*	14,175
				Present value advantage to own =	₹ 4,005

* 12% cost of capital factor.

4. A machine can be purchased for ₹ 20,000. It will be depreciated straight-line over ten years with zero salvage value. The firm could also lease the machine for ₹ 5,500 per year, with payments to be made at the beginning of each year. The firm requires a 10% return on investments and has a 40 % tax rate. Describe whether the firm should purchase or lease.

Solution

The cash inflows which will result from the use of the machine are not given, so the problem can only be solved to the extent of determining which method of acquiring the machine is least costly. There is no way to determine if the machine will yield the 10% rate of return whether leased or purchased.

First, determine the costs involved in purchase. The initial cost is ₹ 20,000. However a tax savings will result from the yearly depreciation of ₹ 2,000. The tax savings will represent a cash inflow of 40% of the depreciation: ₹ 2,000 × .40 = ₹ 800.

The solution table for 10% is shown below:

The Solution Table at 10% for Purchase

Time	*Amount*	*Discount factor*	*Present Value*
Present	–₹ 20,000	1	–₹ 20,007
1-10	800	6.1446	4,916
		NPV =	–₹ 15,084

Next, determine the cost of the lease keeping in mind that the lease payments are tax deductible. The lease payment of ₹ 5,500 will result in a year-end tax savings of ₹ 5,500 × .40 = ₹ 2,200. Hence, during year 1—9, the cost will be ₹ 5,500 – ₹ 2,200 = ₹ 3,300.

Solution Table at 10% for Leasing

Time	*Amount*	*Discount factor*	*Present Value*
Present	–₹ 5,500	1	–₹ 5,500
1-9	–3,300	5.7590	–19,005
	2,200	.3855	8,481
		NPV =	– ₹ 16,024

The NPVs of both the purchase and lease are negative. The one which is least negative is preferred since it represents a lower outflow of funds. Therefore, the purchase would be selected rather than the lease.

5. ABC University needs a new computer. It can either buy it for ₹ 5,20,000 or lease it from Compulease. The lease terms require the University to make five annual payments (first instalment payable immediately) of ₹ 1,40,000. Compulease pays corporation tax at 50% with a 12 month lag and can claim 100% capital allowances for tax purposes. The computer will have no residual value at the end of year 4. The bank has quoted an interest rate of 20% for loan facilities.

(i) Should ABC University lease or buy the equipment?

(ii) How much money is the lessor making from the lease?

Solution

$$\text{NPV leasing} = +520000 - \sum_{t=0}^{4} \frac{1,40,000}{(1+r)^t}$$

Since ABC University does not pay tax, its opportunity cost is the 20% loan interest rate:

$$\text{NPV} = +5,20,000 - 1,40,000 - 1,40,000(2.5887)$$

$$= ₹\ 17,582$$

As leasing has a positive NPV, ABC University should lease rather than buy.

(ii) As the lessor pays tax it can claim the capital allowance and the cost of capital will be reduced to the after-tax rate, i.e. 20(1–0.50) = 10%.

6. XYZ Company is considering a proposal to acquire a new machine. Because of the shortage in cash available to purchase the machine, the lease financing alternative will have to be considered as well. The finance department has been able to provide the following estimates:

Expected useful life	5 years
Purchase price	₹ 2,30,000
Lease payments (per annum)	₹ 72,000
Annual operating costs (if purchased)	₹ 26,000 (fixed for the five years)
Annual operating costs (if leased)	₹ 6,000
Scrap value	NIL

In addition you are given the following additional information: (i) The cashflows take place at the end of each year, except the initial capital expenditure and the lease payments being required at the beginning of the year. (ii) The machine, if purchased, would qualify for a 100% first year capital allowance. (iii) The corporation tax rate is 50%. (iv) There is a 12-month lag in the payment of taxes and in the receipt of tax allowances. (v) The company's cost of capital is 20%, and its current net of tax long-term borrowing rate is 8%. You are required to advise the company whether it should purchase or lease the machine. Show calculations in arriving at your recommendation identifying any important assumption.

Solution

The net present value of leasing can be calculated by enumerating the incremental benefits and costs of leasing and discounting appropriately:

$$\text{NPV}_\text{L} = +2,30,000 - \frac{2,30,000 \times 0.50}{(1+r_1)} - \sum_{t=0}^{4} \frac{72,000}{(1+r_2)^t} - \sum_{t=1}^{5} \frac{72,000 \times 0.50}{(1+r_3)^t}$$

$$-\sum_{t=1}^{5}\frac{20{,}000 \times 0.50}{(1+r_4)^t} \quad -\sum_{t=2}^{6}\frac{20{,}000 \times 0.50}{(1+r_5)^t}$$

In words, NPV of leasing equals purchase price saved, less tax shield forgone on capital allowances, and cost of lease payments, plus tax shield on lease payments and operating costs saved less tax shield on operating costs saved.

It is then necessary to choose appropriate discount rates for r_1–r_5 in the equation. The riskiness of leasing cash flows is usually assumed to approximate that of the stream associated with borrowing. In this case, 8% seems the appropriate rate to use. However, a case could be made for using 20% for r_4 and r_5 as these relate to operating costs.

Using an 8% discount rate:

$$\begin{aligned} NPV_L &= 2{,}30{,}000–1{,}15{,}000(0.9259) –72{,}000(4.3121) + 36{,}000(3.9927) \\ &\quad + 2{,}000\ (3.9927) – 10{,}000\ (3.697) \\ &= +2{,}30{,}000–1{,}03{,}833–3{,}10{,}471 + 1{,}43{,}737 + 79{,}854–36{,}970 \\ &= +2{,}317 \text{ (i.e. leasing is best alternative)} \end{aligned}$$

Note, however, that if a rate of 20% was used for the operating costs and associated tax shield a negative value for leasing would be obtained.

QUESTIONS

1. What is leasing? What roles are played by the lessor and lessee? How are lease payments treated for tax purposes?
2. Indicate why leasing has become a popular method of securing the use of equipment and property in recent years.
3. In what sense is there in effect a down payment on a lease? Is this a greater percentage if the value of the asset of the lease period is short or long, given that the lease payment is made annually in both cases?
4. Critique the notion that leasing is advantageous because additional capital for investment is very difficult for a firm to obtain.
5. Distinguish the following:
   (a) Operating leases and financial leases.
   (b) Net leases and maintenance leases.
   (c) Leverage leases and Sale.
6. Why are the cash outflows associated with both leasing and borrowing discounted at the after-tax cost of debt in evaluating a lease-purchase decision?
7. What are the key advantages and disadvantages of leasing as a source of financing? Which of these advantages and disadvantage are most important in a subjective lease-buy evaluation?
8. How are lease payments timed? What effect might advance payments have on the tax benefits of a lease arrangement and the after-tax cash outflows associated with the lease?
9. What are the major similiarities and the major differences between lease and debt financing? In what circumstances may leasing be most attractive?
10. Leasing is often called a hedge against obsolescence. Under what conditions is this actually true?
11. What sort of companies may act as lessors of asset? Do these lessors generally provide for the renewal of a lease? Under what circumstances may a renewal be offered?
12. What is the main theoretical disagreement between lease-borrow and lease-buy proponents?
13. Why is the matter of cash salvage value important in lease-buy decisions?

14. "The type of equipment best suited for leasing has a long life in relation to the length of the lease, than a removable standard product that could be used by many different firms, and is easily identifiable. In short, it is the kind of equipment that could be repossessed and sold readily. However, we would be quite happy to write a ten-year lease on paper towels for firm such as Premier Motors" Discuss the statement.

PROBLEMS

1. Janata Motors is considering the lease of a new machine. The lease will run for 10 years and will cost ₹ 40,000 per year. It will result in added revenues of ₹ 85,000 and increase operating costs of ₹ 30,000. The company is in the 48% tax bracket. The company requires 15% return on investment Determine whether or not the leased machine will provide this return.

Ans.: Since the NPV is ₹ 94,036, the leased machine yields more than the required 15%.

2. Malwa Rubber is considering either leasing or purchasing a new machine costing ₹ 2,73,550. If the machine is purchased, it will be depreciated straight-line. The lease would entail a 3-year lease requiring annual beginning-of-year payments of ₹ 1,00,000. Alternatively, a ₹ 2,73,550, 10% loan will be used to finance the purchase. The loan would be repaid by three equal payments of ₹ 1,10,000, the first payment being due one period from now.

(a) With a zero tax rate, should the firm buy or lease?

(b) With a 40% tax rate should the firm buy or lease? Assume that the firm uses the after-tax borrowing rate in computing present values.

Ans.: (a) PV (lease) = ₹ 2,73,550 PV (buy-borrow) = ₹ 2,73,550 There is indifference

(b) PV (lease) = ₹ 1,70,000 PV (Buy-borrow) = ₹ 1,76,000 Lease is more desirable.

3. Oswal Spinning has decided to acquire a piece of equipment but has not yet decided to buy or lease. The lease payments would be ₹ 1,40,105 paid annually at the end of each year. If purchased at a cost of ₹ 4,00,000, the equipment would be finance with debt costing 10%, which can be repaid at any time within the four year period. The life of the equipment is four years. The lease is a firm commitment to make four payments. There is no salvage value. Should the firm lease or buy-borrow? There are no taxes.

Ans.: Equal debt payments would result in payments of ₹ 1,26,187 compared with ₹ 1,40,105 if leased; therefore borrow and buy

4. A company decides to acquire an item of equipment which costs ₹ 14,000 and has a useful life of 4 years. Assume that the market value of the equipment at the end of 4 years is expected to be ₹ 4,431. The company required rate of return is 10% and is expected to remain at approximately this rate in the future. The company has the opportunity of either purchasing the equipment outright or obtaining through a financial lease agreement. The lease agreement allows for four lease payments of ₹ 4,000 per year to be paid at the beginning of each year. The company is also able to borrow up to ₹ 20,000 from a financial institution at 6%. Which of the alternatives would you recommend to the company?

Ans.: As net present value of the purchase cost is lower by ₹ 1,849 than the net present value of the investment portion of the lease, the decision to recommend on the basis of quantitative analysis is to purchase the asset and finance the purchase by borrowing at 6%.

5. Bharat Steel Company seeks to acquire the services of a rolling machine, at the lowest possible cost. The choice is to either lease one at ₹ 12,61,870 paid annually at the end of each year or purchase one for ₹ 40,00,000. Their cost of capital is 10% and their tax rate is 40%. The machine has an economic life of four years and no salvage value. The company uses straight-line depreciation. Which is the less costly method of financing.

Ans.: Buying is more desirable as the timing of buy tax deductions is better than ₹ 12,61,870 of tax deductions per year as well be obtained if the firm leases.

6. A level rental plan lease requires a ₹ 45,000 lease payment annually for 15 years on a ₹ 2,25,000 fixed asset. What is the effective interest implied by the lease payment?

Ans.: Approximntely 18 per cent

7. Sirdar Metal Corporation is faced with the decision of whether it should purchase or lease a new equipment. The equipment can be leased at ₹ 1,00,000 per year (first payment on year), hence for 10 years or purchased at a cost of ₹ 5,65,020. The company has weighted average cost of capital of 15 percent. The equipment will have a zero selvage value. A bank has indicated that it would be willing to make the loan (equal payment) of ₹ 5,65,020 at a cost of 10%. There are no taxes. Analyse the buy-borrow versus purchase decision.

Ans.: Because ₹ 5,65,020/6.1446=₹ 91,950, which is less than ₹ 10,00,000, buy-borrow is better than lease.

8. Suman Industries has established a leasing subsidiary. A local firm, Allied Business Machines, has approached the Suman Industries to arrange lease financing for ₹ 10 crore in new machinery. The economic life of the machinery is estimated to be 20 years. The estimated salvage value at the end of 20-years period is ₹ 0. Allied Business Machines has indicated a willingness to pay the Suman Industries ₹ 1 crore per year at the *end* of each year for 20 years under the terms of a financial lease. If Suman Industries depreciates the machinery on a straight-line basis over 20 years to a ₹ 0 estimated salvage value and has a 40 percent marginal tax rate, what *after-tax* rate of return will the Suman Industries earn on the lease?

Ans.: 4.96%

9. Venky Textiles wants to acquire a ₹ 20,00,000 computer. Venky has a 40 percent marginal tax rate. If owned, the computer would be depreciated on a straight-line basis to a *book* salvage value of ₹ 0. The actual cash salvage value is expected to be ₹ 2,00,000 at the end of 10 years. If the computer is purchased, Venky could borrow the needed funds at an annual pretax interest rate of 10 percent. If purchased, Venky will incur annual maintenance expenses of ₹ 10,000. These expenses would not be incurred if the computer is leased. The lease rate would be ₹ 2,80,000 per year, payable at the beginning of each year. Venky's weighted after tax cost of capital is 12 percent. Compute the *net advantage to leasing.*

Ans.: ₹ 1,06,240

10. Gupta Leasing Company (GLC) is considering a leveraged lease agreement involving some mining equipment with the Neelam Mining Corporation. GLC (40 percent tax bracket) will be the lessor; the mining company, the lessee (0 percent tax bracket); and a large private bank, Jamuna Bank, the lender. Neelam Mining Corporation is seeking ₹ 50 crore, and the bank has agreed to lend GLC ₹ 40 crore at 10 percent. GLC has agreed to paying the bank ₹ 4 crore of principal each year plus interest. (The remaining balance will be repaid in a balloon payment at the end of the fifth year). The equipment will be depreciated on a straight-line basis over a 5-year estimated useful life with no expected salvage value. Assuming Neelam has agreed to annual lease payments of ₹ 10 crore, calculate the GLC's initial cash outflows and its first 2 years of cash inflows.

Ans.: Year 1 cash flow : ₹ 3.60 crore

11. RIM Udyog needs to buy a machine for ₹ 4 crore, having 3-year economic life. The machine would be depreciated on a straight-line basis to a zero salvage value The firm is considering the following two financing alternatives:

(i) *Bank Financing:* The firm's bank will give the firm a 3-year loan at an interest rate of 12%. The loan would require three equal annual installment starting one year from now.

(ii) *Sale and Leaseback:* RIM can arrange to purchase the asset, sell it to a third party for ₹ 4 crore, and lease it back for three years. The lease would require three equal lease payments of ₹ 1.40 crore with the first payment due in one year. It would be a net lease and the firm would be given no option to purchase or renew the lease.

Use the IRR method to recommend whether it is cheeper to lease or borrow and buy. Assume the firm has a 40% tax rate.

Ans.: It is cheaper to borrow to buy.

PART - V

THE MANAGEMENT OF WORKING CAPITAL

21

WORKING CAPITAL MANAGEMENT

INTRODUCTION

Working capital typically means the firm's holdings of current, or short-term, assets such as cash, receivables, inventory, and marketable securities. Much academic literature is directed toward gross working capital, i.e., total current or circulating assets. These items are referred to as *circulating assets* because of their cyclical nature. In a retail establishment, cash is initially employed to purchase inventory which is in turn sold on credit and results in accounts receivables. Once the receivables are collected, they become cash-part of which is reinvested in additional inventory and part (i.e., the amount above cost) going to profit or *cash throw-off*.

Corporate executives devote a considerable amount of attention to the management of working capital. An examination of the components of working capital is helpful because of the preoccupation of management with the proper combination of assets and acquired funds, concerted efforts are made to ensure the ability of the firm to meet the short-term obligations. The management must be concerned with proper financial structure, these and other funds must be raised judiciously. The chapter provides a theoretical framework in the risk/return trade-off of various approaches, applied in the firm's working capital management.

CONCEPT OF WORKING CAPITAL

There are two possible interpretations of working capital concept:

(a) Balance Sheet Concept

(b) Operating Cycle Concept

It goes without saying that the pattern of management will be very largely influenced by the approach taken in defining it. Therefore the two concepts are discussed separately in a nutshell.

(A) BALANCE SHEET CONCEPT

There are two interpretations of working capital under the balance sheet concept. It is represented by the excess of current assets over current liabilities and is the amount normally available to finance current operations. On the one hand, economists like Lincoln and Saliers uphold the view that (a) in the long run what matters is the surplus of current assets over current liabilities (b) it is this concept which helps creditors and investors to judge the financial soundness of the enterprise; (c) what can always be relied upon to meet the contingencies, is the excees of current assets over the current liabilities since this amount is not to be returned; and (d) this definition helps to find out the correct financial position of companies having the same amount of current assets. Institute of Chartered Accountants of India also endorsed the former view of working capital when it described net current assets as the difference between current assets and current liabilities. In that case, the excess of current assets over current liabilities is called the *net working capital* or *net current assets.* But some-times working capital is also used as a synonym for gross or total current assets. Economists like Mead, Malott, Baker and Field support the latter view of net working capital. They feel that current assets should be considered as working capital as the whole of it helps to earn profits; and the management is more concerned with the total current assets as they constitute the total funds available for operational purposes.

The conventional definition of working capital in terms of the difference between the current assets and the current liabilities somewhat confusing. Working capital is really what a part of long-term finance is locked in and used for supporting current activities. Consequently, the larger the amount of working capital so derived, greater the proportion of long-term capital sources siphoned off to short-term activities. It is difficult to say whether this is right or wrong. Apparently, when firms are warned about tight working capital situation, the logic of the above definition would perhaps indicate diversion of long-term finances for short-term purposes. For, if short-term bank loans were procured to bring in cash, under the conventional method, working capital would evidently remain unchanged. Liquidation of debtors and inventory into cash would also keep the level of working capital unchanged. Similarly, a relatively large amount of working capital according to this definition may produce a false sense of security at a time when cash resources may be negligible, or when these may be provided increasingly by long-term fund sources in the absence of adequate profits. Again, under the conventional method, cash enters into the computation of working capital. But it may have been more appropriate to exclude cash from such calculations because one compares cash requirements with current assets less current liabilities. The implication of this in conventional working capital computations is that during the financial period current assets get converted into cash which, after paying off the current liabilities, can be used to meet other operational expenses. The paradox, however, is that such current assets as are relied upon to yield cash must themselves to be supported by long-term funds until they are converted into cash.

At least three points seem to emerge from the above. *First,* the balance sheet definition of working capital is perhaps not so meaningful, except as an indication of the firm's current solvency in repaying its creditors. *Secondly,* when firms speak of shortage of working capital, they in fact possible imply scarcity of cash resources. *Thirdly,* in fund flow analysis an increase in working capital, as conventionally defined, represents employment or application of funds.

(B) OPERATING CYCLE CONCEPT

A company's operating cycle typically consists of three primary activities: purchasing resources, producing the product, and distributing (selling) the product. These activities create funds flows that are both unsynchronised and uncertain. They are unsynchronised because cash disbursements (for example, payments for resource purchases) usually take place before cash receipts (for example, collection of receivables). They are uncertain because future sales and costs, which generate the respective receipts and disbursements, cannot be forecasted with complete accuracy. If the firm is to maintain liquidity and function properly, it has to invest funds in various short-term assets (working capital) during this cycle. It has to maintain a *cash balance* to pay the bills as they come due. In addition, the company must invest in *inventories* to fill customer orders promptly. And, finally, the company invests in *accounts receivable* to extend credit to its customers.

FIGURE-1

OPERATING CYCLE OF A TYPICAL COMPANY

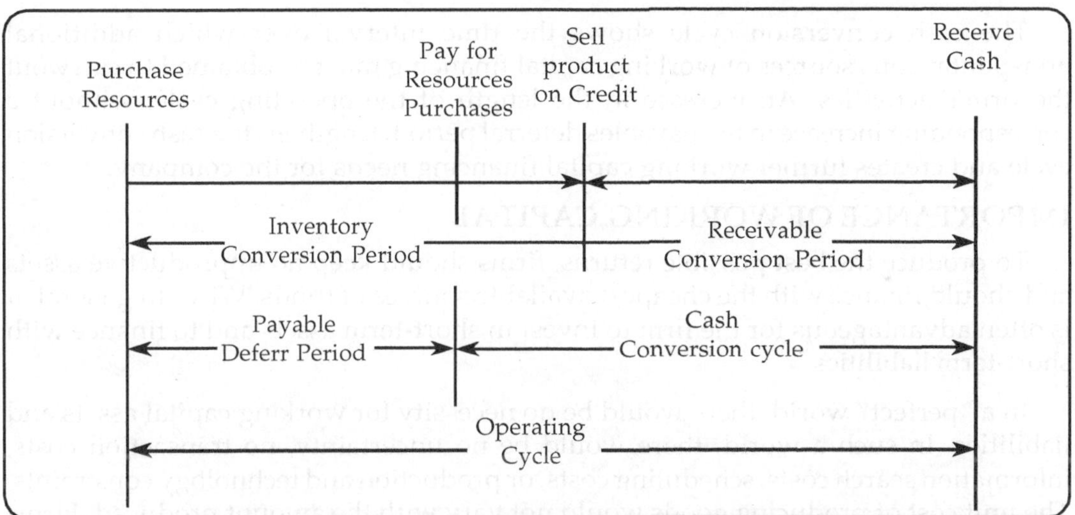

Figure-1 illustrates the operating cycle of a typical firm. The *operating cycle* is equal to the length of the inventory and receivables conversion periods:

$$\text{Operating cycle} = \text{Inventory conversion period} + \text{Receivables conversion period} \quad (1)$$

The *inventory conversion period* is the length of time required to produce and sell the product. It is defined as follows:

$$\textit{Inventory conversion period} = \frac{\text{Average inventory}}{\text{Cost of sales}/365} \quad (2)$$

The *receivables conversion period,* or average collection period, represents the length of time required to collect the sales receipts. It is calculated as follows:

$$Receivables\ conversion\ period = \frac{\text{Accounts receivable}}{\text{Annual credit sales}/365} \quad (3)$$

The *payables deferral period* is the length of time the firm is able to defer payment on its various resource purchases (for example, materials, wages, and taxes). Equation 4 is used to calculate the payables deferral period:

$$Payables\ deferral\ period = \frac{\text{Accounts payable} + \text{Salaries, benefits, and payroll taxes payable}}{(\text{Cost of sales} + \text{Selling, general and administrative expense})/365} \quad (4)$$

Finally, the *cash conversion cycle* represents the net time interval between the collection of cash receipts from product sales and the cash payments for the company's various resource purchases. It is calculated as follows:

$$Cash\ conversion\ cycle = \text{Operating cycle} - \text{payables deferral period} \quad (5)$$

The cash conversion cycle shows the time interval over which additional nonspontaneous sources of working capital financing must be obtained to carry out the firm's activities. An increase in the length of the operating cycle, without a corresponding increase in the payables deferral period, lengthens the cash conversion cycle and creates further working capital financing needs for the company.

IMPORTANCE OF WORKING CAPITAL

To produce the best possible returns, firms should keep no unproductive assets and should finance with the cheapest available sources of funds. Why? In general, it is often advantageous for the firm to invest in short-term assets and to finance with short-term liabilities.

In a "perfect" world, there would be no necessity for working capital assets and liabilities. In such a world, there would be no uncertainty, no transaction costs, information search costs, scheduling costs, or production and technology constraints. The unit cost of producing goods would not vary with the amount produced. Firms would borrow and lend at the same interest rate. Capital, labour, and product markets would reflect all available information and would be perfectly competitive. In such a world, it can be shown that there would be no advantage for firms to invest or finance in the short term.

But the world in which real firms function is not perfect. It is characterized by the firm's considerable uncertainty regarding the demand, market price, quality, and availability of its own products and those of suppliers. There are transaction costs for purchasing or selling goods or securities. Information is costly to obtain, and the firm is faced with limits on the production capacity and technology that it can employ. There are fixed as well as variable costs associated with producing goods for sale, and there are spreads between the borrowing and lending rates for investments and financings of equal risk. Information is not equally distributed and may not be fully reflected in the prices in product and labour markets, and these markets may not be perfectly competitive.

These real-world circumstances introduce problems with which the firm must deal. While the firm has many strategies available to address these circumstances, *strategies that utilise investment or financing with working capital accounts often offer a substantial advantage* over other techniques. For example, assume that the firm is faced with uncertainty regarding the level of its future cash flows and will incur substantial costs if it has insufficient cash to meet expenses. Several strategies may be formulated to address this uncertainty and the costs that it may engender. Among these strategies are some that involve working capital investment or financing such as holding additional cash balances beyond expected needs, holding a reserve of short-term marketable securities, or arranging for the availability of additional short-term borrowing capacity. One of these strategies (or a combination of them) may well be the least costly approach to the problem. Similarly, the existence of fixed set-up costs in the production of goods may be addressed in several ways, but one possible alternative is to hold inventory.

FIGURE-2

RESOURCE FLOWS FOR A MANUFACTURING FIRM

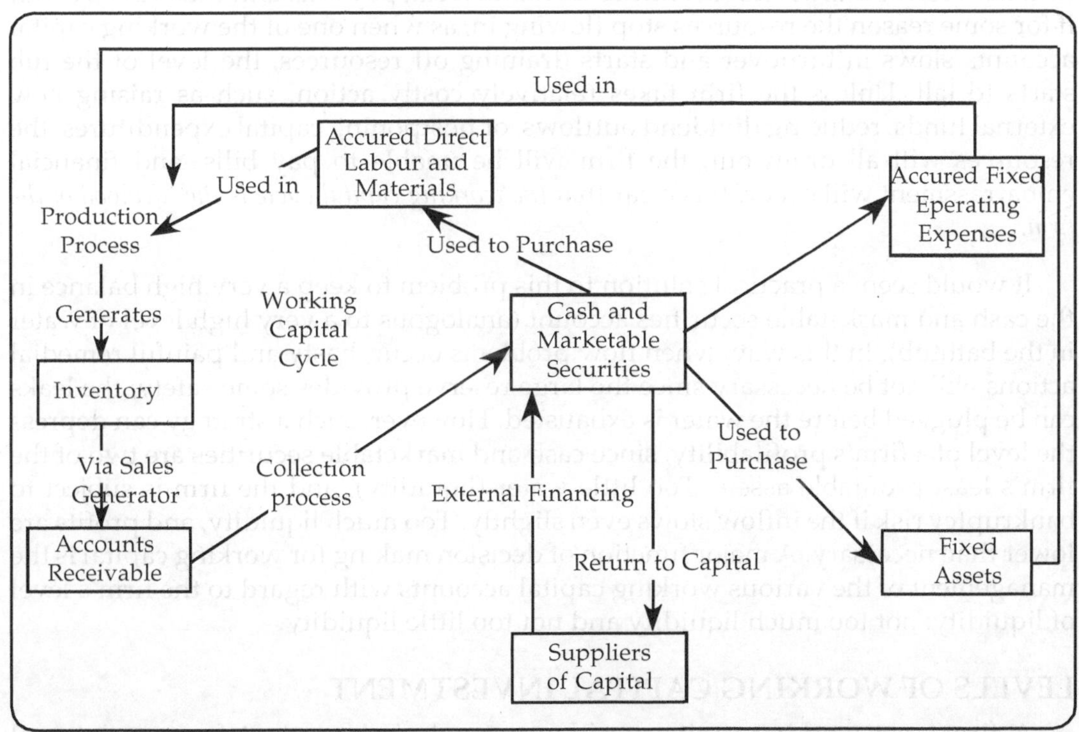

By these examples, we see that strategies using working capital accounts are some of the possible ways firms can respond to many of the problems engendered by the imperfect and constrained world in which they deal. One of the major features of this world is uncertainty (risk), and it is this feature that gives rise to many of the strategies involving working capital accounts.

In addition to its use as a means of handling uncertainty, the management of working capital plays an important role in maintaining the financial health of the firm during the normal course of business. This critical role can be seen by examining Figure-2, which loosely portrays the flow of resources through the firm. By far the major flow, in terms of its yearly magnitude, is the *working capital cycle.* This is the loop which starts at the cash and marketable securities account, goes through the current accruals accounts as direct labour and materials are purchased and used to produce inventory, which is in turn sold and generates accounts receivable, which are finally collected to replenish cash. The major point to notice about this cycle is that *the turnover (or velocity) of resources through this loop is very high* relative to the other inflows and outflows of the cash account.

To see why this cycle is critically important to the firm's survival, visualise the cash account as a bathtub with both the drain and the faucet open. While there are other inflows and outflows, the *major* flow is the working capital cycle. As long as the firm has cash or marketable securities on hand, it can pay bills and thus survive. But if for some reason the resources stop flowing in, as when one of the working capital accounts slows in turnover and starts draining off resources, the level of the tub starts to fall. Unless the firm takes relatively costly action, such as raising new external funds, reducing dividend outflows, or postponing capital expenditures, the resources will all drain out, the firm will be unable to pay bills, and financial embarrassment will occur. It is clear that *the working capital cycle is the lifeblood of the firm.*

It would seem a practical solution to this problem to keep a very high balance in the cash and marketable securities account (analogous to a very high level of water in the bathtub). In this way, when flow problems occur, hasty and painful remedial actions will not be necessary since the large reserve provides some safety; the leaks can be plugged before the water is exhausted. However, such a strategy can depress the level of a firm's profitability, since cash and marketable securities are two of the firm's least profitable assets. Too little water (liquidity), and the firm is subject to bankruptcy risk if the inflow slows even slightly. Too much liquidity, and profits are lower than necessary. A major function of decision making for working capital is the management of the various working capital accounts with regard to the firm's level of liquidity: not too much liquidity and not too little liquidity.

LEVELS OF WORKING CAPITAL INVESTMENT

A firm's net working capital position not only is important from an internal standpoint; it also is widely used as one measure of the firm's *risk. Risk,* as used in this context, deals with the probability that a firm will encounter financial difficulties, such as the inability to pay bills on time. All other things being equal, the more net working capital a firm has, the more likely that it will be able to meet current financial obligations. Because net working capital is one measure of risk, a company's net working capital position affects its ability to obtain debt financing. Many loan agreements with commercial banks and other lending institutions contain a provision requiring the firm on maintain a minimum net working capital position. Likewise, bond indentures also often contain such provisions. The overall policy considers *both* the level of working capital investment and its financing. In practice, the firm has to determine the *joint* impact of these two decisions upon its profitability and risk.

The size and nature of a firm's investment in current assets is a function of a number of different factors, including the type of products manufactured; the length of the operating cycle, the sales level (because higher sales require more investment in inventories and receivables); the inventory policies (for example, the amount of safety stocks maintained; that is, inventories needed to meet higher than expected demand or unanticipated delays in obtaining new inventories); the credit policies; and current assets.

Before deciding on an appropriate level of working capital investment, a firm's management has to evaluate the tradeoff between expected profitability and the risk that it may be unable to meet its financial obligations. Profitability is measured by the rate of (operating) return on total assets; that is, EBIT/total assets. The risk that the firm will encounter financial difficulties is related to the firm's net working capital position.

Figure-3 illustrates three alternative working capital policies. Each curve in the figure demonstrates the relationship between the firm's investment in current assets and sales for that particular policy. Policy C represents a *conservative* approach to working capital management. Under this policy the company holds a relatively large proportion of its total assets in the form of current assets. Because the rate of return on current assets normally is assumed to be less than the rate of return on fixed assets, this policy results in a *lower expected profitability* as measured by the rate of return on the company's total assets. Assuming that current liabilities remain constant, this type of policy also increases the company's net working capital position, resulting in a *lower risk* that the firm will encounter financial difficulties. In contrast to Policy C, Policy A represents an *aggressive* approach. Under this policy the company holds a relatively small proportion of its total assets in the form of lower yielding current assets and thus has relatively less net working capital. As a result, this policy yields a *higher expected profitability* and a *higher risk* that the company will encounter financial difficulties. Finally, Policy B represents a *moderate* approach, because expected profitability and risk levels fall between those of Policy C and Policy A.

Using net working capital as a measure of risk, the aggressive policy is most risky, and the conservative policy is the least risky. The current ratio is another measure of a firm's ability to meet financial obligations as they come due. The aggressive policy would yield the lowest current ratio, and the conservative policy would yield the highest current ratio.

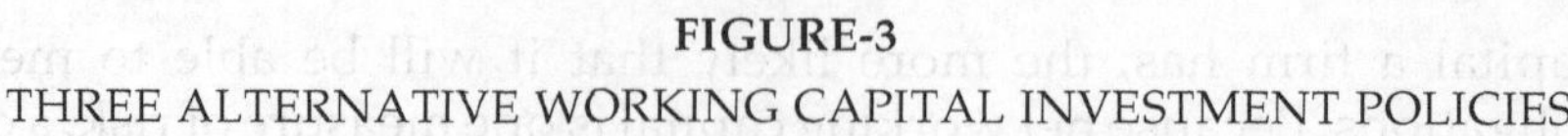

FIGURE-3
THREE ALTERNATIVE WORKING CAPITAL INVESTMENT POLICIES

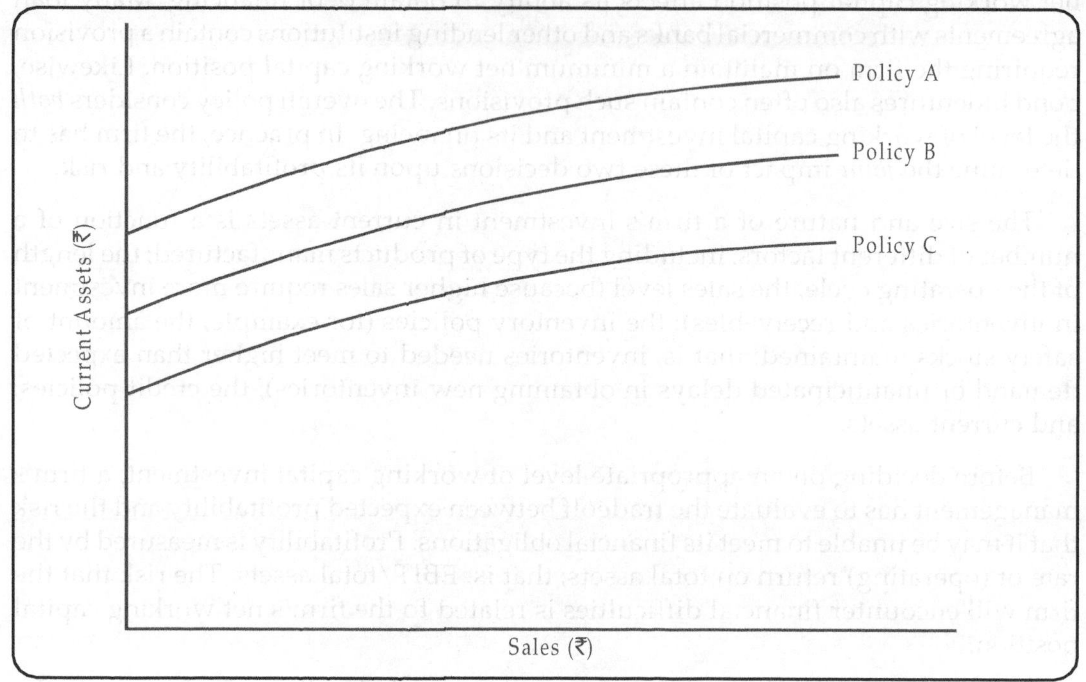

OPTIMAL LEVEL OF WORKING CAPITAL INVESTMENT

The optimal level of working capital investment is the level expected to maximize shareholder wealth. It is a function of several factors, including the variability of sales and cash flows and the degree of operating and financial leverage employed by the firm. Therefore no single working capital investment policy is necessarily optimal for all firms.

Not only does a firm have to be concerned about the *level* of current assets; it also has to determine the *proportions* of short-and long-term debt to use in financing these assets. This decision also involves tradeoffs between profitability and risk.

Sources of debt financing are classified according to their *maturities.* Specifically, they can be categorised as being either *short-term* or *long -term,* with short-term sources having maturities of 1 year or less and long-term sources having maturities of greater than 1 year.

Historically long-term interest rates normally exceeds short-term rates because of the reduced flexibility of long-term borrowing relative to short-term borrowing. Infact, the *effective* cost of long-term debt may be higher than the cost of short-term debt, even when short-term interest rates are equal to or greater than long-term rates. With long-term debt, a firm incurs the interest expense even during times when it has no immediate need for the funds, such as during seasonal or cyclical downturns. With short-term debt, in contrast, the firm can avoid the interest costs on unneeded funds by paying off (or not renewing) the debt. Therefore, the cost of long-term debt generally is higher than the cost of short-term debt.

RISK OF LONG-TERM VERSUS SHORT-TERM DEBT

Borrowing companies have different attitudes toward the relative risk of long-term versus short-term debt than lenders. Whereas lenders normally feel that risk increases with maturity, borrowers feel that there is more risk associated with short-term debt. The reasons for this are twofold. *First*, there is always the chance that a firm will not be able to refund its short-term debt. When a firm's debt matures, it either pays off the debt as part of a debt reduction programme or arranges new financing. At the time of maturity, however, the firm could be faced with financial problems resulting from such events as strikes, natural disasters, or recessions that cause sales and cash inflows to decline. Under these circumstances the firm may find it very difficult or even impossible to obtain the needed funds. This could lead to operating and financial difficulties. The more frequently a firm must refinance debt, the greater is the risk of its not being able to obtain the necessary financing. *Second*, short-term interest rates tend to fluctuate more over time than long-term interest rates. As a result, a firm's interest expenses and expected earnings after interest and taxes are subject to more variation (risk) over time with short-term debt than with long-term debt.

PROFITABILITY VERSUS RISK TRADE-OFF FOR ALTERNATIVE FINANCING PLANS

A company's need for financing is equal to the sum of its fixed and current assets. Current assets can be divided into the following two categories:

- *Permanent* current assets
- *Fluctuating* current assets.

Fluctuating current assets are those affected by the seasonal or cyclical nature of company sales. For example, a firm must make larger investments in inventories and receivables during peak selling periods than during other periods of the year. Permanent current assets are those held to meet the company's minimum long-term needs (for example, "safety stocks" of cash and inventories). Figure-4 illustrates a typical firm's financing needs over time. The fixed assets and permanent current assets lines are upward sloping, indicating that the investment in these assets and, by extension, financing needs tend to increase over time for a firm whose sales are increasing.

FIGURE-4
FINANCING NEEDS OVER TIME

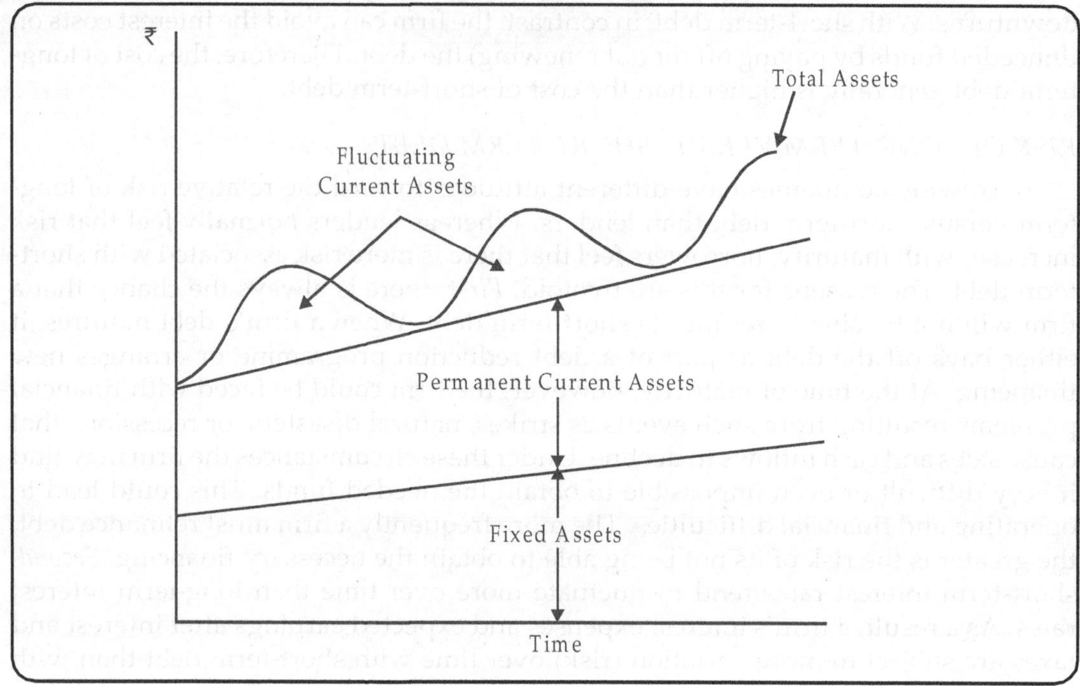

One way in which a firm can meet its financing needs is by using a *matching approach* in which the maturity structure of the firm's liabilities is made to correspond exactly to the life of its assets. This is illustrated in Figure-5. As can be seen, fixed and permanent current assets are financed with long-term debt and equity funds, whereas fluctuating current assets are financed with short-term debt. Application of this approach is not as simple as it appears, however. In practice the uncertainty associated with the lives of individual assets makes the matching approach difficult to implement. Figure-6 and-7 illustrate two other financing plans. Figure6 shows a *conservative* approach, which uses a relatively high proportion of long-term debt. The relatively low proportion of short-term debt in this approach reduces the risk that the company will be unable to refund its debt, and it also reduces the risk associated with interest rate fluctuations. At the same time, however, this approach cuts down on the expected returns available to stockholders, because the cost of long-term debt is generally greater than the cost of short-term debt. Figure-7 illustrates an *aggressive* approach, which uses a relatively high proportion of short-term debt. A firm that uses this particular approach must refund debt more frequently, and this increases the risk that it will be unable to obtain new financing as needed. In addition, the greater possible fluctuations in interest expenses associated with this financing plan also add to the firm's risk (variability in earnings). These higher risks are offset by the higher expected after-tax earnings that result from the lower cost of short-term debt.

FIGURE-5

MATCHING APPROACH TO ASSET FINANCING

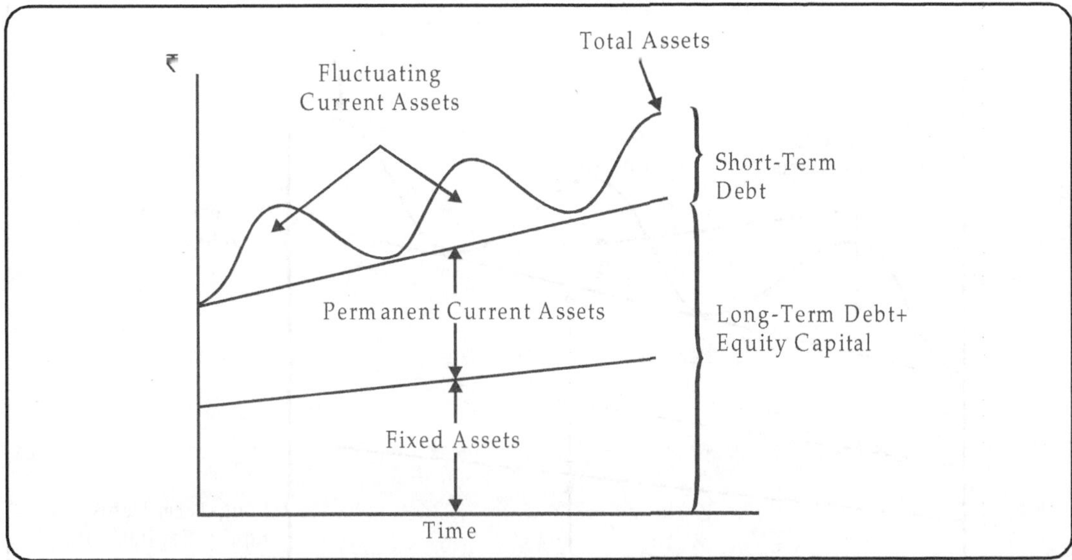

Table-1 shows the data for each of these alternative proposed financing plans. From the standpoint of profitability, the aggressive financing plan would yield the highest expected rate of return to the equity shareholders 14.36 percent—whereas

FIGURE-6

CONSERVATIVE APPROACH TO ASSET FINANCING

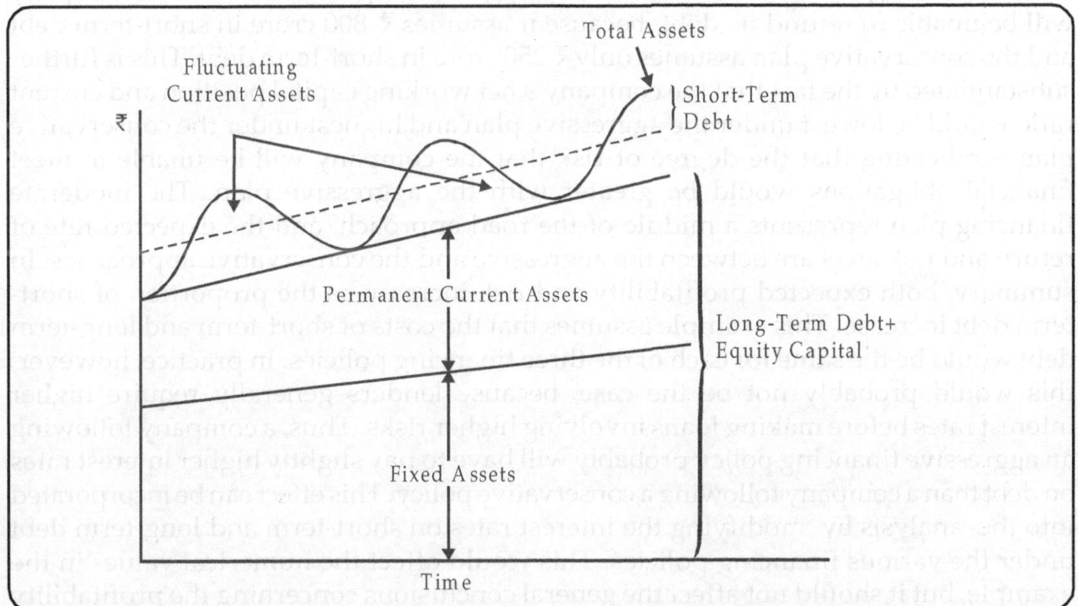

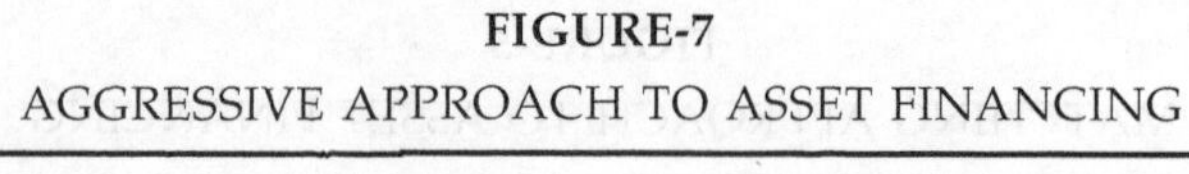

FIGURE-7

AGGRESSIVE APPROACH TO ASSET FINANCING

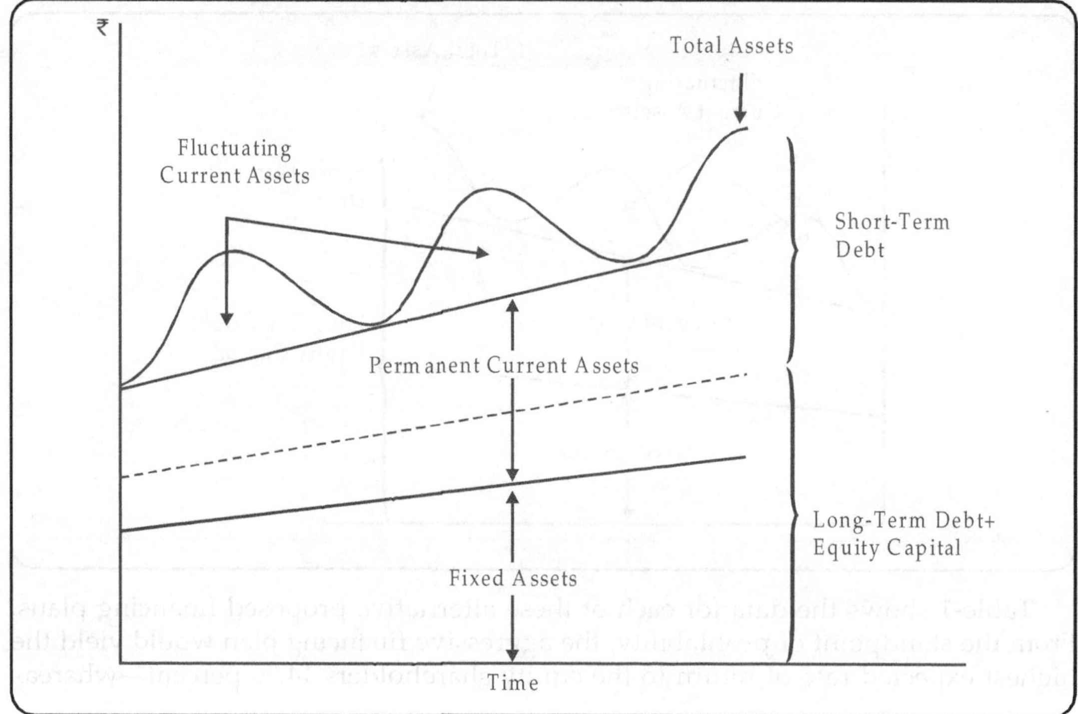

the conservative plan would yield the lowest rate of return—10.56 percent. In contrast, the aggressive plan would involve a greater degree of risk that the company will be unable to refund its debt, because it assumes ₹ 800 crore in short-term debt and the conservative plan assumes only ₹ 250 crore in short-term debt. This is further substantiated by the fact that the company's net working capital position and current ratio would be lowest under the aggressive plan and highest under the conservative plan—indicating that the degree of risk that the company will be unable to meet financial obligations would be greater with the aggressive plan. The moderate financing plan represents a middle-of-the road approach, and the expected rate of return and risk level are between the aggressive and the conservative approaches. In summary, both expected profitability and risk increase as the proportion of short-term debt increase. This example assumes that the costs of short-term and long-term debt would be the same for each of the three financing policies. In practice, however, this would probably not be the case, because lenders generally require higher interest rates before making loans involving higher risks. Thus, a company following an aggressive financing policy probably will have to pay slightly higher interest rates on debt than a company following a conservative policy. This effect can be incorporated into the analysis by modifying the interest rates on short-term and long-term debt under the various financing policies. This would affect the numerical values in the example, but it should not affect the general conclusions concerning the profitability versus risk tradeoffs.

TABLE-1
Working Capital Investment and Financing Policies for XYZ Company (in crores of ₹)

	Aggressive	*Moderate*	*Conservative*
	Relatively Large Amount of Short-term Debt	*Moderate Amount of Short-term Debt*	*Small Amount of Short-term Debt*
Current assets (C/A)	1000	1000	1000
	750	750	750
Total assets (T/A)	1750	1750	1750
Current liabilities (STD) C/L) (interest rate 12%)	800	550	250
Long-term liabilities (LTD) (interest rate 15%)	250	500	850
Total liabilities (60% of T/A)	1050	1050	1050
Equity	700	700	700
Total liabilities and equity	1750	1750	1750
Forecasted sales	2000	2000	2000
Expected EBIT	300	300	300
Less Interest:			
STD,12% / LTD,15%	96 / 37.5 } 133.50	66 / 75 } 141	36 / 127.5 } 163.50
Taxable Income	166.50	150	136.50
Less Taxes (40%)	66.00	63.60	52.60
Net income after taxes	100.50	95.40	73.90
Expected rate of return on equity	14.36	13.63	10.56
Net working capital position (C/A - C/L)	200	450	750
Current ratio (C/A ÷ C/L)	1.25	1.80	4.00

OVERALL WORKING CAPITAL POLICY

Until now this chapter has analysed the working capital investment and financing decisions independent of one another in order to examine the profitability—risk tradeoffs associated with each, assuming that all other factors are held constant. Effective working capital policy, however, also requires the consideration of the *joint* impact of these decisions on the firm's profitability and risk.

Referring to the XYZ Company again, assume that the company is 60 percent debt financed (both short-term and long-term) and 40 percent financed with equity. Also, it is evaluating three alternative working capital investment and financing policies. The *aggressive* policy would require a relatively *small* investment in current assets, ₹ 750 crore, and a relatively *large* amount of short-term debt, ₹ 600 crore. The conservative *policy would require a relatively* large investment in current assets ₹ 1,250 crore and a relatively *small* amount of short-term debt, ₹ 400 crore. The firm also is considering a middle-of-the-road approach, which would involve a *moderate* investment in current assets, ₹ 1000 crore, and a *moderate* amount of shot-term debt, ₹ 500 crore. Table-2 shows the data for each approach. The aggressive working capital policy is expected to yield the highest return on shareholders' equity, 24.66 percent whereas

TABLE-2

Alternative Working Capital Investment and Financing Policies for XYZ Company (in crores of ₹)

	Aggressive	*Moderate*	*Conservative*
	Relatively small Investment in Current Assets; Relatively Large Amount of Short-term Debt	*Moderate Investment in Current Assets; Moderate Amount of Short-term Debt*	*Relatively large Investment in Current Assets; Relatively Small Amount of Short-term Debt*
Current assets (C/A)	750	1000	1250
Fixed assets (F/A)	500	500	500
Total assets (T/A)	1250	1500	1750
Current liabilities (STD)(C/L) (interest rate, 12%)	600	500	400
Long-term liabilities (LTD) (interest rate, 15%)	150	400	650
Total liabilities (60% of T/A)	750	900	1050
Equity	500	600	700
Total liabilities and equity	1250	1500	1750
Forecasted sales	2000	2000	2000
Expected EBIT	300	300	300
Less Interest:			
	STD, 12% LTD, 15%	72 22.50 } 94.50	60 60 } 120
48 97.50 } 145.50			
Taxable income	205.50	180	154.50
Less Taxes (40%)	82.20	72	61.80
Net income after taxes	123.30	108	92.70
Expected rate of return on equity	24.66	18%	13.24%
Net working capital position (C/A – C/L)	250	500	750
Current ratio (C/A ÷ C/L)	1.25	2.0	3.125

the conservative policy is expected to yield the lowest return 13.24 percent. The net working capital and current ratio are lowest under the aggressive policy and highest under the conservative policy, indicating that the aggressive policy is the most risky. The moderate policy yields an expected return and risk level somewhere between the aggressive and the conservative policies.

Whereas this type of analysis will not directly yield the optimal working capital investment and financing policies a company should choose, it can give the financial manager some insight into the profitability—risk tradeoffs of alternative policies. With an understanding of these tradeoffs, the financial manager should be able to make better decisions concerning the working capital policy that will lead to a maximisation of shareholder wealth.

ILLUSTRATIVE PROBLEM

1. Fortune Nurseries is a complete wholesaler of nursery stock—trees, shrubs, vegetable and bedding plants, and many others. Its business is highly cyclical, with the second quarter being its most active period. In the past, management has followed an aggressive financing approach that involves financing fluctuating current asset needs with short-term loans. However, there have been periods of tight money when the availability of credit was questionable. To avoid such cirses, management is presently evaluating a conservative financing approach: negotiating a long-term loan to cover the total current asset needs for the upcoming year. Any surplus funds during the year would be invested in short-term securities, expected to yield 6%. Short- and long-term loans are expected to cost 10% and 14%, respectively. Expected asset and liability totals for the forthcoming year are as follows (the question marks indicate amounts that depend on the financing plan chosen):

	1Q	*2Q*	*3Q*	*4Q*
Cash	₹ 5.0[a]	₹ 5.0	₹ 5.0	₹ 5.0
Marketable securities	?	?	?	?
Inventories	85.0	125.0	65.0	45.0
Total current assets	₹ ?	₹ ?	₹ ?	₹ ?
Short-term loans	₹ ?	₹ ?	₹ ?	₹ ?
Long-term loans	?	?	?	?
Total liabilities	₹ ?	₹ ?	₹ ?	₹ ?

a All amounts are in crore of ₹

What is Fortune's additional annual cost of a conservative financing plan?

Solution

1. With the conservative approach, a long-term loan is negotiated to meet the peak current asset need of ₹ 230, which occurs in 2Q. Excess funds are invested in short-term securities.

   Interest cost = 0.14 x ₹ 230 = ₹ 32.2

Interest earned (marketable securities):	1Q: ₹ 230 – ₹ 130	=	₹ 100
	2Q:		
	3Q: ₹ 230 – ₹ 150	=	80
	4Q: ₹ 230 – ₹ 70	=	160
	Total investment	=	₹ 340
	Average investment	=	₹ 340/4 = ₹ 85
	Annual investment	=	₹ 85 × 0.06 = ₹ 5.1

Net cost of conservative plan = ₹ 32.2 – ₹ 5.1 = ₹ 27.1

2. With the aggressive approach, short-term loans are needed to meet fluctuating current assets and a long-term loan is used to meet the permanent current asset need.
3. The minimum current asset level of ₹ 70 occurs in 4Q. Thus, we can determine seasonal borrowing.

1Q: ₹ 130 – ₹ 70	=	₹ 60
2Q: ₹ 230 – ₹ 70	=	160
3Q: ₹ 150 – ₹ 70	=	80
4Q: ₹ 70 – ₹ 70	=	0
Total borrowing	=	₹ 300
Average borrowing	=	₹ 300/4 = ₹ 75

4. Total interest (financing) cost, then, can be calculated.

₹ 75 × 0.10	=	₹ 7.5
+ ₹ 70 × 0.14	=	9.8
Total interest cost	=	₹ 17.3

5. The conservative plan has a net cost disadvantage of ₹ 9.8 corre a year (₹ 27.1 - ₹ 17.3). Management must decide if the added safety of this arrangement warrants the additional cost.

2. Khalsa Enterprises is a processor of fresh, frozen, and canned fish. Its business is moderately seasonal, being tied somewhat to annual harvest of salmon and other species. To service its customers, Khalsa must maintain a level of current assets. However, to enhance its earnings, a greater investment in fixed assets (processing facilities) is needed. R.D. Sondhi, Khalsa's financial manager, is trying to measure return and risk outcomes associated with different mixes of asset investment and financing arrangements. He has narrowed his choice to the following four plans (A, B, C, and D):

	Plan			
	A	*B*	*C*	*D*
Assets				
Current	₹ 300[a]	₹ 100	₹ 300	₹ 100
Fixed	100	200	100	200

Total	₹ 400	₹ 300	₹ 400	₹ 300
Equities				
Current liabilities	₹ 50	₹ 50	₹ 100	₹ 100
Long-term debt	150	150	100	100
Shareholders' equity	200	100	200	100
Total	₹ 400	₹ 300	₹ 400	₹ 300

[a] All amounts are in crore of ₹.

Sodhi anticipates that the rates of return on current and fixed assets will be 0.10 adn 0.25, respectively. He also believes that financing costs on current liabilities and long-term debt will be 0.08 and 0.15, respectively. Burt intends to measure return with the *ROE* ratio and risk with the *NWC*/total assets ratio.

Evaluate the return and risk characteristics of the four strategies.

Solution

i) Determine the net profit with each strategy, as follows:

Plan	*Return*			*Cost*			*Net Profit*
A	₹ 300 × 0.10	=	₹ 30	₹ 50 × 0.08	=	₹ 4.0	
	100 × 0.25	=	25	150 × 0.15	=	22.5	
			₹ 55	₹ 26.5			₹ 28.5
B	₹ 100 × 0.10	=	₹ 10	same as A = 26.5			
	200 × 0.25	=	50				
			₹ 60				₹ 33.5
C	same as A	=	₹ 55	₹ 100 × 0.08	=	₹ 8.0	
				100 × 0.15	=	15.0	
				₹ 23.0			₹ 32.0
D	same as B = ₹ 60			same as C	=	₹ 23.0	₹ 37.0

ii) Next, determine return (*ROE*) and risk (*NWC*/total assets) estimates, as follows:

Plan	*ROE*			*Rank*	*NWC/Total Assets*			*Rank*
A	₹ 28.5 * ₹ 200	=	0.1425	4	₹ 250 * ₹ 400	=	0.625	1[a]
B	33.5 * 100	=	0.3350	2	50 * 300	=	0.167	3
C	32.0 * 200	=	0.1600	3	200 * 400	=	0.500	2
D	37.0 * 100	=	0.3700	1	0 * 300	=	0,000	4

[a] Ascending numbers indicate increasing risk.

iii) Recalling the low *NWC*/total assets ratio value imply *greater* risk, Sondhi must accept a lower return if he is unwilling to take greater risks. Although we cannot be sure which strategy he will select, it seems unlikely that the relatively small additional return (0.0350 = 0.3700 - 0.3350) with D—relatively small additional return (0.0350 = 0.3700) with D—relative to B—is worth the substantial increase in risk, recognizing that D has zero net working capital.

3. Gitam Press and the Galaxy Publishing Company had the following balance sheets as on March 31, 2013.

(₹ in '000)

	Gitam	*Galaxy*
Current assets	₹ 100,000	₹ 80,000
Fixed assets (net)	100,000	120,000
Total assets	₹ 200,000	₹ 200,000
Current liabilities	₹ 20,000	₹ 80,000
Long-term debt	80,000	20,000
Common stock	50,000	50,000
Retained earnings	50,000	50,000
Total liabilities and equity	₹ 200,000	₹ 200,000

Earnings before interest and taxes for both firms are ₹ 3 crore, and the effective tax is 40 percent.

(a) What is the return on equity for each firm if the interest rate on current liabilities is 10 percent and the rate on long-term debt is 13 percent?

(b) Assume that the short-term rate rises to 20 percent. While the rate on new long-term debt rises to 16 percent, the rate on existing long-term debt remains unchanged. What would be the return on equity for Gitam Press and Galaxy Publishing under these conditions?

(c) Which company is in a riskier position? Why?

Solution

(a) and (b)

Income Statements for Year Ended March 31, 2013

(Thousands of ₹)

	Gitam Press		*Galaxy Publishing*	
	a	*b*	*a*	*b*
EBIT	₹ 30,000	₹ 30,000	₹ 30,000	₹ 30,000
Interest	12,400	14,400	10,600	18,600

Taxable income	₹ 17,600	₹ 15,600	₹ 19,400	₹ 11,400
Taxes (40%)	7,040	6,240	7,760	4,560
Net income	₹ 10,560	₹ 9,360	₹ 11,640	₹ 6,840
Equity	₹ 1,00,00	₹ 1,00,000	₹ 1,00,000	₹ 1,00,000
Return on equity	10.56%	9.36%	11.64%	6.84%

(c) The Gitam Press has a higher ROE when short-term interest rates are high, whereas Galaxy Publishing does better when rates are lower.

Galaxy's position is riskier. First, its profits and return on equity are much more volatile than Gitam's. Second, Galaxy must renew its large short-term loan every year, and if the renewal come up at a time when money is very tight, when its business is depressed, or both, Galaxy could be denied credit, which could put it out of business.

4. Vijay Bharat Company is attempting to establish a current assets policy, Fixed assets are ₹ 6 crore and the firm plans to maintain a 50 percent debt-to-assets ratio. The interest rate is 10 percent on all debt. Three alternative current asset policies are under consideration: 40, 50, and 60 percent of projected sales. The company expects to earn 15 percent before interest and taxes on sales of ₹ 30 crore. The company effective tax rate is 40 percent. What is the expected return on equity under each alternative?

Solution

Vijay Bharat Company: Alternative Balance Sheets

(₹ in '000)

	Restricted (40%)	*Moderate (50%*	*Relaxed (60%)*
Current assets	₹ 1,20,000	₹ 1,50,000	₹ 1,80,000
Fixed assets	60,000	60,000	60,000
Total assets	₹ 1,80,000	₹ 2,10,000	₹ 2,40,000
Debt	₹ 90,000	₹ 1,05,000	₹ 1,20,000
Equity	90,000	1,05,000	1,20,000
Total liabilities and equity	₹ 1,80,000	₹ 2,10,000	₹ 2,40,000

Vijay Bharat Company: Alternative Income Statements

(*₹ in '000*)

	Restricted	*Moderate*	*Relaxed*
Sales	₹ 3,00,000	₹ 3,00,000	₹ 3,00,000
EBIT	45,000	45,000	45,000
Interest (10%)	9,000	10,500	12,000
Earning before taxes	₹ 36,000	₹ 34,500	33,000
Taxes (40%)	14,400	13,800	13,200
Net income	₹ 21,600	20,700	₹ 19,800
ROE	24.0%	19.7%	16.5%

QUESTIONS

1. Define and describe the difference between the operating cycle and cash conversion cycle for a typical manufacturing company.
2. Discuss the profitability versus risk tradeoffs associated with alternative levels of working capital investment.
3. Why is it possible for the effective cost of long-term debt to exceed the cost of short-term debt, even when short-term interest rates are higher than long-term rates?
4. Describe the matching approach for meeting the financing needs of a company. What is the primary difficulty in implementing this approach?
5. Discuss the profitability versus risk tradeoffs associated with alternative combinations of short-term and long-term debt used in financing a company's assets.
6. As the difference between the costs of short-and long-term debt becomes smaller, which financing plan, aggressive or conservative, becomes more attractive?
7. Why is no single working capital investment and financing policy necessarily optimal for all firms? What additional factors need to be considered in establishing a working capital policy?
8. Define and contrast the terms *working capital* and *net working capital.*
9. Why is working capital management considered so important by shareholders, creditors, and the firm's financial manager? What is the definition of net working capital?
10. How can the differences between the returns on current and fixed assets and the cost of current liabilities and long-term funds be used to determine how best to change a firm's net working capital?
11. "Uncertainty makes it difficult for a financial manager to predict the company's requirements for short-term funds". Discuss. What steps can the financial manager take to minimise the resulting risks to the company?

12. Define the following terms: (a) Permanent asset investments; (b) Temporary asset investments; (c) Permanent sources of financing; (d) Temporary sources of financing; (e) Spontaneous sources of financing.
13. Explain why many economists argue that short-term borrowing cost are usually less than long-term borrowing costs.
14. Should a company follow any rule in determining the proportions of short-term and long-term funds that it uses in financing its operations? Justify your answer.
15. It is said that funds tied up in current assets have a detrimental effect on the company's profitability. Why then do companies elect to hold such assets?
16. Is there any reason for a company to use short-term finance to finance current assets and long-term finance fixed assets?
17. Why is an increase in a firm's ratio of current to total assets expected to decrease both profits and risk as measured by net working capital? How can a changes in the ratio of firm's current liabilities to total assets affect its profitability and risk?
18. Define the hedging principle. How can this principle be used in the management of working capital?
19. Explain the advantage of a matching financing plan relative to the financing plan that extensively uses: (a) Long-term financing; (b) Negotiated short-term financing.
20. What is the conservative approach to financing a firm's funds requirements? Why would a firm using the conservative approach be advised to finance no more than its projected peak financial need with long-term funds? What kind of profitability-risk-trade-off is involved?
21. What is the basic premise of the aggressive approach for meeting a firm's funds requirements? What are the effects of this approach on the firm's profitability and risk?
22. As the difference between the cost of short-term financing and long-term financing becomes smaller, which financing plan-aggressive or conservative-becomes more attractive? Would the aggressive or the conservative approach be preferable if the costs were equal? Why?
23. If a firm has a constant funds requirement throughout the year, which, if any, of the three financing plans is preferable? Why?
24. "Current assets are those assets which are turned over and at least partially replaced within the operating cycle of the company". What differences will you usually find between the holdings of current assets of a manufacturer who sells on credit and a retailer who sells only on case basis?
25. (a) Which of the following working capital financing policies subjects the firm to a greater risk? b(i) Financing permanent current assets with long-term debt; (ii) Financing fluctuating current assets with long-term debt. (b) Which policy will produce the higher expected profitability?

PROBLEMS

1. South Industries has forecasted its monthly needs for working capital (net of spontaneous sources such as accounts payable) for 2014 as follows:

Month	*Amount*	*Month*	*Amount*
January	₹ 75,00,000	July	₹ 60,00,000
February	60,00,000	August	75,00,000
March	30,00,000	September	85,00,000
April	25,00,000	October	90,00,000
May	35,00,000	November	95,00,000
June	45,00,000	December	90,00,000

Short-term borrowing (that is, a bank line of credit) costs the company 10 percent, and long-term borrowing (that is, term loans) costs the company 12 percent. Any funds in excess of its monthly needs can be invested in interest-bearing marketable securities to yield 8 percent per annum.

(a) Suppose the company follows a *conservative* policy by financing the *maximum* amount of its working capital requirements for the coming year with long-term borrowing and investing any excess funds in short-term marketable securities. Determine South's *net* interest costs during 2014 under the policy.

(b) Suppose the company follows an *aggressive* policy by financing *all* its working capital requirements for the coming year with short-term borrowing. Determine South's interest costs during 2014 under this policy.

(c) Discuss the profitability versus risk tradeoffs associated with these conservative and aggressive working capital financing policies.

2. Gicky Enterprises is considering two alternative working capital investment and financing policies. *Policy A* requires the firm to keep its current assets at 65 percent of forecasted sales and to finance 70 percent of its debt requirements with long-term debt (and 30 percent with short-term debt.) *Policy B,* on the other hand, requires the firm to keep its current assets at 40 percent of forecasted sales and to finance 40 percent of its debt requirements with long-term debt (and 60 percent with short-term debt). Forecasted sales for next year are ₹ 20 crore. Earnings before interest and taxes are projected to be 15 percent of sales. The firm's corporate income tax rate is 40 percent. Its fixed assets total ₹ 10 crore. The firm desires to maintain its existing financial structure which consists of 50 percent debt and 50 percent equity. Interest rates on short-and long-term debt are 12 and 15 percent respectively.

(a) Determine the expected rate of return on equity next year for Gicky under each of the working capital policies.

(b) Which policy is riskier? Cite specific evidence to support this contention.

3. Banglore Electric Company, manufacturer of various types of electrical equipment, is examining its working capital investment policy for next year. Projected fixed assets and current liabilities for next year are ₹20 crore ₹18 crore, respectively. Sales and EBIT are partially a function of the company's investment in working capital-particularly its investment in inventories and receivables. The company is considering the following three different working capital investment policies:

Working Capital Investment Policy	*Investment in Current Assets (in crore of ₹)*	*Projected Sales (in crore of rupees)*	*EBIT (in crore of ₹)*
Aggressive (small investment in current assets)	₹ 28	₹ 59	₹ 5.9
Moderate (moderate investment in current assets)	30	60	6.0
Conservative (large investment in current assets)	32	61	6.1

(a) Determine the following for each of the working capital investment policies:
   i. Rate of return on total assets (that is, EBIT/total assets).
   ii. Net working capital position.
   iii. Current ratio.

(b) Describe the profitability versus risk tradeoffs of these three policies.

4. Reynolds Equipment Company is investigating the use of various combinations of short-term and long-term debt in financing its assets. Assume that the company has decided to employ ₹30 crore in current assets, along with ₹35 crore in fixed assets, in its operations next year. Given this level of current assets, anticipated sales and EBIT for next year are ₹60 crore and ₹6 crore, respectively. The company's income tax rate is 40 percent. Shareholders' equity will be used to finance ₹40 crore of its assets, with the remainder being financed by short-term and long-term debt. Reynolds is considering implementing one of the following financing policies:

Financing Policy	*Amount of Short-Term Debt (in crore of ₹)*	*Interest Rate*	
		LTD (%)	*STD (%)*
Aggressive (large amount of short-term debt)	₹24	8.5	5.5
Moderate (moderate amount of short-term debt)	18	8.0	5.0
Conservative (small amount of short-term debt)	12	7.5	4.5

(a) Determine the following for each of the financing policies:
   i. Expected rate of return on shareholders' equity.
   ii. Net working capital position.
   iii. Current ratio.

(b) Evaluate the profitability versus risk tradeoffs of these three policies.

5. Superior Brands, Inc., wishes to analyse the *joint impact* of its working capital investment and financing policies on shareholder return and risk. The company has ₹ 40 crore in fixed assets. Also, the firm's financial structure consists of short-term and long-term debt and equity. Superior wishes to maintain a debt to total assets ratio of 50 percent, where debt consists of both short-term and long-term sources. The company's tax rate is 40 percent. The following information was developed for three different policies under consideration:

Working Capital Investment and Financing Policy	*Investment in Current Assets (in crore of rupees)*	*Amount of STD (in crore of rupees)*	*Projected Sales (in crore of rupees)*	*EBIT (in crore of rupees)*	*LTD (%)*	*Interest Rate STD (%)*
Aggressive	₹ 56	₹ 48	₹ 118	₹ 11.8	9.5	6.5
Moderate	60	36	120	12.0	9.0	6.0
Conservative	64	24	122	12.2	8.5	5.5

(a) Determine the following for each of the three working capital investment and financing policies: (i) Expected rate of return on shareholders' equity; (ii) Net working capital position; (iii) Current ratio.

22

MANAGEMENT OF CASH AND MARKETABLE SECURITIES

INTRODUCTION

Cash is the lifeblood of a business firm. It is needed to acquire supplies, resources, equipment, and other assets used in generating the products and services provided by the firm. It is also needed to pay wages and salaries to workers and managers, taxes to governments, interest and principal to creditors, and dividends to shareholders. More fundamentally, cash is the medium of exchange which allows management to carry on the various activities of the business firm from day to day. As long as the firm has the cash to meet these obligations, financial failure is improbable. Without cash, or at least access to it, bankruptcy becomes a grim possibility. Such is the emerging view of modern corporate cash management. On the other hand, marketable securities come in many forms. Their main characteristic is that they represent "near cash" and may be readily sold. Hence marketable securities serve as a back up pool of liquidity that provides cash quickly when needed. Marketable security also provide a short-term investment outlet for excess cash and are also useful for meeting planned outflows of funds. In the previous chapter we introduced the general concepts associated with managing the firm's current assets and liability positions. In this chapter we look in more detail at the problem involved with managing two very important components of current assets; cash and marketable securities.

MOTIVES FOR HOLDING CASH AND MARKETABLE SECURITIES

Cash and short-term, interest-bearing investments (marketable securities) are the firm's least productive assets. They are not required in producing goods or services, unlike the firm's fixed assets. They are not part of the process of selling as are inventory and accounts receivable. When firms hold cash in currency or in non-interest-bearing accounts, they obtain no direct return on their investment. Even if the cash is temporarily invested in marketable securities, its return is much less than the return on other assets held by the firm. So why hold cash or marketable securities at all? Couldn't the firm's resources be better deployed elsewhere?

Despite the seemingly low returns, there are several good reasons why firms hold cash and marketable securities. It is useful to think of the firm's portfolio of cash and marketable securities as comprised of three parts with each part addressing a particular reason for holding these assets.

CASH FOR TRANSACTIONS

One very important reason for holding cash in the form of non-interest-bearing currency and deposits is *transactions demand*. Since debts are settled via the exchange of cash, the firm must hold some cash in the bank to pay suppliers.

CASH AND NEAR-CASH ASSETS AS HEDGES

Unfortunately, the firm's future cash needs for transactions purposes are often quite uncertain; emergencies may arise for which the firm needs immediate cash. The firm must hedge against the possibility of these unexpected needs. Several types of hedges are possible. For example, the firm can arrange to be able to borrow from its bank on short notice should funds suddenly be needed. Another approach is to hold extra cash and near-cash assets beyond what would be needed for transactions purposes. By "near-cash assets," we mean interest-earning marketable assets that have *very* short maturities (a few days or less), and thus can be liquidated to provide funds on short notice with very little risk of loss.

Clearly, the more of this total hedging reserve held in near-cash assets and the less held in cash, the greater the interest earned. However, there is a trade-off between this interest revenue and the transactions costs involved in purchasing and selling such near-cash assets. These transactions costs have a fixed cost component; the firm bears these fixed costs when it buys or sells these assets regardless of the size of investment. Thus, whether it is economical to invest part or all of the hedging reserve in near-cash assets depends on the amount of the reserve. Firms that keep smaller reserves (because their transactions needs are either smaller or more certain) are more likely to hold these reserves in cash, while firms with larger reserves keep them in near-cash assets.

TEMPORARY INVESTMENTS

Many firms experience some seasonality in sales. Often, there will be times during the year when such firms have excess cash that will be needed later in the year. Firms in this situation have several choices. One alternative is to pay out the excess cash to its share holders when this cash is available, and then issue new securities, later in the year when funding is needed. However, the costs of issuing new securities usually make this a disadvantageous strategy. More commonly, firms will temporarily invest the cash in interest-earning marketable securities from the time the cash is available until the time it is needed. Proper planning and investment selection for this strategy can yield a reasonable return on such temporary investment.

All of these are valid reasons for holding cash and marketable securities in response to the needs and uncertainties faced by the firm. In fact, firms generally hold a surprisingly large portion of their assets in these forms, despite the disadvantage of low returns.

CASH MANAGEMENT SYSTEMS

The *cash system* of a firm is the mechanism that provides the linkage between cash flows. The financial manager of the firm has the responsibility, at least in part, of developing and maintaining the policies and procedures necessary to achieve an efficient flow of cash for the firm's operations. The external elements of the cash system include a *collection system* for getting cash into the firm and *disbursement system* for paying the suppliers and other receivers of cash. The internal portion of the cash system consists of a *concentration system* to move cash from the entry point in the firm to the concentration bank and a *disbursement funding system* to move funds from the concentration bank to the disbursement banks so that payments can be made. Since banks are the major institutions involved in the payment system, the financial manager is also responsible for maintaining adequate *banking relations* to ensure the smooth flow of cash into, through, and out of the firm. These activities constitute the *cash management system* of the firm.

COLLECTION SYSTEMS

A collection system is a set of procedures and banking arrangement used to move value from customers or other payers to the payer's deposit bank account, Since finance manager is concerned with value transfer, the analysis of collection system focuses on creating an available balance in the deposit account and not just receiving transfer information (e.g., a cheque). Collection systems must also be concerned with payment information that supports the payment. A payment received without sufficient documentation may incur high search cost for locating information that permits accounts receivable to credit the appropriate customer's account. In short, an efficient collection system performs the functions of mobilising cash, providing accurate cash flow information, providing timely information on sales and customers accounts, and providing an audit trail for goods control.

OBJECTIVE OF A COLLECTION SYSTEM

When a selling firm transfers value to a buyer through the provision of goods or services. There is an opportunity cost incurred if value is not promptly received in return. A primary objective of a collection system is to receive value from the buyer as quickly as possible. A second objective is to receive and process information associated with the payment. A third related factor to consider in designing a collection system is the relationship the firm has with those making payments. Collection procedures have the potential to harm payer-payee relationships. Collection system design must also consider costs associated with receiving payments and the accompanying information. These costs may be associated directly with transaction processing, such as bank costs, postage costs, etc., or may be more administrative in nature. An additional cost factor primarily relates to systems in which coin and currency is the predominant payment vehicle, costs of losses from theft or fraud.

Cost of Collection Float

One of the most important factors in the objective function is to minimise the cost of collection float. To illustrate, assume a company is losing approximately 6 calendar days of interest on ₹ 20,00,000 each week. The annual cost of this float at 12% opportunity cost is:

$$₹\ 20{,}00{,}000 \times 6 \text{ days} \times .12/365 \times 52 = ₹\ 2{,}05{,}150 \text{ per year.}$$

Value of Payment Information

Information accompanying the payment is vital to the firm's accounts receivable function. If payment is received quickly but remittance information is delayed, missing, or garbled, accounts receivable may not be able to post payments to accounts in a timely or accurate manner. In the example, it is important for the company to know which customers' costs are being covered by the weekly payment so that billing can be accurate.

Value of Relationship with Payer

If there are problems in posting payment information to a customer's account, the relationship between the firm and customer may be harmed. For example, suppose the collection system receives a customer's payment very quickly but fails to credit the customer's account for several days. Suppose that an order is held until notice is received from accounts receivable that last month's payment has been made. The delay in posting could cause delay in release of goods and may irreparably harm relations with the customer. What may have been gained in float may be offset many fold by lost business.

Collection System Costs

A collection system incurs costs in processing payments. Some of these costs are direct, such as bank charges for cheque processing or wire transfers. Other costs are indirect, such as administrative effort in managing the collection system. Collection system cost must be traded off with other factors in the objective function. The cost differential must be traded off with the collection float difference.

Costs of Losses from Fraud and Theft

In systems that collect payments primarily through cash, there is a potential for loss due to theft and fraud. It takes only a small number of losses through theft or fraud to counteract an otherwise very efficiently designed collection system the minimises collection float but that fails to deal with security problems.

DESIGN OF A COLLECTIVE SYSTEM

A collection system moves payments from payors to available deposits in the banking system as efficiently as possible. To optimise the collective system, the finance manager is to concentrate on following major elements:

Collection Float

The term *collection float* refers to the total time lag between the mailing of the payment by the payor and the availability of cash in the bank. *Mail float* results from the time that elapse from the mailing of the until is receipt. *Processing float* is due to the processing time before the cheque is deposited in the banking system. The last component of collection float is *availability float,* which is a result of the firm's not being granted immediate availability on all deposit items. These last two elements of collection float were referred as *deposit float*. They represent the difference between the cash that is recorded as a deposit on the company's books and the increase in the available balance at the bank.

Float Measurement

The measurement of float is a function both of the time lag and of the amount involved. Float is usually measured in ₹ amount days, which are calculated by multiplying the time lag in days by the ₹ amount being delayed. Float can be measured either on each item that is processed or on an average daily basis.

Individual Item Float

The float on each item is found by multiplying the amount of the payment by the number of days of delay for that payment. It is the product of these two quantities, and not either one individually, that is important in measuring float. We can see from the calculation of collection float in Exhibit-1 that the float on a ₹ 10,000-item that is delayed for 6 days is identical to the float on a ₹ 20,000 item that is delayed for 3 days.

EXHIBIT-1

CALCULATION OF FLOAT FOR AN INDIVIDUAL ITEM

A Cheque for ₹ 10,000 is mailed from customer A on July 6, a Friday; because of mail, processing, and availability delays, it is not credited as available funds in the bank of Kapoor Enterprises until the following Thursday, 6 days later the float for this cheque is

Float = ₹ 10,000 × 6 days = 60,000 ₹—days.

A Cheque for ₹ 20,000 is mailed from customer B on July 6, but it is available on Monday, 3 days later. The float for this Cheque is

Float = 20,000 × 3 days = 60,000 ₹—days.

Average Daily Float

The analysis of many situations requires the use of a measure of *average daily float* for a set of collection items over some time period, say a month. There are two ways that this measure can be calculated. While they both result in the same average daily float calculation in the end, different insights can be gained from each calculation.

EXHIBIT-2

CALCULATION OF AVERAGE DAILY FLOAT

A firm receives three items each month, as shown in the following table. The float for each item is calculated using the procedure given in Exhibit-1.

Item	*₹ Amount*		*No. of Days Delay*	*₹ Days*
(1)	(2)		(3)	(4) = (2) × (3)
1	45,00,000	×	3	1,35,00,000
2	30,00,000	×	4	1,20,00,000
3	25,00,000	×	7	1,75,00,000
Total	₹ 1,00,00,000			4,30,00,000

A. Following the calculation procedure given in (l), we have

$$\text{Average daily float} = \frac{\text{total float}}{\text{total days}} = \frac{4{,}30{,}00{,}000}{30 \text{ days}} = ₹\ 14{,}33{,}333 \text{ — days.}$$

B. Following the calculation procedure given in (2), we have

$$\text{Average daily receipts} = \frac{\text{total receipts}}{\text{total days}} = \frac{₹\ 1{,}00{,}00{,}000}{30 \text{ days}} = ₹\ 3{,}33{,}333.$$

$$\left[\frac{4.5}{10}\times 3\right]+\left[\frac{3}{10}\times 4\right]+\left[\frac{2.5}{10}\times 7\right]=4.3 \text{ days}$$

Average daily float = average daily receipts × weighted average delay

= 3,33,333 × 4.3 = ₹ 14,33,333 — days.

1. The average daily float is determined by calculating the float for each item, summing the ₹-days of float for the set of items during the period, and dividing this total by the number of days in the period
2. The average daily float is calculated as follows determine the average daily receipts by dividing the total receipts by the number of days in the period. Calculate the weighted average delay by multiplying the delay for each item by that item's proportion of the total receipts during the period. Finally, find the average daily float by multiplying the average daily receipts by the weighted average delay (see Exhibit 2.).

The first method more clearly highlights which individual items contribute most to overall float. For example, Item 3 (the Cheque for ₹ 25,00,000) contributes more float than the other two items.

Determining the Cost of Float

The cost of float represents the opportunity cost because the cash is unavailable for use during the time the payments are tied up in collection. The cost of float is determined by multiplying the average daily float by the opportunity cost. In the previous example, assume that the data represent a typical month and that the annual opportunity cost is 10%. The monthly cost of the collection float is ₹ 14,33,333 × 0.10/12 = ₹ 11,944, while the annual cost is ₹ 14,33,333 × 0.10 = ₹ 1,43,333.

The float results in this being delayed by a total of 1.3 days; the present value (PV) of this delayed cash flows is

$$PV = \frac{₹\ 3,33,333}{(1 + 0.1 \times 4.3/360)} = ₹\ 3,32,935.33$$

Thus we lose in present value ₹ 3,33,333 – ₹ 3,32,935 or ₹ 397.67 for each day's collections. For a 30-day month, this is a loss of value of ₹ 11,930.10. When we compare this figure to the previous result of a cost of ₹ 11,944, we see that the error is only ₹ 14 or 0.1%.

OPTIMISING THE COLLECTION SYSTEM

Potential for Increased Present Value: To optimise mailed payment collection, three elements of collection system design are important:

1. Reducing float costs by speeding the availability of cash in the banking system. This can be done by reducing mail, processing, or availability delay.
2. Reducing the operating costs of the collection system. This may involve a tradeoff between fixed and variable costs and may include the use of outside contractors to perform some of the functions of the collection system.
3. Reducing the administrative costs of managing the system.

Although some of these costs may be hard to identify in many cases, at least the direction is clear; the more complex the system, the more difficult it is to manage and the higher are the administrative costs. The attempt to optimise a system usually involves a tradeoff between these three cost elements; a reduction in one type of cost is available only with an increase in another.

Reducing Mail Float: Mail float can be reduced by careful location of the collection points. In general, the closer the collection points are to the payors, the shorter is the time needed for the item to arrive at the collection point. The geographical dispersion of payors affects the number and location of the collection points. A large number of collection points reduces mail float but increases administrative costs and possibly operating costs associated with the collection points.

Reducing Processing Float: Payments must be processed and conveyed to the deposit bank before the cash can become available in the banking system. The three issues to be considered are speed, accuracy, and security. For reasons of both security and availability, the payments are usually processed and deposited at least once per day. The timing of this processing is a function of the pattern of the receipts during the day, the cutoff times at the bank, whether the processing is done by the firm or by an outside agent, and the schedules of courier services, if used, to transport the deposit to the bank. The number of items received, the form of payment, the average size of an item, and the pattern of arrival are all factors in determining who does the processing and how much automation is used. There is frequently a tradeoff between reducing the float cost by processing the items more rapidly and increasing the cost of processing.

Reducing Availability Float: The form of payment, the location of the bank on which it is drawn, and negotiation with the deposit bank affect the availability float. Cash is immediately available upon deposit into the bank, assuming that the cutoff time for the day is met. The availability granted cheques depends upon the location of the institution on which they are drawn relative to the deposit bank, and the size of the item.

We have seen that the design of a good collection system can enhance the present value of the firm by reducing the opportunity cost of the different types of delay in receiving the funds. An optimal system is one that makes the maximum contribution to the present value of the firm. The nature of the business and the way the receipts arrive affect the type of collection system used.

TYPES OF COLLECTION SYSTEMS

Over-the -Counter Collections

The first specialised collection system that we describe is an *over the counter* collection system, where the payment is received in a face-to-face meeting with the customer. Most retail or consumer businesses receive at least some of their payments on an over-the-counter basis. Since payments are not mailed, an over the counter system does not contain mail float.

The basic components of an over-the-counter collection system include the *field unit* at which the payment is received, a *local deposit bank* that serves as the entry point for the firm's banking system, and an input into the firm's central information system.

In designing an over-the-counter collection system, the issues addressed use the location of the field units, the type of payment accepted, location and compensation of deposit banks, and the reporting system. Some of these elements are solely the function of management decisions, whereas others may be influenced by competition and the institutional arrangements that are available.

Field Office Location: Field units are generally locations where the firm delivers goods or services to the customer and collects payments. In many retail establishments (such as a restaurant) the payments are received when the merchandise or service is delivered to the customer. In most cases, the location of field units is dictated by marketing concerns (an attractive location, good traffic patterns, proximity to competitors, availability of adequate facilities, etc.) and is not an element in collection system design.

Type of Payment Accepted: Over-the-counter payment can be made by cash cheque or third-party credit (debit) card finance. Each form of payment has unique advantages and disadvantages. Cash is often immediately available, is convenient for small purchase amounts, has small handling costs for small quantities, and involves little risk that the payment is invalid. The disadvantages are that it is inconvenient for large payments, requires tight controls in processing, and requires security in handling because it is easy to divert and difficult to trace. A cheque is convenient for large purchase, and security problems are less. The disadvantages are that there is a processing delay (cheques must be deposited before the cash is usable), there may be availability delay before value is received, and there is a risk that the cheque will not be honoured when presented for payment. Third-party credit (debt) cards are convenient, have low security risks, and have a certainty of payment if proper procedures are followed. The disadvantages are the cost, in the form of a discount from the face value, and a possible delay in receipt of value for the payment.

Selection of Deposit Banks: For convenience and safety in handling cash, geographical proximity is a major factor in the choice of banks for deposit of over-the-counter payments. Where regional or statewide branch banking is available, there may be a tradeoff between geographical proximity of a particular branch and administrative and concentration costs of dealing with fewer banks.

Bank Compensation: In addition to acting as an input for deposits into the banking system, some banks, may provide services such as cash replenishment. They must be fairly compensated for these services. Price charged for services, flexibility to pay in balances of in fees, availability on deferred items, and compatibility with the concentration system affect the contribution of the collection system to the net present value of the firm.

Information Gathering: The finance manager must know the amount of deposits and their availability before the money can be put to use. It is usually desirable to have dual reporting of the information for control purposes. One report generally comes from the field manager, containing the amount of receipts and the deposit. Another comes from the deposit bank, containing deposit and availability information. The bank report from small deposit banks is frequently in the form of a monthly statement so it may not be timely enough for the needs. A simple reporting system for timely deposit information is for the manager of the field unit to call headquarters or a third-party information processor and report the deposit information prior to going to the bank to make the deposit.

In a more sophisticated reporting system, the field manager enters the amount of the deposit into a point-of-sale computer that records sales, inventory, and other information. Periodically, perhaps after hours, these data are transmitted directly to the information system at headquarters or to a service bureau for further processing. If the system is set up to gather and transmit information overnight, the treasurer knows exactly how much is available in each bank at the start of the day and the identity of any nonreporting field units.

Mailed Payments Collection System

For many companies, payments, almost always cheques are mailed by the customer in response to an invoice. A mailed payments system contains all three components of collection float: *mail float, processing float,* and *availability float.*

The mailed payments collection system consists of collection centers, deposit banks, and an information system. Payments are mailed by customers to a designated collection center operated either by the company or by an outside agent. Payments are processed at the collection center; cheques are encoded, the deposit is prepared and made, and data are transmitted to the company's information system.

Other Collection Systems

Several other types of collection systems are used. Many of them use electronics and advanced communication systems. Although not widely used at present, they are growing in importance as electronic communications and transactions gain greater acceptance.

Preauthorised cheques (PACs), preauthorised drafts (PADs) etc.

They are sometimes used when the payment amount (or range) and the payment date are specified in advance. On the agreed date, the pay initiates the value transfer from the payer through the banking system, with no need for further action on the part of the payor. Preauthorised payments eliminate mail float, reduce processing and availability float, and improve both parties' forecasting ability.

Electronic Collection Procedures

The time necessary for transmittal of cash from one firm to another revolves largely around the passing from one hand to another of a piece of paper—the remitting firm's cheque. One alternative to this process is to substitute an electronic message of payment for the cheque. This eliminates the need for the paper and thus the various floats associated with taking the paper from one place to another.

Lockbox Systems

A "lockbox" is a post office box number to which some or all of the firm's customers are instructed to send their cheques. The firm grants permission to its bank to take these cheques and immediately start them in the clearing process. In fact, the mail addressed to this "post office box" is actually delivered directly to the firm's lockbox bank. In this way, at firm float is eliminated. Judicious placement of lockboxes and instructions to customers on where to send their cheques can also serve to reduce mail and clearing float substantially.

There is a trade-off between these two sets of costs. As the firm increases the number of lockboxes (properly placed), the opportunity cost of float will be reduced. However, each additional lockbox adds another fixed charge to the costs of the lockbox system. Eventually, the addition of another lockbox increases rather than decreases total costs. This relationship is portrayed in Figure-1.

To solve the lockbox location problem, the firm must collect four sets of data:

1. The mail and clearing times for sending cheques from each part of the firm's geographic sales area to each possible lockbox.

2. The total amount of daily funds and number of cheques received by the firm from each part of the sales area. This is usually collected by an examination of the postmarks on a sample of the firm's incoming cheques. A stratified sample of high-value cheques may be used to reduce collection costs for these data.
3. The required rate of return (for computing opportunity costs).
4. The variable and fixed costs of each proposed lockbox site. To speed clearing times, lockboxes are usually located in cities.

With these data in hand, it is relatively simple to calculate the *one best lockbox* if the firm is constrained to have only one. This optimal solution to the *one-lockbox problem* is simply the lockbox which has the lowest total cost, defined again as the sum of the opportunity cost of float and the costs of the lockbox.

FIGURE-1

COSTS IN LOCKBOX !SYSTEMS !VERSUS NUMBER OF !LOCKBOXES

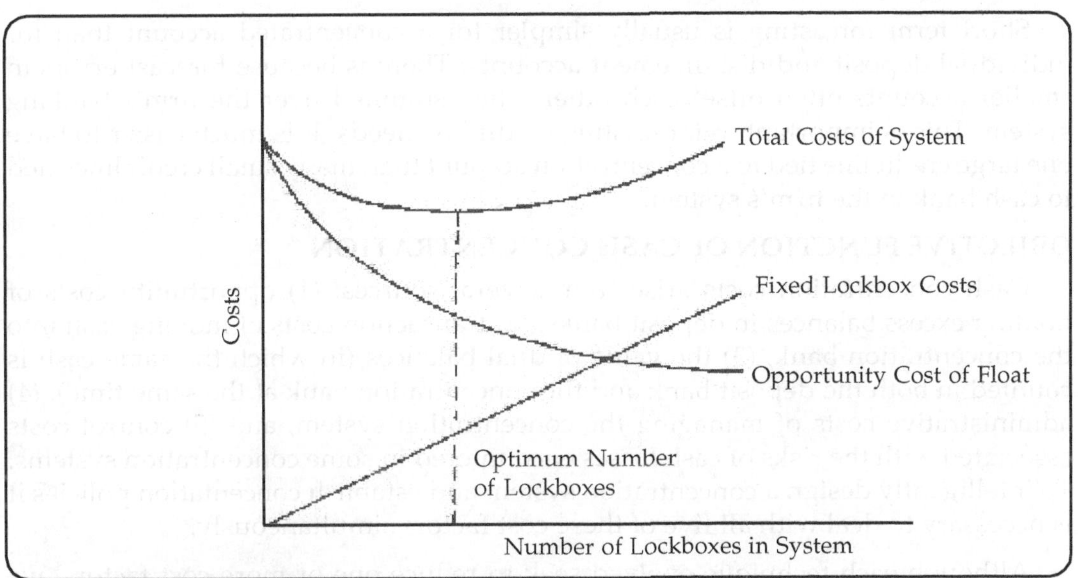

CASH CONCENTRATION STRATEGIES

Concentration is sometimes a neglected part of cash management because firm tend to think that when the cash is in their banking system, the battle is over. Nevertheless there are significant managerial decisions that must still be made to insure that cash is moved efficiently to accounts where it can benefit the firm. Once the remittance from the firm's customers have been received and cleared, the resulting cash balances are available in the firm's lockbox (depository) banks. It is useful for the firm to gather these balances from the lockbox banks into a central bank account. The process of collecting funds is called *cash concentration.* There are two reasons why cash concentration is advantageous. First, the collection process results in a larger pool of funds. The larger pool makes any temporary interest-earning investments more economical because it reduces the transaction costs on investment. For example, if the firm gathers ₹ 10,000 from each of 10 accounts, the firm will have ₹ 1,00,000 to invest, resulting in one purchase of securities rather than 10. Also, the larger amount of funds may enable the firm to take advantage of higher-interest investments that require a larger minimum purchase. Second, with all the cash in a central location, keeping track of the cash (controlling the cash) is considerably simplified.

ADVANTAGES OF CONCENTRATION

Cash concentration simlipfies short-term borrowing and investing decisions. If deposits are more or less routinely transferred to the concentration bank, the finance manager need only make decisions about what to do with cash balances.

Concentrating cash into a central cash pool also facilities investment in short-term securities. Money market securities that give the highest rates are sold in large demonstrations. Accumulating cash in a concentration account provides the quantities needed to purchase such securities.

Short term forcasting is usually simpler for a concentrated account than for individual deposit and disbursement accounts. There is because forecast errors in smaller accounts often offset each other when summed over the firm's banking system. This is important in forecasting credit line needs. It is much easier to have one large credit line tied to a concentration account than many small credit lines tied to cash bank in the firm's system.

OBJECTIVE FUNCTION OF CASH CONCENTRATION

Cash concentration costs arise from several sources: (1) opportunity costs of holding excess balances in deposit banks, (2) transaction costs of moving cash into the concentration bank, (3) the value of dual balances (in which the same cash is counted in both the deposit bank and the concentration bank at the same time). (4) administrative costs of managing the concentration system, and (5) control costs associated with the risks of cash losses encountered in some concentration systems. To intelligently design a concentration system and establish concentation policies it is necessary to deal with all five of these cost factors simultaneously.

Although each technique evolved seek to reduce one or more cost factors, we must keep in mind the other factors may be adversely affected at the same time. The goal is to realise an overall reduction in the objective function.

Reducing Information, Processing, and Clearing Delays

Excess balances are caused primarily by delays in gathering and processing deposit information and by clearing transfers back to the deposit bank.

Information and Processing Delays

Delays often occur in receiving deposit information from field managers. Once firm, for example, requires deposit information to be gathered along with sales and inventory information and processed through several administrative levels. The result is a delay of several days before the cash manager receives deposit information to pass along to the concentration bank. By removing deposit information at an early stage and routing it directly to the cash manager, a significant reduction in excess balances is realised.

Another firm finds frequent delays caused by field managers' irregular reporting habits. This firm begins including reporting promptness as part of its field manager review. Again, excess balances are significantly reduced. Generally, no complex mathematical algorithms are required to trace through information and processing pathways in order to determine ways to shorten the timeline.

Anticipation—Moving Transfer Initiation Forward

Anticipation means initiating a transfer at the concentration bank before cash becomes available at the deposit bank. Thus, by the time the transfer clears the deposit bank, available cash will be there to cover the transfer. This is essentially a method for counteracting information and processing delays. There are two types of anticipation, one less risky than the other.

Ledger anticipation means to initiate a transfer on the basis of ledger deposit information from the deposit bank. Ledger deposits according to an availability schedule. Thus it is known with virtual certainty that a ledger deposit will be converted into an available deposit on a known date and will be able to cover a transfer on that date. There is little risk of overdraft with this form of anticipation. Ledger anticipation presupposes that management has access to ledger deposit information before the ledger deposit becomes available. Many lockbox banks, however, report on next-day basis—that is, they post deposits to accounts late in the evening and let the firm know the next morning about the amount of the ledger deposit. By then, of course, much of the deposit has already become available.

Deposit anticipation means to initiate a concentrating transfer before expected deposits in a deposit bank have been reported. Deposit anticipation, however, is clearly more risky than ledger anticipation, since there is no guarantee that the amount will be deposited. Furthermore, deposit anticipation may require some form of forecast of daily receipts and may entail more complex reconcilement of transfers and deposits.

Faster Transfer Mechanisms

Another way to reduce excess balances is to employ a faster transfer mechanism where excess balances are high. Where excess balances are high, mailed or automated depository transfer cheques (DTC) might be replaced with wire or automated clearing house (ACH) transfers. ACH may be replaced by wires.

Reducing Transfer Costs

Balance Averaging

A way to reduce transfer costs is to transfer less often. Because firms receive deposit information daily, most firms assume that transfers should also occur daily.

This may be unnecessary for some deposit banks. The key is to recognise that compensation is measured by averaging daily balances over some time period. The target compensating balance need not be met daily, but may be met on an average basis. The technique of allowing the balance in the bank to fluctuate above and below the target level is sometimes called *managing about a target of, as we prefer balance averaging*

Reducing Administrative Costs

Administrative costs arise from the management of the concentration system. Several tools are available to assist in concentration management. For instance, third-party information services can assist in gathering deposit information from the field. Besides providing a pure data collection function, such vendors may assist in making concentration decisions, for example, deciding how much to transfer on which days. Some banks already provide relatively simple decision support systems that permit firms to specify which days should be transfer days. This enables firms to depart from the customery—perhaps suboptional—practice making transfers equal deposits and allows them to balance average and perhaps use anticipation. Firms may develop their own concentration administrative control systems that incorporate cash flow forecasts into anticipatory transfers.

Improving Concentration Control

A major component of control in field systems is theft and fraud control. The concentration system should provide safeguards that minimise the possibility of cash being taken from field points before entering the firm's banking system. When complete control is left in the hands of the field manager, this can be a serious problem. One way to reduce the risk of loss is to obtain verifying deposit reports from the deposit bank. Most field banks are not part of balance reporting networks, so a source of information common in lockbox systems is lacking in field systems. To overcome this problem, one firm requires its field banks to inform to a third-party information gatherer with a report of the day's deposits. This provides a confirming source of deposit information to substantiate the report from the field manager.

Unfortunately, most firms rely on insufficient-funds notices from the field bank to alert them to potential problems. If the field manager has not been depositing cash as reported, the only way some firms find out is by eventually overdrafting the account when attempts are made to concentrate the cash. Systems that have large excess balances are likely to take longer to overdraft than systems that exercise more control.

DISBURSEMENT SYSTEMS

Disbursement systems include the banks and the delivery mechanisms and procedures firms use to facilitate the movement of cash from the firm's centralised cash pool to disbursement banks and then on to suppliers and other payers. Disbursement banks are the banks on which disbursement cheques are drawn. A disbursement system may be more complex than a collection system in one sense;

management must choose not only the disbursement banks but also the cheque-issuing points. In contrast, a lockbox bank is the cheque-receiving point, and management has no control over the drawee bank.

OBJECTIVE FUNCTION

The function of a disbursement system is to process the payment obligation to vendors. employees, and creditors. In attempting to maximise the present value of the firm, it is beneficial to delay the time at which value is transferred from the firm in a disbursement system. However, any potential gain in value must be balanced against the costs of delay.

Value of Disbursement Float

All other things equal, a firm would rather pay later than sooner. There is value in delayed payments because the firm can either invest cash for a longer time or put off the cost of obtaining cash from lenders or investors. The main elements of the cash outflow timeline, are payment initiation, mail, vendor processing, and clearing times. Lengthening one or more of these segments may be beneficial to the firm. Usually, the disbursement problem is concerned primarily with the latter three elements of this timeline. Nevertheless, it is useful to consider the payment initiation time as part of the decision process.

Components of Payment Float

The entire outflow timeline is defined as *payment float,* while *disbursement float* is measured from the time the payor mails the cheque to the time of presentment at the payor's bank. Disbursement float consists of (1) *mail float,* measured as the time between the payor's mailing of the cheque and the payee's receipt of it; (2) *processing float,* the time required by the payee to deposit the cheques after it has been received; and (3) *presentation* or *clearing float,* the time required by the banking system to return the cheque and present it against the payor's disbursement account. There is an additional time segment that is not associated with the transfer of value, and so we do not show it as part of the timeline. The segment has to do with reconciling cheque that have cleared and otherwise processing the information associated with value transfer. Most of these activities take place after the value transfer has been affected.

Mail Float Issue: One must be cautious regarding decisions to increase disbursement float by lengthening the mail float component. In part, the decision depends on whether the postmark date or the receipt date is the valid payment date. If the *post-mark date* is used by the payee to determine whether an invoice has been paid on time. The mail time is considered a part of disbursement float. Lengthening the mail time will increase the time value benefit to the firm. On the other hand, if the *receipt* date is considered the valid payment date, lengthening the mail time may have to be accompanied by an offsetting decrease in payment initiation time. There would then be no economic benefit to the firm.

Missed Discounts: Many credit terms permit discounts to be taken if payment is made before a given time period. Disbursement systems must consider the possible costs of missing discounts if payment cannot be made in time.

Excess Balances

Excess balances are defined as available balances above the level necessary to compensate the disbursement bank(s) for its services. Excess balances may be determined from the bank's daily balance report or monthly account analysis if these are provided.

Excess balances arise in disbursement banks primarily because transfers of available funds into the disbursement account may not be synchronized with amounts presented against the account. One cause of excess balances is a timing problem. Banks usually post cheques to accounts late in the day, usually after the cutoff time for accepting transactions for the day. To solve this problem, several alternatives are available.

1. The disbursement bank can sort out cheques drawn on the firm's account and report the totals to the firm in advance of posting. This enables the firm to transfer in enough cash to offset clearings. This is a form of controlled disbursing.
2. At the end of the day, the bank can automatically transfer cash into the account from another account at the same bank.
3. The bank can arrange to sweep any balances left at the end of the day automatically into an interest-bearing account.

Transaction Costs

Transaction costs refer to the costs of transferring value from the concentration account to the disbursement account and to the costs of transferring value to payees. Included in this category are bank charges, third-party vendor information charges, and in-house expenses associated with payment. We also include in transaction costs the costs of overdrafting the disbursement account and any borrowing costs incurred as a result of the overdraft. Some banks permit available overdraft but consider it a loan and charge daily interest. Other banks do not charge interest on available overdrafts.

Dual Balances

Dual balances arise when the disbursement account is funded by a cheque that becomes available at the disbursing account on one day but does not clear the concentration account until a later time. For the time of overlap, available balances exist in both banks at the same time. However, dual balances have been diminishing over time. They occur only sporadically, therefore, most firms do not take them into account when designing disbursement systems.

Payee Relationships

Although they are less important in collection and concentration systems, relationship with other parties are a primary concern in managing a disbursement system. For the collection problem, the seller has provided a good or service to the buyer. Therefore, almost any effort to speed cash inflows is generally considered ethically sound. With disbursement systems, however, the shoe is on the other foot. Now a good or service has already been provided, and payment is due. Efforts by the buyer to delay payment may be considered unfavourable by the seller. Designing disbursement systems that intentionally delay payments are considered by many to be tantamount to stretching payments. The payor benefits at the expense of the payee. The payor, in turn, may find further business dealings with the payee strained or even more expensive as the payee tries to recover some of its costs caused by delayed payments.

Measuring the costs of good supplier relationships is very difficult. Some payment delays may seem virtually costless. But beyond a certain point. consequences may be felt in the form of general ill will, higher prices, delivery holdups, damaged image, and so on. Further delays may even bring legal action and harmed credit ratings.

Administrative Costs

Administrative costs include the management of the disbursement information system and the provision of information support for funding decisions. The objectives of management are to obtain timely information about the disbursed amounts so that disbursements can be covered. In this way, good banking relations can be maintained. Another, perhaps greater, motivation is to preserve the firm's central cash pool and keep it invested as long as possible.

Another administrative cost relates to reconciliation. Disbursements must be reconciled to payables to ensure that payments have actually cleared against the firm's disbursement account. If not, the cheque may have been lost in the mail, misdirected to another party, or lost by the supplier. In any case, inquiries should be made to ensure that valid obligations are honoured.

Control Costs

Costs of control relate to the problem of unauthorised disbursements. Most firms have careful control to minimise this likelihood. Such controls include limiting signature authorisation to only two or three individuals at one site, requiring two signatures per cheque, performing frequent audits, and even removing disbursement control from field personnel.

In addition, it is sometimes necessary to stop a payment after it has been initiated. For a cheque payment, this is done by having the bank issue a stop payment instruction that will flag the cheque when it is presented against the disbursement account. This enables the firm to stop erroneous payments.

TYPES OF DISBURSEMENT DECISIONS

It is convenient to think of disbursement decisions in two categories: strategic and tactical. Strategic decisions are those that have longer-range consequences and are generally more difficult to change on short notice. Tactical decision are the day-to-day operating decisions.

Strategic Decisions

Selection of Disbursement Bank Set: A major strategic decisions involves the selection of one or more disbursement banks. Decisions in this area include the following: How many disbursement banks should be used? Where should they be located? What should be the firm's policy toward intentionally taking advantage of availability and clearing delays?

Selection of Concentration Bank: A second strategic decision is the selection of the concentration bank to fund disbursement banks. This decision, rarely made by field managers, is often not considered an active decision variable. The concentration bank usually already has been selected on the basis of other criteria, and the decision becomes moot. However, if the firm has more than one concentration bank, a choice will have to be made from which concentration bank funds will be drawn.

Disbursement Payment and Account Funding Mechanism A third strategic decision involves selection of the mechanism used for making payments and moving cash from the concentration bank to the disbursement banks. Cheques are by far the most common payment mechanism.

Level of Authority for Authorising Disbursements: Firms must decide who can authorise the release of the firm's cash. Some firms retain close control at headquarters and do not permit disbursements to be authorised in the field. Other firms leave significant authority with field managers. Some set limits: large disbursements can be authorised by certain officers of the firm.

Policies for Determining When and How Much to Pay: Some firms have a simple policy: "Take all discounts and pay on the discount date." Other policies are possible, such as "Take only those discounts that are economically justified" or "Make all payments on the 10th of the month."

Tactical Decisions

Disbursement Authorisation: The first tactical decision is whether to authorise a particular disbursement. Within the authority guidelines already established, someone in the firm must determine if a particular disbursement should be made. Is the invoice valid? Has it already been paid? Have the goods of services actually been received in the amount and quality specified? To assist in making this decision, purchase orders and receiving reports are matched with invoices to ensure that the firm actually owes the amount stated on the invoice.

Funding Amount and Timing: Within strategic policy guidelines, decisions must be made about the amount and timing of transfer from the concentration bank into the disbursement amount. Should cash be transferred daily or nondaily? Can forecast be used? Will the bank permit available overdrafts? This decision is analogous to the cash transfer scheduling problem.

Payment Preparation and Release: A third tactical decision involves the preparation and release of the payment. This includes deciding on the vehicle for making payment and the payment amount. Should payment be in the form of cheque? Should any amount be subtracted for discounts, spoilage during transit, and so on? For some firms these decisions are made in the field, whereas for other they are made at company headquarters.

Drawee Bank Selection: A fourth tactical decision is closely related to the third. The decision involves the selection of a particular drawee bank from the existing set of disbursement bank. It may be possible, either at headquarter or in the field, to draw a cheque on one of several banks, depending on the firm's disbursement policies.

Mail Point: For mailed cheques, a fifth tactical decision is required: from which point to mail the cheque. The mail point and the drawee bank are independent decisions. For most firms, the matter is decided by default and cheques are mailed from the point of the cheque preparation. However, some firms may attempt to extend mail time by mailing cheques from distant locations. To receive any benefits from mail-time extension, one must assume that the postmark date is the valid payment date.

Centralised versus Decentralised Disbursing

More often than not, disbursement control lies between completely, centralised and completely decentralised decision-making. Strategic decisions tend to be made on a centralised basis, whereas tactical decisions may be made in the field. Although some speak of centralised or decentralised systems as if a system must be one or the other, it is generally clever to characterise systems by their degree of centralisation or decentralisation for various disbursement decisions. Most disbursement decisions may be made at either level, depending on the policies of the organisation. Rarely are all decisions made both at headquarters and in the field.

Primarily Decentralised Systems: In a disbursement system in which most tactical decisions are left to the field manager, payment authorisation, preparation, and release are performed at the field level and cheques are drawn on a local bank. This system has some advantages. The field manager retains more autonomy and therefore may be more highly motivated to perform. In addition, relationships with payees may be enhanced because payees receive faster availability of cheques and can resolve disputes more readily.

Primarily Centralised Systems: In a largely centralised disbursement system, payment authorisation, preparation, release, and drawee bank selection are performed by headquarters. The advantages and disadvantages are, of course, the opposite of those in a decentralised system. The advantages are several. The disbursement function may become large enough to warrant the systematic attention of a cash manager who can employ more sophisticated techniques. Excess cash balances at local banks can be moved into centralised cash pools. where they can be more profitably employed. The payment of invoices can be timed and discount policies implemented in the best interest of the firm. Disbursement float can be managed more systematically and unauthorised disbursements can be reduced.

On the other hand, local autonomy is reduced and relationships with payees may be adversely affected. Additional timing delays caused by moving invoice and other data from field units to headquarters may result in missed discounts and delays in resolving payment disputes.

INVESTMENT IN MARKETABLE SECURITIES

The management of the investment in marketable securities is an important financial management responsibility because of the close relationship between cash and marketable securities. One important aspect of this responsibility is determining the amount of marketable securities to hold. Another major aspect of the problem of investment in marketing securities is deciding which securities should the firm invest in ? That is, what should be the composition of the firm's portfolio of securities. A vast array of types and maturities is available, and the financial manager must choose among these alternatives.

GENERAL SELECTION CRITERIA

An assessment of certain criteria can provide the financial manager with a useful framework for selecting a portfolio of marketable securities. The firm will be particularly interested in the safety of the securities, their marketability, and their maturity. Differences in these features are the primary determinants of the yield differences among securities and differences in these features also explain why firms select certain kinds of securities for short-term investments.

Safety : Other things equal, the firm would like to receive as high a yield on its investment in marketable securities as possible. However, seeking higher rates of return leads to accepting larger amounts of risk. Since the firm keeps marketable securities for the precautionary reasons and to men known, scheduled outflows of cash, the firm will tend to invest in very safe marketable securities. Firms tend to buy the highest yielding marketable securities they can find subject to the constraints that the securities have an acceptable risk level. Risk in this context refers to risk of failure. However, failure can have more than one meaning here. At one extreme, a security could default. The issuer fails to redeem the security as per the contract. In a less severe sense the price of the security could fall at a time when the firm needs to liquidate the security (perhaps to replenish the cash account). If the firm sells the security for less than the needed amount, this term is a kind of failure. To minimise the possibilities firm tend to restrict their marketable securities investments to certain "safe" financial instruments, accepting the relatively low yields that accompany such investments as an unavoidable consequences.

Maturity : Since downside price fluctuations are undesirable for safety reasons, the firm will prefer short-lived securities. At the long end of the maturity spectrum, firms prefer marketable securities whose remaining life is no longer than six to nine months. At the short end of the spectrum, firms can and do invest funds overnight.

Marketability : In the present context of managing the marketability of securities portfolio, marketability refers to the ability to transform a security into cash. Should an unforseen event require that a significant amount of cash be immediate available, than a sizeable portion of the portfolio might have to be sold? The financial manager will want to cash *quickly*, and he will not want to accept a large *price concession* in order to convert the securities. Thus, in the formation of preferences for the inclusion of particular instruments in the portfolio, consideration will be given to the time period needed to sell the security and the likelihood that the security can be sold at or near its prevailing market price. The latter element, here means that 'thin' markets, where relatively few transactions take place, or where trades are accomplished only with large price changes between transactions, will be avoided.

TYPES OF MARKETABLE SECURITIES

The securities most commonly held as part of the marketable securities portfolio are divided into two groups : (1) governmental issues and (2) nongovernmental issues. The short-term obligations issued by the central government and available as marketable security are treasury bills. Government securities could have maturities of more or less than one year, at the time of issue. The securities with a maturity of between three to twelve months, at the time of issues, are called treasury bills. The sales are carried out by the RBI, on behalf of the Central Government, to raise short-term finance for the Government and obsorb excess liquidity in the market. The firm can also deposit its excess cash with the commercial banks for some fixed maturity. Deposit scheme are tailored suiting to the needs of the depositors. By various combinations of Demand, Term and Recurring Deposits, banks have brought spectrum of deposit schemes. Bank deposits are very popular due to their safe character. RBI also exercises a strict surveillance over the banking system which also ensures safety of deposits.

MODELS FOR DETERMINING THE OPTIMUM LEVEL OF CASH AND MARKETABLE SECURITIES

In order to invest excess funds, the financial manager must know the minimum amounts that must be kept in the form of cash and marketable securities. Seasonal factors and cyclical requirements make it difficult to ascertain these amounts accurately, and therefore many companies adopt the policy of deliberately erring on the side of conservatism in order not to be exposed to cash deficiencies. Other attempt to ascertain the purposes for which cash is required and to establish methods for estimating the minimum amounts needed for each purposes. A range of cash management models which may be used by the finance manager to help him to maintain approximately enough cash in the company to cover transactions, precautionary and speculative balance are discussed below.

THE BAUMOL MODEL

In this model, the firm is assumed to receive cash periodically but to pay out cash continuously at a steady rate. That is, the firm's inflows are lumpy but its outflows are not. This time pattern of cash balance is portrayed in Panel A of Figure-2. When the cash inflow is received, the firm puts enough cash in its disbursement account to cover outflows until the next inflow is received. There are several types of businesses that experience a time pattern of cash flows similar to this. For example, for firms that manage rental property, rents are often received over a short period early in the month but other expenses (such as maintenance) continue evenly throughout the month.

FIGURE-2

TIME PATTERN OF CASH !BALANCE !FOR !THE BAUMOL MODEL

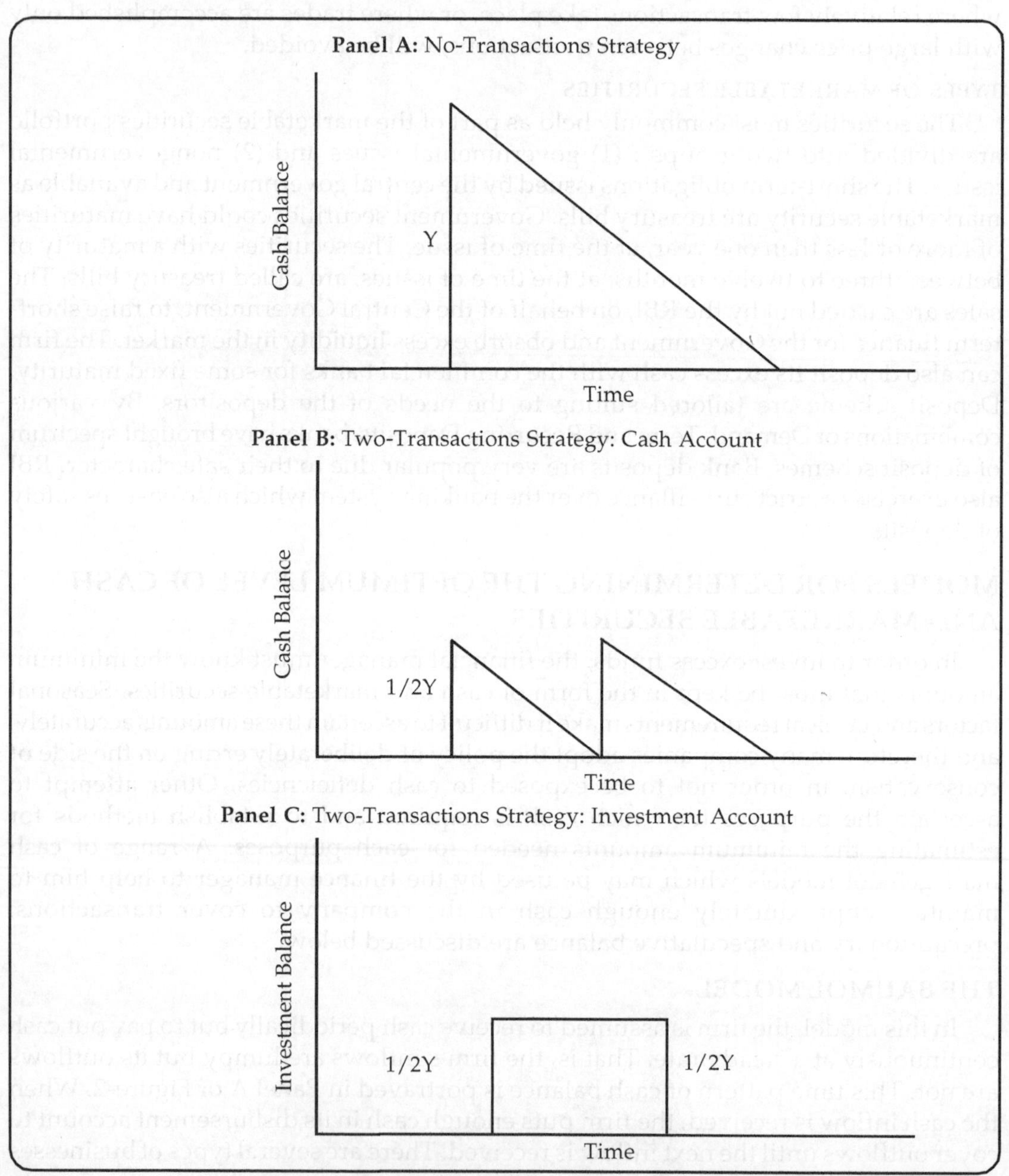

The Baumol model also makes several assumptions about the firm's situation. It assumes that investments yield a fixed rate of return per period, regardless of the length of the investment (that is, it assumes that yield curve effects are small over the time period of investment). This is an appropriate assumption if the firm is limited to investments in money market accounts, negotiated order or withdrawal accounts, or similar small investments. The model assumes that the transaction cost of investing and disinvesting is a fixed cost that is independent of the amount of the investment. These transaction costs consist of all the out-of-pocket costs of making or selling the investment: commissions, postage, telephone charges, the opportunity cost of diverted managerial effort, and so forth.

Given that the firm has periodic inflows and steady outflows, what is the appropriate strategy for investing the funds until they are needed? This is the question addressed by the Baumol model. To understand the tradeoffs in this situation, let us evaluate some possible strategies. One possible strategy is:

1. When the cash inflow is received, invest one-half of the total inflow; put the remaining one-half in the disbursement account.
2. During the first half of the period, pay disbursements from the disbursement account. This account will be drained one-half of the way through the period. At that time, sell the investments and place the resulting funds in the disbursement account.
3. Use these funds to pay disbursements during the remainder of the period.

This is called the *two-transactions strategy because it involves one investment of funds and one disinvestment of funds.* The effects of this strategy on the cash and investment accounts is portrayed in Panels B and C of Figure-2. To see the net gain from this strategy, let Y be the amount of the cash inflow and i be the interest rate per period (that is, the interest rate from one periodic cash inflow to the next). Since in this strategy one-half the inflow is invested for one-half the period, the interest income is:

$$\text{Investment Income} = (1/2)\,(1/2)\,iY = (1/4)iY \qquad (1)$$

But there are two transactions in this strategy: one investment and one disinvestment. If the cost per transaction is a, the transactions cost of this strategy is $2a$, and the profit is:

$$\text{Profit} = (1/4)iY - 2a \qquad (2)$$

While the simple two-transactions strategy captures one-half of the cash inflow into the investment account for one-half the period, other strategies will capture more of this flow for longer periods and thus earn more interest. Consider the *three-transactions strategy:*

1. When the cash flow is received, initially invest two-thirds of it. Place the remaining one-third in the disbursements account.
2. One-third of the way through the period, the disbursements account will be exhausted. At this time, disinvest one-half of the funds in the investment

account [the amount is $(1/2)(2/3)Y = (1/3)Y$] and put this in the disbursement account. Leave the remaining $(1/3)Y$ in the investment account and move the proceeds to the disbursement account. This will fund disbursements through the remainder of the period.

This strategy involves one investment transaction and two disinvestment transactions. The balances in the investment and disbursement accounts are portrayed in Figure-3. This strategy captures a greater portion of the initial cash inflow in the investment account. Two-thirds of the initial cash inflow resides in the investment account for one-third of the period (until the first withdrawal) and one-third of the cash inflow resides in the investment account for the second one-third of the period (until the second withdrawal). The interest income is then:

$$\text{Interest Income} = (2/3)(1/3)iY + (1/3)(1/3)iY = (1/3)iY \quad (3)$$

And since there are now three transactions, the profit is:

$$\text{Profit} = (1/3)iY - 3a \quad (4)$$

FIGURE-3

TIME PATTERN OF CASH BALANCE FOR THE BAUMOL MODEL THREE-TRANSACTIONS STRATEGY

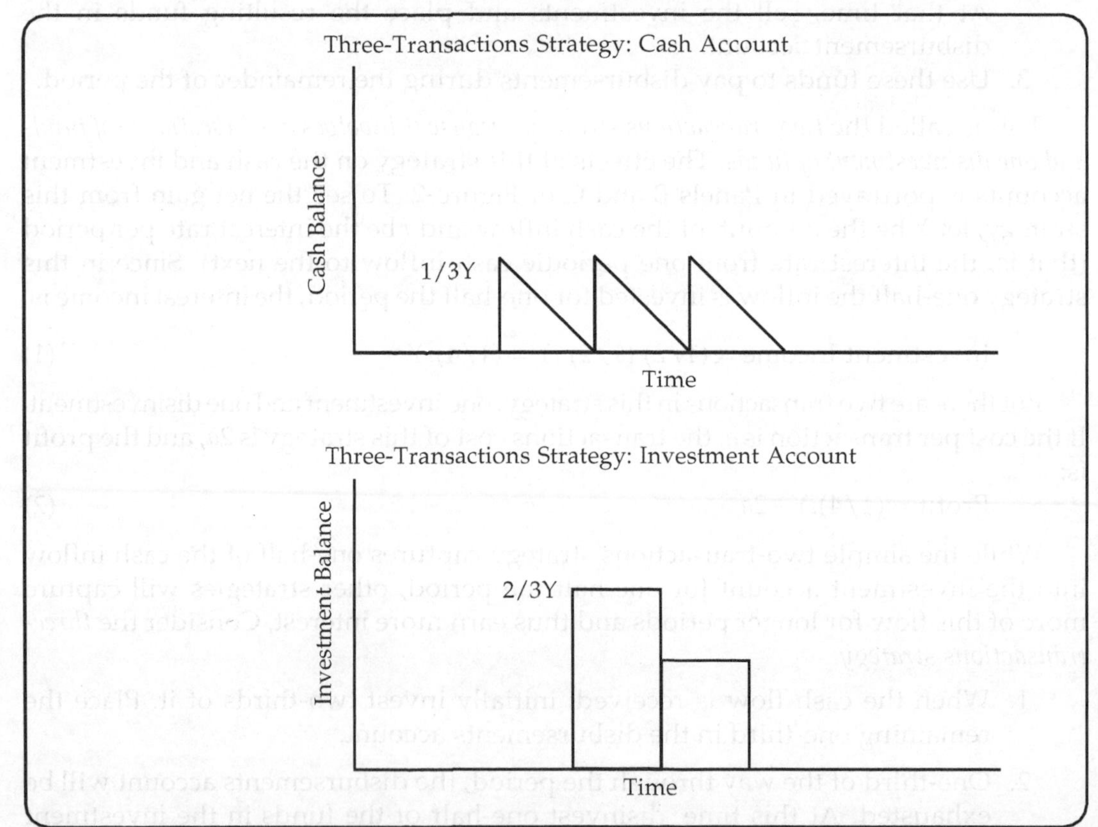

Whether the three-transactions strategy is more profitable than the two-transactions strategy depends on the amount of additional interest earned versus the additional transaction cost paid. The Baumol model addresses the question of the optimal strategy by deriving a general expression for the *optimal number of transactions* for a firm with periodic inflow and steady outflows. In general, the interest income from investment strategies in this situation is:

$$\text{Interest Income} = [(n-1)/2n]iY \qquad (5)$$

where n is the number of transactions. This expression gives the proper income for the two and-three-transactions strategies. Since the transactions cost is na, the profit for n transactions is:

$$\text{Profit} = [(n-1)/2n]iY - na \qquad (6)$$

As the number of transactions increases, the interest income increases but so does the total transactions costs. This relationship is plotted in Figure-4. Since the total interest income is limited to capturing the entire initial cash inflow in the investment account, which would result in an interest income of $(1/2)iY$, the interest income is asymptotic to this level. For some level of n, the profit (equal to the vertical distance between the cost and interest income functions) is at a maximum. To find this, we take the first derivative of the profit function [equation (6)], set this equal to zero, and solve for the optimal n. The result is:

$$n^* = (iY / 2a)^{1/2} \qquad (7)$$

where n^* is the optimal number of transactions. In the Baumol model, the firm will always make one deposit and $n^* - 1$ withdrawals from the investment account. The amount of the initial deposit will be $[(n^* - 1)/n^*]Y$; the amount of the withdrawals will be $(1/n^*)Y$. The profit from this strategy can be computed via equation (6).

FIGURE-4

COSTS AND REVENUES !VERSUS NUMBER OF TRANSACTIONS FOR THE !BAUMOL MODEL

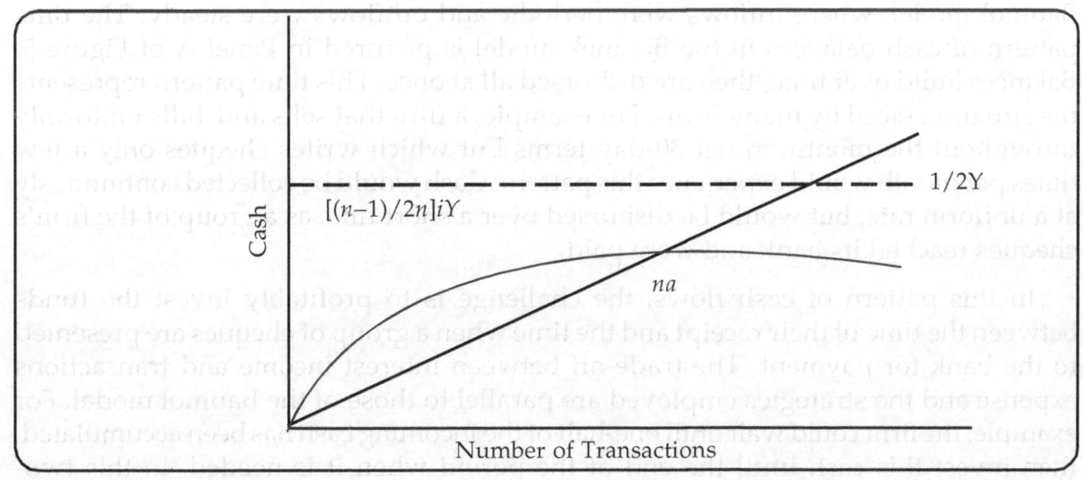

An example in the use of the Baumol model is in order. A firm runs an apartment complex. Cash comes in at the beginning of the month (from rental payments) and is disbursed uniformly throughout the following months. For the upcoming month, the firm expects to have cash expenses of ₹ 2,50,000. By investing in a money market account, it can earn 0.5 percent per month. Transactions costs are estimated at ₹ 25 per transaction. What is the firm's best investment strategy and how much will this earn?

To formulate this strategy, the optimal number of transactions is first computed:

$$n^* = (iY/2a)^{1/2} = [(0.005)\ (2{,}50{,}000)/2(25)]^{1/2} = 5.0 \quad (8)$$

The five-transactions strategy is optimal; there should be one deposit and four withdrawals from the investment account. The amount of the initial deposit will be (4/5) (₹ 2,50,000) = ₹ 2,00,000; each of the four withdrawals will be ₹ 50,000, as will the initial deposit in the disbursement account. This initial deposit will fund the firm for one-fifth of the month (50,000/2,50,000), or about six days; then the first withdrawal will be made from the investment account. Withdrawals will occur every six days (on the sixth, twelfth, eighteenth, and twenty-fourth days of the month). The profit from this strategy will be:

$$\begin{aligned} \text{Profit} &= [(n-1)/2n]iY - na \\ &= [(5-1)/2(5)]\ (0.005)\ (2{,}50{,}000) - 5(25) \\ &= 500 - 125 = ₹\ 375 \end{aligned} \quad (9)$$

Like all the models in this chapter, the applicability of the Baumol model is limited to situations where the cash flow pattern fits that assumed in the model's derivation. Other patterns are addressed by other models, such as the Beranek model.

THE BERANEK MODEL

Beranek hypothesised firms where the cash *inflows* were steady, but the *outflows* were periodic. This is the mirror image of the time pattern OF cash flows within the Baumol model, where inflows were periodic and outflows were steady. The time pattern of cash balances in the Beranek model is pictured in Panel A of Figure-5. Balances build over time, then are disbursed all at once. This time pattern represents the situation faced by many firms. For example, a firm that sells and bills uniformly throughout the month on net 30-day terms but which writes cheques only a few times per month would experience this pattern. Cash would be collected continuously at a uniform rate, but would be disbursed over a short time as a group of the firm's cheques reached its bank and were paid.

In this pattern of cash flows, the challenge is to profitably invest the funds between the time of their receipt and the time when a group of cheques are presented to the bank for payment. The trade-off between interest income and transactions expense and the strategies employed are parallel to those of the Baumol model. For example, the firm could wait until one-half of the incoming cash has been accumulated, then invest this cash until the end of the period when it is needed. In this two-transaction strategy (see panel B of Figure-5), the interest income would be (1/4) iY, as in the Baumol model, and the transaction expense would be $2a$. The formula for the optimum number of transactions is the same as that for the Baumol model, and is given in equation (7). In the Beranek model, however, *the cash is accumulated gradually* (rather than disbursed gradually), so the transactions pattern would involve *a series of investments followed by one disinvestment* at the end of the period.

FIGURE-5

TIME PATTERN OF CASH BALANCE FOR THE BERANEK

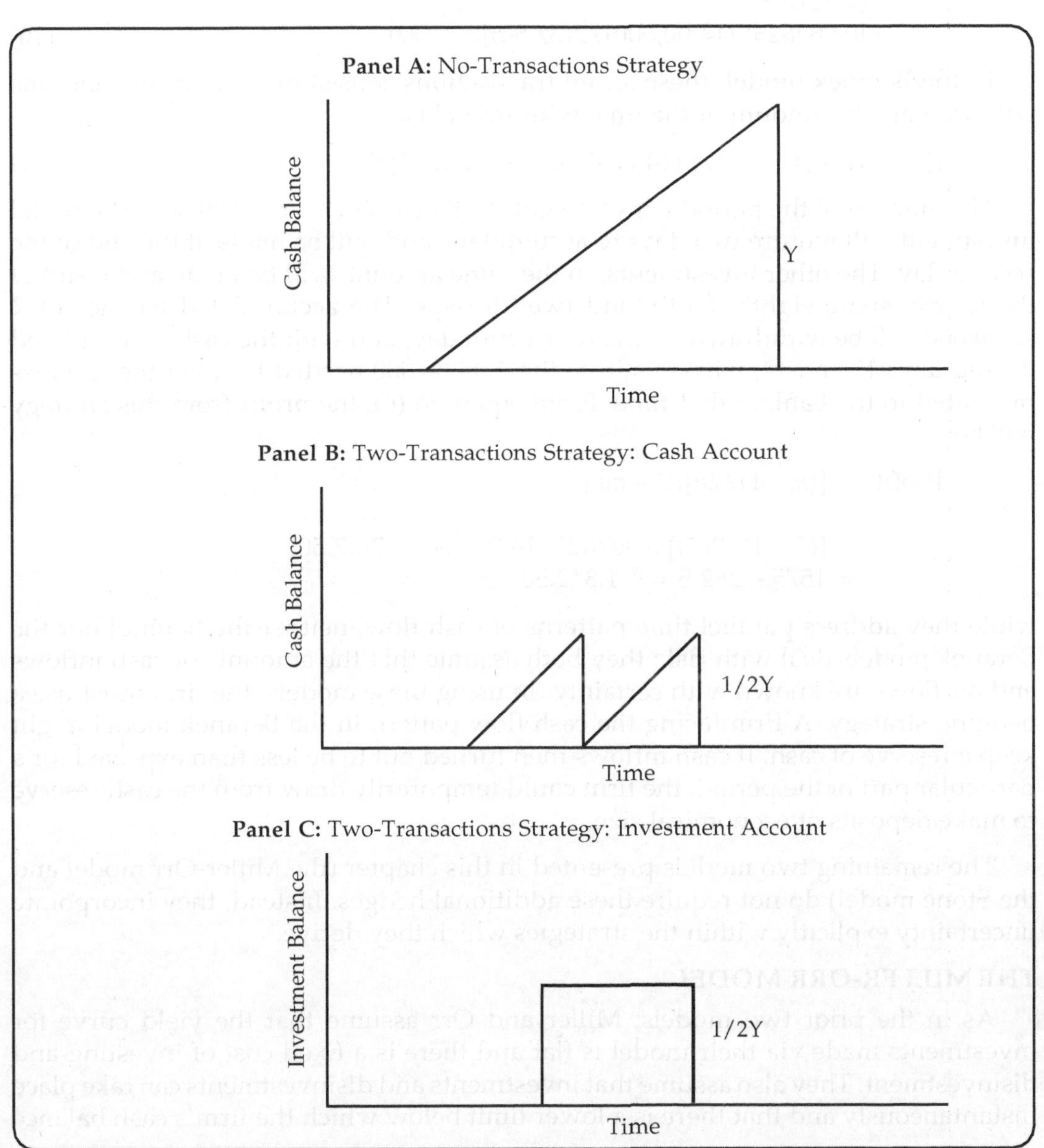

Let us try an example. A firm receives ₹ 1,00,000 per day, which it will eventually need to make disbursements, and follows a policy of writing cheques every two weeks. Over a two-week period, it accumulate ₹ 14,00,000. It can invest at an interest at an interest rate of 6.825 percent per year (0.2625 percent for two weeks). The transaction cost of investment or disinvestment is ₹ 37.50. What investment strategy should the firm follow and how much will this strategy earn?

From equation (7), the optimal number of transactions is:

$$n^* = (iY/2a)^{1/2}$$

$$= [0.002625)\ (14{,}00{,}000)/2(37.50)]^{1/2} = 7.0 \qquad (10)$$

In the Beranek model, these seven transactions consist of six deposits and one withdrawal. The amount of the final withdrawal is:

$$[(n^* - 1)/n]Y = (6/7)\ (14{,}00{,}000) = ₹\ 12{,}00{,}000 \qquad (11)$$

The amount of the periodic investments will be $(1/n)Y$, or ₹ 2,00,000. The initial investment will require two days to accumulate, and will be made at the end of the second day. The other investments, in the same amount, will be made at the end of the fourth, sixth, eighth, tenth, and twelfth days. The accumulated balance of ₹ 12,00,000 will be withdrawn on the fourteenth day, and with the cash accumulated during days 13 and 14, will constitute the ₹ 14,00,000 needed to cover the cheques presented to the bank at that time. From equation (6), the profit from this strategy will be:

$$\text{Profit} = [(n - 1)/2n]iY - na$$

(12)

$$= [(7 - 1)/2(7)]\ 0.002625\ (14{,}00{,}000) - 7(37.50)$$

$$= 1575 - 262.5 = ₹\ 1{,}312.50$$

while they address parallel time patterns of cash flow, neither the Baumol nor the Beranek models deal with risk; they both assume that the amounts of cash inflows and outflows are known with certainty. In using these models, the firm must use a hedging strategy. A firm facing the cash flow pattern in the Beranek model might keep a reserve of cash. If cash inflows then turned out to be less than expected for a particular part of the period, the firm could temporarily draw from the cash reserve to make deposits of economical size.

The remaining two models presented in this chapter (the Miller-Orr model and the Stone model) do not require these additional hedges. Instead, they incorporate uncertainty explicitly within the strategies which they derive.

THE MILLER-ORR MODEL

As in the prior two models, Miller and Orr assume that the yield curve for investments made via their model is flat and there is a fixed cost of investing and disinvestment. They also assume that investments and disinvestments can take place instantaneously and that there is a lower limit below which the firm's cash balance is not to fall. This lower limit is set by management and is not determined within their model; it may be a zero cash balance (so that the firm does not overdraft) or the firm's minimum compensating balance.

The major difference between the Miller-Orr model and the prior two models concerns the assumed time pattern of cash flows. Baumol and Beranek assume a rise-and-fall pattern of net inflows and outflows. Miller and Orr assume that net cash flows are normally distributed with a mean of zero, that the standard deviation of this distribution does not vary across time, and that there is no correlation of the cash flows across time. Under these assumptions, cash flows must follow a random walk around a zero average net flow. Based on these assumptions, and using the advanced mathematical technique of stochastic calculus, they formulate a profit-maximizing strategy based on *control limits.*

This control-limits approach involves exactly the same decision rules as does the control-limits approach in production management theory. In production management theory, a production process is initially adjusted for optimum performance. However, it is recognised that variations in materials. machine wear, and so forth will cause random fluctuations in the output of the process. Since it is costly to adjust the process, control limits are set up based on the expected variation in the process. Only when these limits are breached, the process is adjusted. The Miller-Orr cash management model is basically an application of control-limits theory to the cash/investment decision. Control limits are set up using a formula derived by Miller and Orr. When the firm's total cash goes outside the *upper control limit, investments are made* to bring the cash balance back down to the *return point;* when the firm's cash balance goes below the *lower control limit, disinvestments are made* to bring the balance back up to the return point. The formula developed by Miller and Orr is:

$$R = (3aV/4i)^{1/3} \tag{13}$$

where V is the variance of daily cash flows, i is the daily interest rate on investments, and a is the transactions cost of investing or disinvesting. If L is lower control limit (set by management), the optimal return point is $R + L$ and the optimal upper control limit is $3R + L$.

To see how this model would work in practice, let us address an example problem. A firm has confirmed that its cash flows satisfy the requirements of the Miller-Orr model. It can earn 0.02 percent per day in investments. Based on historic data, the firm has estimated the standard deviation of its daily cash flows at ₹ 50,000 and its transaction costs of investment or disinvestment at ₹ 45.00. It wishes to maintain a minimum cash balance of ₹ 1,00,000 at all times. Based on this data, the R statistic would be calculated as:

$$R = (3aV/4i)^{1/3} = [3(45)(50{,}000)^2 / 4(0.0002)]^{1/3}$$
$$= ₹\ 75{,}000$$

Using this statistic, the firm would set the lower control limit at, ₹ 1,00,000, the return point at ₹ 1,75,000, and the upper control limit at ₹ 3,25,000 = (3(75,000) + 1,00,000). Let us track the effects of this strategy for some example cash flows. Assume that the firm's starting balance was ₹ 1,50,000 and the following cash flows occur:

Day	*Net Cash Flow*
1	–₹ 25,000
2	–₹ 50,000
3	+₹ 1,00,000
4	–₹ 25,000
5	+₹ 1,25,000

The control limits, the return point, and the effects of these cash flows are portrayed in Figure-6. At the end of day 1, the cash balance would be ₹ 1,25,000; since this is between the control limits, no action would be taken. At the end of day 2, however, the cash balance would be reduced to ₹ 75,000 if the firm did nothing. Since this is below the lower control limit, the firm would disinvest sufficient securities to get back the return point. In this case, a disinvestment of ₹ 1,00,000, equal to the return point of ₹ 1,50,000 less the ending cash balance of ₹ 50,000, would be made and the firm would start day 3 at the return point. At the end of days 3 and 4, the cash balance would be ₹ 2,75,000 and 2,50,000 respectively, but no action would be taken since these balances are within the control limits. However, during day 5, ₹ 1,25,000 is collected, and the balance would be ₹ 3,75,000 if no action is taken. However, in the Miller-Orr model, this is a sufficient balance to justify investment, and ₹ 2,00,000 would be invested bringing the cash balance back to the return.

Concerns About the Assumptions of the Miller-Orr Model: While Miller-Orr model has intuitive appeal as a control-limits approach, the time pattern of cash flows hypothesised within the model has been subject to substantial criticism. The random walk nature of this time pattern assumes that management has no knowledge at all about the direction of future cash flows; in reality, management may forecast these flows, but with a substantial error component within the forecast. Also, while existence of the time patterns of cash flows in the Baumol and Beranek models may be suspected by the business patterns and policies of the firm, the assumption of normality in the Miller-Orr model relies on the central limits theorem, and the convergence to normality of a sample under this theorem depends on the shape of the underlying population distribution.

Because of doubts about the normality of firms' cash flows, and about the Miller-Orr assumptions of no correlations in cash flows over time and no changes in standard deviation over time, several empirical studies of the probability distributions of firms' net cash flows have been conducted in finance. These empirical results suggest that a firm should not automatically adopt the Miller-Orr if no discernible time pattern of cash flows is obvious. Instead, the firm needs to perform statistical tests to assess the agreement between the probability distributions of the firm's cash flows and the distributions assumed in the model. Tests for non-normality and for the correlation of the cash flow over time (autocorrelation) are generally sufficient to confirm or deny this agreement.

FIGURE-6

CASH BALANCE !FOR MILLER-ORR EXAMPLE

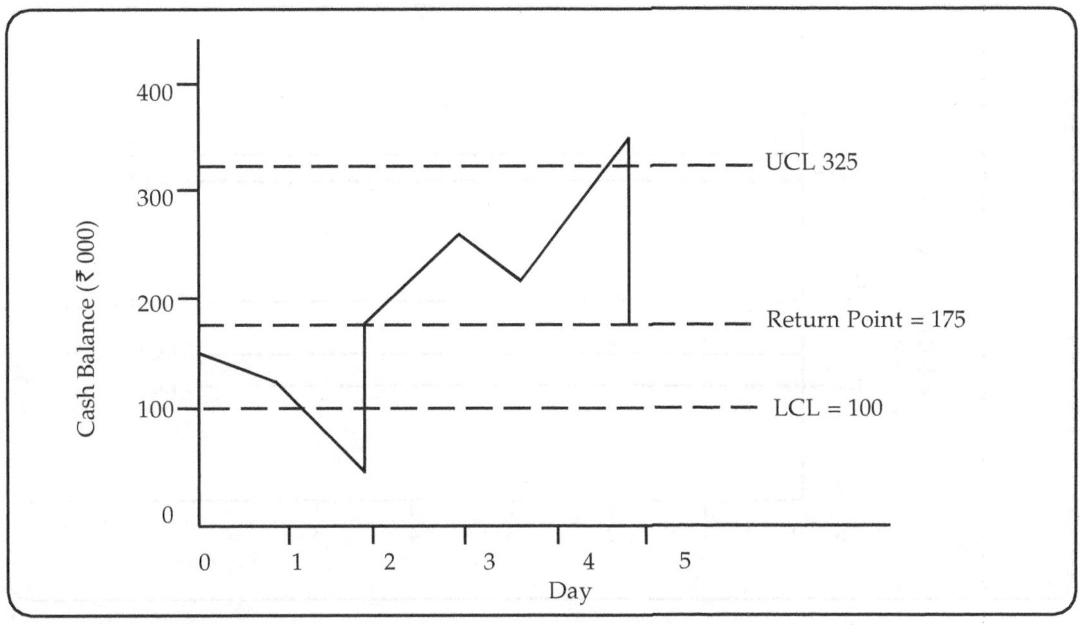

THE STONE MODEL

Like the Miller-Orr model, the Stone model takes a control-limits approach; when cash balances fall outside the control limits, the firm is signaled to do something. But in the Stone model, the signal does not automatically result in an investment or disinvestment: the recommended action depends on management's estimates of future cash flows: that is, the model signals an *evaluation* by management rather than an *action.* To do this, the Stone model uses *two sets* of control limits (see Figure-7); the *inner control limits* (UCL_1 and LCL_1) and the *outer control limits* (UCL_2 and LCL_2).

Under the Stone model, strategy proceeds as follows. The firm performs no evaluation until its cash balance falls outside the *outer* control limits. When this occurs, the firm *looks ahead* by adding the expected cash flows for the next few days to the current balance. If the sum of the current balance and these expected future cash flows (which is the expected cash balance a few days hence) falls outside the *inner* control limits, a transaction is made; otherwise, the transaction is foregone. The transactions are the same as those in the Miller-Orr model. Investments are made sufficient to bring the cash balance back to the return point if the upper control limit is exceeded; corresponding disinvestments are made if the lower control limit is exceeded. Optimal procedures for setting the return point, the two sets of control limits, and the number of days a firm looks ahead are not specific; the outer control limits could be set by the Miller-Orr model or could be based on the cash manager's feeling for the best limits.

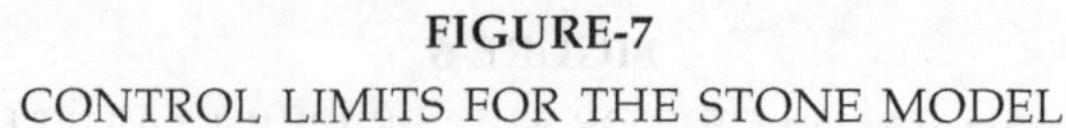

FIGURE-7

CONTROL LIMITS FOR THE STONE MODEL

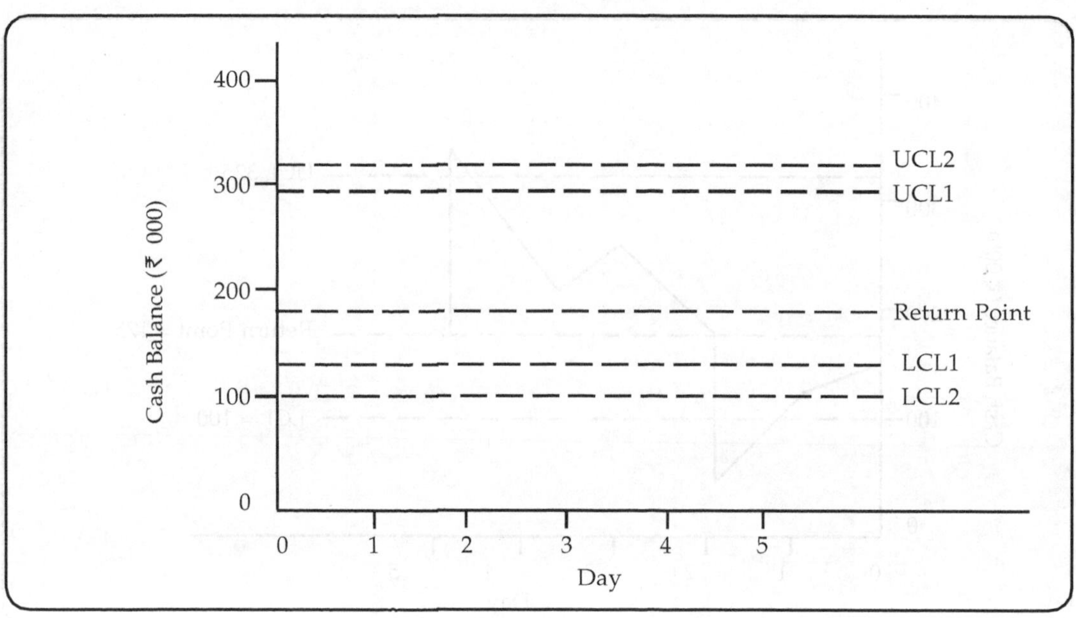

To see how the Stone model would function in practice, let us consider the first example used in the discussion of the Miller-Orr model. In this discussion, the beginning balance was ₹ 1,50,000, the upper control limit was ₹ 3,25,000, the return point was ₹ 1,75,000, the lower control limit was ₹ 1,00,000. The cash flows for the first five days were:

Day	*Net Cash Flow*
1	–₹ 25,000
2	–₹ 50,000
3	+₹ 1,00,000
4	–₹ 25,000
5	+₹ 1,25,000

Let us also assume that the inner control limits are set ₹ 20,000 inside the outer control limits (at ₹ 3,05,000 and ₹ 1,20,000), and that the firm looks ahead at the next two days' cash flows. At the end of day 1, the cash balance is 1,25,000, but since the outer control limits have not been breached, no evaluation is made. At the end of day 2, however, the cash balance has been reduced to ₹ 75,000. At this point, the firm totals the next two days cash flows. Let us assume that this forecast is correct; the total obtained is ₹ 75,000 = (1,00,000–25,000) as the expected future cash flow. Adding this to the current balance of ₹ 75,000 gives an expected balance of ₹ 1,50,000. *Since this expected cash balance is within the inner control limits, no transaction is made.* The pattern of cash balances that would result is illustrated in Figure-8; there are no investments or disinvestments over the five-day period of the example (recall the Miller-Orr model required one investment and one disinvestment).

FIGURE-8

CASH BALANCES FOR THE STONE EXAMPLE

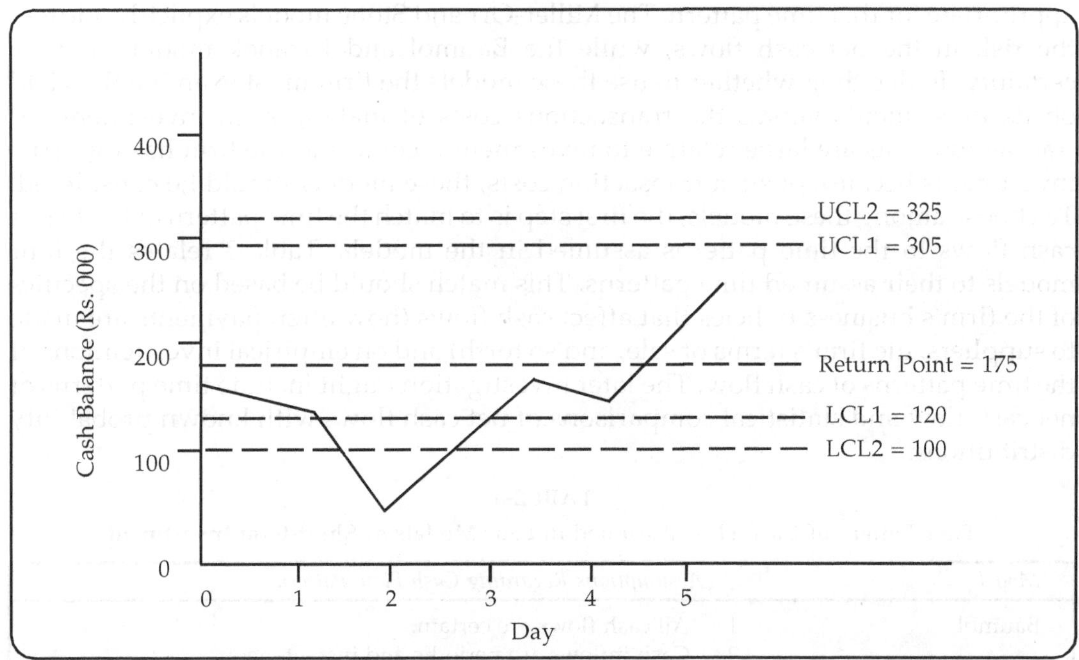

When the firm has some knowledge of future daily cash flows, the Stone model offers an advantage over the Miller-Orr model in reducing the number of investment and disinvestment transactions, though investment income may also be reduced. Also, the Stone model is very flexible in that it does not assume a flat yield curve, and in that the parameters of the model may be changed over time to accommodate the firm's needs. For example, the control limits may be tightened during periods when cash control is critical, or the look-ahead period may be lengthened when the firm has better information about future cash flows. Set against these advantages is a substantial disadvantage; *the model does not specify the optimal levels of the parameters* (the control limits, the return point, and the look-ahead period). Stone states that these parameters should be set by the manager by trying various strategies on past data and observing the results; this is a sensitivity analysis approach. There is no guarantee that this process will lead to optimal (or even near-optimal) strategies. Indeed, though it is flexible and has substantial intuitive appeal, the Stone method might be more properly regarded as an *approach* to the daily management of cash and temporary investments rather than an *optimisation model* for this management.

OPTIMISATION MODELS FOR SHORT-TERM INVESTMENTS IN PERSPECTIVE

All of these models are oriented toward small-and medium-sized firms where the amounts of cash available for investment are sufficiently small that transaction costs are an important consideration in formulating strategy. These models take a similar approach: they first hypothesise a time-pattern of cash flows, then develop a strategy appropriate for that time pattern. The Miller-Orr and Stone models explicitly address the risk in the net cash flows, while the Baumol and Beranek models assume certainty. In deciding whether to use these models the firm must examine the yield on its investments versus the transactions costs of making such investments. If transaction costs are large relative to investment income and the firm has foregone investments because of such transaction costs, these models should be considered. To choose among these models, the first step is to match the time pattern of the firm's cash flows to the time patterns assumed in the models; Table-3 relates the four models to their assumed time patterns. This match should be based on the specifics of the firm's business policies that affect cash flows (how often payments are made to suppliers, the firm's terms of sale, and so forth) and on empirical investigations of the time patterns of cash flow. The later investigation might include time patterns of net cash flow and statistical comparisons of net cash flows with known probability distributions.

TABLE-3

Time Pattern of Cash Flow Assumed in Four Models of Short-term Investment

Model	*Assumptions Regarding Cash Flow Pattern*
Baumol	1. All cash flows are certain.
	2. Cash inflows are periodic and instantaneous.
	3. Cash outflows occur at a constant rate.
Beranek	1. All cash flows are certain.
	2. Cash outflows are periodic and instantaneous.
	3. Cash inflows occur at a constant rate.
Miller-Orr	1. Firm has minimum required cash balance.
	2. Cash flows are normally distributed.
	3. The expected cash flow is zero.
	4. There is no autocorrelation in cash flows.
	5. The standard deviation of cash flows does not change over time.
Stone	1. Firm has minimum required cash balance.
	2. Firm has some knowledge of future cash flows, although this knowledge contains an error component.

While these models provide interesting and useful approaches, their limitations must be stressed. Like all optimisation models, their domain is constrained by the assumptions made in their derivation. While all models are robust to derivations from these assumptions to a greater or lesser extent, the use of an optimisation model outside its intended domain is dangerous, and may lead to uneconomical and perhaps disastrous results. Thus, it makes good sense to pay close attention to the assumptions and derivation of a model in deciding whether to use that model in addressing a particular management decision.

ILLUSTRATIVE PROBLEMS

1. The Mobile Company receives the following cheques during January. Calculate the amount of opportunity costs for January for Mobile if the opportunity cost rate is 12% per annum.

Face Amount	*Days Delay*
₹ 1,00,000	4
1,50,000	5
50,000	3
75,000	6

Solution

To determine the average float for the month we find the total ₹-days of float by multiplying the face amount times the number of days delay and taking the total.

Face Amount	*Days Delay*	*Amount x Delay*
₹ 1,00,000	4	₹ 1,00,000-days
1,50,000	5	₹ 7,50,000-days
50,000	3	₹ 1,50,000-days
75,000	6	₹ 4,50,000-days
Total		₹ 17,50,000-days

The next step is to divide the total by the number of days in the month to determine the average float over the month. Since January has 31 days, the average float is ₹ 56,451.61. Multiplying this by the opportunity cost for the month gives ₹ 56,451.61 × .12 × 31/365 = ₹ 575.34. Note that we could have also just taken the total ₹-days of float for the month of 17,50,000 and multiplied by the daily opportunity costs rate of .12/365 and obtained ₹ 575.34.

2. A firm is currently disbursing from its concentration bank at a cost of ₹ 25 per month for account maintenance and ₹ .10 per cheque processed. The controlled disbursement bank will charge ₹ 75 per month for account maintenance and ₹ .15 per cheque processed. The controlled disbursement account will add 1/2-day float to the disbursements. The company issues 100 cheques of average face amount of ₹ 2,500 per day. The treasurer maintains an overnight portfolio of about ₹ 10,00,000, on which she currently earns about 6% per annum. She estimates that she could earn an additional 25 basis points on the investments if she could invest earlier in the day. Transfers to the controlled disbursement account could be done at a cost of ₹ 1 per transfer. Determine the annual net benefit, or cost, of using the controlled disbursement account instead of the current system.

Solution

(a) The net benefits consists of the float benefits plus the gain on the earlier investment less the additional costs connected with the controlled disbursing account less the transfer costs.

Float benefits are:

annual disbursement x float gain x investment rate

(₹ 2,500 per day × 100 × 250 days) × (.5 days) × (.06/365) = ₹ 5,137

Additional investment benefits are:

amount of the investment portfolio × incremental rate

(₹ 10,00,000) × (.0025) = ₹ 2,500.

Incremental bank charges are:

incremental account maintenance costs + incremental per item charges

(₹ 75 – ₹ 25) × 12 + (₹ .15 × ₹ .10) × 100 × 250 = ₹ 1,850

Transfer costs are:

₹ 1 × 250 = ₹ 250.

The net benefits are:

Float benefits + investment benefits - additional costs - transfer costs

₹ 5,137 + ₹ 2,500 – ₹ 1,850 – ₹ 250 = ₹ 5,537

3. Sadhan Nitro Company currently maintains a centralised billing system at its home office to handle average daily collections of ₹ 4,50,000. The total time for mailing, processing, and clearing has been estimated at 4 days.

(a) If the company's opportunity cost on short-term funds s 15%, how much this time lag of 4 days costing the company?

(b) If management has designed a system of lock-boxes with regional banks that would have reduced the float by 1 1/2 days and home office credit department expense by ₹ 52,000 annually, what is the largest total amount of required compensating balance that the firm should be willing to accept with the lock-box arrangement ?

Solution

(a) Total float = ₹ 4,50,000 (4 days) = ₹ 18,00,000

Cost = .15 (₹ 18,00,000) = ₹ 2,70,000 per year.

(b) Reduced expense of float= 0.15 (1.5 days) (₹ 4,50,000)
= ₹ 1,01,250

Total reduced costs = ₹ 1,01,250 + ₹ 52,000
= ₹ 1,53,250

Maximum acceptable compensating balance
= ₹ 1,53,250/0.15
= ₹ 10,21,666.60

4. Good Luck Enterprises is a manufacturer of cards and party favours. They sell to retail shops in multistate area in the western part of India. Mr. Ashok, the treasurer, is considering the use of a lockbox for the collection of their customers' remittances. Their customers fall into two categories: single outlets and regional chains. During a typical month they receive an average of 5,000 cheques with an average face amount of ₹ 300 from the single-outlet customers and 2,000 cheques with an average face amount of ₹ 2,500 from the regional-chain customers. Currently it takes a total of 7 days for Good Luck to receive the payments, process the deposit, and receive available funds. The XYZ Bank has offered a lockbox service that would reduce the total to 3 days. The cost for the lockbox would be a fixed charge of ₹ 500 per month and ₹ .50 per processed. Currently Good Luck pays ₹ .05 per item deposited at its bank. Ashok does not believe there will be any additional savings to be achieved if the company eliminates the internal processing of the customers' remittances. Good Luck has an opportunity cost rate of 10% per annum.

(a) If Good Luck uses the lockbox, should they have both classes of customers send their remittances to the lockbox.

(b) Should Good Luck use the lockbox?

Solution

(a) The savings achieved on each item sent to the lockbox will be the 4 days saved times the opportunity cost rate times the size of the remitance. The additional cost will be the difference between the deposit cost and the lockbox processing charge. For single-outlet customers Greeting saves ₹ 300 x 4 x.1/365 = ₹ 0.33 for every cheque. For regional-chain customers Good Luck saves ₹ 2,500 x 4 x .1/365 = ₹ 2.74. The additional cost per item processed is ₹ 0.50 - ₹ 0.05 = ₹ 0.45. Thus, if Good Luck uses the lockbox, it is worthwhile to have only the larger cheques sent to the lockbox. The smaller cheques should be processed at the company.

(b) Since only the larger cheques will be sent to the lockbox, the decision depends on whether the total savings from sending the larger cheques to the lockbox out-weights the full cost of using the lockbox. The total opportunity cost savings for the month would be 2,500 × 4 × .1/365 × 2,000 = ₹ 5,476.45. The total cost of using the lockbox for a month would be ₹ 500 + 2,000 × ₹ 0.45 = ₹ 1,400. Thus, Good Luck should use the lockbox to capture the net savings of ₹ 4,076.45 per month.

5. The XYZ Company currently makes payments by cheques. The ABC Company, a supplier, has requested that XYZ allow ABC to debit their account 10 days after the invoice date. XYZ currently pays ABC with a cheque mailed 30 days after the invoice date. It takes an average of 5 days for the cheque to the cleared through XYZ account. The average payment to ABC is ₹ 500. It costs XYZ an average of ₹ 10 to process the invoice through their accounts payables department and to issue a cheque. These costs would be eliminated by the proposed procedure. The opportunity costs of funds to XYZ is 10%.

(a) Should XYZ accept ABC's offer?

(b) XYZ has received a similar offer from TNK Company. Payments to TNK company average ₹ 5,000. All other information is unchanged from the involving ABC. Should XYZ accept TNK's offer?

Solution

(a) Under the current system XYZ loses value from its account on day 35. They also incur internal costs of ₹ 10. (For simplicity assume these costs are incurred on day 35 when the payment is made.) Under the proposed payment terms XYZ will lose value of ₹ 500 on day 10. To compare these two we take the present value (on day 10) of the payment on day 35. This is ₹ 510/(1+.1 × 25/365) = ₹ 506.53. Under the proposed payment terms they will lose value of ₹ 500 on day 10. Since they will be better off by ₹ 6.53 with the payment terms. XYZ should accept ABC's offer.

(b) The present value on day 10 for the payment to TNK under the system is ₹ 5,010/(1+.1 × 25/365) = ₹ 4,975.92. If XYZ accepts TNK's payment terms it will lose value of ₹ 5,000 on day 10. Since XYZ will be worse off by ₹ 24.08, it should reject TNK's offer of the new payment terms.

6. Devise a profit-maximising maturity schedule for investments in marketable securities if the ABC Company expects the following monthly cash balances (net of transaction needs). The precautionary demand for cash is ₹ 1,50,000.

January	₹ 4,50,000	May	₹ 10,50,000	September	₹ 3,00,000
February	7,50,000	June	12,00,000	October	3,00,000
March	9,00,000	July	6,00,000	November	1,50,000
April	7,50,000	August	4,50,000	December	1,50,000

Why might such a schedule not be in the best interest of the shareholders?

Solution

Assuming no speculation demand for cash and an upward sloping yield curve, such a schedule (after subtraction of the ₹ 1,50,000 precautionary demand) might be as follows:

Invest ₹ 1,50,000 for 10 months, January to October
Invest ₹ 1,50,000 for 8 months, January to August
Invest ₹ 1,50,000 for 6 months, February to to July
Invest ₹ 1,50,000 for 5 months, February to June
Invest ₹ 1,50,000 for 2 months, May and June
Invest ₹ 1,50,000 for 1 months, March
Invest ₹ 1,50,000 for 1 months, June

The schedule would not be in the best interests of the shareholders if the return from the investment were:

(a) less than the transaction costs
(b) more than offset by their risk
(c) invested at a rate of return less than the cost of capital (adjusted for risk)

7. Adarsh Chemicals has a weekly pay roll of ₹ 2,50,000 paid on Friday. On average, its employees cash their cheques in the following manner:

Day cheque cleared on Company's account	*Per cent of cheques cashed*
Friday	15
Monday	35
Tuesday	25
Wednesday	15
Thursday	10

As finance manager of the company, how would you arrange your payroll account? Are there any problems involved?

Solution

If the company were certain of the pattern shown, it would wish to have the following on deposit in its payroll account in order to cover the cheques which were cashed:

Friday	₹ 37,500
Monday	87,500
Tuesday	62,500
Wednessday	37,500
Thursday	25,000
	₹ 2,50,000

If employees cheque cashing behaviour is subject to fluctuations, the company will need to maintain "buffer" cash in the account. The greater the uncertainty, the greater the buffer that will be needed.

8. Ram-Laxman Pulp Company has experienced a stochastic demand for its product, with the result that cash balances fluctuate randomly. The standard deviation of daily net cash flows is ₹ 1,000. The company wishes to make the transfer of funds from cash to marketable securities and vice versa as automatic as possible. It has heard that this can be done by imposing upper-and-lower-bound control limits. The current interest rate on marketable securities is 6%. The fixed cost associated with each transfer is ₹ 100, and transfer are instantaneous.

(a) What are the optimal upper-and-lower-bound control limits? (Assume a 360-day year).

(b) What happens at these control limits?

Solution

(a) The return to point, R, is given by Equation-13, i, the interest rate per day, is .06/360 = .0001667

$$R = 3\sqrt{\frac{3a\sigma^2}{4i}}$$

$$R = 3\sqrt{\frac{3(100)(10,00,000)}{4(.0001667)}}$$

$$R = 3\sqrt{4,40,91,00,00,000}$$

The optimal value of the upper control limit is equal to 3R or ₹ 22,989. The lower bound control limit is zero.

(b) At zero cash, R marketable securities are sold and cash becomes ₹ 7,663. At upper control limit ₹ of cash. i.e. at ₹ 22,989 are invested in marketable securities.

9. Jayant Paper currently maintains an account with Bank of India for collections in the southeastern marketing area. The bank handles collections of ₹ 7,50,000 per day in return for a compensating balance of ₹ 5,00,000.

(a) The company is considering an alternative of opening two separate accounts in the southeastern area. It has been projected that total processing time could be reduced by 2 days if accounts are maintained in a Syndicate Bank and in an Andhra Bank, each requiring a ₹ 5,00,000 compensating balance. Would you recommend two bank system to Jayant?

(b) If Bank of India offers to drop the required compensating balance in favour of flat fee, what is the maximum fee Jayant Paper should be willing to pay to leave its business with that bank?

Solution

(a) Additional required balance = ₹ 10,00,000 - ₹ 5,00,000 = ₹ 5,00,000.
Funds freed by earlier collection = 2 (₹ 7,50,000) = ₹ 15,00,000.
The company should change to the two-bank system, since it yields ₹ 15,00,000 – ₹ 5,00,000 = ₹ 10,00,000 in released funds.

(b) There is no fee that would make it worthwhile for Jayant Paper to remain with Bank of India simply because the subsequent freeing up of ₹ 5,00,000 in funds will still be less than the ₹ 10,00,000 in released funds under the two-bank arrangement.

10. Universal Cables currently has a centralised billing system. On an average 5 days are required for customer's mailed payments to reach the central location. An additional 2-days are required for processing payments before a deposit can be made. The firm has a daily average collection of ₹ 8,00,000. The company has recently investigated the possibility of initiating a lock-box system. Such a system would reduce the mailed payments period from five to three days. Further, processing time would be reduced by one day, because each lock-box bank would pick up mailed deposits twice a daily.

(a) Determine the reduction in cash balances that can be achieved through the use of a lock-box system.

(b) Determine the opportunity cost of the present system, assuming a 7.5% return on short-term instruments.

(c) If the annual cost of the lock-box system will be ₹ 1,20,000, should such a system be initiated?

Solution

(a) Total time saving = 3 days

Time saving × daily average collection = reduction in cash balance achieved

3 × ₹ 8,00,000 = ₹ 24,00,000

Reduction in cash balances is ₹ 24,00,000

(b) Opportunity cost of the present system is .075 × ₹ 24,00,000 = ₹ 1,80,000

(c) Since the opportunity cost of the present system (₹ 1,80,000) exceeds the cost of the lock-box system (₹ 1,20,000). The system should be initiated.

11. Indian Tool expects to have ₹ 25,00,000 in cash outlays for next year. The firm believes that it will face an opportunity interest rate of 12.5% and will incur a cost of ₹ 150 each time it borrows (or withdraws). Cash outlays are expected to be steady over the year. Using the inventory model:

(a) Determine the optimal borrowing or withdrawal lot size for the Indian Tool.

(b) What is the total cost for the use of cash needed for transactions demanded?

(c) What will be the cash cycle for the firm (velocity)?

(d) What will be the average cash balance for the firm?

Solution

(a) The optimal borrowing or withdrawal lot size for the Indian tool is:

$$C = \sqrt{\frac{(2)(150)(25,00,000)}{.125}}$$

$$= \sqrt{6,00,00,00,000}$$

C = ₹ 77,460

(b) The total cost for the use of cash needed for transaction:

$$\frac{(150)\,(25,00,000)}{77,460} + \frac{(.125)(77,460)}{2}$$

= 4,841 + 4,841 = ₹ 9,682

(c) Cash cycle will be :

$$\frac{25,00,000}{77,460} = 32.27$$

or $\frac{365}{32.27} = 11.31$ days

(d) Average cash balance will be:

₹ 77,460/2 = ₹ 38,730

12. Refer to Problem-11, assume that the Indian Tool began the year with ₹ 25,00,000 in cash.

(a) How much would initially be invested in securities?

(b) How much would be invested in securities after 113 days?

Solution

(a) Initial investment in securities will be:

₹ 25,00,000 – ₹ 77,460 = ₹ 24,22,540

(b) Investment in securities after 113 days will be:

₹ 25,00,000 – (10+1) (₹ 77,460)

= ₹ 16,47,940

13. The Upton Company is setting up a new account with National Bank. Upton plans to issue cheques in the amount of ₹ 10,00,000 each day and to deduct them from its own records at the close of business on the day they are written. On average, the bank will receive and clear the cheques at 5 P.M. the third day after they are written; for example, a cheque written on Monday will be cleared on Thursday afternoon. The firm's agreement with the bank required it to maintain a ₹ 5,00,000 average compensating balance; this is ₹ 2,50,000 greater than the cash balance the firm would otherwise have on deposit. It makes a ₹ 5,00,000 deposit at the time it opens the account.

(a) Assuming that the firm makes deposits at 4 P.M. each day (and the bank includes them in that day's transactions), how much must it deposit daily in order to maintain a sufficient balance once it reaches a steady state? Indicate the required deposit on Day 1, Day 2, Day 3, if any, and each day thereafter, assuming that the company will write cheques for ₹ 10,00,000 on Day I and each day thereafter.

(b) How many days of float does Upton have?

(c) What ending daily balance should the firm try to maintain (1) on the bank's records and (2) on its own records?

Solution

(a) First, determine the balance on the firm's Cheque book and the banks's records as follows:

	Firms's Cheque Book	*Bank's Records*
Day 1: Deposit ₹ 500,000; write cheque for ₹ 10,00,000	(₹ 5,00,000)	₹ 5,00,000
Day 2: Write cheque for ₹ 10,00,000	(₹ 15,00,000)	₹ 5,00,000
Day 3: Write cheque for ₹ 10,00,000	(₹ 25,00,000)	₹ 5,00,000
Day 4: Write cheque for ₹ 10,00,000; deposit ₹ 10,00,000	(₹ 25,00,000)	₹ 5,00,000

After Upton has reached a steady state, it must deposit ₹ 10,00,000 each day to cover the cheques written 3 days earlier.

(b) The firm has 3 days of float; not until Day 4 does the firm have to make any additional deposits.

(c) As shown above, Upton should try to maintain a balance on the bank's records of ₹ 5,00,000. On its own books it will have a balance of *minus* ₹ 25,00,000

14. Konard Enterprises (KE) has grown from a small Ludhiana firm with customers concentrated in Northern India to a large, national firm serving customers throughout India. It has, however, kept its central billing system in Ludhiana. On average, 5 days elapse from the time customers mail payments until KE is able to receive, process, and deposit them. To shorten the collection period, KE is considering the installation of a lockbox system consisting of 30 local banks, or lockbox operators. The fixed costs of operating the system are estimated to be ₹ 14,000 per month. Under this system, customers' cheques would be received by the lockbox operator I day after there are mailed, and daily collection should average ₹ 30,000 at each location. The collections would be transferred to the regional concentration banks. One transfer mechanism involves having the local banks use "mail depository transfer cheques" or DTCs, to move the funds to the concentration banks; the alternative would be to use electronic (wire) transfers. A DTC would cost only ₹ 0.75 but it would take 2 days before funds were in the concentration bank and thus available to KE. Therefore, float time under the DTC system would be 1 day for mail plus 2 days for tranfers, or 3 days total, down from 5 days. A wire transfer would cost ₹ 11, but funds would be available immediately, so float time would be only 1 day. If KE opportunity cost is 11 percent, should it initiate the lockbox system? If so, which transfer method should be used? (Assume that there are 52 × 5 = 260 working days in a year.)

Solution

First, determine the annual benefit to Konard Enterprises from the reduction in cash balances under each plan:

Average daily collections = (30) (₹ 30,000) = ₹ 9,00,000

DTC:

Current collection float : ₹ 9,00,000 per day × 5 days =	₹ 45,00,000
New collection float: ₹ 9,00,000 per day × 3 days =	27,00,000
Float reduction	₹ 18,00,000

KE can reduce its average cash balances by ₹ 18,00,000 by using DTCs and it can earn 11 percent, which will provide ₹ 1,98,000 of additional income:

Additional income = (₹ 18,00,000)(0.11) = ₹ 1,98,000.

Wire transfer.

Current collection float: ₹ 9,00,000 per day × 5 days =	₹ 45,00,000
New collection float: ₹ 900,000 per day × 1 day =	900,000
Float reduction:	₹ 36,00,000

KE can reduce its cash balances by ₹ 36,00,000 by using wire transfer, which will increase income by ₹ 3,96,000;

Additional income = (₹ 36,00,000)(0.11) = ₹ 3,96,000.

Next, compute the annual cost of each transfer method :

Number of transfers = 30 × 260 = 7,800 per year.

Fixed lockbox cost = ₹ 14,000 × 12 = ₹ 168,000 per year.

DTC:

Total costs = (7,800) (₹0.75) + ₹ 1,68,000 = ₹ 1,73,850.

Wire transfer

Total costs = (7,800)(₹ 11) + ₹ 1,68,000 = ₹ 2,53,800.

Finally, calculate the net additional income resulting from each transfer method:

DTC

₹ 1,98,000 – ₹ 1,73,850 = ₹ 24,150

Wire transfer.

₹ 3,96,00–- ₹ 2,53,800 = ₹ 1,42,200.

Therefore KE should adopt the lockbox system and transfer funds from the lockbox operators to the regional concentration banks using wire transfers.

QUESTIONS

1. What is the objective of the financial manager in cash management? What conditions must be satisfied in meeting this objective?
2. Discuss the motives that a company may have for holding liquid assets. Explain the costs and benefits associated with holding liquid assets.
3. What action can a financial manager take to reduce a company's cash requirements?
4. How do excess balances arise in a disbursement system? Why are ethical problems a greater issue in disbursement than in collection?
5. What are the potential conflicts among the objectives of a disbursement system? Discuss the pros and cons of a disbursement system with local cheques writing and centralised disbursement bank selection.
6. Why is a controlled disbursement system attractive to cash managers even through it may not increase disbursement float?
7. Why do some firms neglect the importance of cash concentration systems in designing a cash management system?
8. Explain how concentrating cash into a central cash pool is superior to managing funds in many smaller balances at various banks.
9. Compare and contrast centralised and decentralised concentration systems, Can a decentralised from have a centralised concentration system?
10. What is meant by *control* in concentration systems? Which types of systems would have more problems with control issue?
11. What factors determine how frequently transfers should be made from a deposit account to a concentration account?
12. Define *collection float* and identify the role of each type of float. How can a collection system affect the amount of collection float? What influences the location of the collection points in an over-the-counter system versus a mailed payments system?
13. Explain how a lockbox works and how the use of a lockbox can increase the present value of a company.
14. Evaluate the following statement: "The only reason lockboxes are used is high interest rates. When rates fall companies stop using lockboxes. They start using them again when rates rise."
15. What role do marketable securities play in fulfilling the firms' overall objective of maximising its owner's wealth? How does the presence of marketable securities in the firm's asset structure affect the risk associated with the firm?
16. Consider the basic inventory model for cash management. If cash is ordered in lot sizes known as the *Optimal Cash Conversion Size,* what does the firm minimise by this action?
17. "It is normal for the financial manager to place great importance on the cash budget in determining the desirable cash holdings for a company." How did Beranek utilise this approach to develop a model suitable for determining the company's optimal cash balance?

18. In the transaction cash balance model, contrast the average cash balance and the return point.
19. Discuss the relative merits of the following inventory models for cash management:
    (a) Baumol (b) Beranek (c) Miller and Orr.

PROBLEMS

1. Amar Dye has an inventory turnover ratio of 12, accounts receivable turnover of 8, and an accounts payable turnover ratio of 9. The firm spends ₹ 10,00,000 per year. Assuming a 360-day, calculate the firm's cash cycle.

Ans.: Cash Cycle = 120 days

2. A firm currently has a weekly payroll of ₹ 80,000. Thus on the average, they have the use of ₹ 40,000 in accrued wages (₹ 80,000/2). If the firm changes to payment every two weeks, and can earn an annual rate of 12% on other investments, what savings if any, could be obtained? Explain.

Ans.: Savings = ₹ 4,800

3. Amba Manufacturing Company pays accounts payable on the 10th day after purchase. The average age of accounts receivable is 30 days and the average of inventory is 40 days. Annual cash outlays are approximately ₹ 1,80,00,000. The firm is considering a plan which would stretch its accounts payable by 20 days. If the firm can earn 7% on its investments, what annual savings can it realise by this plan, assume no discount for early payment of trade credit and a 360-day year.

Ans.: Annual savings = ₹ 70,000

4. Sagar Markets, Inc., a national food chain, is trying to convert as many of its transfers to wire transfers as possible. Presently. Sagar is using draft at cost of ₹ 12 per transfer. A wire transfer would cost ₹ 16.5 and would accelerate collections by 2 days. Excess funds are investable in commercial paper with an average yield of 6.4%. Calculate the minimum amount of a transfer for which the use of a wire would be economically acceptable.

Ans.: ₹ 43,030

5. Royal Products Limited has a credit and collection management policy that calls for centralised billing to and collection from customers. The billing and collection system is costing Royal ₹ 10,00,000 annually in equipment rental and employee expenses. Royal is considering going to a lock-box system that would substantially reduce collection activities at the present location. It is expected that without centralised billings, some personnel and equipment could be assigned to other corporate units, resulting in a saving of ₹ 40,000 annually. The lock-box system that Royal is evaluating would cost ₹ 1,10,000 annually to operate. It would, on the average, reduce by 2 days the amount of time it takes for payments received to become available for investments. Excess funds released through the use of the lock-box system would be temporarily invested in bankers' acceptances with an annualised yield of 6.45%. Royal has been averaging payments of ₹ 7,20,000 daily. Calculate the amount of funds released from using the lock-box system.

Ans.: ₹ 14,40,000

6. Vikrant Paints, which can earn 7% on money-market instrument currently, has a lock-box arrangement with a bank for its northern customers. The bank handles ₹ 3,00,000 a day in return for a compensating balance of ₹ 2,00,000.

(a) Vikrant has discovered that it could divided the northern region into a northeastern region (with ₹ 1,00,000 a day in collections, which could be handled by Bank of Baroda for a ₹ 1,00,000 compensating balance) and a northwestern region (with ₹ 2,00,000 a day in collections, which could be handled by Punjab National Bank for a ₹ 2,00,000 compensating balance). In each case, collections would be one-half day quicker than with the Bank of India arrangement. What would be the annual savings (or cost) of dividing the northern region?

(b) In an effort to retain the business, the Bank of India has offered to handle the collections strictly on a fee basis (no compensating balance). What would be the maximum fee the Bank of India could charge and still retain Vikrant's business?

Ans.: (a) Annual savings = ₹ 3,500; (b) Maximum Bank of India can charge = ₹ 10,500

7. Ambica Mills purchases ₹ 7,50,000 of raw material each year on terms of net 30. The purchasing agent currently is paying each invoice 20 working days after its date to make sure that payment is received by suppliers in 30 days. A study shows that payment could be delayed until the 25th day of working and still leave enough time for receipt by the 30th day. How much would the company save annually by making this change, assuming a 12% cost of funds?

Ans.: Annual savings = ₹ 12,328.77

23

FORECASTING CASH FLOWS

INTRODUCTION

The cash forecast is an estimation of the flows in and out of the firm's cash account over a particular period of time, usually a quarter, month, week, or day. The cash forecast is primarily intended to produce a very useful piece of information : an *estimation of the firm's borrowing and lending needs* and the uncertainties regarding these needs during various future periods.

Cash forecasting is extremely important to most firms. It enables them to *anticipate* periods of surplus cash and periods where financing will be necessary. This anticipation is the reason that cash forecasts are generated. Anticipation enables the firm to *plan* much more effectively for investment and financing, and *via* this planning, produce superior returns. This chapter highlights the objectives and design issues relating to forecasting short-term cash flows. We consider both medium-term monthly and quarterly forecasts and daily cash forecasts. We first discuss the benefits and costs of forecasting and then introduce some of the techniques used in cash forecasting systems.

OBJECTIVES OF CASH FORECASTING

The main objectives of cash forecasting are:

1. *Interest costs and Income.* One major purpose of forecasting is to increase the firm's yield on its investment portfolio or depending on the firm's financial position, to decrease interest costs on its borrowing. Lack of an accurate forecast may force management either to invest in very short-term securities (thereby often earning the lowest yields) or to borrow unexpectedly at higher than usual interest rates.
2. *Excess Balances.* This may be considered a corollary to the first factor. Accurate daily cash forecasts enable management to reduce balances in disbursement and/or deposit accounts and thereby move otherwise non-interest-earning cash into other areas of the firm.
3. *Administrative Costs Benefits.* Forecasting may require extensive administrative efforts to collect and digest data. On the other hand, forecasting may provide

administrative benefits in the form of better planning and more timely management reports.

4. *Control.* Daily cash budgets often provide a standard against which deposit reports from the field can be compared. If actual deposit vary from project deposits, inquiries may be warranted.
5. *Forecast System Costs.* There costs are associated directly with developing, maintaining, and running the forecasting model and associated data bases. Some forecast systems require extensive computer time and information. Others are simple and inexpensive.

DESIGNING FORECASTING SYSTEMS

Designing forecasting systems requires that management make trade off among these five cost factors. For example, an extensive, accurate forecasting system may be costly to build and maintain and may require strong administrative effort. But such a system may enable the firm to achieve better returns on its short-term investments, reduce borrowing costs, and exert better control over cash flows.

Depending on the horizon the forecaster wishes to consider, the cash forecasting may be divided into soughly three horizons. Different techniques and purposes are associated with each horizon.

Long Range Forecasts

Cash forecasts of one or more years into the future are needed primarily to assess the viability of the firm's long-range financing and operating policies. Long-range forecasts give planners an idea of how much cash the firm needs to raise through debt or equity issues, internally generated cash, or other cash sources. These forecasts also assist managers in establishing dividend policies, determining capital investments, and planning a mergers and acquisitions (or divestitures) programme. It is typical for a firm to have a 3 or 5-year forecast that is updated annually.

Long-range forecasts are generally based on accounting projections and typically involved the generation of various scenarios for future economic and technological environments. Such forecasts are considered strategic in the sense that possible major changes are examined.

Medium-Range Forecasts

We consider medium-range forecasts to be those that cover cash flows during the next 12 months. A firm may have, for example, a forecast of quarterly cash flows over the next 4 quarters, with monthly detail over the next 3 months. Medium-range cash forecasting usually takes the firm's existing technology and long-range financing as given. Hence, this kind of forecast is considered tactical rather than strategic. Although it can be accounting based, adjustments are made to focus on cash flows rather than earnings. It is sometimes called *cash budgeting.*

The purpose of medium-range forecasting is to determine the firms need for short-term cash from credit lines, commercial paper sales, or credit and payables policies. It also helps firms to determining the makeup of their short-term investment portfolio. When a firm performs the task called *budgeting*, it generally designates the most likely (or most desirable) scenario of the medium-range forecasts as the *budget*. The budget is used to compare actual performance during the course of the year.

Daily Cash Forecasts

Daily cash forecasts attempt to project cash inflows and outflows on a daily basis 1 or more days into the future. This is perhaps the most difficult forecasting to perform accurately. Even though a firm may know precisely its revenues for the month, it may have difficulty determining specific cash inflows for given days of the month. For some firms, a daily forecast several months into the future is possible. For most, however, a forecast even 2 days into the future is difficult.

The purposes of daily forecasting are to assist management in scheduling transfer in cash concentration, funding disbursement accounts, controlling field deposits, and making short-term investing and borrowing decisions.

METHODS OF FINANCIAL FORECASTING

Financial forecasting is the estimation of the future level of a financial variable, often a cash flow, asset level, or liability level. It is usually assumed that the relationship between the financial variable and other variables is linear. The *general linear model* can then be used.

$$Y_t = a_o + a_1X_1 + a_2X_2......a_nX_n \qquad (1)$$

Here, Y_t is the financial variable *(Y)* to be forecast in period *t*. This *X*'s are the *explanatory variables*, they are assumed to cause the level of *Y* in period *t*. The a_o term represents a constant unaffected by the *X*'s. The other *a* terms are the estimated coefficients of the explanatory X variables. There are *n* terms with *X*'s in them. Any forecast made in this way is subject to some prediction error because of uncertainty about the exact relationship between the explanatory variables (the *X*'s) and the outcome variable (the *Y*; that is, uncertainty about the *a* coefficients). There are four common approaches to forecasting financial variables, but they are all special cases of the general linear model. These four methods are discussed below:

Spot Method: Here it is assumed that the variable to be forecast is independent of all other variables, or alternatively, is predetermined. The variable is forecast by using its expected or predetermined level. All other explanatory variables are presumed to be irrelevant and the formula used is

$$Y_t = a_o \qquad (2)$$

where a_o is the expected or predetermined level of Y_t. For example, if we are doing a cash forecast and we know that the level of particular types of disbursement (such as rental payments) will be ₹ 12,000 in every month because of the firm's lease agreement, it would be reasonable to use the spot method to estimate rental payments as ₹ 12,000 per month.

Proportion of Another Account: This technique is used to project financial variables that are expected to vary directly with the level of another variable. The formula used is:

$$Y_t = a_1 X_1 \tag{3}$$

where X_1 is the other variable to which Y is related and a_1 is the constant of proportionality between the two. The "percent of sales" method is a variation of this technique, wherein X_1 is sales for a particular period and a_1 is the percent. The "proportion of another account" method is widely used, when there is a causal link from the explanatory variable to the variable to be forecast. For example, if sales volume (units sold) increases, it is natural that more units will have to be produced to replenish inventory. It is then reasonable to project certain direct costs of production, such as direct materials, as a percent of sales. In this circumstance, if costs of direct materials have historically been 50 percent of sales, and sales for a particular period have been forecast as ₹ 1,00,000, the firm would normally project direct material purchases at ₹ 50,000 for that period.

Compounded Growth: This method is used when a particular financial variable is expected to grow at a steady growth rate over time. The formula is the same as equation (3), but the explanatory variable X_1 is the *prior period's* level of Y, and a_1 is one plus the expected growth rate. That is:

$$Y_t = (1 + g)\ Y_{t-1} \tag{4}$$

Where g is the period's growth rate. For example, if it is expected that a firm's level of selling expenses will grow at 10 percent per year, and this year's selling expenses are ₹ 10,00,000, we would project next year's selling expenses as ₹ 1,00,000.

Multiple Dependencies: Here the variable is thought to depend on more than one factor; not just sales or some other variable but a combination of several variables. The general linear model as expressed in equation (1) is used, and the statistical technique of *linear regression* is often employed with historic data to estimate which explanatory variables are significant in determining Y_t and to estimate the coefficients of these variables. A classic example of multiple dependency is inventory level. Firms often keep a "base level" or "safety stock" of inventory to hedge uncertainty and vary the remaining portion of inventory in response to demand. In such a system, there are two appropriate variables associated with inventory level:

$$Y_t = a_0 + a_1 X_1 \tag{5}$$

There a_0 term represents the base inventory level, the X_1 the square root of the sales level, and a_1 the proportionality constant. If the firm's base level of inventory is ₹ 50,000, the proportionality constant is 15 and sales are expected to be ₹ 5,00,000, we could estimate inventory as:

$$Y_t = 50{,}000 + (15)\ ((5{,}00{,}000)^{1/2}) = ₹\ 60{,}607$$

In deciding which of these methods to use to forecast a particular variable, a primary consideration is the *term of the forecast:* how far into the future are we projecting? To see this, the concepts of *the short run* and *the long run* from economics can be employed. In the short run, most things are predetermined or pre-planned; very little can be changed. In the long run, almost everything is variable. In terms of financial forecasting, this means that in short-term forecasts, many things will result from plans and events that are already in place (contracts, capital budgets, long-range financing plans, and so forth). But in the long run, most things can vary and are dependent on outside influences such as the firm's long-term growth rate. Since cash forecasts deal mostly with the near future, *many of the items on the cash forecast are estimated by some variation of the spot method.* The bases for these spot estimates are usually the firm's other financial plans. Remaining estimates are mostly on a "proportion of another account" basis, with this "other account" often being a particular period's scales; the other two methods are employed less frequently. This is quite unlike longer-term forecasting. Where compounded growth and multiple dependency methodologies play a more important role.

FORECASTING COLLECTIONS FROM ACCOUNTS RECEIVABLE

The firm's *cash disbursements* are generally forecast in a straightforward fashion using the firm's other plans and a combination of the forecasting methods described previously. However, a major challenge for the analyst comes in estimating the *receipts from the collection of the firm's receivables.* There are two major decisions to be made: the *forecasting methodology* to be used and the *degree of aggregation* of the forecast across the firm's lines of business.

One forecasting methodology used by firms is the *turnover method.* This is a variation of the percent of sales method in which it is assumed that receivables will all be collected based on the average turnover of the receivables of the firm. For example, if the firm's average receivables turnover is 30 days, it is projected that all sales for one month will be collected in the following month. The problem with this system is that it does not do a very good job of capturing the actual process of receivables collection, and therefore it does not produce accurate forecasts except in special cases. This problem stems from the turnover statistic as a *weighted average* of the payment patterns of various customers paying at different times. A better receipt forecasting method is the *payment patterns approach* (also known as payment fractions or payment proportions approach). In this method, the analyst determines (using historical data) the proportion of customers that pay at various times after the date of sale and from this information projects future receipts.

The payment patterns method gives forecasts quite different from the turnover method. To see this, let us develop an example. Assume that last month's sales were ₹ 20,000, that this month's sales are expected to be ₹ 30,000 and that next month's sales are expected to be ₹ 20,000. Assume that 30 percent of the customers purchased products for cash, 40 percent paid in 30 days, and the remaining 30 percent paid in 60 days. These payment patterns would produce a 30-day turnover in periods of constant sales. Forecasts of cash receipts for next month by the turnover and payment patterns methods are presented in Table-1. The forecast of collection made by the turnover method ₹ 30,000 is quite different from the forecast of ₹ 24,000 made by the payment proportions method. Since the payment patterns method is a better representation of the underlying customer remittance habits, the cash receipt forecast associated with this method is likely to be more accurate.

The second issue that must be addressed in forecasting receivables collections is the *level of aggregation* of these forecasts across lines of business for multi-business firms. Firms selling various types of products often employ different terms of sale for their product lines and often sell these different products to customers with quite different payment habits. For example, it would not be expected that a unit of a firm selling on terms of 3 percent 10 days, net 30 days, to a group of very well-financed customers would have the same receipt patterns as a unit selling to less well-financed firms on net 60-days terms. In a situation where the firm is in multiple business lines, the use of *overall* payment patterns to forecast receipts will be accurate *only when the proportions of total sale made in each business line are constant*—an unlikely situation, particularly since the different lines usually have different seasonal variations. In such a multiline situation, the most accurate forecasting result is achieved by forecasting receipts for the *different units of the firm individually* based on their own receipt patterns, then summing these receipt forecasts to obtain total cash receipts for the firm.

TABLE-1

Collections Forecasts by the Turnover and Payment Patterns Methods

Month Sales:	*Last Month ₹ 20,000*	*This Month ₹ 30,000*	*Next Month ₹ 20,000*
Receipts Forecast Based on 30 Days Turnover (Last Month's Sales Figure)		30,000	
Receipts Forecast Based on Payment Patterns:			
Collection from Cash Sales (30 Percent of the Month's Sales)		6,000	
Collections from last Month's Sales (40 Percent of Last Month's Sales)		12,000	
Collection from Sales Two Months Ago (30 Percent of That Month's Sales)		6,000	
Total Collections Forecast by Payment Patterns		₹ 24,000	

SPREADSHEET CASH FORECAST: *AN EXAMPLE*

To see how cash forecasting works, let us generate a hypothetical cash forecast. An analyst for a firm is charged with creating a monthly cash forecast for the next six months. Consultation with the firm's credit manager indicates that, historically, 10 percent of the firm's sales have been for cash, 60 percent used in forecast of receipts by its very nature accounts for the flotation on incoming cheques, assuming that the payment proportions are calculated using cleared items. Table-2 presents the forecast. The spread sheet is started by the "Act." and "Est." notations, where the month abbreviations indicate which sales data are actual and while are projections. Net cash flow is collected as the total receipts minus the total disbursements. Total cash is the net cash flow plus beginning cash. Total cash less desired cash determines the firm's cumulative surpluses of required borrowings (Table-2).

USING THE CASH FORECAST

The cumulative surpluses and required borrowings for the firm is the important result of a cash forecast. This estimate of available funds for investment and needed financing enables the firm to plan so as to obtain the most advantageous borrowing terms for deficits and achieve the greatest interest income on surplus.

TABLE-2
Spreadsheet Cash Forecast

(in ₹)

	May (Act.)	*June (Act.)*	*July (Est.)*	*Aug. (Est.)*	*Sept. (Est.)*	*Oct. (Est.)*	*Nov. (Est.)*	*Dec. (Est.)*
Sales	3,00,000	3,30,000	3,60,000	4,20,000	4,80,000	4,50,000	3,90,000	3,00,000
Cash Receipts Forecast								
Cash Sales			36,000	42,000	48,000	45,000	39,000	30,000
Collection: Ist Prior Month			1,98,000	2,16,000	2,52,000	2,88,000	2,70,000	2,34,000
Collection: 2nd Prior Month			87,000	95,700	1,04,400	1,21,800	1,39,200	1,30,500
Total Receipts			3,21,000	3,53,700	4,04,400	4,54,800	4,48,200	3,94,500
Cash Disbursements Forecast								
Direct Labour Payments			1,22,400	1,42,800	1,63,200	1,57,500	1,36,500	1,05,000
Direct Material Payments			1,26,000	1,38,600	1,51,200	1,76,400	2,01,600	1,89,000
Monthly Fixed Expenses			24,000	24,000	24,000	24,000	24,000	24,000
Tax payments			—	—	1,32,000	—	—	1,32,000
New Construction			—	54,000	—	54,000	—	54,000
Total disbursements			2,72,400	3,59,400	4,70,400	4,11,900	3,62,100	5,04,000
Net Cash Flow			48,600	– 5,700	– 66,000	42,900	86,100	– 1,09,500
Beginning Cash			15,000	63,600	57,900	– 8,100	34,800	1,20,900
Total Cash			63,600	57,900	– 8,100	34,800	1,20,900	11,400
Desired Cash			18,000	21,000	24,000	22,500	19,500	15,000
Surplus or (Borrowings)			45,600	36,900	– 32,100	12,300	1,01,400	– 3,600

Let us assume that the yield curve is upsloping. The firm starts the forecast with no surplus or deficit. During July, a surplus of ₹ 45,600 accumulated. For maximum interest income, these funds should be invested in temporary instruments with the longest possible maturity. In examining the forecast for August we see that the surplus for *this* month is only ₹ 36,900; of July's ₹ 45,600 surplus, ₹ 8,700 will be needed to cover cash outflows and increases in the desired level of cash. Further, there is a deficit in September. Therefore, of the ₹ 45,600 surplus in July, ₹ 36,900 can be invested until these funds are needed in September, the remaining ₹ 8,700 will be needed in August and must be invested in shorter maturity instruments. The firm will need to borrow ₹ 32,100 in September to cover the deficit in this month. They should make arrangements to have these funds available at that time. The entire ₹ 12,300 surplus in October can be invested until December, since the surplus of ₹ 1,04,400 in November is larger than the surplus in October (November being a month of large anticipated cash inflows). The additional ₹ 89,100 surplus in November can be invested at that time until it is needed in December. The firm's maximum borrowing needs over this six month period are ₹ 32,100, reached in September.

Some firms that borrow on short-term credit lines are required to be out of debt for a specific period during the year (often 60 to 90 consecutive days) under these credit agreements. For such firms, the cash forecast has an additional significant benefit: it can help determine whether the firm will fulfill this out-of-debt requirement, given the firm's current plans. For example, examination of Table -2 reveals that the firm in the example will not be out of debt for 90 consecutive days during the July through December period.

FORECASTING DAILY CASH FLOWS

Forecasters typically use scheduling for daily cash forecasts, especially for short horizons. Statistical tools can be helpful for the recurrent, non-major elements in the forecast, however. Many smaller and some medium-sized companies do not even forecast on a daily basis, relying on funding from investments or credit lines to cover shortfalls. The uncertainty of cheque clearing is managed with controlled disbursement accounts. As the opportunity cost for suboptimal investing increases due to increasing interest rates. More companies find it profitable to do daily forecasts.

For most companies doing daily forecasting, the immediate day's flows are simply gathered from balance-reporting systems. For the next day and up to two weeks in the future, historical collection and payment patterns can be used in connection with sales and purchases to project cash flows.

The shorter the horizon, the more detail shown in the cash forecast. Ideally, the format will include columns for the forecast, the actual amount (as it materialises), the budgeted amount, and variances. Typically, actual-versus-forecast and actual-versus-budget variances will be calculated. Explanations of likely causes and corrective actions will accompany the numbers.

With the requirement to present a Statement of Cash Flows, some companies are finding it fruitful to prepare their cash forecasts with separate subtotals for operating, financing, and investing cash flows. While the Statement of Cash Flows format might be more appropriate for a monthly forecast, it can be used for daily forecasts as well.

The major differences when it comes to modeling the daily cash flow are a greater reliance on bank-supplied deposit and cleaning data, an emphasis on scheduling the upcoming cash flows via the receipts and disbursements technique, and a lesser reliance on statistical forecasting techniques. Scheduling upcoming cash receipts and disbursements requires close contact with any corporate personnel having responsibility for or knowledge of impending cash flows.

One area where statistics have been instrumental in achieving accuracy is for spreading out (distributing) cheque clearing or receivable cash effects throughout the days of the week and month. Here regression analysis has been very useful, in that the day-of-the week and even day-of-the month effects can be modeled by assigning each a separate regression coefficient. The regression-based *distribution method* also has been used to model the cash disbursements related to how many business days have elapsed since payroll cheque have been issued. In general, distribution simply refers to spreading out the month's cash forecast into daily flows, thereby showing the intra-month cash flow pattern. We can illustrate this in the disbursements context by assuming that October's total disbursement is forecast to be ₹ 40,00,000 We can forecast the disbursements for Friday, October 13, which is the eleventh work day of the month.

$$CD_{11} = (d_{11} + w_5) \times MDF$$

where CD_{11} = cash disbursement forecast for the eleventh work day of the month
d_{11} = coefficient for eleventh work day (from regression model)
w_5 = coefficient for fifth day of work, Friday (from regression model)
MDF = month's disbursement forecast (from cash budget)

If we assume that d_{11} is (.04, w_5 is .015 and MDF is ₹ 40,00,000, we have:

$$CD_{11} = (.04 + .015) \times (₹\ 40{,}00{,}000) = (.055) \times (₹\ 40{,}00{,}000) = ₹\ 2{,}20{,}000$$

One can think of the work-day coefficient as the effect of the day-of-the-month effect, holding constant the day-of-the-week, and the day-of-week coefficient as to that day's effect holding constant the day-of-the-month.

SOURCES OF UNCERTAINTY IN CASH FORECASTING

Given the short-run nature of the cash forecast, with most things occurring in the near future and the forecast period typically being a year, one would tend to think that most financial transaction, over this period could be forecast very accurately. Unfortunately, this is far from true. Even with this short period there are numerous sources of risk. Among the sources are *sales uncertainty, collection rate uncertainty, production cost uncertainty,* and *capital outflow uncertainty.* Let us look at each one of these in turn.

Sales uncertainty refers to the risk regarding the firm's future levels of sales. Most firms try to forecast accurately enough to hold errors in short-run sales forecasts to less than 10 percent, but are often unsuccessful in these efforts. Sales-projections are a product of two other projections, units to be sold and price per unit. Both are often quite uncertain and depend on economic and competitive conditions. Note that *any errors in sales forecasts have multiple impacts* on the firm's cash flows, they impact on receivable levels (and therefore collections) and also on production expenses (and therefore disbursements).

Collection rate uncertainty is the uncertainty regarding the firm's actual future collection patterns of receivables. The firm may historically have collected an average of a certain percent of its outstanding receivables from a particular period in another particular period, but this average contains considerable variability. Further, changing market and economic conditions may make for chancy extrapolation of post historic data into future period. Because of this and the uncertainties in forecasting sales, forecasts of the collection of future receivables contain at least three sources of uncertainty; uncertainly regarding the number of units that will be sold, uncertainty regarding the price at which these units will be sold, and uncertainty regarding the patterns with which the receivables generated by these sales will be collected.

Production cost uncertainty has to do with the risk of the actual labour and material costs that go into the making of a product of service. Labour productivity may be more or less than expected, making labour costs uncertain. The cost of materials used may vary due to unexpected changes in price or in the amount of materials necessary to produce products and services.

Capital outflow uncertainty is one of the biggest sources of surprises in cash flow forecasting. This is the uncertainty regarding the timing of cash disbursements related to the firm's major capital expenditure and construction programmes. The uncertainty arises from the nature of payments made for new construction. When the firm undertakes to build a new plant or other project of this sort. The total price (subject to specified revisions) is generally agreed upon in advance. The construction firm then starts the project. After a certain percent of the project is done, the construction firm submits a "progress report" to the firm and is paid for what has been completed, less a retainage. For example, assume that the firm has contracted to have built a ₹ 10 crore building with a 10 percent retainage. Once the construction firm completes the first 20 percent of the project, a payment of ₹ 1.8 crore will be due (₹ 10 crore times 20 percent times 90 percent). Such payments are subject to at least two uncertainties. *First,* the weather, a very risky variable, plays a significant part in the rate of construction completion. *Second* construction firms are notorious for filing late progress reports and then expecting immediate payment. While only a small percent of the firm's total bills are from capital construction programmes, the amounts involved are usually very large. One unexpected item of this sort can destroy a carefully planned cash flow management strategy.

ESTIMATING UNCERTAINTY IN CASH FORECASTS

There are two basic approaches to the assessment of risk in cash forecasting. First, we could assess the effects of *individual sources* of uncertainty on important *individual outcome variables.* Second, we could assess the effect of *all the uncertainties* in all the risky estimated variables on *all the important outcome variables* with all the uncertainties allowed to vary simultaneously Both of these methodologies are very useful. The first requires sensitivity analysis; the second requires simulation. The illustrate these, let us return to our cash forecasting example problem, whose solution is contained in Table-2.

Sensitivity Analysis of the Cash Forecast

We know that there are uncertainties in the estimation of sales, collection rates, production and other cost amounts, and the timing and amount of capital disbursements, at the least. Using sensitivity analysis. We can assess some of the effects of these individual sources of uncertainty. For example, recall that the direct labour payments were estimated as 34 percent of sales for the last three months because of a new wage scale. If this new wage scale was the result of a new labour contact that is yet to be negotiated when the forecast is made, the actual wage rate would be subject to uncertainty. Let us assess the effects of variation in the direct labour payments as a percent of sales on the projected surpluses and deficits in October, November, and December. This is done by changing the input variable and observing changes in the output variable. The first step might be to estimate the surpluses and deficits with direct labour at 36 percent of sales. The results are presented in Table-3. The projected surplus in October drops from ₹ 12,300 to ₹

TABLE-3

Sensitivity Analysis of Cash Forecast
(Direct Labour for October Through December Chnged to 36 Percent of Sales)

(in ₹)

	May (Act.)	*June (Act.)*	*July (Est.)*	*Aug. (Est.)*	*Sept. (Est.)*	*Oct. (Est.)*	*Nov. (Est.)*	*Dec. (Est.)*
Sales	3,00,000	3,30,000	3,60,000	4,20,000	4,80,000	4,50,000	3,90,000	3,00,000
Sales	3,00,000	3,30,000	3,60,000	4,20,000	4,80,000	4,50,000	3,90,000	3,00,000
Cash Receipts Forecast								
Cash Sales			36,000	42,000	48,000	45,000	39,000	30,000
Collection : 1st Prior Month		1,98,000	2,16,000	2,52,000	2,88,000	2,70,000	2,34,000	
Collection : 2nd Prior Month		87,000	95,700	1,04,400	1,21,800	1,39,200	1,30,500	
Total Receipts			3,21,000	3,53,700	4,04,400	4,54,800	4,48,200	3,94,500
Cash Disbursements Forecast								
Direct labour Payments			1,22,900	1,42,800	1,63,200	1,62,000	1,40,400	1,08,000
Direct Material Payments		1,26,000	1,38,600	1,51,200	1,76,400	2,01,600	1,89,000	
Monthly Material Payments		24,000	24,000	24,000	24,000	24,000	24,000	
Tax Payments			—	—	1,32,000	—	—	1,32,000
New Construction			—	54,000	—	54,000	—	54,000
Total Disbursements			2,72,400	3,59,400	4,70,400	4,16,400	3,66,000	5,07,000
Net Cash Flow			48,600	–5,700	–66,000	38,400	82,200	– 1,12,500
Beginning Cash			15,000	63,600	57,900	– 8,100	30,300	1,12,500
Cash			63,600	57,900	– 8,100	30,300	1,12,500	0
Total Desired Cash			18,000	21,000	24,000	22,500	19,500	15,000
Surplus or (Borrowings)			45,600	36,900	– 32,100	7,800	93,000	– 15,000

7,800, the surplus in November drops from ₹ 1,01,400 to ₹ 93,000 and the project deficit in December increases from ₹ 3,600 to ₹ 15,000.

Another uncertain variable is the timing of payments for new construction. The weather pays a significant part in the rate of progress of construction. It is possible that the weather may be good and that the firm's construction company may progress ahead of schedule; instead of ₹ 54,000 being due in August. October, and December, this could result in ₹ 81,000 being due in August and October and nothing due in December. The results are presented in Table-4. Other variations in the timing of construction payments could also be investigated.

TABLE-4

Sensitivity Analysis of Cash Forecast: New Construction Payment Accelerates (in ₹)

	May (Act.)	*June (Act.)*	*July (Est.)*	*Aug. (Est.)*	*Sept. (Est.)*	*Oct. (Est.)*	*Nov. (Est.)*	*Dec. (Est.)*
Sales	3,00,000	3,30,000	3,60,000	4,20,000	4,80,000	4,50,000	3,90,000	3,00,000
Cash Receipts Forecast								
Cash Sales			36,000	42,000	48,000	45,000	39,000	30,000
Collection: 1st Prior Month			1,98,000	2,16,000	2,52,000	2,88,000	2,70,000	2,34,000
Collection 2nd Prior Month			87,000	95,700	1,04,400	1,21,800	1,39,200	1,30,500
Total Receipts			3,21,000	3,53,700	4,04,400	4,54,800	4,48,200	3,94,500
Cash Disbursements Forecast								
Direct Labour Payments			1,22,400	1,42,800	1,63,200	1,62,000	1,40,400	1,08,000
Direct receipt Payments			1,26,000	1,38,600	1,51,200	1,76,400	2,01,600	1,89,000
Monthly Fixed Expenses			24,000	24,000	24,000	24,000	24,000	24,000
Tax Payments			—	—	1,32,000	—	—	1,32,000
New Construction			—	81,000	—	81,000	—	—
Total Disbursement			2,72,400	3,86,400	4,70,400	4,43,400	3,66,000	4,50,000
Net Cash Flow			48,600	– 32,700	– 66,000	15,900	86,100	– 55,500
Beginning Cash			15,000	63,600	30,900	– 35,100	19,200	66,900
Total Cash			63,600	30,900	– 35,100	– 19,200	66,900	11,400
Desired Cash			18,000	21,000	24,000	22,500	19,500	15,000
Surplus or (Borrowing)			45,600	9,900	– 59,100	– 41,700	47,400	– 3,600

This kind of analysis provides very useful unformation about the amounts of possible surpluses and deficits in various future periods. With regard to the construction payments example, the expected amounts of surpluses and borrowings in the beginning and ending months are unaffected, but the pattern from September to November is significantly altered. The maximum amount of the firm's necessary borrowings are now ₹ 59,100, not ₹ 32,100 in the original calculation. If there is a significant chance that this speedup of construction may occur, the firm should make far different financing arrangements than were originally anticipated.

Simulation Analysis of the Cash Forecast

While sensitivity analysis methodologies give useful information, it is generally the *overall variation* from the means of the monthly cash deficits and surpluses that concerns management for planning purposes. This information on the probability distributions of cash surpluses and deficits is necessary to plan advantageous strategies. To estimate these probability distributions, a simulation of the overall uncertainty in the ending cash balances for cash of the period within the forecast is needed. To get these, the methods of simulation analysis are used. First, probability distributions for each of the major uncertain variables are developed. For a cash forecast, the variables involved would include sales, collection rates, production costs, and capital expenditures. Statistical estimation procedures or management estimates could be used; discreate or continuous distributions are possible. Then, large number of trials are run. From these trial results, frequency histogrammes of the important outcome variables would be developed and these compared to known probability distributions via goodness-of-fit methods.

To apply simulation analysis in estimating the total uncertainty in a cash forecast, one of the uncertainties that must be quantified is that of the *collection rules on accounts receivable.* Uncertainty in the collection rates of receivables is an important component in the overall uncertainty of the cash forecast. The usual method of estimating these rates is to compute individual collection rates on various period's sales using historic data. Another approach to the problem aids an quantifying the multivariate uncertainty in these rates. The approach estimates all the collection rates simultaneously by regressing past sales figures against past collections. The estimated collection of the sales figures in the regression can be interpreted as the collection proportions and the standard errors of the estimated regression collection as the uncertainty inherent in the estimation of these collection proportion.

ILLUSTRATIVE PROBLEM

1. Global Recreation Centers is attempting to forecast cash receipts from its Eastern Division. Cash is deposited into two field banks on a daily basis. The cash manager has found that deposits follow a fairly strong day-of-week pattern. She used historical data to determine the fraction of each week's total revenues deposited by day-of-week by district. Combined with weekly revenue estimates the fractions help her estimate daily deposits from Eastern Division. The parameters obtained from the past 3 months' deposit data follow:

Day of Week	*District 1 using Deposit Bank 1*	*District 2 using Deposit Bank 2*
Monday	36.0 %	31.0 %
Tuesday	13.0	15.0
Wednesday	17.0	17.0
Thursday	15.0	20.0
Friday	19.0	17.0
	100.0 %	100.0 %

Weekly revenue estimates from the sales department were also obtained:

	District 1	District 2
Week 1	₹ 68,000	₹ 39,000
Week 2	₹ 52,000	₹ 44,000

Solution

To forecast daily deposits into each bank, we simply multiply the weekly revenue by the day-of-week percentage and sum across the two districts.

	District 1 (Bank 1)			District 2 (Bank 2)			Total Daily
Day	Fraction	TOT/Week	Daily	Fraction	TOT/Week	Daily	Deposit
Mon	36.0	₹ 68,000	₹ 24,480	31.0%	₹ 39,000	₹ 12,090	₹ 36,570
Tue	13.0	68,000	8,840	15.0	39,000	5,850	14,690
Wed	17.0	68,000	11,560	17.0	39,000	6,630	18,190
Thu	15.0	68,000	10,200	20.0	39,000	7,800	18,000
Fri	19.0	68,000	12,920	17.0	39,000	6,630	19,550
Mon	36.0	52,000	18,720	31.0	44,000	13,640	32,360
Tue	13.0	52,000	6,760	15.0	44,000	6,600	13,360
Wed	17.0	52,000	8,840	17.0	44,000	7,480	16,320
Thu	15.0	52,000	7,800	20.0	44,000	8,800	16,600
Fri	19.0	52,000	9,880	17.0	44,000	7,480	17,360
Total		₹ 1,20,000	₹ 1,20,000		₹83,000	₹83,000	₹2,03,000

QUESTIONS

1. Why should a financial manager focus on cash flow rather than earnings?
2. What are some of the purposes of long-term, medium-term, and daily cash flow forecasts?
4. What are the elements of the firm's objective function related to cash forecasting?
5. How can days' sales outstanding be computed from a balance sheet and an income statement? What other timing measures can be similarly computed?
6. Why do corporations put so much emphasis on cash forecasts? What would happen if a company continually relied on inaccurate cash forecasts? In what sense do cash forecasts function as a control device?
7. How can a company's cash position be measured for forecasting purposes? Why do manager generally prefer using the available bank balance?
8. Why does top management focus more on the monthly cash forecast than the daily forecast?
9. Define sensitivity analysis, and indicate on what variable you would conduct sensitivity analysis for a simple cash budget.
10. Briefly summarise differences between daily cash forecasting and monthly forecasting.
11. Compare and contrast the scheduling approach with the distribution approach for daily cash forecasting. Which is more useful for which types of cash flows?

PROBLEMS

1. It is June 30 and the treasurer of the ABC Toy Company is trying to forecast cash inflows for the last 6 months of the year. The following credit sales information (in crore of ₹) is available:

Apr	₹ 30	May	₹ 35	Jun	₹ 30 }	Actual
Jul	45	Aug	70	Sep	150 }	
Oct	200	Nov	125	Dec	45 }	Forecast

From prior studies, the treasurer has determined that approximately 85% of the sales for any month are uncollected at the end of the month of the sale, 60% are still uncollected 1 month after the sale, and 10% are uncollected 2 months after the sale. That last 10%, with the exception of bad debts, which average 2% of sales, are collected in the third month after the sale.

a. Forecast the case inflows, by months, for July through December for ABC Toys.

b. Forecast the accounts receivable at the end of each month for July through December, (Assume that bad debts are written off in the third month following the sale rather than through an allowance for doubtful accounts at the time the sale is made.)

2. It is January and the XYZ Company wishes to prepare a monthly cash forecast over the next four months. Sales for December were ₹11,00,000. Expected sales for the next four months are:

Month	*January*	*February*	*March*	*April*
Expected Sales	₹ 6,00,000	₹ 8,00,000	₹ 11,00,000	₹ 8,00,000

Thirty percent of the firm's sales are for cash; the remainder are collected in the month following the sale (there are no bad debts). Disbursements consist of payments for raw materials, direct labour, other operating expenses, purchases of fixed assets, and taxes. Costs of sales are 75 percent of sales. Of these costs of sales, 38 percent are raw material costs and 62 percent are direct labour costs. Direct labour costs are paid in the month incurred, while raw materials are purchased on net 30-day terms. Other operating expenses total ₹ 1,50,000 per month. Expenditures for fixed assets of ₹ 75,000 are to be made in February and April and tax payments of ₹ 1,10,000 are to be made in january and March. As of January 1,there are no surpluses or deficits and the firm's cash balance is ₹ 83,000. The firm keeps a cash balance equal to 10 percent of the month's cost of sales. Generate a monthly cash forecast for the upcoming four months.

3. A firm makes monthly cash forecasts and distributes these forecasts to a daily basis. For the upcoming month, anticipated cash inflows are ₹ 10,00,000. Each of the first two weeks has five working days. Twenty percent of the month's total cash receipts are expected to be received during the first week and 28 percent are expected to be received during the second week. Within each week, receipts are expected to be received as follows:

Day	*Monday*	*Tuesday*	*Wednesday*	*Thursday*	*Friday*
Proportion	0.20	0.23	0.07	0.20	0.30

The firm writes cheques on Tuesday for the entire week's expenses, except for taxes. Ten percent of these cheques are cashed on Tuesday, 5 percent on Wednesday, 60 percent on Thursday, and remainder on Friday. Cheques totaling ₹ 2,50,000 are to be written on Tuesday of the first week, and cheques totaling 2,00,000 are to be written on Tuesday of the second week. A tax payment in the amount ₹ 1,00,000 will be made on Wednesday of the second week via mail transfer. Beginning cash is ₹ 50,000; this is also the desired cash at all times during the first two weeks of the month. Generate the distributed daily cash forecast for the first two weeks of the upcoming months.

4. A firm has performed a simulation of its cash budget, with the following results:

Month	*Expected Surplus Or (Deficit)*	*Standard Deviation of Expected Surplus or (Deficit)*
1	(₹ 80,000)	₹ 1,00,000
2	(₹ 20,000)	₹ 1,50,000
3	₹ 70,000	₹ 2,00,000
4	₹ 20,000	₹ 2,50,000

The firm keeps two hedges against cash flow uncertainty: excess borrowing capacity with its bank and a ₹ 50,000 cash reserve. It must commit to its maximum level of borrowing over the next four months, at a commitment fee of 0.2 percent of the maximum amount of borrowing arranged. The opportunity cost of holding the cash hedge is 10 percent per year (3.33 percent for the upcoming four months). The firm wishes to limit its probability of running out of cash (of exceeding the total available hedge) to a maximum of 5 percent in any month. Calculate the amount of borrowing capacity that the firm should arrange for with its bank and the total cost of its hedges of cash flow uncertainty, assuming that the probability distributions of surpluses and deficits are normal and serially uncorrelated. (Hint: The maximum amount of borrowing required will be the maximum needed for hedging and for expected borrowings less that needed for expected borrowings only.)

24

RECEIVABLES MANAGEMENT

INTRODUCTION

Receivable management refers to the decisions a business makes regarding its overall credit and collection policies and the evaluation of individual credit applicants. In formulating an optional credit policy, finance manager must analyse the marginal benefits and costs associated with changes in credit standards, credit terms, collection efforts etc. Receivables management proves for a firm, both, an asset and a problem : an asset because of the promise of a future cash flow and a problem because of the need to obtain financing while waiting for the future cash flow.

In this chapter, we will investigate the techniques which a company may employ to determine an optimum credit policy. First, a company must decide whether it should sell goods on credit. An affirmative answer will necessitate an evaluation of the credit. Terms which will be consistent with the goal of maximising the value of the company to its shareholders. Once an optimum credit policy is determined, the financial manager must ascertain the effect it will have on the company's current asset requirements. We will carry this analysis to the point of determining the marginal expected return on investment in receivables.

CONCEPTUAL FRAMEWORK

Account receivables are asset accounts representing amounts owed to the firm as a result of the sale of goods and services in the ordinary course of business. The value of these claims is carried on the balance sheet under titles such as accounts receivables, trade receivables or customer receivables. The financial manager can add value to the company's shares by properly influencing *three* areas: the company's aggregate investment in receivables, its credit terms, and its credit standards. Overinvesting in receivables can be costly because the investment is typically financed by short-term borrowing and because it may signal acceptance of late-paying customers. If the credit terms (cash discount and period allowed for payment) are not competitive when compared to other sellers in the same industry or are misaligned with the product line profitability, they can also diminish shareholder value. Setting the credit standard for customers incorrectly can erode shareholder value because of lost sales (when too stringent) or uncollectible sales (when too lenient).

RATIONALE FOR THE EXTENSION OF CREDIT

The rationale for the extension of credit may be found in the following motives:

Financial motive

Sellers charge a higher price when selling on credit, generating a greater present-value profit based on the implicit interest rate charged; sellers raise capital at lower rates than their customers and have cost advantages vis-a-vis banks due to (a) the similarity of customers, (b) the information gathered in the selling process, (c) a lower probability of default (because the purchased goods are part of a product which is an integral part of the buyer's business), and (d) a greater value of collateral to sellers in that they can rework and resell the product without much difficulty or expense.

Operating motive

Here suppliers respond to variable and uncertain demand by the way in which they extend trade credit, instead of using more costly responses such as installing extra capacity, building or depleting inventories, or forcing customers to wait in line.

Contracting Cost motive

Sales contracting costs between buyers and sellers are reduced for buyers because they can inspect the quantity and quality of goods prior to payment and reduce the payment if some goods are missing or defective; sellers have less employee or third party theft because goods are less liquid than cash and collection is not made at the time of delivery, while the separation of collection and delivery allows sellers to achieve efficiency gains due to the specialisation of labour.

Pricing motive

Sellers in certain industries are unable to alter their prices, perhaps because they are part of an oligopoly (and face a kinked demand curve or are part of a collusive agreement) or due to governmental regulation; unpublished variations in credit policy allow these sellers to charge varying amounts to their customers.

Financial market imperfections stand behind all of these motives, which represent company responses to the imperfections. In each case, trade credit is more economical and efficient than using other responses open to the companies. These motives are difficult to test in the real world, and it is very difficult to say which of these motives dominates as the rationale behind most trade credit.

DETERMINING THE APPROPRIATE RECEIVABLE POLICY

How should a financial managers incorporate the costs and benefits, of the receivables into their analysis to achieve the objective of maximising profits without undue risk or to have the return from the extension of credit exceed the cost of capital? The relationship between the components of a company's credit policy and the costs and benefits associated with providing credit helps the financial manager to derive a technique which the company can apply in order to determine an optimum credit policy upon receipt of orders from a new customer or from an existing customer within insufficient preapproved credit. The company is to determine whether to launch a credit investigation of the buyer or not. If it investigates, the company might consult various information sources and tailor the depth of investigation to the size of the account. Credit administration is involved in the establishment of credit policy, only with planning, organising directly, and controlling all aspects of the credit function. Credit policy includes *credit standards, setting credit terms, the company approvals to credit investigation, credit limits, and the collection activity.* As long as payment are received on timely basis the credit-granting process is a continuous flow of alternating orders and payments.

ANALYSIS OF CREDIT STANDARDS

Credit standards have a significant influence on sales as trade credit is one of the many factors that influence the demand for a firm's product. The relaxation of credit terms involve certain costs and the enlarged administrative expense and increased probability of bad debt, and the cost of additional investment in receivables resulting from increased sales and a slow average collection period. There is also the profitability of additional sales, additional demand for the product and the required return on investments.

To illustrate, assume a product sells for ₹ 10 a unit of which ₹ 7 represents variable costs before taxes including administrative costs. Current annual sales are ₹ 24,00,000 represented entirely by credit sales and the firm is considering a more liberal extension of credit, which will result in a slowing in the average collection period from one to two months. However, existing customers are not expected to alter their payment habits. The relaxation in credit side is expected to produce a 25% increase in sales to ₹ 30,00,000 annually. This ₹ 6,00,000 increase represents 60,000 additional units. Assume that the required rate of return on investment in receivable is 20% before taxes.

Present value of receivables = Annual sales/Receivable turnover

= ₹ 24,00,000/12 = ₹ 2,00,000

New level of receivables

= ₹ 30,00,000/6 = ₹ 5,00,000

Additional receivables

= ₹ 3,00,000 = (₹ 5,00,000 – ₹ 2,00,000)

Additional investment in receivables

₹ 3,00,000 × .7 = ₹ 2,10,000

Required return on additional investment

= 0.20 × ₹ 2,10,000 = ₹ 42,000

Profitability on additional sales

= ₹ 3 × 60,000 units = ₹ 1,80,000

As the profitability on additional sales, (i.e., ₹ 1,80,000) exceeds the required rate on the additional investment (i.e., ₹ 42,000) the firm will be advised to relax its credit standards. There are, however, many practical problems in affecting a change in credit policy, particularly in estimating the receivables. It is desirable to attract probability distributions to the increased demand and to the increased sales in receivables and evaluate a range of possible outcomes. Another assumption is that 60,000 additional units can be produced at a variable cost of ₹ 7 a unit (i.e., that plant capacity does not have to be extended). This implies that the firms should vary its credit quality standards in keeping with the level of production and as a capacity is approached, quality standards might be improved. Another assumption is that increased demand as a function of lowering credit quality standards as well as price and cost figures will remain unchanged.

ANALYSIS OF CREDIT TERMS

A company's credit terms specify a credit period (s) and cash discount rate (s) where a cash discount is offered. The *credit period* is the period elapsing between the date when the purchasing company receives its statement of account and the date when payment is due. The *cash discount period* is the period elapsing between the date when the purchasing company receives its statement of account and the date when the cash discount is foregone. The cash *discount rate* expresses, in effect, the reduction in the purchase price that the purchasing company will receive if it pays within the cash discount period. To illustrate, assume a firm with an annual credit sales of ₹ 30,00,000 has an average collection period of 2 months, and the sales terms are net 45 days, with no discount given the annual turnover of receivables is 6 times, so that the average receivable balance is ₹ 5,00,000. If the terms are changed to 2/10-net 45, i.e. a 2% discount is given if the bill is paid before the 10th day after the date of invoice, payment is due by the 45th day, the average collection period is reduced to one month and 50% of customers take advantage of the 2% discount The opportunity cost of the discount to the firm is $0.02 \times 0.5 \times 30{,}00{,}000$ or ₹ 30,000 annually. However, the turnover of receivables has improved to 12 times a year. So that the average receivables are reduced from ₹ 5,00,000 to ₹ 2,50,000. The firm realises ₹ 2,50,000 from accelerated collections and if a 20% rate of return is assumed, the opportunity saving is ₹ 50,000 which is greater than the cost of discount so that the firm should adopt a 3% discount. If the speeding in collections has not resulted in sufficient opportunity saving to offset the cost of discount, the discount policy should not be changed.

When a firm offers a cash discount, its intention is to accelerate the flow of cash into the firm and/or improve its competitive position. Again, the length of the discount period may affect the collection period but the effect is not so clear as two forces then influence the average collection period. If the credit period is held constant, certain customers will be tempted to take the discount where previously they did not do so, a practice which will shorten the average collection period. On the other hand, customers who have been taking the discount and paying at the end of discount period, will now postpone payment until the end of the new discount period, thereby lengthening the average collection period. But for practical purposes, the discount period is variable only within a narrow range, for to increase it significantly beyond 10 days would defeat its purpose.

SEASONAL DATINGS

During slack sales, the firm will sometimes sell without requiring payment for some time to come. Seasonal datings may be employed to stimulate demand from customers who cannot pay until later in the season. The profitability of additional sales should compared with the required return on the additional investment in receivables to determine whether dating are an appropriate means of stimulating demand. Datings also can be used to avoid inventory carrying costs, for if sales are seasonal while production is steady throughout the year, there will be bundles of finished goods inventory during certain time of the year. Storage involves werehousing costs and therefore datings may be profitable. If the warehousing costs plus the required rate of returns in investment in inventory exceed the required rate of return on additional investment in receivable, it is worthwhile to give datings.

DELINQUENCY AND DEFAULT

Delinquency costs are those expenses associated with that portion of total sales which remain uncollected and they force the company to spend an additional amount per account in an attempt to collect. We can express total delinquent costs as follows:

$$DC = AC(N + N^1)\ (Ps)$$

where DC = total delinquency cost

AC = Average collection period

N = the number of units sold

N^1 = the number of additional units sold to the customers because of the discount

Ps = The percentage of total sales that are not paid

In addition to the delinquency cost, we also have to deduct the *default cost* (FC) which arises when the firm gives up trying to collect on the account and charges the entire cost of the goods sold as an expense. A certain portion of the total sales under the 2/10 net 45 policy is expected to default. We can express the *cost of goods* (C) that have to be written off as follows:

$$FC = C(N + N^1)\ (Ps)$$

Capital invested in receivables is exactly the same as that invested in other assets; that is, a cost of associated with the investment, and the value of sales each ₹ sold on terms will be greater if it is received in the immediate future than it would be if it were received at some later date. As a result, both the cost of time value of funds must be given consideration when credit policy is being set. Cash discounts directly affect a firm's cost of capital as that may cause it to increase or decrease. To illustrate, assume that a firm's cost of capital is 1% per month but its cash discount terms are 2% cash, net 30 days. If the discount is taken, the firm's cost of capital doubles — 24% instead of 12% — and the net worth of the firm suffers. If the cash discount is taken, the present value of the sale will be less than it would have been if the account had been collected at the end of 30 days. A simple example illustrate this. Assume an article costing ₹ 0.80 sells for ₹ 1.00 with terms of 2% cash, net 30 days. If the cash discount is taken, the present value will equal ₹ 1.00 with terms of 2% cash, net 30 days. If the cash discount is taken, the present value will equal ₹ 0.18

Sale	₹ 1.00
Cash discount 2%	0.02
Cash or present value	₹ 0.98
Cost (presėnt value)	0.80
Net present value	0.18

If the cash discount is not taken by the customer, the present value of the profit is equal to ₹ 0.19, a gain of ₹ 0.01; the computation is as follows:

Present value of sale 30 days hence, when cost of capital is 1%	₹ 0.99
Cost (present value)	0.80
	₹ 0.19

Since the cost of capital is 1% and the cash discount is 2% the firm will have sustained a loss of 1% (reduction in net worth) if the discount is taken. If the two are equal, it makes no difference to the credit manager whether the discount is taken; however, if the discount is less than the cost of capital and it is taken, the net result will be to raise the present value of the firm's net worth.

Delinquent accounts have the same effect on net worth as an increase in (1) the cash discount, (2) the credit terms, or (3) the cost of capital. If a deterioration in net worth is to be avoided in the event of delinquents accounts, management should do one of three things: 1, eliminate the account by either collecting the account or by eliminating the customer; (2) lower the firm cost of capital, (3) charge the customer an amount equal to the firm's cost of capital for the period of the delinquency.

Factors Affecting Credit Terms

Credit terms vary by industry and even within industries. Differences are linked to product characteristics as well as market structure and market condition. Exhibit-4 highlights some of the factors associated with credit terms. Credit terms of companies are often set based on competitive condition and rarely changed. Analysis of the optimal cash discount has led to the following conclusions.:

(i) The optimal cash discount depends on a product's variable cost: the lower a product's variable set the higher the possible discount. Companies with lower gross margins are the most likely to reduce or eleminate their cash discount.

(ii) Logically the cash discount offered should be based on the offering company's cost of funds when the opportunity cost of funds changes, so should the cash discount.

(iii) Both the timing effect of the payments for discount takers and the effect for those not taking the discount must be considered when setting or changing the discount.

(iv) The size of the cash discount should be based on the product's price elasticity of demand, or, in this context, how responsive sales are to changes in the cash discount.

(iv) The higher the rate of bad debt losses being experienced, the higher the optimal cash discount per cent.

MARGINAL ANALYSIS APPROACH

In determining the appropriate accounts receivable policy, there are number of variables which one analysed in decision making approach. Marginal analysis approach involves a systematic comparison between the marginal returns and the marginal costs from a change in the discount period, the risk class of the customer, or the collection process. The change should be accepted if the marginal return from a proposed change in the management of accounts receivable is greater than the marginal costs on additional investment.

EXHIBIT-1

FACTORS AFFECTING CREDIT TERMS

Factor	*Influence(s)*
Market Share and Industry Structure:	
Competition	1. Meet terms of competition. Less need to do so when the seller has a large market share or prices its output measurably lower than competition.
	2. Offer longer terms in buyer's market.
Product and market Characteristics:	
Operating cycle	Terms should match length of time for customer to process material, sell it, and collect funds from sale.
Type of good	1. Raw material sold to manufacturers on shorter terms than intermediate or finished goods.
	2. Terms generally would not exceed sum of manufacturing time plus storage time.
Perishability	1. Short shelf life is associated with rapid turnover and short selling terms.
	2. Canned goods and processed food products, with a longer turnover period, have longer terms (can be stocked in larger quantities by the retailer).
Seasonality of demand	1. When demand is seasonal, longer terms are given during the off season, as compared to the active sales period.
	2. Supplier trades off financing costs related to these terms with the more even production this policy allows and the lower storage costs during the off season.
Consumer acceptance	More rapidly selling products accorded shorter terms, because of rapid turnover.
Cost and pricing	More expensive items, such as diamonds and jewelry, given 4-6 month terms; relatively inexpensive items, such as drug items, have shorter terms.
Customer type	Same product has different terms depending on whether customer is a retailer, wholesale jobber, or institutional buyer.
Profitability	Higher profit margins allow for longer terms. Competition may prevent the seller from offering longer terms even though output prices are depressed, yielding negligible profits or even losses.

To illustrate the use of marginal analysis, let us assume that the Mukund Steel has annual sales, all credit, of ₹ 50,00,000 and a receivables turnover ratio of six times per year. The current level of bad debt losses is ₹ 1,56,250 and the firm's required rate of return on any new investment in receivables is 14%. Further assume that this firm produces only one product, the variable costs equaling 80% of the selling price. The company is contemplating a relaxation of its credit policy and the expected effects of two proposed policies, A and B are compared below:

TABLE-1

	Present Policy	*Policy A*	*Policy B*
Annuals sales (all credit)	₹ 50,00,000	₹ 54,68,750	₹ 57,81,250
Average collection period	2 months	3 months	4 months
Bad debt losses	₹ 1,56,250	₹ 1,87,500	₹ 3,34,375

To determine the marginal profitability from relaxing the credit policy first from the present policy to policy A and then from policy A to policy B and compare the marginal profitability to the required return on the additional investment in receivable yields, let's apply marginal analysis approach.

The results of the marginal analysis of relaxing credit standards are presented in Table-2. The marginal benefits by shifting from the present policy to policy A is ₹ 62,500 can be observed. In addition, the required return on the increased investment in accounts receivable, which can be thought of as the marginal cost associated with this change, is ₹ 59,791.74. Thus, since the marginal benefit is ₹ 2,708.26 greater than the required return (or marginal cost) a change in the credit policy should be made form the current policy to policy A.

With respect to the change from policy A to policy B, the associated marginal benefit is ₹ 15,625. The required rate of return on the increase in accounts receivable or marginal cost associated with this change is ₹ 62,708.38. Thus , since the marginal benefit is ₹ 47,083.33 less than the required return or marginal cost, the credit policy should not be changed from policy A to policy B.

The logic behind this approach to credit policy is to examine the incremental or marginal benefits, and costs or required returns associated with any change in the credit policy. If the change promises more benefits than costs, the change should be made, if, however, the incremental costs are greater than the benefits, the proposed change should be dropped.

EVALUATING THE CREDIT APPLICANT

Along with the returns to credit extension, the risks are closely associated. The risks of granting credit are of two kinds: the chance that this will be a "slow policy", tying up unwarranted sums in accounts receivable. The magnitude of these risks depends ultimately on the customer's financial strength and willingness to pay. The

TABLE-2

	Present Policy	*Policy A*	*Policy B*
Annual sales	₹ 50,00,000	₹ 54,68,750	₹ 57,81,250
Average collection period	2 months	3 months	4 months
Account receivable turnover ratio	6 times	4 times	3 times
Average level of receivables	₹ 8,33,333	13,67,187.50	19,27,083.30
Step 1: Determine the Marginal Benefits			
Marginal increase in sales (above previous policy)		₹ 4,68,750	3,12,500
Profit on marginal increase in sales (20%)		93,750	62,500
Marginal increase in bad debt loses		31,250	46,875
Profit on marginal increase in sales (less marginal increase in bad debt loss)		62,500	15,625
Step 2: Determine the Required Rate of Return on the Marginal Investment			
Marginal increase in receivables (above previous policy)		₹ 5,33,854.50	₹ 5,59,895.80
Marginal increase in investment in receivables (above previous policy)		₹ 4,27,083.60	₹ 4,47,916.60
Required return (14%) on marginal increase in investment in receivables		₹ 59,791.74	₹ 62,708.33
Step 3: Compare the Marginal Benefits with the Required Return			
Profit on marginal increase in sales (less marginal increase in bad debt loss) less required return (20%) on marginal investment in receivables		₹ 2,708.26	– ₹ 47,083.33

credit evaluation procedure involves three related steps obtaining information on the applicant, analysing this information to determine the applicant's credit-worthiness, and monitorning the accounts receivable policy.

Sources of Credit Information

Though a number of sources supply credit information but for some accounts, especially small ones, the cost of collecting it may outweight the potential profitability of the account. Therefore, a firm extending credit may have to be satisfied with a limited amount of information on which to base a decision. In addition to the cost, the firm must consider the time it takes to investigate credit applicant. Thus, the amount of information collected needs to be considered in relation to the time and expenses required. Depending upon these considerations, the credit analyst may use one or more of the following sources of information.

Financial Statements: By requiring the credit applicant to provide financial statements for the past few years the firm can analyse the applicant's financial stability, liquidity, debt capacity, and profitability. Although no specific information with respect to past payment patterns is shown on a balance sheet or on an income statement, insight into the firm's financial position may indicate the nature of its overall financial management. The willingness of the applicant firm to provide these statements may be indicative of its financial position. Audited financial statements are a must for the analysis of credit applicants desiring to make large credit purchases or to be extended lines of credit.

Bank Reference: It may be possible for the firm's bank to obtain credit information from the applicant's bank. However, the type of information obtained is most likely to be vague unless the applicant aids the firm in obtaining it. This is true since the credit applicant's bank cannot disclose specific information such as account balances, loan balances, and so forth, without the consent of the applicant.

Trade Checking: Credit information frequently is exchanged among companies selling to the same customer. Through various credit organisations, credit people in particular area become a closely knit group. A company can ask other suppliers about their experiences with an account. Useful information includes the length of time they have had the account, the maximum credit is extended, the amount of the line of credit, and whether payment are prompt or slow.

Credit Bureaus: The services of credit bureaus are required in the advanced countries to get a comprehensive and correct information about the applicant. These credit bureaus specialise in consolidating the experiences of other firms with the applicant. Credit bureaus compile a history of the applicant's credit payment performance as reported by the credit granting firms.

In addition to these external sources of credit information, a firm may try to compile its own information. When a firm is approached by a customer desiring credit terms, the firm's credit department typically begins the credit evaluation process by requiring the credit applicant to fill up various forms involving financial and credit information and credit references. Working from the credit application, the firm then obtains additional credit information from other sources. If the firm has previously extended credit to the applicant, it will have its own historical information on the applicant's payment patterns. Alternatively, if the credit request is large enough, it may send a credit department employees to visit personally with the credit applicant and gives as much financial information as possible.

CREDIT ANALYSIS AND DECISION

Having collected credit information, the firm must make a credit analysis of the applicant and determine if the company falls above or below the minimum quality standard. *How does the financial manager evaluate the risk of extending credit to any particular applicant? What standards exist for extending credit?*

Traditional Standards

In the traditional approach to the credit-granting decision on marginal accounts, the credit analyst tries to assess the *creditworthiness* of the applicant. Creditworthiness is a concept related to the positive and negative aspects of granting credit to the applicant. These aspects include the business history of the applicant, the manner in which the applicant makes payments to other trade suppliers, the profitability of the products that the applicant wants to purchase, the applicant's financial position, and so forth. Critical evaluation of the borrower's projected cash budget and most recent statement of cash flows are instrumental here. The general economy and industry environment, as well as reason for loan request, comprise the conditions.

The traditional way of organising this information is to characterise the applicant along five dimensions. These dimensions are called the *Five Cs of Credit—capital , character, collateral, capacity*, and *conditions*. These are discussed below:

Capital

The evaluation of the applicant's capital refers to an analysis of the applicant firm's *financial position*. What are the applicant firm's financial strengths? What are its weaknesses? Overall, is it stronger or weaker than other firms that the seller believes are creditworthy?

To assess the capital dimension, the credit analyst considers the data obtained from the applicant's financial statements. The usual procedure is to perform an extensive ratio analysis, comparing the applicant's financial ratios to ratios for the applicant's industry and performing trend analysis of the applicant's ratios over time. This ratio analysis can be quite sophisticated, using graphical presentations of ratio trends and statistical comparison of the applicant's ratios with industry standards.

Character

In order to make payments to trade suppliers, the applicant must have both the *funds to pay the debts* and the *willingness to pay the debts*. The capital dimension involves the former, while the character dimension involves the latter. In assessing character, the credit analyst considers all the information that relates to willingness to pay be the applicant's management. What is the applicant's history of payments to the trade? Has the firm defaulted to other trade suppliers? Does the applicant's management make a good-faith effort to honor debts as they come due? Information in these areas bears on the analyst's assessment of the applicant's character.

Collateral

If the applicant experiences financial difficulty, it may be forced to liquidate. In such a situation, the recoveries to trade creditors will depend on (1) the recoveries on assets sold, (2) the amount of debt owed by the firm, and (3) the extent to which these debts are secured. If the firm liquidates, the recoveries on assets that are security for debt will go to the holders of that secured debt. That is, the secured creditors get paid first from the revenues of selling the assets that have been granted to them as security. Since, in general, it is very difficult for trade creditors to obtain secured position, this means that the recoveries to trade creditors are significantly lower when the applicant has financed by using secured borrowings. More existing secured financing means lower creditworthiness from the trade creditor's standpoint.

Capacity

This dimension has two aspects: *management's capacity to run the business* and the applicant firm's *plant capacity.* Management's capacity to run the business relates to the competency (ability) of the management personnel in the applicant's operations. Any information relevant to this capacity is assessed, including personal impressions, the history of success or failure by the managers running the applicant business, the number of years that the applicant has been in business, and so forth. The better is management's capacity to run the firm, the lower is the chance of default.

Physical capacity refers to the value and technology of the applicant's production or service facilities. Accounting conventions can paint an unrealistic picture of the value of such assets, particularly if the technology of the applicant's industry is subject to rapid change. The more up-to-date and well-maintained are the applicant's facilities, the more likely that the applicant will be able to stay in business and to take advantage of business upturns.

Conditions

What are the economic conditions in the applicant's industry and in the economy in general? If there is a good deal of foreign and domestic competition in the applicant's industry, the possibility of failure and default to trade creditors is larger, since profit margins are likely to be lower. If the economy in general is undergoing a contraction, failures are more likely to occur than during an expansionary period.

Once the credit analyst has gathered information on these dimensions of the marginal credit applicant and information on the profitability of the product to be purchased, the traditional approach requires that all this information by *analysed* and *synthesised.* By this process, the analyst is to make an *informed judgment* on the overall creditworthiness of the applicant, Unfortunately, there are some problems endemic to this traditional analysis methodology which call its usefulness into substantial question.

Problems With the Traditional Approach

The traditional judgmental approach to credit-granting decisions on marginal accounts is very flexible. In the process of synthesis, the analyst can take into account any and all of the special features that may affect the desirability of the applicant as a customer. Set against this flexibility are several substantial disadvantages inherent in this decision methodology.

No Analytic Framework

Most financial decision methods start with a basic analysis technique, such as net present value. It is then up to the financial analyst to make the necessary estimations to execute the technique. However, there is no such analytic framework in the traditional credit analysis methodology. The analyst is asked to make a *judgment,* with few guidelines on what the appropriate criteria for that judgment should be. Given the large amount of information encompassed in the five Cs and the lack of specific evaluation criteria, this judgment is not easy to make. Consequently, the traditional analysis method is very difficult to execute effectively.

No Link to Shareholder Wealth Maximisation

In most financial decision methods, the analyst starts with a technique that is theoretically and empirically linked to shareholder wealth maximisation. For example, it is known that shareholders value cash flows, so techniques such as net present value concentrate on the evaluation of these flows. The traditional credit-granting decision technique does not contain such an explicit link to the creation of shareholder wealth, so there is no necessity that decisions based on this technique will be consistent with that goal.

No Consistency of Analysis

Because the synthesis process is almost totally judgmental, the results it produces can be inconsistent. The same analyst considering the same applicant on different days can reach different decisions, as can two different analysts considering the same applicant. This inconsistency gives the impression to those outside of the credit department that decision are being made in an arbitrary fashion. This seeming arbitrariness can cause friction between the credit and other departments of the firm.

Difficult for the Inexperienced Analyst to Execute

Over time, a credit analyst, through trial and error, will become experienced at assessing the strengths and weaknesses of applicants, but any judgments will be biased by the analyst's experience. For example, if the analyst grants credit to several applicants who are below-average with respect to a particular ratio and these applicants then default, the analyst will tend to be biased against applicants with such ratios in the future even if the default of these applicants was an aberration, and the particular ratio involved was not truly related to the default. The longer an analyst continues with the traditional method, the larger will be the sample of applicants analysed, and the less will be the likelihood of such bias.

However, the generation of experience through years of wrong decisions is costly to the selling firm. Inexperienced analysts will have great difficulty with the synthesis process and will make numerous costly errors. Credit will be granted to applicants that are not of advantage to the firm, and it will not be granted to many firms that would be advantageous customers.

Heuristic Approach

The heuristic approach described here is based on a manufacturing company's actual experience, The formula or procedure described here has the weight of managerial experience and intuition behind it and therefore is heuristic in nature. To establish a credit limit and grant credit, the following factors need to be considered:

i) *Credit requirements (O)* of the applicant is the first factor to be considered. This factor is measure of the applicant's dependency on the creditor. The applicant will get 0% to the credit line if he plans to buy less than to 25% of his requirements from the creditor. A 5% allowance will be provided if the applicant plans to buy between 25 and 50%. Applicant gets a 10% allowance in case his plan is to buy over 50%. (See Table-3)

ii) *Pay habits (P)* of the applicant is the second factor. It is a measure of the willingness and ability to pay. Payments during the discount period rate are 10%. Payments during the credit period are worth 5%. Habitually late payments rate is minus 5%.

TABLE-3

Heuristic Approach to Establishing the Credit Limit

Contributing Factor	*Rating*	*Contribution to Credit Limits : Per cent of net worth*
Applicant credit requirements (C)	C < 25%	0
	25% <C <50%	5
	C> 50%	10
Pay habits (P)	Takes discount	10
	Pays on time	5
	Pays late	–5
Years in business (Y)	Y <3 years	0
	3 ≤Y ≤10	5
	Y >10	10
Profit Margin (M)	M <5%	0
	5% ≤M ≤14%	5
	M > 14%	10
Current ratio (R)	R < 2.2%	10
	1.5% ≤ R ≤ 2.2%	5
	R ≤ 1.5%	0
Total debt total assets (T)	T < 0.3	10
	0.5 ≤ T ≤ 0.3	5
	T > 0.5	–5
Inventory turnover(I)	I < 10	5
	I > 5	0
Qualitative (Q)	Q = high	10
	Q = average	5
	Q = low	–5

iii) *Year of business (Y)* a third factor, is a measure of the ability of the firm to pay. Less than three years in business has not effect on increasing the limits. The limit is increase by 5% if Y is between 3 and 10 years. For more than 10 years existance in business, the rate is 10%.

iv) *Profit margin (M)* is the fourth measure. Zero per cent is contributed to the credit limit if margins are less than 5%. In case the margin is more than 14%, 10% to be contributed to the credit limit.

v) *Current ratio (R)* is the fifth measure. A current ratio of 2.2 to 1 is considered to be a good indication of ability to pay and helps in contributing 10% towards the credit limit. A current ratio of less than 1.5 : 1 is considered to be relatively weak and does not help in increasing the credit limit.

vi) *Total debt to asset ratio (T)* is the sixth measure. It represents the ability to pay. The applicant is conservative if T is less than 30% and adds 10% to the credit limit. On the other hand a T of over 50% implies higher financial leverage and rates a minus 5% towards the credit limit.

vii) *Inventory turnover (I)* is the seventh factor. A lower inventory turnover implies low efficiency and *vice versa.* Inventory turnover can help contribute anywhere between 0% to 10% towards the credit limit.

viii) *Qualitative factor (Q)* is the last factor and it lets the credit manager to use his discretion in subjective evaluation of the credit applicant's willingness and ability to pay

It should be kept in mind that these factors and their contribution are based on a particular firm's actual experience. However, the factors and their contributions to the credit limit may vary from firm to firm. In addition, other factors such as accounts payable and the economic environment should also be considered in developing a heuristic credit evaluation decision model.

Discriminant Analysis

In quantitative approaches to credit analysis, the firm relies on financial information as well as on the payment record of firms it granted credit in the past. The financial information on customers is used in conjunction with a statistical procedure called multiple discriminant analysis to develop a statistical credit model. *Discriminant analysis is a computer based technique for predicting whether a new credit applicant will prove to be a good or bad credit risk.* To perform a discriminant analysis, suppose the credit analyst has gone back through past credit customers and selected two groups, those that proved to be good accounts and those that proved to be bad ones, either because they defaulted or because they were slow-pays. Assume further that the analyst has *n* pieces of information ($x_1, x_2 \ldots\ldots, x_n$) about each customer from the original credit applications. The objective of discriminant analysis is to find a set of numerical weights $a_1, a_2 \ldots\ldots, a_n$, such that when the weighted sum or credit score,

$$I = a_1x_1 + a_2x_2 + \ldots\ldots + a_nx_n$$

is formed, the I's for the good accounts will be *as different as possible,* from the I's for the had ones. If a substantial difference is attained, the analyst can draw inferences about the credit worthiness of a new applicant by comparing his credit score to those of the test groups. More rigorously, let:

I_g = the mean credit score for the good accounts

I_b = the mean credit score for the bad accounts

$\sigma I = \sigma I_g = \sigma I_b$ = the standard deviation of the I's for groups, which is assumed the same, then the objective of discriminant analysis is to maximise:

$$\frac{I_b - I_g}{\sigma I}$$

Standard Computer programmes are available to achieve this goal.

Figure-1, which presents the relative frequency distributions of the credit scores for the good and bad accounts, provide an intuitive explanation of this objective. Clearly, If I is to discriminate between good and bad accounts, we want the means of these two distributions as far as possible. Hence maximising $I_b - I_g$ is appropriate; but if σI is large, so too will be the overlap between the two distributions. Therefore, our objective should be to maximise the difference in means per unit standard deviation.

FIGURE-1

FREQUENCY DISTRIBUTION OF CREDIT SCORES AMONG PAST ACCOUNT

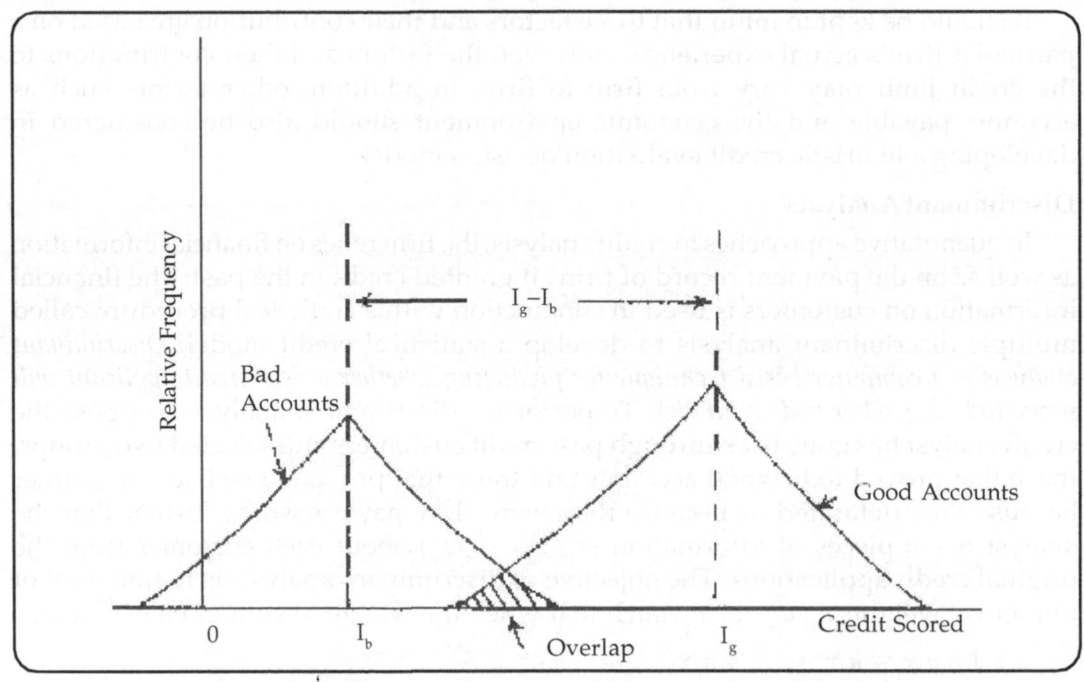

Once the computer has calculated the weights, $a_1, a_2, ..., a_n$ credit scoring becomes a very simple exercise. To illustrate, suppose that the credit analyst has four pieces of information on each applicant:

X_1 = current assets/current liabilities
X_2 = debt/assets
X_3 = years in business
X_4 = net worth

and that after careful analysis of past accounts, a consultant informs the credit department that a_1, a_2, a_3 and a_4 equals 15, – 10, .1 and .000) 1. respectively. Then to evaluate a new credit request from a company with:

$X_1 = 1.5$

$X_2 = .60$
$X_3 = 12$
$X_4 = ₹\ 10,00,000$

the analyst calculates the score

$$I = (15)(1.5) - (10)(.60) + (.1)(12) + (.000001)(10,00,000) = 18.7$$

and compares it with a predetermined critical or cutting score. If 18.7 exceeds the cutting score, the applicant is accepted, otherwise he or she is rejected.

To see how this cutting score is determined, Figure-2 again presents the relative frequency distributions of the credit scores for good and bad accounts in our original samples. We see that good accounts tend to have higher profit scores, than bad ones, so that I is a useful discriminator. However, we also see that the two distributions overlap, and that there is consequently no cutting score that will enable the analyst correctly to classify all new applicants—there will always be some misclassifications. The cross-hatched area to the left of 15 indicates the frequency of good accounts rejected, while the horizontally shaded area to the right indicates the frequency of bad accounts accepted. Since each type of misclassification impose a cost on the firm, the optimal cutting score is the one that minimises these costs. In symbols, if P_1 and P_2 are the relative frequencies of misclassification and C_1 and C_2 are the corresponding cost then optimal cutting score is the one that minimises.

FIGURE-2

FREQUENCY DISTRIBUTION OF CREDIT SCORES AMONG PAST ACCOUNTS

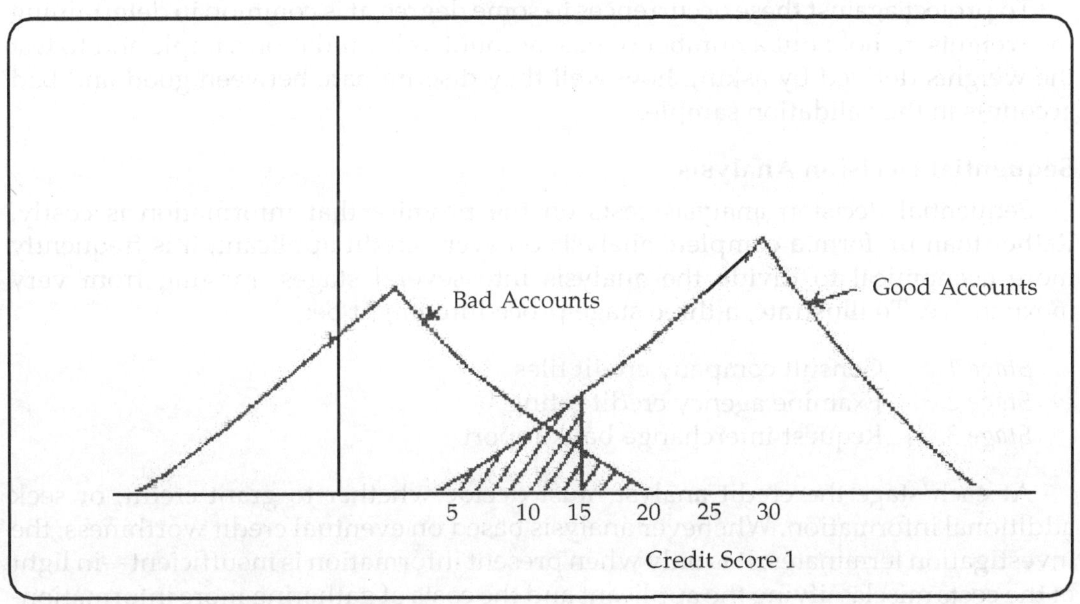

$$\text{Expected cost} = P_1C_1 + P_2C_2$$

Instead of defining a single cutting score, a useful technique in practice is to define all applicants possessing score within the region of overlap as marginal. The credit analyst would then subject these accounts to a more through investigation before making his or her decision. In Figure-2 all applicants with score between 5 and 20 would be marginal according to this criterion.

A useful by-product of discriminant analysis is that it helps the analyst to decide what information to collect. As with regression analysis, there exist statistical technique for estimating the significance of each independent variable in predicting the eventual credit worthiness of the applicant. When these techniques indicate that a particular piece of information is useless or redundant, given other available information, the analyst can save time and money by dropping it from the list of required data.

Although discriminant analysis can greatly simplify the credit decision, its limitations should be recognised. *Firstly*, because a large sample of homogeneous credit applications is necessary to derive the weights in the credit score, the technique is limited to situations in which the company is considering many similar credit requests. *Secondly*, because the analyst is limited in gathering his sample to those past applicants given credit, he has no information on the eventual credit performance of those applicants who were rejected. This introduces a selection bias into the sample and creates the possibility that the weights derived will not be optimal for evaluating new applications. *Third*, the possibility of suboptimal weights is heightend by the fact that the assumption of the same standard deviation for the scores of good and bad accounts may be violated in practice.

To protect against these occurrences to some degree, it is common in determining the weights, to hold out a number of past account as a validation sample and to test the weights derived by asking how well they discriminate between good and bad accounts in the validation sample.

Sequential Decision Analysis

Sequential decision analysis rests on the promise that information is costly. Rather than preform a complete analysis on every credit applicant, it is frequently more economical to divide the analysis into several stages, ranging from very inexpensive. To illustrate, a three stage procedure might be:

Stage 1. Consult company credit files
Stage 2. Examine agency credit rating
Stage 3. Request interchange bank report

At each stage the credit analyst must decide whether to grant credit, or seek additional information. Whenever analysis based on eventual credit worthiness, the investigation terminates. It is only when present information is insufficient—in light of the costs misclassifying the applicant and the costs of gathering more information-that the analyst proceeds to the next stage. Figure-3 shows the first few branches of a tree corresponding to Stage 1. We see that 60% of all credit applicants are former customers with whom the company has had a good credit experience, 5% are poor former customers, and 35% are new customers. For each branch emanating from Stage I, that analyst must decide whether to grant credit, seek more information, or refuse credit. To complete the decision tree it is only necessary to assign benefits to each of these alternatives. For refusal, the benefit is negative and equal to the cost of the credit analysis up to the decision. Calculating the benefits from granting credit at each stage is a little more involved. Letting P equal the probability of receiving payment, the expected profit from accepting an account is

FIGURE-3

PART OF DECISION TREE FOR SEQUENTIAL DECISION ANALYSIS

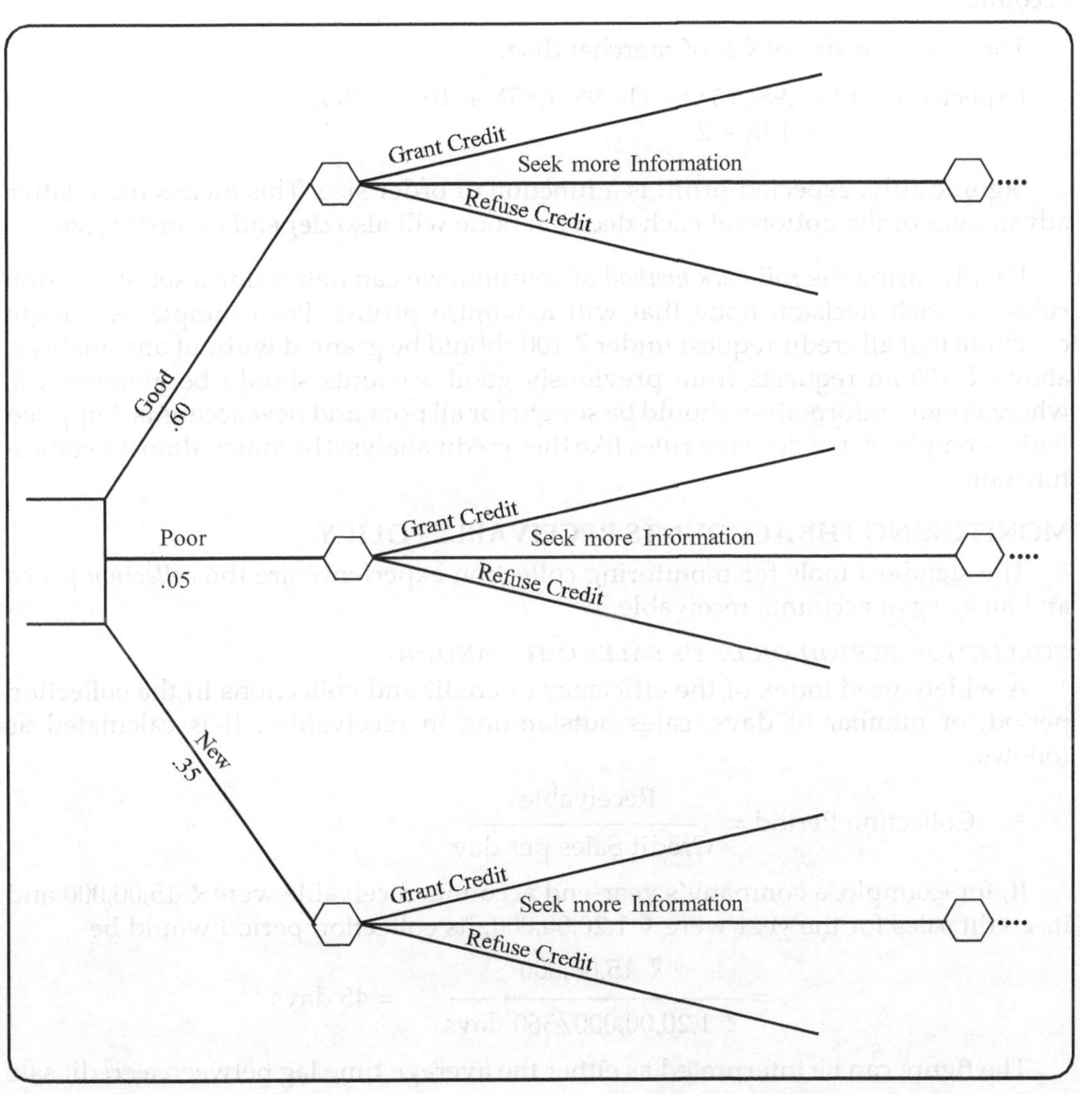

Expected Profit = P (Contribution to profits)–(I–P) *(Cost of failure)*

where the cost of failure includes the variable cost of the merchandise sold on credit, administrative costs of attempting to collect the account, and the opportunity cost of funds committed to accounts receivable. The probability P is determined by examining past records. Thus if 98% of all applicants previously rates good retain this rating on subsequent credit extensions, P for the grant credit branch of the top decision node is 98%. To illustrate the calculation of expected profit when P = 98%, suppose: a firm's variable cost of production is 85% (its contribution margin is 15%); it writes off its receivables as bad debts after three months; the monthly cost of funds invested in receivables is 1%; the firm spends ₹ 100 per account attempting to collect past due accounts.

Then, on an order of ₹ X of merchandise,

$$\begin{aligned}\text{Expected Profit} &= .98(.15X) - (1-.98)\ (.85X + .03X + 100)\\ &= .13X - 2\end{aligned}$$

Significantly, expected profit is a function of order size. This means the relative advantages of the options at each decision node will also depend on order size.

Finally, using the *roll-back method* of solution, we can determine a set of decision rules for each decision node that will maximise profits. For example, we might conclude that all credit request under ₹ 100 should be granted without any analysis; above ₹ 100 all requests from previously good accounts should be given credit, whereas more information should be sought for all poor and new accounts. Supplied with a complex set of decision rules like this, credit analysis becomes almost a clerical function.

MONITORING THE ACCOUNTS RECEIVABLE POLICY

The standard tools for monitoring collection experience are the *collection period* and an *aging* of accounts receivable.

COLLECTION PERIOD OR DAY'S SALES OUTSTANDING

A widely used index of the efficiency of credit and collections in the collection period, or number of days' sales outstanding in receivables. It is calculated as follows:

$$\text{Collection Period} = \frac{\text{Receivables}}{\text{Credit Sales per day}}$$

If, for example, a company's year-end accounts receivable were ₹ 15,00,000 and its credit sales for the year were ₹ 1,20,00,000, its collection period would be

$$= \frac{₹\ 15,00,000}{₹\ 1,20,00,000/360\ \text{days}} = 45\ \text{days}$$

The figure can be interpreted as either the average time lag between a credit sale and payment for the sale or as the average day's worth of credit sales tied up in accounts receivables. Since the collection period measures account receivables per unit sales, a change in the collection period is a rough measure of changing collection experience. However, a major weakness of the ratio for this purpose is that it is quite sensitive to seasonal variations in sales. Consequently, unless sales are quite stable overtime, the collection period can mask fundamental changes in collection experience.

RECEIVABLES AGING

More detailed than the collection period is an aging schedule categories receivables, according to the length of time they have been outstanding. A simple aging of receivables appears below:

Age	*% Accounts Receivable*
0-30 days	52
31-60 days	31
61-90 days	12
91-120 days	5
bad debts	—
	100%

According to this schedule, 52% of the company's receivables on the date of analysis have been outstanding for 30 days or less. Similarly, 5% have been outstanding for 91-120 days; and any accounts older than 120 days are written off as a bad debt.

By comparing aging schedules for different periods, the credit manager can get some idea of any changes in collection experience; additionally, he can pin-point those individual accounts requiring attention. Like the collection period, however, a weakness of the aging schedule is that it is influenced by changes in sales. For instance, if in the month prior to the analysis sales were usually high, it is probable that an inordinately high percentage of accounts will be in the 0-30 days category-even though collection experience may not have improved at all.

COLLECTION-EXPERIENCE MATRIX

Professor Lewellen and Edmister have suggested a control technique that keeps changes in collection experience independent of sales variations. The trick is to age the accounts by months of sale. What we call the *collection-experience matrix,* is the heart of the technique. Suppose that today is June 30, and we wish to construct a collection-experience matrix for the preceding eight months. Our practice is to write-off accounts after they are five months old. Sales for the last eight months have been:

Date:	*Nov.*	*Dec.*	*Jan.*	*Feb.*	*Mar.*	*Apr.*	*May.*	*June*
Sales ('000)	50	200	300	500	100	300	100	100

An examination of the company's receivables ledgers for each of these months allows us to determine the amount of each month's sales which remain uncollected in subsequent months. This information is summarised in the matrix, Table-4.

TABLE-4

Aging of Accounts Receivable by Month of Sale

Sales ('000) *Months of Sales* *Subsequent Months*	*Nov.*	*Dec.*	*Jan.*	*Feb.*	*Mar.*	*Apr.*	*May*	*June*
November	40							
December	25	160						
January	15	100	240					
February	5	60	150	400				
March	2.5	20	90	250	80			
April	0	10	30	150	50	240		
May	0	0	15	50	30	150	80	
June	0	0	0	25	10	90	50	80

According to this matrix, of the ₹ 50,000 in November sales, ₹ 40,000 remained uncollected at the end of the month, ₹ 25,000 was uncollected at the end of December, ₹ 15,000 at the end of January, and so on. The remaining columns are interpreted similarly. Of the ₹ 2,00,000 in sales in December, ₹ 1,60,000 remained uncollected at month end, ₹ 1,00,000 at the end of January and so on.

To construct the collection-experience matrix, we just represent the amount uncollected in each month as a per cent of sales in the month account originated. This is shown in the matrix appearing in Table-4. To illustrate sales in November were ₹ 50,000 of this amount, ₹ 40,000 or 80%, remaining uncollected of month's end. Eighty per cent is, therefore, the first, entry in the Table-5. At the end of December, ₹ 25,000 or 50% of the original total, was still outstanding. 50% is, therefore, the second entry in Column 1. All other entries are determined similarly,

TABLE-5

Collection Experience Matrix

(In % of Sales)

Sales *Months of Sales* *Subsequent Months*	*Nov.*	*Dec.*	*Jan.*	*Feb.*	*Mar.*	*Apr.*	*May*	*June*
November	80							
December	50	80						
January	30	50	80					
February	10	30	50	80				
March	5	10	30	50	80			
April	0	5	10	30	50	80		
May	0	0	5	10	30	50	80	
June	0	0	0	5	10	30	50	80

To use the collection-experience matrix in Table-5 we compare entries along a diagonal. For example, it is apparent that the company's collection experience has remained absolutely stable throughout the entire eight month of observation. In every instance 80% of the month's sales remain uncollected at month end, 50% remain uncollected at the end of second month, 30% after three months, and so on. An increase in these percentages over time would indicate a worsening collection experience, and vice versa.

To see the problem with the collection period, let us calculate a collection period for the most recent four months, based on the preceding five months' sales. Beginning with March, note from the collection-experience matrix in Table-5 that;

Receivable = 80% Mar. sales + 50% Feb. sales + 30% Jan. sales + 10% Dec. sales + 5% Nov. sales

= ₹ 4,42,500

Sales per day, based on the previous five month's sales, are:

Sales per day in March = (Mar. sales + Feb. sales + Jan. sales + Dec. sales + Nov. sales)/150 = ₹ 7,670

The collection period for March, assuming all the sales are on credit, is, therefore,

$$\text{Collection period for March} = \frac{₹\ 4,42,500}{₹\ 7,670} = 58 \text{ days.}$$

A tabulation based on analogous calculations for the other three months appears below:

Month	*Collection Period*
March	58 days
April	51
May	37
June	35

In constrast to the collection-experience matrix, the collection period fallaciously shows a steady improving collection experience, a distortion caused by the usually high sales in January and February. Examination of aging schedules over the period would also evidence this same false trend.

A more sophisticated application of the collection experience matrix uses statistical techniques to set up control limits on the variations in the diagonal entries. Assuming that the entries along a given diagonal vary randomly from month to month, it is possible to define reasonable limits to the extent of this variation. When subsequent variations exceed these limits, the credit manager has important evidence that collection experience is changing.

Another attractive features of the collection-experience matrix is that it greatly simplifies the job of forecasting future accounts receivable. To illustrate, suppose in the above example, we wish to forecast account receivables for next month, July 31, assuming sales in July of ₹ 4,00,000. Looking at the collection-experience matrix, we note that if the evidenced collection experience continues, accounts receivable on July 31 will be:

Receivables July = 80% July sales + 50% June sales + 30% May sales + 10% April sales + 5% March sales

= 80% (₹ 4,00,000) + 50% (₹ 1,00,000) + 30% (₹ 1,00,000) + 10% (₹ 3,00,000) + 5% (₹ 1,00,000)

= ₹ 4,38,000

COLLECTION POLICY

Collection policy refers to the collection procedure as letters, phone calls, personal calls and legal action. The extent to which the company uses each of these will be dependent on its collection policy.

It is to be expected that the incidence of bad debt losses and the average collection period will be reduced as the amount spent on collection expenditure is increased. However, the benefits and costs associated with a particular collection policy are not likely to be linear. It is contended that an initial small level of expenditure is unlikely to have any marked effect in reducing bad debts and the average collection period, while additional expenditure are likely to have a much greater effect. Beyond a certain level of collection expenditure, the benefits will diminish until eventually a saturation point is reached. The expected relationship between bad debt losses and collection expenditure is shown in Figure-4. The relationship between the average collection period and the level of collection expenditure is likely to be similar.

FIGURE-4

RELATIONSHIP BETWEEN THE LEVEL OF COLLECTION EXPENDITURES AND BAD DEBT LOSSES

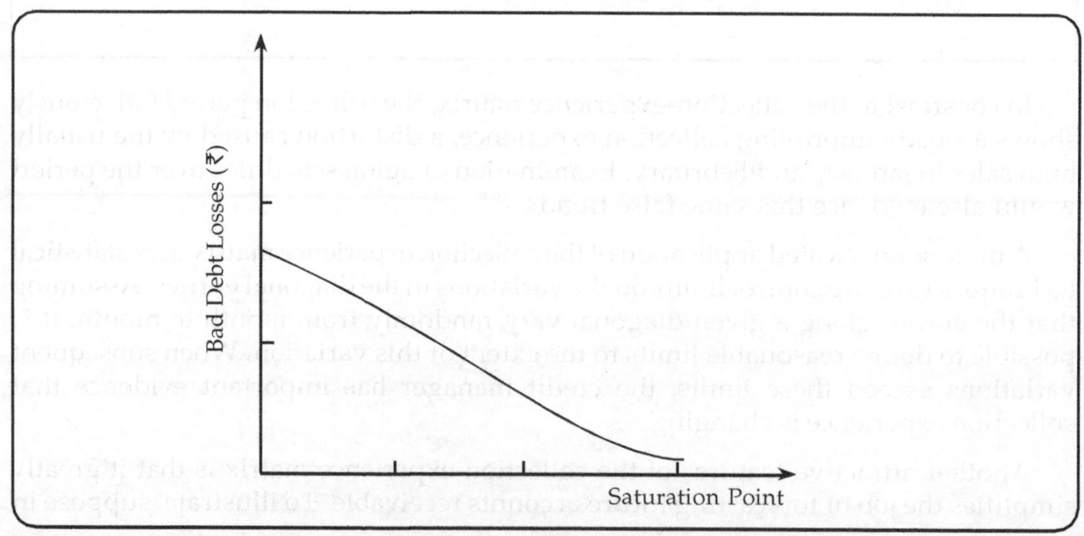

To illustrate, assuming the annual sales of a company to be of ₹ 30,00,000 which are not expected to change with change in the collection effort.

Programme	*Present Programme*	*Programme A*	*Programme B*
Annual Collection expenditures	1,16,000	1,48,000	2,00,000
Collection period	2 months	1½ months	1 month
Percentage of deficit	5	3	1

The collection policy can be seen as a trade-off between collection costs, and the resulting reduction in bad debt losses and shorter average collection period which, in turn will result in a reduction in the company's investment in receivables. Therefore, the collection policy can be evaluated with respect to these associated costs and benefits and an optimum policy determined. However, in seeking this optimum, it is advisable to take account of the effect of any collection policy on sales, as a more forceful collection procedure may adversely affect sales.

The evaluation of collection programmes exhibits that the opportunity saving resulting from a speed up collection plus the reduction in bad debt losses exceeds the additional collection expenditures in going from the present programme to programme A, but not in going from programme A to programme B. (See Table-6.)

TABLE-6

(in ₹)

	Present Programme	*Programme A*	*Programme B*
Annual sales	30,00,000	30,00,000	30,00,000
Turnover of receivables	6	8	12
Average receivables	5,00,000	3,75,000	2,50,000
Reduction in receivable from present programme		1,25,000	
Reduction in receivable from programme A level			1,25,000
Return on reduction in receivable (20%)		25,000	25,000
Bad debt (% of annual sales)	1,50,00	90,000	30,000
Reduction in had debt losses from present losses		60,000	60,000
Opportunity saving on reduced receivables plus reduction in bad-debt losses		85,000	85,000
Additional collection expenditures from present expenditure		32,000	
Additional collection expenditure from programme A expenditures			52,000

In this example the assumption is that demand is independent of the collection effort, but in practice, sales are likely to be affected adversely if the collection efforts of the firm become too intense and customers become increasingly irritated.

EVALUATION OF THE CREDIT DEPARTMENT

Too often credit departments and credit administrators are evaluated primarily according to their bad-debt losses: the lower the losses, the better the preceived performance. It should be obvious, however, that this approach is not consistent with the goals of maximising firm profits, or value. Thus if a credit manager is evaluated solely on the bad-debt losses, he can optimise his observed performance by accepting only the very best credit applicants. Such conservatism will undoubtedly generate lower bad-debt losses, however, in the process it will also eliminate a large number of potentially good accounts. The more logical approach to evaluate credit-department performance accepts a certain amount of bad debts as necessary to effective operations and attempts to look at the profit side of the ledger as well. This involves looking at such yardsticks as the growth in the credit sales and the number of credit requests rejected, in addition to the more traditional bad-debt losses, collection periods, and aging schedules.

ILLUSTRATIVE PROBLEMS

1. Compute the effective interest rate for the failure to take advantage of the prompt payment discount under each of the following credit terms:

(a) 2/10, net 30
(b) 3/30, net 45
(c) 3/30, net 90
(d) 2/20, net 60

Solution

The effective interest rate for the failure to take advantage of the prompt payment discount are:

(a) 2/98 × 365/(30–10) = .0204 × 18.25 = 37.23%
(b) 3/97 × 365/(45–30) = .0309 × 24.33 = 75.18%
(c) 3/97 × 365/(90–30) = .0309 × 6.08 = 18.79%
(d) 2/98 × 365/(60–20) = .204 × 9.13 = 18.63%

2. A firm is considering changing its credit policy from net 20 to 2/10 net 30. Its sales should increase from ₹ 5,00,000 to ₹ 7,00,000, its cost of goods sold will go from 55% to 50% of sales. Miscellaneous administrative costs will remain steady at ₹ 40,000, but collection costs will increase from ₹ 20,000 to ₹ 30,000 and bad debt losses will go from 5 to 10% of its average accounts receivables. 40% of the customers are expected to take the discount. This firm currently has debt of ₹ 2,00,000 at 6%, which include the financing costs for the funds currently tied up in receivables. If the balance in receivables increases or decreases with the new policy, the extra costs of funds tied up will be calculated at the 10% estimated cost of the firm's new debt.

(a) What is the likely receivables balance with each policy?

(b) What will be the forecasted net income after taxes with each policy?

Solution

(a) Likely receivables with net 20 would be ₹ 33,333 and ₹ 50,000 with 2/10 net 30.
(b) ₹ 75,500 with net 20 and ₹ 1,27,500 with 2/10 net 30

	Net 20	*2/10 Net 30*
Sales	₹ 5,00,000	₹ 7,00,000
Cost of goods sold	2,75,000	3,50,000 (55% to 50% sales)
Administrative cost	40,000	40,000
Collection costs	20,000	20,000
Bad-debt losses	2,000	5,000
Discounts taken	0	0
EBIT	₹ 1,63,00	₹ 2,69,000
Interest	12,000	14,000
Taxes	75,500	1,27,500
Net income after taxes	₹ 75,500	₹ 1,27,500

3. Metro Engineering is considering liberalising its credit policies to allow higher risk customers to buy on credit terms of net 30. The credit department has been informed that variable costs will remain at 60% of sales over the new potential sales levels. All new sales will be on credit, and the projected information for each risk class is as shown in the table below:

Risk Class	*Required Return*	*DSO*	*New Sales*
A	0.20	30	₹ 5,00,000
B	0.25	45	4,00,000
C	0.30	60	3,00,000
D	0.35	90	2,50,000

The scale of before-tax required returns reflects the increased risk perceived for each risk class of customers. Which, if any, of the risk classes should Metro allow to buy on credit? (Assume a 360-day year)

Solution

The problem can be approached by comparing the expected return on new sales (0.4 × change in sales) with required return (k) × (changes in investment in accounts receivable), where the change in investment equals.

$$0.6 = \frac{\text{Change in sales}}{(360/\text{Collection period})}$$

For risk class A:

Expected return = 0.4 (₹ 5,00,000) = ₹ 2,00,000
Required return = 0.2(0.6) (₹ 5,00,000) (30/360) = ₹ 5,000

Risk class A should be *allowed to buy on credit.*

For risk class B:

Expected return = 0.4 (₹ 4,00,000) = ₹ 1,60,000
Required return = 0.25(0.6) ₹ 4,00,000) (45/360) = ₹ 7,500

Risk class B should be *allowed to buy on credit.*

For risk class C:

Expected return = 0.4 (₹ 3,00,000) = ₹ 1,20,000
Required return = 0.30 (0.6) (₹ 3,00,000) (60/360) = ₹ 9,000

Risk class C should be *allowed to buy on credit.*

For risk class D:

Expected return = 0.4 (₹ 2,50,000) = ₹ 1,00,000
Required return = 0.35(0.6) (₹ 2,50,000) (90/360) = ₹ 13,125

Risk class D should be *allowed to buy on credit.*

4. Refer to Problem—3, assume the credit department of Metro Engineering realised it had failed to include all the relevant costs in Problem-3, and the following additional information is submitted. Which risk class should Metro allow to buy on credit.

Risk Class	*Default Rate (per cent)*	*Increased Credit Department Expenses*
A	5	₹ 40,000
B	8	40,000
C	15	40,000
D	25	40,000

Solution

The required return remains the same while the expected return declines.

For Risk class A:

Bad debt expense = 0.05 (₹ 5,00,000) = ₹ 25,000
Expected return = ₹ 2,00,000– ₹ 25,000– ₹ 40,000 = ₹ 1,35,000

Risk class A is still *accepted.*

For Risk class B:

Bad debt expenses = 0.08 (₹ 4,00,000) = ₹ 32,000
Expected return = ₹ 1,60,000– ₹ 32,000– ₹ 40,000 = ₹ 88,000

Risk class B is still *accepted.*

For Risk class C:

Bad debt expenses = 0.15 (₹ 3,00,000) = ₹ 45,000
Expected return = ₹ 1,20,000– ₹ 45,000– ₹ 40,000 = ₹ 35,000

Risk class C is still *accepted.*

For Risk class D:

Bad debt expense = 0.25 (₹ 2,50,000) = ₹ 62,500
Expected return = ₹ 1,00,000– ₹ 62,500– ₹ 40,000 = – ₹ 2,500

Risk class D is *rejected.*

5. The credit manager of Finolex Tubes feels that the credit policy of the firm needs to be tightened. In support of his argument to the Chairman, the credit manager contrasts the 90-day terms of Finolex with the 30-day terms of the industry. Finolex is selling ₹ 16,00,000 a year and costs are 80% variable and ₹ 10,000 fixed. On the basis of a survey of Finolex's customers, the credit manager expects the following relationships between terms and sales:

Policy	*Terms*	*Annual Sales*
A	90	₹ 16,00,000
B	75	15,00,000
C	60	14,50,000
D	45	14,25,000
E	30	13,50,000
F	15	13,00,000

If the opportunity cost of capital is 15%, which policy be adopted? (Assume that the average collection period corresponds to the terms given).

Solution

The solution table given below shows that Policy D is optimal since the reduction in profit if more than the reduction in cost of capital E or F is adopted.

TABLE-1

(in ₹ 000's omitted)

Sales	*A*	*B*	*C*	*D*	*E*	*F*
Sales	1600.00	1500.00	1450.00	1425.00	1350.00	1300.00
Variable cost	1280.00	1200.00	1160.00	1140.00	1080.00	1040.00
Fixed cost	100.00	100.00	100.00	100.00	100.00	100.00
Profit	220.00	200.00	190.00	185.00	170.00	160.00
Profit Red.		20.00	10.00	5.00	15.00	10.00
Avg. A/R	400.00	312.50	241.67	178.13	112.50	54.17
Funds freed by charge		87.50	70.83	63.54	65.63	58.33
Cost of capital saving		13.125	10.625	9.521	9.845	8.750

6. Jindal Sports, a manufacturer of atheletic equipment, is currently selling ₹ 50,00,000 annually to dealers on 30-day credit terms. Management believes that sales could be substantially increased if dealers carried more inventory; however dealers are unable to finance their inventory. As a result, the management is considering changing credit policy. The average collection period is now 30 days. Variable cost is 70% and fixed cost is ₹ 5,00,000. Required (pre-tax) rate of return on investment is 20%. The following information is available:

Credit Policy	*Average Collection period*	*Annual Sales*
A	45 days	₹ 56,00,000
B	60 days	60,00,000
C	75 days	65,00,000
D	90 days	72,00,000

(a) Determine which policy Jindal should adopt?
(b) Discuss the implicit assumptions made by the incremental profit/incremental investment approach to decision making.

Solution

(a) Current investment in receivables is:
= (30/360) (₹ 50,00,000)(.70) = ₹ 2,91,666.67

Change in Policy	*A*	*B*	*C*	*D*
Incremental sales	₹ 6,00,000	₹ 4,00,000	₹ 5,00,000	₹ 7,00,000
Incremental cost	4,20,000	2,80,000	3,50,000	4,90,000
Incremental profit	₹ 1,80,000	₹ 1,20,000	₹ 1,50,000	₹ 2,10,000
Average receivables	7,00,000	10,00,000	13,54,167	18,00,000
Investment in receivables	4,90,000	7,00,000	9,47,917	12,60,000
Incremental investment	1,98,333.33	2,10,000	2,47,917	3,13,083
Required return	39,667.67	42,000	89,583	62,617

Policy C is the optimal policy since the required return exceeds the profit generated by going to D.

(b) First, there is a slight inaccuracy in the method since the incremental investment should recognise that the collection of existing accounts is being permanently deferred by changing credit policy. The deferment should be included in the incremental investment figure. More importantly, the implicit assumption in the method is that the new level of sales resulted from a permanent increase in sales.

7. Zenith Steel has annual credit sales of ₹ 40,00,000, the average receivable amount to ₹ 5,00,000. Determine the average collection period.

Solution

Average collection period is:
= ₹ 5,00,000 × 360/ ₹ 40,00,000 = 45 days

8. Universal Tiles has annual sales of ₹ 24,00,000. After 6 months an account is turned over to a collection agency and in the average one per cent of the total receivable volume under the present credit policy is never received by the firm. The current policy and the expected effects of two proposed policies, A and B, are compared in following table:

	Present Policy	Policy A	Policy B
Additional demand (Percentage)	0	25	35
Average collection period	1 month	2 months	3 months
Default losses (Percentage)	1	3	6

Determine the marginal profitability from relaxing the credit policy first from the present policy to policy A and then from policy A to policy B and comparing the marginal profitability to the required rate of return (20%) on additional investment in receivables.

Solution

Policy A should be adopted and credit terms should not be relaxed as far as policy B is concerned for the marginal benefit is positive in moving from the present policy to policy A but negative in going from policy A to policy B. Table-1 gives the solution.

TABLE -1

Profitability Vs. Required Rate of Return and Bad Dabt Losses

	Policy A	Policy B
Annual sales	₹ 30,00,000	₹ 32,40,000
Turnover of receivables	6	4
Level of receivables after change in credit policy	30,00,000/6 = ₹ 5,00,000	32,40,000/4 = ₹ 8,10,000
Additional receivables	3,00,000	3,10,000
Addl. investment in receivables above present investment (Cost per unit/selling price per unit) in Additional receivables	2,10,000	
Additional investment in receivables		217,000
Required return on additional investment (20%)	42,000	43,400
Addl. sales above present sales (units)	60,000	
Addl. sales above Policy A sales (units)		24,000
Profitability of additional sales	1,80,000	72,000
Bad debt losses (per cent of annual sales)	90,000	194,440
Addl. bad debt losses above present losses	24,000	
Addl. bad debt losses above policy A losses (90,000)		104,400
Profitability of additional sales less addl. bad-debt losses	1,14,000	–32,400

Profitability of additional sales less additional bad debt losses, present policy to policy A	1,14,000	
Profitability of addl. sales less addl. bad debt losses policy A to policy B		–34,400
Required return on additional investment	42,000	43,400
	₹ 72,000	– ₹ 75,800

9. Premier Store has annual credit sales of ₹ 24,00,000. Average collection period is of 2 months. Average selling price per unit is ₹ 10 and the average cost per unit of ₹ 8.60. Premier can reduce the average collection period by one month by giving 2% cash discount as 50% of the customers will avail of this cash. The required return for premier is 20%. Should Premier liberalise credit policy?

Solution

Reduction on investment in receivables (₹ 2,00,000 × ₹ 8.60/10)	₹ 1,72,000
Required return on investment	20%
Opportunity saving	₹ 34,400
Opportunity cost of discount (₹ 24,00,000 × .02 × .05)	₹ 24,000
Net savings	₹ 10,400

Since the opportunity savings arising from a speed up in collection is greater than the cost of discount given, the firm can adopt a 2% discount policy'

10. Chanda Enterprises had earnings per share of ₹ 4 last year, and it paid a ₹ 2 dividend. Total retained earnings increased by ₹ 1.20 crore during the year, while book value per share at year-end was ₹ 4 crore. Chanda has no preferred stock, and no new equity was issued during the year. If Chanda's year-end debt (which equals its total liabilities) was ₹ 12 crore what was the company's year-end debt/assets ratio ?

Solution

Chanda paid ₹ 2 in dividends and retained ₹ 2 per share. Since total retained earnings rose by ₹ 1.2 crore there must be 60,00,000 shares outstanding. With a book value of ₹ 40 per share, total equity must be ₹ 40 (0.6 crore) = ₹ 24 crore. Since Chanda has ₹ 12 crore of debt, its debt ratio must be 33.3 per cent:

$$\frac{\text{Debt}}{\text{Assets}} = \frac{\text{Debt}}{\text{Debt + Equity}} = \frac{₹\ 12\ \text{crore}}{₹\ 12\ \text{crore} + ₹\ 24\ \text{crore}}$$

$$= 0.333 = 33.3\%$$

11. Golden Syntex has annual sales of ₹ 24,00,000. The selling price per unit is ₹

10 and the variable cost is 70% of the selling price. Required rate on investment for Golden is 20%. Average cost is ₹ 9 per unit. Annual collection expenditure is ₹ 50,000 and percentage of default is 3%. Credit terms are two months. Golden Syntex is considering the change in credit policy either by following Programme A or Programme B.

	Programme A	*Programme B*
Average collection period	1½ months	1 month
Annual collection expenditure	₹ 75,000	₹ 1,50,000
% of default	2%	1%

Determine which collection programme Golden Syntex should follow?

Solution

The evaluation of the collection programme to be followed by Golden Syntex is present below:

	Present	*Programme Programme*	*Programme A B*
	(₹)	(₹)	(₹)
(1) Annual sales	24,00,000	24,00,000	24,00,000
(2) Turnover of accounts receivable	6 times	8 times	12 times
(3) Average of accounts receivable	4,00,000	3,00,000	2,00,000
(4) Average investment in receivables (at average cost)	3,60,000	2,70,000	1,80,000
(5) Reduction in average investment in receivables		90,000	1,80,000
(6) Required return on investment (20%)		18,000	36,000
(7) Bad debt losses	72,000	48,000	24,000
(8) Cost of bad debt losses	64,800	43,200	21,600
(9) Reduction in cost of bad debt losses from present cost		21,600	43,200
(10) Required return on reduced investment plus reduction in cost of bad debt losses		39,600	79,200
(11) Additional collection expenditure from present expenditure	25,000	1,00,000	
(12) Net savings	14,600	- 20,800	

QUESTIONS

1. What is the general objective of accounts receivable management. In what ways is it similar and different from cash balance management and inventory management?
2. Is there likely to be a conflict of interest between the sales manager and the financial (or credit) manager with regard to the credit policy of the company? Why?

3. Explain the meaning of the credit terms, 2/10, 1/30, 1/45. n/60. Why do companies offer a cash discount?
4. If a credit manager experienced no bad debt losses over the past year, would this be an indication of proper credit management? Why or why not?
5. "A company should determine its attitude to the collection of delinquent accounts by applying marginal analysis." Discuss.
6. What are the principal benefits of a liberal accounts receivable policy? Would you expect the firm's salesmen or shareholders to be more supportive of an easier credit policy?
7. When one firm collects its cash faster, another firm loses cash more rapidly. This is clearly zero-sum game for the system as a whole. If there is no gain to business as a whole, way do firms try to streamline their collection system?
8. What are the five traditional "Cs" the financial manager might consider in evaluating the credit worthiness of a potential customer?
9. Compare and contrast credit standards and credit terms. How can credit standards and credit terms affect the amount invested in receivables and the return on such investments?
10. The management of receivables involves both routine and episodic activities. Contrast and discuss the nature of these activities as they relate to each aspects of credit policy: (1) credit standards, (2) credit terms, and (3) collection activities.
11. Explain why it is important to perform credit analysis on prospective customers even though a firm has well-established credit standards.
    a. What role could credit scoring play in this process? Explain.
    b. Is it necessary to perform credit analysis on existing customers? Explain.
12. Contrast aging accounts receivable with the accounts receivable turnover or average collection period. Are they perfect substitutes for each other? Explain.
13. What key variables should be considered when evaluating possible changes in the firm's credit policy? Briefly explain the possible effects of a more restrictive credit policy on: (a) sales volume; (b) average collection period; (c) investment in receivables; (d) cost of receivables investment; (e) bad debt costs.
14. What role does the firm's required return on investment play in the analytical scheme used to evaluate credit policy decisions?
15. Why must demand elasticities and the possible actions of competitors be considered when evaluating changes in credit policy? Use an increase in the cash discount to illustrate how these two variables can affect the benefits and costs of a pending credit policy change.
16. How does the financial manager evaluate the risk of extending credit to any particular applicant? What standards exists for extending credit?

PROBLEMS

1. For a firm with an average receivables balance of ₹ 5,00,000 and a cost of debt of 15%, what is the cost of funds tied up in receivables?

Ans.: ₹ 75,000

2. A distributor of industrial cleaning products has outstanding accounts receivables of ₹ 1,40,000. The out-of-pocket costs in acquiring, holding, and selling these products amount to 90% of the selling price. What is the actual investments in account receivable for this firm?

Ans.: ₹ 1,26,000

3. Firm ABC, with large daily sales of ₹ 37,500 has ₹ 6,25,000 worth of receivables outstanding during the month of April. It also has an annual turnover rate of 8.25. What is the company's ratio of sales to receivables and how many days, on the average, do its receivables stay outstanding based on its turnover rate?

Ans.: Days receivables outstanding are 44.2

4. Last month National Corporation a huge manufacturer of structural steel, placed large orders for safety shoes glasses, and hard hats, all of which are distributed to new employees in the mill. The bills, totalling ₹ 73,000 arrived on the first of this month and are payable of the 10th. The money to pay these bills is currently invested in short-term securities that yield 8% interest a year. How much can the firm save by not paying the bills until the due date? (Assume a normal 365-day calender year).

Ans.: ₹ 160.

5. Nanak Industries is applying for credit. Its abbreviated balance sheet is given below:

Accounts payable	₹ 4,00,000	Cash and receivable	₹ 7,00,000
Other payables	2,00,000	Inventory	5,00,000
Long-term debt	4,00,000	Net plant	13,00,000
Net worth	₹ 10,00,000	Total assets	₹ 25,00,000

Nanak's most recent income statement showed that it earned ₹ 1,20,000 on total sales of ₹ 36,00,000. Nanak pays on time but does not take the discount all the time. It was incorporated in 1964 and its management is rated excellent. The credit line would be utilised to buy about 30% of Nanak's total raw materials requirements. If you were evaluating Nanak's credit application, would you grant it credit? If not, why? If yes, what is the maximum credit you would allow Nanak. Use Heuristic approach in establishing Nanak's credit limit.

Ans.: Nanak's credit limit is ₹ 6,75,000. Maximum credit is ₹ 2,75,000.

6. Sutlej Cotton Mills Ltd. decides to offer a credit period of 60 days which will result in an increase in sales revenue of ₹ 20,000. The additional costs associated with these sales are ₹ 16,000. There are no costs associated with the provision of credit and the full ₹ 20,000 is received after 60 days. Sutlej's required rate of return is 1% per month. Should the firm extend the credit?

Ans.: As a result of offering 60 days credit, Sutlej has made a profit of ₹ 3,606 in present value terms.

7. Refer to problem-6, consider the case where Sutlej Cotton Mils Ltd. offers credit terms of 1/30, *n*/60. The additional sales revenue and costs thirtieth day. Should Sutlej extend the credit?

Ans.: In this case Sutlej has made a profit expressed in present value terms of ₹ 3,604, so it should extend the credit.

8. Refer to Problem—7, assume that Sutlej offered credit terms of 2/30, 1/60 and as a result obtained an increase in sales of ₹ 30,000. The additional costs associated with these sales total ₹ 24,000. Assume that ₹ 15,000 of the debt is paid on the 30th day and the other ₹ 15,000 after 60 days. What would be the net present value associated with this credit policy?

Ans.: The net present value associated with this credit policy is ₹ 5,111.

9. Refer to Problem-8, assume that Sutlej offers credit terms of 2/30, 1/60 and it has investigated the credit worthiness of a potential creditor (Beas Cotton Mills Ltd.) and has been able to calculate the purchase date and the date Beas pays its account.

Payment by 30 days	*End of 60 days*	*End of 6 months*	*End of*	*No Payment*
Probability	0.40	0.80	0.90	0.10

Bear wishes to purchase goods to the value of ₹ 10,000 each month. The additional costs of making these sales are ₹ 8,000. Ignoring any administrative or collection expenses associated with the provision of credit, should Sutlej be prepared to extend credit to Beas?

Ans.: By extending credit to Beas, Sutlej profits by ₹ 624.

10. Bansal Associates is a consulting firm specialising in office layout and design. Mr. Rakesh Bansal handles the firm's financial affairs and also specialises in colour cordination. The firm bill its clients at the end of an assignment of terms net 30; that is, the customer is supposed to pay within 30 days after the billing date. Lastly Rakesh Bansal has been alarmed about a build-up in account receivables and the pressure placed on the firm's cash position caused by the resulting slowdown in collections. He is also concerned about the bad debt losses the firm has experienced. After analysing the situation with some care, Rakesh is able to classify the firm's clients into two groups, normal risk and high risk. Data for the two classes of clients is shown below:

	Annual Revenues	*Annual Operating costs*	*Annual Bad Debt Losses*	*Current Account Receivable*
Normal risk	₹ 1,20,000	₹ 60,000	₹ 1,000	₹ 10,000
High risk	60,000	40,000	10,000	15,000
Total	₹ 1,80,000	₹ 1,00,000	₹ 11,000	₹ 25,000

The marginal tax rate of the firm's partners is 50%, and they feel that a 15% cost of capital would be appropriate in assessing the desirability of extending credit to high-risk clients. The investment in accounts receivable is difficult to evaluate because the major investment is in time spent by the partners on the client's problems; however, for purposes of analysis Rakesh decided to consider the foregone revenues from the investment of time as being part of the outlay in the accounts receivable. The level of ₹ 15,000 in accounts receivable of high-risk clients is therefore estimated to reflect ₹ 12,000 in investment.

Should Bansal Associates stop extending credit to high-risk clients, assuming that this business would be lost entirely if such a policy were implemented? Base your decision on the "net profit" from accepting high risk clients.

Ans.: Net profit = ₹ 3,200

11. Oriental Dyes has annual sales of ₹ 1,19,25,000 variable costs (two-thirds of sales) of ₹ 79,50,000 and fixed costs (including interest) of ₹ 20,00,000. The company's total assets are ₹ 80,00,000 of which accounts receivable comprise ₹ 7,50,000 and inventory, ₹ 30,00,000. The company has been operating at substantially less than full capacity, and management is eager to increase its sales. The financial manager suggests that sales may be stimulated by a liberalisation of trade-credit terms. His proposal is to modify credit terms from 2/10, *n*/30 to 2/30, *n*/60. The financial manager projects a rise in sales to ₹ 1,52,04,000 under such circumstances but the company must borrow an additional ₹ 20,00,000 at 8.5% to finance its increased accounts receivables (₹ 20,00,000) and inventory (₹ 37,50,000) needs. The total cost related to the trade-credit liberalisation and increased working capital investment are estimated to be ₹ 3,21,000. What return would such a policy change produce?

Ans.: Average return basis 28.63% and Marginal return basis 38.60%.

12. Dinker Company is contemplating a general tightening of its credit policy as a result of the currently high opportunity cost of funds. The tightening is expected to be accomplished by tightening credit standards, shortening credit terms, and increasing collection activity. The key data required to analyse the firm's plan are summarised below:

Current Data

Variable cost rate, 65%; Required rate of return, 25%; Average collection period, 60 days; Sales revenue, ₹ 3,00,00,000; Bad debt percentage for marginal customers, 10%; Average bad debt percentage 8%

Proposed Data

Change in sales, ₹ 40,00,000; Due to elimination of marginal customers,—₹ 25,00,000; Due to shorter credit terms and increased collection activity,—₹ 15,00,000; Average collection period for eliminated marginal customers, 80 days; Average collection period, 45 days; Average bad debt percentage on remaining customers, 5%; Charge in collection cost, + ₹ 40,000

(a) Using the data given, analyse and make a recommendation to Dinker on the proposed tightening of credit policy.

(b) If the required rate of return were 10 per cent and the change in collection cost attributable to the proposed tightening were + ₹ 25,000, what, if any, effect would this have on your conclusions above? Reassess the proposal using these data, and discuss your results in light of the analysis in (a).

13. A credit applicant has placed three orders with a seller, and the seller must make a credit-granting decision regarding the applicant. The first order is to be delivered immediately, the second in 120 days, and the third in 240 days. Each order is for ₹ 10,000. Costs of goods sold are 85 per cent of sales, payable at the time the order is delivered. If the applicant defaults, no recoveries are expected. The applicant is undergoing a period of expansion and is brand loyal. The seller has estimated that the probability of default for the initial order is 20 per cent, and the payment for this order is expected in 75 days if the applicant does not default. If the applicant does not default in paying for the initial order, it is expected that the probability of default for the second order will be 10 per cent and the expected time to pay for that order will be 60 days. If the applicant does not default on the second order, the probability of default on the third order is 5 per cent, and the expected time to pay for that order is 45 days. Indicate whether credit should be granted for the initial order. The seller's cost of capital is 13 per cent; ignore taxes in your calculations and assume that all credit investigation costs have been spent.

14. A selling firm is taxable and wants to evaluate a credit applicant via the one-period, after-tax, net present value approach. The appropriate discount rate for expected future flows is 10 per cent per year. If the applicant does not pay in the normal course of business, it is expected that the applicant will be liquidated. The liquidation process will take two years, and trade creditors are expected to experience a 50 per cent recovery rate, though that average recovery by the seller in such cases is 20 per cent. If the applicant does not default, it is expected that payment will be received in 90 days. Based on a failure-forecasting function estimated with equal sample size of defaulted and nondefaulted firms, a probability of default of 80 per cent of the applicants actually default. The seller is in the 35 per cent tax bracket, and the order amount is ₹ 30,000. The tax cost of the inventory to service the order will be ₹ 27,000, although the actual out-of-pocket cost to replenish inventory when the order is shipped will be only ₹ 26,000. Use a 360-day year.

(a) Calculate the expected net present value of the sale if the firm accrues a reserve for bad debt based on average loss rates.

(b) Calculate the expected net present value of the sale if the firm does not accrue a reserve, but instead writes off bad debts as they occur.

25

INVENTORY MANAGEMENT

INTRODUCTION

Inventory management is concerned with keeping enough product on hand to avoid running out while at the same time maintaining a small enough inventory balance to allow for a reasonable return on investment. Proper inventory management is important to the financial health of the corporation; being out of stock forces customers to turn to competitors or results in a loss of sales. Excessive level of inventory, however, results in large inventory carrying costs, including the cost of the capital tied up in inventory warehouse fees, insurance etc. The objective of the chapter is to examine the impact of inventory on the financial decision-making.

FUNCTIONS OF INVENTORY

The functions of the firm, such as the purchase of raw materials, processing, and having finished goods available for sale, have a sequential, physical dependency. Maintenance of inventories allows the firm to decouple these functions so that each can be planned, scheduled, and operated independently. For retail firms, inventory provides customers with selection choices and decouples the purchasing function from the selling function.

TYPES OF INVENTORIES

Raw Materials

An inventory of raw materials allows separation of production scheduling from arrival of basic inputs to the production process. Factors affecting the amount of the raw materials inventory include proximity to the supplier, relationship with the supplier, predictability of the production process, lead time required to place an order, and transportability and perishability of materials.

Work-in-Process

An inventory of partially completed units allows the separation of different phases of the production process. The amount of work-in-process inventory is in part a function of the type of product, the measurement period, and the nature of the production process. For example, a firm with a very short production process, such as a bakery, may have a work-in-process inventory during the day: kneaded dough that is rising before being backed. However, this work-in-process inventory will not be carried overnight. On the other hand, a firm with a long production process, such as an airframe manufacturer, may have a large work-in-process inventory of partially completed products (airplanes), on a continuing basis. However, even in this latter example, management controls the amount of work-in-process inventory maintained through a choice between working on a few airframes at a time or working on a larger number of planes, to allow more flexibility in scheduling.

Finished Goods

An inventory of finished goods allows separation of production from selling. With a stock of finished merchandise on hand, a firm can fill orders as they are received rather than depend upon the completion of production to satisfy customer demands.

Cash and Marketable Securities

Cash and marketable securities can be thought of as an inventory of liquidity that allows separation of collection from disbursement. Without this liquidity inventory, payment of bills would be tied to collection of accounts, in some cases, with payment delayed until accounts receivable are collected.

MOTIVES FOR HOLDING INVENTORY

Economists have established three motives for holding inventories: a transactions motive, a precautionary motive, and a speculative motive. In addition, there may be a contractual reason for holding some inventories.

Transactions Motive

The *transactions motive* for holding inventory is to satisfy the expected level of activities of the firm. For example, a pizza restaurant receiving its next materials consignment on Monday starts the weekend with enough flour, salt, tomato sauce, sausage, and anchovies to make the number of pizzas anticipated to be ordered over the weekend.

Precautionary Motive

The *precautionary motive* is to provide a cushion in case the actual level of activity is different than anticipated. Again, using a pizza restaurant as an example, in addition to holding enough inventory to make the expected number of pizzas over the weekend, the restaurant may hold additional supplies as a precaution against demand being different than anticipated. If demand exceed expectations (either in total or for a particular ingredient), sales will probably either be lost or, if made, less profitable. It is doubtful that many customers will accept a pie topped with anchovies and pineapple as a substitute simply because the restaurant has run out of sausage and pepperoni.

Speculative Motive

The *speculative motive* for holding inventory might entice a firm to purchase a larger quantity of materials than normal in anticipation of making abnormal profits. Advance purchases of raw materials in inflationary times is one form of speculative behaviour. A second reason for speculative inventory purchases may involve an anticipated change in a product.

Contractual Requirements

Occasionally it may be necessary to carry a certain level of inventory to meet a contractual agreement. Some manufacturers require dealers to maintain a specified level of inventory in order to be the sole representative in a particular territory.

COST OF HOLDING INVENTORIES

The determination of inventory costs is essentially an income measurement problem, a means whereby there is a rational, orderly, systematic interpretation of the effect on the economic progress of the company of expenditures involved in acquiring goods or in maintaining and operating productive facilities. Ability to quantify and develop rigours models of most managerial problems is dependent on the determination of the behaviour of relevant costs. The practical application of such models is also dependent on ability to obtain the cost data. Relevant inventory costs which change with the level of inventory are listed below:

Ordering Costs

Every time an order is placed for stock replenishment, certain costs are involved. The ordering cost may vary, dependent upon the type of item. However, an estimate of ordering cost can be obtained for a given range of items. This cost of ordering includes: paper work costs, typing and despatching an order; follow-up costs—the follow-up required to ensure timely supplies include the travel cost for purchase follow-up, telephone, telex and postal bills; cost involved in receiving the order inspection, checking, and handling to the stores; any set up cost of machines if charged by the supplier, either directly indicated in quotations or assessed through quotations for various quantities; and, the salaries and wages to the purchase department are relevant for consideration if the purchasing function is carried out at the same level with the existing staff. If the level of purchasing activity decreases significantly, obviously a proportional amount of personnel will be transferred to other departments.

Carrying Costs

Carrying costs constitute all the costs of holding items in inventory for a given period of time. They are expressed either in ₹ per unit per period or as a percentage of the inventory value per period. Components of this cost include the following: storage and handling costs; obsolescence and deterioration costs, nsurance; taxes; and, the cost of the funds invested in inventories.

Like ordering costs, inventory carrying costs contain both fixed and variable components. Most carrying costs vary with the inventory level, but a certain portion of them—such as warehouse rent and depreciation on inventory handling equipment—are relatively fixed over the short run. Most of the simple inventory control models, such as the EOQ model, treat the entire carrying cost as variable.

Stockout Costs

Stockout costs are incurred whenever a business is unable to fill orders because the demand for an item is greater than the amount currently available in inventory. When a stockout in raw materials occurs, for example, stockout costs include the expenses of placing special orders (backordering) and expediting incoming orders, in addition to the costs of any resulting production delays. A stockout in work-in-progress inventory results in additional costs of rescheduling and speeding production within the plant, and it also may result in lost production costs if work stoppages occur. Finally, a stockout in finished goods inventory may result in the immediate loss of profits if customers decide to purchase the product from a competitor, and in potential long-term losses if customers decide to order from other companies in the future.

INVENTORY CONTROL MODELS

A number of inventory control models are available that can help in determining the optimal inventory level of each item. These models range from the relatively simple to the extremely complex. Their degree of complexity depends primarily on the assumptions made about the demand or use for the particular item and the lead time required to secure additional stock.

A related question involves the extent of control and the type of inventory model that should be applied to different inventory items. A technique called *ABC inventory classification* can be helpful in this regard. The ABC method divides a company's inventory items into three groups. Group A consists of those items with a relatively large value but a relatively small percentage of the total items, whereas group C contains those items with a small value but a large percentage of the total items. Group B contains the items which are in between groups A and C. A typical result of an ABC analysis is that group A contains roughly 1 to 10 per cent of the total number of items carried in inventory, but these items may represent as high as 80 to 90 per cent of the total value of the inventory. On the other hand, group C may contain about 50 per cent of the total number of items, but these items may constitute less than 10 per cent of the inventory's total value. Group B contains the remaining items. Even though the actual cutoff between the groups is somewhat arbitrary, the ABC method provides management with information that can be used to determine how closely different inventory items should be controlled.

In the "classic" inventory models, which include both the simpler *deterministic* models and the more complex *probabilistic* models, it is assumed that demand is either uniform or dispersed and *independent* over time. In other words, demand is assumed either to be *constant* or to fluctuate over time due to *random* elements. These types of demand situations are common in retailing and some service operations.

The simpler deterministic inventory control models, such as the *economic order quantity* (EOQ) *model,* assume that both demand and lead times are *constant* and known with *certainty.* Thus, deterministic models eliminate the need to consider stockouts. The more complex probabilistic inventory control models assume that demand, lead time, or both are *random variables with known probability distributions.*

Basic EOQ Model

In its simplest form, the EOQ model assumes the annual demand or usage for a particular item is known with certainty. It also assumes that this demand is stationary or uniform throughout the year. In other words, seasonal fluctuations in the rate of demand are ruled out. Finally, the model assumes that orders to replenish the inventory of an item are filled instantaneously. Given a known demand and a zero lead time for replenishing inventories, there is no need for a company to maintain additional inventories, or safety stocks, to protect itself against stockouts.

The assumptions of the EOQ model yield the saw-toothed inventory pattern shown in Figure-1. The vertical lines at the 0, T_1, T_2, and T_3 points in time represent the instantaneous replenishment of the item by the amount of the order quantity, Q, and the negatively sloped lines between the replenishment points represent the use of the item. Because the inventory level varies between 0 and the order quantity, average inventory is equal to one-half of the order quantity, or $Q/2$.

FIGURE-1

CERTAINTY CASE OF THE INVENTORY CYCLE

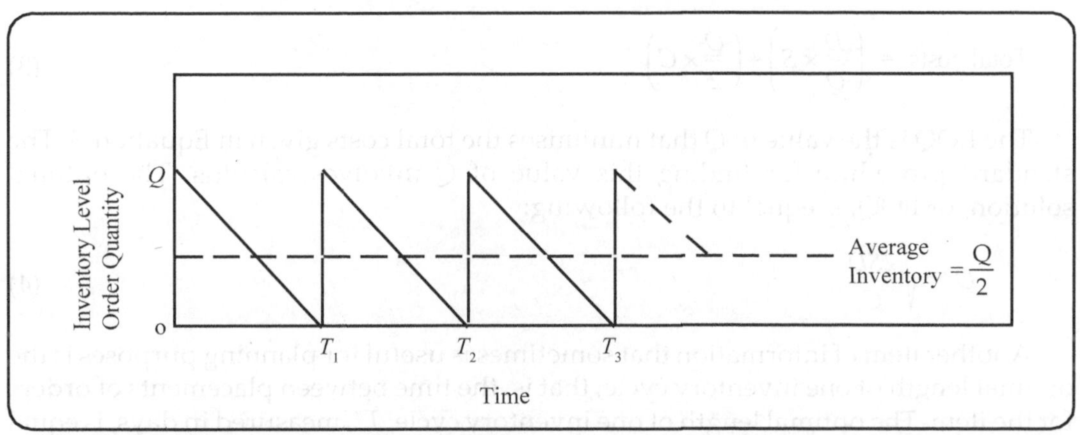

This model assumes that the costs of placing and receiving an order are the same for each order and independent of the number of units ordered. It also assumes that the annual cost of carrying 1 unit of the item in inventory is constant regardless of the inventory level. Total annual inventory costs, then, are the sum of ordering costs and carrying costs. The primary objective of the EOQ model is to find the order quantity, Q, that minimises total annual inventory costs.

Algebraic Solution

In developing the algebraic form of the EOQ model, the following variables are defined

Q = The order *quantity*, in units
D = The annual *demand* for the item, in units
S = The Cost of placing and receiving an order, or *set-up* cost
C = The annual cost of *carrying* 1 unit of the item in inventory

Ordering costs are equal to the number of orders per year multiplied by the cost per order, S. The number of orders per year is equal to annual demand, D, divided by the order quantity, Q. Carrying costs are equal to average inventory, $Q/2$, multiplied by the annual carrying cost per unit, C.

The total annual cost equation is as follows:

Total costs = Ordering costs + Carrying costs (1)

By substituting the variables just defined into Equation-1, the following expression is obtained:

Total costs = (Number of orders per year
× cost per order) + (Average inventory (2)
× annual carrying cost per unit)

or, in algebraic terms,

$$\text{Total costs} = \left(\frac{D}{Q} \times S\right) + \left(\frac{Q}{2} \times C\right) \tag{3}$$

The EOQ is the value of Q that minimises the total costs given in Equation-3. The standard procedure for finding this value of Q involves calculus. The optimal solution, or EOQ, is equal to the following:

$$Q^* = \sqrt{\frac{2SD}{C}} \tag{4}$$

Another item of information that sometimes is useful for planning purposes is the optimal length of one inventory cycle; that is, the time between placements of orders for the item. The optimal length of one inventory cycle, T^*, measured in days, is equal to the economic order quantity, Q^*, divided by the average daily demand, $D/365$ (assuming 365 days per year), as follows

$$T^* = \frac{Q^*}{D/365} \tag{5}$$

This equation can be rewritten as follows:

$$T^* = \frac{365 \times Q^*}{D} \tag{6}$$

The following example illustrates the use of the EOQ model. Suppose that the Novex Company sells Venkat mattresses through its department stores located in

Delhi. All inventories are maintained at the firm's centrally located warehouse. Annual demand for the Venkat standard-sized mattress is 3,600 units and is spread evenly throughout the year. The cost of placing and receiving an order is ₹ 31.25.

Novex annual carrying costs are 20 per cent of the inventory value. Based on a wholesale cost of ₹ 50 per mattress, the annual carrying cost per mattress is 0.20 × ₹ 50 = ₹ 10. Because Venkat maintains a large regional distribution center in Delhi Novex can replenish its inventory virtually instantaneously. The company wishes to determine the number of standard-sized mattresses it should periodically order from Venkat to minimise the total annual inventory costs. Substituting D =3,600, S = ₹ 31.25, and C = ₹ 10 into Equation-4 yields the following EOQ:

$$Q^* = \sqrt{\frac{2 \times ₹\ 31.25 \times 3{,}600}{₹\ 10}} = 150 \text{ mattresses}$$

Using Equation-3, we can calculate the total annual inventory costs of this policy:

$$\text{Total costs}^* = \frac{3{,}600}{150} \times ₹\ 31.25 + \frac{150}{2} \times ₹\ 10 = ₹\ 1{,}500$$

Finally, Equation-6 can be used to determine Novex's optimal inventory cycle for these mattresses:

$$T^* = \frac{365 \times 150}{3{,}600} = 15.2 \text{ days}$$

Thus, the EOQ of 150 mattresses and the optimal inventory cycle of 15.2 days for this item indicate that Novex should place an order for 150 mattresses every 15.2 days.

Graphic Solution

The order quantity that minimises total annual inventory costs can be determined graphically by plotting inventory costs (vertical axis) as a function of the order quantity (horizontal axis). As can be seen in Figure-2, annual ordering costs, DS/Q, vary *inversely* with the order quantity, Q, because the number of orders placed per year, D/Q, decreases as the size of the order quantity increases. Carrying costs, $CQ/2$, vary *directly* with the order quantity, Q, because the average inventory, $Q/2$, increases as the size of the order quantity increases.

The total inventory cost curve is found by vertically summing the heights of the ordering cost and carrying cost functions. The order quantity corresponding to the lowest point on the total cost curve is the optimal solution—that is, the economic order quantity, Q^*.

Extensions of the Basic EOQ Model

The basic EOQ model just described makes a number of simplifying assumptions, including those pertaining to the demand for the item, replenishment lead time, the behaviour of ordering and carrying costs, and quantity discounts. In practical applications of inventory control models, however, some of these assumptions may not be valid. Thus, it is important to understand how different assumptions affect the analysis and the optimal order quantity. The following discussion examines what occurs when some of these assumptions are altered.

FIGURE-2

GRAPHIC SOLUTION OF THE EOQ MODEL

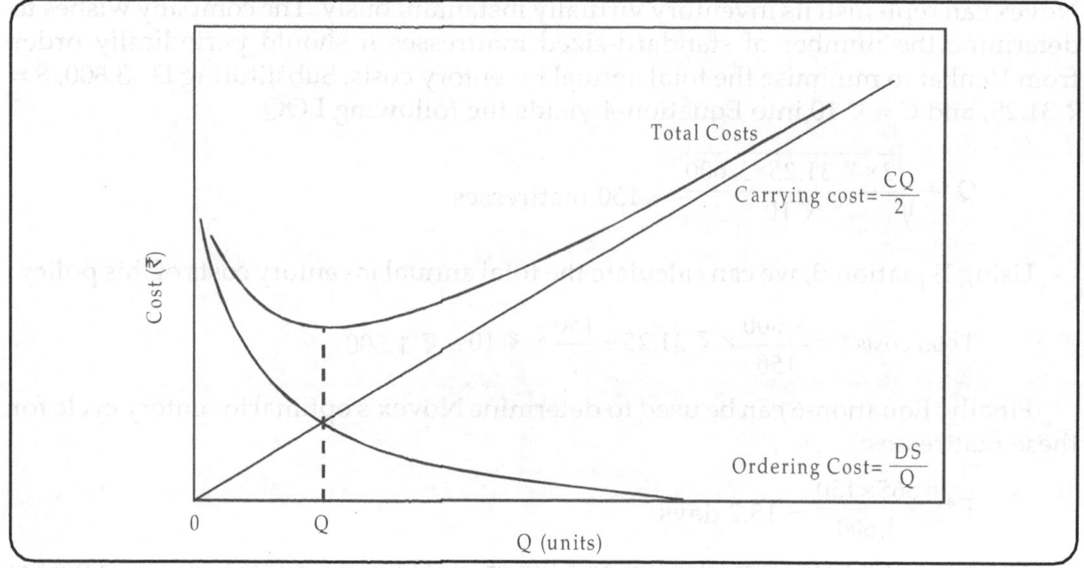

Nonzero Lead Time

The basic EOQ model assumes that orders to replenish the inventory of an item are filled instantaneously; that is, the lead time is zero. In practice, however, some time usually elapses between when a purchase order is placed and when the item actually is received in inventory. This lead time consists of the time it takes to manufacture the item, the time it takes to package and ship the item, or both.

If the lead time is *constant* and *known with certainty*, the optimal order quantity, Q^*, is not affected, although the time when an order should be placed is. Specifically, a company should not wait to reorder until the end of the inventory cycle, when the inventory level reaches zero—such as at points T_1 T_2, and T_3, in Figure-3. Instead, it should place an order *n days prior* to the end of each cycle, *n* being equal to the replenishment lead time measured in days. The *reorder point* is defined as the inventory level at which an order should be placed for replenishment of an item. Assuming that demand is constant over time, the reorder point, Q_r, is equal to the lead time, *n* (measured in days), multiplied by daily demand:

$$Q_r = n \times \frac{D}{365} \tag{7}$$

where $D/365$ is daily demand (based on 365 days per year).

For example, if the lead time for standard-sized mattresses ordered by Novex is 5 days, and annual demand is 3,600 mattresses, an order for 150 mattresses (that is, the economic order quantity) should be placed when the inventory level reaches the following:

$$Q_r = 5 \times \frac{3,600}{365} = 49.3 \text{ mattresses}$$

which occurs during the 10th day of each inventory cycle. Five days later, during the 15th day of the inventory cycle—when the inventory level falls to zero—Novex will receive the order, and the inventory level will again rise to 150.

Quantity Discounts: Large orders often permit a company to realise substantial per-unit savings (that is, economies of scale) in manufacturing, order processing, and transport. Many companies encourage their customers to place large orders by passing on to them a portion of these savings in the form of *quantity discounts.* With a quantity discount, the cost per unit to the customer is variable and depends on the quantity ordered. The following approach can be used to determine the effect of a quantity discount on the optimal order quantity.

FIGURE-3

NORZERO REPLENISHMENT LEAD TIME CASE OF AN INVENTORY CYCLE

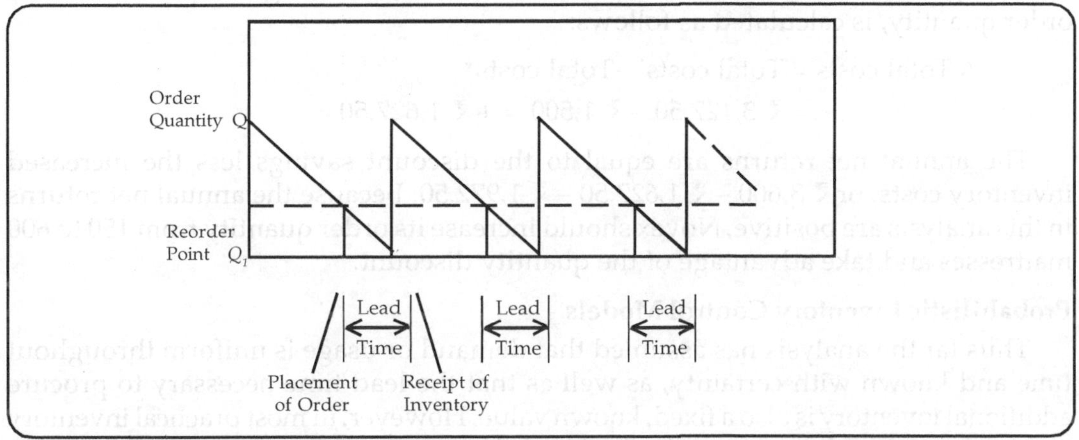

First, the EOQ is determined, using Equation-4. Next, the annual *net* returns when the order quantity is increased from the EOQ level up to the order size necessary to receive the discount are calculated. The annual net returns are equal to the discount savings on the annual demand less any increase in annual inventory costs, as defined in Equation-3. If the annual net returns are *positive,* the optimal order quantity is the order size necessary to receive the discount: if they are not, the optimal order quantity is the smaller EOQ value.

For example, in the Novex example discussed earlier, suppose Venkat offers a 2 per cent, or ₹ 1, quantity discount per mattress on orders of 600 or more standard-sized mattresses. Novex wishes to determine the optimal order quantity under these conditions. Novex EOQ is 150 mattresses. Thus, the annual net returns of increasing the order quantity from 150 to 600 need to be calculated.

The discount savings on annual demand are defined as follows:

Discount savings = Discount per unit × Annual demand (8)

In Novex case, this is calculated as follows:

Discount savings = ₹ 1 × 3,600 = ₹ 3,600

If Novex were to order the discount order quantity, Q^1, of 600 mattresses, the carrying cost per unit, C', would be reduced to ₹ 9.80 (₹ 49 × 0.20). Substituting the appropriate quantities into Equation-3 yields the following total annual inventory costs:

$$\text{Total costs} = \frac{3,600}{600} \times ₹\ 31.25 + \frac{600}{2} \times ₹\ 9.80$$

$$= ₹\ 187.50 + ₹\ 2,940 = ₹\ 3,127.50$$

As calculated earlier, the total annual inventory costs at the EOQ of 150 are ₹ 500. The *change* in annual inventory costs, Δ Total costs, resulting from the increased order quantity, is calculated as follows:

Δ Total costs = Total costs' –Total costs*

= ₹ 3,127.50 – ₹ 1,500 = + ₹ 1,627.50

The annual net returns are equal to the discount savings less the increased inventory costs, or ₹ 3,600 – ₹ 1,627.50 – ₹ 1,972.50. Because the annual net returns in this analysis are positive, Novex should increase its order quantity from 150 to 600 mattresses and take advantage of the quantity discount.

Probabilistic Inventory Control Models

Thus far the analysis has assumed that demand or usage is uniform throughout time and known with certainty, as well as that the lead time necessary to procure additional inventory is also a fixed, known value. However, in most practical inventory management problems either (or both) of these assumptions may not be strictly correct. Typically, demand fluctuates over time due to seasonal, cyclical, and "random" influences, and imprecise forecasts of future demands often are all that can be made. Similarly, lead times are subject to uncertainty because of such factors as transportation delays, strikes, and natural disasters. Under these conditions, the possibility of stockouts exists. To minimise the possibility of stockouts and the associated stockout costs, most companies use a standard approach of adding a *safety stock* to their inventory. A safety stock is maintained to meet unexpectedly high demand during the lead time, unanticipated delays in the lead time, or both.

Figure-4 shows the inventory pattern characterised by these more realistic assumptions. During the first inventory cycle (0 -T_2), an order to replenish the inventory is placed at T_1, when the inventory level reaches the predetermined order point. The order then is received at T_2. The second (T_2 –T_4) is similar to the first, except that demand exceeds the normal inventory of the item, and part of the safety stock is consumed during the lead time prior to receipt of the order at T_4. During cycle 3 (T_4 –T_6), demand exceeds the normal inventory plus the safety stock and, as a result, a stock out occurs during the lead time prior to receipt of the order at T_6.

FIGURE-4

UNCERTAINTY CASE OF INVENTORY CYCLE

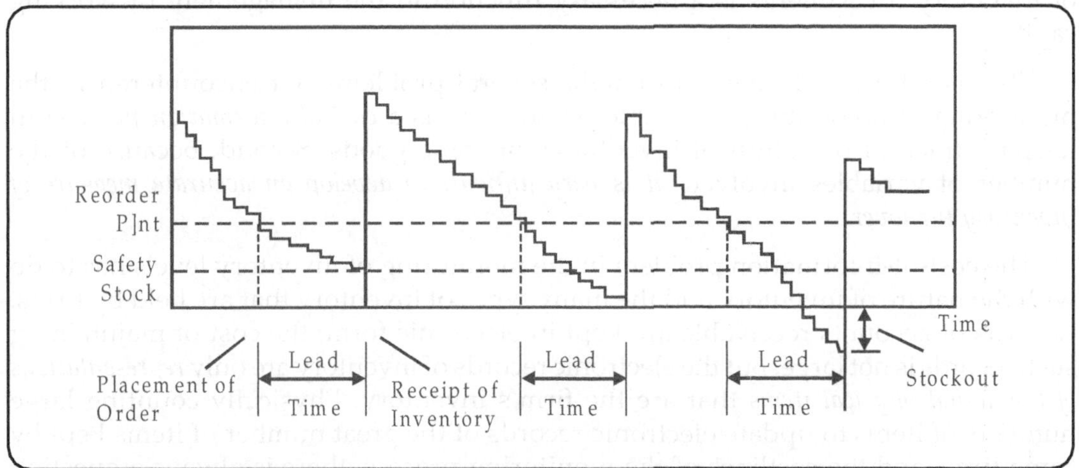

Determining the optimal safety stock and order quantities under these more realistic conditions is a fairly complex process. However, the factors that have to be considered in this type of analysis can be identified briefly. All other things being equal, the optimal safety stock increases as the uncertainty associated with the demand forecasts and lead times increases. Likewise, all other things being equal, the optimal safety stock increases as the cost of stockouts increases. Determining the optimal safety stock involves balancing the *expected* costs of stockouts against the cost of carrying the additional inventory.

Just-In-Time Inventory Management Systems

Just-in-time inventory management systems are part of a manufacturing approach that seeks to reduce the company's operating cycle and associated costs by eliminating wasteful procedures. Just-in-time inventory systems are based on the idea that all required inventory items should be supplied to the production process at exactly the right time and in exactly the right quantities. This approach was first developed by the Toyota Motor Company in the 1950s. In contrast, inventory models used in many plants, which rely on safety stocks, sometimes are referred to as "just-in-case" models.

The just-in-time approach works best for companies engaged in repetitive manufacturing operations. A key part of just-in-time techniques is the replacement of production in large batches with a continuous flow of smaller quantities. The use of a just-in-time inventory system requires close coordination between a company and its suppliers, because any disruption in the flow of parts and materials from the supplier can result in costly production delays and lost sales.

MONITORING INVENTORY BALANCES

As with accounts receivable balances, inventory balances turn over rapidly. Also inventory is a major investment for many firms, particularly firms engaged in manufacturing, retailing, or wholesaling. For these reasons, the continuous monitoring of inventory investments is a necessary function in the management of working capital.

The monitoring of inventory entails several problems not encountered in the monitoring of accounting receivable. First, there is a *cost-of-information problem* in keeping track of the physical inventories of some goods. Second, because of the number of variables involved, *it is very difficult to develop an accurate measure of inventory turnover*.

The cost-of-information problem in the monitoring of inventory levels has to do with the nature of inventory and the many types of inventory that are held by firms. Records of accounts receivable are kept in electronic form; the cost of maintaining such records is not large. But the electronic records of inventory are only *representations of the actual physical items* that are the firm's inventory. Physically counting large numbers of items to update electronic records of the great number of items kept by some firms and the costlines of the monitoring process, there is always a question about how much time and money should be spent on the monitoring of the levels of some inventory items. If the carrying costs and stockout costs associated with holding some types of inventory are small, it makes sense to avoid spending substantial amounts to access the level of these types of inventory; the costs of monitoring outweight the benefits.

The second problem in the monitoring of inventory is developing a procedure to accurately measure the behaviour of inventory. This problem also occurred in the measurement of customer payment patterns of accounts receivable balances. In monitoring accounts receivable, changes in sales caused distortions in turnover-based measures of receivables' quality, such as days' sales outstanding. Measures such as sales-weighted days' sales outstanding were developed to correct for this problem. These measures eliminated the distortion caused by fluctuating sales levels. Unfortunately, the problem of distortion in turnover-based monitoring statistics is even more severe in the management of inventory. For inventory, distortions occur not only because of variations in *sales,* but also variations in *unit investment* in inventory, *usage rates* (unit turnover). and the *mix of different types* of inventory carried by the firm.

To control for price, sales, unit turnover, and mix in assessing behaviour the accounting technique of variances analysis in used. By applying variance analysis to each type of inventory we can separate the effects of mix, sales, turnover, and price. With these effects isolated, investigation of any disadvantageous deviations from expectations can be undertaken.

ILLUSTRATIVE PROBLEMS

1. A firm expects a sale of 90,000 units purchased by the firm for ₹ 10 per unit. The order cost is ₹ 25 and the firm's carrying cost as a percentage of the inventory value has been estimated at 15%. What is the economic order quantity?

Solution

By substituting the values in Equation—4, we get:

$$\text{EOQ} = \sqrt{\frac{2SD}{C}}$$

$$\text{EOQ} = \sqrt{\frac{2(90,000)(25)}{(.15)(10)}} = 1,732$$

The economic order quantity is 1,732 units.

2. Shexilla Products has sales of 2,00,000 units per year. Inventory carrying costs are ₹ 50,000 per unit per year and ordering costs are ₹ 500 per order. What is the optimum order quantity?

Solution

Using Equation—4, we get

$$\text{EOQ} = \sqrt{(2 \times 2,00,000 \times 500)} / 50$$

$$= \sqrt{40,00,000} = 2,000 \text{ units.}$$

The optimum order penalty is 2,000 units.

3. Arisotex Distributors uses an average of 1,000 bags of cement each year. They have an ordering cost per order of ₹ 60, order in quantities of 350 bags and have carrying costs of ₹ 10 per bag each year. Determine their total inventory cost.

Solution

Using Equation—3, we get

$$\text{Total Inventory Cost} = \left(\frac{D}{S} \times S\right) + \left(\frac{Q}{2} \times C\right)$$

$$= \frac{₹\ 10(350)}{2} + \frac{1,000\ (₹\ 60)}{350}$$

= ₹ 1,750 + ₹ 171 = ₹ 1,921

The total cost is ₹ 1,921 per year.

4. Using the information provided in Problem—3, determine the EOQ and the new total inventory cost based on ordering using the economic order quantity.

Solution

First, determine the EOQ by using Equation—4,

$$= \sqrt{\frac{2SD}{C}}$$

$$= \sqrt{\frac{2 \times 1{,}000 \times ₹\ 60}{₹\ 10}}$$

$$= \sqrt{12{,}000}$$

$$= 110$$

It is not economical to place orders in quantities of 110 bags.

Second, determine the total cost based on ordering in 110 bags quantities:

$$\frac{D}{Q} \times S + \frac{Q}{2} \times C$$

$$= \frac{₹\ 10\ (110)}{2} + \frac{1{,}000\ (₹\ 60)}{110} = ₹\ 550 + ₹\ 545 = ₹\ 1{,}095$$

Ordering in 110 bag quantities (the EOQ) instead of 350-bags quantities results in reducing total yearly inventory cost from ₹ 1,921 to ₹ 1,095.

5. Rohit Sportswear Company sells 750 ski parkas each year, which it purchases for ₹ 25 each. It costs Rohit ₹ 6 to place an order for parkas and 10% to carry them in inventory.

(a) What is Rohit's economic order quantity for parkas, and how many orders should it place each year?

(b) What is the total cost of this inventory policy?

Solution

(a) By substituting values in Equation-4, we get:

$$\text{EOQ} = \sqrt{\frac{2(750)(6)}{(.10)(25)}} = 60$$

It should place

$$\frac{750}{60} = 12.5 \text{ orders}$$

(b) Total cost

$$= \frac{60}{2}(25)(.10) \times \frac{750}{60}(6)$$

$$= 75 + 75 = ₹\ 150$$

6. Northast Controls processes orders of 100 units during one half of the months, 200 units during one-quarter of the months. Average inventory carrying costs per month at reorder points of 100, 200, and 300 units are ₹ 50, ₹ 100, and ₹ 175 respectively. Average ordering cost per month is ₹ 50 regardless of reorder point. The lost profit per unit of orders lost due to lack of inventory is ₹ 2. Which reorder point of 100/200/300 will provide the lowest total inventory cost?

Solution

Reorder point	*Order*	*Lost orders*	*Lost order opportunity cost*	*Probability*	*Expected opportunity cost*
	100	0	0	.50	₹ 0
100	200	100	200	.25	50
	300	200	400	.25	100
				Total expected opportunity cost =	₹ 150
	100	0	0	.50	₹ 0
200	200	0	0	.25	0
	300	100	200	.25	50
					₹ 50
	100	0	0	.50	₹ 0
300	200	0	0	.25	0
	300	0	0	.25	0
					₹ 0

Reorder Point	*Expected Total Inventory Cost Per Month*
100	₹ 50 + ₹ 50 + ₹ 150 = ₹ 250
200	₹ 50 + ₹ 100 + ₹ 50 = 200
300	₹ 50 + ₹ 175 + ₹ 0 = ₹ 225

The lowest expected total inventory cost per month occurs at a reorder point of 200 units.

7. A firm expects sales of 90,000 units that cost the firm ₹ 5 per unit. It has policy of 20 days as a safety stock level and has estimated that carrying costs are 20% of inventory value. Order costs are ₹ 25 and lead time is 10 days. What is the reorder point for the firm and how many units should the firm order?

Solution

Reorder point = (90,000/360) (10+20) = 7,500

Reorder point for the firm is 7,500 units.

$$EOQ = \sqrt{\frac{2(90{,}000)\ (25)}{(.20)\ (5)}} = 2{,}121$$

The firm should order 2,121 units.

8. A firm has sales of 18,00,000 units, which are sold at a constant rate throughout the year. The firm's EOQ has been calculated at 50,000 units, the safety stock level is 10 days, and the lead time for orders is 4 days, what is the reorder point for the firm?

Solution

Reorder point = (18,00,000/360) (4+10) = 70,000 units

The reorder point for the firm is 70,000 units.

9. A firm has a ₹ 1,000 per year carrying cost (including costs of financing), on each unit of inventory, an annual usage rate of 40,000 units, and an ordering cost of ₹ 2,000 per order. Ignoring any potential stockout costs:

(a) Calculate the economic order quantity for the firm.

(b) What would be the total annual inventory costs of the firm if it orders in this quantity?

Solution

(a) By substituting the values in Equation—4, we get

$$\text{EOQ} = \sqrt{\frac{2(40,000)\ (₹\ 1,000)}{₹\ 2,000}}$$

$$= 200 \text{ units}$$

(b) Number of orders/year

$$= \frac{40,000}{200} = 200$$

Total ordering cost = 200 (₹ 2,000) = ₹ 4,00,000

$$\text{Average inventory} = \frac{200}{2} = 100 \text{ units}$$

Total carrying cost = ₹ 1,000 (100) = ₹ 1,00,000

Total annual inventory costs = ₹ 1,00,000 + ₹ 4,00,000 = ₹ 5,00,000

10. Refer to Problem-9, assume that the supplier for the firm offers a quantity discount of ₹ 0.10 per unit if the firm orders in lots of 500 units. Should the firm accept the quantity discount?

Solution

If the firm accepts the quantity discount, the annual savings are:

₹ 0.10(40,000) = ₹ 4,000

Purchasing 500 units results in $\frac{40,000}{500}$ = 80orders per year for a total ordering cost of 80 (₹ 2,000) = ₹ 1,60,000. The average inventory of $\frac{500}{2}$ units results in total carrying costs of ₹ 1,000 (250) = ₹ 2,50,000. Thus total inventory costs are ₹ 4,10,000, a ₹ 90,000 decrease. In addition the firm saves ₹ 4,000 on the discounts. Therefore, the advantage to the company is ₹ 94,000. The firm should take the quantity discounts.

11. Bajaj Paints sells an average of 1000 cases of paints each month at a cost of ₹ 90 each. Inventory carrying costs about ₹ 3 per case per month and ordering costs are ₹ 60 per order.

(a) Determine the economic order quantity.
(b) Determine how frequently orders should be placed.
(c) Determine the total inventory costs per month.

Solution

(a) The cost of paints is irrelevant to the problem once the carrying costs are provided. It is assumed that the cost of financing the inventory is included in the carrying cost.

$$\text{EOQ} = \sqrt{\frac{2(1000)\ (₹\,60)}{₹\,3}} = 200$$

Bajaj should order paint in 200 lots.

(b) Since the economic order quantity is 200 cases and only 1000 are used per month, an order should be placed five times a month.

(c) Using Equation-3,

$$= \frac{₹\,3(200)}{3} + \frac{1000(₹\,60)}{200} = ₹\,300 + ₹\,300 = ₹\,600 \text{ per month}$$

Note that the economic order quantity, 200 units, is used as the value of R when calculating the total costs.

QUESTIONS

1. What is the purpose of holding inventory? Name several types of inventory and describe their purpose.
2. Can cash be considered a special type of inventory? If so what functions does it attempt to uncouple?
3. How are the objectives of inventory management and cash balance management are similar?
4. Discuss the primary factors in the control of inventories.
5. How do you determine the expected usage of inventory and which of the various methods is the most advantageous? Why?
6. "For some inventory items, the costs of administering an inventory system may outweigh the benefits." Explain this statement, outlining an approach that a company may follow to overcome this problem.
7. What are the risk-return trade offs associated with inventory management
8. Explain why total ordering costs decline at a decreasing rate as the quantity received with each order increases. Under what conditions might the curve appear differently?
9. Describe the likely effects on inventory levels of the following events; (a) A major supplier announces a 10% price increase; (b) Several major suppliers improve their delivery time of materials to your firm. (c) Demand for the firm's products increases; and, (d) The firm increases its number of styles of products.
10. Explain the purpose of the ABC inventory classification scheme.
11. Define the major categories of inventory costs.
12. What is the significance of Economic Order Quantity to the financial manager?

13. What are the principal components of the analytical framework that give rise to the economic-order-quantity framework?
14. Are quantity discounts a significant factor in the Economic Order Quantity formula? Why or why not?
15. How is the reorder point determined? What is the significance of the reorder points to the financial manager?
16. Distinguish between inventory ordering costs and inventory carrying costs, and give examples of each,
17. How can the EOQ model be modified if demand is not uniform over time?
18. If order costs and the cost of funds are the same for all firm's products, why does the EOQ method of inventory purchasing lead to an optimum investment in inventory.
19. Discuss the use of control limits for inventory management. What assumption must first be made?
20. What is the major difference in underlying assumption between the inventory model and the control limits most for cash management?
21. What factors affect the holding costs for a finished goods inventory?
22. What assumptions are necessary to use the basic economic order quantity (EOQ) model?
23. Contrast the differences in orientation of the EOQ and net present value approaches to inventory control.
24. How would a reduction in replenishment costs affect the net present value of an inventory policy?
25. Contrast the role that inventory plays in a traditional EOQ approach and in a just-in-time approach. Does a just-in-time approach to inventory accomplish anything other than forcing the supplier to carry your raw materials inventory?
26. What is the significance of safety stock to the financial manager? What purpose does safety stock serve? What are some of the benefits and costs associated with safety stock?
27. What factors must a firm consider in deciding how large a buffer stock of inventory to hold?

PROBLEMS

1. A firm uses 800 units of a product per year on a continuous basis. The product has carrying costs of ₹ 2 per unit and fixed costs of ₹ 50 per order. It takes five days to receive a shipmen after an order is placed, and the firm wishes to hold inventory 10 days, usage as a safety stock. Calculate the EOQ and determine reorder point.

Ans.: EOQ = 200 units; Reorder point = 33.33 units

2. DYEA is attempting to determine the optimal order quantity, for a popular book on Indian Economics. The store sells 5,000 copies of this book a year at a retail price of ₹ 12.50, although the publisher allows the store a 20% discount from this price. The store figures that it costs ₹ 1 per year to carry a book in inventory and ₹ 100 to prepare an order for new books.

(a) Determine the total costs associated with ordering five times a year;

(b) Determine the economic order quantity;

(c) Develop the algebraic expression for determining total cost of ordering and holding inventory.

Ans.: (a) ₹ 1,000; (b) 1,000 units; (c) 1,000 units.

3. Sanjay Industries is required to carry 20 days average coal usage, which is 100 tons of coal. It takes 10 days between order and delivery. At which level of coal would Sanjay reorder?

Ans.: The level of coal is 150 tons

4. A firm carries four products, whose annual demands and unit prices are:

Product	*Annual Demand*	*Unit Prices*
A	900	₹ 4
B	600	6
C	500	5
D	300	3

The ordering costs and carrying costs for the four products are the same. Normally, each item is ordered 10 times each year. What is the optimum ordering pattern and total average inventory for the firm?

Ans.: Optimum ordering point = 40; Total average inventory = ₹ 500

5. Bimal Chemicals wants to optimise its inventory management costs for a certain product it handles. It anticipates a demand annual cost of holding the product is expected to be 25% of the retail selling price of ₹ 40.

(a) Calculate the economic order quantity for the product.

(b) Calculate the number of orders placed and average inventory.

(c) Calculate the number of units that Bimal should hold as safety stock if the average lead time to delivery is 3 weeks.

Ans.: (a) EOQ = 11.55 or 12 units; (b) Number of orders = 41; (c) Safety stock = 44.44 or 45 units

6. Kapoor Brothers uses 10,000 units of a raw material per year on a continuous basis. The firm estimates the cost of carrying one unit in inventory is ₹ 25 per year. Placing and processing an order for additional inventory costs ₹ 200 per order. What are the annual order costs, carrying costs, and total costs of inventory if the firm orders in quantities of 1000 and 5000 respectively?

Ans.: For 100 units: Annual order cost = ₹ 2,000; Carrying cost = ₹ 125 and total cost = ₹ 2,125; For 500 units: Annual cost = ₹ 400; Carrying cost = ₹ 625 and total cost = ₹ 1,025

7. Sangam Art Corporation is considering using airfreight rather than express to have one particular item. The annual demand is 600 units and the EOQ model indicates that 25 orders should be placed every year. Average lead time to delivery is 3 weeks with express delivery or 1 week with airfreight delivery. Inventory holding costs are ₹ 100 per unit year. What is the maximum amount of additional freight express that Sangam Art Corporation would be willing to incur to switch from express to airfreight?

Ans.: ₹ 400

8. International Electronics estimates the annual cost of carrying a ₹ of inventory is ₹ .27, while the carrying cost of an equal investment in accounts receivable is ₹ .17. The firm's current balance sheet reflects its average inventory of ₹ 4,00,000 and average investment in accounts receivables of

₹ 1,00,000. If the firm convince its customers to purchase in large quantities, the level of inventory can be reduced by ₹ 2,00,000 and the investment in receivables increased by the same amount. Assuming no change in annual sales, what addition to profits will be generated from this shift?

Ans.: Addition to profit = ₹ 20,000

9. A fairly uniform demand requires Mr. K.N. Behl, a grocery buyer for Avon company, to purchases 6,000 cases of coffee for 12 times a year. He has an opportunity to triple the size of his order and reduce by 1% the present purchase price per case ₹ 8.50. Avon has sufficient warehouse space for the new volume and believe that carrying costs will remain 10% of inventory value. Knowing that the administrative costs of each purchase of coffee are ₹ 10, should Behl take advantage of this purchase discount?

Ans.: As incremental savings, ₹ 6,200 are larger than the incremental cost of ₹ 5,023.50, the opportunity should be accepted.

10. Jain Brothers, Inc., a home-appliance distributer, sells 120 Model 1434 E Refrigerators each month and has recorded a standard deviation in that sales average of 12 refrigerators. The company is reviewing its inventory requirements and has decided that its buffer stock for this item should be enlarged. With a lead time of five weeks, Jain need to plan for at least a two-month period. If sales in any month are not effected by sales in any other month and Jain wants the probability that it will run out of stock to be only 2% (2.0 standard deviation from the mean), what should the new buffer stock be?

Ans.: The new buffer stock should be 35

26

SHORT-TERM FINANCING

INTRODUCTION

Working capital management is the management of the firm's short-term assets and liabilities, individually and in aggregate of all the functional areas of business financial decision making the one that occupies the substantial portion of the financial manager's working day is the management of the problems of current assets and liabilities. These may include such decisions as the level of cash balance to maintain the account of cash to be invested in securities over the weekend, when particular suppliers are to be paid, whether a credit limit for a customer should be increased, or the amount of borrowing to be done under the line of credit for the month. The focus of the chapter is on the major sources of short-term financing for firms, the cost of the short-term credit, and technique (the sequential method) for generating a minimum-cost structure of current liabilities.

TRADE CREDIT

Whenever a business receives merchandise ordered from a supplier and then is permitted to wait a specified period of time before having to pay, it is receiving *trade credit.* In the aggregate, trade credit is the most important source of short-term financing for business firms. Smaller businesses in particular usually rely heavily on trade credit to finance their operations, because they often are unable to obtain funds from banks or other lenders in the financial markets.

Most trade credit is extended on an *open account* basis. A firm sends a purchase order to a supplier, who then evaluates the firm's credit-worthiness using various information sources and decision criteria. If the supplier decides to extend the firm credit, he sells the ordered merchandise to the firm, along with an invoice describing the contents of the sale, the total amount due, and the terms of sale. When the firm accepts the merchandise by the supplier, it in effect agrees to pay the amount due as specified by the terms of sale on the invoice. Once it has been established, trade credit becomes almost automatic and is subject to only periodic reviews by the supplier. Open account trade credit appears on the balance sheet as *accounts payable.*

Promissory notes sometimes are used as an alternative to the open account arrangement. When a company signs a promissory note, which specifies the amount to be paid and the due date, it is formally recognising an obligation to repay the credit. A supplier may require a company to sign a promissory note if it questions the company's credit-worthiness. Promissory notes usually appear on the balance sheet as *notes payable.*

Credit Terms

Credit terms, or terms of sale, specify the conditions under which a business is required to repay the credit that a supplier has extended to it. These conditions include the *length* and the *beginning date* of the credit period, the *cash discount* (if any) given for prompt repayment, and any *special terms,* such as *seasonal datings.*

Cost of Trade Credit

Trade credit is considered a *spontaneous* source of financing, because it normally expands as the volume of a company's purchases increases. For example, suppose a company experiences increased demand for its products. As a result, the company increases purchases from suppliers by 20 per cent from an average of ₹ 10,000 per day to an average of ₹ 12,000 per day. Assuming that these purchases are made on credit terms of "net 30" and that the company waits until the last day of the credit period to make payment, its average accounts payable outstanding (trade credit) automatically will increase by 20 per cent from ₹ 3,00,000 (₹ 10,000 × 30) to ₹ 3,60,000 (₹ 12,000 × 30).

If the terms of sale include a cash discount, the firm must decide whether or not to take it. If the firm *takes the cash discount,* it forgoes the credit offered by the supplier beyond the end of the discount period. Assuming that the firm does not take the cash discount and wants to make maximum use of the credit offered by suppliers, it should pay its bills on the last day of the discount period.

The annual financing cost (AFC) of forgoing a cash discount is equal to the fractional interest cost per period times the number of borrowing periods per year:

$$\text{AFC} = \frac{\text{Percentage discount}}{100 - \text{Percentage discount}} \times \frac{365}{\text{Credit period} - \text{Discount period}} \qquad (1)$$

For example, suppose the XYZ Company has extended ₹ 15,000 of trade credit on terms of "2/10, net 30. The company can either pay the discounted amount ₹ 14,700 by the end of the discount period (day 10) or the full amount of the invoice (₹ 15,000 by the end of the credit period (day 30). By *not* paying on the tenth day—that is, by forgoing the cash discount—the company has the use of ₹ 14,700 (98 per cent of the invoice amount) for an additional 20 days and effectively pays ₹ 300 in interest. Substituting this information into Equation-1 yields the following:

$$\text{AFC} = \frac{2}{100-2} \times \frac{365}{30-10} = 37.2\%$$

As this example shows, the annual cost of forgoing cash discounts can be quite high. Therefore, when making financing decisions, a company should compare this cost to the costs of other sources of credit.

Also, the company that offers credit terms of "2/10, net 30" should consider the annual financing cost of having the use of funds for an additional 20 days. As the preceding calculation illustrates, the annual financing cost of offering cash discounts when the credit terms are "2/10, net 30" is about 37 per cent. Accordingly, a company may want to consider other less expensive methods of encouraging prompt payment of trade credit. However, other benefits may accrue to a company that offers cash discounts. For example, a company actually may increase its sales by offering cash discounts. Or, a company may find that its bad-debt loss ratio is lowered if it offers a discount.

Stretching Accounts Payable

Rather than pay suppliers within the credit period specified in the terms of sale, a firm can postpone payment of the amount due to beyond the end of the credit period. *Stretching* payments in this manner generates additional short-term financing for the firm, but this credit is not cost-free. Not only does the firm incur the costs of forgoing any cash discounts, but its credit rating also may deteriorate, along with its ability to obtain future credit. Late payment penalties or interest charges also may be added to these costs, depending on specific industry practices. Although occasional stretching of payables—for example, to meet a seasonal need for funds—might be tolerated by suppliers and involve little or no cost to the firm, a firm that persistently stretches accounts payable well beyond their due dates may find its trade credit cut off by suppliers, who may adopt a cash before delivery (CBD) or a cash on delivery (COD) policy when dealing with the firm in the future. Finally, when a firm develops a reputation for being consistently slow in meeting financial obligations, banks and other lenders may refuse to loan funds on reasonable terms.

ACCRUED EXPENSES AND DEFERRED INCOME

Accrued expenses and deferred income are additional spontaneous sources of unsecured short-term credit.

Accrued Expenses

Accrued expenses—such as *accrued wages, taxes,* and *interest*—represent liabilities for services rendered to the firm that have not yet been paid for by the firm. As such, they constitute an interest-free source of financing.

Accrued wages represent the money a business owes to its employees. A company can increase the average amount of accrued wages by lengthening the period between paydays. Also, a company can increase accrued expenses by delaying the payment of sales commissions and bonuses. Similarly, the amounts of *accrued taxes and interest* that a firm may accumulate also is determined by the frequency with which these expenses must be paid.

Deferred Income

Deferred income consists of payments received for goods and services that the firm has agreed to deliver at some future date. Because these payments increase the firm's liquidity and assets—namely, cash—they constitute a source of funds.

Advance payments made by customers are the primary sources of deferred income. These payments are common on large, expensive products, such as aircraft. Because these payments are not "earned" by the firm until delivery of the goods or services to the customers, they are recognised on the balance sheet as a liability called *deferred income.*

COMMERCIAL PAPER

Commercial paper consists of short-term unsecured promissory notes issued by major corporations. Maturities on commercial paper at the time of issue range from several days to months. Large issuers of commercial paper normally attempt to tailor the maturity and amounts of an issue to the needs of investors. Only companies with good credit ratings are able to borrow funds through the sale of commercial paper. Purchasers of commercial paper include corporations with excess funds to invest, banks, insurance companies, pension funds, money market mutual funds, and other types of financial institutions.

Commercial paper represents an attractive financing source for large, financially sound firms, because interest rates on commercial paper issues tend to be below the prime lending rate. Commercial paper is sold on a discount basis. This means that the firm receives less than the stated amount of the note at issue and then pays the investor the full face amount at maturity. The annual financing cost of commercial paper depends on the maturity date of the issue and the prevailing short-term interest rates. In addition to the interest costs, borrowers also may pay a 'placement fee' to the commercial paper dealer for arranging the sale of the issue. To successfully market commercial paper, however, the company must normally have unused bank lines of credit equal to the amount of the issue.

The primary disadvantage of this type of financing is that it is not always a reliable source of funds. The commercial paper market is impersonal. A firm that suddenly is faced with temporary financial difficulties may find that investors are unwilling to purchase new issues of commercial paper to replace maturing issues. In addition, the amount of loanable funds available in the commercial paper market is limited to the amount of excess liquidity of the various purchasers of commercial paper. During tight money periods there may not be enough funds available to meet the aggregate needs of corporate issuers of commercial paper at reasonable rates. As a result, a company should maintain adequate lines of bank credit and recognise the risks of relying too heavily on commercial paper. Finally, a commercial paper issue usually cannot be paid off until maturity. Even if a company no longer needs the funds from a commercial paper issue, it still must pay the interest costs.

BANK CREDIT ARRANGEMENTS

Bank borrowing consists of several types of credit arrangements, including lines of credit, term loans, letters of credit, banker's acceptances, etc. Each has a unique combination of maturity, interest rate, fees, indentures (such as the collateral required), and the conditions under which the credit can be called or revoked.

Single-Payment Loan

The simplest credit arrangement is a single-payment loan, or note. It is frequently granted for a specific financial purpose, with a definite beginning and ending time. The note can be either a discount note or an add-on note. For a *discount note,* the amount of cash advanced under the loan agreement is the face value of the loan less the amount of interest for the period covered. For a discount note, the interest rate is fixed at the time the note is originated, since it is necessary to deduct the full interest rate amount at the beginning of the loan period. For example, suppose a company negotiates a ₹ 1,00,000 discount loan for 60 days at a rate of 16%. The amount received from the bank would be

$$₹\,1,00,000 \times \left[1 - \frac{.16(60)}{360}\right] = ₹\,97,333$$

The amount repaid after 60 days would be ₹ 1,00,000.

For a note with interest at maturity, the full principal amount is received when the note is initiated. The interest is added to the principal to determine the cash flow at maturity. For such notes the interest rate can either be fixed or vary over the life of the loan. If the company received a loan with interest at maturity, it would received ₹ 1,00,000 at the beginning. Repayment, assuming a 60-day, fixed-rate 16% loan, would be

$$₹\,1,00,000 \times \left[1 + \frac{.16(60)}{360}\right] = ₹\,1,02,667$$

Even though the single-payment note is the simplest type of loan, it is frequently used in conjunction with another type of credit or a latter of credit.

Line of Credit

A *line of credit* is an agreement between a bank and a firm that permits the firm to borrow up to a specified limit during a particular time period. Once the line of credit is approved at the start of the period, loans taken out against the line are usually approved by the loan officer with a minimum of delay or additional investigation. The agreement specifies the terms and conditions of the loans to be made under the line of credit. Although technically in force for a set time period, usually a year, most credit lines represent an ongoing relationship with the bank and may be renewed. At renewal the rate, credit limit, or other conditions of the line of credit may be altered, depending upon the financial performance, condition, and needs of the borrower. The line of credit provides a very flexible source of short-term financing. The borrower has access to a specified amount of credit, but pays interest only on the actual borrowing.

The primary purpose of a credit line is to supply funds to meet the short-term, frequently seasonal, cash flow needs of the borrower. To ensure that the line is used for short-term purposes, a credit line sometimes includes a requirement of a *cleanup period*, perhaps 30 or 60 days, during which there is no borrowing against the line. Although typical at one time, the cleanup period is a feature that has practically been eliminated. Many small borrowers can't clear the line, while large borrowers negotiate away the cleanup period.

Much of the borrowing under a credit line takes place through specific short-term notes ranging from overnight to 90 days or more. At maturity the interest on the note is paid along with the principal. If funds are needed when, or perhaps before, the note is due, another note is taken down against the line. Thus, actual borrowing is usually through a sequence of short-term notes made under the terms and conditions of the credit line. By rolling over the notes at maturity and by renewing the credit line from year to year, a credit line can be used as a longer-term source of funding.

A second purpose of a line of credit is to provide a backup source of cash to pay off maturing commercial paper. Credit lines used in this way are called *backup lines.* Most organisations issuing commercial paper maintained an unused credit line in an amount sufficient to back up their commercial paper. Of course, the intention is never to have to borrow under this credit line.

A third purpose of a credit line is to provide a liquidity cushion or financial insurance. A financial manager provides for liquidity by obtaining a credit line that, although not intended to be used, is available if needed.

Committed versus Uncommitted Credit Lines

A *committed credit line* is a formal, legal agreement covering the terms and conditions of the credit line. Usually a bank requires some compensation, wither in the form of service credits from balances or cash fees, to make a committed credit line. The bank is legally bound to lend money under the line as long as the terms and conditions are met by the borrower.

An *uncommitted credit line* is simply a verbal or informally written statement from the banker that as long as conditions don't change, the bank is prepared to lend the potential borrower up to the stated amount. Although an uncommitted credit line can be canceled or the terms or conditions changed at any time, it is unusual for a bank not to honour a request for borrowing under the credit line. Competitive pressures and the desire for continuing customer relationships ensure that banks do not treat these agreements lightly. Some banks may try to initiate a relationship with a potential client by offering an uncommitted line of credit for a relatively short period, say 6 months. At the end of this period, the bank reevaluates the prospects of developing an ongoing relationship before deciding whether to renew the line.

Compensation for Credit Lines

Commitment Fee

One element of compensation for a credit line is the *commitment fee,* which is the price for the bank's commitment to keep the line available. On an uncommitted line, there is usually no charge for keeping the line available.

A fee is charged for a committed credit line. The amount may be based on the total credit line or only on the unused portion of the line. The bank may assess the fee in the form of a direct cash charge, usually in the range of ¼% to ½%, but sometimes as low as $^{1}/_{8}$%. The percentage is usually expressed as an annual percentage. The amount of the fee depends upon the quality of the borrower, other products and services being purchased from the bank, and other borrowing opportunities available to the client. For example, suppose a company arranges a ₹ 1,00,000 committed credit line that has a commitment fee of ¼%. During May, the fee charged would be

$$₹\ 1,00,000 \times .0025 \times \frac{1}{12} = ₹\ 20.83$$

If the commitment fee is ¼% on the *unused* portion of the line and the company has ₹ 50,000 in loans outstanding in May, the fee would be

$$(₹\ 1,00,000 - ₹\ 50,000) \times .0025 \times \frac{1}{12} = ₹\ 10.42$$

Compensating Balances

A bank may also charge for maintianing the line by requiring a certain level of demand deposit balances to be held at the bank. The bank may specify the amount of the balances that must be held, either in ₹ or as a percentage of the line, or the balance credits that must be generated by the balances held. Similar to a cash free assessment, required balances may be based either on the total line or on the unused portion of the line. Occasionally a bank offers several options and allows the borrower to choose. At one time, the use of balances was the most common form of compensation for a credit line. Due to competitive pressures and attention to cash management by financial managers, the most common compensation for a credit line today is commitment fees.

Interest Rate

The second element in the compensation for a credit line is the interest rate paid on borrowings against the line. Virtually all credit lines carry a variable interest rate. The base for the rate depends, at least in part, upon the size and financial soundness of the borrower. A small to middle-market borrower is usually charge an interest rate that is based on the prime rate at the bank. The prime rate is an administered price set by the bank. It usually lags and fluctuates less than market rates. The rate on the credit line may range from prime to prime, depending largely on the financial strength of the borrower. Although each bank is free to set its own prime rate, in fact, when one influential bank changes its prime rate, most other banks quickly follow suit.

The line of credit may carry a set of *covenants,* or conditions, that limit the borrower's actions. These covenants may be positive, such as specifying the amount of working capital that must be maintained or certain financial ratios that must be achieved, or they may be negative, such as limiting the amount of capital expenditures, management salaries, or payment of dividends without the bank's prior approval. A common covenant on loans requires the borrower to provide the bank with financial statements on a timely, periodic basis. Covenants are more likely to appear on a line of credit to a small, less financially sound borrower for whose business the bank has little competition. When covenants are violated, the bank may require immediate repayment of outstanding notes. Usually, however, the bank will work with the borrower and attempt to bring about compliance in the near future.

Revolving Credit Agreement

A *revolving credit agreement* is similar to a line of credit but is usually established for more than 1 year. Common maturities extend for 2 or 3 years, during which time the customer may borrow and repay loans several times. Many revolving credit agreements contain a clause that allows the borrower to convert to a term loan. Frequently, the revolving credit agreement is renegotiated prior to its maturity; therefore, it may represent a continuous source of credit. This is sometimes referred to as an *evergreen loan.* The pricing on a revolving credit agreement is similar to that of a credit line. There is a commitment fee, met either by balances or by cash fees. The commitment fee is usually charged only on the unused portion of the credit agreement. The interest rate is almost always variable, based either on the prime rate or on money market rates.

Term Loan

A *term loan* is a more specific loan agreement than either a line of credit or a revolving credit agreement. It has a fixed maturity, usually of 2 to 5 years. The total amount of the loan is forwarded to the borrower on origination, and is repaid in periodic installments over the life of the loan. The repayment schedule may provide for equal payments (a combination of principal and interest), equal payments of principal, or some other schedule that matches the expected cash flow generating capability of the borrower. Repayments can be made monthly, quarterly, or semiannually.

A term loan is frequently obtained to cover a specific financial need that is expected to generate cash for the firm in the future, such as the purchase of a piece of capital equipment. When a tangible asset is financed, it may be pledged as collateral against the loan.

Most term loans carry variable interest rates. The base for these rates can be the same as those for credit lines, although the prime rate tends to be the base more frequently used to price term loans than is true for line of credit. There is seldom a requirement for a compensating balance. Because of the documentation frequently required for a term loan, there may be higher transaction costs, which are charged to the borrower in the form of an origination fee.

Letter of Credit

A *letter of credit* is a guarantee from a bank stating that a loan will be made to the client if specified conditions are met. It is commonly used to finance international trade. Because an exporter does not know an importer or because information, language, and cultural differences make it difficult to perform an adequate credit analysis, the exporter is not willing to sell to the importer on open credit. The importer presents a letter of credit from its bank, stating that the amount necessary for payment of the shipment will be paid on a specified date if conditions are met. This allows the importer to substitute the bank's credit rating for its own credit rating, thereby reducing the risk to the exporter.

Revocablility: A letter of credit can be either *revocable,* in which case the bank has the right to cancel the letter, or *irrevocable,* in which case the bank is bound to honour the terms if the specified conditions are met.

Pricing and Maturity: The maturity of the loan connected to the letter is dictated by the event that evoked the need for the letter. In most instances, it is of relatively short duration, for example, 30 to 90 days. The loan usually has a fixed rate based on the prevailing rate at the time the loan is issued. A commitment fee is usually charged for issuing a letter of credit, whether the loan is issued or not.

Banker's Acceptance: A *banker's acceptance* is generated by a time draft for which a bank is committed to making the payment to the holder at maturity. Banker's acceptances most frequently arise from international transactions when the conditions for a letter of credit have been met. Financing is provided when the bank makes an advance on the time draft issued. Some banks use the term banker's acceptance to refer to a loan issued to finance the purchase of specific good, whether for an international or a domestic transaction.

The loan made under a banker's acceptance is usually a discount loan. The discount from face value advanced to the borrower includes an amount for the interest at prevailing money market rates plus a fee, or a commission, of approximately 1.5%. Because of the commission, the cost to the borrower is usually above the commercial paper rate, but because it is based on money market rates, it may be below the prime rate.

A *reverse repurchase agreement,* or *reverse repo,* is simply the other side of the transaction in a repurchase agreement. The owner of a security needs funds for a shorter period than the maturity on a security held in its marketable securities portfolio. Rather than sell the security and have an investment decision to make when the funds are no longer needed, the firm sells the security with an agreement to repurchase it. This transaction is very similar to a loan with the security used as collateral. Since this is a very secure loan, the rate is usually below that on the other types of loans. The sale and repurchase prices are usually sufficiently below the face value of the secuirty used to ensure that the market value will not drop below the repurchase price during the term of the agreement.

UNSECURED BORROWING

Many lending agreements with commercial banks are unsecured. Lines of credit and revolving credit agreements are usually *unsecured loans,* made on the basis of the general financial strength of the borrower. This type of lending is sometimes referred to as *financial statement lending* because the loan is based on the strength of the income statement and the balance sheet of the organisation. The bank looks at both the cash flow generating capability of the organisation and the liquid resources as repayment sources. If the borrower defaults, the bank is a general creditor and has no specific claim on any assets of the firm. Although every company desires a loan with the fewest number of restrictions, banks make unsecured loans only to those customers for which they perceive little, if any, repayment problem. Unsecured loans are usually granted only to firms that have a long, stable history of solid financial performance.

SECURED BORROWING

A *secured loan* is any loan that, as part of the loan agreement, gives the lender a claim on a specific set of assets in case of default. There are two different approaches to secured lending: a collateralised loan and an asset-based loan.

Collateralised Loan

Under a *Collateralised loan,* the bank still views the credit from a financial statement perspective. However, the customer represents too much risk for the bank to grant credit on an unsecured basis. Just as fire regulations require that there be two exits to any building, the bank wants a second way out of a loan in case the primary "exit" is unavailable. Collateral pledged as security for the loan provides this second exit. If the borrower defaults on one of the conditions of the loan and the loan cannot be paid when it is called, the collateral can be seized, after the appropriate legal steps are taken, and disposed of to generate (hopefully) the funds to retire the loan. Although the collateral is sometimes called a *secondary repayment source,* the bank does not view it as a means of repaying the loan but rather as a way of minimising any potential loss if the loan is not repaid.

Asset-Based Loan

The assets most commonly taken as collateral for a short-term loan are accounts receivable and inventory. The bank wants to ensure that the collateral is adequate to cover the loan if the second way out must be used. There are some costs in attempting to use collateral as a means of repayment. If accounts receivable are taken as collateral, it may be difficult for the bank to collect from some accounts because of the lack of a future supplier relationship influencing the willingness to pay, or because of disputes over returned or defective merchandise. The bank may sell the accounts receivable to a collection agent, but this might be at a substantial discount from the full face value.

If inventory is used as collateral, it is necessary to find someone interested in purchasing it. Clearly, work-in-process inventory has very little value. Raw materials may have commodity value. Finished goods inventory may be converted to cash at a reasonable value. Frequently, the reason the borrower has difficultly in generating cash flows to pay off the loan is that sales are below projections. Under these conditions, the salability of the inventory at anything approaching full value must be questioned.

FINANCE COMPANIES

Finance companies are private companies that make commercial loans. A substantial difference between commercial banks and commercial finance companies is the source of funds. Commercial banks raise much of their funds from the public in the form of deposits, either demand or time. Commercial finance companies raise their funds through direct issuance of securities, such as commercial paper or longer-term notes, equity shares, and bank loans. Commercial finance companies restrict their loans to business firms and do not take deposits.

The loan customers of finance companies are frequently businesses that are considered too risky to be granted credit by a commercial bank. Consequently, commercial finance companies generally charge higher interest rates than banks and concentrate on asset-based lending.

The asset-based loans of commercial finance companies are similar to those of banks. They are based primarily on the underlying value of the assets rather than on the financial strength of the company. The asset most frequently used as collateral is accounts receivable. The loan base is a percentage of the acceptable receivables. Acceptable accounts are those from customers with an acceptable credit risk and a maturity shorter than a designated maturity, often three times normal credit terms. Accounts receivable are usually pledged as collateral on a non-notification, full-recourse basis: receivables customers are not notified of the arrangement, and the borrower has full responsibility for collection. When a receivable is either collected or the maturity exceeds the agreed maturity, it is no longer part of the borrowing base and the funds advanced against the collateral are repaid.

If the amount of acceptable accounts receivable is insufficient to meet the desired financing requirements, inventory and possible machinery and equipment may be used as collateral. The percentage of borrowing against the collateral is adjusted for the expected liquidation value. Commercial finance companies can be expected to take the steps necessary to ensure that the liquidation value of the assets is maintained at a level sufficient to cover the amount of the loan.

FACTORING

Although factoring of accounts receivable appears to be similar to a loan, with accounts receivable pledged as collateral, it is really quite different. *Factoring* is the sale of accounts receivable, usually without recourse, to another party, hereafter called the *factor*. Once the account has been purchased, it is the property and responsibility of the factor. There are three major types of factoring arrangements: (1) maturity factoring, (2) conventional factoring, and (3) maturity factoring with an assignment of equity.

Maturity Factoring

Maturity factoring consists of the sale of accounts receivable to a factor with no advance of funds at the time of sale. When the seller notifies the factor. The factor conducts a credit analysis of the potential customer and, if the risk is acceptable, approves the sale and assumes all responsibility for collection and bad debts. The seller notifies the customer to remit directly to the factor. The factor forwards cash to the seller in the amount of the receivable less the commission on an agreed-upon average maturity date.

Many companies using a factor do not have a credit department; the factor performs all of the credit and collection functions. The cost of using a factor may be less than the cost of establishing a credit department. The factor may be able to achieve economies of scale in credit analysis, administration, and collection of receivables. The factor deals with a broader group of customers than the seller and may have the opportunity to reduce risks through diversification. In industries with many small competitors, the factor may serve several competing manufacturers and have more leverage in collection than would any one company. Due to the nature of the credit function performed, most arrangements with a factor are of long duration, not an emergency sale of accounts receivable.

Conventional Factoring

In *Conventional factoring* the factor performs all of the functions of maturity factoring and also advances funds to the seller prior to the average maturity date of the receivables. The factor charges interest for the actual number of days the funds are advanced. The interest charge is usually tied to the prime rate of money center banks and has a risk premium.

Maturity Factoring with Assignment of Equity

This type of maturity factoring is similar to pledging accounts receivable in commercial bank borrowing. The factor in this case does not purchase receivables but makes loans against them with recourse to the seller if payments are not collected. The factor does provide a credit and collection service not provided when accounts receivable are pledged as collateral. After the factor approves a credit purchase, the factor invoices the customer and makes collections. As payments are received, the loan is paid off.

Cost of Factoring

The cost of using a factor has two distinct elements: (1) the factor's commission and (2) the interest cost of cash advances. Whether the factor's commission is included in the cost of financing depends upon how and why the factor is being used. If the seller is engaged in maturity factoring, the commission is viewed as a substitute for the cost of running a credit department. The correct use of the commission in this case is to compare the cost of using a factor with that of operating a credit department. The factor's commission is not part of the short-term financing cost. If the factor is used only occasionally—an unusual but sometimes employed practice—or if the company maintains its own credit department, the fee is an incremental cost in obtaining the financing. Thus, the factor's fee is considered part of the financing costs and is included in the calculation of the effective cost.

CAPTIVE FINANCE COMPANIES

A captive finance company is a wholly owned subsidiary that provides financing for distributors of the parent company's products, purchases installment receivables, and/or provides direct financing for retail sales. It performs the credit function of the parent company. The receivables appear on the subsidiary's books and not on those of the parent.

Since the consolidated position is the same with or without a subsidiary, the rationale for finance subsidiaries must be something other than the effect on the financial statements. The reasons given for the use of a finance subsidiary are as follows: (1) a captive finance company may stimulate sales by providing easier access to credit for distributors or retail customers; (2) it may be cheaper to operate the financing function separately from the other operations of the company and view the credit arm as a separate profit center; (3) the concentration of accounts receivable in a captive finance company may increase the total debt capacity of the firm or may lower the short-term borrowing costs by clearly defining the assets being financed.

OFF-BALANCE-SHEET FINANCING

Some companies use off-balance-sheet financing as an attempt to keep their financial statements "clean" and not distort financial ratios. Although in efficient markets the theoretical justification is weak, it is an avenue pursued in certain circumstances. The following is an example of how off-balance-sheet finance accounts receivable or to finance temporarily the construction of physical assets with short-term debt.

A company dealing with a highly seasonal supply of raw materials, such as a food processor, finds it worthwhile to purchase a year's supply of product at harvest. If the firm obtains short-term financing to support the purchase, the debt and the inventory appear on the balance sheet. The company will suffer a distortion in several financial ratios—for example inventory turnover, current ratio, quick ratio, and total debt to assets. Instead, the firm enters into a contract with a third party to purchase, warehouse, and sell the raw materials to the processor. The third party obtains financing for the materials purchased through a banker's acceptance. The contract purchase price between the processor and the third is set to cover the cost of the warehousing and financing. The cost of the goods sold is increased by the financing and warehousing costs.

CALCULATING THE COST OF A SOURCE OF SHORT-TERM FINANCING

The first step in structuring the firm's liabilities is to generate a list of the types of short-term debt that are available to the firm. If this listing shows that the minimum levels of the firm's accounts payable and accruals are such that no additional financing is needed and aggregate liquidity targets are satisfied, then the process need go no further; these two sources of financing will comprise the firm's short-term debt package. However, the minimum levels of these liabilities do not provide sufficient short-term financing for most firms. In such cases, it is often useful to calculate measures of the maximum amount of financing and the cost of the alternative sources of short-term debt. We call measures of these characteristics the *net availability* and the *compounded effective annual interest rate.*

Calculating Net Availability

To obtain the net availability from each source, the maximum amount of *net cash provided* by that source is calculated. This calculation is not as simple as it seems. The first thing to remember is that *cash financing* is what the firm requires. Thus, it is the *amount of cash that the firm receives* or the *amount of the delayed cash outflow* that comprises the relevant net availability.

Two problems often occur in determining this net availability from a potential source of financing. The first of these is *up-front expenses* that may make the amount of cash financing different from the face value of the debt. To see this, assume that one option in a firm's short-term financing package is 180-day discounted note with a ₹ 1,000 principal amount. The interest for the 180-day period will be 5 per cent. Such a note *will not provide ₹ 1,000 in financing.* Since the interest is discounted, the ₹ 1,000 note will net the firm only ₹ 950.00 in cash (equal to ₹ 1,000 minus interest of 0.05 (1000)). Similar up-front expenses occur for several other types of current debts, including skipping the discount on accounts payable. Assume that the firm has the option of skipping the discount on invoices with a face value of ₹ 50,000 that have terms of 2 per cent 10 days, net 90 days. If the firm pays in 10 days, the cash outflow will be ₹ 49,000; if it skips the discount, *only this amount of cash outflow is delayed.* The maximum financing from this source is ₹ 49,000, not ₹ 50,000. Any time that interest or other expenses are paid when financing is undertaken, and not at maturity, the net availability will be less than the face value of the liability.

A second problem in calculating the net availability from a liability occurs when *the financing from the liability changes over time.* There are several types of short-term financing with this characteristic, including short maturity term loans and accruals. For example, if the firm takes out a 180-day term loan with monthly amortisation payments, the financing will not be the principal amount of the term loan. Since the principal decreases over time (in a nonlinear fashion), the average financing will be some lesser amount.

For example, assume that the principal amount on such a loan was ₹ 10,000, the interest is 1 per cent per month, and equal monthly amortisation payments are required. An analysis of the net availability from such a loan is given in Table-1. The monthly payment is ₹ 1,725.48. Assuming that the payments on the loans are made at the end of the month, the beginning principal amounts constitute the financing for the month. For example, the financing provided by the loan for the second month is ₹ 8,374.52. The average financing over the term of the loan is ₹ 5,881.70.

TABLE-1

Term Loan:Average Financing

(in ₹)

Month	*Beginning Principal*	*Interest Payment*	*Principal Payment*	*Ending principal*
1	10,000.00	100.00	1,625.48	8,374.52
2	8,374.52	83.75	1,641.74	6,732.78
3	6,732.78	67.33	1,658.16	5,074.62
4	5,074.62	50.75	1,674.74	3,399.88
5	3,399.88	34.00	1,691.48	1,708.40
6	1,708.40	17.08	1,708.40	0.00
Average	5,881.70			

Let us illustrate changing availability over time with another example. Assume that a firm has a quarterly property tax liability with a face value of ₹ 100,000. It may choose to pay this liability on a monthly basis or to make the total payment at the end of the quarter. An analysis of the financing provided appears in Table 3. If the firm elects to pay at the end of each month, no month-end accrual occurs. However, if the firm chooses to pay at the end of the quarter, the accrued balance builds up over time, then is reduced to zero just before the end of the quarter. The delayed payments of ₹ 33,333 for the first and second months provide month-end financing for the next month. That is, the strategy of delaying payments from a monthly to a quarterly basis provides ₹ 33,333 in financing during the second month and ₹ 66,667 in financing during the third month.

TABLE-2

Tax Deferral Financing

(in ₹)

Month	*Outflow for Monthly Payment*	*Month-End Accrual*	*Outflow for Quarterly Payment*	*Month-End Accrual*	*Month-End Financing Provided*
1	33,333	0	0	33,333	33,333
2	33,333	0	0	66,667	66,667
3	33,333	0	1,00,000	0	0

These two types of difficulties must be kept in mind in calculating the maximum amount of financing (the net availability) that is provided by each potential source of current debt. However, as long as the analyst focuses on the *net cash yielded* at various times from a source of financing, errors will be avoided.

Calculating the Compounded Effective Annual Interest (EAI) Rate

Once the firm knows how much financing a source will yield, a second natural question is the cost of this financing. We call this the compounded effective annual interest rate or *compounded EAI* of the funding source. The compounded EAI is calculated the same way for any source of funding: it is the yearly *compounded internal rate of return for the cash flows from the funding source.* To compute this cost statistic, the analyst obtains the cash flows for the funding source and their timing, calculates the internal rate of return (IRR), and compounds this IRR to a yearly basis. This gives a comparative cost statistic for the various available sources of funding which is based on net cash flows and is properly adjusted for the different maturities of the various funding sources. For purposes of this discussion, we will center on before-tax cash flows in calculating this cost measure. To illustrate, consider a firm is selling ₹ 10,00,000 per month on terms of 2 per cent 10 days, net 60 days. Historically, the firm has collected 20 per cent of its receivables on the discount date; an additional 74 per cent of sales are collected on the sixtieth day. Five per cent of sales will be disputed on product quality grounds and will not be collected until 120 days from the date of sale. The remaining 1 per cent are bad debts and are never collected. Credit department costs are 1.2 per cent of sales and are paid 30 days after sales occur. A factor has made an offer of discount factoring. In this offer, the firm will receive the face value of invoices, less a 2.5 per cent factor's fee, 1.75 per cent interest, discount expense, and a 5 per cent product quality hold-back; the cash will go to the seller immediately after sales are made. In this factoring arrangement, the factor absorbs any bad debts. The product quality holdback will be settled on the 120th day, and the borrower will receive the remaining five per cent at that time. What is the effective cost of this factoring?

The necessary analysis is presented in a spreadsheet format in Table-3 The total net cash flow without factoring is ₹ 20,500 greater than that with factoring, but the cash flows from factoring occur earlier in time. The cash flow at day 120 happens to be the same in either case and thus has no bearing on the analysis. Since th last difference in the cash flows occurs at day 60, the present-value interest factors have been computed for a 60-day period using the 60-day rate. The rate of 2.7462 per cent for this 60-day period produces a net present-value of zero in the differential cash flows. The yearly compounded rate is 17.65 per cent.

The computation of the net availabilities and compounded EAIs for each of the firm's potential sources of short-term financing may (under certain circumstances) be used to formulate a financing plan for the firm.

Under some limited conditions, the two parameters the net availability (which measures the maximum cash financing from the source) and the compounded EAI (which measures the costliness of a source alone) may be used to obtain an optimum structure for the firm's current liability package. To be used in this fashion, the net availability and compounded EAI for a source must *completely* capture the relative desirability of that source. For this complete capturing to occur, there must be no interactions among the EAIs and availabilities of the various sources. All sources must be divisible (utilisable in part) without affecting their EAIs. All source must provide funding for one planning period only, or must be refundable at no cost. Finally, the firm must not be concerned with the differential effects of the various sources on aggregate liquidity.

TABLE-3

Discount Factoring : Cost Analysis

Sales	₹ 10,00,000
Discount	.02%
Percentage of taking Discount	20%
Discount Expense	₹ 4,000
Factor Fee	.025 sales
Factor Expense	₹ 25,000 for sales of ₹ 10,00,000
Interest Rate	.0175 sales
Interest Expense	₹ 17,500 for sales of ₹ 10,00,000
Bad Debt Rate	.01 of sales
Credit Department Costs	.012 of sales
60-Day Discount Rate	.027462

Day	*Cash flow, No factoring*	*Cash flow, Discount factoring*	*Difference in Cash Flows*	*PV Factor*	*Contribution to NPV*
0	0	9,03,500	-9,03,500	1.00	-9,03,500
10	1,96,000	0	1,96,000	.995495	1,95,117
30	-12,000	0	12,000	.986545	-11,839
60	7,40,000	0	7,40,000	.973272	7,20,221
120	50,000	50,000	0	.047258	0
Total NCF	9,74,000	9,53,500			NPV 0

Compounded Discount Rate .176507

If these conditions are satisfied, the procedure for generating a minimum-cost plan for the structure of current liabilities is straightforward, and consists of the following steps:

1. List all the potential sources of short-term financing for the firm, starting from the lowest EAI and proceeding to the highest.
2. Starting with the source having the lowest EAI, proceed to utilise sequentially more expensive sources until the firm's financing needs are fulfilled.

We call this method the *sequential method* because source are chosen sequentially based on their costliness, from the cheapest to the most expensive. An illustrative example of this procedure is useful. Assume that a firm needs short-term financing totaling ₹ 6 crore. Five sources of financing are available. Source A has an EAI of 12.75 per cent and a net availability of ₹ 3.14 crore. Source B has an EAI of 11.25 per cent and a net availability of ₹ 1.26 crore. Source C has an EAI of 18.75 per cent and a net availability ₹ 5.50 crore. Source D has EAI of 15.00 per cent and a net availability ₹ 3.50 crore. Source E has an EAI of 10.50 per cent and a net availability of ₹ 2.50crores. There is no interaction among the EAIs or availabilities for these sources (any source may be adopted without affecting the cost or availability of any other source). All the source are completely divisible; the first amount of financing from a source has the same EAI as all other amounts of financing from the source. All the sources are refundable at no cost, and the firm is unconcerned about differences in liquidity among the sources. *What is the minimum-cost financing package?*

The necessary analysis, performed according to the sequential method, is presented in Table-4. Data on the potential short-term financing sources are entered in columns 1through 3, starting with the lowest-cost source and proceeding to the highest-cost source. Columns 4 through 6 determine the financing plan. If the net availability (in column 3) is less than the required financing (in column 4), the net availability is displayed; otherwise, the required financing is displayed. Column 6 contains the remaining financing after the use of the source on that line. For source E, the starting requirement is ₹ 6 crore. The availability is ₹ 2.50 crore. After utilising this source, ₹ 3.50 crores in required financing remains. This amount is also the starting required financing for the next source.

The optimum financing plan appears in column 5, and utilises ₹ 2.50 crore in financing from source E, ₹ 1.36 crore, in financing from source B, and ₹ 2.14 crore from source A. Financing from sources D and C is not utilised. The weighted-average EAI for the plan is calculated in columns 7 and 8. The EAI for this plan is 11.69 per cent, and represents the yearly cost of the minimum-cost financing package from these sources of short-term financing.

TABLE-4

Sequential Method

Source (1)	*Comp-EAI* (2)	*Net Availability* (3)	*Stating Requirement* (4)	*Usage from Source* (5)	*Remaining Requirement* (6)	*Per cent of Total EAI* (7)	*Contri-bution Weighted* (8)
E	10.50	2,50,00,000	6,00,00,000	2,50,00,000	3,50,00,000	.417	4.598
B	11.25	1,36,00,000	3,50,00,000	1,36,00,000	2,14,00,000	.227	2.554
A	12.75	3,14,00,000	2,14,00,000	2,14,00,000	0	.356	4.539
D	15.00	3,50,00,000	0	0	0	0	0
C	18.75	5,50,00,000	0	0	0	0	0
		15,00,00,000		6,00,00,000		1.000	11.691

ILLUSTRATIVE PROBLEMS

1. Madhav Manufacturing is considering entering into an agreement with a factoring company. The main details of the proposed factoring agreement are:

(a) The agreement will be for a minimum period of 2 years, thereafter cancellable at three months notice.

(b) Basic factoring services will be provided for a charge of 1½% of Madhav's annual turnover, the charge payable annually in arrears. Entering into the factoring agreement will enable Madhav to save ₹ 6,00,000 per year in office and other expenses—the savings being effected in a lump sum each year end.

(c) The factor is willing to advance Madhav up to 80% of the invoice value of factored debts immediately a sale is invoiced. A commission of 2½% will be deducted from the gross amount of any funds advanced (i.e. up to 80% of invoice value). The factor will also charge interest at 15% per annum, applied on a simple monthly basis, on the gross funds advanced, i.e. before deduction of the 2½% commission. Both interest charge and commission will be deducted from the funds advanced to Madhav.

(d) The factor is confident that the average collection period will be reduced from the current figure of 90 days to 70 days, or perhaps to only 60 days, although a transition period of up to 6 months will be required before the reduction is fully effected. On receipt of cash from Madhav's invoiced debtors the factor will immediately pay to Madhav all sums outstanding concerning that invoice.

Madhav's annual credit sales amount of ₹ 7.2 crore which are spread evenly throughout the year.

Required

(a) Calculate the effective annual factoring cost, as a percentage of the funds improvement caused by factoring, for a full year after any transition period under each of the following separate conditions:

  (i) Madhav will not take advantage of the factor's willingness to advance funds but the factor will reduce the average collection period to 70 days.

  (ii) Madhav will take full advantage of the factor's willingness to advance funds and the average collection period:

    (a) Remains at 90 days, and

    (b) is reduced to 60 days.

(b) Madhev can borrow at 16% per annum and could, by spending ₹ 3,00,000 per annum payable at the end of each year, reduce the average collection period to 80 days without factoring whereas the factor would reduce the collection period to 70 days. Advise Madhav whether it should enter into the factoring agreement and, if so, whether funds should be obtained from the factor rather than by borrowing.

(You may assume a 360 day year split into 12 equal months. Taxation may be ignored)

Solution

(a) (i)

Current average debtors:	$₹\ 7.2\ \text{crore} \times \frac{90}{360} =$	₹ 1.8 crore
New average debtors:	$₹\ 7.2\ \text{crore} \times \frac{70}{360} =$	1.40
Funds improvement caused by factoring		₹ 4 crore
Cost of factoring:		
Factoring services: 1½% × ₹ 7.2 =		10,80,000
Less: Savings		6,00,000
		₹ 4,80,000
Effective annual cost:	$\frac{₹\ 48,00,000}{₹\ 4\ \text{crore}} \times 100\% =$	12%

(ii) (1)

Funds advanced:

Gross funds advanced: 80% × ₹ 7.2 crore × $\frac{90}{360}$		₹ 1.44 crore
Less: Commission: 2½% × ₹ 1.44 crore =	3,60,000	
Interest: 1.25% × ₹ 1.44 crore × 3 =	5,40,000	
		9,00,000
Funds improvement caused by factoring		₹ 1.35 crore

Total annual cost of factoring:

Factoring services—net cost	4,80,000
Commission: 2½% × 0.8 × ₹ 72 crore m. =	14,40,000
Interest: 15% × ₹ 1.44 crore m. =	21,60,000
Total annual cost	₹ 40,80,000

Effective annual cost: $\frac{₹\ 40,80,000}{₹\ 1,35,00,000} \times 100\% =$ 30.2%

(2)

Funds advanced:

Advance from factor:

Gross funds advanced: 80% × ₹ 7.2 crore m. × $\frac{60}{320}$ =		₹ 96,00,000
Less: Commission: 2½% × ₹ 96,00,000	2,40,000	

Interest: 1.25% × ₹ 96,00,000 × 2 =	₹ 2,40,000	4,80,000
Funds advanced		91,20,000

Improvement in average debtors:

Current average debtors: ₹ 7.2 crore $\times \frac{90}{360}$ =	1.8 crore	
New average debtors: ₹ 7.2 crore $\times \frac{90}{360}$ =	1.2 crore	
Improvement in average debtors		60,00,000
Improvement caused by factoring		₹ 1,51,20,000

Total annual cost of factoring:

Factoring services—net cost		4,80,000
Commission:	2½% × 0.8 × ₹ 7.2 crore m. =	14,40,000
Interest:	15% × ₹ 96,00,000 =	14,40,000
Total annual cost:		₹ 33,60,000

Effective annual cost: $\frac{₹\,33{,}60{,}000}{₹\,1{,}51{,}20{,}000} \times 100\% =$ 22.2%

(b)

Current average debtors: ₹ 7.2 crore $\times \frac{90}{360}$	₹ 1.8 crore
Revised average debtors: ₹ 7.2 crore $\times \frac{80}{360}$ =	₹ 1.6 crore
Funds improvement	₹ 20,00,000

Effective annual cost of improvement: $\frac{₹\,3{,}00{,}000}{₹\,20{,}00{,}000} \times 100\% =$ 15%

Hence as the incremental cost of this internal improvement exceeds the cost of factoring-based finance (calculated in (a)(i), factoring is the cheaper of the two sources of finance and both are less expensive than borrowing.

This may be seen more clearly by examining the incremental costs of the factoring-based benefit compared with this internal improvement:

	Internal improvement	*Factoring based improvement*	*Factoring less internal*
	(1)	*(2)*	*(2)-(1)*
Finance improvement	₹ 20,00,000	₹ 40,00,000	₹ 20,00,000
Cost	₹ 3,00,000	₹ 4,80,000	₹ 1,80,000

$$\frac{₹\ 1{,}80{,}000}{₹\ 20{,}00{,}000} \times 100\% = 9\%$$

Therefore, if Madhav is in need of additional funds, the factoring agreement is the best of the three sources considered.

However, having entered into the factoring agreement, and obtained the benefit of the factor reducing the collection period to 70 days, no further funds should be obtained from the factor as the implicit interest rate always exceeds the 16% borrowing rate. For each ₹ 100 gross borrowed the costs are at least:

Interest	₹ 15 per annum
Commission	₹ 2.5
Total	₹ 17.5

Funds provided : ₹ 100 – ₹ 17.5 = ₹ 82.5

Effective cost: $\frac{₹\ 17.5}{₹\ 82.2} \times 100\% = 21.2\%$

However, this percentage cost will increase with short borrowings as the 2½% commission is a fixed charges irrespective of length of borrowing.

Should Madhev require further finance, it should be borrowed at 16% rather than obtained from the factor.

2. Kunal Ltd. is a small manufacturing company which is experiencing a short-term liquidity crisis during 2011. The company accountant has estimated that by the end of October 2011 a further ₹ 2,00,000 of extra funds will be required. Since the company already has a large overdraft, its banker will not advance any more funds. Three solutions to the problem have been put forward:

(a) *Option 1:* A short term loan of ₹ 2,00,000 could be raised for 6 months from 1 September 2011 at an annual interest rate of 18%. This would be obtained through a finance company, but there would be no costs involved in raising the funds.

(b) *Option 2:* The company could forego cash discounts of 2% which are obtained from suppliers of raw materials for payment within 30 days. The maximum credit which could safely be taken is 90 days. Monthly purchase of raw materials amount to ₹ 1,02,041 before discounts. Kunal Ltd. would forego the discount for 6 months before reviewing the position again.

(c) *Option 3:* The company could factor its trade debtors. A factor has been found who would be prepared, for a period of 6 months from 1 September to advance Kunal Ltd. 75% of the value of its invoices less the deduction of factoring charges, immediately on receipt of the invoices. (You may assume that all invoices are sent out at the end of the month of sale). The factoring charges would consist of:

(i) an interest charge of 15% p.a. on the amount of money advanced, calculated on a day-to-day basis, and deducted in advance;

(ii) a fee for taking on the task of collecting debts, amounting to 2% of the total invoices and deducted in advance. Monthly sales are expected to be ₹ 3,00,000. The factor would pay the balance owing on the invoices on receipt of the money from the debtors. On average, debtors pay at the end of the month following the month of sale. As a result of using the factor, Kunal Ltd. estimates that there would be savings in administration costs of ₹ 4,000 per month.

Any surplus funds in excess of the ₹ 2,00,000 required would be used to reduce the bank overdraft, which costs 1% per month.

Required:

(a) Show which of the three options is cheapest

(b) If the factoring arrangement is the option preferred, what would be the cash flow position for receipts for the period September 2011-April 2012

(c) Briefly explain the other considerations which should be taken into account when choosing between the three options.

Ignore taxation.

Solution

(a) *Cost option 1*

Interest ₹ 2,00,000 × 18% × ½ = ₹ 18,000

Cost option 2

With discount of 2% the monthly payments equal ₹ 1,00,000. Therefore stop paying for supplies of September and October within 30 days. This makes ₹ 2,00,000 available by end-October.

The result is that for each of the six months in which payments are delayed an extra payment of ₹ 2041 has to be made (the discount forgone). This extra payment has an opportunity cost, either cost of extra money borrowed or interest missed. Assume the cost of such opportunities is 18% per annum (i.e. 1½% per month).

The total cost of this policy can be calculated using the terminal value of an annuity table. For six periods it equals ₹ 12,715 (i.e. ₹ 2,041 × 6.2300)

Cost option 3

Basic advance		₹ 2,25,000
Less: Fee	₹ 6000	
interest	₹ 2700	8,700
Net advance		₹ 2,16,300

Interest equals 1.25% per month on amount advanced

Therefore ₹ 2,19,000 (after fee) equals 101.25%

100% equals ₹ 2,16,300. The difference, ₹ 2,700 is the interest charge

The cost of this policy is:

Fee	₹ 6,000

Interest	2,700
	8,700
Less: Administration saving	-4,000
interest at 1% (on balance) (₹ 16,300 + ₹ 4,000)	−200
	₹ 4,500 per month

This is the most expensive of the three alternatives

	In ₹ 000s							
	Sept.	*Oct.*	*Nov.*	*Dec.*	*Jan.*	*Feb.*	*Mar.*	*Apr.*
Investment	-200							
Advance (net)	+216	+216	+216	+216	+216	+216	+216	+216
Balance on sale		+75	+75	+75	+75	+75	+75	+75
Sales (August)	+300							

3. Navin Ltd. has experienced difficulty with the collection of debts from export customers. At present the company makes no special arrangements for export sales. As a result the company is considering either:

(a) employing the services of a non-recourse export factoring company;

(b) insuring its exports against non-payment through a government agency.

The two alternatives also provide new possible ways of financing exports sales.

An export factor will, if required, provide immediate finance of 80% of export credit sales at an interest rate of 2% above bank base rate. The service fee for the debt collection is 2½% of credit sales. If the factor is used administrative savings of ₹ 1,25,000 per year should be possible. The government agency short term comprehensive insurance policy costs ₹ 3.50 per ₹ 1000 insured and covers 90% of the risk of non-payment for exports. For a further payment of ₹ 2.50 per ₹ 1,000 insured the agency will provide its guarantee which enables bank finance for the insured exports to be raised at 5/8% above bank base rate. This finance is only available in conjunction with the government agency comprehensive insurance policy. Navin normally has to pay 2½% above base rate for its overdraft finance.

Navin's annual exports total ₹ 65,00,000. All export orders are subject to a 15% initial deposit. The export sales are on open account terms of 45 days credit, but on average payment has been 30 days late. Approximately ½%, by value, of credit sales result in bad debts which have to be written off. Clearing bank base rate is 10%.

Required:

(a) Determine which combination of export administration and financing Navin Ltd. should use.

(b) Outline the main debt collection techniques with respect to sales in the home market that are available to financial managers.

(c) Discuss how a manufacturing company might devise an effective debt collection system.

Solution

(a) The possible combinations of export administration and financing are: 1.Continue as at present; 2. Agency insurance plus normal overdraft finance; 3. Agency insurance and guarantee with cheaper finance; 4. Factoring with normal overdraft finance; 5. Factoring with finance from the factor (80%) and overdraft finance (20%).

Alternative (4) may be eliminated as normal overdraft finance is more expensive than finance from the factor.

(1) *Continue as at present*

Annual credit sales ₹ 55,25,000

Average credit period taken 75 days

Overdraft cost 12½%

	₹
Annual cost of granting credit ₹ 55,25,000 × $\frac{75}{365}$ × 12½% =	1,41,910
Cost of bad debts	27,620
Total cost	1,69,530

(2) *Agency with normal overdraft*

Annual cost of granting credit, as above	1,41,910
Cost of bad debts (10% risk retained)	2,760
Cost of agency insurance on ₹ 55,25,000 at ₹ 3.50 per ₹ 1,000	19,340
Total cost	1,64,010

(3) *Agency insurance and guarantee*

Interest cost $10\frac{5}{8}$ %

	₹
Annual cost of granting credit ₹ 55,25,000 × $\frac{75}{365}$ × $10\frac{5}{8}$% =	1,20,620
Cost of bad debts	2,760
Cost of agency insurance	19,340
Cost of agency guarantee	13,810
Total cost	1,56,530

(4) *Factoring using factor finance*

80% financed by the factor, 20% by overdraft

	₹
Annual cost of granting credit ₹ 44,20,000 × $\frac{75}{365}$ × 12% =	1,08,990
plus ₹ 11,05,000 × $\frac{75}{365}$ × 12½%	28,380

Service fee		1,38,120
Administrative savings		(1,25,000)
	Total cost	1,50,490

This is the cheapest alternative

(b) Debt collection techniques include: 1. Statements at monthly or other intervals to draw attention to unpaid debts; 2. Reminder letters, either in a standard format or individually produced. A series of standard letters of varying degrees of severity is common; 3. Telephone calls to extract promise of payment; 4. Telex reminders; 5. Customer visits by sales staff. 6. Customer visits by credit control staff. 7. The use of external agencies either: (i) debt collection agencies; (ii) trade protection associations; (iii) factoring companies; 8. Threaten to withdraw normal credit facilities, and cash discounts where they exist unless payment is made; 9. Threaten to withhold future supplies until payment is made. 10. Solicitor's letter threatening legal action; 11. Legal action in the court.

(c) There is no optimal debt collection policy that is applicable to all companies. Debt collection policies will differ according to the nature of the product and the degree of competition.

An effective debt control system is, however, likely to have several features: 1. Good-quality, well-trained credit personnel. 2. Formal set procedures for the collection of overdue debts, including an efficient reminder system. Telephone calls are believed to be more effective than statements or reminder letters. These procedures should be known to all relevant staff, including sales staff, and applied according to an agreed time schedule. The most effective system for an individual company will be established by experience. Key factors will include: (i) *Cost*—the use of legal action, customer visits, and outside agencies may improve debt collection and reduce bad debts, but these measures are very expensive; the cost of debt collection should not normally exceed the debts to be collected, except as a deterrent effect to other customers; (ii) *Customer relationships*—customer goodwill is important and overzealous collection techniques might lose future custom. 3. Use of computerised monitoring systems for overdue accounts. 4. Debt collection policies must not be regarded as completely inflexible, and systems should be modified as circumstances change.

4. Falling interest rates within the past several years has prompted Vivek Kapoor, the Chairman of Mehta Industries, to evaluate the company's current policy of not taking most vendor discounts. Most of Mehta's purchases of raw materials and supplies are made with four vendors (identified as A, B, C, and D, for simplicity). Since the company seldom takes discounts, it purchases from the vendor offering the lowest price, although it maintains some activity with each supplier in order to continue good will. Shortages sometimes occur within the industry, and it is helpful to be an active customer to avoid being cut off completely during tight periods.

Credit terms for the four vendors are as follows:

Vendor	*Terms*
A	2/10; net 60
B	1/20; net 30
C	2/30; net 60
D	3/10; net 30

For the upcoming period, Kapoor believes the vendors will offer identical materials prices. He has decided to allocate Mehta's total purchases of ₹ 200,00,000 as follows: 80% to the vendor offering the lowest-costing credit, 10% to the next lowest, 6% to third lowest, and 4% to the highest. He feels that this will provide Mehta with both reasonably low purchase costs and will maintain its active status with each vendor. To evaluate the situation, Kapoor believes the full cost of negotiated credit will be 20%.

Rank the vendors according to their credit costs, and determine a purchase amount from each.

Solution

1. To determine which vendors offer acceptable discount terms, calculate each vendor's opportunity cost of not taking the discount.

A (2/10; net 60):	(0.02/0.98) × [360/(60 – 10)]	=	0.1469
B (1/20; net 30):	(0.01/0.00) × [360/(30 – 20)]	=	0.3636
C (2/30; net 60):	(0.02/0.98) × [360/(60 – 30)]	=	0.2449
D (3/10; net 30);	(0.03/0.97) × [360/(30 – 10)]	=	0.5567

   Since the cost of alternative credit is 0.20, all purchases from vendors B, C, and D should be paid at the end of their respective discount period. However, purchases from vendor A should not be paid until the end of the credit period.

2. Ranking the vendors is a bit more difficult. Since discounts will be taken from vendors B, C and D, their credit periods are no longer relevant, since all bits will be paid within discount periods. It's clear that C is better than B because the former offers both a greater discount and a longer discount period. C is also better than D because the extra 1 percentage point D offers is not worth paying 20 days sooner; that is, the opportunity cost of forgoing the larger discount is less than the cost of funds (0.20), as follows:

$$\text{Opportunity cost of forgoing D's added discount} = \frac{0.03 - 0.02}{1.0 - (0.03 - 0.02)} \times \frac{360}{30 - 10}$$

$$= \frac{0.01}{0.99} \times \frac{360}{20} = 0.1818$$

3. Also, C is better than A (same discount and longer discount period), and D is better than A (better discount and same discount period). However, is B better than A? No, because B's 1% discount is not worth the additional 40 days (60 - 20) taken to pay A:

$$\frac{0.01}{0.99} \times \frac{360}{40.} = 0.0909$$

4. Thus, the ₹ 2,00,00,000 purchases are allocated as follows:

C:	0.80 × ₹ 2.00 crore	=	₹ 1.60 crore
D:	0.10 × ₹ 2.00 crore	=	₹ 0.20 crore
A:	0.06 × ₹ 2.00 crore	=	₹ 0.12 crore
B:	0.04 × ₹ 2.00 crore	=	₹ 0.08 crore

5. Ajanta Arts has maintained an excellent working relationship with its commercial bank. It has an average monthly balance of about 135,000 and the company typically arranges a revolving credit agreement with a limit of ₹ 10,00,000. Ravinder Jain the Chairman, has made changes recently that cause him to question whether the credit agreement is in the company's best interest. He has initiated cash management techniques that could allow the cash account to be reduced to ₹ 60,000, if possible. It is not possible, however, since the bank insists that a compensating balance be maintained. The requirement is 20% of actual amounts borrowed. Another concern to Jain is the commitment fee, which is 0.005 on the average unused portion of the credit limit.

For the upcoming year, the Company's borrowing needs will be ₹ 600,000 *not including* the borrowing needed to maintain the compensating balance. Jain believes that the bank will charge 8% interest on the average borrowing. He is considering not renewing the agreement and, instead, arranging a series of term loans that will average ₹ 600,000. He expects the interest on these loans will average 9%.

Should the company continue its current arrangement with the bank, or should it select the new credit source?.

Solution

1. Determine the required loan amount (*RLA*) as follows:

$$RLA = ₹\ 6{,}00{,}000 + (0.20\ RLA - ₹\ 60{,}000)$$
$$0.8\ RLA = ₹\ 5{,}40{,}000$$
$$RLA = ₹\ 675{,}000$$

2. Next, determine interest on this average balance: ₹ 675,000 × 0.08 = ₹ 54,000.
3. The average unused portion of the line = ₹ 3,25,000 (₹ 10,00,000 – ₹ 6,75,000), which has a cost of ₹ 1,675 (₹ 325,000 × 0.005).
4. Adding these two and dividing by the usable funds of ₹ 6,00,000 gives the annual percentage cost of 0.09271 (₹ 55,625/₹ 6,00,000).
5. Evaluate the proposal. Since this exceeds the annual cost of 0.090 on the alternative credit arrangement, the alternative is the better choice. However, there are intangibles Jain should consider. First, the credit limit guarantees available credit up to ₹ 10,00,000. Does the alternative have any guarantees? Second, will the company's relationship with the bank weaken if the agreement is not renewed?

QUESTIONS

1. Define and discuss the function of *collateral* in short-term credit arrangements.
2. How is the annual financing cost for a short-term financing source calculated? How does the annual financing cost differ from the true annual percentage rate?
3. Explain the difference between *spontaneous* and *negotiated* sources of short-term credit.
4. Under what condition or conditions is trade credit *not* a "cost-free" source of funds to the firm?

5. Explain the differences between a line of credit and a revolving credit agreement.
6. What are some of the disadvantages of relying too heavily on commercial paper as a source of short-term credit?
7. Explain why the annual financing cost of secured credit frequently is higher than that of unsecured credit.
8. Explain why banks normally include a "clean-up" provision in a line of credit agreement.
9. What savings are realised when accounts receivable are factored rather than pledged?
10. Under what condition or conditions, if any, might a firm find it desirable to borrow funds from a bank or other lending institution in order to take a cash discount?
11. How do cash forecasting and short-term borrowing strategies relate?
12. Compare and contrast the three short-term borrowing strategies. Which strategy would generally result in the lowest borrowing cost? The highest borrowing cost? The most liquidity? The least liquidity?
13. How does the amount of buffer that a treasurer decides to use when establishing a line of credit affect the effective cost of the credit line?
14. What factors cause the nominal rate on a credit line to differ from its effective rate?
15. What factors cause the nominal rate on commercial paper to differ from its effective rate?
16. How does a firm's short-term financing strategy affect its liquidity?

PROBLEMS

1. Sudha Enterprises is considering borrowing ₹ 10,00,000 for 182 days from its bank. Sudha will pay ₹ 60,000 of interest at maturity, and it will repay the ₹ 10,00,000 principal at maturity. (a) Calculate the loan's annual financing cost; (b) Calculate the loan's annual percentage rate.

2. Calculate the *annual percentage rate* of forgoing the cash discount under each of the following credit terms:

(a) 2/10 net 60.
(b) 2/10, net 30.

3. Determine the *annual financing cost* of forgoing the cash discount if the credit terms are "1/10, net 30," and the invoice is not paid until it is 20 days past due.

4. Determine the annual financing cost of a 1-year (365 day), ₹ 10,000 discounted bank loan at a stated annual interest rate of 9.5 per cent. Assume that no compensating balance is required.

5. Ranger Enterprises is considering pledging its receivables to finance a needed increase in working capital. Its commercial bank will lend 75 per cent of the pledged receivables at 1.5 percentage points above the prime rate, which is currently 12 per cent. In addition, the bank charges a service fee equal to 1.0 per cent of the pledged receivables. Both interest and the service fee are payable at the end of the borrowing period. Ranger's average collection period is 50 days, and it has receivables totaling ₹ 5 crore that the bank has indicated are acceptable as collateral. Calculate the annual financing cost for the pledged receivables.

6. Designer Textiles, Inc., is considering factoring its receivable. The company's average collection period is 60 days, and its average level of receivables is ₹ 2.5 crore. Designer's bad-debt losses average ₹ 15,000 a month. If the company factors its receivables, it will save ₹ 4,000 a month by eliminating its credit department. The factor has indicated that it requires a 10 per cent reserve for returns and allowances and charges a 2.5 per cent factoring commission. The factor will advance Designer funds at 4 per cent over prime, which is currently 8 per cent.

(a) Determine the annual financing, *before* considering cost savings and bad-debt losses.

(b) Determine the annual financing cost, *after* considering cost savings and bad-debt losses.

7. The Odessa Supply Company is considering obtaining a loan from a sales finance company secured by inventories under a field warehousing arrangement. Odessa would be permitted to borrow up to ₹ 3,00,000 under such an arrangement at an annual interest rate of 10 per cent. The additional cost of maintaining a field warehouse is ₹ 16,000 per year. Determine the annual financing cost of a loan under this arrangement if Odessa borrows the following amounts: (a) ₹ 3,00,000; (b) ₹ 2,50,000

8. Hari Music Needs to raise ₹ 3,00,000 to increase its working capital. The bank, mindful of Hari's strained financial condition, has refused to loan the firm the needed funds. Hari's is considering *stretching* its accounts payable in order to raise the funds. Current credit terms are "3/ 10, net 30." Payments beyond the credit period are subject to a 1 per cent per month penalty. Hari purchases ₹ 1,25,000 per month from its suppliers and currently takes cash discounts. If Hari is able to raise the ₹ 3,00,000 it needs by stretching its accounts payable, determine the annual financing cost of this source of financing. For this problem, assume that a year consists of twelve 30-day months.

9. As finance manager of your firm, you wish to establish a credit line facility to cover an expected average usable funds of ₹ 16 crore. You have asked two banks to submit proposals for a credit line of ₹ 25 crore. Based on the credit line of ₹ 25 crore, ABC Bank proposes a nominal rate of 10%, a commitment fee of 0.25% on the unused portion of the credit line, and 20% compensating balances on the amount borrowed. XYZ Bank offers a rate of 9% if the size of the credit line is ₹ 40 crore. In addition, the commitment fee on the credit line is 20 basis points and compensating balances of 30% will be required on the amount borrowed.

Calculate the effective cost of both proposals and indicate which proposal should be taken.

PART - VI

SELECTED TOPICS IN CONTEMPORARY FINANCE

27

MERGERS AND ACQUISITIONS

INTRODUCTION

Although growth by itself is not the primary objective of the firm, it often is an important secondary one. Growth usually relates to achievement of the basic corporate goal, maximisation of value of the equity in the long run. Without the expectation of growth, it may be difficult or impossible to attract and hold the aggressive managerial personnel vital to success of the firm. Growth may be attained either internally or externally. Internal growth is achieved through the capital investment process. External growth is accomplished through business combination, commonly known as merger or acquisition. Both types of growth have figured importantly in the development of nearly all major business corporations.

In this chapter we shall first discuss the concept of merger, types of mergers, in economic basis or motives of merging, negotiation process and valuing the target company. Then consolidation and holding companies will be treated.

MERGER

A merger occurs when two or more firms are combined and the resulting firm maintains the identity of one of the firms. Usually, the assets and liabilities of the smaller firms are merged into those of the larger firms. Merger, a form of external expansion, should be undertaken only when they are expected to enhance share value. A merger may take the legal form of either a statutory merger or a purchase of assets (and often assumption of liabilities) of the target firm.

Statutory Merger

In a statutory merger, so called because it is executed under the statutes of the state of incorporation, the stock of the target firm is *directly exchanged* for stock of the acquiring firm, and the legal existence of the target firm automatically ceases. Although the legal form implies a stock-for-stock exchange, the acquiring firm may purchase the stock of the target for cash or by exchanging other securities and then, as the sole stockholder of the target, exchange the stock in a statutory merger.

Purchase of Assets

The acquiring firm might purchase the assets and, usually, assume the liabilities of the target firm. The purchase may be for cash or securities of the acquiring firm. After the purchase, the sole assets of the acquired firm are the cash and/or securities received in the exchange. After any liabilities not assumed by the acquiring firm are paid, the acquired firm is liquidated by distributing its assets (cash and/or securities of the acquiring firm) to its stockholders in a liquidating dividend. Then the acquired corporation is formally dissolved.

Regardless of the legal form used, holders of a stipulated majority of the equity of the acquired firm must approve the merger. Depending on its charter, approval of holders of a majority of the stock of the acquiring firm may or may not be required.

TYPES OF MERGERS

The *four* types of mergers are the (1) *horizontal merger*, (2) *vertical merger*, (3) *congeneric merger*, and (4) *conglomerate merger*. A horizontal merger results when two firms *in the same line of business* are merged. An example would be the merger of two machine-tool manufacturers. This form of merger results in the expansion of a firm's operations in a given product line and at the same time eliminates a competitor. A vertical merger occurs when a firm acquires *a supplier or a customer*. For example, the merger of a machine-tool manufacturer with its supplier of castings would be a vertical merger. The economic benefit of this type of merger stems from the firm's increased control over the acquisition of raw materials or the distribution of finished goods.

A congeneric merger is achieved by acquiring a firm that is *in the same general industry* but neither in the same line of business nor a supplier or customer. An example is the merger of a machine-tool manufacturer with the manufacturer of industrial conveyor systems. The benefit of this type of merger is the resulting ability to use the same sales and distribution channels to reach customers of both businesses. A conglomerate merger involves the combination of firms in *unrelated businesses*. The merger of a machine-tool manufacturer with a chain of fast-food restaurants would be an example of this kind of merger. At first glance it would appear that such a combination could not provide any operating synergism: admittedly, synergism would be relatively small compared to that of most vertical or horizontal combinations. But if the operating profit patterns of the various acquired firms differ as economic changes occur, a portfolio effect might be achieved. This would make the operating risk of the combination smaller than the risk of the firms standing by themselves. If risk is reduced while the combination of cash flows are unchanged, the value of the combination may exceed that of its individual components. There also may be some favourable effects resulting from flexibility of personnel and transfer of technology, even though the firms appear to be engaged in different lines of business. In this sense operating synergy may result from conglomerate growth.

ACQUIRING VERSUS TARGET COMPANIES

The firm in a merger transaction that attempts to acquire another firm is commonly called the **acquiring company**. The firm that the acquiring company is pursuing is referred to as the **target company**. Generally, the acquiring company identifies, evaluates, and negotiates with the management and/or shareholders of the target company. Occasionally, the management of a target company initiates its acquisition by seeking to be acquired.

FRIENDLY VERSUS HOSTILE TAKEOVERS

Mergers can occur on either a friendly or a hostile basis. Typically, after isolating the target company, the acquirer initiates discussions with its management. If the target management is receptive to the acquirer's proposal, it may endorse the merger and recommend shareholder approval. If the shareholders approve the merger, the transaction is typically consummated either through a cash purchase of shares by the acquirer or through an exchange of the acquirer's shares, bonds, or some combination for the target firm's shares. This type of negotiated transaction is known as a friendly merger. If, on the other hand, the takeover target's management does not support the proposed takeover for any of a number of possible reasons, such as too low an offering price, a desire to maintain the firm's autonomy, or a "poor fit," it can fight the acquirer's actions. In this case the acquirer can attempt to gain control of the firm by buying sufficient shares of the target firm in the marketplace. This is typically accomplished by using *tender offers* (i.e., a formal offers to purchase a given number of shares at a specified price). This type of unfriendly transaction is commonly referred to as a *hostile merger*. Clearly, hostile mergers are more difficult to consummate because the target firm's management acts to deter rather than facilitate the acquisitions. Regardless, hostile takeovers are sometimes successful.

STRATEGIC VERSUS FINANCIAL MERGERS

Mergers are undertaken for either strategic or financial reasons. Strategic mergers involve merging firms to achieve various economies of scale by eliminating redundant functions, increasing market share, improving raw material sourcing and finished product distribution, and so on. In these mergers the operations of the acquiring and target firms are somehow combined to achieve economies and thereby cause the performance of the merged firm to exceed that of the premerged firms. An interesting variation of the strategic merger involves the purchase of specific product lines (rather than the whole company) for strategic reasons.

Financial mergers, on the other hand, are based on the acquisition of companies that can be restructured to improve their cash flow. These mergers involve the acquisition of the target firm by an acquirer, which may be another company or a group of investors—often the firm's existing management. The objective of the acquirer is to drastically cut costs and sell of certain unproductive or noncompatible assets to increase the firm's cash flows. The increased cash flows are used to service to the sizable debt that is typically incurred to finance these transactions. Financial mergers are not based on the firm's ability to achieve economies of scale, but rather on the acquirer's belief that through restructuring, the firm's hidden value can be unlocked.

MOTIVES FOR MERGING

Firms merge to fulfill certain objectives. The overriding goal for merging is the maximisation of the owners' wealth as reflected in the acquirer's share price. Specific motives, which includes growth or diversification, synergy, managerial skill or technology, tax considerations, increased ownership liquidity, and defense against takeover, should be pursued when they are believed to be consistent with owner wealth maximisation.

GROWTH OR DIVERSIFICATION

Companies that desire rapid growth in *size* or *market share* or diversification in *the range of their products* may find that a merger can be used to fulfill the objective. Instead of going through the time-consuming process of internal growth or diversification, the firm may achieve the same objective in a short period of time by merging with an existing firm. In addition, such a strategy is often less costly than the alternative of developing the necessary production capability and capacity. If a firm that wants to expand operations in existing or new product area can find a suitable going concern, it may avoid many of risks associated with the design, manufacture, and sale of additional or new products. Moreover, when a firm expands or extends its product line by acquiring another firm, it also remove a potential competitor.

SYNERGISM

The nature of synergism is very simple. *Synergism exists whenever the value of a combination is greater than the sum of the values of its parts.* In other words, synergism is "2 + 2 = 5." But identifying synergism and evaluating it may be difficult; in fact, sometimes its implications may be very subtle. As broadly defined to include any incremental value resulting from business combination, synergism is the basic economic justification of merger. The incremental value may derive from increases in either operational or financial efficiency.

Operating Synergism

Operating synergism may result from economies of scale, some degree of monopoly (or monopsony) power, or increased managerial efficiency. The value may be achieved by increasing sales volume in relation to assets employed (operating asset turnover), increasing profit margins, or decreasing operating risk. Although operating synergy usually is the result of either vertical or horizontal integration, some synergistic effects also may result from conglomerate growth or the integration of technology and/or personnel into a more efficient unit. In addition, sometimes a firm may acquire another to obtain patents, copyrights, technical proficiency, marketing skills, specific fixed assets, customer relationships, or managerial personnel. Operating synergism occurs when these assets, which are intangible, may be combined with the existing assets and organisation of the acquiring firm to produce an incremental value. Although that value may be difficult to appraise, it may be the primary motive behind the acquisition.

Financial Synergism

Synergism may include financial advantages as well as operating ones. Among these are incremental values resulting from complementary internal funds flows more efficient use of financial leverage, increase external financial capability, and income tax advantages.

Complementary internal funds flows: Seasonal or cyclical fluctuations in funds flows sometimes may be reduced or eliminated by merger. If so, financial synergism results in reduction of working capital requirements of the combination compared to those of the firms standing alone.

More efficient use of financial leverage: Financial synergy may result from more efficient use of financial leverage. The acquiring firm may have little debt and wish to use the high debt of an acquired firm to lever earnings of the combination. Or the acquiring firm may borrow to finance an acquisition for cash of a low-debt firm, thus providing additional leverage to the combination. The financial leverage advantage must be weighed against the increased financial risk.

Increased External Financial capability: Many mergers, particularly those of relatively small firms into large ones, occur when the acquired firm simply cannot finance its operations. Typical of this situation is a small growing firm with expanding financial requirements. The firm has exhausted its bank credit and has virtually no access to long-term debt or equity markets. Sometimes the small firm has encountered operating difficulty, and the bank has served notice that its loans will not be renewed. In this type of situation, a large firm with sufficient cash and credit to finance the requirements of the smaller one probably can obtain a good buy by making a merger proposal to the small firm. The only alternative the small firm may have is to try to interest two or more larger firms in proposing merger to introduce competition into their bidding for the acquisition.

The smaller firm's situation might not be so bleak. It may not be threatened by nonrenewal of a maturing loan. But its management may recognise that continued growth to capitalise on its markets will require financing beyond its means. Although its bargaining position will be better, the financial synergy of the acquiring firm's strong financing capability may provide the impetus for the merger.

Sometimes the financing capability is possessed by the acquired firm. The acquisition of a cash-rich firm whose operations have matured may provide additional financing to facilitate growth of the acquiring firm. In some cases, the acquiring firm may be able to recover all or part of the cost of acquiring the cash-rich firm when the merger is consummated and the cash then belongs to it.

A merger also may be based upon the simple fact that the combination will make two small firms with limited access to the capital markets large enough to achieve that access on a reasonable basis. The improved financing capability provides the financial synergy.

Income tax advantages: In some cases, income tax consideration may provide the financial synergy motivating a merger, for example, assume that firm A has earnings before taxes of about ₹ 10 crore per year and firm B, now breaking even, has a loss carryforward of ₹ 20 crore accumulated from unprofitable operations of previous years. The merger of A and B will allow the surviving corporation to utilise the loss carryforward, thereby eliminating income taxes in future periods.

COUNTER SYNERGISM

Certain factors may oppose the synergistic effect contemplated from a merger. Often another layer of overhead costs and bureaucracy is added. Do the advantages outweigh this disadvantage? Some times the acquiring firm agrees to long-term employment contracts with the managers of the acquired firm. Such contracts often are beneficial but they may be the opposite. Personality or policy conflicts may develop that either hamstring operations or require buying out such contracts to remove personnel from position of authority.

Particularly in conglomerate mergers, management of the acquiring firm simply may not have sufficient knowledge of the business to control the acquired firm adequately. Attempts to maintain control may induce resentment by personnel of the acquired firm. The resulting reduction of efficiency may eliminate expected operating synergy or even reduce the postmerger profitability of the acquired firm. The list of possible counter-synergistic factors could go on endlessly; the point is that mergers do not always produce the expected results. Negative factors and the risks related to them also must be considered in appraising a prospective merger.

OTHER MOTIVES FOR MERGER

Mergers may be motivated by two other factors that perhaps should not be classified under synergism. These are the opportunity for an acquiring firm to obtain assets at a bargain price and the desire of shareholders of the acquired firm to increase the liquidity of their holdings.

Purchase of Assets at Bargain Price: Mergers may be explained by the opportunity to acquire assets, particularly land, mineral rights, plant, and equipment, at lower cost than would be incurred if they were purchased or constructed at current market prices. If market price of many stocks have bene considerably below the replacement cost of the assets they represent, expanding firm considering constructing plants, developing mines, or buying equipment often have found that the desired asset could be obtained cheaper by acquiring a firm that already owned and operated the asset. Risk could be reduced because the assets were already in place and an organisation of people knew how to operate them an market their products.

Many of the mergers can be financed by cash tender offers to the acquired firm's shareholders at price substantially above the current market. Even so, the assets can be acquired for less than their current costs of construction. The basic factor underlying this apparently is that inflation in construction costs not fully reflected in stock prices because of high interest rates and limited optimism (or downright pessimism) by stock investors regarding future economic conditions.

Increased Managerial Skill or Technology: Occasionally, a firm will have good potential that it finds itself unable to develop fully because of deficiencies in certain areas of management or an absence of needed product or production technology. If the firm cannot hire the management or develop the technology it needs, it maight combine with a compatible firm that has the needed managerial personnel or technical expertise. of course, any merger, regardless of the specific motive for it, should contribute to the maximisation of owners' wealth.

Increased Ownership Liquidity: The merger of two small firms or a small and a larger firm may provide the owners of the small firm(s) with greater liquidity. This is due to the higher marketability associated with the shares of larger firms. Instead of holding shares in a small firm that has a very "thin" market, the owners will receive shares that are traded in a broader market and can thus be liquidated more readily. Not only does the ability to convert shares into cash quickly have appeal, but owning shares for which market price quotations are readily available provides owners with a better sense of the value of their holdings. Especially in the case of small, closely held firms, the improved liquidity of ownership obtainable through merger with an acceptable firm may have considerable appeal.

Defense Against Takeover: Occasionally, when a firm becomes the target of an unfriendly takeover, it will as a defense acquire another company. Such a strategy typically works like this: the original target firm takes on additional debt to finance its defensive acquisition; because of the debt load, the target firm becomes too large and too highly levered financially to be of any further interest to its suitor. To be effective, a defensive takeover must create greater value for shareholders than they would have realised had the firm been merged with its suitor.

In addition, the stockholder-managers of the acquired firm may be offered attractive management contracts and/or seek the opportunity to rise to positions of greater responsibility in the acquired firm than would be possible within their small one.

LEVERAGED BUYOUTS AND DIVESTITURES

Before addressing the merger negotiation process and mechanics of merger analysis, it is important to understand two topics that are closely related to mergers—LBOs and divestitures. An LBO is a method of structuring a financial merger, whereas divestitures involve the sale of a a firm's assets.

LEVERAGED BUYOUTS (LBOs)

A popular technique that was widely used during the 1980s to make acquisitions is the leveraged buyout (LBO), which involves the use of a large amount of debt to purchase a firm. LBOs are a clear-cut example of *financial merger* undertaken to create a high-debt private corporation with improved cash flow and value. Typically in the LBO 90 per cent or more of the purchase price is financed with debt. A large part of the borrowing is secured by the acquired firm's assets, and the lenders, because of the high risk, take a portion of the firm's equity. *Junk bonds* have been routinely used to raise the large amounts of debt needed to finance LBO transactions. Of course, the purchasers in an LBO expect to use the improved cash flow to service the large amount of junk bond and other debt incurred in the buyout. The acquires in LBOs are other firms or groups of investors that frequently include key members of the firm's existing management.

An attractive candidate for acquisition through leveraged buyout should possess three basic attributes:

1. It must have a good position in its industry with a solid profit history and reasonable expectations of growth.
2. The firm should have a relatively low level of debt and a high level of "bankable" assets that can be used as loan collateral.
3. It must have stable and predictable cash flows that are adequate to meet interest and principal payments on the debt and provide adequate working capital.

Of course, a willingness on the part of existing ownership and management to sell the company on a leveraged basis is also needed.

DIVESTITURES

It is important to recognise that companies often achieve external expansion by acquiring an operating unit—plant, division, product line, subsidiary, etc.—of another company. In such a case the seller generally believes that the value of the firm will be enhanced by converting the unit into cash or some other more productive asset. The selling of some of a firm's assets is called divestiture. Unlike business failure, the motive for divestiture is often positive; to generate cash for expansion of other product lines, to get rid of a poorly performing operation, to streamline the corporation, or to restructure the corporation's business consistent with its strategic goals.

There is a variety of methods by which firms divest themselves of operating units. One involves the *sale of a product line to another firm.* These outright sales can be accomplished on a cash or stock swap basis. A second method that has become quite popular in recent years involves the *sale of the unit to existing management.* This sale is often achieved through the use of *leveraged buyout (LBO).* Sometimes divestiture is achieved through a spin-off, which results in an operating unit becoming an independent company. *A spin-off is accomplished by issuing shares in the operating unit being divested on a prorata basis to the parent company's shareholders.* Such an action allows the unit to be separated from the corporation and to trade as a separate entity. Like outright sale, this approach achieves the divestiture objective, although it does not bring additional cash or stock to the parent company. The final and least popular approach to divestiture involves *liquidation of the operating unit's individual assets.*

Regardless of the method used to divest a firm of an unwanted operating unit, the goal typically is to create a more lean and focused operation that will enhance the efficiency as well as the profitability of the enterprise and create maximum value for shareholders. Recent divestiture seem to suggest that many operating units are worth much more to others than to the firm itself. Comparisons of postdivestiture and predivestiture market value have shown that the "breakup value" of many firms is significantly greater than their combined value. As a result of market valuations, divestiture often creates value in excess of the cash or stock received in the transaction. Unlike LBOs, the use of divestitures in corporate restructuring is expected to remain popular.

THE MERGER NEGOTIATION PROCESS

Mergers are often handled by investment bankers—financial intermediaries hired by acquirers to find suitable target companies and assist in negotiations. A firm seeking a potential acquisition can hire an investment banker to find firm meeting its requirements. Once a target company is selected, the investment banker negotiates with its management or investment banker. Frequently, when management wishes to sell the firm or a division of the firm, it will hire an investment banker to seek out potential buyers.

In the event that attempts to negotiate with the management of target company break down, the acquiring firm, often with the aid of its investment banker, can make direct appeal to shareholders by using *tender offers*. The investment banker is typically compensated with a fixed fee, a commission tied to the transaction price, or with a combination of fees and commission.

A desirable merger candidate usually receives more than a single offer. Normally certain nonfinancial issues relating to the disposition and compensation of the existing management, product-line policies, financing policies, and the independence of the target firm must be resolved. The key factor, of course, is the pre-share price offered in cash or reflected in the ratio of exchange. Although the negotiations are generally based on the expectation of a merger, sometimes negotiations will break down.

TENDER OFFERS

When management negotiations for an acquisition break down, tender offers may then be used to negotiate a "hostile merger" directly with the firm's shareholders. *A tender offer is a formal offer to purchase a given number of shares of a firm's stock at a specified price.* The offer is made to all the shareholders at a premium above the market price. Occasionally, the acquire will make a two-tier offer in which the terms offered are more attractive to those who tender shares early. For example, the acquirer offers to pay ₹ 25 per share of the first 60 per cent of the outstanding shares tendered and only ₹ 23 per share for the remaining shares. The shareholders are advised of a tender offer through announcements in financial newspapers or through direct communications from the offering firm. Sometimes a tender offer is made to add pressure to existing merger negotiations. In other cases the tender offer may be made without warning as an attempt at an abrupt corporate takeover.

FIGHTING HOSTILE TAKEOVERS

If the management of a target firm does not favour a merger or considers the price offered in a proposed merger too low, it is likely to take defensive actions to ward off the hostile tender offer. Such actions are generally developed with the assistance of investment bankers and lawyers who, for generally sizable fees, help the firm to develop and employ effective takeover defenses. Numerous strategies such as informing shareholders of the alleged damaging effects of a takeover, acquiring another company, or attempting to sue the acquiring firm on antitrust or other grounds for fighting hostile takeovers were developed. In addition, many other defenses (some with colourful names) exist—*white knight, poison pills, greenmail, leveraged recapitalisation, golden parachutes,* and *shark repellents.* We now take a brief look at each of these strategies.

The ***white knight*** strategy involves the target firm finding a more suitable acquirer (the "white knight") and prompting it to compete with the initial hostile acquire to takeover the firm. The basic premise of this strategy is that if being taken over is nearly certain, the target firm ought to attempt to be taken over by the firm that is deemed most acceptable to its management. ***Poison pills*** typically involve the creation of securities that give their holders certain rights that become effective when a takeover is attempted. The "pill" allows the shareholders to receive special voting rights or securities that, once issued, cause the firm to be much less desirable to the hostile acquirer. ***Green mail*** is a strategy by which the firm repurchases through private negotiation a large block of stock at a premium from one or more shareholders to end a hostile takeover attempt by those shareholders. Clearly greenmail is a form of corporate blackmail by the holders of a large block of shares. Another hostile takeover defense involves the use of a ***leveraged recapitalisation,*** which is a strategy involving the payment of a large debt-financed cash dividend. This strategy significantly increases the firm's financial leverage, thereby deterring the takeover attempt. In addition, as a further deterrent the recapitalization is often structured to increase the equity and control of the existing management. ***Golden parachutes*** are provisions in the employment contracts of key executives that provide them with sizable compensation if the firm is taken over. Golden parachutes deter hostile takeovers to the extent that the cash outflows required by these contracts are large enough to make the takeover unattractive to the acquirer. Another defense is use of ***shark repellents,*** which are antitakeover amendments to the corporate charter that constrain the firm's ability to transfer managerial control of the firm as a result of a merger. Although this defense could entrench existing management, many firms have had these amendments ratified by shareholders.

Because takeover defenses tend to insulate management from shareholders, the potential for litigation is great when these strategies are employed. Lawsuits are sometimes filed against management by dissident shareholders. In addition, governments frequently intervene when a proposed takeover is deemed to be in violation of law.

VALUING THE TARGET COMPANY

Whether a firm is planning to acquire a target firm for cash or through a stock swap, it must first determine the target firm's value. The value would then be used, along with a proposed financing scheme, to negotiate the transaction—on a friendly or hostile basis. The value of the target would be estimated by using the capital budgeting techniques whether the target firm is being acquired for its assets or as a going concern.

Acquisition of Assets: Occasionally, a firm is acquired not for its income-earning potential but as a collection of assets (generally fixed assets) that the acquiring company needs. The price paid for this type of acquisition depends largely on which assets are being acquired; consideration must also be given to the value of any tax losses. To determine whether the purchase of assets is financially justified, the acquire must estimate both the costs and benefits of the target assets. This is a capital budgeting problem, since an initial cash outlay is made to acquire assets and, as a result, future cash inflows are expected.

Acquisitions of Going Concern: Acquisitions of target companies that are going concerns are best analysed by using capital budgeting techniques similar to those used for asset acquisitions. The basic difficulty in applying the capital budgeting approach to the acquisition of going concern is the *estimation of cash flows* and certain *risk considerations.* The methods of estimating expected cash flows from an acquisition are similar to those used in estimating capital budgeting cash flows. Typically *pro forma income statements* reflecting the post merger revenues and cost attributable to the target company are prepared. They are then adjusted to reflect the expected cash flows over the relevant time period. Whenever a firm considers acquiring a target company that has different risk behaviours, it should adjust the cost of capital appropriately before applying the appropriate capital budgeting techniques.

Stock Swap Transactions

Once the value of the target company is determined, the acquirer must develop a proposed financing package. The simplest, but probably least common, case would be a pure cash purchase. Beyond this extreme case there are virtually an infinite number of financing packages that use various combinations of cash, debt, preference shares, and equity shares. Here we look at the other extreme—*stock swap transactions* in which the acquisition is paid for using an exchange of equity shares. The acquiring firm exchanges its shares for shares of the target company according to a predetermined ratio. The *ratio of exchange* of shares is determined in the merger negotiations. This ratio affects the various financial yardsticks that are used by existing and prospective shareholders to value the merged firm's shares.

Ratio of Exchange: When one firm swaps its stock for the shares of another firm, the firms must determine the number of shares of the acquiring firm to be exchanged for each share of the target firm. The first requirement, of course, is that the acquiring company have sufficient shares available to complete the transaction. Often, a firm's repurchase of shares is necessary to obtain sufficient shares for such a transaction. The acquiring firm generally offers more for each share of the target company than the current market price of its publicly traded shares. The actual *ratio of exchange* is merely the ratio of the amount *paid* per share of the target company to the per-share market price of the acquiring firm. It is calculated in this manner because the acquiring firm pays the target firm in stock, which has a value equal to its market price.

Effect on Earnings Per Share: Ordinarily, the resulting earnings per share differ from the premerger earnings per share for both the acquiring firm and the target firm. They depend largely on the ratio of exchange and the premerger earnings per share of each firm. It is best to view the initial and long-run effect of the ratio of exchange on earnings per share (EPS) separately.

When the ratio of exchange is equal to 1 and both the acquiring firm and the target firm have the *same* premerger earnings per share, the merged firm's earnings per share will initially remain constant. In this rare instance, both the acquiring and target firms would also have equal price/earnings (P/E) ratios. In actuality the earnings per share of the merged firm are generally above the premerger earning per share of one firm and below the premerger earnings per share of the other, after the necessary adjustment has been made for the ratio of exchange.

Effect on Market Price Per Share: The market price per share does not necessarily remain constant after the acquisition of one firm by another. Adjustments occur in the marketplace in response to changes in expected earnings, the dilution of ownership, changes in risk, and certain other operating and financial changes. Using the ratio of exchange, a *ratio of exchange in market price* can be calculated. It indicates the market price per share of the acquiring firm *paid* for market price per share of the target firm. The ratio, the MPR, is defined by:

$$MPR = \frac{MP_{acquiring} \times RE}{MP_{target}}$$

where

MPR = market price ratio of exchange

$MP_{acquiring}$ = market price per share of the acquiring firm

MP_{target} = market price per share of the target firm

RE = ratio of exchange

The postmerger earnings per share of owners of the acquiring and target companies can be explained by comparing the price/earnings (P/E) ratio. By paying more than its current value of earnings to acquire the earnings (P/E paid > P/E of acquiring company), the acquiring firm transfers the claim on a portion of its premerger earnings to the owners of the target firm. Therefore on a postmerger basis the target firm's EPS increases, and the acquiring firm's EPS decrease. Note that this outcome is *almost always* the case, since the acquire typically pays a 50 per cent, on average, premium above the target firm's market price, thereby resulting in the P/E paid being much above its own P/E. If acquiring company were to pay less than its current value of earnings to acquire the earnings (P/E paid < P/E of acquiring company), the opposite effects would result.

The long-run effect of merger on the earnings per share of the merged company depends largely on whether the earnings of the merged firm grow. Often, although a decrease in the per-share earnings of the stock held by the original owners of the acquiring firm is expected initially, the long-run effects of the merger on earnings per share are quite favourable. Since business firms generally expect growth in earnings, the key factor enabling the acquiring company, which initially experiences a decrease in EPS, to experience higher future EPS than it would have without the merger is the fact that the earnings attributable to the target company's assets grow at a faster rate than those resulting from the acquiring company's premerger assets.

The ratio of exchange in market price is normally greater than 1, which indicates that to acquire a firm, the acquire must pay a premium above its market price. Even so, the original owners of the acquiring firm may still gain because the merged firm's stock may sell a price/earning ratio above the individual premerger ratios. This results from the improved risk and return relationship perceived by shareholders and other investors.

The financial manager must recognise that, only with proper management of the merged enterprise can its market value be improved. If the merged firm cannot achieve sufficiently high earnings in view of its risk, there is no guarantee that its market price will reach the forecast value. Nevertheless, a policy of acquiring firms with low P/Es can produce favourable results for the owners of the acquiring firm. Acquisitions are especially attractive when the acquiring firm's stock price is high, since fewer shares must be exchange to acquire a given firm.

TERMS OF MERGERS

Naturally, both firms in the proposed merger/acquisition will seek the best terms possible for their respective shareholders. This involves a negotiation to divide the value between the two sets of shareholders. The ratio of exchange can be determined by a comparison of the two companies in five areas: 1. earnings; 2. growth in earning; 3. dividends; 4. market price; and, 5. book value.

It is clear that if we distribute securities in the new firm in proportion to any one of these basis, there will be a conflict with a distribution that uses any other of the basis except in an extremely fortuitous case. Such a conflict suggests the question of what weight is to be attributed to each of these bases of comparison.

Before we examine the interplay of the different bases of valuation of a firm at a practical level, we must emphasize that if the marger is *synergistic,* the value of both companies for their owners will rise. Thus in a merger negotiation there is always discussion of : 1, the improvement of total receipts that can be anticipated beyond the sum of he separate earnings; 2. The savings or cost reductions expected from the fusion; and 3. The impact of both of these factors on the market value of the securities that would result from the merger. To illustrate the complexity of the problem, even if there were no increase in earnings by fusion and no cost savings, it is quite possible that the merger would result in a price earnings ratio higher than the separate price earnings ratios of the two companies, for example, due to off setting risks. Hence we see that historical earnings or price-earnings ratios are usually inadequate as the principle of merger.

It follows, then that much of the popular analysis of mergers is based on faulty assumptions, namely, that (1) the past record and valuation of each separate entity is indicative of its separate future records and (2) the future record and valuation of the fusion is the sum of the separate (even future) records and valuation of the separate firms.

Let us assume that it is agreed that future valuation of the fused firms is what is to be divided. We might propose that this value should be divided between the two firms in proportion to the present value of each firm (or the market value ratio). But such a proposal assumes that each firm contributes to an improvement in the total value of the new firm in proportion to its separate market value.

Actually one or the other of the merging companies may have more opportunities to merge at high values with other companies. This is sometimes described on bargaining power and it effects not only the division of the increment of the fused value over the sum of the value of the two separate firms but can extend so far as to shift part of the original value of one of the firms to the other as a result of the ratio of shares in the fused firms.

ILLUSTRATION OF THE PROBLEM OF MERGER TERMS

The quantitative data most readily available and most frequently used to evaluate merger terms in the practical world are earnings, dividends, market value, book value, and net current assets.

TABLE-1

Proposal to Merge Company A into Company B

	Company A	*Company B*	*Exchange rate (B for A) indicated if only 1 factor were considered and no increase in earnings or P/E for fused firm*
Total Earnings	₹ 20,000	₹ 50,000	
Shares of equity	10,000	10,000	
Earnings per share	₹ 2.00	₹ 5.00	0.4
Price earnings ratio	₹ 20	₹ 10	
Market value per share	₹ 40	₹ 50.00	0.8
Dividends per share	₹ 0.20	₹ 4.00	0.05
Book value per share	₹ 8.00	₹ 20,00	0.4
Net current assets per share*	₹ 0.50	₹ 3.00	0.17
Expected annual growth rate of earning	10%	5%	

*Net current assets is the same as net working capital i.e., current assets minus current liabilities.

Assuming the data given in Table-1. It is apparent that computations on a per share basis are convenient and this is the customary procedure. A look at the data suggests that company A is a so-called growth company and company B is mature. If an exchange of one for one were to occur and if the market were to place no higher value of the fused operation then on its two separate parts and Company B were the surviving company, the result might be those given in Table-2.

TABLE-2

Possible Results of One for One merger of Company A into Company B

Total earnings	₹ 70,000
Shares of equity	20,000
Earnings per-share	₹ 3.50
Price-earnings ratio	12.85
Market value per share	₹ 45.00
Dividends per share	₹ 2.10
Book value per share	₹ 14.00
Net Current assets per share	₹ 1.75

One thing immediately apparent is that all of the per share figures are the arithmatic means of the separate company figure but that the new price-earnings ratio is not an average of the old price earnings ratio. Price and the earnings ratio is determined by the price and earnings: price is not determined by the price-earning-ratio and earnings.

Notice also that none of the single factor exchange rate is one or greater. The exchange rate of one for one cannot be arrived at by some weighting of the several factors set out. However, in many cases after the exchange rate is established the result can be arithmatically equated to a number of different weighting systems applied to the several factors.

We can determine how long this time period will be by solving the following equation for it:

$$E_1 (1 + g_1)^N = E_2 (1 + g_2)^N$$

Where E_1 and g_1 are the earnings and growth rate before merger and E_2 and g_2 are the earnings and growth rate after merger and is the break-even number of years. The growth rate after merger is the average of the separate growth rates, weighted by the total earnings of each company. In our case g_2 is [0.10 (20,000) + 0.05 (50,000)]/ 70,000, or 6.43 per cent. The company B is trading a current earnings of ₹ 5 per share with a growth rate of 5% for current earnings of ₹ 3.50 per share and a growth rate of 6.43 per cent. Conversely, company A is tracing a current earnings of ₹ 2 per share with a growth rate of 10% for a current earnings of ₹ 3.50 per share and a growth rate of 6.43.

Substituting in this equation, N turns to be 26.4 years for company B and 17 years for company A. Thus as to company B, the decline in earnings in the merger from ₹ 5 per share to ₹ 3.50 per share will be equalised after 26.4 years where the earnings have risen to ₹ 18.13 per share [computed as log 5+26.4 (log. 1.05) or log 3.5 + 26.4 (Log 1.0643)]. Similarly, the increase from ₹ 2 per share to ₹ 3.5 per shares or company A in the merger will be equalised after 17 years when earnings will be at ₹ 10.10 per share [computed as log 2+17 (log 1.1) or log 3.5 + 17 (log 1.0643)].*

FACTORS DOMINATING SITUATIONS

Situations in which each of the five factors is likely to dominate are listed before:

Market Value

Market value will dominate when there are dissenter problems. Great deviation from market value threatens to result in litigation beyond the problem of receiving the cash needed for dissenters. However, when 'market' value represent a thin or even a supported market, only the naive company will be trapped into reorganising market value.

Book Value

Book value is likely to dominate first in the case where liquidity carries a premium. This might occur, for example, at any time when the capital market and/or the economy as a whole have slowed down and new securities of any kind are difficult to market at anything opproximating a reasonable price. A second situation where book value will be dominant is where the market value of the assets of one company is well above the market value of its shares.

Dividends

Dividend rates of the two companies are not likely to influence the terms of the merger but can be expected to affect the form of securities used. Dividends depend on earnings and policy as to payout. But in a merger every effort will be spent to use a type of security which will preserve existing cash dividends for shareholders of the acquired company. The payout policy of fused operation cannot be readily determined in advance except where the policies of both companies have been nearly the same, thus creating an expectation that the same pattern will continue.

Earnings

Earnings are sometimes stated to be the dominant single factor, and 'earnings' in such a statement means historical earnings. The relevant earnings, however, are expected future earnings, and these are reflected in market value. Variability of earnings is a factor to be considered, but his is reflected in market value and appears in the price-earnings ratios, which reflect risk as well as growth prospects.

DISSENTING SHAREHOLDERS

Although a combination generally depends only upon the approval of a required majority of the total number of shares outstanding, minority shareholders can contest the price paid for their share, if a dissenting shareholder and the company fail to agree as to just settlement on a voluntary basis, the shareholder can take his case to court and demand an appraisal of his shares and a settlement in cash. After a fair-market price has been established by the court the dissenting shareholders receives payment in cash for his shares. If the number of dissenting shareholders is large, they can cause considerable trouble. If the transaction is in share, the demands for cash payments on the part of these shareholders may put a severe financial strain on the combination. Thus, most combinations depend not only upon obtaining approval of a required majority of shareholders but also upon minimising the number of dissenting shareholders by making the offer attractive to all. Dissenting shareholders may be able to block the combination if they suspect that fraud is involved, even though the required majority of shareholders has approved it.

BENEFITS AND COSTS

The manager's objective is to maximise the current wealth of A's shareholders. Consequently, he will go ahead with the merger if he can negotiate a deal that makes them richer.

Certain difficulties have to be disposed off before beginning any substantive discussion. In the first place, it is sometimes hard to tell who is purchasing whom, the law makes a distinction between mergers, which are purchased by A of company B's share or assets, and consolidation, in which A and B continue to form a new company, which survives. In the later case buyers and sellers are not legally identified.

The benefits of a merger can be defined as the difference between (1) the total present value of the merged firms and (2) the sum of their values if they do not merge. If V represents a present value, then

$$\text{Benefit} = \Delta V = V_{AB} - V_A - V_B \qquad (1)$$

The implied question is, *"What aspects of the proposed merger make the two firms worth more together than apart?"*

If this definition of benefit is accepted, then cost must be defined as the difference between the amount paid for the acquired firm and the amount it is worth as a separate entity. If B's owners receive case for their shares, for example, then

$$\text{Cost} = \text{Cash} - V_B \qquad (2)$$

Defining benefits in this way focuses attention on the economic value of merger. Estimating this value is indeed just like a capital budgeting problem. Estimating cost, however, requires consideration of how the benefits of merger are shared between A and B's owners. As we will see later that cost can depend on how the merger is financed.

Firms should go ahead with mergers for which benefit exceeds cost. If the merger is financed by cash, this requires that

$$\text{Benefit} - \text{Cost} = \Delta V - (\text{Cash} - V_B) > 0 \qquad (3)$$

It may not be obvious that A's shareholders gain when equation (3) holds. If not, consider the following. If there is no merger, then the aggregate value of their shares is V_a. If the merger goes through, their position is V_{AB} - Cash. Their net gain is exactly as given by equation (3):

$$\begin{aligned}\text{Net Gain} &= V_B - \text{Cash} - V_A \\ &= \Delta V + V_A + V_B - \text{Cash} - V_A \\ &= \Delta V - (\text{Cash} - V_B).\end{aligned}$$

ESTIMATING THE COST OF A MERGER

Cost is the difference between the amount paid for the acquired firm and what it is worth as a seperate entity. Estimating cost is straight forward as long as the merger is financed by cash. However, it is useful to distinguish between I_B, the "intrinsic" value of the acquired firm as a separate entity, and MV_B, the aggregate market value of the firm as observed around the time of the merger, since MV_B, may be affected by information about the merger.

We can rewrite equation (2) as

Cost = (Cash – MV_B)	+ (MV_B – I_B)	(4)
= Premium paid over observed market value of B	Difference between observed market value of B and what it is worth on its own.	

For example, suppose that on the day before A and B's merger is announced, we observe the following"

	Firm A	*Firm B*
Market price per share	₹ 100	₹ 40
Number of shares	1,00,000	50,000
Market value of firm	₹ 1,00,00,000	₹ 20,00,000

Firm A intends to pay ₹ 25,00,000 cash for B. If MV_B reflects only B's seperate value, then

$$\begin{aligned}\text{Cost} &= (\text{Cash} - MV_B) + (MV_B - I_B) \\ &= (25{,}00{,}000 - 20{,}00{,}000) + (20{,}00{,}000 - 20{,}00{,}000) = ₹\ 5{,}00{,}000 + 0 \\ &= ₹\ 5{,}00{,}000.\end{aligned}$$

On the other hand, suppose B's price had risen ₹ 4.00 per share due to rumours about the merger. Then,

$$\begin{aligned}\text{Cost} &= (\text{Cash} - MV_B) + (MV_B - I_B) \\ &= ₹\ 5{,}00{,}000 + ₹\ 2{,}00{,}000 = ₹\ 7{,}00{,}000.\end{aligned}$$

It is also conceivable that A's management has inside information that leads it to believe that B's real value is 20 per cent higher than MV_B. If they are right, B is a *bargain* and the cost is reduced.

$$\text{Cost} = ₹\ 5{,}00{,}000 + (20{,}00{,}000 - 24{,}00{,}000) = ₹\ 1{,}00{,}000.$$

As was noted, the protagonist firm in a merger almost always pays a premium over the market value of the acquired firm.

ESTIMATING THE COST WHEN THE ACQUISITION IS FINANCED BY EQUITY

Estimating cost is tricker when mergers are financed by an exchange of shares. Suppose that firm A offers 25,000 shares, worth ₹ 100 per share before the merger announcement, instead of ₹ 25,00,000 cash. MV_B is ₹ 20,00,000, as before. The apparent cost of the merger is:

$$\text{Apparent cost} = ₹\ 100(25{,}000) - ₹\ 20{,}00{,}000 = ₹\ 5{,}00{,}000$$

However, this is not likely to be the true cost, for three reasons. First, firm B's real value may not be ₹ 20,00,000. Second A's shares may not be valued correctly at ₹ 100. Third, and most important, a portion of the benefits generated by the merger will accrue to B's shareholders—they will be partners of the merged firm.

The true cost is therefore

$$\text{Cost} = \theta V_{AB} - V_B$$

where θ is the proportion of the merged firm that B's shareholders end up owning.

Continuing with out example, consider again A's 25,000 share offer. B's shareholders will end up with one-fifth of the merged firm:

$$\theta = \frac{25{,}000}{1{,}00{,}000 + 25{,}000} = \frac{1}{5}$$

Suppose the market value before the merger announcement accurately reflect the firms' separate values. Also the merger generates benefits worth ₹ 1,00,000, so $V_{AB} = V_A + V_B + \Delta V$ = ₹ 1,00,00,000 + ₹ 20,00,000 + ₹ 10,00,000 = 1,30,00,000. Then the merger's true cost to A's shareholders is $1/5\ V_{AB} - V_B$ or

$$\text{Cost} = \frac{1}{5}\ (₹\ 1{,}30{,}00{,}000) - ₹\ 20{,}00{,}000 = ₹\ 6{,}00{,}000$$

The implication is that A's shareholders are as well of offering ₹ 26,00,000 cash as they are offering shares worth ₹ 25,00,000 before the merger announcement. The larger the benefits generated by the merger, the greater the true cost of the 25,000—share offer.

In making these calculations management is essentially attempting to estimate what B's shares will be worth after the merger agreement is sealed and announced. When this happens, the price of of the 50,000 firm B shares will immediately jump to ₹ 52.00, a ₹ 12.00 capital gain over their initial ₹ 40.00 price. (This assumes the market agrees with the ₹ 10,00,000 estimate of merger benefits). If A's management could wait until the merger terms are announced, estimating cost would be easy.

$$\text{Cost} = ₹\ 52\ (50{,}000) - ₹\ 10{,}00{,}000 = ₹\ 6{,}00{,}000.$$

Why not just announce, tentative merger terms, and then sit back to see how the market reacts before completing the merger negotiations? Would that not avoid these somewhat complicated calculations? The flow in this strategy is that observed market prices will be extremely difficult to interpret if the market knows that the announced terms are tentative and that further negotiations are pending.

CASH VERSUS EQUITY FOR FINANCIAL MERGERS

The key distinction between cash and stock as means of financing mergers is that, if cash is offered, the ultimate pay off to B's shareholders is independent of the success or failure of the merger. Cost can be estimated without reference to the merger's benefits. If share is offered, cost depends on benefits, because they must be shared with B's owners.

It is hard to generalise about whether other financing instruments should be treated like cash or share. For practical purposes, bonds or preference share issued by A will probably be treated like cash. The value of the bonds given to B's shareholders will be essentially independent of the success or failure of the merger, providing A is a good credit risk to start with. Convertible bonds (or convertible preference share) introduced the same problems that equity shares does. The option to convert gives B's shareholders the chance to share in merger benefits. In order to estimate cost, A's management must estimate the bond issue's value once the final merger terms and benefits are known to the market.

What are the consequences of financing mergers with equity rather than cash? Other things being equal, the greater the merger benefits, the greater the cost of equity financing. Also, equity financing mitigates the effect of over-or undervaluation of the acquired firm. If, for example, A's management mistakenly offers more shares for B than that firm is really worth, then the inevitable bad news will fall partly on B's shareholders' shoulders. Finally, equity financing is less advantageous than cash if A's equity is undervalued by the market. If it is observed, then equity financing is cheap. Note, however, there is no necessary connection between high or low price-earnings ratios and over-or undervaluation. A high price-earnings does not mean that equity financing is cheap.

Our analysis of merger costs gives no explanation for the observed association between merger activity and bull markets for share capital. A rapid increase in prices does not imply that shares are generally overvalued. Even if it did, it would not explain a merger wave. Buy B's would gain by financing mergers with over valued shares but lose by acquiring firms that are also overvalued. Mergers can be explained only by assuming differences in valuation errors made by buyers and not sellers. No doubt hindsight can supply some instances where this has happened, but it is a weak theory for explaining merger cycles. Unfortunately, other theories are weak also, which means that responsible management must approach mergers on a case-by-case basis, without any presumption that "the odds are with us."

CONSOLIDATION

A *consolidation* is the combination of two or more firms into a newly created corporation. For example, firms A and B are combined into a new firm C. This usually is accomplished by the exchange of the equity shares of A and B for those of firm C. The assets and liabilities of A and B are transferred to C, and the old corporations, A and B, cease to exist.

Consolidation has not been very widely used in recent years. Its principal disadvantages, as compared to a merger, are that a new corporation must be formed, consent of a stated majority (usually simple or two-thirds) of the shareholders of each combining corporation is required, and there is no possibility of using "pooling of interests" accounting or utilising tax-loss carryforwards.

HOLDING COMPANY

The holding company is a firm which controls one or more other companies (called subsidiaries) through ownership of the subsidiary firm's equity shares. The holding company structure permits the parent firm (the holding company) to control substantial assets with a small investment and also provides earnings that are highly levered. Because of this leverage, the company holding can be a relatively risky enterprise with the opportunity for extraordinary gains if the subsidiaries prosper and large losses if the subsidiaries do poorly.

The difference between the holding company technique for combination and merger and consolidation can be summarised as follows. There are no dissenter rights for minority holders when a holding company gains control. At the same time, there is relatively easy means for the holding company to dispose of the shares where there is a desire to switch investment. Thus, an operating company in a declining industry may first turn itself into an investment company and then become an operating company in another industry over several decades as it recovers depreciation on its plant and phases out its operation.

Advantages of Holding Companies

The primary advantage of the holding company arrangement is the *leverage effect* that permits the firm to control a large amount of assets with a relatively small investment. In other words, the owners of a holding company can *control* significantly larger amounts of assets than they could *acquire* through mergers. The following example illustrates the leverage effect. Suppose, for simplicity, that there are five operational companies each with a Balance Sheet given in Table-3.

Assume that the after-tax income of each operating company is ₹ 2,12,000 of which ₹ 12,000 is due to preference shares. Assume that the equity shares can be bought at book value. Control may require buying at most 51 per cent of the equity. If we create a new company whose assets are the controlling shares of the five operating companies and finance the acquisition with bonds and preference as well as equity shares.

TABLE-3

Balance Sheet of Each Operating Company

Liabilities		*Assets*	
Current liabilities	₹ 2,00,000	Operating assets	₹ 10,00,000
5 per cent bonds	3,00,000		
6 per cent preference share	2,00,000		
Equity share capital	1,00,000		
Surplus	2,00,000		
Total liabilities and net worth	₹ 10,00,000	Total assets	₹ 10,00,000

The Balance Sheet might be given in Table-4, assuming we acquire 50 per cent of the equity shares of each operating company at book value. Now with ₹ 1,50,000 of the holding company's share capital we control ₹ 50,00,000 in assets of the operating companies and claimed ₹ 50,00,000 of earnings of the operating companies (assuming they pay out 100 per cent of earnings). Of the ₹ 5,00,000 we apply ₹ 24,500 to holding company bonds and ₹ 8,000 to the preference shares (both of which carry higher rates than these securities of the operating companies because their income depends on the equity shares earnings of the operating companies). Of the holding company owns 80 per cent or more of the operating company's voting shares, no income tax is due because the intercompany dividends are exempt. But here we own only 50 per cent, and hence only 85 per cent of the intercompany dividends are exempt. At a tax rate of 48 per cent the effective tax rate on the holding company receipts is 0.48×0.15, or 7.2 per cent. Here 15 per cent of the ₹ 5,00,000 is taxable, or ₹ 75,000. But since the bond interest of ₹ 24,500 of the holding company is deductible ₹ 50,500 is taxable. This derive the effective tax rate below 7.2 per cent in this case. Where the equity share capital of the operating companies earns 66 per cent (₹ 2,00,000 of ₹ 3,00,000), the equity of the holding company earns 150 per cent (₹ 4,49,760 on ₹ 3,00,000).

TABLE-4

Balance Sheet of Holding Company

Liabilities		*Assets*	
7 per cent bonds	₹ 3,50,000	Investment in operating companies (₹ 1,50,000 of equity in each of 5 operating companies)	₹ 7,50,000
8 per cent preference share	1,00,000		
Equity share capital	3,00,000		
Total liabilities and net worth	₹ 7,50,000	Total assets	₹ 7,50,000

We have considered the use of only one level of holding company. Above this level leverage increases. The high leverage obtained through a holding company arrangement greatly magnifies earnings and losses for the holding company. Quite often, a pyramiding of holding companies occurs when one holding company controls other holding companies, thereby causing an even greater magnification of earnings and losses. The greater the leverage, the greater the risk involved. The risk-return tradeoff is a key consideration in the holding company decision.

Another commonly cited advantage of the holding company arrangement is the ***risk protection*** resulting from the fact that the failure of one of the companies does not result in the failure of the entire holding company. Since each subsidiary is a separate corporation, the failure of one company should cost the holding company, at maximum, no more than its investment in that subsidiary. Other advantages include the following: (1) certain state *tax benefits* may be realized by each subsidiary in its state of incorporation; (2) *lawsuits or legal actions* against a subsidiary will not threaten the remaining companies; and (3) it is *generally easy to gain control* of a firm, since shareholder or management approval is not generally necessary.

Besides the advantages of avoiding dissenters' rights, minimising the investment needed for control, and achieve leverage, the holding company presents two other advantages: (1) selective insulation of risks and (2) facility in financing. Both of these advantages are not clear cut. If there are inter-company transactions in the system, the courts may easily refuse to recognise the distinction of the corporations. But if the distinction between holding company and the operating companies is maintained, the decline of one operating company may not affect holding company as seriously as it affects the operating company. Facility in financing may follow from the superior standing of the system compared to the lesser status the individual operating companies would have.

A major **disadvantage** of the holding company arrangement is the *increased risk* resulting from the leverage effect. When general economic conditions are unfavorable, a loss by on subsidiary may be magnified. Another disadvantage is *double taxation* Before paying dividends a subsidiary must pay taxes on its earnings. Moreover, the holding companies are generally *high cost of administration* resulting from maintaining each subsidiary company as a separate entity. A merger, on the other hand, would likely result in certain administrative economies of scale. The need for coordination and communication between the holding company and its subsidiaries may further elevate these costs. Finally, the fact that holding companies are difficult *to analyse* is another disadvantage. Security analysts and investors typically have difficulty in understanding holding companies because of their complexity. As a result these firms tend to sell at low multiples, of earnings (P/Es). This means that the shareholder value of holding companies may suffer.

The operating economies that might come from a system would also be available to other forms of combinations.

ACCOUNTING POLICIES: PURCHASE *VERSUS* POOLING OF INTERESTS

There are two general accounting methods for handling mergers and acquisitions. One is called the purchase method, the other the pooling of interest, and they have considerably different effects on post combination EPS.

Goodwill, which occurs when the purchase price of the selling company exceeds its book value, is treated substantially different under the two methods. Under the purchase method the excess of the selling company's purchase price over book value is first assigned, to the extent possible, to tangible assets, the remainder is defined as goodwill. Goodwill is depreciable for investor *reporting* purposes but not for tax purposes. This means that there will be a depreciation charge against earnings each year for goodwill but no commensurate depreciation tax shield. Under the pooling of interest method the books of the combining companies are simply combined or pooled as there is no good-will created and, consequently, no depreciation of goodwill that will reduce reported earnings.

Another aspect of pooling of interest that made it appear favourable was the previously sanctioned accounting practice regarding acquired assets. Assets acquired at book value under pooling could be resold at market value, and the difference would be reflected in higher profits and earnings. These apparent earnings advantages led to widespread preference for the pooling method along with widespread abuses of the method. The accounting profession has attempted to eliminate what are largely artificial advantages of the pooling method by eliminating some of the obvious enticements and by making it more difficult to qualify for pooling of interest.

Example-1

Company XYZ offers ₹ 12,00,000 for ₹ 4,00,000 of ABC's stock at book value. ABC has ₹ 1,00,000 debt. How much goodwill arises? If XYZ has ₹ 20,00,000 equity and ₹ 5,00,000 debt itself, what is the combined balance sheet using the purchase method and the pooling method?

Solution

₹ 8,00,000 goodwill (₹ 12,00,000–₹ 4,00,000). Balance Sheets are as follows:

(per lakh of ₹)

Purchase method				*Pooling of interests method*			
Debt	6	Assets	30	Debt	6	Assets	30
Equity	32	Goodwill	8	Equity	24	Goodwill	0
Total	38	Total	38	Total	30	Total	30

EARN-OUT'S

The deferred payment plan, which has come to be called an earn-out, represents a relatively recent approach to merger financing. The acquiring firm agreed to make a specified initial payment of cash or stock and, if it can maintain or increase earnings, to pay additional compensation.

An earn-out has several benefits for the acquiring organisation. These are tested below:

(1) It provides a logical method of adjusting the difference between the amount of stock the purchaser is willing to issue, and the amount the seller is agreeing to accept for the business.

(2) The merging company will immediately be able to report higher earnings per share because fewer shares of equity will become outstanding at the time of the acquisition. In addition the acquiring company is provided with downside protection in the event that the merged business does not fulfilled its earnings expectations,

(3) The earn-out diminishes the guesswork in establishing an equitable purchase price, because the price is based upon the actual performance of the prospective acquisition after the merger.

Even though several advantages exist for earn-outs, potential problems must also be recognised, these are:

(1) The acquired corporation must be capable of being operated as an autonomous business entity.

(2) The acquiring firm must be willing to allow freedom of operation to the management of the newly acquired business.

(3) The acquiring firm must be willing to contribute toward the future growth of the acquiring company, realising that only by working together with the two firms attain success.

Numerous types of earn-outs have been devised; the various arrangements are limited only by the imagination of the management of the two firms involved. However, the base-period-earn-out may be used as any illustration. Under this plan the shareholders of the acquired company are to receive additional shares in each future year if the firm improves its earnings above the base period profits— that is, earnings in the last year before the acquisition. The amount of the future payments will be determined by three factors:

(1) The amount of earnings in the forthcoming years in excess of the base-period profits.

(2) The capitalisation rate (discount rate) agreed upon by the parties.

(3) The market value of the acquiring organisation at the end of each year. For example, the compensation in shares in future years might be computed by using the following formula:

$$\frac{\text{excess earnings} \times \text{price/earnings multiple}}{\text{equity market price}}$$

To illustrate, company X acquired company Y in 2010, which had base—period earnings of ₹ 8,00,000. At the time of the merger, company Y shareholders received 3,00,000 shares of company X equity. Annual profits subsequent to the merger have been ₹ 8,75,000, ₹ 9,50,000, ₹ 10,50,000 and ₹ 9,00,000. The market value of company X's equity is ₹ 25 per share and the price/earnings ratio is 10. Based upon the formula above, the additional shares to be paid to company stockholders would be:

2011: $\frac{₹\ 75,000 \times 10}{₹\ 25} = 30,000$ shares

2012: $\frac{₹\ 1,50,000 \times 10}{₹\ 25} = 60,000$ shares

2013: $\frac{₹\ 2,50,000 \times 10}{₹\ 25} = 1,00,000$ shares

2014: $\frac{₹\ 1,00,000 \times 10}{₹\ 25} = 40,000$ shares

Total=2,30,000 shares

Therefore, in addition to the down payment of 3,00,000 company X shares, company Y shareholders would receive a total of 2,30,000 shares during the ensuing four years.

The foregoing example, is ovesimplified, since other variables must also be recognised in the development of an earn-out plan. Such factors include

(1) A specified limitation as to the maximum amount of share that can be transferred in any year;

(2) an established range for the share price employed in the computations;

(3) the recognition of yearly earnings increments over the prior year;

(4) the determination of an equitable down payment; and

(5) the succinct definition of earnings for the earn-out computations.

In conclusion, the earn-out technique provides a means by which acquiring business can eliminate part of the guesswork involved in purchasing a firm. In essence, it allows the acquiring management the privilege of hindsight.

ILLUSTRATIVE PROBLEMS

1. The Sony-Tours is in the service sector and is considering merger to achieve

more favourable growth and profit opportunities. After an extensive search of a large number of companies, it narrowed the candidates to a company in the same sector, World-Travellers. As the treasure of Sony Tours you are investigating the possible acquisition of World-Travellers. You have the following basic data to start from:

	Sony-Tours	*World-Travellers*
Earnings per share	₹ 5.00	₹ 1.50
Dividend per share	₹ 3.00	₹ 0.00
Share price	₹ 90.00	₹ 20.00
Number of shares	10,00,000	6,00,000

Further investigations lead you to estimate that investors currently expect a steady compound growth of about 6% each year in World-Travellers' earnings and dividends. Under Sony-Tours' control this growth should increase to about 80% each year, without any additional capital investment and without any change in the riskiness of operations.

Required:

(a) Compute the increase in value resulting from the merger.

(b) What are the gains or losses likely to be to the shareholders in the two companies, assuming Sony-Tours pays ₹ 25 in cash for each share in World-Travellers.

(c) What will be the gain or losses if Sony-Tours offers one of its shares for every three shares of World-Travellers.

(d) Calculate the gains or losses on the assumption that the market does not expect World-Travellers' increased growth rate to materialise. Discuss the theoretical and empirical implications of (d) with respect to (a), (b) and (c) above.

Solution

(a) $\text{Share price} = \dfrac{D}{k_e - g}$

In fact the dividend should be D_1. In this exercise we will take the given dividends as D_1 (not D_o) as the numbers seem to invite this treatment.

For World-Travellers, before the acquisition

$$₹\ 20.00 = \frac{0.08}{k_e - 0.06}$$

therefore k_e, the market capitalisation rate equals 0.10. The acquisition g becomes 0.8, therefore

$$P = \frac{0.80}{0.10 - 0.08} = ₹\ 40.00$$

The increase in value is therefore ₹ 20.00 per share which with 6,00,000 shares, equals ₹ 1,20,00,000

(b) The gains to the shareholders of World-Travellers are straightforward. They give up a share worth ₹ 20 and receive ₹ 25 cash, an immediate gain of ₹ 5.

We will adopt two approaches to calculate the gain to Sony-Tours shareholders. First the total valuation approach:

Existing value of Sony-Tours	₹ 9.0 crore
Valuation of World following merger, 6,00,000 × ₹ 40	2.4 crore
	₹ 11.4 crore
less cash paid to purchase World	1.5 crore
	₹ 9.9 crore

There are 10,00,000 shares in the merged business.

Therefore value per share equals	₹ 99
New price	₹ 99
old price	₹ 90
Gain to Sony-Tours	₹ 9 per share.

There are at least two problems in calculating the gains to Sony-Tours shareholders by the use of a price earnings approach.

(i) We do not know what Sony-Tours has been earning on the ₹ 1.5 crore cash (₹ 25 × 6,00,000) it pays to the shareholders of World-Travellers. In paying this cash it is buying the earnings of World-Travellers but is giving up the return obtained from investing the cash.

(ii) We do not have the market capitalisation rate for the shares of Sony-Tours. We are not given the expected growth rate, nor the market capitalisation rate.

Using the P/E ratio concept, and assuming Sony-Tours was investing its cash to earn 5%, we can estimate the gains:

Existing P/E ratio of Sony-Tours

$$\frac{90}{5} = 18 \text{ to } 1$$

Earnings now	₹ 50,00,000
Earnings of Sony-Tours	9,00,000
	59,00,000
loss of interest on cash	7,50,000
	51,50,000
Number of shares	₹ 10,00,000

Therefore new earnings per share ₹ 5.15 which gives a share price of ₹ 92.70.

The shareholders of Sony-Tours therefore show a gain of ₹ 2.70 per share based on the above assumptions, ignoring the higher expected future growth of World-Travellers, and assuming the P/E ratio of Sony-Tours remains unchanged.

(c) To World-Traveller shareholders immediate gain

Receive share worth	₹ 90
Give up share worth	60
	₹ 30

The gain could be higher if Sony-Tours shares rise in price following merger, which they should:

To Sony-Tours shareholders	
Value of company now	₹ 9.0 crore
Value of World-Traveller	2.4 crore
	₹ 11.4 crore
Number of shares	10,00,000
plus	2,00,000
	12,00,000

This gives a value of ₹ 95 per share in the merged company.

Gain to World-Traveller shareholders	₹ 95 – ₹ 60 = ₹ 35
Gain to Sony Tour Shareholders	₹ 95 – ₹ 90 = ₹ 5

(d) If the market does not expect the higher growth rate in World-Travellers to materialise, the gains are:

Value of Sony-Tours	₹ 9.0 crore
Value of World-Travellers	₹ 1.2 crore
	10.2 crore
Number of shares	12,00,000
Price per share	₹ 85
Gain to World-Traveller shareholders	₹ 85 – 60 = ₹ 25
Loss to Sony-Tour shareholders	₹ 85 – 90 = ₹ –5.00

2. ABC Group wishes to acquire Mukta Arts Ltd. The directors of ABC Group are trying to justify the acquisition to the shareholders of both companies on the grounds that it will increase the wealth of all shareholders.

The supporting financial evidence produced by ABC Group's directors is summarised below:

	ABC	*Mukta Arts*
Operating profit	₹ 124.00 crore	₹ 58.00 crore
Interest payable	44.31	22.00
Profit before tax	₹ 79.69 crore	₹ 36.00 crore
Tax	27.89	12.60
Earnings available to ordinary shareholders	₹ 51.80 crore	₹ 23.40 crore
Earnings per share (pre-acquisition)	₹ 14.80	₹ 29.25
Market price per share (pre-acquisition)	₹ 222	₹ 322
Estimated market price (post-acquisition)	₹ 240	
Estimated equivalent value of one old Mukta Acts share (post-acquisition)		₹ 360

Payment is to be made with ABC Group ordinary shares, at an exchange ratio of 3 ABC Group shares for every 2 Mukta Arts shares.

Required:

(a) Show how the director's of ABC Group produced their estimates of post acquisition value and, if you do not agree with these estimates, produce revised estimates of post-acquisition values.

All calculations must be shown. State clearly any assumptions that you make.

(b) If the acquisition is contested by Mukta Arts Ltd., using ABC Group's estimates of its post-acquisition market price calculate the maximum price that ABC Group could offer without reducing the wealth of its shareholders.

(c) The board of directors of Mukta Arts Ltd. later informally indicate that they are prepared to accept a 2 for 1 share offer.

Further information regarding the effect of the acquisition on ABC Group is given below:

(i) The acquisition will result in an increase in the total pre-acquisition after tx operating cash-flows of ₹ 27.50 crore per year indefinitely.

(ii) Rationalisation will allow machinery with a realisable value of ₹ 72.0 crores to be disposed of at the end of the next year.

(iii) Redundancy payments will total ₹ 35.0 crore immediately and ₹ 84 crore at the end of the next year.

(iv) ABC Group's cost of capital is estimated to be 14%.

All values are after any appropriate taxation. Assume that the pre-acquisition market values of ABC Group and Mukta Arts shares have not changed.

Recommend, using your own estimates of post-acquisition values, whether ABC Group should be prepared to make a 2 for 1 offer for the shares of Mukta Arts.

(d) Assuming no increase in the total post-acquisition earnings, assess whether this acquisition is likely to have any effect on the value of debt and equity of ABC Group.

Solution

(a) The answer to this question depends heavily on what assumptions are made.

The current price/earnings (P/E) ratios of ABC and Mukta Arts are:

$$\text{ABC } \frac{222}{14.80} = 15:1$$

$$\text{Mukta Arts } \frac{322}{29.25} = 11:1$$

Assuming that no synergy occurs, and that the earnings available to ordinary shareholders after the acquisition is the sum of the pre-acquisition earnings for the two companies, post-acquisition earnings total ₹ 75.20 crore.

ABC Group has ₹ 51.80 crore ÷ ₹ 14.8 crore = 3.5 crore shares; Mukta Arts ₹ 23.4 crore ÷ ₹ 29.25 = 0.8 crore shares.

At an exchange ratio of 3 for 2 ABC Group will need to issue 1.2 crore new shares.

ABC's directors have assumed that the post-acquisition P/E ratio will be the same as ABC's pre-acquisition P/E ratio 15:1.

The post-acquisition earnings per share =

$$\frac{₹\ 75.20 \text{ crore}}{4.7 \text{ crore}} = ₹\ 16$$

The estimated post-acquisition market price of ABC shares is ₹ 16.0 × 15 = ₹ 240.

One old Mukta Arts share will be exchanged for 1.5 ABC shares, giving an estimated value per old Mukta Arts share of:

₹ 240 × 1.5 = ₹ 360.

ABC's directors are engaging in what is sometimes referred to as 'bootstrapping' the earnings per share. If no synergy occurs (including synergy through the improved management of Mukta Arts assets) and if Mukta Arts current share price is not under-valued in an inefficient market, it is very unlikely that the market will hold the P/E ratio of ABC constant at 15.1. In the absence of any reasons for shareholders' wealth to increase or decrease in a reasonably efficient market, it is likely that the post-acquisition P/E ratio would be the weighted average of the two pre-acquisition P/E ratios at approx. 14:1.

If there is no change in the total market value post-acquisition, the total value will be:

ABC 3.5 crore share at ₹ 222	=	₹ 7,77,00,00,000
Mukta Arts 80,00,000 shares at ₹ 322	=	₹ 2,57,60,00,000
		₹ 10,34,60,000

The value will be split to $\frac{35}{47}$ existing ABC shareholders

= ₹ 7,70,44,68,100 or ₹ 20 per share

(or the total post-acquisition value divided by the total number of shares = ₹ 1034.60 ÷ 4.7 crore = ₹ 220.

and $\frac{12}{47}$ to existing Mukta Arts shareholders = ₹ 2,64,15,31,900 or ₹ 330 per share.

Mukta Arts shareholders experience a slight increase in wealth because the share exchange ratio of 3 for 2 is more favourable than the ratio of the companies' market prices:

(322 ÷ 222 = 1.45 for 1 or 2.9 for 2).

This gain is at the expense of ABC's shareholders. As ABC is paying more than the current market value for Mukta Arts the wealth of its shareholders will fall.

If any change in expected shareholders wealth occurs because of the acquisition, or if the market is not efficient, different estimated values will result.

(b) Using ABC's estimate of its post-acquisition market price, the total post-acquisition value of the company will be:

4.7 crore × 240 crore	=₹ 1128 crore
ABC's pre-requistion value (found earlier)	= ₹ 777 crore
Gain from acquisition	= ₹ 351 crore

A total of ₹ 351 crore (in cash or the equivalent of this sum in shares or other forms of payment) could be offered without reducing the total wealth of ABC's shareholders.

(c) A 2 for 1 share offer would value one Mukta share at ₹ 444 or the company at ₹ 355.2 crore. The current market value of Mukta Arts is:
₹ 322 × 80,00,000 = ₹ 257.6 crore.

If a 2 for 1 share offer is to be acceptable to ABC, the expected present value of the effects of the new information must exceed ₹ 97.6 crore (₹ 355.2 crore – ₹ 257.6 crore).

After tax, operating cash flows are expected to increase by ₹ 27.5 crore per year indefinitely. The present value to infinity of these cash flows is ₹ 27.5 crore/0.14 = ₹ 196.4 crore.

Alternatively, the present value might be calculated for a finite number of years, for example, 10 years, the present value would be ₹ 27.5 crore x 5.216 = ₹ 143.44 crore.

The present value of redundancy costs is:

₹ 72 crore × 0.877 = ₹ 63.1 crore

The present value of redundancy cost is:

₹ 35 crore + ₹ 84 crore × 0.877 = ₹ 108.7 crore

The expected present value of the effects of the new information is:

₹ 196.4 crore + ₹ 63.1 crore – ₹ 108.7 crore = ₹ 158 crore

This is in excess of the required present value of ₹ 97.6 crore. (even if the 10-year period for operating cash flows is used). On the basis of this data, ABC should be prepared to make a 2 for 1 offer for the shares of Mukta Arts.

(d) As long as the earnings streams of the two companies are not perfectly positively correlated, the riskiness of the combined earnings stream will be reduced, and the post-acquisition company will be less likely to default on its debts. This could be important, in this case, as both ABC and Mukta Arts have large amounts of interest payable and therefore large amounts of debt. As the probability of default is lower, debt is less risky than it was before the acquisition and its value to the lenders of debt increases. This will probably lead to a fall in the cost of new debt for the company.

If the total post-acquisition value is un-changed and the value of debt rises, the value of equity must experience a corresponding decrease. Existing holders of debt are likely to gain at the expense of shareholders.

The shareholders may avoid some of these theoretical losses if the acquisition is partly financed by debt or additional debt is issued and used, where permitted, to repurchase equity—in both cases, making use of the increased debt capacity of the company caused by the greater earnings stability.

A well-diversified shareholder, interested only in systematic risk, will not place a higher value on the company's shares because ABC is now a more diversified company.

3. While scanning through the corporate world performance in recent years, Ashok Dhawan noted the name of Sundran Shipbuilders — a firm built and sold custom yacht and smaller motorized craft. A once prosperous firm, Sundran Shipbuilders had difficulty weathering the reccession that began in 2008. The unexpected death of the firm's founder, S.P. Jain, in March, 2010, further complicated matters and now Southern was on the verge of bankruptcy. It was at this critical time one of Dhawan's friend, R.D. Kapoor, in the same business, approached him and offered him to join hands and purchase control of Sundran Shipbuilders and turn it around. He pointed out that they, in this given situation of the company as the enclosed balance sheet for 2011 indicates, could turn it around by having 52 percent of the shares from the old man's heirs at ₹ 44 per share. Kapoor offered to take 12 percent of shares and for remaining 40 per cent, he asked Dhawan to arrange the funds.

Proforma a Balance Sheet for 2011 : Sundran Shipbuilders

(*₹ in crore*)

Assets		*Liabilities*	
Cash	5.00	Accounts payable	32.00
Marketable securities	3.00	Other current liabilities	17.00
Accounts receivables	27.00	Notes payables	35.00
Inventories	24.00	Bonds	14.00
Machinery	95.00	Equity (₹ 100 per share)	12.00
less accumulated depreciation	(28.00)	Premium	11.00
Plants and fixtures	56.00		
Less accumulated Depreciation	(18.00)	Retained earnings	78.00
Land	35.00		
	₹ 199.00		₹ 199.00

Though the equity price at ₹ 44.00 per share seem to be high considering the firm will have a operating income of ₹ 12.00 crore for 2011 and earnings of ₹ 2.20 per share, Kapoor believes that the deal is not on the current year's earnings but on the 2012 earnings with he himself running the show. In case he took over, his plans are:

(i) Float a 12 per cent bond to immediately pay off the other current liabilities and notes payable. Both can be fully paid off on Dec. 2011 without any penalty.
(ii) Reduce the accounts payable by one-half. To get the cash, the inventories are to be cut in half and the receivables down to ₹ 1.10 crore. The excess cash is to beef up the low cash account.
(iii) Cut costs and adjust prices to raise the return on investment to the 18 per cent. It can be done since he knows the market whereas Jain had lost contact with it.

After having number of meetings with Kapoor, Dhawan decided to check further before taking any final decision. He had not got to be a rich and successful venture capitalist by ignoring promising opportunities. And he did have some money coming in next month from a highly successful deal with the Japanese. After two weeks of investigating, his information supported the facts. He decided to buy deal if it meet his specific guidelines. First, if Kapoor figures were achieved in 2012, he wanted his purchase price per share to be such that he was not paying more than 8/1 price—earnings multiple for his shares. Second, Kapoor must be projecting at least a 300 per cent improvement in EPS. His philosophy was that big risks justified by profits and he would not change that concept under any circumstances.

Required

(a) Prepare the new balance sheet for Sundran Shipbuilders after Kapoor makes the suggested changes.
(b) Calculate the new EPS assuming that Kapoor can achieve the profit goals.
(c) Does Sundran Shipbuilders met Dhawan's guidelines for acquisitions?

Solution

1. Liquidity Charges

(₹ in crore)

Source:	
Reduce receivables by	16
Reduce inventories by	12
Float 12% bonds for	52
Total	80
Uses:	
Increase cash	12
Reduce payables by	16
Eliminate other current liabilities	17
Eliminate notes payables	35
	80

2. New Balance Sheet

(₹ in crore)

Cash	17.00	Accounts Payable	11.00
Marketable Securities	3.00	Bonds (–12.50%)	14.00
Receivables	11.0	Bonds (12%)	52.00
Inventories	12.00		
Machinery	95.00		
(accum. depre.	(28.00)	Equity	12.00
Plant Equip	56.00	Premium	11.00
(accum. depre.)	(18.00)	Retained Earnings	78.00
Land	35.00		
	183.00		183.00

3. New EBIT

An 18% ROI Times ₹ 13 crore assets = ₹ 3.294 crores

4. NEW EPS

EBIT	₹ 32,94,00,000
Interest on 12.5% Bonds	1,75,00,000
Interest on 12% Bond	6,24,00,000
EBIT	24,95,00,000
NIAT	12,47,50,000
Equity Shares Issued	1,20,00,000
EPS	₹ 10.39

EPS increases from ₹ 2.20 to ₹ 10.39, an increase of 372 per cent. At ₹ 44 per share, the P-E ratio is ₹ 44/10.39 = 4.2/1.

Conclusion

Ashok Dhawan is paying less than 8/1 price-earnings multiple and the EPS increases by more the 300 per cent. Thus, Sundran Shipbuilder met his guidelines for acquisition.

4. Bhushan Cotton Textiles (BCT) Ltd. is considering acquiring Gujarat Cotton Textiles (GCT) Ltd. and has made a three-year projections of the firm's financial statements, including the revenue and earnings estimates as follow:

(*₹ in crore)*

	Year			
	0	*1*	*2*	*3*
Revenue	₹ 2250	₹ 2475	₹ 2730	₹ 3000
EAT	150	180	225	270

BCT expects that cash equal to depreciation needs to be reinvested to keep GCT plant operating efficiently. The remaining 60% of the cash generated by operations will need to be invested in growth opportunities. BCT also expects that synergies will net ` 20 crore after tax per year and a 7 % annual growth is expected in all of the target's figures after the third year. Currently the risk free rate is 7.5% and the market return 12% on an average stock. GCT's beta is 1.5 and the firm has shares issued 50 crore, which closed at 18.50 yesterday. How much should BCT pay for GCT's stock? Discuss the quality of the estimate.

Solution:

Using the CAPM approach, the SML yields is:

$$R_i = R_T + (R_m - R_T)\, B_i$$

Where

R_i = Return on security i; R_T = Risk free rate; R_n = Market rate of return; B_i = Beta of security i

By substituting the values, we get.

$$= 7.5\% + (12\% - 7.5\%)\, 1.5$$

$$= 13.75\%$$

13.75% is the appropriate discount rate for the present value calculations. Using the information for the first three years, cash flow estimates for the target are:

GC Textiles Ltd. Estimated Cash Flow

(*₹ in crore)*

	Year			
	0	*1*	*2*	*3*
Revenue	₹ 2250	₹ 2475	₹ 2730	₹ 3000
EAT (Unmerged)	₹ 150	₹ 180	₹ 225	₹ 270

Synergies	20	20	20	20
EAT/Cash flow (Unmerged)*	₹ 170	₹ 200	₹ 245	₹ 290
Reinvested (60%)	102	120	147	174
Cash flow to BCT Ltd.	₹ 68	₹ 80	₹ 98	₹ 116

* Depreciation has not been added back because of the assumption that cash equal to that amount must be reinvested to maintain the plant.

Since BCT Textiles is assuming that the last year flow of ₹ 116 crore will grow at 7% per year indefinitely, the value of a known payment that is to grow at a known rate can be calculated by using the constant growth (Gordon) stock valuation model i.e.,

$$P_0 = \frac{D_0 (1+g)}{k - g}$$

By replacing P_o with the terminal value (TV) and D_o be taken the year 3 cash flow, C_3, we get:

$$TV = \frac{C_3 (1+g)}{k - g}$$

$$= \frac{₹ 116 \text{ crore } (1+.07)}{.1375 - .07}$$

$$= \frac{₹ 116 \text{ crore } (1.07)}{.0675} = \frac{₹ 124.12 \text{ crore}}{.0675}$$

$$= ₹ 1838.81$$

Hence, the cash flow stream in capital budgeting calculations are as:

(₹ in crore)

	Year		
	1	*2*	*3*
Operating cash flow	₹ 80	₹ 98	₹ 116
Terminal Value			1838.81
Total	₹ 80	₹ 98	₹ 1954.81

The present value of the entire stream is

$$PV = \frac{₹ 80}{(1.1375)^1} + \frac{₹ 98}{(1.1375)^2} + \frac{₹ 116}{(1.1375)^3} + \frac{₹ 1838.81}{(1.1375)^3}$$

= ₹ 70.33 + ₹ 75.74!+ ₹ 78.81!+ ₹ 1249.35
= ₹ 1474.23

This shows that GC Textiles is worth ₹ 1474.23 crore to BC Textiles

Since the GC Textiles has issued 50 crore shares, the price per share will be:

$$= \frac{₹\ 1474.23\ \text{crore}}{50\ \text{crore}} = ₹\ 29.48$$

Hence, the maximum price per share is ₹ 29.48. And if the share is currently selling at ₹ 18.50, this represents 59.38% premium over its market price calculated as follows:

(₹ 29.48 - ₹ 18.50) / ₹ 18.50 = 59.38%

Terminal value depend on the highly sensitive assumption made about the long-term future. For example, if 10% long-term growth rate is taken for GCT, the total value of the firm is then:

PV = ₹ 70.33 + ₹ 75.74 + ₹ 78.81 + ₹ 2311.88
= ₹ 2536.76 crore

Under this more aggressive assumption of 10% growth, the terminal value represents 91.13% against the earlier 84.75% of this respective target's final calculated values. The maximum aquisition price will be:

$$= \frac{₹\ 2536.76\ \text{crore}}{50\ \text{crore}} = ₹\ 50.74\ \text{per share}$$

which implies a premium of

(₹ 50.74 - ₹ 18.50) / ₹ 18.50 = 174.24%

Hence, good judgement is called for to avoid basing a high value deal on too high a price.

5. K.K. Enterprise (KKE) is interested in boosting the price of its stock. To do that, management in considering restructuring capital to 60 per cent debt in the hope that the increased EPS will have a positive effect on price. However, the economic outlook is gloomy, and the company's finance manager thinks there is a good chance that deterioration in business conditions will reduce EBIT next year. At the moment KKE's stock sells for its book value of ₹ 10 per share. The selected P & L statement and capital information for the KKE's follow:

(₹ in crore)

		Capital	
Revenue	₹ 748	Debt	₹ 250
Cost/extreme	452	Equity	750\
EBIT	₹ 296	Total	₹ 1,000

KKE pays 12% interest on its debt and currently 75 crore equity shares are issued. If the tax rate is 30%, estimate the effect of the proposed restructuring on EPS. Use the degree of financial leverage to assess the increase in risk that will come along with it.

Solution

The proposed capital structure of KKE will be:

(₹ in crore)

	Current	*Proposed*
Capital		
Debt	₹ 250	₹ 600
Equity	750	400
Total	₹ 1,000	₹ 1,000
Shares issued	75 crore	40 crore

Since equity can be traded at its book value, the restructuring will exchange equity of debt with a proportionate reduction in the number of shares issued. The projected EAT and EPS at the current level of business for both capital structures will be:

(₹ in crore)

	Current	*Proposed*
EBIT	296.0	296.0
Interest (12% of debt)	30.0	72.0
EBT	266.0	224.0
Tax (@ 30%)	79.8	67.2
EAT	186.2	156.8
EPS	2.48	3.92

If the business conditions remain unchanged, the proposed structure will yield a higher EPS by ₹ 1.44 (₹ 3.92 - ₹ 2.48).

DFL under each structure will be:

$$DFL_c = \frac{EBIT}{EBIT - F} = \frac{₹\ 296\ crore}{₹\ 296\ crore - ₹\ 30\ crore} = 1.1$$

$$DFL_p = \frac{EBIT}{EBIT - F} = \frac{₹\ 296\ crore}{₹\ 296\ crore - ₹\ 72\ crore} = 1.32$$

DFL is more volatile under the proposed capital structure than the current. The implication of higher DFL is that if the proposed capital structure is adopted and a substantial downside occurs, the resulting EPS will be lower than the EPS under the existing capital structure. To illustrate, suppose business deteriorates and the EBIT declines by 40%, the EPS decline in percentage under both the existing and the proposed will be:

$\% \Delta EPS_c = DFL_c \times \% \Delta EBIT$

$= 1.1 \times 40\% = 44.4\%$

$\% \Delta EPS_p = DFL_p \times \% \Delta EBIT$

$= 1.32 \times 40\% = 52.8\%$

If these percentage declines are applied to the current and projected EPS to find what they will become under both structures, we get:

Current : ₹ 2.48 (1 - .444) = ₹ 1.40

Project: Rs 3.92 (1 - .528) = ₹ 1.85

The fall in projected EPS of the proposed capital structure by ₹ 2.07 (₹ 3.92 - ₹ 1.85) is clearly substantial.

6. ABC Co. is analysing the XYZ Co. for acquisition. ABC Co. consider 12% rate of interest as appropriate for the analysis. XYZ Co. has 1.5 crore shares issued, and its cash flows including synergies over the next three years in estimated to be as follows:

Year	*Cash flows*
1.	₹ 250 crore
2.	300 crore
3.	400 crore

ABC Co. is fairly conservative and feels that the acquisition be justified by cash flows projected over no more than three years since projection beyond that are too risky to be consider reliable. What is the maximum ABC Co. should pay for a share of XYZ Co.'s stock?

Solution

The present value of XYZ's positive cash flows is calculated below:

Year	*Cash flow*	*$PVF_{12\%}$*	*PV*
1	₹ 250 crore	.8929	223.225
2	300	.7972	239.160
3	400	.7118	284.720
			₹ 747.105 crore

The maximum ABC Co. should pay for all XYZ Co.'s stock is ₹ 747.105 crore. This is the initial outlay which would result in a zero NPV. At this price ABC Co. should be indifferent to the acquisition.

ABC Co. should pay maximum price per share on XYZ Co.'s stock:

$$\text{Maximum Acquisition per share Price} = \frac{₹\ 747.105 \text{ crore}}{1.5 \text{ crore}}$$

$$= ₹\ 498.07$$

7. Apex Industries is considering acquisition of RG Group in an equity for equity exchange. Assume that no immediate synergistic benefits are expected. Table below gives the select financial data on the two companies:

	Apex Industries	*RG Group*
Sales (₹ crore)	₹ 2000	₹ 1500
Earnings after taxes (₹ crore)	₹ 260	₹ 140
Equity issued (in crores)	₹ 100	₹ 60
EPS	₹ 2.50	₹ 3.50
Price per equity share	₹ 50	₹ 40
Dividends per share	₹ 1.50	₹ 1.00

(i) If Apex is not willing to incur an initial dilution in its EPS—that is, not have the postmerger EPS below ₹ 2.50— and if Apex also feels that it will have to offer the RG Group equity shareholders a minimum of 25% over RG Group's current market price, what is the relevant range of RG Group's per equity share price with which Apex is working?

(ii) Calculate Apex's postmerger EPS if the RG Group's shareholders accept an offer by the Apex of ₹ 50 in an equity—for—equity exchange.

Solution

(i) Low end of range:

₹ 40 x 1.25 = ₹ 50

High end of range:

$$P_{max} = (P/E)\,(EPS)$$

$$= (50/2.50)\,(3.50)$$

$$= ₹\ 70$$

$$EPS_{Apex} = \frac{₹260 \text{ crore} + ₹140 \text{ crore} + 0}{100 \text{ crore} + 60 \text{ crore}} = \frac{₹\ 40 \text{ crore}}{160 \text{ crore}}$$

=!₹ !2.50

8. Prem Auto Ltd. is being considered for acquisition by Sonal International Auto Ltd. It can be observed from the table given below on the actual and projected financial statements for Prem Auto Ltd. that the company had ceased growing under present management, and the Sonam's management is of the view that it could, by using its market connections, achieve for the Prem Auto additional growth for several years. The projected financial statements reflect the sales that Sonam expects if the acquisition occurs (see table given below). The risk free rate is 7.4%, and the average risk premium is estimated to be 7% for stocks in general with beta 1.8. From the projected financial statements, the cash flow to equity holders and net cash flow have been estimated. No future growth is estimated after 2017-18, and that new asset acquisition will approximately equal depreciation. Therefore, cash flow will be same as income after 2017-18, and income after 2017-18 will be the same as income in 2017-18. What in the required rate of return?

Financial Statements for Prem Auto Ltd.

(*₹ in crore*)

		PRO FORMA				
Year	*Actual 2012-13*	*2013-14*	*2014-15*	*2015-16*	*2016-17*	*2017-18*
Sales	25,000	27,500	30,250	33,275	36,602	40,263
Cost of good sold	15,000	16,500	18,150	19,965	21,961	24,158
Gross profit	10,000	11,000	12,100	13,310	14,641	16,105
Depreciation	1,150	1,250	1,300	1,350	1,400	1,450
Administrative Costs	5,000	5,450	5,941	6,477	7,061	7,695
Net operating income	3,850	4,300	4,859	5,483	6,180	6,960
Interest	600	630	661	695	729	766
Earnings before tax	3,250	3,670	4,198	3,788	5,451	6,194
Income tax (.40)	1,300	1,468	1,679	1,915	2,180	2,478
Net Income	1,950	2,202	2,519	2,873	3,271	3,716
Current assets	7,500	8,250	9,075	9,982	10,981	12,079
Fixed assets	12,500	13,000	13,500	14,000	14,500	15,000
Total Assets	20,000	21,250	22,575	23,982	25,481	27,079
Current liabilities	3,750	4,125	4,537	4,991	5,490	6,039
Long-term debt	6,000	6,300	6,610	6,940	7,287	7,652
Diferre taxes	1,250	1,375	1,512	1,664	1,830	2,013
Equity	9,000	9,450	9,916	10,387	10,874	11,375
Total liabilities and Net worth	20,000	21,250	22,575	23,982	25,481	27,079

Cash Flow to Equity

Net Income	2,202	2,519	2,873	3,271	3,716
+ Depreciation	1,250	1,300	1,350	1,400	1,450
+ Increased long-term debt	300	310	330	347	375
+ Increase deferred tax	125	137	152	166	183
- Increased net working capital	375	412	452	499	549
- Purchase of fixed assets	1,750	1,800	1,850	1,900	1,950
= Equity residual flow	1,752	2,054	2,401	2,785	3,225

Net Cash Flow

= Equity Residual flow	1,752	2,054	2,401	2,785	3,225
+ Interest x (1 - .40)	378	397	417	437	459
- Increased long-term debt	300	310	330	347	375
= Net Cash flow	1,830	2,141	2,488	2,875	3,309

Solution

Required return on equity = .074 + 1.8 (.07) = 20 percent.

The value of Prem's equity at the end of 2005 is:

V_{2011} = 3716/.20 = ₹ 18,580 crore

Using an equity residual valuation method and assuming that each flows occur at year-end, the value of Prem Auto is:

Equity residual value =

$$\frac{1{,}752}{(1.20)^1} + \frac{2{,}054}{(1.20)^2} + \frac{2{,}401}{(1.20)^3} + \frac{2{,}785}{(1.20)^4} + \frac{3{,}225}{(1.20)^5} + \frac{18{,}580}{(1.20)^5}$$

= 1460.00 + 1426.39 + 1389.47 + 1343.07 + 1296.06 + 7466.88

= ₹ 14,381.87 crore

To use the net cash flow method, the WACC must first be determined. The value of equity has been estimated at ₹ 14,318.87 crore. If the market and book values of the long-term debt are same, the ratio of debt to total capital is:

Debt to Total capital = 6000/(6,000 + 14,381.87) = .2944

The cost of debt (borrowing) is 10%, the after tax cost is .10% (1-.40) = .06. The weighted average cost of capital (WACC) is therefore:

WACC = .2944 (.06) + (1 - .2944) (.20)

= .01766 + 0.14112 = 0.15878

Net cash flow after 2017-18 will be net income flow after tax interest expense 3716

+ 766 (1 - .40) = ₹ 4175.6 crore. The value of capital at the end of 2016 is then ₹ 4,175.6 crore/0.15878 = ₹ 26,298.02 crore. The value of Ashoka's net cash flows is therefore:

Capital value =

$$\frac{1,830}{(1.15878)^1} + \frac{2,141}{(1.15878)2} + \frac{2,488}{(1.15878)^3} + \frac{2,875}{(1.15878)^4} + \frac{3,309}{(1.15878)^5} + \frac{26,298.02}{(1.15878)^5}$$

= 1579.25 + 1594.46 + 1598.99 + 1594.53 + 1584.01 +12588.81

= ₹ 20540 crore

Since the purchaser of the company also accepts a ₹ 6,000 crore debt obligation, the value of the equity is then ₹ 20540.05 crore - ₹ 6,000 crore = ₹ 14,540.05 crore. This is a small difference before the value of equity using the net cash flow and the equity residual cash flow results.

QUESTIONS

1. How would one evaluate the acquisition of a *going concern*? What difficulties are often encountered?
2. What are the important considerations in evaluating the long-run impact of a merger or the combined firm's earnings per share? Why may a long-run view change a merger decision?
3. Often in mergers-especially in conglomerate mergers-tax considerations are a key motive for a business combination. Why and in what situations may the acquisition of a firm with a tax-loss carryforward be quite acceptable?
4. What are acquisitions and mergers? How are they different?
5. What is the justification for the acquisition of companies not as going concerns, but rather for all or part of their assets? What other benefits may result from such acquisitions?
6. Distinguish between a holding company and an operating company. Which appears to be more risky, the use of debt in the holding company's capital structure or the use of debt in the operating company's? Why? Give an example of each.
7. What are the key advantages and disadvantages cited for the holding company arrangement? What is *pyramiding*, and what are its consequences?
8. When an equity exchange type of acquisition is being evaluated, what is normally the key variable considered? Why?
9. Can a merger with a large, stable company serves as an effective way to raise capital for a growth oriented smaller company?
10. Explain: Why the accounting treatment (purchase versus pooling) of the acquisition of a going concern shall be different from the treatment, given the acquisition of any other asset.
11. What is the difference between a merger and a consolidation? How does a holding company arrangement for business combination differ from either?
12. Are the negotiations for merger agreements more difficult if the firms are in different industries or in the same industry? If they are about the same size or quite different in size? If the ages of the firms are about the same or if they are very different? Why?
13. Would the book value of a company's assets be considered the absolute minimum price

to be paid for a firm? Why? Is there any value that would qualify as an absolute minimum?

14. There are many methods by which a company can raise additional capital. Can a merger be considered a means of raising additional equity capital? Explain.
15. Explain the concept of instantaneous merger profit. What assumptions are made about economies of scale in explaining the concept?
16. How would the existence of long-term debt in a company's financial structure affect its valuation for merger purposes? Could the same be said for any debt account regardless of its maturity?
17. Explain the differences among *horizontal, vertical,* and *conglomerate* growth. Which types of growth have the greatest potential for operating synergism?
18. What types of *financial* synergism might economically justify business combination?
19. Under what circumstances might a firm that has been operating at a loss be considered to be a desirable merger partner?
20. What is *countersynergism?* Indicate a few factors that might reduce or nullify the contemplated synergistic effects of a business combination.
21. What is the *ratio of exchange?* Is it based on the current market prices of the shares of the acquiring and target firms? Why may a long-run view of the merged firm's earnings per share change a merger decision?
22. What role do investment bankers often play in the merger negotiation process? What is a tender offer? When and how is it used?
23. Briefly describe each of the following takeover defenses against a hostile merger.
    (a) White knight
    (b) Poison pill
    (c) Greenmail
    (d) Leveraged recapitalisation
    (e) Golden parachutes
    (f) Shark repellents
24. Valuation is the key element in appraising a merger. Explain why. How would you go about establishing the stand-alone value of the closely held stock of a prospective merger candidate firm? How would you appraise the value of that stock if the target firm were merged into your acquiring firm? How would these two values relate to your bargaining with management of the target firm to establish the terms of a friendly merger?
25. Under what circumstances would the following currencies of exchange be appropriate in a merger: *(a)* cash, *(b)* debt securities (bonds or notes), *(c)* convertible stock, and *(d)* equity shares? What sweeteners might be added in a stock-for-stock exchange?
26. What is a *leveraged buyout (LBO)?* What are the three key attributes of an active candidate for acquisition using an LBO?
27. What is a *divestiture?* What is an *operating unit?* What are four common methods used by firms to divest themselves of operating units?

PROBLEMS

1. You have been asked by the directors of Gamma Ltd., a large conglomerate which is involved in a wide range of different activities, to report on the price to be paid for the possible purchase of Bhamma Ltd Bhamma Ltd. is a private company which makes and sells fashion garments- a business which is not currently including among Gamma Ltd.'s activities. Bhamma Ltd. has recently experienced substantial trading difficulties and, if successful in its proposed purchase, Gamma will replace the existing management of Bhamma Ltd.

The directors of Gamma Ltd. are unsure as to how the business of Bhamma Ltd should be valued. They understand that two possibilities exist-either the value of the assets of Bhamma Ltd. or its past earnings could constitute the basis of the purchase price.

You are required to: (a) explain the rationale underlying the assets and the earnings bases of valuation; (b) discuss the practical difficulties which might exist in applying each of the two methods; and, (c) explain how the individual circumstances surrounding the purchase of Bhamma Ltd might determine your choice of method in this case.

2. Hamid Locks manufactures cylinder locks for the Middle-East market. The company's turnover and profits for the past three years and the expected results for the current year are as follows:

Year ended 31 December	*Turnover* ₹ *Crore*	*Net profit after tax* ₹ *Crore*
2010 (actual)	23.0	2.1
2011 (actual)	24.0	2.3
2012 (actual)	21.0	2.0
2013 (estimate)	20.0	2.0

The balance sheet at the end of the current year (31 December 2013) is expected to be as follows:

(₹ *crore)*

Fixed Assets	14.0
Net current assets	6.0
	20.0
Financed by:	
Ordinary share capital (10,00,000) fully paid ordinary share of (₹ 10 each)	10.0
Reserves	5.0
	15.0
Debenture (15%)	5.0
	20.0

The present market price of the shares is ₹ 44 and the price has not fallen below this level since 2007.

The company's directors are concerned about the lack of growth in turnover and profit and are considering ways of improving profitability. The directors feel that there is unlikely to be any significant growth in the construction industry in the foreseeable future and that, in order to improve profitability, the company must either diversify or increase its share of the market. The directors are reluctant to diversify and are exploring the possibility of acquiring a smaller lock manufacturing company as a means of increasing the company's market share. They are particularly interested in Hero Locks Ltd, which manufactures mortise locks, and are considering making a bid for its entire share capital. Hero Locks Ltd. is a publicly quoted company which has in issue 5,00,000 fully paid ordinary shares of ₹ 10.00 each. These shares currently have a market price of ₹ 20 per share.

The company's results for the past three years and its expected results for the current year are as follows:

	Turnover ₹ *crore*	*net profit after tax* ₹ *crore*
2010 (actual)	8.4	0.42
2011 (actual)	9.5	0.54
2012 (actual)	10.8	0.65
2013 (estimate)	12.0	0.75

The balance sheet of Hero Locks Ltd. has reserves of ₹ 5 crore but does not have any preference share capital or long term debt.

The directors of Hamid Locks Ltd. have estimated that, if they acquire Hero Locks Ltd, the combined turnover of the two companies would be ₹ 50 crore and after tax profit would be ₹ 5 crore. In addition they consider the some of the fixed assets of Hero Locks Ltd. would no longer be required and could be sold for ₹ 50,00,000. The financial director has suggested that a bid for the shares in Hero Locks Ltd be made at 120% of their current market price and that, as regards payment of that price, the following three options should be considered:

(a) A new issue of ordinary shares in Hamid Locks Ltd in exchange for the ordinary shares of Hero Locks Ltd.

(b) An issue of 15% convertible debentures, with ₹ 1000 of debentures convertible into 62.50 ordinary shares at the option of the holders in 5 years' time.

(c) An issue of 16% debentures with warrants attached. Each ₹ 1000 of debentures would give the holder a warrant to purchase 10 or ordinary shares at a price ₹ 55.00 per share in 3 years' time.

Required:

(a) Calculate the maximum price that Hamid Locks Ltd should be willing to pay for shares in Hero Locks Ltd.

(b) Briefly discuss the advantages and disadvantages of financing a takeover by an issue of convertible debentures.

(c) Assuming that the takeover of Hero Locks Ltd. is agreed at the price suggested by the financial director and takes place on 1 January 2014, advise the directors of Hamid Locks Ltd of the effect on the company's future earnings per share of each of the alternative financing methods and state, with reasons, which method you would recommend. Assume a corporation tax rate of 50%.

28

BUSINESS FAILURE AND REORGANISATION

INTRODUCTION

A business failure is an unfortunate circumstance. It can be considered from both an *economic* and a *financial* viewpoint. In an economic sense, *business success* is associated with firms that earn an adequate return (equal to or greater than the cost of capital) on their investments. Similarly, *business failure* is associated with firms that earn an inadequate return on their investments. An important aspect of business failure involves the question of whether the failure is *permanent* or *temporary.* For example, suppose a company has ₹ 100 crore invested in assets and only generates operating earnings of ₹ 1 crore. Obviously, this 1 percent return on investment in inadequate. However, the appropriate course of action depends to some extent on whether this business failure is judged to be permanent or temporary. If it is permanent, the company probably should be liquidated. If failure is temporary, the company probably should attempt "to ride out the storm," especially if steps can be taken to speed the company's return to business success. From an economic standpoint, business failure also is said to exist when a firm's revenues are not sufficient to cover the costs of doing business.

TYPES OF BUSINESS FAILURE

A firm may fail because its *returns are negative or low.* A firm that consistently reports operating losses will probably experience a decline in market value. If the firm fails to earn a return that is greater than its cost of capital, it can be viewed as having failed. Negative or low returns, unless remedied, are likely to result eventually in one of the following more serious types of failure.

A second type of failure, *technical insolvency,* occurs when a firm is unable to pay its liabilities as they come due. When a firm is technically insolvent, its assets are still greater than is liabilities, but it is confronted with a *liquidity crisis.* If some of its assets can be converted into cash within a reasonable period, the company may be able to escape complete failure. If not, the result is the third and most serious type of failure, bankruptcy. Bankruptcy occurs when a firm's liabilities exceed the fair market value of its assets. A bankrupt firm has a *negative* shareholders' equity. This means that the claims of creditors cannot be satisfied unless the firm's assets can be liquidated for more than their book value. Although bankruptcy is an obvious form of failure, *the courts treat technical insolvency and bankruptcy in the same way.* They are both considered to indicate the financial failure of the firm.

FREQUENT CAUSES OF FAILURE

Although causes of business failure vary from firm to firm, we can identify several common ones. The predominant cause of failure is managerial incompetence. Also, the following key structural problems within management may appear: (1) An imbalance of skills within the top echelon. A manger tends to attract other managers of similar skills. For example, the corporate management may consist principally of individuals having a background in sales, without anyone having production experience. (2) *A chief executive* who dominates a firm's operations without regard for the inputs of peers. (3) An inactive board of directors. The board of directors' lack of interest in the financial position of the company may lead to insolvency. (4) A deficient finance function within the firm's management. Not infrequently, the only substantial input provided by the financial officer occurs when the budget is submitted to the board. A company may have an effective financial information system, however this information is of no avail if it does not flow to the board through a strong financial officer. (5) The absence of responsibility for the chief executive officer. Although all other managers with a company are responsible to a superior, the chief executive seldom must account of his actions. Conceptually, this person is responsible to the shareholders, the link is tenuous or even missing altogether.

The foregoing deficiencies render the firm vulnerable to several mistakes. *First,* management may be negligent, in developing effective accounting systems. *Second,* the company may be unresponsive to change—unable to adjust to a general recession and unfavourable industry developments. *Third,* management may be inclined to undertake an investment project that is disproportinonately large relative to firm size. If the project fails, the probability of insolvency is greatly increased. *Finally,* management may come to rely so heavily on debt financing that even a minor problem can place the firm in a dangerous position.

SYMPTOMS OF BANKRUPTCY

As a company enters the final stages prior to failure, a pattern may develop in terms of a changing financial ratios have proven to be useful indicators of impending disaster. A study by Altman developed a statistical model that found the financial ratios best predicting bankruptcy. Based upon Altman's sample of bankrupt firms, the study yielded an equation that used five ratios to predict bankruptcy:

$$\text{Bankruptcy score} = 1.2X_1 + 1.4X_2 + 3.3X_3 + .6X_4 + .999X_5$$

where X_1 = (net working capital ÷ total assets)
X_2 = (retained earnings ÷ total assets)
X_3 = (earnings before interest and taxes ÷ total assets)
X_4 = (total market value of stock ÷ book value of total debt)
X_5 = (sales ÷ total assets)

With his equation, the criterion for separating firms with a strong likelihood of bankruptcy from those that probably will not fail should be as follows. If the score exceeds 2.99, no concern should exist that the company is facing bankruptcy in the foreseeable future. On the other hand, a score less than 1.81 suggests that the firm is a likely candidate for failure. Values between 1.81 and 2.99 are difficult to assign to either a "successful" or a "failure" classification. However, although a firm in this "gray area" can easily be misclassified in terms of the final outcome, the best way to set up a dividing line is to predict that a company will fail if its score is less than 2.675. Alternatively, a score exceeding 2.675 may be used as an indicator that success is more likely than failure. These guidelines are shown in Table-1.

TABLE-1

Altman's Bankruptcy Criterion

	Bankruptcy Score	
Less than 1.81	*Between 1.81 and 2.99*	*Greater than 2.99*
Probability of failure is high	Probability of failure is difficult to determine	Probability of failure is remote
Predict failure	Less than 2.675—predict failure Greater than 2.675—predict success	Predict success

We may conclude that a potentially failing corporation begins to invest less in current (X_1). Since X_2 is a cumulative indicator of profitability relative to time, the findings suggest that younger companies have a greater chance of bankruptcy. Variable X_3 reflects the firm's general earnings power. Deterioration in this factor was shown to be the best single indicator that bankruptcy may be forthcoming. Variable X_4 depicts the firm's financial leverage position. Finally, X_5, the asset turnover ratio, measures management's ability to generate sales from the firm's assets.

Although the financial information flowing from a firm helps us identify problems, the predictions we make with it certainly are not perfect. Owing to factors unique to the firm, as well as to the tendency for managements of problem firms to do some "window dressing" of the financial statements, the ratios will not always effectively identify corporations that face bankruptcy within the near future. Even so, they will help us assess the likelihood of bankruptcy.

When a firm faces severe problems, either the problems must be resolved or the firm must be liquidated. At such a point, an important question has to be answered: *Is the firm worth more dead or alive?* A decision to continue operating has to be based upon the feasibility and fairness of reorganising the firm as opposed to the benefits of liquidating the business. As shown in Figure-1, when technical insolvency occurs, management must either modify the operating and financial conditions or terminate the firm's life. If the decision is made to alter the company in the hopes of revitalising its operations, either voluntary agreements with the investors or a formal court-arranged reorganisation must be used. If, on the other hand, the difficulties are believed to be insurmountable, a liquidation will take place, either by assignment of the assets to an independent party for liquidation or by formal bankruptcy proceedings.

FIGURE-1

REORGANISATION VERSUS LIQUIDATION.

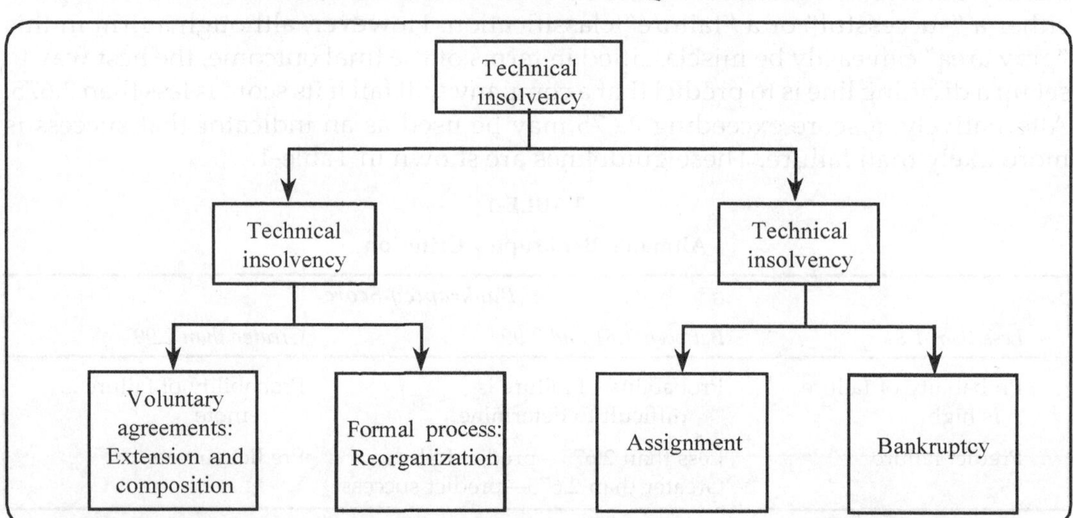

Voluntary Remedies to Insolvency

Once a firm begins encountering these difficulties, the firm's owners and management have to consider the alternatives that are available to failing businesses. In general, a failing company has two alternatives: First, it can attempt to resolve its difficulties with its creditors on *voluntary*, or *informal*, basis. Second, it can petition the courts for assistance and *formally* declare *bankruptcy*. A company's creditors also may petition the courts, and this may result in the company's being involuntarily declared bankrupt.

Regardless of whether a business chooses informal or formal methods to deal with its difficulties, eventually the decision has to be made whether to *reorganise* or *liquidate* the business . Before this decision can be made, both the business's liquidation value and its going-concern value have to be determined. *Liquidation value* equals the proceeds that would be received from the sale of the business assets minus liabilities. *Going-concern value* equals the capitalised value of the company's operating earnings minus its liabilities. Basically, if the going-concern value exceeds the liquidation value, the business should be reorganised; otherwise, it should be liquidated. However, in practice, the determination of the going-concern and liquidation values is not an easy matter. For example, problems may exist in estimating the price the company's assets will bring at auction. In addition, the company's future operating earnings and the appropriate discount rate at which to capitalise the earnings may be difficult to determine. Also, management understandably is not in a position to be completely objective about these values.

Informal Alternatives for Failing Businesses

Regardless of the exact reasons why a business begins to experience difficulties, the result is often the same; namely, cash flow problems. Frequently, the first steps taken by the troubled company involved stretching its payables. In some cases, this action can buy the troubled company up to several weeks of needed time before creditors take action. If the difficulties are more than just minor and very temporary, the company may next turn to its bankers and request additional working capital loans. In some situations, the bankers may make the additional loans, especially if they perceive the situation to be temporary. Another possible action the company's bankers and creditors may take is to restructure the company's debt.

Debt restructuring by bankers and other creditors can be quite complex. However, debt restructuring basically involves either *extension, composition,* or a combination of the two. In an *extension,* the failing company tries to reach an agreement with its creditors that will permit it to lengthen the time it has to meet its obligations. In a *composition,* the firm's creditors accept some percentage amount less than their actual original claims, and the company is permitted to discharge its debt obligations by paying less than the full amounts protected from any further actions on the part of the creditors while it attempts to work out a *plan of reorganisation.* The debtor company has 120 days to work out a plan of reorganisation. After that, the creditors may file a plan of their own. The court has considerable latitude in a bankruptcy case. For example, depending on the nature of the case, it may decide to appoint a *trustee* who will be responsible for running the business and protecting the creditors' interests. Normally, the troubled company is allowed to continue operations. If there is reason to believe that continuing operations will result in further deterioration of the creditors' position, however, the court can order the firm to cease operating.

An important aspect of the bankruptcy procedures involves what to do with the failing firm. Just as in the case of the informal alternatives, a decision has to be made about whether a firm's value as a *going concern* is greater than its *liquidation* value. Generally, if this is the case and a suitable plan of reorganisation can be formulated, the firm is reorganised; otherwise, it is liquidated.

Evaluation of Voluntary Remedies

The primary advantages of voluntary remedies relate to the minimisation of costs and the informality of the process. A significant amount of legal, investigative, and administrative expenses may be avoided, resulting in a higher return to the creditors. Also, the bargaining process is greatly simplified, and a more congenial atmosphere typically prevails than in the bankruptcy courts.

One of the difficulties in arranging a voluntary remedy is that a creditor may refuse to participate. To encourage participation and cooperation of the firm's creditors, a composition generally allows for the payment in full of small claims. For instance, the terms of the agreement may state that all creditors are to receive a certain amount plus a pro rata share of the remaining claim. This provision eliminate the small claims. However, it means that the larger creditors partially underwrite the amounts payable to small creditors.

Another disadvantage, particularly for the extension, is that the debtor maintains control of the business. If the underlying problems confronting the business are not corrected, the company's assets may continue to erode in value, which clearly works to the determent of the creditors. However, controls may be initiated to minimise any potential losses due to continued inefficient management.

REORGANISATION

If a voluntary remedy, such as an extension or composition, is not workable, a company can declare or be forced by its creditors into bankruptcy. As a part of this process, the firm is either reorganised or dissolved. Reorganisation is similar to an extension or composition, the objective being to revitalise the firm by changing its capital structure. The rehabilitation interest the reduction of fixed changes by substituting equity and limited income securities for fixed-income securities.

FINANCIAL DECISIONS IN REORGANISATION

When a business becomes insolvent, a decision must be made whether to dissolve the firm through liquidation or to keep it alive through reorganisation. Fundamentally, this decision depends upon a determination of the value of the firm if it is rehabilitated *versus* the value of the sum of the parts if it is dismembered.

Liquidation values depend upon the degree of specialisation of the capital asset used in the firm and hence their resale value. In addition, liquidation itself involves costs of dismantling, including legal costs. Successful reorganisation also involves costs. Typically, better equipment must be installed, obsolete inventories must be disposed of, and improvements in management must be made.

Net liquidation values are compared with the value of the firm after reorganisation, net of the costs of rehabilitations. The procedure that promises the higher returns to the creditors and owners will be the course of action favoured. Often the greater indicated value of the firm in reorganisation, compared with its value in liquidation, is used to force a compromise agreement among the claimants in a reorganisation, even when they feel that their relative position has not been treated fairly in the reorganising plan.

STANDARDS OF FAIRNESS

The basic doctrine of fairness states that claims must be reorganised in the order of their legal and contractual priority. Junior claimants may participate only to the extent that they have made additional cash contribution to the reorganisation of the firm.

Carrying out this concept of fairness involves the following steps: (1) An estimate of future sales must be made. (2) An analysis of operating conditions must be made so that the future earnings on sales can be estimated. (3) A determination of the capitalisation rate to be applied to these future earnings must be made. (4) The capitalisation rate must be applied to the estimated future earnings to obtain an indicated value of the properties of the company. (5) Provision for distribution to the claimants must then be made.

STANDARD OF FEASIBILITY

The primary test of feasibility is that the fixed charges on the income of the corporation after reorganisation are amply covered by earnings or, if a value for a firm that is to be sold is established; that a buyer can be found at that price. Adequate coverage of fixed charges for a company that is to continue in operation generally requires an improvement in earnings or a reduction of fixed charges, or both.

Policies Required to Improve the Earning Power

Among the actions, that will have to be taken to improve the earning power of the company, the following are: (1) Where the quality of management has been inefficient and inadequate for the task, new talents and abilities must be brought into the company if it is to operate successfully subsequent to the reorganisation. (2) If inventories have become obsolete, they should be disposed of and the operations of the company streamlined. (3) Sometimes the plant and the equipment of the firm need to be modernised before it can operate and compete successfully on a cost basis. (4) Reorganisation may also require an improvement in production, marketing, advertising, and other functions, to enable the firm to compete successfully and earn satisfactory profits. (5) It is sometimes necessary to develop new products so that the firm can move from areas where economic trends have become undesirable into areas where the growth and stability potential is greater.

Example-1

XYZ Corporation is currently undergoing a reorganisation. The firm's balance sheet as of June 30, 2011 is presented in Table-1. The creditors have filed a petition for reorganisation. The court has named a trustee, who is serving to develop a possible plan of reorganisation. Based upon the trustee's evaluation, an internal reorganisation is considered to be both fair and feasible to the existing investors. The trustee has projected the company's earnings, and by using an appropriate price/earnings multiple has estimated the firm's going-concern value to be ₹ 800 crore, as compared to a ₹ 600 crore liquidation value (the approximate amount that would be received if the business were terminated and the assets sold individually).

TABLE-2

XYZ Corporation
Balance Sheet, June 30 2011

(₹ *in crore*)

Assets	
Current assets	200
Net plant and equipment	1550
Other assets	100
Total assets	1850

Liabilities and equity	
Current Liabilities	
Accounts payable	100
Bills payable	300
Total current liabilities	400
Long-term liabilities	
Mortgage bonds (8% due in 2015)	400
Subordinated debentures (9½% due in 2015)	800
Total long-term liabilities:	1200
Total Liabilities	1600
Equity	
Equity Share Capital (par ₹ 10)	50
Paid-up capital	1400
Retained earnings	–1200
Total equity	250
Total liabilities and equity	1850

* Subordinated to the mortgage bonds.

The proposed plan for reorganising the company is shown in Table 3. The first portion of the table specifies the amounts of the distribution to be made to each group of creditors. Since the going-concern value is ₹ 800 crore, only 50 per cent of the ₹ 1600 crore in debt can be honoured. As a result, the equity shareholders will not be entitled to any of the distribution. Also, the subordinated debentures are not to participate in the reorganisation until the mortgage bond holders have been repaid in full. Consequently, the ₹ 400 crore in securities that would have been distributed to the owners of the debentures has to be reduced by ₹ 200 crore. The final distribution, after reorganising the subordination, is shown in the last column of Table 3.

TABLE-3
XYZ Corporation
Reorganisation Plan

(*₹ in crore*)

Creditors	*Amount of claim*	*50 per cent of claim subordination*	*New claim after*
Account payable	100	50	50
Bills payable	300	150	150
Mortgage bonds	400	200	400
Subordinated debentures*	800	400	200
	1600	800	800

* Subordinated to the mortgage bonds.

New Securities Issued in the Reorganisation

(*₹ in crore)*

Old Security	*New Securities*	
Accounts payable	Accounts payable	25
	Equity shares capital	25
Bills payable	Preference shares	75
	Equity shares capital	75
Mortgage bond	Mortgage bond (8%)	200
	Subordinated debentures (9%)	100
	Preference shares (10%)	100
Subordinated debentures	Equity shares capital	200

The lower section of Table-3 reflects the trustee's proposed changes in the firms capital structure. The objective is to reduced the financial leverage to a point commensurate with the company's ability to cover the fixed financial charges from earnings. For example, the original accounts payable balance is reduced to ₹ 50 crore with those creditors having a short-term claim of ₹ 25 crore and receiving ₹ 25 crore in new equity shares. The final capital structure, if the trustee's plan is adopted, is provided in Table-4.

TABLE-4
XYZ Corporation
Liabilities and Equity after Reorganisation

(*₹ in crore)*

Account payable	25
Mortgage-bonds (8%)	200
Subordinated debentures (9½%)	100
Preference shares (10%) capital	175
Equity share capital	300
	800

LIQUIDATION

If for some reason reorganisation is judged unfeasible, a legally declared bankrupt company may be liquidated. In the liquidation procedure, a *referee* normally is appointed to handle the administrative aspects of the bankfuptcy procedure. The referee then arranges for a meeting of the creditors, and they in turn select a *trustee,* who liquidates the business and pays the creditors' claims according to the priority of claims.

PRIORITY OF CLAIMS

It is the trustee's responsibility to liquidate all the firm's assets and to distribute the proceeds to the holders of *provable claims*. The court have established certain procedures for determining the provability of claims. The priority of claims must be maintained by the trustee in distributing the funds from liquidation. It is important to recognise that any secured creditors have specific assets pledged as collateral and, in liquidation, receive proceeds from the sale of those assets. If these proceeds are inadequate to meet their claim, the secured creditors become unsecured, or general, creditors for the unrecovered amount, since specific collateral no longer exists. These and all other unsecured creditors, will divide up, on a pro rata basis, any funds remaining after all prior claims have been satisfied. If the proceeds from the sale of secured assets are in excess of the claims against them, the excess funds become available to meet claims of unsecured creditors. The complete order of priority of claims is as follows: (1) The expenses involved in the administration of the bankruptcy. (2) Business expenses incurred after an involuntary petition has been filed but before a trustee has been appointed. (3) Wages owned for services performed prior to the bankruptcy proceedings. (4) Unpaid employee benefit plan contributions that were to be paid in the period preceding the filing of bankruptcy or the termination of business. (5) Claims of storage. (6) Unsecured customer deposit, resulting from purchasing or leasing a good or service from the failed firm. (7) Taxes legally due and owed by the bankrupt firm to government. (8) Claims of secured creditors, who receive the proceeds form the sale of collateral held, regardless of the priorities above. If the proceeds from the liquidation of the collateral are insufficient to satisfy the secured creditors' claims, the secured creditors become unsecured creditors for the unpaid amount. (9) Claims of unsecured creditors. The claims of unsecured, or general, creditors and insatisfied portions of secured creditors' claims are all treated equally. (10) Preference shareholders, who receive an amount up to the par, or stated, value of heir preference shares. Finally, the equity shareholders who receive any remaining funds, which are distributed on in equal per-share basis.

QUESTIONS

1. What are the primary causes of business failure? What types of actions commonly cause business failure?
2. How can financial analysis be used to forecast the probability of a given firm's failure? Assuming that such analysis is properly applied, can it always predict failure?
3. How can a business firm that meets all its debt obligations technically be considered to have failed? Are firms that just breakeven each period considered failures? Why or why not?
4. It is argued that a small number of bankruptcies is a healthy sign of economic development. Explain.
5. Distinguish between a reorganisation and a bankruptcy. As a creditor of a financial troubled concern, would you prefer liquidation or financial reorganisation? Why? Would you always prefer liquidation if the market value of the firm was less than the liquidation value?
6. Would it be possible to form a profitable company by merging two companies, both of which are business failures? Explain.

7. What is the objective of voluntary liquidation? How is voluntary liquidation process organised? What are: (1) an assignment, (2) an assignee, and (3) a trustee?
8. Explain the difference between the economic and financial definitions of business failure. What alternatives are available to the failing firm?
9. Basically, what determines whether a bankrupt company is reorganised or liquidated?
10. In connection with reorganisation plans, what do *fairness* and *feasibility* mean?
11. What are the three types of business failure? What is the difference between *technical insolvency* and *bankruptcy?* What are the major causes of business failure? Explain how a firm that has failed can be reorganised to operate successfully.
12. Define an *extension* and *composition* in a debt reorganisation. Explain how they might be combined to form a voluntary settlement plan to sustain the firm. How is a voluntary settlement resulting in liquidation handled?

LUXMI PLASTIC INDUSTRIES: *A CASE*

Luxmi Plastic Industries has filed a petition for reorganisation that has been denied. Luxmi is declared a bankrupt firm and is to be liquidated in keeping with Bankruptcy Acts. Its most recent Balance Sheet is given in Table-1

TABLE - 1
Luxmi Plastic Industries
Balance Sheet

Claims		*Assets*	
Accounts payable	₹ 15,00,000	Cash	₹ 2,00,000
Bills payable	10,00,000	Receivable	30,00,000
Accrued wages[1]	1,20,000	Inventory	20,00,000
Taxes Payable	1,80,000	Land	2,00,000
First portgage[2]	30,00,000	Net plant	46,00,000
Subordinated debentures[3]	25,00,000		
		Total assets	₹ 1,00,00,000
Preference shares	5,00,000		
Equity share capital	8,00,000		
Retained earnings	4,00,000		
Total claims	₹ 1,00,00,00		

(a) Average amount due employee is ₹ 400, No. employee is owed more than ₹ 550. All wage were earned in the 3 months preceding filing for bankruptcy.
(b) The first mortgage is secured with land and plant.
(c) Debentures are subordinated to bills payable.

Luxmi has total assets of ₹ 1,00,00,000. The receivables are generally over due and only 80 percent of the ₹ 30,00,000 can be collected. A certain amount of obsolescence is present in the inventory, which can be liquidated at 70 percent of carrying cost. The land and building is to be sold at a package and will bring in ₹ 22,00,000. First, what is the liquidation value of Luxmi's assets? Second, how should the liquidation proceeds be distributed among Luxmi's creditors?

Solution

Liquidation Value

The liquidation value of the firm's assets is calculated as follows:

Cash (100%)	₹ 2,00,000
Receivables (₹ 30 × 0.8)	24,00,000
Inventory (₹ 20 × 0.7)	14,00,000
Land and plant (given)	22,00,000
Total liquidation value	₹ 62,00,000

The total liquidation value is estimated to be ₹ 62,00,000. If we assume that this amount is realised, it will be distributed among the claimants according to the procedure outlined previously.

Distribution of Liquidation Proceeds

Liquidation proceeds equal ₹ 62,00,000 with claims equaling ₹ 1,00,00,000. Assume that expenses related to the administration of bankruptcy proceedings are ₹ 8,00,000. Distribution of the proceeds to the creditors can be divided into two categories to these claimants who are not general creditor and to those who are. The payments to the first group are summarised in Table-2. Net proceeds are ₹ 62,00,000 and bankruptcy expenses are ₹ 8,00,000. Accrued wges are paid in full (since they meet the requirements of the bankruptcy acts). Taxes payable are also paid in full since the remaining proceeds are in excess of taxes payable. The first mortgage is secured by the land and plant, which were sold for ₹ 22,00,000. Since the first mortgage is for ₹ 30,00,000 only ₹ 22,00,000 of the amount can be satisfied. The unsatisfied portion of ₹ 30,00,000–₹ 22,00,000 = ₹ 8,00,000 becomes unsecured credit. Remaining proceeds of ₹ 29,00,000 become available to firm's general condition.

TABLE - 2

Distribution of Liquidation Proceeds (A)

Net proceeds from liquidation	₹ 62,00,000
Expenses related to bankruptcy Administration	8,00,000
Accrued wages	1,20,000
Taxes payable	1,80,000
Portion of first mortgage paid from sale of plant	22,00,000
Proceeds available to general creditors	₹ 29,00,000

Total unsecured claims are the unsatisfied portion of the first mortgage of ₹ 8,00,000 account payable of ₹ 15,00,000 notes payable of ₹ 10,00,000 and subordinated debentures of ₹ 25,00,000 for a total of ₹ 58,00,000. These claims are listed in the second column of Table-3.

Since the total claims of general creditors equal ₹ 58,00,000 and only ₹ 29,00,000 are available for distribution, the general creditors will receive ₹ 29/₹ 58 = 50 percent of their claims before adjustment for subordination. The third column in Table-3 lists payments to the general creditors based on the 50 per cent payments to the general creditors based on the 50 per cent payment figure. The first mortgage receive ₹ 4,00,000. Bills payable would receive payment of ₹ 5,00,000 and holders of subordinated debenture would receive ₹ 12,00,000.

TABLE - 3

Distribution of Liquidation Proceeds (B)

Claimant	*Claim*	*50 % payment*	*Actual payment*[a]	*Percent on original claim*
First mortgage	₹ 8,00,000	₹ 4,00,000	4,00,000	87[b]
Accounts payable	15,00,000	7,50,000	7,50,000	50
Bills payable	10,00,000	5,00,000	10,00,000	100
Subordinated Debentures	25,00,000	12,50,000	7,50,000	30
Total	58,00,000	29,00,000	29,00,000	64[c]

(a) After adjustment for subordination, ₹ 5,00,000 is transferred from debentures to bill payable.

(b) $\frac{₹\ 22,00,000 + ₹\ 4,00,000}{₹\ 30,00,000}$ 87.5%

(c) $\frac{₹\ 29,00,000 + ₹\ 22,00,000}{₹\ 58,00,000 + 22,00,000}$ 64%

Since in the claims the debentures are subordinated to the claims of the bills payable, the amount payable is used first to satisfy the bills payable. To satisfy the ₹ 5,00,000 deficiency, ₹ 5,00,000 from the debentures payment is transferred to bills payable. This adjustment leaves the debentures with a payment of ₹ 12,50,000–₹ 5,00,000 = ₹ 7,50,000. The actual payment after adjustment for subordination is summarised in the fourth column of Table-3.

The last column in Table-3 shows the per cent of payment made on the original claim. Total payment on the mortgage was ₹ 22,00,000 + ₹ 4,00,000 = ₹ 26,00,000 on claims of ₹ 30,00,000 or 87 per cent, 50 per cent was paid on accounts payable. The bills payable were satisfied 100 per cent because of the subordination of the debentures to the bills. The debentures themselves were paid off at the rate of 30 percent. Other than employees and governmental units, the creditors received, on the average, 64 per cent of their claims. Total payment to these creditor were ₹ 22,00,000 + ₹ 29,00,000 = 51,00,000. Total clams were ₹ 58,00,000 + ₹ 22,00,000 = ₹ 80,00,000. Percentage payments on original claims, therefore were ₹ 51,00,000/₹ 80,00,000 = 64 per cent. Since the total proceeds were applied toward paying creditors, no payments are made to either preference or equity shareholders.

Reorganisation and bankruptcy can be an expensive proposition. The debtor and creditors may be better off with a voluntary settlement.

29

CREATING WEALTH: CORPORATE FINANCIAL STRATEGY AND DECISION MAKING

INTRODUCTION

Economic value added (EVA), today's leading idea in corporate finance and one of the most talked about in business, is far from the newest concept. On the contrary: Earnings more than the cost of capital is about the oldest idea in enterprise. But just as Greece's glories were forgotton in the Dark Ages, to be rediscovered in the Renaissance, so the idea behind EVA has often been lost in ever darker muddles of accounting. Managers and investors who come upon it as if they have seen a revelation. Since this is the last chapter in the book, it purports to deal with the corporate financial strategy. In discussing corporate financial strategy, the question can well be asked as to how strategy differs from more modest decision making. There is no completely satisfactory answer to this question, since there is an extensive intersection between those activities that we label decision making and those we label strategy formulation. We could resort to a distinction and have decision making become the application of the basic strategy, but generally decision making has a broader interpretation. Peter Drucker has stated, "The effective executive does not make many decisions. He solves generic problems through policy."[1]

CORPORATE FINANCIAL STRATEGIC PLANNING

Herbert Simon has written that there is a Gresham's law of planning: "Programmed activity tends to drive out non programmed activity."[2] The decision to buy a new energy-saving piece of equipment is a lot easier to discuss and analyze than strategic investment decisions. In the case of the energy-saving equipment, cash flows can be estimated and the decision to buy or not to buy can be made based on well-known capital budgeting techniques. The basic capital budgeting techniques are "programmed activities" in Simon's law. Strategy issues are a lot softer and a lot less satisfactory to

1. J.J. Tarrant, *Drucker: The Man Who Invented the Corporate Society* (Boston: Cahners Books, 1976), p. 258.
2. H.A. Simon, *The New Science of Management Decision* (Englewood Cliffs, N.J.: Prentice-Hall, 1977), p. 53.

write about and to read. However, it may well be that strategy issues are much more important, even if they are not fun to consider.

Strategy leads a firm to enter the energy business. That is the first and most important decision. The firm might then have to value a prospective acquisition as a means of accelerating the entry into the industry, but without the strategy decision it would not be necessary to value the acquisition.

All business decision making is based on abstractions from reality. We have to simplify in order to make decisions. We can delay decision making by insisting- on more information, but when the more information is obtained, there will still be more information that could be obtained if you were willing to defer action. Sooner or later one has to resist the opportunity to get more information, and one has to make the decision.

Herbert Simon has said this best:

> *Administrative theory is peculiarly the theory of intended and bounded rationality—of the behavior of human beings who satisfice because they have not the wits to maximize.*[3]

And as additional explanation:

> *Whereas economic man maximizes—selects the best alternative from among all those available to him, his cousin, administrative man, satisfices—looks for a course of action that is satisfactory or "good enough." Examples of satisficing criteria, familiar enough to businessmen if unfamiliar to most economists, are "share of market," "adequate profit," "fair price."*[4]

The substitution of the word "satisfice" for "maximize" is not necessary if we are willing to consider the costs of information, search, and delay in the decision to maximize. In a sense we can conclude that Simon is suggesting that it is better to make decisions, even imperfect decisions, than to endure the long wait until the perfect information and perfect decision processes are available. "In an important sense, all decision is a matter of compromise."[5]

While Simon's "satisfice" description is an extremely useful device for describing how managers operate, we shall find it convenient to collapse Simon's "satisfice" and profit maximization into one expression. Infact, the profit maximization (where profit is defined in terms of risk-adjusted present value) is deemed to be the primary objective of the firm. More is better. Further, the profit maximization objective includes the information cost and cost of search so that it is consistent with Simon's satisfice (we are not rejecting the satisfice concept). The assumption is that decisions should be made from the point of view of improving the well-being of the stockholders. This is a reasonable point of departure, but it cannot be the entire message. Managers,

---

3. H. A. Simon, *Administrative Behavior,* 3rd ed. (New York: Free Press, 1976), p. xxviii.
4. Ibid., p. xxix.
5. Ibid., p. 6.

employees, customers, and society in general have interests in the results of a firm's operations. We must also consider the impact of decisions on the well-being of these groups. One might object to this conclusion, but realistically such considerations are being included by successful firms.

No manager submits an investment or other decision proposal without carefully considering the impact of the decision being reviewed on his or her well-being. Even the board of directors will consider the well-being of managers if for no other reason than that managers are likely to be on the board. Employees also must be considered, since an obvious and continuous disregard of their interests will cause them to insist on the right to protect their interests. Customers also gain their right to be considered by the economic power they wield, not in the board room directly, but indirectly *via* the right of a consumer to avoid buying a corporation's product.

The rights of society can to some extent be ignored by a corporation for a short period of time, but continuous implementation of a "public be damned" philosophy is likely to bring forth a string of government legislation. The interests of society must be respected if only to avoid such legislation. A corporation should do "right" either because it is the proper thing to do or because it is in its own best interests to behave in such a fashion.[6]

KEY ELEMENTS OF STRATEGIC PLANNING

The five key elements of the strategic planning are listed below:

The *first* element in developing a strategy is the identification of the problems and opportunities that exist. A successful firm will have a fertile idea-generating environment. What problems and opportunities are there? Problem and opportunity identification is one of the more important outputs resulting from good strategic planning. No problem can be solved or an opportunity can be seized unless it exists.

The *second* element is to set goals (*objectives*). Goal setting is not independent of the identification of opportunities. If the goal is to achieve growth in sales of 15% per year, it will be necessary to spend more resources generating ideas than if the goal is to avoid growth. It may be argued that top management should stop with the setting of the goals and leave everything else to the operating managers. For example, top management might set the goals to earn at least 25% return on investment (ROI), to maintain a 15% growth rate per year, and to corner 20% of the total market as the firm's profit goals. Operating management would then establish the details as to how the goals would be achieved. A popular form of managerial style is to "manage by objectives." If one manages by objectives, the goal is set by the top, but the specific method of getting to the goal is not controlled. The results are important, not the method of getting to the results. Performance measurement is substituted for detailed supervision. Thus goal setting becomes a crucially important element in the strategic planning.

6. Christopher D. Ittner and Larcker, David F., Innovations in Performance Measurement: Trends and Research Implications, *Journal of Management Accounting Research,* 1998, vol. 10, p. 205.

We now have problems and goals defined. The *third* element is to have a procedure for providing, possible solutions, or "paths" the firm can follow to find a solution. For example, the current energy situation can be defined as a problem or an opportunity. The goal might be to achieve energy independence or to make a given return on investment. Assume a firm has decided to enter the energy industry and has to decide what kind of energy it will develop and how it will go about it. For example, it might consider solar, wind, tide, and fossil and then decide to go with solar.

Having decided to enter the solar energy industry, the corporation might decide to spend large sums on research or alternatively might decide to acquire a firm that already has valuable know-how and thus accelerate its entry into the industry. The setting of tactics follows the setting of the basic strategy for entering the industry.

The basic decision is to "enter the solar energy industry." The goals that are set can be to earn 25% ROI, increase earnings 15% per year, and gain 20% of the total market. Top management of the corporation might then leave the details of how this is to be achieved to the managers operating the solar energy division. This is an extreme form of decentralization and "bottom line management." The more normal procedure is for top management to oversee the more important decisions that are made, especially those involving large investment outlays or other large commitments.

The *fourth* element of strategic planning is to choose the best solution, given possible solutions and the firm's objectives. On what basis will the best solution be chosen? The goal might have been established to maximize the well being of the stockholders. This is easy to state, but given a large number of ways to enter the energy industry, which method should be chosen? It might be decided to choose the path with the largest net present value. But then risk considerations should enter analysis. Choosing the best solution, even with well-defined goals established, is a difficult job.

The *fifth* and final element of strategic planning is to have some type of review procedures to check how the best solution has actually performed. How this review function is executed will depend on the preferences and style of management.

The above five elements of strategic planning do not reveal anything about the style in which they (and the resulting plans) will be implemented. They are broad enough to encompass a wide range of financial decisions. For example, if the goal is to have reasonable growth but little risk, the amount of risk that is acceptable to the owners of the corporation (or in their absence, to the board of directors) will greatly affect the amount of debt that is used to finance the corporation.

A major planning question not yet answered is to what extent the interests of the organization come ahead of the interests of the different groups of employees. What sort of performance measures will be used, and what happens when goals are not met? Will excuses (explanations) be listened to, or will there be an insistence on performance? Managerial style will circle back and affect things like idea generation.

APPROACH TO STRATEGY

We will consider four approaches to strategy. The first uses brilliance and is unstructured, while the second uses dramatic simplifications and broad generalizations. The third relies heavily on statistical data, and the fourth is a theoretical approach that is correct, but may not always be practical.

Approach 1: Brilliance

Under this approach each situation is unique and the problem solver applies brilliance in arriving at a strategy. There is an unstructured analysis. A systematic approach to thinking about strategy can be learned (one can practice strategy decisions via cases and games), but there are few if any generalizations. A listing of the five elements of strategic planning described above is an illustration of an attempt to systematize thinking about strategy.

One can read a strategy recommendation for a firm and admire its wisdom, but still not be able to tell a computer how to do the next analysis.

Approach 2: Broad Generalizations

The Boston Consulting Group (BCG) has developed an amazingly simple to understand and attractive approach to strategy. In accordance with the model, the best of all worlds is for a product to have a high market share in a high-growth market (be a star). Thus the implication (recommendation?) is that a firm should maintain dominant market position in a growing market (the market segment may be very limited) or the firm should abandon the activity.

To some extent this recommendation is based on theory. To be in a monopolistic position is a desirable state from the point of view of profit maximization. Secondly, if a firm is producing more than the competitors, it is apt to be further along its learning curve, and thus its costs is likely to be less than those of competitor. Here, it is assumed that the incremental costs reduce with the number of units produced, and there is evidence to substantiate this assumption. If the firm has a high market share but slow growth in the market, it has a cash cow. Do not invest in this market, but drain off the cash. And if both the market share and market growth are low, it has a dog, and the advice is to find some fool who will take if off. Finally, if the market growth is high but the market share is low, then there is a question mark. Strategy will depend on the expectation of being able to move from a low market share to a high market share. The firm should either spend to achieve stardom or get out of the market.

Several recommendations follow from this strategy format in addition to the basic strategy of trying to achieve stardom. A firm should plan on growing with the market. Also, a "balanced portfolio" of cash cows and stars is desirable. The cows are used to finance the growth of the stars.

The basic attraction of the BCG approach is that it is simple, it is understandable, and it seems to make sense. It does not bog down in the details of complex models and massive sets of numbers, but rather focuses on the broad strategic considerations. What firm does not want to have essentially a monopolistic (dominant) position in a growth market? With the BCG system resources are allocated to stars and discounted cash flow calculations are largely meaningless. One establishes a growth strategy instead of evaluating individual investments spread over many different product lines.

Approach 3: Statistical Analysis

The third approach is to perform statistical analysis using industry data. Regressing the data, one draws conclusions as to the optimum strategy to be followed. For example, one might conclude that quality is very important in slow-growth markets. This conclusion is intuitively appealing. Customers are apt to become choosy in a situation where there is excess capacity (the market is growing slowly).

The statistical analysis and comparisons should be of some use in setting profit goals. The profits of the other firms can help set the targets of your firm. But the difficulty with this basic approach is that one can determine associative relationships (quality is shown to be important when there is low growth) but not causal relationships, and certainly there is no reliable implication as to the decision that should be followed. If high quality is desirable in a low-growth market, one does not conclude that low quality is desirable in a high-growth market. Further, can the data be used to judge the effects of changes in strategy of a firm? Can the data be used to determine the strategies and decisions that will lead to optimum positions? There are many firms that are betting that the statistical analysis of industry data can be used for these purposes.

Approach 4: A Theoretical Approach

The final approach is a purely theoretical approach. It is consistent with widely accepted economic and financial theory. It bypasses the broad generalizations and focuses on the details of the decisions. The basic strategy is to insist on detailed facts and evaluation of the alternatives, using conventional profitability measures.

Consider the resource allocation decision. Expansion of production in a given market is desirable as long as the marginal revenue of a product is larger than the marginal cost of producing and selling it. A project is undertaken as long as the discounted cash flow is larger than the cost of money (the net present value is positive).

Yes, it is nice to be further down the learning curve than competitors. That is to say, it is better to have some sort of advantage (a good position on the learning curve being one) that leads to lower costs than competitor. This preference is a fact, not a strategy consideration.

In addition to exploiting marketing cost advantages, a firm should take into consideration a wide range of institutional factors. These include the tax laws, trade arrangements, the availability of tax-exempt bonds, and government programmes aimed at helping industry (sometimes the legislation is not aimed at helping an industry but is interpreted in such a manner that it does help).

It is recommended that the definition of diversification be extended from the limited interpretation of obtaining cash from cows to supply stars to a consideration of risk factors arising from different mixes of product line. Based on the details of decisions, one can consider a wide range of different strategy factors. For example, one can focus on the identification of gap in the market and set out to supply a product to fill the need. The need may be in the form of better service or better quality. The strategy is to identify situations where such needs exist.

In evaluating a strategy plan, the first question to be asked about a strategy plant that has been prepared is whether it is understood by the managers who have to implement it. Just because something is said or written does not mean it is understood. The second question is to determine whether the plan is consistent with the firm's resources (e.g., money and managerial talent) and consistent with the objectives of the firm and the capabilities of top management. Recognize that the objectives can range from profit maximization (and there are many ways of measuring profits) The final step in the evaluation is to determine whether any crucial information or consideration has been omitted. For example, is the action legal?

It is easy to fall into the trap of too simple generalizations. Extreme strategies are not likely to be sustained through time. They are apt to change either because management changes its mind or because the composition of management changes. It is noted that generally the extreme strategy positions are frequently the result of one very unusual talented person heavily involved in the organization of the firm. When the genius is replaced by the professional managers, they are more apt to employ normal strategies similar to those employed by other firms in the industry.

Just because the extreme position is not likely to be maintained, a firm should not necessarily move to a so-called normal position. Drucker said it well:

> *The job of management, therefore, is never to be concerned with restoring or maintaining normality, because normality is the condition of yesterday. The real task of management in the effective business is that of re-directing and re-focusing activities towards what are the right economic realities for today and for tomorrow.*[7]

If we were to take all financial decisions out of the set of financial strategy considerations, we would be left with an empty box. If we were to take all strategy considerations out of the set of financial decisions, we would be left with a cookbook (the problems would be simplified so that exact and definite solutions could be obtained). A strategy approach to financial decisions is necessary, since exact normative financial decision recommendations are frequently a fiction based on simplified assumptions. Financial strategy implies that the interconnection between specific decisions be recognized. If debt is added to increase the earnings per share it has to be recognized that risk also increases, and that one has to be careful about not undertaking risky endeavors given the risky capital structure.

7. Peter F. Drucker, *Drucker on Management*, London: Management Publications Limited, 1970, p. 3.

Financial management systems are almost always a spaghetti bowl full of unconnected decision and feedback loops. They are like the internet without a protocol. They amount to internal corporate governance at its worst, and fuzzy finance at its finest. Consider that managers typically rely on cash flow, NPV, IRR and the like for making capital budgeting and valuation decisions, but when it comes time for them to set goals and measure actual performance, they put aside those cash metrics and turn to a separate set of yardsticks.[8] Earnings, growth, margins, market share, unit costs, returns, and earning before interest, taxes, depreciation and amortization (EBITDA) are among the reporting indicators that take center stage for those purposes. In the standard financial model, a wide gulf invariably separates the use of cash flow for capital budgeting on the one side and a long laundry list of accounting measures that are applied on the other. Without really thinking about it, most would have accepted that different measures apply for different purposes, but it should not be so.

To make matters considerably more convoluted, bonuses typically are based on the achievement of certain financial and operational budgetary goals that are negotiated as part of the annual planning process, but which individually and collectively often bear little correlation with shareholder value. And if that were not enough, top management often centers its dialogue with investors around next quarter's earnings-per-share.

Little wonder that when confronted with such a disjointed system, operating managers throw up their hands in exasperation and ask under their breath if not aloud, "So what do the head office so-and-so's really want? They have saddled us with every measure and method under the sun." It is a tyranny of ambiguity and indecision. The finance managers are the ones responsible for this architectural indigestion. Since most of them simply have not brought their financial management systems into sharp focus. Their financial reports and decision procedures know many things but miss really big things, questions like how much value are we creating for our shareholders, and how can we create more? Can a finance manager ever attain the clarity, unity and alignment that is the hallmark of the essence of value-focussed finance? The simple answer is, they should use EVA for everything, as the sun at the center of the financial management universe. They should adopt EVA as their paramount financial goal and corporate performance measure, use it to guide and inform all decisions and plans, and tie everyone's incentive pay to improving it.

ECONOMIC VALUE ADDED (EVA) TO MEASURE PERFORMANCE AND ASSESS STRATEGY

In recent years, **economic value added** (EVA) has already been garnering a following of prominent corporations that feel strongly about its ability to deliver

8. See Ronald E. Shrieves, Wachowicz Jr. John M.: Free Cash Flow (FCF), Economic Value Added (EVA) and Net Present Value (NPV): A Reconciliation of Variations of Discounted Cash Flow (DCF) Valuation, *Engineering Economists,* 2001, Vol. 46, p. 33.

improved company performance. Most EVA adopters allude to **stock price** increases as an outcome of implementing EVA performance measurement in their companies. The two numbers show a remarkable tendency to move up and down together.[9] However, while an individual firm may observe this EVA-**stock price** relationship, the empirical research to date does not support such a generalization. Regardless of actual versus perceived benefits of **stock price** performance, however, companies are embracing the EVA philosophy with a fervor. The idea of comparing profits with the cost of capital used to produce them results in a net measure showing how much **value** has been created or destroyed by the firm during the period. This is an intuitively appealing concept. EVA adopters appear to use some metrics less frequently than nonadopters.

WHAT IS EVA?

EVA is the cornerstone of focussed finance. It is both a measure of the true economic performance of a company and a strategy for creating shareholder wealth. Put more simply, EVA is net operating profit minus an appropriate charge for the opportunity cost of all capital invested in an enterprise. As such, EVA is an estimate of true economic profit,[10] or the amount by which earnings exceed or fall of the required minimum rate of return that shareholders and lenders could get by investing in other securities of comparable risk (see Exhibit-1). Properly implemented, EVA frees the measurement of corporate performance from the vagaries of accounting conventions and aligns the interest of managers with those of shareholders, ending the all too common conflicts of interest.[11]

EXHIBIT-1

What is Economic Value Added (EVA) ?

- A value-based financial performance measure
- A measure reflecting the absolute amount of shareholder value created or destroyed during each year
- A useful tool for choosing the most promising financial investments
- An effective protection against shareholder value destruction
- A tool suitable to control operations
- A measure highly correlated with stock prices
- A measure that can be maximized-EVA has not steering failures like ROI and EPS (maximizing these measures might lead to not optimal outcome; not max. shareholder value)
- An estimator for company's true economic value creation, unlike the **traditional measures** has focus on shareholder value creation

9. Stock prices track EVA far more closely than they track such popular measures as EPS or operating margins or ROE. That's becuase EVA shows what investors really care about—the net cash return on their capital—rather than some other type of performance viewed through the often distorting lens of accounting rules.
10. See Larry M. Prober: EVA: A better financial reporting tool, *Pennsylvanmia CPA Journal,* Fall 2000, Vol. 71, p. 27 and Raj Aggarwal, Using economic profit to asses performance: A metric for modern firm, *Business Horizon,* Feb. 2001, Vol. 44, p. 55.
11. See S. David Young: Some reflections on accounting adjustments and economic value added, *Journal of Financial Statement Analysis,* Winter, 1999, Vol. 4, p. 7.

- A good basis for management compensation systems to motivate managers to create shareholder value
- A tool more useful than rate of return (ROI) in controlling and steering day-to-day operations
- A concept practically the same as Economic Profit (EP), Residual Income (RI) and Economic Value Management (EVM)

The point is, not only *can* EVA be used for everything in the financial management system, it *must* be used for everything. All other metrics must be subordinated to EVA and traced to it in a value-anchored and truly balanced scorecard. Projecting, analyzing and discounting EVA must become the primary decision tool, replacing discounted cash flow analysis wherever it is found. Bonuses should no longer be based on a broad array of performance metrics that vary significantly from level to level; everyone's bonus, from top to bottom, should be strictly funded by a combination of company-wide and business-unit EVA performance.

Experience shows' that, comparatively speaking, the easy part is to add EVA. The hard part is to get managers to give up or subordinate cherished measures and pet goals like EPS, RONA, and margin, and embrace fully the EVA imperative. Most companies that have tried to implement EVA have not been able to do it. They have failed to get the commitment from the top and a mandate that all staff functions collaborate in applying a consistent measure of EVA across the board. If EVA is not implemented in such a cohesive and comprehensive manner—if it is not used to completely revamp the entire financial management system, or if EVA is just added as one more measure to sit alongside existing measures, or if it fails to work its way powerfully into incentives—the management system will turn out worse than before.

EVA BASIC PREMISE

Management most important mission is maximise shareholder wealth. A corporate governance system, based on the performance measure called EVA helps managers make the jump from theory to practice. This system overcomes failure in creating shareholder wealth by converting net present value (NPV), a point-in-time measure of value, with a period measure of performance and integrating it into the financial management and incentives compensation system. The constellation of EVA applications commences with EVA as a performance measure, as simply another — and far better — way to define earnings than taking reported accounting profit at face value. And, because it is just at heart an earnings figure, EVA has the virtue of being relatively simple to explain and to understand, even to the basic shop floor worker. It is neither complicated like cash flow, nor is it a meaningless percentage ratio. It is an exhaustive measure of corporate earnings that anyone can understand and learn to manage.

In simplest terms, EVA is economic profit — profit the way smart shareholders keep score. In contrast to book earnings, EVA subtracts a charge for the use of all capital — equity as well as debt. EVA deducts not just the interest on debt that all can see, but also an invisible charge for the use of equity capital — i.e., the shareholder funds — to recognize that shareholders too expect and deserve a return that compensates them for bearing risk. Unlike EPS, EVA doesn't begin to count profit until the shareholders receive a minimum acceptable return on their investment. Retained earnings are no longer a free form of finance.

To keep it simple, the costs of the debt and equity funds are combined into one overall or blended cost of capital and expressed as an interest rate. The cost of capital is not a cost a company must pay in cash, however. It is an opportunity cost. It is the rate of return that the firm's investors could otherwise expect to earn by purchasing a stock and bond portfolio of risk comparable to that of the company in question. EVA says that until a company earns a profit greater than its investors could earn on their own, it really operates at a loss. As Peter Drucker put the matter in *a Harvard Business Review* article, "Until a business returns a profit that is greater than its cost of capital, it operates at a loss. Never mind that it pays taxes as if it had a genuine profit The ' enterprise still returns less to the economy than it devours in resources...Until then it does not create wealth; it destroys it. EVA corrects this error by explicitly recognizing that when managers employ capital they must pay for it, just as if it were a wage.

EXHIBIT-2

EVA Basic Premise

i) Managers are obliged to create value for their investors
ii) Investors invest money in a company because they expect returns
iii) There is a minimum level of profitability expected from investors, called capital charge
iv) Capital charge is the average equity return on equity markets; investors can achieve this return easily with diversified, long-term equity market investment
v) Thus creating less return (in the long run) than the capital charge is economically not acceptable (especially from shareholders perspective)
vi) Investors can also take their money away from the firm since they have other investment alternatives

By taking all capital costs into account, including the cost of equity, EVA shows the amount of wealth a business has created or destroyed in each reporting period. In other words, EVA is profit the way shareholders define it. If the shareholders expect, say, a 10% return on their investment, they "make money" only to the extent that their share of after-tax operating profits exceeds 10% of equity capital. Everything before that is just building up to the minimum acceptable compensation for investing in a risky enterprise.

EVA by aligning decisions with shareholder wealth help to managers to incorporate two basic principles of finance into their decision making. The first is that the primary financial objective of any company should be to maximize the wealth of its shareholders. The second is that the value of a company depends on the extent to which investors expect future profits to exceed or fall short of the cost of capital. By definition, a sustained increase in EVA will bring an increase in the market value of a company. This approach has proved effective in virtually all types of organizations, from emerging growth companies to turnarounds. This is because the level of EVA isn't what really matters. Current performance already is reflected in share prices. It is the continuous improvement in EVA that brings continuous increases in shareholder wealth.

EVA has the advantage of being conceptually simple and easy to explain to non-financial managers, since it starts with familiar operating profits and simply deducts a charge for the capital invested in the company as a whole, in a business unit, or even in a single plant, office or assembly line. By assessing a charge for using capital, EVA makes managers care about managing assets as well as income, and helps them properly assess the tradeoffs between the two. This broader, more complete view of the economics of a business can make dramatic differences. Further, EVA helps in ending the confusion of multiple goals. As most companies use a numbing array of measures to express financial goals and objectives, their strategic plans often are based on growth in revenues or market share. Companies may evaluate individual products or lines of business on the basis of gross margins or cash flow. Business units may be evaluated in terms of return on assets or against a budgeted profit level. Finance departments usually analyze capital investments in terms of net present value, but weigh prospective acquisitions against the likely contribution to earnings growth. And bonuses for line managers and business-unit heads typically are negotiated annually and are based on a profit plan. The result of the inconsistent standards, goals, and terminology usually is incohesive planning, operating strategy, and decision making. EVA eliminates this confusion by using a single financial measure that links all decision making with a common focus: How do we improve EVA? EVA is the only financial management system that provides a common language for employees across all operating and staff functions and allows all management decisions to be modeled, monitored, communicated and compensated in a single and consistent way-always in terms of the value added to shareholder investment.

Computing Economic Value Added (EVA)

The power of the EVA concept comes from the insight the finance manager can't know if an operation is really creating value until he applies the *true* cost of capital to *all* the capital employed. Most operations with companies—and some companies themselves—have no idea what either amount is. Finding out is fascinating and often startling. The information need to calculate a company's EVA is to be compiled from the company's financial statement. At its most elemental level, EVA requires just a simple, five-line computation:

Sales	₹ 1000 crore
- Operating Costs (including taxes)	750
NOPAT	250
- Capital Costs EVA (₹ 1,000 × 10%)	100
	₹ 150 crore

The cost of capital for all companies starts with the rate of interest on relatively risk free government bonds, but adds to that the premium the market requires to compensate investors for bearing investment risk. The risk premium can vary from firm to firm within the industry and from one industry to another industry.

EVA begins with sales as a measure of customer satisfaction—in this example that is ₹ 1000 crore—and it then subtracts all of the costs required to support the sales. Operating costs, including taxes payable in cash on the operating profit, are deducted first to arrive at a NOPAT, or net operating profit after taxes, which in this case is ₹ 250 crore. Most companies stop there, or near there, when they measure profit, set goals, and pay for performance, but that is a mistake. EVA subtracts one more key cost—the cost of renting the capital employed to run the business.

The capital from debt and equity sources—or what amounts to the same thing, the net assets tied up in working capital, plant and equipment, and other long term assets—is assumed to be a total of ₹ 1,000 crore. Suppose that because of its sector, its business risk and financial structure, the firm faces an overall cost of capital of 10%, which amounts to a 5% risk premium over the 5% government bond rate.[12] The charge the firm must pay to rent the ₹ 1,000 crore of capital is uses at that 10% rate is an even ₹ 100 crore, and the ₹ 150 crore remainder, which is often rightly referred to in the accounting literature as "residual come," is EVA, the economic profit. The example shows that this firm is generating ₹ 150 crore more revenue than is required to cover all of its costs, including the cost of fully financing the capital employed on its balance sheet. Table-1 further illustrates the computation of EVA through the four principal value drivers of EVA.

TABLE-1

The Four Principal EVA Value Drivers

f (₹ in crore)

Initial	*(1)*	*(2)*	*(3)*	*(4)*	
Sales	₹ 1000			-50	+150
- Operating Costs (including taxes)	750		-5	-45	+135
NOPAT	₹ 250		₹ +5	₹ -5	₹ +15
- Capital Costs (₹ 1,000 crore x 10%)	100	₹ -5		₹ -10	₹ +10
EVA	₹ 150	₹ +5	₹ +5	₹ +5	₹ +5

1. **Cost of Capital:** Reduce the overall cost of capital by 0.5% on ₹ 1,000 crore of capital, saving ₹ 5 crore in capital costs. Add ₹ 5 crore to EVA with no change in operations, NOPAT or capital.
2. **Operate Efficiently:** Cut operating costs, after tax, ₹ 5 crore, and increase NOPAT and EVA by ₹ 5 crore.
3. **Manager Assets:** Release ₹ 100 crore in after-tax proceeds from non-productive balance sheet assets, and return the freed funds to investors so they may invest it and earn the 10% cost of capital. The ₹ 10 crore annual profit that investor earn outside the company more than offsets a corresponding ₹ 5 crore NOPAT drop recorded inside the company, leaving them ₹ 5 crore better off a year even though sales and book profit are lower.
4. **Grow Profitably:** Raise ₹ 100 crore in fresh capital at a 10% cost, and invest in a project that earns a 15% rate of return, adding ₹ 15 crore to NOPAT and leaving ₹ 5 crore in net additional EVA profit for the shareholders. The shareholders are better off even though the return on capital and profit margin end up lower.

12. The cost of capital for all companies starts with the rate of interest on relatively risk-free government bonds, but adds to that premium the market requires to compensate investors for bearing investment risk.

Observe that EVA collapses a firm's balance sheet and its income statement into a single profit measure that reflects the quality of operating efficiency and asset management, and over time, profitable growth. No longer are there two financial statements to confuse the non-accountant. There is only one statement—a statement of economic profit and loss. EVA performs this miracle of concision by converting the balance sheet into the equivalent of a profit charge, an operating cost that must be managed like any other cost of doing business.

Uses and Limitations

EVA is rapidly becoming the preferred measure of how well a company is performing. It's also an ideal tool to show how logistics actually benefits a company. Logistics is all about saving money and increasing revenue, and should be integrated into a company's financial strategy. Asset management is no longer something separate and mysterious, but is an integral and natural part of running a business and making a profit. EVA makes it less likely that top executives will succumb to micro-management. By building in a charge for using assets, EVA makes it unnecessary for executive leaders to complicate matters by separately targeting working capital days or cash conversion cycles or plant throughput efficiency. EVA subsumes all those asset management metrics along with profit into one overall score, and thus it frees middle managers to play off earnings and assets in ways that simply cannot be detected from a remove.

Gathering all of the pluses and minuses of business decisions onto one overall score makes it considerably easier for operating people to make intelligent choices, particularly those that involve tradeoffs.[13] EVA easily helps a production manager to figure out whether it is worthwhile to invest capital in automation equipment to save labour costs, for example. The manager simply compares the additional profit against the cost of the additional capital. By the same token, marketing people can readily use EVA to judge a strategy to enhance customer satisfaction by extending payment terms. They set the expected benefit of generating additional sales and profit against the capital cost associated with financing a bigger receivable base. A corporate controller also can look to EVA for answers to more erudite or ad hoc questions, like deciding whether a plant should be sold. The controller examines whether the liquidation proceeds that are subtracted from the balance sheet would reduce the capital enough to offset any on-going reduction in earnings. At whatever level, and for whatever purpose, EVA makes it possible for everyone to make more informed decisions, and to learn more quickly what works and what doesn't in their corner of the value creation game.

Unlike reported accounting profit or operating profit, an EVA profit of zero is not necessarily bad. A company or business unit that just breaks even on EVA is actually earning NOPAT profit large enough to pay the interest it owes on its debts, after taxes, while leaving a bottom line profit remainder large enough to give the shareholders a minimal acceptable return on their equity investment. An EVA of zero is thus not

13. Karen Spinner: *A new tool to measure performance,* Global Finance, Nov. 1997, Vol. 1, p. 24.

bad, but of course, it is not particularly good either. It is the epitome of breaking even. A positive EVA, on the other hand, really is good, and a negative EVA, is not. EVA is the only measure that establishes a searing dividing line between good and bad performance for it is the true measure of profit.

A negative EVA does not necessarily indicate that a business line should be liquidated and management put to pasture, however. That may only make a bad EVA worse. A negative EVA only indicates that capital was misallocated in the misty past, or that prior expectations have not been fully realized, but it is not necessarily an indictment of today's management and current strategy. It may also be due to a recent "strategic" investment that has not yet fully ramped up. If that is the case, EVA will be more accurately measured if part of the capital investment is held back and metered in over the period that the payoff is expected to materialize. A negative EVA, in other words, reflects the impact of prior decisions and sunk costs that are by now irrelevant. A negative EVA is also impounded in the stock market or private market value of a company. As a result, taking an EVA that is negative, and making it less negative, is every bit as valid a way to improve performance, create value and qualify managers for a bonus as would be taking a positive EVA business and making it more positive. It is the continuous sustainable *improvement* in EVA that is the real mission of any true EVA company.

As a result, managers running the best business units cannot rest on their laurels and claim they have hit a triple when they were born on third base. The best are challenged to become even better, and to scale their inherently profitable business models. The managers in charge of tough turnaround situations need not lament their fate. They can be measured and rewarded for making their negative EVA less negative. The mission to increase EVA levels the playing field, makes it unnecessary to waste time and political capital fighting over the allocation of irrelevant sunk costs to get the programme started (such as goodwill from prior acquisitions), and it gives managers all of the right incentives to make the decisions at the margin that will create the most shareholder value.[14]

---

14. Focus on EVA positive is not the most relevant focus. It should be on improving EVA relative to long-term expectations. Fundamental **value** means earning returns in excess of the opportunity cost of capital and how much financial capital is to be exposed to that. Return on capital employed (ROCE) is not the only lever for **value** creation. There are two important levers - time taken to earn returns and the amount of capital to be exposed towards that. An EVA calculation is ROCE less the opportunity cost in a given period. The journey is intrinsic **value** maximising and EVA is a means to the end. Quite often measuring EVA becomes the goal in itself. The focus of any new investment certainly should be on earning positive EVA over the life of the investment. But there are large companies which have invested huge sums of money. Whether or not that amount can earn a positive return on capital employed is an academic question because that investment cannot be undone easily. In many situations businesses find that even though they are in negative EVA, they cannot undo the capital sunk. They have to resort to **value** maximising by continuing with the business and make it less negative EVA. To help senior mangement improve its clarity on what is intrinsic **value**, two broad applications of EVA help. One involves making strategic decisions that impact the intrinsic **value** of the business. The other is managing performance by putting in place performance management systems. In the first, focus is on the types of strategic decisions while making a major investment or divestment. What are the goals they have to set for creating wealth for shareholders? How much improvement in EVA is good enough? For example, assuming a firm in negative EVA and the logical place for that firm to be a zero or positive EVA, what does that say for those who are in psotive EVA? Do they stop the journey? Obviously not.

In fact, the goal to increase EVA shines a bright light on all of the ways that performance can be improved and wealth can be created in any business. While managers can do countless individual things to create value, they must all eventually be measured as an increase in EVA falling into one of these four categories:

1. Reduce the Cost of Capital

The first imperative is to manage financial capital like any other input to the business, and reduce its purchase price. A finance manager must select and put in place the financial policies, risk controls, and pension funding strategies that will minimize the rate the market charges the firm to rent capital. Financial officers also need to think about enhancing transparency and management accountability, strengthening incentives for insiders to maximize the wealth of the owners, and even adopting the EVA Focused Finance platform as ways to increase investor confidence and their willingness to advance funds to the firm on favorable terms.

2. Operate Efficiently

The obvious opportunities to boost EVA in operations are from cutting costs, and saving taxes, and raising NOPAT without using more capital. EVA naturally rewards intelligent expense control, and transforms the tax department into a profit center.

3. Manage Assets and Re-deploy Capital

Management can also cut an EVA expense by reducing the amount of physical and intangible capital it employs. To increase EVA, managers will pare capital tied up in non-productive assets and activities and return the freed cash to investors. Even if operating profit shrinks, so long as the charge for using capital shrinks more, EVA will expand. Managers can use supply chain techniques to step up working capital turns, sell assets they know are worth more to others, or consolidate redundancies and weed out marginal product lines and customer accounts. At a more strategic level, top managers can develop completely new business models that conserve capital by speeding cycles times.

4. Grow Profitably

Costs and capital can only be cut so far. Over the long haul, the only way to increase EVA is to invest, to grow, and to take risks and innovate—but, managers must be sure that they increase operating profit by more the cost of renting the new capital. To maximize EVA they must take on as many positive net present value projects as they possibly can. EVA also tells managers to avoid like the plague investing capital for less than the cost of capital, no matter what other benefits there may appear to be. Increasing market share, for example, while fundamentally decreasing EVA, is a fool's errand. The EVA message is to be profitable first—develop a solid, distinctive operating platform and value proposition—and then step on the next.

EVA is a Better Way to Plan for Value

Whether they are contemplating entering new markets, setting product prices, adding new service lines, or making an acquisition, managers need a way to value the alternatives and choose the ones that will produce the highest stock price. Cash flow analysis can help them to do that, but EVA can help them even more. EVA is preferable because it is a simpler, more informative, and more accountable way to measure and manage value.

An ironclad mathematical formula links EVA to value, and it is this: for a given business case, the present value of the EVA profit is always equal to the net present value of discounted cash flow, or in symbols:

The Present Value of EVA = NPV = Discounted Cash Flow

The equality is a key to unlocking true, value-based management. No longer must managers be held hostage to cash flow. They can feel free to examine all decisions through an EVA lens. To illustrate how this works, consider the aforementioned capital budgeting exercise from an EVA perspective (refer to Table-2).

TABLE 2
Discounted EVA Approach

(₹ in crore)

	Year 0	*Year 1*	*Year 2*	*Year 3*
NOPAT		₹ 250	₹ 250	₹ 250
Investment Capital	₹ 1,000	₹ 1,000	₹ 1,000	₹ 1,000
x Cost of Capital		10%	10%	10%
Capital Charge		₹ 100	₹ 100	₹ 100
EVA		₹ 150	₹ 150	₹ 150
		$(1+10\%)^1$	$(1+10\%)^2$	$(1+10\%)^3$
NPV	₹ 1,500			

Observe that instead of subtracting the proposed ₹ 1,000 crore investment up-front as the cash flow calculation dictates, so that psychologically investments are forgotten the moment they are spent, in the EVA method all investments are converted into amortizing loans paying interest at the firm's cost of capital rate. EVA makes managers accountable for the capital they invest because it memorializes the obligation to the example, the capital charge at the 10% cost of capital on the ₹ 1,000 crore investment is ₹ 100 crore a year.[15] That represents the profit amount that investors could earn by investing the capital on their own, in an equally risky stock and bond portfolio. It is a profit target set by the market, through an objective benchmarking with market available returns. It is the amount the market charges management to rent the capital they say they will need to take on the project and build their business.

15. The ₹ 1,000 crore principal is recouped over time as the depreciation charge that is subtracted from NOPAT. Indeed, the "net" in NOPAT stands for "net of depreciation," so that NOPAT measures sustainable, distributable profit.

Managers will want to be sure they can cover that capital charge, for if they cannot, they will suffer alongside the shareholders by earning a lower bonus (if their bonus is on increasing EVA, as it should be).

In this case, management forecasts that NOPAT will reach ₹ 25 crore amply covering the ₹ 100 crore capital charge and leaving an EVA remainder of ₹ 150 crore which, when discounted to a present value at the 10% cost of capital, is ₹ 1,500 crore—the net present value of the project. The outcome is no coincidence. EVA will always give the same discounting cash flows because EVA subtracts the cost of capital. By its very nature, EVA sets aside the amount of profit that must be earned to recover the value of any capital invested in a project, and so it naturally accounts for any value added or lost relative to that capital.

If management forecasts that a project would earn zero EVA, for instance, then no value would be added from it. Investors would anticipate just breaking even, just earning the return on investment they demand. Accordingly, they would pay a market value that just equaled the book value of the investment, and the net present value difference would be zero. To break even on EVA is to break even on NPV, by definition. Only by exceeding investors' expectations and earning a positive EVA profit can management produce a positive NPV, and vice versa.

This insight leads to a powerful conclusion: *the only way to increase NPV is to increase EVA.* EVA does indeed measure all the ways that performance can be improved and wealth created, in any business. To emphasize this all-important linkage, the firm should rip up their capital budgeting manuals, acquisition valuation procedures and planning reviews that are based on cash flow, and replace them with templates that enable managers to project, analyse and discount EVA. The NPV answers will be the same either way, but the EVA method is far more effective for several reasons.

For one thing, managers can tell at a glance if their business plans are creating value by examining the level and trend in their forecast for EVA. Because it appropriately matches the total cost of generating profit against the profit, EVA reveals, period by period, the amount of value added or lost. If they see sales and earnings growing, margins expanding, and market share soaring in their plan, but no improvement in EVA, the managers know right away they need to go back to the drawing board. They instantly understand that they are spending far too much capital to achieve projected results, and need to rethink the strategy. Cash flow offers no such insights. It concentrates all the pain of an investment up-front with only payoffs to follow. No one period combines the cost and benefit of cash flow in a meaningful way. Cash flow is a highly uninformative measure of value.

EVA is also far easier for line managers to understand and use because it applies so widely. They will encounter EVA not just as an isolated capital budgeting and decision support tool, as is typical with cash flow. They will see EVA at the head of monthly reports and the top of scorecards, as the key driver of their incentive pay, and in the best examples, in shareholder reports and investor communications. One common metric with one common language is a key to simplicity, and it also fosters teamwork when everyone drives toward the same goal.

Accountability also gets a big boost when managers see EVA coming at them from all directions. Managers suddenly become much more grounded when they know that their projects will be approved based upon their projections for EVA and furthermore that their performance will be reviewed and their bonuses will be based on whether they actually deliver it. With EVA, there is no place for them to hide. Transparency and connectivity pervade the management system. All projects, and every initiative, are effectively subject to a natural post audit. Managers quickly realize that if they fail to deliver to plan assumptions or at least cover the cost of capital, they will be the first to feel the pain.

The capital charge plays a vital role in this, for it sets the standard for the NOPAT profit that must be earned before EVA is generated and value is created. Managers know that if they invest more capital into a project, the profit hurdle they must exceed to cover the cost of capital will rise, and vice versa. The NOPAT profit target is automatically reset without the need for top management intervention. If line managers decide to invest another ₹ 50 crore in the example project, for instance, they would be required to earn another ₹ 5 crore in ongoing NOPAT profit[16] just to cover the cost of the capital, and they would know : without the need to touch base with senior executives. The capital charge does the talking for them. More valuable decisions can be made—and made more quickly—when everyone can readily compute the minimum performance standard that is required of them and can work assiduously to beat it.

EVA can be used to value shares as well as decisions. Questions like how much we can afford to pay for an acquisition or whether we should raise or retire stock, require first that market value added (MVA) be unfolded to measure total market value.[17] From that the corresponding share price can be inferred. The trick is to rearrange the formula—MVA equals total value less total capital—to solve for total value. The result is that total value must equal total capital plus MVA, which in turn is just the present value of EVA, and so, in symbols:

Total Value = Total Capital + the Present Value of EVA

The model contains important insights into the factors that underlie the creation of corporate value. The formula says that the total value of a company as a going-concern business enterprise is equal to the commodity cost of its assets as mere tangible assets, plus a premium, or less a discount, that reflects the quality of its asset management. EVA, in other words, is the measure of management's ability to add value to tangible assets by creating and leveraging intangible assets. EVA reflects and implicitly values all forms of innovation and differentiation. It is the value of mind over matter.

---

16. In addition to interest on the capital, the invested in the project would also have to be recouped through the additional depreciation that is subtracted in the measurement of NOPAT.
17. Arnaud Castillo: Using EVA for acquisitions, *Acquisitions Monthly,* Dec. 98, p. 87.

At a more prosaic level, the economic model also can be used to determine share prices. To do that management first prepares a forecast for sales, operating costs, NOPAT, capital and EVA, and then discounts the EVA implied by its business plans to a present value The EVA premium (or discount if the EVA forecast is negative) is then added to the capital already employed on the balance sheet to arrive at the total value of business operations. Capital is added to the value because when investors buy a company's shares, they are acquiring not only their share of the EVA premium; they are also cashing out the capital that the selling shareholders had put or left in the business.

In the next step, the value of non-operating assets like surplus marketable securities is added to the total value, and then the market value of all priority claims—such as debt, pension deficits, and preference stock—is subtracted. The result is the estimated equity shareholder equity value which, when divided by the outstanding equity shares (on a fully diluted basis), is the indicated equity share price. Trace it all the way through and the predicted stock price is, in effect, net equity book value per share, plus the per share value of the EVA premium. Equity shares can be worth more than book value, therefore, only if a company creates and increases its EVA per share.

Such a model is perfectly suited to determining the maximum affordable share price of an acquisition candidate. It implies that for a buyer to come out ahead in a deal, it must limit the purchase price premium to no more than the per share present value of the extra EVA to be created by the combination. The model can also be used to figure out whether a firm's shares are fairly valued in the market, given management's forward plan, and if not, whether it is timely to raise or retire the shares.

The transparent accountability for creating shareholder wealth that the EVA system imposes strongly supports a culture of discipline, which has generally proven a favorable climate for creating value. James Collins found it another attribute shared by the good-to-great companies in his study. Discipline and accountability, however, are not words that inspire fealty from line managers and employees. Some resistance may occur at the outset, and enlightened top executives and board members must be prepared to respond.[18]

18. Performance related pay with coroprate executives is a relatively new trend that began in the 1980s, when companies introduced compensation plans tied directly to stock prices. However, a number of studies found virtually no link between executives' salaries and how well their companies performed for shareholders. So in the early 1990s, corporate boards began making stock options a large part of executive compensation. However, as the market began rising, so too did the executives' pay, without distinguishing between good performance and bad. Alfred Rappaport has found a better way of providing superior total returns to shareholders. He proposes three steps that will bridge the gap between existing compensation practices and those needed to promote higher level of performance at all levels of the organisation. First, reward top managers only when they outperform the competition. Second, determine the real contribution of each business unit to the company's overall share price. And third, involve frontline managers and workers in the quest for higher shareholder value. See Alfreed Rappaport: *New Thinking on How to Link Executive Pay With Performance. Source: Harvard Business Review,* Mar/Apr. 99, Vol. 77, Issue 2, p. 91, 11p, 4 charts 1c.

They must take the time to understand and embrace EVA fully, and become its champion. They must be willing to exert their influence to make sure it is firmly cemented as the keystone of financial management. They must not abrogate their role as the keepers of the value flame and principal architects of the company's internal governance system. But they should employ carrots as well as sticks. They should induce line managers to embrace EVA by freeing them in other ways. They should liberate them to run their businesses as entrepreneurs, and should empower them to make a lot of money if they succeed in creating a lot of EVA. They should, in brief, create a culture of ownership to sit beside the culture of discipline.

Handing out boatloads of stock options is unlikely to be the best solution. The incentive is too remote and too abstract to motivate individual managers and employees who have little influence over aggregate results and little schooling in the factors that truly drive shareholder value. Except for a handful of people at the top, most people would be better off participating in a special kind of bonus plan that simulates the incentives of ownership.

To do that, bonuses should be based exclusively or principally on rewarding company-wide and business-unit EVA. That gives managers a simple and understandable incentive to take the actions they believe will maximize shareholder wealth. The potential bonus should also not be capped. Boards should not constrain managers' willingness to work hard and prosper personally if they can increase EVA and create wealth. With bonuses based on EVA, the bigger the bonuses the better for all concerned.

Managers must, however, be discouraged from gaming the system and gunning short-term results to the detriment of long run value. One workable solution is to hold back a large portion of any very large bonus award and to pay it out over time, subjecting it to the risk that unpaid amounts are forfeited if EVA subsequently deteriorates.

This contingent carry-forward and cancellation clause is essential for an EVA bonus plan for without it, no board could legitimately offer an uncapped bonus. The board must be certain that it links management's incentive pay to improvements in performance and value that can be sustained. The only way to know if improvements are real is to force managers to wait and see. While it is impossible to say for sure, such a provision may tame the opportunistic executive behavior.

The banking system naturally extends managers' decision horizons. They quickly realize there is no point to overreaching and exaggerating short-term results if they cannot hang onto the gains over the long term. With each year's performance connecting to each subsequent year's, managers suddenly care about maximizing the long run stream of EVA and not just the current result. They take on the perspective of an owner. Since EVA bonus plans combine long-term and short-term incentives in one plan, boards can collapse a variety of bonus programs into one cohesive EVA plan. The hedgehog principle demands no less.

By smoothing business cycles and strategic performance gaps, bonus banks also help mitigate the risk of losing good people in bad times. Banks build up in peak performance years and carry over to supplement pay in lean times. The forced savings can be a significant competitive advantage for high tech companies. Even the best-managed companies, occasionally run through a dry spell. Banking bonuses helps retain key research and sales talent until product pipelines are replenished. The bank can also help retain valuable employees in the flush times, incidentally, because they will be forced to surrender their banked bonuses if they join another firm.[19]

The bonus itself should not be tied to meeting budget or exceeding business plan targets. That only encourages managers to sandbag and withhold valuable information. Bonuses should be funded by predictable formulas. One example is to pay a competitive target bonus plus a stated percent of the annual change in EVA —whether positive or negative and without limit in both directions, but subject to the banking feature.[20] Once the formula has been chosen, tested and calibrated, the board should resist changing it for a minimum three-to-five-year period. Adhering to the terms of the bargain, whether the outcome is for better or worse, is crucial to getting managers to take the incentive seriously and motivating them to think and manage for the long term.

When properly constructed, EVA bonus plans are effectively incentive contracts. They give managers a fixed share interest in the value they help to create over a reasonable planning horizon. With that incentive, corporate executives raise their eyes toward building strategic value and look well beyond the quarter-to-quarter earnings.

Line managers no longer find it sensible to hedge expectations and hide information during budget season. They become far more willing to collaborate, share information, and set and achieve ambitious strategic goals for they are compensated not for beating their plans but as a share of the wealth their planning helps them to create.

Incentive compensation by formula also enables the finance department to incorporate bonus computations directly into the templates the company uses to conduct its capital budgeting reviews and planning exercises.[21] Managers can readily simulate how changes in key assumptions will directly affect net present value and their personal net worth. Accepting positive NPV projects and boosting one's incentive pay are transparently joined at the hip.

Managers also realize they have more at stake if things go wrong. With their

---

19. See Dennis G. Uyemura, EVA: A top-down approach to risk management, *The Journal of Lending & Credit Risk Management,* Feb. 1997, Vol. 79, p. 40.
20. Bonus formulas in practice are often more sophisticated, and may involve paying a percent of the current and cumulative increase in EVA measured relative to an "expected improvement" amount that is consistent with market expectations and a realistic assessment of EVA growth opportunities over a 3-5 year horizon.
21. Robert R. Tumble and Delowell, Angela N.: Connecting CEO performance to corporate performance: Examining intangible metrics of shareholder value, *Journal of Compensation and Benefits,* 2001, vol. 17, p. 8.

incentive fixed by a non-negotiable bonus formula, managers are directly exposed to long run investment risks. They naturally take more seriously their responsibility to anticipate risk, control risk, and respond to risk because they are directly exposed to risk. EVA bonus plans, in short, go a long way toward encouraging managers to think and act like owners because the managers can anticipate earning the long-run return of an owner. Setting bonus by formula instead of tying them to budget is a key to making that

> Giving line managers more decision autonomy and spending authority makes more sense once the capital discipline, value guidance, and monetary incentive of EVA are in place. It is to be acknowledged that whereas in the past, capital was essentially free but hard to obtain, with EVA, capital would become readily available but at a market price. Once they truly believe they can access funds when they need it, middle managers' ambition to get their hands on it at all costs dries up overnight. They only want capital when they think they have genuinely valuable uses for the money, in which case it should be made available to them. Such is the reverse psychology of EVA. Private companies that are truly limited in their ability to access equity capital without a public offering may be forced into internally balancing cash sources and uses. If so, EVA should be measured with an artificially high cost of capital, one that is perhaps several percent above the true, open market rate. A higher cost of capital encourages managers to sweat capital out of the balance sheet and to cut off at the knees some of the new projects that they would otherwise want to accept. Faster, more value centric, more decentralized decision making is a clear consequence of imposing the carrot and stick of the EVA financial management system.

In India, the goal of sustainable long term value creation for shareholders is well understood by all the business groups. The companies that have implemented EVA, or another measure of value, credit it with dramatic improvement in operating and financial results. These in turn have been rewarded with the hefty appreciation in stock price. Measures to evaluate business performance and to set targets take into account this concept of value creation.

WHY IS EVA ALSO USEFUL FOR SMALL COMPANIES?

Application of EVA in small companies is useful because traditional performance measures used by small companies, such as sales or profits alone, are unable to describe the company's true business results and sometimes lead to wrong business decisions. Moreover, EVA calculation is simple, since only main data contained in income statement and balance sheet is needed. Along with the simplification of calculation, the EVA reflects company's performance in money. Whereas positive EVA indicates value creation, and the negative EVA indicates value destruction, series of negative EVA is a signal that restructuring in a company may be needed. Particularly in small business, the EVA concept is easy to understand and easy to use. Infact, it helps to understand the concept of profitability even by persons not familiar with finance and accounting. In addition, managers can make the EVA concept transparent to all employees in a short time and a useful tool for allocation of a small company's scarce capital resources. EVA helps to convert a small company's strategy into objectives for all employees. Decisions making process improves small company's business performance because managers having deeper knowledge about capital and capital cost are able to make better decisions.

In implementing EVA in small company, the calculation of EVA is just a starting point. Permanent EVA improvement has to be the main management objective. Further EVA has to be calculated periodically (at least every three months) and changes in EVA have to be analyzed. In small business, EVA development is the basis for a company's financial and business policy.

How can the Management in a Small Company Improve EVA?

The management in a small company can improve EVA by trying to improve returns with no or with only minimal capital investments; by investing new capital only in projects, equipment, machines able to cover capital cost while avoiding investments with low returns; by implementing where capital employment can be reduced; and finally, by identifying where the returns are below the capital cost and divesting those investments when improvements in returns are not feasible. In a small company, EVA is an appropriate tool since it is easy-to-calculate. Periodical EVA calculation and analysis can be done with minimal effort because only few basic data have to be entered in a common spreadsheet. EVA calculation is a starting point for improvement in financial and business policy. Further, scarce capital resources of a small company can be more efficiently allocated using EVA than using intuition or traditional methods. In addition EVA implementation in a small company will result in a better business performance, because of better understanding the objectives (especially near the floor/operating activities)

Since EVA helps the organization to realize that capital is a costly resource the most immediate effect of EVA implementation is in most cases dramatic improvement in capital efficiency (improved capital turnover). Compared to conventional measures, EVA is an epochal measure since it can be maximized: it is the better the bigger EVA is. With traditional measures that is not the case, since ROI can be increased with ignoring below average projects and EPS/Operating Profit/Net Profit can be increased simply investing more money in the company.[22] EVA helps enormously the management and employees to see what should be real objective of the company, since it makes clear to all what profitability really is.

MARKET VALUE ADDED (MVA)

Besides measuring the value of individual projects, EVA also determines a company's overall market value and its stock price via a sister measure called MVA, or market value added. MVA measures the difference between the total market value of a

22. Abuzar MA Eljelly and Khalid, S.A.: Performance measures and wealth creation is an emerging market, *International Journal of Commerce and Management,* Indiana: 2001, Vol. 11, p. 54.

company as reflected in its stock price (and value of its bonds), and the total capital employed on its balance sheet. For example, a firm that has a ₹ 1,000 crore market value and a ₹ 700 crore book value has an MVA of ₹ 300 crore, the difference:

MVA	=	Total Value	-	Total Capital
₹ 300 crore	=	₹ 1,000 crore	-	₹ 700 crore

TABLE-3

MVA and EVA for ABC Co.

(₹ in crore)

	2011	*2010*
MVA Calculation		
1. Price per share	₹ 23.0	₹ 26.0
2. Number of shares (in crores)	50.0	50.0
3. Market value of equity	₹ 1,150	₹ 1,300.0
4. Book value of equity	₹ 896.0	₹ 840.0
5. MVA = Market value – Book value	₹ 254.0	₹ 460.0
EVA Calculation		
6. EBIT	₹ 283.8	₹ 263.0
7. Tax rate	40%	40%
8. NOPAT = EBIT(1–T)	₹ 170.3	₹ 157.8
9. Total investor-supplied operating capital[a]	₹ 1,800.0	₹ 1, 455.0
10. Cost of capital, WACC (%)	11.0%	10.8%
11. Cost of capital = Capital (WACC) (9x10)	₹ 198	₹ 157.1
12. EVA = NOPAT-Capital cost (11–8)	(₹ 27.7)	₹ 0.70
13. ROCE = NOPAT/Operating capital (8/9)	₹ 9.46%	10.85%
14. ROCE-Cost of capital = ROCE-WACC (10–13)	(1.54%)	0.05%
15. EVA = Operating capital (ROCE-WACC)	(₹27.7)	₹ 0.7

a. Investor-supplied operating capital equals the sum of notes payable, long-term debt, preferred stock, and equity, less short-term investments. It could also be calculated as total liabilities and equity minus accounts payable, accruals, and short-term investments.

The MVA spread represents the cumulative amount of wealth that a company has created for its shareholders since the start of the company. It compares the amount of cash that investors have put into a business in the form of capital with the present value of the cash they can expect to take out of it. The investors could withdraw the cash value either by collecting distributions from the company over time, or they could sell their shares and cash in the corporate loans right away. Either way, MVA measures cumulative cash-in versus cash-out value. It measures shareholder wealth, and every company's most important mission is to maximize it.

Table-3 shows how ABC Co. MVA and EVA are calculated. The stock price was ₹ 23 per share at year-end 2011 down from ₹ 26 per share at the end of 2010. Its

WACC, which is the percentage after-tax cost of capital, was 10.8 percent in 2010 and 11.0 percent in 2011, and its tax rate was 40 percent.

Note first that the lower stock price and the higher book value of equity (due to retaining earnings during 2011) combined to reduce the MVA. The 2011 MVA is still positive, but ₹ 460-₹ 254 = ₹ 206 crore of stockholders' value was lost during 2011. EVA for 2010 was just barely positive, and in 2011 it was negative. Operating income (NOPAT) rose, but EVA still declined, primarily because the amount of capital rose more sharply than NOPAT—by about 26 per cent versus 8 per cent—and the cost of this increased capital pulled EVA down. It may be pointed that net income may not reflect the amount of equity capital employed, buy EVA does. Because of this omission, net income is not as useful as EVA for setting corporate goals and measuring managerial performance. From there is a relationship between MVA and EVA, but it is not a direct one. If a company has a history of negative EVAs, then its MVA will probably be negative, and vice versa if it has a history of positive EVAs. However, the stock price, which is the key ingredient in the MVA calculation, depends more on expected future performance than on historical performance. Therefore, a company with a history of negative EVAs could have a positive MVA, provided investors expect a turnaround in the future.

The second observation is that when EVAs or MVAs are used to evaluate managerial performance as part of an incentive compensation program, EVA is the measure that is typically used. The reasons are (1) EVA shows the value added during a given year, whereas MVA reflects performance over the company's entire life, perhaps even including times before the current managers were born, and (2) EVA can be applied to individual divisions or other units of a large corporation, whereas MVA must be applied to the entire corporation.

The simple example illustrates that to increase the wealth of shareholders, managers must adhere to the classic corporate finance textbook rule. They should successfully undertake all positive net present value projects and sidestep the negative ones. It also shows that MVA measures, as no other measure can, how successfully a company has allocated, managed, and re-deployed resources of all kinds so as to maximize net present value and maximize the wealth of its shareholders. MVA is certainly a measure that should/monitor on a regular basis.

Corporate managers cannot manage their stock price or MVA directly, of course, and MVA is quite useless for the managers of private companies and business divisions for which no regular stock price information is available.[23] All managers must drive shareholder wealth by managing a corporate performance proxy that is directly tied to it, and that is the cue for EVA to make a grand entrance once again.

---

23. The most important reason EVA differs from accounting profit is that the cost of equity capital is deducted when EVA is calculated. Other factors that could lead to differences include adjustments that might be made to depreciation, to research and development costs, to inventory valuations, and so on. These other adjustments also can affect the calculation of investor supplied capital, which affects EVA and MVA.

At any point in time, a firm's MVA is mathematically equal to the present value of the stream of EVA profit it can be expected to generate over the its entire future life:

MVA = sum of NPV = discounted corporate cash flows
MVA = present value of consolidated future EVA

Although MVA is based on discounting future projections of EVA, the market often forms expectations from past trends, and thus there often is a strong contemporaneous association between increasing EVA inside a company and increasing the wealth of the shareholders who stand outside the company. It is for this reason that EVA is called "The real key to creating wealth."

Given how strongly EVA ties to MVA in theory and in practice, managers can with confidence use EVA as their primary valuation and decision tool. Questions such as which pricing policies are apt to create and capture the largest value, or whether it is worthwhile to out source a function or to sell a business unit, can all in principle be answered in the same way. Choose the action likely to yield the greatest possible present value of EVA.

QUESTIONS

1. "Financial management systems are almost always a spaghetti bowl full of unconnected decision and feedback loops. They are like the internet without a protocol. They amount to internal corporate governance at its worst, and fuzzy finance at its finest." Comment.
2. "EVA is a better way to plan for value." Discuss.
3. Define the term 'Market Value Added (MVA) and Economic Value Added (EVA). How does EVA differ from accounting profit?
4. You are looking at a ranking of firms based on the economic value added. You notice that the EVA has been computed using the book value cost of capital and that the operating income and capital invested have not been corrected for either operating levels or R&D. What types of firms would be you expect to see at the top of the rankings?
5. Discuss EVA basic premise. How can a financial manager improve EVA?
6. Critically examine the four principal EVA value drivers.
7. The economic value added is the difference between return and capital and the cost of capital, which is already risk adjusted. Thus, EVA fully corrects for risk. Comment.
8. Why might adopting EVA as the measure of management performance be more dangerous in high-growth firm than in a stable-growth firm?
9. "Unlike reported accounting profit or operating profit, an EVA profit of zero is not necessarily bad." Do you agree?
10. Discuss the uses of EVA for small business? How can the management in a small company improve EVA?
11. "Like all corporate buzzwords 'Economic Value Added (EVA)' combines some truth with some chaff." Do you agree?
12. "While Market Value Added (MVA) measures cumulative performance, Economic Value Added (EVA) provides a period to period report card of a firm's success. EVA is economic earning less a charge for all capital invested in the business. A financial performance measure is only effective if it leads managers on an on-going basis to consistently make correct decisions. To this extent, although MVA effectively measures total shareholder wealth creation, it is not practical to use as an internal periodic measurement tool. Among the various performance measures, EVA is the only consistent indicator of shareholder value creation." Discuss.

30

THE WORLD OF FINANCIAL DERIVATIVES

INTRODUCTION

Derivatives, an integral part of the world of finance, use has permeated almost every aspect of domestic and international capital and money markets. They are transforming every aspect of finance from investing to raising capital to manage risk. New products and strategies are being developed at the stunning speed into an enormous, pervasive and controversial force, which is placing an enormous strain on financial professionals who must keep abreast of all the changes. The objective of the chapter is to provide an overview of the developments in the global financial derivatives markets, in terms of variety of products, participants and functions.

DEFINITION OF FINANCIAL DERIVATIVES

Webster's *Ninth New Collegiate Dictionary* (1987) defined derivative thus: 1. A word formed by derivation; 2. Something derived; 3. The limit of the ratio of the change in a function to the corresponding change in its independent variable as the latter change approaches to zero; 4. (a) A chemical substance related structurally to another substance and theoretically derivable from it. (b) A substance that can be made from another substance in one or more steps.

So the use of the word 'derivative' avoids a value judgement on its use. It is instructive to look closely at Webster's definition of 'derivative'.

1. *A word formed by derivation? Derivatiphobia* certainly falls under such a definition!

2. *Something derived?* A financial market derivative is indeed a financial instrument that is derived from a cash market or standard or 'plain vanilla' financial market instrument. A cash market instrument is a financial market instrument that involves paying a principal sum upfront. For this, the buyer obtains the right to interest and return of principal after a period of time (a loan, deposit or a bond) or for a part ownership of a company (a share).

3. *The ratio of the change in a function to the corresponding change in its independent variable?* Curiously, this definition of derivative is similar to that ubiquitous Greek symbol *delta*–δ–an important ratio in the pricing and hedging of options. Delta is the change in the price of an option on a particular financial instrument, relative to the change in the price of the underlying financial instrument.

4. *Are derivatives structurally related to other substances? (b) Can a derivative be made from something else in one or more steps?* We can say that derivatives are structurally related to other substances. The structural relation is driven by financial arbitrage. Although derivatives have taken a life of their own, their prices are structurally related to the prices of their theoretically constituent parts. This does not mean that a derivative has to be derived or created each and every time it is sold from its various bits and pieces. It is just that efficient financial markets monitor the prices of all the financial components of a treasurer's toolbox and if the price of the derivative is too high then others will step in to manufacture the derivative and undercut the price rather than buy one off-the-shelf. If the price of the packaged product is a bargain, then the derivative will be bought for spare parts that could be sold separately or repackaged to form other derivatives. Financial derivatives can also be derived from a combination of cash market instruments or other derivative instruments. In fact, the vast majority of financial instruments are not revolutionary new instruments. They are merely combinations of older generation derivatives and / or standard cash market instruments. This is the *building block approach* first used by a number of financial institutions in the late 1980s to explain financial engineering.

Derivatives are also known as *off-balance sheet instruments* in the 1980s. There is no asset or liability to put on the balance sheet as such. These instruments involve contingent assets or liabilities depending on the movement of market prices. In 80's, transactions and positions in swaps, forwards and options were not recorded on the balance sheet. Such products do not involve the lending or depositing of a principal sum at the time of transaction. Furthermore, there was no requirement to back business in them with capital. They may involve a promise to lend or to exchange currencies some time in the future or provide the right to do so on payment of an insurance premium upfront.

There is considerable debate as to whether *on balance sheet instruments* should be included in the definition of derivatives. Under the *made from something else* definition of derivatives we should also include the sort of products that brought down many of the companies while they were dealing with hedging or risk management instruments. They were not *off-balance-sheet*. They were not contracts for differences. They bought currencies embedded within them. The bonds were thus derivatives, as they were derived from other financial instruments. The structured bonds they bought were a potent cocktail of ordinary bonds, laced with various cross-currency interest rate swaps. The concoction was volatile and the hangover lasting. And, finally, the financial derivatives, or simple, be used to avoid risk or to speculate. They may be called *risk management products, hedging products, off-balance-sheet instruments* etc. In short, *we can define a financial market derivative instrument as a treasury or capital markets instrument that is derived from or bears a close relation to a cash instrument or another derivative instrument.*

BASIC FINANCIAL DERIVATIVES

Derivatives are financial contracts that derive their value from the price of an underlying commodity, asset, rate, index or the occurrence of an event. As instruments for transfer and dispersal of risk, derivatives facilitate socially useful but risky projects, which would not be undertaken in the absence of such risk management framework. Derivatives may either be standard or customized according to the needs of the participants. While the standardized products mostly trade on exchanges, the customized products are traded over the counter. Major exchanges world over have adopted electronic trading platforms that use order-matching technologies to execute trades in a multilateral environment. Trades on exchanges are characterized by anonymity with the exchange clearing house interposing itself as the central counterparty (CCP) along with associated settlement and risk management protocol.

There are two common types of derivative contracts, those patterned on *forwards* and on *options*. Derivatives based on forwards have *linear* payoffs, meaning their payoffs move one-for-one with changes in the underlying price. Such contracts are generally relatively easy to understand, value, and manage. Derivaties based on options have *non-linear* payoffs, meaning their payoffs may move proportionally more or less than the underlying price. Such contracts can be quite difficult to understand, value, and manage.

Options

Options are traded both on organised exchanges and over the counter. The two modes of trading are quite different and lead to important differences in market conventions. The over-the-counter currency and interest rate option markets have become much more liquid in recent years. Many option market participants prefer the over-the-counter markets because of the ease with which option contracts tailored to a particular need can be acquired. The exchanges attract market participants who prefer or are required to minimise the credit risk of derivatives transactions, or who are required to transact in markets with publicly posted prices. There are many types of options. A *European option* can be exercised only at expiration. An *American option* can be exercised at any time between initiation of the contract and expiration. In a market, the basic options are call and put. A *call option* is a contract giving the owner the right, but not the obligation, to purchase, at expiration, an amount of an asset at a specified price called the *strike* or *exercise price.* A *put option* is a contract giving the owner the right, but not the obligation, to sell, at expiration, an amount of an asset at the exercise price. The amount of the underlying asset is called the *notional principal* or *underlying amount.* The price of the option contract is called the *option premium.*

The issuer of the option contract is called the writer and is said to have the short position. The owner the option is said to be long. There are thus several ways to be long an asset: long the spot asset; long a forward on the asset; long a call on the asset; and, short a put on the asset.

A *standard* or *plain vanilla option* has no additional contractual features. An *exotic option* has additional features affective the payoff. Some examples of exotics are: (i) *Barrier options,* in which the option contract is initiated or cancelled if the asset's cash price reaches a specified level; (ii) *Average rate option,* for which the option payoff is based on the average spot price over the duration of the option contract rather than spot price at the time of exercise. (iii) *Binary options,* which have a lump sum option payoff if the spot price is above (call) or below (put) the exercise price at maturity. *Currency options* have an added twist: a domestic currency put is also a foreign currency put.

The *intrinsic value* of a call option is the larger of the exercise price minus the current asset price or zero. The intrinsic value of a put is the larger of the current asset price minus the exercise or zero. Intrinsic value can also be thought of as the value of an option if it were expiring or exercised today. By definition, intrinsic value is always greater than or equal to zero. For this reason, the owner of an option is said to enjoy limited liability, meaning that the worst-case outcome for the owner of the option is to throw it away valueless an unexercised.

The intrinsic value of an option is often described by its *moneyness:* if intrinsic value is positive, the option is said to be *in-the-money;* if the exchange rate is below the exchange rate, a call option is said to be *out-of-the-money;* and, if the intrinsic value is zero, the option is said to be *at-the-money.* If intrinsic value is positive at maturity, the owner of the option will *exercise* it, that is, call the underlying away from writer.

Owning a call option or selling a put option on an asset is like being long the asset. Owning a deep in-the-money call option on a currency is like being long an amount of the asset that is close to the notional underlying value of the option. Owning a deep out-of-the-money call option on a currency is like bing long an amount of the asset that is much smaller than the notional underlying value of the option.

Forward Foreign Exchange

In a Forward foreign exchange, foreign currency is deliverable in the future. Its price is called *forward exchange rate* or the *forward outright rate,* and the differential of the forward minus the spot exchange rate is called the *swap rate* (not to be confused with the rate on plain-vanilla interest rate swaps).

Derivative assets, e.g. **forwards**, can often be constructed from combinations of underlying assets. Such constructed assets are called *synthetic assets.*

In a forward contract, one party agrees to deliver a specified date in the future (the maturity date of the contract) at a specified price (the *forward price*). The commodity may be a commodity in the narrow sense, e.g. gold or wheat, or a financial asset e.g. foreign exchange or shares. The price of the underlying asset for immediate (rather than future) delivery is called the *cash* or *spot price.*

The party obliged to deliver the commodity is said to have a short portion and the party obliged to take delivery of the commodity and pay the forward price for it is said to have a *long position.* A party with no obligation offsetting the forward contract is said to have an *open position.* A party with an open position is sometimes called a *speculator.* A party with an obligation offsetting the forward contract is said to have a *covered portion.* A party with a closed position is sometimes called a *hedger.*

Covered parity or *cost-of-carry* relations are relations between the prices of forward and underlying assets. These relations are enforced by arbitrage and tell us how to determine arbitrage-based forward asset prices. One condition for markets to be termed efficient is the absence of *arbitrage*. The term arbitrage has been used in two very different senses which it is important to distinguish: i) To carry out arbitrage in the first sense, one would simultaneously execute a set of transactions which have zero net cash flow now, but have a non-zero probability of a positive payoff without risk, i.e. with a zero probability of a negative payoff in the futures. ii) Arbitrage in the second sense is related to a model of how asset prices behave. To perform arbitrage in this sense, one carries out a set of transactions with a zero net cash flow now and a positive expected value at some date in the future.

Futures

Futures are similar to forwards in all except two important and related respects *First,* futures trade on organised commodity exchanges. Forwards, in contrast, trade *over-the-counter*, that is, as simple bilateral transactions, conducted as a rule by telephone, without posted prices. *Second,* a forward contract involves only one cash flow, at the maturity of the contract, while futures contracts generally require interim cash flows prior to maturity.

The most important consequence of the restriction of futures contracts to organised exchanges is the radical reduction of credit risk by introducing a *clearinghouse* as the counterparty to each contract. The clearinghouse, composed of exchange members. becomes the counterparty to each contract and provides a guarantee of performance: in practice, default on exchange-traded futures and options is exceedingly rare. Over-the-counter contracts are between two individual counterparties and have as much or as little credit risk as those counterparties.

Clearinghouses bring other advantages as well, such as consolidating payment and delivery obligations of participants with positions in many different contracts. In order to preserve these advantages, exchanges offer only a limited number of contract types and maturities. For example, contracts expire on fixed dates that may or may not coincide precisely with the needs of participants. While there is much standardisation in over-the-counter markets. It is possible in principle to enter into obligations with any maturity date. It is always possible to unwind a futures position via an offsetting transaction, while over-the-counter contracts can be offset at a reasonable price only if there is a liquid market in the offsetting transaction. Settlement of futures contracts may be by net cash amounts or by delivery of the underlying.

In order to guarantee performance while limiting risk to exchange members, the clearinghouse requires performance bond from each counterparty. At the initiation of a contract, both counterparties put up *initial* or *original margin* to cover potential default losses. Both parties put up margin because at the time a contract is initiated, it is not known whether the terminal spot price will favour the long or the short. Each day, at that day's closing price, one counterparty will have gained and the other will have lost a precisely offsetting amount. The loser for that day is obliged to increase his margin account and the gainer is permitted to reduce his margin account by an amount, called *variation margin,* determined by the exchange on the basis of the change in the futures price. Both counterparties earn a short-term rate of interest on their margin accounts.

Margining introduces an importance difference between the structure of futures and forwards. If the contract declines in value, the long will be putting larger and larger amounts into an account that earns essentially the overnight rate, while the short will progressively reduce his money market position. Thus the value of the futures, in contrast to that of a forward, will depend not only on the expected future price of the underlying asset, but also on expected future short-term interest rates and on their correlation with future prices of the underlying asset. The price of a futures contract may therefore be higher or lower than the price of a congruent forward contract. In practice, however, the differences are very small.

Futures prices are expressed in currency units, with a minimum price movement called a tick size. In other words, futures prices cannot be any positive number, but must be rounded off to the nearest tick. The difference between a futures price and the cash price of the commodity is called the *basis* and *basis risk* is the risk that the basis will change unpredictably The qualification unpredictably is important: futures and cash prices converge as expiry date nears, so part of the change in basis is predictable. For market participants using futures to manage exposures in the cash markets, basis risk is the risk that their hedges will offset only a smaller part of losses in the underlying assets.

An expiration, counterparties with a short position are obliged to make *delivery* to the exchange, while the exchange is obliged to make delivery to the longs. The *deliverable* commodities, that is, the assets which the short can deliver to the long to settle the futures contract, are carefully defined. *Squeezes* occur when a large part of the supply of a deliverable commodity is concentrated in a few hands. The shorts can then be forced to pay a high price for the deliverable in order ot avoid defauling on the futures contract.

In most futures markets, a futures contract will be *cash settled* by having the short or long make a cash payment on the difference between the futures price at which the contract was initiated and the cash price at expiry. In practice margining will have seen to it that the contract is already largely cash settled by the expiration date, so only a relatively small cash payment must be made on the expiration date itsellf.

Swap

Swap is an exchange of assets and liabilities. A *plain vanilla interest rate swap* is an agreement between two counterparties to exchange a stream of fixed interest rate payments for a stream of floating interest rate payments. Both streams are denominated in the same currency and are based on a notional principal amount. The notional principal is not exchanged. The design of a swap has three features that determine its price: the maturity of the swap, the maturity of the floating rate. and the frequency of payments.

At initiation, the price of a plain-vanilla swap is set so its current value - the net value of the two interest payment streams, fixed and floating - is zero. The swap can be seen as a portfolio which, from the point of view of the payer of fixed interest (called the *payer* in market parlance) is long a fixed-rate bond and short a floating-rate bond, both in the amount of the notional principal. The payer of floating-rate Interest (called the *receiver* in market parlance) is long the floater and short the fixed-rate bond.

The price of a swap is usually quoted as the *swap rate*, that is as the yield to maturity on a notional par bond. *What determines this rate?* A floating-rate bond always trades at par at the time it is issued, the fixed-rate bond, which represents the payer's commitment in the swap. must then also trade at par if the swap is to have an initial value of zero. In other words, the swap rate is the market-adjusted yield to maturity on a par bond.

Swap rates are also often quoted as a spread over the government bond with a maturity closest to that of the swap. This spread, called the swap-Treasury spread, is almost invariably positive, but varies widely in response to factors such as liquidity and risk appetites in the fixed-income markets.

A *forward swap* is an agreement between two counterparties to commence a swap at some future settlement date. As in the case of a cash swap, the forward swap rate is the market-adjusted par rate on a coupon bond issued at the settlement date. The rate on a forward swap can be calculated from forward rates or spot rates.

Many of these derivative instruments do not, in fact, involve the delivery of a financial instrument in the future. They are *contracts for differences*. If it were not for the purposes of avoiding the gambling laws of various countries, such 'financial instruments' would be more honestly called *bets*. Interest rate futures contracts or Forward Rate Agreements (FRAs) are no less than bets on the future course of a particular interest rating. The price (or implied interest rate) written into the contract is compared with the interest rate outcome at the agreed date or dates in the future and cash is exchanged based on the difference.

PARTICIPANTS AND FUNCTIONS

The three broad categories of *participants*—hedgers, speculators, and arbitrageurs—trade in the derivatives market: *Hedgers* face risk associated with the price of an asset. They use futures or options markets to reduce or eliminate this risk. *Speculators* wish to bet on future movements in the price of an asset. Futures and options contracts can give them an extra leverage; that is, they can increase both the potential gains and potential losses in a speculative ventures. *Arbitrageurs* are in business to take advantage of a discrepancy between prices in two different markets. If, for example, they see the futures price of an asset getting out of line with the cash price, they will take offsetting positions in the two markets to lock in a profit.

The derivatives market performs a number of *economic functions*. *First*, prices in an organised derivatives market reflect the perception of market participants about the future and lead the prices of underlying to the perceived future level. The prices of derivatives converge with the prices of the underlying at the expiration of derivative contract. Thus derivatives help in discovery of future as well as current prices. *Second,* the derivatives market helps to transfer risks from those who have them but may not like them to those who have appetite for them. *Third,* derivatives, due to their inherent nature, are linked to the underlying cash markets. With the introduction of derivatives, the underlying market witnesses higher trading volumes because of participation by more players who would not otherwise participate for lack of an arrangement to transfer risk. *Fourth,* speculative trades shift to a more controlled environment of derivatives market. In the absence of an organised derivatives market, speculators trade in the underlying cash markets. Margining, monitoring and surveillance of the activities of various participants become extremely difficult in these kind of mixed markets. *Fifth,* an important incidental benefit that flows from derivatives trading is that it acts as a catalyst for new entrepreneurial activity. The derivatives have a history of attracting many bright' creative, well-educated people with an entrepreneurial attitude. They often energise others to create new business, new products and new employment opportunities, the benefit of which are immense. *Sixth,* derivatives markets help increase savings and investment in the long run. Transfer of risk enables market participants to expand their volume of activity.

THE GROWTH OF WORLD DERIVATIVES MARKET

Some of the earliest derivatives were linked to tulip bulbs in Holland and to rice in Japan in the 17th century. But derivatives markets were small until the 1970s, when economic conditions, along with advances in the pricing of derivatives, led to spectacular growth. In that decade, the volatility of interest rates and currency-exchange rates increased sharply, making it imperative to find efficient ways to hedge related risks. Meanwhile, deregulation in a variety of industries, along with soaring international trade and capital flows, added to the demand for financial products to manage risk.

Development of the Black-Scholes formula in the early 1970s, along with the introduction of cheaper, faster computers to manage the computations, changed the trading of derivatives forever. Thereafter, financial engineers could invent new derivatives and easily find their value.

Until the 1970s, derivatives mostly took the form of option, forward and futures contracts. Except for futures contracts on commodities, the trading of derivatives had been done "over the counter," meaning without intermediation by an organized exchange. But in 1972, the Chicago Mercantile Exchange started trading futures contracts on currencies. The Chicago Board Options Exchange, where stock options are traded, was founded in 1973. In the late 1970s and early 1980s, the swaps market took off. Exotic derivatives trading exploded a few years later.

The OTC derivatives markets are decentralized and unregulated (except by contract law), and the parties are not required to report transactions. However, since an OTC derivative trade typically involves a bank or a regulated broker, the quasi-governmental Bank for International Settlements has been able to estimate the size of the OTC market for derivatives by surveying financial firms.

In June 2004, the total notional amount of derivatives traded over the counter was $220 trillion. This figure is a proxy for the value of the underlyings against which claims are traded in the derivatives markets. The euro forward contract example discussed earlier had a notional value of $118 million, while the interest-rate swap had a notional amount of $200,000. Interest-rate swaps represent 56 percent of the derivatives market.

In 1987, the notional amount of interest-rate swaps outstanding was $865 billion; 17 years later, it was $127 trillion, implying growth at an average annual rate of 34 percent. The notional amount of exchange-traded derivatives (futures and options) grew from $616 billion in December 1986 to $50 trillion in mid-2003, for an average annual growth rate of 29 percent.

Adding up the OTC market and the exchanges, the notional amount of derivatives was some $270 trillion at the end of June 2004. To put this number in perspective, the capitalization of all the markets for corporate debt and equity in the world was $31 trillion at the end of 2003.

A second way to look at the size of the derivatives market is as follows: Suppose that every party and counterparty had to write off all derivatives contracts. For each swap contract, one party would write off an asset, the positive value of the contract at that time, and the counterparty would write off a liability. Now, just add up the positive value of all contracts at that time. By this net measure, the aggregate value of OTC derivatives outstanding in June 2003 was $6.4 trillion - a big number, but nothing compared to the notional amount of contracts outstanding.

The past decade has witnessed an explosive growth in the use of financial derivatives by a wide range of corporate and financial institutions. The following factors which have generally been identified as the major driving force behind growth of financial derivatives are the (i) increased volatility in asset prices in financial markets; the increased integration of national financial markets with the international markets; the marked improvement in communication facilities and sharp decline in their costs; the development of more sophisticated risk management strategies; and the innovations in the derivatives markets, which optimally combine the risk and returns over a large number of financial assets, leading to higher returns, reduced risk as well as transaction costs as compared to individual financial assets. The growth in derivatives has run in parallel with the increasing direct reliance of companies on the capital markets as the major source of long-term funding. In this respect, derivatives have a vital role to play in enhancing shareholder value by ensuring access to the cheapest source of funds. Furthermore, active use of derivative instruments allows the overall business risk profile to be modified, thereby providing the potential to improve earnings quality by offsetting undesired risks.

In the Foreign Exchange and Derivatives Market and the OTC derivatives segment, the average daily turnover of interest rate and non-traditional foreign exchange contracts increased by 71 % to $2.1 trillion in April 2007 over April 2004, maintaining an annual compound growth of 20 per cent witnessed since 1995. The growing investor interest in emerging market economies along with foreign exchange convertibility restrictions have led to the development of an offshore foreign exchange market, called the non-deliverable forward (NDF) market in several emerging market currencies (Box 1). Turnover of foreign exchange options and cross-currency swaps more than doubled to $0.3 trillion per day, thus outpacing the growth in 'traditional' instruments such as spot trades, forwards or plain foreign exchange swaps. The traditional instruments also show an unprecedented rise in activity in traditional foreign exchange markets compared to 2004. Average daily turnover rose to $3.2 trillion in April 2007, an increase of 71% at current exchange rates and 65% at constant exchange rates. Relatively moderate growth was recorded in the much larger interest rate segment, where average daily turnover increased by 64 per cent to $1.7 trillion. While the dollar and euro clearly dominate activity in OTC interest rate derivatives, their combined share has fallen by nearly 10 percentage points since the 2004 survey, to 70 per cent in April 2007, as turnover growth in several non-core markets outstripped that in the two leading currencies.

BOX 1

Non-Deliverable Forward Market

With controls imposed by local financial regulators and consequently the non-existence of a natural forward market for non-domestic players, private companies and investors investing in some economies such as China, India and South Korea look for alternative avenues to hedge their exposure to such currencies. In this context, non-deliverable forwards (NDFs) have become popular derivative instruments for meeting the offshore investors' demand for hedging. NDFs are types of derivatives for trading in non-convertible or restricted currencies without delivery of the underlying currency.

The NDF market for Asian currencies is largely concentrated in Singapore, although their existence is found in London and New York as well. The major trading currencies in the NDF market are the Chinese renminbi, the Korean won, the New Taiwan dollar, the Indian rupees, the Indonesian rupiah and the Philippine peso. The volatility and bid-ask spread in the NDF market for Asian currencies are found to be lower for shorter maturities than for longer maturities.

The NDF market in the Indian rupee (INR NDF) has been in existence for around 10 years or so, reflecting onshore exchange controls and regulations. Besides, the INR NDF market also derives its liquidity from (i) non-residents wishing to speculate on the Indian rupee without any exposure to the country; and (ii) arbitrageurs who try to exploit the differentials in the prices in two markets. The spread as well as volatility of the INR NDF is higher than that of onshore spot and forward markets. Though an accurate assessment of the volumes is difficult, estimated daily INR NDF turnover was around US $ 100 million in 2003/2004. NDF volumes have reportedly grown substantially since then. While these volumes are not large enough to affect the domestic onshore market under regular market conditions, in volatile market conditions, however, these may impact the domestic spot market. The NDF turnover for the Indian rupee is estimated to be lower than that in the Chinese renminbi, the Korean won and the New Taiwan dollar. This could be attributed to the gradual relaxation of exchange controls and reasonable hedging facilities available to offshore non-residents with exposures to the Indian rupee.

In the second half of 2008, the financial crisis resulted in a decline in the total notional amounts outstanding of over-the-counter (OTC) derivatives to $592 trillion at end-year, an indication of reduced market activity. Foreign exchange and interest rate derivatives markets both recorded their first significant contractions. Against a background of severely strained credit markets and efforts to improve multilateral netting of offsetting contracts, credit default swap (CDS) markets continued to contract, with outstanding amounts decreasing by more than 25%. Facing significant price drops, outstanding commodity and equity derivatives also declined notably.

Despite the drop in amounts outstanding, significant price movements resulted in notably higher gross market values, which increased to $34 trillion at end-2008. Gross market values, which measure the cost of replacing all existing contracts, can be used to capture derivativesrelated exposures. The higher market values were also reflected in gross replacement costs after taking into account bilateral netting agreements, also referred to as gross credit exposures, which grew by nearly one third to $5 trillion.

The market for interest rate derivatives contracted for the first time in the second half of 2008, with notional amounts outstanding of these instruments falling to $419 trillion. Nonetheless, declining interest rates resulted in almost a doubling of the gross market value. The gross market value of interest rate swaps, by far the largest market segment, reached $17 trillion. The most significant increase took place in the US dollar swap market, where the gross market value nearly tripled.

Amounts outstanding of CDS contracts fell to $42 trillion against a background of severely strained credit markets and increased multilateral netting of offsetting positions by market participants. This was a continuation of the developments which began in the first half of 2008. Single-name contracts outstanding declined to $26 trillion while multi-name contracts, including CDS indices and CDS index tranches, saw a more pronounced decrease to $16 trillion. The composition of market activity across counterparties also changed in the second half of 2008. Outstanding contracts between dealers and other financial institutions as well as between dealers and non-financial institutions saw large declines relative to the inter-dealer market. Despite the lower outstanding amounts, the gross market value of CDS contracts also increased significantly as a result of the credit market turmoil.

Notional amounts outstanding of foreign exchange derivatives decreased to $50 trillion, while their gross market value rose to $4 trillion. The dollar and the euro remained the most important vehicle currencies, followed by the yen and the pound sterling.

Amounts outstanding of commodity derivatives fell by two thirds to $4.4 trillion. The continued declines in commodity prices during the second half of 2008 also had a substantial impact on the gross market value of commodity contracts, which fell to $1.0 trillion.

Outstanding equity derivatives decreased to $6 trillion, well below the levels seen in recent years and a notable change of pace from the increase in the first half of 2008.

Reflecting lower outstanding positions and significantly lower equity prices, the gross market values of outstanding equity derivatives saw only a moderate decline.

The first quarter of 2009 saw a continued but limited decline of activity on the international derivatives exchanges. Total turnover based on notional amounts decreased further, to $367 trillion from $380 trillion in the previous quarter. Consistent with a gradual return of risk appetite, however, trading activity on a monthly basis did start to increase towards the end of the quarter. Overall turnover in interest rate derivatives remained largely unchanged at $324 trillion compared to the previous quarter. The moderate change in overall turnover nonetheless reflects differences across regions, with turnover in North America declining notably relative to the previous quarter, while European turnover increased.

In contrast to interest derivatives markets, equity derivatives turnover fell for all contract types and all major currencies, including the euro. Against a background of negative economic growth and uncertainty about growth recovery, activity in equity index derivatives declined significantly to $38 trillion. Foreign exchange derivatives turnover also continued to slide. The decrease in activity among the main currencies was most pronounced for the yen and US dollar segments. Turnover in Australian and New Zealand dollar futures, possibly driven by renewed interest in FX carry trades, increased substantially relative to the previous quarter.

The second quarter of 2009 saw a small rebound in activity on the international derivatives exchanges, although trading volumes were still well below the pre-crisis level two years before. Total turnover based on notional amounts increased to $426 trillion from $366 trillion in the previous quarter, consistent with a return of risk appetite.

The increase was mostly accounted for by derivatives on short-term interest rates. Turnover in this segment rose to $344 trillion in the second quarter, compared to $294 trillion in the previous one. The increase was most marked in US dollar contracts, followed by euro, sterling and yen contracts. In particular, turnover in futures on three-month eurodollar rates picked up sharply to $115 trillion from $96 trillion in the previous quarter, possibly due to stabilising money market conditions amid a gradual retreat of concerns over the financial system.

Turnover in equity index derivatives also increased in the second quarter, from $37 trillion to $43 trillion. The increase was attributable in large part to the Korean market, where trading volumes rose significantly from $7.6 trillion to $12.0 trillion in the second quarter chiefly as a result of rising equity valuations. Global turnover measured in the number of contracts traded rose only by less than 100 billion.

Activity in foreign exchange derivatives began to recover as well with turnover increasing to $5.9 trillion from $4.8 trillion in the previous quarter. The gain in activity among the main currencies was particularly marked for contracts with one leg in sterling. A significant increase in notional amounts of futures contracts in such currency segments as the Australian and Canadian dollar, Swiss franc and New

Zealand dollar possibly reflected renewed interest in FX carry trades as investors' confidence returned.

Trading in commodity futures and options increased slightly in the second quarter. Global turnover in commodity derivatives measured in numbers of contracts (notional amounts are not available) stood at 446 million, compared to 423 million in the previous quarter. Major contributors were contracts on agricultural products and non-precious metals, while trading in energy derivatives fell.

INDIAN DERIVATIVES MARKET: GROWTH AND REGULATORY FRAMEWORK

In India, OTC derivatives, *viz.*, Interest Rate Swaps (IRS) and Forward Rate Agreements (FRAs) were introduced in July 1999, while one exchange traded derivative, *viz.*, Stock Index Futures was introduced by the two largest stock exchanges in June 2000. The FRA is an off-balance sheet contract between two parties under which one party agrees on the start date (or trade date) that on a specified future date (the settlement date) that party, *viz.*, the party that agrees, would lodge a notional deposit with the other for a specified sum of money for a specified period of time (the FRA period) at a specified rate of interest (the contract rate). The party that has agreed to make the notional deposit has, thus, sold the FRA to the other party who has bought it. The IRS is a contract between two counterparties for exchanging interest payment for a specified period based on a notional principal amount. The notional principal is used to calculate interest payments but is not exchanged. Only interest payments are exchanged. The IRS and FRA were introduced with a view to deepening the money market as also to enable banks, Primary Dealers and financial institutions to hedge interest rate risks. The IRS has emerged as the more popular of the two instruments In the Indian market, accounting for nearly all of the 928 outstanding deals, amounting to Rs. 12,620 crore of notional principal as on November 17, 2000. The overnight call money rates and the forex forward rates have emerged as the most popular benchmark rates.

A resident of India who has borrowed foreign exchange in accordance with the FEMA, may enter into an interest rate swap or currency swap or coupon swap or foreign currency option or interest rate cap/collar or Forward Rate Agreement (FRA) contract with an authorised dealer (AD) in India or with a branch outside India of an authorised dealer for hedging his loan exposure and unwinding from such hedges provided that (i) the contract does not involve rupee, (ii) foreign currency borrowing has been duly approved, (iii) the notional principal amount of the hedge does not exceed the outstanding amount of the loan, and (iv) the maturity of the hedge does not exceed the un-expired maturity of the underlying loan. ADs in India may remit foreign exchange related to such foreign exchange derivative contracts. No resident In India can enter legally into a foreign exchange derivative contract without the prior permission of the Reserve Bank. Among the non-residents, while FIIs may enter into a forward contract with rupee as one of the currencies with an AD in India, non-resident Indians and Overseas Corporate Bodies could take forward cover with an AD to hedge (i) dividend due on shares held in India, (ii) balances in FCNR (B) and NR (E) A, and (iii) the amount of investment made under portfolio scheme. The Reserve Bank may also consider allowing residents to hedge their commodity price risk (including gold but excluding oil and petroleum products) subject to certain conditions.

Forward contracts market has emerged as an important segment of the forex market in India in the recent years. It comprises customers, such as, corporates, exporters, importers, and individuals. Authorised Dealers (ADs) and the Reserve Bank. Of late, FIIs have emerged as major participants in this segment. The market operates from major centres with Mumbai accounting for bulk of the transactions. Till February 1992, forward contracts were permitted only against trade related exposures and these contracts could not be cancelled except where the underlying transactions failed to materialise. In March 1992, in order to provide operational freedom to corporate entitles, unrestricted booking and cancellation of forward contracts for all *genuine* exposures, whether trade related or not, were permitted. At present, the forward contracts market is active up to six months where two-way quotes are available. The maturity profile has recently elongated with quotes available up 10 one year. With the gradual opening up of the capital account, forward premium is now increasingly getting aligned with the interest rate differential. Importers and exporters also influence the forward market in many ways. Besides, banks are allowed to grant foreign currency loans out of FCNR (B) liabilities and this too facilitated Integration of the forex and the money markets, affecting the forward premium.

Market turnover has also increased during the current year. In the cash segment of the equity market, the total turnover of the BSE and NSE stood at ₹ 4,10,230 crore and ₹ 19,73,624 crore during 2012-13 (April-December) as compared to ₹ 6,67,498 crore and ₹ 28,10,893 crore respectively in 2011-12 (Table-1).

TABLE 1

Market Turnover

(₹ *crore)*

Market	*2009-10*	*2010-11*	*2011-12*	*2012-13#*
BSE				
Cash	1378809	1105027	667498	410230
Equity Derivatives	234	154	808476	5741593
NSE				
Cash	4138024	3577410	2810893	1973624
Equity Derivatives	17663665	29248221	31349732	22879486

Source: BSE and NSE.

Note: # As on 31 December 2012.

In the equity derivatives segment, the NSE witnessed a total turnover of ₹ 2,28,79,486 crore during 2012-13 (April-December) as compared to ₹ 3,13,49732 crore during 2011-12. The total turnover in the equity derivatives segment of the BSE stood at ₹ 57,41,593 crore in 2011-12 (April-December).

In the currency derivatives segment, the NSE witnessed a turnover of ₹ 37,25,842 crore in 2012-13 (April-December). The turnover in the currency derivatives segment of the Multi-Commodity Exchange (MCX-SX) stood at ₹ 23,63,819 crore in 2012-13 (April-December). Further, the United Stock Exchange (USE) witnessed a turnover of ₹ 32,109 crore during the same period (Table-2).

TABLE 2
Trends in Currency Derivatives

Year	*NSE*		*MCX-SX*		*USE*	
	2011-12	*2012-13#*	*2011-12*	*2012-13#*	*2011-12*	*2012-13#*
No. of contrcts (lakh)	9733	6772	7703	4272	3153	57
Trading Value (₹ crore)	4674990	3725842	3732446	2363819	1488978	32109
Average Daily Trading Value (₹ crore)	18775	20140	14990	12777	5980	174

Source: NSE, MCX-SX, and USE.
Note: # As on 30 November 2010.

Curent Regulatory Framework

In the light of increasing use of structured products and to ensure that customers understand the nature of the risk in these complex instruments, RBI after extensive consultations with market participants issued comprehensive guidelines on derivatives in April 2007, which cover the following aspects:

i) Participants have been generically classified into two functional categories, namely, market-makers and users, which would be specific to the position taken by the participant in a transaction.!This categorisation was felt important from the perspective of ensuring Suitability & Appropriateness compliance by market makers on users.

ii) The guidelines also define the purpose for undertaking derivative transactions by various participants. While Market-makers can undertake derivative transactions to act as counterparties in derivative transactions with users and also amongst themselves, Users can undertake derivative transactions to hedge - specifically reduce or extinguish an existing identified risk on an ongoing basis during the life of the derivative transaction - or for transformation of risk exposure, as specifically permitted by RBI.

iii) The guidelines clearly enunciate the broad principles for undertaking derivative transactions:

a) Any derivative structure is permitted as long as it is a combination of two or more of the generic instruments permitted by RBI and

b) Market-makers should be in a position to mark to market or demonstrate valuation of these products based on observable market prices.

c) Further, it is to be ensured that structured products do not contain derivative(s), which is/ are not allowed on a stand alone basis. This will also apply in case the structure contains 'cash' instrument(s).

d) All permitted derivative transactions shall be contracted only at prevailing market rates.

iv) The guidelines set out the basic principles of a prudent system to control the risks in derivatives activities. It is required that all risks arising from derivatives exposures should be analysed and documented and the management of derivative activities should be integrated into the bank's overall risk management system using a conceptual framework common to the bank's other activities.

v) The critical importance of 'suitability' and 'appropriateness' policies within banks for derivative products being offered to customers (users) have been underlined. It is imperative that market-makers offer derivative products in general, and structured products, in particular only to those users who understand the nature of the risks inherent in these transactions and further that products being offered are consistent with users' internal policies as well as risk appetite.

Within the above broad framework, the specifics of the forex and interest rate derivatives permitted are explained below:

Forex Derivatives

Economic entities in India currently have a menu of OTC products, such as forwards, swaps and options, for hedging their currency risk and the markets for the same are fairly deep and liquid, as reflected in the volumes and bid-offer spreads. The origin of the forex market development in India could be traced back to 1978 when banks were permitted to undertake intra-day trades. However, the market witnessed major activities only in the 1990's with the floating of the currency in March 1993. Cross currency derivatives with the rupeee as one leg were introduced with some restrictions in April 1997 Rupee-foreign exchange options were allowed in July 2003. The foreign exchange derivative products that are now available in Indian financial markets can be grouped into three broad segments, viz., forwards, options (foreign currency rupee options and cross currency options) and currency swaps (foreign currency rupee swaps and cross currency swaps) (Box-2).

In respect of forex derivatives involving rupee, residents have access to foreign exchange forward contracts, foreign currency-rupee swap instruments and currency options – both cross currency as well as foreign currency-rupee. In the case of derivatives involving only foreign currency, a range of products such as IRS, FRAs,

BOX 2

Foreign Exchange Derivative Instruments in India

Foreign Exchange Forwards

Authorised Dealers (ADs) (Category-1) are permitted to issue forward contracts to persons resident in India with crystallised foreign currency/foreign interest rate exposure and based on past performance/actual import-export turnover, as permitted by the Reserve Bank and to persons resident outside India with genuine currency exposure to the rupee, as permitted by the Reserve Bank. The residents in India generally hedge crystallised foreign currency/foreign interest rate exposure or transform exposure from one currency to another permitted currency. Residents outside India enter into such contracts to hedge or transform permitted foreign currency exposure to the rupee, as permitted by the Reserve Bank.

Foreign Currency Rupee Swap

A person resident in India who has a long-term foreign currency or rupee liability is permitted to enter into such a swap transaction with ADs (Category-1) to hedge or transform exposure in foreign currency/foreign interest rate to rupee/rupee interest rate.

Foreign Currency Rupee Options

ADs (Category-1) approved by the Reserve Bank and ADs (Category-1) who are not market makers are allowed to sell foreign currency rupee options to their customers on a back-to-back basis, provided they have a capital to risk-weighted assets ratio (CRAR) of 9 per cent of above. These options are used by customers who have genuine foreign currency exposures, as permitted by the Reserve Bank and by ADs (Category-1) for the purpose of hedging trading books and balance sheet exposures.

Cross-Currency Options

ADs (Category-1) are permitted to issue cross-currency options to a person resident in India with crystallised foreign currency exposure, as permitted by the Reserve Bank. The clients use this instrument to hedge or transform foreign currency exposure arising out of current account transactions. ADs use this instrument to cover the risks arising out of market-making in foreign currency rupee options as well as cross currency options, as permitted by the Reserve Bank.

Cross-Currency Swaps

Entities with borrowings in foreign currency under external commercial borrowing (ECB) are permitted to use cross currency swaps for transformation of and/or hedging foreign currency and interest rate risks. Use of this product in a structured product not conforming to the specific purposes is not permitted.

option are allowed. While these products can be used for a variety of purposes, the fundamental requirement is the existence of an underlying exposure to foreign exchange risk whether on current or capital account. While initially the forward contracts could not be rebooked once cancelled, greater flexibility has now been given for booking cancellation and rebooking of forward contracts. In the case of exporters and importers, they are also allowed to book forward contracts based on past performance and the delivery condition has also been gradually liberalized.

In order to simplify procedural requirements for Small and Medium Enterprises (SME) sector, RBI has recently granted flexibility for hedging both underlying as well as anticipated and economic exposures without going through the rigours of complex documentation formalities. In order to ensure that SMEs understand the risks of these products, only banks with whom they have credit relationship are allowed to offer such facilities. These facilities should also have some relationship with the turnover of the entity. Similarly, individuals have been permitted to hedge upto USD 100,000 on self declaration basis.

AD banks may also enter into forward contracts with residents in respect of transactions denominated in foreign currency but settled in Indian Rupees including hedging the currency indexed exposure of importers in respect of customs duty payable on imports. ADs have been delegated powers to allow residents engaged in import and export trade to hedge the price risk on all commodities in international commodity exchanges, with few exceptions like gold, silver, and petroleum. Domestic producers/users are allowed to hedge their price risk on aluminum, copper, lead, nickel and zinc as well as aviation turbine fuel in international commodity exchanges based on their underlying economic exposures.

Facilities for Non-residents

Foreign Institutional Investors (FII), persons resident outside India having Foreign Direct Investment (FDI) in India and Non-resident Indians (NRI) are allowed access to the forwards market to the extent of their exposure in the cash market. FIIs are permitted to hedge currency risk on the market value of entire investment in equity and/or debt in India as on a particular date using forwards. For FDI investors, forwards are permitted to (i) hedge exchange rate risk on the market value of investments made in India since January 1, 1993 (ii) hedge exchange rate risk on dividend receivable on the investments in Indian companies and (iii) hedge exchange rate risk on proposed investment in India. NRIs can hedge balances/amounts in NRE accounts using forwards and FCNR (B) accounts using rupee forwards as well as cross currency forwards.

Currency Futures

In the context of growing integration of the Indian economy with the rest of the world, as also the continued development of financial markets, there is a need to allow other hedging instruments to manage exchange risk like currency futures. The Committee on Fuller Capital Account Convertibility had recommended that currency futures may be introduced subject to risks being contained through proper trading mechanism, structure of contracts and regulatory environment. Accordingly, Reserve Bank of India in the Annual Policy Statement for the Year 2007-08 proposed to set up a Working Group on Currency Futures to study the international experience and suggest a suitable framework to operationalise the proposal, in line with the current legal and regulatory framework.

The group has had extensive consultations with a cross section of market participants including bankers associations, banks, brokers, exchanges, both Indian and international, and is in the process of finalizing its report. Given that India is not yet fully convertible on capital account, various options are available to deal with the issue of reconciling the regulatory framework in the cash and OTC forward market with the currency futures segment. The international experience in this regard is mostly from OECD countries except for one single exception of South Africa which has very recently introduced domestic currency futures.

Rupee Interest Rate Derivatives

Rupee derivatives in India were introduced in July 1999 when RBI permitted banks/FIs/PDs to undertake Interest rate swaps and Forward rate agreements. These institutions were allowed to offer these products to corporates for hedging interest rate risk as well as deal in these instruments for their own balance sheet hedging and trading purposes. Since then, many initiatives have been undertaken to deepen and broaden the market.

The rupee interest rate derivatives presently permissible are Forward Rate Agreements (FRA), Interest Rate Swaps (IRS) and Interest Rate Futures (IRF). The permitted benchmarks for FRA/IRS are any domestic money or debt market rupee interest rate; or, rupee interest rate implied in the forward foreign exchange rates, as permitted in respect of MIFOR swaps. While both banks and PDs are allowed as market makers in the swap market, all business entities (including banks and PDs) are permitted to hedge their underlying exposures using these instruments. PDs have been also permitted to hold trading position in IRF, subject to internal guidelines in this regard. The interest rate swap market has grown rapidly with participation from banks and corporates. The market is liquid and bid-offer spreads are narrow.

In order to have a mechanism for transparent capture and dissemination of trade information, the Clearing Corporation of India, at the instance of RBI, has recently developed a reporting system for OTC interest rate swaps. The reported deals are processed by CCIL which also offers certain post trade processing services like resetting interest rates, providing settlement values etc. to the reporting members. Once things stabilize, the next phase could be development of post-trade processing infrastructure to address some of the attendant risks. While FRA/IRS markets have shown phenomenal growth, the interest rate futures, first introduced on NSE in 2003, have not picked up on account of certain structural factors. A sub-group of the RBI Technical Advisory Committee on Markets having representatives from the industry and academia, has been constituted to examine the issues, including the following: (i) Review the experience with the Interest Rate Futures so far, with particular reference to product design issues and make recommendations for activating the Interest Rate Futures. (ii) Examine whether regulatory guidelines for banks for Interest Rate Futures need to be aligned with those for their participation in Interest Rate Swaps. (iii) Examine the scope and extent of the participation of non-residents, including Foreign Institutional Investors (FIIs), in Interest Rate Futures, consistent with the policy applicable to the underlying cash bond market.

VALUE-AT-RISK (VAR): A BIRD'S EYE VIEW

Value at risk (VaR) is a new approach to risk management that has been accepted by practitioners and regulators as the "right" way to measure risk. For example, the

Bank for International Settlements (BIS) has allowed banks to use their own models of VaR to set the capital requirements for market risk. This measure of risk focuses on the tail of the distribution of the rate of return (or the profit/loss or the percentage change in the exchange rate), which means that the emphasis is placed on the worst given percentages of outcomes. In what follows, a brief (and perhaps superficial) treatment of VaR is presented.

Essentially, this approach is used to answer the question *"over a given period of time with a given probability, how much money might be lost?"*. The money lost pertains to the decline in the value of a portfolio, which may consist of a single asset or a large number of assets. The measurement of VaR requires the choice of: (i) a measurement unit, normally the base currency; (ii) a time horizon, which could be a day, a week or longer provided that the composition of the portfolio does not change during this period; and (iii) a probability, which normally ranges between 1% and 5%. Hence VaR is the maximum expected loss over a given holding period at a given level of confidence (that is, with a given probability).

FIGURE 1

VALUE AT RISK ASSUME A NORMAL DISTRIBUTION OF EXPOSURE, WHICH IS AN APPROXIMATION

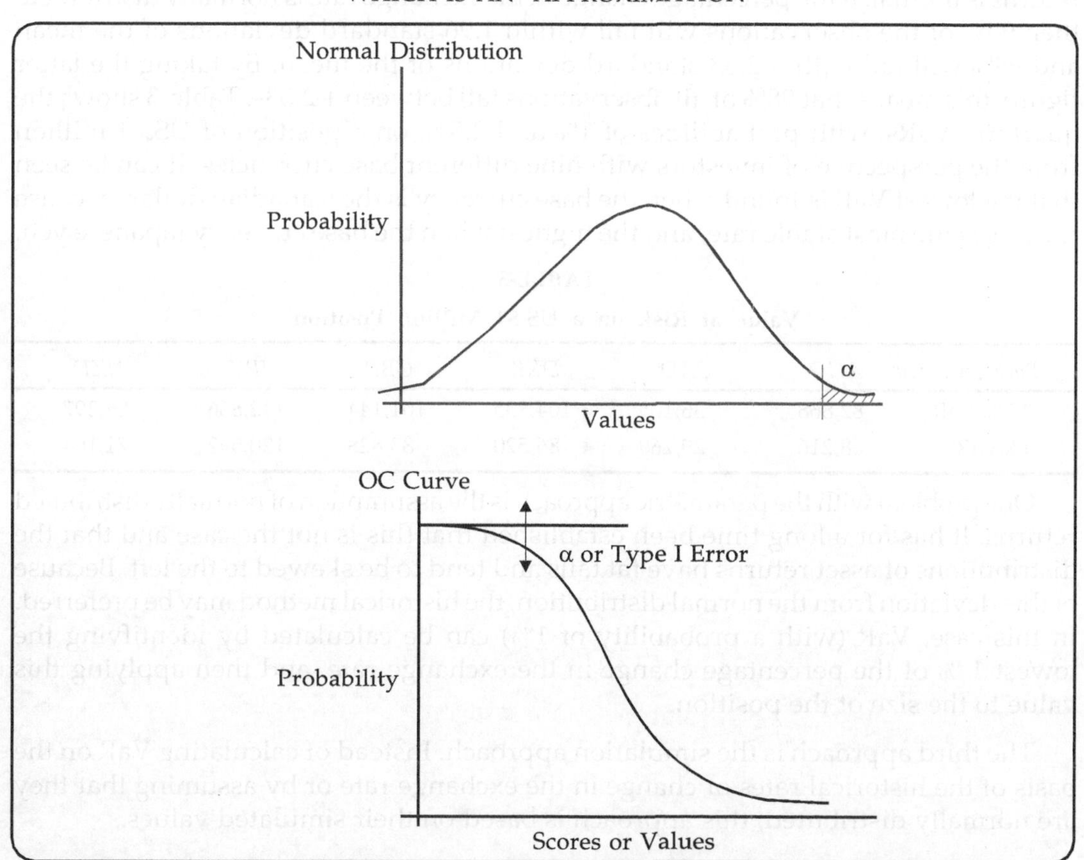

VaR as a measure of risk is illustrated in Figure-1 for a position in currency y, when the base currency is x. This figure shows a probability distribution (or frequency distribution) for the percentage change in the exchange rate over a chosen holding period.The calculation of value at risk assumes a normal distribution of exposures, which is evidently an approximation, whether we talk of individual instruments or of the contents of the whole trading book. A positive aftermath of this approximation is that we can use the concept underpinning the operating characteristics curve (lower part of Figure 1) to estimate the 99 per cent probability that the worst case will not exceed the value derived from computation. This 99 percent level of confidence corresponds to a Type 1 error, on the OC curve, of 1 percent. This is known as α. In the long run, in 1 percent of cases the VaR estimate will not cover the worst case.

Implementation of VaR Analysis

There are at least three approaches to the implementation of VaR analysis, all of which involve the estimation of the statistical distribution of asset returns: these are the parametric (or analytical) approach, the historical approach and the simulation approach. These approaches will be discussed briefly here,

The main assumption of the parametric VaR is that the distribution of asset returns is normal. If the percentage change in the exchange rate is normally distributed, then 95% of the observations will fall within 1.96 standard deviations of the mean and 98% will fall within 2.33 standard deviations of the mean. By taking the latter figure, this means that 98% of all observations fall between + 2.33s. Table-3 shows the quarterly VaRs, with probabilities of 1% and 2.5%, on a position of US$ 1 million from the perspective of investors with nine different base currencies. It can be seen that the lowest VaR is found when the base currency is the Canadian dollar, because the rate is the most stable rate, and the highest when the base currency Japanese yen.

TABLE-3

Value at Risk on a US $1 Million Position

Base Currency	*AUD*	*CAD*	*DKK*	*GBP*	*JPY*	*NZD*
2.5% VaR	82,868	36,105	104,835	101,144	142,866	86,297
1%VaR	68,216	29,260	86,520	83,828	120,592	71,164

One problem with the parametric approach is the assumption of normally distributed returns. It has for a long time been established that this is not the case and that the distributions of asset returns have fat tails and tend to be skewed to the left. Because of this deviation from the normal distribution, the historical method may be preferred. In this case, VaR (with a probability of 1%) can be calculated by identifying the lowest 1 % of the percentage change in the exchange rate, and then applying this value to the size of the position.

The third approach is the simulation approach. Instead of calculating VaR on the basis of the historical rates of change in the exchange rate or by assuming that they are normally distributed, this approach is based on their simulated values.

Pros and Cons of the VaR Methodology

Value at risk has become a widely used method for measuring financial risk, and justifiably so. The attractiveness of the concept lies in its simplicity, as it represents the market risk of the entire portfolio by one number that is easy to comprehend. It thus conveys a simple message on the risk borne by a firm or an individual. The concept is also suitable for risk limit setting and for measuring performance based on the correlation between the return earned and the risk assumed. Moreover, it can take account of complex movements such as non-parallel yield curve shifts. In general, it has two important characteristics: (i) it provides a common consistent measure of risk across different positions and risk factors; and (ii) it takes into account the correlations between different risk factors (for example, different currencies).

VaR is useful, but it should be handled with care and should be used in conjunction with other measures of risk.Sophisticated experimental approaches, however, require handling nonlinear distributions for daily changes in market variables; using Monte Carlo simulation; and employing Taylor Series expansion to calculate VaR when distributions are non-normal.

Senior management finds these issues awfully technical. Yet, they are crucial in defining and measuring market risk in an accurate way. Just as important is that the board and senior management understand the role of backtesting for tuning the parameters of VaR calculations, as well as the importance of using stress scenarios for measurement of catastrophic market risk. It is imperative, however, that VaR should not be viewed as a strict upper bound on the portfolio losses that can occur.

Backtesting is required by the 1996 Market Risk Amendment, and institutions have to present the results to the regulators. The results essentially consist of how well the VaR model has prognosticated the real-life exposure. Depending on these results, the prognostification falls in the green, yellow, or red zone. The green zone is the best.

Stress testing is not required at present by the Basle Committee, but institutions are well advised to learn how to do it. The study of catastrophic scenarios is an added value to VaR. Rigorous models can help in distinguishing levels of exposure in terms of expected business risk, unexpected risk, and catastrophic risk.

These differ in both their measurement and management; therefore, they require appropriate solutions to testing and reporting. In an information technology sense, typical business risks can be served through "pull" software (the classical approach where the user asks to be informed on results), while "push" software supported by agents is needed for catastrophic and near catastrophic risks.

There are, however, several shortcomings associated with the VaR methodology. First, it can be misleading to the extent of giving rise to unwarranted complacency. The VaR is highly sensitive to the assumptions used to calculate it. Moreover, the VaR is a number that itself is measured with some error or estimation risk. Thus, the VaR results must be interpreted with reference to the underlying statistical methodology.

Infact, this approach to risk management cannot cope with sudden and sharp changes in market conditions. It neglects the possibility of discrete, large jumps in financial prices (such as exchange rates), which occur quite often. Losses resulting from catastrophic occurrences are overlooked due to dependence on symmetric statistical measures that treat upside and downside risk in a similar manner. From a statistical viewpoint, VaR is a scalar estimate of an unknown parameter of the loss distribution. Sampling errors can affect the accuracy of point estimates so institutions using VaR must be careful with the hypotheses that they make and the way these hypotheses influence the outcome.

In the computation of VaR there may be other errors too that are not statistical in nature, but depend on assumptions and on the correlations. Empirically derived correlations are used for aggregation within each of three basic risk classes: currency exchange, interest rates, and equities. Other classes, too, can be distinguished depending on the business of the bank. Across risk classes, cumulative exposure is computed assuming zero correlation among highly defined risk classes. This is, of course, another approximation reflecting the diversification that might or might not exist in business areas. Hence, depending on the institution and its trading habits, this hypothesis may be weak or outright false.

In real life risk and returns are not normally distributed-as it is assumed. When markets are calm the bell shaped distribution may be acceptable, but in nervous markets it leads to implementation flaws: *Firstly*, VaR models are particularly weak at the edges, because of extreme movements, *Secondly*, outliers occur much more frequently than suggested by the normal distribution. *Thirdly*, VaR fails to account for fat fails. Yet, leptokyrtotic distributions very commonly appear with financial time series. The discarding of extreme or repetitive values weakens the benefits obtained from the model.Fourthly, VaR incorporates a significant probability of financial disaster-particularly if the 95 per cent level of confidence is used instead of the regulatory 99 percent. Neither the parametric VaR nor the simulation VaR say anything about extreme values: precisely what might happen in the "other" 1 percent, beyond the 99 percent confidence limit. It was found out that in the case of LTCM's near-bankruptcy this other 1 per cent showed a loss of $1.36 billion. Banks should be very careful with extreme events. Fifthly ,the expected tail loss (ETL) is a measure of risk that is also known as expected shortfall, conditional VaR, tail conditional expectation, and worst conditional expectation. The concept is very simple: ETL is the expected value of a loss that is in excess of VaR. While the VaR tells us the most that can be expected to be lost if a bad event does occur, the ETL tells us what we can expect to lose if a bad event does occur. Infact, to view risk in terms of the probability of a given loss or the amount that can be lost with a given probability at the end of the investment horizon is wrong. This view of risk considers only the final result.The investors should perceive risk differently because they are affected by risk and exposed to loss throughout the investment period. In addition, the investors must consider risk and the possibility of loss throughout the investment horizon; otherwise, their wealth may not survive to the end of the investment horizon. As a result of this , two new measures of risk— within-horizon probability of loss and continuous VaR — — should be used to demonstrate that the possibility of making loss is substantially greater than what investors normally assume. Finally, another major weakness with the method (but not necessarily with the model) is the use of meager databases, which leads to meaningless if not outright misleading results.

Satisfying Regulatory and Managerial Requirements

The 1996 Market Risk Amendment outlines regulatory specifications for VaR. These are the 99 percent confidence interval a 10-day holding period; a historical observation period of at least one year; a minimum three-month frequency for the update of data sets; and the recognition of correlations across broad risk factors categories, interest rate, currency exchange, equities, and commodities. Another regulatory requirement is a scaling factor for VaR results.

For internal management accounting reasons the bank may also follow another list of "musts". Many institutions have started to internally differentiate between value at risk and capital at risk. Also, for internal management control purposes VaR has started to be endowed with delta/gamma hedging to calculate risk based on a one-day holding period, exponential moving average volatilities, and correlations within risk factors.

This enlarges the implementation horizon of value at risk, and the use of estimates of potential losses in the bank's portfolio for a predetermined probability and holding period. Attention must be paid to the methodology employed to capture all significant risks and meet or exceed industry standards in terms of accuracy and timeliness.

Challenges with the Test of Hypothesis Used in the Model

Analysts with experience in modeling, and in the computation of credit risk and market risk, have evidence that mapping the market into the computer and doing a rigorous experimentation allows divesification. This brings up a number of other issues relating to management culture, skills requirements, the hypotheses being made, and technological leadership.

A basic but not always appreciated policy is that, in principle, the more diversified is the trading book, the lower the corresponding capital requirements will be. There are regulatory measures, however, that do not permit this flexibility; neither are the available eigenmodels able to serve reliably all sorts of diversification moves.

Beyond the pricing models and the risk models for derivatives, an institution also needs optimisation models that address the contents of the trading book for diversification reasons. Since the algorithms being used most often rest on the normal distribution and its confidence intervals, one of the concerns is the existence of correlations, outliers, and spike volatilities.

Usually spike patterns see to it that data are not normally distributed. Therefore the hypotheses are not substantiated by market facts. Furthermore, because the way to bet is that every distribution has outliers, one of the critical questions is how well model will cope with them. Is it really sensitive to extreme events? Will such events upset its behaviour? For this methods for estimating conditional probabilities that account for fat tails are required. An institution may incur a loss beyond VaR; but how far can it expect it to go? The study of extreme events can be done through extreme value theory. Because extreme events matter, in all likelihood this theory will become an important part of methodology.

The best way to judge models is by what they deliver. Sometime down the line the current linear models based on the normal distribution will become inaccurate. Then they will become unacceptable, if we have not been careful enough to test for outliers in a dual sense; as predictors and as deviators of model behaviour. A similar point can be made about correlations. Usually the algorithms we develop are based on a hypothesis of independent events. This rarely happens in real life, and if we have not been careful about the existence of correlations or their neutralisation, the model will give inadequate results.

The opposite is also true. Fairly frequently the assumption of th existence of correlation is made without the appropriate study and associated tests. It is, for instance, often assumed that the G-10 stock markets move in synergy and that they highly correlate because of globalisation. Yet, a recent study by the Bank of England documents that from 1988 onward the market behaviors of the London Stock Exchange and of the Tokyo Stock Exchange don't positively correlate in any significant manner. Indeed, if intraday statistics are considered, then sometimes the correlation is negative. Such findings invalidate the hypotheses we sometimes make. They also impact model behaviour, and for this reason they should be kept in perspective. Other issues, too, influence the choice of value at-risk algorithms to be used.

Is VaR Used in Practice?

VaR is widely used by major companies in real life. Microsoft, for example, uses VaR as a management tool to estimate its exposure to market risk, reporting the estimated VaR figures in its annual reports. For the purpose of calculating VAR, Microsoft uses a time horizon of 20 days, which is longer than what is typically used by banks. Another difference is that Microsoft uses a confidence level of 97.5% rather than 99%, which is what is used by banks.

In 1999, Moosa and Knight conducted a survey of the practices of Australian public shareholding companies with respect to the use of value at risk analysis. The results of the survey reveal significant unfamiliarity with VaR analysis, as half of the respondents indicated that they were unaware of the existence of this technique. Financial institutions, those involved in international operations and those using derivatives tend to be more familiar with the technique. Moreover, not all of the companies with VaR awareness actually use the technique for measuring risk. The results of the survey produced several findings, including the following: (i) companies that do not use VaR mostly employ scenario analysis; (ii) those not using VaR claim that it is not relevant to their operations; (iii) those using VaR predominantly employ the parametric approach; and (iv) the majority of users employ back testing and stress testing. The results also revealed that financial institutions, companies involved in international operations and those using derivatives are more aware of the existence of VaR analysis and more inclined to use it, and that companies not using VaR but intending to use it are predominantly those involved in international operations and those using derivatives.

According to the Reserve Bank of Australia , the VaR of major Australian banks was 0.02% of their capital base, much lower than the corresponding figures in other countries. In Germany, for example, the corresponding figure was 0.15%. The 1999 figures are shown in Table-4.

TABLE-4

VaR of Major Banks

Country	*Foreign exchange risk (% of capital)*	*Total market risk (% of capital)*
Australia	0.02	0.08
Canada	0.02	0.12
Germany	0.15	0.71
Japan	0.07	0.31
Netherlands	0.02	0.20
UK	0.03	0.16
USA	0.03	0.15

Source: Reserve Bank of Australia (2000)

QUESTIONS

1. Discuss the growth of financial derivatives in the global financial markets.
2. "The changing nature of financial industry, especially as reflected in developments in the financial derivatives market, provides a considerable opportunities for risk sharing or inter-temporal smothering." What actions can be taken to control or plan for these risks? Can value be produced through risk management strategies? Explain.
3. Discuss the various financial derivatives instruments traded on organised exchanges in world financial markets.
4. Critically examine the global positions in OTC derivatives markets by type of risk instrument.
5. "Global networking is no longer a mere metaphor for worldwide activities but now describes in very literal terms the advances in information and communication technology which have been a major driving force behind internationalisation in many areas of life, but especially in the economy. Within the economic sector, in turn, it is in the financial markets that globalisation has been particularly dynamic." Comment.

6. Examine the impact of growth of the financial derivatives on the financial system.
7. Discuss the emerging derivatives market structure in India.
8. Discuss the primary risks and vulneralitities in the global financial market.
9. Critically examine the Value-at-Risk (VaR) approach.
10. Critically examine the several variants of financial derivative contracts.
11. Discuss the regulatory framework evolved for derivatives market in India.
12. "Derivatives are sometimes deliberately mispriced in order to conceal losses or to make profits by fraud"" Comment.

31

INTERNATIONAL FINANCIAL MANAGEMENT

INTRODUCTION

The importance of multinational corporations and the globalisation of production are now well recognised. Multinational corporations have become central actors of the world economy and, in linking foreign direct investment, trade, technology and finance, they are a driving force of economic growth. Since the world is reduced to an electronic village and global finance has become a reality, therefore in a contemporary global corporation financial capital is one of the most fungible assets to cross national boundaries. The determinants of the way in which transnational corporation acquire, organise and manage those assets is of critical importance, not only to the success of those corporations, but also to the development and industrial restructuring of nation states. The task of international financial manager is to make the best possible tactical decision that the market has to offer on liabilities, within the strategic funding constraints set by currency denomination, maturity, and capital structure.

THEORETICAL DEVELOPMENTS IN THE INTERNATIONAL FINANCIAL MANAGEMENT

From the perspective of international corporate financial management, the definition of international business and—by implication—the international firm, is quite comprehensive: it includes all business activities on which management must make financial decisions, taking into account simultaneously: (1) the conditions prevailing in *two or more financial markets,* (2) regulatory and institutional *barriers* to the international movement of funds, and (3) the changes in the *exchange rates* of national monies. To illustrate, instead of taking into account one set of national tax rules, one rate of inflation, one set of interest rates, one integrated system of money and capital markets and the assorted institutions, management must now take into account the complex interactions of at least two tax systems, two interest rate structures, and two sets of financial institutions when making decisions. Obviously, this entails additional complications and risks. However—and this represents the other side of the coin—management has available more alternatives and, therefore, better opportunities to attain the firm's objectives: to enhance the value of the business enterprise by minimising the cost of funds and the risk to the firm.

Thus the range of enterprises for which the practice and theory of international financial management is relevant is much more inclusive than the traditional concepts of the multinational corporation (MNC), which is defined typically as a firm having a substantial portion of its activities and assets deployed in different countries. The concept relevant for financial management comprises all firms that are involved in international business, directly or indirectly, to such an extent that the managerial process must take into account the complexities of a *multimarket, multicurrency environment*. The objective of international financial management is the same as that of domestically oriented financial management i.e. the maximisation of the value of the firm. The differences arise because of the term's exposure to international and multinational environments. The common thread of international aspects of financial management is found in the following: What aspects of the issue are peculiarly international, and what opportunities does a firm have by virtue of its being international? The clues to an answer lie in the basic understanding of the management of the cross border financial assets and liabilities and cash flows. From a corporate perspective, the most important theoretical developments in international financial management can be captured by concentrating on the following areas:

The Foreign Exchange Markets

What is foreign exchange? Foreign exchange is simply a *payment or a deposit* in some national currency (or artificial currency) that is exchanged for a payment in another currency. Thus any money can become foreign exchange by surprise and the moment after it has been exchanged it forgets it was foreign exchange. Once more, it is national money.

Unlike the money and capital markets, the foreign exchange market deals not in *credit* but in *means of payment*. This brings one to a fundamental point: While foreign exchange deals frequently take place between residents of different countries, the money being traded never actually leaves the country of the currency. Thus when German deutsche marks are exchanged for U.S. dollars in London, the deutsche marks and dollars stay in Germany and the United States respectively. The act of trading only effects a *change of ownership* of the money. The money itself, in the form of bank deposits, merely gets shifted from one deposit to another through the country's interbank payments system.

In contrast to a *spot transaction, a forward foreign exchange contract* calls for delivery at a fixed future date of a specified amount of one currency for a specified amount of another currency. By *borrowing* money in one currency, buying a second currency *spot*, placing the funds in a *deposit* in the foreign currency, and simultaneously selling the foreign currency forward, an arbitrageur can profit if the domestic interest rate does not equal the foreign interest rate, adjusted for the *forward premium or discount* (the difference between the spot and forward exchange rate, expressed as an annualised percentage). This means that arbitrage will insure *interest rate parity—the* forward premium or discount always equals the interest rate differential between two currencies.

Covered interest arbitrage of this kind represents the fundamental link between Euro currency deposits or loans denominated in different currencies, and also between national capital markets—though, as will be shown, the last are imperfectly linked because of national controls on financial markets and because of exchange controls.

Doing business across national boundaries means dealing with more than one currency and therefore involves exchange risk. *Exchange risk* is the additional systematic risk to a firm's flows arising from exchange rate changes. The three main types of foreign exchange-risk management which are of special interest to MNCs fall under the heading of *economic, transaction* and *translation*—exposure management. The foreign exchange economic exposure is defined as the likelihood that the net present value of a firm's future cash flows will change due to an unexpected change in exchange rates. When exchange rates change unexpectedly, a transnational corporation's sales volume, price and costs are likely to be affected.

Effort by the firm to manage exchange rate changes are really the macroeconomic version of what is happening at the macroeconomic level. International economics literature is rich in discussions of how countries adjust to exchange rate changes. For example, the concept of a "real (inflation-adjusted) exchange rate" is well understood in economics literature and by government policy makers. However, neither economic exposure nor the real effective exchange rate are well understood by top management. Instead, they often assume that any foreign exchange issue is the responsibility of the treasurer or financial vice president. In reality, managing economic exposure is best accomplished by internationally diversifying sales, production and financing by currency. These are strategic decisions that must be approved by top management and the board of directors, as well as by the financial officers.

Foreign exchange transaction exposure is defined as the change in domestic (reporting) currency value of outstanding financial accounts which are denominated in a foreign currency. Typical accounts which are exposed are foreign currency denominated accounts receivable, accounts payable and dividends which have been declared but not yet paid from foreign affiliates. Transaction exposure can be managed by both operating policies, such as leads and lags in payments, and by contractual hedging instruments such as forward contracts, money market hedges, swaps and foreign currency future and option contracts.

Exchange rate determination and the use of contractual hedges have long been the domain of the international economics literature. Therefore the corporate finance literature has focused more on a derivative question: are exchange rate changes predictable and, if so, can a firm (engaged in international transactions) benefit from the prediction? The answer to that question depends on whether or not foreign exchange markets are efficient and how much risk aversion management can tolerate. Reported hedging of all transaction exposure can be more costly than the expected loss or gain from remaining unhedged, especially if foreign exchange markets are efficient. However, if the markets are inefficient, and the size of a transaction exposure is large compared to the size of the firm, most managers would probably hedge all or some of the exposure in order to reduce variability of cash flows and earnings.

Cost of Capital

A number of transnational corporations have been able to lower their cost of capital by raising funds in international capital markets and by cross-listing on foreign stock exchanges. As a result of the efforts of those firms to internationalise their cost of capital, segmented capital markets have gradually become more integrated and international portfolio investment has flourished. In addition, the investors may purchaser the shares of firms which are resident in segmented capital markets. This could further lower the cost of capital of transnational firms.

If capital markets are partially segmented, investors cannot gain the full benefit from international portfolio diversification, and firms cannot fully lower their cost of capital by selling their securities to foreign investors. A national capital market can be segmented because of government interference and/or because of investor perceptions. An example of government interference is restrictions on the free movement of capital, either by limiting what domestic securities foreign investors can buy, or by limiting what foreign securities domestic investors can buy. Other examples are discriminatory tax policies, rationing of foreign exchange, and policies which increase transactions costs in domestic securities markets. Investor perceptions are shaped by the quality of financial disclosures, familiarity with foreign securities markets and institutions, alternative portfolio possibilities, foreign exchange risk and political risk.

If a country's capital market is segmented, investors resident in that country may not be able to hold an efficient internationally diversified portfolio, and firms resident in that country may not enjoy the lowest possible cost of capital. However, with the proper strategies, transnational firms may be able to raise their funds abroad and gain an international pricing of their securities even though their home market remains segmented. On the other hand, firms which are too small to tap international capital markets are forced to continue to accept the higher cost of capital typical of their domestic markets.

The "small firm" bias is even more of a deterrent when it comes to interesting international equity investors in holding the shares of a small firm. Most institutional investors are very concerned about their ability to sell as well as to buy a firm's shares. The market for shares in a small firm is perceived as being illiquid, whether that firm is transnational or domestic.

To what extent can the shares of a transnational corporation serve as a substitute for investors who wish to diversify their portfolios internationally but cannot find or purchase the shares of firms which are resident in segmented capital markets? Considerable evidence exists to suggest that transnational firms should have a lower cost of capital than their domestic counterparts. Because of that, they may receive a higher valuation by investors who are using their shares for international diversification into segmented markets that they cannot tap themselves. Listing on foreign securities exchanges has a favourable liquidity effect because more investors are available to buy the limited number of a firm's shares outstanding. Tapping foreign markets is also a way for firms which are resident in segmented markets to escape the lower valuation of their shares in that market. Normally a firm must be transnational, or at least extremely visible abroad, to succeed in attracting a significant following of foreign investors.

Financial Structure

Modigliani and Miller launched the great debate about whether or not an optimal financial structure for a firm exists. Their original contention was that, under certain very restrictive assumptions about perfect competition, financial structure was irrelevant. They later modified this assertion by recognising that the tax advantages of debt biases the firm towards a much higher use of debt. Later theorists suggested that agency and bankruptcy costs place an upper limit on the desirable portion of debt.

The "traditionalists" always felt that an optimal debt ratio exists in the form of a U-shaped cost of capital curve. As a firm takes on debt, the weighted average cost of capital is reduced due to the tax advantages of debt; but when the debt ratio becomes too high, agency and bankruptcy costs, as well as the reticence of lenders, raises the cost of capital. Therefore, the optimal debt ratio is a flat range at the bottom of the U-shaped cost of capital curve.

Capital structure decisions are particularly important when financial structure decisions dealing with leverage (or gearing) must be made. To the extent that any priorities can be established among the complex, interrelated steps of a funding decision in MNC, such strategic considerations probably take first place. Of course, the reason why the debt/equity ratio matters so much is that it determines the financial risk of the enterprise. because of the contractually fixed nature of payments to debt holders, returns to the owners of equity will fluctuate more in response to given, unanticipated fluctuations of operating returns the higher the proportion of debt relative to equity. Thus a positive partial relationship between the risk of equity returns and leverage ratios can be documented. Because of nontrivial default costs one can also find that a firm's leverage ratios and enterprise risk are negatively related. The interaction between the tax shield provided by debt and the various costs associated with default provide the theoretical support for an optimal capital structure. And to the extent that these factors are influenced by environmental factors such as tax laws and factors affecting the cost and probability of bankruptcy. one finds significant country factors in the capital structure of MNCs based in various countries.

This rationale is often mistakenly applied in the analysis of funding decisions involving individual, wholly owned affiliates. What is usually overlooked is the fact that such wholly owned affiliates of MNC's have a distinct and separate debt/equity ratio only if the parent is prepared to allow the affiliate in question to default on its debt without coming to its rescue. On the other hand, as long as the rest of the MNC group has a *legal* (loan guarantees) or an effective *moral obligation* to prevent the affiliate from defaulting—even if this threatens the survival of the remainder of the group—the individual affiliate has *no independent debt/equity ratio.* Its true leverage ratio is equal to that of the consolidated group.

Since virtually all MNC's feel obliged to their wholly owned (and sometimes even partially owned) affiliates, simply because they cannot afford to lose their financial respectability, the debt/equity ratio of the affiliate is determined by purely institutional factors. Most prominent among such are (i) *Statutory laws,* which prescribe a required minimum equity level in many countries; (2) *tax laws,* which often treat interest payments differently than payments on equity (dividends): (3) *exchange control regulations,* which are usually less restrictive when interest payments are concerned: (4) expropriation risk, *which can be lessened if the parent expects to default on its local debt in the specific case that the lending institutions have also been taken over by the government in question, or the lending institutions are state-owned already.*

Thus the debt/equity decision for foreign affiliates is either a purely legal one—as opposed to a financial decision—or it involves *strategic questions of ownership* to the extent that third-party investors, local or otherwise, own a part of the affiliate's equity.

When it comes to making debt/equity decisions for the parent, or rather the group as a whole, a very difficult issue arises: which market's standards will govern its "acceptable" debt/equity ratio? For domestic firms, the answer is usually quite clear. In different national capital markets, certain target debt/equity ratios have been established by market forces for different kinds of firms. These acceptable debt/equity ratios are influenced by the nature of the firm. To illustrate, public utilities, whose operating risk is relatively low, are permitted to have a much higher proportion of debt before the market begins to penalise these enterprises by increasing the required rate of return on equity or the interest on their debt relative to for example, capital goods producers, whose return on assets is very much subject to the vagaries of the business cycle. The problem for the multinational firm is that different national markets differ quite a bit in terms of standards for acceptable debt/equity ratios, and to the extent that MNCs sell their equity or borrow funds in many countries they must choose a reference market.

Theoretically, this question is largely unsolved because empirical work in finance has not sufficiently progressed to answer the question. "Precisely how are financial assets priced internationally?" That is, which is a more correct approximation of reality, that markets are separated or that they are integrated? In practice, most MNCs do not have to face this problem head on because the great bulk of the equity is usually held by investors of a national market whose standards dominate the applicable debt/equity ratio. However, as more and more companies make an effort to broaden their stockholder base internationally (e.g., by listing their stock on the exchanges of two or more countries) this issue will become more and more acute.

Next to capital structure decisions, the issue of *debt denomination* is probably the most important strategic aspect of the funding decision. In the absence of specific and identifiable market imperfections, currency decisions cannot be made on the basis of financial market factors alone. They must be coordinated with an analysis of the impact of *currency fluctuations* on the firm's operating cash flows (i.e., *corporate exchange risk*).

Capital Budgeting

Capital budgeting for a foreign project uses the same discounted cash-flow techniques as are used to evaluate domestic projects. In a true transnational corporation, all projects, foreign and domestic, compete on an equal footing for a piece of the capital budget. However, the analysis of a foreign project is considerably more complex than for a domestic project for the following reasons:

(i) Parent cash flows must be distinguished form project cash flows. Each of these two types of flow contributes to a different view of value.

(ii) Parent cash flows often depend on the form of financing. Thus cash flows cannot be clearly separated from financing decisions, as is done in domestic capital budgeting.

(iii) Remittance of funds to the parent must be explicitly recognised because of differing tax systems, legal and political constraints on the movement of funds, local business norms, and differences in how financial markets and institutions function.

(iv) Cash flows from affiliates to parent can be generated by an array of non-financial payments, including payment of license fees and payments for imports from the parent.

(v) Differing rates of national inflation must be anticipated because of their importance in causing changes in competitive position, and thus in cash flows over a period of time.

(vi) The possibility of unanticipated foreign exchange rate changes must be remembered because of possible direct effects on the value to the parent of local cash flows, as well as an indirect effect on the competitive position of the foreign affiliate.

(vii) Use of segmented national capital markets may create an opportunity for financial gains or may lead to additional financial costs.

(viii) Use of host government subsidised loans complicates both capital structure and the ability to determine an appropriate weighted average cost of capital for discounting purposes.

(ix) Political risk must be evaluated because political events can drastically reduce the value or availability of expected cash flows.

(x) Terminal value is more difficult to estimate because potential purchasers from the host, parent, or third countries, or from the private or public sector, may have widely divergent perspectives on the value to them of acquiring the project.

Since the same theoretical capital budgeting framework is used to choose among competing foreign and domestic projects, a common standard is critical. Thus all foreign complexities must be quantified as modifications to either expected cash flow or the rate of discount. Although in practice many firms make such modifications arbitrarily, readily available information, theoretical deduction, or just plain common sense can be used to make less arbitrary and more reasonable choices.

International Financial Markets

The capital markets of the world consist of sources of finance, and uses for finance, in a number of different countries. Each of these is a capital market on its own. On the other hand, *national capital markets* are partially linked, and partially segmented.

This fact is what makes international finance so exciting. Because national capital markets are of very different stages of development and size and depth, they have very different prices and availability of capital. Hence, the international financier has great opportunities for *arbitrage*—finding the cheapest source of funds, and the highest return, without adding to risk. And because markets are imperfectly linked, the means and channels by which foreigners enter domestic capital markets, and domestic sources or users of funds go abroad, are the essence of this aspect of international financial management. The other aspect is the fact that domestic claims and liabilities are denominated in national currencies. These must be exchanged for one another for capital to flow internationally; since relative values depend on supply and demand, the international financier faces *exchange risk*. Finally, the past

FIGURE-1

MARKETS OF INTERNATIONAL FINANCE

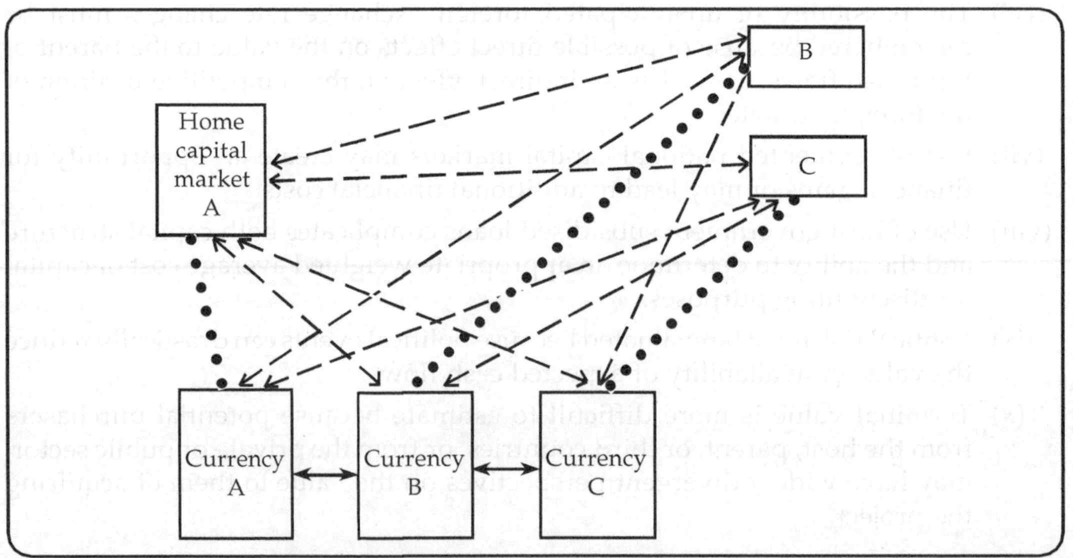

Key: Solid lines, prefect linkages; dotted lines, partial linkages; arrow, foreign exchange linkages.

few decades have seen a new phenomenon: the separation of *currency of denomination* of assets and liabilities from *country of jurisdiction.* This removal of currencies from their home countries is the *Euromarket* phenomenon.

Figure-1 illustrates *the three sets* of markets—home, foreign and Euromarket—faced by every investor or borrower, plus the fourth market, the foreign currency market, which must be crossed as one enters the world of finance. Each country has more or less imperfect linkages with every other country and with the Euromarket, both the segment in its own currency and Euromarket segments in other currencies. The *linkages of each country with its Euromarket* segment are very important, since domestic and Euromarket instrument are close substitutes and no foreign exchange market comes between them. The *links among segments of the Euromarket* are also very important, since no national controls come between them—in other words, linkages within the Euromarket are perfect, being differentiated only by currency of denomination. They are linked through the *spot* and *forward foreign exchange markets.*

This scheme provides a picture of the contents herein as well as that of the environment of international finance. International finance is thus concerned with:

Domestic capital markets and their linkages with Euromarkets and other domestic markets.

Euromarkets and their linkages' with other Euromarkets and domestic markets.

Foreign exchange markets that link domestic markets and Euromarkets in different currencies.

The *techniques* of borrowing, investing, moving; and exchanging funds internationally: international financial management.

Domestic Capital Markets and their Linkages

The *international role* of a capital market and. the *regulatory climate* that prevails are closely related. Appropriate regulation can and does make markets more attractive (e.g., by minimising the risk of losses through fraud, through conflicts of interest, and through a lack of adequate disclosure). However, the dividing line between regulatory measures that improve markets and those that have just the opposite effect is very thin. When governments pursue other objectives, such' as *credit allocation* according to political criteria, or when they discriminate against non-residents, markets can quickly become inefficient. The result is that both foreign and domestic market participants use markets in other jurisdictions.

Foreign Financial Markets

Most of the savings and investments of a country take place in that country's domestic financial market. However, many financial markets have extensive links abroad—domestic investors purchase foreign securities and invest funds in foreign financial institutions. Conversely, domestic banks can lend to foreign residents, and foreign residents can issue securities in the national market or deposit funds with resident financial intermediaries. These are the *traditional foreign markets* for international financial transactions.

The significant aspect of traditional foreign lending and borrowing is that all transactions take place under the rules, usances, and institutional arrangements prevailing in the respective national market. Most important, all these transactions are directly subject to public policy governing foreign transactions in a particular market. To illustrate, when savers purchase securities in a foreign market, they do so according to the rules, market practices, and regulatory precepts that govern such transactions in that particular market. The same applies to those who invest their funds with foreign financial intermediaries.

Likewise, foreign borrowers who wish to issue securities in a national market must follow the rules and regulations of that market. Frequently, these rules are *discriminatory* and *restrictive.* The same is true with respect to financial intermediaries; the borrower who approaches a foreign financial institution for a loan obtains funds at rates and conditions imposed by the financial institutions of the foreign country and is directly affected by the authorities' policy towards lending to foreign residents.

The Euromarkets and Their Linkages

Eurocurrencies—which are neither currencies (they are deposits, loans, or securities) nor are they necessarily connected with Europe—represent the separation of currency of denomination from the country of jurisdiction.

Banks and clients make this separation simply by locating the market for credit denominated in a particular currency outside the country where that currency is legal tender (i.e. the locus is in a jurisdiction that offers a more hospitable regulatory climate for such transactions).

To illustrate, markets for dollar-denominated loans, deposits, and securities in jurisdictions other than in the United States effectively avoid U.S. banking and securities regulations. These markets are referred to as "Euro" or, more properly, as "external" markets in order to indicate that they are not part of the domestic or national financial system. Thus the essence of this classification criterion is the nature of regulation. Differences in interest rates, practices and regulations that exist between domestic and external markets arise primarily from the extent to which regulatory constraints are different.

As in the domestic markets, the Euromarket consists of *intermediated funds* and *direct funds.* Intermediated credit in channel through banks is called the "Eurocurrency market". Direct credit—in particular, bonds—can be arranged by banks but it represents the direct liability of the borrower. The Eurobond market is such a market.

Figure-2 summarises the three-tiered structure of capital markets. Capital markets consist of:

A *domestic market,* usually with special and unique aspects and institutions stemming from historical and regulatory differences.

FIGURE - 2
INTERNATIONAL CREDIT MARKETS
A SCHEMATIC PRESENTATION

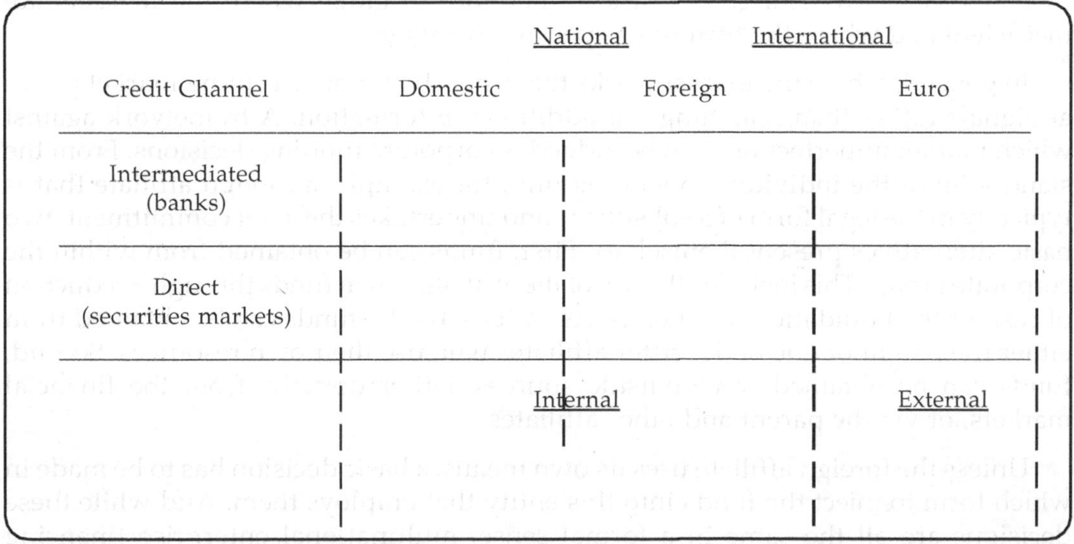

A *foreign segment* attached to the national market, where non-residents participate as suppliers and takers of funds, frequently playing both roles simultaneously, but always under the specific conditions, rules and regulations established for foreign participants in a particular national market.

An *external segment* that is characterised by being in a different political jurisdiction, with only the currency used to denominate the financial claims being the essential link to the national market.

As a result, the various external markets have more features in common with each other than with the respective national markets. Therefore, they are properly discussed as a common, integrated market where claims denominated in different currencies are exchanged.

International business is subject to *capital and credit controls.* International managers should know how to respond to governments' attempts to restrict the movement of funds into or out of countries and to manipulate the allocation of funds in domestic capital markets.

The multinational enterprise, by virtue of its foreign origin and international character, has special *monopolistically held advantages* that enable it to create and take advantage of imperfections in markets for factors, products and financial capital.

As the last suggests, much of what international financial management is about is taking advantage of the international firm's ability to exploit market imperfections. The crux of this is the ability to distinguish between situations where market imperfections truly exist and those where the profit opportunities have been eliminated by the workings of the market. A prime example is in the foreign exchange forecasting area—in currency markets that are likely to be efficient, no gain is to be had from exchange rate forecasting. The task is therefore to judge where the markets are inefficient and where the firm has a special advantage.

In general, where the market works the firm is better off accepting market prices as signals rather than searching out additional information. A framework against which market imperfections can be judged is corporate funding decisions. From the standpoint of the individual operating unit, for example, a foreign affiliate that is typically in the legal form of a subsidiary and undertakes the asset commitment, two basic alternatives present themselves. First, funds can be obtained from within the corporate group. This includes the use of the affiliate's own funds through a reduction of cash or the liquidation of other assets. Alternatively, funds can be obtained from either the parent or one of the sister affiliates who use their own resources. Second, funds can be obtained from outside sources, either directly, from the financial markets, or via the parent and other affiliates.

Unless the foreign affiliate uses its own means, a basic decision has to be made in which form to inject the funds into this entity that employs them. And while these decisions are all the same in a formal sense, multinational enterprise financing requires careful *distinction between outside relations and intragroup transactions.* This while the labels might look alike, the economic significance of the decision is quite different, except when joint ventures are involved. In this case, complex managerial and financial control issues result that are typical for joint ventures. And while both corporate managements are normally unwilling to tackle such problems, strong nationalistic tendencies in many countries make this form of foreign operation much more prevalent than business conditions would suggest.

Limiting the discussion to wholly owned affiliates, it must be pointed out that unlike the case of transactions, the distinction between inside and outside funds is of limited significance. This is because ultimately all funds are outside funds *in an opportunity cost sense;* the alternative use for retained profits is always to repay loans and/or to increase dividends to stockholders. Thus the only difference between the cost of external and internal funds (capital) can be attributed to agency costs (issuing and underwriting fees), restrictive covenants, and/or tax-related costs. To illustrate, a number of countries apply a lower tax rate to distributed earnings than to funds retained within the corporation. In the absence of specific institutional costs or incentives, the cost of internally generated funds in a multinational firm and its affiliates is equal to the cost of capital for the group as a whole.

INTERNATIONAL FINANCIAL MANAGEMENT AND IMPERFECTIONS IN FINANCIAL MARKETS

The equilibrium relationships and market linkages provide a point of departure for decision making. One can think of the expected relationships—in particular, the *unbiased forward rate* theory—as providing *market-based forecasts* of the exchange rate and other conditions.

Such forecasts can be used as a *benchmark* against which to judge the firm's own ability to forecast or to exploit market imperfections. Given the market-based forecasts, one can distinguish three situations, each with distinct implications for the currency aspects of financial planning:

1. *When the financial markets in question are reasonably efficient, and financial planners know of no systematic biases or constraints on market rates, then market-based forecasts should be accepted as valid.* Under these conditions, which probably hold for most financial decisions involving the major international financial markets, no expected gain will result from manipulating the timing or currency of borrowing or investing, and financial management's energies should be directed toward matching borrowings and investments with the timing and currency of the funds needed or generated by the firm's operations. The use of market-based forecasts then implies planning for the deviations, or forecasting errors, that will probably occur.

> Specifically, what one wants to know is how cash flows from operations (return on assets) will change for any given deviation of the interest or exchange rate from the value predicted. As long as the return on assets is contractually fixed and denominated in a particular currency, as would be a portfolio of bonds or loans, the analysis is quite straightforward. A rise in interest rates will cause a proportional fall in the value of such a fixed-interest portfolio; a given fall in the exchange rate will lead to an equal drop in the dollar value of the portfolio. Protecting the value of such assets, therefore, requires funding the liabilities of the firm in the same currency and maturity as the assets.
>
> This *efficient market financial planning framework* assumes the market's forecasts unbiased predictions of future exchange rates. Often, specific market imperfections will not allow this assumption to hold. The next two situations consider the Implications of such biases.

2. *When the term structure of interest or exchange rates deviates in a systematic way from the market's actual expectations because of government controls, or because of other specific market imperfections, financial management has profit opportunities.* The exploitation of these opportunities requires first, a flexible legal and operational structure, and second, *an* explicit trade-off function that permits management to decide whether the gains are worth the increase in risk and the exploitation of market imperfections might involve.

> Government controls tend to be always partial, never comprehensive. The reason is simple; controls on all borrowing or lending, and all international transfers of funds, would cause economic activity to come to a grinding halt. Therefore, with regulations permitting certain transactions, and funds being fungible, international firms with diverse legal structures and a multitude of intercompany links usually are in a privileged position to *exploit the financial*

windfalls that government distortions provide by keeping interest rates low and preventing exchange rates from adjusting to market pressures.

3. *When the market-based forecasts deviate from forecasted rates, not because of* market *imperfections but because the firm has some proprietary information or unusual forecasting ability, then financial managers should act on their forecasts only when the risks of doing so are offset by the expected gains.* When financial planners can confidently answer the questions, "Why do we believe we can predict interest or exchange rates better than the market"? Their focus should be on the proper perspective on the risks involved in speculative actions, and on a rapid response to opportunities when action is warranted.

> Few financial managers can consistently resist the temptation to base financing decisions on their own judgements rather than those of the market. In most cases little harm is done, for unless the firm really goes out on a limb, position and negative forecasting errors tend to cancel out over time. But the mark of a good financial manager is not a knack for occasionally outguessing the market's forecasts, but rather an ability to obtain the highest return on invested assets, for a given level of risk, and the best long-run terms and conditions on debt, irrespective of the tend of interest rates or exchange rates. It is important for the integrity of the financial management process to keep these aspects of the function strictly separate. Otherwise, the inability of financial management out perform the markets tends to be hidden in the results of the risk management function.

The imperfections and linkages of domestic financial markets, Euromarkets, and foreign exchange markets provide both risks and opportunities for the international financial management. Management attention should be concentrated on those markets and channels in which the firm has a competitive advantage, and should rely on banks, partners, and markets themselves to do what they can do more cheaply and efficiently. In the area of foreign exchange risk management, the market's forecasts of future exchange rates are readily available in the form of the forward exchange rates. On the other hand, where financial managers feel they have a peculiar advantage in financial markets, resulting from the firm's legal structure, geographical locations, or because of an unusual forecasting ability, then the timing, maturity, and currency of borrowing and investment decisions should be based on the firm's own forecasts whenever the expected gains justify the risks.

ROLE OF THE INTERNATIONAL FINANCIAL MANAGER

The chief tasks of the international financial manager are summarised as under:

Forecasting the financial environment—prices, inflation rates, interest rates and exchange rates.

Management of assets—from cash management to international capital budgeting, at home and abroad, in domestic and foreign currencies.

Management of liabilities—borrowing relationships and decisions, in domestic and foreign currencies and markets, short-term and long-term.

Exchange risk management—measuring the effect of exchange rate changes on balance sheets, income, and cash flows, and managing these risks.

Performance evaluation and control—accounting for outsiders, the tax authorities, and for management, and doing so across countries and currencies without distortion.

Sounds like a Herculean agenda? Yes, but domestic financial management is difficult too, and many of the techniques are transferable. The place to start learning about international financial management is therefore to gain a basic understanding of what and how financial decisions affect the value of the firm.

ECONOMIC FRAMEWORK OF INTERNATIONAL FINANCIAL MANAGEMENT

Much of received international financial management doctrine consists of techniques for borrowing, investing, or hedging decisions in one currency or another. However, many of these

FIGURE-3
DISEQUILIBRIUM CONDITIONS

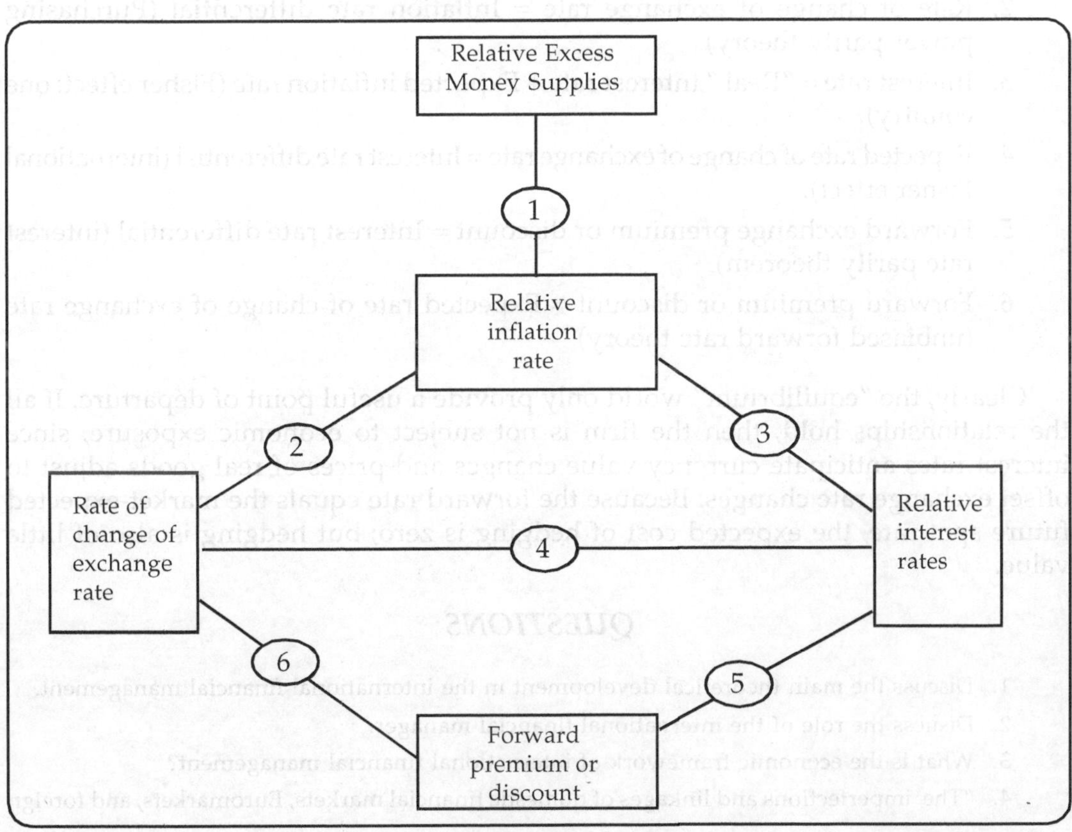

techniques work only under certain macroeconomic conditions, and the rules of thumb do not apply under other, quite plausible, conditions. In order to see how a number of the techniques of international finance are applicable only under conditions of disequilibrium. Figure-3 illustrates a framework showing the linkages among prices, exchange rates, interest rates, and other variables.

Figure-5 is interpreted as follows International differences in the extent to which the growth of the money supply exceeds the growth of real income result in international differences in inflation rates. Through the purchasing power parity relationship the inflation rate differential causes a corresponding rate of change of the exchange rate. If the foreign exchange market is efficient, the forward exchange rate equals the market's expected future exchange rate. Hence, the expected rate of change of the exchange rate equals the forward premium or discount, which in turn equals the interest rate differential while the interest rate differential equals the expected inflation rate differential.

These six relations are stated more explicit:

1. Inflation rate = Rate of growth of money supply – Rate of growth of real gross national product (too much money chasing too few goods).
2. Rate of change of exchange rate = Inflation rate differential (Purchasing power parity theory).
3. Interest rate = "Real " interest rate + Expected inflation rate (Fisher effect: one country).
4. Expected rate of change of exchange rate = Interest rate differential (international Fisher effect).
5. Forward exchange premium or discount = Interest rate differential (interest rate parity theorem).
6. Forward premium or discount = Expected rate of change of exchange rate (unbiased forward rate theory).

Clearly, the "equilibrium" world only provide a useful point of departure. If all the relationships hold, then the firm is not subject to economic exposure, since interest rates anticipate currency value changes and prices of real goods adjust to offset exchange rate changes. Because the forward rate equals the market-expected future spot rate, the expected cost of hedging is zero; but hedging is also of little value.

QUESTIONS

1. Discuss the main theoretical development in the international financial management.
2. Disucss the role of the international financial manager.
3. What is the economic framework of international financial management?
4. "The imperfections and linkages of domestic financial markets, Euromarkets, and foreign

exchange markets provide both risks and opportunities for the international financial manager." Comment.

5. Discuss the effect of market segmentation on a corporation's cost of capital.
6. If domestic securities are inaccessible to foreign investors would they commands super-risk permium?
7. Disucss the effects of international operations on the market value of the multinational firm.

32

GLOBAL FINANCIAL CRISIS

INTRODUCTION

The financial turmoil which began in the summer of 2007 has developed into a global financial crisis. With the end of the boom in the US housing market and increasing interest rates on sub-prime mortgages, delinquency rates on mortgage loans rose. The value of mortgage- backed securities dropped heavily. Crisis in sub-prime market segment gradually spilled over to most other asset markets, in particular the credit derivatives markets, corporate bond and equity markets, and also to the money markets, not only in the US but also in the Euro area and elsewhere. The combined strength of the various shocks affecting the global financial system has been broadly unexpected, started to move the global economy into a recession. On an annual basis, global growth is expected to moderate from 5.0 percent in 2007 to 3.9 percent in 2008 and 3.0 percent in 2009. Great uncertainty surrounds the implications of this crisis for developing countries. However, the crisis as such cannot be regarded as a complete surprise. It did not build up overnight but instead has developed gradually over several years. Governments in both developed and developing countries have started to put together fiscal and monetary stimulus packages in order to prevent the global financial crisis from turning into another Great Depression.

THE INGREDIENTS OF THE CRISIS

The pre-crisis global macroeconomic environment was characterised by low interest rates, low inflation and sustained economic growth. The apparent growth pattern that emerged from the 2000s came with high risks. Growth was driven to a significant extent by strong consumer demand in the United States, stimulated by easy credit and underpinned by booming house prices, and by very high rates of investment demand and strong export growth in some developing countries, notably China. Growing United States deficits in this period were financed by increasing trade surpluses in China, Japan and other countries accumulating large foreign-exchange reserves and willing to buy dollar-denominated assets. At the same time, increasing financial deregulation, along with a flurry of new financial instruments and risk-management techniques (mortgage-backed securities, collateralized debt obligations, credit default swaps, and so on), encouraged a massive accumulation of financial assets supported by growing levels of debt in the household, corporate and public sectors. In some countries, both developed and developing, domestic financial debt has risen four- or fivefold as a share of national income since the early 1980s. Also fuelling the credit growth through the period was a shift of the major US and European banks away from the traditional "originate to hold" banking model towards an "originate to distribute" model, which for a range of reasons was seen as more profitable. In "originate to hold", mortgage and other credit originations typically stay on the originating bank's balance sheet until maturity. In "originate to distribute", the credit originations are securitised and sold, removing them from the originating bank's balance sheet. A typical securitisation would involve, along the way, the creation and sale of derivatives based on the securitised exposures, further increasing the fee-earning potential of the underlying origination in an environment of voracious demand for risk.

In the event, the rapid growth and diversity of financial institutions and products ran well ahead of the ability of financial institutions to understand their risk positions, of rating agencies to translate the new exposures that were created, and of regulators to ensure that financial institutions were managing risk prudently. Long-standing, well-conceived banking practices were abandoned as financial institutions focused on maximising short-term profitability. For example, *compensation structures* at the top management level are based on the comparison of latest results vis- -vis those of their peers and thus tend to encourage short-termism and risk-taking by managers keen on avoiding underperformance. The pressure to deliver quick profits makes it more difficult for *risk management* departments that are often viewed as "party spoilers", to curb excessive risk taking in their financial institutions. The job of risk managers is also complicated by the fact that certain risks are hard to quantify and measure (for example, tail risks) and that commonly agreed valuation models are missing for more complex securities.

The mutually reinforcing strengths of real and financial demand showed up first in rising prices in the commodity and asset markets. As debt-funded consumption and investment in the developed world surged, generalised inflation pressure began rising. Leverage ratios of some institutions went up to as high as 30, well above the ceiling of 10 generally imposed on deposit banks , indicating strengthened investors' risk appetite and contributed to the underestimation and under-pricing of risk. All parties seemed to benefit from the boom, particularly the major financial players in the rich economies, while the risks were conveniently ignored, despite repeated warnings that mounting household, public sector and financial sector indebtedness in the United States and elsewhere would not be sustainable over time. As strains in the United States mortgage market were transmitted to the wider financial sector, fears of a meltdown escalated and spread around the world.

The first obvious signs of credit over-extension appeared in mid-2007, as credit impairment on US subprime mortgage exposures began to surface. Money market spreads rose quickly in the US and Europe as frictions emerged in the cash markets. Soon, the credit quality and liquidity of other types of asset-backed securities and derivative instruments became subject to doubt. The frictions spread further and markets in which risk is traded away became dysfunctional. Financial institutions became increasingly unwilling to deal with each other as uncertainty about who was exposed, and how badly, became more and more enlarged.

This fragility set the stage for the turbulence in financial markets. It is no accident that the massive simultaneous surges in the prices of commodities, equities, housing and other real estate around the world since the mid-2000s until 2007 matches the surge in credit. In hindsight, this correlation can be explained fairly simply as the mutual reinforcement of a number of powerful factors. Emerging market countries, especially in Asia, ran high rates of national savings out of the earnings from strong export-led growth. As world oil prices surged, national savings in oil exporting countries also increased rapidly. Finally, the developed world ran fairly loose monetary policy as part of the recovery from the 2000-01 recession. In this environment, the premium charged for credit risk fell to low levels through the middle part of the decade . The growth in asset prices in the latter part of this period increased capacity for secured borrowing, adding further stimulus for credit growth.

As 2008 progressed, it became obvious that the financial dysfunction was taking a lot longer to clear than expected. Innovative products with strong credit ratings proved less than robust. Unanticipated concentrations and correlations of risk were suddenly revealed – including within the largest global banks and credit insurers. The substantial increase in the diversity and sophistication of financial products and institutions turned out not to have reduced systemic risk through diversification. The fragmentation of risk had not enabled individual institutions efficiently to isolate, hedge and transfer risk. Understanding of risk had become lost in translation as risk was traded across institutions and national borders. Measured regulatory capital that had seemed bountiful up until 2007, now looked thoroughly inadequate.

A number of large financial institutions came under severe financial stress and were cut off from access to long-term capital and short-term funding markets. In the United States, these included the two government-sponsored enterprises (GSEs), Fannie Mae and Freddie Mac, as well as Lehman Brothers, American International Group (AIG), Inc. and Washington Mutual. The financial turmoil deepened in the weeks following the collapse of the Lehman Brothers in mid-September 2008, more than a year after the onset of the crisis, eventually developing into a full-blown crisis with adverse spillovers into real activity. Within two weeks from the bankruptcy of Lehman Brothers, mounting losses from the sub-prime mortgage markets led to both the US largest insurance company (AIG) and largest savings and loan institution (Washington Mutual) being seized by the government. Widespread concerns about the solvency of financial institutions ensued and spread to Europe, where government assistance was needed to avert the collapse of several institutions.

Despite massive liquidity injections and an increasingly loose monetary policy stance in the United States, Japan and parts of Europe, the turmoil continued into 2008. Major warning signs came with the collapse of Bear Stearns, the fifth-largest investment bank in the United States, which had to be rescued by joint action of the United States Federal Reserve (Fed) and JP Morgan Chase. In September 2008, the financial turmoil intensified once again, this time turning into a global financial tsunami characterized by a severe credit freeze, a precipitous sell-off in stock markets worldwide and the collapse or near collapse of major financial institutions in the United States and Europe. Several developed countries, including Iceland and Hungary, needed massive emergency loans from the International Monetary Fund (IMF) to cope with their financial problems.

The credit crisis quickly spread to Europe, with a number of large European financial institutions teetering on the edge of collapse, such as the French- Belgian Dexia, the British mortgage lender Bradford & Bingley, Germany's Hypo Real Estate, as well as the Dutch bank and insurance company ING and the Dutch insurance giant Aegon. In Iceland, three major banks collapsed, dragging the country to the brink of bankruptcy as the total external liabilities of the three banks accounted for five times Iceland's annual GDP. The contagion effects of the crisis also spread rapidly to emerging economies. Hungary was among the first of the emerging market countries to suffer. Both Iceland and Hungary had to recur to the IMF (and other sources) to alleviate the immediate financial market stress, becoming the first two European countries to do so in over 30 years. Ukraine also ran into acute liquidity problems, as its access to international capital markets was curtailed sharply, its currency was sold off and the credit-rating agencies downgraded the country's debt. Ukraine also had to recur to the IMF for a $16.4 billion loan. Belarus and Serbia also filed requests for substantial emergency support from the IMF. Pakistan also entered into acute balance-of-payments' problems and filed for IMF support, as its foreign reserve level dropped to less than a few weeks worth of imports.

September 2008 marked a sea change in the international financial landscape, including the end of independent investment banking in the United States and an end to previous faith in the virtues of unfettered financial markets. Investment banks either went bankrupt, merged with other commercial banks, or converted themselves into commercial banks. Between September 2007 and October 2008, 16 banks in the United States filed for bankruptcy, and more than 100 out of some 7,000 banks are on the Fed's watch list. While this proportion is still small compared with the Great Depression, when about 700 out of a total of 9,000 banks failed, its ramifications in an integrated financial world are every bit as big. In November, the United States Government also had to come to the rescue of Citigroup, backing about $306 billion in loans and securities and investing $20 billion directly in the financial institution considered "too big to fail".

The continued housing slump in the United States triggered the collapse of this financial house of cards. House prices continued to decline in 2008 at an annual rate of about 17 per cent. Mortgage delinquency rates surged, particularly for sub-prime loans. No less than 40 per cent of the sub- prime mortgage loans originated in 2006 were delinquent by the second half of 2008. As a result, the value of mortgage-related assets deteriorated significantly. By the third quarter of 2008, financial institutions worldwide had written down a total value of about $700 billion worth of asset-backed securities, of which more than $500 billion related to the commercial banking sector. Many more write-downs are forthcoming as the prices of these securities continue to drop, leading to an accelerated erosion of the capital base of financial institutions and severely constraining their ability to lend.

The complex way in which those asset-backed securities were constructed made it difficult to assess their value. Having been cavalier about risk during the boom years, investors have become extremely risk averse along with the plummeting market confidence, resulting in further declines in asset prices and a further drying up of liquidity in a number of funding markets. Banks have become extremely reluctant to lend to each other, losing confidence in the credit worthiness of counterparties. The credit market stress was reflected in the surge of the spread between the interest rate on interbank lending and the interest rate on Treasury bills. In late September and early October, 2008 this spread reached its highest level in decades. It had soared to nearly 400 basis points, whereas under normal market conditions, the spread would be about 20 to 30 basis points.

The credit crunch has become widespread, and even some large, financially sound non- financial corporations were unable to roll over their commercial paper in the money market to fund working capital needs. A fire sale in asset markets followed the collapse of major financial institutions in the United States and Europe. Prices of financial companies' stocks were under tremendous pressure even before September,2008, but a further erosion of investor confidence, combined with a significant downgrading of the outlook for the real economic sector, triggered another round of asset sell-offs worldwide in late September and October, 2008. Equity markets remained highly volatile thereafter. In the first ten day of October, 2008 alone, equity markets worldwide plummeted by about 20 per cent on average, losing roughly $10 trillion worth of equity. Many markets, including those of the United States and some Asian countries, experienced the worst sell-off recorded in a single week. For the year, global equity markets have declined by about 40 per cent on average. In several emerging markets, the decline has been even steeper, with stock exchanges dropping by more than 60 per cent in China and the Russian Federation, for example.

The intensification of the global financial crisis from late September-October 2008 onwards heightened the risk of a complete collapse of the global financial system. In response, policymakers worldwide, particularly those in major developed countries, drastically scaled up their policy measures in October, 2008. Most importantly, they made two strategic changes in the way they deal with the crisis. First, the initial piecemeal approach was abandoned and replaced with a more comprehensive one. Second, unilateral national approaches have given way to more international cooperation and coordination. These policy measures aimed at unfreezing credit and money markets by recapitalizing banks with public funds, guaranteeing bank lending and insuring bank deposits. Interbank lending rates retreated somewhat following the start of the large-scale bailout. However, congestion and dysfunction remain in important segments of the credit markets. Meanwhile, great uncertainty remains in credit derivatives, with $400 trillion to $500 trillion in notional value of derivatives outstanding.

Three key features emerged from the ongoing financial turbulence: excessive and hidden leverage; excessive complexity; and imprudent financial alchemy. The first key feature was excessive and hidden leverage. The 2007 global credit crisis was preceded by a sizeable credit boom. What was new was that the boom was amplified and so to speak leveraged by financial innovation. Indeed, the leverage in the global financial system was much greater than one would think when looking only at the balance sheets of regulated financial institutions, mainly because of the new leverage possibilities provided by the "shadow banking system".The second key feature was the excessive complexity of new structured finance products, which exceeded the comprehension of bankers, investors and regulators. As a result, disclosure about the risk exposure of financial institutions turned out to be inadequate and difficult to interpret, especially regarding their off- balance sheet holdings and credit risk transfer activities. The third feature was imprudent financial alchemy. With the benefit of hindsight, it was a fundamental illusion to believe that financial engineering can create complex instruments that are both tailored to the needs of individual investors and, at the same time, tradable in liquid markets. It also proved an illusion to believe that structured finance would be able to offer, in a sustainable way, high yields without the corresponding risks—in other words, to break the traditional relationship between risk and return, like alchemists thinking they could magically transform lead into gold. These developments produced strong incentives to increase leverage in the system, as investors were attracted by these new higher- yielding but apparently still low-risk instruments.

The main ingredients that emerged in the years 2000–08 which led to global credit excesses are accommodative monetary policies; large global imbalances and forex reserve accumulation; and very rapid financial innovation. The first ingredient is the accommodative monetary policy in the G3 countries, as manifested in low policy rates and low long-term rates. These low interest rates precipitated a search for yield and a high risk appetite, in a context of low volatility and low risk premia. What was new and unprecedented was that accommodative monetary policy had become a global (worldwide) phenomenon. Moreover, a large number of EMEs implemented a strategy aiming at resisting exchange rate appreciation by keeping interest rates at a level sufficiently low to avoid excessive short-term capital inflows. In addition, excess global saving relative to investment may also have contributed to exceptionally low real long-term interest rates. The second ingredient which led to the global credit crisis was the sharp increase in global imbalances. The massive rise in the US current account deficit has been largely financed by reserve accumulation by emerging market economies, possibly related to a global savings glut. A key element was that the strong increase in US net external liabilities in recent years reflected a large decline in US households' saving rate, which in turn was associated with rising US household leverage and buoyant US housing markets. Hence, the US current account deficit and the US housing credit bubble have been two faces of the same reality ("twin imbalances"). On the financing side of this deficit, those emerging market central banks willing to resist exchange rate appreciation through foreign reserve accumulation as well as commodity-exporting countries had a rapidly growing pool of dollar reserves to invest each year .At the global level, these foreign exchange reserves were mainly invested in sovereign securities, reinforcing downward pressures on long-term interest rates. At the domestic level, to the extent that reserve accumulation was not fully sterilised, it led to an expansion of money supply and therefore easy credit at home; and sterilisation cannot always be perfect. In a nutshell, the resistance to exchange rate appreciation in emerging countries and the associated reserve accumulation contributed to the persistence of global imbalances and provided financing for US financial liabilities.The third ingredient of the credit excesses was financial innovation in the form of securitisation, credit derivatives and structured finance. Financial engineering offering relatively high yields with high credit ratings proved to be a kind of imprudent alchemy whose exponents believed that they could transform lead into gold. This third ingredient was a key element of surprise in the 2007 financial turmoil. No one had anticipated the securitisation crisis and the structured finance crisis, or their spillover to the money markets and interbank markets. Financial innovation allowed the repackaging of mortgages— traditionally, illiquid assets originated and held by local banks – into higher-yielding complex securities with triple-A rating. Mortgage backed securities or more complex products based on those securities were in high demand by banks and investors around the world who were *"searching for yield"* in an environment characterised by low interest rates. The situation endured, as sustained appetite of foreign investors for debt securities issued by the US government and government- sponsored agencies as well as by the corporate sector allowed the country to smoothly finance its current account deficit. And the "search for yield" fostered the demand for more complex forms of securitisation, which led to the creation of instruments that entailed risks that were difficult to assess and price. No active secondary market existed for many of the new instruments, and the associated *opacity* of the credit risk distribution made it difficult to keep track of the exposures.

A key question is why investors did not look more closely into the risks associated with the securities purchased, thereby playing a disciplining role in the securitisation process. The answer leads us to an important microeconomic factor behind the current crisis: the existence of *agency problems* associated with the implementation of the "originate and distribute" model. This model – that became prevalent among large banks over the past twenty years – was designed to deliver a more efficient allocation and distribution of risks in the economy. However, because of information asymmetries and frictions, the "originate and distribute" model in practice gave rise to inefficient outcomes and distorted the behaviour of the various parties involved in the securitisation process: investors, rating agencies, intermediaries, and originators. The main reason for this is that the goals of the parties involved differed, and in some instances may even have been in conflict. Besides, the different categories did not fully internalise the consequences of their individual actions in the overall process, and therefore did not have the right incentives to share information efficiently.

In particular, *investors* became over-reliant on the ratings provided by the rating agencies and often did not properly conduct their due diligence. The fact that regulators gave *ratings* a prominent role in the risk assessment framework might have indirectly affected investors' incentives. Investors often ignored the fact that rating agencies' risk measures offer only a partial account of the risks embedded in the securities, as they focus primarily on the expected loss and do not take into account the tail of the loss distribution. In addition, they do not take liquidity risks into account. Moreover, rating agencies were themselves subject to potential *conflicts of interest* that may have diminished their incentives to undertake timely downgrades of structured products and provide adequate information to investors regarding the analysis underlying the rating decision. In fact, because ratings are paid for by issuers, rating agencies may have incentives to expand coverage to products whose risk assessment is difficult and, potentially unreliable, in order to maximise their revenues. Besides, agencies may also provide commercial advice to the issuers of those securities that are then requested to rate.

As regards *originators of loans*, their incentives to screen and monitor borrowers may have been reduced under the "originate and distribute" model, once they sold the originated assets to intermediaries that subsequently took care of repackaging them into securities. Instead, the loan originators may have concentrated on expanding volumes of loans originated to boost their profits. The diminished incentive to screen and monitor borrowers implies that investors may have ultimately acquired assets of relatively lower quality and performance.

Two paradoxes relating to capital and liquidity have been revealed by the global financial turmoil. The first is that, after several years of high profits, the global banking sector was thought to be well capitalised. In fact, banks' actual capital buffers and provisioning proved to be thinner than desirable. Widely used VaR indicators of risk underestimated the rise in underlying position-taking during the period of low volatility. The second paradox is that bouts of massive illiquidity occurred in certain financial market segments (such as those for complex structured products) within a context of overall excess liquidity worldwide. However, the observers are divided into two groups when assessing the underlying causes of the current financial turmoil and understanding the two aforementioned paradoxes. The first type of explanation observers come up with is the general macrofinancial explanation. The turmoil is seen as the long-run consequence of the easy global money and credit conditions that prevailed particularly from early 2002: accommodative monetary policies, accumulation of global reserves amplifying excess liquidity, and advances in financial technology. These elements led to a persistent rise in risk-taking and financial leverage. The second type of explanation is the idiosyncratic or microfinancial explanation. The turmoil is the result of shortcomings in specific types of financial products and entities that have come into being in recent years:

subprime mortgages, associated structured products, and bank-related structured investment vehicles (SIVs) and asset-backed commercial paper (ABCP) conduits. It is a securitisation crisis, risk management techniques having lagged behind overly rapid financial innovation.

THE GLOBAL FINANCIAL CRISIS AND BEYOND

Six years ago, in mid-2007, cracks started to appear in the financial system. Little more than a year later, Lehman Brothers failed, bringing advanced economies to the verge of collapse. Throughout the ensuing half-decade of recession and slow recovery, central banks in these economies have been forced to look for ways to increase their degree of accommodation. First they lowered the policy rate to essentially zero, where it has been ever since in the United States, United Kingdom and euro area. (And where it has stood in Japan since the mid-1990s!) Next, these central banks began expanding their balance sheets, which are now collectively at roughly three times their pre-crisis level – and rising.

Originally forged as a description of central bank actions to prevent financial collapse, the phrase "whatever it takes" has become a rallying cry for central banks to continue their extraordinary actions. But central banks the height of the crisis, and the goal of policy has changed – to return still-sluggish economies to strong and sustainable growth. Can central banks now really do "whatever it takes" to achieve that goal? As each day goes by, it seems less and less likely. Central banks cannot repair the balance sheets of households and financial institutions. Central banks cannot ensure the sustainability of fiscal finances. And, most of all, central banks cannot enact the structural economic and financial reforms needed to return economies to the real growth paths authorities and their publics both want and expect.

What central bank accommodation has done during the recovery is to borrow time – time for balance sheet repair, time for fiscal consolidation, and time for reforms to restore productivity growth. But the time has not been well used, as continued low interest rates and unconventional policies have made it easy for the private sector to postpone deleveraging, easy for the government to finance deficits, and easy for the authorities to delay needed reforms in the real economy and in the financial system. After all, cheap money makes it easier to borrow than to save, easier to spend than to tax, easier to remain the same than to change.

Yes, in some countries the household sector has made headway with the gruelling task of deleveraging. Some financial institutions are better capitalised. Some fiscal authorities have begun painful but essential consolidation. And yes, much of the difficult work of financial reform has been completed. But overall, progress has been slow, halting and uneven across countries. Households and firms continue to hope that if they wait, asset values and revenues will rise and their balance sheets improve. Governments hope that if they wait, the economy will grow, driving down the ratio of debt to GDP. And politicians hope that if they wait, incomes and profits will start to grow again, making the reform of labour and product markets less urgent. But waiting will not make things any easier, particularly as public support and patience erode.

Alas, central banks cannot do more without compounding the risks they have already created. Instead, they must re-emphasise their traditional focus – albeit expanded to include financial stability – and thereby encourage needed adjustments rather than retard them with near-zero interest rates and purchases of ever larger quantities of government securities. And they must urge authorities to speed up reforms in labour and product markets, reforms that will enhance productivity and encourage employment growth rather than provide the false comfort that it will be easier later. Countries need to examine the labour and product market reforms to boost productivity and unlock growth; the private sector must deleverage and the public sector needs to ensure fiscal sustainability; risks in the financial system need to be managed; and the expectation that monetary policy can solve these problems is a recipe for failure. This cells for pro-active approach on the part of counries since only a forceful programme of repair and reform will return economies to strong and sustainable real growth.

ENHANCING FLEXIBILITY: A KEY TO GROWTH

Sustained and balanced growth remains elusive in the global economy. In many advanced economies, growth rates have only partially recovered, and unemployment remains stubbornly high. Rigidities in labour and product markets are among the most important obstacles standing in the way of long-term economic health. The financial crisis and its aftermath showed that such structural problems are exacerbated when the cycle turns and the boom becomes a bust. As a result, the recovery has been disappointing in many economies.

When a housing sector boom turns into a bust, as it did in a number of countries, rigidities limit the mobility of people across sectors. Tight employment protections slow the recovery and the growth of employment in economies that go into recessions with significant sectoral imbalances. The implication is obvious: countries stand to reap substantial benefits from moving towards less regulated and more growth-friendly labour and product markets.

Measures that make labour and product markets more flexible allow resources to flow more easily from low- to high-productivity sectors, with obvious gains for growth. In parallel, such reforms help foster entrepreneurship, paving the way for firms to boost productivity, grow and hire more workers. This means that simplifying regulations and reducing the power of special interests that are impeding productivity enhancements are essential for raising sustainable growth. To be sure, basic worker and consumer protections must be preserved, and the extent of desirable regulation will vary from country to country. But the costs of overly regulated labour and product markets are clear: they reduce flexibility to the point where long-run growth will suffer.

Given the evidence that structural rigidities are particularly harmful in the aftermath of a crisis, there is a strong case for undertaking reforms in good times instead of under pressure. Although such cases of pre-emptive reform are rare, countries that came through the financial crisis relatively unscathed have every reason to address labour and product market flexibility sooner rather than later.

FISCAL POLICY: THREATS REMAIN

As governments responded to the financial crisis with bank bailouts and fiscal stimulus, their indebtedness rose to new highs. And in countries that experienced a housing bubble in the run-up to the crisis, households had already accumulated large debts. In the half-decade since the peak of the crisis, the hope was that significant progress would be made in the necessary deleveraging process, thereby enabling a self-sustaining recovery.

Instead, the debt of households, non-financial corporations and government *increased* as a share of GDP in most large advanced and emerging market economies from 2007 to 2012. For the countries, this debt has risen by about 20 percentage points of GDP. And over the same period, some countries, including a number of emerging market economies, have seen their total debt ratios rise even faster. Clearly, this is unsustainable. Overindebtedness is one of the major barriers on the path to growth after a financial crisis. Borrowing more year after year is not the cure.

In a majority of the countries, public debt is principally responsible for the increase. Although countercyclical fiscal policy was needed to combat the threat of depression at the height of the financial crisis, the situation is different today. As government debt surpasses about 80% of GDP, it starts to become a drag on growth. With public debt now above 100% of GDP in most advanced economies, and the prospect of large increases in age-related spending, finding the way to medium- and long-term fiscal sustainability remains a key challenge.

Ultimately, outsize public debt reduces sovereign creditworthiness and erodes confidence. By putting their fiscal house in order, governments can help restore the virtuous cycle between the financial system and the real economy. And, with low levels of debt, governments will again have the capacity to respond when the next financial or economic crisis inevitably hits.

Although the need for fiscal consolidation has become more and more pressing, tangible results have been meagre. In a number of countries, the cheap financing made available by low short- and long-term interest rates has taken the pressure off governments to make fiscal adjustments. But the relief is temporary and not without risks. To see why, recall that in the two decades preceding the crisis, long-term interest rates in many advanced economies averaged about 6%. Today, long-term bond yields in major advanced economies are around 2% – in Japan, they are well below. When interest rates and bond yields start to rise, investors holding government bonds stand to lose huge amounts of money.

And while sophisticated hedging strategies can protect individual investors, someone must ultimately hold the interest rate risk. Indeed, the potential loss in relation to GDP is at a record high in most advanced economies. As foreign and domestic banks would be among those experiencing the losses, interest rate increases pose risks to the stability of the financial system if not executed with great care. Clear central bank communication well in advance of any moves to tighten will be critical in this regard.

Governments must redouble their efforts to ensure that their fiscal trajectories are sustainable. Growth will simply not be high enough for fiscal consolidation to happen on its own; that is, the denominator of the debt-to-GDP ratio will not grow faster than the numerator. Postponing the pain carries the risk of forcing consolidation under stress – which is the current situation in a number of countries in southern Europe. Structural fiscal problems have to be tackled early. Doing so means avoiding much more pain later.

At the same time, the quality of fiscal adjustment is as important as the quantity. Waiting has not paid dividends. Some laggard countries have been forced to make drastic, indiscriminate cuts, slicing away at productive public investment and raising growth-unfriendly taxes. Those that still have the wherewithal to do so should focus their efforts on cutting expenditures by reducing government consumption and transfers. In countries where tax rates are still low, revenue increases should also play a role.

Importantly, many countries need to do more now to reduce future age related spending. While long-term in nature, these measures will bring immediate positive effects as they strengthen perceptions of fiscal sustainability.

Public finances in many emerging market economies have remained well in hand, partly because those regions were not at the centre of the crisis. But the fiscal positions of some, while currently bright, have been buoyed by revenues from rising asset and commodity prices. Unlikely to be sustainable, these situations call for caution. In other cases, weakening global demand has reduced revenue and induced higher spending, driving up public debt levels. These early threats to fiscal sustainability, along with the possibility of age-related increases in public spending, will require policymakers in emerging market economies to remain vigilant.

THE FINANCIAL SYSTEM: INCREASING RESILIENCE

The complexity of the financial system presents a continuing challenge for the prudential framework. Ensuring systemic stability requires adequate capital, liquidity and resolution regimes. All financial institutions must have ample, high-quality capital buffers to protect against losses and sufficient liquidity buffers to protect them from sudden collapses in market confidence. And we need resolution regimes to make it possible for large, complex institutions to fail in an orderly way.

Still, finding the best way to manage the risks arising from an increasingly global and intricate financial system remains a challenge for the world's policymakers. In fact, the measurement and management of these risks is central to creating a safer prudential framework. A simple rule, such as a leverage ratio, and a more complex risk-weighted metric each have their advantages and limitations as a barometer of bank strength. But they are complementary. Used in combination, the two reinforce each other, generating more information on the riskiness of a bank than does either of them alone. On top of that, manipulating these measures is much more difficult when they are used simultaneously. The policy response to the recent debate on the complexity of regulation should therefore rest on the mutually reinforcing ability of risk-sensitive metrics and simple balance sheet rules to monitor and mitigate financial system risk.

Limiting the permissible range of banking activities may help reduce systemic risk, but that is not likely to be a silver bullet. The limits will do little to reduce the complexity of banks, and even if they simplify the firm-level organisation of banks, their impact on system-wide risk is ambiguous.

The evolving standards governing the global financial system must be based on simple principles: internalise systemic risks; require enough capital and liquidity to align private incentives with the public interest; set risk sensitivity to reduce shifts into high-risk assets; extend prudential reach to keep risks within view of supervisors (and managers); and allow the regulatory system to evolve along with the financial system. But what is simple in principle will usually be complicated in fact. This means that the success of financial reforms hinges on long and complex definitions and processes. And the reason for that is a simple, practical one: details are enforceable, principles are not.

MONETARY POLICY: BORROWING TIME

Since the outbreak of the financial crisis, central banks have found themselves pushing deeper into unconventional territory. Having hit the lower bound for interest rates, central banks in major advanced economies turned to amassing assets, which now stand at 25% of their countries' collective GDP. Meanwhile, central banks in emerging market economies have also expanded their balance sheets, and now hold assets worth more than 40% of GDP. Combined, central bank assets across advanced and emerging market economies have risen from $10.4 trillion in 2007 to more than $20.5 trillion today, and central banks remain pressured to do even more.

But despite all the monetary accommodation, economic growth remains lacklustre, and job creation has yet to gain firm traction. Moreover, the low interest rates in advanced economies create international spillovers. These include capital flows to fast-growing emerging market economies and to some small advanced economies. The resulting upward pressure on the value of the currencies in those economies has hampered the domestic stabilisation efforts of their central banks.

Delivering further extraordinary monetary stimulus is becoming increasingly perilous, as the balance between its benefits and costs is shifting. The policy frameworks anchored to price stability remain the foundation for growth. Without price stability, you have nothing. But, as the crisis has taught us, narrow near-term price stability is not enough: financial stability is also essential for long-term macroeconomic stability.

The challenge is to modify traditional monetary policy frameworks to include financial stability considerations effectively and symmetrically.

All of this puts monetary policymakers in the largest advanced economies in a delicate position. How can central banks encourage those responsible for structural adjustment to implement reforms? How can they avoid making the economy too dependent on monetary stimulus? When is the right time for them to pull back from their expansionary policies? And in pulling back, how can they avoid sparking a sharp rise in bond yields? It is time for monetary policy to begin answering these questions.

POLICY RESPONSE : *THE ROAD AHEAD*

Systemic risks have been substantially reduced following unprecedented policy actions and nascent signs of improvement in the real economy. There is growing confidence that the global economy has turned the corner, underpinning the improvements in financial markets. Nonetheless, the risk of a reintensification of the adverse feedback loop between the real and financial sectors remains significant as long as banks remain under strain and households and financial institutions need to reduce leverage. Although indicators of sovereign risk are lower than six months ago, the transfer of financial risks to fiscal authorities, combined with the financing burden of fiscal stimulus, has raised concerns over crowding out the private sector and the sustainability of public sector finances. These vulnerabilities underscore the need to strengthen financial intermediation, restore health to the financial system, and eventually reduce the private risks now borne by sovereign balance sheets. Great care in disengaging from public support will be necessary to avoid either sparking a secondary crisis through premature withdrawal or endangering monetary and fiscal credibility through a belated exit. Complacency now becomes a risk—banking system problems could go unresolved and much-needed regulatory reforms may be delayed or diluted. Policymakers should promptly provide a plan for the future regulatory framework that mitigates the buildup of systemic risks, grounds expectations, and underpins confidence, thereby contributing to sustained economic growth.

With growing international linkages and gathering momentum of the transaction from guided or controlled economies to deregulated and decentralised ones- not only in the industrial world but also in a number of developing countries, the liberalisation has been in the making over the years in an increasingly interdependent, open and competitive, world. The trends towards globalisation and liberalisation are seen mostly in the financial flows and direct investment. Taken together, innovation, technology and deregulation have smashed the barriers both within and among national financial markets.

Changes in international financial systems have mirrored these changes and all evidence points to continued internationalization of domestic financial systems. The links between money and capital markets have become as close as it to make futile to concentrate on any individual part. The consequences of events in the stock markets and interest rates of one country immediately show up around the globe, which has become an increasingly integrated and interdependent financial environment. Investors also gain from the efficient allocation of capital: when capital is allocated to its best uses on a global scale overall returns are higher, and these additional returns can be shared among the global investors. There has been tremendous growth in foreign investment in the money market, the bond market, the stock market, the real-estate market, and the market for operating businesses. At times, the importance of foreign investments and investors has swelled to overshadow that of domestic investments and investors. In catering to the expanding horizons of investors and borrowers, there has been an explosion of internationally oriented financial products , such as internationally diversified ,global ,and single foreign country institutional investors. The popularity of these products is a sign of the widening internationalisation of financial markets.

The volatility of capital flows is central to the problem of instability in international financial markets.Private and public institutions can facilitate the growth and strength of the financial system. Government agencies such as the Securities and Exchange Commission, Securities Exchange Board Of India, etc. perform both regulatory and market development functions. Rules that insure the smooth functioning of the markets are developed and enforced. As the globalization of financial markets continues, so does the need to understand that crisis that have plagued them and the policies best suited to preventing such crises.

The immediate outlook for the financial system has improved markedly and extreme tail risks have abated. Current investment policies at the national and international levels are being shaped by a number of important developments, which are likely to also define future policy directions:

i) There are simultaneous moves to (i) further liberalize investment regimes and promote foreign investment in response to intensified competition for foreign direct investment (FDI) on the one hand, and (ii) regulate and harness FDI in pursuit of broader policy objectives on the other.

ii) At the national level, there is an increasing emphasis on the rights of the State and the obligations of the investors, including through new entry and operational measures. Economic stimulus packages and State aids have impacted on foreign investment, while instances of investment protectionism have so far not been observed.

iii) Rebalancing is also emerging within the rapidly growing multifaceted and multilayered network of international investment agreements (IIAs). In addition, the systemic evolution of the IIA regime in content and structure points towards achieving greater coherence.

iv) Other international investment initiatives—including those addressing broader economic, social and environmental issues—also point towards a greater emphasis on the role of regulation.

Overall, pendulum swing towards a more balanced approach to the rights and obligations between investors and the State can be observed. Financial markets have rebounded, emerging market risks have eased, banks have raised capital, and wholesale funding markets have reopened. Even so, credit channels are still impaired and the economic recovery is likely to be slow.

Extreme systemic risks have abated, but complacency about banking system repair is still a concern. Recently, bank balance sheets have benefited from capital-raising efforts and positive earnings. Nonetheless, there are still serious concerns that credit deterioration will continue to put pressure on banks' balance sheets. Moreover, steady-state earnings are likely to be lower in the post-crisis environment. Stronger action to address impaired assets will help bolster bank earning capability and support lending. The tightening of bank regulation under way is expected to reduce net revenues and require more costly self-insurance through higher levels of capital and liquidity.

*Crisis risks in emerging markets have subsided, but vulnerabilities remain.*Tail risks in emerging markets have declined as a result of strong policy measures—including increased IMF resources. Financial stresses have eased substantially in emerging Europe, but vulnerabilities remain high. Western European banks appear able to absorb deteriorating credit conditions in emerging Europe, but may lack sufficient capital to support a recovery in the region. Asia and Latin America have benefited most from the stabilization of core markets and a recovery in portfolio inflows. Although international flows into emerging market debt have recovered, they have been skewed toward higher quality borrowers, leaving many corporates facing substantial rollover risks, particularly in emerging Europe. Financial policies should continue to foster an orderly adjustment of bank, corporate, and household balance sheets. Extending agreements to maintain or even increase sustainable cross-border bank funding channels would also help.

*Impaired credit channels may face difficulty meeting even tepid private sector demand.*With ongoing bank deleveraging pressure and dislocations in securitization markets, it appears that ex ante supply may fall short of even anemic private sector demand.As a result, pressure on funding rates could increase and the flow of credit to support recovery could be curtailed.

*The transfer of private risks to sovereign balance sheets needs careful management.*The transfer of risk to public balance sheets as a result of financial system rescues and fiscal stimulus packages has raised concerns that record sovereign issuance could push up interest rates and hurt the nascent recovery. In this context, credit capacity could struggle to meet even tepid private sector demand, while deteriorating public finances may compromise sovereign creditworthiness. Countries should mitigate this risk by designing and articulating medium-term fiscal consolidation plans that take into account their financial sector stabilization policies and contingent liabilities.

*Financial institutions need further restructuring to ensure their ability to lend and support economic recovery.*Credit capacity constraints suggest little room for complacency in cleansing bank balance sheets of impaired and illiquid assets and resuscitating securitization. Deeper financial reform and the resolution of weak banks will be needed before authorities in many jurisdictions can fully exit from liquidity and funding provision. This calls for renewed efforts to increase bank capital and cleanse troubled assets from bank balance sheets. Official stress tests are important instruments through which the condition of banks can be diagnosed in order to design appropriate strategies for recapitalization of viable banks and for careful resolution of nonviable banks. However, the public release of bank-by-bank outcomes should be considered only if effective remedies to address any capital shortfalls can also be presented. Nondisclosure should not imply the absence of such remedies, if needed.

Incentives are critical to repair and restart securitization. A combination of new regulation and better private sector practice will be needed to align incentives of those institutions taking part in securitization and avoid it contributing to systemic instability once more. In redesigning regulation and market practices, the benefits of transferring credit risk outside the banking system and the ability of lenders to diversify funding sources need to be retained.

Policies Needed to Underpin Financial System Recovery and Reform. The policy response to dislocations in funding and credit markets has been unprecedented and, though definitive conclusions are difficult to make on the longer-term benefits, the initial evidence is generally positive.

Some unconventional policies have provided support better than others. Those aimed at supporting liquidity were most effective prior to the Lehman Brothers event, but were less so once it was evident that the financial crisis had become one of solvency rather than liquidity risk in a number of countries. Correspondingly, announcements of capital injections were most effective in reducing the default risk of banks in the post-Lehman period, as was the announcement of the potential use of asset purchases. Another important result is that interventions aimed at domestic institutions or markets had important spillover effects to other countries, with magnitudes sometimes larger than in the home country. This underlines the critical importance of coordinating policy responses.

*It is too early to withdraw official support policies, but a strategy for disengagement is needed.*While the time is not ripe for a full-fledged disengagement from all the unconventional policies undertaken—indeed in some countries additional public resources may still be needed—it is time for policymakers to consider and articulate how and in what sequence policies may be unwound. Timing is complicated by the fact that some policies may be effective even if their usage is limited, as they may be bolstering confidence or acting as a backstop to a class of institutions or investors.

*A clear vision of future financial system regulation is needed to provide clarity and boost confidence.*In addition to a well-defined strategy for unwinding unconventional policies, confidence in the financial system will be bolstered by clarity over future regulatory reforms needed to address systemic risks. The recent easing of tail risks should not prompt authorities to relax their efforts to map out the path to a more robust financial system. A holistic, understandable approach needs to be formulated so that the private sector can plan appropriately.

The priority should be to reform the regulatory environment so that the probability of a recurrence of a systemic crisis is significantly reduced. This includes not only defining the extent to which capital, provisions, and liquidity buffers are to rise, but also how market discipline is to be reestablished following extensive public sector support of systemic institutions in many countries. There are already proposals that will go some way toward removing procyclicality in the financial system and increasing buffers against losses and liquidity dislocations. But hard work lies ahead in devising capital penalties, insurance premiums, supervisory and resolution regimes, and competition policies to ensure that no institution is believed to be "too big to fail."

A macroprudential approach to global policymaking is needed to restore market discipline and ensure that the benefits of financial integration are preserved. The further challenge is to place these reforms in the context of an integrated macroprudential policy framework in which both domestic and cross-border institutions can operate securely. There is now recognition that a combination of microprudential and macroeconomic policies operated procyclically and led to a buildup of leverage and systemic risk. Policymakers will need to address ways in which their own actions exacerbate systemic risks, regardless of whether they oversee monetary, fiscal, or financial policy.

Cooperation and consistency in the policy field must extend across borders. Cross-border relationships between institutions and markets have made it impossible for policymakers to act unilaterally without consequences for others. Following the crisis, however, there is a danger that some countries will want to ring-fence their institutions and withdraw from global markets to protect their domestic economies from external shocks. What is needed instead is a way to benefit from increasing financial integration, while ensuring that potential negative spillovers are contained and clarity exists about the roles of home and host authorities. As policymakers move forward on this difficult task, the IMF can play a catalytic role through its surveillance activities and work on global macrofinancial linkages.

QUESTIONS

1. Discuss the main ingredients of current global meltdown.
2. Critically examine the key elements on which the policy response to current global meltdown depend.
3. Explain the factors which contribute to asset price bubbles in emerging economics.
4. What steps should be taken to reform the international financial options?
5. Discuss the factors underlying the stronger-than-expected start of the global recovery.
6. "Great case in disengaging from public support is necessary to avoid either sparking a secondary financial crisis through premature withdrawal or endangering monetary and fiscal credibility through a belated exit." Comment.

33

FINANCIAL SECTOR REFORMS: ACCOMPLISHMENTS, PITFALLS AND PROSPECTS

INTRODUCTION

The financial crisis severely tested banking systems, and the deficiencies it revealed warranted a swift and comprehensive official response. The Basel Committee and the FSB introduced a series of strong international measures, capped by the Basel III framework issued in December 2010. The crisis revealed that risk can be transmitted through unexpected channels. Thus, while Basel III responded to the lessons learned from the recent financial crisis, it is primarily designed to improve the resilience of all banks regardless of complexity and size and in all jurisdictions. Moreover, while the global regulatory reform programme will impose some transitional costs but the medium- and long-term investment in improving banking system resilience will yield benefits that far outweigh the costs. Banks have already begun to adjust to the new requirements, although they have also resumed taking on higher levels of risk.

Achieving international agreement on stronger policy frameworks was the first step in global regulatory reform. The next step is full and timely implementation of the new global standards and all other prudential standards. More intensive and intrusive supervision will be needed to help ensure that banks implement these standards and that all jurisdictions enforce them in a coordinated, consistent manner.

The policy response to the weaknesses revealed by the crisis continues. Outstanding issues include dealing with systemically important institutions, designing more effective cross-border bank resolution regimes, and addressing the risks relating to shadow banking activities. Meeting these challenges will be the focus of the final chapter.

BASEL III AND FINANCIAL STABILITY

There is a wide body of evidence that banking crises are associated with much deeper economic and financial downturns. The reason is obvious: banks are at the centre of the credit intermediation process, both directly and indirectly through their role as lenders, market makers, providers of backstop liquidity, and payment services.

Moreover, banking crises have been much more frequent than we would like, occurring on average about every 20 to 25 years in both industrial and emerging market countries. That is an annual probability of about 4-5%, which is simply unacceptable.

The crisis has entered a dangerous new phase in which weak public finances have interacted with remaining fragilities in financial institutions to open up fault lines in both the financial system and the economy. This is evident particularly—though not exclusively – in the euro zone. This new phase has also reopened some debates about: how fast the full transition to Basel III should be made; about how far some banks need to be recapitalized; about how sovereigns should be treated in the regulatory framework for capital and liquidity; and about how consistently the new rules should be applied, both the formal adoption of the rules and their actual implementation in national jurisdictions.

Full, timely and global implementation of Basel III and other reforms is essential for strengthening the financial system. Responsibility for Basel III does not rest only with the regulatory community. Bank boards, senior management and risk managers all have a clear role in adapting to the new framework. Auditors also play a key part in providing independent and disciplined review and feedback on management's efforts. But regulation is only part of the broader public policy agenda. Continuous effort should be made to finalize and implement regulatory reforms Safeguarding financial stability, however, requires action in all areas of public policy—including fiscal, monetary and macroprudential measures. These policies need to take a long-term view and to better internalize systemic risk. And, lastly, various institutional reforms and private sector reforms are essential if confidence in the financial system is to be restored. The private sector also has a vital part to play in building a more resilient financial system.

KEY ELEMENTS OF BASEL III FRAMEWORK

"Basel III" is a comprehensive set of reform measures, developed by the Basel Committee on Banking Supervision, to strengthen the regulation, supervision and risk management of the banking sector.

These measures aim to:

i) improve the banking sector's ability to absorb shocks arising from financial and economic stress, whatever the source

ii) improve risk management and governance

iii) strengthen banks' transparency and disclosures.

The reforms target:

i) bank-level, or microprudential regulation, which will help raise the resilience of individual banking institutions to periods of stress.

ii) Macroprudential, system wide risks that can build up across the banking sector as well as the procyclical amplification of these risks over time.

Table 1
Banking Supervision Reform – Basel III
(Strenthens microprudential regulation and supervision, and adds a macroprodential overlay that includes capital buffers)

	Capital				
	Pillar 1			Pillar 2	Pillar 3
	Capital	Risk coverage	Containing leverage	Risk management and supervision	Market discipline
All Banks	**Quality and level of capital** Greater focus on concern equity. The minimum will be raised to 4.5% of risk-weighted assets, after deductions **"Gone concern" contingent capital** "Gone concern" capital proposal would requires contractual terms of capital instruments to include a allowing at the direction of the relevant authority write off the conversion to common shares if the bank is judged to be non-viable "Gone concern" contingent capital increases the contribution of the private sector to revolving future banking crises and thereby reduces moral hazard. **Capital conservation buffer** Comprising common equity 2.5% of risk-weighed assets, bringing the total common equity standard to 7% constraint on a bank's discretionary distributions will be imposed when banks fall into the buffer range. **Countercyclical buffer** Imposed within a range of 0-2.5% comprising common equity, when authorities judge credit growth is resulting in an unacceptable build up of systematic risk.	**Securitisations** Strengthens the capital treatment for certain complex securitisations requires banks to conduct more rigorous credit analyses of externally rated securitization exposures. **Trading book** Significantly higher capital for treading and derivatives activities, as well as complex securitization of a stressed value-at-risk framework to help mitigate procyclicality. **Counterparty credit risk** Substantial strengthening of the counterparty credit risk framework. Includes more stringent requirements for measuring for banks to use central counterparties for derivatives, and higher capital for inter-financial sector exposures.	**Leverage ratio** A Non-risk-based leverage ratio that includes off-balance sheet exposures will serve as a backstop to the risk-based capital requirement Also helps contain system wide build up of leverage.	**Supplemental Pillar 2 requirements.** Address firm-wide governance and risk management capturing the risk of off-balance sheet exposures and securitization activities, managing risk concentrations; providing incentives for banks to better manage risk and returns over the long term sound compensation practices, stress testing, accounting standard for financial instruments corporate governance, and supervisory colleges.	**Revised Pillar 3 Disclosures requirements** The requirements introduced relate to securitization exposures and sponsorship of off-balance sheet vehicles Enhanced disclosures on the detail of the components of regulatory capital and their reconciliation to the reported accounts will be required, including a comprehensive explanation of how a bank calculates its regulatory capital ratios.
SIFIs	In addition to meeting the Basel III requirements, global systemically important financial institutions (SIFIS) must have higher loss absorbency capacity to reflect the greater risks that they pose to the financial system. The Committee has developed a methodology that includes both quantitative indicators and qualitative elements to identify global SIFIs. The additional loss absorbency requirements are to be met a progressive Common Equity Tier 1 (CET1) capital requirement ranging from 1% to 2.5% depending on a bank's systemic importance.				

These two approaches to supervision are complementary as greater resilience at the individual bank level reduces the risk of system wide shocks.

The basel III framework is summarized in Table-1 which provides an overview of the various measures taken by the Committee.

BASEL III AND FINANCIAL REGULATORY FRAMEWORK

As the source of credit intermediation between lenders and borrowers, banks provide essential domestic and international financial services to consumers, businesses and government. A strong and resilient banking system is thus the foundation for sustainable economic growth. Throughout history, however, financial crises have occurred at one time or another in every region of the world and for a wide range of reasons. The most recent crisis, in 2007–09, revealed fundamental shortcomings in the operation and regulation of the banking system in many countries.

The crisis had its roots in the United States and spread primarily to other advanced economies, having originated in the imprudent use and inadequate regulation of complex securitisations by large banks. However, in a broader sense, the causes and evolution of the crisis reflect deficiencies that are typical of financial crises in general: investors chasing yield, too much credit, weak underwriting standards, an underpricing of risk, excessive leverage, and contagion.

Given the speed at which crises can arise and be transmitted around the globe, and given ever more rapid financial innovation, banks in all countries need to hold higher capital and liquidity buffers to protect the global banking system and economy from unforeseen risks. Unfortunately, memories tend to be short, and significant risks to the banking sector generally emerge after a period of complacency bred of apparent calm. Thus, the work to strengthen banking systems must be carried through now, when the crisis is still fresh in people's minds and policymakers and the wider public understand the urgency of an effective response.

With its release of the Basel III rules on 16 December 2010, the Basel Committee on Banking Supervision set out new global regulatory standards on bank capital adequacy and liquidity to correct the deficiencies revealed by the crisis. Some of the new rules represent a significant overhaul of existing global standards, others introduce rules where none previously existed. Taken together, they strengthen capital and liquidity regulation to promote more resilience in global banking. Thus fortified by Basel III, the international regulatory framework will better shield the financial sector from the next crisis, whatever its origin, and reduce the risk of spillover from the financial sector to the real economy. As risk-taking in the financial sector resumes, banks have started to accumulate capital and to adapt their funding strategies and broader business models to the new regulatory framework, which will call on them to target lower, more stable returns on equity.

HOW THE FINANCIAL CRISIS IS SHAPING REGULATORY REFORM

The severity of the crisis owed much to the fact that the banking sector in many countries had taken on too much risk without a commensurate increase in capital.

Furthermore, this inadequate *level* of capital was of insufficient *quality*, as the latter had gradually eroded. Basel III tightens capital requirements, encompasses a broader array of risks, and explicitly addresses macroprudential aspects of banking system stability.

Bank Capital

The leverage ratio will provide a backstop to the risk-basedmeasures and help curb the build-up of excessive leverage. Basel III substantially raises the quality as well as the quantity of capital, with a much greater emphasis on common equity (Box-1). During the crisis, losses reduced banks' common equity. However, some banks maintained deceptively high ratios of Tier 1 capital to risk-weighted assets through the inclusion of other forms of financial instruments in the capital base. Moreover, non-common Tier 1 capital instruments often did not share in banks' losses through reduced coupon or principal payments and so did not contribute to maintaining the institutions as going concerns in any meaningful way. The artificially high Tier 1 risk-based ratios also meant that banks were building up high levels of leverage. Basel III therefore also introduces a simple leverage ratio that provides a backstop to the risk-based regime. The supplementary ratio, which is a measure of a bank's Tier 1 capital as a percentage of its assets plus off-balance sheet exposures and

BOX -1
Capital instruments

The global banking system entered the crisis with an insufficient level of high-quality capital. The crisis revealed an inconsistency in how regulatory capital is defined across jurisdictions and the lack of disclosure that would have enabled the market to fully assess and compare the quality of banks' capital. In response, Basel III introduces a harmonised definition of capital that comprises the following components:

- **Common Equity Tier 1** – consists of the bank's common shares and retained earnings less regulatory adjustments (eg the deduction of goodwill). This component of capital fully absorbs losses while the bank remains a going concern. It is therefore the highest-quality component of a bank's capital. A key element of the new definition of capital is the greater focus on Common Equity Tier 1.
- **Additional Tier 1 capital** – consists of preferred shares and other capital instruments that comply with a set of criteria to ensure they can absorb losses while the issuing bank remains a going concern. These criteria include requirements that the instruments be subordinated, have fully discretionary non-cumulative dividends or coupons and have neither a maturity date nor an incentive to redeem.
- **Tier 2 capital** – consists of debt instruments that comply with a set of criteria to ensure they are able to absorb losses when a bank fails (ie when it has become a "gone concern"). These criteria include requirements that the instruments be subordinated, have a minimum original maturity of at least five years and contain no step-ups or other incentives to redeem. Regulatory recognition of these instruments is amortised over the five years before maturity.

During the crisis, a number of distressed banks were rescued by the injection of public sector funds in the form of common equity and other forms of Tier 1 capital. While this had the effect of supporting depositors, it also meant that certain capital instruments did not absorb losses. Therefore, in addition to the characteristics noted above, instruments in Additional Tier 1 and in Tier 2 must have a feature ensuring that they can be written off or converted to common equity when the issuing bank reaches the point of non-viability (ie the point at which the bank is unable to support itself in the private market) as determined by the relevant authority.

The Basel III definition of capital phases out innovative hybrid capital instruments, which provided an incentive to redeem through features such as step-up clauses. It also eliminates Tier 3 capital, which was short-term subordinated debt that was previously permitted to cover market risk.

In addition to the Basel III elements of capital, certain other instruments are being considered in the context of systemically important banks:

- **Contingent capital** (also called cocos) – debt instruments that convert to Common Equity Tier 1 capital through a write-off or conversion to common shares before a bank reaches the point of non-viability.
- **Bail-in-able debt** – debt instruments that convert to Common Equity Tier 1 capital through a write- off or conversion to common shares when a bank reaches the point of non-viability.

derivatives, will serve as an additional safeguard against attempts to "game" the risk-based requirements, and will mitigate model risk (Table-2). By helping contain the build-up of excessive leverage, the leverage ratio will also complement other macroprudential measures, discussed below, to reduce systemic risk.

TABLE 2

Strengthened Capital Framework: From Basel II to Basel III

In percentage of risk-weighted assets	*Capital requirement*								*Additional macroprudential overlay*
	Common Equity			*Tier 1 capital*		*Total capital*		*Counter-cyclical buffer*	*Additional loss absorbing capacity for SIFI*
	Minimum	*Conservation buffer*	*Required*	*Minimum*	*Required*	*Minimum*	*Required*	*Range*	
Basel II	2			4		8			
Memo	*Equivalent to around 1% for an average international bank under the new definition*			*Evuivalent to around 2% for an average international bank under the new definition*					
Basel III									
New definition and calibration	4.5	2.5	7.0	6	8.5	8	10.5	0-2.5	Capital surcharge for SIFLs?

*Modalities to be defined.

Turning to the minimum capital requirements, the higher minimums for common equity and tier 1 capital will be phased in beginning in 2013, and will become effective at the beginning of 2015. The schedule will be as follows:

- The minimum common equity and Tier 1 requirements will increase from the current 2% and 4% levels to 3.5% and 4.5%, respectively, at the beginning of 2013.
- The minimum common equity and Tier 1 requirements will be 4% and 5.5%, respectively, starting in 2014.
- The final requirements for common equity and Tier 1 capital will be 4.5% and 6%, respectively, beginning in 2015.

The 2.5% capital conservation buffer, which will be comprised of common equity and is in addition to the 4.5% minimum requirement, will be phased in progressively starting on 1 January 2016, and will become fully effective by 1 January 2019.

Finally, the leverage ratio will also be phased in. The test (the so-called "parallel run period") will begin in 2013 and run until 2017, with a view to migrating to a Pillar 1 treatment on 1 January 2018 based on review and appropriate calibration.

Risk Coverage

The Basel Committee has also improved the risk coverage of the regulatory capital framework for capital market activities – a salient feature of the recent crisis, where trading exposures accounted for much of the build-up of leverage and were an important source of losses. (Trading exposures include positions in financial instruments and commodities held either with the intent to trade them or to hedge other trading activities. For purposes of calculating regulatory capital, such positions are subject to the Basel Committee's market risk rules and are said to be held in the "trading book"). Weak capital, excessive leverage and inadequate risk coverage prevented the banking system from fully absorbing systemic trading and credit losses. Nor could it cope with the reintermediation of large off-balance sheet exposures that had built up in the shadow banking system. Under Basel III, banks will have to hold more capital against their less liquid, credit-sensitive assets whose holding periods are much longer than traditional trading positions. Trading activities will also be subject to a stressed value-at-risk requirement. In addition, securitisation exposures in the trading book will be subject to capital charges more consistent with those for the banking book. Basel III also imposes higher capital requirements for counterparty credit risk, that is, for the amount that would be lost in the event of default by a counterparty to a financial contract. Moreover, Basel III creates incentives for banks to increase the use of central counterparties (CCPs) – financial institutions that act as intermediaries between market participants (see Box -2) – while ensuring that the risk arising from banks' exposures to CCPs is adequately capitalised.

Liquidity

During the build-up to the crisis, many banks had operated with increasingly thin liquidity margins, placing undue reliance on easy access to market liquidity. At the height of the crisis, counterparties lost confidence in the liquidity of many banking institutions, severely straining their access to funding. Basel III addresses the liquidity deficiencies that the crisis laid bare. The internationally harmonised liquidity framework consists of two minimum regulatory standards: the liquidity coverage ratio (LCR) and the net stable funding ratio (NSFR). They have complementary objectives.

Box-2

The role of financial market infrastructures

Transactions in financial markets are conducted either on organised exchanges or over the counter (OTC). After the transaction is concluded, it is passed on to what is commonly known as the post-trade infrastructure. This process starts with the matching of the transaction and ends with its settlement. Settlement typically involves the transfer of money against the delivery of an asset or a financial instrument such as a derivative. In modern financial systems, settlement takes place in financial market infrastructures like large-value payment systems, securities settlement systems and central counterparties (CCPs).

The way these post-trade infrastructures are designed and how they function has important implications for financial stability because they can act as a channel through which disruptions can spread among financial market participants. Put differently, these infrastructures can serve as an important means to mitigate the risks arising from the "interconnectedness" of market participants and can reduce the risk of contagion.

The financial crisis revealed a striking weakness in the way important OTC derivatives, in particular credit default swaps, were processed in the post-trade phase. Many of these transactions were inadequately reported, and the bilateral exposures between counterparties were insufficiently collateralised.

Against this background, authorities from around the world are pushing for two significant changes in the post-trade infrastructure for OTC derivatives. Both should be implemented by the end of 2012. First, OTC derivatives will need to be reported to a trade repository (TR). A TR is an electronic registry that keeps a record of all relevant details of an OTC derivative transaction over its lifetime. This information can be used in various ways by the reporting institutions, authorities and the public. If all trades are reported to a TR, and the information is made available to the relevant supervisory authorities, then these authorities will be able to attain an overall view of the OTC derivatives markets, including the most important (gross and net) positions taken by the major dealers in these markets. If TRs had existed before the crisis, the build-up of huge derivative positions, such as those at American International Group (AIG), would have been observed much earlier.

Second, clearing OTC derivatives through a CCP instead of bilaterally can bring about several benefits from a financial stability perspective. A CCP interposes itself between the two original counterparties of a financial transaction, becoming the buyer to the seller and the seller to the buyer. In other words, the CCP isolates the original counterparties from each other should one of them default. Thus, it makes financial institutions less interconnected. However, since risks become concentrated in the CCP, the CCP itself needs to be highly robust: it must protect itself against the default of one or more of its members. To that end, the CCP requires its members to adjust their collateral at the CCP at least daily in accordance with the price movements of their positions.

The LCR is designed to bolster the short-term resilience of a bank's liquidity risk profile by ensuring that it has high-quality liquid assets in sufficient quantity to survive a plausibly severe stress scenario lasting for 30 calendar days. The stress scenario, designed by the Basel Committee, incorporates many of the shocks experienced during the crisis. It includes a partial run-off of retail deposits, a partial or complete drying-up of wholesale funding sources, a need to post additional collateral due to a credit rating downgrade, and unscheduled draws on unused credit and liquidity facilities.

The NSFR is designed to promote resilience over a longer time horizon by creating additional incentives for banks to use more stable sources of funding on an ongoing basis. These standards complement the Committee's 2008 *Principles for sound liquidity risk management and supervision*, the implementation of which will be assessed in the near term.

Macroprudential Aspects

Basel III was designed to enhance both bank-specific soundness and wider banking sector stability. Thus, besides its firm-specific approaches, it incorporates macroprudential measures to explicitly address systemic risk.

During the crisis, mounting losses and the resulting strain on capital impaired banks' ability to lend – precisely at the time when economies were most in need of credit. This tendency for the financial system to amplify cyclical effects in the real economy, or procyclicality, combined with the interconnectedness of financial institutions that were considered too big to fail, exacerbated the crisis.

To help mitigate procyclicality in banking and the broader financial system, the new regulatory capital framework provides for building up capital in good times to levels above the minimum requirement. The resulting *capital conservation buffer* will help banks absorb losses during periods of financial and economic stress. As a bank's capital level moves closer to the minimum requirement, the conservation buffer imposes a progressively tightened constraint on the bank's discretionary distributions, such as dividends. Retaining a bigger proportion of earnings during a downturn will help ensure that capital remains available to support banks' ongoing business operations during the period of stress.

Basel III also introduces a *countercyclical buffer*. It is based on the observation that private sector credit growth that is out of line with historical experience often ultimately imposes losses on the lenders. The ratio of aggregate credit to GDP will serve as the reference for the build-up of the buffer, which will be implemented through restrictions on capital distributions identical to those that apply to the conservation buffer. Within countries, the authorities will impose this buffer only when they judge that credit growth is resulting in an unacceptable build-up of system-wide risk. Conversely, the buffer will be released when, in the judgment of the authorities, the capital can help absorb banking system losses that pose a risk to financial stability. The ability to run down the buffer without penalties will help reduce the risk of constraining the availability of credit.

The macroprudential elements of Basel III contribute significantly to the development of the broader macroprudential policy framework. The BIS has advocated such a framework for some time and is encouraged to see the growth of national and international efforts to develop and implement it (see Box-3). However, while much

BOX -3

National and international progress on implementing macroprudential policy frameworks

One of the key lessons of the recent financial crisis is that regulatory policy must have an enhanced macroprudential orientation to comprehensively address systemic financial risks. The national and international work to develop such a macroprudential policy has intensified and continues to grow, building on conceptual efforts by the BIS since the apparent coining of the term "macroprudential" by the Cooke Committee, the forerunner of the Basel Committee, in 1979.

Recent initiatives in a number of international forums, have aided the formation of a clear consensus regarding the key features of an effective macroprudential framework. These include:

- effective integration of supervisory information, market intelligence and aggregate indicator data;
- recognition of the importance of domestic and cross-border interlinkages across financial institutions and markets;
- macroprudential instruments matched to the particular risks or imbalances diagnosed;
- macroprudential policy responsibility assigned to an independent central agency or formal committee, either within the central bank or involving the central bank in a key role;
- clarity of mandate, adequacy of powers and strong accountability; and
- clear macroprudential policy communications that link financial stability assessments to policy decisions and that manage public expectations about the capabilities of macroprudential policy. Formal macroprudential policy arrangements that will enable these principles to be realised have

been established or are well in train in many jurisdictions, including the United States, the United Kingdom and the European Union. In many cases, operations under new arrangements have begun. The emerging frameworks feature advancements in the structured, regular diagnosis of systemic risk. For example, these diagnoses are conducted at the international level by the Committee on the Global Financial System (CGFS), the Financial Stability Board (FSB) Standing Committee on the Assessment of Vulnerabilities, and the IMF-FSB Early Warning Exercise; and national financial stability reports are progressively strengthening their support of macroprudential policy. Basel III incorporates macroprudential capital elements, and many jurisdictions continue to accumulate practical experience with macroprudential instruments such as loan-to-value ratio caps and reserve requirements.

The powers, tools and accountability requirements for macroprudential policy are either well defined or in an advanced stage of development. The imperative now is to get actual policy operations up and running. To do so, key operational issues must be resolved, including the selection, design and calibration of instruments, the translation of risk indicators to instrument settings, and arranging for efficient decision-making by committees encompassing diverse policy interests and knowledge. In short, the development of macroprudential policy is moving from conceptual issues of design to practical questions of implementation.

The more technical phase of macroprudential policy development is being facilitated by increasingly useful data generated by the growing number of actual macroprudential interventions and improvements to statistical coverage. Nonetheless, a substantial amount of trial and error is likely to be needed for the time being, given the still-limited history of macroprudential policy usage. Sharing of practical experiences among macroprudential policymakers, including through the BIS and FSB processes, will promote the development of the international dimension of macroprudential policy and the refinement of national frameworks.

has been accomplished, more needs to be done, especially on practical implementation of the broad consensus now evident around the framework's core concepts.

IMPACT OF THE NEW REQUIREMENTS

A stronger, safer banking system allocates credit more efficiently, reduces the risk of a costly financial crisis and stabilises the environment for long-term business decisions. These benefits will begin to be reaped when the reforms are implemented. But the process of implementing the new framework will also impose some costs on banks and their customers as banks adjust their balance sheets and business models.

How much adjustment will be needed? The answer varies substantially across institutions and jurisdictions. In some economies, particularly those affected by the financial crisis, banks are still rebuilding capital and running off certain assets. In others, capital and liquidity levels already meet the new requirements. Regardless of their starting point, all economies will see some adjustment, given the significant qualitative and quantitative changes in supervisory definitions and approaches in Basel III.

OUTSTANDING ISSUES AND FUTURE WORK

The reform agenda now encompasses implementation of regulations complemented by more intensive and intrusive supervision; more extensive regulation and supervision of systemically important financial institutions (SIFIs) and development of effective cross-border resolution regimes; and broader consideration of non-bank financial firms and the shadow banking system. The Basel Committee is also reviewing the distinction between the regulatory banking book and the trading book.

Implementation

The Basel III rules need to be implemented in a timely and globally consistent manner. All member countries of the Basel Committee must now translate the Basel III texts into national regulations and legislation in time to meet the 2013 deadline.

The Committee and its oversight body of Governors and Heads of Supervision have consistently stated that the new standards will be introduced in a manner that does not impede the economic recovery. Thus, they have chosen a staggered timeline for implementation . For example, the July 2009 enhancements that strengthen regulatory capital and disclosure requirements are due to take effect no later than the end of 2011. The Basel III requirements themselves begin to take effect from the beginning of 2013 and will be phased in by 2019. This time frame includes an observation period to review the implications of the liquidity standards for individual banks, the banking sector and financial markets, with a view to addressing any unintended consequences. Similarly, the Committee will assess the impact of the leverage ratio on business models during the transition period in order to ensure that it achieves its objectives.

Like all Basel Committee standards, Basel III sets out *minimum* requirements, and the transitional arrangements are the deadlines for adopting the new standards.

Countries should move faster if their banks are profitable and are able to apply the standards without having to restrict credit. Banks should not be permitted to increase their capital distributions simply because the deadline for achieving the minimum standards is still some way off, particularly if there are signs of growing macroeconomic risks and imbalances. Therefore, banks, for their part, must also begin to plan and to prepare.

Basel III is the core regulatory response to problems revealed by the financial crisis. Delay or weakening of the agreements would jeopardise financial stability and the robustness of the recovery over the long term. The full, timely and consistent implementation of *all* relevant standards by banks, along with rigorous enforcement by supervisors, is critical. Ultimately, both the official and the private sector will reap the benefits of a more stable financial system.

More Intensive and More Intrusive Supervision

Implementation efforts need to be supplemented by strong and enhanced supervision of individual banks. Strong supervision is needed to ensure that banks operate with capital levels, liquidity buffers and risk management practices that are commensurate with the risks taken. It must also address the consequences of financial innovation or risks of regulatory arbitrage that regulation cannot fully capture and, more generally, address the firm-level consequences of emerging risks and economic developments. National authorities must supervise in a more intensive and more intrusive fashion, especially for the largest and most complex banks. It will also be important to reinforce both the firm-specific and macroprudential dimensions of supervision and the way they interact.

In particular, as it carries forward its work on the implementation of the supervisory review process under Basel II (ie Pillar 2), the Basel Committee will foster the adoption of better supervisory practices.

Systemically Important Financial Institutions

Reducing the risks posed by financial institutions that are systemic in a global context (global systemically important financial institutions, or G-SIFIs) is a high priority for the international regulatory community. Basel III will enhance the quality and quantity of capital for all banks, but it does not fully address the externalities or spillover effects that G-SIFIs generate. Additional policy tools are necessary.

In November 2010, the FSB introduced a policy framework for these institutions. It recommends that G-SIFIs have higher loss-absorbing capacity to reflect the greater risks that they pose to the global financial system and that these institutions be subject to more intensive and coordinated resolution planning to reduce the probability and impact of their failure. This will help ensure that G-SIFIs can be closed or wound up quickly without destabilising the financial system or exposing the taxpayer to the risk of loss. In addition, the FSB calls for enhanced supervision of SIFIs that will be more intensive and effective than in the past.

The Basel Committee has developed quantitative indicators and qualitative elements to identify G-SIFIs. Work is also continuing on calibrating the additional loss absorbency that G-SIFIs should have, which could be met through some combination of common equity and contingent capital. The Committee will pursue this work in close cooperation with the FSB in the coming months.

More Effective Cross-border Bank Resolution

Higher loss-absorbing capacity for G-SIFIs and their effective resolution complement each other, but neither by itself is sufficient. The financial crisis also illustrated the importance of effective cross-border crisis management. The scope, scale and complexity of international financial transactions expanded at an unprecedented pace in the years preceding the crisis, while the tools and techniques for handling cross-border bank resolution have hardly evolved. Some of the events during the crisis revealed gaps in intervention techniques and, in many countries, a lack of appropriate resolution tools. Actions taken to resolve cross-border institutions during the crisis tended to be ad hoc, severely constrained by time, and dependent on a significant amount of official support.

In March 2010, the Basel Committee issued recommendations to strengthen national resolution powers and their cross-border implementation. The recommendations also covered firm-specific contingency planning for banks and home and host country authorities. Contagion can be reduced through risk mitigation mechanisms such as netting arrangements, collateralisation practices and the use of regulated central counterparties. These and other measures would help limit the market impact of a bank failure. The recommendations should lead to practical and credible plans to promote resilience in periods of severe financial distress and to facilitate a rapid resolution if necessary.

Building on the recommendations, the Basel Committee and the FSB are assessing progress in national and multinational efforts to enhance authorities' ability to manage and resolve distressed banking institutions in a manner that minimises disruptions to the financial system. The two bodies are evaluating legal and policy changes that would assist authorities in addressing future needs for crisis management and bank resolution.

Other Financial Sectors and Firms

Work to strengthen the regulation of SIFIs also needs to take account of differences across financial sectors. The FSB will review how the different regulatory measures fit together and whether there are inconsistencies or contradictions among the standards. For instance, deeper consideration is needed to assess the systemic importance of insurance companies and their role in financial stability. Insurance companies tend to have very different risk characteristics from those of banks, particularly regarding liquidity. Insurance company balance sheets also differ considerably across countries, for example in terms of the exposure to equity markets . Except for unusual cases such as American International Group (AIG) and the monoline insurers, these institutions proved broadly resilient during the financial crisis .

Hedge funds are another set of firms for which regulatory instruments and objectives differ sharply from those appropriate to banks. Despite major investment losses and outflows during the crisis, assets and leverage in the hedge fund sector have been broadly stable in the post-crisis period.

Shadow Banking

Shadow banking refers to credit intermediation that takes place outside the traditional banking system and involves maturity or liquidity transformation. Examples include the activities of money market funds, lending by unregulated finance companies, the issuance by specialised conduits and investment vehicles of commercial paper backed by longer-term assets, and the funding of securitisation activities through repo markets. The shadow banking system is, however, closely intertwined with the regulated system. Large banks typically draw substantial income from shadow banking activities and retain both direct and indirect credit and operational exposures to them through business lines such as loan origination, credit enhancements, backup liquidity lines, brokerage services, warehousing and credit insurance.

Shadow banking can perform valuable functions, including facilitating credit extension to certain sectors and providing banks and investors with a range of vehicles for managing credit, liquidity and maturity risks. However, the financial crisis demonstrated that shadow banking can also give rise to a number of risks in the broader financial sector. Some of these risks (such as those related to bank exposures through contingent credit lines) are being addressed through the improvements in bank regulation as well as through initiatives such as stronger regulation of credit rating agencies and money market funds. Other aspects are more difficult to deal with, especially those that call for a high degree of coordination across regulatory agencies, both within and across national boundaries. For example, judging the extent of liquidity mismatch in a bank-sponsored investment vehicle may require input from banking and market regulators in several jurisdictions.

Another lesson of the crisis was that activities in the shadow banking system need to be monitored in order to improve the ability of authorities and market participants to understand and anticipate the build-up of systemic risks. For example, in the years leading up to the crisis, US money market funds were important providers of funding to European banks. As a result, the disruption to the US money market fund sector in the aftermath of the Lehman Brothers bankruptcy in September 2008 had knock-on implications for European bank funding as well as for foreign exchange swap markets because the banks had used these instruments to swap their funding from dollars into local currencies. Existing statistical frameworks do not provide adequate information for assessing these risks .

Shadow banking's potential threats to financial stability must be reduced. First, firm-level disclosure and system-wide statistical frameworks need to be improved to ensure that the build-up of risks can be monitored properly. Improved data need to be accompanied by regular monitoring of those indicators that can be informative about the nature and locus of potential systemic risks. Second, gaps in regulation need to be identified and addressed, with the goal of reducing risky build-ups of leverage and maturity and liquidity mismatches, wherever these occur in the financial system. Rules that mitigate these risks in a consistent way across different entities and activities would reduce the scope for regulatory arbitrage. Given the global nature of many shadow banking activities, these efforts need to be coordinated at the international level.

Other Regulatory and Supervisory Initiatives

The financial crisis exposed significant flaws in the existing regulatory capital approach to market risk and trading activities. The most immediate shortcomings were remedied in the July 2009 enhancements to the regulatory capital framework. The Basel Committee is now also carrying out a fundamental review of the trading book framework and expects to conduct a public consultation on its findings around end-2011.

There are a number of key questions: how to remove opportunities for arbitrage across the banking book and trading book, how to define trading activities, and how to capture risks in trading books (and possibly market risk more generally). Under the current regime, banking book exposures are subject to capital charges against credit risk (through the Basel II credit risk framework) and also against foreign exchange risk and commodities risk (through the market risk framework). Positions in the trading book are subject to capital charges against interest rate risk, foreign exchange risk, equity position risk and commodities risk (through the market risk framework).

ROAD TO A MORE RESILIENT BANKING SECTOR

The financial system is gradually recovering from the crisis, and banks are moving forward in strengthening their balance sheets, albeit at an uneven pace across countries. The future stability of the system depends on banks' completing this process. It also depends on policymakers' completing the regulatory reform agenda and ensuring its consistent implementation across jurisdictions.

Although bank profits have generally recovered from the low levels of the crisis, earnings capacity is still weak and unreliable in a number of countries. In adapting their business models to the post-crisis environment, successful banks will be those that purge crisis-weakened assets, convincingly repair their balance sheets and establish a reliable earnings base.

The progress to date in regulatory reform is providing the foundations for a more resilient financial system. New standards address gaps identified in the crisis and more general weaknesses in the financial system. Success hinges on rapid implementation, however, and so international standard setters are paying increased attention to progress in individual jurisdictions.

In ensuring systemic stability, the prudential framework must address the increasingly intricate organisation of financial firms, and it must stay abreast of the growing complexities of financial transactions and risk assessment. Policies that simplify the organisational structure of institutions can deal with only one aspect of the problem. A more general and effective approach sets prudential capital and liquidity requirements that are aligned with bank risk.

Given the uncertainties of risk measurement, simple gauges of bank solvency risk used in combination with more elaborate risk-sensitive metrics can improve risk capture. Regulation can also improve risk assessment by setting higher standards of quality for banks' internal risk models. Finally, the supervisory framework can strengthen market discipline by requiring more specific disclosures of the characteristics and performance of those internal models.

CAPITAL, PROFITABILITY AND BALANCE SHEET REPAIR

The need to repair balance sheets has dominated banking sector developments in recent years. Banks' financial strength deteriorated abruptly after the prolonged financial boom turned to a bust and the economy entered a balance sheet recession. The disruption to financial intermediation highlighted the need to restore bank solvency and profitability. The repair of banks' balance sheets involves the recognition of legacy losses, the disposal of impaired assets, and the build-up of robust capital buffers supported by a reliable earnings capacity.

Banks have made progress in charging off bad loans, with US banks generally leading their European peers. Uncertainty about asset quality remains a greater concern in Europe. The forthcoming asset quality review and stress tests of European banks will be critical in ensuring completion of the loss recognition and balance sheet repair process, which will also require that appropriate backstops be put in place.

At the same time, banks worldwide have improved their capital ratios at a faster pace than set out in the Basel III phase-in arrangements. In the 12 months to mid-2012, the average Common Equity Tier 1 (CET1) capital of large, internationally active banks had risen from 7.1% of risk-weighted assets to 8.5%. It was thus considerably higher than the 2019 minimum of 4.5% CET1 plus a 2.5% conservation buffer.

During the same period, banks still below the 2019 benchmark reduced their capital shortfall by almost 60%, to 208.2 billion. That remaining gap is roughly equivalent to half of their collective profits (after tax and before distributions) for the period. For a group of smaller banks, the corresponding capital shortfall was 16 billion, or 70% of the same profit measure.

Retained earnings are at present the main source of capital for banks. A stable earnings environment would be instrumental in closing the gap in required capital before the 2019 deadline. Retained earnings of major global banks have generally risen above pre-crisis levels and have made a major contribution to capital, although in many cases with the help of volatile trading income. By contrast, new capital offerings have played a lesser role. In the euro area, sovereign debt problems have been seen as potentially limiting the ability of lenders there to access new capital.

Stable profits will be critical to the resilience of the banking sector. Profits have rebounded from the lows registered during the financial crisis, but recovery remains uneven across countries (Table 3). In the United States, pre-tax bank profits improved further last year, in large part because of a fall in loan loss provisions. However, the combination of accommodative monetary policy and competitive lending conditions continued to squeeze net interest margins. The profits of banks in China and India increased substantially, owing to higher net interest margins and strong loan growth. In Australia, Canada and Sweden, banks consolidated the gains made in previous years. Profitability in Russia improved mainly because of a sharp drop in loan loss provisions.

Profits in other jurisdictions remained lacklustre. In the euro area, sovereign debt strains compromised asset quality, while a stagnating economy lowered revenues. Non-performing loans increased, especially in Italy and Spain, leading to a sharp rise in loan loss provisions. Profits in Brazil continued to slide, in line with larger loan loss provisions and despite lower costs.

TABLE 3

Profitability of Major Banks[1]

As a percentage of total assets

	Pre-tax profits			*Net interest margin*			*Loan loss provisions*			*Operating costs[3]*		
Country[2]	*2000–07*	*2008–11*	*2012*	*2000–07*	*2008–11*	*2012*	*2000–07*	*2008–11*	*2012*	*2000–07*	*2008–11*	*2012*
Australia (4)	1.58	1.07	1.18	1.96	1.81	1.82	0.19	0.33	0.21	1.99	1.20	1.19
Canada (6)	1.03	0.80	1.07	1.74	1.57	1.65	0.24	0.27	0.19	2.73	1.87	1.77
France (4)	0.66	0.29	0.19	0.81	0.96	0.90	0.13	0.26	0.20	1.60	1.10	1.06
Germany (4)	0.26	0.06	0.09	0.68	0.81	0.83	0.18	0.17	0.13	1.38	1.10	1.33
Italy (3)	0.83	–0.03	–0.06	1.69	1.86	1.65	0.40	0.60	0.95	2.27	1.83	1.63
Japan (5)[4]	0.21	0.36	0.56	1.03	0.92	0.84	0.56	0.19	0.07	0.99	0.84	0.75
Spain (3)	1.29	0.94	0.08	2.04	2.31	2.36	0.37	0.81	1.49	2.29	1.58	1.73
Sweden (4)	0.92	0.56	0.68	1.25	0.93	0.92	0.05	0.18	0.09	1.34	0.88	0.81
Switzerland (3)	0.52	–0.05	0.03	0.64	0.52	0.60	0.05	0.06	0.01	2.39	1.82	2.02
United Kingdom (6)	1.09	0.19	0.20	1.75	1.14	1.08	0.31	0.59	0.34	2.02	1.24	1.37
United States (9)	1.74	0.42	0.96	2.71	2.53	2.34	0.45	1.23	0.41	3.58	3.00	3.06
Brazil (3)	2.23	1.61	1.50	6.56	4.77	4.42	1.24	1.42	1.46	6.21	3.79	3.33
China (4)[5]	1.62	1.56	1.83	2.74	2.32	2.39	0.31	0.30	0.25	1.12	1.02	1.01
India (3)[6]	1.26	1.34	1.45	2.67	2.35	2.90	0.88	0.46	0.60	2.48	2.52	2.25
Russia (3)	3.03	1.46	2.39	4.86	4.70	4.09	0.87	1.90	0.36	4.95	2.72	2.78

1. Values for multi-year periods are simple averages. Cross-country comparisons may be limited by differences in accounting standards.
2. In parentheses, number of banks included in 2012.
3. Includes personnel and other operating costs.
4. Excludes personnel costs; 2012 figures for one of the banks are estimated on the basis of half-year results.
5. Data start in 2007.
6. Data start in 2002.

Sources: Bankscope; BIS calculations.

Since the onset of the crisis, banks have also been improving their regulatory capital ratios by reducing risk-weighted assets through a combination of divestments and portfolio reallocations. The process broadly stabilised in 2012 for most major banks. Global banks have reportedly sold about $720 billion in assets since the start of 2007, with European banks accounting for more than half that amount. The crisis in the euro area has weighed heavily: European banks have been net sellers of assets, while banks from the United States and other advanced economies have been net buyers. At the same time, banks have increased their holdings of low risk-weight assets, including government guaranteed debt. By so doing, however, they have become more sensitive to changes in the valuation of government debt.

Moreover, the continued reduction in risk-weighted assets through the postcrisis period suggests that impaired assets have still not been fully recognised. Market commentary has suggested that much of this trend reflects banks' optimisation of risk-weighted assets – the redesign of transactions in order to lower capital requirements – rather than a genuine increase in loss absorption capacity.

Such window-dressing raises questions about the use of internal risk assessments for the determination of regulatory capital requirements.

The progress in balance sheet repair has also resulted in a steady decline in leverage, especially for those banks that have made considerable progress in the resolution of legacy assets. The pressure from regulators and investors has been a key factor in driving leverage down.

Balance sheet restructuring is necessary to improve banks' willingness and ability to provide new lending. By the same token, it lays the basis for a stronger economic recovery. In fact, the cost and availability of credit are more favourable in those jurisdictions where banks have been most successful in rebuilding capital.

PROGRESS WITH GLOBAL REGULATORY FINANCIAL REFORM

The Basel III framework, developed by the Basel Committee on Banking Supervision, is a central element of the reform agenda. It sets significantly higher requirements for loss absorption, puts greater emphasis on a higher quality of capital, and better captures the full scope of bank risk. Innovative aspects of the framework include a leverage ratio, a capital overlay for systemically important banks, a countercyclical capital buffer and standards for a liquidity coverage ratio (LCR). The final version of the LCR was published in January 2013.

The LCR promotes the resilience of banks by ensuring that they maintain an adequate stock of high-quality liquid assets to withstand reversals in funding conditions. The LCR requirements are being phased in, like the new capital adequacy requirements, to support the gradual strengthening of the banking system and the supply of finance for economic activity. Work is progressing on other elements, including a net stable funding ratio, the review of trading book rules, the treatment of securitisation, and large exposures.

A globalised banking system will reap the benefits of the framework only through its full, timely and consistent implementation across all jurisdictions. Basel Committee members have agreed to assess both the alignment of national regulations with the Basel III standards and the consistency of the framework's outcomes on banks. The Committee's implementation monitoring programme assesses the timeliness of adoption of Basel III; domestic regulatory consistency; and the consistency of outcomes, including banks' calculations of risk-weighted assets.

Weaknesses in the resolution procedures for banks at the point of failure, especially for those with more complex business models and international operations, significantly increased the costs of the global crisis. Resolution schemes that enable authorities to quickly deal with failing financial institutions would reduce spillovers to the financial system and the exposure of taxpayers to losses. The Financial Stability Board (FSB) provided guidance with its November 2011 publication *Key attributes of effective resolution regimes for financial institutions*. The implementation of the FSB guidance is at an early stage. Many countries still need to adopt legislation to enable the efficient resolution of global systemically important banks and other internationally active banks.

Another major area of regulatory reform focuses on financial market infrastructure. The crisis revealed major shortcomings in the post-trade processing of OTC derivatives, notably the inadequate reporting of transactions and an insufficient collateralisation of bilateral counterparty exposures. Commitments to improve standards in OTC derivatives markets have covered three principal areas. *First,* the centralised clearing of standardised contracts: robust legal and regulatory frameworks that place a central counterparty (CCP) between transacting parties will reduce interconnectedness across the financial system. *Second,* mandatory reporting of customised transactions: reporting to trade repositories of transactions not channelled through a CCP will improve transparency in OTC markets. *Third,* noncentrally cleared contracts: these will be singled out and subjected to more exacting prudential capital requirements.

In 2009, the G20 agreed to implement central clearing and electronic trading of standardised derivatives instruments by the end of 2012. Few jurisdictions have met this deadline, but legislative frameworks are in place in key jurisdictions, and some progress has been made in implementing the necessary standards. Market regulators are developing detailed rules and addressing issues of cross-border consistency and applicability.

The reform agenda is also advancing with regard to applying oversight and regulation to the shadow banking system, which provides financial services that complement those of regulated banks. Reforms focused on banks may spur the migration of certain financial activities to the shadow banking sector, producing a build-up of systemic vulnerabilities in the form of leverage and liquidity mismatches. The FSB has provided policy recommendations and guidance for further regulatory steps aimed at mitigating this risk. Specific areas include money market funds; banks' exposures to shadow banks; and measures to address risks in repurchase agreements and securities lending.

NATIONAL INITIATIVES ON BANK STRUCTURE REGULATION

Acting parallel to the international regulatory reform process, a number of individual jurisdictions are implementing or considering initiatives on the regulation of bank structure.

The various initiatives involve different ways of separating commercial banking activities – deposit-taking and credit intermediation in the real economy – from the risks inherent in investment banking (see Box-4). The initiatives have implications not only for the business models of universal banks but also for the effectiveness of the global prudential framework as they interact with international regulatory standards.

The proposals would protect commercial banking directly by shielding it from losses incurred elsewhere. The structural separation that achieves this shielding can itself provide an indirect form of protection for commercial banks by reducing their complexity and, arguably, also their size. Separation also makes them easier to manage, supervise and resolve, as well as more transparent to outside stakeholders. In addition, structural separation may prevent the aggressive risk-taking culture of investment bankers from infecting the more utility-like business of commercial banking. And it can reduce moral hazard because it prevents public sector support of protected activities (deposit guarantees and central bank lending) from indirectly subsidising other business activities.

Structural reform initiatives are not without challenges. Defining and enforcing the lines that separate commercial and investment banking activities is a notoriously difficult task, and it is rendered more so by an increasingly complex financial marketplace. Another challenge is to avoid an unintended shift of intermediation activities outside the perimeter of consolidated supervision. An open question is how structural reform initiatives would interact with each other. In particular, will national differences in structural regulation complicate the supervision and resolution of internationally active banks? Avoiding that outcome puts a premium on international coordination in order to ensure a level playing field.

Structural banking reforms proposed at the national level differ from international regulation, notably Basel III. The former impose constraints on specific activities, while the latter takes banks' business models and structure as given and sets capital and liquidity requirements that depend on the riskiness of the consolidated group. From this perspective, the two approaches can be seen as complementary. Indeed, certain aspects of structural regulation – restrictions on leverage for ring-fenced institutions – may reinforce elements of Basel III.

However, structural regulation could lead to different capital and liquidity requirements for the core banking and trading entities within a single banking group. Although this may be intended, it complicates regulation at the consolidated level. Hence, there are limits to the substitutability between structural reform regulation on the one hand, and capital and liquidity regulation on the other. Restrictions in bank structure may support the stability of individual firms, but their benefits are less clear for the system as a whole. Buffers that are robust to uncertainty and reflect the complexities in risk assessment can help at the level of both the firm and the system.

BOX-4

Recent Proposals for the Structural Reform of Banking

Proposals for changing the structure of banking activities are in varying stages of implementation across jurisdictions. They include the Volcker rule (United States); the proposals of the Vickers Report (United Kingdom); and the Liikanen Report (European Union).* The common rationale of these initiatives is to protect financial stability by shielding core functions of commercial banks from losses related to investment banking and securities markets activities. The initiatives vary, however, in their diagnoses and prescriptions.

A stylised comparison of selected structural reform proposals

	Volcker: institutional separation	Liikanen: subsidiarisation	Vickers: ring-fencing
Permissible activity and structure	Remove certain investment activities from bank holding companies	Proprietary and higherrisk trading activity have to be placed in a separate legal entity	Structural separa tion of activities via a ring fence for retail banks
Deposit-taking institution			
• deal as principal in securities and derivatives	No	No	No
• invest in hedge funds and private equity	No	No	No
• engage in market-making	Yes	No	No
• provide underwriting	Yes[1]	Yes	Restricted
• hold non-trading exposures to other financial intermediaries	Unrestricted	Unrestricted	Restricted (inside the group)
Holding company with banking and trading subsidiaries	Not permitted	Permitted	Permitted
Geographic scope	Unrestricted	Unrestricted	Limitations on the ability of UK ringfenced banks to provide services outside the European Economic Area[2]

[1] Underwriting in response to demand from clients and counterparties.

[2] The European Economic Area is the Europen Union plus Iceland, Liechenstein and Norway.

The Volcker rule considers that certain trading operations are non-core activities and therefore should be kept outside the financial sector safety net. It prohibits proprietary trading by commercial banks and prevents them from investing in or sponsoring hedge funds and private equity funds, even within the same business group. A holding company with a commercial bank subsidiary would not be permitted to also have a trading subsidiary.

The proposals in the Liikanen Report are mainly designed to address the too-big-to-fail problem. The report sees the growing investment banking and wholesale funding activities of universal banks as the root cause of banking system distress. It strives to prevent contagion and cross-subsidisation within banking groups by compartmentalising risk. It recommends placing riskier trading activities in specific subsidiaries within the same holding company, thus improving the resolvability of banking firms.

Like the Volcker rule, the Vickers Report considers core banking activity to be like a public utility – an essential but low-return business that should be shielded from excessive risk. In contrast, however, it proposes ring-fencing of core banking activities and moving trading and underwriting activities to separate entities within the same holding company.

* Draft legislation with similar objectives has been proposed in France and Germany.

COMPLEXITY IN RISK MEASUREMENT AND PRUDENTIAL RULES

Policymakers are working to improve consistency in the application of the new, more stringent capital standards. The monitoring of how the regulatory framework is performing in practice has revealed a higher than expected range of variation in risk weights across banks. These differences are both systematic and persistent. The range of variation indicates that the interaction of risk-sensitive rules with the complexity of risk modelling has created a wide scope for inconsistency, which can seriously weaken both the credibility and the effectiveness of the framework.

The relevance of the concern and possible remedies depend on the factors that drive this variation in internal risk measurement outcomes. Some factors are inherent in statistical risk modelling; others largely reflect the practicalities of risk measurement and the specifics of implementing the prudential framework. Both types of factors can hinder the ability of outsiders to interpret the predictions of risk models and to understand differences between banks. The response of policy, including the calibration of the balance between risk-based and risk-insensitive elements of the prudential framework, should reflect the relative importance of these factors.

SOURCES OF VARIABILITY IN INTERNAL RISK MODELS

The calculation of regulatory capital largely depends on banks' internal risk models. However, the outcomes of these models can differ across banks at a given time and within a bank across time for reasons other than changes in underlying risk. The sources of these differences can be classified into five broad categories, which differ in their transparency (their observability by an outsider) and in the extent to which they distort risk measurement in ways detrimental to financial stability.

The *first* category consists of differences in what risk models actually measure – that is, the risk parameter of interest. For example, in calculating the probability of default, some banks may measure the ability of the borrower to repay in the prevailing macroeconomic environment; others may assess the average ability to repay over the course of the cycle. Likewise, the tail risk in trading portfolios could be estimated under either prevailing or stressed market conditions, and the probability of tail losses can be set at more or less stringent levels. If not clearly flagged, such differences can produce spurious variation in the calculated size of safety buffers across banks and reduce comparability.

The *second* category consists of more fundamental differences in the structure of the risk models. Models are stylised descriptions of the real world that rely on assumptions and statistical estimation. While some models may be inferior to others, no single model is unambiguously better than the rest. Models based on different assumptions can provide different risk assessments even when applied to the same data. This does not invalidate their outcomes. On the contrary, two models both fully supported by existing evidence can produce two different assessments of risk, and the difference will simply reflect a legitimate diversity in views.

In the absence of a single objective gauge of risk, such diversity is desirable: the ability of market participants to form independent judgments on risk and to base business decisions on those judgments is a key source of market liquidity and systemic resilience. From a financial stability perspective, imposing a single view on risk can be counterproductive, as the market provides a mechanism to balance the views of bulls and bears.

A *third* category is estimation noise.* Statistical noise in the data used to estimate risk models can produce different outcomes even for models that are quite similar in structure. Depending on the underlying risk characteristics and the size of the sample used to estimate the model, the magnitude of the range of estimates can match the underlying risk being measured.

Variation due to estimation noise is unavoidable. While the noise can be reduced, for instance through the use of larger samples of historical data, it cannot be eliminated. This means that the prudential framework must account for this source of variability. Fortunately from the perspective of systemic stability, the noise in statistical estimation is by nature unbiased: deviations across banks and over time tend to cancel out, thus mitigating the impact on systemwide behaviour.

A *fourth* source of variation in outcomes stems from bankers' incentives, which favour optimistic views on risk and low regulatory capital. The natural entrepreneurial proclivity for risk-taking can inject an optimistic bias in model calibration, as the views of the risk management units may take a back seat to those of the front office. More importantly, banks want to economise on their funding costs. While in theory the mix between debt and equity should not affect the overall cost of funding, in reality a number of distortions make debt cheaper. The tax deductibility of debt costs and the funding advantages from the presence of the safety net are cases in point. In addition, banks have specific incentives to economise on regulatory capital. For any given level of bank capital, the lower the regulatory capital requirement, the less likely it is that the supervisory judgment will constrain business decisions. Moreover, a capital level higher than the regulatory minimum projects an image of a safe and sound bank.

Differences due to strategic choices by banks are unwelcome because they undermine

---

* Risk measurement is subject to estimation noise, which can be quite significant when estimation focuses on rare events such as extreme losses in a securities portfolio or the default of highly rated borrowers.

regulatory efforts. Unlike the effect of purely statistical factors such as estimation noise, the effects of which cancel out across banks, management interventions in the models skew risk assessments downwards by understating potential loss. They arguably account, at least in part, for the secular decline in the industry-wide ratio of risk-weighted assets to total assets.

Finally, variations in model outcomes can reflect supervisors' scope for intervention in setting specific model attributes. For instance, the supervisordetermined multiplier for estimates of market risk can range from 3 to 5.5 times the model outcome and is not always disclosed. Similarly, weaknesses in a bank's process of risk measurement and management, or peculiarities in the local economic environment, can lead supervisors to make compensatory changes in model outcomes. Like definitional differences in models, supervisory interventions that are not transparent can frustrate analysts' ability to compare outcomes across banks and over time.

This suggests that, in theory, if the contribution of each source of variation could be identified, it should be treated separately according to its effect on financial stability. But detecting a bias in risk measurement is quite difficult in practice. Real-time estimates of future risks always have a strong element of judgment, and there are limits to model validation based on the model's historical track record. True, the requirement that banks use the same model for internal and regulatory purposes aims at limiting the scope for misrepresentation, but it cannot fully address the problem of incentives. And given the absence of objective benchmarks, peer comparison may be of limited help: market participants tend to form similarly optimistic views of the future during a boom, only to be collectively disappointed by the bust.

THE RISK SENSITIVITY OF THE PRUDENTIAL FRAMEWORK

The difficulties of risk measurement raise the question of whether the prudential framework puts too much emphasis on internal measures of risk. Many commentators have argued that minimum prudential requirements should have a less easily manipulated basis, namely the simple ratio of regulatory capital to total assets – the leverage ratio – instead of the ratio of regulatory capital to riskweighted assets. Indeed, simplicity and transparency are important advantages of the leverage ratio. Nevertheless, the issue hinges on its ability to capture the solvency risk of banks and on how it interacts with incentives.

Risk capture is a key consideration if the prudential framework is to achieve its objective of ensuring a minimum level of solvency for banks. In an ideal world in which risk can be measured objectively and accurately, the minimum ratio of capital to assets will vary across banks depending on their risk profile. In an alternative hypothetical world in which risk measurement is impossible, the prudential requirements will be based on a risk-insensitive metric of solvency such as the leverage ratio. The real world is somewhere between these two ends of the spectrum.

Common equity measured against both risk-weighted and unweighted assets, which are proxies of the corresponding regulatory ratios, can give advance signals of bank weakness. A low ratio of common equity to risk-weighted assets (CE/RWA) is strongly associated with the likelihood that the bank's operations, net of any external support, will receive a credit rating equivalent to distress or default within one year. A drop in CE/RWA from 8% to 6% would increase the likelihood of distress from less than 8% to almost 11%; a further drop of the ratio to 4% would boost the distress likelihood to 14%. Since rating agencies' assessments of distress and the capitalisation ratios differ from supervisory definitions, these numbers can only be interpreted as being indicative.

The link between the proxy of the leverage ratio – common equity to total (unweighted) assets (CE/TA) – and the likelihood of bank distress shows a similar pattern. A drop in CE/TA (an increase in leverage) from 4% to 2% raises the likelihood of distress from below 8% to almost 12%. In addition, predictions based on the proxy leverage ratio appear more precise than those based on the risk-weighted measure, as evidenced by their narrower confidence band.

Importantly, the two ratios provide signals that are complementary to each other, so when used jointly they improve risk capture. In particular, the combination of low values for each ratio (a low level of risk-weighted capital and high leverage) shows a much higher likelihood of future distress than does the same low value for each ratio considered separately. For instance, 14% of the banks with common equity equal to 6% of its risk-weighted assets and 4% of its total assets would be in distress within a year's time. This is a higher likelihood than that signalled by either capitalisation ratio in isolation, and it jumps to 30% for the banks with respective proxy capitalisation ratios of 4% and 2%.

Each ratio interacts differently with bank incentives and market discipline. In the ideal world of objective, accurate risk measures, prudential rules based on riskweighted metrics of solvency deal effectively with bankers' incentives. In the real world, measurement relies on judgment and is subject to estimation noise and model error. Complexity gives rise to uncertainty and distorts the final outcome by providing more room for regulatory arbitrage and optimistic assessments of risk. In turn, this puts a premium on the ability of supervisors to detect such bias in validating a model, and it strengthens the case for the use of risk-insensitive metrics.

That said, the leverage ratio does not address the problem of incentives because it lumps together positions of very different risk profiles. For a given ratio, banks seeking to minimise regulatory capital can simply reallocate their portfolios towards riskier activities, or shrink their balance sheet without necessarily reducing their potential losses. In order to ensure a minimum level of solvency for all banks, risk-insensitive rules must require higher capital at all banks. Put differently, the simplicity of the leverage ratio improves comparability in the application of prudential rules, but at the cost of not providing information to the market about the underlying risk profile of the bank. Simplicity in this case weakens market discipline.

POLICY RESPONSES TO UNCERTAINTY IN RISK MEASUREMENT

The policy response to the challenges posed by variability in risk model outcomes must be multifaceted. The overarching objective is to strengthen financial stability by supporting an adequate and credible solvency standard for banks. To fulfil that objective, the policy response needs to seek a balance between several specific but somewhat conflicting goals: enhance the quality of risk measurement in banks by preserving the legitimate diversity of individual firm perspectives; narrow the scope for regulatory arbitrage; and empower market discipline by supporting the ability of outside stakeholders to compare the performance of banks.

The first element of a multifaceted policy response is to strengthen the risk sensitivity of the prudential framework. Somewhat paradoxically, the incorporation of a leverage ratio as an additional element of the framework strengthens its risk capture. Harnessing the complementary strengths of the two ratios provides an effective response to the practical and theoretical shortcomings in risk measurement. The argument for a framework that combines the two metrics is also supported by the fact that it is difficult to manipulate one without affecting the other, typically in the opposite direction. For example, an upward shift in portfolio risk might leave the leverage ratio unaffected, but it should increase riskweighted assets. Conversely, investments in assets with underestimated risk, such as highly rated tranches of collateralised debt obligations prior to the crisis, would increase the denominator of a leverage ratio that incorporates derivatives exposures.

A second facet of the response would be to improve the reliability of internal risk measurement in banks through more stringent requirements for model approval. Tighter requirements can mitigate some of the variability that arises from statistical factors. An obvious example is a minimum length of time over which the model must be estimated, possibly conditioned on whether the sample covers a full credit cycle. Other standards could address the quality of the data and performance when the model is applied to stylised portfolios supplied by the supervisor. More demanding standards of approval also strengthen the confidence of outsiders in model estimates.

A third facet of the policy response is to enhance market discipline by improving outsiders' understanding of risk weight calculations. Doing so requires greater transparency regarding the characteristics of internal models. Greater comparability in the disclosures that banks make about the structure and performance of their internal models will help analysts and outside stakeholders assess the relative strength of banks. Such comparability can be improved with more specific information about the risk measurement technology used by the bank, including its calibration. More importantly, greater standardisation of information allows outsiders to better compare model performance. This information could include more detailed results of historical performance (comparing model assessments with eventual portfolio performance) and the assessment of the model as applied to standardised portfolios supplied by the supervisor. Greater transparency by supervisors concerning the application of addons and multipliers to individual bank outcomes would also work in this direction.

Thus ensuring the stability of an evolving financial system requires continual adaptation by the prudential framework. In response to the crisis, the authorities have tightened prudential rules, and banks are working to meet higher solvency standards. The combined effect of these efforts can make banks more resilient. Banks need to rebuild their franchise on business lines that play to their individual strengths and deliver a steady stream of earnings. Repairing their balance sheets through loss recognition and the build-up of capital are key to future success.

Policy responses to complexity are also important for the overall outcome. Rules that simplify the organisational structure of banks may reduce the complexity at the level of the firm, but their impact on system-wide risk can be ambiguous. This is especially true if national rules take different approaches and result in conflicting requirements for global banks.

Prudential standards that strengthen the capacity of banks to deal with risks represent the most reliable defence against financial instability. Rules requiring ample capital and liquidity buffers that are linked to the underlying risks are key elements of these standards. These rules need to address the complexities of risk measurement in a way that improves transparency and comparability in the financial system. A key step towards that goal is harnessing the mutually reinforcing nature of risk-sensitive and risk-insensitive metrics of solvency. Buffers that are robust to uncertainty and reflect the complexities in risk assessment will enhance the resilience of individual banks and of the financial system as a whole.

QUESTIONS

1. Discuss the key elements of Basel III framework.
2. Critically examine the role of financial crisis in shaping the current regulatory reform.
3. Critically examine the financial regulatory framework under Basel III.
4. What steps have been recently initiated to promote broader financial stability?
5. Discuss the steps taken to strengthen the capital framework from Basel II to Basel III.
6. "Balance-sheet restructuring in necessary to improve banks, willingness and ability to provide new lending. By the same token, it lays the basis for a stronger economic recovery. Substantiate the statement."
7. Critically examine the progress made in implementing the global regulatory financial reform agenda to address weaknesses highlighted by the financial crisis.
8. Discuss the initiatives taken by various national authorities on bank structure regulation.
9. "Risk-based and risk-insensitive elements of the prudential framework should reflect the relative importance of the factors that drive the variation in internal risk measurement outcomes. Some factors are inherent in statistical risk-modelling; others largely reflect the practicalities of risk measurement and the specific implementing the prudential framework." Comment.

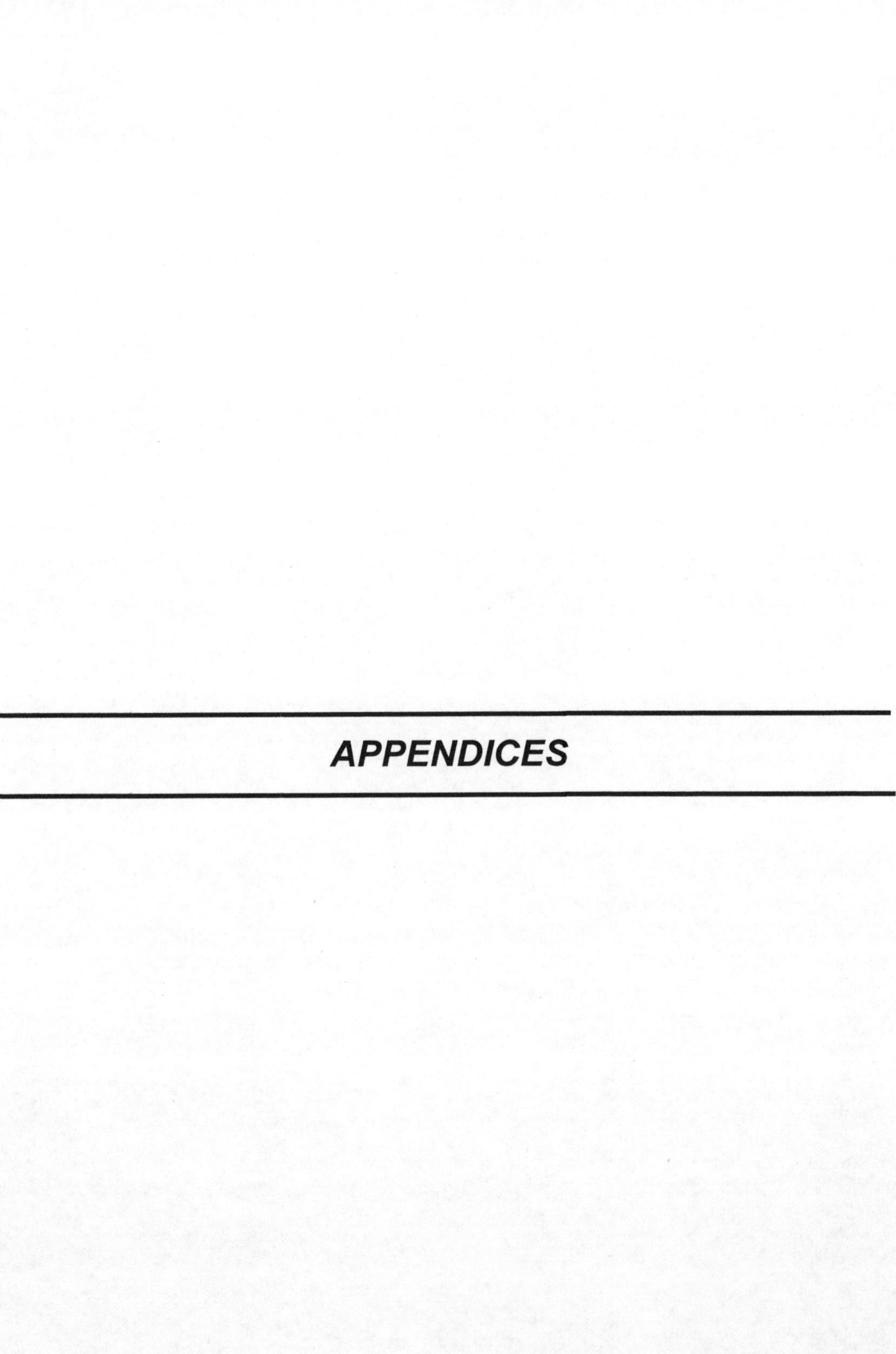

APPENDICES

This Page has been intentionally left blank

TABLE-1

Future Value of ₹ 1.00

n/i	1.0	1.5	2.0	2.5	3.0	3.5	4.0	4.5	5.0	5.5
1	1.01000	1.01500	1.02000	1.02500	1.03500	1.04000	1.04500	1.04500	1.05000	1.05500
2	1.02010	1.03022	1.04040	1.05062	1.06090	1.07122	1.08160	1.09202	1.10250	1.11302
3	1.03030	1.04568	1.06121	1.07689	1.09273	1.10872	1.12486	1.14117	1.15762	1.17424
4	1.04060	1.06136	1.08243	1.10381	1.12551	1.14752	1.16986	1.19252	1.21551	1.23882
5	1.05101	1.07728	1.10408	1.13141	1.15927	1.18769	1.21665	1.24618	1.27628	1.30696
6	1.06152	1.09344	1.12616	1.15969	1.19405	1.22926	1.26532	1.30226	1.34010	1.37884
7	1.07214	1.10984	1.14869	1.18869	1.22987	1.27228	1.31593	1.36086	1.40710	1.45468
8	1.08286	1.12649	1.17166	1.21840	1.26677	1.31681	1.36857	1.42210	1.47746	1.53469
9	1.09369	1.14339	1.19509	1.24886	1.30477	1.36290	1.42331	1.48609	1.55133	1.61909
10	1.10462	1.16054	1.21899	1.28008	1.34392	1.41060	1.48024	1.55297	1.62889	1.70814
11	1.11567	1.17795	1.24337	1.31209	1.38423	1.45997	1.53945	1.62285	1.71034	1.80209
12	1.12682	1.19562	1.26824	1.34489	1.42576	1.51107	1.60103	1.69588	1.79586	1.90121
13	1.13809	1.21355	1.29361	1.37851	1.46853	1.56396	1.66507	1.77220	1.88565	2.00577
14	1.14947	1.23176	1.31948	1.41297	1.51259	1.61869	1.73168	1.85194	1.97993	2.11609
15	1.16097	1.25023	1.34587	1.44830	1.55797	1.67535	1.80094	1.93528	1.07893	2.23248
16	1.17258	1.26899	1.37279	1.48451	1.60471	1.73399	1.87298	2.02237	2.18287	2.35526
17	1.18430	1.28802	1.40024	1.52162	1.65285	1.79468	1.94790	2.11338	2.29202	2.48480
18	1.19615	1.30734	1.42825	1.55966	1.70243	1.85749	2.02582	2.20848	2.40662	2.62147
19	1.20811	1.32695	1.45681	1.59865	1.75351	1.92250	2.10685	2.30786	2.52695	2.76565
20	1.22019	1.34685	1.48595	1.63862	1.80611	1.98979	2.19112	2.41171	2.65330	2.91776

* n = number of time periods: i = rate of interest in per cent.

contd....

Table-1 continue

Future Value of ₹ 1.00

n/i	6.0	6.5	7.0	7.5	8.0	8.5	9.0	9.5	10.0	10.5
1	1.06000	1.06500	1.07000	1.07500	1.08000	1.08500	1.09000	1.09500	1.10000	1.10500
2	1.12360	1.13422	1.24490	1.15562	1.16640	1.17722	1.18810	1.19902	1.21000	1.22102
3	1.19102	1.20795	1.22504	1.24230	1.15971	1.27729	1.19503	1.31293	1.33100	1.34923
4	1.26248	1.28647	1.31080	1.33547	1.36049	1.38586	1.41158	1.43766	1.46401	1.49090
5	1.33823	1.37009	1.40255	1.43563	1.46933	1.50366	1.53862	1.57424	1.61051	1.64745
6	1.41851	1.45914	1.50073	1.54330	1.58687	1.63147	1.67710	1.72379	1.77156	1.82043
7	1.50363	1.55399	1.60578	1.65905	1.71382	1.77014	1.82804	1.88755	1.94872	2.01157
8	1.59385	1.65500	1.71819	1.78348	1.85093	1.92060	1.99256	2.06687	2.14359	2.22279
9	1.68948	1.76257	1.83846	1.91724	1.99900	2.08386	2.17189	2.26322	2.35795	2.45618
10	1.79085	1.87714	1.96715	2.06103	2.15892	2.26098	2.36736	2.47823	2.59374	2.71408
11	1.89830	1.99915	2.10485	2.21561	2.33164	2.45317	2.58043	2.71366	2.85312	2.99906
12	2.01220	2.12910	2.25219	2.38178	2.51817	2.66169	2.81266	2.97146	3.13843	3.31396
13	2.13293	2.26749	2.40984	2.56041	2.71962	2.88793	3.06580	3.25374	3.45227	3.66193
14	2.26090	2.41487	2.57853	2.75244	2.93719	3.13340	3.34173	3.56285	3.79750	4.04643
15	2.39656	2.57184	2.75903	2.95888	3.17217	3.39974	3.64248	3.90132	4.17725	4.47130
16	2.54035	2.73901	2.95216	3.18079	3.42594	3.68872	3.97030	4.27195	4.59497	4.94079
17	2.69277	2.91705	3.15881	3.41935	3.70002	4.00226	4.32763	4.67778	5.05447	5.45957
18	2.85434	3.10663	3.37993	3.67580	3.99602	4.34245	4.71712	5.12217	5.55992	6.03283
19	3.02560	3.30859	3.61653	3.95149	4.31570	4.71156	5.14466	5.60878	6.11591	6.66627
20	3.20713	3.52364	3.86968	4.24785	4.66096	5.11204	5.60441	6.14161	6.72750	7.36623

Table-1 continue

Future Value of ₹ 1.00

n/i	11.0	11.5	12.0	12.5	13.0	13.5	14.0	14.5	15.0	15.5
1	1.11000	1.11500	1.12000	1.12500	1.13000	1.13500	1.14000	1.14500	1.15000	1.15500
2	1.23210	1.24322	1.25440	1.26562	1.27690	1.28822	1.29960	1.31102	1.32250	1.33402
3	1.36763	1.38620	1.40493	1.42383	1.44290	1.46214	1.48154	1.50112	1.52087	1.54080
4	1.51807	1.54561	1.57352	1.60181	1.63047	1.65952	1.68896	1.71879	1.74901	1.77962
5	1.68506	1.72335	1.76234	1.80203	1.84244	1.88356	1.92541	1.96801	2.01136	2.05546
6	1.87041	1.92154	1.97382	2.02729	2.08195	2.13784	2.19497	2.25337	2.31306	2.37406
7	2.07616	2.14252	2.21068	2.28070	2.35261	2.42645	2.50227	2.58011	2.66002	2.74204
8	2.30454	2.38891	2.47596	2.56578	2.65844	2.75402	2.85259	2.95423	3.05902	3.16706
9	2.55804	2.66363	2.77308	2.88651	3.00404	3.12581	3.25195	3.38259	3.51788	3.65795
10	2.83942	2.96995	3.10585	3.24732	3.39457	3.54780	3.70722	3.87306	4.04556	4.22493
11	3.15176	3.31149	3.47855	3.65324	3.83586	4.02675	4.22623	4.43466	4.65236	4.87980
12	3.49845	3.69231	3.89598	4.10989	4.33452	4.57036	4.81790	5.07768	5.35025	5.63617
13	3.88328	4.11693	4.36349	4.62363	4.89801	5.18736	5.49241	5.81395	6.15279	6.50977
14	4.31044	4.59037	4.88711	5.20158	5.53475	5.88765	6.26135	6.65697	7.07570	7.51879
15	4.78459	5.11827	5.47356	5.85178	6.25427	6.68248	7.13794	7.62223	8.13706	8.68420
16	5.31089	5.70687	6.13039	6.58325	7.06732	7.58462	8.13725	8.72746	9.35762	10.03025
17	5.89509	6.36316	6.86604	7.40615	7.98608	8.60854	9.27646	9.99294	10.76126	11.58494
18	6.54355	7.09492	7.68996	8.33192	9.02427	9.77069	10.57517	11.44191	12.37545	13.38060
19	7.26334	7.91084	8.61276	9.37341	10.19742	11.08974	12.05569	13.10099	14.23177	15.45459
20	8.06231	8.82058	9.64629	10.54509	11.52309	12.58685	13.74348	15.00963	16.36653	17.85005

contd....

Table-1 continue

Future Value of ₹ 1.00

n/i	16.0	16.5	17.0	17.5	18.0	18.5	19.0	19.5	20.0	20.5
1	1.16000	1.16500	1.17000	1.17500	1.18000	1.18500	1.19000	1.19500	1.20000	1.20500
2	1.34560	1.35722	1.36890	1.38062	1.39240	1.40422	1.41610	1.42802	1.44000	1.45202
3	1.56090	1.58117	1.60161	1.62223	1.64303	1.66401	1.68516	1.70649	1.72800	1.74969
4	1.81064	1.84206	1.87389	1.90613	1.93878	1.97185	2.00534	2.03926	2.07360	2.10838
5	2.10034	2.14600	2.19245	2.23970	2.28776	2.33664	2.38635	2.43691	2.48832	2.54059
6	2.43640	2.50009	2.56516	2.63164	2.69955	2.76892	2.83976	2.91211	2.98598	3.06141
7	2.82622	2.91260	3.00124	3.09218	3.18547	3.28117	3.37931	3.47997	3.58318	3.68900
8	3.27841	3.39318	3.51145	3.63331	3.75886	3.88818	4.02138	4.15856	4.29982	4.44525
9	3.80296	3.95306	4.10840	4.26914	4.43545	4.60750	4.78545	4.96948	5.15978	5.35635
10	4.41143	4.60531	4.80683	5.01624	5.23383	5.45988	5.69468	5.93853	6.19173	6.45461
11	5.11726	5.36519	5.62399	5.89409	6.17592	6.46996	6.77667	7.09654	7.43008	7.77781
12	5.93603	6.25045	6.58007	6.92555	7.28759	7.66690	8.06424	8.48037	8.91610	9.37226
13	6.88579	7.28177	7.69868	8.13752	8.59936	9.08528	9.59645	10.13404	10.69932	11.27357
14	7.98752	8.48326	9.00745	9.56159	10.14724	10.76606	11.41977	12.11018	12.83918	13.60876
15	9.26552	9.88300	10.53872	11.23487	11.97374	12.75778	13.58953	14.47166	15.40701	16.39855
16	10.74800	11.51369	12.33030	13.20097	14.12902	15.11797	16.17154	17.29364	18.48842	19.76025
17	12.46768	13.41345	14.42645	15.51114	16.67224	17.91479	19.24413	20.66589	22.18610	23.81111
18	14.46251	1562667	16.87895	18.22558	19.67324	21.22903	22.90051	24.69574	26.62332	28.69238
19	16.77651	18.20507	19.74837	21.41506	23.21443	25.15640	27.25161	29.51141	31.94798	34.57432
20	19.46075	21.20891	23.10559	25.16270	27.39302	29.81033	32.42941	35.26614	38.33758	41.66205

Table-1 continue

Future Value of ₹ 1.00

n/i	21.0	21.5	22.0	22.5	23.0	23.5	24.0	24.5	25.0	25.5
1	1.21000	1.21500	1.22000	1.22500	1.23000	1.23500	1.24000	1.24500	1.25000	1.25500
2	1.46410	1.47622	1.48840	1.50062	1.51290	1.52522	1.53760	1.55002	1.56250	1.57502
3	1.77156	1.79361	1.81585	1.83827	1.86087	1.88365	1.90662	1.92978	1.95312	1.97666
4	2.14359	2.17924	2.21533	2.25188	2.28887	2.32631	2.36421	2.40258	2.44141	2.48070
5	2.59374	2.64778	2.70271	2.75855	2.81531	2.87299	2.93162	3.99121	3.05176	3.11328
6	3.13843	3.21705	3.29730	3.37922	3.46283	3.54815	3.63521	3.72405	3.81470	3.90717
7	3.79750	3.90871	4.02271	4.13954	4.25928	4.38196	4.50767	4.63645	4.76837	4.90350
8	4.59497	4.74909	4.90771	5.07094	5.23891	5.41172	5.58951	5.77238	5.96046	6.15389
9	5.55992	5.77014	5.98740	6.21190	6.44386	6.68348	6.93099	7.18661	7.45058	7.72313
10	6.72750	7.01072	7.30463	7.60958	7.92594	8.25409	8.59442	8.94733	9.31322	9.69253
11	8.14027	8.51803	8.91165	9.32174	9.74891	10.19381	10.65708	11.13942	11.64153	12.16412
12	9.84973	10.34940	10.87221	11.41913	11.99116	12.58935	13.21478	13.86858	14.55191	15.26597
13	11.91817	12.57452	13.26410	13.98843	14.74913	15.54785	16.38633	17.26638	18.18989	19.15880
14	14.42099	15.27804	16.18220	17.13583	18.14143	19.20159	20.31905	21.49665	22.73736	24.04429
15	17.44940	18.56282	19.74228	20.99139	22.31395	23.71397	25.19562	26.76332	28.42170	30.17558
16	21.11377	22.55383	24.08558	25.71445	27.44616	29.28675	31.24257	33.32034	35.52712	37.87036
17	25.54766	27.40290	29.38441	31.50020	33.75878	36.16913	38.74078	41.48382	44.40890	47.52730
18	30.91267	33.29452	35.84897	38.58774	41.52330	44.66888	48.03857	51.64735	55.51113	59.64675
19	37.40433	40.45284	43.72575	47.26998	51.07365	55.16606	59.56783	64.30095	69.38891	74.85667

contd....

Table-1 continue

Future Value of ₹ 1.00

20	45.25924	49.15020	53.35761	57.90572	62.82059	68.13008	73.86410	80.05468	86.73613	93.94512
n/i	**26.0**	**26.5**	**27.0**	**27.5**	**28.0**	**28.5**	**29.0**	**29.5**	**30.0**	**30.5**
1	1.26000	1.26500	1.27000	1.27500	1.28000	1.28500	1.29000	1.29500	1.30000	1.30500
2	1.58760	1.60022	1.61290	1.62562	1.63840	1.65122	1.66410	1.67702	1.69000	1.70302
3	2.00038	2.02428	2.04838	2.07267	2.09715	2.12182	2.14669	2.17175	2.19700	2.22245
4	2.52047	2.56072	2.60145	2.64266	2.68435	2.72654	2.76923	2.81241	2.85610	2.90029
5	3.17580	3.23931	3.30384	3.36939	3.43597	3.50361	3.57230	3.64207	3.71293	3.78488
6	4.00150	4.09773	4.19587	4.29597	4.39805	4.50214	4.60827	4.71649	4.82681	4.93927
7	5.04189	5.18362	5.32876	5.47736	5.62950	5.78525	5.94467	6.10785	6.27485	6.44575
8	6.35279	6.55729	6.76752	6.98363	7.20576	7.43404	7.66863	7.90966	8.15730	8.41170
9	8.00451	8.29497	8.59475	8.90413	9.22337	9.55274	9.89253	10.24301	10.60450	10.97727
10	10.08568	10.49313	10.91533	11.35277	11.80591	12.27527	12.76136	13.26470	13.78584	14.32534
11	12.70796	13.27381	13.86247	14.47478	15.11157	15.77372	16.46215	17.17779	17.92160	18.69457
12	16.01203	16.79137	17.60534	18.45534	19.34280	20.26923	21.23618	22.24524	23.29807	24.39641
13	20.17515	21.24108	22.35878	23.53056	24.75879	26.04596	27.39467	28.80758	30.28749	31.83731
14	25.42069	26.86997	28.39565	30.00146	31.69125	33.46906	35.33912	37.30582	39.37374	41.54769
15	32.03007	33.99051	36.06248	38.25186	40.56480	43.00774	45.58746	48.31103	51.18586	54.21973
16	40.35789	42.99799	45.79935	48.77112	51.92294	55.26495	58.80783	62.56278	66.54161	70.75675
17	50.85094	54.39245	58.16517	62.18318	66.46136	71.01545	75.86209	81.01880	86.50410	92.33755
18	64.07218	68.80645	73.86976	79.28355	85.07053	91.25485	97.86210	104.91934	112.45532	120.50050
19	80.73095	87.04016	93.81460	101.08652	108.89028	117.26248	126.24210	135.87054	146.19191	157.25314
20	101.72099	110.10579	119.11453	128.88531	139.37955	150.68228	162.85230	175.95234	190.04947	205.21534

Table-1 continue

Future Value of ₹ 1.00

n/i	31.0	31.5	32.0	32.5	33.0	33.5	34.0	34.5	35.0	35.5
1	1.31000	1.31500	1.32000	1.32500	1.33000	1.33500	1.34000	1.34500	1.35000	1.35500
2	1.71610	1.72922	1.74240	1.75562	1.76890	1.78222	1.79560	1.80902	1.82250	1.83602
3	2.24809	2.27393	2.29997	2.32620	2.35264	2.37927	2.40610	2.43314	2.46037	2.48781
4	2.94500	2.99022	3.03596	3.08222	3.12901	3.17633	3.22418	3.27257	3.32151	3.37099
5	3.85795	3.93214	4.00746	4.08394	4.16158	4.24039	4.32040	4.40161	4.48403	4.56769
6	5.05391	5.17076	5.28985	5.41122	5.53490	5.66093	5.78933	5.92016	6.05344	6.18922
7	6.62062	6.79955	6.98260	7.16987	7.36142	7.55734	7.75771	7.96262	8.17215	8.38639
8	8.67302	8.94141	9.21704	9.50007	9.79068	10.08904	10.39533	10.70972	11.03240	11.39355
9	11.36164	11.75795	12.16649	12.58759	13.02161	13.46887	13.92974	14.40457	14.89374	15.39762
10	14.88376	15.46170	16.05976	16.67856	17.31874	17.98094	18.66585	19.37415	20.10655	20.86377
11	19.49773	20.33214	21.19889	22.09909	23.03392	24.00456	25.01224	26.05823	27.14384	28.27040
12	25.54203	26.73676	27.98253	29.28130	30.63511	32.04608	33.51640	35.04832	36.64418	38.30640
13	33.46005	35.15884	36.93694	38.79772	40.74470	42.78152	44.91197	47.13998	49.46964	51.90516
14	43.83267	46.23388	48.75675	51.40697	54.19045	57.11333	60.18204	63.40327	66.78401	70.33149
15	57.42079	60.79755	64.35891	68.11423	72.07329	76.24629	80.64393	85.27740	90.15841	95.29917
16	75.22124	79.94877	84.95376	90.25136	95.85748	101.06286	108.06286	114.69809	121.71385	129.13037
17	98.53982	105.13263	112.13896	119.58304	127.49044	135.88803	144.80422	154.26893	164.31370	174.97164
18	129.10417	181.79795	195.39090	158.44752	169.56228	181.41051	194.03765	207.49170	221.82348	237.08656
19	169.10417	181.79795	195.39090	209.94296	225.51782	242.18302	260.01044	279.07632	299.46169	321.25228
20	221.52645	239.06430	257.91598	278.17440	299.93869	323.31432	348.41398	375.35764	404.27326	435.29682

contd....

Table-1 continue

Future Value of ₹ 1.00

n/i	36.0	36.5	37.0	37.5	38.0	38.5	39.0	39.5	40.0	40.5
1	1.36000	1.36500	1.37000	1.37500	1.18000	1.38500	1.39000	1.39500	1.40000	1.40500
2	1.84960	1.86322	1.87690	1.89062	1.90440	1.91822	1.93210	1.94602	1.96000	1.97402
3	2.51546	2.54330	2.57135	2.59961	2.62807	2.65674	2.68562	2.71470	2.74400	2.77350
4	3.42102	3.47161	3.52275	3.57446	3.62674	3.67959	3.73301	3.78701	3.84160	3.89677
5	4.65259	4.73874	4.82617	4.91489	5.00490	5.09623	5.18888	5.28288	5.37824	5.47497
6	6.32752	6.46838	6.61185	6.75797	6.90676	7.05827	7.21255	7.36962	7.52953	7.69233
7	8.60542	8.82934	9.05824	9.29220	9.53133	9.77571	10.02544	10.28062	10.54135	10.80772
8	11.70337	12.05205	12.40979	12.77678	13.15323	13.53936	13.93536	14.34146	14.75788	15.18485
9	15.91659	16.45105	17.00141	17.56807	18.15146	18.75201	19.37015	20.00634	20.66104	21.33471
10	21.64656	22.45568	23.29193	24.15610	25.04901	25.97153	26.92451	27.90885	28.92545	29.97526
11	29.43932	30.65201	31.90994	33.21463	34.56764	35.97056	37.42507	38.93284	40.49563	42.11524
12	40.03747	41.83999	43.71662	45.67012	47.70334	49.81923	52.02084	54.31131	56.69388	59.17191
13	54.45096	57.11158	59.89177	62.79641	65.83060	6899963	72.30897	75.76427	79.37142	83.13653
14	74.05330	77.95730	82.05172	86.34506	90.84623	95.56448	100.50946	105.69115	111.11999	116.80682
15	100.71248	106.41171	112.41085	118.72445	125.36779	132.35679	139.70814	147.43914	155.56797	164.11357
16	136.96897	145.25198	154.00285	163.24611	173.00754	183.31415	194.19431	205.67759	217.79515	230.57956
17	186.27779	198.26894	210.98390	224.46340	238.75039	253.89008	269.93007	286.92023	304.91319	323.96426
18	253.33778	270.63709	289.04792	308.63716	329.47552	351.63774	375.20278	400.25370	426.87845	455.16976
19	344.53936	369.41961	395.99564	424.37607	454.67620	487.01825	521.53185	558.35388	597.62980	639.51347
20	468.57351	504.25774	542.51400	583.51707	627.45312	674.52024	724.92923	778.90363	836.68167	898.51638

TABLE-2

Present Value of ₹ 1.00*

n/i	1.0	1.5	2.0	2.5	3.0	3.5	4.0	4.5	5.0	5.5
1	0.99010	0.98522	0.98039	0.97561	0.97087	0.96618	0.96154	0.95694	0.95238	0.94787
2	0.98030	0.97066	0.96117	0.95181	0.94260	0.93351	0.92456	0.91573	0.90703	0.89845
3	0.97059	0.95632	0.94232	0.92860	0.91514	0.90194	0.88900	0.87630	0.86384	0.85161
4	0.96098	0.94218	0.92385	0.90595	0.88849	0.87114	0.85480	0.83856	0.82270	0.80722
5	0.95147	0.92826	0.90573	0.88385	0.86261	0.84197	0.82193	0.80245	0.78353	0.76513
6	0.94205	0.91454	0.88797	0.86230	0.83748	0.81350	0.79031	0.76790	0.74622	0.72525
7	0.93272	0.90103	0.87056	0.84127	0.81309	0.78599	0.75992	0.73483	0.71068	0.68744
8	0.92348	0.88771	0.85349	0.82075	0.78941	0.75941	0.73069	0.70319	0.67684	0.65160
9	0.91434	0.87459	0.83676	0.80073	0.76642	0.73373	0.70259	0.67290	0.64461	0.61763
10	0.90529	0.86167	0.82035	0.78120	0.74409	0.70892	0.67556	0.64393	0.61391	0.58543
11	0.89632	0.84893	0.80426	0.76214	0.72242	0.68495	0.64958	0.61620	0.58468	0.55491
12	0.88745	0.83639	0.78849	0.74356	0.70138	0.66178	0.62460	0.58966	0.55684	0.52598
13	0.87866	0.82403	0.77303	0.72542	0.68095	0.63940	0.60057	0.56427	0.53032	0.49856
14	0.86996	0.81185	0.75788	0.70773	0.66112	0.61778	0.57748	0.53997	0.50507	0.47257
15	0.86135	0.79985	0.74301	0.69047	0.64186	0.59689	0.55526	0.51672	0.48102	0.44793
16	0.85282	0.78803	0.72845	0.67362	0.62317	0.57671	0.53391	0.49447	0.45811	0.42458
17	0.84438	0.77639	0.71416	0.65720	0.60502	0.55720	0.51337	0.47318	0.43630	0.40245
18	0.83602	0.76491	0.70016	0.64117	0.58739	0.53836	0.49363	0.45280	0.41552	0.38147
19	0.82774	0.75361	0.68643	0.62553	0.57029	0.52016	0.47464	0.43330	0.39573	0.36158
20	0.81954	0.74247	0.67297	0.61027	0.55368	0.50257	0.45639	0.41464	0.37689	0.34273

* n = number of time periods; i = rate of interest in per cent.

contd....

Table-2 continue

Present Value of ₹ 1.00*

n/i	6.0	6.5	7.0	7.5	8.0	8.45	9.0	9.5	10.0	10.5
1	0.94340	0.93897	0.93458	0.93023	0.92593	0.92166	0.91743	0.91324	0.90909	0.90498
2	0.89000	0.88166	0.87344	0.86533	0.85734	0.84946	0.84168	0.83401	0.83645	0.81898
3	0.83962	0.82785	0.81630	0.80496	0.79383	0.78291	0.77218	0.76165	0.75131	0.74116
4	0.79209	0.77732	0.76290	0.74880	0.73503	0.72157	0.70843	0.69557	0.68301	0.67073
5	0.74726	0.72988	0.71299	0.69656	0.68058	0.66505	0.64993	0.63523	0.62092	0.60700
6	0.70496	0.68533	0.66634	0.64796	0.63017	0.61295	0.59627	0.58012	0.56447	0.54932
7	0.66506	0.64351	0.62275	0.60275	0.58349	0.56493	0.54703	0.52979	0.51316	0.47912
8	0.62741	0.60423	0.58201	0.56070	0.54027	0.52067	0.50187	0.48382	0.46651	0.44989
9	0.59190	0.56735	0.54393	0.52158	0.50025	0.47988	0.46043	0.44185	0.42410	0.40714
10	0.55839	0.53273	0.50835	0.48519	0.46319	0.44229	0.42241	0.40351	0.38554	0.36845
11	0.52679	0.50021	0.47509	0.45134	0.42888	0.40764	0.38753	0.36851	0.35049	0.33344
12	0.49697	0.46968	0.44401	0.41985	0.39711	0.37570	0.35553	0.33654	0.31863	0.30175
13	0.46884	0.44102	0.41496	0.39056	0.36770	0.34627	0.32618	0.30734	0.28966	0.27308
14	0.44230	0.41410	0.38782	0.36331	0.34046	0.31914	0.29925	0.28067	0.26333	0.24713
15	0.41727	0.38883	0.36245	0.33797	0.31524	0.29414	0.27454	0.25632	0.23939	0.22365
16	0.39365	0.36510	0.33873	0.31439	0.29189	0.27110	0.25187	0.23409	0.21763	0.20240
17	0.37136	0.34281	0.31657	0.29245	0.27027	0.24986	0.23107	0.21378	0.19784	0.18316
18	0.35034	0.32189	0.29586	0.27205	0.25025	0.23028	0.21199	0.19523	0.17986	0.16576
19	0.33051	0.30224	0.27651	0.25307	0.23171	0.21224	0.19449	0.17829	0.16351	0.15001
20	0.31180	0.28380	0.25842	0.23541	0.21455	0.19562	0.17843	0.16282	0.14864	0.13575

Table-2 continue

Present Value of ₹ 1.00*

n/i	11.0	11.5	12.0	12.5	13.0	13.5	14.0	14.5	15.0	15.5
1	0.90090	0.89686	0.89286	0.88889	0.88496	0.88106	0.87719	0.87336	0.86957	0.86580
2	0.81162	0.80436	0.79719	0.79012	0.78315	0.77626	0.76947	0.76276	0.75614	0.74961
3	0.73119	0.72140	0.71178	0.70233	0.69305	0.68393	0.67497	0.66617	0.65752	0.64901
4	0.65873	0.64699	0.63552	0.62430	0.61332	0.60258	0.59208	0.58181	0.57175	0.56192
5	0.59345	0.58026	0.56743	0.55493	0.54276	0.53091	0.51937	0.50813	0.49718	0.48651
6	0.53464	0.52042	0.50663	0.49372	0.48032	0.46776	0.45559	0.44378	0.43233	0.42122
7	0.48166	0.46674	0.45235	0.43846	0.42506	0.41213	0.39964	0.38758	0.37594	0.36469
8	0.43393	0.41860	0.40388	0.38974	0.37616	0.36311	0.35056	0.33850	0.32690	0.31575
9	0.39092	0.37543	0.36061	0.34644	0.33288	0.31992	0.30751	0.29563	0.28426	0.27338
10	0.35218	0.33671	0.32197	0.30795	0.29459	0.28187	0.26974	0.25819	0.24718	0.23669
11	0.31728	0.30198	0.28748	0.27373	0.26070	0.24834	0.23662	0.22550	0.21494	0.20493
12	0.28584	0.27083	0.25668	0.24332	0.23071	0.21880	0.20756	0.17694	0.18691	0.17743
13	0.25751	0.24290	0.22917	0.21628	0.20416	0.19278	0.18207	0.17200	0.16253	0.15362
14	0.23199	0.21785	0.20462	0.19225	0.18068	0.16985	0.15971	0.15022	0.14133	0.13300
15	0.20900	0.19538	0.18270	0.17089	0.15989	0.14964	0.14010	0.13120	0.12289	0.11515
16	0.18829	0.17523	0.16312	0.15190	0.14150	0.13185	0.12289	0.11458	0.10686	0.09970
17	0.16963	0.15715	0.14564	0.13502	0.12522	0.11616	0.10780	0.10007	0.09293	0.08632
18	0.15282	0.14095	0.13004	0.12002	0.11081	0.10235	0.09456	0.08740	0.08081	0.07474
19	0.13768	0.12641	0.11611	0.10668	0.09806	0.09017	0.08295	0.07633	0.07027	0.06471
20	0.12403	0.11337	0.10367	0.09483	0.08678	0.07945	0.07276	0.06666	0.06110	0.05602

contd....

Table-2 continue

Present Value of ₹ 1.00*

n/i	16.0	16.5	17.0	17.5	18.0	18.5	19.0	19.5	20.0	20.5
1	0.86207	0.85837	0.85470	0.85106	0.84746	0.84388	0.84034	0.83682	0.83333	0.82988
2	0.74316	0.73680	0.73051	0.72431	0.71818	0.71214	0.70616	0.70027	0.6944	0.68869
3	0.64066	0.63244	0.62437	0.61643	0.60863	0.60096	0.59342	0.58600	0.57870	0.57153
4	0.55229	0.54287	0.53365	0.52462	0.51579	0.50714	0.49867	0.49038	0.48225	0.47430
5	0.47611	0.466598	0.45611	0.44649	0.43711	0.42797	0.41905	0.41036	0.40188	0.39361
6	0.41044	0.399999	0.38984	0.37999	0.37043	0.36115	0.35214	0.34339	0.33490	0.32665
7	0.35383	0.34334	0.33320	0.32340	0.31393	0.30477	0.29592	0.28736	0.2908	0.27108
8	0.30503	0.29471	0.28478	0.27523	0.26604	0.25719	0.24867	0.24047	0.23257	0.22496
9	0.26295	0.25297	0.24340	0.23424	0.22546	0.217704	0.20897	0.20123	0.19381	0.18669
10	0.22668	0.21714	0.20804	0.19935	0.19106	0.18315	0.17560	0.16839	0.16151	0.15493
11	0.19542	0.18639	0.17781	0.16966	0.16192	0.15456	0.14757	0.14091	0.13459	0.12857
12	0.16846	0.15999	0.15197	0.14439	0.13722	0.13043	0.12400	0.11792	0.11216	0.10670
13	0.14523	0.13733	0.12989	0.12289	0.11629	0.11007	0.10421	0.09868	0.09346	0.08855
14	0.12520	0.11788	0.11102	0.10459	0.09855	0.09288	0.8757	0.08258	0.07789	0.07348
15	0.10793	0.10118	0.09489	0.08901	0.08352	0.07838	0.07359	0.06910	0.06491	0.06098
16	0.09304	0.08685	0.08110	0.07575	0.07078	0.06615	0.06184	0.05782	0.05409	0.05061
17	0.08021	0.08685	0.08110	0.07575	0.07078	0.06615	0.06184	0.05782	0.05409	0.05061
18	0.06914	0.06399	0.05925	0.05487	0.05083	0.04711	0.04367	0.04049	0.03756	0.03485
19	0.05961	0.05493	0.05064	0.04670	0.04308	0.03975	0.03670	0.3389	0.03130	0.02892
20	0.05139	0.04715	0.04328	0.03974	0.03651	0.03355	0.03084	0.02836	0.02608	0.02400

Table-2 continue

Present Value of ₹ 1.00*

n/i	21.0	21.5	22.0	22.5	23.0	23.5	24.0	24.5	25.0	25.5
1	0.82645	0.82305	0.81967	0.81633	0.81301	0.80972	0.80645	0.80321	0.80000	0.79681
2	0.68301	0.67740	0.67186	0.66639	0.66098	0.65564	0.65036	0.64515	0.64000	0.63491
3	0.56447	0.55753	0.55071	0.54399	0.53738	0.53088	0.52449	0.51819	0.51200	0.50590
4	0.46651	0.45888	0.45140	0.44407	0.43690	0.42987	0.42297	0.41622	0.40960	0.40311
5	0.38554	0.37768	0.37000	0.36251	0.35520	0.34807	0.34111	0.33431	0.32768	0.32120
6	0.31863	0.31084	0.30328	0.29593	0.28878	0.28184	0.27509	0.26852	0.26214	0.25594
7	0.26333	0.25584	0.24859	0.24157	0.23478	0.22821	0.22184	0.21568	0.20972	0.20394
8	0.21763	0.21057	0.20376	0.19720	0.19088	0.18478	0.17891	0.17324	0.16777	0.16250
9	0.17986	0.17331	0.16702	0.16098	0.15519	0.14962	0.14428	0.13915	0.13422	0.12948
10	0.14864	0.14264	0.13690	0.13141	0.12617	0.12115	0.11635	0.11177	0.10733	0.10317
11	0.12285	0.11740	0.11221	0.10728	0.10258	0.09810	0.09383	0.08977	0.08590	0.08221
12	0.10153	0.09662	0.09198	0.08757	0.08339	0.07943	0.07567	0.07211	0.06872	0.06551
13	0.08391	0.07953	0.07539	0.07149	0.06780	0.06432	0.06103	0.05792	0.05498	0.05220
14	0.06934	0.06545	0.06180	0.05836	0.05512	0.05208	0.04921	0.04652	0.04398	0.04159
15	0.05731	0.05387	0.05065	0.04764	0.04482	0.04217	0.03969	0.03736	0.03518	0.03314
16	0.04736	0.04434	0.04152	0.03889	0.03643	0.03415	0.03201	0.03001	0.02815	0.02641
17	0.03914	0.03649	0.03403	0.03175	0.02962	0.02765	0.02581	0.02411	0.02252	0.02104
18	0.03235	0.03649	0.03403	0.03175	0.02962	0.02765	0.02581	0.02411	0.02252	0.02104
19	0.02673	0.02472	0.02286	0.02116	0.01958	0.01813	0.01979	0.01555	0.01441	0.01336
20	0.02209	0.02035	0.01874	0.01727	0.01592	0.01468	0.01354	0.01249	0.01153	0.01064

contd....

Table-2 continue

Present Value of ₹ 1.00*

n/i/	26.0	26.5	27.0	27.5	28.0	28.5	29.0	29.5	30.0	30.5
1	0.79365	0.79051	0.78740	0.78431	0.78125	0.77821	0.77519	0.77220	0.76923	0.76628
2	0.62988	0.62491	0.62000	0.61515	0.61035	0.60561	0.60093	0.59629	0.59172	0.58719
3	0.49991	0.49400	0.48819	0.48247	0.47684	0.47129	0.46583	0.46046	0.45517	0.44995
4	0.39675	0.39052	0.38440	0.37841	0.37253	0.36676	0.36111	0.35557	0.35013	0.34479
5	0.31488	0.30871	0.30268	0.29679	0.29104	0.28542	0.27993	0.27457	0.26933	0.26421
6	0.24991	0.24404	0.23833	0.23278	0.22737	0.22212	0.21700	0.21202	0.20718	0.20246
7	0.19834	0.19292	0.18766	0.18257	0.17764	0.17285	0.16822	0.16372	0.15937	0.15514
8	0.15741	0.15250	0.14776	0.14319	0.13878	0.13452	0.13040	0.12643	0.12259	0.11888
9	0.12493	0.12056	0.11635	0.11231	0.10842	0.10468	0.10109	0.09763	0.09430	0.09110
10	0.09915	0.09530	0.09161	0.08808	0.08470	0.08146	0.07836	0.07539	0.07254	0.06981
11	0.07869	0.07534	0.07214	0.06909	0.06617	0.06340	0.06075	0.05821	0.05580	0.05349
12	0.06245	0.05955	0.05680	0.05418	0.05170	0.04934	0.04709	0.04495	0.04292	0.04099
13	0.04957	0.04708	0.04473	0.04250	0.04039	0.03839	0.03650	0.03471	0.03302	0.03141
14	0.03934	0.03722	0.03522	0.03333	0.03155	0.02988	0.02830	0.02681	0.02540	0.02407
15	0.03122	0.02942	0.02773	0.02614	0.02465	0.02325	0.02194	0.02070	0.01954	0.01844
16	0.02478	0.02326	0.02183	0.02030	0.01926	0.01809	0.01700	0.01598	0.01503	0.01413
17	0.01967	0.01838	0.01719	0.01608	0.01505	0.01408	0.01318	0.01234	0.01156	0.01083
18	0.01561	0.01453	0.01354	0.01261	0.01175	0.01096	0.01022	0.00953	0.00889	0.00830
19	0.01239	0.01149	0.01066	0.00989	0.00918	0.00853	0.00792	0.00736	0.00684	0.00636
20	0.00983	0.00908	0.00839	0.00776	0.00717	0.00664	0.00614	0.00568	0.00526	0.00487

Table-2 continue

Present Value of ₹ 1.00*

n/i	31.0	31.5	32.0	32.5	33.0	33.5	34.0	34.5	35.0	35.5
1	0.76336	0.76046	0.75758	0.75472	0.75188	0.74906	0.74627	0.74349	0.74074	0.73801
2	0.58272	0.57829	0.57392	0.56960	0.56532	0.56110	0.55692	0.55278	0.54870	0.54465
3	0.44482	0.43977	0.43479	0.42989	0.42505	0.42030	0.41561	0.41099	0.40644	0.40196
4	0.33956	0.33442	0.32939	0.32444	0.31959	0.31483	0.31016	0.30557	0.30107	0.29665
5	0.25921	0.25431	0.24953	0.24486	0.24029	0.23583	0.23146	0.22719	0.22301	0.21893
6	0.19787	0.19340	0.18904	0.18480	0.18067	0.17665	0.17273	0.16891	0.16520	0.16157
7	0.15104	0.14707	0.14321	0.13947	0.13584	0.13232	0.12890	0.12559	0.12237	0.11924
8	0.11530	0.11184	0.10849	0.10526	0.10214	0.09912	0.09620	0.09337	0.09064	0.08800
9	0.08802	0.08505	0.08219	0.07944	0.07680	0.07425	0.07179	0.06942	0.06714	0.06495
10	0.06719	0.06468	0.06227	0.05996	0.05774	0.05561	0.05357	0.05162	0.04974	0.04793
11	0.05129	0.04918	0.04717	0.04525	0.04341	0.04166	0.03998	0.03838	0.03684	0.03537
12	0.03915	0.03740	0.03574	0.03415	0.03264	0.03121	0.02984	0.02853	0.02729	0.02611
13	0.02989	0.02844	0.02707	0.02577	0.02454	0.02337	0.02227	0.02121	0.02021	0.01927
14	0.02281	0.02163	0.02051	0.01945	0.01845	0.01751	0.01662	0.01577	0.01497	0.01422
15	0.01742	0.01645	0.01554	0.01468	0.01387	0.01312	0.01240	0.01173	0.01109	0.01049
16	0.01329	0.01251	0.01177	0.01108	0.01043	0.00982	0.00925	0.00872	0.00822	0.00774
17	0.01015	0.00951	0.00892	0.00836	0.00784	0.00736	0.00691	0.00648	0.00609	0.00572
18	0.00775	0.00723	0.00676	0.00631	0.00590	0.00551	0.00515	0.00481	0.00451	0.00422
19	0.00591	0.00550	0.00512	0.00476	0.00443	0.00413	0.00385	0.00358	0.00334	0.00311
20	0.00451	0.00418	0.00388	0.00359	0.00333	0.00309	0.00287	0.00266	0.00247	0.00230

contd....

Table-2 continue

Present Value of ₹ 1.00*

n/i	36.0	36.5	37.0	37.5	38.0	38.5	39.0	30.5	40.0	40.5
1	0.73529	0.73260	0.72993	0.72727	0.71464	0.72202	0.71942	0.71685	0.71429	0.71174
2	0.54066	0.53670	0.53279	0.52893	0.52510	0.52132	0.51757	0.51387	0.51020	0.50658
3	0.39754	0.39319	0.38890	0.38467	0.38051	0.37640	0.37235	0.36836	0.36443	0.36055
4	0.29231	0.28805	0.28387	0.27976	0.27573	0.27177	0.26788	0.26406	0.26031	0.25662
5	0.21493	0.21103	0.20720	0.20346	0.19980	0.19622	0.19272	0.18929	0.18593	0.18265
6	0.15804	0.15460	0.15124	0.14797	0.14479	0.14168	0.13865	0.13569	0.13281	0.13000
7	0.11621	0.11326	0.11040	0.10762	0.10492	0.10229	0.09975	0.09727	0..09486	0.09353
8	0.08545	0.08297	0.08058	0.07827	0.07603	0.07386	0.07176	0.06973	0.06776	0.06586
9	0.06283	0.06079	0.05882	0.05692	0.05509	0.05333	0.05163	0.04998	0.04840	0.04687
10	0.04620	0.04453	0.04293	0.04140	0.03992	0.03850	0.03714	0.03583	0.03457	0.03336
11	0.03397	0.03262	0.03134	0.03011	0.02893	0.02780	0.02672	0.02569	0.02469	0.02374
12	0.02498	0.02390	0.02287	0.02190	0.02096	0.02007	0.01922	0.01841	0.01764	0.01690
13	0.01837	0.01751	0.01670	0.01592	0.01519	0.01449	0.01383	0.01320	0.01260	0.01203
14	0.01350	0.01285	0.01219	0.01158	0.01101	0.01046	0.00995	0.00946	0.00900	0.00856
15	0.00993	0.00940	0.00890	0.00842	0.00798	0.00756	0.00761	0.00678	0.00643	0.00609
16	0.00730	0.00688	0.00649	0.00613	0.00578	0.00546	0.00515	0.00486	0.00459	0.00434
17	0.00537	0.00504	0.00474	0.00446	0.00419	0.00394	0.00370	0.00349	0.00328	0.00309
18	0.00395	0.00369	0.00346	0.00324	0.00304	0.00284	0.00267	0.00250	0.00234	0.00220
19	0.00290	0.00271	0.00253	0.00236	0.00220	0.00205	0.00192	0.00179	0.00167	0.00156
20	0.00213	0.00198	0.00184	0.00171	0.00159	0.00148	0.00138	0.00128	0.00120	0.00111

TABLE-3

Future Value of an Annuity of ₹ 1.00*

n/i	1.0	1.5	2.0	2.5	3.0	3.5	4.0	4.5	5.0	5.5
1	1.00000	1.00000	1.00000	1.00000	1.00000	1.00000	1.00000	1.00000	1.00000	1.00000
2	2.01000	2.01500	2.02000	2.02500	2.03000	2.03500	2.04000	2.04500	2.05000	2.05500
3	3.03010	3.04522	3.06040	3.07562	3.09090	3.10622	3.12160	3.13702	3.15250	3.16802
4	4.06040	4.09090	4.12161	4.15252	4.18363	4.21494	4.24646	4.27819	4.31012	4.34227
5	5.10100	5.15227	5.20404	5.25633	5.30914	5.36247	5.41632	5.47071	5.52563	5.58109
6	6.15201	6.22955	6.30812	6.38774	6.46841	6.55015	6.63298	6.71689	6.80191	6.88805
7	7.21353	7.32299	7.43428	7.54743	7.66246	7.77941	7.89829	8.01915	8.14201	8.26689
8	8.28567	8.43284	8.58297	8.73612	8.89234	9.05169	9.21423	9.38001	9.54911	9.72157
9	9.36853	9.55933	9.75463	9.95452	10.15911	10.36850	10.58279	10.80211	10.02656	11.25626
10	10.46221	10.70272	10.94972	11.20338	11.46388	11.73139	12.00611	12.28821	12.57789	12.87535
11	11.56683	11.86326	12.16871	12.48347	12.80779	13.14199	13.48635	13.84118	14.20679	14.58350
12	12.68250	13.04121	13.41209	13.79555	14.19203	14.60196	15.02580	15.46403	15.91713	16.38559
13	13.80933	14.23683	14.68033	15.14044	15.61779	16.11303	16.62684	17.15991	17.71298	18.28680
14	14.94742	15.45038	15.97394	16.51895	17.08632	17.67699	18.29191	18.93211	19.59863	20.29257
15	16.09689	16.68214	17.29342	17.93192	18.59891	19.29568	20.02359	20.78405	21.57856	22.40866
16	17.25786	17.93237	18.63928	19.38022	20.15688	20.97103	21.82453	22.71933	23.65749	24.64114
17	18.43044	19.20135	20.01207	20.86473	21.76158	22.70501	23.69751	24.74170	25.84036	26.99640
18	19.61474	20.48937	21.41231	22.38635	23.41443	24.49969	25.64541	26.85508	28.13238	29.48120
19	20.81089	21.79671	22.84056	23.94600	25.11686	26.35718	27.67123	29.06356	30.53900	32.10267
20	22.01900	23.12366	24.29737	25.54465	26.87037	28.27968	29.77807	31.37142	33.06595	34.86831

*n = number of time periods : i = rate of interest in per cent.

contd....

Table-3 continue

Future Value of an Annuity of ₹ 1.00*

n/i	6.0	6.5	7.0	7.5	8.0	8.5	9.0	9.5	10.0	10.5
1	1.00000	1.00000	1.00000	1.00000	1.00000	1.00000	1.00000	1.00000	1.00000	1.00000
2	2.06000	2.06500	2.07000	2.07500	2.08000	2.08500	2.09000	2.09500	2.10000	2.10500
3	3.18360	1.19922	3.21490	3.23062	3.24640	3.26222	3.27810	3.29402	3.31000	3.32602
4	4.37462	4.40717	4.43994	4.47292	4.50611	4.53951	4.57313	4.60696	4.64100	4.67526
5	5.63709	5.69364	5.75074	5.80839	5.86660	5.92537	5.98471	6.04462	6.10510	6.16616
6	6.97532	7.06373	7.15329	7.24402	7.33593	7.42903	7.52333	7.61886	7.71561	7.81361
7	8.39384	8.52287	8.65402	8.78732	8.92280	9.06050	9.20043	9.34265	9.48717	9.63403
8	9.89747	10.07686	10.25980	10.44637	10.63663	10.83064	11.02847	11.23020	11.43589	11.64561
9	11.49132	11.73185	11.97799	12.22985	12.48756	12.75124	13.02104	13.29707	13.57948	13.86840
10	13.18079	13.49442	13.81645	14.14709	14.48656	14.83510	15.19293	15.56029	15.93742	16.32458
11	14.97164	15.37156	15.78360	16.20812	16.64549	17.09608	17.56029	18.03852	18.53117	19.03866
12	16.86994	17.37071	17.88845	18.42373	18.97713	1954925	20.14072	20.75217	21.38428	22.03772
13	18.88214	19.49981	20.14064	20.80551	2149530	22.21093	22.95338	23.72363	24.52271	25.35168
14	21.01506	21.76729	22.55049	23.36592	24.21492	25.09886	26.01919	26.97738	27.97498	29.01360
15	23.27597	24.18217	25.12902	26.11836	27.15211	28.23227	29.36091	30.54023	31.77248	33.06003
16	25.67252	26.75401	27.88805	29.07724	30.32428	31.63201	33.00339	34.44155	35.94973	37.53133
17	28.21287	29.49302	30.84021	32.25803	33.75022	35.32073	36.97370	38.71349	40.54470	42.47212
18	30.90565	32.41006	33.99903	35.67738	37.45024	39.32299	41.30133	43.39127	45.59917	47.93169
19	33.75998	35.51672	37.37896	39.35318	41.44626	4366544	46.01845	48.51344	51.15908	53.96452
20	36.78558	38.82530	40.99549	43.30467	45.76196	48.37701	51.16011	54.12222	57.27499	60.63080

Table-3 continue

Future Value of an Annuity of ₹ 1.00*

n/i	11.0	11.5	12.0	12.5	13.0	13.5	14.0	14.4	15.0	15.5
1	1.00000	1.00000	1.00000	1.00000	1.00000	1.00000	1.00000	1.00000	1.00000	1.00000
2	2.11000	2.11500	2.12000	2.12500	2.13000	2.13500	2.14000	2.14500	2.15000	2.15500
3	3.34210	3.35822	3.37440	3.39062	3.40690	3.42322	3.43960	3.45602	3.47250	3.48902
4	4.70973	4.74442	4.77933	4.81445	4.84980	4.88536	4.92114	4.95715	4.99337	5.02982
5	6.22780	6.29003	6.35285	6.41626	6.48027	6.54488	6.61010	6.67593	6.74238	6.80945
6	7.91286	8.01338	8.11519	8.21829	8.32271	8.42844	8.53552	8.64395	8.75374	8.86491
7	9.78327	9.93492	10.08901	10.24558	10.40466	10.56628	10.73049	10.89732	11.06680	11.23897
8	11.85943	12.07744	12.29969	12.52628	12.75726	12.99273	13.23276	13.47743	13.72682	13.98101
9	14.16397	14.46634	14.77566	15.09206	15.41571	15.74675	16.08535	16.43165	16.78584	17.14807
10	16.72201	17.12997	17.54873	17.97857	18.41975	18.87256	19.33729	19.81424	20.30372	20.80602
11	19.56143	20.09992	20.65458	21.22589	21.81432	22.42036	23.04451	23.68731	24.34927	25.03095
12	22.71318	23.41141	24.13313	24.87912	25.65018	26.44710	27.27074	28.12197	29.00166	29.91075
13	26.21163	27.10372	28.02911	28.98901	29.98470	31.01746	32.08865	33.19965	34.35191	35.54691
14	30.09491	31.22065	32.39260	33.61264	34.88271	36.20482	37.58106	39.01360	40.50470	42.05668
15	34.40535	35.81102	37.27971	38.81422	40.41746	42.09247	43.84241	45.67057	47.58041	49.57547
16	39.18994	40.92929	42.75327	44.66599	46.67173	48.77495	50.98034	53.29280	55.71747	58.25967
17	44.50085	46.63616	48.88367	51.24924	53.73906	56.35957	59.11759	62.02026	65.07508	68.28991
18	50.39592	52.99931	55.74971	58.65540	61.72513	64.96811	68.39405	72.01320	75.83635	79.87485
19	56.93947	60.09423	63,43967	66.98732	70.74940	74.73880	78.96922	83.45511	88.21180	93.25545
20	64.20282	68.00507	72.05243	76.36073	80.94682	85.82824	91.02491	96.55610	102.44357	108.71004

contd....

Table-3 continue

Future Value of an Annuity of ₹ 1.00*

n/i	16.0	16.5	17.0	17.5	18.0	18.5	19.0	19.5	20.0	20.5
1	1.00000	1.00000	1.00000	1.00000	1.00000	1.00000	1.00000	1.00000	1.00000	1.00000
2	2.16000	2.16500	2.17000	2.17500	2.18000	2.18500	2.19000	2.19500	1.20000	2.20500
3	3.50560	3.52222	3.53890	3.55562	3.57240	3.58922	3.60610	3.62302	3.64000	3.65702
4	5.06650	5.10339	5.14051	5.17786	5.21543	5.25323	5.29126	5.32951	5.36800	5.40671
5	6.87714	6.94545	7.01440	7.08398	7.15421	7.22508	7.29660	7.36877	7.44160	7.51509
6	8.97748	9.09145	9.20685	9.32368	9.44197	9.56172	9.68295	9.80568	9.92992	10.05568
7	11.41387	11.59154	11.77201	11.95533	12.14152	12.33064	12.52271	12.71779	12.91590	13.11710
8	14.24009	14.50414	14.77325	15.04751	15.32699	15.61180	15.90203	16.19775	16.49908	16.80610
9	17.51851	17.89733	18.28471	18.68082	19.08585	19.49999	19.92341	20.35632	20.79890	21.25135
10	21.32147	21.85039	22.39311	22.94996	23.52131	24.10748	24.70886	25.32580	25.95868	26.60788
11	25.73290	26.45570	27.19993	27.96621	28.75514	29.56737	30.40354	31.26433	32.15041	33.06250
12	30.85016	31.82089	32.32392	33.86029	34.93106	36.03733	37.18021	38.36087	39.58049	40.84031
13	2678619	38.07133	39.40399	40.78584	42.21865	43.70423	45.24445	46.84124	48.49659	50.21257
14	43.67198	45.35310	47.10266	48.92336	50.81801	52.78952	54.84090	56.97528	59.19591	61.50614
15	51.65949	53.83636	56.11012	58.48495	60.96525	63.55557	66.26067	69.08546	72.03509	75.11490
16	60.92501	63.71936	66.64883	69.71982	72.93899	76.31335	79.85019	83.55712	87.44210	91.51345
17	71.67301	75.23305	78.97913	82.92078	87.06801	91.43132	96.02173	100.85076	105.93052	111.27371
18	84.14069	88.64650	93.40559	98.43192	103.75025	109.34611	115.26585	121.51665	128.11662	135.08481
19	98.60320	104.27318	110.28453	116.65750	123.41349	130.57514	138.16636	146.21239	154.73994	163.77719
20	115.37971	122.47825	130.03290	138.07256	146.62792	155.73153	165.41797	175.72381	186.68792	198.35151

Table-3 continue

Future Value of an Annuity of ₹ 1.00

n/i	21.0	21.5	22.0	22.5	23.0	23.5	24.0	24.5	25.0	25.5
1	1.00000	1.00000	1.00000	1.00000	1.00000	1.00000	1.00000	1.00000	1.00000	1.00000
2	2.21000	2.21500	2.22000	2.22500	2.23000	2.23500	2.24000	2.24500	2.25000	2.25500
3	3.67410	3.69122	3.70840	3.72562	3.74290	3.76022	3.77760	3.79502	3.81250	3.83002
4	5.44566	5.48484	5.52425	5.56389	5.60377	5.64388	5.68422	5.72481	5.76562	5.80668
5	7.58925	7.66408	7.73958	7.81577	7.89263	7.97019	8.04844	8.12738	8.20703	8.28738
6	10.18299	10.31185	10.44229	10.57431	10.70794	10.84318	10.98006	11.11859	11.25879	11.40067
7	13.32142	13.52890	13.73959	13.95353	14.17076	14.39133	14.61528	14.84265	15.07348	15.30784
8	17.11892	17.43762	17.76230	18.09308	18.43004	18.77329	19.12294	19.47909	19.84186	20.21133
9	21.71389	22.18670	22.67001	23.16402	23.66895	24.18502	24.71245	25.25147	25.80232	26.36522
10	27.27381	27.95684	28.65741	29.37592	30.11280	30.86849	31.64343	32.43808	33.25290	34.08835
11	34.00130	34.96757	35.96204	36.98550	38.03875	39.12259	40.23786	41.38541	42.56612	43.78088
12	42.14158	43.48559	44.87369	46.30724	47.78766	49.31639	50.89494	52.52483	54.20765	55.94501
13	51.99131	53.83499	55.74590	57.72636	59.77882	61.90575	64.10972	66.39341	68.75956	71.21098
14	63.90948	66.40951	69.00999	71.71479	74.52795	77.45359	80.49605	83.65979	86.94945	90.36978
15	78.33047	81.68756	85.19219	88.85062	92.66937	69.65518	100.81510	105.15644	10968680	114.41407
16	95.77987	100.25038	104.93447	109.84200	114.98332	120.36915	126.01072	131.91976	138.10850	144.58965
17	116.89364	122.80420	129.02004	135.55645	142.42948	149.65589	157.25329	165.24010	173.63562	182.46001
18	142.44130	150.20711	158.40445	167.05664	176.18826	185.82502	195.99407	206.72391	218.04452	229.98730
19	173.35396	183.50163	194.25342	205.64438	217.71155	230.49390	244.03264	258.37126	273.55564	289.63405
20	210.75829	223.95447	237.98917	252.91436	268.78520	285.65995	303.60047	322.67220	342.94455	364.49072

contd....

Table-3 continue

Future Value of an Annuity of ₹ 1.00*

n/i	26.0	26.5	27.0	27.5	28.0	28.5	29.0	29.5	30.0	30.5
1	1.00000	1.00000	1.00000	1.00000	1.00000	1.00000	1.00000	1.00000	1.00000	1.00000
2	2.26000	2.26500	2.27000	2.27500	2.28000	2.28500	2.29000	2.29500	2.30000	2.30500
3	3.84760	3.86522	3.88290	3.90092	3.91840	3.93622	3.95410	3.97202	3.99000	4.00802
4	5.84798	5.88951	5.93128	5.97330	6.01555	6.05805	6.10079	6.14377	6.18700	6.23047
5	8.36845	8.45023	8.53273	8.61595	8.69991	8.78459	8.87002	8.95618	9.04310	9.13077
6	11.54425	11.68954	11.83657	11.98534	12.13588	12.28820	12.44232	12.59826	12.75603	12.91565
7	15.54575	15.78727	16.03244	16.28131	16.53392	16.79034	17.05059	17.31474	17.58284	17.85492
8	20.58764	20.97089	21.36119	21.75867	22.16342	22.57558	22.99527	23.42259	23.85769	24.30067
9	26.94043	27.52818	28.12872	28.74230	29.36918	30.00962	30.66389	31.33226	32.01499	32.71237
10	34.94494	35.82314	36.72347	37.64643	38.59255	39.56236	40.55642	41.57527	42.61949	43.68965
11	45.03062	46.31627	47.63880	48.99919	50.39846	51.83763	53.31778	54.83997	56.40533	58.01499
12	57.73858	59.59008	61.50128	63.47397	65.51003	67.61136	69.77993	72.01776	74.32693	76.70955
13	73.75061	76.38145	79.10662	81.92931	84.85283	87.88059	91.01611	94.26300	97.62500	101.10596
14	93.92576	97.62253	101.46541	105.45987	109.61162	113.92655	118.41078	123.07058	127.91249	132.94327
15	119.34646	124.49250	129.86106	135.46132	141.30286	147.39561	153.74990	160.37639	167.28623	174.49096
16	151.37653	158.48300	165.92354	173.71318	181.86766	190.40335	199.33736	208.68742	218.47210	228.71070
17	191.73442	201.48099	211.72289	222.48430	233.79059	24566830	258.14518	271.25020	285.01371	299.46745
18	242.58536	255.87344	269.88806	284.66747	300.25195	316.68375	334.00727	352.26899	371.51781	391.80500
19	306.65755	324.67989	343.75783	363.95101	385.32248	407.93861	431.86937	457.18833	483.97313	512.30550
20	387.38850	411.72004	437.57243	465.03753	494.21275	525.20109	558.11147	593.05886	630.16504	669.55865

Table-3 continue

Future Value of an Annuity of ₹ 1.00*

n/i	31.0	31.5	32.0	32.5	33.0	33.5	34.0	34.5	35.0	35.5
1	1.00000	1.00000	1.00000	1.00000	1.00000	1.00000	1.00000	1.00000	1.00000	1.00000
2	2.31000	2.31500	2.32000	2.32500	2.33000	2.33500	2.34000	2.34500	2.35000	2.35500
3	4.02610	4.04422	4.06240	4.08062	4.09890	4.11722	4.13560	4.15402	4.17250	4.19102
4	6.27419	6.31816	6.36237	6.40683	6.45154	6.49649	6.54170	6.58716	6.63287	6.67884
5	9.21919	9.30837	9.39832	9.48905	9.58054	9.67282	9.67588	9.85973	9.95438	10.04983
6	13.07714	13.24051	13.40579	13.57299	13.74212	13.91321	14.08628	14.26134	14.43841	14.61751
7	18.13105	18.41127	18.69564	18.98421	19.27702	19.57414	19.87562	20.18150	20.49186	20.80673
8	24.75167	25.21082	25.67824	26.15407	26.63844	27.13148	27.63332	28.14412	28.66400	29.19312
9	33.42469	34.15223	34.89528	35.65414	36.42912	37.22052	38.02865	38.85384	39.69640	40.55667
10	44.78634	45.91018	47.06177	48.24173	49.45073	50.78939	51.95839	53.25841	54.59014	55.95429
11	59.67011	61.37188	63.12153	64.92030	66.76947	68.67033	70.62424	72.63256	74.69669	76.81805
12	79.16784	81.70402	84.32041	87.01939	89.80339	92.67489	95.63648	98.69079	101.84053	105.08846
13	104.70987	108.44079	112.30294	116.30068	120.43850	124.72098	129.15288	133.73911	138.48470	143.39486
14	138.16992	143.59963	149.23988	155.09840	161.18320	167.50250	174.06485	180.87909	187.95434	195.30002
15	182.00259	189.83350	197.99663	206.50537	215.37364	224.61583	234.24689	244.28236	254.73835	265.63152
16	239.42338	250.63105	262.35554	274.61960	287.44693	300.86211	314.89081	329.55976	344.89676	360.93069
17	314.64462	330.57981	347.30930	364.87095	383.30441	402.65091	422.95367	444.25785	466.61061	490.06106
18	413.18444	435.71244	459.44825	484.45398	510.79484	538.53893	567.75789	598.52678	630.92430	665.03270
19	542.27159	573.96184	607.47166	642.90150	680.35711	719.94945	761.79553	806.01848	852.74777	902.11927
20	711.37576	755.75979	802.86256	852.84444	905.87492	962.13247	1021.8060	1085.0948	1152.2094	1223.3716

contd....

Table-3 continue

Future Value of an Annuity of ₹ 1.00*

n/i	36.0	36.5	37.0	37.5	38.0	38.5	39.0	39.5	40.0	40.5
1	1.00000	1.00000	1.00000	1.00000	1.00000	1.00000	1.00000	1.00000	1.00000	1.00000
2	2.36000	2.36500	2.37000	2.37500	2.38000	2.38500	2.39000	2.39500	2.40000	2.40500
3	4.20960	4.22822	4.24690	4.26562	4.28440	4.30322	4.32210	4.34102	4.36000	4.37902
4	6.72507	6.77153	6.81825	6.86523	6.91247	6.95997	7.00772	7.05573	7.10400	7.15253
5	10.14607	10.24313	10.34101	10.43970	10.53921	10.63955	10.74073	10.84274	10.94560	11.04930
6	14.79866	14.98188	15.16718	15.35458	15.54411	15.73578	15.92961	16.12562	16.32384	16.52427
7	21.12618	21.45026	21.77903	22.11255	22.45087	22.79405	23.14216	23.49524	23.85337	24.21660
8	29.73160	30.27960	30.83727	31.40475	31.98220	32.56976	33.16760	33.77586	34.39472	35.02432
9	41.43498	42.33166	43.24706	44.18153	45.13543	46.10912	47.10296	48.11723	49.15260	50.20916
10	57.35156	58.78271	60.24847	61.74960	63.28689	64.86112	66.47311	68.12367	69.81364	71.54387
11	78.99812	81.23839	83.54040	85.90570	88.33591	90.83265	93.39762	96.03251	98.73909	101.51913
12	108.43744	111.89040	115.45034	119.12033	122.90354	126.80321	130.82269	134.96535	139.23471	143.63438
14	202.92587	210.84196	219.05873	227.58686	236.43748	245.62207	255.15249	265.04091	275.30001	258.94282
15	276.97917	288.79926	301.11044	313.93192	327.28371	341.18655	355.66195	370.73206	386.41999	402.74964
16	377.69165	395.21097	413.52129	432.65637	452.65150	473.54334	495.37008	518.17119	541.98795	566.86320
17	514.66062	540.46294	567.52414	595.90247	625.65903	656.85749	689.56438	723.84877	759.78310	797.44276
18	700.93841	738.73188	778.50803	820.36586	864.40942	910.74757	959.49445	1010.7690	1064.6963	1121.4070
19	954.27681	1009.3696	1067.5564	1129.0038	1193.8857	1262.3861	1334.6978	1411.0236	1491.5757	1576.5777
20	1298.81640	1378.7896	1463.5523	1553.3802	1648.5622	1749.4047	1856.2299	1969.3780	2089.2059	2216.0917

TABLE-4

Present Value of an Annuity of ₹ 1.00*

n/i	1.0	1.5	2.0	2.5	3.0	3.5	4.0	4.5	5.0	5.5
1	0.99019	0.98522	0.98039	0.97561	0.97087	0.96618	0.96154	0.95694	0.95238	0.94787
2	1.97039	1.95588	1.94156	1.92742	1.91347	1.89969	1.88609	1.87267	1.85941	1.84632
3	2.94098	2.91220	2.88388	2.85602	2.82861	2.80164	2.77509	2.74896	2.72352	2.69793
4	3.90197	3.85438	3.80773	3.76197	3.71710	3.67308	3.62990	3.58753	3.54595	3.50515
5	4.85343	4.78264	4.71346	4.64583	4.57971	4.51505	4.45182	4.38998	4.32948	4.27028
6	5.79548	5.69719	5.60143	5.50812	5.41719	5.32855	5.24214	5.15787	5.07569	4.99553
7	6.72819	6.59821	6.47199	6.34939	6.23028	6.11455	6.00206	5.89270	5.78637	5.68297
8	7.65168	7.48592	7.32548	7.17014	7.01969	6.87396	6.73275	6.59589	6.46321	6.33457
9	8.56602	8.36051	8.16224	7.97086	7.78611	7.60769	7.43533	7.26879	7.10782	6.95220
10	9.47130	9.22218	8.98259	8.75206	8.53020	8.31661	8.11090	7.91272	7.72174	7.53763
11	10.36763	10.07112	9.78685	9.51421	9.25262	9.00155	8.76048	8.52892	8.30642	8.09254
12	11.25508	10.90750	9.78685	9.51421	9.25262	9.00155	8.76048	8.52892	8.30642	8.09254
13	12.13374	11.73153	11.34837	10.98318	10.63495	10.30274	9.98565	9.68285	9.39357	9.11708
14	13.00370	12.54338	12.10625	11.69091	11.29607	10.92052	10.56312	10.22282	9.89864	9.58965
15	13.86505	13.34323	12.84926	12.38138	11.93793	11.51741	11.11839	10.73955	10.37966	10.03758
16	14.71787	14.13126	13.57771	13.05500	12.56110	12.09412	11.65230	11.23401	10.83777	10.46216
17	15.56225	14.90765	14.29187	13.71220	13.16612	12.65132	12.16567	11.70719	11.27407	10.86461
18	16.39827	15.67256	14.99203	14.35336	13.75351	13.18968	12.65930	12.15999	11.68959	11.24607
19	17.22601	16.42616	15.67846	14.97889	14.32380	13.70984	13.13394	12.59329	12.08532	11.60765
20	18.04555	17.16863	16.35143	15.58916	14.87747	14.21241	13.59033	13.00794	12.46221	11.95038

**n* = number of time periods; *i* = rate of interest in per cent.

contd....

Table-4 continue

Present Value of an Annuity of ₹ 1.00*

n/i	6.0	6.5	7.0	7.5	8.0	8.5	9.0	9.5	10.0	10.5
1	0.94340	0.93897	0.93458	0.93023	0.92593	0.92166	0.91743	0.91324	0.90909	0.90498
2	1.83339	1.82063	1.80802	1.79557	1.78326	1.77111	1.75911	1.74725	1.73554	1.72396
3	2.67301	2.64848	2.62432	2.60053	2.57710	2.55402	2.53129	2.50891	2.48685	2.46512
4	3.46511	3.42580	3.38721	3.34933	3.31213	3.27560	3.23972	3.20448	3.16987	3.13586
5	4.21236	4.15568	4.10020	4.04588	3.99271	3.94064	3.88965	3.83971	3.79079	3.74286
6	4.91732	4.84101	4.76654	4.69385	4.62288	4.55359	4.48592	4.41983	4.35526	4.29218
7	5.58238	5.48452	5.38929	5.29660	5.20637	5.11851	5.03295	4.94961	4.86842	4.78930
8	6.20979	6.08875	5.97130	5.85730	5.74664	5.63918	5.53482	5.43344	5.33493	5.23919
9	6.80169	6.65611	6.51523	6.37889	6.24689	6.11906	5.99525	5.87528	5.75902	5.64632
10	7.36009	7.18883	7.02358	6.86408	6.71008	6.56135	641766	6.27880	6.14457	6.01477
11	7.88687	7.68904	7.49867	7.31542	7.13896	6.96898	6.80519	6.64730	6.49506	6.34821
12	8.38384	8.15873	7.94269	7.73528	7.53608	7.34469	7.16073	6.98384	6.81369	6.64996
13	8.85268	8.59974	8.35765	8.12584	7.90378	7.69096	7.48690	7.29118	7.10336	6.92304
14	9.29498	9.01384	8.74547	8.48915	8.24424	8.01010	7.78615	7.57185	7.36669	7.17018
15	9.71225	9.40267	9.01791	8.82712	8.55948	8.30424	8.06069	7.82817	7.60608	7.39382
16	10.10590	9.76777	9.44665	9.14151	8.85137	8.57533	8.31256	8.06226	7.82371	7.59622
17	10.47726	10.11058	9.76322	9.43396	9.12164	8.82519	8.54363	8.27604	8.02155	7.77939
18	10.82760	10.43247	10.05909	9.70601	9.37189	9.05548	8.75563	8.47127	8.20141	7.94515
19	11.15812	10.73471	10.33560	9.95908	9.60360	9.26772	8.95011	8.64956	8.36492	8.09515
20	11.46992	11.01851	10.59401	10.19449	9.81815	9.46334	9.12855	8.81238	8.51356	8.23091

Table-4 continue

Present Value of an Annuity of ₹ 1.00*

n/i	11.0	11.5	12.0	12.5	13.0	13.5	14.0	14.5	15.0	15.5
1	0.90090	0.89686	0.89286	0.88889	0.88496	0.88106	0.87719	0.86957	0.86057	0.86580
2	1.71252	1.70122	1.69005	1.67901	1.66810	1.65732	1.64666	1.63612	1.62571	1.61541
3	2.44371	2.42262	2.40183	2.38134	2.36115	2.34125	2.32163	2.30229	2.28323	2.26443
4	3.10245	3.06961	3.03735	3.00564	2.97447	2.94383	2.91371	2.88410	2.85498	2.82634
5	3.69590	3.64988	3.60478	3.56057	3.51723	3.47474	3.43308	3.39223	3.35216	3.31285
6	4.23054	4.17029	4.11141	4.05384	3.99755	3.94250	3.88867	3.83600	3.78448	3.73407
7	4.71200	4.63704	4.56376	4.49230	4.42261	4.35463	4.28830	4.22358	4.16042	4.09876
8	5.14612	5.05564	4.96764	4.88205	4.79877	4.71774	4.63886	4.56208	4.48732	4.41451
9	5.53705	5.43106	5.32825	5.32848	5.13166	5.03765	4.94637	4.85771	4.77158	4.68789
10	5.88923	5.76777	5.65022	5.53643	5.42624	5.31952	5.21612	5.11591	5.01877	4.92458
11	6.20652	6.06975	5.93770	5.81016	5.68694	5.56786	5.45273	5.34140	5.23371	5.12951
12	6.49236	6.34058	6.19437	6.05348	5.91765	5.78666	5.66029	5.53834	5.42062	5.30693
13	6.74987	6.58348	6.42355	6.29976	6.12181	5.97943	5.84236	5.71034	5.58315	5.46055
14	6.98187	6.80133	6.62817	6.46201	6.30249	6.14228	6.00207	5.86056	5.72448	5.59355
15	7.19087	6.99671	6.81086	6.63289	6.46238	6.29893	6.14217	5.99176	5.84737	5.70870
16	7.37916	7.17194	6.97399	6.78479	6.60388	6.43077	6.26506	6.10634	5.95424	5.80840
17	7.54879	7.32909	7.11963	6.91982	6.72909	6.54694	6.37286	6.20641	6.04716	5.89472
18	7.70162	7.47004	7.24967	7.03984	6.83991	6.64928	6.46742	6.29381	6.12797	5.96945
19	7.83929	7.59644	7.36578	7.14652	6.93797	6.73946	6.55037	6.37014	6.19823	6.03416
20	7.96333	7.70982	7.46944	7.24135	7.02475	6.81890	6.62313	6.43680	6.25933	6.09018

contd....

Table-4 continue

Present Value of an Annuity of ₹ 1.00*

n/i	16.0	16.5	17.0	17.5	18.0	18.5	19.0	19.5	20.0	20.5
1	0.86207	0.85837	0.85470	0.85106	0.84746	0.84388	0.84034	0.83682	0.83333	0.89988
2	1.60523	1.59517	1.58521	1.57537	1.56564	1.55602	1.54650	1.53709	1.52778	1.51858
3	2.24589	2.22761	2.20959	2.19181	2.17427	2.15698	2.13992	2.12309	2.10648	2.09010
4	2.79818	2.77084	2.74324	2.71643	2.69006	2.66412	2.63859	2.61346	2.58873	2.56440
5	3.27429	3.23646	3.19935	3.16292	3.12717	3.09208	3.05764	3.02382	2.99061	2.95801
6	3.68474	3.63645	3.58918	3.54291	3.49760	3.45323	3.40978	3.36721	3.32551	3.28465
7	4.03857	3.97979	3.92238	3.86631	3.81153	3.75800	3.70570	3.65457	3.60459	3.55573
8	4.34359	4.27449	4.20716	4.14154	4.07757	4.01519	3.95437	3.89504	3.83716	3.78069
9	4.60654	4.52746	4.45057	4.37578	4.30302	4.23223	4.16333	4.09627	4.03097	3.96738
10	4.83323	4.74460	4.65860	4.57513	4.49409	4.41538	4.33894	4.26466	4.19247	4.12230
11	5.02864	4.93099	4.83641	4.74479	4.65601	4.56994	4.48650	4.40557	4.32706	4.25087
12	5.19711	5.09098	4.98839	4.88918	4.79323	4.70037	4.61050	4.52349	4.43922	4.35757
13	5.34233	5.22831	5.11288	5.01207	4.90951	4.81044	4.71471	4.62217	4.53268	4.44612
14	5.46753	5.34619	5.22930	5.11666	5.00806	4.90333	4.80228	4.70474	4.61057	4.51960
15	5.57546	5.44737	5.32419	5.20567	5.09158	4.98171	4.87586	4.77384	4.67547	4.58058
16	5.66850	5.53422	5.40529	5.28142	5.16235	5.04786	4.93770	4.83167	4.72956	4.63119
17	5.74840	5.36878	5.47461	5.34589	5.22233	5.10368	4.98966	4.88006	4.77463	4.67318
18	5.81785	5.67377	5.53385	5.40076	5.27316	5.15078	5.03333	4.92055	4.81220	4.70804
19	5.87746	5.72770	5.58449	5.44745	5.31624	5.19053	5.07003	4.95444	4.84350	4.73696
20	5.92884	5.77485	5.62777	5.48719	5.35275	5.22408	5.10086	4.98279	4.86958	4.76096

Table-4 continue

Present Value of an Annuity of ₹ 1.00*

n/j	21.0	21.5	22.0	22.5	23.0	23.5	24.0	24.5	25.0	25.5
1	0.82645	0.82305	0.81967	0.81633	0.81301	0.80972	0.80645	0.80321	0.80000	0.79681
2	1.50946	1.50045	1.49153	1.48272	1.47399	1.46536	1.45682	1.44836	1.44000	1.43172
3	2.07393	2.05798	2.04224	2.02671	2.01137	1.99624	1.98130	1.96656	1.95200	1.93763
4	2.54044	2.51686	2.49364	2.47078	2.44827	2.42611	2.40428	2.38278	2.36160	2.34074
5	2.92598	2.89453	2.86364	2.83329	2.80347	2.77418	2.74538	2.71709	2.68928	2.66194
6	3.24462	3.20538	3.16692	3.12922	3.09225	3.05601	3.02047	2.98561	2.95142	2.91788
7	3.50795	3.46122	3.41551	3.37079	3.32704	3.28422	3.24232	3.20130	3.16114	3.12182
8	3.72558	3.67178	3.61927	3.56799	3.51792	3.46900	3.42122	3.37454	3.32891	3.28432
9	3.90543	3.84509	3.78629	3.72897	3.67310	3.61863	3.56550	3.51368	3.46313	3.41380
10	4.05408	3.98773	3.92318	3.86039	3.79927	3.73978	3.68186	3.62545	3.57050	3.51697
11	4.17692	4.10513	4.03540	3.96766	3.90185	3.83788	3.77569	3.71522	3.65640	3.59918
12	4.27845	4.20175	4.12737	4.05523	3.98524	3.91731	3.85136	3.78733	3.75512	3.66469
13	4.36236	4.28128	4.20277	4.12672	4.05304	3.98163	3.91239	3.84524	3.78010	3.71688
14	4.43170	4.34673	4.26456	4.18508	4.10816	4.03371	3.96160	3.89176	3.82408	3.75847
15	4.48901	4.40060	4.31522	4.23272	4.15298	4.07588	4.00129	3.92912	3.85926	3.79161
16	4.53637	4.44494	4.35673	4.27161	4.18941	4.11002	4.03330	3.95914	3.88741	3.81802
17	4.57551	4.48143	4.39077	4.30335	4.21904	4.13767	4.05911	3.98324	3.90993	3.83903
18	4.60786	4.51147	4.41866	4.32927	4.24312	4.16006	4.07993	4.00260	3.92794	3.85582
19	4.63460	4.53619	4.44152	4.35042	4.26270	4.17818	4.09672	4.01816	3.94235	3.86918
20	4.65669	4.55653	4.46027	4.36769	4.27862	4.19286	4.11026	4.03065	3.95388	3.87983

contd....

Table-4 continue

Present Value of an Annuity of ₹ 1.00*

n/j	26.0	26.5	27.0	27.5	28.0	28.5	29.0	29.5	30.0	30.5
1	0.79365	0.79051	0.78740	0.78431	0.78125	0.77821	0.77519	0.77220	0.76923	0.76628
2	1.42353	1.41543	1.40740	1.39946	1.39160	1.38382	1.37612	1.36849	1.36095	1.35347
3	1.92344	1.90943	1.89559	1.88193	1.86844	1.85511	1.84195	1.82895	1.81611	1.80343
4	2.32019	2.29994	2.27999	2.26034	2.24097	2.22188	2.20306	2.18452	2.16624	2.14822
5	2.63507	2.60865	2.58267	2.55713	2.53201	2.50730	2.48300	2.45909	2.43557	2.41243
6	2.88498	2.85269	2.82100	2.78990	2.75938	2.72942	2.70000	2.67111	2.64275	2.61489
7	3.08332	3.04560	3.00866	2.97247	2.93702	2.90227	2.86821	2.83484	2.80211	2.77003
8	3.24073	3.19811	3.15643	3.11567	3.07579	3.03679	2.99862	2.96126	2.92470	2.88891
9	3.36566	3.31866	3.27278	3.22797	3.18421	3.14147	3.09970	3.05889	3.01900	2.98001
10	3.46481	3.41396	3.36439	3.31606	3.26892	3.22293	3.17806	3.13428	3.09154	3.04982
11	3.54350	3.48930	3.43653	3.38514	3.33509	3.28633	3.23881	3.19249	3.14734	3.10331
12	3.60595	3.54885	3.49333	3.43933	3.38679	3.33566	3.28590	3.23745	3.19026	3.14430
13	3.65552	3.59593	3.53806	3.48183	3.42718	3.37406	3.2240	3.27216	3.22328	3.17571
14	3.69485	3.63315	3.57327	3.51516	3.45873	3.40394	3.35070	3.29896	3.24867	3.19978
15	3.72607	3.66257	3.60100	3.54130	3.48339	3.42719	3.37264	3.31966	3.26821	3.21822
16	3.75085	3.68582	3.62284	3.56180	3.50265	3.44528	3.38964	3.33565	3.28324	3.23235
17	3.77052	3.70421	3.64003	3.57789	3.51769	3.45936	3.40282	3.34799	3.29480	3.24318
18	3.78613	3.71874	3.65357	3.59050	3.52945	3.47032	3.41304	3.35752	3.30369	3.25148
19	3.79851	3.73023	3.66423	3.60039	3.53863	3.47885	3.42096	3.36488	3.31053	3.25784
20	3.80824	3.73931	3.67262	3.60815	3.54581	3.48549	3.42710	3.37057	3.31579	3.26271

Table-4 continue

Present Value of an Annuity of ₹ 1.00*

n/j	31.0	31.5	32.0	32.5	23.0	33.5	34.0	34.5	35.0	35.5
1	0.76336	0.76046	0.75758	0.75472	0.75188	0.74906	0.74627	0.74349	0.74074	0.73801
2	1.34608	1.33875	1.33150	1.32431	1.31720	1.31016	1.30319	1.29628	1.28944	1.28266
3	1.79090	1.77852	1.76629	1.75420	1.74226	1.73046	1.71880	1.70227	1.69588	1.68462
4	2.13046	2.11294	2.09567	2.07864	2.06185	2.04529	2.02895	2.01284	1.99695	1.98127
5	2.38966	2.36726	2.34521	2.32350	2.30214	2.28111	2.26041	2.24003	2.21998	2.20020
6	2.58753	2.56065	2.53425	2.50830	2.48281	2.45776	2.43314	2.40894	2.38516	2.36177
7	2.73857	2.70772	2.67746	2.64778	2.61866	2.59008	2.56205	2.53453	2.50752	2.48101
8	2.85387	2.81956	2.78595	2.75304	2.72079	2.68920	2.65824	2.62790	2.59817	2.56901
9	2.94189	2.90461	2.86815	2.83248	2.79759	2.76345	2.73003	2.69733	2.66531	2.63396
10	3.00907	2.96928	2.93041	2.89244	2.85533	2.81906	2.78361	2.74894	2.71504	2.68189
11	3.06036	3.01847	2.97759	2.93769	2.89875	2.86072	2.82359	2.78732	2.75188	2.71726
12	3.09951	3.05587	3.01332	2.97184	2.93139	2.89193	2.85342	2.81585	2.77917	2.74337
13	3.12940	3.05587	3.01332	2.97184	2.93139	2.89193	2.85342	2.81585	2.77917	2.74337
14	3.15221	3.10594	3.06091	3.01707	2.97438	2.93281	2.89231	2.85283	2.81436	2.77685
15	3.16963	3.12239	3.07644	3.03175	2.98826	2.94592	2.90471	2.86456	2.82545	2.78734
16	3.18292	3.13490	3.08822	3.04283	2.99869	2.95575	2.91396	2.87328	2.83367	2.79509
17	3.10307	3.14441	3.09713	3.05119	3.00653	2.96311	2.92087	2.87976	2.83975	2.80080
18	3.20082	3.15164	3.10389	3.05750	3.01243	2.96862	2.92602	2.88458	2.84426	2.80502
19	3.20673	3.15714	3.10901	3.06227	3.01687	2.97275	2.92987	2.88816	2.84760	2.80813
20	3.21125	3.16132	3.11288	3.06585	3.02020	2.97584	2.93274	2.89083	2.85008	2.81043

contd

Table-4 continue

Present Value of an Annuity of ₹ 1.00*

n/j	36.0	36.5	37.0	37.5	38.0	38.5	39.0	39.5	40.0	40.5
1	0.73529	0.73260	0.72993	0.72727	0.72464	0.72202	0.71942	0.71685	0.71429	0.71174
2	1.27595	1.26930	1.26272	1.25620	1.24974	1.24334	1.23700	1.23071	1.22449	1.21832
3	1.67349	1.66249	1.65162	1.64087	1.63024	1.61974	1.60935	1.59908	1.58892	1.57888
4	1.96580	1.95055	1.93549	1.92063	1.90597	1.89151	1.87723	1.86314	1.84923	1.83550
5	2.18074	2.16157	2.14269	2.12410	2.10578	2.08773	2.06995	2.05243	2.03516	2.01815
6	2.33878	2.31617	2.29394	2.27207	2.25056	2.22941	2.20860	2.18812	2.16797	2.14815
7	2.45498	2.42943	2.40433	2.37969	2.35548	2.33170	2.30834	2.28539	2.26284	2.24068
8	2.54043	2.51240	2.48492	2.45796	2.43151	2.40556	2.38010	2.35512	2.33060	2.30653
9	2.60326	2.57319	2.54373	2.51488	2.48660	2.45889	2.43173	2.40510	2.37900	2.35340
10	2.64945	2.61772	2.58667	2.55627	2.52652	2.49739	2.46887	2.44093	2.41357	2.38676
11	2.68342	2.65034	2.61801	2.58638	2.55545	2.52519	2.49559	2.46662	2.43827	2.41051
12	2.70840	2.67425	2.64088	2.60828	2.57641	2.54527	2.51481	2.48503	2.45590	2.42741
13	2.72676	2.69175	2.65758	2.62420	2.59160	2.55979	2.52864	2.49823	2.46850	2.43944
14	2.74027	2.70458	2.66976	2.63578	2.60261	2.57022	2.53859	2.50769	2.47750	2.44800
15	2.75020	2.71398	2.67866	2.64421	2.61059	2.57778	2.54575	2.51448	2.48393	2.45409
16	2.75750	2.72086	2.68515	2.65033	2.61637	2.58323	2.55090	2.51934	2.48852	2.45843
17	2.76287	2.72591	2.68989	2.65479	2.62056	2.58717	2.55460	2.52282	2.49180	2.46151
18	2.76681	2.72960	2.69335	2.65803	2.62359	2.59002	2.55727	2.52532	2.49414	2.46371
19	2.76972	2.73231	2.69588	2.66038	2.62579	2.59207	2.55919	2.52771	2.49582	2.46528
20	2.77185	2.73429	2.69772	2.66210	2.62739	2.59355	2.56057	2.52840	2.49701	2.46639

TABLE-5

Areas Under the Normal Curve

$$\left[z = \frac{X-\mu}{\sigma} : P[z>1] = 0.1587 : P[z>1.96] = 0.0250\right]$$

Normal Deviate z.	.00	.01	.02	.03	.04.	.05	.06	.07	.08	.09
0.0	.5000	.4960	.4920	.4880	.4840	.4801	.4761	.4721	.4681	.4641
0.1	.4602	.4562	.4522	.4483	.4443	.4404	.4364	.4325	.4286	.4247
0.2	.4207	.4168	.4129	.4090	.4052	.4013	.3974	.3936	.3897	.3859
0.3	.3821	.3783	.3745	.3707	.3669	.3632	.3594	.3557	.3520	.3483
0.4	.3446	.3409	.3372	.3336	.3300	.3264	.3228	.3192	.3156	.3121
0.5	.3085	.3050	.3015	.2981	.2946	.2912	.2877	.2842	.2810	.2776
0.6	.2743	2709	.2676	.2643	.2611	.2578	.2546	.2514	.2483	.2451
0.7	.2420	.2389	.2358	.2327	.2296	.2266	.2236	.2206	.2177	.2148
0.8	.2119	.2090	.2061	.2033	.2005	.1977	.1949	.1922	.1894	.1867
0.9	.1841	.1814	.1788	.1762	.1736	.1711	.1685	.1660	.1635	.1611
1.0	.1587	.1562	.1539	.1515	.1492	.1469	.1446	.1423	.1401	.1379
1.1	. 1357	.1335	.1314	.1292	.1271	.1251	.1230	.1210	.1190	.1170
1.2	.1151	.1131	.1112	.1093	.1075	.1056	.1038	.1020	.1003	.0985
1.3	.0968	.0951	.0934	.0918	.0901	.0885	.0869	.0853	.0838	.0823
1.4	.0808	.0793	.0778	.0764	.0749	.0735	.0721	.0708	.0694	.0681
1.5	.0668	.0655	.0643	.0630	.0618	.0606	.0594	.0582	.0571	.0559
1.6	.0548	.0537	.0526	.0516	.0505	.0495	.0485	.0475	.0465	.0455
1.7	.0446	.0436	.0427	.0418	.0409	.0401	.0392	.0384	.0375	.0367
1.8	.0359	.0351	.0344	.0336	.0329	.0322	.0314	.0307	.0301	.0294
1.9	.0287	.0281	.0274	.0268	.0262	.0256	.0250	.0244	.0239	.0233
2.0	.0228	.0222	.0217	.0212	.0207	.0202	.0197	.0192	.0188	.0183
2.1	.0179	.0174	.0170	.0166	.0162	.0158	.0154	.0150	.0146	.0143
2.2	.0139	.0136	.0132	.0129	.0125	.0122	.0119	.0116	.0113	.0110
2.3	.0107	.0104	.0102	.0099	.0096	.0094	.0091	.0089	.0087	.0084
2.4	.0082	.0080	.0078	.0075	.0073	.0071	.0069	.0068	.0066	.0064
2.5	.0062	.0060	.0059	.0057	.0055	.0054	.0052	.0051	.0049	.0048
2.6	.0047	.0045	.0044	.0043	.0041	.0040	.0039	.0038	.0037	.0036
2.7	.0035	.0034	.0033	.0032	.0031	.0030	.0029	.0028	.0027	.0026
2.8	.0026	.0025	.0024	.0023	.0023	.0022	.0021	.0021	.0020	.0019
2.9	.0019	.0018	.0018	.0017	.0016	.0016	.0015	.0015	.0014	.0014
3.0	.0013	.0013	.0013	.0012	.0012	.0011	.0011	.0011	.0010	.0010

INDEX

A

B

C

D

M

N

O

P

T

U

V

W

Y

Z